Praise for
An Army at Dawn

"A monumental history of the overshadowed combat in North Africa during World War II that brings soldiers, generals, and bloody battles alive through masterful storytelling."
— citation for the 2003 Pulitzer Prize for History

"A book that stands shoulder to shoulder with the other major books about the war, such as the fine writing of Cornelius Ryan and John Keegan."
— Associated Press

"Atkinson's writing is lucid, vivid. . . . Among the many pleasures of *An Army at Dawn* are the carefully placed details—shells that whistle into the water with a smoky hiss; a colonel with 'slicked hair and a wolfish mustache'; a man dying before he can fire the pistols strapped in his holster."
— *Milwaukee Journal Sentinel*

"One of the most compelling pieces of military history I've ever read, *An Army at Dawn* will become a military history and strategy studies classic. Atkinson writes with incredible insight and mastery of the details, and he is always mindful of the larger picture. He goes from the highest political levels to the deepest foxhole without missing a beat. This is history at its finest."
— General Wesley K. Clark, U.S.A. (ret.), former NATO supreme commander

"An engrossing narrative . . . Atkinson has an impressive command of words, a flair for simplifying complex issues, and a vast reservoir of information. . . . This is a fascinating work which any reader can enjoy, and professional historians will find perusal of it eminently worth their while."
— Arthur L. Funk, *Journal of Military History*

"A masterpiece. Rick Atkinson strikes the right balance between minor tactical engagements and high strategic direction, and he brings soldiers at every level to life, from private to general. *An Army at Dawn* is history with a soldier's face."
— General Gordon R. Sullivan, U.S.A. (ret.), former Army chief of staff

"What distinguishes his narrative is the way he fuses the generals' war . . . with the experiences of front-line combat soldiers."
— *Raleigh News & Observer*

"Atkinson's book is eminently friendly and readable, but without compromising normal standards of accuracy and objectivity. More than a military history, it is a social and psychological inquiry as well. His account of the Kasserine Pass disaster alone is worth the price of the book and stands as an exciting preview of the rich volumes to come. I heartily recommend this human, sensitive, unpretentious work."
—Paul Fussell, author of *Doing Battle* and *Wartime*

"Rick Atkinson's *An Army at Dawn* is a superb account of the Allied invasion of North Africa. From the foxhole to Eisenhower's supreme headquarters, Atkinson has captured the essence of war in one of the most neglected campaigns of World War II."
—Carlo D'Este, author of *Patton* and *Eisenhower*

"Given his success with modern military history, the penetrating historical insights Atkinson brings to bear on America's 1942–43 invasion of the North African coast are not surprising. . . . The most thorough and satisfying history yet of the campaigns in North Africa."
—*Kirkus Reviews* (starred review)

"This is a wonderful book—popular history at its best. It is impressively researched and superbly written, and it brings to life in full detail one of the vitally important but relatively 'forgotten' campaigns of World War II. What Bruce Catton and Shelby Foote did for the Civil War in their trilogies, Rick Atkinson is doing for World War II in the European Theater." —Professor Mark A. Stoler, author of *Allies and Adversaries*

"Atkinson's book puts him on a fast track toward becoming one of our most ambitious and distinguished military chroniclers. . . . [He] has unpacked facts that will lift many eyebrows." —*Bookpage*

"For sheer drama, the Tunisian campaign far overshadowed any other phase of the Second World War. Rick Atkinson has told the story with zest and brutal realism. His account will be a monument among accounts of World War II."
—John S. D. Eisenhower, author of *Allies* and *The Bitter Woods*

"*An Army at Dawn* is an absolute masterpiece. Atkinson conveys both the human drama and historical significance of this campaign with a power and intensity that is nothing short of electrifying. This book is storytelling—and history—at its most riveting."

—Andrew Carroll, editor of *War Letters: Extraordinary Correspondence from American Wars*

"Rick Atkinson has done a beautiful job of research and writing in *An Army at Dawn*. This is the North African campaign—warts, snafus, feuding allies, incompetents, barely competents—unvarnished. It whets my appetite for the rest of the Liberation Trilogy Atkinson has promised us."

—Joseph L. Galloway, coauthor of *We Were Soldiers Once . . . and Young*

"Rick Atkinson combines meticulous research and attention to detail with an extraordinary ability to tell a story. It is a rich and powerful narrative which is certain to become a classic."

—Ronald Spector, author of *At War at Sea* and *Eagle against the Sun*

Also by Rick Atkinson

The Long Gray Line

Crusade

An Army at Dawn

An Army at Dawn

THE WAR IN NORTH AFRICA,

1942–1943

VOLUME ONE OF THE LIBERATION TRILOGY

Rick Atkinson

A Holt Paperback

HENRY HOLT AND COMPANY

NEW YORK

To my mother and father

Holt Paperbacks
Henry Holt and Company, LLC
Publishers since 1866
175 Fifth Avenue
New York, New York 10010
www.henryholt.com

Library of Congress Cataloging-in-Publication Data
Atkinson, Rick.
    An army at dawn : the war in North Africa, 1942–1943 / Rick Atkinson.—1st ed.
        p.   cm.
    Includes bibliographical references and index.
    ISBN-13: 978-0-8050-8724-6
    ISBN-10: 0-8050-8724-9
        1. World War, 1939–1945—Campaigns—Africa, North. 2. Operation Torch. 3. Africa,
    North—History, Military. I. Title.
D766.82 .A82 2002
940.54'23—dc21   2002024130

Henry Holt books are available for special promotions and premiums.
For details contact: Director, Special Markets.

Originally published in hardcover in 2002 by Henry Holt and Company

First Holt Paperbacks Edition 2003

Designed by Fritz Metsch

Maps by Gene Thorp

Printed in the United States of America
5   7   9   10   8   6

At last the armies clashed at one strategic point,
They slammed their shields together, pike scraped pike
With the grappling strength of fighters armed in bronze
And their round shields pounded, boss on welded boss,
And the sound of struggle roared and rocked the earth.

The Iliad, Book 4

Gene Thorp

CONTENTS

PART TWO

PART THREE

MAPS

MAP LEGEND

River/Stream

HIGHWAY/MAJOR ROAD

MINOR ROAD/TRAIL

RAILROAD

Swamp

Salt Flat

Terrain

Hill/Mountain

City/town/village with urban area

Capital city

Airfield

Clash

UNITED STATES

UNITED KINGDOM

FRANCE

GERMANY

ITALY

AXIS		**ALLIED**
	Front line	
	ship	
	gun emplacement	
	Advance	
	Retreat	
	Infantry	
	Armor	
	Mechanized	
	Airborne	
I	**Company**	
II	**Battalion**	
III	**Regiment**	
X	**Brigade**	
XX	**Division**	
XXX	**Corps**	
XXXX	**Army**	

ALLIED CHAIN OF COMMAND
TUNISIAN CAMPAIGN, 1942–43

Commander-in-Chief: EISENHOWER

Deputy: CLARK
ALEXANDER (Feb 1943)
Chief of staff: SMITH

Commander, Naval Forces: CUNNINGHAM

Commander, Air Forces: TEDDER
NW Africa AF: SPAATZ
Tactical AF: CONINGHAM

18th Army Group: ALEXANDER (Feb 1943)

U.S. Fifth Army: CLARK (Jan 1943)
2nd Armored Div
3rd Infantry Div

French Forces: GIRAUD
French Army: JUIN

British First Army: ANDERSON

British Eighth Army: MONTGOMERY

V Corps: ALLFREY
78th Div
6th Arm Div (Jan 1943)
1st Div (March 1943)
4th Div (Apr 1943)

IX Corps: (Mar 1943)
CROCKER
HORROCKS (APR 1943)
46th Div
1st Arm Div
7th Arm Div
4th Ind Div
201st Guards Bde
(all Apr–May 1943)
6th Arm Div
(March 1943)

X Corps:
HORROCKS
FREYBERG (Apr 1943)
1st Arm Div
7th Arm Div
56th Div

XXX Corps:
LEESE

2nd NZ Div
50th Div
4th Ind Div
201st Gds Bde

U.S. II Corps: FREDENDALL
PATTON (March 1943)
BRADLEY (Apr 1943)

French XIX Corps: KOELTZ

1ST Arm Div: WARD
HARMON (Apr 1943)
1st Inf Div: ALLEN
9th Inf Div: EDDY
34th Inf Div: RYDER

An Army at Dawn

PROLOGUE

TWENTY-SEVEN acres of headstones fill the American military cemetery at Carthage, Tunisia. There are no obelisks, no tombs, no ostentatious monuments, just 2,841 bone-white marble markers, two feet high and arrayed in ranks as straight as gunshots. Only the chiseled names and dates of death suggest singularity. Four sets of brothers lie side by side. Some 240 stones are inscribed with thirteen of the saddest words in our language: "Here rests in honored glory a comrade in arms known but to God." A long limestone wall contains the names of another 3,724 men still missing, and a benediction: "Into Thy hands, O Lord."

This is an ancient place, built on the ruins of Roman Carthage and a stone's throw from the even older Punic city. It is incomparably serene. The scents of eucalyptus and of the briny Mediterranean barely two miles away carry on the morning air, and the African light is flat and shimmering, as if worked by a silversmith. Tunisian lovers stroll hand in hand across the kikuyu grass or sit on benches in the bowers, framed by orangeberry and scarlet hibiscus. Cypress and Russian olive trees ring the yard, with scattered acacia and Aleppo pine and Jerusalem thorn. A carillon plays hymns on the hour, and the chimes sometimes mingle with a muezzin's call to prayer from a nearby minaret. Another wall is inscribed with the battles where these boys died in 1942 and 1943—Casablanca, Algiers, Oran, Kasserine, El Guettar, Sidi Nsir, Bizerte—along with a line from Shelley's "Adonais": "He has outsoared the shadow of our night."

In the tradition of government-issue graves, the stones are devoid of epitaphs, parting endearments, even dates of birth. But visitors familiar with the American and British invasion of North Africa in November 1942, and the subsequent seven-month struggle to expel the Axis powers there, can make reasonable conjectures. We can surmise that Willett H. Wallace, a private first class in the 26th Infantry Regiment who died on November 9, 1942, was killed at St. Cloud, Algeria, during the three days of hard fighting against, improbably, the French. Ward H. Osmun and his brother Wilbur W., both privates from New Jersey in the 18th Infantry and both killed on Christmas Eve 1942, surely died in the brutal battle of Longstop Hill, where the initial Allied drive in Tunisia was stopped—for more than five months, as it turned out—within sight of Tunis. Ignatius Glovach, a private first class in the 701st Tank Destroyer Battalion who died on Valentine's Day, 1943, certainly was killed in the opening hours of the great German counteroffensive known as the battle of Kasserine Pass. And Jacob Feinstein, a sergeant from Maryland in the 135th Infantry who died on April 29, 1943, no doubt passed during the epic battle for Hill 609, where the American Army came of age.

A visit to the Tunisian battlefields tells a bit more. For more than half a century, time and weather have purified the ground at El Guettar and Kasserine and Longstop. But the slit trenches remain, and rusty C-ration cans, and shell fragments scattered like seed corn. The lay of the land also remains—the vulnerable low ground, the superior high ground: incessant reminders of how, in battle, topography is fate.

Yet even when the choreography of armies is understood, or the movement of this battalion or that rifle squad, we crave intimate detail, of individual men in individual foxholes. Where, precisely, was Private Anthony N. Marfione when he died on December 24, 1942? What were the last conscious thoughts of Lieutenant Hill P. Cooper before he left this earth on April 9, 1943? Was Sergeant Harry K. Midkiff alone when he crossed over on November 25, 1942, or did some good soul squeeze his hand and caress his forehead?

The dead resist such intimacy. The closer we try to approach, the farther they draw back, like rainbows or mirages. They *have* outsoared the shadow of our night, to reside in the wild uplands of the past. History can take us there, almost. Their diaries and letters, their official reports and unofficial chronicles—including documents that, until now, have been hidden from view since the war—reveal many moments of exquisite clarity over a distance of sixty years. Memory, too, has transcendent power, even as we swiftly move toward the day when not a single participant remains alive to tell his tale, and the epic of World War II forever slips into national mythology. The author's task is to authenticate: to warrant that history and memory give integrity to the story, to aver that all this really happened.

But the final few steps must be the reader's. For among mortal powers, only imagination can bring back the dead.

No twenty-first-century reader can understand the ultimate triumph of the Allied powers in World War II in 1945 without a grasp of the large drama that unfolded in North Africa in 1942 and 1943. The liberation of western Europe is a triptych, each panel informing the others: first, North Africa; then, Italy; and finally the invasion of Normandy and the subsequent campaigns across France, the Low Countries, and Germany.

From a distance of sixty years, we can see that North Africa was a pivot point in American history, the place where the United States began to act like a great power—militarily, diplomatically, strategically, tactically. Along with Stalingrad and Midway, North Africa is where the Axis enemy forever lost the initiative in World War II. It is where Great Britain slipped into the role of junior partner in the Anglo-American alliance, and where the United States first emerged as the dominant force it would remain into the next millennium.

None of it was inevitable—not the individual deaths, nor the ultimate Allied victory, nor eventual American hegemony. History, like particular fates, hung in the balance, waiting to be tipped.

Measured by the proportions of the later war—of Normandy or the Bulge—the first engagements in North Africa were tiny, skirmishes between platoons and companies involving at most a few hundred men. Within six months, the campaign metastasized to battles between army groups comprising hundreds of thousands of soldiers; that scale persisted for the duration. North Africa gave the European war its immense canvas and implied—through 70,000 Allied killed, wounded, and missing—the casualties to come.

No large operation in World War II surpassed the invasion of North Africa in complexity, daring, risk, or—as the official U.S. Army Air Forces history concludes—"the degree of strategic surprise achieved." Moreover, this was the first campaign undertaken by the Anglo-American alliance; North Africa defined the coalition and its strategic course, prescribing how and where the Allies would fight for the rest of the war.

North Africa established the patterns and motifs of the next two years, including the tension between coalition unity and disunity. Here were staged the first substantial tests of Allied landpower against Axis landpower, and the initial clashes between American troops and German troops. Like the first battles in virtually every American war, this campaign revealed a nation and an army unready to fight and unsure of their martial skills, yet willful and inventive enough finally to prevail.

North Africa is where the prodigious weight of American industrial might began to tell, where brute strength emerged as the most conspicuous feature of the Allied arsenal—although not, as some historians suggest, its only redeeming feature. Here the Americans in particular first recognized, viscerally, the importance of generalship and audacity, guile and celerity, initiative and tenacity.

North Africa is where the the Allies agreed on unconditional surrender as the only circumstance under which the war could end.

It is where the controversial strategy of first contesting the Axis in a peripheral theater—the Mediterranean—was effected at the expense of an immediate assault on northwest Europe, with the campaigns in Sicily, Italy, and southern France following in train.

It is where Allied soldiers figured out, tactically, how to destroy Germans; where the fable of the Third Reich's invincibility dissolved; where, as one senior German general later acknowledged, many Axis soldiers lost confidence in their commanders and "were no longer willing to fight to the last man."

It is where most of the West's great battle captains emerged, including men whose names would remain familiar generations later—Eisenhower, Patton, Bradley, Montgomery, Rommel—and others who deserve rescue from obscurity. It is where the truth of William Tecumseh Sherman's postulate on command was reaffirmed: "There is a soul to an army as well as to the individual man, and no general can accomplish the full work of his army unless he commands the soul of his men, as well as their bodies and legs." Here men capable of such leadership stepped forward, and those incapable fell by the wayside.

North Africa is where American soldiers became killing mad, where the hard truth about combat was first revealed to many. "It is a very, very horrible war, dirty and dishonest, not at all that glamour war that we read about in the hometown papers," one soldier wrote his mother in Ohio. "For myself and the other men here, we will show no mercy. We have seen too much for that." The correspondent Ernie Pyle noted a "new professional outlook, where killing is a craft." North Africa is where irony and skepticism, the twin lenses of modern consciousness, began refracting the experiences of countless ordinary soldiers. "The last war was a war to end war. This war's to start 'em up again," said a British Tommy, thus perfectly capturing the ironic spirit that flowered in North Africa.

Sixty years after the invasion of North Africa, a gauzy mythology has settled over World War II and its warriors. The veterans are lionized as "the Greatest Generation," an accolade none sought and many dismiss as twaddle. They are condemned to sentimental hagiography, in which all the brothers are valiant and all the sisters virtuous. The brave and the virtuous appear throughout the North African campaign, to be sure, but so do the cowardly, the venal, and the foolish. The ugliness common in later campaigns also appears in North Africa: the murder and rape of civilians; the killing of prisoners; the falsification of body counts.

It was a time of cunning and miscalculation, of sacrifice and self-indulgence, of ambiguity, love, malice, and mass murder. There were heroes, but it was not an age of heroes as clean and lifeless as alabaster; at Carthage, demigods and poltroons lie side by side.

The United States would send sixty-one combat divisions into Europe, nearly 2 million soldiers. These were the first. We can fairly surmise that not a single man interred at the Carthage cemetery sensed on September 1, 1939, that he would find an African grave. Yet it was with the invasion of Poland on that date that the road to North Africa began, and it is then and there that our story must begin.

September 1, 1939, was the first day of a war that would last for 2,174 days, and it brought the first dead in a war that would claim an average of 27,600 lives every day, or 1,150 an hour, or 19 a minute, or one death every 3 seconds. Within four weeks of the blitzkrieg attack on Poland by sixty German divisions, the lightning war had killed more than 100,000 Polish soldiers, and 25,000 civilians had perished in bombing attacks. Another 10,000 civilians—mostly middle-class professionals—had been rounded up and murdered, and 22 million Poles now belonged to the Third Reich. "Take a good look around Warsaw," Adolf Hitler told journalists during a visit to the shattered Polish capital. "That is how I can deal with any European city."

France and Great Britain had declared war against the German aggressors on September 3, but fighting subsided for six months while Hitler consolidated his winnings and plotted his next move. That came in early April 1940, when Wehrmacht troops seized Denmark and attacked Norway. A month later, 136 German divisions swept into the Netherlands, Belgium, Luxembourg, and France. Winston S. Churchill—a short, stout, lisping politician of indomitable will and oratorical genius, who on May 10 became both Britain's prime minister and defense minister— told President Franklin D. Roosevelt, "The small countries are simply smashed up, one by one, like matchwood." It was the first of 950 personal messages Churchill would send Roosevelt in the most fateful correspondence of the twentieth century.

France was not small, but it *was* smashed up. German tactical miscalculation allowed the British to evacuate 338,000 troops on 900 vessels from the northern port of Dunkirk, but on June 14 the German spearhead swept across the Place de la Concorde in Paris and unfurled an enormous swastika flag from the Arc de Triomphe. As the French tottered, Germany's partner in the Axis alliance, the Italian government of Benito Mussolini, also declared war on France and Britain. "First they were too cowardly to take part," Hitler said. "Now they are in a hurry so that they can share in the spoils."

After the French cabinet fled to Bordeaux in shocked disarray, a venerable figure emerged to lead the rump government. Marshal Philippe Pétain, the hero of Verdun in World War I and now a laconic, enigmatic eighty-four-year-old, had once asserted, "They call me only in catastrophes." Even Pétain had never seen a catastrophe like this one, and he sued for terms. Berlin obliged. Rather than risk having the French fight on from their colonies in North Africa, Hitler devised a clever armistice: the southern 40 percent of France—excluding Paris—would remain under the sovereignty of the Pétain government and unoccupied by German troops. From a new capital in the resort town of Vichy, France would also continue to administer her overseas empire, including the colonies of Morocco, Algeria, and Tunisia, which together covered a million square miles and included 17 million people, mostly Arab or Berber. France could keep her substantial fleet and an army of 120,000 men in North Africa by pledging to fight all invaders, particularly the British. To enforce the agreement, Germany would keep 1½ million French prisoners-of-war as collateral.

Pétain so pledged. He was supported by most of France's senior military officers and civil servants, who swore oaths of fidelity to him. A few refused, including a forty-nine-year-old maverick brigadier general named Charles André Joseph Marie de Gaulle, who took refuge in London, denounced all deals with the devil, and declared, in the name of Free France: "Whatever happens, the flame of French resistance must not and shall not die." Hitler now controlled Europe from the North Cape to the Pyrenees, from the Atlantic Ocean to the River Bug. In September, Germany and Italy signed a tripartite pact with Japan, which had been prosecuting its own murderous campaign in Asia. The Axis assumed a global span. "The war is won," the Führer told Mussolini. "The rest is only a question of time."

That seemed a fair boast. Britain battled on, alone. "We are fighting for life, and survive from day to day and hour to hour," Churchill told the House of Commons. But German plans to invade across the English Channel were postponed, repeatedly, after the Luftwaffe failed to subdue the Royal Air Force. Instead, the bombardment known as the Blitz continued through 1940 and beyond, slaughtering thousands and then tens of thousands of British civilians, even as RAF pilots shot down nearly

2,500 German planes in three months, killing 6,000 Luftwaffe crewmen and saving the nation.

Churchill also received help from Roosevelt, who nudged the United States away from neutrality even as he promised to keep Americans out of the war. Roosevelt's true sympathies were given voice by his closest aide, Harry Hopkins. "Whither thou goest, I will go," Hopkins told Churchill in January 1941, quoting the Book of Ruth. "And where thou lodgest, I will lodge; thy people shall be my people, and thy God my God." Hopkins added softly, "Even to the end." Roosevelt sent Churchill fifty U.S. Navy destroyers in exchange for the use of British bases in the Caribbean and western Atlantic, and by the spring of 1941 had pushed through Congress a vast program of Lend-Lease assistance under the charade of "renting" out the matériel. By war's end the United States had sent its allies 37,000 tanks, 800,000 trucks, nearly 2 million rifles, and 43,000 planes—so many that U.S. pilot training was curtailed because of aircraft shortages. In 1941, though, the British were "hanging on by our eyelids," as General Alan Brooke, chief of the Imperial General Staff, put it.

Hitler faced other annoying disappointments. Spain refused to join the Axis or abandon her neutrality to permit a German attack against the British fortress at Gibraltar, which controlled the mouth of the Mediterranean. Italian troops invaded Greece without warning on October 28, 1940—"Führer, we are on the march!" Mussolini exclaimed—and immediately found themselves so overmatched that Wehrmacht divisions were needed to complete the conquest and rout an ill-conceived British expeditionary force sent to save the Balkans. Greece fell in April 1941, a week after Yugoslavia, where 17,000 people had been killed in a single day of Luftwaffe bombing.

Mussolini's legions had also been on the march in Africa, attacking from the Italian colony of Libya into Egypt, a former British protectorate still occupied by British troops. A British and Australian counteroffensive in December 1940 smashed an Italian army twice its size, eventually inflicting 150,000 casualties. With the Axis southern flank imperiled, Hitler again came to Mussolini's rescue, dispatching a new Afrika Korps to Libya under a charismatic tank officer who had previously commanded the Führer's headquarters troops in Poland. General Erwin Rommel reached Tripoli in mid-February 1941 and launched a campaign that would surge back and forth across the North African littoral for the next two years, first against the British and then against the Americans.

Two monumental events in 1941 changed the calculus of the war. On

June 22, nearly 200 German divisions invaded the Soviet Union in abrogation of the nonaggression pact that Hitler and Soviet leader Joseph Stalin had signed in 1939, which had allowed a division of spoils in eastern Europe. Within a day, German attacks had demolished one-quarter of the Soviet air force. Within four months, the Germans had occupied 600,000 square miles of Russian soil, captured 3 million Red Army troops, butchered countless Jews and other civilians, and closed to within sixty-five miles of Moscow. But four months after that, more than 200,000 Wehrmacht troops had been killed, 726,000 wounded, 400,000 captured, and another 113,000 had been incapacitated by frostbite.

The second event occurred on the other side of the world. On December 7, Japanese aircraft carriers launched 366 aircraft in a sneak attack on the U.S. Navy Pacific Fleet at Pearl Harbor, sinking or damaging eight battleships at their moorings, destroying or crippling eleven other warships, and killing 2,400 Americans. Simultaneous attacks were launched on Malaya, Hong Kong, and the Philippines. In solidarity with their Japanese ally, Hitler and Mussolini quickly declared war on the United States. It was perhaps the Führer's gravest miscalculation and, as the British historian Martin Gilbert later wrote, "the single most decisive act of the Second World War." America would now certainly return to Europe as a belligerent, just as it had in 1917, during the Great War.

"I knew the United States was in the war, up to the neck and in to the death," Churchill later wrote. "I went to bed and slept the sleep of the saved and thankful."

Two years, three months, and seven days had passed since the invasion of Poland, and the United States had needed every minute of that grace period to prepare for war. Churchill's chief military representative in Washington, Field Marshal Sir John Dill, told London that, notwithstanding the long prelude, American forces "are more unready for war than it is possible to imagine."

In September 1939, the U.S. Army had ranked seventeenth in the world in size and combat power, just behind Romania. When those 136 German divisions conquered western Europe nine months later, the War Department reported that it could field just five divisions. Even the homeland was vulnerable: some coastal defense guns had not been test-fired in twenty years, and the Army lacked enough anti-aircraft guns to protect even a single American city. The building of the armed forces was likened to "the reconstruction of a dinosaur around an ulna and three vertebrae."

That task had started with the 16 million men who registered for the draft in the fall of 1940, and who would expand Regular Army and National Guard divisions. By law, however, the draftees and newly federalized Guard units were restricted to twelve months of service—and only in the western hemisphere or U.S. territories. Physical standards remained fairly rigorous; soon enough, the day would come when new recruits claimed the Army no longer examined eyes, just counted them. A conscript had to stand at least five feet tall and weigh 105 pounds; possess twelve or more of his natural thirty-two teeth; and be free of flat feet, venereal disease, and hernias. More than forty of every hundred men were rejected, a grim testament to the toll taken on the nation's health by the Great Depression. Under the rules of conscription, the Army drafted no fathers, no felons, and no eighteen-year-olds; those standards, too, would fall away. Nearly two million men had been rejected for psychiatric reasons, although screening sessions sometimes went no further than questions such as "Do you like girls?" The rejection rate, one wit suggested, was high because "the Army doesn't want maladjusted soldiers, at least below the rank of major."

Jeremiads frequently derided the nation's martial potential. A Gallup poll of October 1940 found a prevailing view of American youth as "a flabby, pacifistic, yellow, cynical, discouraged, and leftist lot." A social scientist concluded that "to make a soldier out of the average free American citizen is not unlike domesticating a very wild species of animal," and many a drill sergeant agreed. Certainly no hate yet lodged in the bones of American troops, no urge to close with an enemy who before December 7, 1941, seemed abstract and far away. *Time* magazine reported on the eve of Pearl Harbor that soldiers were booing newsreel shots of Roosevelt and General George C. Marshall, the Army chief of staff, while cheering outspoken isolationists.

Equipment and weaponry were pathetic. Soldiers trained with drainpipes for antitank guns, stovepipes for mortar tubes, and brooms for rifles. Money was short, and little guns were cheaper than big ones; no guns were cheapest of all. Only six medium tanks had been built in 1939. A sardonic ditty observed: "Tanks are tanks and tanks are dear / There will be no tanks again this year." That in part reflected an enduring loyalty to the horse. "The idea of huge armies rolling along roads at a fast pace is a dream," *Cavalry Journal* warned in 1940, even after the German blitzkrieg signaled the arrival of mechanized warfare. "Oil and tires cannot like forage be obtained locally." The Army's cavalry chief assured Congress in 1941 that four well-spaced horsemen could charge half a mile across an open field to destroy an enemy machine-gun nest without sustaining a scratch. "The motor-mad advocates are obsessed with a mania for excluding the horse from war," he told the Horse and Mule Association of America, four days before Pearl Harbor. The last Regular Army cavalry regiment would slaughter its mounts to feed the starving garrison on Bataan in the Philippines, ending the cavalry era not with a bang but with a dinner bell.

To lead the eventual host of 8 million men, the Army had only 14,000 professional officers when mobilization began in 1940. The interwar officer corps was so thick with deadwood that one authority called it a fire hazard; swagger sticks, talisman of the Old Army, could serve for kindling. Secret War Department committees known as plucking boards began purging hundreds of officers who were too old, too tired, too inept. Not a single officer on duty in 1941 had commanded a unit as large as a division in World War I; the average age of majors was forty-eight. The National Guard was even more ossified, with nearly one-quarter of Guard first lieutenants over forty, and senior ranks dominated by political hacks of certifiable military incompetence. Moreover, Guard units in eighteen states were stained with scandal—embezzlement, forgery, kickbacks, and nepotism.

Yet slowly the giant stirred. Congress in 1940 had given the Army $9 billion, more than all the money spent by the War Department since 1920. The fabled arsenal of democracy began to build steam, although nearly half of all military production in 1941 went to Lend-Lease recipients (including 15,000 amputation saws and 20,000 amputation knives to the Soviets). A remarkable cadre of promising professional officers began to emerge. The two-year, three-month, and seven-day preparation period was over. It was time to fight.

But where? American strategists since the early 1920s had considered Tokyo the most likely enemy, as the United States and Japan vied for dominance in the Pacific. But in 1938 a series of informal conversations with the British marked the start of an increasing Anglo-American intimacy, nurtured by a growing conviction in Washington that Germany was mortally dangerous and that the Atlantic sea-lanes must always be controlled by friendly forces. Among potential adversaries, Germany had the largest industrial base and the greatest military capacity, and therefore posed the biggest threat. A U.S. strategy paper of November 1940 concluded that if Britain lost the war "the problem confronting us would be very great; and while we might not lose everywhere, we might, possibly, not win anywhere."

An evolving series of American war plans culminated in a strategic scheme called RAINBOW 5, which in the spring of 1941 posited joint action by the United States, Britain, and France in the event of America's entry into war, with the early dispatch of U.S. troops "to effect the decisive defeat of Germany, or Italy, or both." Forces in the Pacific would remain on the strategic defensive until European adversaries had been clubbed into submission. Even the debacle at Pearl Harbor failed to shake the conviction of Roosevelt and his military brain trust that "Germany first" was conceptually sound, and this remained the most critical strategic principle of the Second World War.

The smoke had hardly cleared from Pearl Harbor when Churchill arrived in Washington for extensive talks. The conference, code-named ARCADIA, failed to produce a specific Anglo-American plan of attack, but the prime minister and president reaffirmed the Germany-first decision. Moreover, on January 1, 1942, twenty-six countries calling themselves the "united nations" signed an agreement to forswear any separate peace without mutual concurrence and to make a common cause of "life, liberty, independence, and religious freedom, and to preserve the rights of man and justice."

The American idea of how to defeat the Third Reich was simple and obvious: drive straight for Berlin. "Through France passes our shortest route to the heart of Germany," declared Marshall, the Army chief of staff. It was only 550 miles from the northwest coast of France to the German capital, over flat terrain with a sophisticated road and rail network that also sliced through the core of Germany's war industry. If Hitler was the objective, the American instinct was to "go for him bald-headed and as soon as possible, by the shortest and most direct route," a British general later noted. The Yanks, another British officer agreed, "wanted revenge, they wanted results, and they wanted to fight."

Direct, concentrated attack was an American strategic tradition often linked to Ulysses S. Grant in the Civil War. The surest route to victory was to obliterate the enemy's army and destroy his capacity to make war. As the world's greatest industrial power, with a military expanding to 12 million men, the United States could do that—particularly now that the nation belonged to a powerful alliance that included the British empire, the Soviet Union, and China. The prevailing impatience to get on with it was voiced by a young American general from Kansas, whose diligence, organizational acumen, and incandescent grin had made him a rising star in the War Department. "We've got to go to Europe and fight," Dwight David Eisenhower scribbled in a note to himself on January 22, 1942. "And we've got to quit wasting resources all over the world—and still worse—wasting time."

As the new chief of war plans for the Army's General Staff, Eisenhower helped draft the blueprint that would convert these strategic impulses into action. A three-part American proposal evolved in the spring of 1942. Under a plan code-named BOLERO, the United States would ferry troops and matériel across the Atlantic for more than a year to staging bases in Britain. This massing of forces would be followed in April 1943 by ROUNDUP, an invasion across the English Channel to the coast of France by forty-eight American and British divisions supported by 5,800 aircraft. The spearhead would then seize the Belgian port of Antwerp before wheeling toward the Rhine. If Germany abruptly weakened before that invasion, or if Soviet forces in the east appeared in danger of collapse and needed diversionary help, a smaller, "emergency" assault by five to ten divisions—code-named SLEDGEHAMMER—would be launched in the fall of 1942 to secure a beachhead in France, perhaps at Cherbourg or Calais, and tie up as many German soldiers as possible.

Churchill and his commanders concurred in principle with this strategy in April 1942, then immediately began backing away. The British already had been expelled from the Continent three times in this war—from Dunkirk, from Norway, and from Greece—and they were reluctant to risk a fourth drubbing with a hasty cross-Channel attack. "We shall be pushed out again," warned Alan Brooke. More than two dozen German divisions were now based in France, and the Germans could operate on interior lines to shift additional forces from the east and seal off any Allied beachhead.

SLEDGEHAMMER particularly discomfited the British, who would have to provide most of the troops for the operation while American units were still making their way across the Atlantic. Studies of Channel weather over the previous decade showed the frequency of autumn gales that could dismast an Allied expeditionary force as surely as the Spanish Armada had been wrecked in 1588. The Axis enemy would also have a 6-to-1 air advantage and could reinforce the point of attack three times faster than the Allies could; in all likelihood, the Wehrmacht defenders in France would need no reinforcement from the Russian front to bottle up or even massacre an Allied bridgehead that would be so weak some skeptics called the plan TACKHAMMER. Hitler had begun constructing formidable coastal fortifications from above the Arctic Circle to the Spanish border on the Bay of Biscay, and a few planners considered *Festung Europa*, Fortress Europe, impregnable: in their view, the Allies would have to land in Liberia—midway down the west coast of Africa—and fight their way up.

Churchill shared his military commanders' misgivings. "He recoiled in horror from any suggestion of a direct approach" in attacking Europe, one British general later recalled. A disastrous Allied defeat on the French coast, the prime minister warned, was "the only way in which we could possibly lose this war." If eager to accommodate his American saviors, he was also mindful of the million British dead in World War I. A French invasion, he believed, could cost another half million and, if it failed, accomplish nothing. "Bodies floating in the Channel haunted him," George Marshall later acknowledged. Marshall's own reference to SLEDGEHAMMER as a "sacrifice play" to help the Russians hardly was comforting.

Whereas the dominant American strategic impulse was a direct campaign of mass and concentration, the British instinctively avoided large-scale land campaigns. For centuries, Britain had relied on superior naval power to protect the Home Islands and advance her global interests. She was accustomed to protracted wars in which she minimized her losses and her risks, outmaneuvering opponents and restricting combat to the periphery of the empire. The catastrophic stalemate in the trenches from 1914 to 1918 was an exception to the wisdom of the strategic rule. Churchill even hoped that, by encircling and squeezing Hitler's empire, Allied forces could foster rebellions by the subjugated peoples of Europe; with the Wehrmacht enervated by such revolts, an Anglo-American force could swiftly dispatch a depleted, exhausted Germany.

North Africa seemed a plausible place to start. British officers had first floated the possibility of joint Anglo-American action there in August 1941. Churchill raised the notion again during the ARCADIA conference in Washington at the end of the year, when the plan was assigned the code-name SUPER GYMNAST, and he continued to bring it up throughout the spring with the dogged enthusiasm of a missionary.

Punctuating each point with a stab of his trademark cigar, the prime minister ticked off the advantages to anyone within earshot: the occupation of Morocco, Algeria, and Tunisia could trap the Afrika Korps between the new Anglo-American force and the British Eighth Army already fighting Rommel in Egypt; Allied possession of North Africa would reopen the Mediterranean routes through the Suez Canal, shortening the current trip around the Cape of Good Hope by thousands of miles and saving a million tons of shipping; green American soldiers would get combat experience in conditions less harrowing than a frontal assault on France; the operation would require fewer landing craft and other battle resources than a cross-Channel attack; the Vichy government might be lured back into the Allied camp; and the operation could be mounted in 1942, in keeping with Roosevelt's wishes to help the Soviets as soon as possible and to expedite the entry of American soldiers into the war.

"This has all along been in harmony with your ideas," Churchill told the president. "In fact, it is your commanding idea. Here is the true second front of 1942."

The American military disagreed, adamantly and then bitterly. North Africa was a defeatist sideshow, a diversion, a peck at the periphery. Even before Pearl Harbor, a War Department memo warned that an attack in Africa would provide only an "indirect contribution to the defeat of the Nazis." That obdurate conviction hardened through the first six months of 1942. Another memo, in June 1942, concluded that the invasion of North Africa "probably will not result in removing one German soldier, tank, or plane from the Russian front."

To many American officers, the British proposal seemed designed to further London's imperial ambitions rather than win the war quickly. The Mediterranean for centuries had linked the United Kingdom with British interests in Egypt, the Persian Gulf, India, Australia, and the Far East. Old suspicions resurfaced in Washington that American blood was to be shed in defense of the British empire, particularly after Japanese armies swept across Hong Kong, Singapore, and Burma to threaten India. U.S. Army officers recalled a bitter joke from 1917: that "AEF" stood not for "American Expeditionary Force" but for "After England Failed."

Following another visit by Churchill to Washington in mid-June 1942, the fraternal bickering intensified and the Anglo-Americans entered what turned out to be the most fractious weeks of their wartime marriage. On July 10, Marshall and the chief of naval operations, Admiral Ernest J. King, suggested to Roosevelt that if the British continued to insist on "scatterization" in North Africa, "the U.S. should turn to the Pacific for decisive action against Japan." The irascible King, who had once been accused by Roosevelt of shaving with a blowtorch, went so far as to predict that the British would never invade Europe "except behind a Scotch bagpipe band." Roosevelt likened this repudiation of Germany-first as "taking up your dishes and going away"; he asked Marshall and King to send detailed plans for "your Pacific Ocean alternative" that very afternoon—knowing that no such plans existed.

Roosevelt was so enigmatic and opaque that his own military chiefs often had to rely on the British for clues to his inner deliberations. But increasingly he seemed beguiled by Churchill's arguments rather than those of his own uniformed advisers. Although Roosevelt never had to enunciate his war principles—and they could surely have been scribbled on a matchbook cover—foremost among them was "the simple fact that the Russian armies are killing more Axis personnel and destroying more

Axis matériel than all the other twenty-five United Nations put together," as he had observed in May. The War Department now estimated that the Red Army confronted 225 German divisions; six faced the British in Egypt. If Soviet resistance collapsed, Hitler would gain access to limitless oil reserves in the Caucasus and Middle East, and scores of Wehrmacht divisions now fighting in the east could be shifted to reinforce the west. The war could last a decade, War Department analysts believed, and the United States would have to field at least 200 divisions, even though it was now hard pressed to raise fewer than half that number. A gesture of Anglo-American good faith beyond Lend-Lease was vital to encouraging the Soviets. After promising Moscow in May that the United States "expected" to open a second front before the end of the year, Roosevelt in July told his lieutenants that "it is of the highest importance that U.S. ground troops be brought into action against the enemy in 1942."

Other factors also influenced the president's thinking. More than half a year after Pearl Harbor, restive Americans wanted to know why the country had yet to counterpunch against the Axis; November's congressional elections would provide a referendum on Roosevelt's war leadership, and polls indicated that he and his Democratic Party could take a drubbing. Demonstrators in London's Trafalgar Square and elsewhere were chanting "Second front, *now!*" in sympathy with the besieged Russians. By seizing Africa, the Allies would deny the Axis potential bases for attacking shipping lanes in the South Atlantic or even striking the Americas. The Pacific campaign, although hardly swinging in the Allies' favor, had stabilized, permitting the strategic defensive envisioned in the RAIN-BOW 5 plan; but unless another battlefront opened across the Atlantic, U.S. forces would drain into the Pacific. In May, the U.S. Navy in the Coral Sea had attacked a Japanese fleet escorting invasion troops bound for the Solomon Islands and New Guinea; losses on the two sides had been nearly equal. A month later, four Japanese aircraft carriers were sunk at the battle of Midway, marking the first unambiguous American victory of the war. Operation WATCHTOWER, the first Allied counteroffensive against Japan, was about to unfold with the landing of 16,000 American troops on an island in the Solomons: Guadalcanal.

The campaign against Germany and Italy, on the other hand, was faltering. Wehrmacht troops had overrun the Don River in southern Russia and were approaching Stalingrad, on the Volga. Except for Britain and neutrals such as Spain, Sweden, and Switzerland, all Europe belonged to the Axis. In Egypt, the Afrika Korps was only sixty miles from Alexandria and the Nile valley, gateway to the Suez Canal and Middle East oil fields.

In Cairo, refugees jammed the rail stations, and panicky British officers burned secret papers in their gardens. After a long siege, Rommel had captured 30,000 British Commonwealth troops in the Libyan port garrison of Tobruk. Hitler rewarded him with a field marshal's baton, to which prize Rommel replied, "I am going on to Suez."

By chance, the bad news from Tobruk reached Churchill on June 21, 1942, while he stood next to Roosevelt's desk in the Oval Office. Marshall's face was grimmer than usual as he strode in with a pink dispatch sheet. Churchill read the message and took a half step back, his ruddy face gone ashen. Roosevelt's response was a thrilling gesture of magnanimity to a friend in need. "What can we do to help?" the president asked.

In the short run, the Americans could, and did, strip 300 new Sherman tanks from the newly outfitted U.S. 1st Armored Division for shipment to British troops in Egypt. Marshall, Admiral King, and Harry Hopkins returned Churchill's visit by flying as a delegation to London for more strategic negotiations, but the talks bogged down even as the Americans conceded that an attack across the Channel that year was unlikely. In a limp gesture of mollification, the British took the three Yanks to see Oliver Cromwell's death mask and Queen Elizabeth's ring before they flew home.

Roosevelt had had enough. The time had come to end the protracted stalemate and get on with the war. After informing both Churchill and his own senior military advisers on July 25 that he intended to invade North Africa, he slammed the door on further discussion. At 8:30 P.M. on Thursday, July 30, he summoned his lieutenants to the White House and announced that, as he was commander-in-chief, his decision was final. North Africa was "now our principal objective." There would be no SLEDGEHAMMER against France. The African offensive was to occur "at the earliest possible date," preferably within two months.

The president had made the most profound American strategic decision of the European war in direct contravention of his generals and admirals. He had cast his lot with the British rather than with his countrymen. He had repudiated an American military tradition of annihilation, choosing to encircle the enemy and hack at his limbs rather than thrust directly at his heart. And he had based his fiat on instinct and a political calculation that the time was ripe.

In choosing Operation TORCH, as the North Africa invasion was now called, Roosevelt made several miscalculations. Despite Marshall's warnings, he refused to believe that a diversion to North Africa in 1942 precluded a cross-Channel invasion in 1943. He failed to see that the

Mediterranean strategy of encirclement precluded other strategies, or that more than a million American soldiers, and millions of tons of matériel, would be sucked into the Mediterranean in the next three years, utterly eviscerating the buildup in Britain. He continued to argue that "defeat of Germany means defeat of Japan, probably without firing a shot or losing a life."

Yet the president's decision was plausible, if not precisely wise. As Brooke had observed of the proposed cross-Channel attack: "The prospects of success are small and dependent on a mass of unknowns, whilst the chances of disaster are great." American planners considered the British argument for TORCH "persuasive rather than rational," but the American argument for SLEDGEHAMMER and ROUNDUP had been neither. Direct attack was premature; its adherents exemplified an amateurish quality in American strategic thinking that would ripen only as the war ripened.

The American military had been animated mostly by can-do zeal and a desire to win expeditiously; these traits eventually would help carry the day, but only when tempered with battle experience and strategic sensibility. One general later claimed that Army logisticians kept insisting they could support ten Allied divisions in Cherbourg although they were not certain where the French port was, much less what the condition of the docks might be or whence those divisions would come. Moving a single armored division required forty-five troopships and cargo ships, plus warship escorts, and moving the fifty divisions needed to sustain an invasion required far more ships than the Allies now possessed. Similarly, the critical issue of landing craft had been blithely ignored. "Who is responsible for building landing craft?" Eisenhower had asked in a May 1942 memo. With some planners estimating that an invasion of France required at least 7,000 landing craft, and others believing the number was really triple that, the hard truth was that by the fall of 1942 all the landing craft in Britain could carry only 20,000 men. Yet a U.S. War Department study had concluded that to draw significant numbers of German troops from the Russian front required at least 600,000 Allied soldiers in France. "One might think we were going across the Channel to play baccarat at Le Touquet, or to bathe at the Paris Plage!" Brooke fumed.

Roosevelt had saved his countrymen from their own ardor. His decision provoked dismay, even disgust, and would remain controversial for decades. "We failed to see," Marshall later said of his fellow generals, "that the leader in a democracy has to keep the people entertained." Eisenhower believed the cancellation of SLEDGEHAMMER might be remembered as the "blackest day in history"—a silly hyperbole, given the blackness of other days. The alienation many senior American officers felt from their British cousins could be seen in a War Department message of late August, proposing that "the Middle East should be held if possible, but its loss might prove to be a blessing in disguise" by giving the British their comeuppance and bringing them to their senses.

But the decision was made. The "thrashing around in the dark," as Eisenhower called it, was over; the dangerous impasse had been breached.

Much, much remained to be done. Problems ranging from the size and composition of the invasion force to the timing and location of the landings required solutions. In early August, TORCH planners moved into offices at Norfolk House on St. James's Square in London under the supervision of Eisenhower, who had recently been sent from Washington to Britain as commanding general of the European Theater of Operations. As a gesture of reconciliation, and in anticipation of the eventual American preponderance, the British proposed that the Allied expedition be commanded by an American. Churchill nominated Marshall, but Roosevelt was reluctant to give up his indispensable Army chief. Eisenhower, already overseas, had demonstrated impressive diligence and energy, and on August 13 he was named commander-in-chief of TORCH.

As the days grew shorter and the summer of 1942 came to an end, few could feel buoyed by news from the front:

Wehrmacht troops had reached the Volga, and the first shots were exchanged in the battle for Stalingrad. German U-boats, traveling in predatory "wolfpacks," were sinking ships faster than Allied yards could build them; a supply convoy to northern Russia lost thirteen of forty vessels, despite an escort of seventy-seven ships. The Chinese war effort against the Japanese had disintegrated. The fighting over the Solomon Islands had made Guadalcanal a shambles. The fall of Suez seemed imminent. Four of the seven aircraft carriers in the American fleet when the United States entered the war had been sunk. And antipathy between British and American confederates threatened to weaken the alliance even before the fight against their common enemy was joined.

Only seers or purblind optimists could guess that these portents foreshadowed victory. The Allies were not yet winning, but they were about to begin winning. Night would end, the tide would turn, and on that turning tide an army would wash ashore in Africa, ready to right a world gone wrong.

Part One

1. PASSAGE

A Meeting with the Dutchman

A FEW minutes past 10 A.M. on Wednesday, October 21, 1942, a twin-engine Navy passenger plane broke through the low overcast blanketing Washington, D.C., then banked over the Potomac River for the final approach to Anacostia Field. As the white dome of the Capitol loomed into view, Rear Admiral Henry Kent Hewitt allowed himself a small sigh of relief. Before dawn, Hewitt had decided to fly to Washington from his headquarters near Norfolk rather than endure the five-hour drive across Virginia. But thick weather abruptly closed in, and for an anxious hour the aircraft had circled the capital, probing for a break in the clouds. Usually a man of genial forbearance, Hewitt chafed with impatience at the delay. President Roosevelt himself had summoned him to the White House for this secret meeting, and although the session was likely to be little more than a courtesy call, it would never do for the man chosen to strike the first American blow in the liberation of Europe to keep his commander-in-chief waiting.

Kent Hewitt seemed an unlikely warrior. Now fifty-five, he had a high, bookish forehead and graying hair. Double chins formed a fleshy creel at his throat, and on a ship's bridge, in his everyday uniform, he appeared "a fat, bedraggled figure in khaki," as a British admiral once observed with more accuracy than kindness. Even the fine uniform he wore this morning fit like blue rummage, notwithstanding the flag officer's gold braid that trimmed his cuffs. A native of Hackensack, New Jersey, Hewitt was the son of a mechanical engineer and the grandson of a former president of the Trenton Iron Works. One uncle had been mayor of New York, another the superintendent of the Metropolitan Museum of Art. Kent chose the Navy, but as a midshipman in the Annapolis sail loft he was said to have been so frightened of heights that he "squeezed the tar out of the rigging." As a young swain he had enjoyed dancing the turkey trot; in recent decades, though, he was more likely to be fiddling with his slide rule or attending a meeting of his Masonic lodge.

Yet Hewitt had become a formidable sea dog. Aboard the battleship U.S.S. *Missouri*, he circled the globe for fifteen months with Theodore Roosevelt's Great White Fleet, displaying such a knack for navigation that the stars seemed to eat from his hand. As a destroyer captain in World War I, he had won the Navy Cross for heroism. Later he chaired the Naval Academy's mathematics department, and for two years after the invasion of Poland he ran convoy escorts between Newfoundland and Iceland, ferrying war matériel across the North Atlantic.

In April 1942, Hewitt had been ordered to Hampton Roads to command the Atlantic Fleet's new Amphibious Force; late that summer came Roosevelt's decision to seize North Africa in Operation TORCH. Two great armadas would carry more than 100,000 troops to the invasion beaches. One fleet would sail 2,800 miles from Britain to Algeria, with mostly British ships ferrying mostly American soldiers. The other fleet, designated Task Force 34, was Hewitt's. He was to sail 4,500 miles to Morocco from Hampton Roads and other U.S. ports with more than 100 American ships bearing 33,843 American soldiers. In a message on October 13, General Eisenhower, the TORCH commander, had reduced the mission to twenty-six words: "The object of the operations as a whole is to occupy French Morocco and Algeria with a view to the earliest possible subsequent occupation of Tunisia." The Allies' larger ambition in TORCH had been spelled out by Roosevelt and Churchill: "complete control of North Africa from the Atlantic to the Red Sea."

Through a tiny window over the plane's wing, Hewitt could see the full glory of Indian summer in the nation's capital. Great smears of color—crimson and orange, amber and dying green—extended from the elms around the Lincoln Memorial to the oaks and maples beyond the National Cathedral. Across the Potomac, the new Pentagon building filled Hell's Bottom between Arlington Cemetery and the river. Jokes had already begun circulating about the immense five-sided maze, including the story of a Western Union boy who entered the Pentagon on a Friday and emerged on Monday as a lieutenant colonel. Though it now owned the world's largest building, the Army was still leasing thirty-five other office complexes around the city, and cynics quipped that if the military were to seize enemy territory as quickly as it had conquered Washington, the war could end in a week.

The plane settled onto the runway and taxied to a hangar. Hewitt buttoned his jacket and hurried down the steps to the Navy staff car waiting on the tarmac. The car sped through the airfield gate and across the Anacostia River to Pennsylvania Avenue. Hewitt had enough time to swing by the Navy Department building downtown and check there for messages before heading to the White House.

"You do everything you can," he liked to say, "then you hope for the best." Since receiving the first top-secret orders for Task Force 34, he had done everything he could, to the verge of exhaustion. Every day brought new problems to solve, mistakes to fix, anxieties to quell. Rehearsals for the TORCH landings had been hurried and slipshod. With Axis predators sinking nearly 200 Allied vessels a month, including many along the American coast, all amphibious training had been moved inside the Chesapeake Bay, whose modest tides and gentle waves resembled not at all the ferocious surf typical of the Moroccan coast. During one exercise, only a single boat arrived on the designated beach, even though a lighthouse had provided a beacon on a clear night with a calm sea; the rest of the craft were scattered for miles along the Maryland shore. In another exercise, at Cove Point, ninety miles north of Norfolk, security broke down and the men stormed the beach to be greeted by an enterprising ice cream vendor. In Scotland, the training by troops bound for Algeria was going no better; sometimes it was conducted without the encumbrance of actual ships, because none were available. Troops moved on foot across an imaginary ocean toward an imaginary coast.

Would the eight Vichy French divisions in North Africa fight? No one knew. Allied intelligence estimated that if those troops resisted stoutly, it could take Eisenhower's forces three months just to begin the advance toward Tunisia. If U-boats torpedoed a transport during the Atlantic passage, how many destroyers should be left behind to pick up survivors? Hewitt was not certain he could spare *any* without jeopardizing the task force, and the prospect of abandoning men in the water gnawed at him. Had word of the expedition leaked? Every day he received reports that someone, somewhere had been talking too much. For the first months after its creation, the Amphibious Force was so secret that it used a New York City post office box as its mailing address. Only a select few now knew Hewitt's destination, but the existence of a large American fleet designed to seize a hostile shore could hardly be kept secret anymore. A few weeks earlier, Hewitt had received a letter from Walt Disney—written on stationery with the embossed letterhead "Bambi: A Great Love Story"—who offered to design a logo for the Amphibious Force. Ever the gentleman, Hewitt wrote back on October 7 with polite, noncommittal thanks.

The staff car crawled past Capitol Hill to Independence Avenue. Nationwide gasoline rationing would begin soon, but Washington's

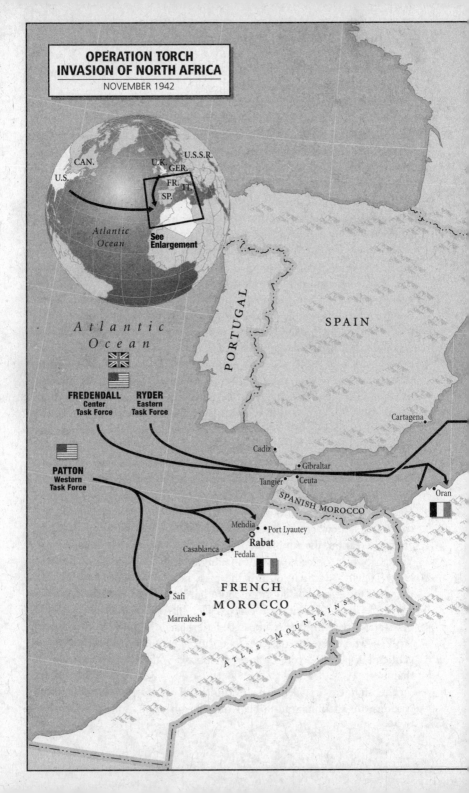

population had nearly doubled in the last three years, and for now the streets were jammed. Coffee rationing would begin even sooner—one cup per person per day—and diners had started hoarding for special customers, like speakeasies stocking up on liquor just before Prohibition. Bawling newsboys on street corners shouted the day's headlines from the various war fronts: fighting on Guadalcanal ebbs; Red Army at Stalingrad stops Nazi tank attacks; another American merchantman sunk in the Atlantic, the 500th U.S. ship lost to U-boats since Pearl Harbor. The domestic news was also war-related, if less febrile: the first meatless Tuesday had gone well in New York; penitentiary inmates with only one felony conviction were urged to apply for parole so they could serve in the Army; and a survey of department stores in Washington revealed that "there aren't any nylon stockings to be had for love or money."

The car pulled up to the Navy Department's blocky gray building, just south of the Mall. Hewitt climbed from the rear seat and hurried up the steps. *He* knew where all those stockings had gone. Flying from Norfolk that morning, he could see stevedores on the docks still trying to wedge 50,000 tons of food, gasoline, and munitions into the holds of ships moored across Hampton Roads. Among the secret cargoes in sealed crates were six tons of women's stockings and lingerie, to be used for barter with Moroccan natives. Clandestine military buyers had swept clean the store shelves all along the Eastern Seaboard.

For Hewitt, it was just another secret to keep.

Since Roosevelt's final decision on July 30, TORCH had grown so complex that planning documents now filled a pair of mail sacks, each weighing fifty pounds. Two issues in particular had occupied Anglo-American strategists, and in both instances the president—who referred to himself as "a pig-headed Dutchman"—had pressed his views relentlessly.

First, he insisted that almost no British troops participate in the initial landings. A seething Anglophobia had spread through Vichy France in the past two years as a consequence of several unhappy incidents: Royal Air Force bombers had accidentally killed 500 French civilians while attacking a Renault plant outside Paris. British forces had intervened in the French overseas dependencies of Syria and Madagascar. Britain had also sponsored a failed attack on the French port at Dakar, Senegal, by the Free French forces of Charles de Gaulle, whom Marshal Pétain and many French officers considered an impertinent renegade. And worst of all, in July 1940 British warships had issued an ultimatum to the Vichy fleet at Mers el-Kébir, near Oran, Algeria: lest the French ships fall into

German hands, the captains were told to sail for Britain or a neutral port. When the ultimatum was rejected, the British opened fire. In five minutes, they slaughtered 1,200 French sailors.

"I am reasonably sure a simultaneous landing by British and Americans would result in full resistance by all French in Africa, whereas an initial landing without British ground forces offers a real chance that there would be no French resistance or only a token resistance," Roosevelt cabled Churchill on August 30. To test this theory, the president commissioned a Princeton, New Jersey, firm to discreetly survey public opinion in North Africa. The poll results—drawn from a scientifically dubious sample of fewer than 150 respondents—reinforced Roosevelt's conviction.

There was skepticism in London. One British diplomat believed that Roosevelt's "spirit of Lafayette" merely reflected a sentimental Yankee affection for Paris, "where all good Americans hoped to go in the afterlife." But, having won on the larger issue of whether to invade Africa or France, Churchill chose to concur with the president. "I consider myself your lieutenant," he cabled Roosevelt. "This is an American enterprise in which we are your help mates." The president's further suggestion that British forces wait a full month after the invasion before coming to North Africa was gently rebuffed; the plan now called for Tommies to follow hard on the heels of their Yank cousins in Algeria.

The second vital issue involved where to land. Most British strategists, supported by Eisenhower, had stressed the importance of controlling Tunisia within two weeks of the invasion, before Axis troops from nearby Sicily and the Italian mainland could establish a bridgehead. "The whole conception of TORCH may stand or fall on this question of early Allied occupation of Tunisia," a British message advised. Once Tunisia was held, Allied control of Mediterranean shipping was all but assured. Rommel's Afrika Korps would be trapped in Libya, and the Allies would possess a southern springboard for further operations, against Sicily or the European continent.

These considerations argued for putting invasion forces from both armadas onto Mediterranean beaches in Algeria, and perhaps even as far east as the principal Tunisian port of Bizerte. "We should take great risks" to reach Tunis first, the British military chiefs of staff urged. Landings too far west should be avoided "like the plague" because of the hazard that the subsequent advance "eastward will be so slow as to allow Germans to reach Tunisia in force." In late August, Eisenhower's preliminary TORCH plan called for landings entirely within the Mediterranean, at the Algerian ports of Oran, Algiers, and Bône.

But General Marshall and War Department planners had other ideas. Tunisia and eastern Algeria lay within range of Axis warplanes on Sicily and beyond range of Allied fighters at Gibraltar. Landings at sites vulnerable to Luftwaffe attack would be extraordinarily perilous. Furthermore, the Americans feared that Hitler might lunge through neutral Spain and close the Straits of Gibraltar, trapping them in the Mediterranean as if cinching the drawstring of a sack. That argued for at least one landing on Morocco's Atlantic coast to guarantee an open supply line across the Atlantic.

For weeks, cables had fluttered back and forth in what Eisenhower called "a transatlantic essay contest." The Royal Navy believed that although the Strait of Gibraltar at its narrowest was just eight miles wide, it could not be controlled by enemy forces any more than the English Channel had been controlled. British planners also calculated that even with Madrid's consent to cross Spain—consent that, London insisted, was unlikely to be given—the Germans would need at least six divisions and more than two months to overpower Gibraltar.

In the American view, however, the risks were too great. The TORCH landings must succeed, Marshall argued, because failure in the first big American offensive of the war would "only bring ridicule and loss of confidence."

Roosevelt agreed, and again he intervened. "I want to emphasize," he cabled Churchill on August 30, "that under any circumstances one of our landings must be on the Atlantic." The president blithely dismissed the notion that Axis forces might build a Tunisian redoubt before the Allies arrived. In another message to the prime minister, he reiterated "our belief that German air and parachute troops cannot get to Algiers or Tunis any large force for at least two weeks after [the] initial attack."

Again Churchill acquiesced, not least because General Brooke, chief of the Imperial General Staff, shared the American disquiet and believed that diverting Hewitt's armada to Morocco "is a much wiser plan."

If not wiser, it was safer in the short run. But rarely are wars won in the short run. The Americans had been audacious to the point of folly in advocating SLEDGEHAMMER, the sacrificial landing of a mostly British force on the French coast. Now, with American soldiers predominant in TORCH, caution prevailed and audacity stole away. Hewitt's Task Force 34 would deposit one-third of the invasion force more than a thousand miles from Tunis. The invaders would bifurcate themselves by facing east *and* west, violating the hallowed principle of concentration and weakening their Sunday punch. In London, Eisenhower changed the odds of quickly capturing Tunis from "the realm of the probable to the remotely possible."

On September 5, the final decision was made to attempt landings at three sites in Morocco and at half a dozen beaches around Algiers and Oran. "Please make it before election day," Roosevelt asked Marshall. In this, the president would be disappointed. Various delays intruded, and on September 21, Eisenhower fixed the invasion date for Sunday morning, November 8, five days after the U.S. congressional elections.

TORCH remained breathtakingly bold, an enterprise of imagination and power. But at a critical moment, the Allies had taken counsel of their fears.

His business done at the Navy Department, Hewitt emerged at 1 P.M. to find that the day had turned warm and humid, with temperatures edging into the low seventies. The staff car picked him up and headed east on Independence Avenue before angling north across the Mall on 15th Street.

At the White House, a Secret Service agent directed his driver through the southeast gate, then led Hewitt on a circuitous route to avoid nosy reporters. Walking through the narrow corridors, the admiral saw that the mansion was battened down for combat. Blackout curtains draped the windows, and skylights had been painted black. Every room in the old tinderbox was equipped with a bucket of sand and a shovel, along with folded gas masks. The cluttered Fish Room, where Roosevelt kept trophies from his angling expeditions, was a reminder of the admiral's last encounter with the president. In December 1936, as skipper of the U.S.S. *Indianapolis,* Hewitt had taken Roosevelt on a monthlong trip to South America. He fondly remembered his passenger casting from the boat deck, then chortling with glee as he hauled in two fish. Roosevelt named them "Maine" and "Vermont," for the two states he had failed to carry in his recent reelection.

Waiting, as planned, in a small, vaulted antechamber of the Oval Office was the battle captain who would command the American troops in Morocco once Hewitt put them ashore: Major General George S. Patton, Jr. He, too, had been escorted by a roundabout route to avoid the press, but Patton was incapable of looking inconspicuous. Tall and immaculate in his starched pinks-and-greens, the crease in his trousers bayonet sharp, gloves folded just so in his left hand, Patton seemed every inch the warrior looking for a war.

Even as he shook Patton's hand and returned his broad smile, Hewitt remained uncertain what to make of this strange man. That he was a gifted and charismatic officer bound for glory seemed obvious. But, thoughtful and utterly charming one moment, he could be profane and truculent the next. Later in the war, military planners were to recommend at least six months' preparation from the day an invasion order was issued to the day the fleet sailed; the belated decision to invade Morocco had given Task Force 34 only seven weeks to ready one of the most complex military operations in American history. George Patton seemed determined to make every hour as difficult as possible.

Rather than move his headquarters to Hampton Roads, Patton had remained in his capacious office loft in the Munitions Building on the Mall, even as he railed against the "goddam fools in Washington." "By all means, as I have already written you, come see us as soon as you can," Hewitt wrote in exasperation. Without consulting the Navy, Army planners proposed Moroccan landing sites, one of which had no beach and another of which was boobytrapped with shoals. In recent days Patton had finally traded Washington for Norfolk, yet he still seemed deeply suspicious of naval officers in general—"that bunch of rattlesnakes," he called them—and of Hewitt in particular. Hewitt had been puzzled, then annoyed, then alarmed, and his mild complaints of August had escalated by mid-September to a formal protest at "the Army's failure to cooperate." Only Eisenhower's personal warrant to the War Department of his old friend's virtues had prevented Patton from being sacked and ending a luminous career before it began. Marshall added his own admonition in a private meeting with Patton: "Don't scare the Navy."

Another tense moment came when Hewitt proposed delaying TORCH a week to give the invaders a rising tide rather than risk having their boats stranded on the beaches by the ebb tide forecast for dawn on November 8. Patton objected with arm-flapping vigor, and even Hewitt's Navy superiors agreed that a postponement was impossible. Oddly, Patton seemed to take personally neither Hewitt's complaints about him nor their professional disagreements. Odder still, Hewitt found himself liking the man, and he suspected that Patton liked him, too. Hewitt could only chuckle at the shotgun marriages made by war.

At precisely two, the wide door to the Oval Office opened and Roosevelt spoke: "Come in, skipper and old cavalryman, and give me the good news." The president sat in his armless wheelchair, beaming and gesturing to a pair of empty chairs. Patton, unaware that Hewitt and Roosevelt had been shipmates six years earlier, looked nonplussed to find himself introduced to the president by the admiral.

"Well, gentlemen," Roosevelt asked with a wave of his cigarette, "what have you got on your minds?"

Hewitt had a great deal on his mind, but he tried to summarize the TORCH plan as succinctly as possible. Three hundred warships and nearly 400 transports and cargo vessels would land more than 100,000 troops—three-quarters of them American, the rest British—in North Africa. Task Force 34 would sail for Morocco on Saturday morning. The other armada would leave Britain shortly thereafter for Algeria. With luck, the Vichy French controlling North Africa would not oppose the landings. Regardless, the Allies were to pivot east for a dash into Tunisia before the enemy arrived.

The gray-green walls of the Oval Office gave the room a nautical air. Patton waited for a lull, then in his shrill, nasal voice said, "Sir, all I want to tell you is this—I will leave the beaches either a conqueror or a corpse."

Roosevelt smiled and deflected the remark with that jaunty toss of the head that George Marshall privately called the "cigarette-holder gesture." Did the general plan to mount his old cavalry saddle on a tank turret? the president asked Patton. Would he charge into action with his saber drawn?

The conversation rambled on, with much more left unsaid than said. Hewitt chose not to dwell on TORCH's risks. Unlike most senior officers, he had felt only relief upon learning that there would be no frontal assault against the French coast; even zealous advocates of SLEDGEHAMMER had been chastened in mid-August, when a raid by 6,000 Canadian and British troops on the German-occupied French port of Dieppe ended in catastrophe. Hewitt had watched a rehearsal for Dieppe during a visit to England, and he still found it hard to accept that half of those eager young men were now dead or in German prison camps.

But TORCH had its own hazards. Except for the Guadalcanal landings in August, it was the first large amphibious operation by the United States in forty-five years, and the most audacious ever. Some believed it to be the greatest amphibious gamble since Xerxes crossed the Hellespont in the fifth century B.C. The only modern precedent for landing on a hostile shore after a long sea voyage through perilous waters was the British disaster at Gallipoli in 1915, which cost a quarter of a million Allied casualties. The initial mission of seizing three port cities—Casablanca, Algiers, and Oran—was complicated by the need to land at nine coastal sites scattered across 900 miles. And not only U-boats menaced Task Force 34: so would the sea, for the long fetch across the Atlantic often brought mountainous waves to the Moroccan coast.

For his part, Roosevelt chose not to mention the War Department's lingering resentment of TORCH—even his secretary of war, Henry L. Stimson, had accused him of the "wildest kind of dispersion debauch," and called North Africa "the president's great secret baby." Nor did the president complain about delays in the invasion date, although he must have suspected how badly his party would fare in the elections, less than two weeks away. (The Democrats were to lose almost sixty congressional seats to a disgruntled electorate unaware that their nation was about to strike back.)

After half an hour, the conversation drifted into trivialities. Roosevelt offered Hewitt detailed advice on how to moor a ship with a stern anchor to keep her head into the wind, a tactic he had once employed with a yacht. Patton made a final effort to pull the discussion back to TORCH. "The admiral and I feel that we must get ashore regardless of cost, as the fate of the war hinges on our success," he told the president. But the meeting was over. "Of course you must," Roosevelt replied with a final cigarette-holder gesture. He ushered them out the door with handshakes and a hearty "Godspeed."

Patton returned to the Munitions Building. Hewitt drove directly to Anacostia Field and flew to Hampton Roads. By late afternoon he was back in his office, a tiny converted bedroom in the Hotel Nansemond at Ocean View. He had been gone only ten hours, but a thick stack of papers awaited him, including weather reports for Africa and the Atlantic, and the latest intelligence on German U-boats.

You do everything you can, then you hope for the best. Night had fallen by the time he stepped into his admiral's barge at the Willoughby Spit boat landing. The coxswain steered across Hampton Roads toward the Hotel Chamberlin at Fortress Monroe, where Hewitt had a suite with his wife, Floride. He studied the silhouettes of the ships moored in the great bay. Their superstructures loomed against the skyline, inky black but for the occasional orange glow of cigarettes on the weather decks. In two days, this fleet would carry 33,843 soldiers, every last one of them his responsibility.

Hewitt ate a quick supper at the Chamberlin, then moved to an arm-chair in the sitting room and unfolded the afternoon newspaper. A few minutes later, Floride Hewitt looked in on her husband and screamed: he lay crumpled on the floor. Hewitt sat up slowly, more bemused than shaken. "I guess I just dropped off," he said. The barge was dispatched for a medical officer, who examined Hewitt and pronounced him healthy but exhausted. The admiral, he admonished, really should get more rest.

Gathering the Ships

A N unholy din rolled across Hampton Roads at dawn on October 22. Aboard a dozen ships at five sets of piers, sailors in dungarees and white pillbox caps ripped out linoleum decks, wood paneling, and cork insulation. Hundreds of other swabs with hammers and chisels scraped the painted bulkheads to bare metal. Raging ship fires in the Solomon Islands earlier that fall had convinced the Navy to strip Task Force 34 of all combustible furnishings, giving the fleet the fighting trim of an unfinished garage.

From Norfolk and Portsmouth on the southern rim of the Roads, to Newport News and Hampton in the north, tugboats bullied another clutch of cargo ships into the wharves. Stevedore battalions swarmed onto each vessel, stacking hatch covers on an aft deck and swinging a boom over the exposed hold. Gangwaymen clipped the cargo sling to a pallet on the dock, and chuffing steam winches hoisted another load onto the ship. Above the cacophony of welders and riveters and that infernal scraping, the strains of "Over There" drifted from a warehouse where the port band practiced its war repertoire. *The Yanks are coming, the Yanks are coming. . . .*

Into the holds went tanks and cannons, rubber boats and outboard motors, ammunition and machine guns, magnifying glasses and step-ladders, alarm clocks and bicycles. Into the holds went: tractors, cement, asphalt, and more than a million gallons of gasoline, mostly in five-gallon tins. Into the holds went: thousands of miles of wire, well-digging machinery, railroad cars, 750,000 bottles of insect repellent, and 7,000 tons of coal in burlap bags. Into the holds went: black basketball shoes, 3,000 vehicles, loudspeakers, 16,000 feet of cotton rope, and $100,000 in gold coins, entrusted to George Patton personally. And into the holds went: a platoon of carrier pigeons, six flyswatters and sixty rolls of fly-paper for each 1,000 soldiers, plus five pounds of rat poison per company.

A special crate, requisitioned in a frantic message to the War Department on October 18, held a thousand Purple Hearts.

In theory, only 800 people in the world knew the destination of the TORCH armadas; many boxes had been sealed and placed under guard to avoid leaking any hint of French North Africa. Phrase books with pronunciation keys, to be distributed at sea, perfectly captured Allied ambivalence, giving the French for both "I am your friend" and "I will shoot you if you resist." A propaganda radio station, cobbled together with a transmitter salvaged in Jersey City and a generator from a South Carolina cotton mill, was secretly installed in the U.S.S. *Texas,* along with a script to be broadcast to Berber tribes: "Behold, we the American holy warriors have arrived. . . . We have come to set you free."

Quartermasters had rounded up not only all that lingerie but also 70,000 pairs of goggles and a comparable number of havelocks—neck cloths—sewn at a secret plant in Philadelphia, as well as 10 million salt tablets and 67,000 American-flag armbands, with 138,000 safety pins to secure them to uniform sleeves. Black-lettered labels on the boxes warned: "Do not open until destination is reached." A thirty-day supply of poison gas bombs, shells, and mines had been tentatively consigned to a follow-up convoy, then canceled in late September after Allied commanders deemed it "most unlikely" that an enemy would use chemical weapons early in the North Africa campaign.

Using a Michelin commercial road guide to Morocco, a government printing plant outside Washington had spent weeks reproducing sixty tons of maps, which were manhandled into the holds along with sealed bundles of Baedekers, old issues of *National Geograpic,* French tourist guidebooks, and volume "M" of various encyclopedias. Armed couriers brought aboard plaster-of-Paris relief maps of Moroccan ports and coasts; the War Department had found that men drafted from the confectioners' and bakers' union became the best model makers. Other secret crates contained peculiar fifty-four-inch open tubes and three-pound darts—along with instruction sheets, because almost no one in the task force had ever heard of a "launcher, rocket, antitank, 2.36-inch, M9," soon to be known as a bazooka.

All cargo was supposed to be combat loaded, a key principle of assault in which equipment is stowed in reverse order of the sequence needed upon landing under fire. Instead, the only principle in effect was chaos. Matériel had been cascading into port since late September, in rail cars so poorly marked that at one point all loading stopped while soldiers pawed through 700 mysterious boxcars that had been diverted to a Richmond siding.

Different railroads served different piers, so that misdirected freight had to be lightered across the bay. Docks grew cluttered with dunnage; cargo holds were packed so haphazardly that soldiers climbing over vehicles in search of their kit broke nearly a third of the windshields. Ammunition needed for ballast arrived late, forcing some ships to warp back to the docks for reloading. Artillery shells, loose grenades, and TNT were simply dumped on the decks, or in passageways, staterooms, and troop holds. The captain of U.S.S. *Lakehurst* confided that a torpedo would sink his ship in five minutes—unless the stocks of gasoline and ammo were hit, in which case it would be quicker.

An officer with a twisted mind and a classical education had borrowed the motto for Hampton Roads Port of Embarkation from the *Aeneid*: "*Forsan et haec olim meminissee iuvabit.*" "Someday, perhaps, the memory of even these things will be pleasant." Someday, perhaps, but not soon.

On this disorderly Thursday, Patton flew to Norfolk from Washington in a C-47 transport plane with his tin suitcase and an entourage of eight staff officers. In his slashing, runic handwriting he had written his will and a long treatise to his wife, Bea, on how to care for their horses in his absence. He also wrote several farewell letters. To his brother-in-law: "My proverbial luck will have to be working all out. All my life I have wanted to lead a lot of men in a desperate battle; I am going to do it." To a family friend, he noted that by the time she read his letter, "I will either be dead or not. If I am, please put on a good Irish wake." Now, striding from ship to ship along the wharves, Patton inspected the cargo with the possessive eye of a man who intended to use every last bullet, bomb, and basketball shoe: When he asked a young quartermaster captain how the loading was proceeding, the officer replied, "I don't know, but my trucks are getting on all right." Patton took a moment to scribble in his diary: "That is the answer. If everyone does his part, these seemingly impossible tasks get done. When I think of the greatness of my job and realize that I am what I am, I am amazed, but on reflection, who is as good as I am? I know of no one."

It was a fair self-assessment by a man who had spent the past four decades preparing for this moment, since the day he had arrived as a plebe at West Point. More than a quarter-century had gone by since his first intoxicating taste of battle and fame, during the Punitive Expedition to Mexico in 1916, when he had briefly become a national hero for killing three banditos and strapping their bodies to his automobile running boards like game trophies. He had been a temporary colonel at age thirty-two in the Great War, and a founding father of armored warfare. Then, his career had seemed all but over, mired in the lethargy of the interwar Army. At the age of fifty, upon reading J.F.C. Fuller's classic *Generalship: Its Diseases and Their Cures*, Patton had wept bitterly because eighty-nine of the one hundred great commanders profiled were younger than he. Now, when he was fifty-six, his hour had come round.

He was a paradox and would always remain one, a great tangle of calculated mannerisms and raw, uncalculated emotion. Well-read, fluent in French, and the wealthy child of privilege, he could be crude, rude, and plain foolish. He had reduced his extensive study of history and military art to a five-word manifesto of war: "violent attacks everywhere with everything." In less than three years he would be the most celebrated American battle captain of the twentieth century, a man whose name—like those of Jeb Stuart and Phil Sheridan—evoked the dash and brio of a cavalry charge. In less than four years he would be dead, and the *New York Times* obituary would offer the perfect epitaph: "He was not a man of peace."

"Give me generals who are lucky," Roosevelt had recently told a British officer. In their encounter in the Oval Office the previous afternoon, the president had shrewdly sized up Patton as a man who was lucky and who also believed in his luck. "Patton is a joy," Roosevelt had written after the meeting. For his part, typically, Patton dwelt on his disappointment at the president's failure to deliver a more stirring victory-or-death speech to Admiral Hewitt, whose resolve Patton still doubted. "A great politician," Patton told his diary after leaving the White House, "is not of necessity a great military leader."

Nor was a great military leader of necessity a great politician, as Patton had repeatedly demonstrated during the preparations for TORCH. While Hewitt readied his ships, Patton readied his men, and he had approached the task by imposing his will on everything and everyone in his path.

His command for TORCH consisted of three divisions pieced together from other units—the 9th Infantry, the 3rd Infantry, and the 2nd Armored; eight other divisions had been so ransacked of troops and equipment to fill out the departing force that six months would pass before they recovered. In the past two weeks, Patton had traveled to staging areas across Virginia and North Carolina to inspect the troops and "put iron in their souls." One commander later recalled that he always knew when Patton had visited because the units so honored invariably called to report that assorted officers "had been ordered into arrest after incurring his wrath." On October 14, Patton sent identical letters to all his senior commanders: "If you don't succeed, I don't want to see you alive," he advised. "I see no point in surviving defeat, and I am sure that if all of you enter into battle with equal resolution, we shall conquer, and live long, and gain more glory."

In a dinner toast at one base, Patton declared, "Here's to the wives. My, what pretty widows you're going to make." His advice to the 9th Division for defeating the Germans was: "Grab those pusillanimous sons-a-bitches by the nose and kick 'em in the balls." To others, he spoke of slaughtering "lousy Hun bastards by the bushel." At Fort Bragg, while he was addressing troops he had once commanded in the 2nd Armored Division, tears coursed down his cheeks and he stalked from the stage without a word. The men roared their approval. In his diary, Patton had once rebuked himself for being "inclined to show emotion, a most unmilitary trait."

On Friday morning, October 23, more than 150 troop commanders, ship captains, and senior staff officers filed into a tightly guarded Army warehouse in Norfolk. Hewitt spoke briefly, revealing to most for the first time that they were bound for Africa. For more than four hours, the TORCH planners reviewed the operation in intricate detail. They finished with the proper procedures for burying the dead and registering their graves.

Then Patton took the stage in breeches and riding boots, ivory-handled pistols on either hip. He roused the men from their torpor by announcing that he would shoot any American soldier molesting a Moroccan woman.

"If you have any doubts as to what you're to do, I can put it very simply," he said in his jarring falsetto. "The idea is to move ahead, and you usually know where the front is by the sound of gunfire. To make it perfectly clear to you: suppose you lose a hand or an ear is shot off, or perhaps a piece of your nose, and you think you should go back to get first aid. If I see you, it will be the last goddamn walk you'll ever take. As an officer, you're expected to move ahead."

Then he challenged the Navy to emulate Admiral David Farragut, who had damned the torpedoes at Mobile Bay in 1864. But, Patton continued, "I'm under no illusion that the goddamn Navy will get us within a hundred miles of the beach or within a week of the date set for landing. It doesn't matter. Put us on Africa. We'll walk."

He finished with a flourish: "We shall attack for sixty days and then, if we have to, for sixty more. If we go forward with desperation, if we go forward with utmost speed and fight, these people cannot stand against us."

The men came to attention as Patton strode from the room. Most of the Navy officers, and even some of their Army counterparts, had never heard of George S. Patton before. Now they knew who he was.

As the hour of departure drew near, anarchy ruled the docks. Sometimes Patton contributed to the disorder. On one especially hellish morning his quartermasters changed the loading plan six times between eight and nine A.M.

More usually however, Patton, Hewitt, and their lieutenants demonstrated the inventive resolve that would characterize the American way of war for the duration. At the eleventh hour, medical officers abruptly realized that Task Force 34 had stockpiled only a small fraction of the blood plasma required. Recent experience had shown that plasma—the fluid remaining after removing red and white blood cells—was highly effective in keeping wounded soldiers alive, and when dried it could be stored without refrigeration for weeks. With authority from the War Department, the port surgeon by day's end had requisitioned virtually all the plasma east of the Mississippi River and organized three bombers to deliver it. When bad weather closed in on Norfolk, ground crews lit flares to guide home the pilots. Trucks raced from the airfield to the port with a thousand precious units just before the fleet weighed anchor.

No less dramatic was the saga of the S.S. *Contessa*. The War Department for weeks had sought a shallow-draft ship capable of navigating a dozen miles up a serpentine Moroccan river to the Port Lyautey airfield, one of Patton's prime objectives. A worldwide search turned up the *Contessa*, a salt-caked, rust-stained scow that drew just over seventeen feet and had spent most of her undistinguished career hauling bananas and coconuts from the Caribbean. She was ordered to Newport News. There the skipper, Captain William H. John, a thick-browed Briton with an untended mustache and a long, saggy face, learned he was to load more than a thousand tons of bombs, depth charges, and high-octane aviation fuel for a destination to be named later. The crew promptly jumped ship.

The *Contessa* was emptied of bananas and winched into dry dock on October 24 for a quick caulking of her leaky seams. Captain John and a Navy reserve lieutenant named A. V. Leslie then headed for the Norfolk jail, which state corrections officials recently had identified as the most squalid lockup in all Virginia. John and Leslie interviewed fifty inmates. Many were bibulous seamen, said to be "bleary-eyed and unsteady on their pins," but game for a voyage described only as high-paying, dangerous, and far from any Norfolk cellblock. Fifteen men were chosen and their sentences commuted. Navy guards with riot guns escorted them to the *Contessa*. Pumped dry and heavily patched, the fruiter slid from the dry dock with a clean bottom and made for Pier X, the ammunition wharf, to begin loading her cargo.

All the confusion that characterized the cargo loading now attended the convergence of 34,000 soldiers on Hampton Roads. Troop trains with blinds drawn rolled through Norfolk and Portsmouth, sometimes finding the proper pier and sometimes not. Many men were exhausted, having traveled all night or even all week. One artillery commander, suspecting they were bound for a tropical battlefield, had decided to acclimate his troops by sealing the windows on their train, transforming it into what one surviving officer described as "a sweltering inferno."

Military policemen patrolled the tracks and bus stations to watch for deserters. The Army in the past six months had charged more than 2,600 soldiers with desertion and convicted 90 percent of them. Indiscipline also plagued units that had been staging in southeast Virginia for weeks. So many men were sentenced to the crowded brig at Solomon's Island in Chesapeake Bay during amphibious training that there was a waiting list to serve time; on October 3 alone, thirty men had been court-martialed for various infractions. Sensing they were going to war, many troops drank until they were "knee-walkin' tight." Commanders distributed pamphlets warning, "The truth is that using the sex glands too much exhausts them and weakens a man." Many a weak man dragged himself to the pier.

Naughty Norfolk catered to those looking for sin before shipping out, notwithstanding the occasional sign that read "No dogs or sailors allowed." The town's iniquity grew with the arrival of each new regiment. Every night, thousands of men swarmed down East Main Street, described as "the largest, most solid block of beer joints in the world." Taxis became rolling brothels, and fleets of "girlie trailers" served the concupiscent. On October 18, vice officers arrested 115 people in the "largest morals raid in local history." His jail cells bulging, Norfolk's police chief asked the federal government to "give me a concentration camp . . . a camp large enough to handle two or three thousand women." The strains of war—including many U-boat attacks along the Virginia coast—pushed the town toward hysteria. Widespread rumor had it that local Negroes planned to massacre white citizens during a blackout; the plotters were even said to have purchased 300 icepicks at a downtown hardware store.

Sober and otherwise, the troops found their way to the twenty-eight transport ships. All public telephones at the wharves were disconnected, and port engineers erected a high fence around each dock area. "If you tell where you are going, you may never get there," security posters warned—pointlessly, because few men had any inkling of their destination. Some soldiers inflated condoms with natural gas from tent heaters and floated them toward town, with notes attached inviting any girl willing to comfort a departing warrior to infiltrate the security area. In a final, senseless act of confusion, the Army insisted the men board alphabetically rather than by tactical unit. Thousands struggled up the ramps with heavy barracks bags and wandered the companionways for hours in search of their comrades. Others disembarked at night, to re-form on the dock by platoon and then reboard.

Eight to twelve officers shared each stateroom. The ranks wedged into holds with bunks stacked four high and hammocks slung in every open space. "God must love enlisted men," they told one another; "he made so many of them." Poker and dice games raged in the stairwells. Sailors scraped and scraped. Boys barely old enough to shave lay in their bunks and stared vacantly at the bulkheads, or struggled to articulate in letters home what every one of them felt: *I'm scared. I miss you. I love you.*

A distant clatter of winches signaled the lifting of the last cargo slings. And a new sound joined the racket: the harsh grind of a thousand whetstones as soldiers put an edge on their bayonets and trench knives.

Dawn on October 24 revealed a forest of masts and fighting tops across Hampton Roads, where the greatest war fleet ever to sail from American waters made ready. Brief squalls blew in from the Atlantic, shrouding the ships in gray mist. Launches with hooded lanterns carried a few officers from a final night with their wives in the Chamberlin Hotel. Wrapped in a boat cloak, Hewitt boarded his flagship, the U.S.S. *Augusta.* The rising trill of a bosun's whistle announced the admiral's arrival.

From this very anchorage, dispatched with patriotic huzzahs and guided from the Roads by Theodore Roosevelt aboard his yacht, *Mayflower,* Hewitt had sailed the world with sixteen battleships in the Great White Fleet in 1907. To make the current departure less conspicuous, Hewitt arranged for a mid-ocean rendezvous with several of his biggest warships, including the new dreadnought *Massachusetts,* which had sortied from Maine. An even larger contingent awaited the task force near Bermuda. This group included the *Ranger,* his only true aircraft carrier, and four "escort" carriers—oil tankers overlaid with flight decks. None of the carriers had more than half a dozen experienced aviators; the Navy also reported that some crews included "a bare handful of officers and men who had previously seen salt water." But of the 102 ships in the fleet, only *Contessa* was seriously delayed. Still loading fuel and bombs at Pier X, she would follow the convoy in two days, alone.

Patton settled into the comfortable captain's cabin aboard *Augusta.* A stack of mystery novels lay on the table by his bunk, along with the Koran, which he planned to read during the passage. He had often practiced a fierce martial scowl in the mirror, but there was no need for dramatics now. He was alone, as only a battle commander could be, bound for the sharp corners of the world.

"This is my last night in America," he had written in his diary the previous evening. "It may be years and it may be forever. God grant that I do my full duty to my men and myself." He thought of his Wednesday morning in Washington three days earlier. Before going to the White House, he had driven up 16th Street to Walter Reed Army Hospital to call on his ancient hero, General John J. Pershing. A feeble eighty-two, Pershing had reminisced about their adventures in Mexico, where Patton had served as an unofficial aide-de-camp. "I can always pick a fighting man," Pershing said. "I like generals so bold they are dangerous." Patton kissed Pershing's hand, as desiccated as a fallen leaf, and asked for his blessing. "Good-bye, George," the old general replied. "God bless you and keep you and give you victory."

Generals so bold they are dangerous. He would take that challenge. To his old friend Eisenhower in London he had written, "We should plan either to conquer or to be destroyed at Casablanca." He also scribbled two notes to Bea. "It will probably be some time before you get a letter from me but I will be thinking of you and loving you," he wrote in one. In the other, to be opened only "when and if I am definitely reported dead," he confessed how difficult it was to convey his feelings for a woman he had known since they were both sixteen years old. He addressed her as if from beyond the grave: "Your confidence in me was the only sure thing in a world of dreadful uncertainty."

Shortly before seven A.M., the *Joseph T. Dickman* slipped her lines and moved into the stream, joined by the *Thomas Jefferson,* the *Leonard Wood,* and a stately procession of other transports. Destroyers darted ahead into the seaward mists—the lead ship in the position known as Dead Man's Corner—as the transports threaded the antisubmarine nets protecting Hampton Roads. With radio silence imposed, course adjustments swept across the fleet in an ecstasy of signal lamps and semaphore flags. Patrol planes and two silver blimps scouted the swept channel that angled eastward between Cape Henry and Cape Charles. Building to fourteen knots, the transports steamed out the drowned mouth of the James River, across Thimble Shoals and Tail of the Horseshoe. Soldiers cinched their life jackets and lined the weather-deck rails, staring in silence at Old Point Comfort.

The dawn was bright and blowing. Angels perched unseen on the shrouds and crosstrees. Young men, fated to survive and become old men dying abed half a century hence, would forever remember this hour, when an army at dawn made for the open sea in a cause none could yet comprehend. Ashore, as the great fleet glided past, dreams of them stepped, like men alive, into the rooms where their loved ones lay sleeping.

Rendezvous at Cherchel

EVEN before the fleet weighed anchor in Virginia, a small invasion van-guard had arrived off the African coast. This party comprised fewer than a dozen men; their mission—both courageous and daft—would become one of the most celebrated clandestine operations of the war.

It began with a single light. Major General Mark W. Clark stood on the bridge of the submarine H.M.S. *Seraph* at ten P.M. on October 21, peering through his binoculars at a bright beacon on the Algerian coast. Braced to absorb the submarine's roll, he raked the lenses across the white line of surf two miles away. After several days of creeping sub-merged across the Mediterranean from Gibraltar at four knots, Clark was desperate to get ashore. Though *Seraph* surfaced every night to recharge her batteries, the fetid air inside grew so stale each day that a struck match would not light. Clark and the four other American officers had passed the time playing countless rubbers of bridge or, after lessons from the British commandos aboard, hands of cribbage. Small bruises covered Clark's head; at six foot three inches tall, he found it impossible to dodge the sub's innumerable pipes and knobs.

"There's the sugar-loaf hill to the left. I can see its outline against the sky," Clark told *Seraph*'s commander, Lieutenant Norman L. A. Jewell. A pale glow to the east marked the fishing port of Cherchel, said to have been founded by Selene, daughter of Mark Antony and Cleopatra. Algiers lay another sixty miles up the coast. Clark focused again on the light burning in the seaward gable of an isolated farmhouse. "There's a beach below the house. A black splotch behind the beach—that's the grove of trees," Clark said. "Yessir, this is the place we're looking for."

Jewell ordered the diesel engines started. *Seraph* edged forward to within 400 yards of the breakers and hove to. A rising moon silvered the deck and dark sea. The commandos deftly assembled the folbots—two-man kayaks made with hickory frames and canvas skins. Clark and the other Americans rechecked their inventory, including money belts stuffed with greenbacks and $1,000 in Canadian gold pieces, which had been obtained with difficulty from the Bank of England vault in central London on Sunday afternoon. Every man wore his military uniform; six German saboteurs, captured in civilian clothes after being put ashore by U-boat in New York and Florida, had died in the District of Columbia electric chair two months earlier. No one on this mission wanted to be executed as a spy.

The first three pairs of men successfully grabbed the folbot rails and eased themselves into the waist holes. But as Clark was about to step from the submarine, the heavy lop flipped his boat and the commando already in it, Captain Godfrey B. Courtney. "I've got to get off!" Clark shouted. "I've got to go *now*." Another folbot was recalled and one of the Americans surrendered his seat to Clark. The submarine crew righted the capsized craft and fished Courtney from the sea. Ready at last, the men feathered away from *Seraph* with their double-scoop paddles, then turned in a V formation toward the beckoning light above the beach.

Mark Clark—Wayne, to his friends—was an odd choice to lead a clandestine mission behind enemy lines. As Eisenhower's deputy and chief planner, he knew more about Operation TORCH than any man alive. He also was among the few Americans privy to Ultra, the intelligence gathered through British decipherment of coded German radio messages—a secret so profound it was jokingly known as BBR, "burn before reading." Should Vichy forces capture Clark and surrender him to the Gestapo, the consequences would be incalculable, for both TORCH and the Allied cause.

That Eisenhower had entrusted this mission to Clark despite the hazards was a sign of both his naïveté as the new Allied commander-in-chief and his faith in Clark, who had become his indispensable alter ego. Clark's parents were an Army officer and the daughter of an immigrant Romanian Jew; as a West Point cadet, he had had himself baptized an Episcopalian, the creed considered most expedient for aspiring generals. At the academy he was known as Contraband for his guile in smuggling forbidden sweets into the barracks. More important, he fashioned a friendship with the company sergeant, an older cadet named Ike Eisenhower. Seriously wounded by shrapnel in 1918, Clark as a young captain between the world wars had been detailed to a Chautauqua tour, spreading the gospel of Army life with an ensemble of ventriloquists, roadcompany Macbeths, and Swiss bell ringers.

More recently, while serving as a War Department staff officer, he had been credited with designing the Army's assembly-line techniques for mass-producing divisions. In June 1941, his superior officer described him as "a rare combination of a most attractive personality with a stout heart and fine tact and intelligence." George Marshall had asked him, after Pearl Harbor, for a list of ten able brigadier generals from among whom to select a new war plans chief. "I'll give you one name and nine dittos," Clark replied. "Dwight D. Eisenhower." Years later Eisenhower would tell Clark, "You are more responsible than anybody in this country for giving me my opportunity."

The debt was repaid in August 1942, when Eisenhower made Clark his chief planner in London and the deputy TORCH commander. Soon the two Americans were favorites of Churchill, frequently summoned to No. 10 Downing Street or the prime minister's country home at Chequers for midnight skull sessions. Clark vividly described Churchill, dressed in his baggy smock and carpet slippers, expounding on strategy while drinking brandy or devouring a late supper:

> When the soup was put before him, he tackled it vigorously, his mouth about two inches from the liquid and his shoulders hunched over. He ate with a purring and slurping and the spoon went from mouth to plate so rapidly you could hardly see it until he was scraping the bottom of the bowl and bawling lustily, "More soup!" Turning to his guests, he'd say, "Fine soup, ain't it?"

Like Eisenhower, Clark had vaulted over hundreds of more senior officers in the past two years, during his ascent from major to major general. Meticulous and shrewd, he was also given to a relentless self-promotion that vexed his friends and outraged his rivals. Among the latter was Patton, who confided to his diary in late September: "He seems to me more preoccupied with bettering his own future than in winning the war." Another general called Clark the "evil genius" of the Allied force, but that epithet both diminished and caricatured his role. In truth, he was a gifted organizer—his daily memos to Eisenhower are tiny masterpieces of precision and efficiency—bedeviled by insecurities. "The more stars you have, the higher you climb the flagpole, the more of your ass is exposed," he once asserted. "People are always watching for opportunities to misconstrue your actions."

The voyage to Cherchel had been hastily organized at the secret request of General Charles Emmanuel Mast, a senior Vichy commander in Algiers. Mast had sent word that he wanted to confer with a high-ranking American about how the Allies might "gain entry practically without firing a shot." Clark insisted on leading the mission, "happy as a boy with a new knife" at both the prospective adventure and the chance to consummate the greatest American diplomatic coup of the war.

In addition to collecting intelligence through Ultra, the Allies had managed—by seduction and burglary—to purloin various Italian, Vichy French, and Spanish diplomatic codes. Washington also had an espionage network in North Africa: a dozen American vice consuls, known as the Twelve Apostles, who technically served as "food control officers" under a trade agreement still in effect between Vichy and Washington. But the Apostles were hardly professional spies. One had been a Coca-

Cola salesman in Mississippi, and another was described as "an orna-ment of Harry's Bar in Paris." A third later confessed, "I didn't even know how to pry open a desk drawer." The Apostle Kenneth Pendar, a former Harvard archaeologist, acknowledged, "We flew over . . . to drop like so many Alices into the African Wonderland." A dismissive German agent reported to Berlin: "All their thoughts are centered on their social, sexual, and culinary interests." Although the Apostles in fact collected useful information about ports, beaches, and coastal defenses, they could not answer the most fundamental question: Would the French fight? Clark intended to find out.

Only a howling dog and the murmuring surf broke the stillness as Clark and Captain Courtney waited 200 yards offshore. It was now shortly after midnight on October 22. Moonlight and that naked bulb dangling in the dormer revealed that the farmhouse on the bluff had a red tile mansard roof and stucco walls draped with vines. From the beach came the all-clear signal: the dash-dot-dash of a Morse "k." Leaning into their paddles, the two men skimmed neatly across the breakers and joined the others, who were already dragging their boats across the sand.

From an olive grove at the edge of the bluff stepped a tall, stooped man wearing a turtleneck sweater, sneakers, and a baseball cap. Robert Murphy was the top American diplomat in Algiers, as well as the Apos-tles' spymaster. "Welcome to North Africa," he said, with the insou-ciance of an experienced host greeting dinner guests. Clark abandoned the grand speech he had prepared in French and replied simply, "I'm damned glad we made it." The men shouldered the folbots and followed Murphy up the hill and through a large green gate. Entering a courtyard lined with palm trees, they passed the villa's owner, a French patriot named Henri Teissier, who stood watching nervously from the shadows. Eyeing Clark with his carbine, another Frenchman muttered, "A general with a rifle! What sort of army is this?" After hiding the boats in a kitchen storeroom, they settled into a small, untidy room in the farmhouse, toasting their good fortune with glasses of whiskey before stretching out for a nap.

Murphy was too excited to sleep. This rendezvous was his doing, and he believed that if it succeeded he could deliver North Africa into the Allied camp without bloodshed. Now forty-seven, with pale Irish skin and "a gaiety that brought out gaiety in others," he had grown up in Mil-waukee. A foot crushed in an elevator accident had kept him out of the military in World War I; instead, he studied law before joining the diplo-matic corps. Fluent in German and French, genial and cultured, he spent a decade in Paris; when the Germans marched in, he followed the rump government to Vichy on orders from Washington. He had helped arrange the secret shipment of nearly 2,000 tons of gold from the Bank of France to Dakar on an American cruiser, and Roosevelt, who always appreciated a charming operator, appointed Murphy his personal representative to French Africa with the admonition "Don't bother going through State Department channels." For months Murphy had shuttled between Washington and London, occasionally disguised as a lieutenant colonel because, as General Marshall noted, "nobody ever pays any attention to a lieutenant colonel." On frequent trips to North Africa, he smuggled radio transmitters in his diplomatic pouches.

By nature drawn to the conservative status quo, Murphy was distrusted by the Free French of Charles de Gaulle, who dismissed him as "inclined to believe that France consisted of the people he dined with in town." The British diplomat Harold Macmillan concluded that Murphy "has an incurable habit of seeing every kind of person and agreeing with them all in turn." Bob Murphy shrugged off such derision with an impish smile, secure in the conviction that he was doing Roosevelt's bidding.

At six A.M., General Mast arrived by car from Algiers with five staff officers. Murphy roused Clark and the others for introductions, followed by a breakfast of coffee and sardines in the living room. Short, burly, and fluent in English, Mast had been captured by the Germans in 1940 and repatriated after months in Saxony's notorious Königstein prison. His post as deputy commander of the Vichy army's XIX Corps notwithstanding, he had the heart of an insurrectionist. If the Americans were to invade North Africa, Mast told Clark, they should consider doing it in the spring, when rebel officers would be fully ready to help. Clark had strict orders not to disclose that TORCH was actually under way; he replied vaguely that it was "best to do something soon. We have the army and the means."

For more than four hours, the two generals exchanged mendacities. Mast urged the Americans to align themselves with his patron, Henri Giraud, a senior general whose bold recent escape from Königstein had galvanized French resistance. If you bring Giraud to Algiers from his hiding place in southern France, Mast promised, all North Africa will "flame into revolt" and rally around him as a symbol of French resurgence. With sufficient weapons—Mast nearly wept, describing the bedraggled Vichy troops—North Africa could field an army of 300,000 in common cause with the Allies, all under Giraud's inspiring generalship. He also urged a simultaneous invasion of southern France to prevent the Germans from seizing the fragment of the country controlled by Vichy.

Clark carefully sifted through Mast's proposals. He pledged immediate delivery of 2,000 automatic weapons to North Africa, a promise that would not be kept. In a rare show of candor, he admitted that simultaneous invasions of North Africa and metropolitan France exceeded Allied means. But he assured Mast that any assault would be more than a hit-and-run raid like that at Dieppe in August. An African invasion force would involve half a million men with 2,000 aircraft. This was a fivefold exaggeration.

"Where are these five hundred thousand men to come from?" Mast asked. "Where are they?"

"In the U.S. and U.K.," Clark replied.

"Rather far, isn't it?"

"No."

Perhaps lies and misunderstandings were inevitable: Clark could hardly disclose the imminence of TORCH, even if Mast's good faith seemed genuine. But by mid-morning tiny seeds of confusion and distrust had been sown over the timing of the invasion, the political realities of Vichy North Africa, the extent to which each side could aid the other, and, most important, who would command whom. At eleven, Mast stood and announced that he must return to Algiers before his absence aroused suspicions. Before walking to his car, he warned Clark, "The French navy is not with us. The army and the air force are."

Mast also repeated his earlier assertion that General Giraud intended to command all forces in North Africa, including any Allied troops. Clark was noncommittal, and Mast left in a flurry of salutes. He drove slowly past the café card players and old men bowling on the public square in Cherchel, taking with him the pleasant delusion that he had weeks or even months to properly prepare for an Allied invasion.

After twelve hours of hosting this cabal, M. Teissier had become visibly anxious. Nevertheless, he served the conspirators a fortifying lunch of peppery chicken with red wine and oranges. Several of General Mast's staff officers had remained at the farmhouse for further talks. They handed over maps and charts pinpointing gasoline and ammunition caches, airfields, troop strengths, and other military secrets. Clark swapped uniform blouses with one of the Frenchmen and took a stroll in the courtyard for some fresh air.

The happy colloquy ended abruptly with the jangling of the telephone early that evening. Teissier answered, then slammed down the receiver with a shriek. "The police will be here in five minutes!" This news, Clark later observed, had the effect of "fifty dead skunks thrown on the table." One French officer bolted out the door with his satchel. Others leaped through the windows and vanished into the brush. Gold pieces clattered across the floor as the Americans flung francs, Canadian dollars, and greenbacks at Murphy to use for possible bribes. Clark rousted the British commandos and sent one packing toward the beach with a walkie-talkie to alert the *Seraph*. With six others, he then scrambled into a dank wine cellar beneath the patio. "I don't want you to lock me up," he called. Teissier slammed the trapdoor anyway. The men crouched in darkness, clutching their rifles and musette bags full of documents.

Murphy and Teissier agreed to feign an inebriated revel, with much slurred singing and clinking of wine bottles. At 9:30 P.M., a coast guard cadet loyal to Teissier arrived at the green gate to explain his earlier telephone warning: an off-duty servant had reported odd activity at the farmhouse, and the police, suspecting smugglers, were organizing a raid. Murphy urged the cadet to stall the authorities as long as possible. "We had a little party down here. We had some girls, a little liquor, and food," Murphy said. "Everybody's left now, but I can assure you that no harm was done."

Clark and the others soon emerged from the cellar. "Get the hell down to the beach as fast as you can," Murphy urged. Collecting the folbots, the men clattered down the bluff. The brisk clacking of a nearby windmill signaled a freshening sea breeze, and to Clark's dismay waves five to seven feet high now crashed onto the shore. He stripped to his undershorts, tucking the money belt and his rolled-up trousers in the boat's waisthole. After a short sprint into the surf, he and one of the commandos leaped aboard, paddling furiously. An immense comber lifted the nose of the kayak until the craft was nearly vertical, then pitched it backward into the foaming sea. "To hell with the pants," someone yelled from shore, "save the paddles."

Cold, drenched, and trouserless, Clark requisitioned an underling's pants and hiked to the villa, where he was confronted by a horrified Teissier. "Please, for God's sake," the Frenchman begged, "get out of the house." Clark snapped, "I don't like to be hurried." Wrapped in a silk tablecloth, he hobbled barefoot back to the beach with a loaf of bread, two borrowed sweaters, and several bottles of wine. To keep warm, Clark bobbed up and down in a frenzy of deep-knee bends; meanwhile, the men reviewed their options. Should they storm Cherchel to steal a fishing boat? Perhaps they could buy one instead; Murphy suggested offering 200,000 francs. A French officer pointed out that either gambit would likely bring the police if not the army. The Americans agreed that if any Arab blundered onto the beach, they would lasso and strangle him.

At four A.M., someone noticed a sheltered spot where the surf seemed a bit calmer. Clark and a comrade mounted their kayak. Four others carried the boat to shoulder depth and shoved it seaward. Again the craft nosed up nearly perpendicular to the shore, but this time it crested the wave. Aboard *Seraph*, Lieutenant Jewell eased the submarine so close to shore that her keel shivered from proximity to the sea floor. The other boats, after capsizing at least once each, finally cleared the surf and made for the silhouetted conning tower. Murphy capered along the beach, kissing the French officers in glee as they collected the commandos' abandoned tommy guns and raked all footprints from the sand.

Clark's men spread their sopping documents in the engine room to dry. Fortified with a double tot of Nelson's blood from *Seraph*'s rum cask, Clark composed a message for London:

> Eisenhower eyes only... All questions were settled satisfactorily except for the time the French would assume supreme command.... Anticipate that the bulk of the French army and air forces will offer little resistance.... Initial resistance by French navy and coastal defenses indicated by naval information which also indicates that this resistance will fall off rapidly as our forces land.

Jewell swung the submarine due west, toward Gibraltar, and sounded the dive klaxon.

On the Knees of the Gods

As Hewitt's Task Force 34 zigged and zagged toward Morocco with Patton's legions aboard, more than 300 other ships bound for Algeria steamed from anchorages on the Clyde and along England's west coast. For all these vessels to shoot the Strait of Gibraltar in sequence and arrive punctually at various Barbary coast beaches, the two-week voyage must, in Churchill's phrase, "fit together like a jewelled bracelet." The challenge had roused the Royal Navy to its keenest pitch of seamanship, and the convoys held such perfect alignment that "only the boiling white foam thrown up by the screws betrayed that the ships were moving."

Eight distinct deception plans had been adopted by the Allies to suggest that this armada was bound for Scandinavia, or France, or the Middle East. The ploys included noisy searches for Norwegian currency; public lectures on frostbite; the conspicuous loading of cold-weather clothing; bulk purchases of French dictionaries; and instruction for army cooks on how to prepare rice dishes. A platoon of reporters was shunted to northern Scotland for ski and snowshoe training. Whatever their effect on Axis intelligence, these clues so confounded American troops that many simply concluded they were sailing for home, especially when the fleet first veered far west to evade U-boat wolfpacks before looping southeast toward the Mediterranean.

Like Hewitt's ships, those loaded in Britain carried tens of thousands of tons of war supplies. The cargo manifests also included $500,000 worth of tea, hand tools for 5,000 North African natives, 390,000 pairs of socks, and $5 million in gold, packed in thirty small safes at a Bank of England vault in Threadneedle Street. Complementing all those French lexicons, a special glossary translated British into American, noting, for example, that an "accumulator" is a battery, that "indent" means requisition, and that a "dixie" is a bucket for brewing tea.

The loading at British ports made even the Hampton Roads ordeal seem a model of logistical simplicity. On September 8, Eisenhower had sent Washington a fifteen-page cable confessing that his quartermasters in Britain were profoundly confused. Roughly 260,000 tons of supplies, ammunition, and weapons—enough to fight for a month and a half—had been misplaced after arriving in the United Kingdom. Would the War Department consider sending a duplicate shipment? The cable explained that the American system for marking and dispatching the cargo was poor—one U.S. Army regiment and its kit arrived in England on fifty-five different ships—and British warehouse procedures worse. Pilferage topped 20 percent, and many crates were buried beyond retrieval in a thousand dockside sheds. Eisenhower, not as embarrassed as perhaps he should have been, also asked that, as long as Army logisticians were rummaging about, would they please send various additional items, including barber chairs and a "bullet-proof, seven-passenger automobile of normal appearance."

The cable stirred grave doubts about Eisenhower's management acumen among the few senior officers permitted to see it. Both he and Patton seemed to be improvising to an alarming extent. A tart message from the War Department to London in October noted, "It appears that we have shipped all items at least twice and most items three times." But with TORCH on the tightest of schedules, logisticians had little recourse. By October 16, another 186,000 tons had been shipped across the Atlantic—and 11 million rounds of ammunition were borrowed from the British. Much of this cargo was now Africa-bound.

Few of the 72,000 troops embarked in Britain knew or cared about these travails. Outnumbering their British comrades two to one, the Americans were mostly drawn from three divisions staging in England, Scotland, and Northern Ireland: the 1st Infantry, the 1st Armored, and the 34th Infantry. After a few days at sea, convoy life took on a monotony only partly relieved by topside boxing matches in makeshift rings, where pugilists in sleeveless shirts pummeled one another into insensibility. An Army booklet, "What to Do Aboard a Transport," contained sections on "seasickness, cold, and balance" and "malaria and other plagues." An equally dispiriting essay, on "mental matters," warned, "One of the deep-down urges that must be controlled is that of sex"—advice that failed to curb the troops' endless reliving of amorous conquests, real and imagined. (Belfast's Belgravia Hotel, dubbed the Belgravia Riding Academy, was a favorite fantasy site of the 34th Division.) The mandatory "short-arm inspections" for venereal disease gave many a Lothario his comeuppance.

Regimental bands organized afternoon concerts of college fight songs and Sousa marches, always ending with "The Star-Spangled Banner," "God Save the King," and the "Marseillaise," in rotating order. The Argyll and Sutherland Highlanders marched fore and aft aboard the *Cathay*, loudly accompanied by bagpipers; although all soldiers had been ordered to remove their unit insignia, it was widely agreed that any potential enemy should know that Highland troops were afoot. Yanks with guitars or harmonicas played "Marching Through Georgia" or a ribald ballad about the medically exempt called "4-F Charley." For their part, Tommies sang, "There'll be no promotion this side of the ocean / Fuck them all, fuck them all, fuck them all." More refined entertainment was provided 34th Division troops on *Otranto* by a soldier-thespian who delivered soliloquies from *Hamlet* over the ship's public address system.

For the officers, the voyage was weirdly languorous, as if they were going to war on a Cunard cruise. Stewards awakened them with cups of tea each morning. Waiters posted printed menus in the dining rooms before every meal. An American officer on the *Durban Castle* later recalled, "Blouses were worn for dinner, [with] coffee in the lounge afterwards." Slender Indian cabin boys in black-and-white livery filled the tubs with hot seawater each evening and asked, "Bath, sahib?" On the *Monarch of Bermuda*, Brigadier General Theodore Roosevelt, Jr., assistant commander of the 1st Infantry Division, entertained his staff officers by reciting long passages of Kipling from memory after they challenged him with a succession of first lines. He further cheered the men by observing that the division's headquarters ship, several hundred yards abaft, appeared to be rolling twice as much as the *Monarch*. "Cleared for strange ports—that's what we are," Roosevelt wrote to his wife on October 26. "Here I am off again on the great adventure."

Below the waterline, in the troop holds known as Torpedo Heaven, the adventure seemed less thrilling. The stench of sweat, oil, and wool blankets filled the nostrils, while the ear heard an incessant clicking of dice and snoring so loud it was likened to the ripping of branches from a tree. Bunks on some tubs were stacked six high; a soldier in one top berth passed the time by penciling poetry on the steel overhead—a few inches above his nose—and sketching tourist maps of his native Philadelphia. To preserve the blackout, hatches had to be closed at night; the air grew so foul that some Coldstream Guards rigged a canvas airshaft, to little avail. Amid heavy seas mid-voyage, the large drums for the use of seasick soldiers slid across the deck with unpleasant splashings. Mess kits, washed in seawater, produced mass dysentery. Long queues formed at the sick bays and heads, and abject soldiers lined the rails.

Troops caught nibbling their emergency D-ration chocolate bars were dubbed Chocolate Soldiers and punished by forfeiting two meals. This was a happy penance. The galleys served so much fatty mutton that derisive bleating could be heard throughout the convoy and the 13th Armored Regiment proposed a new battle cry: "Baaa!" Crunchy raisins in the bread proved to be weevils; soldiers learned to hold up slices to the light, as if candling eggs. The 1st Infantry Division on *Reine de Pacifico* organized troop details to sift flour through mesh screens in a search for insects. Wormy meat aboard the *Keren* so provoked 34th Division soldiers that officers were dispatched to keep order in the mess hall. When soldiers aboard *Letitia* challenged the culinary honor of one French cook, he "became quite wild and threatened to jump overboard."

Morale suffered as much as stomachs. Relations between the cousins grew testy. Yanks resented the British food, if not the war itself. Tommies, who had long been entitled to rum rations, were shocked to get nothing stronger than ginger ale aboard ship. To monitor morale, American censors collected excerpts from more than eight thousand letters home: "The British are nothing but sorry sons of bitches, feed us stuff a hog wouldn't eat," one disgruntled soldier wrote. Another confided: "Don't mind my continual bitching. It's only that I hate myself & hate this life & I'm sick of it all."

"To make a good army out of the best men will take three years," Sylvanus Thayer, father of the U.S. Military Academy at West Point, concluded in the early nineteenth century. Most American soldiers bound for Africa in October 1942 had been in the Army for less than three years, some for less than three months. They were fine men, but not yet a good army. Indeed, they were not an army at all, but a hodgepodge of units cobbled together after the decision to launch TORCH. Mighty hosts are rarely made from expedients.

The 1st Armored Division—formed in 1940 and known as Old Ironsides—was a case in point. More than half its strength had been left behind in Britain for a later convoy. Most of the division's medium tanks had also remained behind, after they proved a couple of inches too big for the bow openings on the only landing ships available. Instead, the crews manned light tanks, with a puny 37mm gun, and some units still carried equipment from horse cavalry days. Even before crossing the Atlantic to Northern Ireland earlier in the year, Old Ironsides had been dislocated by frequent moves. Mackerel fishing in the Bay of Dundrum and fresh lobsters at fifty cents apiece were pleasant enough, but training on Britain's narrow lanes and stone-fence fields was limited. (British officers trailed the American tanks and paid local farmers a shilling for each sixteen feet of fence destroyed.) Many of the division's best soldiers volunteered for new Ranger, paratrooper, and commando units, to be sometimes replaced by men of lesser mettle with no armor training. Some crews had fired as few as three tank rounds. The War Department had long assumed that the division was destined for combat in northern Europe, and little thought was given to other possible battlefields. Old Ironsides, the only American tank division to see desert combat in World War II, was the only one to get no desert training. Hamilton H. Howze, the 1st Armored operations officer and a future four-star general, later asserted, "None of the division was worth a damn."

This harsh secret, suspected by few and believed by fewer, was equally true of other units. The 34th Infantry merits particular scrutiny because it had been the first American division dispatched to the European theater and because the division's saga, in North Africa and beyond, would embody the tribulations and triumphs of the U.S. Army as fully as any of the eighty-nine divisions ultimately mustered in World War II.

Twenty months earlier, the 34th had existed only in principle, as regiments of the Iowa National Guard and sister Guard units from Minnesota. Guardsmen in peacetime met once a week, usually on Monday evenings. For two hours of close-order drill they earned a dollar. Training in the art of war was limited to bayonet assaults against a football goalpost and skirmishes across the town square, where platoons practiced outflanking the local Civil War monument. Training in more sophisticated martial skills was limited to a couple weeks of summer camp. Troops were pressed into civil service for floods, or harvests, or strike-breaking at the

Swift meatpacking plant in Sioux City, where Guardsmen in 1938 had pierced the workers' cordon with a flying wedge before setting up their machine guns on a loading dock. That was the closest to combat most had ever come.

On February 10, 1941, after nine false alarms, the War Department federalized the Iowa and Minnesota regiments to form the 34th Division. It was among the last of eighteen Guard divisions swept into the Army under the congressional act that limited Guardsmen to a year of service in defense of the western hemisphere. Regiments staged hasty recruiting drives to fill out their ranks before heading to Louisiana for further training. The 151st Field Artillery, headquartered in Minneapolis, offered new recruits $21 a month and a chance to "go south with the Gopher Gunners." Those who signed up gathered on the balcony of the state armory, where a Guard major general told them, "I hope you return with Hitler and Mussolini on your shield"—disconcerting words to troops who had enlisted for twelve months of homeland defense. Many preferred to heed President Roosevelt, who had promised a crowd in Boston, "I have said this before but I shall say it again and again and again: Your boys are not going to be sent into foreign wars." Newspaper editorials across the Midwest caught the same spirit of denial. "World War II is a battle of airplanes and naval units," the *Daily Freeman Journal* of Webster City, Iowa, intoned on February 27, 1941. "No one expects the United States Infantry to leave the borders of the United States, even if this country should get into war."

Ten months later, war came, and not the pleasant war that required no infantrymen. The 34th Division was rushed to Britain in January 1942 as a symbol of American commitment to the Allied cause. In Britain, the troops unloaded supplies and guarded various headquarters, with little opportunity for garrison soldiers to become combat killers. The division missed large-scale maneuvers in Louisiana and the Carolinas that benefited many other U.S. units. As with the 1st Armored, hundreds of the division's best men left to form other units; the new 1st Ranger Battalion had been carved mostly from the 34th Division. With the decision to undertake TORCH, the 34th—already in Britain and thus deemed available even if ill-prepared—was consigned to Algeria. The lower ranks were still flush with boys from Iowa and Minnesota, but not the division's officer cadre: thanks to a general purge of National Guard officers from the Army, the 34th retained few of the leaders who had led them out of the Midwest. Once begun, the turmoil snowballed. In the past year alone, for example, the officers in the division's 168th Infantry Regiment had been cashiered almost wholesale three times.

Among those who survived the purges was an engaging citizen-soldier named Robert R. Moore. Now aboard the *Keren*, Moore had spent the days since sailing from Britain quelling mutiny in the mess hall and keeping his men occupied with calisthenics and busywork. Of average height, with a broad Irish face and a toothy grin, Moore had gray eyes and a forelock that hung from his crown like a pelt. He hailed from the southwest Iowa town of Villisca, population 2,011, where he owned the local drugstore, a homey place with a striped retractable awning and Meadow Gold ice cream signs in the window. Moore had joined the Iowa Guard in 1922 at the age of seventeen, and six years later took command of Company F of the 168th Infantry's 2nd Battalion. Known as Cap'n Bob or the Boy Captain, Moore was obstinate, charming, and unsparing, purging the company of those he deemed "no-accounts" and working hard to prepare his Guardsmen for the war no one expected to fight.

Fourteen years later, Bob Moore was thirty-seven. No longer a boy, he was also no longer a captain, having been promoted to major and appointed executive officer—second in command—of the 2nd Battalion. At night on the *Keren*, in his crowded cabin or by moonlight on the weather deck, Moore scribbled letters home and thought often of the last days in Iowa, in February 1941, as the regiment had prepared to leave for what everyone believed was a year's training. Those days were the benchmark against which all subsequent progress could be measured in the transmutation of ordinary American boys into troops capable of crushing the Third Reich. Moore remembered how the men had plucked the brass "Iowa" insignia from their uniforms and replaced it with a brass "U.S." He still had the letter he had sent to the 114 men in Company F, ordering them to report to the Villisca armory with "3 suits of underwear (either long or short, whichever you wear); 6 handkerchefs; 6 pair of socks (*no silk*); 1 white shirt (if you have one. It is not necessary, however)." For three weeks they had practiced the manual of arms in the same soup-bowl helmets their fathers had worn at the Meuse-Argonne, with the same Springfield bolt-action rifles. They pitched tents on the town square, grousing about their four-buckle shoes, which they swore the Army had deliberately designed to be an inch shorter than the average depth of mud; then they ate chicken-fried steak in the Presbyterian church basement. The Methodists organized a town banquet honoring the departing warriors with roast turkey served by home economics students in red, white, and blue uniforms. The after-supper program included a solo, "If I'm Not at the Roll Call," and a reading of "Old Glory" by Miss Eva Arbuckle. A local booster supplied a tune with these encouraging lyrics: "The boys are okay, you need have no fears / For they've drilled each week for the last three years." The splendid evening ended with the townfolk on their feet singing "God Bless America," followed by the mournful notes of "Taps" from the company bugler.

Then the time had come to leave, and in thirty-two Iowa towns during the first week of March 1941 the troops gathered at their armories while citizens lined the streets leading to the train depots. Aging veterans of the Great War, their shadows stretching long and blue across the snow, stamped their frozen feet and reminisced about their own call to the colors nearly a quarter century before. In Des Moines, a live radio broadcast covered the progress of 600 men of the 168th Infantry from East First Street across the Grand Avenue Bridge to Union Station. When the band launched into Sousa's "Field Artillery March," a haunting anthem of World War I, a mother marching with her son had shrieked, "Those bastards! They promised they'd never play that again!" At Clarinda, the high school band played "God Be with You Until We Meet Again" as the anti-tank company boarded the Burlington special. At Red Oak, where officers from Company M had urged mothers to stay home and "avoid any emotional display as the men leave for their year's training," scores of tearful mothers thronged the platform, clinging to their sons in a last embrace.

And in Villisca, on March 2, cars lined the village square and 1,500 people spilled from the little depot into the adjacent streets. "Most cars I ever saw in Villisca on Sunday morning," said the graybeards, before launching into another account of the departure of '17. Shortly before eight A.M., someone spotted the flash of the drum majorette's baton on Third Avenue. "Here they come!" the crowd murmured. Behind the Company F guidon, Bob Moore led his men across the viaduct in perfect march step. At the station, he commanded them to halt and fall out for final hugs and handshakes and murmured words of reassurance no one quite believed. An airplane circled overhead. "There's a German bomber!" a prankster shouted. A nervous titter rippled through the crowd. Then the fatal order was given, and the men disentangled themselves to heave their packs into the coaches, blowing kisses through the windows. With a shudder, the train lurched forward, and a great cry formed in the lungs of those standing on the platform, a roar of pride and hope and dread of all that was yet to come.

The boys are okay, you need have no fears. Eighty-seven weeks had passed since that moment, far short of the three years Sylvanus Thayer deemed necessary to make a good army from the best men. Bob Moore knew he was a better officer now, and that his men were better soldiers. But whether the division was worth a damn remained to be seen.

* * *

As the convoy neared the Mediterranean in early November, the men finally learned their destination: Algeria. Grumbling subsided. A new sense of mission obtained as the troops realized they were soon to attempt the most daring amphibious operation in the history of warfare.

"Everyone was excited and trying to be calm," one private wrote. Someone from the 1st Ranger Battalion on H.M.S. *Ulster Monarch* mistook two frolicking porpoises for torpedoes and a brief, if intense panic ensued. Francophone officers in the 1st Infantry Division offered French lessons, only to emerge from their wardroom classes shrouded in chalk dust, with expressions of despair. American soldiers in yellow Mae Wests did jumping jacks on deck while chanting, *"Nous sommes soldats américains, nous sommes vos amis."* To obscure the British role in TORCH, each Tommy sewed an American flag on his sleeve. "Long as it saves lives we don't care if we wear the bloody Chinese flag," a British officer said. A newly uncrated fifteen-page pamphlet advised, "Never smoke or spit in front of a mosque" and "When you see grown men walking hand in hand, ignore it. They are not queer." Repeated lectures stressed such respect for Arab dignity that many GIs were said to think of the North Africans as the "First Families of Virginia, in bathrobes."

Shortly after sunset on November 5, the convoy began to swing east, past the Pillars of Hercules. Soon the fleet would split apart, with 33,000 soldiers bound for Algiers and 39,000 for Oran. Wisps of mist drifted across the forecastles. Anti-aircraft gunners flipped up the collars on their peacoats, scanning a sky teeming with stars but still empty of enemy planes. Gibraltar loomed off the port bow. The lights of Algeciras, on the Spanish coast to the north, and Ceuta, in Spanish Morocco to the south, brought thousands of men on deck. Most had not seen a city illuminated at night in months or even years; the vision made them yearn for home and peace.

"The die is cast," Ted Roosevelt wrote his wife, "and the result is on the knees of the gods."

A Man Must Believe in His Luck

KNOWN as TUXFORD in British codebooks and as DURBAR in the American, Gibraltar by any name was formidable. Guns bristled like needles from the great slab of Jurassic limestone, three miles long and a mile wide. British sentries patrolled the perimeter against all enemies of empire, keeping an especially keen eye on the surveillance teams—

known to the Tommies as Der Führer's Snoopers—that watched the Rock from La Línea on the Spanish side of the border. Canadian miners bored relentlessly with gelignite explosives and special drill bits, designed for the obdurate Rockies and edged with nine carats of industrial diamonds. Thirty miles of tunnel now wormed through Gibraltar. Compressed-air shovels removed the spoil, which engineers tamped into the sea to extend the airfield's runway another 250 yards. Oilers, freighters, and refueling men-of-war filled the harbor, "as thick as logs behind a mill dam." Tars on liberty wandered the narrow cobblestoned streets of Gibraltar town, delighted to learn that liquor was still just ten shillings a bottle.

The Snoopers had much to observe. Fourteen squadrons of fighter planes that had arrived by sea in crates over the past few weeks now stood assembled, wing to wing, around the colonial cemetery. The Gibraltar racecourse starter's box had been converted into one of the world's busiest control towers. Several hundred pilots took turns flying patrols in their Spitfires and Hurricanes to master local conditions; winds shearing off the cliffs could be so treacherous that windsocks at either end of the runway often pointed at each other.

Late in the afternoon of November 5, 1942, as the convoys bound for Algeria first nosed into the Mediterranean, five B-17 Flying Fortresses touched down on the airfield after a harrowing flight from England. Their departure from Bournemouth had twice been postponed by heavy fog on the Channel coast; as one pilot reported, "even the birds were walking." Having flown only a hundred feet above the Atlantic, to evade enemy fighters, the planes then circled Gibraltar for an hour until the crowded runway could be cleared.

Staff cars pulled up to the stairs beneath each bomber to shield the arriving passengers from prying eyes. Their leader, disembarking from a plane named *Red Gremlin,* traveled under the nom de guerre of "General Howe." But the baggage carted through town to the former convent now known as Government House was stenciled "Lieutenant General Dwight D. Eisenhower." At eight P.M. Greenwich time, he cabled London, "Command post opens Gibraltar, 2000 Zulu, 5 November. Notify all concerned."

Eisenhower left the guest suite on the second floor, ignoring the fat cask of sherry in the governor-general's drawing room, and immediately headed for the tunnel angling into Mount Misery above the harbor. A guard in the sentry box snapped a salute as the TORCH commander and his staff marched past on their way to the command center. In the future Eisenhower would jog the half mile, but this evening the ten-minute walk allowed his British hosts to describe the underground lair that would be his headquarters for the next three weeks.

It was a subterranean village, with sewers, heating pipes, and water mains threading the tunnels. Signposts pointed down oblique shafts to a laundry and Monkey's Cave Convalescent Hospital. A naked bulb burned every twenty-five feet, casting eerie shadows on the weeping limestone walls. Duckboards bridged the puddles, and clattering ventilation fans discouraged conversation. Rats were a nuisance; they even ate uncovered bars of soap. Galleries had been cut for three dozen offices built with corrugated sheeting. Jerry cans caught the dripping water.

Eisenhower's brisk stroll also let the British take his measure. There was that incandescent grin, of course, said to be "worth an army corps in any campaign." His eyes were wide-set and unwavering, his head broad-browed and perfectly centered over squared shoulders. Both his face and his hands moved perpetually, and he exuded a magnetic amiability that made most men want to please him. Perhaps that was because, as one admirer asserted, they intuited he was "good and right in the moral sense," or perhaps it was because, as a British air marshal concluded, "Ike has the qualities of a little boy which make you love him."

In his rapid rise, talent, opportunity, and fortune converged improbably—to many, it seemed, providentially. Patton—who earlier in the year had told Eisenhower, "You are my oldest friend"—privately claimed the initials "D.D." stood for "Divine Destiny." Thirty months earlier, Eisenhower had been a lieutenant colonel who had never commanded even a platoon in combat. Young Ike, the third son of a failed Midwestern merchant turned creamery worker, had chosen a military career because West Point provided a free education. After an indifferent cadetship he embarked on an ordinary career as a staff officer, stalled at the middling rank of major for sixteen years. Even his first venture into the rarefied circles he would inhabit for two decades was inauspicious: the White House usher's log for February 9, 1942, recorded the initial visit to the Oval Office of one "P. D. Eisenhauer."

His worldview seemed conventional, his gifts commensurate with the modesty he exuded. He was a true believer in Allied righteousness: "If [the Axis] should win we would really learn something about slavery, forced labor, and loss of individual freedom." Congenitally willing to make decisions and shoulder responsibilities, he had limited opportunities for either in the interwar Army. "There's a lot of big talk and desk hammering around this place—but very few *doers!*" he wrote in frustration. He took pride in being apolitical, as required of American Army officers, and he impressed others—as one British admiral later noted—as "completely sincere, straightforward, and very modest," but "not very sure of himself."

Yet he possessed depths enough to resist easy plumbing. "I have the feeling," the war correspondent Don Whitehead later wrote, "that he was a far more complicated man than he seemed to be—a man who shaped events with such subtlety that he left others thinking they were the architects of those events. And he was satisfied to leave it that way." Eisenhower's sincerity and native fairness were so transparent that they obscured an incisive intellect. He had read much and thought much, concluding soon after the first world war that a second was inevitable—friends called him Alarmist Ike—and that the winning side must fight as a coalition under a unified command. He graduated first in his class at the Army's staff college and served six years—in Washington and the Philippines—on the staff of that American Machiavelli, Douglas A. MacArthur, learning courtier's arts best displayed in a palace or a headquarters.

His capacity for hard work was heroic; in the past eleven months, he had taken just one day off, which he spent practicing pistol marksmanship outside London. He wrote well and spoke very well; the infamous "wandering syntax" of his White House years, one historian concluded, was "contrived for presidential purposes." His frequent "Dear General" letters to Marshall were dictated with clarity, precision, and occasional obsequiousness, as in this of October 20, 1942:

> Whenever I'm tempted to droop a bit over the burdens cast upon us here, I think of the infinitely greater ones you have to bear and express to myself a fervent wish that the Army may be fortunate enough to keep you at its head until the final victory is chalked up.

To Mark Clark and other intimates, Eisenhower claimed he would rather be leading a division into combat, but the bravado rang hollow. So, too, did his posture of steely ruthlessness, a quality he had yet to develop. "I find," he wrote in October, "that all my senior commanders are still inclined to regard inexcusable failures and errors with too tolerant an eye." As if fearing his own exposure, he had written a friend, "Fake reputations, habits of glib and clever speech, and glittering surface performance are going to be discovered and kicked overboard."

As D-Day for TORCH drew near he affected a hearty confidence. "Never felt better in my life," he wrote on October 12, two days before his fifty-second birthday, "and, as the big day approaches, feel that I could lick Tarzan." In fact he had been irritable and often depressed, smoking up to four packs of Camel cigarettes a day. To Marshall he would concede only that "it has been a trifle difficult to keep up, in front of every-body, a proper attitude of confidence and optimism." Not until years later did he acknowledge "the sober, even fearful, atmosphere of those days." For now, the concealment of his anxieties was part of the art of generalship.

Inside Gibraltar, just off Green Lane and Great North Road, several Nissen huts housed the operations center. The armada from Britain inched eastward on the charts of the Mediterranean that covered the wall. A map of the eastern Atlantic charted the estimated position of Hewitt's fleet. A chagrined British officer showed Eisenhower the dank office he would share with Clark. It was an eight-foot-square cell, with a wall clock, maps of Europe and North Africa, and several straight-backed chairs. The plain desk held a water carafe, a pen set, and an ancient telephone of the sort surmounted with dual bells. Eisenhower was so amazed to find himself in command of Fortress Gibraltar that he hardly noticed the drab setting.

For forty-eight hours he paced and smoked. Communications with London and Washington, via ocean cable, were good, but he had noth-ing to report. The convoys from Britain kept radio silence, and of Hewitt's task force virtually nothing was known—except that meteorol-ogists forecast bad conditions in Morocco, with fifteen-foot swells. "Dear Kent," Eisenhower radioed Hewitt, "here is wishing you all the glory there is and greatest success to you and Gen. Patton. . . . I'll be around close if you need me. . . . As always, Ike."

On November 6, Eisenhower had time to ask London about the health of his black Scottie dog, Telek. Privately, to Clark, he again grum-bled about the decision to invade Africa rather than France. Whether the French in North Africa would resist was still unclear. Although General Mast had guaranteed that there would be no resistance at airfields near Oran and other key sites, on November 4 Robert Murphy in Algiers had relayed a warning from a top French commander, who revealed "orders to defend French Africa at all costs, so that we should not make the mis-take of attacking." Murphy sent another panicky cable insisting that TORCH be delayed at least two weeks to sort out Vichy politics, and was brusquely dismissed; the proposal was "inconceivable," said Eisenhower. He and Clark agreed that Murphy had "the big and little jitters."

On November 7, Eisenhower drove in a Ford to view the Barbary apes. An "officer-in-charge of Rock apes" was responsible for their survival—a heavy burden, given the British conviction that without its apes, the Rock would be lost to the empire. Eisenhower petted one for good luck. As the afternoon shadows lengthened, blue searchlights played over the airfield and the Spanish frontier. Fourteen hundred feet below, tiny ships milled about the harbor. Fifteen miles beyond Point Europa lay Africa, a tawny smudge on the southern horizon.

"We are standing of course on the brink and must take the jump," he had cabled Marshall that morning. "We have worked our best to assure a successful landing, no matter what we encounter."

His head cleared, Eisenhower returned to the tunnel and jogged down the Great North Road. The first substantive news from the TORCH transports had arrived. It was bad.

Not until reconnaissance planes finally detected the armada in the western Mediterranean had the Axis high command begun to suspect an invasion. Speculation about landing sites ranged from southern France to Egypt; the German navy considered French North Africa the least likely destination. Hitler believed the Allied ships were bound for Tripoli or Benghazi in an attempt to trap Rommel's Afrika Korps, which had begun retreating from El Alamein after a thrashing from Montgomery's Eighth Army. Hoping to annihilate the Allied fleet in the Sicilian Straits, Hitler ordered his available forces—thirty-five submarines and seventy-six aircraft—to concentrate at the narrows. "I await a ruthless, victorious attack," he proclaimed. Too late, the Führer would realize that nearly all of his ambush force had been positioned too far east.

But not all. At daybreak on Saturday, November 7, U.S.S. *Thomas Stone* was making eleven knots in the left column of ships, thirty-three miles off the Spanish coast. *Stone* was among the few American transports in the armada. She carried 1,400 soldiers from the 2nd Battalion of the 39th Infantry, 9th Division regiment; Eisenhower had added them late to the Algiers assault, although they had little amphibious training. An alert officer on the bridge spotted the white runnel of a torpedo wake several hundred yards off the port side. "Hard right rudder!" he ordered the helmsman, then rang up flank speed. The ship tacked ninety degrees and was nearly parallel to the torpedo's path when the blast ripped through her stern, so hard that sailors on *Samuel Chase*, 600 yards ahead, thought *they* had been struck.

Men already about their morning duties were flung to the deck. Captain B. Frank Cochran, the chaplain of the 39th Infantry, had risen early to read his Bible; now he heard the screams of dying sailors and shouts from a fire brigade heaving ammunition crates over the side. The blast demolished the fantail, snapped *Stone*'s propeller shaft, and killed nine men. Her rudder jammed at hard right, the ship drifted in a languid arc before stopping dead in the water, 160 miles from Algiers. Two white rockets burst above the superstructure, the signal for "I have been torpedoed." As ordered, other ships in the formation steamed past without slowing; swabs watched wide-eyed from the rails.

The 2nd Battalion commander was an obstinate thirty-seven-year-old major named Walter M. Oakes. With *Stone* in no danger of sinking and help summoned from Gibraltar, Oakes assembled his men on deck and announced to lusty hurrahs that they would continue on to Algiers—in twenty-four landing craft. Chaplain Cochran, who was to remain aboard the *Stone*, offered the departing mariners his benediction, and at three P.M. the troops clambered down the boarding nets into the flimsy boats. Among them was a galley cook who stowed away in a landing craft rather than be left behind. "The men in this battalion," he told his new comrades, "are lousy with courage."

Soon enough, they were also desperately seasick. After wallowing about until dark, the matchwood fleet motored south in three columns at eight knots. At eight P.M., the first boat broke down. Ninety minutes later, the flotilla made way again, only to have two more boats stall. Overheated engines and ruptured oil lines now spread like the pox, with all boats forced to stop during each repair. An east wind rose, and with it the sea, forcing the men to bail with their helmets. At eleven P.M., the corvette H.M.S. *Spey*, assigned to guide the craft to Algiers Bay, darted off to investigate a mysterious radar contact four miles to the east. As the puttering boats waited, a white flare and the roar of 20mm cannon fire tore open the night. When the corvette returned, her chastened captain explained that his men had mistaken landing boat No. 28—lost and headed the wrong way—for an enemy submarine. Fortunately, the shots missed.

Shortly after midnight, boat No. 9 reported she was sinking after colliding with another craft. The men scrambled off and the seacocks were opened. By this time, the flotilla was making less than four knots, with a hundred miles still to cover. Tow ropes broke, engines seized up, retching soldiers by the hundreds hung their heads over the gunwales and prayed for land. Major Oakes agreed to cram the men into seven seaworthy boats and scuttle the rest, a task *Spey*'s gunners undertook with uncommon zeal.

Even then the cause was lost—the sea too great, the craft too frail. Sodden and miserable, the battalion and its stowaway cook gingerly boarded the *Spey*. With all deliberation, to avoid shipping seas that would wash men overboard, the corvette steamed south, nearly foundered by the burden of an extra 700 men, but determined to invade Algiers, however belatedly.

* * *

Some hours passed before Eisenhower learned that the first dire reports about the *Stone,* like most first dire reports, were exaggerated. She was not sinking; her troops had not perished. By the time an accurate account reached Gibraltar, however, he was occupied with a challenge to his generalship more distressing than a mere torpedo strike. The French had arrived.

General Henri Honoré Giraud had been plucked from the Côte d'Azur two days earlier by the ubiquitous H.M.S. *Seraph.* He wore a gray fedora and a wrinkled herringbone suit, with field glasses around his neck; stubble filled the hollows of his cheeks. Nor had his appearance been improved by a partial ducking during the perilous transfer from a fishing smack to the submarine. But his bearing was imperious and his handlebar mustache magnificent. Tall and lean, he marched down the Great North Road tunnel as though it were the Champs Élysées. It was then five P.M. on November 7.

In a briefcase, Giraud carried his own plans for the invasion of North Africa, the liberation of France, and final victory over Germany. He stepped into the tiny office where Eisenhower and Clark waited, and as the red do-not-disturb light flashed on outside the closed door, he proclaimed, "General Giraud has arrived." Then: "As I understand it, when I land in North Africa, I am to assume command of all Allied forces and become the supreme Allied commander in North Africa." Clark gasped, and Eisenhower managed only a feeble "There must be some misunderstanding."

Indeed there was. Eisenhower had tried to avoid this meeting in part because the issue of command remained unresolved, and he had even written Giraud an apology for not seeing him, postdated with a phony London letterhead. But when the general showed up at Gibraltar demanding answers, Eisenhower relented.

Giraud was without doubt intrepid. U.S. intelligence reported that his last message before being captured in 1940 was this: "Surrounded by a hundred enemy tanks. I am destroying them in detail." One officer described him flinging men into battle with a rousing *"Allez, mes enfants!"* Thrusting one hand into his tunic like Napoleon, he used the other to point heavenward whenever he spoke of the noble French army. In German captivity, he signed his letters "Resolution, Patience, Decision."

But valor has its limits. Giraud, one of his countrymen observed, had the uncomprehending eyes of a porcelain cat. "So stately and stupid," Harold Macmillan wrote, adding that the general was ever willing to "swallow down any amount of flattery and Bénédictine." Privately, the Americans called Giraud "Papa Snooks."

The general's greatest genius appeared to be a knack for getting captured and then escaping. He had been taken prisoner in 1914, too, but soon made his way to Holland and then England, disguised as a butcher, a stableboy, a coal merchant, and a magician in a traveling circus. His April 1942 flight from Königstein, after two years' imprisonment with ninety other French generals, was even more flamboyant. Saving string used to wrap gift packages, he plaited a rope reinforced with strips of wire smuggled in lard tins; after shaving his mustache and darkening his hair with brick dust, he tossed the rope over a parapet and—at age sixty-three—climbed down 150 feet to the Elbe River. Posing as an Alsatian engineer, he traveled by train to Prague, Munich, and Strasbourg with a 100,000-mark reward on his head, before slipping across the Swiss border and then into Vichy France.

Now he was in Eisenhower's office, demanding Eisenhower's job. Giraud spoke no English, and Clark, hardly fluent in French, labored with help from an American colonel to translate the words of a man who habitually referred to himself in the third person. "General Giraud cannot accept a subordinate position in this command. His countrymen would not understand and his honor as a soldier would be tarnished." Eisenhower explained that the Allies, under the murky agreement negotiated at Cherchel and approved by Roosevelt, expected Giraud to command only French forces; acceding to his demand to command all Allied troops was impossible. To ease Giraud's burden, the U.S. military attaché in Switzerland had made available 10 million francs in a numbered account. A staff officer with a map was summoned to describe the landings about to begin in Algeria and Morocco.

Giraud would not be deflected. The plan impressed him, but what about the bridgehead in southern France? He believed twenty armored divisions there should suffice. Were they ready? And was Eisenhower aware that Giraud outranked him, four stars to three? But the heart of the matter was supreme command of any landing on French soil. "Giraud," he said, "cannot accept less."

After four hours of this, Eisenhower emerged from what he now called "my dungeon," his face as crimson as the light over the door. He had agreed to dine in the British admiralty mess while Giraud enjoyed the governor-general's hospitality at Government House. Several days earlier, Eisenhower had warned Marshall: "The question of overall command is going to be a delicate one. . . . I will have to ride a rather slippery rail on this matter, but believe that I can manage it without giving serious offense." Unfortunately, Clark had ended this first meeting by telling Giraud, "Old gentleman, I hope you know that from now on your ass is out in the snow." Eisenhower dashed off a quick message to Marshall, closing with the simple confession: "I'm weary."

Dinner at Government House, where the sherry cask was always full and the larder well provisioned, softened Giraud not a whit. Back in Eisenhower's office at 10:30 P.M., with the red light again burning, he again refused all appeals. After two hours of circular argument, Giraud retired from the field. The impasse remained: Giraud wanted supreme command, not the limited command of French troops offered by the Americans. His favorite joke was that generals rose early to do nothing all day, while diplomats rose late for the same purpose; tomorrow's dawn would bring another opportunity for inaction, and he announced plans to shop for underwear and shoes in the town bazaar. Clark threatened him again, although less crudely this time. "We would like the honorable general to know that the time of his usefulness to the Americans for the restoration of the glory that was France is *now*," he said through the interpreter. "We do not need you after tonight."

Giraud took his leave with a shrug and a final third-person declaration: "Giraud will be a spectator in this affair." Eisenhower muttered a sour joke about arranging "a little airplane accident" for their guest, then headed outside for a few moments of meditation.

From the face of the Rock the Mediterranean stretched away to merge with the night sky in a thousand shades of indigo. Eisenhower was a gifted cardplayer and he sensed a bluff. Perhaps Giraud was playing for time, waiting to see how successful the invasion was. Eisenhower suspected he would come around once events had played out a bit.

Otherwise, the news was heartening. After more than two weeks of battle at El Alamein, Rommel was in full retreat from Egypt; the British Eighth Army could either destroy the Afrika Korps piecemeal, or drive Rommel into the TORCH forces that would soon occupy Tunisia. And not only had the Axis ambush in the Mediterranean been laid too far east, but a German wolfpack in the Atlantic had been lured away from Morocco by a British merchant convoy sailing from Sierra Leone. More than a dozen cargo ships were sunk, but Hewitt's transports in Task Force 34 remained unscathed. Was it possible that the great secret would hold until morning? There had been some horrifying security breaches—secret papers, for instance, consigned to a blazing fire at Allied headquarters in London, had been sucked up the chimney, unsinged. Staff officers had scampered across St. James's Square for an hour, spearing every scrap of white in sight. Still, the Axis forces appeared to have been caught unawares by TORCH.

To Marshall, Eisenhower had written: "I do not need to tell you that the past weeks have been a period of strain and anxiety. I think we've taken this in our stride. . . . If a man permitted himself to do so, he could get absolutely frantic about questions of weather, politics, personalities in France and Morocco and so on."

Eisenhower headed back to his catacomb, dragging on another Camel. He spread his bedroll, determined not to stray from the operations center as he awaited reports from the front. "I fear nothing except bad weather and possibly large losses to submarines," he had asserted with the bravado of a man obliged by his job to fear everything. Years later, after he was crowned with laurels by the civilized world he had helped save, Eisenhower would remember these hours as the most excruciating of the entire war. In the message to Marshall he had added a poignant postscript.

"To a certain extent," he wrote, "a man must merely believe in his luck."

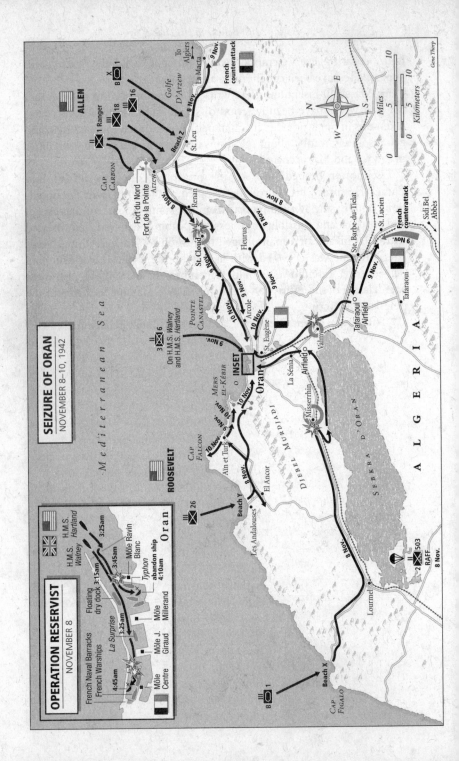

SEIZURE OF ORAN
NOVEMBER 8–10, 1942

OPERATION RESERVIST
NOVEMBER 8

Oran

French Naval Barracks
French Warships
Floating dry dock 3:15am
3:25am
La Surprise
3:45am
Môle Ravin
Blanc
Typhon
abandon ship
4:10am
3:25am
4:45am
Môle
Centre
Môle J.
Giraud
Môle
Millerand

H.M.S.
Walney
H.M.S.
Hartland

ALLEN
ROOSEVELT

Gene Thorp

Mediterranean Sea

To Algiers
9 Nov.
La Macta
Golfe D'Arzew
8 Nov.
La Leu
Beach 2
St. Leu
Arzew
Cap Carbon
Fort du Nord
Fort de la Pointe
8 Nov.
Renan
St. Cloud
9 Nov.
Fleurus
8 Nov.
8 Nov.
Ste. Barbe-du-Tlelat
St. Lucien
Sidi Bel Abbes
9 Nov.
Tafaraoui
Tafaraoui Airfield
9 Nov.
Valmy
9 Nov.
Arcole
9 Nov.
St. Eugène
10 Nov.
10 Nov.
9 Nov.
St. Eugène
ORAN
INSET
Oran
Mers El-Kébir
10 Nov.
10 Nov.
10 Nov.
Misserhin
La Sénia Airfield
Pointe Canastel
On H.M.S. Walney and H.M.S. Hartland
9 Nov.
Aïn et Turk
8 Nov.
El Ancor
Cap Falcon
Les Andalouses
Beach Y
Beach X
Cap Figalo
Lourmel
8 Nov.
8 Nov.
RAFF
8 Nov.
Djebel Murdjadj
Sebkra d'Oran

ALGERIA

French counterattack
French counterattack
French counterattack

N E W S

Miles
0 5 10
Kilometers
0 5 10

2. LANDING

"In the Night, All Cats Are Grey"

Two hundred and thirty nautical miles southeast of Gibraltar, Oran perched above the sea, a splinter of Europe cast onto the African shore. Of the 200,000 residents, three-quarters were European, and the town was believed to have been founded in the tenth century by Moorish merchants from southern Spain. Sacked, rebuilt, and sacked again, Oran eventually found enduring prosperity in piracy; ransom paid for Christian slaves had built the Grand Mosque. Even with its corsairs long gone, the seaport remained, after Algiers, the greatest on the old Pirate Coast. Immense barrels of red wine and tangerine crates by the thousands awaited export on the docks, where white letters painted on a jetty proclaimed Marshal Pétain's inane slogan: *"Travail, Famille, Patrie."* A greasy, swashbuckling ambience pervaded the port's many grogshops. Quays and breakwaters shaped the busy harbor into a narrow rectangle 1½ miles long, overwatched by forts and shore batteries that swept the sea to the horizon and made Oran among the most ferociously defended ports in the Mediterranean.

Here the Allies had chosen to begin their invasion of North Africa, with a frontal assault by two flimsy Coast Guard cutters and half an American battalion. While Kent Hewitt's Task Force 34 approached the Moroccan coast, the fleet from Britain had split. Half had turned toward three invasion beaches around Algiers, while the other half steamed for three beaches around Oran. Since the reaction of French defenders in Africa remained uncertain, in both Morocco and Algeria quick success for the Allies required that the ports be seized to expedite the landing of men and supplies. Oran was considered so vital that Eisenhower personally had approved a proposal to take the docks in a bold coup de main before dawn on November 8, 1942.

The plan was British. Concocted in August and code-named RESERVIST, the attack—similar to a successful British operation six months earlier against Vichy forces in Madagascar—was designed to forestall the sabotage of Oran's port. British intelligence estimated that French sailors would need only three hours to scuttle all merchant ships at their quays, and another twelve to sink the huge floating dock across from the harbor entrance. To encourage a friendly reception from Anglophobic defenders, the British also proposed using mostly American troops aboard two Great Lakes cutters. Once used to chase rum-runners, the boats had been deeded to the Royal Navy under Lend-Lease and renamed H.M.S. *Walney* and H.M.S. *Hartland*. How French gunners would recognize the American complexion of the assault in utter darkness was never clarified, notwithstanding Churchill's warning that "in the night, all cats are grey." Each cutter—250 feet long and built to withstand North Atlantic storms but not shell fire—was fitted with iron plating around the wheelhouse and lower bridge. Code words drawn from an exotic palette were assigned to various docks, barracks, and other objectives to be seized: Magenta, Lemon, Claret, Fawn, Heliotrope, and Scarlet.

To command RESERVIST, the British chose a voluble fifty-three-year-old salt named Frederick Thornton Peters. Thin lipped, with arching half-moon eyebrows, Captain Peters had returned to the Royal Navy in 1939 following a twenty-year hiatus. After commanding a destroyer flotilla on convoy duty, he headed a training school for intelligence agents in Hertford; his students included Kim Philby and Guy Burgess, who would be notorious soon enough as British traitors. Peters razored his jowls so vigorously that they had a blood sheen. He favored slender black cheroots, preferably lit by a toady with a ready match. "Rain, darkness, and secrecy followed him," one acquaintance wrote. Now glory was his goal. Peters meant not only to prevent sabotage of the port but also to capture the fortifications and accept Oran's surrender. "This," he confided, "is the opportunity I have been waiting for."

Peters worried the Americans, and so did his plan. Even Churchill acknowledged that the catastrophe at Dieppe in August had "showed how a frontal assault on a defended port was doomed to failure." Naval wisdom since Admiral Horatio Nelson's day held that "a ship's a fool to fight a fort." At a minimum, one British theorist argued, "defenders must be drenched with fire and reduced to a state of gibbering." No drenching bombardment would precede RESERVIST, and no defenders would gibber. An intelligence report warned, "The number of naval vessels in the Oran harbor varies daily, and [they] are capable of delivering heavy, long range fire." The timing of the attack caused particular consternation. Originally, RESERVIST was to coincide with the first beach landings east and west of Oran. But now the cutters were to enter the harbor two hours after the landings had started, allowing time to cancel the mission if the French appeared either particularly inflamed or conveniently supine. The Royal Navy insisted RESERVIST was "more a Trojan horse operation than an assault."

Convinced that Peters planned to attack regardless of conditions ashore, the senior U.S. Navy officer in the Oran task force, Rear Admiral Andrew C. Bennett, protested to Eisenhower. "If determined resistance is met from the French navy, which seems to be the general opinion, it is believed that this small force will be wiped out," Bennett wrote on October 17. "If resistance is determined, then I am convinced that five times the number of troops would be insufficient." RESERVIST was "suicidal and absolutely unsound."

Another American admiral working in London, Bernhard H. Bieri, also protested. But Eisenhower felt obliged in the interests of Allied harmony to heed the British, particularly the four-star admiral Bertram H. Ramsay. "I can't take your advice on this thing," Eisenhower told Bieri. "I have to get my advice from Ramsay." Bieri then approached Ramsay, who replied, "If it doesn't do anything else, it's good for the spirit of the people to carry out one of these operations. If successful, it's a wonderful boost for morale." Further objection from Major General Orlando Ward, whose 1st Armored Division was to provide the troops for RESERVIST, brought only a rebuke from Mark Clark, who had become an enthusiast. "If these craft are fired on by coast defenses, they are to retire," Clark assured Eisenhower on October 13. Ward's misgivings persisted, but, he wrote a subordinate, "My conscience is clear in this matter."

The honor of storming Oran port went to Ward's 3rd Battalion of the 6th Armored Infantry Regiment. First organized in 1789, the 6th Infantry carried battle streamers from Chapultepec and Chancellorsville, San Juan Hill and Saint-Mihiel. The regimental rolls had included Jefferson Davis, Zachary Taylor, and a particularly gallant commander mortally wounded while fighting the Seminoles in a Florida swamp on Christmas Day 1837. "Keep steady, men," he advised before expiring. "Charge the hummock." The current 3rd Battalion commander was a thirty-one-year-old Floridian named George F. Marshall. A West Pointer whose domed forehead crowned a long face and a strong jaw, Marshall had served in the Philippine Scouts and married the daughter of an Army doctor. He had jumped from captain to lieutenant colonel in recent months. If he had doubts about RESERVIST, he kept them private: the mission, he told a division staff officer, was "the finest assignment" possible. He would charge the hummock.

After a few days' training in Britain with grappling hooks and boarding

ladders, Marshall and 392 of his men—all that the cutters could carry—
sailed to Gibraltar on a Royal Navy cruiser. Arriving on November 5, in
time to witness the landing of Eisenhower and his staff aboard the B-17s,
the men were ferried to the *Walney* and *Hartland,* which had sailed sep-
arately from Northern Ireland. They joined antisabotage specialists,
including twenty-six U.S. Navy officers and seamen, six U.S. Marines,
fifty-two Royal Navy officers and ratings, and the cutters' British crews.
At noon on November 7, the enlisted men and junior officers learned
their destination.

The overloaded cutters wallowed so badly during the short trip across
the Mediterranean that soup sloshed from the mess bowls. Neither
Peters nor Marshall knew that in Oran a coup organized by Robert
Murphy's Twelve Apostles and the Office of Strategic Services (OSS)—
the American spy agency—was collapsing. Although a plucky cabal of
royalists, Jews, Freemasons, and Communists remained eager to seize
the port and other installations, a key conspirator in the army high command had lost his nerve. A coded alert sent to Gibraltar from a secret
radio transmitter in Oran—"Expect resistance everywhere"—was not
relayed to the Allied task force.

Each cutter flew an American flag the size of a tablecloth. Both boats
also hoisted the White Ensign, emblem of the Royal Navy. The British
crews had insisted on sailing under their own flag, deception be damned.
Peters met his fellow officers for a final briefing in the *Walney* wardroom. "I think," he said, "we've got a good chance of carrying out our
mission without firing a shot."

At one minute past midnight on November 8, the cutters' crews took
battle stations. Tars stacked extra ammunition in the quarterdeck lock-
ers and the laundry, close to the guns. Scrambling nets were draped over
the bows. On *Walney*'s darkened upper bridge, Lieutenant Paul E. A.
Duncan of the Royal Navy stood in American battle dress with two pistols strapped low on his hips and a tommy gun clutched across his chest.
He was Captain Peters's linguist, and he practiced speaking French with
an American accent, murmuring words he would soon bellow over the
boat's public address system.

With *Hartland* trailing 600 yards behind, *Walney* stalked the Algerian
coast at six knots, carving a brilliant green furrow in the phosphorescent
sea. Colonel Marshall's men waited on the mess deck below, sipping coffee and listening to the water hiss along the hull. Physician's assistants
spread white sheets over makeshift operating tables. Among them was

Marvin P. Clemons, a former coal mine brakeman from Eccles, West Virginia. The battalion surgeon, Captain Robert Fuller, had recently busted his rambunctious assistant from sergeant to private, and Clemons planned to desert after the first payday in Oran. He helped Fuller lay out the surgical instruments, while privately plotting his flight.

Peters, Duncan, and fifteen other men crowded the bridge. Their faces were so blackened with camouflage that close friends could not recognize one another. The amber lights of Oran spilled down the dark hills, then abruptly, at 2:45 A.M., began to wink out. The distant moan of air raid sirens carried across the water. *Walney*'s skipper, Lieutenant Commander P. C. Meyrick, read aloud an equivocal radio message from the task force command ship, H.M.S. *Largs*: "No shooting thus far. Landings unopposed. Don't start a fight unless you have to." The men on the bridge laughed. Their disembodied cackling died away as a flare soared lazily above the docks off the starboard bow. For the first time, Peters saw that a double boom stretched 200 yards across the harbor mouth.

Meyrick ordered the helmsman to swing beneath the shadow of the cliffs east of the port. Two small motor launches that had accompanied the cutters from Gibraltar prepared to lay down a smoke screen. *Walney*'s propellers wrenched at the water as Meyrick came about at fifteen knots for a run at the booms. At a nod from Peters—it was precisely three A.M.—Duncan gripped the microphone and in his faux American accent bawled into the dark: *"Ne tirez pas. Nous sommes vos amis. Ne tirez pas."*

Red tracers arced across the water and the stutter of a machine gun echoed from the Môle Ravin Blanc. Tongues of flame erupted from shore batteries at Fort Laumone above the harbor entrance. Violent splashes sounded from out on the dark water. "Lie flat for crash," Meyrick ordered. "We are approaching boom." With hardly a shudder, *Walney* sliced the first cable and then, "like a wire through cheese," parted the string of coal barges that formed the second boom. She was in the harbor.

A splintering crash cut short all congratulatory banter. One of the motor launches, swerving to escape its own asphyxiating smoke, had collided with *Walney*. No one was injured, but the launch—her bow crushed—fled into the night. Smoke lay across the docks like the densest fog, billowing white beneath the many flares now burning over the length of the port. A searchlight beam swung wildly across the water. Small-arms fire crackled from the docks and jetties, muffled by the deeper roar of the Batterie de Gambetta. An explosion ripped through

Walney's bridge, and Lieutenant Duncan fell dead at the microphone, his plea for a cease-fire strangled in mid-sentence, his pistols unfired in their holsters.

Then, silence descended for a long minute as *Walney* crept past the Môle Ravin Blanc and the Môle Millerand toward her objectives at the harbor's west end. French gunners swiveled their attention to *Hartland*, now five minutes behind and caught in the searchlight. On *Walney*'s mess deck, 200 American soldiers had listened to the battle strains above, first with enthusiasm, then with alarm as machine-gun bullets stippled the hull. Several men writhed in pain on the deck. Medics crouched over them and fumbled for morphine. Colonel Marshall darted among his troops, rallying them with stout words, then headed toward the forecastle. As planned, British tars lowered three canoes over the side. One had been holed; it sank immediately, spilling soldiers into the water. Anti-sabotage teams in the other two paddled furiously toward the docks in Basin Maroc.

As suddenly as it had descended, the lull lifted. Peering through the shattered windows of the bridge, Peters saw the French sloop *La Surprise* gathering speed dead ahead. He ordered Meyrick to swerve and ram the ship, but the French captain was quicker. The first salvo, at 300 yards, smashed the iron plate girdling *Walney*'s bridge, killing the helmsman and others around him. Blinded in the left eye, Peters shouted another rudder command, but he was issuing orders to dead men. *Walney* drifted past at four knots and French gunners raked her decks with another broadside from twenty-five yards, the terrible muzzles almost close enough to stroke.

Worse was to come. As the cutter passed Môle Jules Giraud, a shell detonated in the engine room, causing heavy casualties and wrecking the lubricating-oil tanks. The automatic stop valve closed, the engines seized, and *Walney* was adrift. More shells destroyed both boilers, scalding the crewmen. Two berthed submarines, a coastal battery above the harbor, and French snipers peppered the *Walney* fore and aft. Shells slammed into the wardroom flat, the captain's cabin, the steering compartment. Topside, the dead were piled three deep. Below, the mess deck resembled a charnel house, scarlet with the blood of butchered infantrymen.

Drifting to the Môle Centre at the western end of the harbor, *Walney* came abeam of the moored destroyer *Epervier*. Survivors in a boarding party managed to fling a grappling hook between the destroyer's funnels, but with no steam to turn the capstans the men could not winch the cutter close enough for boarding. Instead, *Epervier* swept *Walney* with her deck guns, killing Meyrick on the bridge, killing the surgeon Fuller in his sickbay, and killing Colonel Marshall, last seen on the forecastle with a dozen of his doomed men, flinging grenades at the French destroyer. Fire now licked the deck. Of the seventeen men who had stood on the bridge an hour earlier, a solitary survivor stepped among the dead in the red glare of the spreading flames. It was Peters.

Hartland fared no better. Trailing too far behind the motor launches to be screened with their smoke, *Hartland* attracted the initial fury of French fire from Fort Laumone. Tracers danced along her deck, killing most of the cutter's gunners even before she reached the harbor. Shrapnel severed a steam pipe, and a banshee shriek pierced the battle din. Shrapnel also temporarily blinded *Hartland*'s captain at the most inopportune moment, causing the cutter to veer to port and strike the jetty six feet from the harbor entrance. Pinned by the searchlight beam and momentarily aground, *Hartland* was holed and burning by the time she heaved herself from the rocks and made port on the second try. The captain, Lieutenant Commander Godfrey Philip Billot, ordered his gun crews to return fire, but he too was commanding the dead at their breeches. *Hartland* managed only three rounds from her three-inch battery before the guns fell silent for good.

Rounding the Môle Ravin Blanc and approaching the Quai de Dunkerque, the cutter now passed beneath the destroyer *Typhon*. A broadside from 100 feet ripped through *Hartland*'s unarmored hull; she staggered sideways. Shrapnel scythed the bridge, the forward messing compartments, and the dressing station in the wardroom, where medicos and patients alike fell dead. In the engine room, cordite fumes churned with steam from the fractured pipes. Teenage stokers died clutching their shovels. On deck, machine-gun fire swept back and forth monotonously, like a garden sprinkler; the dead were piled so high that survivors could not reach the fire hoses. Sailors helped wounded infantrymen into the unfamiliar life jackets, then heaved them over the side. *Typhon* cased her guns only when the four-inch shells—blowing through *Hartland* like blue flame—threatened other French vessels behind her. At four A.M., Commander Billot dropped anchor and stepped from the bridge; he was immediately wounded in the shoulder and both legs. With ammunition detonating, with flames now funnel high, and with decks glowing red from the inferno below, Billot ordered all survivors to abandon ship.

A mile to the west, *Walney* too was dying. Life trickled across the deck and spilled into the water. Sergeant Ralph Gower clawed his way topside, lost consciousness near the rail, and awoke to find himself pinned beneath a stack of corpses. "Them dead men wouldn't move much," he later said. Marvin Clemons, the demoted physician's assistant, would not have to desert after all: Captain Fuller was dead, and Clemons took four bullets in the right leg before struggling through the water to refuge on a dock. Leo S. Disher, Jr., a journalist aboard *Walney*, struggled to safety despite twenty-five wounds and a life preserver shredded by shell fire. An American soldier yanked Disher from the water with one hand: the other had been shot away.

Men paddled through the oily scum, clinging to flotsam and shielding their heads from hot shrapnel hissing into the water all around. Some French sailors on the docks and aboard the *Epervier* helped rescue survivors. Others murdered the men as they swam, picking them off with rifle and machine-gun fire.

At 4:15 A.M., an explosion tore through *Walney*. Already holed by more than fifty shells, she heeled gracefully and sank. Both the Stars and Stripes and the White Ensign were still flying. Peters, who had been helping with the aft mooring lines, managed to reach shore on a raft with ten other men. French sailors took him prisoner.

Hartland burned into the morning, flames licking at her flags. A final, thunderous explosion blew her to flinders and damaged warehouses around the Môle Ravin Blanc. Of the 200 soldiers aboard, only two had reached shore with their weapons. They were promptly captured.

Dawn brought a strange tranquility. The hollow *pock pock pock* of rifle fire ebbed, then died completely. Clumps of floating debris burned like campfires. Far above, at the shrine of Notre Dame de Santa Cruz, a weathered stone madonna extended her hand toward the harbor, as if to offer absolution for all that she had witnessed.

French marines rounded up the survivors. The badly wounded, groaning and bloody, were hoisted into trucks and ambulances. Others had to walk. Barefoot or in tattered plimsolls, clad only in their underwear and coated with oil, they shuffled in a gray drizzle through the streets of Oran for two miles to a military prison. Weeping Frenchmen lined the sidewalks; jeering Arabs spat and threw stones. Casualties in the RESERVIST force topped 90 percent, about half of whom were killed. Of Marshall's 393 men, 189 were dead and 157 wounded. The toll also included 113 Royal Navy dead and 86 wounded, plus 5 U.S. Navy dead and 7 wounded.

The British would claim that the gallantry of RESERVIST so impressed the French navy that it "contributed to the half-hearted manner" with which the port was sabotaged. But there was nothing halfhearted about it. Even as the bedraggled survivors trudged off to jail, the port commandant ordered the seacocks opened. Within hours, twenty-seven French hulks joined *Walney* and *Hartland* on the harbor floor. Masts and funnels broke the surface at cockeyed angles. Three floating dry docks were scuttled, including the 25,000-ton Grand Dock, which blocked the harbor entrance and later required two months to raise. The Royal Navy took small revenge by sinking or driving aground five French warships that had sortied from Oran; among them, *La Surprise* went down with her captain and fifty crewmen at dawn, while *Epervier*— engulfed in flame—beached herself, and *Typhon* was scuttled in the harbor fairway.

Corpses bobbed to the surface for weeks. They were hauled ashore and wrapped in blankets by men in rowboats with grappling hooks. More than 300 Allied dead confounded the living; the task force had included no mortuary team in the initial landing. Unseemly dickering over who would bury the fallen, and where, would persist for days after Oran had fallen. Finally, Army engineers selected a hilltop outside town and dug long trenches from the chalky hardpan with jackhammers and air compressors. Twenty-nine of those buried remained unidentified. Many men were never found, including George Marshall, who left a widow and two young sons.

Ostensibly to avoid antagonizing the French, Eisenhower's senior British naval commander, Admiral Andrew Browne Cunningham, would insist that "silence is the best policy" regarding RESERVIST. The top British planners overseeing the Oran assault each won commendations. Peters, described by one witness as a dejected, hatless buccaneer wearing a black eye patch, won the Victoria Cross—Britain's highest valor award—and the Distinguished Service Cross, the Americans' second-highest award. Five days after RESERVIST, the fickle winds at Gibraltar brought down his plane and Peters, who was en route to see Churchill, was killed. The French with breathtaking cheek billed the Allies for pilotage fees for *Walney* and *Hartland,* citing a local law requiring payment from every vessel entering Oran harbor.

Eisenhower eventually accepted blame for the debacle during a private meeting with the combined British and American Chiefs of Staff. No consequence attended the gesture. But Andrew Bennett, the American admiral most strident in opposing the operation, persisted in his criticism; he infuriated both the British and Eisenhower, who declared he was "going to get that fellow out of there immediately." Unrepentant, Bennett soon found himself in Iceland.

As for Major General Orlando Ward, still in England with the bulk of his 1st Armored Division, news of the battalion's destruction moved him to scrawl in his diary a fragment from *The Rubáiyát of Omar Khayyám*:

> For some we loved, the loveliest and the best
> That from his Vintage rolling Time hath prest,
> Have drunk their Cup a Round or two before,
> And one by one, crept silently to rest.

In Barbary

FAINT odors of Barbary—charcoal smoke, damp earth, decay—drifted seaward to the nearly 40,000 assault troops preparing to envelop Oran from east and west on the early morning of November 8. Ignorant of the disaster unfolding at the port, the soldiers emptied their pockets of any scraps that could identify their units. The sad detritus of men leaving the world of peace formed little piles in the transport lounges: love letters, dance cards, railroad ticket stubs, lodge pins, driver's licenses. The much maligned cooks roused themselves for a final meal "sumptuous as a condemned man's, and as little appreciated." An enterprising shortwave radio operator managed to pick up the Army–Notre Dame football game and broadcast it to the 16th Infantry Regiment over the ship's public address system. Colonel Alexander N. Stark, Jr., commander of the 26th Infantry Regiment, told his men in a final address, "Let's give them every chance to surrender peacefully with honor, instead of forcing them to fight. This could be a terrific mess if bungled, so let's think clearly." A voice heard in the gloom on one boat deck spoke for many: "Sure I'm scared, you dope. Don't tell me you're not." Soldiers from the 1st Battalion of the 6th Armored Infantry—a sister unit of Colonel Marshall's battalion—stared at the dark coast six miles away. The shoreline was tranquil except for some curious flashes near the harbor. "Looks as if they're not going to fight," the men assured one another.

Under the plan approved by Eisenhower and Clark, Oran was to be captured by a double envelopment of American troops landing on three beachheads—designated X, Y, and Z—spread across fifty miles of coastline and under the overall command of Major General Lloyd R. Fredendall. Tanks beached at X and Z were to race inland before dawn in a pincer movement to help capture two airfields south of Oran while Operation RESERVIST supposedly secured the port. Infantrymen would also encircle the city, preventing any reinforcements from reaching Oran if the French chose to fight. Allied intelligence reported that four thousand French sailors crewed the thirteen batteries of coastal guns protecting the city, and 10,000 soldiers formed the Oran Division.

The largest contingent of invaders—drawn from the U.S. 1st Infantry and 1st Armored divisions aboard thirty-four transport ships—would storm ashore at Beach Z near Arzew, a fishing town sixteen miles east of Oran. Two forts protected Arzew's shingle; the task of capturing them before the main landing fell to the 1st Ranger Battalion. Trained for the past six months by British commandos, the Rangers sported wax-tip mustaches and Vandyke beards in emulation of their tutors. Their lineage dated to French and Indian War irregulars long celebrated for their stealth, their vigor, and their fratricidal brawls. The ranks now included former steelworkers, farmers, a bullfighter, a lion tamer, a stockbroker, and the treasurer of a burlesque theater. Their tough-as-a-boot commander was William O. Darby, a charismatic thirty-one-year-old artilleryman from Arkansas.

From the *Ulster Monarch, Royal Ulsterman,* and *Royal Scotsman,* 500 Rangers packed into landing boats like spoons in a drawer, pale faces peering from beneath their helmet brims. Rather than climb down nets, most men on these particular transports were loaded in their landing craft, which were then lowered from the boat decks by davits and squealing winches. Coxswains cranked the muffled V-8 engines and made for shore, the hulls slapping every ripple. The forward davit cable on one boat snapped as it was being lowered, dumping Rangers, rifles, and Darby's radio into the sea. Amused tars rescued the sputtering men, whose roaring curses filled the night until a louder Cockney voice boomed, "Be bloody thankful our lads dipped you out of the deep."

Two companies, led by Major W. H. Dammer, made straight for Arzew port. They found the French garrison slumbering like a children's nursery. Barrels of sardines curing in brine lined the docks. Eight landing craft lowered their bow ramps, but the sloping seawall was higher than expected and the Rangers slipped back down the slimy stones again and again before finally gaining purchase atop the Grand Quay. Fifteen minutes later they crouched outside Fort de la Pointe, an ancient, moated battery above the harbor. Spotting a French sailor carrying laundry on his head, the lead squad trailed him through the front gate. A few shots rang out, followed by the splat of lead on paving stones and the convulsive jerks of a dying soldier. Rangers took the commandant and his wife into custody, along with sixty sleepy troops. From the landing craft below, a jubilant British sailor bellowed, "For King and country!" Fort de la Pointe had fallen.

Darby meanwhile led his other four companies across a stony beach a mile north of the harbor. Breathing hard, with the land seeming to rise and fall around them after weeks at sea, the Rangers scrambled up a steep ravine to outflank Fort du Nord. Three companies abreast cut their way through a thick belt of barbed wire, rousting a trio of French soldiers from the dugout they were sharing with an Algerian strumpet. A sudden burst of gunfire forced Darby to pull back his men and dump eighty mortar rounds on the fort. Howling Rangers then rushed the sunken emplacements and shoved bangalore torpedoes—steel pipes packed with explosives—into the muzzles of the four big shore guns. Others dumped grenades down ventilator shafts, flushing out gunners who had barricaded themselves in a powder magazine.

Soon the battery commander emerged, a peacoat over his pajamas and carpet slippers. Another sixty sailors trailed behind, carrying a white flag. At Darby's insistence, the commander phoned a nearby garrison used as a Foreign Legion convalescent home and urged surrender; the Legionnaires obliged by flinging their rifles down a well and getting drunk. The mayor of Arzew, his teeth clacking in terror as he clutched the phone receiver with two trembling hands, also agreed to surrender his town.

Darby hurried to a rocky knob overlooking the sea. The Royal Navy would not move the troop transports closer than five miles from shore until assured that the Arzew guns had been spiked. The prearranged success signal was four green flares followed by four sets of double white star clusters. But Darby's white flares had all gone to the bottom with his radio. Frantically, he fired one green rocket after another. Admiring murmurs ran through the troops packing the ships' decks on the horizon. After confused debate, the task force commanders decided the signal meant what indeed it did mean: that in the land of Hannibal and Scipio Africanus, the Allies had captured their first town.

On the weather deck of S.S. *Reina del Pacifico,* a leathery, lantern-jawed major general paced the rail with the bowed stride of a horseman saddle-hardened as a child. Hair the color of gunmetal bristled from his crown. His thick neck and sloping shoulders implied his uncommon strength, fortified with Indian clubs and a medicine ball during the long passage from Britain. He often jogged three miles after breakfast, then spent the rest of the day cadging cigarettes from subordinates by elaborately patting his empty pockets. Two symmetrical scars dimpled his cheeks: a bullet through the face in the Argonne had removed his molars along with an annoying adolescent stutter. When he was intense—and he was intense now—the old wound caused an odd hissing, like a leaky tire. Pacing the rail, wheezing, he paused long enough to study the lime-green threads of phosphorescence trailing the landing craft below. As the first wave of troops beat toward the horizon, he murmured, "The shore."

Terry de la Mesa Allen: even his name swaggered, an admirer once wrote. Commander of the 1st Infantry Division, Terry Allen embodied the unofficial motto of the Big Red One: "Work hard and drink much, for somewhere they're dreamin' up a battle for the First." His exotic middle name came from his mother, daughter of a Spaniard who fought as a Union colonel in the Civil War. From his father, an artillery officer posted mostly in Texas, Allen derived extraordinary equestrian abilities as well as a proclivity for chewing, drinking, and shooting dice. After flunking ordnance and gunnery his final year at West Point, Allen left the academy, graduated from Catholic University, and took a commission in 1912. Wounded at Saint-Mihiel in 1918 and carried from the field on a stretcher, he regained consciousness, ripped off the first-aid tag, and dashed back to rally his men. The next bullet drilled him through the jaw, right to left, but not before he had broken his fist on a German machine-gunner's head.

The drowsy interwar years were hard on an officer later described by an aide as "the fightingest man I ever met." One triumph occurred in January 1922, when the Texas Cattlemen's Association proposed a marathon horse race to determine whether a doughboy could compete with a real cowboy. Major Allen was chosen to represent the Army against Key Dunne, a world champion bronco buster and wagon boss of a 4-million-acre ranch in Chihuahua. Both men were to ride 300 miles to the finish line at the Alamo in San Antonio, Allen from Dallas and Dunne from Fort Worth.

Averaging sixty miles a day, they clattered across the state, Dunne in chaps and sombrero on a blaze-faced mustang named AWOL, and Allen in his snug Army riding uniform on a big black named Coronado. Crowds and banner headlines greeted each rider as he galloped across Texas. "Enough money was bet on the contest to build a battleship," one commentator noted. Upon hearing mid-race that Dunne was short of fodder for his horse, Allen sent him a carload of hay and oats. After 101 hours and 56 minutes in the saddle, the young officer cantered across the finish line, more than seven hours ahead of his rival. Allen accepted the crowd's huzzahs, then trotted off to play polo.

Less successful was Allen's tenure at the Army staff college at Fort Leavenworth: he finished near the bottom of the class in which Major Eisenhower graduated first, and was denounced by the commandant as "the most indifferent student ever enrolled." But as an instructor at the Fort Benning Infantry School, he impressed the assistant commandant, Lieutenant Colonel George C. Marshall, who rated Allen superior or excellent in nine of ten categories on his 1932 efficiency report (he was only satisfactory in "dignity of demeanor"). His gorgeous young wife, Mary Frances, concluded that horses were Terry's second love, after fighting. When Allen's photograph appeared in a Missouri newspaper article about promising young officers, the caption identified him as a "champion rioter and rebel."

With war, the rioters came into their own. In contemplating who should command the Army's multiplying regiments and divisions, Marshall and his training chief, Lesley J. McNair, kept a list in a safe of more than 400 colonels with perfect efficiency reports. Allen, neither a full colonel nor perfect, was not on it. Rather, he was facing court-martial for insubordination in 1940 when word arrived of his double promotion, from lieutenant colonel to brigadier general. He was the first man in his former West Point class to wear a general's stars. No man better exemplified the American military leadership's ability to identify, promote, and in some cases forgive those officers best capable of commanding men in battle. Among the encomiums that followed Allen's promotion was a penciled note: "Us guys in the guardhouse want to congratulate you, too."

After receiving his second star, Allen announced his arrival at the 1st Division by marching down the street crooning "Deep in the Heart of Texas." The oldest division in the Army, the Big Red One had remained largely intact between the wars; it also retained a high proportion of West Pointers and other Regular Army officers. Its "work hard and drink much" philosophy blossomed under Allen, who received a private warning from Marshall about "drinking in the daytime. . . . Be on your guard." Before leaving London, Eisenhower issued a tart memorandum noting that of all American soldiers arrested the previous month in Britain for being drunk and disorderly, two-thirds came from the Fighting First.

Proud, self-absorbed, and ornery, the division was as much a warring tribe as a military unit. "Men of the 18th," Colonel Frank U. Greer proclaimed to his infantry regiment, "we're goin' a-fightin'!" When his superiors sent Allen a warning on the eve of TORCH that the French should not be considered hostile, he had it burned. "You should forget you ever saw this message," he told his intelligence officer. "It would be very dangerous for us at this late hour to begin telling our troops that the French are going to be with us." The fervent loyalty the division felt toward its unorthodox commander was fully reciprocated. "Have never had quite so many perplexing problems to overcome," Allen had recently written Mary Fran and their young son. But, he added, the men were trained and ready to fight. "I now have a really intensive faith in the First Division. They are 1,000 percent better than they were. . . . They are young but are hard and fit. Please remember that I am thinking of you and Sonny all the time."

He swung a leg over the side of the *Reina del Pacifico* and with a gymnast's grace scrambled down the net to the waiting boat below.

Chaos awaited him on the beaches near Arzew. An unanticipated westerly set had pushed the transports and landing craft off course. Dozens of confused coxswains tacked up and down the coast in the dark, looking for the right beaches. Most of the soldiers carried more than 100 pounds of equipment; one likened himself to a medieval knight in armor who had to be winched into the saddle. Once ashore, feeling the effect of weeks aboard ship with a poor diet and little exercise, they staggered into the dunes, shedding gas capes, goggles, wool undershirts, and grenades. Landing craft stranded by an ebb tide so jammed the beaches that bull-dozers had to push them off, ruining their propellers and rudders.

The flat-bottomed oil tankers that were supposed to haul light tanks onto the beach instead ran aground 300 feet from shore; engineers spent hours building a causeway through the surf. As British sailors sounded the depths with a leadline, an American officer barked, "Men, this is what we've been waiting for. Let's have at it!" Stepping over the side of the landing craft with his boots tied around his neck, he promptly sank from sight; his troops hauled him back into the boat as the coxswain edged toward firmer ground.

Linguists holding bullhorns hollered, "*A bas les Boches! A bas les Marcon!* Down with the Boches! Down with the Macaronis! *Vive la France!*" A mortar crew with the 18th Infantry fired a special shell the size of an ostrich egg. It soared 200 feet into the night, detonated with dazzling pyrotechnic sparkle, and unfurled an American flag, which floated to earth; given a clear target at last, French gunners replied with eager fire. "Okay, boys, it's open season," one battalion commander ordered. "Fire at will."

Some fired, others balked. Decanted onto a strange, dark shore, many men feared shooting their own. The hillsides hissed with the night's challenge and countersign: "Hi yo, Silver!" and "Awaaay!" General Allen's pugnacity notwithstanding, many officers had been so indoctrinated not to fire first that French resistance simply baffled them. "They're not shooting at us, they're not shooting at us," one infantry commander insisted, even as French artillery plastered his battalion. Others fired indiscriminately, as one soldier near Arzew later confessed, shooting up "half the grapevines in North Africa." Hunting snipers outside Arzew, soldiers from Company K of the 18th Infantry killed an Arab civilian, who tumbled down a hillside with his robes flying about him. Soldiers from the 2nd Battalion of the 16th Infantry shuffled inland with their equipment piled onto a few commandeered mules and oxcarts until mortar fire forced them into a ditch. When some men moved back to reorganize as ordered, panic took hold, and troops fled down the road in disarray.

Confusion and error, valor and misdeed marked this first night of green troops in combat. Hearing an ominous clanking and a motor roar outside Arzew, 1st Infantry troops whispered hoarsely, "Tank coming!" Someone ordered, "Hold your fire." But a volley from twenty riflemen ripped the night, followed by gurgling: the troops had riddled a wine delivery truck, killing the driver in his cab. "The image of that first casualty, an old truck driver caught in the dark, would be with us always," one soldier later wrote. When a captured French colonial soldier reached into his jacket for his identity papers during interrogation, a skittish American guard ran him through with a bayonet. For some, the war would just last a few hours. A soldier from the 18th Infantry, who had been machine-gunned in the legs, arrived at the field hospital in St. Leu murmuring, "Everything's all right." A chaplain lay next to him until he died. "They're French and always will be French," a wounded correspondent observed of those who had shot him. "The French die hard."

Terry Allen had seen worse. As a battalion commander in France, it was said, he had once pulled a pistol on a hesitant junior officer and shot him in the buttocks. "There," Allen said. "You're out. You're wounded." Such gestures would be unnecessary here. Allen's flamboyance made him easy to caricature—he detested the nickname "Terrible Terry" because it made "me appear like a mountebank"—but during thirty years in the Army he had reduced his philosophy of war to a few commonsense precepts. In attacking, he urged his troops to "ride around 'em, over 'em, and through 'em." And he instructed his officers: "A soldier doesn't fight to save suffering humanity or any other nonsense. He fights to prove that his unit is the best in the Army and that he has as much guts as anybody else in the unit."

Using a flashlight with red tissue over the lens, Allen studied the map and saw that his 18th Infantry Regiment was moving toward St. Cloud, steadily if not quickly. The 16th Infantry was angling farther south to outflank Oran. Initial reports regarding Operation RESERVIST sounded grim, but if the landings west of Oran succeeded, the entire task force could expect to have 18,000 men ashore within twenty-four hours, almost as many as the planners in London had hoped.

His "intensive faith in the First Division" remained as unshaken as his faith in God. "I believe if your cause is just," he often said, "you get divine help." So far the Lord appeared to be behind the Fighting First, just as Allen had requested in his prayers before leaving the *Reina del Pacifico.* Spotting an empty, bloodstained litter near his command post, he lay down and took a nap.

On the other side of Oran, the landings unfolded with the same mix of anarchy and success. At Beach X, nearly thirty miles west of the city, a flying column of light tanks managed to cross the strand and clank inland by mid-morning despite lost boats, unexpected sandbars, and an engine fire that caused one landing craft to burn through the dawn.

At Beach Y, a European seaside resort midway between Beach X and Oran, more than 5,000 infantrymen began staggering ashore along the broad bay at Les Andalouses. Behind the empty cabanas, a short, wrinkled figure clutching a riding crop stood in a jeep with "Rough Rider" stenciled on the fender, shouting "Get on your feet! Keep moving!" Brigadier General Ted Roosevelt had a voice like a foghorn. Prone men on Beach Y blinked hard, picked themselves up, and staggered inland. When Roosevelt spotted a French cavalry patrol working around the flank, he ordered his driver forward in hot pursuit. Bracing a carbine against his shoulder, he dropped one horseman and scattered the others.

Bookmakers in the 1st Division had fixed the odds at 10 to 1 against their assistant division commander surviving more than two weeks in combat. When he learned of the wager months later, Roosevelt bought one losing bettor a $10 meal and lectured him on the evils of gambling. Despite his antique disregard for personal safety, Ted Roosevelt was hard to kill. Like Allen, he was a force of nature. "T.R. and you are very much of the same type as to enthusiasm," George C. Marshall had written Allen. "I am a little fearful." Spotting some old sergeant, Roosevelt would bellow, "Goddam it, but you're ugly! You're uglier every day!" The sergeant, beaming at the recognition, would bark back, "The general isn't a handsome man himself!" Roaring his approval and whacking his leg with the riding crop, Roosevelt then motored down the road in search of another comrade to charm.

Handsome he was not, with his gamecock walk, fibrillating heart, weak and vaguely crossed eyes, and arthritis so severe he needed a cane. In tattered fatigues and a wool cap worn like a cheap wig, he could have been taken for a battalion cook. "He was," an aide allowed, "the most disreputable-looking general I ever met." He was also, in Marshall's estimation, "an A–No. 1 fighting man with rare courage, and what is rarer, unlimited fortitude." Along with Allen and Patton, Ted Roosevelt was said to be the chief of staff's "favorite swashbuckler."

His father, the twenty-sixth president, had warned he would "never amount to more than a $25-a-week clerk," and indeed he took a job out of Harvard working in a carpet factory for a dollar a day. But young T.R. became a rich investment banker by 1914, when he was twenty-seven. As a battalion commander in the 26th Infantry, he was gassed and shot; he finished the Great War as a lieutenant colonel with a permanent limp. He had believed war's "unity of purpose" would "sweat the softness off our bones," but came to disavow that fatuous notion, just as he eventually repudiated his ties to the isolationist group America First. After the war he helped found the American Legion; became a successful writer; and served as assistant secretary of the Navy, governor general of Puerto Rico, colonial governor of the Philippines, chairman of American Express, and vice president of the Doubleday publishing house, where he sponsored wholesome books "as American as Indian corn." In 1941, at the age of fifty-four, he returned to active duty. He and Allen, who was seven months younger, were still working out their command relationship; as Marshall sensed, the two men were far too similar to be entirely comfortable with each other.

Now Roosevelt was ashore with his former regiment, the 26th Infantry, a copy of *The Pilgrim's Progress* crammed in one pocket and a history of medieval England in his kit bag. He had landed in darkness with the first assault wave—"little, scarcely seen black shapes" scuttling out of the sea—and immediately began urging the fainthearted to "march to the sound of the guns." Sometimes, writing home to Oyster Bay, he yearned for "the piping days of peace." But not today. His crowded hour had come, and this spectacle was too magnificent to wish away. Glowing shells whirred overhead, and tracers skipped among the hills until their burning magnesium winked out. Artillerymen—including his son Quentin, a battery commander—hauled pack howitzers across the beach. "With their tow ropes over their shoulders they look like the illustrations in the children's Bibles of building the pyramids," Roosevelt wrote.

The French counterattacked with fourteen ancient Renault tanks, five of them so broken down they had to be towed into battle. All were destroyed in minutes, and their return fire barely smudged the American armor. The first colonial prisoners, Senegalese riflemen with rolling eyes and tribal scars notched in their cheeks, marched past to a freighter converted into a prison ship. A forward patrol reported capturing a French headquarters near La Sénia, five miles south of Oran, but the office safe yielded only two brassieres and a volume of risqué tales.

"Soldier, what in the hell are you doing there?" Roosevelt bellowed to a private cowering behind a hillock. "Come on, follow me." The soldier followed, machine-gun bullets pinging about. Breathing hard, Roosevelt stopped his jeep just long enough to announce that he was heading to the front line in search of a French commander ready to surrender. "If I'm not back in two hours, give it all you've got," he said, then jounced down the road.

"Would God I might die with my sword in hand," he had once written in a poem submitted to *Harper's*, "ringed by dead foes all around." But not today.

VILLAIN

THE American soldiers investing Oran from east and west on this Sunday morning knew no more than their five senses told them, minus the half-truths, untruths, and honest errors spread by rumor on every battlefield. The French had obviously chosen to fight, but how hard and for how long no one could guess. Exhaustion, dislocation, and sudden death seemed as much a part of the Algerian landscape as the sand dunes and *djebels*—rocky hills—that now echoed with cries of "Hi, yo, Silver!" and "Away!" Even the commanders had only the sketchiest notion of how the overall battle for Oran was unfolding: troops ashore at X, Y, and Z; modest progress toward double envelopment of the city; apparent catastrophe at the harbor. Of the simultaneous landings at Algiers and in Morocco, they knew nothing.

One final element in the Oran invasion remained to play out: the first American airborne operation of the war. It was also among the most daring before or since. On the previous afternoon—Saturday, November 7—556 U.S. paratroopers had gathered at two airfields in Cornwall, on England's southwest coast. Faces darkened with camouflage paint, the men had received printed orders specifying where in their jump suits to carry everything from two pencils (left chest pocket) and toilet paper (right hip pocket), to a razor with four blades (right thigh pocket) and four grenades (field jacket pockets). Slips of rice paper—edible, in case the men were captured—contained secret radio code words, including BLACKBIRD ("paratroops have been dropped") and DUCK ("paratroops have been dropped, cannot find airport"). The soldiers taped their bulging pants pockets to keep them from snagging and prepared to board thirty-nine C-47 transport planes.

The objective of Operation VILLAIN was simple enough: to seize two airfields, Tafaraoui and La Sénia, south of Oran, and hold on until reinforcements arrived from the beach landing forces. Simplicity stopped there. The flight from Cornwall covered 1,100 miles—nearly three times as far as any previous combat jump—at night, across neutral Spain with inexperienced pilots and navigators flying for nine hours at 10,000 feet. Beguiled by German parachute operations in Holland and Crete, Allied planners failed to appreciate the high casualties. British commanders opposed the operation, and had told Churchill they preferred to husband the planes and troops for a quick strike into Tunisia. Even the U.S. Army planners responsible for capturing Oran concluded that VILLAIN would make "no material difference." Eisenhower had shared their skepticism. "That's a long ways," he said dryly, but ultimately yielded to Clark, who urged audacity. "The British just want to take our airplanes and use them for something else," Clark had told Eisenhower.

The 2nd Battalion of the 509th Parachute Regiment, commanded by a short, bullet-headed West Pointer named Edson D. Raff, trained hard. But their practice jumps had occurred in daylight and good weather, using large drop zones. Only four sets of navigation instruments could be found for the 60th Troop Carrier Group. Another thirty-five sets, sent from the United States after urgent pleas, had reportedly "miscarried" in transit. At the last minute, navigators received British instruments, with which they were unfamiliar and which would not work in American planes anyway. Maps and charts were so scarce that only flight leaders received them. Some planes had arrived in Cornwall just a few hours before the scheduled takeoff, and crew briefings were limited to a "few minutes of distracted conversation." The frenetic activity left many pilots so tired they could barely keep their eyes open.

Clark had approved one last complication before leaving London for Gibraltar. Because of uncertainty over the French reaction in Algeria, parallel plans were drafted. If resistance appeared likely, Plan A called for the paratroopers to take off from England at five P.M., jump before dawn, and overpower the two airfields. If the French appeared passive, Plan B called for the battalion to leave four hours later, land at La Sénia in daylight, and prepare for another mission toward Tunisia. Lieutenant Colonel Raff and his men were to listen for a broadcast from Gibraltar on November 7, relayed by the Royal Air Force, indicating which plan to use. The phrase "Advance Alexis" meant: carry out Plan A and expect to fight. "Advance Napoleon" meant: carry out Plan B and expect a docile reception.

In the quiet asylum of a London headquarters, this arrangement perhaps made perfect sense. But in the event it miscarried. Distracted by their negotiations with General Giraud at Gibraltar, Eisenhower and Clark paid insufficient heed to the conflicting reports from Algeria regarding French intentions. Notwithstanding Murphy's warnings and other omens, optimism had prevailed at Gibraltar.

At 4:15 P.M. on November 7, Eisenhower's signal arrived at the Cornish airfields near St. Eval and Predannack: "Advance Napoleon." Peace was at hand. Pilots who had been warming their engines now cut the ignition and strolled to the control tower for another cup of coffee. Four hours later, the paratroopers settled into the bucket seats and tugged the blackout curtains over the windows, chattering about the warm weather that surely awaited them in Algeria. Seventy-eight engines coughed once, twice, and caught. The lead aircraft lifted into the thin fog at 9:05 P.M. Captain Carlos C. Alden, a thirty-one-year-old battalion surgeon flying in a plane named *Shark Bait,* scribbled in his pocket diary, "Dear God, in Thy wisdom help me to come back."

After takeoff, almost nothing went right. Fair weather yielded to squalls over the Bay of Biscay. In dodging thunderheads, the pilots lost sight of one another. Soon, of the thirty-nine aircraft flying over Spain, the largest formation still intact was a mere three airplanes. Few of the navigators were proficient in celestial navigation, which thick clouds made difficult anyway, so the planes flew by dead reckoning. A strong east wind, which meteorologists in Britain had failed to detect, steadily shoved the C-47s westward; within a few hours, the unwitting crews were at least fifty miles off course. Colonel Raff's paratroopers—still expecting a docile reception—huddled beneath wool blankets in the frigid cabins, nibbling British army biscuits and chewing wads of gum to ward off airsickness.

Two navigation aids dispatched to help the aircraft find Oran also failed. The British ship *Alynbank,* thirty-five miles off the coast, was supposed to provide a homing beacon by transmitting a radio signal at 440 kilocycles. For reasons never adequately explained, she instead broadcast, unheard, at 460 kilocycles. The second aid was more elaborate. An electronic signaling device code-named REBECCA had been smuggled from Gibraltar to Tangiers to Oran in two heavy suitcases. Before midnight on November 7, an American OSS agent named Gordon H. Browne rode in the back of a French ambulance to a deserted pasture near Tafaraoui airfield. After struggling in the dark to erect a nine-foot mast antenna and guy wires, Browne switched on the apparatus and waited all night in the brush among the cooing plovers, unaware that the paratroopers had delayed their departure on the false expectation of peace. At five A.M., with dawn approaching and the gunfire near Oran now audible, Browne abandoned his vigil. He disassembled the antenna and dragged REBECCA into a cactus patch, where he blew her to pieces.

The sun rose on November 8 at precisely 6:30 A.M. to reveal a scatter of paratroopers across the western Mediterranean. One plane landed at Gibraltar and two at Fez in French Morocco. Four others touched down in Spanish Morocco, where the men—banging their fists against a wall in frustration and shouting, "Fuck! Fuck!"—would be interned for three months. Three more planes miraculously found La Sénia airfield, only to be greeted with a barrage of anti-aircraft fire. This awkward welcome, strongly suggestive of peace gone bad, provoked panicky radio chatter among the pilots, who were down to a very few gallons of fuel. On *Shark Bait*, soldiers began pumping up their life rafts. Colonel William C. Bentley, Jr., the senior airman on the mission and pilot of Raff's plane, landed in a grain field to confirm—through the Socratic quizzing of some bemused Arabs—that he was on the right continent. They had at least found Africa.

Airborne once again, Bentley at eight A.M. spotted more than a dozen C-47s clustered on the western fringe of the Sebkra d'Oran, a dry lake bed stretching for twenty miles south of the coast. An armored column nearby appeared to be preparing to attack the grounded paratroopers. Raff ordered troops in the nine planes now straggling after Bentley to parachute behind the tanks. First out the door, Raff landed hard, cracked a rib, and was spitting blood when he learned that the tanks belonged to the U.S. 1st Armored Division. After landing at Beach X, they were heading for the airfields the paratroopers had failed to seize. Several hundred of Raff's men spent the balance of the morning dodging sniper fire. Bentley meanwhile flew on with his gaggle and landed at the east end of the *sebkra*, where he was immediately captured. French guards marched him to a cellblock at Fort St. Philippe, where he was locked up with several hundred other Allied prisoners, including oil-coated survivors of RESERVIST.

The final act of VILLAIN was no more glorious. With permission from Raff, a resolute band under Major William P. Yarborough decided to capture Tafaraoui airfield on foot. They had hardly walked a furlong before realizing that mud beneath the *sebkra*'s dry crust made crossing the pan like marching through molasses. Shedding ammunition and wool underwear in a conspicuous trail, the men made for the southern rim of the lake bed. Exhausted, they dug shallow trenches with their helmets and collapsed beneath a blanket of weeds. Yarborough radioed for three C-47s to siphon the remaining fuel from the other stranded aircraft and then come fetch him and his men. No sooner had the planes taken off with Yarborough's group aboard for the short hop to Tafaraoui than cannon fire from six French Dewoitine fighters riddled the fuselages. The American pilots spun around, lowered their wheels, and crash-landed onto the *sebkra* at 130 miles per hour. The Dewoitines made three more strafing passes, killing five soldiers and wounding fifteen. When the marauders finally flew away, a dead platoon leader dangled head down from the doorway of Yarborough's plane, the copilot was slumped dead in his cockpit, and even the most audacious paratrooper was discouraged.

Most of Raff's surviving men arrived at Tafaraoui by truck on November 9. The surgeon Carlos Alden, who had petitioned God's protection in Cornwall, was the sole man in the battalion to reach the field by air on the morning of November 8. He had remained on *Shark Bait* after the other paratroopers got out to walk across the *sebkra*.

British skepticism of VILLAIN had been well founded. The operation contributed nothing to the invasion while expending half of all Allied parachute forces. Just fourteen of the thirty-nine planes could fly again immediately. At a time when every infantry squad was precious to the Allied cause, only fifteen paratroopers were judged fit for another mission within three days.

On the first day of their invasion, the Allies had nearly surrounded Oran. They had put thousands of soldiers ashore with only light casualties. The Royal Navy controlled the sea if not the port. But VILLAIN had demonstrated, like RESERVIST before it, that temerity untempered by judgment would exact a heavy price in this war.

To the Last Man

VIEWED from the great half-moon bay that cradled the city, Algiers spread up the verdant hills like an alabaster vision. Distance lent an enchantment not wholly dispelled by the stench of the Arab quarter or the vaguer odor of French colonial rule. Cinemas, emporiums, and chic cafés lined shady avenues enlivened each evening by promenading boulevardiers. Algiers had been an inconsequential hamlet until Moors expelled from Spain in 1492 took sanctuary there. Like Oran, the city soon thrived on piracy, and for more than three centuries sheltered corsair fleets that terrorized the Mediterranean basin. Barbarossa's

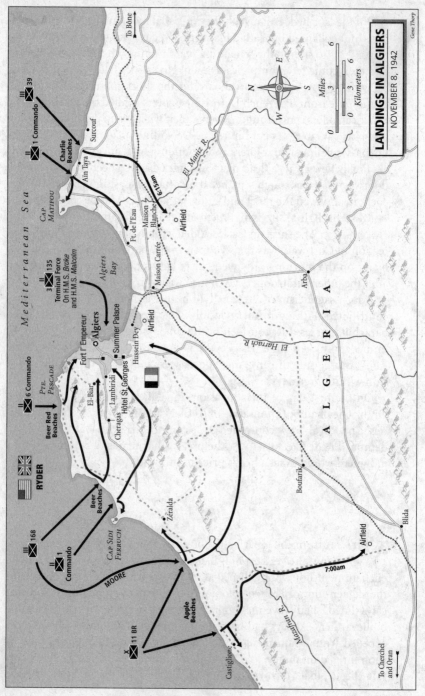

LANDINGS IN ALGIERS
NOVEMBER 8, 1942

Gene Thorp

sixteenth-century palace still crowned the skyline 400 feet above the harbor; a Western traveler in the 1920s fancied that the old heap "resounded to the groans of Christian slaves."

For more than a century, Algiers had been the epicenter of France's North African empire, a "white-walled city of flies and beggars and the best Parisian scent." To one Frenchman, the old pirate haven now resembled "a reclining woman, white and naked, leaning on her elbow." To Eisenhower and his planners, Algiers was the key to Algeria if not the entire African littoral. As the easternmost landing site in TORCH, the city was to provide a springboard for the subsequent drive into Tunisia. The Anglo-American invaders—thinly disguised as an all-American force—would be followed immediately by British troops who were to pivot ninety degrees to the east and make for Tunis.

So it was that Robert Murphy in the earliest minutes of November 8 pelted through the city's affluent suburbs in his big Buick on the most important diplomatic mission of his life. The American envoy had remained in his office until early Saturday evening, affecting a placidity he did not feel. "Two years of hopeful soundings and schemings," as he put it, were about to be tested. Murphy had been stung by the sharp rebuff from Eisenhower and the White House to his proposed delay of the TORCH landings. "I am convinced," he had cabled Roosevelt, "that the invasion of North Africa without favorable French high command will be a catastrophe." The reply from Washington had been unequivocal: "The decision of the president is that the operation will be carried out as now planned." Murphy was instructed "to secure the understanding and cooperation of the French officials with whom you are now in contact."

He had done his best. Trusted French rebels, including General Mast, had been given several days' advance warning of the invasion. Upon hearing a prearranged radio message from London on Saturday night—"*Allo, Robert. Franklin arrivé*"—Murphy alerted the rebels that the landings were about to begin. The coup in Oran had evidently miscarried, but in Algiers several hundred French partisans began to seize key installations despite the failure of Clark to deliver the modern weapons he had promised at Cherchel; the intent, a French historian later wrote, was "to chloroform the city." By ruse and by force, the insurgents soon controlled police and power stations, Radio Algiers, telephone switchboards, and army headquarters, where the French corps commander was held incommunicado. Some Vichy officers happily acquiesced in their arrests—"it saved them," one observer noted, "any painful search of their conscience." As for Murphy's repeated radio query to Gibraltar—"Where is Giraud?"—there had been no satisfactory answer.

At 12:45 A.M. on Sunday he arrived at the Villa des Oliviers, a blocky, mustard-hued Arab palace in the well-heeled enclave of el-Biar; brushing past the tall Senegalese sentries, Murphy rapped on the door. A swarthy, mustachioed man in a foul mood came to the foyer. General Alphonse Pierre Juin, commander of all Vichy ground troops in North Africa, usually favored a Basque beret and a mud-spattered cape; at this moment he wore pink-striped pajamas. Maimed in 1915, Juin had been authorized to salute with his left hand, but he offered Murphy neither salute nor handshake.

"I am happy to say that I have been instructed by my government to inform you that American and British armies of liberation are about to land," Murphy said.

"What! You mean the convoy we have seen in the Mediterranean is going to land here?"

Murphy nodded, unable to suppress a nervous grin.

"But you told me only a week ago that the United States would not attack us."

"We are coming by invitation," Murphy said.

"By whose invitation?"

"By the invitation of General Giraud."

"Is he here?"

Preferring not to disclose that Giraud was sulking in a Gibraltar cave, Murphy waved aside the question. "He will be here soon."

Murphy described the invasion forces lurking off the African coast, multiplying their size severalfold. "Our talks over the years have convinced me," he told Juin, "that you desire above all else to see the liberation of France, which can come about only through cooperation with the United States."

Now the opéra bouffe began in earnest. General Juin voiced sympathy with the Allied cause but was hindered by the unexpected presence in Algiers of his superior officer. "He can immediately countermand any orders I issue," Juin said. "If he does, the commands will respect his orders, not mine." Twenty minutes later, after a quick phone call and the hurried dispatch of a driver with the Buick, one of the war's most reviled figures strolled into the Villa des Oliviers.

In a truncated nation of small men, Admiral Jean Louis Xavier François Darlan stood among the smallest. Stumpy and pigeon-breasted, given to jocose vulgarity and monologues on the efficiency of the German army, he was the sixty-one-year-old scion of French sailors. The death of his great-grandfather at Trafalgar supposedly fed Darlan's pathological hatred of the British, although it was the Americans who called him Popeye. The French fleet was his fiefdom, but he also served as Marshal Pétain's dauphin and commander of all Vichy armed forces. His favors to the Nazis had included the use of Vichy airports in Syria and resupply aid to Rommel through Tunisia. Churchill called him "a bad man with a narrow outlook and a shifty eye."

By a coincidence that would forever seem either contrived or divine, Darlan was in Algiers to attend his son, Alain, who lay in the Hôpital Maillot so reduced by polio that his coffin had been ordered. Several times in the past two years, the admiral had privately hinted at supporting the Allies if circumstances warranted. Just before Eisenhower left London for Gibraltar, Churchill had told him, "If I could meet Darlan, much as I hate him, I would cheerfully crawl on my hands and knees for a mile if by doing so I could get him to bring that fleet of his into the circle of Allied forces." Roosevelt on October 17 had sent Murphy similar if less histrionic instructions, authorizing any arrangement with the Vichy admiral that might help TORCH.

But Darlan seemed disinclined to parley. Upon learning of the imminent invasion, he flushed and replied, "I have known for a long time that the British are stupid, but I have always believed Americans were more intelligent. Apparently you have the same genius as the British for making massive blunders."

For fifteen minutes, Darlan paced the room and sucked on his pipe. Murphy shortened his stride and paced beside him, insisting, "The moment has now arrived!" The admiral waved off the entreaties. "I have given my oath to Pétain," he insisted. "I cannot revoke that now." But he agreed to radio Vichy for guidance. Upon stepping outside, however, the men found that the Senegalese guards had been replaced by forty rebels wearing white armbands and armed with long-barreled rifles dating to the Franco-Prussian War. Juin was incredulous. "Does this mean we are prisoners?" he asked.

It did. Murphy's colleague, the Apostle Kenneth Pendar, was dispatched to the Admiralty office downtown with Darlan's sealed message for Vichy, which Pendar promptly opened, read, and discarded as insufficiently zealous for the Allied cause. Returning to the villa, Pendar told Darlan cryptically, "The necessary has been done."

As the impasse dragged on with no word from Vichy and no sign of the Allied invaders, Murphy dimly wondered whether he had confused the date and launched his putsch a day early. The hours ticked past. Dawn approached. Darlan stopped pacing and puffing long enough to offer some thoughtful political advice. "Giraud is not your man," he said. "Politically he is a child. He is just a good division commander, nothing more."

The insurrection, in fact, was collapsing. Loyalist forces gathered their composure—"This isn't just a civil defense drill?" one perplexed Vichy officer asked—and recaptured the strong points one by one. At army headquarters, insurgents and loyalists sang the "Marseillaise" together before the rebels stacked their arms and filed from the building. Upon learning of the events in Algiers and Oran, Pétain in Vichy sent President Roosevelt a curt message: "France and her honor are at stake. We have been attacked. We will defend ourselves."

A loyalist patrol with three tanks arrived at the gates of the Villa des Oliviers, dispersing the rebels and locking Murphy and Pendar in the porter's lodge. Juin's aide rushed about waving an enormous revolver at the Americans, crying, "What have you done? What have you done?" Pendar wondered if he had blundered into a production of *Pirates of Penzance*. A Senegalese sentry offered each American a Gitane cigarette, the customary courtesy to those about to face a firing squad.

Regrettably, the Allies had planned a frontal assault on Algiers harbor that was identical to RESERVIST in folly. Again the mission was concocted and commanded by the British, with a predominately American supporting cast. Code-named TERMINAL and designed to capture the port intact, the attack featured two antiquated destroyers, H.M.S. *Broke* and H.M.S. *Malcolm*, under Captain H. L. St. J. Fancourt of the Royal Navy. Engineers welded quarter-inch iron sheeting, three feet high, around the upper deck of each ship as a thin shield against sniper fire. Forward compartments in the bow were filled with concrete, and heavy armor plates covered the prow. About the time Murphy began wondering whether he had confused the invasion date, these floating rams reached the eleven-fathom line in the Bay of Algiers and swung west toward the boom blocking the harbor entrance.

The 686 soldiers aboard *Broke* and *Malcolm* came from the 3rd Battalion of the 135th Infantry, which had left Minnesota almost two years earlier to join her sister regiments from Iowa in the 34th Division. The regiment's motto—"To the last man"—had been hard won at Gettysburg. The 3rd Battalion called itself "the Singing 3rd," and had mastered an impressive repertoire of barracks ballads, including one bawdy British ditty called "There's a Troopship Now Leaving Bombay." The unit retained its Minnesota accent, and the ranks were full of Ericksens, Carlsons, and Andersens. The battalion commander, Lieutenant Colonel

Edwin T. Swenson, was a former assistant warden of the Minnesota State Penitentiary at Stillwater.

Witty and bighearted, with the craggy face of a prizefighter, Colonel Swenson was reputedly capable of swearing fluently for hours without ever repeating an expletive; he had told the British that his battalion's top sergeant was whoever could whip him in a fistfight. Captain Fancourt in turn told Swenson that Allied commandos would capture French batteries overlooking the port; that several of the French guns could not be tilted low enough to hit targets below anyway; and that initial landings east and west of Algiers, which would start before the TERMINAL attack, would likely draw defenders away from the harbor. None of this proved true.

The lights of Algiers twinkled as the destroyers made for the boom extending from the crescent seawall. American flags flapped from the masts. Then the city lights went out and searchlight beams scissored across the water. Swenson briefly believed they were meant to direct the intruders toward the harbor entrance. But the beams found and fixed both ships, blinding those on the bridge. Sporadic gunfire opened as *Broke*, with *Malcolm* a mile astern, sheered to starboard to avoid a breakwater and then came about under a thick screen of smoke. A second try to find and sever the boom also failed, as did efforts to shoot out the searchlights and to illuminate the harbor mouth with flares, which were swallowed by the destroyers' own smoke.

By this time, French gunners had ranged *Malcolm*. Beginning at 4:06 A.M., shells smacked through the hull, perforating the boilers and reducing the destroyer to four knots. Swathed in white steam, she made an easy target. Other shells hit the funnels. Fragments sprayed across the deck, where 300 infantrymen had flattened out behind the useless sniper shields. Fire broke out amidships among the pasteboard crates of mortar ammunition stacked on the center hatch. With the ship listing so badly to starboard that her weather deck was only six inches from the water, soldiers hurled flaming mortar crates over the deck rail. *Malcolm* managed to get under way again and limped seaward, where the crew spent the next several hours hosing blood and brains from the deck and heaving the dead overboard in weighted shrouds fashioned from mattress covers.

Then, on his fourth try for the port, *Broke*'s skipper, Lieutenant Commander A.F.C. Layard, spotted a pair of dim green buoy lights marking the harbor entrance. He increased speed to twenty knots and easily sliced through the boom of chained timber baulks. Layard berthed at the Môle Louis Billiard while the destroyer's guns silenced sniper fire from the docks.

Badly shaken, Colonel Swenson and the Singing 3rd were slow to rise from the deck, but eventually scurried across the extended brows to the quay. Swenson instructed his men to "light out like stripey-assed baboons up the wharf until you can get some cover, then fight like hell." But little fighting was necessary. As dawn broke over Algiers, the Americans controlled the electric power station, Morey's Oil Depot, and several warehouses on the southern wharves near the seaplane base. Round objects that had resembled coastal defense guns in aerial photos proved to be latrines. Church bells across the city pealed out the Angelus call to Sunday mass. A preternatural peace settled over the quays and the handsome white houses stretching up to the Rue Michelet. Soldiers joked about how Algiers smelled like a saloon, the consequence of gasoline shortages that forced most vehicles to burn alcohol. Swenson strained to hear the tramp of boots from the 168th Infantry—the sister regiment from southwest Iowa—marching downhill to relieve their comrades on the docks after landing west of the city.

Instead, he heard the abrupt rush of artillery shells from a battery at Jetée du Nord a mile to the north. French sailors had dismantled an old wall to give the casemate guns a clear field of fire along the waterfront. The third round clipped *Broke*'s forepeak and burst against the quay wall in a great splash of smoke and masonry. With permission from Captain Fancourt, Layard parted all lines and moved the destroyer to a new berth in the lee of a French freighter along the Quai de Dunkerque. Calm returned until 9:20 A.M., when French gunners again opened fire with a howitzer battery above the port. The first six shots missed the destroyer; the next five hit. Shells burst in the chart house and the wardroom. Another blew through the sick bay, killing one physician and tearing the right arm from another, who kept himself conscious with morphine long enough to advise an American medic on how to perform several urgent amputations.

Fancourt sounded the recall siren. But with Swenson's troops scattered across the docks under sniper fire, only sixty men had scrambled back to *Broke* before she again parted lines and zigzagged from the harbor, smoke trailing her like a veil. Private First Class Harold Cullum, shot in the arm and abdomen earlier in the morning, crawled to the end of the pier too late to board; he lay in the sun munching sulfa tablets and sipping from his canteen, watching *Broke* steam from sight. "The morale effect of a destroyer sunk in the port in full view of the town might have an adverse effect on the situation," Fancourt explained three days later. The morale effect of stranding 250 soldiers ashore was not addressed. Holed twenty-two times, *Broke* soon sank anyway, after all hands had leaped to the deck of a rescue ship.

Even with the ship gone, Swenson kept heart. He estimated that four French infantry companies surrounded Môle Louis Billiard—imposing numbers, but not overwhelming. He hesitated to use his mortars and machine guns for fear of killing the civilians who could be seen peering from doorways and intersections. But Royal Navy bombers pummeled the noisome battery on the Jetée du Nord, and Swenson continued to hope that the 168th Infantry would soon arrive as planned. Fashioning breastworks from hay bales and shipping crates, he organized an outer perimeter to keep French troops beyond hand grenade range and an inner defense to shield his wounded and his heavy weapons.

Then the unmistakable creak of armored tracks echoed through the quays. Several Renault light tanks peppered the breastworks with machine-gun and 37mm cannon fire. Swenson gathered the few anti-armor grenades available and positioned his gunners to ambush the approaching tanks; every grenade missed. Hay bales ignited, and fire spread to the warehouses. Two more Renaults arrived to set up a cross-fire, backing the Americans to the water's edge. Mortar rounds detonated as flames reached stacks of ammunition cases. With his riflemen low on cartridges, Swenson instructed the men to fix bayonets, then thought better of the order. Already, TERMINAL had cost twenty-four Allied dead and fifty-five wounded. Complete annihilation of the men on the dock would serve no cause. At 12:30 P.M., Swenson raised a white flag and surrendered.

Stretcher bearers quickly trundled away the wounded; encroaching flames threatened to ignite their bandages. Lining up Swenson and his men, Senegalese troops were stripping them of watches, rings, and billfolds when a French officer stepped in, ordered the booty returned, and threatened to shoot the looters. A diehard sniper fired a final shot as the Americans marched uphill to prison. The bullet killed Corporal Alvin Ronning, a tall blond farm boy from Milan, Minnesota: So jubilant were the French defenders at repelling the assault that they neglected to scuttle the port, unlike the wrecked harbor at Oran. For the Americans in TERMINAL, this accidental victory nearly redeemed their ordeal.

Thirty-three thousand Allied troops stumbled onto the beaches east and west of Algiers on November 8 without grace, finesse, or agility. Overloaded landing craft shipped water and sank. Others foundered when their bow ramps opened prematurely, or broached from an inexperienced hand on the tiller. Some scrambling nets proved too short, requiring soldiers to leap six feet into the waiting boats. Despite orders to preserve utter silence, the pandemonium was such that "I should have thought the Germans in Berlin could have heard us," one officer later wrote. The East Surreys and Royal West Kents finally got their rum ration, with the result that at least two officers ostensibly "testing for salt" staggered semiconscious to their bunks while the merry troops embarked for the Barbary shore in full throat.

Finding the right beach at night in Algiers proved even harder than at Oran. Boats puttered for hours, pursuing one signal light after another like children chasing fireflies. Seasickness so immobilized strong men that they envisioned being court-martialed for cowardice. Shouted queries across the water—"Who are you? Where are you going?"— brought incoherent moans or the rudest invective. A British beach-master, wearing white cuffs to be better seen in the dark, greeted boat after boat with a cheerful demurral: "I'm sorry to tell you, but you're on the wrong beach!" Six landing craft drifted two miles off course to fall within range of a French battery at Ilot de la Marine; four were sunk. So many other boats were mishandled that only six of 104 in the Algiers flotilla survived the initial trip to shore. The half-dozen survivors put to sea again to pick up a second wave, only to find their mother ships gone; an unexpected 2½-knot westward set had pushed the convoy eleven miles to leeward in four hours.

Outnumbered five to one, the French defenders offered little coherent resistance. Near Cap Matifou on the eastern lip of the Bay of Algiers, sol-diers unloaded by error on a sandbar clung to a toggle rope and bounced into the beach like kangaroos, springing off the sandy bottom through water over their heads. British and American commandos at Matifou found the coastal battery they were seeking, then threw grenades down an ammunition elevator. The dull detonations were followed by screams and a sharp, accented reproach: "Why don't you go fight the Germans?" British naval gunfire fell short, hitting civilians and Allied troops alike; a French farmer trudged past on the coastal road, carrying the body of his dead twelve-year-old son. Other French families walked to early mass in their fine clothes, gazes averted from the Allied soldiers tramping past. In the town square at Aïn Taya, troops who had been dumped into the surf warmed themselves at a huge bonfire while an enterprising wine mer-chant unshuttered his shop, and villagers still in their nightclothes gath-ered to gawk at what the sea had heaved up on this strangest of Sunday mornings.

On the far western fringe of the Allied landings, the British 11th Brigade landed 7,000 men at Castiglione to find that a sympathetic French officer had declined to issue ammunition to his troops. At Sidi Ferruch, where in 1830 a French army had claimed Algeria for

Napoleon II, the garrison capitulated in minutes. A French artillery major stepped from the shadows near the beach and declared, "You gentlemen are late."

The 168th Infantry of the U.S. 34th Division, which was supposed to hurry east to reinforce Swenson's beleaguered TERMINAL force at Algiers harbor, was both late and lost. Four thousand Americans in the regiment were scattered along fifteen miles of coastline. Officers raced up and down narrow country lanes in confiscated autos, searching for their commands. Among the displaced was Major Robert Moore, the former Boy Captain from Villisca, Iowa, now second-in-command of the regiment's 2nd Battalion. Launched before midnight from the *Keren,* Moore led two companies in nine landing craft to an assembly area several hundred yards from the ship. After futilely waiting almost an hour for the rest of the battalion flotilla to arrive, Moore ordered the coxswain to turn toward land.

A naval officer motoring through the swell a mile offshore assured Moore that he was on course. But after beaching the boats and dragging their equipment across the sand, the men were chagrined to see British 11th Brigade troops. Moore quickly deduced that instead of landing at the beach code-named Beer White, the boat crews had veered eight miles down the coast to *Apple* White. Moore sent a scouting party inland; when it failed to return, he rousted the remaining 200 men from their bivouac and set out to find the rest of his battalion.

The deficiencies of the past two years in preparing the 34th Division for war now began to tell. The amateurish football field maneuvers and town-square drilling by the Iowa National Guard seemed irrelevant in the scrub pines of coastal Algeria. The hurried dispatch of the 34th to Britain ten months earlier, the dispersal of regiments across Northern Ireland, the poor training facilities, the rapid turnover in commanders, and the diversion of troops for use as laborers and headquarters guards meant that most of the infantry units arriving in Africa "were not prepared for combat service," as a division history acknowledged. Like other regiments in the division, the 168th had a proud history, including five battle ribbons won in the Great War. But old ribbons would not take Algiers, nor infuse the men with combat experience, nor tell Bob Moore where he was.

Moore marched his two companies for more than a mile through vineyards and pine copses along the coastal hills before concluding that he was on the wrong road. He halted the men and ordered a counter-march, but the lieutenant at the head of the column failed to get word and instead continued unawares with a small vanguard. At mid-morning,

200 French colonial troops in a dozen trucks drove past Moore and his men, who stared wide-eyed and silent until the convoy disappeared from sight without a shot.

Hours after landing, footsore and thirsty, Moore heard gunfire in Lambiridi, just west of Algiers. A French machine gun on a knoll overlooking the road had killed two soldiers from Company G and wounded two others. Moore ordered three platoons to outflank the position; after a flurry of shots, seven enemy soldiers surrendered. French sniper bullets chewed into masonry walls and gouged divots from the pavement while children with outstretched palms begged cigarettes from American soldiers huddled in the doorways. Arabs in grimy robes and blackened sandals ambled across the square, acknowledging neither the snipers nor their American targets.

Moore hurried across an exposed intersection by mingling with the pedestrians, then tried to organize another flanking assault. He now commanded fragments from all three of the regiment's battalions, including scores of stragglers. A second machine gun, firing from an upper floor, killed a lieutenant and wounded a captain. Moore worked his way along a hill overlooking the house. Squirming forward on his belly, he carefully rose up for a better look.

Suddenly he was on his back, stunned and confused. A private next to him was bleeding from a gunshot wound. Moore unsnapped his own chin strap and removed his helmet. A deep groove from a sniper's bullet ran across the crest like a black scar. An inch lower and the first round ever fired at the Boy Captain would have killed him.

For the first time, Moore realized how frightened he was. Even nameless skirmishes could be lethal. "I thought the fight with the snipers was quite a battle," he would say months later, after receiving the Silver Star for his valor at Lambiridi. "Now I know it was just a comic-opera war." Still, good men lay as dead as if at Antietam or the Meuse-Argonne. When he had time to scribble a letter home, Moore wrote, "I got my helmet creased and set back on my butt before I realized that I was being shot at. Outside of that and being scared, I came out okay."

In these first hours of the war, Moore had learned several vital lessons that thousands of other American soldiers were also learning around the rim of Africa. Some lessons were fundamental: stay low; take a few extra moments to study the map before setting off. But others involved the nature of combat and leadership: a realization that battlefields were inherently chaotic; that improvisation was a necessary virtue; that speed and stealth and firepower won small skirmishes as well as big battles; that every moment held risk and every man was mortal.

Moore shoved the helmet back onto his head and summoned a medic to attend the wounded private. The living awaited orders, and the white roofs of Algiers gleamed in the distance. Bob Moore, unhurt but now blooded, pressed on.

"Glory Enough for Us All"

THE stars had once again eaten from Kent Hewitt's hand. Four thousand miles from Hampton Roads, Task Force 34 approached the Moroccan coast on the night of November 7 with celestial precision, eight minutes ahead of schedule.

More than 100 ships in nine columns had steamed across the Atlantic in a box measuring twenty miles by thirty, zigzagging so vigorously that each wake was said to resemble the path "of a reeling drunk in the snow." Following a sharp rebuke from Admiral Hewitt for radio chatter that sounded "more like a Chinese laundry at New Year's than a fleet going to war," the convoy had fallen silent for two weeks; expertly tossed semaphore signals now flew from one side of the armada to the other in ten minutes. Sailors still scraped the painted bulkheads to bare metal. Hundreds of new soldiers had been virtually press-ganged for the invasion; sergeants taught them how to load, aim, and fire a rifle from the fantail. Other troops broke out the newfangled bazookas. After pondering the stovepipe design, a volunteer clad in an asbestos firefighter's suit squeezed the trigger and launched a round into a wave. The roaring back blast flung hot debris to the rear, and the wounded whitecap swept on. But troops at the rail cheered as though a dragon had been slain.

A gale born south of Iceland had struck the fleet on November 4 near Madeira, with seas so foul that even heavy cruisers rolled thirty degrees. Battalion surgeons treating the seasick exhausted their stocks of belladonna and phenobarbital. The captain of the transport *Charles Carroll* studied his clinometer and, with a dispassion that terrified every landlubber in earshot, mused, "I can't believe a ship can roll so far without turning over." The four top-heavy escort carriers, known collectively as the Old Indispensables, wallowed so grievously that during each perilous yaw sailors took bets on whether the ships would recover.

For Hewitt, the storm posed the greatest challenge of his naval career. Surf higher than five feet was considered lethal to amphibious landings; seas up to eighteen feet now pounded the Moroccan coast. For weeks, meteorologists had repeatedly flown from Gibraltar to the Azores, taking measurements and jotting cabalistic symbols in their notebooks in an effort to better understand weather patterns in the eastern Atlantic. Reconnaissance pilots had photographed the Moroccan surf so often they could now report that waves averaged ten feet in height, even without a northeaster blowing, and broke in thirty-second sets of seven. A radio transmission from the War Department included a forecast of landing conditions on November 8: "Very poor."

Hewitt paced *Augusta*'s heaving bridge, studying the forecast and similarly disheartening messages from the Navy Department and the British Admiralty. The lives of 34,000 soldiers weighed heavily in his musings; history had often punished invaders who disregarded the weather. But a decision was required by dawn on November 7, to allow time for the fleet to split and take station off the three landing sites along the Moroccan coast. American troops were to seize an all-weather airfield at Port Lyautey in the north and, through landings above and below Casablanca, envelop the city and capture her port. Hewitt reduced his problem thus: he could wait for surer seas, but with fuel supplies dwindling, U-boats threatening, and the French surely alert at their guns; he could divert into the Mediterranean in search of a shoreline that was more benign yet far from the crucial port at Casablanca; or he could launch the landing craft as planned and hope for the best. Lord Louis Mountbatten, commander of British amphibious forces, had been reading the same grim weather forecasts in London. "I hope to God," Mountbatten said, "Admiral Hewitt will have the guts to go through with it."

The choice was Hewitt's, but Patton, who would assume command of the expedition once the troops were ashore, urged him forward. Patton had spent the long passage reading the Koran, exercising in his cabin by holding the dresser and running in place—480 steps, he calculated, made a quarter-mile—and issuing proclamations.

"We are to be congratulated because we have been chosen," he told his troops. "You must succeed, for to retreat is as cowardly as it is fatal. Americans do not surrender." Soldiers should prepare for battle with "daily calisthentics of as violent a nature as the facilities of the ship permit." He briefly terrorized his staff upon discovering that propaganda leaflets prepared by the War Department were written in bad French. The *accent grave* in *fidèle,* for example, was missing. "Some goddam fool in the States forgot to put the accents in this thing," Patton told his intelligence officer. "Get a bunch of your men and put them to work. Let them put the accents where they belong, or none of these goddam leaflets will be dropped. Or do you expect me to land on French soil introduced by such illiterate calling cards?" Thousands of leaflets had been restored to literacy by a platoon of soldiers with pencils.

Despite their early antipathy, Patton and Hewitt had grown closer during the voyage, and their partnership now verged on real friendship. Yet Patton still suspected the Navy would avoid a fight if possible. "War is the only place where a man really lives," he liked to say; the thought of flinching from combat was excruciating. Before leaving Norfolk, Patton had asked Eisenhower for secret authority to force Hewitt to bombard Casablanca if the admiral showed weakness in the knees. Eisenhower promptly replied that "no, repeat no, bombardment will be executed without prior authority from me. . . . In the unlikely event of a complete failure in signal communications, you will use your own discretion as to the action to be taken." Thus shackled, Patton blithely dismissed the danger that landing craft would capsize in high surf: "You know what happens when things get overturned. They get washed ashore. If that happens, the men will get washed ashore, and then they'll be there ready to fight."

In the smallest hours of November 7, Hewitt was dozing on a cot in his command post on *Augusta*'s flag bridge when his aerologist woke him. Lieutenant Commander R. C. Steere carried a smudged weather map and a flashlight. Steere had concluded that the War Department and Navy forecasts were wrong. The storm would abate. He handed Hewitt a typed sheet of paper with his own prediction: "Swell and surf will be much reduced by offshore winds. Saturday night waves will be of the order of two to four feet."

Hewitt studied Steere's report and barometric charts. High seas would likely return on Monday, November 9, giving the invaders a day to gain a beachhead. One of Kent Hewitt's favorite concepts was that of "velvet," a sufficient margin of safety to allow for unexpected reverses. Divine Providence, he now believed, had given him some velvet. Without betraying the turmoil churning within him, Hewitt issued his orders: "Gentlemen, we will execute Plan One, as scheduled. Be prepared to make that signal to the task force at first daylight." In London, Mountbatten judged this "one of the most important decisions of the war . . . a brave decision, the decision of a commander."

At dawn on November 7, twenty-six ships carrying 6,000 assault troops peeled away from the convoy and headed toward Safi, in southern Morocco. Eight hours later, twenty-seven other ships with 9,000 soldiers veered north toward Mehdia, a coastal village near Port Lyautey. Hewitt's main force, with almost 20,000 troops under Patton's oversight, continued on toward Fedala, just north of Casablanca. A solitary banana boat spotted on the western horizon proved to be the intrepid *Contessa*; rolling deep in the water from her cargo of bombs and high-octane aviation fuel, she had crossed alone. Wary of being gunned down by trigger-happy

American sailors, the jailhouse crew hoisted the Honduran flag and a vivid assortment of signals, including "I am a straggler." Hewitt dispatched a destroyer to escort *Contessa* to Mehdia, and bluntly warned the explosive scow to keep her distance from the rest of the fleet.

With new urgency, soldiers studied the coastline recognition silhouettes painted on wardroom bulkheads. Medical officers believed that clean soldiers had a better chance of surviving wounds and infections, and they ordered every man going ashore to shower. The troop holds "resembled a fraternity house before a big dance," one sailor reported. "All hands were scrubbing down." No one told the men that the Army had secretly projected first-day battle casualties in Morocco of 1,700 killed or drowned, and 4,000 wounded. Sailors tested their winches, regreased the blocks and running gear, and shifted deck cargo off the hatch covers. Others wetted down wooden decks and manila lines to make them less combustible. Many soldiers were puzzled at the notion of combat against the French. "Come on, boys," a gunner's mate suggested, "let's pretend they're Japs."

Commanders with an impulse to declaim offered the men the solace of their rhetoric. The skipper of *Massachusetts* uttered the Latin motto of the state for which his battleship was named: *"Ense petit placidam sub libertate quietem,"* which every swab no doubt could translate as "With the sword she seeks peace under liberty." Rear Admiral Robert C. Giffen, who commanded the warship escorts under Hewitt, declared, "Hit hard and break clean. There is glory enough for us all." *Brooklyn*'s captain summoned the ship's chaplain and confided, "I'm not a praying man myself, but here's the sentiment I want to put into language appropriate for the Almighty: 'O, Lord, gangway for a fighting ship.'"

Patton napped briefly before appearing on *Augusta*'s bridge in the early hours of November 8. His own final words had included sound advice for the infantry: "Get off that damned beach as fast as you can." He was still leery of orders, passed from Marshall to Eisenhower to Allied commanders, to "avoid firing the first shot." Patton had told his commanders, "Do not risk the lives of thirty thousand men trying to decide who wants to surrender and who doesn't. . . . If they show white flags, don't attack. But I doubt if you can see the white flags." American soldiers "must have a superiority complex," he insisted, and letting the French shoot first did not contribute to that elevated mentality.

On the darkened bridge Patton's temper flared anew at the sound of Roosevelt's voice over the ship's public address system. The president's appeal to the Vichy government, secretly recorded at the White House in English and French, was being broadcast every half hour by the BBC.

"We come among you solely to destroy your enemies and not to harm you," Roosevelt proclaimed. "Do not obstruct, I beg of you, this great purpose." Patton had pleaded in vain with Eisenhower to forestall this broadcast, since the Moroccan invasion would begin several hours after those in Algeria. (The delay was intended to prevent Moroccan defenders from spotting Hewitt's ships before nightfall on November 7.) *"Vive la France eternelle!"* Roosevelt concluded. Men listening on *Augusta* and other ships were aghast. Not a single landing craft had yet been launched. Patton paced the bridge, mimicking Roosevelt's stringy French: *"Mes amis . . . Mes amis."*

He paused in his fuming to study the sea. The wind had died and the swell was flattening. Aerologist Steere had been right. By dawn the Atlantic would be calm as a millpond. "I guess," Patton said, "I must be God's most favorite person."

Down the length of Morocco, the French slept unawares. Fuel shortages had long grounded Vichy coastal air patrols, and no one monitored the BBC, which was disdained as mere propaganda. Roosevelt's appeal went unheard, Hewitt's ships undetected, Patton's pique unsuspected.

Only rebels were afoot. For more than two years, British and American agents had tried to organize a fifth column in Morocco. The results had been mixed. A scheme by Moroccan Jews to blow up 5,000 tons of rubber on the Casablanca docks came to naught; but the insertion of an eavesdropping microphone at the German armistice commission succeeded admirably. The Apostles had formed several cells of secret agents with exotic noms de guerre (Mr. Fish, Sea Slug, Leroy the Badger) and imaginative covers (a onetime Foreign Legionnaire known as Pinkeye ostensibly worked as a black-market macaroni salesman). Leading the insurrectionists was "Black Beast," Major General Émile Béthouart. The commander of the Casablanca division and a hero of the Franco-Polish expeditionary force that fought in Norway in 1940, Béthouart had been enlisted as a conspirator by Robert Murphy and General Mast. At eight P.M. on November 7, he informed ten trusted officers of the imminent Allied landing and dispatched them to secure various garrisons and landing fields. They rushed off, Béthouart later recalled, "with almost a juvenile enthusiasm." Six hours later he awoke the sleeping resident-general of Morocco, General Auguste Paul Noguès, in Rabat, and informed him that the country was being delivered to the Allies. He also arrested the chief of Vichy air forces in Morocco, urging him, "Have a seat in a good arm chair."

After that, nothing went right. Noguès was a slippery equivocator known to the Allies as "No-Yes"; he barricaded himself in his palace and declined to believe that a hundred American ships could sneak up on his country undiscovered. On a secret phone line that he had just installed between the palace and the Admiralty in Casablanca, Noguès called his naval chief and told him of the putsch. Vice Admiral François Michelier peered seaward, then assured the resident-general that no Allied fleet lurked offshore and that such an expedition was "not technically possible." Michelier phoned back to confirm this assessment at three A.M., four A.M., and five A.M. Gathering the fortitude needed to assure his own preservation, Noguès accused Béthouart of being duped by a "group of idiots" and ordered a general alert. Béthouart lost heart and surrendered; he was promptly jailed, consoled only by the two bottles of champagne smuggled into his cell by a prison doctor.

In Casablanca, squads of Senegalese soldiers set up their machine guns with languid gestures. Platoons of spahi cavalrymen in heavy capes cantered from their barracks. Sleepy naval officers hurried toward the port and coastal batteries by Citroën, motor scooter, and bicycle. Allied agents kindled their codebooks. Apart from kidnapping the commander of the Fez garrison out of his mistress's bed, the insurrectionists had achieved nothing but to give Vichy authorities several hours' advance warning of possible trouble.

"The sky is dark," a young Army lieutenant scribbled in a hasty letter before heading to the boat deck, "and everything looks perfect."

The lieutenant was deceived. Not only was trouble brewing ashore but Hewitt's ships had thoroughly deranged themselves. Two weeks of flawless navigation collapsed almost within sight of land. Even before half the force peeled off for Ṣafi to the south and Mehdia to the north, disagreement erupted among the captains over the convoy's precise position. One plot showed that the fleet had actually sailed into the Moroccan hills. The dispute persisted through the early evening of November 7, even though the sky was clear enough to shoot the stars and even after the great lighthouse beacon at El Hank was spotted. The lights of Casablanca burned so brilliantly that one submarine captain likened surfacing seven miles from the city to coming up "in the center of Times Square."

Despite this irrefutable evidence that land was near, commanders in the main convoy bound for Fedala failed to make the course corrections needed to prevent straggling and align the transports. Just before 11:30 P.M., the fleet tried to set itself right with a 45-degree turn to starboard, followed by another sharp turn fifteen minutes later. On this moonless night, many of the red and green lights used to order these maneuvers went unseen. Whistle signals were unheard or miscounted. El Hank and other shore lights abruptly winked out "as though one switch had been pulled." By the time the drop-anchor whistle sounded, not a single transport could be found in the right location, and some were 10,000 yards—six miles—out of position. "To be perfectly honest," one naval officer confessed, "I am not right sure exactly where we are."

Destroyers tacked back and forth to seaward, sniffing for enemy submarines. A light offshore wind carried the loamy scent of land. Above the patchy clouds, Cassiopeia set and the Great Bear rose on his tail. The relentless throb of ships' engines died away, bringing a silence not heard since Norfolk. Then the metallic rattle of anchor chains broke the spell. Crewmen peeled back the hatch covers, and wheezing donkey engines began to winch cargo from the holds. Bells clanged and clanged again to no purpose discernible to landsmen. In the packed troop compartments, blue cigarette smoke curled around the dim battle lights. Soldiers in green herringbone twill shifted their creaky rucksacks and awaited orders.

Orders came. Men shuffled onto the boat decks. Color-coded cargo nets now draped the sides like spiderwebs. A loadmaster with a bullhorn called to a landing craft sputtering below, "Personnel boat come alongside Red!" Coxswains in yellow oilskin coats and capacious pantaloons eased close, squinting to distinguish red from blue and trying not to foul their propellers in the nets. Officers climbed over the sides, their tommy guns and map cases banging against them all the way down. On some transports, after countless rehearsed departures from the starboard rail, the men were inexplicably ordered over the port side. Chaos attended. Others were told to fix bayonets—until the first man on the net impaled his thigh and was hoisted back on deck as a casualty. The feeble, obscene strains of "4-F Charley" sounded from troops waiting their turn. A veteran of the Great War revived a line often uttered before going over the top: "Don't harass the shock troops."

Then the loadmasters bellowed, "Shove off!" Coxswains gunned their engines and sheered away in a green blaze of phosphorescence, studying the heavens with a faint hope that Polaris or Sirius would tell them where to find land.

At Fedala, the first wave of twenty-six landing craft headed vaguely east just after five A.M. Misguided boats missed the beach and struck a reef with, as an official account later lamented, "indescribable confusion." Men from the 30th Infantry Regiment struggled toward shore in

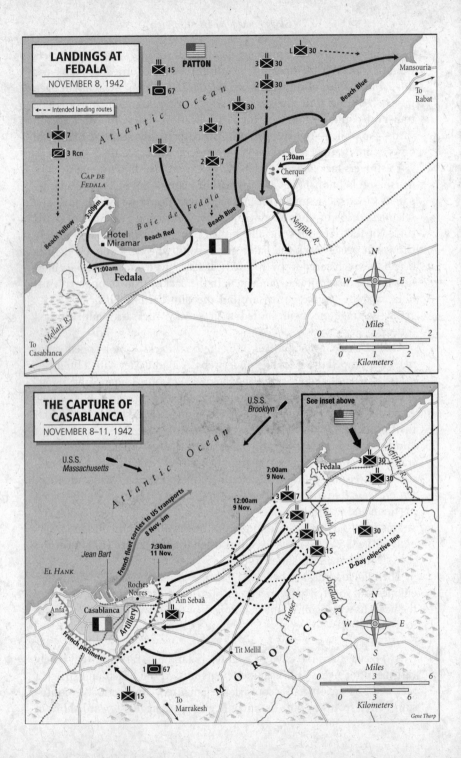

LANDINGS AT FEDALA
NOVEMBER 8, 1942

◄--- Intended landing routes

PATTON

Atlantic Ocean

III 15
1 ☐ 67

III 3 ☒ 30
II 2 ☒ 30
L ☒ 30
To Mansouria
To Rabat

Beach Blue

II 1 ☒ 30
III 3 ☒ 7

L ☒ 7
☒ 3 Rcn

III 1 ☒ 7
II 2 ☒ 7

1:30am
Cherqui

CAP DE FEDALA

Beach Yellow 3:00pm

Baie de Fedala

Beach Blue

Nefifikh R.

Hotel Miramar Beach Red

11:00am Fedala

Mellah R.

To Casablanca

N
W E
S

Miles
0   1   2

Kilometers
0   1   2

THE CAPTURE OF CASABLANCA
NOVEMBER 8–11, 1942

U.S.S. Brooklyn

See inset above

Atlantic Ocean

U.S.S. Massachusetts

French fleet sorties to US transports 8 Nov. am

Fedala

II 3 ☒ 30
II 2 ☒ 30

Nefifikh R.

7:00am 9 Nov.
III 3 ☒ 7
12:00am 9 Nov.
II 2 ☒ 7
II 2 ☒ 15
☒ 15

II 1 ☒ 30

Mellah R.

D-Day objective line

Jean Bart

7:30am 11 Nov.

EL HANK

Roches Noires

Ain Sebaâ

III 1 ☒ 7

Hasser R.

Mellah R.

Anfa

Casablanca

Artillery

Tit Mellil

French perimeter

1 ☐ 67

M O R O C C O

III 3 ☒ 15

To Marrakesh

N
W E
S

Miles
0   3   6

Kilometers
0   3   6

Gene Thorp

water chin deep, their hands and legs a fretwork of coral cuts. Dead-weighted with entrenching tools, rifles, grenades, wire cutters, gas masks, ammo magazines, and K rations, those knocked from their feet by the modest waves rarely rose again. The coxswain of a fifty-foot lighter strayed too far in front of a breaker; the bow caught the seafloor 200 yards from the beach and the boat cartwheeled, flinging men, guns, and a jeep into the surf. Only six soldiers emerged alive. Troops flopped onto the sand, shooting wildly at searchlights from the coastal battery at Cherqui while Arabs on spavined donkeys trotted along the water's edge, scavenging life jackets and canteens. The task force challenge and counter-sign soon echoed through the dune grass like a taunt: "George!" and "Patton!"

Eighty miles north, at Mehdia, troops from eight transports were to push six miles inland to capture the Port Lyautey airfield. Brigadier General Lucian K. Truscott, Jr., climbed down a cargo net on the *Henry T. Allen* and motored from transport to transport, trying to convince suspicious sailors that he was indeed commander of the Mehdia force. A ragged flotilla of landing craft eventually made for shore with American flags snapping from each stern "like a yacht race." The crack of gunfire carried across the water, once, twice, then twice more: four soldiers were wounded accidentally by comrades loading their rifles in the boats. Several landing craft snagged on sandbars or capsized as soldiers rolled over the gunwales in their haste to reach land. Sodden bodies washed ashore, facedown in a tangle of rifle slings and uninflated lifebelts. But at 5:40 A.M., 100 minutes late, the first troops from the 60th Infantry Regiment scrambled un-opposed across Green Beach, eyeing the sixteenth-century Portuguese fort that blocked their path to the airfield.

The third and final frontal assault against a defended port in Operation TORCH was planned for Safi, 140 miles south of Casablanca. A Portuguese trading post in the age of Columbus, Safi had once earned fame for horse breeding and then as the world's largest sardine fishery. Now it was an unlovely phosphate-exporting town of 25,000, famous for nothing. Much of the American battle planning was based on a yellowed 1906 French nautical chart, as well as on picture postcards from the Navy's hoard of tourist snapshots and other memorabilia showing various ocean frontages. Jew's Cliff, a sheltered beach outside Safi, had been identified through just such a faded postcard; renamed Yellow Beach, it was designated as a prime landing site.

To seize Safi port itself, the Navy chose a pair of ancient destroyers, the U.S.S. *Cole*, which in 1921 had been the world's fastest ship, capable of forty-two knots, and the U.S.S. *Bernadou*. A secret refitting in Bermuda intended to lighten the vessels and lower their profiles by amputating all masts and funnels had left them "sawed-off and hammered-down." Each destroyer would carry 200 assault troops from the 47th Infantry Regiment, who received American flag armbands and two cartons of cigarettes apiece with which to buy French amity. Capturing the little harbor would allow Patton to land a battalion of fifty-four Sherman tanks, which could then outflank Casablanca from the south without exposure to the city's formidable coastal guns.

The Safi assault, known as BLACKSTONE, differed in key details from the port attacks at Oran and Algiers. Safi's defenses were less sturdy than those in the Algerian cities, and American warships stood ready to pulverize any resistance. Also, to avoid alerting the defenders, the attack would slightly precede the beach landings. Commanding the 47th Infantry was Colonel Edwin H. Randle, an Indiana native with slicked hair and a wolfish mustache. "Violent, rapid, ruthless combat is the only way to win," Randle told his men. "Fire low—richochets may kill the enemy and they certainly will scare him. . . . Make it tough and make it violent."

The usual muddle obtained during disembarkation, delaying the attack for half an hour. Loadmasters finally stretched a huge net at an angle from the transport *Lyon* to the destroyers' decks and rolled the troops down into their comrades' waiting arms. Only one soldier tumbled into the Atlantic, never to be seen again. At 3:50 A.M., *Bernadou* headed for shore, with *Cole* trailing. As the lead destroyer glided toward the granite breakwater, a sharp-eyed French sentry challenged her by flashing two Morse letters: "VH." *Bernadou*'s captain answered by semaphore with precisely the same signal. The ruse befuddled the defenders for eighteen minutes until *Bernadou* rounded the bell buoy and announced her presence in the harbor at 4:28 A.M. by firing a pyrotechnic gadget designed to unfurl an illuminated American flag. The stubborn flag stayed furled, and the French opened fire.

Machine-gun rounds cracked overhead and 75mm shells whistled into the water with a smoky hiss. *Bernadou* answered, sweeping the jetties with cannon and mortar fire, then ran aground so hard that her bow lurched thirty feet onto the fish wharf. The assault troops in Company K were flung to the deck.

At sea, two radio messages ran through the American fleet. "Batter up" announced French resistance. "Play ball," at 4:38 A.M., authorized retaliatory fire. With a tremendous roar, the battleship *New York* and cruiser *Philadelphia* complied, aiming at muzzle flashes nine miles away.

Mesmerized soldiers and sailors watched the glowing crimson shells arc across the sky before smashing into the shore batteries north of Safi. One of *New York*'s fourteen-inch shells caught the lip of the three hundred-foot cliff at Pointe de la Tour, dug a furrow twenty feet long, then ricocheted up through the fire control tower at Batterie la Railleuse, killing everyone inside. Scraps of scalp and the battery commander's shredded uniform painted the shattered walls.

Unsettled, the troops on *Bernadou* were slow to leave her. They flopped back to the deck with each new shell burst until rousted by their officers and shoved toward the single scrambling net now draped over the bow. Canteens and cigarette cartons snagged in the webbing, leaving soldiers caught like seined fish. The men finally found their valor on solid ground. French troops clattered down a jetty with a small field gun pulled by a donkey; sheets of American bullets sent them fleeing. The *Cole* managed to berth at the phosphate quay at five A.M. Company L swarmed ashore, chasing Foreign Legionnaires from the docks and seizing the railroad station, post office, and Shell Oil depot.

Three more waves of infantrymen landed, remarkably, where they were supposed to land. White-robed Arabs crowded balconies above the harbor to watch. An American major later reported to the War Department:

> A soldier would snake his way painfully through rocks and rubble to set up a light machine gun, raise his head cautiously to aim, and find a dozen natives clustered solemnly around him. Street intersections were crowded with head-turning natives, like a tennis gallery, following the whining flight of bullets over their heads.

By early afternoon, the invaders held a beachhead five miles wide and half a mile deep. American sharpshooters knocked out three Renault tanks with rifle grenades, then turned the tank guns on a French barracks. Three hundred colonial troops surrendered. A solitary Vichy bomber made a feeble pass at the port; American anti-aircraft gunners, with zeal far eclipsing their marksmanship, shot up warehouse roofs and their own deck booms so vigorously that ricocheting .50-caliber tracers resembled "someone trying to cut the cranes with a welder's torch."

It was all too much for the French garrison commander. American troops stormed his headquarters at Front de Mer, capturing him and seven staff officers without a struggle. Their combined arsenal consisted of two revolvers. Except for a few snipers, Safi had fallen. U.S. casualties totaled four dead and twenty-five wounded.

Eisenhower had trusted in his luck, and so far his luck had held. Only by the clock on his office wall in the Gibraltar tunnel did the commander-in-chief know that dawn had come on November 8. He neither heard the church bells in Gibraltar town on this balmy Sunday morning nor saw the Spitfires lift from the runway to patrol the approaches from Spain and Italy. Eisenhower rose from his cot and padded down to the lavatory for a cold-water shave. To Marshall, he reported:

> Everything appears to be going ahead about as anticipated. . . . Information directly from task forces is meager, but I do not care to worry commanders at this stage by demanding reports. But I'd give a month's pay for an accurate report this minute from each sector. We do know that we are fairly solidly ashore at eastern and central points, and that western attack began as scheduled.

Besides that, he knew very little. The message center at Gibraltar had fallen hours behind in decoding the dispatches pouring in from Algeria and Morocco, as well as from Washington and London. Sketchy reports from Algiers and Oran indicated troops were ashore at all six Algerian landing sites. As for Task Force 34, almost nothing was known beyond a brief message from Hewitt reporting that he was proceeding apace. Eavesdroppers had picked up radio broadcasts of "The Star-Spangled Banner" and the "Marseillaise" from Patton's propaganda station aboard the *Texas,* but not a word had been heard from Patton himself.

"When you get to high places in the Army," Eisenhower had recently written to his son, John, a cadet at West Point, "this business of warfare is no longer just a question of getting out and teaching the soldiers how to shoot or how to crawl up a ravine or dig a foxhole—it is partly politics, partly public-speaking, partly essay-writing, partly social contact. . . . A fellow wishes he could just get into a hammock under a nice shade tree and read a few wild west magazines!"

"This business of warfare" was also partly about waiting. As the hours ticked by, a few more dispatches dribbled in, including vague accounts of "trouble in Algiers harbor" and resistance at the Oran port. By nine A.M., one airfield outside Algiers was supposedly in Allied hands, but except for reports that three transport aircraft from Operation VILLAIN had been forced down, nothing was heard regarding the airborne operation. Eisenhower's naval aide and confidant, a former CBS executive named

Harry C. Butcher, wrote in his diary, "What becomes of thirty-six paratroop planes?" Another garbled dispatch indicated that at one Moroccan
beach, Patton was re-embarking the landing craft under a truce flag.
"That I do *not* believe," Eisenhower wrote to his chief of staff, Major
General Walter B. Smith, who was still in London. "Unless my opinion
of Georgie is 100 percent wrong, he wouldn't re-embark anything,
including himself."

Lighting another Camel, Eisenhower retreated into his tiny office. He
had agreed to another negotiating session with Giraud in an hour. That
unpleasant prospect now was complicated by perplexing reports that
Admiral Darlan was in Algiers talking to Robert Murphy. Eisenhower
remembered Churchill's advice: "Kiss Darlan's stern if you have to, but
get the French navy." But what about Giraud?

He uncapped a fountain pen and in his tight cursive wrote at the top
of a sheet of notepaper: "Worries of a Commander." Beginning with
"Spain is so ominously quiet," he listed ten anxieties. Number three:
"Defensive fighting, which seemed halfhearted and spiritless this morning, has blazed up, and in many places resistance is stubborn." Number
six: "Giraud is difficult to deal with—wants much in power, equipment,
etc., but seems little disposed to do his part to stop fighting." Number
nine: "We don't know whereabouts or conditions of airborne force."
And number ten: "We cannot find out anything."

Having unburdened himself, he capped the pen and reviewed the
message traffic once again. Casualties seemed modest, pending further
word on RESERVIST, TERMINAL, and VILLAIN. It was tragic that France
felt compelled to fight, but the defenders had displayed remarkable lassitude in failing to lay mines, conduct reconnaissance, or to sortie Vichy
submarine and air fleets.

Yet if politically ambivalent and militarily inert, the French had *not*
capitulated. Vichy resistance near Casablanca and Mehdia appeared to
be stiffening. Darlan's intentions remained opaque. Giraud was brooding somewhere in this Gibraltar grotto. Murphy apparently was under
arrest. Many French rebels were in irons. German and Italian forces
would not likely remain quiescent for long. And Tunisia—the reason for
launching the most ambitious seaborne invasion in history—remained
far, far away.

Sometimes a fellow just wished he could crawl in a hammock and
read a few wild west magazines.

3. BEACHHEAD

A Sword in Algiers

EISENHOWER'S uncertainty over the progress of Operation TORCH was shared by every soldier in the Algerian and Moroccan beachheads. No man knew anything irrefutably except what he had witnessed. Sailors at sea could see nothing except gun flashes ashore. Soldiers ashore remained ignorant of what was beyond the next *djebel*. Commanders received fragmentary reports that proved to be incomplete, or contradictory, or wrong. This was war, "our condition and our history, the place we had to live in," as one correspondent wrote, but to many it seemed like a street brawl with artillery. For neophyte troops, this first combat experience was revealing: war *was* fought by ignorant armies on a darkling plain.

The fighting between Anglo-American invaders and Vichy French defenders would last just over three days; sometimes it was a matter of halfhearted potshots, but there were pitched firefights on a dozen battlefields across two countries. This little war between ancient friends— many Americans still could not believe they were fighting the French—was complicated by concomitant diplomatic maneuvers and the first attacks from Axis forces. All this happened more or less simultaneously, from Sunday morning through Tuesday night—November 8 to 10, 1942—but for narrative simplicity the action can unfold counterclockwise around the northwest rim of Africa, beginning in Algiers and ending in Morocco.

East of the Algerian capital, a battalion from the U.S. 39th Infantry had appeared at the gates of the Maison Blanche airfield just after dawn on November 8. French soldiers fired a few wild shots for honor's sake and then surrendered. At ten A.M. the first Hurricane fighters, launched hours earlier from Gibraltar with no guarantee of a place to land in Africa, touched down on the runway.

From Castiglione on the western edge of the beachhead, where industrious Algerians were stripping abandoned landing craft of their compasses and propellers, British troops captured another airfield at Blida and looped into Algiers from the south. One impatient commander seized half a dozen hostages—whom he described as "all very friendly and matey"—then drove to the docks, put a pistol to the head of the concierge, and hoisted a British ensign above a French command post. "Cheers rent the welkin," he reported.

Lieutenant Colonel Edward J. Doyle, commander of the 1st Battalion of the 168th Infantry, also grew impatient with his unit's dawdling progress against French snipers in the western suburb of Lambiridi—the same gunmen who had clipped Robert Moore's helmet earlier that morning. Ignoring orders to hold in place, Doyle flanked the skirmishers with two dozen men and sprinted through Algiers. Soon he was rattling the gates of the governor-general's Summer Palace. A watchman refused to admit him. "The governor," the Frenchman advised, "is at the beach." American troops responded by shooting out the tires of a well-heeled gentleman leaving the German consulate across the street. The driver's rage—good tires were particularly dear—was interrupted by the crack of a sniper's rifle. Doyle pitched to the pavement, mortally wounded by a bullet below his left shoulder blade. After Colonel Marshall in Operation RESERVIST, he was the second American battalion commander to die that morning.

Luftwaffe pilots flying from Italy on Sunday afternoon made their first appearance off Cap Matifou, where a covey of transport ships lay at anchor. An enemy Ju-88 dodged Allied flak and launched two torpedoes from an altitude of fifty feet. One missed. The second caught U.S.S. *Leedstown* on the starboard flank, carrying away her rudder. Dead in the water and listing with 500 men still aboard, the ship was easy prey. Near misses by dive-bombers opened her seams; then two more torpedoes amidships caused her to quickly settle by the head. Men leaped overboard, only to be sucked back into the ship through the torpedo holes; they scrambled topside and leaped again. Castaways on rafts paddled toward shore, singing with lusty abandon until they saw the heavy surf at Aïn Taya. The locals stopped their looting long enough to cut tall reeds, with which they pulled capsized survivors from the foaming water. Led to an abandoned theater, the shivering men were bedded in straw and revived with brandy. *Leedstown* sank in twenty fathoms.

Pleasing as such retaliatory Axis raids may have been, Admiral Darlan recognized with the discernment of a professional survivor that the jig was nearly up. The Vichy commander-in-chief had only 7,000 badly armed troops in Algiers; both major airfields had been captured, his fleet was bottled up by British men-of-war, and the city was surrounded by 30,000 soldiers. At three P.M. on Sunday, Darlan reappeared at the Villa des Oliviers, where Robert Murphy and Kenneth Pendar had been spared execution through the timely clemency of General Juin. The admiral found the American diplomats at lunch, watching the port warehouses burn and dive-bombers pirouette over Algiers Bay. Darlan announced that he was ready to parley. Would M. Murphy find the American commander, who was said to be on the beach ten miles west of Algiers?

In Juin's limousine with a white flag and the French tricolor flapping from the fender, the diplomats threaded their way through straggling columns of American soldiers west of Algiers. At Beach Beer White, they discovered Major General Charles W. Ryder, commander of the 34th Infantry Division, sitting on a large rock. A fellow Kansan and West Point classmate of Eisenhower's, Ryder—Doc, to his friends—was a tall, angular infantryman, highly decorated in the Great War. Asked if he would discuss terms with the French, he replied evenly, "I will go anywhere to talk to anyone who wishes to surrender Algiers to me." He then went nowhere. Sitting his rock, fussing about the need for a fresh uniform, he composed a one-paragraph report to Gibraltar with the speed of a man dictating to a stonecutter. "You will have to forgive me," he told Murphy. "I haven't slept in a week." Murphy stopped pacing, took the general by the arm, and bundled him into the limousine.

A bugler perched on the running board blew "Cease Fire" as they careered through Lambiridi to the Avenue Maréchal Joffre. Outside Fort l'Empereur, headquarters of the Vichy military, Juin's chief of staff stood at rigid attention in the street. Behind him were spaced six soldiers in a V formation. "I don't like blood," Murphy confided to Ryder as they climbed from the limousine. With the precise gestures of a man practiced in capitulation, the French chief of staff extended his sword to Ryder, hilt first, "like a historical painting in some museum," Pendar observed. Murmuring a few words of abdication, he wheeled smartly and marched into the fort.

Ryder and Murphy followed. They entered a cavernous hall where stuffed hunting trophies and booty from ancient battlefields hung from the wainscoting. Fifty French officers stood along the walls, glancing between the Americans and General Juin, who stood at the head of a long table swathed in green baize. Juin had exchanged his pink-striped pajamas from the previous night for the bemedaled splendor of his finest uniform. The distant mutter of small-arms fire was swallowed by the roar of bombs from Royal Navy planes attacking French targets barely a hundred yards distant. "How wonderful!" Ryder exclaimed. "This is the first time since World War One that I have been under fire." Icy silence greeted this remark.

"Are you the senior commander?" Juin finally asked, tossing his left-handed salute.

"I am."

"Will you assume responsibility for keeping law and order in Algiers if it is surrendered to your force?"

"Yes," Ryder answered, "provided I may have the services of the French gendarmes acting under my orders."

"When will you be ready to do this?"

"Immediately."

"Would you permit French troops to retain their arms?"

Ryder hesitated for an instant. "Yes, provided the troops are assembled in their barracks."

The deed was done. Allied units would enter the city at eight P.M. Prisoners were to be freed immediately, including survivors from Operation TERMINAL. French officers dispatched cars through every precinct of Algiers to herald the city's surrender with a fugato of bugles.

Algiers had fallen, but not the rest of French North Africa, and there was the rub. The Americans soon learned that Darlan had formally divested himself of all power outside the city. He professed, with an infuriating shrug, to have no negotiating authority for the rest of the Vichy empire. Another meeting at Fort l'Empereur, this time with Darlan present, yielded only an agreement to move Allied ships into Algiers harbor.

At dawn on Monday, the task force flagship, H.M.S. *Bulolo*, steamed with imperial dignity toward the Railway Jetty, unaware that an earlier near-miss from a Luftwaffe bomb had damaged her engine room telegraphs. A routine docking order from the bridge for full steam astern went unheard. The French welcoming committee on the jetty watched with mounting alarm as the ship loomed nearer at twelve knots. Officers on the bridge debated whether *Bulolo*'s masts would more likely shear off forward or backward upon impact. Shrieking bystanders scattered; the captain yelled "Everyone lie down!" to his crew; and the great bow heaved up onto a fortuitous mudbank, demolishing the seawall and nicking a waterfront house before settling back into the harbor, intact. Applauding spectators recovered their wits and agreed that the Royal Navy knew how to make an entrance.

So, too, did General Giraud. On Monday morning, November 9, he left Gibraltar for Algiers in a French plane with intentions of elbowing

Darlan aside and establishing himself as the new Allied satrap in North Africa. As Eisenhower had shrewdly anticipated, Giraud had come around after sensing TORCH's early success; with histrionic sighs he agreed to serve as commander of the French military in North Africa and chief civil administrator there. Eisenhower packed him off, then publicly proclaimed that "his presence there will bring about a cessation of scattered resistance." (To Marshall he privately confessed, "I find myself getting absolutely furious with these stupid Frogs.")

The authorities in Vichy greeted Eisenhower's proclamation by denouncing the French general as "a rebel chief and a felon." Giraud landed at Blida airfield to be met not by the honor guard and whooping throng he had envisioned, but by a few furtive supporters who warned of assassins. Worse yet, his luggage and uniform had gone missing. Giraud could hardly stage a proper coup in rumpled gabardine. Despondent and out of costume, he climbed into a borrowed car and headed for the serpentine alleys of Algiers's Ruisseau quarter, where a sympathetic family had offered sanctuary.

Three hours later, Mark Clark arrived by B-17 at Maison Blanche airfield with orders from Eisenhower to help Giraud take command of French forces and secure a general armistice. Instead, he found his putative viceroy in hiding, Admiral Darlan in firm command of Vichy loyalties, and fighting continuing everywhere except Algiers proper. "This," Clark told Murphy, "really messes things up!"

In his retinue, Clark had included a former *Rin Tin Tin* screen writer and 20th Century–Fox executive named Darryl F. Zanuck; now a Signal Corps colonel, Zanuck emerged from the plane with a 16mm movie camera and ten rolls of film with which to document Clark's triumphant entry into Algiers. The cinematic moment was disrupted, however, by the appearance of a dozen Luftwaffe raiders. As Spitfires and Junkerses tangled overhead, gabbling civilians thronged the streets to watch the dogfights. Clark and his men crammed into two British half-tracks and clanked through the city. Every wall, they noticed, seemed plastered with large posters of Marshal Pétain. The invasion of North Africa was barely twenty-four hours old but already it had descended into French farce.

The Hôtel St. Georges was a rambling, bone-white hostel on Rue Michelet, the most fashionable avenue in Algiers's most fashionable neighborhood. Long favored for its gorgeous sea vistas by wealthy spinsters touring the Mediterranean, the St. Georges now served as headquarters for the French navy. Marines had tracked the lobby's intricate mosaic floor with mud. It was here that the Americans agreed to meet Darlan and his lieutenants early Tuesday morning, November 10.

Clark found General Ryder exhausted from hours of fruitless dickering. "I've stalled them about as long as I can," Ryder said. A rifle company had been posted among the palm trees outside with orders to "shoot their butts off" if the French made trouble. Murphy led Clark through the hotel foyer to a small, stuffy room with blue Moorish tile and a view of the sun-dappled Mediterranean. Five French admirals and four generals awaited them. Darlan wore elevated heels and a black, double-breasted admiral's tunic that accentuated his pasty complexion. He greeted the Americans cordially, but the French refused to shake hands with the solitary British officer in Clark's delegation. Clark folded himself into a chair at the head of the table with Darlan on his left, Juin on his right, and Murphy translating.

"We have work to do to meet the common enemy," Clark said.

"All my associates and I feel hostilities are fruitless," Darlan replied. But beyond surrendering Algiers, he had no authority to sign an armistice. "I can simply obey the orders of Pétain."

"The problem is bigger than that," Clark insisted. He gestured vaguely toward Tunisia. "Will the French troops east of Algiers resist as we pass through to meet the common enemy?"

Darlan's watery blue eyes avoided Clark's stare. "I have asked Vichy to give me an answer to your terms as soon as possible."

Clark thumped the table with his fist. "It will be necessary to retain you in protective custody. I hope you understand. We must move east. I will go to General Giraud. He will sign the terms and issue the necessary orders."

Darlan mopped his pate, and the faintest trace of a smile crossed his lips. "I am not certain the troops will obey."

"If you think Pétain will agree with you that hostilies must cease, why can't you issue that order now?"

"It would result," Darlan said slowly, "in the immediate occupation of southern France by the Germans."

Clark's fist again crashed onto the table. "What you are doing now means the killing of more French and Americans. This is the time when we must lean on our inclinations and not on our orders. Here is an opportunity for all Frenchmen to rally and win the war. Here is your last chance."

"That is your decision," Darlan said.

"Tell him," Clark said to Murphy, "that Pétain is nothing in our young lives." He pushed back his chair to leave, but Juin held up his hand. "Give us five minutes."

As the Allied delegates filed from the room, Darlan murmured to Murphy, "Would you mind suggesting to Major General Clark that I am a five-star admiral? He should stop talking to me like a lieutenant junior grade."

The Americans retreated to a remote corridor across the foyer. The sound of raised French voices drifted from the closed door. Clark paced, muttering about "YBSOBs," the private acronym he and Eisenhower had invented for "yellow-bellied sons of bitches." Clark's tacit threat to declare martial law in North Africa horrified Murphy. He could hardly imagine administering railroads, mail, water supply, and other civil functions across a million square miles with nearly 20 million people, few of whom shared a language with any American. If the Allies were to lunge toward Tunisia without fear of a stab in the back, they needed French help.

The door swung open. Darlan's pudgy confidant and his host in Algiers, Vice Admiral Raymond Fenard, smiled and gestured. As Clark and the others took their seats, Darlan turned to Murphy and said, "*J'accepte.*"

He laid a draft order before Clark announcing to all French troops that further battle was futile. A proposed message to Pétain suggested that continued fighting would likely cost France its African possessions. Darlan took up a pen and scratched an order "in the name of the Marshal" ordering all land, sea, and air forces in North Africa to cease fire, return to their bases, and observe a strict neutrality. Darlan again mopped his head. "This will stand," Clark declared.

He immediately cabled word of the agreement to Gibraltar. "I deemed it of the utmost importance," he told Eisenhower, "to do anything to secure an order which would be obeyed to cease hostilities." Giraud resurfaced in his kepi, jodhpurs, gold braid, and gleaming cavalry boots. "He appeared to have emerged directly from the barber's shop," journalist Alan Moorehead later wrote. "His small, bird-like head was beautifully groomed." With his misplaced uniform restored and his pride swallowed, Giraud announced that for the greater glory of France he would serve under Darlan in fighting the Germans.

Yet no sooner was the deal made than it collapsed. Within hours, news came from Vichy that Marshal Pétain had sacked Darlan as his military commander and repudiated any agreement with the Americans rather than risk the German occupation of Vichy France and seizure of the large Vichy fleet anchored at Toulon. "I issued the order to defend

North Africa," Pétain decreed. More diminished than ever, Darlan moped around Admiral Fenard's villa like a disinherited heir. "I am lost," he said. "I can only give myself up."

At three P.M. on Tuesday afternoon Clark and Murphy arrived at the villa, alarmed by reports that their new protégé intended to renege on the armistice he had signed six hours earlier.

"Pétain is the mouthpiece of Hitler," Clark insisted.

Darlan shrugged. "There is nothing I can do but revoke the order which I signed this morning."

"Damned if you do!" Clark drew himself to his full, imposing height. "You are now a prisoner."

"Then I must be taken prisoner."

Furious, Clark ordered two infantry platoons to throw a cordon around Fenard's compound. An American colonel, Benjamin A. Dickson, shoved past Darlan's aides to confront him directly. "Mon Admiral, by order of the supreme commander you are hereby under arrest in these quarters. Guards have been posted with orders to shoot if you attempt to escape."

Dickson returned to the front gate. "Our prisoner in that house is Admiral Darlan," he told the captain of the guard. "He is a short, bald-headed, pink-faced, needle-nosed, sharp-chinned little weasel. If he tries to get away in uniform or civilian clothes, he is to be shot."

At Gibraltar, Eisenhower thumbed through the dispatches from Africa and tried to make sense of the front. "War brings about strange, sometimes ridiculous situations," he had written in another longhand memo to himself on Monday afternoon. With each passing hour this war seemed to get stranger and more ridiculous. In a scribbled note he titled "Inconsequential thoughts of a commander during one of the interminable waiting periods," Eisenhower added, "I'm anxiously waiting word of: west coast operations. Oran operations. Giraud's movements and intentions. Darlan's proposals. Movements of Italian air. Intentions of Spain."

Darlan appeared to have capitulated twice and reneged twice under countervailing pressure from Vichy and Clark. Giraud's influence in North Africa seemed to be nil. Eisenhower had greeted one of Clark's cables by wailing, "Jeee-sus Ch-e-rist! What I need around here is a damned good assassin." He wondered whether bribery would help. Should the Allies, he asked Clark, consider depositing a large sum "in a neutral country such as Switzerland?"

As the seat of French authority in North Africa, Algiers was crucial to the Allied cause and the staging ground for the push toward Tunisia. British troops still waited offshore to begin that eastward drive once Clark was certain of French neutrality if not collaboration. Morocco also was vital as the conduit for supplies and reinforcements from the United States. Yet Eisenhower still had heard virtually nothing from Hewitt and Patton.

But it was Oran that had preoccupied the commander-in-chief in a message to Marshall late on Monday. The airfields in western Algeria were critical to building up Allied power, and so were the port at Oran and the nearby naval base at Mers el-Kébir. "My biggest operational difficulty at the moment is the slowness in straightening out the Oran region," Eisenhower wrote. "I must get it soon."

A Blue Flag over Oran

ESENHOWER was about to get his wish.

American soldiers had converged on Oran all day Sunday, November 8, driving 9,000 French defenders into a bowl twenty miles in diameter. From the west, Ted Roosevelt and the 26th Infantry marched through Algerian villages given code names drawn from soldiers' home-towns—Brooklyn, Brockton, Syracuse—along roads named for pas-times from a former life: Baseball, Golf, Lacrosse.

Terry Allen and a larger portion of his 1st Division descended on Oran from the sandstone hills above St. Cloud, a key crossroads east of the city, and the salt lakes farther south. Children in dirty kaftans shouted "Hi yo, Silver!" or flung stiff-arm Fascist salutes to liberators they presumed to be German. Veiled Berber women with indigo tattoos peered through casement shutters, and in cafés men wearing fezzes looked up from their tea glasses long enough to applaud the passing troops, African-style: arms extended, clapping hands hinged at the wrists, no pretense of sincerity. A war correspondent seeking adjectives to describe the locals settled on "scrofulous, unpicturesque, ophthal-mic, lamentable."

Exhausted soldiers who could elude their officers skulked into the underbrush; soon the thorn bushes themselves seemed to be snoring. The raspy trundle of artillery shells sometimes woke the men, and often did not. Other troops threw their shoulders behind farm carts used as cais-sons. Sweating like horses beneath the molten sun, they plodded toward the unseen city beyond the horizon. Abandoned cartridge belts and field jackets blazed a broad, sad trail all the way back to Arzew. Occasionally a wood-burning bus rattled past, carrying unshaven French prisoners to cages on the beach. A cook from the 18th Infantry commandeered a brown mule and a two-wheeled cart to haul his field kitchen. When the mule bolted past a column of hooting GIs toward French lines, the cook threw aside the useless reins, dropped the animal with a single rifle shot, and forced the men, hooting no longer, to haul the kitchen themselves.

A wounded soldier lay in the tall grass, waiting for an ambulance and pleading with passersby, "Don't kick my legs, please don't kick my legs." During a mortar barrage, four soldiers from Company E of the 16th Infantry took cover in an irrigation ditch. When the shelling lifted, a lieutenant across the road noticed a luminous blue glow and found that a shell fragment had severed the power line overhead. The fallen wire had electrocuted all four men.

So this is war, soldiers told one another: misfortune at every bend in the road. Misery and murdered mules and sudden death in a ditch.

St. Cloud was a buff-tinted farm town of 3,500, surrounded by vine-yards, with sturdy stone houses and—because by November grapevines had been trimmed to mere nubs—fields of fire extending half a mile in all directions. Straddling the main road to Oran from the east, St. Cloud had been reinforced with the 16th Tunisian Infantry Regiment, the 1st Battalion of the Foreign Legion, an artillery battalion, and paramilitary troops of the Service d'Ordre Légionnaire, French Fascists who modeled themselves on the German SS. American intelligence rated the defenders "second- or third-class fighting troops." But before noon on November 8, Company C of Terry Allen's 18th Infantry had been ambushed, driven off, then driven off again when it returned to St. Cloud with the bulk of the 1st Battalion.

At 3:30 P.M., the battalion attacked once more down the road from Renan, joined by the 2nd Battalion trying to outflank the defenders on the south. Long, smoky ribbons of French machine-gun fire lashed the grapevines, killing the Company A first sergeant with a bullet in the fore-head and mortally wounding the commander in the throat. A clock in the stone steeple looming above St. Cloud tolled four o'clock. From the belfry a sniper's orange muzzle flashes winked insolently. American .50-caliber bullets gnawed at the steeple and clanged off the bells. Discordant pealing carried across the tile rooftops.

Men from both U.S. battalions crawled on their bellies through the vineyards toward the whitewashed stone wall encircling the St. Cloud cemetery 200 yards south of town. French and American riflemen flitted among the tombs and obelisks like shades in the fading gray light. Bullets pinged off gravestones and chipped the wings of marble cherubim. Gunfire roared in the crypts.

Lieutenant Edward McGregor formed a skirmish line from Company B, blew three blasts on his whistle, then leaped the cemetery wall to lead a platoon rush on the town. Three men leaped with him; forty others cowered behind the wall. McGregor spun around and rallied the troops with a wild-eyed vow to shoot every shirker in the back. This time the platoon followed until a bullet ripped the face from the B Company commander. "Keep going, Mac," the officer urged, and fell dead. McGregor and eight others were captured. St. Cloud was not.

Now French artillerymen opened with their field pieces. The barrage sent American soldiers by the score into full flight. Officers pursued them bellowing, "Stop! Stop!" A wounded lieutenant beside the road pleaded, "Please, please, don't leave me." He was left. Medics would find him at dawn, dead white and still alive, his shattered arm too far gone to save. French guns also sniffed out a battery from the 32nd Field Artillery, which had set up behind a ridge north of town. Shells screamed down as a terrified herd of goats stampeded through the howitzer positions twice, each time knocking American gunners to the ground.

Night slipped down on St. Cloud, transforming the farm town into a dark, sinister redoubt. Bodies lay like bloody rugs among the stubby vines. Gunfire rippled from nervous sentries, and it was worth a man's life to move about before dawn.

At seven A.M., on November 9, the 18th Infantry attacked again, with nearly 7,000 troops. By noon the attack had failed, with heavy casualties. For Colonel Frank Greer, the regimental commander, St. Cloud had become a grudge fight. The entire Allied drive on Oran was stalled because of this town's resistance. Greer stood on the concrete loading ramp of the winery that served as his command post, studying St. Cloud through field glasses. Half the church steeple was gone now, and with it the clock chimes. Palm trees had been sheared off mid-trunk, and yawning holes could be seen in several house roofs. A riderless black mount, wearing a French cavalry saddle and dragging its bridle, grazed at the edge of town. A dozen other horses lay dead, their legs in the air, like upended tables.

"I'm going to put a creeping artillery barrage through that town, starting at this end and working right over it," Greer said. Two hundred shells had been fuzed and stacked at each battery; the barrage of 1,500 rounds would begin at one P.M., followed thirty minutes later by a three-battalion assault. Scouts reported that hundreds of women and children were in the town, huddling in shuttered rooms as the world detonated around them. Some had already been killed, and many more no doubt would die in the bombardment.

At that moment a hatless, weathered figure in shirtsleeves pulled up to the winery in a jeep. Terry Allen had spent the night in a Tourville schoolhouse, wedged into a child's desk with a gasoline lantern illuminating photos of Pétain and colorful wall maps of France's colonial empire. Battle reports indicated that Roosevelt's men were on Djebel Murdjadjo, the high ground west of Oran; T.R. himself was said to be chasing French hussars with a carbine. Tafaraoui airfield had fallen quickly, and 5,000 troops from the 1st Armored Division, having skirted a French strong point at Misserrhin, had just captured La Sénia airfield. Little was known of the VILLAIN paratroopers or the RESERVIST raiders, but a Foreign Legion counterattack from Sidi Bel Abbès in the southern desert was collapsing. "Boys," Allen said, "I've just sent a signal to the French to put in their first team." To an exhausted rifle company huddled in a ditch, he urged, "There are a lot of good-looking girls in that town ready to welcome the liberating Americans." Others he simply warned, "Take Oran or you don't eat."

Standing beneath a fig tree, a cigarette dangling from his lips, Allen swiveled his head from side to side to keep the smoke from his eyes. Greer explained his intentions; a soft hiss leaked from Allen's cheeks as he studied St. Cloud in the middle distance. The division staff opposed Greer's plan. It took little imagination to picture terrified civilians mumbling their Hail Marys and fingering their rosaries in preparation for the next world. Terry Allen himself had prayed this morning, as he did before every battle.

He studied the map and took a long, final gaze at St. Cloud. Allen had been in a dozen provincial French towns like it during the Great War. Among his idiosyncrasies was a disdain for all foreign names more complicated than "Paris," and he routinely substituted "Whatever-the-Hell-They-Call-It" for any polysyllabic place. But in St. Cloud he could picture the greengrocer, the dressmaker's shop, the scruffy taverns with their Dubonnet signs and bored waiters in cummerbunds.

He turned to Greer. "There will not be any general artillery concentration," he said. "If we bombard the town and then fail to take it by attack, it would be disastrous."

Obliterating a French town "would make a bad political impression," he added. And it would use too much ammunition. "We don't need the damned place anyway. We can bypass St. Cloud and take Oran by night maneuver." Leave one battalion as a holding force, Allen said, then swing the rest of your men wide of the town and get them moving toward Oran. Greer saluted, disappointment etched on his face.

If the order to sidestep St. Cloud seems obvious in retrospect, at the time it was not. By leaving a large armed force in his rear, and suppressing the impulse of his men to avenge their losses and win the town at any cost, Allen had taken a calculated risk. He had calibrated political and battlefield variables to make the first singular tactical decision by an American general in the liberation of Europe.

"I just couldn't do it," Allen later mused. "Just couldn't. There were civilians in that goddam place. I couldn't blast hell outta all of them."

The circumvention of St. Cloud and the capture of La Sénia unhinged French defenses. Oran was encircled. For the final assault on the city, Allen at 7:15 A.M. on November 10 dictated "field order No. 3," which ended: "Nothing in hell must delay or stop this attack."

The French in fact delayed them, at Arcole and then at St. Eugène, but not for long. When a young major complained that his tired, hungry men needed rest, the 16th Infantry commander rounded on him and snapped, "You will not talk that way. You will attack." By dawn on November 10, following a night of sleet and wild wind, the converging U.S. forces faced little more than sniper fire. Lieutenant Colonel John Todd, known in the 1st Armored Division as Daddy Rabbit, was told, "Take your tanks in and mill around." Shoving the road barricades aside, Todd's tanks rolled down the Boulevard de Mascarad and reached the blue bight of Oran bay; they were too late to prevent the harbor sabotage that followed RESERVIST, but they thwarted a French scheme to flood the port with fuel oil and set it ablaze. Lieutenant Colonel John K. Waters, commander of another armored battalion (and Patton's son-in-law), put on an intimidating show of force along Boulevard Paul Doumer— although the tanks seemed less fearsome after some ran out of gas near the cathedral.

Festive crowds filled the sidewalks, flashing Vs with their fingers and flinching at occasional sniper fire. The pretty girls Allen had promised blew kisses from balconies on Boulevard Joffre and dropped hibiscus garlands onto the tank turrets. A potbellied burgher with a black felt hat and a white flag rapped on a tank hull, introduced himself as Oran's mayor, and offered to surrender his town. The 1st Battalion of the 6th Armored Infantry—sister unit of the battalion destroyed in RESERVIST— stormed the gates of Fort St. Philippe to free more than 500 Allied prisoners: paratroopers, pilots, British tars, and American infantrymen from *Walney* and *Hartland*. Liberators and liberated wept alike. French camp guards formed up, stacked arms, and marched smartly to confinement in their own barracks.

For more than five hours, St. Cloud resisted a final attack—sans artillery barrage—by the 1st Battalion of the 18th Infantry and Darby's Ranger battalion. The town finally capitulated after house-to-house combat, yielding 400 French prisoners, fourteen artillery tubes, and twenty-three machine guns. No one counted the bodies. At Château-Neuf, where golden carp swam in a tinkling fountain amid syringa and pepper trees, General Robert Boisseau surrendered his Oran division at noon on Tuesday, November 10. A large blue pennant was hoisted above the city, the prearranged American signal of Oran's fall.

Beyond the killed and wounded of RESERVIST, the Big Red One alone suffered more than 300 casualties at Oran. Allen and Roosevelt also relieved two of their division's nine infantry battalion commanders for various inadequacies. The tally of French dead in defending the city was put at 165.

The liberators immediately set to work converting Oran into a vast supply depot. Quartermasters requisitioned the local bullring for a food warehouse, then realized that it reeked, indelibly, of bulls. The provost marshal built a fenced compound in which to quarantine 150 soldiers who had developed venereal disease during the passage from Britain. Troops named the camp Casanova Park; the barbed wire, one commander explained, was "to make them feel like heels." Lieutenant Colonel Waters, showing the initiative that would one day lead him to four-star rank, liberated ten barrels of red wine from the Oran docks and filled the helmet of every soldier in his battalion. A tank destroyer unit threw a jolly party for Allen and Roosevelt, who upheld Fighting First tradition by getting pie-eyed drunk.

Almost 37,000 men now occupied a beachhead seventy miles wide and fifteen miles deep. With the surrender of Algiers, the capture of Oran gave the Allies virtual possession of Algeria, although Morocco was still contested and North African politics remained more tangled than ever. Still, the dispatch sent from Oran to Eisenhower at dusk on November 10 summed up the prevailing sentiment, however ephemeral: "Everything is rosy." After three days of fretful confusion this news proved bracing. "Now we must get ports in shape and rush eastward without delay," Eisenhower cabled London that same Tuesday.

"This business of battle is just rush and rush," he added. "But I like it."

"An Orgy of Disorder"

CASABLANCA provided Vichy with its best anchorage south of Toulon, and the French navy had chosen to defend the Moroccan port with valor worthy of a better cause. Not one French sailor in a thousand knew the identity of the hostile fleet that appeared in the morning haze at dawn on November 8. But just after seven A.M., the great coastal battery at El Hank had opened fire, followed moments later by the four fifteen-inch guns on the front turret of the berthed battleship *Jean Bart*. Searing plumes of orange flame and cylindrical smoke rings blossomed from the muzzles. At eighteen thousand yards—ten miles—El Hank's first salvo straddled the battleship *Massachusetts*, whose skipper the previous evening had uttered those fine Latin words about seeking peace with a sword. *Jean Bart*'s shells then lifted immense gouts of seawater 600 yards off the starboard bow. *Massachusetts* and her sisters soon answered, and what the U.S. Navy cheerfully called "an old-fashioned fire-away Flannagan" had begun.

Kent Hewitt was on *Augusta*'s flag bridge when excited calls of "Batter up!" and "Play ball!" began spilling from the radios, signaling, respectively, hostile fire and the authorization to reply in kind. After two weeks of relative indolence during the passage from Hampton Roads, during which he had eaten too much, exercised too little, and put on weight, Hewitt had been relentlessly busy since deciding to trust his aerologist's weather eye and proceed with the three Moroccan landings. He knew that the assault on Safi in the south was going well, although only the sketchiest reports had come from General Truscott's force at Mehdia in the north. The cloak-and-dagger efforts by the OSS to stage a coup through the rebel general Émile Béthouart had evidently failed; Hewitt could only guess that the resident-general, Auguste Noguès, had chosen to resist the invasion. At Fedala, just above Casablanca, where 20,000 of the Army's 33,000 assault troops aimed at Morocco were to land, the first craft had reached shore two hours earlier. Despite calm seas and mild surf, many boats had broached or capsized, but at least some soldiers were on the beach and preparing to advance on Casablanca. Hewitt had dutifully reported these developments in coded dispatches every couple of hours, unaware that, because Navy signalmen had neglected to classify the messages as urgent, Eisenhower had received hardly a syllable.

Hewitt considered that Divine Providence was still with him, but he had begun to fret about his "velvet." The aerologist, Steere, warned that the weather was likely to begin deteriorating within a day. Enemy submarines would hardly remain at bay forever, despite the destroyers patrolling the fleet's flanks and the eight minelayers scattering sea mines around the troop transports. Another large convoy from Hampton Roads was scheduled to arrive on Friday, November 13, despite Hewitt's efforts to persuade the Army to delay the follow-on force until he could guarantee enough secure berths in Casablanca harbor.

Now it appeared the French intended not just to fight but to fight with passion. At first the defensive fire on the beaches had seemed sporadic, more symbolic than lethal. The captain of the cruiser U.S.S. *Brooklyn* had signaled Hewitt at 5:39 A.M.: "Have noticed gunfire and am moving into position to take care of eventualities." But the shells from El Hank and the *Jean Bart* were ship-killers; they opened what became one of the most intense naval battles of the Atlantic war.

Within ten minutes of the first salvos, the sky seemed to leak steel across Casablanca's moles and harbor basins. American shells gouged great divots from the docks, spraying concrete shrapnel against hulls and across decks. Ten merchantmen lay defenseless at their moorings, and there they would sink, along with three French submarines. The last of 2,000 civilian refugees who had arrived from Dakar on three passenger ships the previous evening fled down piers soon pounded to rubble. Dozens of sailors, including several captains, died on the docks short of their gangplanks and the dignity of a seagoing death.

The *Jean Bart*—France's newest dreadnought, with turrets heavy as a frigate—was still unfinished: she could not leave her slip. A sixteen-inch shell from *Massachusetts* burrowed through the battleship's forward turret. Another hit the turret's armored apron, immobilizing the guns. After firing just seven rounds, *Jean Bart* fell silent. Three other shells from *Massachusetts* punched through the armored decks, the side, and the keel, and *Jean Bart* settled on the bottom along the Môle du Commerce. Oddly, not one of the shells exploded; they, along with more than fifty other American duds—the consequence in part of fuzes dating to 1918—spared Casablanca worse destruction.

The commander of the French 2nd Light Squadron, Rear Admiral Gervais de Lafond, was as ignorant as his seamen of the enemy's identity. Haze prevented him from making out the battle pennants on the enemy ships, and he had received no authoritative reports from his superiors or from the beaches. But Lafond clearly saw a disaster in the making. Only by putting to sea and slipping along the coastline under the blinding glare of the rising sun could his squadron escape obliteration.

Lafond failed to realize that his foes had radar. The admiral issued his orders, boarded the destroyer *Milan,* and headed for the harbor entrance at 8:15 A.M. Attacking dive-bombers struck the commercial basin even as

French submarine crews muscled a few final torpedoes aboard before casting off. A brave figure in a black cassock, the fleet chaplain, sprinted through the bombardment to the end of the pier, where he waved the sign of the cross at each warship as it sortied past. Along the corniche the wives and children of French sailors gathered on rooftops to cheer the sixteen ships into battle. They would have an unobstructed view as American fire whittled away the familiar silhouettes of the Casablanca fleet.

French shells were dye-loaded to help gunners see the fall of shot. Majestic geysers of green, purple, magenta, and yellow erupted around the American ships. On the presumption that no two enemy rounds would land in the same spot, helmsmen were ordered to "chase the splashes"—an especially difficult maneuver when gunfire straddled a ship. Cruisers, destroyers, and the *Massachusetts* swerved to and fro, battle ensigns snapping. The battleship was hit once, suffering little damage; another shell tore her colors to tatters. The concussion of their own big guns knocked out the radar range finders on *Tuscaloosa* and *Massachusetts,* so the gun teams had to aim crudely, by sight, wasting quantities of shells. Shock waves from *Augusta*'s number three turret jarred a radio receiver from its mountings. It smashed to the deck, thus producing one among many communications problems that by noon led to the sacking of several signal operators for incompetence.

Concussion from the flagship's aft turret claimed another victim: the landing craft Patton intended to ride to the beach had its bottom blown out while hanging from davits over the port rail. His kit—except for the ivory-handled Colt Peacemaker and Smith & Wesson .357, which he had just strapped on—plunged into the Atlantic. In Norfolk Patton had vowed to land with the first wave and die at the head of his troops; now, immaculately dressed in his shiny two-star helmet and cavalry boots, he was trapped on *Augusta.* "Goddammit," he barked at an aide. "I hope you have a spare toothbruth with you I can use to clean my foul mouth. I don't have a thing left in the world, thanks to the United States Navy."

He stopped fuming long enough to scribble a letter to Bea—"It is flat calm. God was with us"—and record the morning events in his diary:

> I was on the main deck just back of number two turret, leaning on the rail, when one [French shell] hit so close that it splashed water all over me. When I was on the bridge later, one hit closer but I was too high to get wet. It was hazy and the enemy used smoke well. I could just see them and make out our splashes. We had the [*Massachusetts*], the *Brooklyn,* the *Augusta* and some others all fir-

ing and going like hell in big zig-zags. . . . You have to put cotton in your ears. Some of the people got white but it did not seem very dangerous to me—sort of impersonal.

Hewitt was too busy to fret over Patton's impatience or his snippy assessment of naval combat. This sea battle would certainly dispel any doubts Patton still held about the Navy's desire to fight. So engrossed was the Navy in the duel with *Jean Bart* and the shore batteries that the warships soon found themselves nearly thirty miles south of Fedala— with Admiral Lafond's squadron angling straight for the vulnerable American transports. A report from a spotter plane alerted Hewitt to the French sortie from the harbor, and shortly before 8:30 A.M. he ordered *Augusta, Brooklyn,* and two destroyers to intercept the French at flank speed. The historian Samuel Eliot Morison, aboard *Brooklyn* as a naval reserve officer, reported that "the four ships went tearing into action like a pack of dogs unleashed."

It was a near-run thing. The rising sun, the glare, and the sporadically malfunctioning Navy radar reduced the French ships to black dots dancing on the horizon. Visibility was further cut by the pall from oil tanks blazing ashore and by the French squadron's smoke generators. Shooting at the agile Vichy destroyers was likened to "trying to hit a grasshopper with a rock." Shells from a shore battery holed the destroyer U.S.S. *Palmer*—one blew through a galley trash can without scratching the two sailors carrying it—and severed the mainmast; she fled west at twenty-seven knots. The destroyer U.S.S. *Ludlow,* firing so furiously that her deck guns appeared to be squirting a solid stream of tracers, hit Lafond's flagship, *Milan,* and set her ablaze, only to be answered with a six-inch shell that wrecked the wardrooms and ventilated the port bow. Every swatch of unchipped paint seemed to burn like tar paper. *Ludlow* also fled. Those French submarines that escaped the carnage of the harbor nearly took their revenge: *Massachusetts* threaded a four-torpedo spread, with number four missing the starboard paravane by fifteen feet. Several minutes later *Tuscaloosa* avoided another four torpedoes, from *Méduse,* and *Brooklyn* dodged five others, fired by the *Amazone.*

Four miles from the transports, French luck ran out for good at eleven A.M. The carrier *Ranger* and the escort carrier *Suwannee* had been plagued by light winds that complicated takeoffs and landings. Both ships tacked aggressively, searching for the riffled water that signaled stiffer breezes needed for sufficient lift. A squadron of Grumman Wildcats finally launched from the *Ranger* and tangled with Vichy fighters in a dogfight that cost four American and eight French aircraft. Fuselage and aileron fragments rained down on Casablanca's minarets. Planes damaged beyond saving flipped belly-up so the pilots could more easily parachute out. The repair crews on *Ranger* mended so many bullet holes in the Wildcats that they ran short of adhesive tape and broadcast an appeal throughout the carrier for personal supplies of Scotch tape.

Patched and vengeful, the American planes swarmed out of the sun from 8,000 feet. Fighters do not fight, the French writer Antoine de St.-Exupéry once observed: they murder. Each Wildcat carried six .50-caliber guns, and each barrel fired 800 rounds per minute—some armor-piercing, some incendiary, and some tracer rounds. Working from fantail to forecastle, pilots strafed Lafond's flotilla so savagely that the French ships glittered from all the bullets richocheting off their superstructures. "The first pass was, I believe, devastating," one flier reported. Flying bridges disintegrated, and the men on them were sliced to ribbons. A single strafing run against one destroyer killed every sailor on deck, except for the gunners crouched in the armored turrets. Their gun ports smudged with carbon, the planes returned to the carrier decks to reload and launch again.

The air attacks and weight of American gunfire soon told, although none of the forty-one bombs dropped on El Hank scored a direct hit. Green- and red-dyed Navy shells rained down by the score, then by the hundreds. *Brooklyn* alone fired 2,600 rounds; *Massachusetts* used more than half her supply of sixteen-inch shells. One shattered French destroyer "heeled over as if she had been pushed by the smokestacks," a pilot noted. The *Fougueux* sank by the bow even as her stern guns continued to fire. *Frondeur*, her engine room flooded, limped back to port and capsized; *Brestois*, too, returned to a jetty only to roll over and sink. The destroyer *Boulonnais*, hit eight times as she maneuvered to launch torpedoes, went down so quickly that a final green shell from *Massachusetts* simply marked the grave. With her bow crushed and all hands on the bridge wounded, including Lafond, *Milan* beached herself. *Albatros* was hit twice, then shelled and strafed while under tow back to Casablanca; she, too, was beached, with more than a hundred casualties. One by one, the green flecks vanished from American radar screens.

The most operatic death was left to the largest ship in the 2nd Light Squadron, the *Primauguet*. When the American attack began, all four of the cruiser's gun turrets had been in various states of undress. By nine A.M., three of the four had been reassembled, a crew of 553 men was aboard, and with help from two tugs *Primauguet* had sortied to join the mêlée. Building to twenty-one knots, she was soon in a running gunfight with *Massachusetts* and both American cruisers. Three shells hit *Primau-*

guet without exploding before a strong shock, then another, staggered the ship. Holed five times below the waterline, her boilers winking out, she hemorrhaged smoke and wallowed back toward Casablanca at four knots. Wildcats caught her off the beach at Roches Noires, killing the captain and twenty-eight other men on the bridge. A laconic distress call reported that fire had become "conspicuous." Men plunged overboard to escape the flames. Terrified pigs broke loose from a pen in the hold and savaged the helpless wounded lying on deck. With more than half her crew dead or injured, *Primauguet* burned for more than a day.

Of the French ships that had sortied, only *Alcyon* returned to port unscathed, and it was left to her to search for survivors. She found little more than whiffs of cordite and brine. Sixteen other vessels—including eight submarines—had been sunk or crippled, with 490 men dead and 969 wounded. Four American ships had taken a single shell each, and *Ludlow* took two. Navy casualties totaled three killed in action and twenty-five wounded. Among the dead was a gunner on a dive-bomber who had rejected more than $200 from a comrade eager to buy a seat in the first wave; with his leg severed at the knee by anti-aircraft fire, the gunner died trying to knot his silk muffler into a tourniquet. He was buried at sea from *Ranger*'s hangar deck as the carrier made a sweeping, ceremonial turn to starboard. A few downed American pilots were captured. From their prison window in Casablanca, they cheered each successive bombing wave, then bathed in champagne purchased from their jailors in a desperate effort to rid themselves of the fleas infesting the cell.

Diehard French officers tried to form another battle fleet, but with only two sloops intact, the rally quickly petered out. Sailors hauled a sixteen-inch American dud from the port to Admiralty headquarters, where it was displayed near the entrance with a placard, in French: "We Come As Friends!" Surviving crewmen were rounded up, issued a rifle and five cartridges, and formed into infantry companies for the defense of Casablanca. Leaning on a cane, the wounded Admiral Lafond took the salutes of his sailors as they passed in review before heading to the front.

Patton finally reached Fedala's Beach Red 1 by crash boat at 1:20 P.M. Sunday afternoon. In better times, the fishing port of 16,000 residents catered to swells from nearby Casablanca who came to enjoy the racetrack and seafront casino. Now the town was almost deserted. Soaked to the waist and escorted by bodyguards cradling submachine guns, Patton scuffed across the sand to a cabana at the seawall. His leather jacket was stained with yellow dye from the French shell that had splashed him on

Augusta that morning. At last, after so many years of preparing himself for war, he was in the fight. Large and unhasty, he took stock.

"I cannot stomach fighting the French if there is a way to avoid it," Patton had confessed to another officer on *Augusta*. That deep Francophilia would now have to be put aside. As ignorant as virtually every other commander in TORCH, Patton knew little of what was happening beyond this beach at this hour. Unlike many, he was comfortable with ambiguity: that trait would inform his generalship for the next two and a half days and then the next two and a half years. A message received on the *Augusta* at noon reported that the French garrison in Safi had surrendered almost seven hours earlier, but it would take at least a day or two for the Sherman tanks unloaded there to travel the 140 miles north to Casablanca. At Mehdia, fifty miles north of Fedala, Truscott had signalled "Play ball!" at 7:15 A.M., but nothing had been heard since, in part because the Army's tactical radios on *Augusta* had also been knocked out by concussion from the ship's guns. The immediate challenge was to organize the three regiments from the 3rd Infantry Division landing at Fedala to capture the town's little harbor, then swing into position for the assault on Casablanca ten miles to the north.

That would be no easy task. Patton had once described combat as "an orgy of disorder," and Fedala confirmed that view. Instead of being concentrated on a four-mile beachhead, troops were sprinkled up and down the coast for forty-two miles. Of seventy-seven light tanks in the convoy, only five had reached shore. Of nine fire control parties landed, just two could communicate with the Navy ships whose guns they were supposed to direct. Inexperienced radio operators tried to extend their range by increasing transmitter power, but succeeded only in jamming other channels. Pilfering natives worked the strand like beachcombers, shouting the passwords "George!" and "Patton!" and wondering why—as they surmised on seeing the big white stars on the invaders' vehicles—a Jewish army had come to Morocco. Soldiers flung away their cumbersome bazookas, and when confronted by Senegalese infantry some just pointed to the American flags pinned to their sleeves, as if that should explain everything. "Had the landings been opposed by Germans," Patton later conceded, "we would never have gotten ashore."

While trapped on Hewitt's bridge during the naval battle, Patton had lamented, "I wish I were a second lieutenant again." Now he acted like one. Flailing and cursing, he scattered Moroccans and timid soldiers alike. He sprinted past the cabanas, rousting slackers from the dunes. "If I see another American soldier lying down on this beach," he roared, "I'll court-martial him!" Patton believed in "words of fire which [would] electrify his chessmen into frenzied heroes," one of his colonels later said. Electrified if not yet heroic, the troops shambled inland. A useful rumor that Berber tribesmen were castrating prisoners tended to curb straggling.

Five French infantry battalions with 2,500 men and forty-six artillery pieces faced nearly 20,000 Americans. Confused and disorganized though they were, the landings at Fedala effectively bisected the French forces defending the coast above Casablanca. The Army's first success came against a four-gun coastal battery at Pont Blondin, three miles northeast of Fedala. Soldiers from the 30th Infantry Regiment dumped mortar shells onto the fort, while a platoon leader shouted, "Rendezvous!" over and over, in the conviction that it meant "Surrender." Several Navy ships contributed a brutal bombardment, which killed four French defenders and drove others into the shelter of a sturdy stone toilet. The shells also killed six Americans in a glade along the Nefifikh River. "When our own naval barrage is falling into our position it is most demoralizing," a major reported. After yellow smoke grenades—the signal to cease firing—failed to halt the Navy's cannonade, an Army officer radioed, "For God's sake stop shelling Fedala! You're killing our own men. . . . The shells are falling all over town. If you stop, they will surrender."

The shelling stopped. A white handkerchief fluttered from a window on the point of a bayonet, and seventy-one dazed French defenders emerged from the fort. An American captain offered water and a cigarette to a French sailor who lay in a stairwell, both legs severed. A Catholic chaplain gave last rites to the dead and dying from each side.

Patrols pushing into Fedala captured ten members of the German Armistice Commission—some still in pajamas—as they trotted across the municipal golf course toward a waiting airplane. Their rooms at the Miramar Hotel yielded stacks of secret documents and an ornate Prussian military helmet. The helmet's owner, General Erich von Wulisch, the head of the commission, had escaped to Spanish Morocco, although not before a weepy farewell phone call to General Noguès: "This is the greatest setback to German arms since 1918. The Americans will take Rommel in the rear, and we shall be expelled from Africa."

Rommel was still 2,000 miles away and the Americans had yet to take even Casablanca. To offer the French "the choice of peace or getting hell knocked out of them," Patton dispatched a francophone colonel, William Hale Wilbur, in a jeep with a white flag. Wilbur, whose negotiating credentials included captaincy of the West Point fencing team thirty years earlier, set off in search of General Béthouart, unaware that he was immured in a Meknès prison and had been charged with treason. Wilbur motored through French defenses, greeting Senegalese machine-gunners with a chipper, "Good day, my friends! You're well this morning?" At the Admiralty building, where wounded French marines sprawled across the bloody courtyard cobblestones, Wilbur was sent packing. Dodging his own navy's gunfire, he drove back to American lines, joined a tank attack on a coastal battery, and later was awarded the Congressional Medal of Honor. A second emissary also made it to the Admiralty building just as El Hank loosed another salvo at two P.M. "*Voilà votre réponse,*" a disdainful French officer said, and shut the gate. "The French navy," a staff officer told Patton, "is determined to slug it out with us."

The fight would be to the finish. Patton was sad, but not very. While still trapped on *Augusta,* he had felt the singular loneliness of command, compounded by his frustrating inability to reach the battlefield. Now he was in his element. "My theory is that an army commander does what is necessary to accomplish his mission and that nearly 80 percent of his mission is to arouse morale in his men," he once wrote. On Sunday night, as his aide barked "At-*ten*-tion!" to staff officers in the candlelit Miramar Hotel dining room, Patton strolled to the table wearing his pistols, polished cavalry boots, and von Wulisch's shiny white casque emblazoned with a Prussian double eagle. To gales of laughter he announced over champagne, "I shall wear it for our entrance into Berlin."

That night, before falling asleep, he scribbled in his diary, "God was very good to me today."

God withdrew his beneficence on Monday. Following what one Fedala resident described as "the calmest day in sixty-eight years," the Atlantic turned nasty with six-foot waves before dawn on November 9. Unloading slowed, then nearly stopped. Although 40 percent of the invasion force was ashore, barely one percent of the 15,000 tons of cargo had left Hewitt's ships. Of 378 landing craft and tank lighters, more than half were breached, sunk, or stranded. Navy cooks lowered lard pails full of coffee to exhausted boat crews. Sloppy loading in Norfolk, and Patton's chronic neglect of logistics—"Let's do it and think about it afterwards," in his chief engineer's tart phrase—now cost him dearly.

Shore parties lacked forklifts, pallets, rope, and acetylene torches. Soaked cardboard boxes disintegrated. Guns arrived on the beach with no gun sights; guns arrived with no ammunition; guns arrived with no gunners. Critical radio equipment had been stowed as ballast in the most inaccessible depths of the holds simply because it was heavy. Medical supplies remained shipbound for thirty-six hours. Boat and vehicle shortages left dozens of wounded soldiers stranded on the beaches, along with the trussed-up dead. Ammo was so desperately scarce that it was towed to shore on life rafts. Patton had imprudently relegated his chief logistician to the follow-on convoy, which was still days from Morocco. Press-ganging Moroccans to work as stevedores—at a wage of one cigarette per hour—simply gave many locals a better chance to steal.

A company of 113 military policemen was dispatched in four boats from the *Leonard Wood* with instructions to "bring order out of chaos on the beaches." In the predawn gloom on Monday, the lead coxswain mistook the burning *Primauguet* for his intended navigation beacon, an oil fire near Beach Yellow in Fedala. The boats puttered fifteen miles down the coast and into the fairway of Casablanca harbor, where an M.P. hailed what he thought was a U.S. Navy destroyer. "We are Americans!"

At a range of fifty yards, the French vessel opened with machine-gun fire, killing the company commander. The astonished soldiers in the lead boat stood with raised hands, some ripping off their undershirts to wave in frantic surrender. The French bore down, answering with 20mm cannon fire and a three-inch shell that shattered the motor and sank the boat in less than a minute. The second craft, only twenty yards behind, swerved to escape, but a shell blew off the coxswain's leg and machine-gun fire crippled a lieutenant who jumped up to take the wheel. "The air," one survivor recalled, "was full of metal." Burning gasoline spread from the stern in a crackling blue sheet. Those still alive leaped over the side as the two trailing boats fled through swarms of tracer fire. Twenty-eight Americans were killed or wounded; French sailors fished forty-five prisoners from the sea. A few men swam to shore, vomiting oily seawater. French civilians dragged them to the seawall and wrapped them in overcoats.

Two hours later, Patton reappeared on the Fedala beach with a determination "to flay the idle, rebuke the incompetent, and drive the timid." After wading through the surf to help reel in corpses from another overturned boat—"they were a nasty blue color," he later reported—Patton halted further unloading except in Fedala's tiny harbor. "The beach was a mess and the officers were doing nothing," he told his diary. Upon spotting a soldier gibbering on the beach, "I kicked him in arse with all my might. . . . Some way to boost morale. As a whole the men were poor, the officers worse. No drive. It is very sad."

One officer quoted Patton in waist-deep water summoning soldiers to help him shoulder a stranded landing craft from a sandbar: "Come back here! Yes, I mean *you!* All of you! Drop that stuff and come back here. Faster than that, goddamit. On the double! . . . Lift and push. Now! Push, goddamit, *push!*"

Scourging would not calm the sea or replenish empty caissons. The 3rd Infantry Division on November 8 had barely pushed south from Fedala toward Casablanca when troops were halted for lack of supplies. By late morning on November 9, the motor pool of the 15th Infantry Regiment still consisted of only a few camels, a few donkeys, and five jeeps, hardly the makings of a blitzkrieg. A four-battalion attack that began at seven A.M. on Monday stopped several hours later, again for want of wheels and munitions. At day's end Patton gave his customary acknowledgment to the Creator, but this time the diary entry had a perfunctory tone: "Again God has been good."

As dawn broke on November 10, the Americans were still five miles from Casablanca. The 7th Infantry on the right, and the 15th Infantry on the left, tramped forward to the sound of scuffing boots and howls from mongrel dogs flanking the columns. French sailors, dismasted but dangerous, appeared in skirmish lines with their five cartridges. On a distant ridgeline spahi cavalrymen in brilliant robes could be seen with their long battle pennants and longer rifles. "Enemy cavalry!" an American officer shouted. "Direct front!" Horses pranced in the morning sun, the silver fittings on their bridles flashing; American sharpshooters debated whether to aim at horse or man, only to have the targets vanish in the haze. Then artillery fire fell from at least a dozen French 75s, and a battalion from the 7th Infantry broke for the rear until steadied by their officers 500 yards back.

"Today has been bad," Patton told his diary late Tuesday. A message from Eisenhower at Gibraltar added to his vexation: "Dear Georgie— Algiers has been ours for two days. Oran defenses crumbling rapidly. . . . The only tough nut left is in your hands. Crack it open quickly."

To his diary entry on November 10, Patton added, "God favors the bold, victory is to the audacious." He now believed that only by flattening Casablanca could he take it. Sherman tanks from Safi had nearly reached the southern suburbs. Hewitt's ships and carrier planes had sovereignty at sea and in the air. Third Division troops invested the city from north and east. The road to Marrakesh had been cut.

Patton notified his staff and subordinate commanders: at first light on Wednesday they would crack open the city, quickly and terribly.

Battle for the Kasbah

OF the nine major landing sites chosen for TORCH in Algeria and Morocco, a beach that American planners had considered among the easiest was proving the most difficult. Eighty miles north of Casablanca, the seaside resort of Mehdia had confounded Brigadier General Lucian Truscott's best efforts to subdue it. Landed badly but without serious opposition, Truscott's 9,000 troops were supposed to capture the modern airfield at Port Lyautey, a few miles up the serpentine Sebou River. Once the field had fallen, aircraft from Gibraltar, and seventy-seven Army P-40s now parked on the escort carrier *Chenango*, would give Patton formidable airpower in Morocco—with bombs and fuel provided by the *Contessa*. Facing only 3,000 French defenders, Truscott had assured Mark Clark that the field "should not be too difficult to capture." American troops believed the French defenders would be so cowed that they would greet the invaders "with brass bands," as one sergeant put it. George Marshall told Eisenhower that he expected the airfield to fall by "noon Dog Day," November 8. The assurance proved rash, and the expectations hollow.

"Beloved Wife," Truscott had written from Norfolk two weeks earlier, "my greatest ambition is to justify your confidence and to deserve your love." Sentimental and uxorious, he was also brusque, profane, and capable of hocking tobacco with the most unlettered private in the Army. "Polo games and wars aren't won by gentlemen," he said. "No sonofabitch, no commander." Chesty and, at forty-seven, slightly stooped, he had protruding gray eyes, a moon face, and a voice as raspy as a wood file. His hands were huge, with fingers like tent pegs. He made his own polo mallets and trimmed his nails, obsessively, with a pocket knife. In uniform, Truscott was almost foppish: enameled helmet, silk scarf, red leather jacket, riding breeches. Before joining the cavalry in 1917, he had spent six years as a teacher in one-room schoolhouses. Until the disaster at Dieppe, which he attended as an American observer, he had never heard a shot fired in anger; he spent the grim return voyage to England belowdecks rolling cigarettes for the wounded from his plug of Bull Durham and wondering how to avoid a similar catastrophe in TORCH, for which he was a planner. "I am just a little worried about ability of Truscott," Patton told his diary. "It may be nerves."

Truscott's opening gambit at Mehdia was to dispatch a pair of emissaries bearing a parchment scroll adorned with red ribbon and wax seals. In elegant calligraphy it urged the French commander to give up. Carrying this document were two aviators, Colonel Demas T. Craw, who had

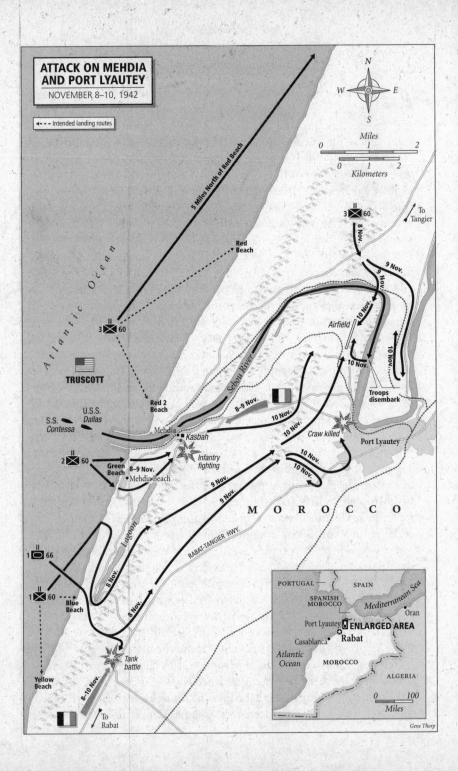

ATTACK ON MEHDIA AND PORT LYAUTEY

NOVEMBER 8–10, 1942

◄--- Intended landing routes

N
W E
S

Miles
0   1   2

Kilometers
0   1   2

To Tangier

3 ⊠ 60
8 Nov.

9 Nov.
9 Nov.

10 Nov.

Airfield

10 Nov.

10 Nov.

Troops
disembark

5 Miles North of Red Beach

Red Beach

Atlantic Ocean

3 ⊠ 60

🇺🇸
TRUSCOTT

Red 2 Beach

8–9 Nov.

10 Nov.

10 Nov.

Craw killed

10 Nov.

Port Lyautey

Sebou River

S.S. *Contessa*

U.S.S. *Dallas*

Mehdia

Kasbah

Infantry fighting

10 Nov.

2 ⊠ 60

Green Beach   8–9 Nov.

• Mehdia Beach

9 Nov.

9 Nov.

10 Nov.

10 Nov.

10 Nov.

M O R O C C O

Lagoon

RABAT-TANGIER HWY.

1 ▭ 66

8 Nov.

1 ⊠ 60

Blue Beach

8 Nov.

Yellow Beach

Tank battle

8–10 Nov.

To Rabat

PORTUGAL   SPAIN

SPANISH MOROCCO

Mediterranean Sea

Port Lyautey 🏛 **ENLARGED AREA**

• Oran

• Casablanca   ★ **Rabat**

Atlantic Ocean

MOROCCO

ALGERIA

0   100
Miles

Gene Thorp

captained the West Point polo team for the class of 1924, and Major Pier-pont M. Hamilton of Tuxedo, New York, a product of Groton, Harvard, and years of living in Paris as an international banker. In their finest pinks-and-greens the two men had hit the beach Sunday morning, boarded a jeep, and headed inland. Holding a French tricolor and the Stars and Stripes, Craw sat in front next to the driver. Hamilton, seated in back on an ammunition box, carried a white truce flag.

The road from Mehdia angled past a sixteenth-century Portuguese fortress overlooking the turquoise Sebou where it emptied into the blue-black Atlantic. Already misnamed the Kasbah by the Americans, the citadel occupied the site of a Carthaginian trading post of the sixth cen-tury B.C. High-prowed fishing smacks bobbed at their moorings along the riverbank, nets draped over the gunwales to dry. Stork nests, intri-cately thatched and big as a queen's bed, crowned utility poles along the road. Hamilton waved to Moroccan infantrymen, who waved back. A few artillery rounds burst in front and then behind. "Damn it," Craw radioed, "we're being shelled by both you and the French." Three miles ahead, they spied the airfield's concrete runway tucked into an oxbow bend of the Sebou. Beyond lay Port Lyautey.

The jeep climbed a low hill. Without warning, a machine gun stut-tered twenty yards away. Craw slumped against the driver, instantly dead, his chest embroidered with bullets. A French lieutenant rushed forward, disarmed Hamilton and the driver, and then, leaving Craw folded in the jeep, delivered his prisoners to Colonel Jean Petit, com-mander of the 1st Regiment of Moroccan Tirailleurs. Petit expressed sympathy for the dead man, but less for the cause of French capitulation. "A decision of this kind," he explained after studying the scroll, "is not within my jurisdiction." While awaiting instructions from his superiors in Rabat, Petit offered Major Hamilton a private room and a seat in the officers' mess, where the American spent the next three days thrilling his captors with vivid accounts of the secret bazooka and other new terrors in the invaders' arsenal.

The failed diplomatic mission—for which Craw, posthumously, and Hamilton would win the Medal of Honor—proved Truscott's last, best hope for a quick victory. Troops from the 60th Infantry closed on the Kasbah only to be driven back to the Mehdia lighthouse by wild shellfire from their own navy. With massive gates and masonry walls a yard thick, the fort proved impregnable. Eighty-five French soldiers inside at the time of the American landings were reinforced Sunday evening by 200 others, all peppering the invaders with fire from the battlements and rifle ports. The 60th Infantry commander ordered the Kasbah bypassed, then belatedly realized that nothing could move upriver until the fort's big guns had been spiked. With more élan than sense, Truscott ordered the Kasbah taken "with cold steel" rather than reduced by U.S. warships. A French counterattack with three decrepit Renault tanks routed Truscott's 2nd Battalion and scattered the Americans so effectively that company musters produced as few as thirty men. "Officers as well as men were absolutely dumbfounded at their first taste of battle," one major later told the War Department.

Nightfall made matters worse. After repeatedly yelling "George!" at a suspicious shadow to no effect, a skittish sentry heaved a grenade and killed the lighthouse keeper's donkey. Sepulchral moaning from a lagoon terrorized several tank crewmen until they realized it was the croaking of giant African toads. The French ambushed a patrol near a fish cannery along the river, wounding an officer and shooting six of his men in the head. Skittish troops on the beaches and ships shot down a twin-engine plane in a wild fusillade before realizing that it was a British aircraft dispatched from Gibraltar to monitor the landings. A burst of machine-gun fire from a jumpy American soldier missed Truscott's head by an inch.

On the broad white shingle at Mehdia, Truscott cupped a cigarette in his big hands. He was violating his own blackout order but he desperately needed a smoke. The orange ember illuminated a face fissured with worry. "It came to me that even with hundreds all around me, I was utterly alone," he later wrote of that "grim and lonely" Sunday night.

> As far as I could see along the beach, there was chaos. Landing craft were beaching in the pounding surf, broaching to the waves, and spilling men and equipment into the water. Men wandered about aimlessly, hopelessly lost, calling to each other and for their units, swearing at each other and at nothing.

The troops ducked as one whenever a sniper round cracked overhead. Artillery crumped in the distance: certainly it was French; the Americans had been unable to get their guns ashore. The rising sea that tormented Patton at Fedala was worse here, with waves now cresting at fifteen feet. Ammunition, water, and half of Truscott's troops remained on the ships. Wary of the Kasbah batteries, the Navy had moved its transports over the horizon—"halfway to Bermuda," Truscott fumed—adding thirty miles to each round-trip for lighters and landing craft.

Like Patton, Truscott concluded that the landing would have been a "disaster against a well-armed enemy intent upon resistance." So few American soldiers seemed to be shooting, and so many were willing to give up. Truscott suspected that peacetime training had taught them how to surrender better than how to fight. "One of the first lessons that battle impresses upon one," he later observed, "is that no matter how large the force engaged, every battle is made up of small actions by individuals and small units."

He drew on his cigarette and picked up a rifle. Every battle also was made up of small actions by generals. Bellowing over the crashing surf, Truscott ordered straggling infantrymen, stranded coxswains, and anyone else within earshot to grab a weapon and move inland. Here, he said, thrusting an abandoned bazooka at a Navy boat crew. The first tint of Monday's dawn glowed in the east behind the Kasbah. There would be no Dieppe in Africa. Lucian Truscott would not permit it. No sonofabitch, no commander.

Yet only luck, valor, and French hesitation prevented the Americans at Mehdia from being thrown back into the Atlantic. Just seven of the fifty-four light tanks in Truscott's armor battalion reached shore, but they were enough—with timely gunfire from the cruiser *Savannah*—to repulse French armored reinforcements heading toward Mehdia from Rabat on November 9. French Renaults and American Stuarts swapped fire at a hundred yards' range, scooting up and back without exposing the thin armor on their flanks. When shell ejectors jammed, tank commanders tore out their fingernails clawing spent brass from the gun breeches. French bullets wedged between the turret and hull on several tanks, jamming the swivel mechanisms; crewmen leaped from their hatches and yanked out the slugs with pliers, as if extracting teeth. Navy pilots dropped fifty depth charges—designed to combat submarines—on French tanks and artillery.

By nightfall on November 9, the beachhead was no longer imperiled, although French snipers continued to kill men careless with their silhouettes. A U.S. infantry battalion that had been marooned on a beach far to the north hacked a trail through dense juniper to appear on the north bank of the Sebou across from the airfield. Stuart tanks approached Port Lyautey from the southwest. The night was "not a cheerful one," Truscott later recalled, "although for me it was less grim and dismal than the night before."

At first light on November 10, the U.S.S. *Dallas* approached the twin rock jetties bracketing the mouth of the Sebou. Seventy-five American commandos were aboard the World War I–era destroyer, whose stacks and superstructure had been whittled down to reduce her draft as she eased upriver to the airfield. At the helm was the former chief pilot of

Port Lyautey, René Malvergne. A French patriot who had briefly been jailed for his Gaullist sympathies, Malvergne earlier in the year had been smuggled by the OSS to Tangier in a trailer pulled by a Chevrolet; every few miles the driver had stopped to hear Malvergne's muffled assurances, *"Tout va bien—pas trop de monoxide!"* From Gibraltar, Malvergne had made his way to London—where he introduced himself at Allied headquarters as "Mr. Jones" and asked personally for Eisenhower—before being spirited to an OSS safe house in Washington, where he was known simply as the Shark. George Marshall had been furious upon learning of the escapade, and pointed out that Malvergne's conspicuous absence from Port Lyautey would "rivet attention on this particular area." Yet here he was, almost home, at the wheel of an American destroyer, wearing U.S. Army herringbone, and straining to recall the seasonal shift of sandbars in a treacherous pilotage he had not negotiated in many months.

Dallas yawed wildly against an ebb tide in violent rain that spattered the deck like gravel. Thirty-foot swells swept between the jetties, curling over the destroyer's stern in great emerald tubes. Spindrift whipped past the bridge as Malvergne felt for the channel, narrowly missing the breakwater rocks. Seamen called the diminishing depths with a hand lead improvised from a steel shackle. The Sebou's mucky bottom sucked at the destroyer's hull, then abruptly held her fast near the cannery. Swells pounded *Dallas* from behind, and great splashes of turquoise blossomed around the ship as gunfire from the Kasbah began smacking into the water.

Malvergne ordered flank speed. *Dallas*'s propellers chopped at the river with such fury that her engine-room dials showed twenty-five knots when in fact she was barely creeping, her keel carving a trench in the silt. A mile upstream, the prow sliced through a cable boom stretched across the Sebou. The destroyer's three-inch guns popped away at the Kasbah and French machine-gunners on the encroaching hills. Malvergne threaded a path between two scuttled steamers and traced the oxbow loop to the eastern flank of the runway. There, at 7:37 A.M., *Dallas* ran aground for good. The commandos launched their rubber boats, and within twenty minutes the airfield had been seized.

Two hours later, Truscott crouched in the shadow of the cannery below the Kasbah. He had captured the airfield, but the Mehdia garrison refused to capitulate. Another infantry assault on the fortress had been repulsed, then another, then two more. Over 200 wounded soldiers lay in aid stations near the beach, and dozens of dead lay in a makeshift morgue. All ship-to-shore movement had been halted by high seas, and water, ammunition, and medical supplies were now desperately short. Truscott was also running out of troops, and a message from Patton warned him that no reinforcements were available. A provisional assault company of cooks, clerks, and drivers met behind a dune for hasty instruction in how to use the Thompson submachine gun, then filtered into trenches north of the Mehdia lighthouse.

In the teeming rain, gunners wheeled a pair of 105mm howitzers up to the Kasbah walls and opened fire at point-blank range. The masonry yielded, but French counterattacks with grenades and machine-gun fire again drove the Americans back 200 yards. At 10:30 A.M., as Truscott scanned the enemy battlements with his field glasses, eight Navy dive-bombers appeared overhead. Howitzer gunners marked the targets with smoke shells, and moments later the Kasbah erupted in flame and dust.

"It was a beautiful sight for a soldier's eyes," Truscott later wrote. Whooping infantrymen boiled through the main gate and broken wall, chasing snipers through the labyrinthine *fondouk* with bayonets fixed, shoving grenades into firing ports at the commandant's headquarters. Combat engineers forced the lower gate along the river, and the Kasbah surrendered. The garrison commander had been killed. More than 200 French troops emerged with their hands raised, and another 150 were captured in nearby trenches and mud huts. "The final assault," an Army account acknowledged, "had touches of *Beau Geste*."

Enemy resistance was broken, but sniping and sporadic shelling—including more than 200 high-explosive rounds from the *Texas*—continued until Tuesday evening. At 10:30 P.M., a French officer drove toward American lines in a staff car with a tricolor lashed to the radiator and a bugler repeatedly tooting "Cease Fire." American sentries mistook the stirring call for "Charge" and opened fire, wounding the automobile grillwork but no passengers. After more hours of delay and confusion, Truscott received word at his command post on the beach that French commanders wanted to parley. A brief conference at the Kasbah, described in one account as "a brightly colored pageant of varied French and colonial uniforms, Arab costumes, and flags," led to a formal cease-fire. French troops stacked arms and returned to their barracks. "Our parley," Truscott reported, "ended with another interchange of stiff salutes."

The three-day fight for Mehdia and Port Lyautey had cost seventy-nine American lives and 250 men wounded. The French, with pardonable imprecision, estimated their dead at 250 to 300. Colonel Craw and other fallen soldiers from both sides were buried together in a new cemetery on the bluff above the Sebou, a few yards from the Kasbah. Late on

November 10, René Malvergne was ferried from the *Dallas* out to the *Contessa* for another run up the river. Scraping hard across the bar at the Sebou's mouth, the scow sheared into the southern jetty with a grinding crash that seemed certain to detonate her 1,000 tons of munitions and fuel. Instead, *Contessa* simply settled in the mud, her bow plates crushed and the forward hold flooded, in under two minutes, with thirteen feet of water.

Both ship and pilot had come too far to give up now. Awaiting a rising tide, Malvergne swung *Contessa*'s bow downriver, rang up full steam astern, and backed up the river ten miles to the airfield. Unloading took three days. Malvergne returned home to his wife and children with a Silver Star on his chest.

In a final twist, of the seventy-seven P-40s launched from *Chenango*, one crashed into the sea, one vanished into the fog, and seventeen were damaged while landing at the hard-won Port Lyautey runway. Many of the mishaps reflected elementary pilot errors, which were attributed to "war hysteria." None of the surviving planes saw action in TORCH.

"It's All Over for Now"

GRAY with fatigue, Patton had returned to the *Augusta* in his crash boat to make final plans for the reduction of Casablanca. His struggles in climbing the boarding net so alarmed Hewitt that the admiral fell to his knees on the well deck and hauled Patton over the side. "Doctor, I think the general is very tired," Hewitt told the ship's surgeon. "I wish you would prescribe for him. You might prescribe for me, too." The doctor measured out two bracing shots from a liquor bottle. Patton and Hewitt still addressed each other as "General" and "Admiral"—not until Sicily, nine months later, did they mutually agree to "George" and "Kent"—but this small episode, so charged with the stress and isolation of command, was another important moment in their ripening cama-raderie. Duly revived, they finished planning their battle, and Patton motored back to his army.

Hewitt resumed his station on the bridge on November 10 just as the mighty *Jean Bart*—considered hors de combat for the past two days—returned to life. French crewmen had secretly repaired her damaged turret but left the guns cockeyed as a ruse. An officer in the battleship's cramped crow's nest had been watching *Augusta* for hours, beckoning with a crooked finger and murmuring, "Come a little closer, come a little closer." At 14,000 yards—eight miles—*Jean Bart* opened with a two-gun salvo. A pair of orange geysers heaved sixty feet out of the sea, splattering those on *Augusta*'s bridge with dyed water.

Nine more salvos followed. The bridge rang up flank speed, hard right rudder, and smoke. *Augusta* fled like a goddess in her own fog bank, chased by shells that straddled the cruiser but failed to strike home. *Ranger*'s aircraft retaliated promptly with a barrage of thousand-pound bombs that gouged a ten-foot hole in *Jean Bart*'s main deck near the bow and blew a twenty-foot length from the stern. The flight leader radioed back to the carrier, "No more *Jean Bart*," and this time it was true.

For Patton, enough was enough. Eisenhower had explicitly ordered that "no bombardment will be executed without prior authority from me," but Patton—citing balky communications—intended to raze Casablanca without even notifying Gibraltar, much less awaiting permission. At his headquarters in Fedala, engineers put the final touches on plans to blow up aqueducts and power lines. Pilots studied aerial photos of their targets. Gunners built pyramids of extra ammunition. Infantrymen honed their bayonets and edged forward for an assault now fixed for 7:30 A.M. on Wednesday, November 11.

At two A.M., about the time that Truscott learned of Port Lyautey's capitulation, a French car approached a 30th Infantry picket with the usual bragging bugle and a truce flag lit with a flashlight. Two French officers and four enlisted men carried a dispatch from General Noguès's headquarters. At the Hotel Miramar, Patton rose, dressed, and marched through the double doors of a smoking room off the lobby. As later recounted by Patton's aide Charles R. Codman, a French major wearing a black leather helmet and a khaki uniform white with dust handed the general a flimsy onionskin. Patton sat on a banquette and by candlelight studied the scribbled message. More negotiating by Darlan and Clark in Algiers, Pétain in Vichy, and Noguès in Rabat appeared to have resulted in a cease-fire across North Africa. At any rate, the French army in Morocco had been ordered to stop fighting.

Patton looked at the major sitting rigid in a straightback chair. "Unless the French navy immediately signifies that it is bound by this ceasefire order," he warned, "the attack on Casablanca jumps off as scheduled." That gave the French three hours. Patton dismissed the officer and his delegation with a safe-conduct through American lines into Casablanca. "Staff wanted me to call off attack but I would not yet," he wrote in his diary. "It was too late, and besides it is bad to change plans."

At dawn, the guns were loaded and elevated, with fingers poised on triggers and firing keys. Navy dive-bombers vaulted from the *Ranger* and circled toward the city with full bomb racks. Hewitt dispatched a truculent if syntactically suspect message to Admiral Michelier, the Vichy naval chief: "Report whether you intend forcing me destroy your ship and shore installations and spill the blood of your people. The decision is your individual responsibility."

At 6:40 A.M. the French reply reached Patton at the command post of the 3rd Infantry Division. He ordered his deputy over a walkie-talkie, "Call it off. The French navy has capitulated." Then to Hewitt: "Urgent to *Augusta*. Cease fire immediately. Acknowledge immediately. Patton." A Wildcat flight leader radioed, "Boys, it's all over for now. Let's go back." The pilots jettisoned their bombs in the sea and returned to the carrier.

Franco-American amity—part of the natural order, in Yankee eyes—was quickly reestablished. The bloodletting of the past three days, if neither forgotten nor quite forgiven, was set aside, just as a marital indiscretion might be glossed over for the sake of the children. An unshaven American colonel toting a tommy gun and assorted pistols arrived at Admiralty headquarters, where a French officer threw up his hands in mock terror and cried, "Chicago, I give up!" The Americans claimed their dead from a French morgue and buried them on the beach in pits powdered with lime. Just past noon on November 11, Patton and Hewitt hosted a luncheon at a Fedala brasserie for their French counterparts, lubricating the pleasantries with Bordeaux and cognac.

At the Miramar later that afternoon, Noguès, Michelier, and other French commanders drove past the coconut palms and banana trees lining the driveway to find that Patton had posted a welcoming honor guard. In the smoking room he complimented his adversaries on their gallantry and proposed a gentlemen's agreement under which French troops could keep their arms. Details of the cease-fire would be left to Eisenhower and Darlan in Algiers. Patton sealed the deal with a toast to "our future victory over a common enemy."

"They drank $40 worth of champagne," he later told Washington, "but it was worth it." Hewitt shook Admiral Michelier's outstretched hand and told him that the U.S. Navy, which had dumped 19,000 shells on Morocco in the past three days, regretted firing on the tricolor. "You had your orders and you carried them out. I had mine and I carried them out," Michelier replied. "Now I am ready to cooperate in every way possible."

The conquest of Morocco cost the United States more than 1,100 casualties: 337 killed, 637 wounded, 122 missing, and 71 captured. The Allies had secured an Atlantic base in Africa, strengthening the sea-lanes, tightening control of the Strait of Gibraltar, and discouraging any Axis expedition through Spain. "We are in Casa[blanca] and have the harbor and airport," Patton told his diary on November 11. "To God be the praise." In a letter to Eisenhower he added, "If you adhere to your plan things usually work for you."

Press dispatches from Morocco, if sketchy and distorted, made Patton a national hero. The seventy-four-hour battle had given him a chance to display his most conspicuous command attributes: energy, will, a capacity to see the enemy's perspective, and bloodlust. "Of course, as a Christian I was glad to avoid the further [ef]fusion of blood," he wrote the secretary of war, Henry Stimson, "but as a soldier I would have given a good deal to have the fight go on."

Yet Patton's defects also were revealed: a wanton disregard of logistics; a childish propensity to feud with other services; an incapacity to empathize with frightened young soldiers; a willingness to disregard the spirit if not the letter of orders from his superiors; and an archaic tendency to assess his own generalship on the basis of personal courage under fire. He relied on charm and half-truth in explaining to Eisenhower his readiness to bombard Casablanca without authorization: "I cannot control interstellar space, and our radio simply would not work. The only person who lost by it was myself, since the press was probably unable to recount my heroic deeds." But Patton was too discerning a professional soldier to be wholly satisfied. "Unfortunately I did not get a chance to distinguish myself except not to lay down a couple of times when we got strafed," he wrote Bea.

Perhaps the shrewdest assessment came in Bea's return letter, written on November 8: "I realize that there are months and perhaps years of waiting and anxiety ahead of me, yet today all I can think of is your triumph, and the thought that rings through my mind like a peal of bells is that the first jump is taken and you will never have to take it again."

After leaving the Miramar late Wednesday afternoon, Hewitt returned to *Augusta* in a quandary. Fifteen transports and cargo ships remained in the vulnerable anchorage off Fedala. Although almost all Army troops had disembarked, three-quarters of their supplies—11,000 tons— remained in the holds. The Army was pleading for food, fuel, medical supplies, tentage, everything. An obvious solution was to move the ships into Casablanca harbor for unloading; a staff officer reported to Hewitt with sketches and notes showing five berths available along the Jetée Transversale and room for at least ten more ships in various basins. But when Hewitt had asked Michelier at lunch about the port, the French admiral threw up his hands. *"C'est un cimetière!"* Herding the ships in at night among the submerged wrecks would be hazardous, Hewitt agreed. More to the point, the next convoy from Norfolk—with twenty-four ships and 32,000 soldiers—would arrive in two days, on November 13, with expectations of a safe harbor. The port was far too small to accommodate everyone, and the arriving ships were more precious since they still carried all of their troops and cargo.

And yet. Hewitt studied the secret intelligence message received that afternoon. An estimated fourteen German submarines were heading toward Casablanca, including an eight-boat wolfpack designated *Schlag-tot:* "Death Blow." "Go after them, full attack," the U-boats had been ordered. "Let nothing hold you back." All U.S. ships and aircraft had been alerted to the danger. A minefield was laid along the northeast flank of the transport anchorage despite a shortage of sea mines. Eleven destroyers patrolled the other approaches. The Army had been asked repeatedly to extinguish all lights in Casablanca because their glare silhouetted the ships against the coast.

"Good lads," Hewitt often told his staff officers. "You make it so easy for me. All I have to do is decide." Yet with all the factors carefully considered, this decision was difficult. Hewitt knew that detecting even a surfaced submarine was hard—many cloud shadows had been bombed and shelled in recent days. Spotting a "feather," the thin wake made by an extended periscope, was virtually impossible at night. And killing submerged U-boats with depth charges was like trying to hit a fish with a stone. At six P.M. Hewitt gathered his staff again on *Augusta,* then sent another message to Patton once more asking him to turn out the lights. All vessels would remain at anchorage overnight. He would revisit the issue in the morning.

Blackout drapes covered the tall windows of the Miramar's dining room. Outside, the faint scent of bougainvillea sweetened the air. A sea breeze stirred the bamboo thickets that screened a croquet green from the beach casino. Patton and two dozen staff officers dined on duck, very credibly prepared by a French chef who had been informally conscripted into the American Army hours before. Many a glass of wine was raised to toast the coincident occasion of Patton's fifty-seventh birthday, his triumph in Morocco, and the twenty-fourth anniversary of the armistice ending the Great War.

At 7:48 P.M., the festivities were interrupted by a muffled detonation that rattled the seaward windows. As Patton and his men hurried to the veranda or climbed five stories to the hotel roof, two more explosions carried across the water. Three miles off the beach, yellow flames licked from one ship; brilliant orange fireballs floated into the sky as stocks of gasoline and ammunition exploded. Two other vessels also appeared to be in distress. Frantic blinkering flashed from the signal lamps on two dozen ships in an arc stretching to the horizon. With field glasses it was possible to see men flailing in the water, backlit by fire. "That," Patton's chief engineer later recalled, "ended the party."

The German submarine *U-173* had slipped through the destroyer screen and sprayed half a dozen torpedoes at the concentrated American ships. Three vessels had been struck, each in the port side. *Joseph Hewes* sank by the bow in twenty-six minutes, taking her captain and several seamen to the bottom. An officer aboard the tanker *Winooski* had spotted a torpedo wake slide past his prow, then turned his head just in time to see a second torpedo burrow into the hull between the bridge and poopdeck house; the detonation wounded seven men and gashed a twenty-five-foot hole in a fuel tank that was fortunately empty and ballasted with seawater. The destroyer *Hambleton,* waiting to refuel, was struck in the forward engine room, four feet below the waterline. The blast killed twenty men and broke the back of the ship so completely that "you could see her working her bow and stern, which were no longer rigidly attached," a witness reported. Survivors huddled on deck and sang "Don't Give Up the Ship." Another destroyer spotted *U-173* making for the open sea just before 8:30. But, owing to momentary confusion over whether the submarine was in fact an American landing craft, the killer slipped away. (Pressing her luck, the U-boat would be trapped off Casablanca five days later and sunk by depth charges, with all fifty-seven hands lost.)

The "goosing" of three ships, in the Army's impudent phrase, cost Hewitt a sleepless night. Red-eyed and rumpled, he convened his top commanders aboard *Augusta* early on Thursday, November 12, in the cramped cabin of his chief of staff. Two hours after the attack, he had sent a superfluous warning to all ships: "Be especially vigilant against Axis submarines." *Winooski* had been righted with hard pumping, and the swayback *Hambleton* was towed to sanctuary in Casablanca harbor. But for the rest of the fleet the issues remained unchanged: Tens of thousands of additional soldiers were scheduled to arrive tomorrow in the second convoy, and there was no room in the harbor for both Hewitt's original cargo ships and the newcomers.

Hewitt was furious. For months he had warned the Army that this follow-on convoy would arrive almost a week too early, putting itself and the invasion force at risk. But Patton and other generals had worn him down by insisting that more troops and cargo would be needed in

Morocco immediately. Hewitt had finally concurred, "with extreme reluctance and misgivings."

For more than an hour he reviewed his options. *All I have to do is decide.* He could move the invasion transports into Casablanca immediately and let the arriving convoy wait at sea. For a victorious fleet, the measure seemed defensive, even embarrassing, and it would imperil the newcomers. Hewitt was more tempted by a proposal to continue unloading by lighter and at Fedala's tiny harbor during the day, repairing to the relative safety of the open sea at night and ceding Casablanca to the new arrivals. But that would add days to the unloading, and blue water was hardly a refuge: this very morning, fifty miles off the coast, *Ranger* had narrowly escaped an attack by U-boats.

Finally, he could continue unloading day and night at Fedala, and hope that last night's attack had been a fluke. Hewitt's transport commander, Captain Robert R. M. Emmet, argued loudly for this third option. The Navy's primary obligation at Casablanca was to support the Army, Emmet insisted. Even with a cease-fire in place, Patton and his commanders howled at the Navy's delays in unloading.

Hewitt slumped in a chair. Emmet's arguments had force. Surely the Navy could protect itself. And if a ship was torpedoed close to shore, the chance of salvaging at least some cargo was better than if it was hit far out at sea.

Augusta would move into Casablanca and berth at the stinking phosphate pier. The rest of the fleet would remain off Fedala, unloading as fast as possible. The admiral dismissed his men and headed toward the bridge with a churning sense of unease. If ever he needed a bit more velvet, it was now. But Kent Hewitt had been at sea for too many years and was too fine a sailor to deceive himself. His velvet was gone.

As dusk sifted over Fedala, and Patton's staff gathered at the Miramar for Thursday's supper, Captain Ernst Kals eased *U-130* down the Moroccan coast from the northeast in water so shallow the submarine's hull scraped bottom. Kals knew the Americans well: he had won the Knight's Cross after sinking nine ships in a two-week spree along the East Coast earlier in the year. *U-130* slipped at dead slow between the beach and the American minefield. The unseen feather purled the sea like a shark's fin. Shortly before six P.M. the U-boat fired four torpedoes from her bow tubes, then nimbly pirouetted to let fly a fifth from the stern tube.

Each hit home. Three laden transports—*Hugh L. Scott, Edward Rutledge,* and *Tasker H. Bliss*—burst into flame. The 12,000-ton *Scott,* struck twice on the starboard flank, heaved from the sea like a beast harpooned, then promptly settled aft with a 30-degree list. Flimsy wooden partitions exploded into a thousand arrows, impaling sailors in the mess hall and cooks in the galley. Concrete slabs installed to protect the bridge fell through the buckled deck and flattened the compartments below. Lights went dead. Flame loped down the starboard companionway, and oil sloshed along the canted passages so that sailors slipped and fell in a tangle. Boiler number two exploded, sluicing scalding water through the engine room; men who touched the glowing bulkheads drew back a palmful of blisters. Sailors dragged their buddies from the sick bay and freed the lone occupant of the brig. The shout "Abandon ship!" echoed above the tumult. Those still able scrambled over the side before *Scott* sank by the stern with a hiss.

Her two sisters fared no better. *Rutledge,* hit twice, immediately went dark and mute. Captain M. W. Hutchinson, Jr., slipped anchor in the futile hope that wind and tide would nudge the ship ashore. She burned like a furnace and sank stern first, precisely seventy-eight minutes after being torpedoed. *Bliss* lingered for hours, and a weird keening rose from her fiery hull, where nearly three dozen sailors were reduced to carbon ash. An officer on *Augusta*'s bridge watched the *Bliss* and murmured, ambiguously, "The damned fools, the damned fools."

Hewitt's intelligence officer handed him a handwritten message at 8:25 P.M.: "*Rutledge* sunk. *Bliss* burning. *Scott* listing and abandoned. . . . Search for survivors will continue all night." Hewitt stared at the dispatch. He ordered a tug to tow *Bliss* into the shallows, but no tug was available. At 2:30 Friday morning the transport slid beneath the waves. A few russet puffs of smoke marked her descent.

Fifteen hundred survivors struggled to reach the beach. A flotilla of landing craft and French fishing smacks hauled in sailors coated with oil but for the whites of their eyes. Five hundred men required medical treatment, overwhelming doctors still busy from the previous night's attack. A camel barn on the Fedala dock was converted into a triage center. In the drafty wooden casino outside the Miramar, more than 150 litters were wedged between the baccarat tables. Men with strips of skin hanging like bark from a gum tree wandered through the door to ask, politely, for morphine.

Surgeons operated by Signal Corps torches. Corpsmen fumbled by candlelight to set fractures and stanch wounds. Of 400 burn cases, one in four—Patton described them as "pieces of bacon"—required multiple blood plasma transfusions. Most of the precious 1,000 units rushed to the fleet at Norfolk in late October had been saved, and so, in consequence, were at least twenty lives. But critical medical equipment was missing, including vital pieces of anesthesia machines. And so were lives lost.

Friday's dawn brought the flat African light and full illumination of the catastrophe. Wounded sailors sprawled in the pews of the Catholic church and on classroom floors. Barges ferried the worst cases to shipboard sick bays, where some died and some lived and some loitered in the netherworld. An unidentified sailor taken to the *Leonard Wood*, clothed only in third-degree burns, regained consciousness long enough to spell out, mysteriously, K-E-N-S-T-K, then slid into a coma and died three days later, known only to God.

Soldiers looking seaward were unsettled by the ships' missing silhouettes, as if teeth had been knocked from a familiar smile. Hewitt soon ordered all surviving vessels away from the coast. A day later, five transports berthed in Casablanca harbor, where they finished unloading and took on a ballast of wounded men for the return trip to America. The approaching convoy was waved away; it steamed aimlessly and without incident here and there in the eastern Atlantic for five days until being summoned into Casablanca on November 18, the precise date Hewitt had proposed months earlier. *U-130*, which had sunk twenty-five Allied ships, escaped for four months. Then she was cornered off the Azores and destroyed with all hands.

On November 17 Hewitt and *Augusta* sailed for Norfolk. He would return in triumph to Hampton Roads, as he had after the Great White Fleet's circumnavigation thirty-three years earlier, more convinced than ever that the world was round but imperfectly so. Yet a certain melancholy attended, fed by the suspicion that 140 men had forfeited their lives because, among a dozen vital decisions, he made one that was simply wrong. Hewitt would be back—for Sicily, Salerno, Anzio, southern France—a large figure in a large war. But that November night off the coast of Casablanca remained, forever, a small and tender scar on his strong sailor's heart.

If the shooting between Anglo-Americans and Frenchmen had stopped, the political scuffling had not. The brief final act of Operation TORCH played out in Algiers, where the invasion ended as raggedly as it began.

General Clark's arrest of Darlan was rescinded on November 11 when the admiral pledged his conversion to the Allied cause—again—after learning that ten German and six Italian divisions had invaded Vichy France. With an Allied army in North Africa, Hitler could not risk an exposed flank on the French Mediterranean, so Operation ANTON gobbled up Vichy in hours. Darlan telephoned French commanders in Tunisia—while Clark eavesdropped—and ordered them to resist any Axis intrusion. He also cabled the commander of the Vichy fleet at Toulon, Admiral Jean Laborde, and invited him to weigh anchor for French North Africa. Laborde loathed Darlan as only one old salt can detest another, and he replied with scatological concision: *"Merde!"*

However, Clark went to bed and enjoyed the deep slumber of self-approbation until five A.M. on November 12, when he was awakened and told that Darlan had reneged yet again. The order to Tunisian commanders had been suspended pending approval by General Noguès, whom the besieged Pétain had designated as his plenipotentiary in North Africa. A familiar scene followed in the St. Georges conference room: threats, table-thumping, bad French.

"Not once have you shown me that you are working in our interests!" Clark shouted at Darlan. "I'm sick and tired of the way you have been conducting yourself. I think you are weak."

The admiral meticulously creased several strips of scrap paper, then folded them into pleasing shapes.

"I want to fight the Germans," General Juin declared. "I am with you."

"No. You're not."

"I am with you," Juin repeated. "I'm not being treated right. This puts me in a very difficult spot."

Darlan tore the paper into tiny pieces.

"I know it, but I'm in a worse way," Clark said. "I am not sure who my friends are. I can't afford to make mistakes."

At noon on November 13, Eisenhower arrived from Gibraltar in hopes of breaking the impasse. Clark picked him up at Maison Blanche airfield in two commandeered French cars with tires so frayed the drivers were told not to exceed eight miles per hour. Even at that snail's pace, Eisenhower was happy to escape, if only for a few hours, what he described as his "badly ventilated office six hundred feet underground."

"We have had many hours of strain," he had written Walter Bedell (Beetle) Smith two days earlier, "and the events through which we have passed will be classed as quite important." If the assessment seemed dispassionate, nonchalance verging on apathy would be characteristic of Eisenhower after later battlefield victories, too. In part, he was looking ahead, determined "to rush pell mell to the east." He had written Marshall of his "burning ambition" to "make the Allied governments an early present of Tunis and the French fleet" at Toulon. In part, he may have been emotionally distancing himself from the casualties for which he was, as commander-in-chief, inescapably responsible. The losses, he had told Churchill in a letter, were "insignificant compared to the advantages we have so far won." Few commanders in this war could function without arriving at a sensibility in which thousands of dead and wounded men could be waved away as "insignificant."

At the St. Georges, Clark and Robert Murphy recounted the latest developments: General Noguès had arrived from Morocco and promptly called General Giraud a coward and a liar; Noguès had then ceded his powers back to Darlan; orders to resist the Axis in Tunisia had been reinstated, but to uncertain effect; Clark had again threatened reprisals ranging from shackles to the scaffold. Yet, after hours of loud bickering among themselves, the French this morning had agreed to an arrangement that Clark believed might serve: Darlan would become high commissioner in French North Africa, with Giraud as chief of the French armed forces, Juin as army commander, and Noguès remaining as governor-general in Morocco.

Eisenhower sighed. These political machinations perplexed and annoyed him. "Do these men want to become marshals of a greater and more glorious France or do they want to sink into miserable oblivion?" he had asked Clark. In a message to Marshall, he was even blunter: "If these stupid French would only realize what side their bread is buttered on, what a chance they now have to execute a master stroke. They seem completely inert." Still, the new agreement looked like a path out of this "maze of political and personal intrigue." Eisenhower had intended, he told Clark, to "lay down the law with a bit of table pounding," but now that appeared unnecessary.

In the hotel conference room, Darlan had exchanged his uniform for a three-piece civilian suit. He and the others stood when the Americans entered at two P.M. Eisenhower shook hands and after a few pleasantries uttered only eleven sentences, including: "What you propose is completely acceptable to me. From this day on, Admiral Darlan heads the French North African state. In this attitude I am supported by President Roosevelt. . . . We all must agree to put together all means to whip the Germans." He shook hands again and marched from the room.

Before boarding the B-17 at Maison Blanche, Eisenhower fished out a five-pointed star from his pocket and pinned it next to the other two on Clark's shoulder, making him a lieutenant general. "When you are away and out of touch," he had told Clark two days before, "I feel like I've lost my right arm."

Feeling expansive, Clark returned to the St. Georges and summoned reporters. "Now we can proceed in a business-like way," he told them. "Things look good."

* * *

Sixty years after TORCH, a precise count of Allied casualties remains elusive. Official U.S. tallies, which clearly undercounted British losses, put the combined Anglo-American figure at 1,469, including 526 American dead. British figures, which include minor actions on November 12 and 13, calculate Allied losses at 2,225, including nearly 1,100 dead.

The number of French killed and wounded probably approached 3,000. In three days, Vichy forces in North Africa also lost more than half their tanks, armored cars, and airplanes—matériel so sorely missed in the weeks ahead that Eisenhower considered eighteen French battalions equivalent in combat power to a single American battalion. Allied commanders initially suppressed news regarding the intensity of the TORCH fighting so the French would not "remain embittered against us for having to fight them into submission."

TORCH had lured more Frenchmen—including many who had been morally deranged by invasion, occupation, and partition—back to the side of the angels. But the naïveté of Eisenhower and his lieutenants was such that none foresaw the consequence of embracing Darlan, whose purported villainy had been relentlessly denounced by Allied leaders for' two years. "It's not very pretty," Charles de Gaulle wrote in mid-November. "I think that before long the retching will take place." American military officers who had spent the past two decades perfecting cavalry charges on windswept posts in the middle of nowhere could be pardoned for having limited political acuity. The truth was that a callow, clumsy army had arrived in North Africa with little notion of how to act as a world power. The balance of the campaign—indeed, the balance of the war—would require learning not only how to fight but how to rule. Eisenhower sensed it; he wrote Beetle Smith, "We are just started on a great venture."

The war's momentum was shifting to the Allies, but in mid-November 1942, few men could see how irrevocable, how tectonic that shift was. Churchill, who a month earlier had warned, "If TORCH fails then I'm done for," assessed the moment most elegantly: "Now this is not the end. It is not even the beginning of the end. But it is, perhaps, the end of the beginning."

As for combat, TORCH revealed profound shortcomings in leadership, tactics, equipment, martial élan, and common sense. Certain features of the invasion, such as amphibious assaults and attacks on an enemy's flanks, would be polished by harsh experience and provide a template for Allied offensives throughout the war. But the U.S. Army was simply inept at combined arms—the essence of modern warfare, which requires skillful choreography of infantry, armor, artillery, airpower, and other combat forces. Most soldiers also remained wedged in the twilight between the "habits of peace and [the] ruthlessness of war."

Worse yet, few realized it. Tens of thousands of American soldiers had heard the bullets sing, and any number believed, in George Washington's fatuous phrase, that there was something charming in the sound. That was only because they had not heard many. Those who had seen American tank shells punch through the French Renaults swaggered through their bivouacs with helmets full of Algerian wine, crowing "Bring on the panzers!" Such confidence was so infectious that the British and American chiefs of staff suggested paring down the TORCH forces in order to undertake other Mediterranean adventures, such as an invasion of Sardinia. "For God's sake," Eisenhower replied, "let's get one job done at a time." But even the cautious commander felt a little cocky: the White House was told to expect the occupation of Tunis and Bizerte in December and the fall of Tripoli in late January.

They believed they had been blooded. They believed that overpowering the feeble French meant something. They believed in the righteousness of their cause, the inevitability of their victory, and the immortality of their young souls. And as they wheeled around to the east and pulled out their Michelin maps of Tunisia, they believed they had actually been to war.

Part Two

4. Pushing East

"We Live in Tragic Hours"

At two A.M. on November 8, the American consul-general in Tunis, Hooker A. Doolittle, had rapped on the front gate of the governor's palace, demanding to see the Vichy resident-general. Vice Admiral Jean-Pierre Estéva soon appeared, immaculate if unorthodox in full naval uniform and bedroom slippers. An elfin bachelor with a square-cut white beard, Estéva was known as the Monk for his ascetic habits, which included rising before dawn each morning to attend mass, and eating nothing before noon except dry toast and an orange. The son of a cork merchant from Reims, Estéva at the age of sixty-two was looking toward retirement so he could devote himself to his greatest passion: the magnificent Cathédrale Notre-Dame in his native town, where twenty-six French kings had been crowned. Doolittle's breathless annunciation of the Allied assault seemed unlikely to smooth Estéva's path to old age.

The admiral listened as Doolittle, whom one acquaintance described as "an *Esquire* fashion plate gone seedy," predicted the imminent arrival in Tunisia of Allied legions so vast they would darken the sky with aircraft. "They had better hurry up, because the others will be here within forty-eight hours," Estéva said dryly, and escorted his guest to the door.

Posing as a French farmer on his way home, Doolittle soon fled Tunis in a borrowed car with his Spanish maids and Pekingese dogs. Upon reaching the Allied lines he told anyone who would listen: "Hurry, hurry, hurry."

There was no need for Admiral Estéva to specify who "the others" were, and he had actually underestimated German agility. Tunisia was only "a panther's leap" from Axis bases in Italy, as the deputy Führer, Hermann Göring, had observed. At 10:55 A.M. on November 9, the first Luftwaffe fighters touched down at the El Aouina airfield northeast of Tunis. Dive-bombers and transport planes soon followed, after making a low, intimidating pass over the city. Hastily mustered German troops—many of them only marginally fit for combat—stumbled down the ramps.

French troops ringed the field, and French armored cars on the runway greeted each landing plane with guns trained at the cockpit. This impasse lasted several hours until a Luftwaffe security force set up machine guns behind a hangar and laid mines around the French vehicles. Choosing to heed directives from Vichy rather than the confused gabble coming out of Algiers, Estéva ordered the cordon removed. By dusk, ninety planes had landed. German troops marched from the tarmac to bivouacs along the narrow Carthage road, singing "Lili Marlene" as they dug their revetments.

The Wehrmacht's entrenchment in Tunis set the stage for a confrontation between German and Anglo-American armies that was to scorch two continents over the next two and a half years and cost several million lives. Here began the struggle for possession of the earth itself, or at least the western earth, an unremitting series of titanic land battles that would sweep across Salerno and Anzio, Normandy and the Bulge, broken only by brief interludes to cart away the dead and revivify the living.

Hitler had learned the full extent of the Allied invasion while stopped at a remote rail siding in Thuringia: he was on his way to Munich for a reunion of the old beer-hall *Kämpfer*. Within hours he recognized that if the Allies seized North Africa they could transform a peripheral expedition into a platform for the invasion of southern Europe. That would imperil Italy, his closest ally, and Axis possessions from France to Greece. "To give up Africa means to give up the Mediterranean," he declared. It "would mean not only the ruin of our revolutions, but also the ruin of our peoples' future," Hitler subsequently wrote Mussolini. He signed the letter, "Yours in indissoluble unity."

Already 230 of Germany's 260 divisions were on the defensive. Some German strategists sensed that their war's arc had swung from expansion to contraction, but Hitler refused to accept that Germany had lost the strategic initiative. Tunisia was to be the "cornerstone of our conduct of the war on the southern flank of Europe." If secondary to the eastern crusade against Bolshevism, it was vital nonetheless. At his most grandiose, Hitler conjured new African offensives—to the west, to drive the TORCH invaders from Algeria and Morocco, and to the east, to drive the British Eighth Army across the Suez Canal. By late November, the Führer's strategic vision would be articulated in a one-sentence order: "North Africa, being the approach to Europe, must be held at all costs." That sentence condemned a million men from both sides to seven months of torment.

On Tuesday, November 10, Wehrmacht paratroopers arrived in numbers for the first time. A platoon from the 5th Parachute Regiment flew from Naples and immediately fortified the main road leading to Tunis from the west. Guns earmarked for Rommel's army in Egypt were diverted to Tunisia and dragged forward, still wrapped in shipping paper. Fuel was so scarce that troops eventually used heating pellets made from grass and the residue from olive presses. Commanders hired French taxis as staff cars. Messengers traveled by Tunis street tram—a young *Gefreiter* carrying dispatches reported with delight that no one had made him buy a ticket.

Weak as the German vanguard was, the leaders of Vichy France's 30,000 troops in North Africa were weaker. Ambivalence racked the French high command. On November 11, Hitler ordered German and Italian troops to occupy Vichy France; that same day, Admiral Louis Derrien, commander of the Vichy naval base at Bizerte, forty miles north of Tunis, told his subordinates, "I count on everyone to keep his calm, his sang-froid, and his dignity." That night, after receiving new orders from Darlan in Algiers, Derrien decreed, "The enemy is the German and Italian. . . . Blaze away with all your heart against the foe of 1940. We have a revenge to take. *Vive la France!*" French officers drank champagne toasts, and all ranks sang the "Marseillaise" on the Bizerte docks.

This jubilation lasted less than an hour. At midnight, forty minutes after Derrien had issued his battle cry, he annulled it by order of Vichy. "November 8, we fight everybody," he wrote privately. "November 9, we fight the Germans. November 10, we fight nobody. November 10 (noon), we fight the Germans. November 11 (night), we fight nobody." Perhaps no passage written during the war better captured the agony of France and the moral gyrations to which her sons were subject.

On November 12, Derrien phoned Admiral Darlan, then still gripped by indecision, but received no clear direction. The increasingly listless Estéva was even more in thrall to Vichy. A German officer concluded that Estéva was capable "of only nodding his head. It seems that he is not quite equal to the tense situation." Estéva agreed: "After forty years of obedience, I cannot begin to disobey orders now." The first sea shipments of German troops and equipment—including seventeen tanks and forty tons of ammunition—arrived November 12. Derrien was scheduled to retire in a month, after forty-two years of service. Now, he predicted, "I shall be known as the admiral who delivered Bizerte to the Germans."

Sadly, yes. By November 14, the Germans had inserted 3,000 men into Bizerte alone. They controlled all the important buildings in Tunis, where troops marched four abreast to occupy the Marshal Foch bar-racks downtown. The abandoned U.S. consulate became the Axis com-mand post, notwithstanding German grumbling that Tunisian "office personnel cannot read or write." To make the German contingent appear even larger, paratroopers were driven in circles around the city in armored cars loaned by helpful French commanders. The Tunisian bey—whose family had long ruled the country beneath the firm hand of French guardians—quickly pledged loyalty to Berlin. In gorgeous uniforms of scarlet, black, and gold, his bodyguard marched from the royal palace, using the newly fashionable goose step.

Soon enough, Derrien would receive a German ultimatum: surrender all French troops and ships in Bizerte within thirty minutes, or see 6,000 French sailors shot. He capitulated after extracting a single concession: the retention of a French company under arms to lower the garrison tri-color with honors. Derrien's request to keep his own sword was denied.

A French court after the war would convict and imprison Estéva for "national unworthiness." Although the admiral once asserted that "it is an honor to suffer for the high ideals of civilization," his own suffering derived from baser stuff. Derrien, too, eventually drew life in prison; he would be freed less than two weeks before his death. After killing hun-dreds of American and British soldiers during TORCH, the French had failed to so much as scratch a single German invader. Only the French commander of the Tunis Division, General Georges Barré, refused to kowtow. With 9,000 troops and fifteen ancient tanks, Barré sidled west-ward into Tunisia's wild hills, there to await developments.

The fire that consumed proud Carthage after Romans sacked it in 146 B.C. was said to have burned for seventeen days. French Tunis was a cold ember from the moment the first German shadow loomed. "We live in tragic hours," Pétain observed. "Disorder reigns in our spirits."

Conviviality reigned in the spirit of Field Marshal Albert Kesselring, known as Smiling Albert for his toothy grin and unquenchable opti-mism. On the morning after the Anglo-American invasion, Hitler had phoned Kesselring to give him "a free hand" in Tunisia. This was the Allies' misfortune.

The son of a Bayreuth schoolmaster, Kesselring belonged to an ancient Bavarian clan whose fortune had been lost in the hyperinflation following World War I. Courtly and fluent in Italian, he had broad hips and a hairline in full retreat. He had been an artilleryman and balloon observer in the Great War, then had learned to fly at the age of forty-eight and soon ranked high in the Luftwaffe. One of the Reich's ablest commanders, he was both daring—shot down five times in his career—and brutal, having orchestrated the terror bombings of Warsaw, Coventry, and many cities in between, as well as the air campaign against Russia. When German anti-aircraft gunners in Tunis fired at his plane by mistake, Kesselring rebuked them—for missing an easy target.

On November 10, Hitler formally seconded Kesselring to Rome as Mussolini's deputy. With authority over Axis air and ground forces in the Mediterranean, the field marshal politely rebuffed Il Duce's proposals to attack the Allies with poison gas and to transport war stocks in hospital ships. Instead, he focused on building a bridgehead around Tunis and Bizerte, dismissing complaints from subordinates that the Axis forces amounted to only "a drop of water on a hot stone" compared to the Allied host.

The Allies had achieved strategic surprise, Kesselring conceded, but could they exploit it? Why had they not also landed in Tunisia, which had nearly 800 miles of coastline? Kesselring approved the conscription of Tunisian civilians to build fortifications and unload Axis ships. But an impenetrable bridgehead was not enough. On November 13, he ordered his lieutenants to plan an offensive to the west. The only way to forestall the loss of Africa was to counterattack across the Tunisian mountains into Algeria. Smiling Albert meant to chase the Anglo-Americans back to their ships.

A Cold Country with a Hot Sun

FIVE hundred and sixty road miles separated Algiers from Tunis, and the first Allied troops cantered eastward in the rollicking high spirits obligatory at the beginning of all military debacles. Virtually everyone from private to general presumed the expedition would be a promenade. Much chatter was devoted to the likely date of arrival in Tripoli or even Naples. One soldier spoke for many in his bravado toward the Germans: "Those squareheads can't fight. Hell, leave *them* to the Limeys, we'll finish the Japs." A young officer reported that the only anxiety in his tank battalion was "that all of the Germans would escape" before the Americans could prove their mettle.

Town mayors donned their frock coats and top hats to greet the Allied convoys with warm, incomprehensible welcoming speeches. Cheering crowds offered rough Algerian wine and hampers of tangerines. Jeep drivers, in vehicles named *Kidney Buster, Miss Conduct,* and *Miss Demeanor,* twined winter roses around their radio antennas, and pretended to enjoy the proffered local cigarettes, soon dubbed "Dung d'Algerie." "*Vive l'Amérique!*" shouted the Arab children, to mostly British troops. To deal with the inevitable traffic fatalities a sliding scale of reparations was established, paid in the oversize French currency GIs called wallpaper: 25,000 francs ($500) for a dead camel; 15,000 for a dead boy; 10,000 for a dead donkey; 500 for a dead girl.

British troops dominated the initial convoys, camouflage cloths knotted in big bows atop their helmets like "Edwardian motoring veil[s]." The Algerian villages reminded some veterans of Flanders, with their shuttered hotels and their fishmongers in striped sweaters. For those traveling by rail, the narrow-gauge boxcars with neatly lettered signs— "*Hommes 40, chevaux 8*"—brought memories of the Western Front: there, too, the French railcars had fitted forty men or eight horses. So slowly did the Algerian trains chuff uphill that soldiers often hopped off to walk, brewing their tea from hot water in the engines as they ambled alongside.

For the Yanks, it was all new: the skinned goat carcasses dripping blood in roadside stalls; the Algerians hawking grass mats and bolts of blue silk; the cursing muleteers; the peasants leaning into their iron-shod plows; the buses propelled by charcoal engines lashed to the bumper and stirred by each driver with a poker. American units chosen for the vanguard strutted with pride. The 2nd Battalion of the 13th Armored Regiment rolled out of Arzew toward Algiers and beyond, their tanks stuffed with eggs and hidden bottles of Old Grandad. The 5th Field Artillery Battalion swung onto the road with guidons snapping; each battery presented arms to the 1st Division color guard, and "When the Caissons Go Rolling Along" crashed from the division band.

Eastward the caissons rolled, past Algerian villages with adobe walls loopholed for muskets, past groves of mandarin oranges "hanging like red lamps." Past clopping French army columns of hay carts drawn by crow-bait horses, past mounted artillery officers in double-breasted tunics. Past stubbly wheatfields that had once served as Rome's granary, and past aqueducts dismembered during the Vandals' century of anarchic misrule and now bleaching like stone bones in the sun.

At dusk they bivouacked. Soldiers swam in the chill Mediterranean or washed from their helmets in the delicate ritual called a whore's bath. They staged scorpion fights in gasoline flimsies or spooned whiskey into pet lizards to watch them stagger about. The evening mist rose from fields with a scent like fresh-mowed hay, which troops had been taught was the odor of deadly phosgene; at least one unit panicked, with shrieks of "Gas! Gas!" and a mad fumbling for masks before reason returned.

Soldiers sharpened their bartering skills with hand gestures, talking loudly in the distinctively American belief that volume obviates all language barriers; one sharp trader swapped a box of candy, piece by piece, for three bottles of perfume, a dozen eggs, a large portrait of Pétain, and a small burro named Rommel.

Pilfering by the impoverished locals was epidemic. Troops smeared fuel cans with bacon rind in hopes that the Koranic prohibition against contact with pork might deter thieves. *"Allez!"* the soldiers would shout—often their only French except for the hugely popular, *"C'est la guerre"*—after discovering that thieves had slashed the canvas top from a jeep to make shoes. A single parachute canopy was said to yield more than 500 sets of silk drawers. "If they could have carried it away," a division history declared, "they'd have stolen the air out of tires." Disdain for the Arabs grew by the hour. The Army's chief quartermaster described his native workforce as "useless, worthless, illiterate, dishonest, and diseased."

At dawn, the promenade resumed. One sergeant, perhaps confounded by the stink of human waste widely used as fertilizer, wrote home, "Every town over here smells like something dead." The day would come when that was literally true. For now, though, the benign sun and doughboy camaraderie moved some men to lyricism. "The sky is almost unbelievably blue," wrote an officer in the 1st Division, "and the nights are a poet's dream." In the gnarled hills that steadily mounted toward the Tunisian frontier, shepherds watched the columns draw near and heard the chorus of a battle hymn sung with sufficient verve to carry above the harsh grind of truck gears:

> *She'll be coming 'round the mountain,*
> *She'll be coming 'round the mountain,*
> *She'll be coming 'round the mountain when she comes.*

Thanks to Ultra's decipherment of Axis codes, Eisenhower and his lieutenants knew precisely how many German and Italian troops were flooding into Tunisia. But poor understanding of these deployments' significance compounded other, earlier miscalculations. Allied intelligence had predicted that up to 10,000 Axis soldiers could reach Tunisia within two weeks, but that these would be troops of "low category and without motor transport." The Allied forecast as to "the probable scale of Axis intervention turned out to be an underestimate in every respect," a British intelligence study later concluded, "with results that were to say the least unfortunate." After a fortnight, the actual number approached

11,000; they included crack paratroopers and panzer grenadiers with heavy equipment and trucks, and they were soon followed by the tanks of the 10th Panzer Division.

There was much talk in Allied councils of speed in countering the Axis intervention, but little speed was applied. Eisenhower and Clark had planned that the seizure of Tunisia would fall primarily to the British. Having carried most of the load in TORCH, the Americans would provide an occupation force and reserves to guard against a German thrust through Spain into Morocco. Scant thought had been given to actions after the initial landings, and only sketchy staff work was available on terrain, logistics, and air support in Tunisia. But given German celerity in occupying Tunis and Bizerte, Allied leaders decided to hasten the move of American troops eastward to bolster the British. Three U.S. armored battalions and other units were to be dispatched disparately and then farmed out—fragmented—to British commanders who possessed scant armored forces of their own. This American muscle would add more than 100 tanks to the Tunisian front.

Proverbially, no military plan survives contact with the enemy. That is never truer than when there is no plan to begin with. No scheme existed for integrating U.S. units into British organizations, or for provisioning them, or for getting them to the front in the first place. Eisenhower would complain that his ad hoc orders to support the British with American troops "were not clearly understood nor vigorously executed." To his brother Edgar he confided, "I suffer from the usual difficulty that besets the higher commander—things can be ordered and started, but actual execution at the front has to be turned over to someone else."

"I get so impatient to get ahead that I want to be at a place where there is some chance to push a soldier a little faster or hurry up the unloading of a boat," Eisenhower cabled Beetle Smith on November 16. Yet he remained in his Gibraltar grotto for nearly two weeks after the French surrender—far from Algiers and far, far from the battlefield. From his office, he railed against Estéva and other French commanders in Tunisia, who "without the slightest trouble could cut the throat of every German and Italian in the area and get away with it." The Allies "could take all sorts of reckless chances," Eisenhower added, but only if Estéva resisted and the French took chances of their own. His denunciations of the enemy were often mild, even prissy. "We will all be together in a fine headquarters one of these days," he told Smith, "and really set out in earnest to whip these blankety-blank Huns!" Rarely did he convey savage determination to overcome all obstacles; to smash, to destroy, to butcher. He professed "a violent hatred of the Axis and all that it stands for," but no hate lodged in his bones. He was not yet ruthless.

Nor was he yet much of a field marshal. Air and naval attacks were poorly planned and indifferently carried out. Few Allied aircraft had been allocated for reconnaissance or for assaults on Axis forces arriving by sea. Strategic bombing was launched only against targets in Italy and elsewhere outside North Africa, with no bombers initially available to batter Axis concentrations in Tunis or Bizerte. No naval attacks were launched against Axis convoys for three weeks. Not a single Axis ship was sunk on the run to Tunis in November.

Perhaps the biggest deficiency was transportation. Ignoring their logisticians, Eisenhower and Clark had chosen to devote the limited TORCH shipping space to tens of thousands of extra troops at the expense of vehicles and arms. For an American force designed as an occupation army, the decision was plausible. But the Oran convoy alone was pared by 10,000 vehicles before leaving Britain. Unloading snarls made matters worse: by November 12, 8,700 vehicles were planned to be ashore in Oran, the actual number was 1,800. Now, with the ostensible occupation army transformed into a strike force, most units were immobile. "Inevitably there was chaos," the correspondent Philip Jordan wrote, "that sort of amateur bungling to which the army is liable when it tries to organize something outside routine."

Ordnance officers wandered through Oran with $5,000 in silver ingots to buy trucks fueled with charcoal, or to hire horse-powered livery for hauling ammunition. The North African rail system proved particularly frail. Half the rolling stock was paralyzed for lack of fuel. Few French railcars were strong enough to carry medium tanks such as the American Sherman. Of the nine small trains that crept eastward from Algiers every day, two were required to haul coal for the railroad itself and one carried provisions to keep the local civilians from starvation; French, British, and American logisticians fought over the remaining six, which usually took nearly a week just to reach the Tunisian border.

Even success in snaring a train was no guarantee of movement. To demonstrate the new fraternity between former adversaries, U.S. Army public relations officers organized a festive departure in Oran for a French battalion heading to Tunisia. As newsreel photographers recorded the scene, American soldiers crowded the rail siding to exchange cigarettes with their French comrades and wave bon voyage— only to hear the stationmaster announce that delays in the east meant the train could not leave for at least another day. The engine and cars rolled

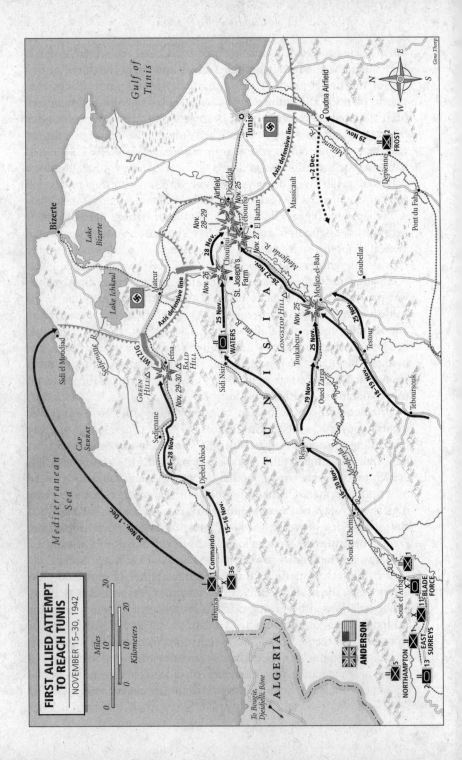

FIRST ALLIED ATTEMPT TO REACH TUNIS
NOVEMBER 15–30, 1942

Miles
0   10   20

Kilometers
0   10   20

Gene Thorp

Mediterranean Sea

Gulf of Tunis

ALGERIA

To Bougie;
Djedjelli; Bône

30 Nov. – 1 Dec.

Tabarka

Cap Serrat

Bizerte

Lake Ichkeul

Lake Bizerte

Sidi el Moudjad

Sedjenane R.

Mateur

Sedjenane

Djebel Abiod

15–16 Nov.

26–28 Nov.

Green Hill

Jefna

Bald Hill

Nov. 29–30

Axis defensive line

WITZIG

Axis defensive line

Sidi Nsir

Beja

Oued Zarga

Toukabeur

Souk el Khemis

Souk el Arba

Medjerda R.

Medjez-el-Bab

Longstop Hill

Nov. 25

St. Joseph's Farm

Tine R.

Chouigui

Nov. 26

28 Nov.

26–27 Nov.

Nov. 28–29

Djedeida

Airfield

Tebourba

Nov. 25

Nov. 27 El Bathan

19 Nov.

25 Nov.

23 Nov.

18–19 Nov.

Testour

Teboursouk

Goubellat

Massicault

Tunis

Oudna Airfield

29 Nov.

1–2 Dec.

Depienne

Pont du Fahs

Miliane R.

T U N I S I A

N E W S

ANDERSON

NORTHAMPTON 5

2 13

EAST
SURREYS

BLADE
FORCE

1/1

1 1 WATERS

25 Nov.

1 Commando

36

2 FROST

a few hundred yards down the tracks, gayly huzzahed for the benefit of the cameras, then backed up after dark to await a better day to go to war.

This muddle greeted Lieutenant General Kenneth A. N. Anderson, who on November 11 took command in Algiers of the newborn British First Army with orders to hie east. "I applaud your dash and energy," Eisenhower cabled him on the twelfth. "Boldness is now more important than numbers. Good luck."

For a commander of congenital pessimism—and Anderson's was bred in the bone—this dismissal of mere "numbers" rang hollow. First Army comprised hardly a division, with four British brigades and a hodgepodge of American units. Even so, Anderson moved from the command ship *Bulolo* into the Hotel Albert and announced plans to "kick Rommel in the pants as soon as possible." Then, alarmed that the phrase implied an insouciance he did not feel, he circulated a written addendum to correspondents: "The German is a good soldier and I expect hard fighting."

Anderson had been born in India on Christmas Day, 1891, son of a knighted railroad executive who eventually packed him off to Sandhurst. Badly wounded on the Somme, he also had fought in Palestine, in Syria, on the Indian frontier, and at Dunkirk, where he commanded a division during the evacuation. He was clean-shaven, thin-lipped, and deeply religious, with untidy gray hair, small eyes, and—one American officer noted—"an air of grinning preoccupation." He was said to lack "the jutting chin that gives force to personality"; a British acquaintance wrote that "he looks more like a moderately successful surgeon" than a soldier. In dress he favored old-fashioned breeches and puttees; as his troops moved east, he could occasionally be seen peering under the tarpaulin of a rail flatcar to see what the train had brought him.

One British general damned Anderson with faint praise as a "good plain cook," a bon mot that soon circulated through all the right clubs. Certainly he was the sort of gauche, abrasive Scot invariably described as "dour." A sardonic subordinate nicknamed him Sunshine, while his American code name was GROUCH. Fluent in French and Italian, he could be silent in any language. Even his rare utterances were to remain private: he soon threatened to expel from North Africa any correspondent who quoted him. Eisenhower remarked that "he studies the written word until he practically burns through the paper." Few guessed at Anderson's perpetual struggle against what he called "a queer sort of inhibition, or shyness, which prevents me coming out of my shell. . . . Often I would like to expand, but find it very difficult. A queer thing, human nature." It was no doubt God's will, and he very much believed in God, just as he also believed "it is good medicine to one's self-esteem to meet with serious setbacks at timely intervals." Such palliatives awaited him on the road to Tunis.

Anderson's most ambitious timetable on the eve of TORCH called for Allied paratroopers to be in Tunis and Bizerte by November 12, with reinforcements following immediately. The exigencies of invasion— including French resistance and the broadcast of American paratroops across half the continent—knocked that schedule askew. Instead, the slow overland movement of troops by road and rail would be paralleled in a series of shallow envelopments by seaborne forces along the Mediterranean coast.

A battalion of the Royal West Kent Regiment landed without opposition early on November 11, 100 miles east of Algiers, at Bougie, where the candle was said to have been invented. But heavy surf caused the Royal Navy to scuttle a similiar landing thirty miles farther east, at Djidjelli. This small setback carried large consequences. The inability to bring fuel to the Djidjelli airfield kept RAF Spitfires there grounded for two days, leaving the exposed force at Bougie virtually without air cover.

At 4:40 P.M. on November 11, thirty Ju-88s attacked Bougie harbor from the cover of low clouds, closely followed by German torpedo planes. Four bombs punctured the transport *Awatea*, followed by a torpedo that lanced her port side; at a 40-degree list she soon burned with greater fury than any Bougie chandler could have imagined. The destroyer *Bicester* picked up twenty-five survivors and played hoses on the transport's glowing plates, pressing so close that flames caressed the destroyer and *Awatea*'s portside davits briefly fouled the bridge. After twenty minutes, even the doughty *Bicester* stood off. Gutted by a colossal final explosion, *Awatea* sank at eleven P.M.

Two bombs hit the monitor *Roberts*, wounding her badly. Worse befell the transport *Cathay*, which had 1,200 British soldiers aboard. Battered by near misses that dimpled her hull, *Cathay* then took a dud in the galley. That was enough to panic the quailing crew; they lowered boats without orders and rowed away from the abandoned and terrified troops. A rescue flotilla of landing craft managed to get nearly everyone off, although one lighter was bombed and a surgeon reported seeing a soldier with both legs blown off "swimming frantically using only his arms." Shortly before midnight, *Cathay* caught fire; she burned all night before sinking.

November 12 was also bad. To better prepare for more air attacks at dawn, the anti-aircraft ship *Tynwald* weighed anchor at 4:45 A.M., only to strike a mine sown by a German plane. She sank in seven fathoms. A dawn attack *did* materialize. Bombs hit the transport *Karanja*, whose decks were packed with survivors from the *Cathay*; they again promptly lowered boats without orders. Sensing that the morning belonged to the enemy, *Karanja*'s captain ordered his vessel abandoned at 8:30 A.M. She soon sank.

Most soldiers and sailors demonstrated pluck. But no élan could obscure the fact that four British ships had been sunk and a fifth damaged before the strike force was barely beyond Algiers. Several vessels pressed into duty as hospital ships returned to Algiers harbor with the dead sewed up in canvas sacks and the wounded making a shambles of the mess deck tables. The British troops ashore at Bougie pivoted eastward with an occasional wistful look over their shoulders; among other losses, their greatcoats lay at the bottom of Bougie bight—with the wintry Tunisian Atlas looming ahead.

Things went better at Bône, 125 miles east of Bougie, where in the year 393 a council of bishops had first recognized the canon of the New Testament. Two destroyer transports landed an unopposed force of British and American commandos who sang the French anthem as they disembarked. Three hundred paratroopers, commanded by the infelicitously named Major R. G. Pine-Coffin, soon leaped to join them; a hard landing killed one man and injured a dozen others, including a concussed paratroop officer who would lie in a coma for four days, murmuring, "I'll have a little more of the turbot, waiter." As the sun set on November 12, this Allied force was only 185 road miles from Bizerte.

Unfortunately, Bône was also comparably close to Kesselring's airfields in Sicily and Sardinia. Bombs blew up the rail station, the cinema, and the sidewalk bistro with its striped umbrellas. Bombs eviscerated the port elevator—a golden cascade of grain spilled across the wharf—and sent mothers scurrying for shelter across the cobbled streets with their grocery bags and perambulators. Of twenty-two piers in the port, eighteen were soon wrecked. The attacks so terrorized the locals that when six Allied coasters put in later in the week no Tunisian labor could be found to unload them. British soldiers pressed into service as stevedores composed a bit of doggerel for the occasion:

> *In this force we've just one moan:*
> *Too little meat—and too much Bône.*

Having chased Napoleon Bonaparte into exile, the British Army perhaps felt justified in ignoring certain of l'Empereur's precepts. For example: the dictum that the most difficult maneuver involves marching widely separated columns against an enemy who has time to strike at them one by one before they can converge. Such an assault across a broad front was precisely what General Anderson and his lieutenants proposed. Moreover, they intended to do so with few tanks and little artillery in hilly terrain congenial to defense and ambush.

On November 14, Anderson ordered all available Allied troops eastward in hopes of attacking Bizerte and Tunis within a week. The British 36th Brigade—4,500 men from the 78th Division—would hug the coast on the Allied left. An equivalent contingent in the 11th Brigade would follow a parallel route twenty-five miles to the south, on the Allied right. In the Allied center a patchwork group of 2,600 tankers, riflemen, and parachutists, known as Blade Force, was to work the broken high ground between the two brigades.

The British plan would cut the Axis bridgehead in half and isolate Bizerte, which was to be captured after Tunis had fallen. American units would be fed into the attack as they arrived. For now, Anderson's army numbered just over 12,000 men; "all available" troops amounted to barely one-tenth of those landed in TORCH. British armor featured the Valentine tank, an obsolete can with a three-man crew, a cross-country speed of eight miles per hour, and a gun that fired two-pound shells comparable to heaving loaves of hard bread at the enemy.

The plan was made; the plan was fixed; and amending the plan— despite evidence that thousands of veteran Axis troops were extending their bridgehead westward—"had no appeal to the orderly British mind." Precisely what Anderson could have done otherwise, given his paltry force and stringy logistics, is debatable; but gathering his scattered troops into a compact, clenched fist would have been a start.

And then, they were in Tunisia. Crossing out of Algeria along the ancient border between Numidia and Carthage, the road switchbacked through stands of cork oak and mountain ash rich with the mossy scent of mist and wood smoke. The nights turned bitter, with icy winds and hail that forced men to tip their helmets over their faces like a knight's beaver. Letters home began stressing the "north" in North Africa, which soldiers now described as "a cold country with a hot sun." Slightly larger than the state of Georgia, Tunisia in winter seemed more like Michigan. On the rare occasions when open fires were allowed, the Americans huddled close in their blankets, dusted with snow. The shivering British pined for their lost greatcoats.

As marauding Messerschmitts became increasingly common, campfires vanished. Breakfast was eaten facing east, so every man could scan for fighters on strafing runs out of the sun. Supply was patchy, with absurd surpluses of hair oil and other inessentials, and desperate shortages of artillery rounds, fresh food, and commodities like cutlery. "The most important thing," a British tanker advised, "is *never* to be parted from your spoon."

To protect Anderson's far southern flank, Eisenhower dispatched Edson Raff, whose American paratrooper battalion had regrouped after its dispersion across the Mediterranean in Operation VILLAIN. Raff's Ruffians jumped—successfully this time—from thirty-three planes on the east Algerian town of Tébessa. He then herded them onto green passenger buses fueled by charcoal and placed a machine gun in each rooftop baggage rack. On a perfectly plumb Roman road they drove past pink stucco farms and neo-Palladian French villas to the remote Tunisian oasis of Gafsa, where the force soon grew to 2,500 men. Behind them, American combat engineers heading through the mountain pass called Kasserine found themselves detained at a border post by French customs officials who demanded that duty be paid on all matériel. After realizing that Frenchman and Arab alike were mesmerized by the power of official stamps, the engineers fabricated their own rubber imprimatur and "just stamped the hell out of everything."

But most of the Allied force was farther north, in the two brigades lurching in loose tandem toward Tunis. Lancashire millworkers, Kentish clerks, laborers from Surrey—all came under the British 78th Division commander, Major General Vyvyan Evelegh. Known as Santa Claus for his ruddy face and imposing girth, Evelegh was a saddle-nosed, gap-toothed man in a beret, with the obligatory English officer's mustache worn on his upper lip like a campaign ribbon. He was mercurial, with a loud, braying laugh that could quickly give way to scalding invective untrammeled by his tendency to stutter when enraged. Evelegh was said to be feuding with one of his subordinates, the commander of the elite 1st Guards Brigade, over the b-b-b-bloody foolish issue of seniority. It was also said that he was keen to seize Tunis before others of higher rank could swoop in and claim credit.

With Anderson's approval, Evelegh decided to leapfrog 500 paratroopers ahead of the meandering brigades. The British 1st Battalion boarded planes in Algiers and on November 16 jumped on the border town of Souk el Arba. Five soldiers were wounded when a fumbled Sten gun accidentally discharged, and another was garrotted in midair by his own shroud lines; the entire town turned out for the dead man's funeral and, following local custom, all 3,000 people insisted on shaking hands with the battalion officer designated as chief mourner.

They hurried onward by bus, forty miles to Béja, a hilltop town dotted with ruins from the days when local grain fields provided the bread to complement Rome's circuses. After a miserable night in filthy weather, the battalion moved its command post into the local slaughterhouse on November 17. Five hundred men marched through Béja's narrow streets in their soup-bowl helmets, then discreetly changed to red berets and marched around some more to simulate "a non-existent preponderance" for the benefit of any Frenchman or Arab of wavering loyalties. Fooled or not, the locals cheered from the balconies of their white houses and the parapets of Béja's Byzantine towers.

They cheered again on November 18, when a British patrol to the northeast ambushed a small German column, killing six enemy soldiers before returning to Béja with nine scuffling prisoners and a captured German staff car paraded like a centurion's booty. The ambush had occurred barely ten miles from Mateur, the gateway city to Bizerte. How close they were now! To British and American paratroopers, and to the two brigades slogging behind them, the prize seemed within grasp.

Then Stuka dive-bombers found Béja for the first of many, many raids—the Tommies called the attacks "bouncing"—and the cheers stopped. Bombs gilded the town with fire and peeled back the French mansard roofs along the Avenue de la Gare, exposing charred rafters and scorched wallpaper like something publicly naked and shameful. Bombs plowed the little gardens and reduced mud-wattle Arab houses to dust. Bombs ruined the ruins, Roman and Byzantine, and it became hard to tell antique reliquiae from modern wreckage. Béja was bounced so often that by the end of the week 300 Frenchmen and Arabs had been killed, and there was not enough lime in all Tunisia to unstink the dead.

Local enthusiasm faded for the Allied cause, or *any* cause, and even the shadow of a large bird sufficed to send citizens howling through the streets, in search of a refuge that did not exist. As Bône and Bougie had been and a thousand other towns between here and Berlin would be, Béja was caught in the crossfire between the Allies and their Axis enemies, victimized by the total war that had begun, this week, in this place.

Medjez-el-Bab

"WHOEVER has Medjez-el-Bab has the key to the door, and is the master of all Tunisia," Hannibal supposedly declared. The quotation has the tin ring of apocrypha, but the sentiment had been true in the centuries before Christ and it was true in 1942. Modern Medjez-el-

Bab was a dusty market town smelling of rosemary and juniper and fed by roads from every compass point, a place for flinty merchants to sell French *colons* the tobacco and salt with which they paid their Arab farm-workers. Traces of Rome, Byzantium, and even seventeenth-century Spain could be found in the town, whose name means "Ford by the Gateway." It was in Medjez that Allied and Axis forces would first collide "with the grappling strength of fighters armed in bronze," in Homer's phrase, and it was around Medjez that much of the struggle over the next seven months would revolve.

Medjez-el-Bab's strategic value derived from its position straddling the Medjerda River, thirty air miles from Tunis. Rising in the Algerian highlands, the Medjerda was a serpentine ditch wandering vaguely northeast for 125 miles before spilling into the Gulf of Tunis between Bizerte and the capital. It provided a rare portal through the Eastern Dorsal, the rugged mountain chain that stretched southward to wall off the coastal plain of eastern Tunisia. The Medjerda valley at Medjez was said to be among the half-dozen most fertile on earth: the fecund fields and irrigation ditches resembled California's Central Valley. Shallow and mustard-hued, the river was less than a hundred yards wide, with sheer banks twenty feet high and dense rush brakes in the bottoms. An eight-arch bridge, built in the eighteenth century with stones from the original Roman viaduct, crossed the Medjerda at Med-jez. It was the grandest of nine bridges spanning the river at intervals of six to ten miles.

At this bucolic place, the commander of the Tunis Division, General Barré, chose to make his stand. After declining to follow the collabora-tionist path of the Vichy admirals Estéva and Derrien, Barré had tempo-rized, for a week, teasing the Germans with hints of capitulation while trading space for time. His 9,000 men had eased westward from Tunis into the hills, where they retrieved small caches of fuel and ammunition hidden two years earlier as a precaution after the German invasion of France. Badly armed with a few creaky tanks and a half-dozen artillery pieces pulled by mules, they were pinched between Allied forces approaching from the west and Axis troops pressing from the east—a perfect metaphor for the Vichy commanders collectively.

As British paratroopers on November 18 paraded their spoils through Béja, twenty miles away, the 3rd Battalion of the German 5th Parachute Regiment closed to within sight of Medjez-el-Bab. Troops in field-gray coats and coal-scuttle helmets fanned out along Highway 50, a narrow blacktop that hugged the Medjerda all the way to the stone bridge in Medjez. They drifted through eucalyptus brakes lining the river and skirted the cactus hedges that fenced the little farms east of town. Many had wrapped their rifle muzzles with newspaper to keep out the mud.

Although they were veteran soldiers who two weeks earlier had been training in Normandy for a possible invasion of Malta, the Germans were hardly more mobile or robustly armed than the plodding British or French. Messages to headquarters in Tunis complained at the lack of shovels, radios, hot food, machine guns, and field glasses. The battalion commander was a dark, heavy-browed captain named Wilhelm Knoche, who liked quoting Frederick the Great: "I have no need in my army for officers who lack luck." Knoche's luck had held so far in several parleys with French officers; after reviewing a map on which he had charted the positions of entirely fictitious regiments, the French had ceded to German forces the Medjerda valley towns of Djedeïda and Tébourba. But Barré refused to forsake Medjez. Now German patience, never robust, had expired. Field Marshal Kesselring issued new demands to "throw the enemy back to Bône" and to "end an intolerable situation by sending in the Stukas against the French divisions." Knoche warned in a final parley: "Think what's at stake. When I go, the apple falls."

At four A.M. on November 19, a German diplomat carrying a truce flag drove into Medjez to a stucco house perched above the river. This time there was no parley, only an ultimatum. The French were given until seven A.M. to strike their colors. A French colonel replied in a theatrical huff that his honor and that of France had been insulted. Although Barré's men were scattered across the Eastern Dorsal and only a few hundred troops defended Medjez, they would fight. The French had enough ammunition for a day of combat, provided that they were not required to shoot much.

Barré passed word to a British armored-car squadron near Medjez that an attack was likely in several hours. He also phoned French army headquarters in Algiers, announcing both his return to the Allied fold and the imminent destruction of his command.

A bad British plan promptly got worse. On November 18, Anderson had ordered General Evelegh not to commit his 78th Division until he finished concentrating the force. But in a flurry of frantic, pleading calls, French generals now demanded reinforcement. Shortly before six A.M. on November 19, Anderson's headquarters told Giraud that "while everything will be done to assist," fighter aircraft based at Bône were too far away to effectively intercede and no tanks were available.

Santa Claus was in a tight spot. The strategic worth of the Medjerda valley was evident. But German troops with tanks had also appeared on his left flank, a few miles from the Mediterranean coast. The fragmented

Allied force was about to fragment further. Evelegh shoved several units toward Medjez, including the 500 paratroopers from Béja and twelve American howitzers of the 175th Field Artillery Battalion.

An apricot dawn spread through the valley, heralding a gorgeous autumn day. Farmers shambled out to feed their livestock, casting anxious glances at the 200 gray-clad Germans who in the night had entrenched along the Medjerda's east bank, a thousand yards from Medjez. Captain Knoche moved his command post into a cemetery on high ground east of town. Seven A.M. passed, then eight, then nine, and the ultimatum began to resemble a bluff. But at 9:15 rifle fire crackled, followed by the brisk notes of a machine gun. Bullets swarmed back and forth across the river. Terrified residents ran from the town. "The war," an American artillerist recalled cheerfully, "was on!"

West of town, several British soldiers waited roadside to guide an American artillery battery into firing positions. At a fair distance, they spied a churning column of dust. Soon the column resolved into four bouncing howitzers and their gun teams hurtling up to and then past the frantically waving Tommies. Over a small rise they boiled, and down the forward slope overlooking Medjez, where they lurched to a stop in full view of the Germans. Shooting that had been brisk now became furious. A British officer reported "guns of all calibers firing."

British paratroopers and Derbyshire Yeomen hurried forward to extract their cousins. The mêlée subsided only when the truculent Yank gunners were persuaded of the merits of defilade. The British paratrooper commander, Lieutenant Colonel S.J.L. Hill, upon inquiring about the eccentric American approach, learned that the "gun teams had worked it out that one of them would be the first American to fire the first shot against the Germans in this world war. They had all started jockeying for position and racing each other down the road." Colonel Hill accepted this explanation philosophically, as he did the reply from a young American who, when asked why he was firing at a church steeple in Medjez, said it was because he could "see if he hit it." The answer, Hill concluded, "seemed fair enough."

The balance of the day was less risible. At 10:45 A.M., 120 spahis appeared in crimson capes and turbans bound in camel's hair. With a rumble of hooves and an ululant war cry, the double column broke into a gallop toward the stone bridge just as the first German dive-bombers appeared overhead. "Poor buggers were cut off by Stukas and ruined," an American gunner noted. The planes heeled over in a nearly vertical dive, sirens screaming and silver bombs tumbling. In a swirl of smoke and flapping capes, fragments of horses and riders blew into the air.

What the Stukas failed to destroy, German machine guns and mortars finished. A witness counted the bodies of ninety-six cavalrymen.

By late afternoon the Germans held everything east of the river except the train station. French colonials fought until their ammunition was gone and then the station fell, too. Yet even with Stukas attacking punctually every two hours, the Germans failed to dislodge Barré's troops from the shops and houses on the west bank. Galling fire from the American 25-pounders curtained the bridge and repulsed each attempt to force it. Knoche, the German battalion commander, ordered a large patrol from his Number 10 Company to ford the river and outflank the defenders from the south. Wading through icy water to their necks, the Germans overran a French machine gun and captured several prisoners.

But the patrol was trapped, exposed to enfilading fire and unable to reach the bridge abutments. Now it was the Germans' turn to be murdered. Venturing from the shelter of the riverbank, the company commander soon pitched to the pavement with a bullet in his brain. Allied machine guns scythed the rushes until the water ran red and German corpses drifted downstream like a gray flotilla. Only four men returned to the east bank.

Night fell. A German mortar hooted, and a few seconds later yet another detonation struck a town more hideous by the hour. Allied soldiers lay in their slit trenches studying the rectangular roof of sky overhead and the stars in their courses. French commanders tallied the butcher's bill—nearly a quarter of Barré's force had fallen—and issued another futile plea for armor, ammunition, and fresh troops.

At one A.M. on November 20, a staccato series of blasts ripped through four sectors of Medjez. Reinforced by two companies of Italian infantry, ten German patrols had swum the river with satchel charges and grenades. German machine pistols fired at every flitting shadow. Allied troops fell back, leaving intact the bridge, which they had prepared for detonation. Flames guttered in the dying town.

Colonel Hill summoned the senior French officer in Medjez and informed him that a general withdrawal would begin immediately. By 4:30 A.M. the town was abandoned. American gunners, along with British and French infantrymen, scuttled westward to a steep ridge halfway to Béja. Knoche's troops, who had suffered only twenty-two casualties, swept into Medjez as soon as the Allies decamped. By dawn, the key to the door was in a German pocket.

This disagreeable news jarred General Anderson, whose grand assault on Tunis and Bizerte was scheduled to begin November 21. Anderson had resisted sending more Americans into Tunisia for fear that First

Army's fragile logistics would buckle beneath the strain, and now he doubted that the Allies could reach Tunis without heavy reinforcement. Given persistent supply problems and the difficulty in massing Allied combat power, he ordered a three-day postponement.

Anderson's native pessimism was reinforced by a quick tour of the front, where he found irrefutable evidence of an Axis buildup that was swifter and stronger than anything anticipated in London or Washington. Neither side, however, could yet launch a sustained offensive. "Bits of war were threaded . . . like beads on a string," wrote the reporter A. J. Liebling. Tunisia had become "a funny sort of front," an American major said. "It's about fifty feet wide—just across the road and a little on each side of it."

But Axis forces were pressing in the north and infiltrating the southern flank, where the oasis at Gafsa had been recaptured. Kesselring's new commander in Tunisia, Generalleutnant Walther K. Nehring—a veteran of Poland, France, and Russia, as well as Rommel's Afrika Korps—declared, with an urgency rarely detected in Allied actions, "There is no time to lose. . . . Each man must be saturated with the fact that he must fight for his position to the last man." Nehring now had 16,000 German and 9,000 Italian troops in Tunisia; they had swept in so fast that Allied intelligence, despite Ultra, had temporarily lost count and believed the number to be less than half that. The Allies for their part had forfeited surprise with a plodding, tactically suspect use of the Tunisian terrain; precious tanks, for example, had been diverted to the left flank, where mountains rendered them useless.

A churlish frustration took hold. British troops began referring to American soldiers collectively as "Alice," and it was not a compliment. Anderson cabled Eisenhower at Gibraltar: "Roseate picture of speedy aid by an efficient French army is a figment of imagination." Eisenhower's naval chief, Admiral Andrew B. Cunningham, wrote to a friend, "Tunis is anyone's who cares to walk in. But the Huns are beating us in the race."

Never hesitant to play the field marshal, Churchill impatiently accused his military commanders of timidity and undue deference to logistics. "The Army is like a peacock—nearly all tail," he grumbled. To which the chief of the Imperial General Staff, General Brooke, replied sharply, "The peacock would be a very badly balanced bird without its tail." Unpersuaded, Churchill simply switched metaphors. "I intended North Africa to be a springboard, not a sofa," he complained. While British commanders voiced doubts about the Yanks' fighting qualities, some also harbored secret qualms about their own ranks. Churchill earlier in the year had expressed concern "that our soldiers are not as good fighters as their fathers were," and Brooke worried that "half our corps and divisional commanders are totally unfit" because of "the losses we sustained in the last war of all our best officers."

Eisenhower maintained a brave face, though nagged by a suspicion that the campaign was slipping away. "My biggest worry at this moment is that the Axis reinforcements, pouring into Tunisia from Sicily and Italy, are coming faster than I can kick troops up the line to the eastward," he wrote General Henry H. "Hap" Arnold, commander of the Army Air Forces, on November 21. A day later, in a memo to himself, Eisenhower added, "It would be wrong at present to assume that the Axis forces, now estimated to be 12,000, will be rapidly destroyed." It was wronger than he knew: Nehring's actual strength by November 25 was 25,000. The consequences of failure were hard to contemplate, but Eisenhower summed them up in a note to Beetle Smith: "If we don't get Tunisia quickly, we surrender initiative, give the Axis time to do as it pleases in that region, encourage all our enemies in the area, individually and collectively. . . . This battle is not, repeat *not* won."

Most disheartening was enemy air superiority. Axis planes in Tunisia already had available seven good airfields, in addition to bases on Sicily, Sardinia, and the Italian boot. Kesselring had assembled twenty squadrons of Stukas and fighters. They attacked relentlessly.

Allied fighters, by contrast, operated from crude dirt fields at such a distance—Bône, for example, lay 135 air miles from Tunis—that they could rarely loiter more than ten minutes over the battlefield. A Luftwaffe raid on November 21 destroyed more than a dozen planes on the ground in Algiers and forced all Flying Fortresses to safer fields near Oran; that meant a 1,200-mile round-trip bombing run to Tunis. Among the planes shot down was Eisenhower's personal B-17, which he had donated to the bombing campaign.

Field conditions were primitive. Pilots often had to refuel their own fighters from five-gallon tins, using a chamois to filter the badly refined French gasoline. Few radar sets had been shipped to Africa, so the Allied early-warning network consisted of French gendarmes with telephones. By late November, only half the Allied planes in North Africa were still airworthy; American pilots also lost nearly twice as many aircraft to crashes and other mishaps than to combat, a ratio described by one commander as "rather appalling." The Allied air command was disorganized, poorly coordinated, and split by rivalry and national chauvinism.

Troops learned to their sorrow that North Africa was not only cold but wet: Tunisia's sixteen yearly inches of rain fell almost exclusively between November and March. Crews wielded sticks and shovels to scrape mud off aircraft wheels so pilots could at least taxi onto the runways. To keep the nose from burrowing into the muck, crew chiefs sat on the horizontal stabilizer, then hopped off as the plane gained speed. Aviation engineers tried laying matting of cork, bamboo, and steel; mud ate them all. "Such a loving type of mud works its way up to your arm pits," a British soldier wrote.

On November 24, Anderson ordered General Evelegh to resume his advance on Tunis and Bizerte as swiftly as possible. Again the two brigades lurched eastward with Blade Force between them. On the left wing, eight miles from the Mediterranean coast, the 36th Brigade found an enemy reluctant to play its assigned role. Rather than remain fixed on the narrow road and await the British blow, German paratroopers simply backed up, sowing mines as they went. The Allies found themselves striking at thin air. Again the brigade surged forward; again the Germans backed up, as precisely as a minuet partner. So it went for more than two days, at a pachydermal pace of several hundred yards per hour.

Thirty miles to the south, on the Allied right flank, three British battalions in the 11th Brigade again closed on Medjez-el-Bab in a two-pronged assault reinforced by American gunners. Officers wagged their blackthorn sticks to inspirit the troops as they darkened their faces with burnt cork. From the southwest, the 5th Battalion of the Northamptonshire Regiment and the U.S. 175th Field Artillery attacked before dawn on November 25. Three miles from Medjez, they killed a dozen Italians and seized the heights called Djebel Bou Mouss—soon renamed Grenadier Hill. The new name stuck; Allied troops did not. A counterattack by German tanks from Medjez cleared the ridge in several hours. Brits and Yanks again retreated, this time to await reinforcement from an American armored battalion expected to arrive the next day.

The other prong of the Allied attack on Medjez came from the northwest. The 2nd Battalion of the Lancashire Fusiliers moved forward in trucks, then climbed out close to town. Blued by a hunter's moon, the men marched along the road and rail embankment, silent except for their bootsteps and the creak of their kit. At 4:30 A.M., the Medjerda came into view, a quicksilver runnel beneath the black arches of the bridge. Across the river a first hint of dawn limned the horizon. Lieutenant Colonel L. A. Manly, the British battalion commander, strolled to the point and after an exchange of hand gestures and hoarse whispers pressed ahead to reconnoiter. Five hundred shadows in flawless assault formation followed across an open field.

All this was seen. Captain Knoche's battalion watched from its emplacements, now reinforced with two 88mm guns and tanks from the 190th Panzer Battalion. Fighting in Crete and the Low Countries had made the German paratroopers expert in gauging distance at night. Mortar crewmen eyed the drifting shadows and adjusted their elevation knobs with the delicacy of safecrackers.

The first burst of machine-gun fire killed Colonel Manly. Five hundred British soldiers dropped as one, slithering across the ground in search of cover. Mortar tubes coughed, and German shells exploded behind the field, discouraging retreat. Then the shells walked forward, discouraging men inclined to stay put. Bullets gouged the earth with a plopping sound. Like doughboys going over the top—"jumping the bags," their fathers had called it at the Somme—the Lancashires rose up and charged a German line glittering with muzzle flashes. Crashing through hedges near the bridge, they made for the river, plunging down the muddy slope and into the Medjerda, splashing chest-deep to the far bank with rifles held high.

They found no more sanctuary here than had Knoche's Number 10 Company five days earlier. Bullets and mortar fragments frothed the water, and the ominous whipcrack of German 88mm shells sounded overhead. Wounded men pitched into the river; sometimes their comrades hauled them back to the bank, and sometimes they did not. Though badly disorganized by the fall of Manly and other leaders, two companies managed to scale the east bank and resume their charge across no-man's-land in a din of shouts and tweetering whistles.

They were hacked to pieces. The sun, now fully risen and flush in their faces, so blinded the Tommies that they could no longer pick out even muzzle flashes. Officers bellowed orders that were only partly heard above the roar, as if the tail end of each sentence was shot away. Squinting men faltered and fell back, tumbling down the bank to the bullet-whipped Medjerda. There the Lancashires' third company had fared just as poorly by remaining in the ditch; machine-gun and shell fire exterminated one platoon almost to a man. Bodies again drifted on the current, this time clad in British serge.

The attack was finished. An Allied artillery barrage provided covering fire for those still alive to recross the river and scramble up the west bank. They dragged the wounded by their collars in wide, bloody slicks. From the stucco husks that had once been houses, counterattacking German tanks and infantry hurried the retreating Tommies on their way. Along both sides of the Medjerda they left behind—another image from the Somme—"a landscape of dead buttocks." This time the butcher's bill came to 144 Lancashires, dead and wounded.

Fat Geese on a Pond

WITH both brigades stymied on the flanks, any hope for a breakthrough by the British First Army now fell to the provisional Blade Force in the center. Puny in size, with fewer than 3,000 troops, the unit nevertheless boasted more than a hundred tanks, half of them American. Now Blade Force hurried forward, crying, "Armor for Tunis!" and accompanied by Senegalese *tirailleurs,* "great ebony warriors with enormous teeth and bayonets a yard long." Sensing softness in the Axis line east of the hill town of Sidi Nsir, Blade Force planned to rip the seam with its two tank battalions, the British 17th/21st Lancers and the U.S. 1st Battalion of the 1st Armored Regiment. Both were directed to create "a tank-infested area" in the Tine River valley, ten miles north of the Medjerda and roughly parallel to it.

This order greatly pleased the Americans, even if no one was quite sure what "tank-infested" meant or how to effect such a teeming condition. The 1st Battalion—part of a regiment created in the 1830s for the Black Hawk War and still heavily drawn from Kentucky, Tennessee, and West Virginia—was commanded by the handsome thirty-five-year-old John Knight Waters. The son of a Baltimore banker, Waters had attended Johns Hopkins University for two years before persuading a Chicago congressman, in whose district he had spent a single day, to appoint him to the West Point class of 1931. Waters's ambition to be a pilot was thwarted by imperfect eyesight; he settled for the cavalry and betrothal to the daughter of a crotchety major named Patton. "Waters, I don't know you. Come back in three years," Patton told the young lieutenant when asked for permission to marry. Waters bided his time, eventually winning both Patton's deep affection and his daughter.

Waters's fifty-four light tanks formed the spearhead of Blade Force because the larger American medium tanks landed in Oran would not fit through the narrow Tunisian rail tunnels and were en route to the front by sea. The "light," fourteen-ton M-3 General Stuart was a fast, agile deathtrap with a 37mm gun known to American tankers as the "squirrel rifle." Oddly top-heavy, like "a hat box about to fall from the top shelf of the hall closet," the Stuart had a manually rotated turret and an engine that required a dozen vigorous turns with a hand crank to start. The four-man crew was cramped and virtually blind, viewing the hostile world through narrow glass-prism peepholes. On the frequent occasions when the intercom radio failed, tank commanders in the turret signaled direction changes to the drivers in the hull below with little kicks to the left or right shoulder; a kick between the shoulders meant "Stop," a sharper kick meant "Advance." A kick to the head meant "Back up."

The battalion rolled northeast through the narrow Tine valley along a rough braid of goat trails. Whenever Stukas appeared overhead, Waters shooed the Stuarts into the nearest stand of cactus, where his driver vaulted from the hatch to hide in a ditch, muttering, "I'm scared to death, I'm scared to death." On the afternoon of November 25, along the right bank of the Tine, scouts spotted enemy soldiers in a French farm compound that had been built to withstand Arab banditry. Gum trees rose above a rectangular courtyard enclosed by a thick stone-and-concrete wall with fighting parapets and musket loopholes. Outside the wall, Italian infantrymen peered from a network of trenches and saps.

Company A's tanks dashed forward, circling the compound in a dusty, shrieking assault. Machine-gun fire chewed through the trenches and killed a few infantrymen, but the squirrel gun hardly blemished the stone wall. Waters ordered his mortar platoon and assault guns into action, and soon the crump and boom of mortar and field tubes joined the rippling tank fire. The cannonade broke a few red terra-cotta roof tiles and fired two haystacks, but otherwise had little effect. The defenders peppered the Stuarts with rifle and machine-gun fire, shattering many of the glass vision ports. Tank commanders furiously toed their drivers—left shoulder, right shoulder, left shoulder—but without infantry and artillery support the attack soon lost momentum. Waters pulled the company back down the valley, where the crews spent the late afternoon manicuring tank hulls that bristled with hundreds of embedded enemy bullets. The effect, one officer wrote, gave the armor plates a manly texture, "like a three-day growth of beard."

Farther north, a British Lancers battalion rounded up 140 Axis prisoners, accepted a bleating sheep from a grateful farmer, then broke for tea. Stuka pilots evidently confused German signal flares with Allied anti-aircraft fire: a Lancer reported that Wehrmacht infantrymen repeatedly "sent up a stream of Very lights, which had the satisfying effect of bringing the bombs down amongst themselves, whilst we watched." Mateur, the linchpin to the defense of Bizerte, lay only ten miles away.

But it was on the southern fringe of a landscape now properly tank-infested that the day's strangest events unfolded. As his attack on the farm compound petered out, Waters ordered the seventeen tanks from his Company C to reconnoiter the bridges over the Medjerda River. Angling east from the Tine valley, a mile-long defile named Chouïgui Pass gave onto the flat, fertile plains, twenty miles from Tunis. The paved road through the pass veered southeast for five miles to the grain fields and orchards of the Medjerda valley. It was this route that Major Rudolph Barlow followed with the three platoons of Company C.

At thirty-five miles an hour, Barlow and his men skirted the town of Tébourba and followed Highway 55 for two miles to the narrow bridge spanning the Medjerda at El Bathan. A few bursts of coaxial machine-gun fire scattered the sentries; the Allies, so roughly handled at Medjez-el-Bab, now owned their own Medjerda bridge, twenty-two miles downstream from Medjez and deep behind the German line.

Suffused with cavalry panache, Barlow pressed ahead. His tanks rumbled northeast for seven miles along the left bank of the Medjerda, sheltered by olive groves, to the village of Djedeïda. Behind a ridge a few hundred yards ahead, a German plane lifted into the air, followed by another. Barlow sent forward a platoon under Lieutenant Wilbor H. Hooker while the rest of the company remained secluded in the olive trees.

Hooker and his tankers soon came galloping back. A new airfield "packed with planes" lay on the other side of the rise, Hooker reported. No sentries had been posted and the Luftwaffe seemed oblivious of the approaching Americans. Barlow ordered the tanks into a forage line, with two platoons abreast and a third trailing slightly behind. He radioed Waters and relayed Hooker's report in a voice pitched to the occasion:

"Right in front of me is an airport full of German airplanes, sitting there, the men all sitting out on the gasoline barrels, shooting the breeze in the sunlight. What should I do?"

Waters had spent much of the day hiding in the cactus from these very aircraft. Now he nearly leaped in the air with incredulity. "For God's sake, attack them! Go after them!"

Seventeen Stuarts surged up and over the crest of the hill, tracks churning the wheat stubble as they barreled down the front slope from the northwest. Tank commanders craned for a better view from the open turret hatches and spurred their drivers forward. Several dozen Messerschmitts, Stukas, and Junkerses crowded around the dirt airstrip, reminding one American officer of "fat geese on a small pond." Some were taking gas at a makeshift fuel dump; others were being rearmed with bombs and belts of machine-gun bullets. Late-afternoon shadows stretched before the charging Stuarts as if racing the tanks to the bottom of the slope. A few Luftwaffe crewmen turned and waved, evidently believing the tanks were Italian.

Then the first bursts of machine-gun fire struck the parked planes and the mêlée began. Fuel drums exploded, spreading sheets of fire across the runway and engulfing German soldiers and planes alike. The boom of seventeen tank guns reverberated in the hills, as Barlow's gunners hit their fire buttons as fast as loaders could shove rounds into the breech. Gunfire from the tanks created its own hot wind, flattening the brush and blowing a dark cloud of debris before the hulls.

The squirrel guns proved lethal to aircraft sheet metal. Planes blew up, planes disintegrated, planes collided with other planes making for the end of the runway. A Messerschmitt gained enough speed to lift off, only to be raked by machine-gun bullets and cartwheel, burning, to earth. Mud slowed the taxiing Junkerses long enough for American gunners to take languid aim and machine-gun the fuselages from propeller to vertical stabilizer. As for those still able to build speed, a tank commander at the far end of the runway raked departing planes with fire until a nearby grainfield was full of burning cruciforms.

Tanks lunged onto the runway. Terrified pilots in their leather headgear fled zigzag across the field, only to be shot down or crushed beneath the tracks. Several Stuarts rolled behind a row of parked aircraft, methodically shearing off their tails. Desultory German rifle fire, one tank crewman later recalled, hit the turrets and "bounced off like peas." A few defenders tried to turn their 20mm anti-aircraft weapons into tank killers, but the Stuarts were too agile and the gunners died at their guns.

Tanks tacked back and forth across the airfield looking for things to kill. Spent brass rained down on the Stuart drivers and bow gunners, who wrapped towels around their necks and kept their collars buttoned tight to avoid burns from the hot casings. A few fighters had managed to get airborne when the attack began, and now they circled back for low strafing runs that ignited bedrolls and clothing bags lashed to the American hulls. Crewmen climbed from their hatches to beat at the flames, then pressed forward to kill some more.

In half an hour the fight was over. Barlow pulled his whooping tankers back up the hill. The raid had cost him one tank destroyed, several damaged, and two men killed by strafing, including a platoon leader.

He paused for a final look at the carnage below. Wreckage from more than twenty German planes lay scattered in a burning swath longer than a mile. Spikes of flame from detonating fuel and ammunition flared the length of the runway, illuminating scattered propellers, wheels, and fuselages. Bodies lay sprawled across the field. Barlow briefly considered pressing on to Tunis even at the risk of being cut off, but night had closed completely over the countryside and Waters wanted C Company to return. The tanks turned back toward Chouïgui Pass. Behind them, to the east, a pale orange glow reflected off the belly of the clouds above Djedeïda, like a false dawn.

Panicky, exaggerated reports that American tanks were nine kilometers—five miles—from Tunis vexed General Nehring to the point of despair on the night of November 25. Only a few irrigation ditches and two 88mm guns stood between Allied forces and Tunis harbor. From his command post in the erstwhile American consulate, Nehring spoke by phone to Kesselring in Rome and warned that he was forced "to tear open one tactical hole in order to stop another more serious one." A panzer battalion that had been protecting Mateur would have to move south in the face of this latest threat to the capital. That opened the road to Bizerte. German commanders across the bridgehead were rifling through files and preparing to burn their secret papers.

Kesselring voiced sympathy for his field commander's "state of understandable excitement." The raid at Djedeïda, he agreed, "made a beautiful mess of things" and "suggested a certain limpness in German defenses." But Nehring should not overreact. "It was a rather unpleasant incident, to be sure," Kesselring said, yet their predicament was less bleak than Nehring believed. The field marshal now had a sense of his Allied foes: they were cautious and tentative, disinclined to bold tactical gambles. Remain calm, Kesselring urged. He promised to fly to Tunisia in the morning for a closer look.

Smiling Albert's assurances seemed plausible. Recovery from a battlefield victory could sometimes be more difficult than recovery from defeat, and indeed the Djedeïda success found the Allies unprepared to exploit their winnings. Eisenhower, who had just moved his headquarters from Gibraltar to Algiers, showed no inclination to rush to the front to strike the coup de grâce that Kesselring was rushing to prevent. Anderson and Evelegh had locked themselves into a tactical disadvantage by failing to concentrate their forces for a single hammer blow at the brittle Axis defense. Logistical woes, airpower weaknesses, shortages of infantrymen, disintegrating weather—all conspired to bring the Allied advance up short. There was even confusion about whether the primary objective should be Bizerte, now code-named DIZZY, or Tunis, known as INCUR.

Yet Kesselring's certitude failed to persuade Nehring, who concluded that the field marshal did not understand how precarious Tunisia had become. Luftwaffe pilots reported thirty enemy tanks heading north toward Mateur. Nehring had shown impeccable courage and combat skills both as an infantryman in the last world war and as a panzer leader in this one. But as commander of the Afrika Korps under Rommel, he had been badly wounded in an air attack two months earlier; the posting to Tunisia had disrupted his physical and mental convalescence, and his recovery was hardly expedited by the crash of the plane carrying him to Tunis.

Now Nehring's confidence flagged. Shortly after hanging up on Kesselring, he ordered a general contraction of his line, into a tighter, more defensible bridgehead. In the Medjerda valley the line would shift seven miles, from Tébourba to Djedeïda; troops in the north would fall back to Mateur. All along the front, German and Italian soldiers gathered their weapons and ammunition, and silently began trudging east.

At daybreak on Thursday, November 26, Allied sentries in the hills west of Medjez-el-Bab were startled by a deep boom from the center of town. A white cloud corkscrewed above the river. Led by British infantrymen, a newly arrived battalion of American tanks cautiously pushed through the battered outskirts of Medjez. At the Medjerda, a forty-foot section of the humpback masonry bridge lay in the river where Wehrmacht demolitionists had just dropped it. The town was empty except for a few stray cats and a stamping mule. Unspeakable odors seeped from the rubble. American tankers were shocked to see that dead British soldiers from the failed assault earlier in the week had been stripped of every stitch by Arab looters. One soldier explained this behavior in a letter home: "It's because they never had any bringing up."

The key to the door was back in an Allied pocket. Battered though the town was—and it would look only worse in the succeeding months—American and British soldiers gaped in astonishment at their good fortune. Burial details dug graves for the dead. Combat engineers studied the broken span and began moving up a portable Bailey bridge, which would take less than ten hours to erect. Infantry and armored troops followed the river northeast toward Tébourba. The spoor of a retreating enemy—ration tins, empty ammunition clips, and bloody bandages—littered Highway 50. White concrete kilometer markers, two feet high and capped in red paint, counted down the distance to Tunis. Battalion cooks bustled about in their field kitchens, rummaging for something beyond the dreary daily hash and bully beef to mark the occasion: Thanksgiving Day, 1942.

A new confidence took root. For two weeks Eisenhower had bounced between hope and despair, and he seized on the news from Medjez to rekindle his optimism. "At this moment," he wrote Patton, "our situation throughout [the] theater appears better than we had calculated it would." In a message to Beetle Smith, he went even further. "I believe," he predicted, "the enemy will be forced shortly to abandon either DIZZY or INCUR, so as to concentrate on the other."

5. PRIMUS IN CARTHAGO

"Go for the Swine with a Blithe Heart"

FROM the tall windows of his corner office in the Hôtel St. Georges, Eisenhower stared out at a city going about its business with little regard to war. The shrill whine of electric trolleys muffled the muezzins' call to prayer and the chatter of schoolgirls in blue uniforms pouring from the École Ste. Geneviève. In the *salon de coiffure* outside the hotel's front entrance, Arabs worked their worry beads and sipped coffee with extended pinky fingers; the solitary barber's chair displayed a manufacturer's stamp showing it had been made in St. Louis. Algerian cavalrymen clopped past on their white chargers, followed by an open truck with bandaged soldiers just arrived from Tunisia. In the hotel corridors squads of barefoot, broom-wielding Arab women whisked furiously at muddy bootprints, to small effect. The rich odor of Thanksgiving dinner wafted from the St. Georges dining room: roasted peacock, cabbage, and peas, served with a credible Algerian rosé.

For officers long trapped in Gibraltar's subterranean gloom—such wraiths were marked by their pallor and hacking coughs—sunny Algiers offered a pleasant respite. Purple bougainvillea, pink oleander, and bright blue plumbago lent the city a Tropic of Cancer palette. Eisenhower was happier than most to escape the Rock; the damp lingered in his bones, afflicting him with a catarrh that would linger for months. The commander-in-chief had intended to move his headquarters on November 10 or 11, but loitered until November 23 because the undersea cable from Gibraltar gave him better communications to Britain and the United States than he would have in Algiers. That propinquity now seemed like a mixed blessing. "How weary I am of this long-distance essay contest with London and Washington," he had written Clark on November 20. A day later he added, "I've been pounded all week from the rear. Sometimes it seems that none of us in the field can do anything to the satisfaction of Washington and London."

He was hardly out of reach in Algiers, but the War Department and

Downing Street seemed far more distant, if only because communications remained primitive. In the signal offices at the east end of the St. Georges's second floor, cryptographic machines were balanced on a wooden frame over a bathtub. The British code room occupied a cramped Quonset hut in the garden, while American coding and teletype operators worked among the scattered ottomans and brass tables in the hotel lounge.

Eisenhower's own office was spare but functional. Three hotel bedrooms and a sitting room at the end of a long corridor had been converted into a suite. The many windows admitted ample light, but the only heat in the old hotel came from a few small fireplaces, which left him and his staff scented with wood smoke. Nights in the St. Georges could be bitter, especially for soldiers temporarily housed on the hallway floors. The hotel shook violently during the frequent attacks by German bombers against the nearby port and airfields. After a sleepless first night in the office, Eisenhower, who had since moved his sleeping quarters to a more isolated villa, fumed at the limp Allied air defenses and berated his air commanders for their inadequacies.

A few days before leaving Gibraltar, Eisenhower had proposed limiting his headquarters to 150 officers. "Am particularly anxious that we strip down to a working basis and cut down on all of the folderol," he told Clark. Algiers was to be a temporary billet, with Allied Forces Headquarters moving closer to the battlefield in a couple of months. But already AFHQ was expanding wildly. Within a fortnight, the headquarters would occupy nearly 400 offices scattered through eleven buildings. Three hundred officers now devoured as much meat as rationing allocated to 15,000 French civilians. Eisenhower's signal officer proposed that the formula for staffing a headquarters should be "a reasonable estimate, multiplied by five." AFHQ would remain in Algiers for years, expanding into a "huge, chairborne force" of more than 1,000 officers and 15,000 enlisted troops occupying 2,000 pieces of real estate. A popular aphorism soon circulated among frontline troops: "Never were so few commanded by so many from so far." Asked why the Germans failed to bomb AFHQ headquarters, a cynical American major replied, "Because it's worth fifty divisions to them."

Algiers already showed the strains of occupation. So many electric razors buzzed in the morning that they interfered with radio transmissions. Prostitutes working the Aletti Hotel now charged £10 sterling per trick. A French newspaper began printing English-language lessons, including the sentence: "No, sir, I am married, and I am hurrying home where my husband is awaiting me." In Oran, officers in their pinks-and-greens ate in a mess with green leather chairs while musicians in evening dress played Big Band melodies. A supply major proposed creating a medal inscribed "Valor, Patience, Indigestion," which would be awarded for exemplary "paperwork connected with the social struggle."

Oranges that had been fifteen cents a bushel in Algiers jumped to fifteen cents a dozen. Beer went from two cents a schooner to a dollar. Nightclubs with names like La Belle Rose and Bucket of Blood were always jammed, while battalion sergeant majors inspected various brothels and chose several of the least odious for licensing. Discovering huge wine barrels awaiting export on the wharves, soldiers tapped them with rifle fire and caught the drainage in their canteen cups; a drunken brawl led to a waterfront firefight suppressed by military policemen who then disarmed all dockworkers. Indiscipline overwhelmed the military justice system: in Oran alone, hundreds of American soldiers had been arrested for various infractions in the two weeks after the invasion, but less than 2 percent of them were prosecuted. A summary court was established to restore order; nearly 300 soldiers would be tried in the first part of December, with a total of 9 acquittals. A third of the cases involved drunkenness. Serious offenses drew harsh sentences: four years for a self-inflicted gunshot to the big toe to avoid combat; eight years at hard labor for kicking a superior officer; life in prison for a soldier who shot and killed an Algerian woman with his rifle.

There was folderol aplenty, despite Eisenhower's wishes, and it all rested on the commander-in-chief's squared shoulders. Many of the distractions were fatuous. A rumor in Arab neighborhoods that Eisenhower was a Jew sent by the Jew Roosevelt to establish a Jewish state in North Africa required a leaflet campaign stressing the general's German Protestant ancestry. The War Department tried to inflate his dignity by urging reporters not to refer to him as "Ike," and thus ensured that the nickname would stick forever. Ever eager to see his own name in headlines, Clark gave an interview full of breezy predictions about the imminent fall of Tunis and Bizerte; Eisenhower had killed the story just before leaving Gibraltar. Draconian censorship was soon imposed, with correspondents advised that no dispatches would be allowed that made people at home feel unhappy. Equally rigorous censorship of letters home inspired one soldier to write his parents:

> After leaving where we were before we left for here, not knowing we were coming here from there, we couldn't tell whether we had arrived here or not. Nevertheless, we now are here and not there.

The weather here is just as it always is at this season. The people here are just like they look.

On this page a censor scribbled simply, "Amen."

In a message on November 22, Churchill voiced hopes that Eisenhower had "not been too much preoccupied with the political aspect." As for the Germans in Tunisia, the prime minister advised, "Go for the swine with a blithe heart." But blitheness was hard to come by. "It seems difficult for people at home ... to understand that we are in a dirty battle, with Germans pouring into Tunisia and with us having need for every man we can get to the front," Eisenhower wrote Clark. To Beetle Smith he added, "My whole interest is Tunisia."

In truth, he spent at least three-quarters of his time worrying about political issues, and that preoccupation poorly served the Allied cause. Had he shunted aside all distractions to focus on seizing Tunis with a battle captain's fixed purpose, the coming months might have been different. But a quarter-century as a staff officer, with a staff officer's meticulous attention to detail and instinctive concern for pleasing his superiors, did not slough away easily. Eisenhower had yet to bend events to his iron will, to impose as well as implore, to become a commander in action as well as in rank.

No distraction tormented him more than the French. While disdainful of "these Frogs" and their "morbid sense of honor," he remained convinced that French cooperation was critical to civil order and equivalent to ten divisions in safeguarding Allied supply lines. General Giraud, who now commanded all French forces in North Africa, still routinely requested control over all Allied troops as well. Eisenhower considered him "volatile rather than stable," a megalomaniac who "knows no more about logistics than a dog about religion."

But the commander-in-chief lacked the confidence or stature to insist that French soldiers—many of whom now wore decorations awarded for resisting the Anglo-American invaders—cooperate fully with General Anderson. As a result, the movement of troops and supplies to the front, as well as the assault on the enemy bridgehead, remained ill coordinated. Particularly suspect were French troops in Tunisia whose families lived in the German occupation zone; a single battalion reported 132 desertions. Many troops were worse equipped than those who had fought seventy years earlier in the Franco-Prussian War. A French soldier claimed his boot soles were so thin he could step on a wad of chewing gum and tell the flavor; some colonial soldiers had no boots at all, although their bare feet were so dirty they looked shod. Yet French supply requests to the Americans included large quantities of table and bed linen, china, and gold braid for officers' uniforms.

More distracting by far was the public outcry at home over the "Darlan deal." The North African political morass was "covered like a Tammany scandal by most of the American press," one correspondent acknowledged, and a scandal it had become. The Allied marriage of convenience with the quisling Darlan was deemed a sordid betrayal of fundamental united nations' principles. "What the hell is this all about? Are we fighting Nazis or sleeping with them?" asked Edward R. Murrow, the most influential broadcaster in America.

British public and parliamentary opinion was even more intense. Eisenhower's aide Harry Butcher wrote in his diary that Darlan was considered "a stinking skunk" in London. The British Foreign Office cabled its embassy in Washington, "We are fighting for international decency and Darlan is the antithesis of this." The outrage was fed by the adroit public relations apparatus of Charles de Gaulle's London-based Free French, which demonized Darlan relentlessly.

Darlan's repressive actions as high commissioner hardly mollified his critics. Thousands were imprisoned in North African camps, including men who had helped the Anglo-American invaders. The anti-Semitic laws of Vichy remained in effect for fear of provoking the Arabs. Four hundred press censors now worked for Darlan, and BBC broadcasts were jammed, so that North Africans failed to hear allegations that 500 pounds of hoarded coffee and 800 pounds of sugar had been confiscated at the admiral's home in metropolitan France.

Eisenhower averted his gaze. In a Thanksgiving Day note he told Patton, "We did not come here to interfere in someone else's business. We are on a military mission." He became defensive and shrill. "We are making the best of a rather bad bargain," he informed Marshall, and to the combined chiefs he added, "I realize that there may be a feeling at home that we have been sold a bill of goods," but Darlan offered "the only possible workable arrangement for securing advantages and avoiding disadvantages." At times his exasperation boiled over. "The authorities in London and Washington continue to suffer a bit from delusion as to the extent of our military control over this country," he told Smith. "It will be a long time before we can get up on our high horse and tell everybody in the world to go to hell."

Roosevelt had authorized the Darlan deal, but in his public statement supporting it he used the word "temporary" five times. Sensing the impermanence of his utility to the Allies, Darlan wrote Eisenhower on November 21: "Information coming from various parts tends to give credit to the opinion that I am but a lemon which the Americans will drop after it is crushed."

All this was folderol of the most noxious sort, and it both preoccupied Eisenhower and preyed on him. "For Christ's sake, do you think I want to talk politics? Goddam it, I hate 'em," he declared. "I'm sick to death of this goddam political question." Although he had no way of knowing that Roosevelt harbored private doubts about his commanding general's judgment, Eisenhower sensed that he, too, was expendable. Referring to his permanent, pre-war rank—to which he would return if cashiered as a three-star general—he once muttered, "Tell [Roosevelt] I am the best damn lieutenant colonel in the U.S. Army." He was particularly incensed by unfair suggestions in the newspapers that his indifference to civil liberties made him a fascist (as he pronounced it, "fatchist"). In his long career of public service, his skin would never be thinner nor his temper more volatile than it was in Algiers in the winter of 1942. Press criticism particularly was a chafing new experience for military officers accustomed to anonymity in a peacetime army. "I'm no reactionary!" Eisenhower exploded after a flurry of accusatory articles. "Christ on the mountain! I'm idealistic as hell!"

At the end of a very long day he returned to Villa dar el Ouard—"Villa of the Family"—for some supper. Axis bombers had again knocked out the heat, gas, and water, forcing an orderly to cook over an open wood fire in the dining room hearth. The tessellated stone floor was as cold as a meat locker. The drafty villa had seven bedrooms, a library with a Ping-Pong table, and a music room with a grand piano. Sometimes Eisenhower picked out "Chopsticks" or joined his staff in belting out West Point songs or cowboy tunes. On more somber evenings, however, he put a record on the phonograph and listened to his favorite passage from Verdi's *Il Trovatore, "Vedi! le fosche notturne spoglie,"* also known as the Anvil Chorus. The villa echoed with the sound of singing Gypsies working their forge. Eisenhower's Scottie puppy, Telek, newly arrived from London, chased his own tail round and round.

Even an officer as strong and selfless as Eisenhower at times felt overwhelmed. "It would be idle of me to say that I have not felt some degree of strain," he had written Marshall a few days earlier. One acquaintance described him as a "lonely man who worried, worried, worried." Eisenhower rarely yielded to self-pity, but occasionally a bitter tone crept into his letters, as when he told General Arnold, "I have literally slaved like a dog." The Darlan uproar eclipsed the extraordinary accomplishments of his soldiers in TORCH, and he regretted that.

He regretted, too, not devoting himself more robustly to the battle for Tunisia. "I live ten years each week, of which at least nine are absorbed in political and economic matters," he told Marshall. Some British generals, who were to supply three-quarters of the combat troops in Tunisia, had growing reservations about a man who had never led a battalion in action but now commanded armies.

"Eisenhower far too busy with political matters. . . . Not paying enough attention to the Germans," Brooke, the British Army chief, would write in his diary on December 7. Eisenhower possessed charm, an evenhanded knack for uniting allies, and "more than his share of luck," Brooke conceded. But he seemed "unable to grasp the urgency of pushing on to Tunis before Germans build up their resistance there." Eisenhower had no illusions about his responsibilities. Harry Butcher wrote in his diary entry for Thanksgiving Day: "The whole thing in Algiers and to the east needs vigorous coordination that only Ike himself can arrange."

The low moan of air raid sirens sounded. Above Algiers harbor he could see crimson anti-aircraft shells coiling into a purple sky crisscrossed with tracers and searchlight beams. Every gun battery and warship within ten miles appeared to be firing. Smoke generators around the port churned out an oily fudge that blanketed parts of the city. Barrage fire and smoke were the only real defenses. Of the mere half-dozen Allied fighters available to intercept enemy planes at night over Algiers, three had been destroyed on the ground by Axis bombs or shot down by overzealous Allied gunners.

Concussions rattled the windows. Eisenhower would have his air commanders on the carpet again tomorrow; among other consequences, bumbling air defenses threatened to provoke a revolt by terrified French and Arab civilians. He walked into the master bedroom at the back of the villa. Fragments of spent anti-aircraft shells rattled on the roof like hailstones.

To his son, John, at West Point, Eisenhower had recently written, "I hope that you occasionally are brushing up on your Mediterranean geography because some day I will want to talk over this campaign with you and get your ideas as to whether or not we did it correctly." But for the moment the general was tired of thinking large thoughts. From a stack of paperbacks next to his bed he plucked a pulp Western and for a few placid minutes lost himself in a world of rustlers and cowpokes and dance-hall doxies before drifting off to sleep.

"The Dead Salute the Gods"

THERE was no roasted peacock for Thanksgiving in John Waters's 1st Battalion. Tucked once again into the Tine River valley, twenty-five miles west of Tunis, his tank crews settled for a breakfast of greasy mutton stew with hardtack, heated over gasoline-soaked dirt and washed down with thick tea. Their cigarettes long gone, the men rolled dried eucalyptus leaves in toilet paper and pretended they were Chesterfields.

Each soldier habitually watched the sky as he ate, smoked, scribbled a letter, or cleaned his weapon. Luftwaffe pilots now attacked on average once an hour, and the Americans had renamed the Tine glen "Happy Valley." German troops had reoccupied Djedeïda airfield just hours after Wednesday evening's raid, and once again Stukas landed and took off with the crisp efficiency of a taxi rank. Their plummeting attacks reminded one reporter of "swallows diving after midges on an evening at home." Captain Evelyn Waugh of the British Army wrote of the Stuka, "Like all things German, it is very efficient and goes on much too long."

German Me-109 fighters also lurked in the clouds or slipped along an adjacent valley before suddenly popping over the ridgeline in a terrifying whirlwind of bombs and bullets that bounced like scarlet marbles off the macadam. Officers tweeted their air-attack whistles and every man dove for the nearest slit trench. Virtually all road traffic now moved at night: a cavalcade of burned-out vehicles suggested the hazards of daylight driving. The relentless attacks so infuriated the U.S. troops that they fired at enemy aircraft "with any weapon we had in our hands, including a mortar," one soldier reported. A gallows humor took hold: "Famous last words: 'Don't worry, boys, those are our Spitfires.'" The unofficial motto of Allied forces in Tunisia soon became "Dig or die."

On the rare occasions when Allied planes dominated the skies, fratricide added to the ground troops' torment. Word soon spread of an incident near Medjez-el-Bab, where a company of American tank destroyers was helping secure the town on Thanksgiving morning when eleven U.S. P-38 Lightnings flew over. Jubilant at the unexpected help from friendly fighters, the tank destroyer crews raced across the open terrain, waving and smiling. Built with distinctive twin fuselages, the P-38s languidly circled until the sun was behind them, then dropped to fifty feet and executed five textbook strafing runs in three minutes.

The attack all but destroyed the shocked company, which fired not a single retaliatory shot. Five men were killed—including the unit's only World War I veteran—and sixteen wounded; nearly every vehicle and antitank weapon was destroyed or damaged. One outraged company commander in the 1st Armored Division ordered his men to shoot any airborne object larger than a goose. And another bromide circulated among American soldiers: "If it flies, it dies." Allied pilots grew so accustomed to being fired upon by their own troops that the formula for recognizing enemy aircraft from the ground, "WEFT"—check the Wings, Engines, Fuselage, Tail—was said to mean "Wrong every fucking time."

Despite such demoralizing episodes, the contraction of the Axis line permitted General Evelegh's two brigades to nudge eastward a few miles along the Mediterranean road on the Allied left flank, and down the Medjerda valley from Medjez-el-Bab on the Allied right. But neither brigade lunged forward to rock the Germans back on their heels before they could dig in. In the Allied center, Blade Force remained static. Waters drove forty miles to Béja for consultations with the Blade commander, who told him to keep 1st Battalion in defensive positions along a three-mile stretch of Happy Valley. There were to be no more forays onto the plains of Tunis without orders.

Before dawn on November 26, Waters returned by jeep to his command post in a gritty walled enclosure known as St. Joseph's Farm, half a mile south of the Tine. A brisk wind tossed the gum trees lining the river; on the far bank, an Arab farmer harrowed his field behind a brace of oxen. The tinkle of collar bells carried across the water. Camouflage netting and haystacks hid the American jeeps and radio antennae in the farm compound.

Blue grease pencil on a crude map showed the disposition of the battalion's fifty-two surviving Stuart tanks: Rudolph Barlow's Company C, still reveling in the previous day's airfield rumble, plugged the eastern entrance to Chouïgui Pass, which angled to the right from Happy Valley two miles downstream of St. Joseph's Farm; Major William R. Tuck's Company B was hidden behind a low hill overlooking the Tine, just north of the pass; Major Carl Siglin's Company A waited on a cactus-covered ridge a mile south of the pass, almost within hailing distance of Waters's headquarters.

Shortly before noon, a sentry using a pair of French naval binoculars spotted a nimbus of dust several miles downriver. Waters loped up a hill and confirmed the approach of what he called "a beautiful column, preceded by some pathetic Italian reconnaissance armored vehicles." Three German companies, including armor from the 190th Panzer Battalion, were rolling from Mateur to reinforce Axis troops retreating from Medjez-el-Bab. No sooner had Waters begun counting the enemy tanks than rounds came screaming into St. Joseph's Farm. Men yanked down the camouflage netting, cranked the engines of their Stuarts, and heaved their bedrolls to the ground. The first tank battle of World War II between German and American forces had begun.

To buy time, Waters ordered three 75mm assault guns to occupy an olive grove along the river road. Mounted on armored half-tracks, they opened with a brisk cannonade of thirty rounds at a thousand yards' range: the only effect was to raise more dust and provoke a retaliatory volley through the olive branches. On Waters's order the howitzers hurried back to the farm, masking their retreat with a few smoke rounds. The approaching Mk IV Panzer tanks, Waters soon realized, had a new, long-barreled 75mm gun unknown to Allied intelligence. The new gun's muzzle velocity of nearly 3,000 feet per second was twice that of American tank guns and had correspondingly greater penetrating power.

From the ridge southeast of the farm, Major Siglin, in a tank named *Iron Horse,* and eleven other Stuarts from Company A now charged down the hill to the valley floor. Machine-gun tracer rounds lashed the air in crimson flails. The Stuarts' main guns barked and barked. An Italian armored car was struck, and lurched to a smoky stop.

Then the German panzers answered with a deep roar and a Stuart abruptly lurched up. Less than a hundred yards away, Lieutenant Freeland A. Daubin, Jr., commanding a platoon of three tanks on Company A's right flank, saw "long searing tongues of orange flame" erupt from every hatch of the shattered tank and "silver rivulets of aluminum" puddle beneath the engine block. Sparks spouted from the barrel as ammunition began to cook. Thick black smoke boiled from the burning rubber tracks and bogey wheels.

Another Stuart was hit, and another. They brewed up like the first. Crewmen tumbled from the hatches, their hair and uniforms brilliant with flame, and they rolled across the dirt and tore away their jackets in burning shreds. Others were trapped in their tanks with fractured limbs, and their cries could be heard above the booming tumult as they burned to death in fire so intense it softened the armor plates. Even near misses from the German guns were devastating. A shell that failed to penetrate the hull still carried enough force—thousands of g's—to shear off a Stuart's rivet heads, which then richocheted inside the tank like machine-gun bullets. One tank commander later reported that a glancing shot gouged metal from the side of his turret "like a finger rubbing along a pat of butter, producing a brief rosy glow on the inside of the turret wall as the steel became white hot at the point of impact."

Wreathed in gray smoke, the panzers closed to within 300 yards. Siglin's *Iron Horse* and the other surviving Stuarts scooted up and back, their drivers blinded by smoke and dust as they wrestled their gearshifts and steering levers. Compared to the German tank guns, the Stuart 37mm "snapped like a cap pistol," a platoon leader observed. "Jerry seemed annoyed." Lieutenant Daubin on the right flank pumped more than eighteen rounds at a single German Mk IV; the shells simply bounced off the bard plates, which shed "sparks like a power-driven grindstone." Daubin tap-danced furiously on his driver's shoulders and shouted instructions to zigzag backward. At less than fifty yards, a panzer round struck the forward hatch and the Stuart's front end buckled like a tin can hit with a hammer. The blast killed the driver and blinded the bow gunner. Bullets cut down the loader as he climbed from the hatch. Wounded but alive, Daubin tumbled to the ground and crawled into a ditch. His tank continued to roll backward from the battlefield, swallowed in flames.

In ten minutes half of Captain Siglin's twelve tanks had been destroyed. But now Waters sprang the trap for which Company A had been bait. In their zeal to attack Siglin's Stuarts, the Germans failed to notice Major Tuck's Company B hidden behind the ridge just north of the entrance to Chouïgui Pass. As the Axis formation passed, less than a hundred yards away, Tuck and his tanks came pounding over the crest of the hill to fall on the enemy flank and rear. At point-blank range even the squirrel gun's two-pound shell could punch through the thin armor on panzer engine doors and docks. The enemy tried to wheel around but it was too late. Dozens of American rounds ripped into the German tanks. Seven panzers were destroyed, including a half-dozen of the new Mk IVs.

The Axis survivors fled down the Tine, pursued by yelling, vengeful Americans. German infantry and two surviving tanks took refuge in the walled farm compound that Siglin's company had unsuccessfully attacked the day before. This time the Americans forced the gates and rampaged through the garrison, shooting up the parapets before retreating back outside the wall. Other Axis troops were hunted down and killed in the vineyards above the river. After dark, the German commander withdrew the remnant of his force eight miles north to Mateur, where he was sacked and court-martialed for retreating without orders. "Our losses," the German war diary for November 26 noted, "were considerable."

So, too, were American losses, although Waters had essentially traded tank for tank. This first armored battle had ended in a draw. In the final mêlée at the farm compound, the intrepid Major Siglin had been killed by a tank round through the turret of *Iron Horse*. His body was returned to St. Joseph's Farm for burial, a stark refutation of the old lie that the weakest fruit drops to the ground first. Perhaps the greatest tribute came from the British Lancers who arrived after the skirmish to find Happy Valley choked with pillars of black smoke from burning tanks. "The Americans had done well," the Lancers' historian later wrote. "A gallant effort."

Once again the Allies had a sense of momentum. On the left flank, the 36th Brigade broke loose and cantered forward. In the center, Blade Force had cleaned out the Tine valley; Mateur, the key to Bizerte, lay just over the horizon. And on the right flank the race for Tunis would be decided by a series of pitched battles that now began almost within artillery range of the capital.

Ten miles south of Happy Valley, British infantrymen from the 1st Battalion of the East Surreys captured the Medjerda valley town of Tébourba before daylight on Friday, November 27. Tommies found half-cooked eggs and a beefsteak still sizzling in a police station kitchen vacated by enemy pickets. Two weeks earlier, Tébourba's population had been 4,000; now a quick census tallied half a dozen Arabs, three Italians, a pig, a donkey, and some chickens. Bombs and artillery had smashed every building except for a few squat hovels and the Hôtel de France, facing the central square. Tébourba, the correspondent Drew Middleton reported, was "dusty and empty, as such towns are when war has rolled through them."

Tucked into an oxbow of the Medjerda, Tébourba lay midway between Medjez-el-Bab and Tunis, within olive groves of beguiling geometric precision. The Surreys posted a company at the stone Medjerda bridge a mile south of town. Another company scrambled up Djebel Maïana, a steep, barren hill a mile to the east and soon renamed Point 186 for its height in meters. From it, the railway, the river, and Highway 50 could be seen running roughly parallel toward Djedeïda and beyond, as could Stukas landing at the reoccupied Luftwaffe airfield less than four miles away. The distant minarets of Tunis were also visible with the naked eye: thin, graceful fingers poking through the Mediterranean haze. Officers trooped up the hill amid the thistles and darting bank swallows to behold a view that "was to remain a haunting memory through many tough days ahead," an American armor commander later wrote.

The Surreys were spread thin across a seven-mile arc, but euphoria was the order of the day. General Evelegh spoke of entering Tunis in twelve hours. Another British brigade—the 1st Guards—would soon arrive from Algiers with three battalions to fill out Evelegh's 78th Division, and more American units from the 1st Armored Division were drawing close from Oran. The Surreys grabbed their blankets from trucks in the olive groves and agreed that a short rest was warranted before they pushed on. Visiting officers were guided up the hill for the inspirational vista. Among the tourists was the prime minister's son, Randoph Churchill, a plumpish toff in a commando uniform who paused long enough to rebuke a soldier digging a foxhole in an olive grove: "My good man, do you realize that by digging a trench in that spot you may be killing a tree well over a thousand years old?"

At 11:30 A.M. the Germans returned—"Tanks! Tanks!" someone yelled—and euphoria vanished with the tourists. Seventeen panzers swarmed through the olive groves on both sides of Point 186 and shot up the Surreys' trucks. For two hours, fighting raged from ranges of a hundred yards to a few feet. Shell fire and machine-gun bullets chewed through branches and into Tébourba, riddling the high cactus hedges and the few hovels previously spared. Eight British field guns defended the town; one by one they fell silent. So did the smaller 2- and 6-pounders. Welsh gunners danced over the dead to shove another shell into the breech and yank the lanyard. A Tommy promised a mortally wounded comrade: "We'll be in Tunis eating bloody great oranges in a week.".

The British line buckled, then held, and at two P.M. the firing ebbed. Seven of eight guns had been knocked out, with the sole functioning 25-pounder now manned by a single sergeant. Eight wrecked panzers stood in a semicircle, the bent barrel of one just a few feet from the muzzle of the shattered British gun that had destroyed it. Debris littered the ground, including Chianti bottles and tins of Portuguese sardines blown from the German hulls. Nine surviving panzers lumbered back down the railway line toward Djedeïda, and Wehrmacht tankers who had escaped their burning wrecks darted among the cactus patches, firing pistols over their shoulders like fleeing robbers. Wreckage discomposed the perfect groves, and the shell-riddled corpses of thousand-year-old olive trees lay among those of Surreys killed in action.

There was not a moment to be lost, but a day passed before a counterattack could be organized. As the Surreys buried their dead, two more battalions—one British, one American—pushed forward. Their orders were to seize Djedeïda—the troops now called it "Deedahdeedah"—and punch on to Mateur the same day. Many soldiers skipped breakfast and lunch, believing that an empty digestive tract lessened the chance of contaminating a gut wound. At one P.M. on Saturday, November 28, two companies from the 5th Battalion of the Northamptonshire Regiment, known as the Northants, climbed onto nineteen tanks from the U.S. 2nd Battalion of the 13th Armored Regiment. A dozen or more Tommies clung precariously to each tank, and two more companies of Northants trailed on foot, 300 yards behind. They set off for Djedeïda along the rail embankment the retreating Germans had followed the day before.

For two miles the Anglo-Americans rolled in an attack wedge across undulating terrain dotted with orchards and gum trees. Larks and red partridges flushed from the underbrush in a whir of wings, but the only sign of human life was the clutch of officers watching with field glasses from Point 186, like spectators at a racetrack. Troops on the right flank almost brushed the Medjerda with their sleeves as the low, white profile of Djedeïda came into view. The American tankers drove General Lees— double the Stuart's weight, with a 75mm gun in the hull, a 37mm squirrel rifle in the turret, and four machine guns. If bigger and more lethal, the Lee had distinct flaws. At more than ten feet tall "it looked like a damned cathedral coming down the road," as one tanker complained. The larger gun could traverse just a few degrees—which meant it could fire only in the direction the tank was heading—and was set so low that virtually the entire hull had to be exposed in order to shoot.

Perfectly camouflaged, the German ambushers waited until the lead American platoon—four tanks abreast—drew to within three hundred yards. Then gashes of fire leaped from the hidden revetments. Half a dozen antitank guns rocked the General Lees and the cackle of machine guns swept the landscape. Tommies dove from the tanks; some ran for a shallow ditch fifty yards behind, while others sheltered behind the armor hulls or simply fell dead. Soon five Lees were burning and the rest pulled back, firing at cactus copses and gun flashes. Major Henry E. Gardiner, a thirty-seven-year-old Montanan commanding the tank force, dashed forward in a half-track with a medic to one of the stricken tanks. Opening the rear door, they dragged out one boy—he was "horribly wounded," Gardiner reported, "having a huge chunk torn from his back and shoulder"—then retreated under searing fire when other wounded men on the battlefield waved them away.

The Northants swung to the right to outflank the enemy through the gum trees by the river. Gusts of German fire stopped them cold, and Stukas drove them to cover. Several tanks sought to force the same flank by following the rail line hugging the north bank of the Medjerda. As Lieutenant Eugene F. Jehlik searched for enemy gun pits from his open hatch, a German shell decapitated him. His headless corpse toppled into the tank onto his horrified crew, and the flanking attack collapsed. The ubiquitous Major Gardiner laid Jehlik behind a hillock, marking the body with a pair of upright shell casings for later retrieval.

There was nothing for it but retreat. The counterattack had failed completely, undone by a lack of surprise, of airpower, of artillery, of tactical nuance. Brits and Yanks "fought in each other's presence rather than in close coordination," the 1st Armored Division later concluded. After nightfall, Gardiner led two British medics and several stretcher bearers back onto a battlefield so well illuminated by burning General Lees that ambulances immediately drew German fire. Each tank, an American soldier observed, "burns like twenty haystacks." The smell of charred flesh enveloped the flaming hulls—medics had yet to learn to approach these crematories from upwind—and across the killing ground, pleas for water mingled with whimpers from men too ruined even for thirst.

At an aid station in Tébourba, the dead were stacked in the shadows, and ranks of stretchers with wounded soldiers awaited evacuation. Burn victims lay with faces raw and black, their eyebrows gone and their skin hanging in curly shreds. Among those Gardiner brought out was Private Roy Bates, a twenty-two-year-old West Virginian who had waited nine hours for rescue in the company of dead crewmates. From a four-inch hole in his right thigh, a surgeon pulled a one-pound shell fragment, which Bates now clutched. "As soon as I get well," he promised, "I'm going back up there and cram this down somebody's throat."

British soldiers, stone deaf from the din and with tears streaking their grimy cheeks, drifted back to a farm west of Point 186 designated as a rallying point for the Northants. "When they reached the farm they stumbled blindly toward the barn and pitched forward on their faces," Middleton reported. An infantryman tormented by Stukas all afternoon shouted, "Who'll give sixpence for a Spitfire?"—cynically echoing a Battle of Britain slogan that had encouraged schoolboys to donate pocket money for more fighters. Soldiers listening to the BBC hooted at reports that Allied troops were surging toward Tunis. One listener compared such communiqués to *Alice in Wonderland*: "a pack of lies but very interesting in spots." Correspondent A. D. Divine reported seeing on a Roman column the inscription "D.M.S.," an abbreviated supplication which he translated as "The dead salute the gods." The sentiment seemed germane.

Toward midnight, a feeble attempt was made to reorganize the Northants for a night attack on Djedeïda, but the order was recognized as witless and soon cancelled. Evelegh's two brigades had already suffered 580 casualties, exclusive of the Americans killed, wounded, and missing, and he considered it prudent to wait until morning before he tried again.

*   *   *

The commander-in-chief of Allied forces in North Africa, General Dwight D. Eisenhower, photographed in Algiers in early 1943

Unless otherwise noted, all photographs are from
U.S. Army Signal Corps archives.

LEFT: Rear Admiral H. Kent Hewitt, commander of Task Force 34, during the American invasion of Morocco in November 1942. At fifty-five, with a high, bookish forehead and mild demeanor, Hewitt was nevertheless a formidable fighting admiral.

RIGHT: Lieutenant General Kenneth A. N. Anderson, commander of the British First Army, in northern Tunisia. A sardonic subordinate nicknamed him "Sunshine," while his American code name was "Grouch"; fluent in French and Italian, he could be silent in any language. (*Imperial War Museum*)

BELOW: General Henri Giraud inspects spahi cavalrymen and colonial riflemen in Algiers. Intrepid and brave, with a knack for escaping from German prisons, he also possessed what one Frenchman described as the uncomprehending eyes of a porcelain cat.

Lieutenant Colonel Robert R. Moore, a druggist from Villisca, Iowa, rose from the "Boy Captain" of his National Guard company to command the 2nd Battalion of the 168th Infantry Regiment during the German counteroffensive east of Kasserine Pass. (*Courtesy of the Moore family*)

Four days before the American landings in Morocco, Signal Corps soldiers aboard ship initiate another member into the Bald-Head Club. All troops were also ordered to shower before the invasion to lessen the chance of wounds becoming infected.

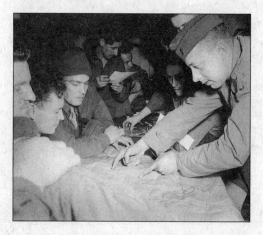

Men from the 1st Ranger Battalion review a map of Arzew aboard ship, November 7, 1942, hours before they captured the Algerian harbor at the beginning of the TORCH invasion.

The harsh sound of steel on whetstones could be heard throughout the convoys as soldiers put an edge on their bayonets and trench knives during the passage to Morocco and Algeria. This photograph was taken on November 7, 1942, invasion eve.

American troops landing at Fedala, Morocco, on Sunday, November 8, 1942. After what local residents described as the calmest day in decades, the Atlantic surf soon turned ferocious.

ABOVE LEFT: Major General Terry de la Mesa Allen, commander of the 1st Infantry Division, with French officers on the Tunisian front in early 1943. With the bowed stride of a horseman who had been saddle-hardened as a child, Allen was, an aide later observed, "the fightingest man I ever met."

ABOVE RIGHT: Brigadier General Theodore Roosevelt, Jr., assistant commander of the 1st Infantry Division, seen here at the Tunisian front. An accomplished author, diplomat, businessman, and soldier, he was erudite and valorous; but in tattered fatigues and wool cap he could be mistaken for a battalion cook.

Robert Murphy, the senior American diplomat in Algiers, and General Alphonse Juin, commander of French ground forces in North Africa, seen here after the armistice between Vichy troops and the Allies. Murphy is wearing his new Distinguished Service Medal, awarded for his part in Operation TORCH.

ABOVE: Two soldiers guard a broached landing craft on the Moroccan coast in the early hours of the American invasion. Despite uncommonly calm seas, hundreds of landing craft and lighters were lost in Morocco and Algeria during the operation.

LEFT: Lieutenant Colonel William O. Darby, commander of the 1st Ranger Battalion, outside Arzew, Algeria. No one who met him ever doubted that he was born to lead other men in the dark of night.

BELOW: The 1st Ranger Battalion captures a French coastal gun at Arzew, east of Oran, in the early hours of November 8, 1942.

Two Ranger corporals, Robert Bevin and Earl Drost, both from Iowa, cover a French gun battery above Arzew harbor in Algeria on November 8.

Oran harbor. In Operation RESERVIST, the British cutters *Walney* and *Hartland* carried hundreds of American soldiers into the teeth of French defenses before dawn on November 8. The port entrance is visible in the upper center of this photograph, taken six months later.

LEFT: Major General Lloyd R. Fredendall, who later commanded the U.S. II Corps in Tunisia, pins a Purple Heart on correspondent Leo "Bill" Disher. The reporter survived twenty-five wounds—eleven from gunshots and fourteen from shell fragments—during Operation RESERVIST, and later composed a brilliant account of the debacle.

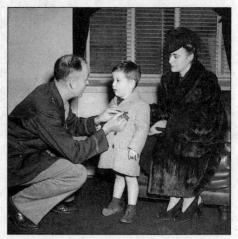

RIGHT: The widow and son of Lieutenant Colonel George F. Marshall receive his posthumous Distinguished Service Cross in a Pentagon ceremony. The senior American commander during Operation RESERVIST, Marshall was last seen on the bow of the British cutter *Walney*, throwing hand grenades at a French destroyer.

Burying U.S. soldiers killed in action in early December 1942. This temporary cemetery was at Les Andalouses, near Algiers.

The mouth of the Sebou River, opening onto the Atlantic, as seen from the north wall of the old fortress dubbed the Kasbah. On the road to Port Lyautey, seen passing beneath the fort, Colonel Demas T. Craw was killed in a French ambush. (*Collection of the author*)

After three days of shelling and dive bombing by U.S. Navy planes, the Kasbah lies in ruins. The U.S. Army, which suffered more than three hundred casualties in the attack on Mehdia and Port Lyautey, conceded that "the final assault had touches of *Beau Geste.*"

Brigadier General Lucian K. Truscott, Jr., commanded the attack force that invaded Mehdia in northern Morocco and later ran General Eisenhower's forward headquarters during the battle for Tunisia. Chesty and slightly stooped, he had protruding gray eyes, a moon face, and a voice as raspy as a wood file.

Admiral Jean Darlan (*left*), commander of the Vichy French armed forces, shares a cup of coffee in Algiers on November 22, 1942, with Lieutenant General Mark W. Clark after the formal signing of a controversial armistice between Allied and Vichy forces in North Africa. A photograph of Marshal Pétain looks over Clark's shoulder.

Darlan shaking hands with Major General Charles W. Ryder, commander of the U.S. 34th Infantry Division, during a ceremony in Algiers on December 1, 1942. Between them in the background is Brigadier General Lyman L. Lemnitzer, a staff officer who later became chairman of the U.S. Joint Chiefs of Staff.

Correspondent Ernie Pyle, slender as a thread at one hundred pounds and given to drink and melancholy, arrived in North Africa with a typewriter to educate America about the war. Here he is seen with wounded soldiers at a hospital near St. Cloud, Algeria, in early December 1942.

General Auguste Paul Noguès (*left*), the French resident-general of Morocco, and Major General George S. Patton, Jr., at a parade in Rabat after the armistice between Allied and Vichy forces. Noguès, a slippery equivocator known to the Allies as "No-Yes," had led French resistance to the American invasion in three days of bloody fighting.

Field Marshal Albert Kesselring was given a "free hand" by Hitler in repelling the Allied invasion of North Africa. Known as Smiling Albert for his toothy grin and unquenchable optimism, he had orchestrated the terror bombings of Warsaw, Coventry, and many cities in between.

Major General Jimmy Doolittle, commander of U.S. air forces in North Africa and winner of the Congressional Medal of Honor for his raid on Japan in April 1942. Seen here in a Spitfire cockpit before a reconnaissance flight from Algiers on December 21, 1942, Doolittle initially was disliked by Eisenhower, who also resented the amount of time he spent flying.

A few of the eight thousand mourners who filed past Admiral Darlan's bier on Christmas Day, 1942, a day after his assassination. "Not a tear was shed," one correspondent wrote. Darlan's naval cap is perched on the casket.

Picking through the wreckage of an American B-17 Flying Fortress destroyed in a Luftwaffe raid on an Algerian airfield, January 9, 1943. Costly German raids forced all B-17s westward to safer fields near Oran, which meant a twelve hundred–mile roundtrip bombing run to Tunis.

The 1st Ranger Battalion marching over hilly Algerian terrain in late January 1943, shortly before the raid against an Italian outpost at Sened Station in southern Tunisia.

An American tank crew from the 2nd Battalion of the 1st Armored Regiment, in Tunisia, February 1943. At more than ten feet tall, the M-3 General Lee "looked like a damned cathedral coming down the road," one tanker complained.

The Anglo-American combined chiefs of staff in the Anfa Hotel conference room outside Casablanca, January 1943. Visible from the left are the American chiefs: Admiral Ernest J. King, General George C. Marshall, and General H. H. "Hap" Arnold. On the far right is Field Marshall John Dill, the senior British officer in Washington, and then the British chiefs: Air Marshal Charles F. A. Portal; General Sir Alan Brooke, chief of the Imperial General Staff; Admiral Dudley Pound; and Vice Admiral Louis Mountbatten, commander of British combined operations.

President Roosevelt inspects U.S. troops during the Casablanca Conference, January 21, 1943. Lieutenant General Mark W. Clark is in the rear seat of the jeep, which is followed by Secret Service agents. "They are a bunch of cheap detectives," Patton complained of the agents, "always smelling of drink."

The handshake seen round the world: on January 24, 1943, at the end of the Casablanca Conference, General Henri Giraud (*left*) and General Charles de Gaulle, who detested each other, pose for the cameras at the insistence of Roosevelt, partly obscured between them, and to the amusement of Prime Minister Winston S. Churchill.

Correspondents and photographers gather on the lawn outside Villa Dar es Saada on January 24, 1943, to hear Roosevelt and Churchill discuss the Casablanca Conference, which had just ended. The president, to Churchill's surprise, has just announced that "unconditional surrender" by the Axis powers was the only acceptable way to end the war.

Regrettably, this decision by the British commander was not relayed to the U.S. 5th Field Artillery Battalion, which hurried toward the battlefield on November 28 with a dozen badly needed long-range howitzers and the conviction that Djedeïda belonged to the Allies. Luftwaffe pilots above Highway 50 dropped flares "so evenly spaced they looked like street lights," an American officer wrote. A command tent outside Tébourba reminded one battery commander of "an old Frederic Remington painting my father had of the Civil War, all done in black and gray, of tense, hard-faced officers poring over a map." There, at nine P.M., the gunners learned that German troops still held Djedeïda. But the British artillery chief, under whose command the Yanks now fell, insisted the town would capitulate by midnight. Lieutenant Colonel Warren C. Stout, commander of the 5th Field Artillery, was told to reconnoiter the terrain north of Djedeïda with an eye to placing his guns near the airfield.

At 9:30, Stout drove forward in a small convoy with four staff officers, three battery commanders, and ten enlisted men. His orders were clipped and precise: "Radio silence. Come forward on foot at all halts. This is our first mission under British command." A rising moon in the east drenched the olive groves with light. In a stand of trees beyond Point 186, a British sentry flagged them down with a warning: "Tank battle at the next turn. Bad show, sir." Moonlight glinted off Stout's spectacles and gave his face a greenish hue. He told his men to "move forward according to plan." A mile farther east the convoy halted again. Several charred General Lees burned south of the road. "It looks as if there's been a major change in the situation," a staff officer observed. Stout shook his head with the resignation of a man embracing his fate. "I have my orders," he said.

Less than a mile from Djedeïda, Stout told his battery commanders to wait in the olive trees while he scouted ahead with a driver and two staff officers. The dim shape of his command car melted into the night. Half a minute later, the distant tree line "erupted in blue-white sheets of flame," one of the battery commanders, Captain Joseph S. Frelinghuysen, later recalled. Yellow tracers converged on the road from both flanks. The wide-eyed officers heard the crack of an antitank gun, then silence. For forty-five minutes they waited, debating their course in voices pinched with anxiety, unable to raise Stout on the radio and unaware that in Tébourba, moments before the rest of the battalion was to start toward Djedeïda, the British had canceled the move on grounds that "the town was unsafe."

At midnight, three gallant, foolish captains agreed to press ahead to search for Colonel Stout. Each took a jeep with a driver and a machine-gunner. A fourth officer declined to follow. "I wish you luck," he said, "but I sure as hell disagree with you." Creeping into the tree line, the jeeps had nearly reached the wreckage of Stout's car when German gunners opened up again from both flanks.

"The world exploded in my face," Captain Frelinghuysen later wrote. "The air reeked with raw gasoline mixed with cordite and TNT." In less than a minute, the ambush was over. Several dozen German soldiers surrounded the jeeps. To Frelinghuysen, who had miraculously survived without injury, "their deep-flanged helmets and gray faces had a death's head aspect."

He and nine others were taken prisoner. Colonel Stout, his driver, and the two staff officers with him lay dead. The 5th Field Artillery had been stripped of its leaders before firing a single shell. The Germans also captured the 1st Armored Division's radio frequencies, as well as secret recognition signals and documents detailing the American order of battle.

Dawn on November 29 brought a renewed attempt by Evelegh to punch through to Djedeïda. The battered Northants again attacked past Point 186 with a dozen American tanks. German defenders yielded the high ground they had occupied the previous day, but when the American tankers rushed forward, an ambush of antitank guns set four General Lees aflame and scattered the rest. On the left the Northants' D Company took a ridge and disappeared; nothing more was seen of the unit until a few men strayed back an hour later. "Drag ass outta here," a tall American gunner hollered. "There's thirty German tanks comin' this way."

Not yet, but the point was taken. Bloody and bent, the Anglo-Americans fell back. The tank battalion had been reduced to twenty-five Lees, less than half strength, and the Northants were as undone as the Surreys had been two days earlier.

This Sunday—precisely three weeks after the TORCH landings began—marked the apogee of the Allied offensive for the next six months. For now, Tunis would come no closer than that mesmerizing white vision on the horizon. The attackers had been too few, too weak, too dispersed, too tardy. Now they were dispossessed of the initiative, which slipped like a turncoat across the battlefield from west to east. Churchill in London declared that Djedeïda had been captured. Soldiers who had failed to do just that guffawed at the BBC again, and the Tunisian theater edged into that inevitable condition of war in which anything might be believed, except what was uttered by persons in authority.

Captain Frelinghuysen and other artillerymen captured in the

Djedeïda ambush huddled in the back of a German armored car during the short ride into Tunis. Down the tree-lined avenues they rode, sniffing the rich odors of coal smoke and animal dung. "We had achieved General Eisenhower's objective," Frelinghuysen observed dryly, "of reaching Tunis as fast as possible."

At El Aouina airport, whence the captives were to be flown to prison camps in Italy, the Americans watched as Allied bombers briefly pummeled the field and flew away. At the all-clear signal, German soldiers heaved grappling hooks into a burning Junkers transport plane bombed moments after landing from Italy. Bulldozers dragged the wreckage off the runway. Landings resumed instantly, and Wehrmacht troops clattered down the aircraft ramps before the propellers stopped spinning. Only then did an ambulance pull up to the burning Junkers, and German rescue workers in asbestos suits begin pulling injured men from the wreckage.

Another captured officer turned to Frelinghuysen. "People who fight a war like that," he said, "will be hard to beat."

The southern prong of the First Army's drive on Tunis had been parried, but the northern thrust toward Bizerte still offered hope. After more than a week of little progress, Evelegh's 36th Brigade abruptly found itself racing eastward through the village of Sedjenane on November 27 and into the wild heath of the coastal uplands. At dawn on the twenty-eighth, the brigade was told to seize a crossroads ten miles west of Mateur by sunset; the order meant covering twenty-six miles on Route 7 at speeds unprecedented if not improvident.

Four thousand British troops gobbled a breakfast of bully beef and quickly broke camp. Led by the 8th Battalion of the Argyll and Sutherland Highlanders, they climbed through the morning on a road barely as wide as a single lorry and tortured with hairpin turns. The cork harvest had left black scars around the tree trunks; stacks of curing bark awaited transport to market. Women in magenta robes thrashed their laundry in trickling creeks, while children wearing filthy kaftans rode the rumps of spavined donkeys. Squalls blew in from the Mediterranean, thickening a mud the Argylls likened to "a mixture of putty and glue." Every few hundred yards, soldiers with shovels climbed down from their personnel carriers to scrape the wheel wells. Sappers exhumed a few mines planted by the retreating Germans. Despite such delays, the column had traveled fifteen miles by midday, pleasing the officers. Dotted with isolated crofts beneath a scudding sky, the countryside resembled the dramatic terrain at Inverness or Fort William. The Highlanders felt much at home.

Shortly before one P.M., the battalion pushed into a valley formed by two imposing hills on either side of Highway 7. On the left, Djebel el Azzag rose 1,300 feet. Olive trees covered the lower flanks, yielding at altitude to grasses through which the wind snaked like a thing alive. Lieutenant Colonel J. G. Mackellar, the Argylls' commander, christened this slope Green Hill. On the right, south of the road, Djebel el Ajred soared even higher, to 1,800 feet, its summit shingled with bare rock. This, Mackellar called Bald Hill. At the far end of the valley the hamlet of Jefna perched in the crotch between the hills where the narrow-gauge rail line vanished into a tunnel. It was there that British scouts spied a few figures in field gray scurry into foxholes. The hills seemed "no more menacing than those previously passed that day," an Argyll wrote, and the enemy troops appeared to be a small patrol of the sort seen all week.

Both presumptions were fatally wrong. Jefna and the adjacent hills had been meticulously prepared for battle with sheltered gun pits, interlocking fields of fire, and excellent camouflage. A German account called it "a Tunisian Verdun on a minor scale." The valley was defended by five Italian antitank guns and the 21st Parachute Engineer Battalion, commanded by Major Rudolf Witzig. Boyish and rosy-cheeked, with eyes set so deep he appeared to be squinting from the cavern of his skull, Witzig had fought on Crete, in Russia, and in France. His greatest exploit, for which Hitler had personally handed him the Knight's Cross, was the May 1940 assault on Eben Emael, a supposedly impregnable fortress vital to Belgian defenses. With several dozen new explosive devices called shaped charges, Witzig and seventy-seven men landed on the fort in ten gliders, and in twenty minutes routed the garrison of 800 defenders at a cost of twenty-six casualties. The fall of Eben Emael allowed German panzers to surge through a gap in the Belgian line, driving British and French forces toward Dunkirk. Now Witzig and his paratroops waited in ambush at Jefna and on the flanks of both hills.

The Argylls stopped for lunch. At 1:30 P.M., Colonel Mackellar, a chipper man with a dimpled chin, ordered A Company to push into the valley. Because of the stress on speed and on reaching the crossroads by dark, the Argylls sent no pickets up to the heights and ordered no reconnaissance scouts—precautions even the greenest subaltern should have taken. A few machine-gun bursts at suspected enemy positions failed to stir the disciplined Germans. The Argylls' A Company edged down the draw with eight armored Bren carriers on the road and dismounted infantry stumping through a plowed field on the left. Mackellar followed with his other company commanders.

The column had nearly reached Jefna when, on Witzig's signal, a solitary antitank round ripped into the lead carrier and the fusillade began. An Italian gun destroyed the last carrier, blocking retreat. Then machine-gun and mortar fire raked the column from west to east and back again, quickly demolishing the rest of the carriers and laying Argylls in bloody windrows. Within ten minutes, A Company was destroyed; only eight men would return to fight another day. Mackellar ordered his Y Company into the valley, where it was immediately pinned down. B Company then surged forward on the left with ambitions of cresting Green Hill, but it, too, was immobilized by fire, as was X Company after brief progress on the skirts of Bald Hill. With his entire battalion imperiled, Mackellar inched back down the road. There, in one of those winsome moments characteristic of British men-at-arms for centuries, his second-in-command whispered cheerfully, "Look, George, partridges!" A covey of seven birds fled into the brush.

Only darkness saved the Argylls from obliteration. Mackellar ordered his companies to rally half a mile back of the western mouth of the valley. Among the 150 casualties were three company commanders, shot respectively in the shoulder, chest, and thigh. A courageous battalion medical officer walked down Highway 7 with his stretcher bearers, calling into the gloom: "Is anyone there?" They brought back eight men, including a driver found in a carrier cab with both feet shot away. "If only I had even one foot, I could drive this damn thing out," he said, and died, faithful to his stripes.

The brigade regrouped for a day, then tried again with a two-battalion assault at dawn on November 30. Shouting and waving, the Royal West Kents reached the scalded peak of Bald Hill at a cost of 161 casualties, only to be driven off by Witzig's men, who had been reinforced during the lull. On Green Hill, a commando battalion failed even to reach the crest. Fighting was bitter, and some bayonets were thrust with such ferocity that they could not be pulled out again.

A British brigade of more than four thousand had been stopped by a force one-tenth its size. German casualties totaled fourteen killed, twenty wounded, and a man missing. Another high-water mark could now be chalked on Allied maps. For six months, the Jefna position would remain as impregnable in fact as Eben Emael had been in reputation.

Exhausted Tommies collapsed in their open bivouacs and slept on their arms in the streaming rain, slack-mouthed and undreaming. On Green Hill and Bald Hill, the scent of juniper and damp earth soon soured with rotting bodies; by spring they would be bleached clean, speaking bone to bone. Eight Bren carriers stood rusting on Highway 7 for half a year, spaced as evenly as kilometer posts. The 36th Brigade commander, described as a "gaunt and gangling figure who lacked joviality," was sent home for being too old and too tired. He was fifty-three. Given the dual setbacks at Djedeïda in the south and Jefna in the north, General Anderson authorized Evelegh to suspend his attack while the First Army tried to gather itself, again.

Word of the aborted offensive reached every Allied unit except those that needed the information most.

In a pretty moment of optimism during the first drive on Djedeïda, Evelegh conceived two flanking attacks intended to distract an enemy believed to be buckling. On the north coast, 500 seaborne British and American commandos would land near Bizerte on various missions of mayhem. South of Tunis, a paratrooper battalion was to overrun an airfield and shield the right wing of the Allied drive into the capital. Both forces set off in buoyant spirits, unaware that the offensive had been canceled and that the brigades they were relying on for reinforcement would be nowhere near.

The commandos departed at last light on November 30 from the mossy fortress at Tabarka, on the coast near the Algerian border. Six British and four American troops, each comprising fifty men—plus eight Algerian donkeys engaged to carry the mortars—filled thirteen landing craft. Recruited mostly from the Iowa and Minnesota men of the 34th Division, the American commandos had trained with their British mentors so long that they smoked Players, drank Twinings, and wore British battle dress like lads from Yorkshire or Chelsea.

"Never give the enemy a chance," the British *Handbook of Irregular Warfare* advised. "Every soldier must be a potential gangster." Major Jack A. Marshall, an American troop leader, later recalled, "Commando duty attracted malcontents. About half of my men had been court-martialed at least once. . . . Several had been busted more than once." The requirements for commandos included fitness, intelligence, the ability to swim, and immunity to seasickness.

Unfortunately none of these manly virtues inhered in the donkeys, which after sixty miles across choppy seas in a small boat were in no condition to walk, much less pack mortar tubes up the coastal hills. As the landing craft neared the beach at Sidi el Moudjad, the braying, biting, kicking, vomiting beasts were heaved over the side with commando curses so vivid that even the coxswains blushed. Three donkeys promptly sank; the rest somehow made shore, where they contributed nothing to the expedition.

Sixteen miles west of Bizerte, soaked to the armpits, the commandos headed inland at 3:15 A.M. on December 1. After being assigned sectors on the map in which to operate, the ten troops split up. Within minutes, they discovered what no map had disclosed: the hills were covered with heather so dense that one soldier likened himself to "an ant in a hairbrush." Only by dropping to all fours and nosing along trails made by wild goats could the men cover even a mile in an hour.

For three days, the commandos blundered along the north coast, waiting for an Allied juggernaut that never arrived. Tipped off by locals to the intruders, German troops reacted with swift fury. Two troops—one British and one American—were ambushed shortly after landing, and only five Americans escaped. A German officer reported to Tunis that the commandos "were decimated in a short fire fight. We took fifty-two prisoners." So impenetrable was the undergrowth that men simply knelt and fired by earshot, like Civil War soldiers in the Wilderness. Four commando teams raided a Bizerte airfield, destroying gasoline stocks and several parked aircraft; German soldiers newly arrived from Italy, still wearing their fine uniforms and singing as they counterattacked, drove them away. A troop captain who had edged to within four miles of downtown Bizerte was killed on the second afternoon; another was shot a day later. Unable to move his legs, he was carried on a stretcher rigged from two rifles and cotton rope. "Get the men away from this position," he urged, and then died. His soldiers buried him on a lonely ridge.

The captain's advice was finally heeded by Lieutenant Colonel Claire Trevor, the expedition commander, "a tall, Dracula-like figure with a bushy mustache" who "treated all men with equal contempt." The surviving commandos rendezvoused north of Garaet Ichkeul, a shallow salt lake outside Bizerte. "Failure of the British attack from the south left us in confusion," reported Jack Marshall, the American troop commander. "Radio silence could not be broken." The men were exhausted and reduced to emergency rations. Soldiers listening to a radio receiver heard the propagandist Axis Sally promise the annihilation of "renegade U.S. and British commandos" in northern Tunisia; more disturbing was her accurate recitation of the names of men captured or killed in the past three days. Colonel Trevor proposed a final night raid on Bizerte, but after heated debate his troop commanders balked. On December 4, the men turned west, walking at night along a track so faint they sometimes had to grope for it with their hands. Two days later the commandos closed within Allied lines. The raid had cost 134 men killed or captured, more than half of them American.

If the commando foray had been "essentially fruitless," in Major Marshall's phrase, the paratrooper mission south of Tunis was a foolish, wanton mistake. Five hundred and thirty British paratroopers, dropped from forty-four American transport planes, were to "spread alarm and despondency." Aerial reconnaissance, however, failed to disclose that the targeted German airfield had been abandoned, and no attempt was made to ring up sympathetic French farmers for intelligence even though the telephone system worked well. Nor could Anderson or Evelegh explain why an entire battalion should be risked on a target that could easily be bombed from the relative safety of 20,000 feet. "The fact of the matter was that the British army had no idea of how or when the new airborne capability should be used," the mission commander subsequently concluded.

That commander was Lieutenant Colonel John D. Frost, who two years later would win renown at the disastrous "bridge too far" in the Dutch town of Arnhem. "We were not the least worried," the tall, mustachioed Frost later wrote. "We imagined ourselves being *Primus in Carthago*, gloriously."

There was no glory, of course, no triumphant entry into Carthage at the head of the Allied legions. Parachuting twenty-five miles below Tunis on November 29, the battalion then headed northward with a few commandeered donkey carts—"looking like a fucking traveling circus rather than a parachute battalion," as one soldier later recalled. "There was a medieval look about us," another man wrote, "with helmets slung at saddle bow, the jerkin-look of our belted smocks, and my Sten slung over my back like a crossbow." Within hours, German panzers had cornered the paratroopers, who escaped one predicament only to fall into another and then another, each time losing more men to enemy fire. Tormented by thirst, Frost's men licked split cactus leaves and sucked rainwater from their uniforms as they tacked to the west for three days in search of the Allied line.

Down to less than a hundred rifle rounds among them, the surviving Tommies at noon on December 3 flagged down an American patrol eight miles from Medjez-el-Bab. "Dr. Livingston, I presume?" Frost asked a puzzled Yank. At five P.M., the 180 men still able to stand formed ranks and marched into Medjez. Two hundred and eighty-nine paratroopers were dead, wounded, or missing. More than half the battalion had been destroyed in what would be the last significant airborne mission in the North African campaign, a harrowing, heroic gesture of singular futility.

"Jerry Is Counterattacking!"

IN late November, Eisenhower and Clark made a two-day visit to what they stoutly referred to as "the front," although getting there did not even involve venturing into Tunisia. The expedition—Clark called it "a Boy Scout trip"—began badly on November 28, when the jeep leading the generals' armored Cadillac struck and killed a twelve-year-old Algerian boy who stepped into traffic. Regrets were issued, and the convoy drove on. Unable to find Anderson's headquarters before sunset, the group blundered about in the dark until the same star-crossed jeep skidded into a ditch, injuring five soldiers. Eisenhower and Clark spent the night with a bewildered French family in Guelma, forty miles south of Bône, then tracked down Anderson at first light. After several hours of earnest discussions in a farmhouse, the American generals piled back into the Cadillac and returned to Algiers. Miserably ill and wheezing like a man who had been gassed, Eisenhower fell into bed to run the war from his room at the Villa dar el Ouard.

He had much to think about. Foremost was the shocking news from the Toulon naval base, where seventy-seven French ships had been scuttled in one of the greatest acts of self-immolation in military history. In occupying Vichy France on November 11, German forces had stopped short of the base and, for more than two weeks, sought the fleet's voluntary submission. Darlan at the same time continued to urge his old rival, Admiral Jean de Laborde, to sail his fleet to North Africa and throw in his lot with the Allies. De Laborde temporized until German patience snapped. In the early hours of November 27, SS panzer troops stormed the Toulon base gates. De Laborde ordered signal blinkers on the yardarms to flash the fatal message: "Scuttle! Scuttle! Scuttle!"

French sailors opened the sea cocks, grenaded their boilers, and smashed all radios and navigation instruments. The intruders finally reached the fleet flagship at Jetty No. 6, where an interpreter on the wharf yelled in broken French: "Admiral, my commander asks you to give up your ship intact." An indignant de Laborde gestured to the deck settling beneath his feet and roared, "The ship is sunk!" Among the vessels lost were three battleships, seven cruisers, and thirty-two destroyers. Eisenhower characteristically saw the silver lining: at least the prize had not fallen into enemy hands.

Of greater concern to the commander-in-chief was the Tunisian front, which he better understood after viewing it, albeit from a distance of 120 miles. Eisenhower concurred in Anderson's decision to suspend the offensive, but he harbored doubts about his First Army commander.

He could look past Anderson's brooding reticence—that "queer thing, human nature," in the Scottish general's phrase. But Anderson's Caledonian pessimism cut against the American grain and contributed to the mood swings that so buffeted the Allied camp. Anderson "is apparently imbued with the will to win, but blows hot and cold by turns, in his estimates and resulting demands," Eisenhower wrote Marshall on November 30. Clark had been particularly offended by what he called "the Anderson setup." American troops, Clark urged, "should be withdrawn from his command and organized in a separate sector of the front under their own commander." For now, Eisenhower resisted such a blow to Allied unity. He was learning, as he would later write, that "nothing is more difficult in war than to adhere to a single strategic plan" and to resist the "constant temptation to desert the chosen line of action in favor of another one." To Marshall he added, "Everything is coordinated to the single objective of taking Tunisia. We are devoting everything to Anderson's support."

Some things about the war had become clearer, including Allied intelligence miscalculations. Before TORCH, planners had estimated that the Germans would have 515 warplanes available to help defend Tunisia; the actual number exceeded 850, plus nearly 700 transport planes. By contrast, Anglo-Americans in the forward areas had only two small British fields and, at Tébessa, fifty-four U.S. P-38s, of which only forty could actually fly. A new battlefield ditty, sung to the tune of "The White Cliffs of Dover," included this verse:

> There'll be Stukas over the vale of Tébourba
> Tomorrow when I'm having tea.
> There'll be Spitfires after, ten minutes after,
> When they're no bloody use to me.

To Eisenhower's surprise, American tanks and armored tactics also seemed wanting. U.S. Army doctrine held that tanks ought not fight other tanks, but should leave that job to specialized tank destroyers while armored formations tore through defenses and ripped up the enemy rear. Regulations had prohibited the development of tanks heavier than thirty tons, and until 1941 tank armor was constructed only to stop small-arms fire. Allied armor was simply overmatched. The inconsequential M-3 Stuart caused one American general to muse that "the only way to hurt a Kraut with a 37mm is to catch him and give him an enema with it"; the half-track mounted with a 75mm gun was already known as a "Purple Heart box." American tanks were so flammable they were dubbed Ronsons, after a popular cigarette lighter advertised with the slogan "They light every time." American armor crews, moreover, knew little about reconnaissance, worked poorly with the infantry, and showed an alarming propensity for blind charges, now known as "rat racing."

All of these issues required the commander-in-chief's urgent attention, as soon as he could rise from his sickbed. For the moment, he dictated a wheezy message to Marshall: "My immediate aim is to keep pushing hard, with a first intention of pinning the enemy back in the fortress of Bizerte and confining him so closely that the danger of a breakout or a heavy counter-offensive will be minimized."

Even as this pretty delusion flew to the office of the Army chief of staff in Washington, the "heavy counter-offensive" Eisenhower intended to forestall was already in motion. On the same day that he and Clark drove east from Algiers, Kesselring flew south from Rome. In Tunis, he upbraided Nehring for excessive caution and for the abandonment of Medjez-el-Bab, which he called "a definite change for the worse." Axis troops were pouring into Tunisia at a rate of a thousand a day, but aerial reconnaissance on November 29 counted 135 British and American tanks in Tunisia east of Béja. Soon the Allies would be too strong to unseat. After inspecting the Medjerda valley on the afternoon of the twenty-ninth, Kesselring issued orders at 5:45 P.M. that "every foot of ground must be defended to the utmost, even dying for it." The bridgehead must be widened, he added, to "play for time."

Nehring gave the task to the newly arrived commander of the 10th Panzer Division, Major General Wolfgang Fischer, who had been training in France after combat duty in Russia. "Attack the enemy troops in the vicinity of Tébourba," Nehring told Fischer, "and destroy them." Tanks rolled directly from the Bizerte quays to the front. Mules and horses pulled captured French 75s toward Djedeïda. German 88mm guns used for anti-aircraft protection were stripped from the airfields, to be used as antitank weapons in the west. Fischer scurried about the countryside in an armored car that served as his command post; his staff rode motorcycles. Quickly they fashioned four strike groups with sixty-four tanks and fourteen armored cars for a spoiling attack scheduled to open on December 1. Only thirty German soldiers remained in Tunis. Everything would be risked on this throw of the dice.

From decrypted German messages on Monday, November 30, Anderson learned that the Germans intended to take the offensive. At 4:52 on Tuesday morning, a "special priority signal" notified Allied commanders

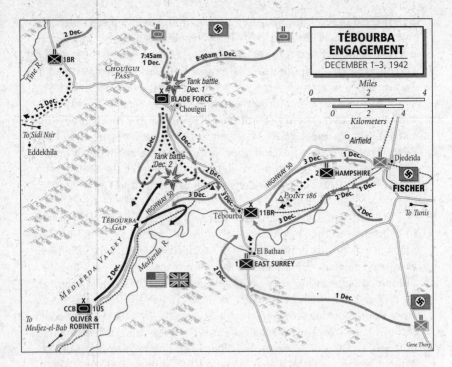

that the 10th Panzer Division had been ordered to attack Tébourba at dawn. If the warning ever reached frontline troops, it had little effect. At eight A.M., two V-shaped German formations personally led by Fischer slammed into the village of Chouïgui from the north and northeast. Blade Force—including John Waters's tank battalion—crumpled under the assault and fled south to the Medjerda valley.

"All around us men were running back down the road shouting, 'Jerry is counterattacking!'" a British private recalled. Fischer followed with the deliberation of a natural killer. From a hill to the west, the journalist A. D. Divine watched the approaching dust clouds—"incandescent, enormous, and beautiful"—and listened as the heavy throb of engines drew closer. Then the panzers lurched over a ridgeline and, "using the folding of the ground, raced from one dead area to another" as they spilled into the river valley.

Fischer's tanks had closed to within a few hundred yards of Highway 50 west of Tébourba when British artillery opened fire. Standing outside their tanks for a cigarette break, German crews cocked an ear at the tearing-silk sound of incoming shells; unhurried, they stubbed out their butts, remounted, and trundled off in search of defilade. At least for the moment, Fischer's attack from the north had been checked.

Two German infantry groups attacked Tébourba early Monday afternoon from the east and southeast. The first pushed out of Djedeïda only to be stopped by the 2nd Battalion of the Royal Hampshire Regiment, which had replaced the decimated Northants two days earlier. Fischer vented his disgust at the Wehrmacht infantry in a scathing message to Nehring: "Not the slightest interest existed, no aggressive spirit, no readiness for action. . . . It is impossible to fight successfully with such troops." Nor did the attack from the southeast succeed in capturing the stone Medjez bridge at El Bathan. There the East Surreys held their ground, with little help from the American 5th Field Artillery Battalion, whose officers now mostly lived in a German prison camp. Out of ammunition and unable to raise the British artillery commander for orders, the Americans retreated to Medjez-el-Bab without permission rather than risk the capture of their guns.

As darkness fell on December 1, the Allied hold on Tébourba was more precarious than Fischer's pique implied. German forces invested the town from three sides. If the panzers from the north severed Route 50, three Allied battalions around Tébourba would be cut off. To forestall such a disaster, Evelegh ordered forward 4,000 troops from Combat Command B (CCB) of the 1st Armored Division, the first sizable American force to reach the Tunisian front.

They came running. After two tedious weeks on the road from Oran, the CCB troops were truculent and confident, even though most of the division was still en route from Liverpool. For 700 miles across Algiers and into Tunisia, wherever British traffic controllers had posted road signs warning of soft shoulders—"Keep clear of the verges"—pranksters with black paint altered them to "Keep clear of the virgins." As reinforcements poured into Medjez-el-Bab, a British staff officer thrust his head into a command vehicle and exclaimed, "Thank God you've arrived!" Yes, reinforcements had arrived in strength, including the Americans: Germans and virgins beware.

The CCB commander was Brigadier General Lunsford E. Oliver, a fifty-three-year-old, Nebraska-born, West Point–trained engineer known as Bugs. His brigade—designated a "combat command" as part of an Army organizational brainstorm—comprised six battalions, two of which were already in northeast Tunisia as part of Evelegh's armored spearhead. Oliver put his headquarters in a red-roofed farmhouse five miles north of Medjez. John Deere machinery stood in the barnyard, and the irrigated fields were full of lemon, almond, and apricot trees. On the morning of December 2, he dispatched the commander of his 13th Armored Regiment, Colonel Paul McD. Robinett, with orders to organize Allied tank units around Tébourba and repulse the German counterattack.

Robinett was delighted to take over. Battlefield command would give him a chance to demonstrate his personal credo: "Always do whatever you can to keep your superior from making a mistake." At five feet four inches, with a cavalry strut and a cowcatcher chin, he was known alternately as Little Napoleon, Little Caesar, and Robbie. His Army career included membership on the Olympic equestrian team, study at the French cavalry school at Saumur, and service as a strategic planner and intelligence officer for George Marshall. He had long offered a dollar to any soldier who could outshoot him; only one man—a deadeye pistoleer from the 3rd Infantry—had ever collected. A prodigious cusser in his youth, Robinett now prided himself on having "learned to cleanse my mouth." A forty-eight-year-old bachelor from the Ozark foothills of Missouri, he was arrogant and querulous—"fussy like an old maid," a 1st Armored officer said. "He annoyed everyone." Within days he would annoy the British high command, which considered him "all talk and grouse." The dismissal sold him short: for all his niggling, he was a capable tactician who knew the art of war.

Robinett arrived on a ridgeline four miles west of Tébourba just in time to see the Americans butchered. Before General Fischer could resume his attack, thirty Stuart tanks had barreled forward without artillery support. German pilots saw them coming, and the attack was repulsed with heavy losses at a cost of only four panzers. Then a company of General Lees had been ordered by a battalion commander to make a frontal assault despite the bitter objections of the company commander. Following the rail line two miles west of Tébourba, the tanks charged at midday across open ground without reconnaissance against an enemy of uncertain strength.

Within twenty minutes, eight Lees stood in flames. So efficient were German antitank gunners that panzer crews stood in the open, pulling on their meerschaums without bothering to mount their own tanks. "They appeared to be watching the show," one lieutenant reported. German 88mm rounds—already known as "demoralizers"—zipped chest-high across the ground, leaving a trail of spinning dust devils. Survivors gathered the wounded and left the dead to burn. Apart from stirring British admiration—"the most intrepid chaps I ever saw," one Tommy said—the attack had accomplished nothing. Upon hearing the news, Bugs Oliver commented, "The boys stuck their necks into a noose."

Now the noose was cinched around Tébourba, as Robinett could see from his ridgetop command post. Plumes of oily smoke spiraled from the wrecked Lees a mile below and from the wrecked Stuarts farther north; the Germans would tally Allied thirty-four tanks and six armored cars destroyed that day, and 200 Anglo-Americans captured. Every few minutes another enemy gun jounced down the road from the north, then vanished into a haystack or a farm shed. Robinett counted at least twenty-five panzers, and many more no doubt remained hidden. The roar of new German machine guns—each MG 42 could spit 1,500 rounds a minute—carried up the ridge with a sound one soldier likened to "the hammers of the devil."

Robinett had seen enough. As John Waters and other commanders reported in, he realized that two of the three American tank battalions had been reduced to half strength. Blade Force apparently no longer existed. With timely, vigorous leadership—Robinett had himself in mind, of course—and the proper massing of armor, the Allies might well have blunted the German attack before it gained momentum. But this infernal rat racing and confused command structure had crippled First Army. Without sufficient airpower, the capture of Tunis remained a pipe dream. Robinett also concluded that Anderson, Evelegh, and now Oliver lingered too far in the rear to control the battlefield.

He scrambled down the hill for the careening drive through the olives back to Medjez. He would recommend an Allied retreat. Tébourba must be abandoned.

Oliver agreed, and so did the British; but not until the next day, after more men had been lost and the task had become harder. Tébourba was held by Lieutenant Colonel James Lee with nearly 700 Hampshires and 500 East Surreys. While American tanks were being roughly handled north of town on December 2, British infantrymen fought for their lives 2,000 yards west of Djedeïda. General Fischer himself led the German infantry, personally capturing fifteen soldiers, whom he drove to a Bizerte prison camp before returning to the front with two fresh companies of panzer grenadiers.

Fischer also deployed the Wehrmacht's latest secret weapon, sent by Hitler with a guarantee that it would be "decisive" in the Tunisian campaign. No one had ever seen a tank like the Mk VI Tiger: developed as a birthday present for the Führer the previous spring, it was a sixty-ton monster with an 88mm main gun and frontal armor four inches thick. The first Tiger to arrive at Bizerte seized up on the dock; the second broke down on the road west. But four others rumbled to Djedeïda under Captain Nikolai Baron von Nolde, who sported the gym shoes he always wore in combat. Crushing everything in their paths, at midmorning on December 2 the Tigers and several smaller tanks slammed into the British line.

From a range of twenty yards, a Tiger obliterated a platoon on Colonel Lee's left flank; one corporal ringed by Germans was last seen "swinging round and spraying them with a tommy gun." The panzers then wheeled south to rake the battalion headquarters at White Farm, killing six signalmen. On the British right, a company holding the north bank of the Medjerda counterattacked with bayonets, but by midday they, too, had been overrun. Seven men survived. German losses also were heavy. When Nolde stepped into the open to deliver an order to another captain, a British antitank round ripped away both of the baron's legs in their gym shoes; a sniper's bullet killed the second German captain. "The situation is very unpleasant," a Wehrmacht lieutenant wrote in his diary. "A wounded Tommy is lying fifty meters in front of us in the branches and leaves, but it is only possible to bring him in after dark. He has been shot through the lung." At midnight, the Hampshires pulled back two miles to form another line between the river and Point 186. Surreys anchored both flanks.

If Wednesday had been unpleasant, Thursday was worse. Marking their own lines with white flares, the Germans greeted the day with Stuka attacks and four hours of artillery and mortar fire. By noon they had outflanked and captured Point 186. "Throughout the morning extremely fierce and confused fighting took place," a Hampshire captain reported. Fischer's dispatch to Tunis concluded: "Indications are that the enemy is being softened and is beginning to yield."

A British major, H. W. Le Patourel, led a futile counterattack to retake the hill; last seen in heroic silhouette with a pistol and grenade, he would posthumously win the Victoria Cross only to reappear, wounded but alive, in an Italian prison hospital. At dusk on December 3, two German pincers met at the Tébourba train station to complete their double envelopment. Reduced to forty officers and 200 men, Lee formed a defensive square around the battalion command post. "It was Dunkirk all over again," a Surrey later recalled.

General Anderson had, in fact, commanded the Surreys at Dunkirk as a brigadier, and perturbations seized him, too. In a message to Evelegh he declared:

Commander is dissatisfied with the position 78th Division is getting itself into. It is not sufficient, indeed it is highly dangerous, for it to allow itself to become hemmed-in in a narrow sector round Tébourba. . . . To allow the enemy to entrench themselves on the Chouïgui ridge, overlooking Tébourba, would be very nearly fatal.

"More elbow room," Anderson added, "or he will have us out."

Too late. At seven P.M. Lee ordered his surviving men to fix bayonets and strip the dead for extra weapons. Disembodied German voices called for surrender— "We will treat you well." A Hampshire answered: "Bollocks!" Beneath the frosty brilliance of Very flares, the men pivoted to the west and formed a line with their right flank on the rail tracks. "Give it to them when you're close enough," Lee advised. Then, firing his Bren, he loosed a great roar—"Charge!"—and they plunged toward Tébourba. Two German panzers and an infantry company cut down the first screaming ranks before yielding to the surge. Tommies swept past the roofless church and into the broken town. Pausing long enough to form ranks they marched down the deserted main street counting cadence— "Left, right, left!"—only to discover that enemy troops had severed Highway 50 to the west. Tébourba had been abandoned at Evelegh's behest, but once again critical orders had failed to reach those who most needed to know them.

Even Colonel Lee was deflated. He ordered the men to cut their way out in small groups. Into the darkness they slipped in twos and threes. Some drowned in the Medjerda; others crawled along the railbed cinders beneath the vermilion arcs of machine-gun bullets. "Looking back to Tébourba," an officer later wrote, "we could see many fires and the streaks of tracer as the enemy tried to shoot up what survivors remained." The once handsome market town was now as ugly as an exit wound.

At noon on December 4, Fischer phoned his division headquarters. "Tébourba taken," he reported tersely. "Heavy losses inflicted on the enemy. Valuable booty." An American lieutenant who watched the Tommies drift into Medjez-el-Bab over the next couple of days reported to Robinett: "But for occasional curses and groans of the wounded, they came on in silence—damn well-trained." A reporter for *The Times* of London found the survivors "savagely angry with the enemy." "One night in Glasgow," a soldier proposed, "and then I'll go back to the bastards."

At a field hospital in the rear, dying men arrived so pale that the dirt on their foreheads stood out as vividly as Lenten ashes. Surgeons worked without pause through the night and the next day, donating their own blood for transfusions when stocks ran low. Henry Gardiner, the American major whose tankers had been fighting around Tébourba for a week, arrived with an arm full of shrapnel from the latest battle. He found a foul-smelling ward tent "illuminated by candlelight. The shadows were long and grotesque. Two men in adjoining cots were completely swathed in bandages except for one small hole" for their mouths. "From time to time they would feebly paw the air." One soldier borrowed a long cigarette holder, "and this enabled him to smoke, since the cigarette was kept just beyond the range of the gauze."

Several miles to the east, a German doctor called, "Next up!" from his table, then lopped off the leg of another ruined boy. A British prisoner working in an Axis surgery later described how "with delicate respect they placed the amputated limb among the severed members in the darkest corner."

The East Surreys had departed England six weeks earlier with 793 men; they returned to Medjez with 343. The Hampshires, even more undone, counted 194 survivors out of 689. Yet another foreign field would remain forever England. Among the casualties was Colonel Lee, who had been wounded and captured in the final debacle. Of 74 British field guns around Tébourba, 53 were lost. Fischer's tally of Allied losses during the three-day fight included 55 tanks, 300 other vehicles, and more than 1,000 prisoners. Reporter Philip Jordan wrote, "There is an air of uncertainty up here at advance H.Q. and staff officers half-laughingly—but only half—are wondering if we are going to be surrounded. . . . How rapidly the atmosphere changes."

Colonel Robinett, insufferably eager as always to preserve his superiors from their own folly, took it upon himself to inform George Marshall directly of Allied failings. Sitting in his command post on the heights west of Tébourba, he wrote the chief a confidential letter that would eventually find its way to an angry Eisenhower:

> The coordination of tank attacks with infantry and air attacks has been perfect on the German side. On our own it is yet to be achieved. . . . Men cannot stand the mental and physical strain of constant aerial bombings without feeling that all possible is being done to beat back the enemy air effort. . . . They know what they see, and at present there is little of our air to be seen.

Yet for all his bumptious gall, Robinett possessed an unsparing analytical mind. He recognized that he himself was culpable in the rout, having failed to organize a night counterattack that might have saved more Surreys, Hampshires, and Americans. He "had not foreseen the possibility and had no plan for such a contingency," he later admitted. "Frankly, I was too new at the game."

"My dear C-in-C," Anderson wrote Eisenhower on December 5, "the fighting on 3 December resulted in a nasty setback for us." With the thin satisfaction of a pessimist whose apprehensions have been confirmed, Sunshine catalogued his army's infirmities: "heavy dive bombing attacks"; "faulty use of the field artillery"; "faulty handling of the U.S. medium tanks."

"There was abroad a sense of careless dash and a failure to adopt proper action and tactics when faced by a serious assault by tanks, until too late," he added. "The affair at Chouïgui the day before with Blade Force should have shown the red light, but evidently did not do so." Some battalions now mustered fewer than 350 men, while the "enemy has already [reinforced] and can continue to reinforce far more rapidly than I can." Logistics remained spotty, with a "collection of wheezy French lorries" hauling supplies. In consequence the offensive must again be suspended for at least four days.

"I am very sorry," Anderson concluded, "but there it is."

Fischer and his 10th Panzer Division had no intention of waiting. Sensing a weak link in CCB, the Germans attacked along a one-mile front at seven o'clock on the cool, clear morning of December 6. Two waves of Stukas hammered the 1st Battalion of the 6th Armored Infantry Regiment, which had dug in three miles southeast of Tébourba, below the crest of Djebel el Guessa. Wehrmacht paratroopers worked up a saddle to gain the ridgeline, and in twenty-five minutes the American left flank had been turned. A confused, terrified .50-caliber gunner turned his weapon against one of his own platoons, and dead soldiers soon lay like sprats in a tin; a single man survived. Then panzers struck the American right, crushing soldiers in their foxholes and mortally wounding a company commander. He would die in a German ambulance and be buried in a shallow grave on the road to Tunis.

As the battalion commander, Lieutenant Colonel William B. Kern, struggled to save his unit from extermination, Battery C of the 27th Armored Field Artillery Battalion opened fire on twenty panzers at a range of just under a mile. This sally distracted the Germans, who now slewed on the gunners. Giving ground slowly, the artillerymen retreated into a rocky amphitheater with their half-track-mounted howitzers. The panzers came on, each tank trailed by a field-gray cloud of infantrymen on foot or motorcycle. At 10:50 A.M. the battery commander, Captain William H. Harrison, first radioed for help. His frantic pleas ended at 11:20 with this transmission:

> For Christ's sake, isn't there anything besides C Battery in this First Armored Division? We're putting up a helluva fight, but we can't hold out all day. Please, *please* send help!

Help had been ordered forward by General Oliver at eight A.M., but for unexplained reasons the 2nd Battalion of the 13th Armored Regiment failed to get word. Not until one P.M. did Lieutenant Colonel Hyman Bruss and his tanks cover the six miles along the Medjerda to Djebel el Guessa. Compounding tardiness with tomfoolery, Bruss split his force, conducted no reconnaissance, and ordered the tanks to "charge up the valley as quickly as possible." Reinforced with five new Shermans from Patton's units in Morocco, the General Lees arrived at flank speed with no inkling of where Colonel Kern's men were, much less the enemy. German gunners waited until the Shermans, five abreast, closed to a quarter mile.

Fifteen minutes later every Sherman and most of the General Lees stood in flames. "Shells were cutting through the wheat on either side of us," Lieutenant Philip G. Walker later wrote. "I walked from tank to tank trying to make them fire and retire. They seemed petrified. I cursed and insulted, climbing on tanks and shouting." An explosion killed a soldier in the turret beneath Walker's feet. Shell fragments peppered his arm, eyelid, and right temple. "I was swearing and crying from frustration and pain. Took a shot of morphine and felt better."

More American tanks blundered into the kill zone after giving German gunners time to reposition and reload. The disaster was complete. Wearing full-length sandwich boards painted with huge red crosses, Wehrmacht medics traipsed from hulk to flaming hulk, salvaging a few wounded. In the confusion, Kern's battalion had escaped destruction, but still suffered 219 casualties. All five Battery C howitzers were destroyed, the last at ranges of twenty yards or less, with thirty-nine casualties among the gunners including the valiant and now captured Captain Harrison. Eighteen tanks were lost. On Robinett's recommendation, Oliver sacked Colonel Bruss. His crippled battalion would go to Henry Gardiner, as soon as the major returned from the hospital.

Rain began that night and fell incessantly for three days. Cold, sodden soldiers wondered, as their fathers had in the Great War, whether the Germans could make it rain whenever they pleased. Although Fischer's

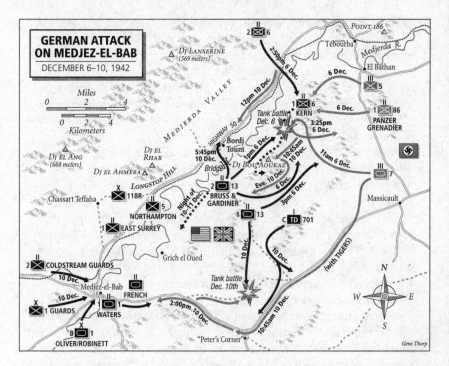

troops had also been stung, the galling defeat at Djebel el Guessa infected First Army with a despondency that spread at viral speed. Now known as Stuka Valley, the Medjerda glen seemed sinister, even demonic. German psychological operations spooked the men further, especially the tactic of firing all small arms at dusk and lofting flare after flare as if in prelude to an attack. The "total effect was in fact terrifying and this was a factor in the combat," the CCB intelligence officer noted.

Latrine rumors became virulent: the Germans had shot prisoners, used poison gas, enlisted Arab cannibals. More and more Arab looters and collaborators were shot or had their houses blown up by Allied vigilantes; rarely was there a legal process that did credit to Anglo-American jurisprudence. French troops hanged Arab bodies from balcony rails in Béja as a crude warning, and commandos burned an entire Arab village in retaliation for the alleged shooting of a French forester. Anxious soldiers exchanged stories of things they had seen, or at least heard about: of a bushwhacked sentry found with his eyeballs strung like beads; of a British soldier who had dared chat up an Arab woman and was found sliced into fleshy strips laid out to spell "Beware"; of a jeep driver who, decapitated by an 88mm shell, drove for another thirty feet, fifty feet, half a mile, clutching the steering wheel in a death grip. German panzers were reported "like an escaping murderer, at a score of points at once," one correspondent wrote. Infiltrating enemy tank crews were said to be master sculptors, capable of disguising a Mk IV as a Sherman with a few handfuls of mud. Soldiers collected good-luck amulets—shrapnel was especially popular, the view being that like repelled like—and every pocket became a potential reliquary.

"In an attack half the men on a firing line are in terror and the other half are unnerved," the British theorist J.F.C. Fuller had written. Some First Army troops confused smoke shells with billowing enemy parachutes; others betrayed their positions by trying to shoot down German flares. Disquiet seeped into the upper ranks as well. Evelegh had pulled back British and American troops another four miles closer to Medjez-el-Bab, but Oliver protested daily that CCB was too vulnerable. Anderson was ready to quit Stuka Valley altogether. He floated the idea in a "most secret" message to Eisenhower on December 8.

"Reason is necessity to rest and refit troops and make them ready to resume offensive," Anderson wrote. "Present positions are too exposed and widespread." Building a new line fifteen miles west of Medjez could "prove to be the wisest course," he suggested, although "I regret giving up Medjez-el-Bab." In a subsequent note late that night, Anderson told Eisenhower, "There are limits to human endurance." Lest the commander-in-chief miss the point, Anderson added in another message on December 9: "The spirit is willing but the flesh has reached its limit."

Even before Eisenhower's reply came back from Algiers, CCB was told to prepare to retreat toward Béja under Operation HAIRSPRING. Thirty minutes later, the retreat was canceled. Juin and Barré had learned of the British plan. The French generals were horrified. Did General Anderson not know the strategic value of Medjez? Had he not heard the wisdom of Hannibal—that Medjez was the key to the door? Throwing his left-handed salute, Juin stalked off to phone Giraud, who then hectored Eisenhower into countermanding the order.

A new plan emerged: the British 1st Guards Brigade would move up to occupy Medjez, while CCB and Evelegh's troops pulled back just west of the town to be, in Anderson's phrase, "reinforced, rested, reclothed, and refitted." The move was scheduled for the night of December 10.

Omens and auguries haunted the valley. Villagers with a few pathetic possessions bundled on their backs fled into the hills from farm hamlets near Djebel el Guessa. A drunk German deserter blundered into Allied lines with tales of grenadiers massing in the hollows. The rain stopped, but standing water drowned the trails. Every field became a quagmire. The air was heavy and unstirring.

At eight A.M. on December 10, General Oliver went forward to reconnoiter. Soon afterward, French pickets came pelting through the lines bellowing, *"Tank Boche! Tank Boche!"* Two panzer columns with an estimated total of sixty tanks advanced on either side of the Medjerda. By noon the enemy on Route 50 had been stopped by American tanks and a dense minefield near the village of Bordj Toum, ten miles downriver from Medjez-el-Bab. The parallel force on the south side of the river clumped through the mud to attack Colonel Kern's 1st Battalion, now retrenched midway between Tébourba and Medjez on the craggy heights of Djebel Bou Aoukaz, known as the Bou. Kern held, and the Bou remained in American hands.

But a greater threat loomed from the southeast. Fischer dispatched his 7th Panzer Regiment with artillery and thirty tanks on a bold flanking sweep to take Medjez from the rear. Through Massicault they rolled, Tigers among them, smashing ten of John Waters's remaining Stuarts and half-tracks. Waters retreated with his remnants through Medjez-el-Bab and across the Bailey bridge spanning the Medjerda. By early afternoon the enemy was at the gates, two miles from town, with a chance to bag the whole of Combat Command B. Only an intrepid French force of zouaves, *tirailleurs*, and artillerymen held them at bay.

Holding a poor map in his lap and a capricious radio microphone in his left hand, Robinett sat in a farmhouse three miles southwest of Medjez, trying to piece together a battle he could neither see nor hear. He had been unable to reach Oliver, and repeated pleas to Evelegh's headquarters for reinforcement by American Shermans went unanswered. Medjez appeared doomed, but at 1:30 P.M. Robinett ordered the 1st Battalion of his 13th Armored Regiment to attack due south from the Bou in an effort to catch the flanking Germans from behind.

It nearly worked. A company of Stuarts fell on seven surprised enemy armored scout cars and destroyed them with a smoking broadside at fifty yards. But then the panzers appeared—"the whole top of the high ground was alive with them," an American captain remarked—and the counterblow stopped in mid-career. Squirrel-gun rounds bounced off the panzer glacis as usual, and the wider German tracks provided more purchase in the mud. Outmaneuvered and outgunned, American commanders were reduced to aiming at the panzers' gun sights in a futile effort to blind them.

Nineteen Stuarts were lost, their crewmen machine-gunned as they climbed out of their stricken tanks. Two dozen surviving Yanks hid in a ravine, then scuttled north to swim the Medjerda. At 4:30 P.M., Robinett ordered all remaining American troops around the Bou to cross the one-lane bridge at Bordj Toum after dark and pull back to Medjez on Highway 50.

Moments after this order went out, Oliver returned to the command post, muddy and exhausted from a harrowing day spent dodging German patrols. Collapsing into a chair, he listened in anguish to Robinett's account of 1st Battalion's counterattack. His eyes brimmed with tears. "My God, why did you attack with the light tanks?" Oliver said. "You have ruined me!"

Robinett pulled himself to his full, unimposing height, jaw thrust out, gaze level and unblinking. "No, General," he answered. "I have saved you."

He had indeed, although salvation was ephemeral on the night of December 10. Medjez had been preserved for the moment, but more than three battalions of American troops remained at risk. Oliver chose not to venture down the valley again; bucking the traffic that would soon jam the road from Bordj Toum to Medjez seemed more than his frayed nerves could handle. Instead, the evacuation was left to the senior officer on the Bou, a forty-three-year-old West Pointer from Ohio, Lieutenant Colonel John R. McGinness. Oliver lay down on a straw mat pulled from an olive press and dozed off.

Rain was falling again, heavy as birdshot, as the long columns debouched from the ravines around the Bou. Blackout lights—cat's-eye slits—gleamed from the trucks and half-tracks inching toward the river and the macadam highway that would carry them to safety. A flare arced across the sky a mile to the northeast, hissing for half a minute before winking out. Somewhere in the dark near the Bordj Toum rail station, 300 German infantrymen and two dozen panzers had bivouacked after a day of brutal combat so close that artillery gunners fought with rifles as infantrymen. Somewhere also in the dark two platoons of British soldiers waited for the Americans; Evelegh had first pledged to hold the bridge until at least 10:30 P.M., then, under pleas from CCB, had extended the deadline to four A.M. and eventually to dawn.

A CCB infantry platoon crossed the narrow Bordj Toum bridge, followed by a company of General Lees. Tank tracks creaked across the plank deck only inches from the edge on both sides. As the Lees swung onto Highway 50, German voices sang out near the rail station. A few yellow muzzle flashes stabbed the darkness, followed by a machine gun's stutter. An officer ordered his infantrymen back toward the bridge for better cover until the gunfire could be sorted out.

But panic had been building for a week, fed by stories of headless drivers and eyeballs on strings. Another sputtering flare projected—as Robinett later observed—"new terrors into the minds of the weak." If minds were weak, legs remained strong: the cold light revealed silhouetted men sprinting back across the bridge, their eyes glazed with fear. "The Krauts! The Krauts!" Fear raced down the column like a lit fuze. A panting officer splashed through the mud to Colonel McGinness's jeep. His words tumbled out: Germans had broken through; no Brits could be seen; panzers were said to block the bridge already.

A casual stroll to the front of the column would have disproved it all. No breakthrough had occurred. The British, while modest in strength, were standing their ground not far from the bridge. The panzers were wrecks, knocked out in earlier fighting. The shots had been inconsequential.

But McGinness was not the man to vanquish bogeys. Ignoring reasoned pleas from his subordinates and taking counsel only of his fears, he issued the fateful order: "Turn the column around." The battalions would return to Medjez on an unpaved goat path along the south bank of the river.

The first few vehicles at the column's tail, now its head, managed to reverse course and plow west through bumper-deep mud. But each passing set of wheels and armored tracks churned the mire more. After a few hundred yards, vehicles began to bog down—first the tanks, then the half-tracks and guns and jeeps and trucks. Swearing, sweating soldiers stuffed bedrolls and ration cases beneath the wheels and tracks. They hacked at the mud with shovels and picks until their hands bled, while drivers gunned the engines and groped for traction in the muck. Clutches burned out. Axles and transmission rods broke. Tracks slipped from their bogey wheels. Gas tanks ran dry.

At 1:30 A.M. an aide shook Oliver awake. Smelling faintly of olive residue, the general read with disbelief the radio transmission from McGinness. The column had mired. Most vehicles were stuck, and McGinness had "ordered their abandonment and destruction." Oliver tried to raise the column by radio. No one answered.

The sopping dawn revealed a spectral, half-buried procession strung out for three miles along the swollen Medjerda. Thermite grenades had melted through engine blocks, leaving silver puddles of metal congealing in the mud. A few soldiers, ignoring the abandon-ship order, continued to rock their trucks back and forth in a stubborn search for grip. Some troops had tossed away their rifles and wandered into a boggy field; like dead men they slept where they fell, swaddled in mud. Hundreds of others staggered westward eight miles into Medjez, too weary even to watch for Stukas. Officers organized foraging parties to gather straw for the shivering troops.

McGinness stumbled in at noon, spattered and bedraggled. Although Patton, upon hearing of the debacle, proposed a firing squad, Oliver simply sacked him—making McGinness the second battalion commander from the 13th Armored Regiment relieved in three days. "I never felt so bad in my life," Oliver said. Eisenhower also considered firing Oliver, but would instead send him home for promotion and eventual division command. Robinett, promoted to brigadier general, soon succeeded him as CCB commander.

He would take over a ghost unit. The miring at Bordj Toum had cost eighteen tanks, forty-one guns, and 132 half-tracks and wheeled vehicles. Buried to the headlights, most of the carcasses were too deep for even the Germans to salvage. With more disbelief than anger, Anderson observed, "It was a crippling loss." In two weeks at the front, CCB had lost three-quarters of its tanks and howitzers, and comparable portions of half-tracks and trucks. Never having anticipated such grievous losses—especially not the destruction of 124 tanks and the complete wearing out of the rest—the Americans had no system to provide quick replacements. Many dismounted armor crews were reduced to traffic duty for weeks; one battalion had six tanks left. Two days after Bordj Toum, Anderson declared CCB no longer combat worthy.

It was humiliating, and nearly past imagining for the cocky young men who had rolled out of Oran and Algiers only a month before. A. D. Divine, the South African–born journalist who had spent many weeks with the Americans, shrewdly assessed their shortcomings:

> The faults were clear enough: the greatest of them was an initial lack of appreciation of the possibilities of the enemy; a certain indiscipline of mind; a tendency towards exaggeration. . . . Men used the skyline because the view was better from there. Men neglected camouflage because it might smack of overanxiety. Men failed to dig slit trenches because the work was hard.

Other deficiencies could hardly be blamed on green soldiers. Virtually no bazookas had been shipped to Tunisia; Patton had plenty in Morocco, a thousand miles from the front, where he was testing their penetrating power against live goats placed in a light tank. Another three weeks would pass before ordnance officers discovered that American tank crews had gone into combat with training ammunition rather than more explosive, more lethal armor-piercing rounds. And not only had German tanks, tactics, and airpower proved superior, so too had the enemy's field glasses, tank sights, smokeless powder, and machine guns.

Even more important, little cohesion obtained among Allied formations or even between American units. They had fought not as an army, but as a disjointed confederation. Neither leaders nor the led had yet proven themselves, despite flashes of competence and many acts of valor. British command had been as deficient as American command. In a crucial phase of the campaign, when every rifle squad counted—infantrymen were particularly valuable in seizing hilly redoubts and holding passes—whole battalions had been thrown away, beginning with those in Operations RESERVIST, TERMINAL, and VILLAIN, and extending through the destruction of the Argylls, the Hampshires, the Surreys, the commandos, Frost's paratroopers, and now McGinness's 2nd Battalion, which lost all but ten vehicles.

Eisenhower again chose to be optimistic. "We are having our troubles; so is the enemy," he wrote in a note to himself on December 10. "If we can make up our minds to endure more and go farther and work harder than he does . . . we can certainly win." History would reveal the correctness of his appraisal, but he could hardly foresee the pain implicit in the phrase "endure more and go farther." A month of fighting had ended, the first in what would be thirty months of pitched battle between the Allies and the Axis. All the players were now onstage. Although the combat in these initial weeks had been small scale—companies and battalions hurled against other companies and battalions—soon the bloody epic would embroil regiments, divisions, corps, and, eventually, armies.

There was yet time for the Allies to regroup, to punch through, to seize the whole of the African shore and avoid the deadlock of World War I trench warfare. But that time was short.

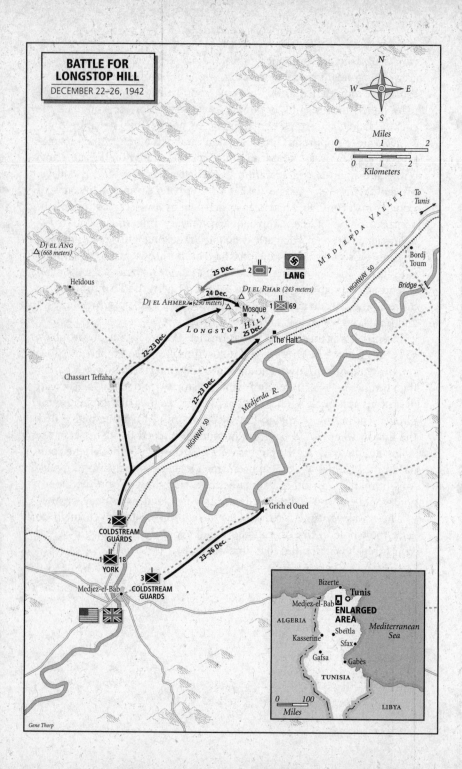

BATTLE FOR LONGSTOP HILL
DECEMBER 22–26, 1942

Miles
0   1   2
0   1   2
Kilometers

MEDJERDA VALLEY

To Tunis

Dj el Ang (668 meters)

Heïdous

Bordj Toum

25 Dec.   2 ▨ 7

LANG

HIGHWAY 50

Bridge

24 Dec.

Dj el Rhar (243 meters)

Dj el Ahmera (290 meters)   Mosque   1 ▨ 69

LONGSTOP HILL

22–23 Dec.

25 Dec.

"The Halt"

Chassart Teffaha

22–23 Dec.

HIGHWAY 50

Medjerda R.

Grich el Oued

2 ▨
COLDSTREAM GUARDS

1 ▨ 18
YORK

3 ▨
COLDSTREAM GUARDS

23–26 Dec.

Medjez-el-Bab

Gene Thorp

ENLARGED AREA

Bizerte

Tunis

Medjez-el-Bab

ALGERIA

Sbeïtla

Mediterranean Sea

Kasserine

Sfax

Gafsa   Gabès

TUNISIA

LIBYA

0   100
Miles

6. A Country of Defiles

Longstop

FOR eleven days in mid-December, both sides licked their wounds along the Medjerda valley. War clawed out a no-man's-land between Medjez-el-Bab and Bordj Toum, seven miles wide and crowded with shades. Patrols went out and patrols came back, or failed to. Sniper bullets whizzed about like small, vexing birds. Shells rustled overhead, and smoke drifted from the gun muzzles in stately gray hoops above poplar groves now smashed to splinters. Concussion ghosts rippled the pup tents, like pebbles in a pond. Anything that moved drew fire, but Arab farmers still scratched their fields with ancient plows, veering around the shell craters; sentries squinted from their dugouts and debated whether the furrows were shaped like an arrow to signal enemy pilots. "Hovering there on that borderland that divided the two hostile armies," a correspondent later wrote, "was like standing on a window ledge of a high building waiting to commit suicide."

Medjez was wrecked, but German guns continued to make the rubble dance—the British called it "their shelling programme." Whenever a dud landed, French soldiers murmured, *"Fabriqué à Paris!"* in tribute to saboteurs toiling among the forced laborers at home. Life moved underground. A Grenadier Guard battalion occupied the shaft of an abandoned lead mine, and "it was only after some days that they discovered a complete family of Arabs living in darkness at the far end." Foxholes and trenches—"coffin slits," to the Tommies—scarred the landscape like pox. British sappers proudly turned the eastern approaches to Medjez into "one bloody great mine."

By December, 180,000 American troops had arrived in northwest Africa. Yet fewer than 12,000 of them could be found at the Tunisian front, plus 20,000 British and 30,000 ill-equipped French (who now counted as 7,000 in the Allied calculus). Together they lived at the sharp end. Blackout rules for the long winter nights meant everyone turned in at six P.M. and rose at four A.M. Canned stew and biscuits were "donkey dung" and "armor plating." Soldiers softened their hardtack by dipping it into ersatz coffee brewed from pulverized dates, with the color and taste of ink. GI toilet paper was rough-hewn enough to be used for double-sided stationery, and troops caught up on their correspondence even as they battled ferocious dysentery.

"No shave, no bath, very little food, no beds, no liquor, no women, no fun, no nothing," an American soldier wrote his sister. A platoon leader in the 18th Infantry Regiment apologized for not sending Christmas presents; he had spent his last $50 on eyeglasses for nine of his men after Army stocks ran short. "Thanks for giving me the grandest gifts of all," added Lieutenant Robert M. Mullen, "faith and love." In three months he would be dead. Mail finally arrived for some troops—many had received nothing for two months or more—and Christmas packages often implied a certain homefront incomprehension of life in the combat zone: bathrobes, slippers, and phonograph records were particularly popular.

A redhead in a knit cap, slender as a thread at 100 pounds and given to drink and melancholy, showed up with a typewriter to educate America. Ernest Taylor Pyle had recently become a war correspondent after writing more than 2 million words as a roving reporter during the Depression. From Tunisia he wrote:

> There are none of the little things that make life normal back home. There are no chairs, lights, floors, or tables. There isn't any place to set anything, or any store to buy things. There are no newspapers, milk, beds, sheets, radiators, beer, ice cream, or hot water. A man just sort of exists. . . . The velvet is all gone from living.

The lull allowed Brits and Yanks to take each others' measure in circumstances other than abject bloodletting. Scruffy GIs noticed that no matter how foul the weather, the Tommies shaved every morning, religiously; in their trousers, collarless shirts, and broad suspenders, they reminded one American officer of "old-fashioned workingmen cleaning up on a Saturday night." Every British officers' mess seemed to have a Christmas goose fund, to which each man contributed 200 francs and extensive advice. Yanks soon adopted the expression "Good show!"— although always uttered sardonically. Because British sutlers provided many staples for both armies, the Americans at times fed on treacle pudding and oxtail stew with jointed bones. Steak-and-kidney pie in British "compo" rations inspired a field kitchen ditty:

We've eaten British compo,
We like the meat the best,
We know a cow has kidney,
But where in hell's the rest?

Across the killing fields, the Germans and Italians also took stock. Axis troop strength in the Tunisian bridgehead had reached 56,000, with 160 tanks, roughly equal to the Allies but with the added benefit of Luftwaffe air superiority and good defensive terrain. From the Mediterranean coast twenty miles west of Bizerte, the line extended just east of Medjez-el-Bab and then down the entire length of Tunisia. German soldiers held the northern sector, with the 10th Panzer Division shielding Tunis, and the Italian Superga Division held the south. Nowhere was the enclave deeper than forty miles, and no shoulder-to-shoulder manning of such a long front would have been possible even if Nehring had been so inclined.

General Nehring's success in blunting the Allied offensive failed to atone for the abandonment of Medjez and his persistent pessimism. Without warning, his replacement had arrived on December 8: Colonel-General Hans-Jürgen von Arnim, whom Hitler whisked from a corps command in Russia to take over the newly formed Fifth Panzer Army in Tunis. Nehring flew home. With a bird of prey's beaked nose and stern countenance, the fifty-three-year-old Arnim issued from a Prussian family that had been producing officers for the Fatherland since the fourteenth century. Having compiled a distinguished record in both the Great War and this one, he gave Kesselring a diligent, quick-thinking field commander. On December 13, Arnim announced that since Allied forces around Tébourba had been obliterated, the Fifth Panzer Army would go over to the defensive to await the next blow.

Defense meant fortifications, and fortifications required laborers. Sixty thousand Jews served nicely. Mostly artisans and tradesmen, Tunisian Jews were a tiny minority with a long pedigree; on the island of Djerba—said to be the original of Homer's Land of the Lotus Eaters—tradition held that the small Jewish community had arrived after the sack of Jerusalem by Nebuchadnezzar II in 586 B.C. Under a Vichy-inspired statute, Tunisian Jews had been banned from teaching, banking, and other professions since 1940. When the Axis invaded, life soured even more.

On November 23, German troops had arrested a number of Jews in Tunis, including the president of the Council of the Jewish Community. On December 9, the city's grand rabbi was ordered to provide overnight a list of 2,000 young Jews for a labor corps; when the rabbi requested a delay, the quota was increased to 3,000. All were to appear with tools. After only 120 workers showed up, Axis troops rampaged through the streets and synagogues in various Jewish quarters, seizing hostages. A secret OSS assessment reported: "Equipped with tools and food by the Jewish community, 3,600 laborers were finally drafted." Hundreds worked under Allied bombardment in Bizerte and at the Tunis airfield. Hundreds more dug defensive trenches for Major Witzig near Green and Bald Hills, and for General Fischer's men west of Tébourba. Others were press-ganged to tend the horses and mules that hauled ammunition.

In mid-December, the Council of the Jewish Community was told that as "allies of the Anglo-Saxons," Jews were expected to provide 20 million francs to cover bomb damage in Tunis. A rapacious Tunisian bank loaned the money at 8 percent interest, taking Jewish land and property as collateral. The Germans also began plundering Jewish gold, jewelry, and bank deposits. Meanwhile, the clang of picks and shovels could be heard in the rugged hills above the Medjerda valley.

Prodded by Eisenhower, Anderson sent word to Algiers that the Allied offensive would resume on the night of December 23–24. By then, enough supplies could be stockpiled at the Tunisian railhead for a week of hard fighting, and a full moon would light the way. Evelegh's 78th Division, with American help, would secure the left flank on the high ground above the Medjerda, while the British 6th Armoured Division, just arrived from Britain, blasted through to Tunis on the southern lip of the Medjerda valley.

"This means a most un-Christian Christmas, but perhaps this will be forgiven in view of all the facts," Anderson told the commander-in-chief. He agreed with Eisenhower that the Allies could not allow "passive acceptance of a strong Hun bridgehead," although he put the odds of seizing Tunis at "not more than 50–50, I think. But it is also certainly not an impossible task. Far from it. With good planning and execution, stout hearts and fair weather, we will do our utmost to gain success. If we deserve God's help, we will gain it."

At the same time, Anderson urged Eisenhower to keep his eye fixed on Tunis. Several schemes had floated from Allied Forces Headquarters for operations in southern Tunisia; none would contribute to the paramount objective of capturing the capital and severing the Axis lifeline to Italy. First Army was already "living hand to mouth, with reserves temporarily exhausted," Anderson warned, and he planned to throw 80 percent of his strength into the Christmas Eve offensive. "The essence of any plan," he advised Eisenhower, "must be to *concentrate maximum strength* at the chosen point of attack."

Before launching his offensive, Anderson first had to capture an annoying German outpost on an annoying Tunisian hill six miles down the Medjerda valley from Medjez-el-Bab. Djebel el Ahmera had been seized by Fischer's men after the debacle at Bordj Toum bridge. Two miles long and 800 feet high, the hogback ridge appeared to have been welded at a right angle onto the prevailing hill mass: it jutted into the valley within a few hundred yards of the river, creating a bottleneck at the gap where Highway 50 and the rail line to Tunis passed. The British named the hill Longstop, a cricket term.

Longstop offered omniscience. From its crest, nothing in the Medjerda valley could move undetected—not a rabbit, not a man, certainly not a tank. Scented with thyme, covered with heather and scrub juniper, the hill had a dark and forbidding mien even in sunlight. It was so rocky as to seem bony, with powdery soil that covered a climber as flour covers a miller. Although modest in height, Longstop was intricately complex, with a thousand secret folds and dips. Olive groves bearded the lower flanks; a few gum trees stood sentinel on the crest. One British officer considered the terrain "so foul, broken, blasted, and inhospitable that the Devil himself was surely the principal agent in its creation." Longstop exemplified why another officer called Tunisia "a country of defiles."

Had the British spent less time execrating the hill and more time studying it, subsequent events might have been different. For two critical errors preceded the attack by the 2nd Battalion of the Coldstream Guards. First, Allied intelligence believed the hill was held by a single German company with four to eight machine guns; in fact, enemy strength approached a battalion and included three companies from the 69th Panzer Grenadier Regiment commanded by Colonel Rudolf Lang, another sinewy veteran of Eben Emael.

Worse yet, the British had misread both ground and map. Longstop was actually two hills: Djebel el Ahmera dominated the main crest, separated by a ravine from the slightly lower Djebel el Rhar to the northeast. To capture one without the other was to capture neither. This second knoll was unseen by British reconnaissance, which was conducted by telescope at a distance of seven miles. Even so, Djebel el Rhar was plainly marked on Allied maps, and infantrymen had rambled across the hills for two weeks in November and early December. "We failed to realize its tactical importance," the Coldstreams later acknowledged. The error proved most unfortunate.

* * *

As required by the unwritten rules of military calamity, the initial attack went well. Nearly a week of fine weather had dried the ground and lifted spirits. The Coldstreams were keen to close with the enemy in their first fight since Dunkirk two and a half years earlier, and they tramped forward in bright moonlight that filtered through scudding clouds. At 11:15 P.M., on Tuesday, December 22, a barrage by sixteen British guns confirmed for the Germans the Allied assault that Luftwaffe reconnaissance had detected earlier. For fifteen minutes the artillery barked. Muzzle flashes reddened the olive leaves and white smoke spiraled up like spun moonbeams where the shells struck Longstop's crest. Then the cannonade lifted, and four Coldstream companies pushed off.

An undefended col on the northwest face of the hill fell immediately. The crest proved tougher. A sudden constellation of German flares was followed by machine-gun bursts and grenades that cascaded down the slope. Slipping on the scree and shooting from the hip, the Coldstreams scrambled toward the top even as a company commander and sergeant major fell dead. German pickets from the green 754th Infantry Regiment counterattacked with bayonets, then scuttled back through the heather with a few parting shots. Coldstreams followed—the terrain was so jumbled that some tried to navigate by stars glimpsed behind the thickening clouds—then dug in among the rocks. On the right flank of the hill, next to Highway 50, another Coldstream company seized a rail station known as the Halt, then promptly lost it to a German counterattack.

No matter: Coldstreams held the high ground, including the highest, at Point 290. All major objectives on Longstop had been taken in two hours. The Coldstream commander chose not to bring forward his reserve company or to reattack the Halt. Soon, as planned, an American battalion from Terry Allen's 1st Infantry Division would arrive to relieve the Coldstreams, who would get a day's rest in Medjez before joining the main attack down the valley.

Officers set their command post beside a small white mosque on Longstop's south face. Word arrived that the Yanks were making their way up the hill, slowly. Occasional mortar rounds gave way to silence broken only by the raspy whispers of British sergeants and the chink of entrenching tools in the bony ground. Djebel el Rhar squatted in the darkness, unseen and unsensed, 800 yards beyond Point 290. Rain began to fall.

An hour passed, then two. The moon set, the darkness deepened, the rain intensified. Finally, at three A.M. on December 23, the sound of the

American challenge and countersign carried up the hill in stage whispers: "Brooklyn?" "Dodgers." "Brooklyn?" "Dodgers." A Coldstream sergeant shushed the newcomers as they emerged from the gloom. Bulling through the waist-high heather, each GI was as wet as if he had fallen into a lake. The Americans, one Tommy complained, always seemed as noisy as "Blackpool beach on a summer Sunday afternoon."

The relief in combat of one battalion by another is difficult for kindred units in daylight and fine weather; between strangers of different nationalities at night in a downpour, the task is infinitely harder. The British guides posted to intercept the American companies either missed them completely or were uncertain where they should go. The commander of the 1st Battalion of the 18th Infantry Regiment, Lieutenant Colonel Robert H. York, lost his way near the Halt and was pinned down by enemy machine-gun fire. He eventually stumbled into the Coldstream command post near the white mosque, but with his staff officers still wandering the night and 800 of his infantrymen scattered across the hill. At 4:30 A.M., their duty done as they defined it, the Coldstreams decamped. Back through Medjez-el-Bab they hiked in squelching boots, sleepless and hungry. A thousand men sang "Good King Wenceslas" as they marched.

Dawn on Longstop revealed the full peril of the American battalion. Half the hogback remained in German hands. The Coldstreams had abandoned several forward positions before American troops arrived, and enemy soldiers quickly reoccupied them. Told by the British that only a few Wehrmacht troops remained to be mopped up, Colonel York learned from enemy prisoners that in fact an entire battalion of panzer grenadiers invested Longstop, with reinforcements coming. Flashes of field gray and an occasional coal-scuttle helmet could be glimpsed among the boulders to the east.

Then the enemy struck. "They just appeared out of nowhere," Captain Irving Yarock later recalled. Panzer grenadiers on the right flank near the Halt surrounded Company A, which in the night had become separated from the rest of 1st Battalion. Grenadiers built fire lanes with their mortar and machine-gun fire, paring away and destroying one piece of the company at a time before starting on another wedge. One American officer and thirteen enlisted men escaped death or capture.

Along the hill crest, German gunfire rattled "like a boy drumming a stick along an endless iron fence," wrote one chronicler. Brown mortar smoke foamed over ridges "leaping with light" from enemy artillery. Rock splinters sliced the eyes and noses of men unable to dig in more than a few inches. Shell fire severed telephone wire; messengers dispatched from the battalion command post simply vanished. "The mud would foul your rifle after a few clips, and you'd throw it down and crawl around hollering for another rifle," Sergeant Charles C. Perry of Company C later said. "There were extra rifles—by the dozens—after the first day and night of Longstop."

Pinned in a cactus patch a thousand yards behind his Company B, York pleaded for artillery counterfire. British gunners responded slowly, uncertain of the Yank positions and hampered by the incompatibility of British and American radios. A few shells finally detonated in delicate white puffs that reminded an observer of "a gigantic white chrysanthemum." Hardly deterred, the Germans by three P.M. had seized all positions held before the original Coldstream attack, including Point 290. By last light, the 1st Battalion had edged back into defensive positions on Longstop's west and south faces.

The Coldstreams had just finished a late breakfast on December 23 when the first call for help came from the Americans. Disbelief yielded to angry disgust. Couldn't the Yanks even hold a hill that had been gift-wrapped for them? Impenitent, the 18th Infantry commander, Colonel Frank Greer, appeared at the British command post near Medjez-el-Bab to warn that York's exhausted, depleted men were at risk of losing the hill altogether. There was no alternative: the only available reserves were the exhausted, depleted 2nd Coldstreams, who trudged back toward Longstop with what one man described as "the . . . bored indifference of a man who goes to work he does not love."

Not until dusk did the British vanguard reach the col below Longstop's northwest face. Rain had transformed the Medjerda valley into a vast brown sea too quaggy even for mules. A brace of bullocks was harnessed to pull a few guns forward. Wheeled vehicles bogged down 5,000 yards from the hill. Even tracked carriers could get no closer than Chassart Teffaha, a farm hamlet two miles away. There, in a damp cellar that stank like a slaughterhouse, surgeons worked by candlelight over boys beyond surgeoning; stretcher bearers dumped another load and headed back into the night without even bothering to fold stretchers stiff with blood. One in every four riflemen was converted into a coolie, shouldering heavy green ammunition boxes and crates of mortar rounds. Up the scree they trudged in the rain. Dead men slumped in their shallow trenches, some already green and bloated, others as alabaster and dignified as lunar princes. A Coldstream officer later in the war would speak for the living in describing "the release of fear, the release of the bird under the ribs" that every sane man felt on the slopes of Longstop Hill that night.

A lull persisted past dawn and into Thursday afternoon, December 24. Then Allied artillery opened again, with a barrage calculated to dump 750 shells in a hundred-yard square around Point 290. In the valley below, one witness wrote, "guns flashed from every cluster of trees. The shells shrieked through the rain and clouds." At five P.M., the Cold-streams attacked on a 1,200-yard front with modest help from American riflemen. Stalking and grenading, the troops swept across the ridgeline, bellowing at the enemy, who bellowed back. Those watching from below followed the Coldstreams' progress by the ascending rivulets of red trac-ers. Tiny figures vanished into hollows, then reappeared, climbing steadily. A white flare bright as a nativity star signaled the recapture of Point 290.

From that pinnacle, in the failing light, the Coldstreams at last saw Djebel el Rhar: half a mile across a deep gully. The final peak, a Cold-stream major lamented, "had never been appreciated." There was noth-ing for it but to press on. A gallant platoon skittered down the ravine and up the far slope to the crest. German defenders killed the officers and sergeants, and shredded the rest with mortar fire.

The German shelling paused briefly, then resumed with a cannonade that would continue until morning. Too much had been wagered to stop now. Eight British and American companies occupied all of Djebel el Ahmera and one flank of Djebel el Rhar, ground that had cost them more than five hundred casualties, including the Coldstream battalion commander and adjutant. German losses also had been heavy, but Arnim and Fischer drove to Colonel Lang's command post east of the hill to demand resistance to the last man: the Tunisian bridgehead itself was at stake. More Wehrmacht infantrymen, and tanks from the 7th Panzer Regiment, had been ordered forward.

At 7:15 P.M., General Evelegh reported to the British high command that Longstop was "in our possession, in most places." He was confi-dent—as only Santa Claus could be—that the rest of the hill would fall by Christmas morning.

The rain slowed to a drizzle, then stopped for the first time in two days. A monstrous, blood-orange moon drifted behind the breaking clouds. Backlit by desultory shell fire, British victualers darted up with tins of cold plum pudding for men who spooned it down behind their pathetic fieldstone parapets. Flares rose to define the dead. Another mor-tar barrage crumped across Point 290—German gunners had the range to the inch—and a Cockney voice shrieked, "Get this man out! Get this man out!" Medics hurried forward with stretchers rigged from rifles and phone-wire lashings.

A hunched figure in a trench coat scuttled from foxhole to foxhole, handing out razor blades. "Muddy Christmas," the American chaplain murmured. "Muddy Christmas."

Eisenhower had yet to set foot in Tunisia, but an acerbic message from Marshall on December 22 had sent him hurrying eastward:

> Delegate your international problems to your subordinates and give your complete attention to the battle in Tunisia.

At 6:15 A.M. on the twenty-third, unable to fly because of foul weather, Eisenhower climbed into the armored Cadillac and sped from Algiers in a five-vehicle convoy. Rain tattooed the highway blacktop, already slick with mud from trucks shuttling to the front. The commander-in-chief wore what he called his goop suit: overalls hiked to the armpits, with cuffs buttoned around his shoes; a heavy field jacket; and a knit cap with a hooded visor. He carried a zippered purse with his lucky coins, and a swagger stick that concealed a wicked dagger in the handle. Slumped in the rear seat with reading glasses perched on his nose, he flipped through a stack of reports or stared morosely at the sopping countryside.

He suspected that the Tunisian campaign had already stalemated. The thought grieved him: deadlock would be broken only by a static, protracted slugging match. That was precisely what the combined British and American chiefs had urged him to avoid in a message earlier in December: "Losses in the initial assault may be heavy but should be less than those that are bound to occur if you become involved in a long, drawn-out attrition battle." Did anyone in Washington or London really understand what a close-run thing the race for Tunis had been? In a note to Churchill, Eisenhower suggested that if the Allies had landed in Africa with an extra half-dozen transport companies—perhaps 600 additional trucks—"this battle could have been over."

He hardly bothered defending the deficiencies in his army and his own generalship. "The best way to describe our operations to date," he wrote his friend Major General Thomas Handy, ". . . is that they have violated every recognized principle of war, are in conflict with all operational and logistic methods laid down in textbooks, and will be condemned, in their entirety, by all Leavenworth and war college classes for the next twenty-five years."

Even so, he continued "praying steadily to all the Gods-of-War." Perhaps Anderson's new offensive would turn the tide. If not, he would have to consider the advice Churchill had offered in a private message on

December 16: "Engage and wear [the Germans] down, like Grant and the Confederates in 1864." Grant's casualties in 1864, as Eisenhower well knew, had exceeded 200,000. Was the prime minister ready for the Wilderness? Spotsylvania Courthouse? Cold Harbor?

As always, he contemplated the art of generalship through the lens of his own shortcomings. "Through all this I am learning many things," he wrote in a mid-December note to himself. One lesson was "that waiting for other people to produce is one of the hardest things a commander has to do." Even more important, "an orderly, logical mind [is] absolutely essential to success":

> The flashy, publicity-seeking type of adventurer can grab the headlines and be a hero in the eyes of the public, but he simply can't deliver the goods in high command. On the other hand, the slow, methodical, ritualistic person is absolutely valueless in a key position. There must be a fine balance. . . . To find a few persons of the kind that I have roughly described is the real job of the commander.

Shortly after noon, the convoy rolled into Constantine, ancient seat of Numidian kings. The city resembled a Tibetan lamasery, with great limestone walls—described by one visitor as "cubes of frozen moonlight"—and a thousand-foot gorge, the most dramatic in the Atlas Mountains. Constantine supposedly had withstood eighty sieges in antiquity, but it was helpless before the onslaught of Allied clerks, camp followers, and brass hats who were building a vast supply dump. Eisenhower stretched his legs, gaped at the ravine—the stench of tanneries wafted from the bottom—and drove on.

Even as they neared the Tunisian border, the worries of Algiers were hard to leave behind. His problems with the French persisted, despite Marshall's facile advice to "delegate your international problems." On December 17, General Giraud had again demanded supreme command in North Africa; he still refused to allow French soldiers to obey Anderson's orders, and without informing Eisenhower he kept shipping colonial troops to a front that could not sustain them. The logistics pipeline was so sclerotic that all rail loadings at ports and supply depots had been suspended for four days in mid-December. Inventories were hopelessly muddled, a problem compounded by the mingling of British and American units. To calculate ammunition needs, World War I data had been used until ordnance officers discovered that modern divisions, although comprising half the manpower of their Great War counterparts, used more than twice as many shells and bullets. And absurd problems continued to arise. A convoy had just arrived from Britain with a huge consignment of tent pegs—and no tents. One AFHQ message to Washington pleaded, "Stop sending stockings and nail polish." As if Eisenhower did not have enough worries, Marshall this very day had asked him to find a suitable meeting place in Morocco for Roosevelt, Churchill, and the Allied military brain trust. "Do *not* discuss any of this with British until clearance is given from here," the chief added.

Increasingly, the strain showed in the furrows on Eisenhower's broad brow and in the violet rings beneath his eyes. "It is easy for a man to be a newspaper hero one day and a bum the next," he wrote his son on December 20. One aide described him as "a caged tiger, snarling and clawing to get things done." Staff officers treated him with the hushed deference usually reserved for convalescents or lunatics. "I am very much worried over the terrific pressure being put on him more or less to do the impossible," Marshall had written the week before. Privately the chief wondered whether Eisenhower hesitated to drive his troops because a majority of casualties would necessarily be British. Roosevelt's impatience was less nuanced: "Why are they so slow?" he asked.

The strain on Eisenhower also revealed itself more sharply. When the American air chief, Major General James H. Doolittle, who had won the Medal of Honor for leading a retaliatory raid against Japan earlier in the year, tried to explain why Axis planes dominated the Tunisian battlefield, Eisenhower snapped, "Those are your troubles—go and cure them. Don't you think I've got a lot of troubles, too?" During a recent lunch at the Hôtel St. Georges, Eisenhower had asked a staff officer to call diners and waiters to attention. "Tell everybody here," he added, "that anyone who wants my job can damned well have it." On December 17—the day Giraud had demanded his job and a day after Churchill's Civil War analogy—he told his aide Harry Butcher, "Damned if I'm not about ready to quit. If I could just command a battalion and get into a bullet battle, it would all be so simple."

Following an overnight stop at Guelma, the motorcade pressed into Tunisia the next morning. At two P.M. on Thursday, December 24, after picking up General Anderson in Aïn Seymour, Eisenhower arrived at a remote farmhouse outside Souk el Khémis on the north bank of the Medjerda, twenty miles west of Béja. Soldiers peered through teeming rain from their haystack burrows. Harrows and a tractor had been conspicuously positioned to suggest agricultural rather than military purposes. Jeeps and the Cadillac were banned from the barnyard lest their tracks betray the headquarters of V Corps, formed earlier in the month under Anderson's subordinate, Lieutenant General Charles W. Allfrey, to coordinate the Allied advance on Tunis.

Eisenhower and Anderson clumped through mud ankle deep to find the farmhouse parlor crowded with wet, spattered officers. Robinett and his CCB battalion commanders had been invited for a pep talk, which Anderson now delivered in a grim monotone. ("He seemed greatly depressed," Robinett commented later.) Eisenhower appeared no happier. Groping for words, he offered neither censure nor praise for CCB's earlier travails, nor inspiration for battles yet to come. Robinett and his men filed past to shake hands with the generals, then vanished into the rain to wonder why their leaders seemed so gloomy.

The same melancholy prevailed for the next two hours, as Anderson and Allfrey spread a large map to review the battlefront for the commander-in-chief. Winter rains would worsen in January and February, Anderson said. Interrogated "natives" told him so. He had "ordered trials of moving various sizes of equipment" through the mud, but "nothing could be moved satisfactorily." No offensive was likely for at least six weeks, until the ground dried.

Eisenhower nodded. Earlier in the day, he had seen four soldiers futilely try to wrestle a motorcycle from the muck. There was no avoiding the obvious: a winter stalemate was at hand. Sensing the commander-in-chief's bitter disappointment, Anderson offered to resign. A successor, someone with a brighter outlook, might have more luck with the Germans and the French. Eisenhower dismissed the proposal.

Perhaps CCB could move south, Eisenhower suggested, where the weather was drier and the ground firmer. Robinett could be reunited with the rest of the 1st Armored Division, which would soon reach Tunisia. Anderson's earlier plea "to *concentrate maximum strength* at the chosen point of attack" was ignored, along with his Presbyterian musings about only the deserving earning God's help.

The current offensive would be postponed indefinitely—with the exception of the current attack on Longstop Hill. The hill must be captured to eliminate the German salient near Medjez. The First Army log noted: "Decision was made to defer advance on Tunis owing to weather." Eisenhower excused himself from the conference to dictate a message to London and Washington: "Due to continual rain there will be no hope of immediate attack on Tunis. May be possible later by methodical infantry advance. Am attempting to organize and maintain a force to operate aggressively on southern flank."

Rain drummed off the farmhouse roof. Soldiers wrapped themselves in their gas capes and burrowed deeper into the haystacks. The dark afternoon slid toward dusk, and a wet, cold, miserable Holy Night.

"They Shot the Little Son of a Bitch"

ALGIERS on Christmas Eve was festive if not quite spiritual. The white houses spilling down the hills gleamed beneath a mild winter sun. Palm fronds stirred in the sea breeze. French mothers bustled from shop to shop in search of toys and sweets for their children. The price of Algerian champagne—Mousse d'Islam—doubled during the morning. Outside the city, soldiers decorated scrawny evergreens with grenades, mess kits, and ammunition bandoliers. Security had relaxed to the point that a sentry's challenge was answered not with the daily countersign but rather with "It's us, you daft bugger!" Nipping from hidden casks of wine, troops washed their uniforms in gasoline and gave one another haircuts in preparation for midnight chapel services. A signalman in the 1st Division picked up a BBC broadcast of Bing Crosby singing "White Christmas"; men from the Fighting First huddled around the radio and wept. Those of a more cynical persuasion, tired of looking at veiled women, composed a parody: "I'm Dreaming of a White Mistress."

Morale officers in Algiers and Oran had worked hard to keep thousands of soldiers diverted after the initial weeks of an occupation characterized by "extremely bad discipline and long lines of soldiers at the houses of ill-fame." Activities now ranged from French-language classes to chaperoned mixers. ("I have seen cases where a Jewess or a girl of easy virtue was present, and the chaperones took all the girls home," an officer reported with evident approval.) Engineers emptied local swimming pools and converted them to basketball courts. Softball and volleyball leagues were organized—more than 20,000 softballs and 3,000 basketballs would be requisitioned for the war theater in the next ten months—although, owing to occasional sniping by disaffected Algerians, some games were said to be played "at high tension." Moviegoers in Algiers could see *Yankee Doodle Dandy* or *Mutiny on the Bounty,* and the Oran opera house was transformed into an American service club. The first variety show performance, scheduled for Christmas Eve, featured an act billed as the Robert Taileur Troupe and His Spanish Twins. None of the troupers spoke English, so a bilingual captain had agreed to stand on stage and translate the punch lines.

Alas, there would be no troupe, no Spanish Twins, no delayed guffaws at ribald jokes. Nor would there be midnight mass, brothel visits, or mixers with girls of virtue impeccable or otherwise. Admiral Darlan's hour had come round.

The Little Fellow, as Clark and Murphy called him, had become littler in Allied eyes. Not only was Darlan an international embarrassment, he had failed to lure the now-scuttled Toulon fleet into the Anglo-American camp. Many of his acts as high commissioner caused irritation if not outrage, including his demand for 200 Coldstream and Grenadier Guards to serve as an honor company for the annual celebration of Napoleon's victory at Austerlitz. Graffiti scrawled on the walls of Algiers demanded, "Death to the traitor Darlan!" His recent attempt to win over Allied correspondents with a champagne reception only intensified their vilification.

Darlan seemed weary of it all. "His small blue eyes looked incredibly sad," reporter John MacVane noted. At a luncheon for Allied officers on December 23, the admiral voiced interest in joining his son, who had nearly died of polio and was recuperating, at Roosevelt's invitation, in Warm Springs, Georgia. "I would like to turn this thing over to General Giraud," Darlan told Clark. "He likes it here and I don't." Clark pulled Murphy aside and said, "You know, the Little Fellow may do it." Murphy nodded. "Yes, he might." After lunch Darlan ushered Murphy into his office and confided, "There are four plots in existence to assassinate me."

One would suffice. At 2:30 P.M. on the twenty-fourth, the bells in the English chapel on Rue Michelet struck the half hour as a tall young man with a shock of dark hair stepped from a Peugeot sedan. Dressed in black and wearing a brown overcoat, he strolled to the south gate of the whitewashed Summer Palace, where he signed the registry under the name Morand. Asking to see Admiral Darlan on a personal matter, he was directed to a small anteroom in a Moorish arcade where the high commissioner kept his office. He lit a cigarette and waited on a threadbare couch.

Fernand Bonnier de la Chapelle was the son of a French journalist father and an Italian mother. An antifascist monarchist, he had returned to his native Algiers from metropolitan France after the German invasion of 1940 and had fallen in with a royalist cabal keen to transform the pretender to the French throne, the exiled count of Paris, into Henri

VIII. Precisely how the plot evolved, or why an attack on Darlan was expected to advance the cause of a French monarchy, would never be known. But shortly after three P.M. Bonnier heard the crunch of tires on the gravel drive in the garden outside. From his coat he pulled a Rubis 7.65mm revolver, which he had test-fired that morning at a nearby golf course after receiving absolution for his sins from a priest involved in the conspiracy.

Returning from lunch, Darlan walked slowly down the narrow corridor. He had spent another difficult morning with Murphy, who had pressed him on the prickly issues of political prisoners and restoring the rights of Algerian Jews. The spa in Warm Springs sounded ever more inviting.

As he opened the door to his study, the admiral heard the snick of a cocking pistol behind him. He whirled. Bonnier fired twice at point-blank range into his victim's face and abdomen. Darlan collapsed across the threshhold, eyes wide and unblinking, blood streaming from his mouth. An aide rushed in to seize the assassin by the throat, only to take a bullet in the thigh for his trouble. Bonnier bolted toward a window to escape through the palace grounds, but a spahi cavalryman dragged him back into the room. Another clubbed him with a chair, knocking away the pistol.

Half a mile away, at the Hôtel St. Georges, Clark was clearing his office desk before leaving for Christmas Eve dinner when he heard running feet in the hallway. The door flew open and Murphy burst into the office. "They shot the little son of a bitch!" he exclaimed. "He's on his way to the hospital."

A voluble mob of Frenchmen had already gathered in the waiting room when Clark and Murphy arrived at Maillot Hospital. Pushing through the crowd and into the surgical suite, the Americans found that the admiral had just been pronounced dead on the operating table. "The Little Fellow," Clark later said, "looked calm and quiet."

Clark handled bloodshed with his usual brisk efficiency. Affecting a turn-out-the-guard scowl, he doubled the pickets at the St. Georges and ordered all officers to arm themselves. Machine-gun posts were set up in the hotel gardens and outside other important Allied buildings. "The whole headquarters is in an uproar," one officer reported. Trucks jammed with armed soldiers carrying gas masks rumbled back and forth through the streets. Holy Night festivities were canceled, and in camps across Algeria troops were ordered to stand to in the mud with their weapons in the event of a "native uprising."

While Clark considered that Darlan's death was "like the lancing of a troublesome boil," he moved quickly to score propaganda points by implying Axis complicity in the murder, An official AFHQ statement declared, "Complete order reigns in Algiers notwithstanding general indignation caused by the event." The suggestion that the citizenry might riot in pique at Darlan's demise struck many as ludicrous. One correspondent observed that he had "never seen happier faces in Algiers."

Eisenhower had insisted that no Signal Corps officers accompany him eastward on his inspection tour and for hours after the shooting he remained beyond reach at the V Corps command post in Souk el Khemis, 400 miles away. The first frantic radio message went out from Algiers at four P.M., but a courier failed to find the commander-in-chief. A phone call from AFHQ to First Army headquarters at five P.M. obliquely reported that the "most serious thing has happened"; less than an hour later, another message disclosed that Darlan had met with an accident and that the AFHQ staff was "very anxious to get in touch with C-in-C who is in forward area. Get him to ring General Clark immediately." None of these dispatches reached Eisenhower in timely fashion.

A long afternoon of meetings stretched into a long evening. General Evelegh's message at 7:15 P.M. suggesting that Longstop Hill would fall by Christmas morning was the first good news Eisenhower had heard all day. At eleven P.M. he was just about to sit down with Anderson and Juin for a late Christmas Eve supper when a radio officer stumbled in with a message from Clark: "Have just returned from hospital. Darlan is dead."

The Cadillac pulled across the muddy barnyard to the farmhouse. Someone would erase the tracks before dawn. Just forty miles south, Eisenhower's boyhood hero, Hannibal, had been smashed at Zama by Scipio Africanus to close the Second Punic War in 202 B.C. He hoped to visit the site someday, to understand by walking the ground what had gone wrong for the Carthaginians. But not now. The trip back to Algiers would take thirty hours. Always a more subtle political thinker than Clark, Eisenhower expected that the assassination would carry unforeseen consequences. Darlan's death ended one problem, he mused aloud in the back of the car, but no doubt created many more.

General Evelegh's prediction proved all too accurate. Longstop Hill *did* fall on Christmas morning.

Badly reduced, with his main force driven into a vulnerable swale southeast of Djebel el Rhar, Colonel Lang chose to gamble. A small detachment would pin down the Anglo-Americans with frontal fire while a tank company looped around the hill to the north and grenadiers, led by Lang personally, swung along the south face above the Halt. The counterattack was set for first light on Friday, the twenty-fifth.

More than a hundred Algerian *tirailleurs* with horse-drawn caissons and not a syllable of English among them had reinforced the 18th Infantry's Company B during the night. With grunts and gestures, an American lieutenant positioned the company along the col on Longstop's northwest slope. For reasons unclear, artillery observers had left their posts on Longstop during the night and returned to the hamlet at Chassart Teffaha. An appalled officer ordered them back on the hill as the eastern sky lightened with Christmas dawn.

Too late. At seven A.M. the German attack opened, with shelling so intense an American officer described being simply "blasted all around." Colored signal rockets soared over Djebel el Rhar to launch the flank assaults. Ten panzers negotiated the mud north of the hill and slammed into the French. Lacking antitank weapons, the *tirailleurs* broke. From 800 yards, panzer volleys enfiladed the left flank of the American line on Djebel el Ahmera. Without artillery, the Yank reply was a paltry spatter of light mortar and rifle fire, along with a few grenades tossed more in defiance than as a military response. Unable to reach Colonel York at the battalion command post, the B Company commander announced darkly: "We will fight to the last man." His executive officer, Lieutenant Edward McGregor, found himself thinking obsessively of the Little Big Horn.

The right flank also crumpled under an assault from the Halt by Lang and his grenadiers. Enemy fire began falling in the rear, suggesting encirclement from both wings. American and British officers would each claim to have been left in the lurch by the unannounced withdrawal of their allies along various Longstop knobs. But without doubt, the Coldstreams holding forward positions at the crest of Djebel el Ahmera now faced annihilation.

At nine A.M., after learning that the Germans had once again captured Point 290, General Allfrey authorized Evelegh to abandon Longstop. Runners darted forward with orders to retreat. Platoons leapfrogged back to Chassart Teffaha for the rest of the morning, sowing mines to discourage German pursuit. The ammunition and medical supplies so laboriously hauled forward were now loaded on carts and carriers for the return to Medjez-el-Bab.

Rain fell again as the survivors trudged back, at the last pitch of exhaustion. As Christmas night descended, officers walked ahead of the jeeps and trucks waving white handkerchiefs for drivers to follow; some were so weary they veered off the road every few hundred yards anyway. Men sheltered in Chassart or Medjez and "clung together like sick kittens on a hot brick," in the phrase of the infantryman-turned-cartoonist Bill Mauldin. Christmas dinner consisted of British compo, supplemented with "a few scraggy chickens boiled in the muddy water of the Medjerda."

Word soon circulated of who was missing and who was known to be dead. As always after a fight, infantrymen checked to see if their closest buddies had survived before tabulating the battle's net worth. British casualties totaled 178 men; officers had been hit especially hard, and of a dozen Coldstream platoon sergeants on Longstop, one still stood. American losses were precisely twice as heavy: 9 officers and 347 enlisted men killed, wounded, or missing. With 40 percent of the 1st Battalion gone, the 18th Infantry levied replacements, picking random names from a regimental roster to prevent commanders from simply dumping their shirkers and misfits. Platoons voted on whether to keep Christmas packages addressed to the dead, or send them home unopened.

Longstop belonged to the Germans, who renamed it Weihnachts-hügel, Christmas Hill. There was much celebrating in the handsome house on the corner of Place de Pasteur in Tunis, where Arnim lived, with toasts of Tunisian red wine hoisted in honor of Lang's *Kämpfer;* sentries even set up a small Christmas tree, decorated with garlands and white candles. The revels came to a rude end at 10:30 P.M. on the twenty-sixth, when an American bomber, damaged by flak and losing altitude, jettisoned its 4,000-pound bomb before crashing on the western fringe of Tunis. The bomb detonated in the dense Arab neighborhood along Rue el Mekhtar, demolishing every house in a 16,000-square-foot area and killing eighty-four civilians.

Of the Tommies and Yanks who had held Longstop, some held it still: six months later, skeletons in moldering battle dress were found facing east on Point 290 with their kit intact, oddly unmolested by scavengers. Such constancy from the dead offered small comfort to the living; the enemy resumed his "shelling programme," ventilating parts of Medjez so completely that one man likened the town to "a cheese-grater." Upon hearing the bitter news about the destruction of his battalion on Longstop, Terry Allen reduced four days of fighting to four words: "Objective lost, mission unaccomplished."

"This Is the Hand of God"

F OR a man who had just lost a critical battle and spent thirty hours in the rear seat of a car, Eisenhower was in buoyant spirits on Christmas night. Stiff and pallid after the long drive, he soon revived upon reaching AFHQ headquarters at six P.M. A quick staff meeting; a quicker, handwritten sympathy note to Madame Darlan ("You have the consolation of knowing that he died in the service of his country and that we view his passing with regret"); and then it was off to Beetle Smith's mosaic-floored villa. Eisenhower ambled into the foyer singing in his fine deep voice:

> *God rest ye merry, gentlemen,*
> *Let nothing you dismay.*

With a small clique of officers, the commander-in-chief tucked into a Christmas feast of plum pudding, champagne, and roast turkey. Patton had sent from Casablanca two live birds, one of which survived the journey long enough to be stuffed, cooked, and devoured. So merry and undismayed did the gentlemen celebrate that at breakfast the next morning Harry Butcher requested only "a bowl of cold aspirin."

The investigation by French authorities into Darlan's murder was conducted with such brisk efficiency that a coffin was ordered for Bonnier de la Chapelle even before his trial began. A perfunctory prosecution followed by a perfunctory defense—"I have brought to justice a traitor," Bonnier proposed—led to the foreordained sentence of death from a secret military tribunal. The defendant seemed so certain of reprieve that he discussed with police interrogators his future career in diplomacy. "They will not shoot me. I have liberated France," he told a priest. "The bullets will be blank cartridges." At 7:45 A.M. on Saturday, December 26, Bonnier was trussed to a stake in the courtyard of a police barracks and executed even before he finished murmuring his prayers. "He was," Churchill later noted, "surprised to be shot."

As his assassin was being dispatched in squalid anonymity, Darlan was about to receive a funeral worthy of a North African potentate. On Christmas Day, 8,000 people had filed through Government House in downtown Algiers, where the admiral lay in state on a catafalque blanketed in floral wreaths, and guarded by spahis and *tirailleurs* with bared halberds. "Not a tear was shed," one correspondent insisted. Another witness claimed that General Giraud's eyes moistened. Perhaps it was in gratitude: he would now succeed Darlan as high commissioner.

Bereaved or otherwise, the genuflecting mourners—including the assassin's father—paid homage at the bier, which was crowned with the admiral's little billed cap. Then sailors in snowy white puttees hoisted the coffin into a black hearse and the cortège wove through the city to the Cathédrale St. Philippe.

As the funeral service began, at nine A.M. on Saturday, French officials packed the right side of the vast nave; on the left sat a large delegation of Allied officers who had been instructed to forgo "all sidearms and mourning badges."

The requiem mass droned on. At one point the principal mourners were supposed to walk to the bier, make the sign of the cross, and sprinkle the coffin with a cedar sprig dipped in holy water. Ever the Kansas Protestant, Eisenhower remained in his pew. Clearly enjoying the commander-in-chief's discomfiture at these papist rituals, his naval chief, Admiral Andrew B. Cunningham, punched him playfully in the shoulder. "Go ahead," Cunningham whispered.

"I can't do it."

Cunningham gestured with a tilt of his head. "Go ahead."

Eisenhower trudged up the aisle, declined to genuflect, then dunked the sprig and splattered "enough water to drown the man in the coffin," as Cunningham later recounted. The commander-in-chief stomped back to his seat, glowering, while his amused lieutenants could hardly contain their mirth.

It was over except for the final review. Mourners filed from the church to stand on the cathedral steps. Pulling on his white gloves and glancing at the sky as if expecting heavy weather, Eisenhower took his place next to Giraud. Then a French navy band played the "Marseillaise" at a somber tempo; a Signal Corps movie cameraman recorded the Allied officers holding their salutes amid sidelong glances and eye-darting worthy of a Borgia wedding. Eight sailors emerged from the church with the casket on their shoulders. Zouaves marched past on the Chemin du Thelmely, followed by spahis on white chargers, a British color guard, and a company from the 34th Division. An Army officer with a clipboard noted "the following errors, which should be avoided the next time: American company failed to fix bayonets before passing in review. Also, they failed to do 'eyes right.' Dispersal was not properly organized." Who the critiquing officer expected the corpse to be "the next time" was not recorded.

The procession wound down the Rue Michelet to the Summer Palace. Here, at the scene of the crime, the unlamented admiral would remain in a private chapel pending his burial in the Sailors' Cemetery. Now the

Little Fellow was carrion for every epitaph writer in Christendom. De Gaulle saw Darlan as a symptom of "the long disease of the state." Harold Macmillan, who had just arrived in Algiers as Churchill's political representative at AFHQ, was slightly more generous: "Once bought, he stayed bought."

But perhaps the shrewdest assessment came from David Hunt, a British intelligence officer. "The murder fell like a stone into a small pond and the ripples were only brief," Hunt wrote. "It was as if Darlan had never been."

Finger-pointing occupied Allied high councils for weeks after the offensive stalled on Longstop Hill. Anglo-American ties in particular showed signs of corrosion. A charming, divided-by-a-common-language mutual incomprehension had long characterized relations between the armies, as for example in the American aphorism that "Britain is a country where somebody is for ever lovingly bringing you a cup of tea up six flights of stairs." Or the story of the American head-quarters clerk who took a phone call from a British officer with such a thick accent that the Yank asked his officemates, "Is there anyone here who understands French?" Many an Englishman was appalled at the long initial "A" common in American pronunciation of the word "Arab"—"very ugly this, but done in the best circles," one reporter sniffed. Harold Macmillan, whose mother was from Indiana ("I am a Hoosier," he declared with perfect Oxbridge diction upon introducing himself to Eisenhower), advised a British officer: "You will find the Americans much as the Greeks found the Romans—great big vulgar, bustling people, more vigorous than we are and also more idle, with more unspoiled virtues, but also more corrupt. We must run AFHQ as the Greeks ran the operations of the Emperor Claudius."

Yet a harsher, toxic tone now seeped into the alliance. Britain had long benefited from American bounty, and only indebtedness breeds contempt quicker than familiarity. British Army references to the Americans as "our Italians" could be heard for the first time; a British correspondent voiced the widespread view that "the Americans were frivolous about the war—gifted amateurs." A senior British general told a colleague that he considered the Yanks "crashing bores. Their hospitality and generosity were boundless, [but] their business efficiency and hustle, pure baloney." For their part, the Americans coined another bromide: "The British cope, we fix."

Longstop—the first protracted, cheek-by-jowl infantry combat shared by the cousins—intensified the enmity. A 1st Guards Brigade after-action account of the battle excoriated the 18th Infantry:

> The plain facts are that the Americans did not retain possession of the key points, and did not really make a major effort to get them back. . . . I have nothing whatever to say against the Americans myself, except that they were unfitted and unprepared for the task they were asked to perform, which would, in fact, have been difficult for any battalion.

To Major General Terry Allen, that American Hotspur, those were fighting words. Since the capture of Oran six weeks earlier, Allen had impatiently waited in an Algerian bivouac with his 1st Division, watching from afar as the British struggled in Tunisia. He had put his affairs in order, preparing himself for whatever ordeal lay ahead.

"Please always remember that I love you more than anyone has ever loved anyone," he wrote to his wife, Mary Fran. As if to shed the skin of a previous life, he burned various personal records, including the July 30 letter in which Marshall had warned Allen to "be on your guard" against excessive drinking. (Allen dismissed such "ridiculous allegations made against my personal habits.") By incinerating "all that stuff," Allen told Mary Fran, he hoped to purge all "rancor or ill-will in my mind or in my heart." The little bonfire provided a rite of purification; only the enemy deserved his malice. As Ernie Pyle observed, "He hated Germans and Italians like vermin."

Yet as the weeks passed he had grown incredulous, for the Big Red One remained idle while Anderson built a logistical network that could support more troops at the front. Allen and Ted Roosevelt continued to train their men hard, but garrison life suited the Fighting First no better than it did its commander. Clutching his zippered leather valise, on which he had written "Hands off! Please return" three times in blue ink, Allen swept into AFHQ headquarters in Algiers. "Is this a private war," he was said to have demanded, his perforated cheeks hissing with indignation, "or can anybody get in?"

Frustration turned to outrage as pieces of the division were shaved off and shipped east. First the 5th Field Artillery had been sent to the British at Tébourba, where most of the battalion's officers were promptly captured. Then a battalion from the 26th Infantry was dispatched to southern Tunisia. Allen believed that "infantry, like whiskey, loses potency when diluted"; moreover, fragmenting the division undermined morale.

Men did not risk their lives in battle for cause or country, Allen insisted, but to keep faith with their buddies. "A man fights to help the man next to him, just as a company fights to keep pace with its flanks," he insisted. "Things have to be that simple."

The last straw had been the dispatch of his 18th Infantry—one-third of the Big Red One's infantry strength—and the subsequent mauling of the regiment's 1st Battalion on Longstop. Grieving for his dead men and furious at the British slur against them, Allen had no intention of ignoring the charge that his troops were "unfitted and unprepared." He ordered the division intelligence officer to investigate the 18th Infantry's performance during Longstop. Predictably, the subsequent account painted a far different picture, of British malfeasance as well as American failings. British commanders had "completely misused" York's battalion, the investigation concluded. Allen stuffed the report in his valise and set off for British V Corps headquarters in Tunisia.

General Allfrey read the paper over breakfast while Allen sucked on a cigarette, eyes narrowed against the smoke.

"I can't understand the rumors that I hear from Beetle Smith and General Eisenhower of the Americans being incompetent soldiers," Allen said when Allfrey finished. "Particularly the reports from the higher echelons of command in your army."

The blood had drained from Allfrey's face. "I have no apologies," he said with a shrug. "I haven't heard anything like this from the commander of the Guards brigade or the division commander." He gestured with the sheaf of papers in his hand. "What are you going to do with this?"

Allen kept his gaze steady, then reached across the table, took the report from Allfrey, and tore it in half. "I hope this will be a lesson to the British high command on how to deal with the Americans," he said. "I am not going to cause an international incident over this, but I expect that if I get any British troops under my command, I'll give them a lot better treatment than you have given my men." He saluted and walked out.

If not precisely gracious, the gesture was generous. Allen had averted a row and cauterized an ugly wound. But many more such flourishes would be necessary before the war approached the Allied ideal of a righteous crusade in which good men dared to trust one another.

The bottom of the year had come, and with it the nadir of Allied fortunes in Africa. The abandonment of the drive on Tunis "has been the severest disappointment I have suffered to date," Eisenhower confessed in a cable to the combined chiefs on the twenty-sixth. His original orders from London and Washington had directed him to carry the TORCH offensive "to the east through Libya against the rear of the Axis forces in the Western Desert." In this he had failed, and no bowl of cold aspirin would set it right.

There would be no trapping of Rommel's rump army in Libya between Anderson's First Army and Bernard Montgomery's Eighth Army, now lumbering westward out of Egypt. Rather than crushing Axis forces in the jaws of a vise, the failed Allied strategy gave interior lines to the enemy and all but guaranteed that four armies—Anderson and Montgomery, Arnim and Rommel—would slug it out in a campaign of attrition not unlike that on the Western Front a quarter century before.

An enormous siege loomed, and perspicacious strategists could begin to see that a fast, mobile campaign of maneuver would never come easily against Fortress Europe. An armed *Gefreiter* dug into a hillside was harder to remove than an impacted molar. Someone with perfect prescience might have seen that failure at the gates of Tunis had cascading consequences: delaying the invasion of the Italian boot by several months, preventing Allied armies from breaching the Gustav Line south of Rome until 1944, and extending the Italian campaign until the end of the war. But all that lay in the future, and was impossible to know.

For now, there were deficiencies to address. The tactical shortcomings of the U.S. Army had been all too evident, and they were meticulously catalogued by observers dispatched from the War Department. One report declared:

> The German army makes war better than we are now making it. The prevailing attitude is that the North African operation is just another maneuver with live ammunition. The enemy is regarded as the visiting team, and this is *not* a major game. Even units suffering heavy casualties did not evince hatred of the enemy. . . . Both officers and men are psychologically unprepared for war.

In another assessment, a colonel concluded, "More than discipline, I believe, [is] the lack of valor, the desire to kill or be killed; the will to fight is missing." A major general indicted junior officers in particular for "not leading their men well, which is evidenced by the comparatively large proportion of casualties among field officers who have to supply the impetus to their juniors to move forward."

All this was terribly true, but subtle changes could be sensed in the Americans. They were learning fieldcraft: how to keep off ridgelines, how to camouflage slit trenches, how to flush German crews from their tanks with white phosphorus smoke sucked into the engines. At first, few had known what many now knew: that battle is incessant noise, confusion, danger, and misery. Ernie Pyle was right: the velvet *was* all gone from living. They had seen things no man should see: incineration; evisceration; the soldier, killed by a booby trap, whose face resembled the "cracked porcelain surface of an old vase—thousands of small splits from the concussion."

They were becoming hard-bitten. They were wary of excessively gung-ho leaders—known as "questers for glory"—but appreciative of those who remained calm and tactically alert. They had learned that combat was slower than expected, a choreography of feint, thrust, withdrawal, and parry; that the battlefield often seemed empty and lonely; that death was ubiquitous, a fifth element added to air, fire, water, and earth. True, they did not hate yet; but they were developing the capacity for hatred, which required a nihilistic core of resignation and rage. C. Russ Martin, a sergeant in the 1st Division, hinted at this upon hearing of the death of his twin brother in North Africa: "Twins, we feel for one another, and the minute he got killed, I knew it, a sensation and a kind of relief from worrying about him. I didn't have to worry about him anymore."

In the wake of Longstop, another weary general sat down to explain himself. Marked "personal and most secret," Anderson's lengthy Christmas Day letter to Alan Brooke was indeed both. "Things have not gone well and all my plans have had to be scrapped," Anderson wrote. "I am very disappointed, as I am convinced we had an excellent chance of smashing our way into Tunis with my concentrated force, the Boche being rather widely spread." But he and Eisenhower had agreed "to bow to *force majeure*. . . . This is the hand of God."

He flicked through other campaign issues: Eisenhower seemed determined to shift the battle to southern Tunisia; the Americans had chosen not to give the British the remaining Sherman and Lee tanks from CCB; Darlan's murder was probably "for the best," although to strengthen Giraud further by making him commander-in-chief "would be disastrous. The man lives in the clouds."

But Anderson's great theme was the manifestation of the divine in this muddy, embattled world. He returned to that motif as he finished his dispatch. "I feel deflated and disappointed, but it is no use getting depressed. It would be too easy if we all attempted everything and succeeded.

"The Almighty," he added, "is much too wise to spoil us mortals that way."

Part Three

7. CASABLANCA

The Ice-Cream Front

AT 10:30 P.M. on Saturday, January 9, 1943, the presidential limousine rolled through the White House gates and turned south past the rime-glazed Ellipse and the Washington Monument. Only four blocks from the executive mansion, the car veered down a guarded ramp on the east side of Fourteenth Street and vanished beneath the Bureau of Engraving and Printing. The new presidential rail coach, *Ferdinand Magellan*, stood on a secret spur built two months earlier to allow secure shipments of newly printed paper money from the government presses overhead. Secret Service agents opened the limousine door and carried the president half a dozen steps to the railcar, gently setting him into an armless wheelchair. Gray and haggard from another war winter in Washington, Roosevelt nevertheless grinned broadly as he slipped a cigarette into his holder. The great adventure had begun.

A few final items were hoisted onto the train, including gas masks and a rack of M-1 carbines. To avoid suspicious piles of luggage at the White House, agents had picked up the suitcases of the president's thirty traveling companions at their houses. The porters and waiters who normally staffed the presidential train had been replaced by Filipino mess stewards from the White House yacht. Custom built by the Pullman Company, the *Ferdinand Magellan* was a plush, wheeled fortress with window glass three inches thick and an armored rear door that weighed nearly a ton. The main coach had four staterooms, an observation deck, a dining room that could seat twelve, and a galley stocked with presidential favorites, including wild duck, terrapin, and vintage wines. A baggage car behind the engine had been converted into a communications center, with a coding machine and four transmitters powered by a pair of 10,000-watt generators capable of lighting a small town.

With a steamy sigh, the train lurched forward, clacking past the Navy Yard. Not until half an hour before departure had the engineer been given any inkling of their destination: feint north into Maryland as if heading to the Roosevelt home in Hyde Park, New York, he was told, then turn around on a siding at Fort Meade and head south. So secret was the trip that Roosevelt was listed on the manifest simply as "Register Number 1." His press secretary would learn that the president had left Washington only upon walking into his empty bedroom on Monday morning.

Roosevelt loved maps, and he had pored over the route of their five-day journey: twenty-seven hours by train to Miami—the stewards would burn incense to mask the ripening odor of dirty laundry—then a chartered Pan Am flying boat to Trinidad, followed by another flight to Brazil, and a third leg 2,000 miles across the Atlantic, to Gambia on Africa's west coast. Navy ships had been posted along the water route in case the plane went down; all crews were sworn to secrecy. This would be Roosevelt's first flight since 1932, and the first time an American president had ever left the country during war.

But their final destination still remained secret even from some members of the traveling party. With his affection for the clandestine, Roosevelt had dropped a clue yet to be deciphered. At the usual White House party for family and friends on New Year's Eve, before his champagne toast "to the united nations' victory," the president had shown his guests a new film directed by Michael Curtiz. Starring Humphrey Bogart and Ingrid Bergman, the melodrama told the story of an American expatriate struggling with his conscience and his heart in Vichy North Africa in 1941.

> Capitaine Renault: What in heaven's name brought you to
>   Casablanca?
> Rick: My health. I came to Casablanca for the waters.
> Renault: The waters? What waters? We're in the desert.
> Rick: I was misinformed.

No one had guessed that *Casablanca* was anything but a movie.

There was no Rick in Casablanca, no Ilsa, no Nazi goons or tinkling piano in the Café Américain. But of intrigue there was plenty, and not even Hollywood could imagine the goings-on in the well-heeled suburb of Anfa. A kind of Roman camp was under construction, roughly a mile square and enclosed by concertina wire hung with pebble-filled tin cans. At the center of the camp stood a white four-story hotel that resembled a riverboat stranded amid date palms. German Armistice Commission members had lived here before November 8; the rooms had since been cleansed of canned *Schweinebraten* and photographs of toothy, buxom girls on skis. The Signal Corps had installed three switchboards, a message center, and forty-one miles of phone cable.

Fragrant with begonias and mimosa, the lush grounds swept down to the sea, where roaring surf heaved against a black breakwater. Eighteen villas dotted the Anfa landscape, each recently appropriated from a wealthy French *colon*. Secret Service agents removed eavesdropping microphones from several villas, but left the volumes of Boccaccio illustrated with fine pornographic woodcuts. The grandest of the houses, Dar es Saada, had a living room with a twenty-eight-foot cathedral ceiling and zebra-hide sofas; steel shutters protected the tall windows. Engineers converted the swimming pool into a bomb shelter reinforced with steel plates stripped from the late *Jean Bart*. As ordered, Army carpenters built a wooden ramp up the steps to the villa's front door. They wondered why.

Supplies and personnel poured into the camp, including officers dragooned as hotel desk clerks. American soldiers prowled the area with mine detectors and Geiger counters. Physicians tested food and bottled water for poisons before the provisions were placed under armed guard. A pallet of fine brandy arrived from London. From Algiers, as requested, Eisenhower shipped three cases of gin, three cases of Scotch, and five young captains from the Women's Army Auxiliary Corps. With excruciating indirection, a protocol officer tried to find out whether a regimental band from the 2nd Armored Division knew how to play "Hail to the Chief." Belated attempts were made to teach American soldiers some decorum: on posters in company billets, George Washington on horseback admonished them not to curse.

Overseeing this feverish activity was the putative viceroy of Morocco, George Patton. In the two months since TORCH's end, Patton had converted Casablanca into a vast supply depot and a port of debarkation for the thousands of troops pouring into Africa every week. "Every other four-wheeler horse cab had two or three Americans on board," author A. B. Austin wrote. "You could see them strolling through the parks, sitting with French girls in cafés, riding on bicycles and in jeeps, playing baseball." Soldiers firing tommy guns chased quail through the cork forests outside town, while officers hunted wild boar with platoons of Moroccan bush-beaters. French municipal officials assured American generals that venereal disease in Moroccan brothels had long been "absolutely steady"—at 100 percent. So comfortable was life in Casablanca, with its nut-cake patisseries and sleeve-tugging flesh merchants, that it became known as "the Ice-Cream Front."

Patton was miserable. Whether careering about in his huge Packard limousine or staring at the sea from his office atop the Shell Oil building, he brooded at being shunted into this backwater also known as Boring Acres. During a brief visit to Tunisia he strutted about, crowing, "Where are the Germans? I want to get shot at." Later he scribbled, "I want to be Top Dog and only battle can give me that." Favorable press clippings fed his vanity—Bea had collected more than a thousand articles about her husband since November 8. Yet such meretricious laurels only whetted his thirst for real glory. "Personally," he wrote in a letter home, "I wish I could get out and kill someone."

Patton discharged much of his frustration at his immediate superiors. He had been heartsick to learn of Clark's promotion to lieutenant general, which gave him three stars to Patton's two. Clark was "too damned slick," Patton declared, and "makes my flesh creep." He railed at Eisenhower's perceived tilt toward the British and his use of English colloquialisms such as "tiffin" and "petrol." "I don't think he or Clark have any idea what they are going to do next," he said. Patton sensed a growing rift between the two men and happily encouraged it by offering a sympathetic ear to each. Clark for more than an hour "spent his time cutting Ike's throat," Patton told his diary on January 10, "[and] feels that Ike has sold out to British." For his part, Eisenhower confided worries about Clark's loyalty. "He and Clark are at outs," Patton wrote privately.

But high-command politics would have to wait. The first of a hundred high-ranking guests had begun to filter into Casablanca for the conference now code-named SYMBOL. Patton was their host, and his full attention was needed to keep his visitors happy.

Arriving from Washington, London, Gibraltar, and Algiers, the conferees landed at a new airfield ten miles inland, where they were quickly bundled into waiting limousines. To confound prying eyes during the drive to Anfa, the car windows were smeared with mud. A diplomat reported seeing GIs around the runway "working up mud like nursery children, and slinging it with infinite satisfaction at a clean, polished sedan."

The American chiefs of staff had departed Washington on January 9 in a pair of transport planes carrying six steamer trunks of trinkets for trading with the locals, as well as parkas, snowshoes, and other arctic gear in the unlikely event the aircraft missed Africa and crash-landed on the Russian steppe. They had not even left the Western Hemisphere when a protocol squabble erupted over whether the plane carrying Admiral Ernest J. King, the flinty chief of naval operations, should remain airborne at Puerto Rico until George Marshall landed first, as befitted the senior officer in the delegation. This flapdoodle was followed, on the leg to Gambia, by such dire warnings from the quarter-master general about malevolent African mosquitoes that each passenger was encouraged to take full malaria prophylaxis. When the plane taxied to a stop at the Gambian seaport of Bathurst, Marshall was first down the stairs—in mosquito boots, gloves, and a floppy veiled hat like a bee-keeper's—only to be greeted by nonplused British officers in khaki shorts and shirtsleeves.

Now, finally, they were in Casablanca.

Churchill and his entourage arrived after a ten-hour flight in an unheated bomber from a field near Oxford. As was his custom on long plane trips, the prime minister wore a silk vest and nothing else. Each passenger had been issued a parachute, currency from every country in which the plane might conceivably crash, and a device for catching the dew so as not to die of thirst—if "we were clever enough to use it prop-erly," one passenger wrote. Churchill, who adored skullduggery no less than Roosevelt did, sometimes traveled disguised in a false beard; on this trip, he settled for an RAF uniform. Upon landing in Casablanca, he dodged security officers trying to shoo him into a car and instead marched around the tarmac, smoking a cigar and shaking hands while his twenty suitcases were unloaded. "Any fool can see that is an air com-modore disguised as the prime minister," a British general quipped. One admirer thought he resembled "a big English bulldog who had been taught to give his paw."

He was perhaps more fox than dog. The Casablanca conference, while reviewing progress of the campaign in Africa, was primarily intended to chart the Allied course for the rest of the war, although in Stalin's absence: he refused to leave the Soviet Union while the battle for Stalin-grad continued. Roosevelt had warned his lieutenants that "at the con-ference the British will have a plan and stick to it."

True enough. Churchill was no keener on a frontal assault across the English Channel than he had been six months earlier, during the TORCH debate; on November 9, even with the African landings still in progress, he had begun agitating for "a decisive attack on Italy, or, better still, southern France." To help build the British case for a continuing Mediterranean campaign, he had ordered a headquarters ship, H.M.S. *Bulolo*, to Casablanca. With its war room full of planning studies bound in red leather dispatch folders, *Bulolo* symbolized the British empire's formidable bureaucratic firepower.

On the evening of his arrival at Anfa Camp, Churchill gathered his mil-itary chieftains in Villa Mirador, a stone's throw from the slightly grander Dar es Saada, which awaited Roosevelt's arrival. The prime minister knew that the American military considered the Mediterranean "a kind of dark hole," where additional "periphery pecking" would simply delay the cross-Channel invasion needed to attack the Nazi jugular. The Americans also believed the British had little sympathy for their struggle in the Pacific against the Japanese. But for Churchill, as his physician Lord Moran put it, "the control of the Mediterranean meant . . . control of the Western world." The Middle Sea was critical to British imperial fortunes in Egypt, the Middle East, and India; Churchill also deemed it the Axis's most vulnerable point.

The prime minister quickly outlined the British plan for Casablanca: he would lobby Roosevelt; the British chiefs would lobby their American counterparts; all issues would be discussed fully, without reference to clock or calendar. The relentless logic of the British position would eventually win through, Churchill promised, like "the dripping of water on a stone."

The task involved nothing less than the future of civilization. To Harold Macmillan, Churchill and Roosevelt were, respectively, the Emperor of the East and the Emperor of the West. The former had a plan, indeed he did, and he intended to stick to it. Now all that remained before SYMBOL began in earnest was for the Emperor of the West to arrive with whatever thoughts he had on how to win the war.

Speedy Valley

As the Allied brain trust gathered in Casablanca to plot future campaigns, the current campaign in Tunisia sputtered. Baleful weather and tenacious Germans had thwarted the Allied drive toward Tunis. Eisenhower now expected his troops to remain stalled for at least two months, and he shifted his attention farther south, with an attack plan that required the first big military operation launched in a Tunisian winter since the Punic Wars.

Operation SATIN envisioned a quick lunge across southern Tunisia to the coastal town of Gabès, 260 miles south of Tunis. A rear guard laying minefields would then block any counterattack by Rommel's army driving from Libya into Tunisia, while the main force pushed eighty miles up the coast to capture Sfax, a small port now defended by 2,700 Axis troops with fifteen tanks. The attack was intended to prevent Rommel's army from joining Arnim's; it also would lure the defenders of Tunis from their breastworks and give Anderson's mired First Army another chance to spring forward. SATIN was to be an American production, undertaken by the U.S. II Corps, which now included the 1st Armored Division, one of Terry Allen's infantry regiments, and various other units.

SATIN was bold but also perilous, and it constituted an abrupt change in theater strategy. No longer was the immediate Allied objective the capture of Tunis and Bizerte, but rather the destruction of Rommel's army by Montgomery's hammer bashing the enemy against the SATIN anvil. Although 437,000 soldiers and 42,000 vehicles had been landed in North Africa since November 8, Anglo-American forces in Tunisia remained thin and undersupplied. To lengthen the Tunisian battlefield would stretch Axis troops—still flowing into the bridgehead at a rate of 1,000 a day—but also the Allies. "The Allied forces now appear to be extended over a very wide front, with practically no depth to their position," the combined chiefs observed in early January with undisguised anxiety. "This situation is fraught with danger." A SATIN spearhead to the coast might sever Rommel from Arnim, or it might be crushed between those two German grindstones. "It looks as if the II Corps is to be bait, a sheep tied to a post," an American staff officer wrote in early January.

Eisenhower and his staff concocted SATIN, then paid it little attention as the impending Casablanca conference and other diversions intruded. In the first two weeks of January, the proposed SATIN force grew from 20,000 men to 38,000; that meant pushing forward not 450 tons of provisions daily, but 800 tons, a task beyond the frail Allied supply system. The plan had grown "logistically out of hand," a senior supply officer warned. Bickering persisted over the operation's ultimate objective, and whether swinging as far south as Gabès made sense. But Eisenhower was adamant that "it was fatal to do nothing." The attack was scheduled for the fourth week of January.

Eisenhower made several moves intended to exert tighter command over the newly configured front, none satisfactory and one ultimately disastrous. In a former Constantine orphanage, he established a forward command post from which he assumed "personal command of the battle area" despite remaining 200 miles from any fighting. As his proxy in Constantine when he was back in Algiers, which was almost always, Eisenhower summoned Lucian Truscott, the conqueror of Port Lyautey and a new major general. Because Truscott lacked the commander-in-chief's rank and stature, his influence over the British, French, and even American contingents was largely limited to passing messages to and from AFHQ headquarters.

Mark Clark was a candidate to command American forces in southern Tunisia, but in early January he received a post "for which he has begged and pleaded for a long time," in Eisenhower's tart phrase: the new U.S. Fifth Army, comprising all those underemployed troops in Morocco and Algeria. George Marshall, still obsessed with the nonexistent threat from Spain, insisted the new army remain on guard against Spanish treachery, leaving the Tunisian campaign to others. "Ike doesn't think Clark is disappointed—in fact thinks he is rather relieved as he hadn't wanted the [Tunisian command] particularly," Harry Butcher wrote in his diary. Some believed that Clark was indeed happy not to risk his reputation in actual combat; the British, who despised him—"very ambitious and unscrupulous," Alan Brooke wrote privately—were happy to see him leave AFHQ headquarters.

No sooner had he taken Fifth Army—"his own manure pile," Eisenhower called it—than Clark began fretting over his future and whether the Mediterranean war would end before he had proven himself in a battle command. At the same time, his relentless self-aggrandizement again discomfited his superiors. Eisenhower this winter had twice privately warned his old friend about the hazards of overweening ambition, and Marshall—as furrow-browed as any prophet—lectured him against self-promotion. "Clark admitted he had perhaps been overly ambitious, and would knuckle down and do the job assigned to him like the good soldier he is," Butcher told his diary.

But who would command II Corps? Eisenhower had just the man, and in him the makings of a disaster.

"I bless the day you urged Fredendall upon me, and cheerfully acknowledge that my earlier doubts of him were completely unfounded," Eisenhower had cabled Marshall in November. This unctuous poppycock soon would yield to resurgent doubt and then bitter regret, but for now Major General Lloyd R. Fredendall remained in good odor, not least because he was perceived to be "a Marshall man," and of all the officers in all the world *he* had been chosen by the U.S. Army to lead its inaugural corps in combat against the Third Reich.

At fifty-nine, with periwinkle-blue eyes and hair the color of gunmetal, he was second oldest of the thirty-four men who would be entrusted with American corps command in World War II. Short, stocky, and opinionated, Fredendall had earned a reputation in the prewar Army as a capable trainer and a skilled handler of troops. Reporters liked him for his hail-fellow accessibility and imperturbable air—he liked to sit cross-legged on the floor at two A.M. playing solitaire, like

Grant's whittling during the Wilderness carnage. His father had been a pioneer in Wyoming Territory, eventually serving as the sheriff of Laramie and a scourge of cattle rustlers before accepting an Army commission in the Spanish-American War. Young Lloyd went off to West Point in 1901, only to flunk mathematics and depart after six months. Reappointed by a Wyoming senator, he again lasted just a semester. "A very soldierly little fellow, but extremely goaty at mathematics," his academy roommate observed. After earning a degree, improbably, at MIT, Fredendall took an infantry commission in 1907.

Thirty-five years later he arrived in Oran during TORCH with a peaked cap perched at his trademark rakish angle, and a conviction that neither Eisenhower nor Clark wanted him in Africa since he outranked both in pre-war, permanent grade. As de facto military governor in Oran, Fredendall showed exceptional tolerance for Vichy thuggery; a prominent French Fascist received the American contract for airport reconstruction despite pronouncing himself against "the Jews, the Negroes, and the British." When an American diplomat protested, Fredendall threatened him with arrest, thundering, "Lay off that stuff! What the hell do you know about it?" Orders issued from his headquarters in Oran's Grand Hotel were headed, "II Corps—In the field," which provoked hoots from those living in tents and slit trenches.

Unencumbered with charisma, Fredendall substituted bristling obstinacy. Truscott found him "outspoken in his opinions and critical of superiors and subordinates alike." On the telephone, Fredendall employed a baffling code, which he often abandoned in mid-conversation whenever he and his auditor had become sufficiently confused. During a mid-January conversation with Truscott—whose stenographer eavesdropped on an extension—Fredendall reported:

> I do not have enough MENUS. . . . Relative to the force at Oussel-
> tia, it has been passed from the head ASH TRAY to a second ASH
> TRAY. . . . Everything DAGWOOD of GARDEN has been withdrawn
> or collapsed. I cannot spare any CLOUDS.

Translation: He was short of infantry. A unit that had been serving under a French commander was now under a different Frenchman. Forces north of Pichon had been routed. Fredendall had no extra battalions.

Fredendall also harbored the Anglophobia so common in senior American officers; II Corps became a hotbed of anti-British sentiment to the point of mocking English accents and perpetuating the calumny that

"Ike is the best commander the British have." As the corps staff checked out of the Grand Hotel for the front—the real front—a ditty circulated among them:

> *When the British First got stuck in the mud*
> *And settled down for tea,*
> *They up and beckoned for the Fighting Second*
> *To help in Tunisee.*

Lloyd Fredendall's chosen avenue for Operation SATIN started on the eastern border of Algeria in ancient Tébessa, the walled city of Solomon the Eunuch and headquarters of Rome's Third Legion. Nine miles southeast of Tébessa, in a sunless gulch accessible only by a serpentine gravel road, II Corps planted its flag and began staging for the grand march to the sea that would cleave the Axis armies in half. Soon Fredendall and sixty-eight staff officers had established residence in the ravine, officially called Speedy Valley but also known as "Lloyd's Very Last Resort" and "Shangri-La, a million miles from nowhere." Inexperienced and unusually young, the II Corps staff was dubbed "Fredendall's kindergarten"; their commander had thrown up his hands in mock horror, exclaiming, "My God, I am going to war surrounded by children!" Three thousand support soldiers—signalers, anti-aircraft gunners, engineers—infested the fir copses around Speedy Valley. "The woods are stiff with troops, and it sounds like the Battle of the Marne though no enemy is within many miles," a lieutenant wrote. Combat units mustered farther east, toward Bou Chebka and Kasserine.

Tébessa's high plateau was "cold as a snake," one officer reported, adding, a few days later, "Everyone is freezing." Perpetual shade and frequent snow squalls made Speedy Valley particularly inhospitable. Officers lived and worked in "igloos"—frigid tents with crushed stone floors—wearing every stitch they owned, including wool watch caps that "made the place look like a lumber camp," a reporter commented. Wearing a knit balaclava with an upturned visor, Fredendall slouched in his canvas chair near a potbelly stove and studied the map, played solitaire, or gabbed with passing correspondents like a cracker-barrel clerk in a country store. He had ordered a bulletproof Cadillac similar to Eisenhower's, and periodically called Oran to find out why the car had not arrived.

Day and night, Speedy Valley was a bedlam of pneumatic drills and jackhammers. In a most perplexing decision, Fredendall had commanded the 19th Engineer Regiment to shelter his headquarters by boring a pair of immense, double-shafted tunnels in the ravine wall. The project was like "the digging of the New York subway," Fredendall's aide reported. Working from a blueprint labeled "II Corps Tunnel Job," engineers began excavating two complexes fifty yards apart, each with parallel shafts six and a half feet high, five feet wide, and braced every four feet with timbers ten inches thick. Walls and ceilings were lined with planks milled in the nearby forest and overlapped like shingles. Each complex was to be U-shaped, running 160 feet into the hillside with the parallel shafts joined at the rear by ample galleries designed for offices and a magazine. Fredendall supervised the construction with pharaonic intensity, and the gloomy ravine soon assumed a Valley of the Kings ambience. The work occupied a valuable engineering company for weeks.

Some officers believed the tunnels a prudent precaution against enemy air attack. Others—noting that Speedy Valley was seventy miles from the front, well concealed, and protected by an anti-aircraft battalion—considered the project a ludicrous embarrassment. Some questioned Fredendall's courage. Breaking off a chat with visiting reporters at the sound of airplanes overhead, he would roll his eyes heavenward and mumble, "Some of ours, I hope." Fredendall's chief engineer, Lieutenant Colonel William A. Carter, later recalled, "We had no proper explosives to use for tunneling, and our men had no experience in tunneling. . . . But I could not convince him that it would take a long time to do what he wanted.

"To make the digging as unpopular as possible in an effort to have it stopped, I made sure the blasting was done at night to keep everyone awake," Carter added. "But that did not stop it."

As the Tunisian front lengthened from north to south, Allied and Axis troops jostled each other in a fringe of a fire that extended 200 miles from the Mediterranean to the Sahara. In the far south, Colonel Raff's task force recaptured the oasis town of Gafsa, gateway to the great desert. Suspected Tunisian collaborators and looters, who sometimes could be identified by the stolen light fixtures hanging from their burnooses, were rounded up outside the pink-walled kasbah and remanded to French troops.

"Of the thirty-nine Arabs slated to be shot, only one escaped," Raff reported. "One of them didn't die immediately so a member of the firing squad pulled out his pistol and pumped four bullets into the man's head at close range. . . . They lay in the Tunisian sunlight on view for the whole town to see."

In the muddy north, Allied troops of different nationalities were mingled even more as Eisenhower tried piecemeal reinforcement of desperately weak French segments of the line below the Medjerda valley. Confusion was the result. Ted Roosevelt, who had been peeled away from the 1st Division on temporary duty to help the French, initially was charmed by the Byronic landscape of ancient ruins on a wind-swept tell. "You and I could have a lovely time here were it the piping days of peace," he wrote Eleanor on January 16. But this romanticism soon clouded over. In the course of a single month, the Fighting First's 26th Infantry had thirty-three other units attached to it, while the regiment's 3rd Battalion noted in the daily log, "We have served under everything but the Rising Sun and the swastika." Roosevelt wrote:

> The units are all mixed—French, English, American. That makes command and coordination a major problem. To mix and fragment units is a military crime of the gravest sort. . . . I have done all that lies in my power. Man does what he can and bears what he must.

Among the most active outposts were five camps run by the Special Operations Executive, a British organization established in 1940 to nurture indigenous resistance groups, with help from the American OSS. Intended to bolster Anderson's First Army and Fredendall's II Corps, each camp was commanded by a British officer who supervised recruits drawn from Vichy concentration camps and other seedbeds of disaffection. Collectively they were known as the "Bad-Eyes Brigade," for the unusual number of brigands in bifocals.

The senior American in the operation, Carleton S. Coon, was a corpulent Harvard anthropologist who had run guns to pre-TORCH Morocco and invented "detonating mule turds," artistically sculpted plastic explosives that were liberally scattered on Tunisian roads to flatten German tires. Fluent in Arabic and French, Coon had taught the fine art of blowing things up to French irregulars in Aïn Taya until one of his pupils, Bonnier de la Chapelle, showed extracurricular initiative by shooting Admiral Darlan; although Coon had no discernible role in the assassination, he was given leave to disappear until Algiers cooled down. Thus had he appeared at the SOE's northernmost post on remote Cap Serrat, forty miles west of Bizerte, under the nom de guerre Captain Retinitis and dressed in a British Army uniform with phony officer's pips cut from the green felt of a billiard table. "Now," a fellow saboteur observed, "the company of rogues and cutthroats is complete."

Leading a band of fifty desperadoes, Coon blew up a railroad bridge, harassed the local Italian garrison, and scattered mule turds by the bushel. His freebooters soon specialized in seizing hostages, usually the sons of elders in villages of doubtful loyalty. The boys were imprisoned in the Cap Serrat lighthouse until their fathers provided authenticated information about enemy positions. "This use of hostages was our chief source of intelligence aside from the work of our own patrols," Coon reported. Less successful were booby traps, which according to the professor's accounting claimed only two casualties: "one Arab and one cow."

From Cap Serrat to Gafsa and at all points in between, the Tunisian winter proved crueler than most Allied soldiers had imagined possible in Africa. "It is still bitterly cold and as our military with its customary dumbness did not envisage this and considered Africa as a tropical country, we are not well prepared," Roosevelt wrote. Disclosing that "I have not changed my underclothes for twelve days," T.R. catalogued what he was wearing: "wool union suit, then my wool trousers and shirt, then a sweater, then a lined field jacket, then my lined combat overalls, then a muffler, then my heavy short coat." Disheveled as always, he was still freezing.

So were the tens of thousands of other soldiers whom Ernie Pyle christened the "mud-rain-frost-and-wind boys." Supply trains could not keep pace with the battalions flooding into Tunisia, and II Corps was short of field glasses, machine guns, truck parts, and especially hot food. "If you don't eat for three days, canned Army grub tastes like chicken," one resigned soldier wrote home. Another offered an improvised recipe for gruel: cracked wheat and condensed milk boiled together with two rolls of Life Savers. An officer in the 1st Division reported that the battalion cook had been nicknamed Hitler. "We often wonder if all the hogs in America have been turned into Spam and all the cows into corned beef," he added. Cattle rustling flourished; soldiers claimed that grilled beefsteak was actually "Tunisian deer" or "German chicken."

Dysentery, parasites, trench foot, and bad teeth bedeviled those living in the open in mid-winter. So did Luftwaffe fighters. Soldiers joked bitterly about "Stuka time"—comprising nearly all daylight hours—and "Spitfire time"—the half hour or so each day during which friendly aircraft appeared. Slit trenches were dug deeper with each strafing until they became caves. Skittish soldiers often confused migrating "Messerstorks" with approaching enemy planes. After strafing caused 250 Allied casualties in one week along a six-mile stretch of road outside Medjez-el-

Bab, Evelegh ordered that all vehicles destroyed in air attacks be removed from sight immediately to avoid lowering morale. Morale sank anyway.

"Never out of artillery range, mail weeks catching up, warm rations one time. . . . An old man at twenty," one private wrote. Day by miserable day the troops eased themselves into combat "like an old man with chilblains getting into a hot bath," A. J. Liebling observed. The troops also edged toward that timeless state common to veteran armies in which the men trusted no one less wretched than themselves. Still they did not hate. But each time they had to bundle up unopened mail for the dead and return it to the rear, their blood rose. An officer noticed that American artillery barrages now elicited raucous cheers. "Lay it on them!" the men yelled. "Give it to the bastards!" And the poignancy of young men dying young intruded every hour of every day. This farewell note was found in a dead pilot's sunglasses case:

> Mother, please do not grieve but rather console yourself in the fact that I am happy. Try to enjoy the remainder of your life as best you can and have no regrets, for you have been a wonderful mother and I love you. Jim.

It was enough to incite a man to murder.

As the day for SATIN drew nearer, the man who would lead the armored thrust to the coast finally stepped onto the Tunisian stage. Major General Orlando Ward, commander of "Old Ironsides"— the 1st Armored Division—had waited first in Britain and then in Oran for permission to unify his force at last. Ward had been no less irked than Terry Allen at the splintering of his division. He held Mark Clark responsible for keeping him in England while CCB landed in TORCH and headed east. "I should have begged to go instead of taking orders," he told his diary in mid-November. Paul Robinett, eager as ever to prevent his superiors from making a mistake, fueled Ward's anguish by telling him, "I would either go or be relieved of my command." But Ward played the dutiful soldier, and now his moment had arrived.

Ward was a quiet, genteel man, with large sensitive eyes set in an oval face; some thought he resembled a schoolmaster more than a tank commander. Known as Dan to his family, he was Pinky to everyone else, though only graying wisps remained of his crop of red hair. "I am fifty and at times feel my age," he had confessed a year earlier. A residual reddish cowlick grated so on George Marshall's mania for order when Ward worked for him in the late 1930s that the Army chief had demanded, "Ward, make that hair lie down."

Born in Missouri and raised in Denver, Ward had graduated from West Point a year ahead of Eisenhower, invaded Mexico with the 7th Cavalry in 1916, and fought five battles in France. Homesick for his new bride, Edith, he wondered whether he was better suited to farming. "The husband in me tends to make me not much of a soldier," he told his diary. Transfer to the field artillery put to rest the farmer in him (although not the horticulturalist: as commander of a frontier post in Wyoming in the 1920s, he planted 25,000 trees). His innovations in gunnery at Fort Sill in the 1930s became the stuff of legend, including a technique that reduced the time required to concentrate the fire of twelve battalion howitzers from several hours to six minutes. ("Like squirting a hose," he said with a shrug.) As secretary of the Army General Staff before the war, Ward so impressed the phlegmatic Marshall that the chief recommended he be immediately promoted two grades, from colonel to major general, cowlick be damned.

Ward was honest, ambitious, and emotional. "If the sermon moved him, the pew would shake," his daughter Robin recalled. He could be irreverent, often quoting *Alice in Wonderland*: "Sentence first, verdict afterwards!" To a group of younger officers he had recently confessed, "It has been my observation that most generals are generally unaware of their most peculiar peculiarities." While working in Washington, he had often visited the National Zoo to study the monkeys on the theory that their behavior would illuminate that of the primates in the War Department. An imperishable grief also marked him: When his daughter Katherine, just eighteen, had died of cancer on Christmas Day, 1938, Ward entered "a period of numbness from which I will never recover."

Ward had two peculiarities of his own that informed his generalship. The first was a picayune Anglophobia. He likened the U.S. Army to "a pointer pup. If someone with a red mustache, a swagger stick, and a British accent speaks to us, we lie down on the ground and wiggle." On invasion day, November 8, he wrote in his diary, "Went to church. They prayed for Empire, and the King, but not the Allies." The destruction in Oran harbor of his armored infantry battalion during the British-led Operation RESERVIST simply fed his prejudice. "I hate to serve under the British," he wrote. "They have misused my troops enough already."

The other peculiar trait was an instant willingness to take offense from General Fredendall, his superior officer. Arriving in Constantine on January 15, Ward wrote in his diary, "Went [to] corps HQ to see Fredendall. Did not see fit to see me as I waited over an hour. . . . Corps does not look with favor on matters I suggest." Ward urged the concentration of Old Ironsides for maximum combat power in SATIN, but his advice was brushed aside in favor of what Ward considered a "dribbling commitment" of the division. Fredendall seemed "prone to make map judgment *sans* advice" by issuing orders without reconnoitering the terrain to determine if his map corresponded to reality. Ward soon concluded that Fredendall and the II Corps staff were not even studying the map carefully before drafting deployment orders "on absurd lines."

Even as Allied leaders in Casablanca were struggling to resolve their differences in pursuit of a common purpose, the senior American commander in Tunisia and his top armor lieutenant had, with remarkable speed, cultivated a deep mutual hostility. Staff officers were surprised, then perplexed, then alarmed at this inauspicious development, explicable only in terms of personal chemistry and human folly.

"The Touch of the World"

THE Emperor of the West arrived in Casablanca at 6:20 P.M. on Thursday, January 14, 1943, tired but exhilarated after the five-day journey from Washington. With the gray in his cheeks offset by the glint in his eye, Roosevelt was bundled into a mud-smeared sedan for the circuitous drive to Anfa Camp. Installed in Villa Dar es Saada, the president welcomed Churchill for the first of ten meals and forty-three hours of conversation they would share in Casablanca. An air-raid warning after midnight required them to finish the colloquy by candlelight before Roosevelt finally went to bed at three A.M. "Winnie is a great man for the status quo," he mused, smoking a final cigarette in his uptilted holder. "He even *looks* like the status quo, doesn't he?"

Preserving the *status quo ante bellum*—particularly in maintaining His Majesty's empire—was very much part of the British scheme and, in keeping with Churchill's plan, the prime minister wooed Roosevelt while his military lieutenants wooed the American joint chiefs. At 2:30 P.M. on January 15, a dozen of the most senior generals and admirals in the Anglo-American alliance strolled back from lunch to a high-ceilinged, semicircular banquet room off the main corridor of the Anfa Hotel. Full of sunbeams and the fragrance of cut flowers, the room was dominated by a large rectangular table. Sentries guarded the door, where a neatly printed placard read: "Business: Chiefs of Staff Conference." This would be the third session of the combined chiefs in Casablanca, and before returning to the paramount issue of a global war strategy they were to hear from General Eisenhower this afternoon on the Tunisian campaign and his plan for Operation SATIN.

Poor Eisenhower: yet another room filled with bemedaled generals whose military plumage bespoke battlefield exploits greater than his own. He looked haggard, thanks to his high blood pressure, the purple bags beneath his eyes, and the lingering grippe—exacerbated by chain smoking—that had kept him in bed for four days after Christmas. "Ike seems jittery," Roosevelt later commented. The flight from Algiers this morning had hardly been restful. Two engines on Eisenhower's Flying Fortress had failed and the passengers spent the last fifty miles of the flight standing at the exits with parachutes on, ready to jump. As he strode to the head of the table the British eyed him curiously, still intrigued by how such a man could emerge from lowborn obscurity to hold this high command.

He spoke without notes. Yes, there had been setbacks in Tunisia, unfortunate delays. The roads were bad, the weather horrid, the mud unspeakable. A single dirt runway needed 2,000 tons of perforated steel matting to make it mud-proof, but to carry that matting required the total cargo capacity of the North African rail system for at least a day. British and American soldiers had learned valuable combat lessons. As for the French—and here Eisenhower took his revenge for those long hours in the Gibraltar tunnel—they had the misfortune of being led by General Giraud, who "might be a good division commander but has no political sense and no idea of administration." In a final plunge of the knife, Eisenhower added that dealing with the late Darlan had been easier.

The SATIN offensive, scheduled to begin in a week, looked promising. "At first, operations on the right flank were looked upon primarily as a diversion," Eisenhower said. "But it now seems probable that it will be possible to advance on Sfax and hold it with infantry, while withdrawing the 1st Armored Division as a mobile reserve further to the rear." If successful, SATIN would cut the Axis forces in half.

Watching this performance with heavily lidded eyes was General Sir Alan Brooke, chief of the Imperial General Staff and among the greatest soldiers of the war. Immaculate, punctilious, utterly fluent in French, Brooke came from a family of Northern Ireland baronets known as "the fighting Brookes." With brilliantine-black hair and a face as pinched as an ax blade, he had narrow shoulders, spindly legs, and the unnerving habit—as described by an admirer—of "shooting his tongue out and round his lips with the speed of a chameleon." He had been mentioned in dispatches six times in the Great War, but his charmed life had changed in April 1925 when he rolled his Bentley on a slippery road, breaking his own leg and his wife's spine; she died a few days later.

"I very much wish I could have been finished off myself at the same time," Brooke wrote. Increasingly taciturn and withdrawn, he developed a pronounced stoop and a perpetual frown. Remarriage brought new happiness—for decades, Brooke wrote his second wife lyrical love letters, always signed "Your devoted old Alan"—without rectifying the stoop, the frown, or the taciturnity. "Colonel Shrapnel" 's signature phrase was a blunt "I flatly disagree," often accompanied by the snap of a pencil. In January 1943, he was fifty-nine years old. Birding was his greatest civil passion, and he could treat *The Truth About the Cuckoo* like Holy Writ. This very morning, prowling the beach with his field glasses, Brooke had jubilantly spied a goldfinch, a stonechat, sanderlings, and a ring plover, all carefully recorded in his journal.

Such sightings did not distract him from the task at hand. As the officer largely responsible for extracting the British Expeditionary Force from Dunkirk in 1940, Brooke was disinclined to underestimate German ferocity, and he flatly disagreed with what he privately described as Eisenhower's "ridiculous plan" for SATIN. As for Brooke's opinion of the commander-in-chief himself, his diary entry for December 28, 1942, was unsparing: "Eisenhower as a general is hopeless! He submerges himself in politics and neglects his military duties, partly, I am afraid, because he knows little if anything about military matters."

Now Brooke pounced on Eisenhower like a hawk on a pigeon. How, he asked, would the II Corps drive to the sea be coordinated with Anderson's First Army in the north and Montgomery's Eighth Army in Libya? If Anderson was bogged down for two more months, would not Arnim's forces "thin out in the north and defeat the Sfax forces in detail?" Montgomery was still a week from reaching Tripoli, and Eighth Army would be "quite immobilized" until the shattered port there could be reopened. Rommel no doubt "would react like lightning" to any attack on Sfax that threatened his logistics lifeline. The Desert Fox still had an estimated 80,000 German and Italian troops, Arnim 65,000. Would not II Corps risk being trapped between Arnim and Rommel, with little prospect of help from Anderson or Montgomery? In fact, an Ultra decrypt today had disclosed that Rommel's 21st Panzer Division had already begun moving north into Tunisia.

Eisenhower tried to regroup in the face of this onslaught, but he got no help from the American chiefs, Hap Arnold, Ernest King, and Marshall. The latter appeared somnolent after a heavy lunch and had yet to open his mouth. "Fredendall's plan," as Eisenhower called it, envisioned

Ward's 1st Armored Division as a counterpunching force to stave off Rommel. Eisenhower faced "the dilemma of either allowing the troops in the north to deteriorate by remaining inactive in the mud, or suffering some losses through keeping them active." The latter, he believed, "was the lesser of the two evils." Even so, he looked forward to discussing the issue further and "to make any necessary adjustments in the plan."

Eisenhower saluted and left the room with the grim look of a man in full retreat.

The British and American chiefs of staff or their deputies had met fifty-six times since an initial strategy session in January 1942, but Casablanca revealed that they were still not speaking the same language. They reached quick agreement at Anfa on several matters, including the need to bolster Stalin's Red Army, to concentrate air attacks against the German homeland, and to suppress marauding U-boats, whose number had doubled in 1942. But the preeminent issues were how to divide Allied war resources between the Pacific and Atlantic wars, and where the next blow should fall. On these vital questions, no unity obtained. It is axiomatic that commanders in conference tend to be on their best behavior and therefore at their least useful. The first few days of SYMBOL demonstrated that they could also accomplish little while behaving badly.

No sooner had Eisenhower left the conference room than Brooke resumed the dripping of water on stone that Churchill required. He believed that "final victory in the European theater before the end of 1943" was possible. Repeating arguments he had made in earlier sessions, he also maintained that Japan's offensive power had already been blunted and that Tokyo's defeat was certain once Germany surrendered. But if the Germans were allowed to defeat the Soviet Union, the Third Reich could become impregnable. Therefore, the Allied strategy should be not just to defeat Germany first, as Roosevelt and Churchill had agreed a year earlier, but to put the overwhelming weight of Allied resources into the European theater.

But where to strike next? The American inclination was to "strike directly at the heart of the enemy over the shortest possible route": a cross-Channel assault on the north coast of France aimed at Berlin. Yet—and here those red leather folders from the *Bulolo* reappeared, to reveal wondrously precise studies and statistics—the Germans had forty-six divisions in France and the Low Countries, plus another eleven available nearby in Germany. Moreover, good east-west rail lines in northern Europe would allow the Wehrmacht to shuttle seven more divisions from the Russian front to the west in two weeks. By September 1943, the latest prudent date for a cross-Channel invasion before bad weather intruded, the Allies could stage twenty-five divisions at most in Britain, hardly an invincible force; also, shipping and landing craft shortages meant that the initial assault wave against the fortified Atlantic Wall would be limited to six divisions, although Eisenhower's own planners in London had recently recommended at least twelve.

All of which argued for further Mediterranean operations, starting in Sicily. The island had five hundred miles of mostly unfortified coastline. As Churchill had told Stalin, "Why stick your head in the alligator's mouth at Brest when you can go to the Mediterranean and rip his soft underbelly?" Owing to the flimsiness of the Italian rails, vulnerable to Allied air attack, the Wehrmacht could move only one reinforcing division south in two weeks. Knocking Italy out of the war, the British estimated, would cost Germany fifty-four divisions and more than 2,000 planes. And reopening the Mediterranean and the Suez Canal would save the Allies the equivalent of 225 ships, Brooke concluded—a huge bonus in a global war where shipping was often more precious than manpower. The red folders snapped shut.

As Brooke had listened to Eisenhower with predatory patience, so Admiral King listened to Brooke. Easily the most pugnacious of the three American chiefs—fittingly, he had an anchor tattooed on one forearm and a dagger on the other—he had been described by one admirer as "a formidable old crustacean." Bibulous and lecherous, with a foghorn voice that could be heard the length of a carrier deck, King was "always ready to find Albion perfidious," in Marshall's phrase, and the admiral smelled perfidy in this room amid the hibiscus and hair oil. The Pacific was *his* theater, and he would not step back. King has "his eye on the Pacific. That is his eastern policy," a British admiral concluded. "Occasionally he throws a rock over his shoulder. That's his western policy."

King threw a rock. He did not object to Sicily per se, but he believed that the British did "not seem to have an overall plan for the conduct of the war." Their dismissal of the Pacific was simply anathema. Tokyo was replenishing its empire with raw materials from conquered territories, he asserted, and fortifying an inner defensive ring in the East Indies and the Philippines. Bitter fighting with flamethrowers and grenades would persist on Guadalcanal for nearly another month, and a comparably bitter campaign was just ending in Papua New Guinea, where American and Australian casualties exceeded 8,000. In the far north, a small American force had just landed on Amchitka to begin reclaiming the Aleutians; that campaign would last until summer.

Like Brooke, King recycled arguments made in earlier sessions; the discussions were beginning to seem circular. The admiral considered it "necessary for the united nations to prevent the Japanese having time to consolidate their gains." Of nine fronts now engaged by Allied forces, four were in the Pacific. Were the British aware that only 15 percent of the Allied war effort was being channeled into the Pacific? That proportion, King believed, should be doubled.

If not precisely a lie, the 15 percent statistic was certainly not the truth. More than half of U.S. Army forces overseas and one-third of the combat air groups were arrayed against Japan; virtually all U.S. Marines overseas—now four divisions, and growing—also served in the Pacific. At least three times as many ships were required to transport and sustain troops in the vast Pacific as were needed in the Atlantic.

No matter: it was "essential to maintain the initiative against the Japanese and not wait for them to come against us," King argued. As for Brooke's rebuttal—that the Allies lacked sufficient resources to wage all-out war against both Japan and the European Axis—King shrugged. Hap Arnold and Marshall remained silent. The session broke up before five P.M.

Battle lines had been drawn. Brigadier General Albert C. Wedemeyer, a War Department planner who so distrusted the British that he secretly tape-recorded meetings with their officers, bitterly opposed further dabbling in the Mediterranean. "If we subscribed to the British concept," Wedemeyer warned the American chiefs after the meeting, "we should disperse our forces in an area which is neither vital nor final." But a cross-Channel invasion in 1943 looked unlikely without a change of heart in London.

Brooke recorded his assessment of the day's events later that night. In an uncharacteristically fraternal diary entry, he wrote: "There is no doubt that we are too closely related to the Americans to make cooperation between us anything but easy."

Casablanca lay a thousand miles from any battlefield, but the casualty roll here was growing. SATIN had been mortally wounded; Eisenhower's reputation was injured, if less grievously. "Deficient of experience and of limited ability," Brooke concluded in his diary. Word soon circulated that the Tunisian offensive had been scrubbed. Clark told Patton that the British were simply trying to garner all the glory in Tunisia by excluding Americans from the final kill. "If so," Patton wrote in *his* diary, "it is too terrible for words."

After his humiliating performance in the hotel conference room, Eisenhower slowly walked beneath the coconut palms to Villa Dar es

Saada. The president wanted to see him at four P.M. Precisely what Eisenhower should do now in Tunisia, particularly with II Corps, was as uncertain as his own future. "His neck is in a noose and he knows it," Butcher would write two days later. Despite Marshall's efforts to give Eisenhower rank comparable to the senior British field generals', Roosevelt balked at awarding him a fourth star. Harry Hopkins recorded the private exchange at Anfa:

> The President told General Marshall that he would not promote Eisenhower until there was some damn good reason for doing it, that he was going to make it a rule that promotions should go to people who had done some fighting, that while Eisenhower had done a good job, he hasn't knocked the Germans out of Tunisia.

And now Marshall himself was irked at Eisenhower's limp showing before the combined chiefs.

Sitting in his zebra-skin living room, Roosevelt ruminated at length on the improbability of France regaining her prewar stature. After wondering aloud "what I'm going to do with Tunisia after the war," he quizzed Eisenhower on the campaign.

"Well? What about it? What's your guess?"

"Sir?"

"How long it'll take to finish the job?"

Eisenhower hesitated. The president seemed far too sanguine about fighting in the Tunisian winter.

"With any kind of break in the weather, sir, we'll have 'em all either in the bag or in the sea by late spring."

"What's late spring mean? June?"

Eisenhower nodded. "Maybe as early as the middle of May. June at the latest."

He had committed himself. Victory in Africa by mid-May.

That night Eisenhower lingered in Patton's villa until 1:30 A.M., confiding his anxieties. "He thinks his thread is about to be cut," Patton wrote in his diary. "I told him he had to go to the front. He feels that he cannot, due to politics."

Brooke's deputy, General Sir John Kennedy, observed of Churchill: "He is difficult enough when things are going badly, more difficult when nothing is happening, and quite unmanageable when all is going well." Despite frictions within the military councils, SYMBOL was going very well in the prime minister's estimation; if not unmanageable, he was certainly ubiquitous. Escaping from the Anfa compound on January 16, he was found strolling the beach near the El Hank lighthouse, pockets bulging with seashells. During another beachfront expedition, he came upon several American sailors with a guitar; at his request, they serenaded him with "You Are My Sunshine." Walking back to Villa Mirador after a late-night dinner, Churchill was challenged at three A.M. by a young sentry from North Carolina who bellowed, "Corporal of the guard! I have a feller down here who claims he is the prime minister of Great Britain. I think he is a goddamn liar."

Mornings, he lounged about in a pink gown, nipping breakfast from a wine bottle or studying his traveling collection of military maps. Eventually dressing in his coverall "zip rompers," he played countless hands of bezique, or watched field marshals build sand castles and skip stones into the surf. "Come and see my maps," he urged. "Will you have a whiskey?" Long past midnight he debated issues large and small with his minions, whose bleary yawns he dismissed: "Very well, if you don't care about winning the war, go to sleep." He tended "to view with contempt suggestions that did not originate with himself," a British general observed, and when challenged he huffily replied, "You have grown fat in honors from your country, and now you betray her. All you want is to draw your pay, eat your rations, and sleep." Excessive civility annoyed him, too. "We don't get paid to be polite to each other," he snapped. All in all, he was having a wonderful time.

Roosevelt also found Anfa a great tonic. He lunched in the villa garden, drank old-fashioneds, and read a popular play, *The Man Who Came to Dinner.* Two of his sons, both in uniform, stayed with him at Dar es Saada; the president guffawed at their two A.M. account of touring Casablanca's cobble-paved souk and red-light district—a walled village where visitors sipped sweet mint tea as dusky harlots lifted their skirts and ground their hips like a prurient vision from Burton's *Arabian Nights.*

A state dinner for the sultan of Morocco and his grand vizier went well, though Churchill grumbled because, in deference to Muslim sensibilities, no alcohol was served. The prime minister insisted on a postprandial open bar so he could recover from the pernicious effects of teetotalism. At noon on January 17, Roosevelt received General Noguès, still clinging to power as Moroccan resident-general. When Noguès complained that Jews in Morocco and Algeria were demanding restored suffrage, Roosevelt jauntily replied, "The answer to that is very simple, namely, that there just aren't going to *be* any elections, so the Jews need not worry about the privilege of voting." The president also proposed restricting Jewish participation in law, medicine, and other professions to reflect Jewish percentages in "the whole of the North African population." This, he told Noguès, would "eliminate the specific and understandable complaints which the Germans bore towards the Jews in Germany" for disproportionately dominating certain occupations. Despite his commitment to the large freedoms underpinning the Allied cause, Roosevelt no less than Churchill could be "a great man for the status quo."

Around and around went the chiefs. Debate descended into dithering, then regained the altitude needed for earnest dialogue, which still led nowhere. On Saturday, January 16, the morning after Eisenhower's rout by Brooke, Marshall opened the session with a dozen rapid-fire questions, some incisive and all legitimate. The American chiefs, he said, were curious "to learn the British concept as to how Germany is to be defeated." Would Sicily be "merely a means towards an end, or an end in itself?" American strategists believed that if Mussolini's government showed signs of collapse, Hitler would send Wehrmacht troops to reinforce the easily defended Italian boot. What then? What should be the Allies' "main plot" for winning the war? "Every diversion or side issue from the main plot acts as a suction pump," Marshall added.

Brooke had spotted a whimbrel, a yellow wagtail, and five small owls. He had also seen this American argument winging around Anfa many times by now. Out came the red leather folders. "The Germans have forty-four divisions in France," he said in a monotone that implied exasperation. "That is sufficient strength to overwhelm us on the ground and perhaps hem us in with wire or concrete. . . . Since we cannot go into the Continent in force until Germany weakens, we should try to make the Germans disperse their forces as much as possible."

There it was, and there it remained. The Americans, whose delegation included but a single logistician frantically thumbing through three loose-leaf notebooks, tended toward observation and generality. British statements bulged with facts and statistics from *Bulolo*'s humming war room. The Americans had an inclination; the British had a plan. The American chiefs also lacked a viable alternative to Churchill's "soft underbelly": Roosevelt had held but a single planning session with his military brain trust before Casablanca, and if the president held strong views on the timetable and strategic trajectory of the war he had yet to share them with his chiefs.

That evening, Marshall told Roosevelt that the American chiefs intended to endorse the British plan for the invasion of Sicily, now code-named HUSKY. As selfless as he was austere, Marshall was enough of a poker player to know when to fold his hand. The new requirement for twelve assault divisions in a cross-Channel invasion rather than the anticipated six; the need for more robust amphibious training, so amply revealed during TORCH; a decision to cut back landing-craft production in favor of more urgently needed convoy escort warships; and the simple need for Allied unity: all played into his decision. The British, moreover, were "not interested in occupying Italy," Marshall told the president. "This would add to our burdens without commensurate returns." Roosevelt agreed.

The Army chief also knew the strategic value of a good bluff, and for two days he kept his change of heart from the British. More sparring followed, more circular squabbling, especially over the Pacific. "We cannot defeat Germany and Japan simultaneously," Brooke pleaded on Monday morning, January 18. "Because of the distances involved, the British chiefs of staff believe that the defeat of Japan first is impossible, and if we attempt to do so we shall lose the war." Marshall simply reiterated his opposition "to interminable operations in the Mediterranean."

After two stormy hours, the meeting broke up at one P.M. Despondency etched Brooke's narrow face. "It is no use, we shall never get agreement with them," he told Field Marshal Sir John Dill, the senior British officer in Washington. Dill urged resolve. "You cannot bring the unsolved problem up to the prime minister and the president," he warned. "You know as well as I do what a mess they would make of it!"

And then the logjam broke. The British proposed a compromise in which the Allies agreed to retain the initiative against Japan without undermining "any opportunity that may present itself for the decisive defeat of Germany in 1943." Marshall, King, and Arnold pored over the paragraph, scratched a few minor amendments, and pronounced themselves satisfied. Roosevelt and Churchill blessed the agreement at 5:30 P.M. in Dar es Saada and returned to their cocktails. The document, Admiral King suggested, "goes a long way toward establishing a policy of how we are to win the war."

The plan indeed affirmed the primacy of the war against Germany. It enshrined a Mediterranean strategy, while confirming the American determination to punish Japan without mercy. It also demonstrated the ability of the British to outmaneuver and outmuscle their American allies. The experience had been chastening. "They swarmed down upon us like locusts," Albert Wedemeyer told the War Department.

"We lost our shirts," Wedemeyer added. "We came, we listened, and we were conquered."

* * *

If Roosevelt shared these sentiments, he kept them to himself, perhaps because he recognized the inevitability of American dominion. The old imperial order was cracking under the pressure of global war, and all the red leather folders in the British Commonwealth would not preserve the status quo forever.

Besides, the president had pressing business. At 9:20 A.M. on January 21, dressed in a felt hat and gray suit, he set off in an olive-drab Daimler limousine escorted by motorcycles, reconnaissance cars, and a pair of jeeps bristling with Secret Service agents. North they sped through the blustery morning, eighty-five miles to Rabat. "Roadsides were a panorama of Arabs and Moors in their flowing robes and burnooses, veiled women, French *poilus,* large bearded natives astride the rumps of tiny burros . . . and innumerable cyclists," a captain in the motorcade reported. To distract curious onlookers from the Daimler, Secret Service agents stood in their jeeps and pointed at the sky or pretended to tumble halfway out of the vehicles. Outside Rabat, agents erected a privacy screen and lifted Roosevelt from the car into the front seat of a jeep.

Patton, immaculate in jodhpurs and gloves, greeted him with a salute and a crinkled grin. Though he hid it well, the strain of guaranteeing security for SYMBOL had exhausted him. At three one morning Patton barged into the Secret Service command post at Anfa. "The Heinies know the president is here and they're coming to get him!" he warned. Agents calmed him down and sent him packing—"They are a bunch of cheap detectives always smelling of drink," Patton fumed. The demands of this inspection trip further inflamed him. First, Clark had ordered him to find some "Negro troops who had participated in our landings" to show the president, who was considered partial to Negroes. Then the Secret Service insisted that all 20,000 troops under review be disarmed and kept 300 feet from the road; soldiers could keep their rifles but no bullets. Now as the motorcade rolled through the 2nd Armored Division, a dozen agents kept their submachine guns trained on the docile troops standing at attention. Patton was furious.

Rumors that FDR was in Africa had provoked derisive scoffs. "Anything is possible," the 2nd Armored Division chaplain said, "but this story to our mind reaches the height of fantasy." Then the order "eyes right" was given and there he was, sitting sidesaddle in the jeep: the leonine head, the big shoulders, the jaunty cant of the cigarette holder clenched between his teeth. From deep in the ranks came a plainly audible "Jesus!" The president waved, and the motorcade swept on to the 3rd Infantry Division.

They stopped for a lunch of boiled ham and sweet potatoes at an Army field kitchen while a band played "Chattanooga Choo-Choo." Next came the 9th Infantry Division—Clark drew Roosevelt's attention to a conspicuously placed contingent of black soldiers—before the procession sped through Port Lyautey to Mehdia. Precise rows of American and French graves overlooked the turquoise Sebou River below the Kasbah walls. A bugler blew "Taps" as aides propped two wreaths against a plaque commemorating the "Battle of Mehdia, November 8–11, 1942." His bared head bowed, Roosevelt contemplated the dead for a long, long moment.

Cold rain drenched the Secret Service agents in their jeeps on the return to Casablanca. The sight pleased Patton, who was riding in the Daimler with the president. Roosevelt "says India is lost" to the British empire, Patton wrote in his diary that night, "and that Germany and Japan must be destroyed." For his part, Roosevelt later noted that Patton had told him "at least five times that he hoped to die with his boots on."

Back in his villa, Roosevelt ate a quick supper and went to bed at 9:30. This had been a long day for the Emperor of the West, but a gratifying one. He had seen the future: the legions of democracy in serried ranks of herringbone twill, brave men who would unshackle a continent.

The distant roar of surf rolled over Anfa's green lawn like a dreamy cannonade. Translucent with African light, a cloudless sky domed the camp, and only a frond-tossing breeze off the sea restrained the midday sun from overbearing intensity. At fifteen minutes past noon on Sunday, January 24, twenty-seven reporters and almost as many photographers were herded through two rows of barbed wire toward Dar es Saada. They had spent the morning in an empty bungalow used as a holding pen, amusing themselves with a French edition of the *Decameron* and swapping conjectures on why they had been summoned to Casablanca.

Sitting cross-legged on the damp Bermuda grass, the scribes glared at an officious press officer who bustled among them warning, "No questions, no questions." Purple sprays of bougainvillea climbed the white columns of a loggia leading from the villa's rear door to the terrace, where a pair of leather drawing-room chairs stood before a microphone. "We'll need *four* chairs," a young officer called. Two more quickly appeared. A dozen admirals and generals drifted through the shrubs or leaned against the orange trees, and no sooner had the reporters voiced their surprise—Was that Marshall? What the devil was Brooke doing here?—than they fell silent in astonishment at the sight of the prime minister and the president emerging from the villa, escorted by the khaki-clad figures of Generals Giraud and De Gaulle.

Immense effort had been devoted to getting these two French rivals to share the same stage. Giraud considered "petit De Gaulle," as he called him, "a self-seeker and a bad general." De Gaulle, the £70 million his Free French movement had received from the British notwithstanding, considered Giraud an Anglo-American puppet. When Roosevelt summoned Giraud to Casablanca for a public display of French unity, he came running, only to find that his stock had tumbled since those heady hours at Gibraltar when Eisenhower had begged for his help. After their first meeting at Anfa, Roosevelt had dismissed him as "a dud" and "a very thin reed," and the Army's supply chief opened his own session with Giraud by instructing the translator, "I want you to begin by telling this Frog that Uncle Sam is no Santa Claus."

For his part, De Gaulle refused to leave London for Casablanca until Churchill, livid and embarrassed, threatened him with financial excommunication. "We call him Jeanne d'Arc and we're looking for some bishops to burn him," the prime minister said sourly. Roosevelt had long considered De Gaulle an aspiring tyrant, and he found no reason to reform his opinion during their meeting in the Dar es Saada living room. To forestall any Gallic treachery, the entire Secret Service detail—a dozen of them cradling submachine guns—had secretly taken positions behind drapes and doorways throughout the villa.

But here they were on the Dar es Saada terrace, two immensely tall Frenchmen wearing identical expressions of peevish disgruntlement. Two agents hoisted Roosevelt from his wheelchair and set him as gently as a porcelain figurine on one of the leather chairs. Eleven days of sun had bleached the dark hollows beneath his eyes. He removed the cigarette from his lips and called greetings to several reporters he knew; to the rest, he offered a broad grin. Churchill, dressed in gray pinstripes and carrying a cane, slumped into another chair. A black cigar swiveled in his face. Photographers trampled the bird-of-paradise beds in a frenzy of clicking shutters.

"You'll run out of ammunition before we've finished," the prime minister warned. He had objected to a noon photo session on grounds that it was far too early for him to appear at his best, but had agreed to "put on a very warlike look" for the occasion. Now he scowled at the sun and tugged the brim of his homburg. One reporter thought he resembled "Peter Pan with a cigar stuck in his mouth"; to another, he seemed "a rather malicious Buddha." Roosevelt asked if he would care to remove his hat for the cameras.

"I wear a hat to keep the sun from my eyes," Churchill replied. "*You* should wear one."

"I was born without a hat," the president said with a chuckle. "I don't see any reason for wearing one now."

As the generals took their chairs—Giraud stiff as a tin soldier, De Gaulle slouching, cigarette between his thumb and forefinger—Roosevelt offered a few sketchy words about the conference just ended. Details must remain secret, he said, but the meeting had been "unprecedented in history. The chiefs of staff have been in intimate touch. They have lived in the same hotel. Each man has become a definite personal friend of his opposite number on the other side."

The chiefs stared impassively from their foliage redoubts.

So, too, had Generals Giraud and De Gaulle been in intimate touch, the president added. (In truth their brief dialogue had been limited, as one diplomat noted, to each offering "the other the privilege of serving under him.") Asking in fractured French for the two generals to demonstrate their commitment to the liberation of France, Roosevelt grasped each by the elbow and almost physically lifted them from their seats. They stood, they shook, they sat—so quickly that the photographers howled and they had to repeat the pose with grim, waxwork smiles. "This is an historic moment," the president declared. The generals then stalked off through the banana trees, leaving their minions to release a joint statement of haikulike concision: "We have seen each other. We have discussed." Roosevelt waved and called after them, "Bon voyage!"

"It was all rather embarrassing," reporter Alan Moorehead later recalled, "like the first rehearsal of an amateur play."

Now the president had another issue he wanted to raise.

"I think we have all had it in our hearts and heads before, but I don't think that it has ever been put down on paper by the prime minister and myself, and that is the determination that peace can come to the world only by the total elimination of German and Japanese war power," he said. Perhaps even the British journalists knew the story of U. S. Grant, who at Appomattox in April 1865 had demanded unconditional surrender from Robert E. Lee?

Similar terms seemed fitting in this war, Roosevelt said. "The elimination of German, Japanese, and Italian war power means the unconditional surrender of Germany, Italy, and Japan." He glanced at a sheaf of notes. "It does *not* mean the destruction of the population of Germany, Italy, or Japan, but it does mean the destruction of the philosophies in those countries which are based on conquest and subjugation of other people."

The reporters might even consider calling this conference the "unconditional surrender meeting," he added. Churchill nodded. "I agree with everything that the president has said." The Allies must insist upon "the unconditional surrender of the criminal forces who plunged the world into storm and ruin."

No one scrutinizing that Buddha-like countenance guessed that Roosevelt's proclamation had caught the prime minister short. After the war, Churchill suggested that the unconditional surrender demand had taken him completely by surprise, but that was disingenuous; the issue had been raised by Roosevelt on the evening of January 18, when Churchill even proposed a joint statement "to the effect that the united nations are resolved to pursue the war to the bitter end." He had then cabled London for advice from his war cabinet, which on January 21 unanimously endorsed the concept and, unlike the prime minister, also favored extending the surrender demand to cover Italy. What Churchill had not expected was that Roosevelt would make such a blunt declaration here and now.

For his part, the president later said the notion "just popped into my mind"—a ludicrous claim: in the notes he referred to at the press conference, the term "unconditional surrender" appeared three times. After contemplating the concept for over six months, Roosevelt had broached it with his military chiefs at the White House on January 7; none of them objected and, what is more remarkable, neither Marshall nor any other chief thought to initiate staff studies of what the demand might mean for the conduct of the war. At Anfa, the American chiefs had briefly discussed the issue among themselves, listening without comment to General Wedemeyer's impassioned warning that "unconditional surrender would unquestionably compel the Germans to fight to the very last" and would "weld all of the Germans together."

What was done was done, and much debate would be devoted in the coming months and years to the consequences of such a grand action taken with so little forethought. Clearly, Roosevelt was eager to avoid the mistakes of 1918; the ambiguous armistice signed then had later allowed the Nazis to claim that political betrayal rather than battlefield reverses caused Germany's defeat in World War I. But the president's Civil War analogy was flawed: Grant had issued his famous terms in 1862 during the siege of Fort Donelson in Tennessee, not three years later in Virginia. Nor was unconditional surrender a feature of Britain's wars: none of the fifteen since the end of the sixteenth century had ended thus. Perhaps a closer parallel lay in the Third Punic War, when

Rome demanded that Carthage unconditionally surrender all her "territory, cities, and citizens," as scholar Anne Armstrong has observed; the Carthaginians refused, and the war ultimately ended with their city's obliteration in 146 B.C.

What was done was done indeed. The reporters had their story. Soon they would repair to the same airy room where the chiefs had met, collectively churning out 100,000 words on their typewriters, while censors scrutinized each new page before passing it to Signal Corps radiomen for transmission. But first the two leaders invited the correspondents to come forward and shake hands. Squinting from under his hat brim, Churchill extended a hand to each in turn, asking, "What's your paper, eh? What's your paper?" Next to him Roosevelt canted his head and beamed like a ward heeler cadging votes. "Pleased to meet you," he said. "Pleased to meet you."

As a Scottish reporter strolled toward the hotel with an American colleague, he cocked a thumb toward the president. "Ah," said the Scot, "he has the touch, the touch of the world, has he not?"

The Sinners' Concourse

EARLY that afternoon, while the hacks pounded their keyboards, Roosevelt and Churchill slipped out of Anfa in the olive-drab Daimler. For four hours they drove due south on Highway 9, stopping only for a roadside picnic of boiled eggs, mincemeat tarts, and Scotch packed in a wicker hamper. American fighter planes patrolled overhead and Patton's sentries stood guard every hundred yards for 150 miles. Late-afternoon shadows stretched toward the Atlas Mountains as the motorcade pulled into Marrakesh in a moil of dust, luggage, and swaggering Secret Service agents.

Churchill had beguiled the president with tales of the thousand-year-old "Paris of the Sahara," a red adobe caravanserai of desert nomads and snake charmers and "the largest and most elaborately organized brothels in the African continent." General Marshall's stern demand that Roosevelt "refuse any invitation of the prime minister" to visit this suspected nest of Axis agents had been ignored. For a few sweet hours president and prime minister, respectively code-named A-1 and B-1, would retreat as far from the war as possible.

Their refuge was the estate of La Saadia, loaned for the occasion by the rich American widow who owned it. The russet stucco villa (fifteen bedrooms) was embellished with intricate Moorish carvings, sunken baths, and ceiling frescoes in gold and royal blue. Five gardeners tended the lush grounds and the immense emerald-green swimming pool. As at Anfa, Army engineers had feverishly installed wheelchair ramps, secure scrambler phones, and extra electrical transformers. The villa's French butlers were supplanted by American soldiers who received a quick course in dining room etiquette and practice in serving food from huge platters to other GIs pretending to be the president, the prime minister, and their courtiers. It was all too much for the supervising American lieutenant, who suffered a nervous breakdown and was locked in a bedroom after heavy sedation with a bottle of bourbon.

Looming above La Saadia was a six-story observation tower with a winding staircase. At Churchill's insistence, two aides fashioned a chair with their clasped hands and carried Roosevelt up sixty steps to a wicker chair on the open terrace; Lord Moran, the prime minister's physician, later recalled the president's "paralyzed legs dangling like the limbs of a ventriloquist dummy." The Atlas soared ten miles distant, a mesmerizing spectacle of pinks and violets that deepened as the sun sank. "It's the most lovely spot in the whole world," Churchill murmured. He sent down for the president's coat and draped it across Roosevelt's shoulders tenderly.

They sat in reverent silence. Arabs rode their swaying camels through the city gate called Bab Khemis. The red walls of Marrakesh dissolved to an oxblood hue. Electric lights twinkled around the great souk and the square known as the Sinners' Concourse, where shackled slaves from central Africa once stood at auction and where sultans had staged mass executions to discourage revolt. From every minaret in Marrakesh the muezzins' cry called believers to evening prayer as the Atlas darkened and the mingled scents of honeysuckle and orange rose on the evening airs, wafting across the little terrace like the precise odor of piety.

Darkness and hunger finally drove them down. The president took a last wistful look at the indigo mountains before hooking his arms around the necks of his porters. Churchill followed, softly singing a tuneless ditty of his own composition: "Oh, there ain't no war, there ain't no war."

In the world where there *was* a war, the transactions at Casablanca would help chart its course until, thirty-two months later, Berlin and Tokyo lay in ruins. The main strategic consequence of the eighteen meetings held by the combined chiefs at Anfa was a year's postponement of a cross-Channel invasion, a delay that probably saved the Allies from catastrophe. The weight of numbers accumulating in North Africa, and the decisions taken in the TORCH debates the previous summer, gave the Mediterranean strategy a certain inevitability, which Casablanca simply confirmed.

But what should happen after Sicily remained unclear; the British no less than the Americans lacked a comprehensive vision for winning the war. American chiefs so frequently asked, "Where do we go from here?" that the British grew huffy. The danger inherent in a Mediterranean strategy was that war against the European Axis would veer into a protracted fight against Germany's junior partner, Italy; the soft underbelly might also have "chrome steel baseboards," in Marshall's ominous phrase. And as Admiral King had observed at Anfa, for at least another year "our main reliance in Europe is on Russia." That would hardly please the Russians, who were still locked in titanic struggle at Stalingrad. "Nothing in the world will be accepted by Stalin as an alternative to our placing fifty or sixty divisions in France by the spring of this year," Churchill acknowledged.

The compromises at Anfa had been greased with ambiguity, and the coming months would show that some of the chiefs' plans were either unsound, unfeasible, or simply undone by events. Schemes to invade Burma and attack the Japanese naval base at Rabaul died a-borning. Shipping shortages—an arcane subject understood by almost no one outside a small, briny priesthood—put "a stranglehold on all offensive operations," in Brooke's words. To refit eleven French divisions, as Roosevelt had blithely promised Giraud, would require 325 cargo vessels the Americans simply could not spare.

Hopes for an Anglo-American bomber offensive to pummel German targets had also faltered. "I note that the Americans have not yet succeeded in dropping a single bomb on Germany," Churchill observed in early January. That was unfair: not only had more than 600 planes been diverted from the U.S. Eighth Air Force in Britain for use in Africa, but nearly all aircrews and support units had been stripped bare; the paltry force of American bombers and fighters remaining in the United Kingdom pounded German submarine pens in France, as the British wanted. Many months would pass before air commanders could fulfill the chiefs' January 21 order to wreak "the progressive destruction of the German military, industrial, and economic systems, and [undermine] the morale of the German people to a point where their armed resistance is fatally weakened."

Many months would also pass before the demand for unconditional surrender seemed germane. Some strategists agreed with J.F.C. Fuller that the term would "hang like a putrefying albatross around the necks of America and Britain," needlessly prolonging the war and turning its end into an Armageddon. Yet certain clear advantages accrued, as Roosevelt knew. The unambiguous demand reflected Allied public opinion, provided a moral lode star, and seemed a natural corollary of total war. Britain now was committed to smashing Japan even after Germany collapsed. Most important, the Russians would worry less that their Western allies might sign a separate peace of the sort made with Admiral Darlan. Little evidence ever emerged that the declaration fundamentally altered the military course of the war; perhaps it discouraged membership in German resistance cabals, which remained pitifully weak. If uttered without sober reflection, the demand could also be considered "a word of encouragement and exhortation addressed by companions to each other at a turning point on a journey which promised still to be long and arduous," as the British historian Michael Howard has concluded.

A sense of companionship *was* among the most enduring legacies of Casablanca. True, the Americans had been outgeneraled at the conference table. British guile and imperial heft had won through on most issues—"We were a reluctant tail to the British kite," Robert Murphy lamented. The wariness that characterized the Roosevelt-Churchill relationship throughout the war persisted. British commanders remained supercilious. "[Americans] are difficult though charming people to work with," Brooke told his diary, and "Marshall . . . arrived here without a single real strategic concept." American resentment could be seen even in a typed British transcript of the daily meetings: before the document was sent to Washington, some pencil turned aerodromes to airdromes, defence to defense, and honour to honor.

Yet Roosevelt's assertion that "each man has become a definite personal friend of his opposite number" sold the real relationships short. Something closer to kinship was developing, albeit with all the fraternal squabbles and envies to which brothers are heir.

Vice President Henry Wallace had observed that Franklin Roosevelt was a great waterman who could look in one direction while rowing a straight line in another. The president was at the oars with Churchill but he was looking at other horizons. Roosevelt recognized that the prime minister was "pretty much a 19th century colonialist," as the diplomat Averell Harriman put it, and "that the old order could not last." The war was a fault line. American strength was here for all to see, even in those bored soldiers lining the road for 150 miles to Marrakesh. Yes, the Yanks had been outgeneraled, and their shortcomings as strategic planners revealed—to none more clearly than themselves. But the British would never impose their will so easily again. Casablanca, like the African campaign as a whole, was part of the American coming of age, a hinge on which world history would swing for the next half century.

Dinner at La Saadia that Sunday night was fabulous, served without a faux pas by the GI butlers. The president and prime minister began with cocktails at eight in the salon. Their host was the senior American diplomat in Marrakesh, Kenneth Pendar, who as one of the Twelve Apostles had briefly been held under arrest with Murphy in Algiers during those early hours of TORCH. Sprawled on a divan with his arm extended, Roosevelt joked to Pendar, "I am the pasha. You may kiss my hand." At table, filet mignon and lobster were followed by a three-foot-high nougat sculpture of a Moorish tower; a candle flickered inside to dramatic effect, and spun sugar on the platter's edge approximated the distant mountains.

Many a toast was drunk—to king, to country, to president, to unconditional surrender—and many a song was sung. At midnight Roosevelt and Churchill repaired to two cleared tables in an adjoining room to write their communiqués to Stalin and to Chiang Kai-shek, the generalissimo who led the Chinese resistance against the Japanese. When the dispatches were finished at 3:30 A.M., they contained a "catching quality" of optimism, Pendar later wrote. "The prime minister seemed much more in the present and more of an extrovert," he added. "The president on the other hand often sat gazing into space as he worked. That night he had a look that was not exactly sad, yet it was the look of someone who comprehended sadness."

Four hours later, Roosevelt was wheeled to La Saadia's front steps and carried to the Daimler for the short drive to the airport. It was time to go home. Churchill planned to linger in Marrakesh for another two days, but insisted on accompanying the president to the plane. "I love these Americans," he told the physician Moran. "They have behaved so generously." Now the bleary prime minister appeared wearing monogrammed black velvet slippers, a quilted dressing gown embellished with red dragons, and an RAF air marshal's cap, which only partly concealed his deranged hair. Brandishing his cigar at the photographers on the runway, he grumbled, "You simply cannot do this to me."

Good-byes exchanged, Roosevelt settled into his seat for the long journey. He scribbled a note of thanks to be mailed to Pendar from the White House: "Marrakesh seemed far from wars and rumors of wars." A cordon of American troops ringed the airfield. Wispy morning fog drifted across the tarmac. To the southeast, the mountains blazed like the thrones of angels in the rising sun. Churchill climbed back into the car. "Don't tell me when they take off. It makes me too nervous," he said. The prime minister clutched Pendar's arm. "If anything happened to that man, I couldn't stand it. He is the truest friend. He has the farthest vision. He is the greatest man I have ever known."

8. A Bits and Pieces War

"Goats Set Out to Lure a Tiger"

THE almond trees bloomed early in central Tunisia, sweetening the January air with white blossoms that soon carpeted the ground as if strewn for a wedding. Arabs trotted to market on their braying donkeys, carrying faggots of firewood or panniers heaped with green onions. Veiled women peered through the iron grilles in their front doors at soldiers hurrying along the roads. War and rumors of war flared along the Eastern Dorsal, but mostly there was an intense bustle, as though scenewrights were building a proscenium on which great battles were to be staged once the curtain lifted. Men died—in firefights and in minefields and in plane crashes; at the temporary American cemetery in Maktar, grave markers were fashioned from the wooden slats of ration crates after the stack of crosses purchased from a local monastery ran out. But deaths remained few enough for the fallen to be unique and even flamboyant, like the American officer shot dead by a sniper in his jeep outside the Ousseltia Valley: while the jeep was being towed back to Allied lines, its brakes stuck, the vehicle caught fire, and soldiers for miles along the front could see what appeared to be a corpse riding a comet across the Tunisian pan.

As a first line of defense in extending the Allied battle lines south of the Medjerda River, the Anglo-Americans had entrusted the Eastern Dorsal to the French. General Juin's 35,000 troops formed a frayed picket line for 200 miles down to the Saharan oasis at Tozeur. Relations between the French and British were even more strained than those between Brits and Yanks. "British senior officers are what they are," Juin wrote Giraud. "What we think in them is stupidity or obstruction is often only the result of a slowness in, or absence of, imagination." A British colonel described his French counterpart in Tunisia as "a comic-opera soldier on the stage, 45 years' service in the Foreign Legion, covered with medals held on to his tunic by two bits of cotton. . . . We get on like fighting cocks."

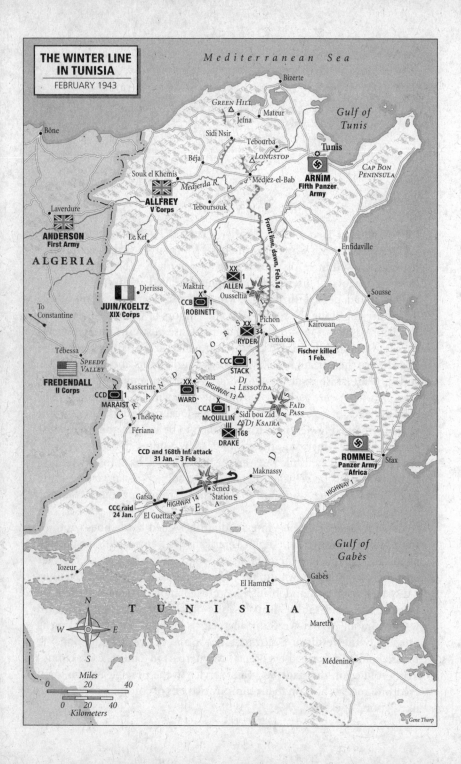

THE WINTER LINE
IN TUNISIA

FEBRUARY 1943

Mediterranean Sea

Bône

Gulf of Tunis

Bizerte

GREEN HILL
Jefna   Mateur

Sidi Nsir   Tébourba

Béja   LONGSTOP   Tunis

Souk el Khemis   Medjéz-el-Bab   ARNIM
                                         Fifth Panzer
ALLFREY   *Medjerda R.*   Army
V Corps
Laverdure   Teboursouk   CAP BON
                                                        PENINSULA
ANDERSON
First Army
                Le Kef   Enfidaville

ALGERIA
                                                        Sousse
                Djerissa   Maktar

JUIN/KOELTZ   XX 1
XIX Corps   ALLEN
To   Ousseltia
Constantine   X   1
                CCB 1   Pichon   Kairouan
Tébessa   ROBINETT
        SPEEDY   XX 34   Fondouk
        VALLEY   RYDER
FREDENDALL   Fischer killed
II Corps   X   1   1 Feb.
                               CCC
                Kasserine   STACK
        X   1   Sbeïtla   DJ
        CCD   LESSOUDA
MARAIST   XX 1   HIGHWAY 13
                WARD
        Thélepte   FAÏD
                               X   1   Sidi bou Zid PASS
        Fériana   CCA
                               McQUILLIN DJ KSAIRA
                               III 168
                               DRAKE
                CCD and 168th Inf. attack   ROMMEL
                31 Jan. – 3 Feb   Panzer Army
                                Maknassy   Africa
                                                   Sfax
        Gafsa   Sened
        CCC raid   Station
        24 Jan. HIGHWAY 14
        El Guettar
                                              HIGHWAY 1
                                                   *Gulf of
                                                   Gabès*
        Tozeur
                                        Gabès

                El Hamma
        N
                T U N I S I A
W   E
        S   Mareth

        Miles
        0   20   40   Médenine

        0   20   40
        Kilometers

                                              Gene Thorp

The French possessed almost no antitank weapons, but Allied planners considered most of the Eastern Dorsal too mountainous for German armor. Besides, the French lacked almost everything else, too: ammunition, artillery, uniforms, boots. Horses pulled trucks, men pulled wagons. Artillerymen wagged signal flags to communicate between batteries, as their forefathers had in Napoleon's legions. Morale slumped; some French soldiers pleaded for American helmets, to fool the Germans into thinking they were facing better-armed U.S. troops. Scattered on the lonely ridgelines, A. J. Liebling wrote, the French units resembled "goats set out to lure a tiger." An American liaison officer reported to Eisenhower that the French were "somewhat discouraged" because "it seems to be a question of running or being overrun."

"This past week has been a succession of disappointments," Eisenhower confessed to his diary after returning to Algiers from Casablanca. "I'm just writing some of them down so as to forget them." The abandonment of SATIN was one; he cited, as well, the "signs of complete collapse" by the French.

Other disappointments went unlisted. Neither Roosevelt nor Churchill had been effusive in his praise at Casablanca, and Eisenhower felt unappreciated. "His work and leadership had been taken rather for granted," Butcher wrote on January 17. The "absence of clear-cut words of thanks from the president or prime minister showed that they had their noses to the political winds." Harry Hopkins told Butcher at Casablanca that taking Tunisia would prove Eisenhower "one of the world's greatest generals," but without such a victory his fate was uncertain. "Such is the life of generals," Butcher mused. Some British journalists had begun speculating that the commander-in-chief might be sacked, and editorial writers at home also voiced impatience. "Mud is a silly alibi [for the] failure of the Allied forces to deliver a knockout blow," an Oklahoma newspaper opined. In a note to a West Point classmate, Eisenhower wrote, "There is no use denying that at times discouragement has piled on top of discouragement."

The abrupt scuttling of SATIN sent Allied planners back to the drawing board. There would be no drive to the sea, at least not until Montgomery's Eighth Army was in Tunisia to lend support. Instead, Fredendall's II Corps was to conduct raids and keep the enemy off-balance until better weather allowed a coordinated offensive. "We must keep up a bold, aggressive front," Eisenhower wrote Marshall, "and try to keep the Axis forces back on their heels."

At a commanders' meeting in the Constantine orphanage on January 18, the commander-in-chief laid out this new strategy, calling it "offensively defensive." Juin listened closely, then warned, "The Germans will not remain inactive." Eisenhower replied with the exasperation of a man who had had a difficult week: "I don't want anything quiescent on this goddam front during the next two months."

In this the Germans accommodated him, beginning that very day. Axis troops already occupied the mountain passes in the north, including the portals at Jefna and Longstop Hill that gave on to Bizerte and Tunis. Now they set out to capture the four main gaps through the Eastern Dorsal in central and southern Tunisia. Control of the passes would enlarge the Axis bridgehead and safeguard the coastal corridor linking Arnim's Fifth Panzer Army and Rommel's troops, who were closing into Tunisia from Libya. It would also guarantee Tunis's water supply—a reservoir forty miles southeast of Medjez-el-Bab—and keep the initiative in the Axis camp. (Eisenhower on January 11 had asked his staff about cutting off drinking water to the capital; he was told that because of heavy rains and multiple sources "no action can be taken against the water supply of Tunis.") Field Marshal Kesselring had not abandoned his ambition of driving the Anglo-Americans back through Constantine and Bône, but first he needed firm possession of the Eastern Dorsal.

On the afternoon of January 18, after a feint by fifty panzers toward British lines in the north, Tiger tanks and 5,000 Axis infantrymen slammed into the French around the reservoir. The enemy swarmed like wasps into the Ousseltia Valley, which controlled the critical pass to the holy city of Kairouan. Reporter A. D. Divine described French troops "retiring from crest to crest, fighting like mountain goats in an area of rock and shaley slopes." Within a day the equivalent of seven French infantry battalions had been cut off on the ridgelines. Juin reported that he was "not hopeful."

General Anderson ordered a British infantry brigade to counterattack from the north, then asked Fredendall to dispatch Robinett's CCB from the 1st Armored Division to block further Axis advance in the south. At 5:15 P.M. on January 19, from his lair in Speedy Valley, Fredendall phoned Robinett with an order so circumspect it seemed delphic:

> Move your command, i.e., the walking boys, pop guns, Baker's outfit and the outfit which is the reverse of Baker's outfit, and the big fellows to "M," which is due north of where you are now, as soon as possible. Have your boss report to the French gentleman whose name begins with "J" at a place which begins with "D," which is five grid squares to the left of "M."

Robinett later observed that translating this message, so freighted with mystery and confusion, probably took "about as much of my time as it did of the opposing German commander's." The corps commander's desires having at last been divined, 3,400 men and three dozen CCB tanks marched fifty miles to Maktar while Robinett reported to Juin at Djerissa. On the morning of January 21, American tanks rumbled down a perilous corkscrew road into the Ousseltia Valley, filled with "a lake of morning mist, beautiful, almost ethereal," Divine reported.

Three days of desultory fighting followed, with neither side robust enough to win a decisive advantage. Five battalions from Terry Allen's Big Red One joined Robinett, who theoretically was under French command but continued to receive contradictory orders from Fredendall, including one message that required nine hours to decode. "An excellent example of lack of coordination in the high command," a CCB assessment concluded, although the maverick Robinett was never wholly displeased at any confusion among his superiors that enlarged his autonomy.

By January 24 the battlefield had stabilized with the German line three to eight miles west of where it had been a week earlier. American casualties exceeded two hundred. Jubilation swept Speedy Valley at a report that more than four hundred Germans had been captured, but the whooping subsided when a second dispatch reduced the figure to fewer than forty.

French casualties were catastrophic, with prisoner-of-war losses alone close to 3,500 and some battalions pared to 200 men. "The French can no longer be counted on for much," Truscott reported.

Even Giraud now recognized the idiocy of his refusal to integrate French units into the Allied command structure. On January 24, with French concurrence, Eisenhower gave Anderson command of the entire Tunisian front, including French and American units. Fredendall's 32,000 men in II Corps would join the 67,000 British and American soldiers already in First Army, rather than reporting directly to Eisenhower through Truscott.

Until dry weather arrived in the north, and the drive on Tunis resumed, II Corps was to "act defensively" in protecting the Allied right wing. Eisenhower had decreed on January 18—and he repeated the order on January 26 and February 1—that the 1st Armored Division was to remain concentrated in a tight fist as "a mobile reserve" capable of countering any Axis attack in lower Tunisia.

He had no sooner issued these orders than he undercut them by authorizing the extended diversion of CCB to reinforce the Ousseltia

Valley and by encouraging Fredendall to "blood" the rest of Old Ironsides in various raids. Instead of being "well concentrated," as Eisenhower advised, the division was soon scattered across southern Tunisia.

As in the initial planning for SATIN, Eisenhower had issued ambiguous directives and then failed to ensure that his orders were properly executed. Again he was distracted by matters large and small: planning had begun for the invasion of Sicily, with Patton chosen to command the American forces; Churchill and his retinue intended to visit Algiers in early February, despite warnings of a plot to assassinate "the Big Cigar Man"; a variety show produced by Irving Berlin was scheduled to tour North Africa with 300 troupers; some American officers were drinking excessively, and, Eisenhower wrote Beetle Smith on January 26, "barracks used by our soldiers are not kept as neat and homelike in appearance at they could be."

Some of these issues required a supreme commander's attention, but they compromised Eisenhower's efficacy as a field general. Once again he considered moving to Constantine to take direct command of the front; once again he decided that the press of business in Algiers precluded the move. Instead he watched from afar and issued plaintive edicts urging that "every man do his best."

"As much as we preach simplicity in the Army," he wrote a friend in Washington in late January, "I sometimes feel it is the one thing most frequently violated in my own thinking."

Orlando Ward, who ostensibly commanded the 1st Armored Division, watched the splintering—again—of Old Ironsides with deepening dismay. Orders to Robinett in the Ousseltia counterattack had bypassed Ward completely. He had little to do except draft plans that the corps commander seemed determined to ignore. "Fredendall and his staff continue to command this division in detail—even arranging platoons," Ward scribbled in his diary.

Ward proposed recapturing another of the key Eastern Dorsal passes with a strong attack on Maknassy, nearly a hundred miles south of the Ousseltia fight and fifty miles due east of Gafsa on the road and rail line to Sfax. On January 23 Fredendall summoned Ward to Speedy Valley, where the clamor of pneumatic drills from the tunnel project echoed through the frozen hills. Fredendall in fact liked the Maknassy proposal, which would put American troops in striking distance of Rommel's line of retreat up the Tunisian coast, and he scheduled the attack for January 30. But first he wanted to launch a raid against Sened Station, a miserable whistle-stop in a shallow bowl midway between Gafsa and Maknassy.

Ward shifted uneasily. Such a raid would "give our hand away" and alert the Germans to American designs on Maknassy, he warned. Fredendall dismissed the objection with an impatient wave and told Ward to "knock the shit out of the Italians at Sened Station" the next day. Ward saluted, uttered a terse "Will do," and left Speedy Valley to return to his headquarters, six miles to the southeast.

At four A.M. on January 24, a raiding party of 2,000 American troops departed Gafsa in trucks for the twenty-eight-mile trip to Sened Station. Shortly before noon, artillery fire opened on the crossroads. Within three hours, the village had fallen, a hundred Italians lay dead or wounded, and nearly a hundred other bewildered prisoners had been rounded up. The raiders returned to Gafsa in time for dinner. American casualties totaled two wounded.

Fredendall was in high feather. At 3:30 P.M. he phoned Truscott in Constantine. "Remember that force I sent toward Maknassy looking for trouble? They ran into some stuff and smeared it. As soon as I get the details I will give them to you. I thought you might like to have some cheerful information from down here." At 9:30 P.M., Fredendall called again to boast that among the enemy captured was an Italian brigadier general. (Under closer scrutiny, he proved to be a lieutenant.) "Trump that if you can, damn it!" the corps commander exclaimed.

There was little celebrating at Ward's command post. A few prisoners had been captured, but now the Germans were aware of American eyes on Maknassy. Moreover, the 1st Armored Division was currently split into three parts and scattered across a hundred miles; Allen's Big Red One covered an even bigger arc. Allied units were so fragmented that Jack Thompson, a reporter for the *Chicago Tribune,* had begun calling the Tunisian campaign "a bits and pieces war."

"Whole staff completely disgusted with the high command as inefficient and meddlesome," Ward confided to his diary on January 28. "I agree, but we can't talk that way. We must absorb and hide our misgivings no matter what they are."

As a postscript he added: "Fed up but conscience is very clean."

General von Arnim duly noted the dustup in the far south and immediately reinforced both Maknassy Pass and the unfortunate garrison at Sened Station. But the mountain pass thirty miles north of Maknassy worried him more. Bisected by Highway 13 as it angled from Kasserine in the west to Sfax on the eastern coast, Faïd Pass was a narrow defile between razorback ridges and red shale chimneys twisted into fantastic shapes. French strategists considered Faïd vital in controlling central

Tunisia, as Medjez-el-Bab was in controlling the north. Arnim called it "my nightmare": barely 500 yards deep and half a mile wide, the pass gave on to the broad, flat coastal plain to the east and the broad, arid Tunisian plateau to the west. The ubiquitous Colonel Raff had seized Faïd from 200 Axis defenders in early December; more than a thousand French troops held it now, the last significant gap in the Eastern Dorsal still in Allied hands.

That was about to change. The 21st Panzer Division had rearmed after repairing to Tunisia from El Alamein at the van of Rommel's retreating army. On January 30, battle groups from the division struck Faïd Pass in a three-pronged attack as precise as a pitchfork. One French outpost reported being duped by Germans wearing U.S. Army uniforms and shouting, "Do not fire. We are Americans." Rippling fire from thirty panzers drove the French back yard by yard, and body by body, until by late afternoon the valiant defenders were encircled.

In the noisy perpetual shade of Speedy Valley, tearful French officers pleaded with Fredendall for help. The two battalions besieged at Faïd could hold out only a few hours more. The Americans must counterattack immediately, in force. "This is the most important point in the line," one French officer said. "It must be held."

Fredendall was reluctant to abandon his planned drive on Maknassy, which was scheduled to begin in a few hours with another 2000-man raiding party. He believed that the attack would siphon Axis troops away from Faïd. But French pleas, and a vague directive at mid-morning from Anderson to "restore" the situation at Faïd, forced his hand.

Prompt, decisive action could well have saved Faïd Pass and altered the grim course of the Tunisian campaign in the coming weeks. Fredendall instead ordered a mincing sequence of half-measures destined to make a bad predicament truly dire. He began at 9:30 A.M. by ordering the 1st Armored Division's Combat Command A to counterattack Faïd Pass but without weakening defenses around the town of Sbeïtla on the road to Kasserine. Part of CCA headed east along Highway 13, but at a glacial pace slowed further by air attacks—first by Stukas, then by misdirected American fighters. At 2:30 P.M., still seven miles short of the pass, the CCA commander, Brigadier General Raymond E. McQuillin, decided to bivouac for the night and delay his attack until the next morning.

McQuillin's nickname was Old Mac, and it was all too apt. Born in 1887, he was placid and fusty, with a snowy crown and the straight posture of a Kentucky long rifle. A bachelor cavalryman, McQuillin in a long career had served as a White House aide in the 1920s and later commanded the Signal Corps Buzzer School. "As a man he was wonderful and warm, but as a commander he was a 20th-century George Armstrong Custer, in many ways a genuine blockhead," one 1st Armored officer said.

Having granted the enemy an extra half day to winkle out the remaining French, Old Mac spent the night pondering the maps and blaring radios in his cramped command half-track. He was joined by Truscott, who had come forward from Constantine as Eisenhower's man on the ground, and Ward, a spectator in his own division's fight. Neither visitor sensed trouble, although portents abounded: McQuillin's tardiness; French distemper at the sluggish American response; and feuding between McQuillin and the senior infantry officer assigned to the counterattack, Colonel Alexander N. Stark, Jr. Stark, commander of the 26th Infantry from Allen's Big Red One, was known as Old Stark for reasons no more flattering than those informing Old Mac's moniker. He had won the Distinguished Service Cross in World War I, but was a heavy drinker, and staff officers routinely searched his jeep for hidden bottles. "It was nerve-racking," his operations officer later recalled. "I thought, 'This man has got to be sober.' . . . He should never have been in a position like that."

The American assault began at seven A.M. on Sunday, January 31, just late enough for the sun peeping over the Eastern Dorsal to catch the attacking GIs flush in the face. An intelligence officer warned McQuillin that the Germans had emplaced 88mm anti-aircraft guns as antitank weapons above the western approaches to Faïd Pass, but Old Mac "strongly rejected the validity of the report," a 26th Infantry officer recorded.

Truscott and Ward drove 800 yards north to climb Djebel Lessouda. A mile long and 2,000 feet high, the hill lay on the desert pan like a whale on a beach. Prickly pears planted for livestock fodder covered the lower slopes in neat rows. Breathing hard, the two generals climbed a steep shale incline glittering with flecks of mica. The crowing of cocks and a cur's insistent bark carried from the shabby hamlet of Poste de Lessouda, where McQuillin's command post occupied a cactus patch along Highway 13.

In the panorama from Lessouda's eastern flank, both Truscott and Ward noted similarities to the terrain of the American high plains. Here in Tunisia, reporter Philip Jordan wrote, was "that half-world where cultivation does not quite know where to cease or the desert to begin." Seven miles to the south lay the dark green cedars and white stucco houses of Sidi bou Zid, once an important camel market and now a somnolent town of 500 Arabs and a few French farmers. Seven miles to the east, the Eastern Dorsal rose like an ocean swell. From Poste de Lessouda the blacktop ran taut as a bowstring through the nick in the ridgeline that marked Faïd Pass.

Gazing east with their field glasses through the morning haze, Truscott and Ward saw a dozen Sherman tanks and a battalion of Stark's infantrymen following Highway 13 toward the pass; pushing out of Sidi bou Zid farther south, a battalion from Ward's 6th Armored Infantry tramped across irrigated vegetable fields cut by the narrow ravines, or wadis. An artillery battery spoke just below Djebel Lessouda, and moments later white puffs flowered around Faïd.

The American force looked puny in the expanse of the Tunisian plain, and puniness against Germans in the desert usually proved fatal. Given ample time to entrench, the enemy had fortified Faïd Pass with machine guns, mortars, and the 88mm guns whose existence McQuillin had denied. Lieutenant Colonel Gerald C. Kelleher, commanding the 1st Battalion of the 26th Infantry, led his 700 men to within a mile of the pass and then veered left to outflank Faïd from the north. Gunfire rippled from the hills. The battalion scaled one ridge, then a second, only to be pinned down for the rest of the day by an impenetrable wall of Axis fire from the third crest. After dark, Kelleher ordered his men to creep back down to the plain. American cannoneers found the exhausted battalion commander wandering across the desert and revived him with a supper of French toast and syrup, commodities hoarded for just such an emergency.

For Company H of Ward's 1st Armored Regiment the day was shorter but worse. In this, their first combat, the tankers were ordered to stage a frontal assault on the pass with seventeen Sherman tanks and a few tank destroyers. Strafed by Messerschmitts roaring down the defile, the tanks pressed into the pass, firing through the morning glare at muzzle flashes real and imagined.

Then the trap was sprung. German antitank gunners opened up from three sides. "The velocity of the enemy shells was so great that the suction created by the passing projectiles pulled the dirt, sand, and dust from the desert floor and formed a wall that traced the course of each shell," Lieutenant Laurence Robertson later recalled. Shells zipped through the American formation, trailed by thick coils of dust tinted bright green by the tracer magnesium burning on the German rounds. Within ten minutes, more than half the American tanks were ablaze; flames licked from the hatches and exhaust vents, and each wounded Sherman frothed with its thirty pounds of chemical fire retardant.

Back the surviving tanks raced, as fast as reverse gear could carry them, swerving to keep their thick frontal armor toward the German muzzles. Wounded soldiers lay like trophy deer on the hull decks. Tankless tankers clumped through the mud, chased by swarms of green tracers. When two self-propelled howitzers sank in quicksand to their barrels during the retreat, gunners detonated thermite grenades on the engine blocks within view of the disheartened brass watching from Djebel Lessouda. The survivors shambled into Sidi bou Zid, where French troops shared out a dinner of dates and heavy black bread sliced with a bayonet.

The failed counterattack had cost nine tanks, 100 casualties, and whatever mutual trust had existed between tankers and infantrymen. The enmity between McQuillin and Stark carried into the lower ranks, with each unit convinced the other had left it in the lurch. The parallel attack farther south had also collapsed under Stuka attacks and heavy panzer fire. McQuillin swallowed his discouragement and scheduled another attack for February 1 at one P.M., when the sun would be at a less hostile angle. "McQuillin, put everything into it tomorrow and accomplish your mission," Ward urged in a message at 9:15 P.M. on Sunday. "I am counting on you."

No use. Two infantry battalions surged up the ridgeline three miles south of the pass early Monday afternoon. German gunners "held their fire until we were practically at the foot of the objective," an officer wrote. "The men got a terrific raking over by the enemy as they fell back." One commander signaled McQuillin, "Too much tank and gun fire. . . . Infantry can not go on without great loss." Fifteen panzers swung out from Faïd Pass and enfiladed the infantry with fire on the left flank until checked by countercharging American Shermans. "They shook us like we had been dragged over a plowed field," one sergeant wrote. McQuillin's message to Ward was equally terse: "Failed to accomplish mission."

Faïd Pass was gone, and with it the Eastern Dorsal. More than 900 French defenders were dead or missing; the 1st Armored alone suffered 210 casualties. Recriminations followed. McQuillin bitterly accused Stark of ineptitude, although his own generalship was wanting. General Giraud dispatched a scathing message to Fredendall, protesting the butchery of French troops. The II Corps commander parried a proposal for yet another assault by telling Anderson, "To retake it will be too expensive, but I can contain the pass." Anderson concurred.

About the only solace for the Allies on this Monday afternoon was the fatal wounding of General Wolfgang Fischer, whose leadership of the 10th Panzer Division had helped win the day for the Axis at Tébourba and Longstop Hill in December. Wandering into an improperly marked minefield west of Kairouan, Fischer's staff car detonated an Italian "devil's egg" that blew off both the general's legs and his left arm. He called for a notebook and managed to scribble a page and a half to his wife, of which the last words were "It will soon be over."

"This Can't Happen to Us"

FREDENDALL's attention remained riveted in the south, and he entertained the belief that triumph at Maknassy could compensate for debacle at Faïd. Sitting in his canvas chair by the stove in Speedy Valley, he told reporters he intended to press "on to Maknassy, at least, and draw the pucker string tight."

Instead of concentrating the 1st Armored's two combat commands as Eisenhower desired, Fredendall even further fractured the division. The recently concocted Combat Command C had staged the glorious raid on Sened Station a week earlier, and now an even newer Combat Command D was created to seize Maknassy. On January 30 at one P.M., as the Axis attack on Faïd Pass developed, Fredendall by telephone—again bypassing Ward—had ordered CCC to march northeast from Gafsa toward Sidi bou Zid in order to aid McQuillin by hitting the enemy in the flank. Two thousand men tramped all night to within a dozen miles of Faïd Pass, but at four P.M. on January 31, Fredendall countermanded himself. Persuaded that Old Mac's counterattack at Faïd was succeeding—a hundred miles' distance from the battlefield encouraged such delusions— the corps commander ordered CCC to "turn south and join in coordinated effort . . . on Maknassy."

CCC swung south for ten miles, and by mid-afternoon on February 1 was poised thirteen miles north of Maknassy. There another barrage of conflicting orders fell, ending with a directive to march north yet again, this time toward Sbeïtla and the road to Kasserine. Greater confusion could scarcely be imagined.

That left Maknassy to CCD, now reinforced with the first units in Tunisia from the 34th Infantry Division and specifically the Iowa boys of the 168th Infantry Regiment. The plan drawn by Colonel Robert V. Maraist—Ward's artillery chief, pressed into service as the CCD commander—was straightforward: artillery, tanks, and infantry would again fall on Sened Station in an attack similar to the January 24 raid, and then press on twenty miles to Maknassy.

Infantrymen from the 1st Battalion of the 168th packed into open trucks late Sunday morning, January 31, for the trip from Gafsa to Sened

Station. Having just arrived from Algeria, many still carried their bulky barracks bags. Hundreds of orange cigarette embers glowed from the truck beds. Sened Station had been a walkover a week earlier, the men told one another; the village still was said to be defended only by Austrians and Italians. An engineer officer detected "a sort of Sunday School picnic atmosphere in the morning as we started out."

Then the Stukas came. Eight rolled out of the sun in the first wave, one trailing another with sirens shrieking as bombs tumbled among trucks bunched nose to tail. "All down the road men were lying, some terribly hurt, some dead, some shocked beyond control," one witness wrote. "We sent messages for doctors, ambulances, and stretcher parties, [and] did what we could for men who were bleeding to death." Fifty soldiers had been killed or wounded, the worst toll from a Stuka attack in the entire Tunisian campaign. Another officer wrote:

> It was the most terrible thing I had ever seen, not the bodies and parts of bodies near smoking vehicles, some sitting, some scattered, some blue from powder burns—it was the expressions on the faces of those [who] wandered listlessly around the wreckage, not knowing where to go or what to do, saying, "This can't happen to us."

Sergeants herded the troops back into the remaining trucks, but the planes soon returned, this time with Messerschmitts that dimpled the road with cannon fire. Terrified men pelted into the desert. "Maimed and twisted bodies, some of them still burning, made the men overcautious," wrote Lieutenant Lauren E. McBride. Again the men were loaded on their trucks, only to flee with each rumor of approaching aircraft; finally, the trucks were abandoned and the battalion staggered toward Sened Station in two parallel columns 500 yards on either side of Highway 14. Arriving at dusk in an olive grove three miles from the village, too late to attack at five P.M. as planned, the battalion bivouacked for the night. "My God," the engineer officer reflected, "this Sunday School picnic has really turned into something."

Three different colonels had led the 3,600 men of the 168th Infantry in the last six months of 1942, and a fourth took command in January. Thomas D. Drake, raised in a West Virginia coal town, had enlisted at sixteen, won a Distinguished Service Cross and two Silver Stars in World War I, then served as the first sergeant of Pershing's honor guard. After leaving the Army for college, Drake had returned as an officer in 1923. Now forty-two, he was short, brave, and crotchety, incessantly yelling "Allez!" at Tunisian date merchants along the road. Two weeks earlier he had issued regimental mess regulations forbidding officers from bolting their meals. "Neither will good table manners tolerate placing elbows on the table and consuming food in a reclining position," he added. The men privately called him Quack-Quack.

As his 1st Battalion huddled in the Sened Station olive groves on the evening of January 31, Drake stood with Fredendall in Speedy Valley before a map of southern Tunisia. Drake was to support the thrust to the east by Colonel Maraist's CCD, Fredendall said. "You will attack tomorrow morning and seize this high ground," he added, pointing to the ridges east of Maknassy. "After taking up an all-around defensive position you will conduct raids into Rommel's lines of communications, doing all the damage you can and preventing his uninterrupted movement north."

But first, Sened Station must fall. Colonel Drake left Speedy Valley and reached Gafsa a few minutes past midnight on Monday, February 1. He planned to reinforce 1st Battalion's morning attack, and an armor captain named Frederick K. Hughes had been assigned to lead the 2nd Battalion that night to a staging area outside Sened Station, where Maraist's force was already hidden in ravines and orchards. Drake cautioned Captain Hughes against "overrunning the front line" in the dark. As the first trace of dawn smudged the eastern horizon, Drake followed in a jeep, ready for a fight.

Except that he could not find 2nd Battalion. Daybreak stole across the flat desert where 800 men should have been fixing their bayonets: the ground was empty but for tuft grass and a few of Maraist's tanks. Military policemen on Highway 14 reported that eighty trucks, including the 2nd Battalion's field kitchens, had barreled through roadside checkpoints and into no-man's-land outside Sened Station. A subsequent investigation revealed that Captain Hughes had led his charges into the heavily reinforced enemy defenses.

Hysterical shooting and a constellation of parachute flares in the east confirmed the worst. The 2nd Battalion was pinned down less than a mile from Sened Station, and would remain so for the next ten hours. Hughes was captured. Soldiers tumbled from the truck beds to scoop shallow foxholes with helmets and hands. Enemy mortars crumped, and machine guns stuttered "like old sewing machines being cranked." The fusillade destroyed seventeen vehicles. Ebony smoke spiraled from burning rubber and gasoline. "They were," an officer in another unit later noted, "in a very bad spot."

Intended to be a cakewalk on the way to Maknassy, Sened Station turned into a daylong pitched battle. At 9:30 A.M., Drake rallied the 1st

Battalion from its olive grove. Tromping about in his cavalry boots with field glasses banging against his chest, he roared, "Go on up there! They can't hurt you! They're nothing but black Dagos, and you're Americans!"

By noon the troops remained more than a mile from the village, harassed by Stukas and swarms of bullets that prompted one chaste young private to ask if anyone else could hear "all those bees buzzing?" Men lay on their backs kicking at jammed rifle bolts with their boots. "We learned in that battle that sand and oil don't mix," a lieutenant recalled. The 1st Battalion commander, Lieutenant Colonel John C. Petty, was firing from his knees when enemy bullets tore open his stomach; he would cling to life for twelve days before passing. Petty's executive officer bled so profusely from a head wound that his submachine gun clogged with blood. An enemy shell blew through the battalion intelligence officer, Lieutenant Woodrow N. Nance. "I saw his canteen fly up in the air," another officer reported. "He was on his back and gurgling incoherently. He was torn almost in two at the middle." Drake later wrote: "Men were dying everywhere. The sand was kicked up in clouds and the air was filled with whining bullets."

At midafternoon, as Maraist directed artillery and tank fire on the village, Drake ordered a flanking attack on the right by 1st Battalion's Company B. Three rifle platoons fixed bayonets, fanned out in a skirmish line, and surged toward the village. Charred corpses were splayed across the turrets of three smoldering American tanks. A platoon leader whose leg had been reduced to a bloody stump screamed at the passing infantrymen, "Kill them! Kill them all!"

Sened Station buckled and then fell at four P.M. beneath the weight of 1st Battalion's assault. An enemy counterattack reclaimed the town long enough to capture the 2nd Battalion surgeon and fifteen medics who had rushed in prematurely. In a final spasm of grenades and bayonets, the village fell for good to the Americans at 5:30. The captured booty included 152 prisoners and a fleet of Axis reconnaissance bicycles. Most enemy troops melted back toward Maknassy.

Fredendall was considerably less charmed by this excursion into Sened Station than he had been by the one a week earlier. In a message to Colonel Maraist—yet again bypassing Ward, who issued contradictory orders of his own—Fredendall declared, "Too much time has been wasted already. . . . Use your tanks and shove."

Shove they did, on Tuesday, February 2. By noon CCD held a ridgeline six miles east of Sened Station. Then Stukas attacked in earnest at four P.M. Twenty-four dive-bombers dropped from the western sun in the rear, unnerving Drake's already shaky infantrymen, and the subsequent appearance of panzers on the left flank completed their unmanning. An officer in the 2nd Battalion of the 168th Infantry came pelting through the lines. "There has been a breakthrough!" he bellowed. "Save yourselves! Save yourselves!"

Hundreds obeyed. Rising from their holes, they ran toward the rear or vaulted into fleeing vehicles. Drake reported that the men "were wild-eyed as they roared along at full speed. The column was made up of half-ton weapon carriers, jeeps, halftracks, tanks—anything that would roll." An artillery battalion commander later recalled, "A sort of hysteria took hold of everyone. The [enemy] tanks were knocked out, but the hysteria continued." A combat engineer added, "All of the infantry soldiers I could see anywhere around were hightailing it to the rear." His troops fled, too.

Officers cobbled together a straggler line from north to south across Highway 14 at Sened Station to snare those fleeing. There the stampede was finally turned by armed guards as unyielding as those in the Civil War who had demanded, "Show blood!" before admitting any soldier to the rear. Sergeant James McGuiness of Company F wrote his parents:

> Some of the fellows have run off and leave us fighting and don't think for one minute that I haven't had the urge to get up and leave. A fellow isn't yellow, but those shells bursting above and around you day in and day out is really tough.

The American attack was spent. A few tank destroyers edged to within six miles of Maknassy on February 3, but American planes mistakenly bombed U.S. positions in Sened Station that afternoon, discouraging further initiative. "Your outfit is a bunch of darn poor map readers," Drake complained in a message to the Army Air Forces. "They just bombed my service train bivouac instead of the enemy concentration. Besides that, they are poor bombers as they missed that target by five hundred yards." By dawn on the fourth all of CCD had pulled back to Gafsa, abandoning Sened Station for the second time in ten days.

The offensive had failed to seize Maknassy, failed to relieve enemy pressure on Faïd Pass, failed to help McQuillin's CCA. A 1st Armored Division account concluded that "no decisive objective was gained." American losses totaled 331, among them the 2nd Battalion commander. Lightly nicked in the hand, but psychologically unhinged by the Tuesday afternoon panic, he was replaced by his executive officer, Lieutenant Colonel Robert Moore, the onetime Boy Captain and druggist of Villisca, Iowa.

Mistrust cascaded like a rock slide. General Anderson and the French doubted the Americans. Eisenhower doubted Fredendall. Fredendall doubted Ward. McQuillin doubted Stark. Stark doubted McQuillin. Fredendall on February 5 summoned Ward to Speedy Valley and read portions of a letter Eisenhower had sent him the previous day:

> One of the things that gives me the most concern is the habit of some of our generals in staying too close to their command posts. Please watch this very, very carefully among all your subordinates. . . . Generals are expendable just as is any other item in an army; and, moreover, the importance of having the general constantly present in his command post is frequently overemphasized.

With cocked eyebrow and knowing nod Fredendall implied that the cutting reference was to McQuillin, or perhaps to Ward himself. In fact, the letter as a whole made clear that the commander-in-chief's deeper reservations concerned his II Corps commander's Anglophobia and other shortcomings. Eisenhower had confided to Truscott his fear that Fredendall was too rash, inclined to throw away men in "futile rushing around."

Ward sensed Fredendall's game. "He is a spherical SOB. No doubt. Two-faced at that," Ward told his diary. The corps commander "has no loyalty in him for his subordinates."

As recently as February 1, Eisenhower had considered abandoning the Eastern Dorsal and pulling back toward the higher, western mountain range known as the Grand Dorsal. But now he thought better of such a retrenchment: the ethos of the U.S. Army resisted surrendering even an acre of ground fairly won. New orders called for clinging to as much forward territory as possible while the Allied armies prepared for "sustained, aggressive action in the month of March."

Meanwhile the troops buried their dead and again dug in down the length of Tunisia. One company war diary spoke for many brave men: "We could not help wondering whether the officers directing the American effort knew what they were doing."

"The Mortal Dangers That Beset Us"

ERWIN Rommel did know what he was doing. And he would not wait until March.

At eight A.M. on February 12, musicians from the 8th Panzer Regiment band gathered outside a dusty yellow trailer parked beneath camouflage netting near coastal Highway 1 south of Sfax. Citrus perfumed the morning air, masking the usual army odors of canvas and hot oil. Hoisting their tubas and cornets, the bandsmen struck up a serenade for their commander to mark the second anniverary of his arrival in Africa. Then they switched to a brisk march inspired by the struggle of the past two years: "We are the men of the Afrika Korps . . ."

The trailer door swung open and Field Marshal Rommel stepped into the sun. Against the morning chill he wore a soldier's greatcoat with red lapel facings, gold buttons, and "Afrikakorps" stitched on the cuffs. He was lean and sunburned, like his men, with lips perpetually cracked and crow's-feet etched around eyes long accustomed to squinting. Hatless, he looked older than his fifty-one years. A widow's peak jagged across his broad cranium, and the hair brushed back above his ears lay sleek as feathers. Every soldier in the encampment could see the toll of the past two years in Rommel's face, the anguish of 10,000 German and Italian graves left behind in Egypt and Libya when Panzer Army Africa had crossed into Tunisia two weeks earlier.

"My dear young friend," Rommel had told a staff officer a few days before, "if you only knew how long it's been since I've been able to sleep." Kesselring, who considered Rommel's nerves all but shot, later observed, "The very last armored infantryman knew of the doubts that were rending the heart of his commanding general." So few of Rommel's original "Africans" remained—only 4 of the 1,000 who had come with the 8th Machine Gun Battalion, for example. After the impromptu band concert, the field marshal returned to the trailer to write to his wife, Lucie-Maria:

> It's two years to-day since I arrived on African soil. Two years of heavy and stubborn fighting, most of the time with a far superior enemy. . . . I have endeavoured to do my duty, both in my own sphere and for the cause as a whole. . . . We must do our utmost to beat off the mortal dangers that beset us. Unfortunately it's all a matter of supplies. I hope that my decision to remain with my troops to the end will be confirmed. You will understand my attitude. As a soldier one cannot do otherwise.

"Rommel, Rommel, Rommel!" Churchill had exclaimed the previous summer. "What else matters but beating him?" Like most of history's conspicuously successful commanders, he had an uncanny ability to dominate the minds of his adversaries. The son and grandson of school-teachers, he was short and a bit jowly; his face had a bronzed reserve, as if he were already wearing his death mask. A Württemberger from Swabia in the German southwest, with neither Prussian blood nor the crimson trouser stripe of a General Staff alumnus, he embodied several traits of his native region: self-reliance, thrift, decency, and a dour common sense. A much decorated infantryman in the Great War, he remained skeptical of the newfangled tank until the blitzkrieg in Poland imbued him with a convert's passion. He rocketed from lieutenant colonel to field marshal in four years, his reputation burnished by Goebbels's Propaganda Ministry; the young division commander's dash across Flanders and down the French coast to Spain in 1940 was featured in the film *Victory in the West,* which Rommel also helped direct. He still carried one of Goebbels's flunkies on his staff in Africa to stoke his own mystique, which Kesselring considered "the equivalent of one good division."

Rommel's first successes in Africa manifested the audacity, tactical brilliance, and personal style—he occasionally hunted gazelle with a submachine gun from a staff car—that contrasted so invidiously with British lumpishness and won him the sobriquet of Desert Fox. The campaign had seesawed back and forth across 1,500 miles of the African littoral, with Rommel eventually chasing the British Eighth Army back toward the Nile in the summer of 1942. Then came El Alamein, that clanging defeat. Ever since, he had been retreating, under languid but insistent pressure from Montgomery. *Life* magazine called him "a fugitive leading a fugitive army."

"Day and night I'm tormented by the thought that things might go really wrong here in Africa," he had written Lucie a few hours before crossing into Tunisia at dawn on January 26. "I'm so depressed that I can hardly do my work." Insomnia, headaches, low blood pressure, rheumatism, exhaustion, intestinal distress: he was not a well man. Before hurrying back to Egypt for the emergency at El Alamein, Rommel had been medically evacuated to convalesce in the Fatherland; in the four months since then his health had not returned.

At a recent staff conference, a subordinate thought the field marshal "gave the impression of a broken man. We hardly recognized him." Only in the past few days had he showed renewed signs of aggression; his lieutenants hoped that the greening hills of Tunisia would lift him from his torpor. But the real tonic for the old fox was a scent of fresh prey from beyond the Eastern Dorsal: the Americans.

Rommel understood more than most how tenuous the Axis grasp on North Africa was. Through the end of January, more than 100,000 German and Italian troops had arrived in Tunisia from Europe, with reinforcements of roughly a thousand a day still coming. As Rommel's

Panzer Army Africa finished moving into southern Tunisia, the bridge-head numbers would swell to 190,000 soldiers and over 300 tanks, a temporary advantage of fourteen Axis divisions to nine for the Allies.

Yet many of Rommel's German units were at far less than half strength, with barely 30,000 combat soldiers; in January alone, he suffered more than 2,000 casualties in rearguard fighting against the British—and a total of five soldiers had arrived as replacements. Some units were pitifully weak: the 90th Light Africa Division reported only 2,400 troops, the 164th Light just 3,800. Equipment shortages were even more grievous. Authorized 386 tanks, he had but 129, of which only half were ready for combat. Instead of 747 antitank guns, his men had 182; instead of 3,797 machine guns, they had 1,411. Only one-sixth of his artillery strength remained intact.

Rommel may have "exercised an almost hypnotic influence on Hitler," in Kesselring's words, but the Führer was not so beguiled as to provide anything like the quantities of arms and fuel needed for his army. The demands of Stalingrad, now entering its epic final act, as well as an increasingly lethal Allied interdiction campaign in the Mediterranean, meant that only a fraction of the necessary matériel and manpower made it to Africa. As Rommel had told Lucie, it was all a matter of supplies.

True, Rommel's army included almost 50,000 Italian troops, the remnants of Mussolini's imperial force in Libya. Thirty thousand more had been shipped to Tunisia from Italy. But the bridgehead also included a huge number of noncombatants, including colonial civil administrators and camp followers swept along by the retreating army. An official German account estimated that by late February 350,000 Axis men would be in Tunisia, of whom barely one-third could be considered true combat soldiers.

Rommel increasingly blamed the Italians for his woes, and his disdain reflected the attitude of the German high command. Easily caricatured, Italian soldiers in fact showed flashes of ferocity and tactical competence in North Africa, particularly in infantry skirmishes. Yet most Italian troops were badly trained, ill equipped, and poorly led. The best Italian divisions had already been smashed in Russia or while fighting the British in Africa. Il Duce's army, one German general concluded, "was in agony." The standard Italian rifle dated to 1891; Italian grenades were so capricious that British troops were warned never to use them; troops moved by foot or not at all, because there were few trucks. Many Italian recruits were so unlettered that drill instructors tied bandannas around their left arms to teach them left from right. Even an Italophile like Kesselring asserted, "The Italian is easily contented. He actually has only three fashionable passions: coffee, cigarettes, and women. . . . The Italian soldier is not a soldier from within." The Panzer Army Africa war diary for February 11 noted, "Combat value of the almost totally untried Italian units is the great question. . . . Experience has unfortunately shown that any optimism is uncalled for."

In these and other matters, Rommel had a natural ally in Arnim. A meeting at a recent conference south of Gabès had been their first since both were young captains in the Weimar Republic eighteen years earlier. They had not cared much for each other then, and that distaste lingered. But Rommel's strategic assessment had a blunt simplicity: the high command must either provide sufficient supplies to the two African armies or abandon Tunisia altogether. The Axis cause in Africa was "a house of cards." He fervently hoped that "sober calculations would win over political dreams."

Arnim agreed. Hitler had promised him six to seven additional divisions, which had yet to materialize. A quarter of his combat strength was Italian, and of the 150,000 tons of supplies he and Rommel estimated they needed jointly every month, far less than half was actually arriving. There had even been talk of shipping to North Africa a penal brigade of homosexuals. "We cannot afford a second Stalingrad," Arnim told Rommel. "Right now the Italian fleet could transport us back."

But such talk of decampment fell on hostile ears in Berlin and Rome, where relinquishing North Africa was seen as inviting an Allied invasion of southern Europe. Kesselring considered Rommel a weary defeatist eager to repair to Tunis or perhaps the Italian Alps. Promises of more guns, more men, more this and more that, trickled south from the Axis capitals; there would be no abandonment of Tunisia. Hitler in mid-February left for his Eastern Front command post in the Ukraine, where thoughts of North Africa rarely penetrated. Some officers in the Wehrmacht high command had voluntarily placed themselves on restricted rations as a gesture of solidarity with the encircled army at Stalingrad: 2½ ounces of bread a day, 6½ ounces of horsemeat, a half-ounce of sugar, and a single cigarette.

If the troops in Tunisia were to avoid a similar diet, the bridgehead would have to be widened beyond the current fifty-mile coastal strip. Soon Rommel and Arnim would have to defend a 400-mile front against an enemy steadily growing in power, with new tanks, heavy howitzers, antitank guns, and fighters. Allied strength would quickly grow from nine divisions to twenty. In the past month the Anglo-Americans had flown more than 11,000 air sorties over Tunisia, an intimation of things to come.

On January 19, the high command in Berlin had first floated the idea of attacking through Gafsa and Sbeïtla toward Tébessa and from there "either by an advance on Bône or Constantine bring on a collapse of the hostile northern front." Rommel believed the greatest potential threat to the entire Tunisian bridgehead was an American lunge from Gafsa toward Gabès to sever the two Axis armies. If the Germans were to survive in Tunisia—and the field marshal had such grave doubts that he had privately ordered an English dictionary—they must "break up the American assembly area in southwest Tunisia." The leisurely pace of Montgomery's pursuit would allow Rommel's troops at least a fortnight of mischief in Tunisia while a rear guard barricaded the door at Mareth, a fortified line near the Libyan border. After crushing the Americans, Panzer Army Africa could swing back south to repel the British Eighth Army.

Kesselring agreed, and the attack plan quickly coalesced. Arnim's Fifth Panzer Army would strike first in Operation FRÜHLINGSWIND—Spring Breeze—a thrust by two panzer divisions through Faïd Pass on Sidi bou Zid. Spearheaded by more than 200 Mark III and Mark IV tanks, plus a dozen Tigers, FRÜHLINGSWIND was designed to "weaken the American by destroying some of his elements and thereby confuse and delay his advance." Rommel's Panzer Army Africa, including the Afrika Korps, would then strike farther south through Gafsa in Operation MORGENLUFT, Morning Air. When reinforced by a portion of Arnim's army, Rommel—who had designs on the vast Allied dumps at Tébessa and Speedy Valley—would have 160 tanks. "We are going to go all out for the total destruction of the Americans," Kesselring declared.

On February 12, as the panzer regiment band played for Rommel, Arnim fixed his initial attack for dawn on Sunday, February 14, Valentine's Day. It would fall precisely thirteen weeks—a quarter of a year—after the first TORCH landings. In his own encampment, Rommel finished writing orders to shift several units from the Libyan border to a staging area northwest of Gabès that night.

The predatory glint had returned to his eyes. He again emerged from the trailer to greet the officers who had come to Africa with him in February 1941 and were still fighting under his command; now numbering but nineteen, they had been invited to pay their respects in a brief, sentimental reunion. The band once again struck up the familiar march, and the old fighters sang, in voices thick with emotion:

> In the scorching sands of Africa, the German panzers struggle,
> For our people and for our Fatherland. . . .
> We are the men of the Afrika Korps.

* * *

The front remained preternaturally quiet for more than a week after the Maknassy expedition collapsed. For a few francs, Tunisian boys carried messages between American and Italian sentries encouraging each other to surrender; the Italians sometimes did, slipping through the lines with a battered suitcase, a sheaf of pornographic photos, and the address of a cousin in Brooklyn or Detroit. A circuit-riding U.S. Army chaplain conducted services in the shadow of the Eastern Dorsal for troops whose devotions had fallen into arrears; his assistant played "Rock of Ages" on a portable piano and handed each congregant a few sticks of chewing gum, as if they were communion wafers. Red Cross volunteers appeared in blinding snow and dust storms with drums of hot coffee dispensed from a rattletrap truck known as Clubmobile California.

II Corps had suffered more than 700 casualties in the past month, and the first replacement troops filtered into Tunisia from depots in Casablanca and Oran. Many lacked rifles or entrenching tools. One group of 190 replacements included 130 charged with absence without leave or other offenses. A number of "involuntary AWOLs" also showed up—misfits deliberately dumped by their officers, often in a bar or brothel, shortly before their units had sailed from Virginia or Britain.

Some 450 replacements arrived in the 168th Infantry. Very few were trained infantrymen. As the new commander of the 2nd Battalion, Robert Moore took 125 of them to make good his losses at Sened Station only to find that some lacked even rudimentary marksmanship training. When Moore asked one private if he could shoot a Browning Automatic Rifle, the soldier replied, "Hell, no, I've never even seen one." The 168th also received six truckloads of bazookas the night of February 12. "We had never heard of them before," an ordnance officer later recalled, "but we had a piece of paper that explained how to fire them." Colonel Drake scheduled the first rocket-gun training class for Sunday morning, February 14.

Quiescence at the front gave Allied generals a chance to ponder the tangled command structure in North Africa. On February 10, Eisenhower and others at the Hôtel St. Georges each tried to sketch an organizational chart of AFHQ. Every attempt failed in a barrage of crumpled paper. Eisenhower glumly suggested that the organization had become "too complicated to be placed on paper." But the muddle seemed more annoying than lethal. Ultra intercepts of messages from Rommel and Arnim revealed the depth of Axis supply difficulties. Allied intelligence concluded that although Axis infantry battalions outnumbered Allied battalions fifty-five to forty-two in Tunisia, the Allies held a 381–241 advantage in artillery tubes and a 551–430 advantage in tanks. The enemy seemed more likely to improve his defenses and husband his reserves than take the offensive. This judgment, shared by Eisenhower and Anderson, was measured, reasonable, and wrong. Among other defects, it failed to consider the native aggressiveness of Kesselring and Rommel.

Commanders in Tunisia of course took nothing for granted, and seven possible counterattack plans had been drafted in case of a German offensive. To devise a common strategy, Generals Allen and Roosevelt hosted a conference in a French farmhouse in the Ousseltia Valley with Paul Robinett and French officers. Allen was in high dudgeon, his division still splintered and now broadcast the length of Tunisia. "He sucked in his breath as he talked, making a hissing sound familiar to all who knew him," Robinett reported. "The conference was far from orderly, for everyone was trying to talk at once. . . . Allen was doing very well with his sketchy French, but Roosevelt tried to improve it." Robinett came away shaking his head. "We can't win a war with a debating society," he told his intelligence officer. "We're just asking for trouble." Ready as usual to speak his mind, Robinett wrote to Anderson on February 9, criticizing Allied dispositions and warning that "the enemy could probably concentrate four armored divisions in Tunisia." He also told Fredendall that armor should be fought in mass, "not daubed all over the landscape."

Daubed it was. Anderson still had the British V Corps under General Evelegh in the north. Below Evelegh, the French sector had been shored up by British and American confrères, including the 133rd and 135th Infantry Regiments of the 34th Division. Part of the Big Red One remained with the French in Ousseltia, and Robinett's Combat Command B covered the French southern flank with 110 tanks. Even farther south were CCC and then McQuillin's CCA, responsible for blocking Faïd Pass with help from Drake's 168th Infantry, which had moved north after the fiasco at Sened Station. "The generals of three nations had borrowed, divided, and commanded one another's troops until the troops were never quite certain who was commanding them," a 1st Armored officer observed.

Nor were commanders certain whom they were commanding. On February 6, Orlando Ward drove eighty miles to Speedy Valley from his new headquarters in a cactus patch outside Sbeïtla. Fredendall and many staff officers had shaved their heads, perhaps in defiance of the piercing cold. ("They seemed to expect to be admired," one II Corps lieutenant wrote.) Ward had begun to wonder whether Fredendall drank too much; nevertheless, he was delighted to hear—between TNT detonations in the ever deepening tunnels—that he was to oversee American defenses at

Faïd Pass. He returned to his cactus redoubt to learn that the appointment had been revoked without explanation. As his aide recorded in a diary, Ward "was both angry and disappointed."

With good faith gone, hostility spread between Speedy Valley and the 1st Armored encampment. "Infuriated, insulted, disappointed—there's no contrary emotion that I did not have," Ward's operations officer, Lieutenant Colonel Hamilton H. Howze, later said. "One of the most miserable experiences of my life. . . . It was an unholy mess." Howze, destined for four-star rank, recalled developing "such a detestation for Fredendall that it was hard to control, simply because of the way he treated General Ward."

The greatest insult arrived February 11, in an order entitled "Defense of Faïd Position." Feeling pressure from Anderson to avoid yielding more ground, Fredendall explicitly dictated the positioning of units down to individual companies. Two prominent hills within sight of the pass were to be occupied, Fredendall wrote: "Djebel Ksaira on the south and Djebel Lessouda on the north are the key terrain features in the defense of Faïd. These two features must be strongly held, with a mobile reserve in the vicinity of Sidi bou Zid." In a postscript scribbled in longhand, he added: "In other words I want a very strong active defense and not just a passive one. The enemy must be harassed at every opportunity. Reconnaissance must never be relaxed—especially at night. Positions *must* be wired and mined *now*. L.R.F."

Standing in his small command tent, Ward held up the paper to catch the light. He read the order carefully, then slapped the field table with the flat of his hand. "It's wrong," he said. "It's wrong. He's telling me how to suck eggs."

Fredendall had visited Sbeïtla only once and his knowledge of the Faïd terrain was derived almost exclusively from a map. When the commander of Ward's 1st Armored Regiment, Colonel Peter C. Hains III, saw Fredendall's plan he said simply: "Good God." Troops placed on the two hills would be marooned if a fast-moving attack swept around them. The hills were mutually visible ten miles across the desert but not close enough for defenders on one to help their comrades on the other. These directions resembled a World War I defense, Hains thought, without an appreciation for the speed and power of modern tank divisions.

Ward's objections to "Defense of Faïd Position" seemed to have more to do with the protocol breach of a superior dictating minute troop dispositions than with the tactical plan itself. He protested, but not loudly. "Neither he nor I perceived with sufficient alarm the bad dispositions," Howze later acknowledged.

Orders were orders. Poring over the directive, McQuillin instructed his engineers to lay barbed wire and mines across the entire CCA front, roughly forty miles. "Hell," observed a perplexed young lieutenant, "there isn't that much barbed wire in all of North Africa." Lieutenant Colonel John Waters was given command of the new outpost on Djebel Lessouda. Patton's son-in-law had become executive officer of the 1st Armored Regiment after his battalion, eviscerated in the fighting before Christmas, had retired toward Algeria for refitting. To convert Djebel Lessouda into a Tunisian redoubt, Waters would receive 900 troops, including a company of fifteen tanks, a four-gun artillery battery, and Robert Moore's 2nd Battalion.

On February 12, Ward drove to Lessouda, where he and Truscott had watched the failed attack against the Faïd Pass two weeks earlier. The chink of shovels on rock echoed along the escarpment as Moore's infantrymen clawed out fighting positions in crevices and behind shale parapets. Moore considered the battle plan "excellent to defend against a flood," less useful in stopping Wehrmacht tanks; having commanded the battalion for barely a week, he kept the thought to himself. His Company E had been peeled away and placed on the desert floor as a forward picket line. Each day the brass shoved the company farther east until it now spanned a five-mile front in the shadow of Faïd Pass, more than an entire battalion should have covered. McQuillin advised stringing empty ration cans filled with rocks as an alarm tripwire. "Sir," Moore replied, "you can hear tanks coming for miles. How would you hear rocks in a can?" When Moore suggested that certain signs presaged an Axis offensive, McQuillin lost his temper. "Poppycock!" he replied. "The attack is not coming through Faïd Pass."

Ward found Waters's command post tucked into a ravine halfway up the slope, with a view of Sidi bou Zid to the south and the pass in the east. "Waters, I've got orders here from Fredendall directing where you're supposed to put all your platoons on and around this mountain," Ward began. "Never have I seen anything like this before. Here I'm a division commander . . ."

Ward paused, groping for words. "My division has been taken away from me. All I have left is a medical battalion. I have no command. I can't tell you what to do."

Waters nodded sympathetically. Intelligence analysts seemed to think that any attack would likely fall forty miles to the north, again aimed at the French near Pichon or the Ousseltia Valley, but Waters had doubts. Enemy activity seemed to be increasing across the Eastern Dorsal. "General McQuillin, let me ask you a question, sir," Waters had said after returning from a reconnaissance mission. "Suppose tomorrow morning I wake up and find that I'm being attacked by an armored division coming through Faïd Pass?" Old Mac had scoffed. "Oh, Waters, don't suggest that."

Now Ward was pouring his heart out. "I've never seen anything like it in my life," Ward repeated. "I'm desperate. I don't know what to do."

There was nothing for it but to entrench and hope for the best. Ten miles southeast of Djebel Lessouda and east of Sidi bou Zid, Moore's sister unit—the 3rd Battalion of the 168th Infantry Regiment—dug in under the stern eye of Colonel Drake on Djebel Ksaira. Bent like a horseshoe, with the open end facing north toward Highway 14 and Faïd Pass, Ksaira had been shelled so punctually each day by enemy howitzers—at eight A.M., one P.M., and six P.M.—that Drake's troops joked about German gunners being union men working a daytime shift. To complement Waters's 900 men on Lessouda, Drake in the vicinity of Ksaira had nearly 1,700, including the regimental band and a fair number of soldiers without rifles.

The last hot food had been served February 10. The men were restricted to cold rations and a single canteen of water per day. Drake no longer issued edicts against eating with elbows on the table: his thoughts had become less culinary than sanguinary. Any soldier leaving the line under fire without permission was to be "killed at once," he ordered. There would be no quarter for the enemy, either. "Teach all personnel to hate the Germans and to kill them at every opportunity," he declared. "I will notify you when I want prisoners taken."

Engineers laid mines along the base of Ksaira. Artillerymen near Lessouda registered their guns on known features around Faïd. Patrols ventured into the Eastern Dorsal each night, poking at the pass and smaller cuts in the ridgeline. At the tip of the spear, in front of Company E, a single strand of barbed wire was hung with rock-filled cans.

"A Good Night for a Mass Murder"

As commander-in-chief of Allied forces, Eisenhower had been given far greater powers than Marshal Foch possessed in 1918. Yet adjustments made at Casablanca in the Allied command structure threatened to circumscribe that authority in ways Eisenhower had only begun to appreciate. The lifelong staff officer with impeccable instincts about where real power lay—the master bridge player who always knew how many trump remained in play—had nevertheless been slow to realize that the British had outflanked him.

Under a proposal from General Brooke, the combined chiefs on January 20 had agreed that a single general would command both Anderson's First Army and Montgomery's soon-to-arrive Eighth Army in Tunisia. That commander would be Eisenhower; but three British deputies would handle daily sea, air, and ground operations since Eisenhower, as Brooke confided to his diary, had neither "the tactical or strategical experience required for such a task." Admiral Cunningham and Air Marshal Sir Arthur W. Tedder took the sea and air jobs respectively. The ground commander, due to assume command in February, would be General Harold R. L. G. Alexander, who since August had been Montgomery's superior as head of the British Near East Command. This arrangement cheered the Americans, especially Marshall, since Eisenhower remained top dog.

It pleased the British more. In his diary entry for January 20, Brooke wrote:

We were pushing Eisenhower up into the stratosphere and rarified atmosphere of a supreme commander, where he would be free to devote his time to the political and inter-allied problems, whilst we inserted under him our own commanders to deal with the military situations and to restore the necessary drive and co-ordination which had been so seriously lacking of late!

Unaware of Brooke's disparagement, Eisenhower was happy to have help. But two subsequent decrees from the combined chiefs undercut the commander-in-chief by empowering his subordinates with independent authority. Like a patsy suddenly aware that he has been duped, Eisenhower composed a furious message of protest; only after pleading by Beetle Smith did he tone it down.

But on February 8 he sent two cables to Marshall, warning against "a popular impression of an overriding British control of this great area and operation. . . . I believe that such publicity as is given in the U.S. should stress the American grip on the whole affair." The empowering of his subordinates, he added, smacked of British rule-by-committee; it violated the sacred U.S. Army principle of unity of command under a single authority; and it threatened to reduce Eisenhower to a figurehead.

"As far as I am concerned, no attention will be paid" to such intrusions from Washington or London into the AFHQ command arrangements, he wrote, because "I would consider it a definite invasion of my own proper field." With that off his chest, Eisenhower wanted to see how the new structure worked in practice. In a press conference on February 10, he briefed reporters and graciously praised his new British deputies. In truth, as Butcher noted, he was "burning inside."

Promotion helped mollify him. On February 11, Eisenhower received his fourth star, becoming the twelfth full general in the history of the U.S. Army; Ulysses S. Grant had been the first. Marshall's prodding had overcome Roosevelt's reluctance despite the lack of progress in Tunisia. The promotion was political, reflecting a grudging need to give the American commander-in-chief stature at least equivalent to his British deputies.

Upon hearing the news, Eisenhower summoned his domestic staff to the living room at Villa dar el Ouard. Orderly, houseboy, cook, and two waiters braced at attention on the cold tile floor as he promoted each on the spot. That night he sat by a crackling fire, sipping a highball and accepting congratulatory toasts from his new American logistics deputy, Brigadier General Everett S. Hughes, a pouchy-eyed artilleryman. On the phonograph Eisenhower repeatedly played his favorite record, "One Dozen Roses," crooning the lyrics:

> Give me one dozen roses
> Put my heart in beside them
> And send them to the girl I love.

He had weathered Darlan, Casablanca, and the disappointing winter campaign. But given palace intrigue in Algiers—not to mention London and Washington—some believed his neck remained on the block no matter how many stars peppered his shoulders. "I think Ike is doomed," Hughes had confided to his diary in late January. "Too many conflicting forces at play."

Then there was *that* woman. Tongues had begun to wag about Eisenhower and his willowy driver, Kay Summersby. Nicknamed Skibereen after her Irish hometown, Summersby had worked in England as a model and movie extra before enlisting as a military driver in London; she had been assigned to Eisenhower the previous summer, joining him in Algiers in mid-January after surviving the U-boat sinking of her transport ship off the African coast. At thirty-four, discreet, divorced, and comely, she served not only as the commander-in-chief's "chauffeuse," but also as his bridge partner and riding companion. When she turned out in boots, flying jacket, and helmet, Eisenhower teasingly accused her of trying to look like Patton. She was engaged to one of Fredendall's staff officers, a young engineering colonel from New York, but tongues wagged anyway. One drollery circulating in North Africa had the commander-in-chief's sedan stalling on a lonely road. Summersby tinkers under the hood until Eisenhower appears with the toolbox from the trunk. "Screwdriver?" he supposedly asks, to which she supposedly replies, "We might as well. I can't get the goddam motor fixed."

"Discussed Kay," Everett Hughes had written in his diary. "I don't know whether Ike is alibi-ing or not. Says he wants to hold her hand, accompanies her to house, doesn't sleep with her. He doth protest too much, especially in view of the gal's reputation in London." On February 12, after the "Dozen Roses" performance the previous evening, Hughes scribbled, "Maybe Kay will help Ike win the war."

Skibereen was behind the wheel of Eisenhower's armored sedan when his eleven-vehicle convoy slipped from Algiers shortly after midnight on February 12. "You're taking too many trips to the front," Marshall had cautioned Eisenhower after Casablanca, eight weeks after rebuking him for inattention to the Tunisian campaign. "You ought to depend more on reports." In fact, this was only the commander-in-chief's second visit to Tunisia, and the first time he would be close to enemy artillery range. Heavy rain drummed off the car roof. A fierce winter storm lashed the Atlas, knocking down tents and filling slit trenches with icy water. Soldiers burrowed into their bedrolls and dreamed of spring. "I never knew the wind and sand could really be so miserable," Corporal Charles M. Thomas of the 19th Engineer Regiment wrote in his diary on February 13.

The cavalcade stopped for the night in Constantine before pressing on toward Tébessa at dawn. The conversation in the Cadillac's rear seat centered on whether to retreat to the Grand Dorsal in the event of an enemy attack. Truscott, who had joined the convoy in Constantine, advised against it. He believed Gafsa and Sidi bou Zid should be defended to protect the American airfields now operating south of Kasserine.

"In one respect only have Axis forces demonstrated superiority: the ability to concentrate superior means in local areas and to retain the initiative," he had written Eisenhower in a recent memo. Truscott meant to be encouraging, but the ability to concentrate combat power and keep the initiative lies at the heart of modern warfare. By Truscott's own analysis, the Axis was winning. In other respects he was simply wrong: German armor, tactical airpower, and battlefield leadership had also been superior. But Truscott's reluctance to concede acreage had influenced Eisenhower's decision to overextend the Allied line.

At 1:45 P.M. on Saturday, February 13, the convoy eased down the serpentine gravel road into Speedy Valley. The rain and sleet had stopped, but heavy overcast lent the encampment a monochromatic melancholy. II Corps officers dashed about, throwing salutes and ducking in and out of the tent igloos. Eisenhower climbed from the sedan and stretched his cramped limbs. No one seemed certain where to find General Fredendall or General Anderson, who had agreed to rendezvous here.

Eisenhower cocked an ear. A deafening clamor of pneumatic drills washed through the gulch. Little railcars brimming with rock spoil rolled from several shafts punched into the ravine wall. Soldiers in mining helmets lugged heavy timbers and stacks of wooden shingles. A staff officer explained how engineers for several weeks had been excavating a corps headquarters that would be impervious to air attack. The project was nearly three-quarters complete. Nonplussed, Eisenhower asked whether they had first helped construct frontline defenses to the east. "Oh," the officer answered cheerfully, "the divisions have their own engineers for that!" Muttering to himself, Eisenhower stalked into a briefing tent. A lieutenant colonel used a pointer and a large map streaked with blue and red crayon to show how II Corps was arrayed.

Fifteen minutes later Fredendall strolled in, his boots crunching the crushed stone floor. He was in high spirits with a bounce in his step and a smile on his face. Bill Darby's 1st Ranger Battalion had just conducted a nearly flawless raid on an Italian outpost near Sened Station, the sort of nugatory jab Fredendall loved. At 1:30 in the morning, after a twelve-mile hike across the desert, the Rangers crept to within 200 yards of the enemy camp. One of Darby's company commanders had told his men, "We've got to leave our mark on these people. . . . Every man uses his bayonet as much as he can—those are our orders. And remember this: We're only bringing ten prisoners back—no more and no less."

Screaming Rangers had attacked on a half-mile front, ignoring Italian pleas of *"Non fiermati!"* as they raced among the tents gunning down men struggling to pull on their trousers. The Americans suffered only one killed and twenty wounded, with enemy casualties estimated at seventy-five. Eleven Italians had been captured—someone miscounted—and, by one participant's account, at least one wounded prisoner was executed during the return march to avoid slowing the column. ("I did what I was ordered to do," one Ranger explained years later. "That was a long time ago. I get a little nervous sometimes when I start telling about some of it.") Fredendall had just returned from Gafsa, where he had passed out to the participants a dozen Silver Stars. The Rangers joked about how it had been "a good night for a mass murder."

Anderson walked in right behind Fredendall. The British commander looked even more morose than usual. He had spent the past half hour in another frigid igloo with Fredendall's G-2—intelligence chief—who had minced no words in telling Anderson why First Army's estimates of enemy intentions were misguided. Tall and athletic, with brooding eyes and a hussar's mustache, Colonel Benjamin Abbott Dickson possessed an extraordinary mind and a relentless impiety. At West Point, Dickson had been nicknamed Monk because of his middle name and his atheist resistance to mandatory chapel. Resigning his infantry officer's commission after World War I, he had studied mechanical engineering at MIT, held several inventor patents for laundry equipment and warehousing machinery, then reentered the Army in 1940 as an intelligence officer. Monk Dickson was able, loyal to Fredendall, and, now, convinced that bad things were brewing in southern Tunisia.

"Rommel can be expected to act offensively in southern Tunisia as soon as rested and rearmed," Dickson had warned on January 25. He further cautioned that Axis infantry could hold off Montgomery's pursuing Eighth Army near the Libyan border, allowing Rommel to use his tanks "as a striking force" against the Americans. Dickson believed any attack was likely to come through Gafsa or perhaps Faïd Pass, rather than farther north as AFHQ and First Army intelligence insisted, and it was this divergence of views that had led Anderson to seek out Dickson for cross-examination. Before joining Eisenhower, the British general ended the interview with a sour compliment: "Well, young man, at least I can't shake you." Anderson later told Fredendall, "You have an alarmist and a pessimist for a G-2."

For over two hours, Anderson reviewed the disposition of his army for Eisenhower: British V Corps in the north; the French in the center, stiffened by Anglo-Americans; Fredendall's II Corps in the south. Enemy ambitions remained obscure. Bad weather and Luftwaffe air superiority had prevented extensive air reconnaissance. Ultra decrypts from earlier in the month suggested a possible Axis attack out of Kairouan against French forces, but that was likely to be a limited operation intended to grab better defensive terrain. As a precaution, Anderson was keeping his reserves concentrated in the north, including Robinett's CCB and much of Allen's Big Red One. Any thrust through Faïd Pass or Gafsa was likely to be a diversion.

Eisenhower nodded. "General disposition of forces was satisfactory to General Eisenhower on 13 February," Fredendall's operations officer later reported. The commander-in-chief himself would cable Marshall that Anderson's plan was "as good as could be made pending the development of an actual attack and in view of the great value of holding the forward regions." As for Fredendall, Eisenhower was impressed "by his thorough knowledge of his battlefront."

"He seems keen and fit," Eisenhower added, "and I am placing a lot of confidence in him."

An urgent phone call summoning Anderson back to his headquarters in northern Tunisia broke up the conference as late-afternoon shadows swallowed Speedy Valley. Eisenhower and Truscott pared their motorcade to four vehicles; Kay Summersby, a bit awkwardly, remained at II Corps with her affianced colonel. At six P.M., after some quick sightseeing around Tébessa—it was not every day a man could contemplate the ruins of Solomon the Eunuch—the convoy sped southeast forty-five miles for a view of the American airfields at Thélepte and Fériana, then swung northeast another forty miles to the 1st Armored Division command post at Sbeïtla.

Ward and Robinett waited in a small tent tucked into a cactus patch. Old comrades greeted one another by candlelight with affection accrued through years of keeping faith in the feeble interwar Army and now enhanced by a sense of common destiny in this perilous land. Ward and Eisenhower had been a year apart at West Point. As for Robinett, upon first meeting Eisenhower in 1929 he had been so smitten by the engaging young major that, he later confessed, "I hoped to win your friendship."

Ward quickly sketched the disposition of the 1st Armored, including the marooning of Drake and Waters on the two hills near Faïd Pass. He was cheerful and precise, masking the turmoil churning within. Earlier in the evening Ward had poured out his heart to Robinett about II Corps' meddling, but to Eisenhower he avoided criticizing Fredendall even as he made clear that he had been stripped of virtually all authority in his own division; Ward had last controlled CCB, for example, in Northern Ireland. With 294 tanks and substantial artillery, the division was hardly impotent, but the units were scattered along a sixty-mile crescent.

Then Robinett took the floor, jaw jutting. He had scouted the approaches at Fondouk enough to curtly dismiss Anderson's preoccupation with an enemy thrust in the north. "The only evidence of an attack in this area is nervousness in higher headquarters," he told Fredendall in a message on February 12. He repeated that to Eisenhower, then condemned the current placement of CCA troops around Faïd Pass. They were isolated, "in no sense mutually supporting," Robinett said. The

Eastern Dorsal had "lost its importance for the time being and should be given up without squandering additional means in the hope of covering up past losses.

"Only a question of prestige gives the position any importance," Robinett added, "and prestige is little compared with the troops." Given superior German tanks and antitank guns, the entire Allied position was "impossible." In short, the situation was grave. He sat down.

This analysis was greeted with the politesse reserved for an idiot savant or a tiresome house pet. Eisenhower looked thoughtful and said nothing. Truscott glowered and said nothing. A French officer who had joined the conference broke the silence: "Now that General Eisenhower is here and the Americans are in force, the situation will be restored." But even he seemed unconvinced.

The conference ended with salutes and farewells. Robinett mounted his jeep for the frigid drive north to CCB's bivouac in Maktar. Eisenhower promised to take up the issues he had raised—tomorrow. "The yielding of ground," Robinett later observed, "even worthless, untenable ground, involved too much loss of face." Eisenhower and Truscott climbed back into the Cadillac, this time with Ward wedged between them, for the thirty-mile drive east to Sidi bou Zid. It was eleven P.M.

Another cactus patch, another command post, another briefing. In a cramped personnel carrier roofed with a tarpaulin, McQuillin offered a brief summary of the latest intelligence. No changes had been observed in German positions around Faïd Pass; the enemy had "not been very active." Colonel Hains, commander of the 1st Armored Regiment, followed with a more detailed sketch of CCA's dispositions. Hains pointed out that the 1,700 men around Djebel Ksaira were especially vulnerable. A few portents could be divined, Hains added. For example, small scouting parties south of Faïd Pass had been attacked by German aircraft, suggesting that the enemy was hiding something. A French farmer reported that Axis pickets had prevented Arab field hands living across the Eastern Dorsal from traveling west to work. Allied pilots flying over the coastal plain earlier in the day had strafed a fleet of more than 300 enemy trucks—enough to carry an infantry regiment—but the trucks had been empty.

Eisenhower had sensed enough unease among his commanders in the past twelve hours to feel perturbations himself. ("Ike would swap stars for divisions," Ward scribbled in his diary.) But he limited his comments to the issue of minefields around American positions. Why had it taken so long to lay mines? Why were there so few? The Germans needed only two hours to prepare a new position against counterattack. Here it had taken more than two days. "Get your mine fields out first thing in the morning," he snapped. Sidi bou Zid must be held.

Otherwise he said nothing. The CCA war log noted that Eisenhower "listened to a description of our situation and dispositions without comment."

He stepped from the personnel carrier. The overcast sky had brightened, with clouds backlit by the moon. A few hundred yards to the northwest stood the vaguely biblical silhouettes of palm trees and squat, flat-roofed buildings in Sidi bou Zid. As Eisenhower listened, an infantry captain addressed his men: "We do not pray for victory, nor even for our individual safety. But we pray for help that none of us may let a comrade down—that each of us may do his duty to himself, his comrades, and his country, and so be worthy of our American heritage." Eisenhower's eyes welled with tears.

Colonel Drake appeared, summoned by McQuillin from Djebel Ksaira to be decorated for his valor at Sened Station two weeks earlier. While waiting for the ceremony to begin, Drake asked McQuillin, "General, what will we do if the enemy attacks from the pass in the east?" McQuillin shushed him. "Don't bring that up." Now Drake stood at rigid attention as Eisenhower plucked a Silver Star from his pocket and pinned it to the colonel's fatigue jacket. "Drake," he said, "I think you're going to go a long ways." It was the most prescient remark he had made all day.

At 1:30 on Sunday morning, Eisenhower took a brief stroll in the desert, mindful of the prickly pears. Even his zippered goop suit and heavy gloves could not repel the high desert cold. It would take the rest of the night to drop Ward at Sbeïtla and return to Speedy Valley, and another long day to reach Algiers. He had much to contemplate. Ten miles to the east, he could barely discern a serrated notch in the black ridgeline where Faïd Pass pierced the Eastern Dorsal. He climbed into the warm sedan and headed in the opposite direction.

A week later, when the moment for excuses and scapegoats had arrived, Eisenhower would remind Marshall that it "would naturally be a delicate matter for me to interfere directly into tactical dispositions." No one asked whether it was not less delicate to permit the destruction of his men. In truth, Eisenhower—preoccupied with strategic and political issues, and having no personal combat experience—had simply failed to grasp the tactical peril on that Valentine's Day morning. In trying to serve as both supreme commander and field general, he had mastered neither job. The fault was his, and it would enlarge him for bigger battles on future fields. But it was not his fault alone. Mistakes clattered down the line, along with bad luck, bad timing, and the other handmaidens of havoc.

A dearth of frontline intelligence from patrols, pilots, and prisoners meant that since February 8 virtually all information about enemy intentions had come from Ultra decrypts. Yet the Germans had changed plans several times, and much of the scheming by Kesselring, Rommel, and Arnim had been done tête-à-tête, without resort to radio transmissions vulnerable to Allied interception. On February 13, Ultra disclosed that the 21st Panzer Division had been ordered forward, and that Sunday was to be "A-day" for an operation by Arnim's Fifth Panzer Army. Having rushed back to his headquarters from Speedy Valley to assess this news, Anderson issued a warning, which arrived at II Corps as coded message No. 915 at 1:29 A.M., just as Eisenhower was pinning the Silver Star on Drake: "Urgent. Absolute priority. Information from First Army leads to belief attack will take place tomorrow." Alerts flashed through the Allied command.

But the warning did not specify the avenue of attack. Other intercepted messages revealing that Luftwaffe fighters would arrive Sunday morning at Kairouan reinforced the near certitude in AFHQ and First Army that the attack would come in the north. Yet another message circulated through II Corps that "Rommel has been reported critically ill in a Tunisian hospital and was probably thereafter evacuated from Tunis by air."

Fantasy obscured fact; small errors compounded large. More than 100 enemy tanks from the 10th Panzer Division had moved south toward Faïd Pass without Allied pilots seeing them. American scouts reported that a small defile below Faïd Pass was "impassable for armored vehicles," but they had failed to detect enemy engineers feverishly regrading the trail. Lieutenant Colonel Waters, before snatching a few hours of sleep in his rocky den on Djebel Lessouda, sent a patrol with a radio to Faïd Pass, but the patrol stopped three miles short of the Eastern Dorsal. "I didn't go out to check them," Waters later admitted. "My error." Despite a stiff wind blowing from the west, the patrol soon heard a faint rumble from the direction of the pass, like the slow roll of kettledrums— or the thunder of massing tanks. Dutifully reported, the noise was dutifully noted, and a few CCA supply vehicles were dutifully dispatched toward the safety of the rear.

A cold drizzle added to the misery of soldiers huddled without campfires, hot food, or hope in a better tomorrow. GIs stuffed rags in their rifle muzzles and wrapped the bolts in oilskin. Skittish sentries barked the code-word challenge—"Snafu!"—at suspicious shadows and strained to hear the proper countersign: "Damned right!" Southeast of Djebel Ksaira a patrol of five tanks and two dozen men led by Lieutenant Laurence P. Robertson laagered for the night in the lee of the Eastern Dorsal with their Shermans parked back-to-back like the spokes of a wheel. Robertson ordered the engines switched off one by one at ten-minute intervals to create the illusion that the platoon was drawing farther away rather than stopping.

Below Djebel Lessouda, ammunition handlers dumped an extra hundred rounds at each howitzer in Battery B of the 91st Field Artillery Battalion. The battery commander, Captain W. Bruce Pirnie, Jr., thought the gesture "seemed sort of silly. We had spent a quiet ten days in our position." Everyone hoped that any disturbance of the peace would be brief. General Eisenhower himself had predicted as much in a message to the War Department earlier in the day: "Axis cannot risk at this moment to embark on operation which might mean heavy losses of men and equipment."

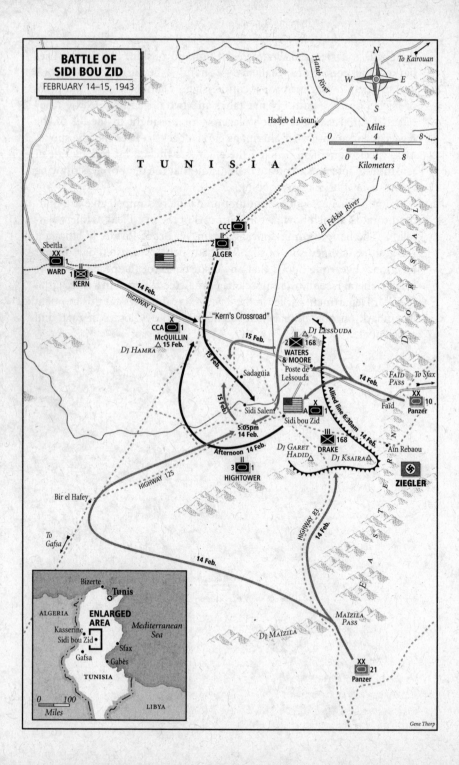

BATTLE OF SIDI BOU ZID
FEBRUARY 14–15, 1943

To Kairouan

N
W E
S

T U N I S I A

Hadjeb el Aioun

Hatab River

El Fekka River

Miles
0 4 8

Kilometers
0 4 8

CCC 1

Sbeïtla

XX 1
WARD

1 6
KERN

ALGER 2 1

14 Feb.
HIGHWAY 13

"Kern's Crossroad"

CCA 1
McQUILLIN
15 Feb.

Dj HAMRA

15 Feb.

15 Feb.

Dj LESSOUDA

WATERS
& MOORE 2 168

Poste de
Lessouda

Sadaguia

Sidi Salem

15 Feb.

A 1

Sidi bou Zid

5:05pm
14 Feb.

Afternoon 14 Feb.

3 1
HIGHTOWER

Bir el Hafey

HIGHWAY 125

To
Gafsa

Dj GARET
HADID

DRAKE 168

Dj KSAIRA

Allied line 6:30am 14 Feb.

FAÏD
PASS   To Sfax

Faïd

XX 10
Panzer

Aïn Rebaou

ZIEGLER

HIGHWAY 83
14 Feb.

D O R S A L

E A S T E R N

MAÏZILA
PASS

14 Feb.

Dj MAÏZILA

XX 21
Panzer

Bizerte

Tunis

ALGERIA

ENLARGED
AREA

Mediterranean
Sea

Kasserine
Sidi bou Zid

Sfax

Gafsa   Gabès

TUNISIA

LIBYA

0   100
Miles

Gene Thorp

9. KASSERINE

A Hostile Debouchment

A BRIEF, howling sandstorm swept across the Tunisian plain early Sunday morning, February 14. German sappers cinched bandannas across their noses and finished lifting the last American mines from the western mouth of Faïd Pass. At four A.M. a bobbing procession of lights, almost ecclesiastical in grandeur, emerged from an olive grove east of the gap. Soldiers in black tunics tramped down Highway 13 carrying lanterns to guide more than a hundred tanks—a dozen Tigers among them—and as many infantry lorries and half-tracks. Exhaust stink and the creak of armor tracks filled the defile.

As dawn spread behind him, the commander of Operation FRÜH-LINGSWIND, General Heinz Ziegler—a Russian Front veteran who now served as Arnim's chief of staff—climbed a rocky parapet above the squalid hamlet of Faïd. Light seeped across the desert, exposing the odd humps of Djebel Lessouda on Ziegler's right and Djebel Ksaira on his left. Ziegler liked what he saw: nothing. The Americans did not appear aroused, nor even alert. At precisely 6:30 A.M. the drivers shifted into gear and panzers spilled from the Eastern Dorsal onto the plain. Behind them the sun rose through the dust in an enormous, molten orb.

They came down like the wolf on the fold. First to fall victim was the infantry squad dispatched by John Waters the previous night, now obliterated by German tanks three miles from Faïd. The Americans sent no radio warning; the prearranged rocket signal intended to trigger an artillery barrage on the pass went unfired. Every man in the squad was killed or captured. Two miles on, the 10th Panzer Division slammed into ten tanks from Company G of Colonel Hains's 1st Armored Regiment. This morning, as on every morning, the tankers had left their night bivouac in a ravine near Sidi bou Zid and moved to a squat hillock east of Djebel Lessouda known as the Oasis. Having watched the routine each dawn for a week, the Germans knew precisely where to find them. Several crews had dismounted and were fixing breakfast when a swarm of green fireballs blew through the picket line at half a mile per second, trailing fantails of brown dust. One astonished sergeant likened the noise to "half of the Krupp Iron Works moving out of the German Ruhr valley." Within minutes the American tanks were annihilated; so were half a dozen others from the same company rushing forward to help. Sixteen columns of black smoke corkscrewed into the sky. It was barely 7:30 A.M.

Three miles east of Djebel Lessouda, the attackers split up. One pack of eighty tanks and trucks veered north and then west to encircle the hill; two others angled south toward Sidi bou Zid. Captain Bruce Pirnie, who the night before had considered the provision of extra shells for his Battery B an extravagance, reported "a tremendous force of tanks and infantry approaching us, not more than two thousand yards away. . . . Scarlet and white flashes." Gun captains shortened the range of their shells by reducing their powder from charge 7 to charge 5 to charge 3 as the enemy drew near. The smaller charges "really changed the sound of the howitzers," Pirnie later wrote. "They sounded impotent, just a little pop and hardly any recoil. We were scared and green." The gunners fired until "the Germans were so close that our fire couldn't clear the crest in front of us." Pirnie radioed Waters on Djebel Lessouda behind him. "We can't hit them," Pirnie said. "They've gotten in under us." "If you can't fire," Waters replied evenly, "move back to where you can."

Crews broke for the rear, belatedly. Only one of four guns escaped, jouncing across the desert. Pirnie followed at the wheel of a careering ammunition half-track. The Germans reminded him of wild dogs hunting in a pack. When they again drew close he sabotaged his last tube with thermite grenades stuffed down the muzzle. As in every catastrophe, petty inconvenience would remain as vivid in memory as the blackest strokes of tragedy: Pirnie would always recall his shoes, purchased from an Irish cobbler before TORCH. They hurt like the devil.

One after another the American units fell. A platoon of tank destroyers was itself destroyed by tanks. The 2nd Battalion of the 17th Field Artillery—armed with eighteen World War I–vintage 155mm howitzers and somehow forgotten in the confusion—waited east of Sidi bou Zid for orders to decamp. The German attack on the battalion "erased it, getting every gun and most of the men," a staff officer reported. Battery A of the 91st Field Artillery fired in a smoking frenzy from Sidi bou Zid until all forward observers were killed or wounded, blinding the gunners. "We didn't know exactly where to fire," one lieutenant said. "There was artillery fire, machine gun fire, armor-piercing tank shells whizzing through the town." Tossing their dead into an empty trailer, the artillerymen leapfrogged west.

Enemy bullets and tank shells sheeted across the desert. Soldiers scooped shallow foxholes with their helmets or clawed at the ground until their fingers bled. "All around me comrades were being machine-gunned from tanks," one soldier recalled. "Their screams were faintly heard due to the terrific explosions." Another soldier stumbled upon a cowering group of troops too frightened even to speak. "I broke down and went off by myself," he later confessed. A third soldier leaped into a jeep and cranked the ignition so insistently the key snapped in half. An anti-aircraft platoon leader, having "lost his sense of direction in the confusion and stampede of other units," unwittingly bolted southeast to deliver himself and his men into German hands. Enemy outriders also seized four ambulances, each jammed with wounded GIs; most of the medical detachment of the 168th Infantry and the collecting company of the 109th Medical Battalion would fall prey, with the loss of 100 men, including ten physicians. Wehrmacht medics passed out oranges to sav-agely burned American prisoners.

The enemy without question had made "a hostile debouchment," as a clerk scribbled in the CCA war diary. General McQuillin, trying from his command post on the southeast edge of Sidi bou Zid to make sense of the shrieking radios and billowing smoke, believed the morning could still be made right with a brisk counterattack. At 7:30 A.M. he ordered the commander of the 3rd Battalion of the 1st Armored Regiment to "clear up the situation." Lieutenant Colonel Louis V. Hightower, a thirty-three-year-old West Point classmate of John Waters, emerged from McQuillin's tent with his briefcase in hand. He climbed onto his Sher-man tank—named *Texas*, she flew the Lone Star flag from a radio antenna—and cantered toward the Oasis. With the early destruction of Company G, he had three dozen Shermans left.

Two miles north of Sidi bou Zid, the first Stukas attacked. Little dam-age was done to Hightower's tanks, but the bombs "smoked us up so that we couldn't see through the dust," he later recounted. Then green fire-balls ripped into the formation, "close to the ground like a ricocheting stone in water." Shermans left and right burst into flame. "Sometimes two or three men got out," one sergeant reported. "Sometimes no one got out. Most of the tanks burned when hit." A shell snipped the head of the H Company commander from his shoulders. The platoon com-manded by Lieutenant Laurence Robertson, sent on patrol to the south-east the previous night, abruptly roared through a gap in an American minefield to join the mêlée. Chased for miles by thirty panzers, Robert-son had bought enough time to escape by firing smoke rounds at his pursuers to simulate artillery fire. It was now apparent that the attack from Faïd Pass was complemented by the 21st Panzer Division spilling from Maïzila Pass twenty miles south. The enemy intended to snare all of CCA in a double envelopment.

Hightower pulled the remnants of his battalion back into Sidi bou Zid in a zigzagging retreat, and clattered out the south side on the Gafsa road. Behind them, Luftwaffe squadrons methodically obliterated the town. A captain in a jeep raced through the olive groves that sheltered the CCA supply trains. "Take off, men!" he bellowed. "You are on your own." Some bolted; others desperately cranked engines that refused to start—lint from camouflage nets had clogged the fuel filters on many jeeps and trucks. A major sprayed the Sidi bou Zid fuel dump with machine-gun bullets as appalled tankers, their Shermans nearly dry, darted among the flames to salvage a few five-gallon tins.

Uncertainty yielded to confusion, confusion to panic. A horizontal avalanche of men and vehicles slid west across the desert, making for the intersection of Highways 13 and 3, ten miles from Sidi bou Zid and almost halfway to Sbeïtla. (This junction soon would be known as Kern's Crossroad after the battalion commander sent to secure it, Lieutenant Colonel William B. Kern.) Thomas E. Hannum, an artillery lieutenant, was reminded of the Oklahoma land rush, except that "the air was full of whistles" from enemy projectiles. Another gunner watched as several half-tracks "suddenly blossomed out with red and black, like the first puff of fire in oil, and then seemed to settle down like a sinking ship." Indefatigable Tunisian peddlers stood along the road holding up eggs, tangerines, and tiny gasoline stoves.

Now reduced to a dozen tanks, Hightower's battalion also swung west at fourteen miles per hour to provide a screen for those in flight. Hightower soon spotted panzers half a mile to the south; one pincer from the 21st Panzer Division was closing in on Sidi bou Zid. An even larger enemy tank force—the number swelled with each report—bore down from the north after looping around Djebel Lessouda. "It looks," suggested one tanker, "like a dryland Dunkirk."

Hightower angled south with four Shermans to buy time while the rest of his force continued toward the crossroads. At 700 yards, *Texas* hit two enemy tanks with well-aimed shots from her 75mm main gun. Watching with field glasses from an open hatch, Hightower cheerfully reported that a panzer turret "broke into flame like a flower." A German shell drilled *Texas* through the bogey wheels, and darted out the other side "like a rabbit." Other rounds glanced off the Sherman's turret and hull. "Each shell that hit sounded like a giant anvil or tremendous bell,"

Hightower later recalled. After shooting two more panzers, *Texas* was struck from the left by a round that punctured the fuel tank and landed spinning on a hatch cover. Above the crackle of flaming gasoline Hightower roared, "Let's get the hell out of here!" The crew "boiled out like peas from a hot pod before the tank had stopped running." Five men sprinted west as their tank blew up behind them.

Of fifty-two Shermans in action, six survived the afternoon. At 1:45 P.M. half a dozen Tigers bulled through the rubble on Sidi bou Zid's northern outskirts. At 5:05 P.M., tanks from the 21st Panzer in the south and those from the 10th Panzer in the north met two miles east of town on Highway 125. The double envelopment had taken less than twelve hours.

The disaster was all too evident from the shaley brow of Djebel Lessouda, where John Waters watched the attack with both dismay and professional discernment. The folly of the Allied battle plan was clear: after losing Faïd Pass in late January, the Americans should have either recaptured the Eastern Dorsal—at whatever cost—or retired to defensible terrain on the Grand Dorsal. Instead they had dispersed across a vulnerable open plain where the enemy could defeat them in detail. Lessouda, like Djebel Ksaira in the hazy distance, was so steep, with such a commanding vista of the dun world below, that the Americans had been bewitched by an illusion of security. In fact, the hill provided Waters only with a panorama of his own imminent destruction.

When the first wave of eighty German tanks and half-tracks had looped north around the hill at dawn, a combination of glare, dust, and wishful thinking prevented Robert Moore and his 900 infantrymen from shooting, on the remote chance that the force was friendly. Colonel Hains had radioed Waters from Sidi bou Zid. "There must be something going on," Hains said in one of the war's premier understatements. "There is an awful lot of firing out there in front of you now."

Better visibility and dire reports from routed forces to the east soon clarified the predicament. By 8:30 A.M., German officers in peaked caps stood on their tank turrets just beyond rifle range, raking Lessouda with field glasses. Led by motorcycle troops, an enemy column on the east pressed up the lower slopes through a narrow wadi. At a range of 300 yards Moore gave the command to fire. A stabbing red volley rippled from the rocks and the Germans fell back, leaving a trail of dead and wounded. Two Wehrmacht officers and six enlisted men were taken prisoner.

At noon the enemy tried again, this time pressing up the southern face where Waters's command post was tucked into a gulch. Gray-clad figures darted through the olive trees and tuft grass below. Unable to reach Moore by radio, Waters sent his driver up the hill to find him. A few minutes later the soldier stumbled back, ashen, blood bubbling from a hole drilled through his chest by one of Moore's nervous infantrymen. "Sir, I couldn't get up there," he told Waters, "and I got shot." Waters wrapped him in a bedroll with two shots of morphine, and soon the young man was dead.

Waters radioed Hains. "Pete, I'm going to shut this thing off," he said. "They are all around here and looking for me now, but I don't think they've discovered this half-track yet." Not only were German patrols closing in, but locals had begun combing the battlefield to strip the dead and betray the living. Moore was marooned with his infantry on the upper slope. "I'm going to dismantle the radio and I'll hide the parts," Waters added. "I will go into the next little ditch and hide out there until dark."

Try to hold on, Hains urged. "Good luck to you, John."

"Never mind about me," Waters said. "Just kill those bastards at the bottom of the hill."

At four P.M. Waters heard footsteps on shale. Assuming that it was one of his own officers, he rose from his hiding place beneath an overhanging ledge. Fifteen feet away, seven German soldiers led by two Arabs whirled around; a short burst of Schmeisser bullets fired from the hip missed Waters by inches and pinged off the rocks. Delighted to capture such a high-ranking officer—soon enough the enemy would learn he was also Patton's son-in-law—the Germans marched him half a mile down the hill. Several Wehrmacht officers sat in a makeshift command post listening to dance music on a big radio. Waters was plopped in a motorcycle sidecar and driven through Faïd Pass to begin a voyage that would take him to Tunis by truck, to Italy by transport plane, and finally over the Alps by train to a Bavarian prison camp. For John Waters, the war was over.

Ten miles to the southeast the war went on, badly, for Drake and his men. With nearly a thousand troops already dug in on Djebel Ksaira, Drake decided to herd the rest of his command—now bivouacked in various wadis southeast of Sidi bou Zid—onto Garet Hadid, a slightly loftier escarpment four miles west of Ksaira. Soon 950 riflemen, musicians, cooks, and clerks were perched on the barren rock like nesting birds. Nearly one-third lacked weapons. After watching the artillery flee near Djebel Lessouda, Drake had called McQuillin at eight A.M. on a field phone to report the makings of a rout. When Old Mac disputed his characterization, Drake snapped, "I know what I'm talking about. I know panic when I see it." McQuillin hesitated, then told Drake: "You are on the spot. Take command and stop it."

The arrival of the 21st Panzer Division precluded any chance to "stop it." Half the panzers swung cross-country far to the west for the back-door attack on Sidi bou Zid, which Hightower would only briefly disrupt. The rest drove straight north along Highway 83, into the gap between Djebel Garet Hadid and Djebel Ksaira. American troops on the two hills spattered the enemy with enough steel to delay this prong of the German advance six miles from Sidi bou Zid. Enemy gunners answered with artillery, mortar, and tank fire. "It seems like everything the enemy uses is designed to harass a man," one American private concluded.

Drake soon recognized that his position was desperate if not hopeless. Enemy tanks near Sidi bou Zid appeared to be methodically pirouetting over the slit trenches to crush the remaining defenders. Several American units around Djebel Ksaira tried to steal away before officers hectored them back into the line with threats and curses. At 11:30, McQuillin at Sidi bou Zid reported by radio to General Ward's headquarters in Sbeïtla: "Enemy tanks closing in and threatening both flanks and . . . Drake. Any orders?" Ward replied: "Continue your mission." At 12:08 P.M. McQuillin reported: "Enemy right on top of us."

Drake was scanning the battlefield from a rocky knob on Garet Hadid when a staff officer approached. "General McQuillin is on the telephone," the officer said. "He is pulling out and you are to stay here." Drake flew to the phone only to find the line dead. Two signalmen followed the wire to the abandoned CCA headquarters outside Sidi bou Zid. The command post had temporarily moved seven miles west, then joined the ragged exodus toward Sbeïtla. McQuillin "fled so fast he even left the codebook" behind, Drake later complained.

At two P.M., Drake reached McQuillin by radio. Swallowing his anger, he asked permission to pull his men off Djebel Ksaira. McQuillin passed the request to Ward, who relayed it to Fredendall. At Speedy Valley, a hundred miles from the shooting, life looked less bleak. Within eight minutes, McQuillin was told: "Too early to give Drake permission to withdraw." McQuillin radioed the message to Garet Hadid: "Continue to hold your position."

A few minutes later Drake dictated a ninety-three-word message directly to Ward. Scribbled on three sheets of British toilet paper, the note ended: "Talked to McQuillan [*sic*] once by radio, said had requested help. Germans have absolute superiority ground and air. . . . Unless help from air and armor comes immediately, infantry will lose immeasurably."

A young lieutenant folded the message and slid it into the breast pocket of his fatigue shirt. He scrambled down the back slope of Garet Hadid and headed west in a jeep, a dispatch rider in search of the cavalry.

Eisenhower and Truscott had returned to Speedy Valley from Sidi bou Zid at dawn on Sunday morning, the fourteenth. In his goop suit, with a wool hat pulled over his eyes, the commander-in-chief "looked pinched with cold," Kay Summersby reported. "He was very tired and very depressed." He crawled into a tent near Fredendall's command post and slept for two hours in a sleeping bag spread across a cot, snoring loudly.

Rising at midmorning, Eisenhower conferred with Fredendall and Anderson. Both affected a bluff élan. Information was sketchy, they admitted, but the enemy attack appeared to be a local affair. "There was no reason to think that McQuillin would not be able to hold his own," Truscott later wrote. No other enemy activity was reported along the front, but Anderson wanted to evacuate exposed Gafsa in the far south as a precaution, retracting the Allied right flank to the more defensible foothills of the Grand Dorsal. Eisenhower agreed. He told Marshall in a subsequent message, "I really believe that the fighting of today will show that our troops are giving a very fine account of themselves even though we must give up part of our extended line."

The truth would soon out. Some troops indeed were fighting with uncommon valor; many were not fighting at all. Most were befuddled and frightened. Hightower's gallantry, coupled with resistance around Djebel Ksaira, had allowed hundreds of McQuillin's men to escape, but several thousand others were trapped, captured, or dead. Of the five battalions controlled by CCA, two were surrounded and three were on the way to obliteration. Nine Axis battalions had slammed into the Americans, and although the depleted German units barely added up to a full-strength armored division, they included two of the Wehrmacht's most celebrated formations: the 10th Panzer Division, spearhead of General Heinz Guderian's breakthrough at Sedan in May 1940, and the 21st Panzer, the first German division in Africa and perhaps the most experienced desert fighters on earth. Moreover, the second phase of the offensive, MORGENLUFT—Rommel's attack in the south—had yet to begin.

No sense of urgency gripped Speedy Valley. There was concern, yes, and vexation at an annoying foe who refused to relinquish the initiative.

But no commander seemed to have an inkling that life-and-death consequences derived from decisions made *right now*. Anderson's eyes remained fixed on the north, peering for enemy columns that did not exist. CCA had yet to identify 10th Panzer as the agent of its destruction; consequently, Anderson surmised that the division remained poised to strike the French near Kairouan. Not only was Ward's 1st Armored Division too dispersed to throw an effective counterpunch, but the division artillery chief's diversion to command the improvised CCD two weeks earlier had deprived the most lethal American defensive arm—massed howitzers—of its leader and his staff.

Eisenhower summoned reinforcements from Morocco and Algeria, but not many; the Americans remained as fixated on the fantasy of an Axis strike through Spain as the British did on a prospective blow in northern Tunisia. Those who heard the trumpet came slowly: the U.S. 9th Infantry Division, for example, was missing half its vehicles, which had been left at home in TORCH or sent as replacements to the Tunisian front. Other troops, unaccountably, were left on the sidelines, including more than 4,000 gunners in the 13th Field Artillery Brigade, who had landed with tubes and full transport in Algeria in December and would remain there until mid-March.

With Summersby again behind the wheel, Eisenhower left Speedy Valley at 11:30 A.M. Sunday for the return to Algiers. Fifty-five miles northeast of Tébessa, while Hightower fought for his life and Waters hid under a rock, Eisenhower ordered the motorcade to stop at the ancient city of Timgad. Built by Rome's Third Legion in A.D. 100 the town had been consigned to oblivion for centuries until French archaeologists excavated the site in the 1880s.

For more than an hour, the Allied commander-in-chief and his band wandered through streets paved in blue limestone and lined with Doric colonnades. The white bones of Timgad ribbed a hillside dominated by the Emperor Trajan's forty-foot triumphal arch. Commode seats were still graced with marble arms in the shape of frolicking dolphins. Little imagination was needed to hear the clatter of chariot wheels, or to smell cedar burning on the altars of Jupiter Capitolinus. A guidebook invited visitors to conjure "barbarians from the outer desert in paint and feathers flitting along the narrow byways," and the scuffing cadence of Roman soldiers helmed in bronze. Eisenhower and Truscott studied an inscription chiseled between two columns in the great forum: *"Venari lavari ludere ridere hoc est vivere"*: To hunt, to bathe, to play, to laugh—that is to live.

"When you remember me in your prayers, that's the special thing I want—always to do my duty to the extreme limit of my ability," Eisenhower wrote his wife a few hours later, during a stop in Constantine. Finally returning to Villa dar el Ouard after the long last leg to Algiers, he sat at the grand piano in the room where a few nights before he had belted out "One Dozen Roses." Sometimes Eisenhower amused himself at the keyboard by plunking "Chopsticks" with two fingers. This night, weary and morose at the increasingly bad news from Tunisia, he instead, very slowly, picked out "Taps," then stood without a word and went to bed. To err, to fret, to grieve, to learn—that, too, was to live.

None Returned

WITH Anderson's decision to shorten his southern flank and evacuate Gafsa, GIs took a last quick wash in the hot-spring Roman baths and headed northwest. It was Sunday night, February 14. Soon Highway 15 was jammed with overloaded refugee carts, bleating livestock, and 180 Army trucks. A tearful bordello owner who introduced herself as Madame LaZonga pleaded with American officers for deliverance. Deliverance came. At midnight Madame rode out of town on the back of a General Stuart with six young women she identified as her daughters, all waving like beauty queens on a Columbus Day parade float. Combat engineers blew up the power station, "plunging us into total and rather sinister darkness," one British officer noted. Then they wedged six tons of ammonal, plastic explosives, bangalore torpedoes, guncotton, and "great quantities of cortex" into a subterranean gallery beneath Gafsa's sixteenth-century citadel. The blast, at six on Monday morning, was audible for thirty miles. "Rocks three feet in diameter flew more than a hundred feet into the air," an engineer captain reported proudly. The explosion also demolished nearly three dozen houses; the bodies of thirty residents were recovered immediately, and eighty people remained missing when Axis troops arrived a day later.

The sprawling air bases at Fériana and Thélepte, forty-five miles up Highway 15, were next to be abandoned on Anderson's order. Evacuation of the 3,500 troops had begun at eleven on Sunday night. For the benefit of future German occupants, a departing officer tacked up a large wall map showing the latest battle lines around Stalingrad, where Field Marshal Friedrich Paulus of the Wehrmacht's Sixth Army had just surrendered.

Thirty-four Allied airplanes grounded for repairs were scuttled with thermite grenades. An engineer who had been detailed to destroy 50,000 gallons of gasoline recounted, "Before I finished the Germans were attacking the field. I was the last one out. . . . They were shooting at me, but there was an awful lot of smoke and they couldn't see me very well." The enemy nevertheless captured fifty tons of aviation gas and oil, and the engineer was not, it so happened, the last one out. The evacuation order failed to reach Company C of the 805th Tank Destroyer Battalion, which instead heeded a previous command to attack the approaching enemy. Repulsed, utterly, the company suffered seventy-five casualties and lost all twelve tank destroyers along with sixteen other vehicles.

A battlefield bromide cautions: "Never believe a straggler and rarely believe a casualty." Both breeds had begun trickling in to 1st Armored Division headquarters, and their collective tale of prodigious German strength fell on deaf ears. Colonel Hightower arrived at Ward's command post in the Sbeïtla cactus patch on Sunday night. He was, a witness reported, "badly used up and declared that his battalion had been wiped out." Hightower confirmed that Tigers were involved in the attack along with scores of other panzers. Messages from Djebel Lessouda and Djebel Ksaira provided detailed if fragmentary intelligence about enemy tanks, guns, and troop concentrations.

Yet a mood of benighted denial had settled over the Allied high command, which no eyewitness testimony could dislodge. Anderson visited Robinett at Maktar and proposed borrowing a single tank battalion to drive the enemy from Sidi bou Zid. A French proposal to fling *all* of CCB into the counterattack was rejected by the British as imprudent given the suspected German legions waiting to pounce in the north. Shortly after eight P.M. on Sunday night, Anderson sent Fredendall a message:

> As regards action in Sidi bou Zid: concentrate tomorrow on clearing up situation there and destroying enemy. . . . Army Commander deeply regrets losses suffered by CCA, but he congratulates them on their fine fight, is confident they will decisively defeat the enemy tomorrow, and is sure that the enemy must have suffered losses at least as heavy as their own.

This hallucination whisked through Speedy Valley without challenge and on to Ward. He and his operations officer, Hamilton Howze, then wrote the order to counterattack with a force weaker than the one already routed: a tank battalion, a tank destroyer company, an infantry battalion from CCC, and a few artillery tubes. "I didn't like it much," Ward told his diary, but he neither protested the order nor tried to enlarge the contingent. Howze, who admitted to knowing little about armor tactics, later acknowledged an enduring shame "for not contesting the order more strongly, even at the cost of my commission."

The tank battalion chosen to lead the counterblow had never seen combat. Fitted with new Shermans and commanded by Lieutenant Colonel James D. Alger, a twenty-nine-year-old West Pointer from Massachusetts, the 2nd Battalion of the 1st Armored Regiment held battle honors dating to the Black Hawk War. But in this war the unit was green as grass. Ward told his diary: "Alger was more or less on his own."

Robinett stood by the road in Maktar as the tanks rolled south, stripped for battle. "Off we went across the desert," a lieutenant later recalled. "We knew not what we were getting into." As for young Alger, Robinett reported that he "saluted and smiled as he passed."

Half a mile south of Highway 13 and midway between Sidi bou Zid and Sbeïtla, Djebel Hamra provided a fine grandstand from which to watch the enemy get his comeuppance, and by midmorning on Monday, February 15, a covey of officers and correspondents had scaled the 2,000-foot crest. McQuillin arrived along with the CCC commander, Colonel Robert I. Stack. So did Hains and Hightower and the ubiquitous Ernie Pyle, with his "signature belch, inventive profanity, [and] wondrous hypochondria." At Ward's headquarters in Sbeïtla that morning, an officer had assured Pyle, "We are going to kick hell out of them today and we've got the stuff to do it with."

The day was dry and sunny. A mirage shimmered like spilled mercury around Sidi bou Zid, a dark green smear thirteen miles distant. Beyond the town, the hazy lavender trapezoid of Djebel Ksaira sat on the horizon. Djebel Lessouda loomed to the left, tethered to the long ribbon of Highway 13. A landscape that from a distance seemed flat as a billiard table was in fact corrugated with subtle folds and dips. Even from Hamra's Olympian summit the plain teemed with Arab farmers plowing their fields behind plodding black bullocks. Birdsong and the smell of dung rose on the morning thermals.

Just before one P.M., Alger's battalion appeared on a camel track from the north. The column wheeled with parade-ground precision around a lone gum tree and headed southeast for Sidi bou Zid at eight miles per hour. Dust plumed behind each Sherman. Tank destroyers flared to the flanks, and an infantry battalion followed in trucks and half-tracks, trailed in turn by a dozen artillery tubes. From a radio truck blared "The Stars and Stripes Forever," clearly audible on the hillcrest, where a lieutenant who was immune to the prevailing confidence of his seniors murmured, " 'Into the valley of death rode the six hundred.' "

Alger had been told to push beyond Lessouda and Ksaira "and then hold until friendly infantry could withdraw" from the hills where they were trapped. Ward's staff drew his route with blue pencil and a straight edge on the only map available, a 1-to-100,000 scale sheet on which each mile of terrain was represented by less than an inch of paper. Drivers were to use Ksaira's north nose as a homing beacon. No reconnaissance was conducted, and Allied intelligence put enemy strength at only sixty tanks. This was less than half their actual number.

At 1:40 P.M., twenty Stukas materialized like swallows in the brilliant air; they caused little damage but deranged Alger's formation and confirmed that German commanders knew of the counterattack. Alger again paused after hearing a radioed warning that American planes planned a counterstrike on Sidi bou Zid. When no friendly planes appeared, he pressed on, neatly overrunning a half-dozen enemy antitank guns hidden along a wadi near the hamlet of Sadaguia.

Ward sat in his command post listening to radio traffic and eating lunch from a wooden tray. At 2:45 he heard CCC report: "Tanks now approaching Sidi bou Zid. . . . Enemy's lack of reaction suspicious but, on present indications, enemy force must be small or sucking us in." On a sheet of lined paper he scribbled a message for Drake to be dropped by airplane: "Daisy Mae join Lil Abner in the moonlight. He will give you a lift. Ward." Howze also sent a radio message alerting the men on Djebel Ksaira to their imminent salvation: "Keep your eye peeled and be ready to jump on the bandwagon."

No sooner did these optimistic messages go forth than a flare arced over Sidi bou Zid, "like a bright diamond in the afternoon sun," A. D. Divine reported from Djebel Hamra. Muzzle flashes winked near the town; twenty seconds later, enemy artillery airbursts spattered the American gun batteries. Alger reported the telltale dust feathers of approaching enemy tanks on his left and, ten minutes later, his right.

Into the trap they had ridden, into the valley. "Brown geysers of earth and smoke began to spout," wrote Pyle. He was astonished to see Arabs go on plowing, as if declining to acknowledge disfigurement of the day's tranquility. An ammunition carrier detonated, "with flames leaping and swaying. Every few seconds one of its shells would go off, and the projectile would tear into the sky with a weird *swhang-zing* sort of noise." Divine, standing at McQuillin's elbow, reported that "within a matter of minutes the golden dust that trailed [Alger's tanks] like banners had turned black. Blue smoke and red smoke from the German signals mingled with it. . . . We saw the counterattack falter and break and shatter."

The killing was confined mostly to an onion field a thousand yards square and two miles west of Sidi bou Zid. Tank rounds by the hundreds skipped across the furrows, many of them striking armor plates with electric blue flashes. By 4:30, American tanks were brewing up from Company D in the north, Company E in the center, and Company F in the south. Subsequent tests would show that the Sherman's main gun could not penetrate a Tiger's frontal armor even at point-blank range, while a Tiger could puncture a Sherman a mile away. Less scientific but no less relevant was the calculation by an American soldier that medium tanks once holed took twenty minutes to burn up and that "it takes ten minutes for a hearty man within to perish." Battle din muffled the sounds of those hearty men within, as if they were screaming underwater.

At 4:50 P.M., Colonel Stack radioed Alger. What was happening? What did the battalion need? "Still pretty busy," Alger answered laconically. "Situation is hard. No answer to second question. Further details later." Moments later a German round severed his radio antenna. Another struck the gun barrel and jammed the turret; four more in quick succession blew through the engine and turret, killing the radio operator and triggering dreamy clouds of fire retardant. Leaping from the hatch with two crewmen, Alger sprinted north across the desert. Within half an hour he was a prisoner, soon to join John Waters in a German camp.

Stack warned Ward that getting to Lessouda and Ksaira looked doubtful: "May not be able to reach position indicated to you by sundown." Five minutes later he ordered his infantry battalion to hold in place rather than risk encirclement. At six P.M., the attack was canceled outright, and all survivors began pulling back. Four Sherman tanks kept in reserve rallied below Djebel Hamra to await their fifty-two sisters. But, as the battalion war diary recorded, "None returned."

"As dusk began to settle, the sunset showed red on the dust of the Sidi bou Zid area," McQuillin later reported. "There was no wind, and the frequent black smoke pillars scattered over the terrain marked locations of burning tanks." He counted twenty-seven tanks aflame, but "the heavier dust cloud near Sidi bou Zid no doubt obscured more that were afire. It was easy to recognize a burning tank due to the vertical shaft of smoke." Throughout the evening the desert leaked beaten, smoke-stained tankers. "I found myself all alone wandering amongst the dead and wreckage," recounted one soldier. "The night had a dead silence except for a few howling dogs." German salvage teams fanned across the shell-plowed field, scavenging weapons by the light of flaming tanks and hosing brains and gore from the few Shermans that had failed to burn.

By morning, CCA would estimate casualties from the past two days at

1,600 men. Nearly a hundred tanks had been sacrificed, along with fifty-seven half-tracks and twenty-nine artillery pieces. Also lost, after such obviously inept generalship, was whatever confidence the ranks still held in the high command.

Listening to the bray of voices from the radio, Ward refused to give up hope. At 10:30 Monday night, he told Fredendall, "We might have walloped them or they might have walloped us."

Anderson had no illusions. "We are dangerously dispersed," he warned Eisenhower in a message. "It is wise to consider in good time whether we should not voluntarily withdraw to the main ridge of the Grand Dorsal." The "awful nights of fleeing, crawling, and hiding from death," in Ernie Pyle's words, had begun.

"Sometimes That Is Not Good Enough"

THE immolation of Alger's battalion had also been visible from Djebel Lessouda, which provided bleacher seats for Robert Moore and his trapped infantrymen. Except for mortar barrages every two hours, the enemy seemed content to starve the Americans on Lessouda into surrender. At dusk on Monday evening, a lone P-40 flew over the hill and dropped a U.S. mail sack tied to a small parachute. Inside, Moore found a message to John Waters, whose fate was still unknown: "You are to withdraw to road west of Blid Chegas where guides will meet you. Bring everything you can. Ward." Suspecting a trick, Moore radioed McQuillin's command post for authentication. What was the division commander's nickname? "Message okay," came the reply, then added: "Pinky."

At 10:30 P.M. Moore gathered his men on Lessouda's southwestern slope. Hundreds of faces, blued by starlight, turned to hear his instructions. Heavy weapons would be spiked and abandoned. Moore himself was taking only his cherished English sleeping bag and his helmet, with its crease from the French machine-gun bullet in Algiers. They would march in two columns, thirty yards apart, parallel to and a mile north of Highway 13. The rendezvous point lay nine miles west, near the crossroads below Djebel Hamra on the road to Sbeïtla. Wounded men would be carried on litters. If any German prisoner uttered a sound, he was to be bayoneted.

Off they went beneath a full, ascending moon, two snaking lines led by Company F, which Moore had commanded so long ago in Villisca. At the base of the hill the men passed an 88mm gun, "so close that we could have easily reached out and touched it," one officer later reported. A German gunner called out. Moore shushed his men and pressed on. The gunner shrugged and lay back down.

Half an hour later, Moore heard voices in bushes to his left. Perhaps Ward's guides were searching for them. He veered from the column toward the trees, and a dark figure thirty yards away hailed him *auf deutsch*. Moore circled back to the column. "He didn't speak our language," he whispered to a young captain. The voice called out again, insistent this time, and then machine-gun fire ripped across the desert.

"Scatter!" Moore yelled. "Run like hell." Like hell they ran, to all directions of the compass. The first German rounds flew high but within twenty seconds men began to fall. Moore ordered them to flatten out and crawl. In a frenzy they crawled. Artillery from the western edge of Lessouda boomed, followed by the crump of German mortars blindly gouging the desert. The battalion chaplain, Lieutenant Eugene L. Daniels, told the litter bearers and medics to flee while he remained with the wounded to await capture.

At five o'clock on Tuesday morning, February 16, Moore and a small band from Company F reached the crossroads where Ward had posted sentries. Haggard and red-eyed, lacerated by cactus thorns and desperately thirsty, they found nearly three dozen men from the company already there. Fifteen minutes later, part of Company H staggered in with a dozen German prisoners, followed by Company G. By sunrise, Moore counted 231 men. Others arrived throughout the day in Sbeïtla, where a quartermaster passed out blankets and overcoats. After another head count, Moore reported that of the 904 men he had commanded two days before, 432 remained.

Drake's ordeal was even more hideous. Nearly twice as far from friendly lines, he and his 1,900 men had been squeezed into an ever shrinking perimeter on the crests of Djebel Ksaira and Garet Hadid. "Besieged, good strength, good morale," Drake radioed Ward. Only the first was true. Hunger gnawed at troops whose tongues were swollen with thirst and who repeatedly wandered back from fighting positions on various pretexts. Drake authorized the regimental bandleader to form firing squads if necessary to keep the lines intact.

German intelligence mistakenly believed that only a company occupied each hill—the American force equaled roughly two battalions—and efforts to winkle out the defenders grew increasingly bold. By sunset on February 15, an estimated 300 grenadiers backed by panzers had infiltrated the lower slopes of Ksaira. German machine-gunners and snipers fired at any movement; the band's bass drummer fell dead while carrying extra ammunition to the perimeter, and a clarinetist was killed trying to avenge him. Wounded men died for want of medical aid; dead men lay unburied for want of grave diggers. American counterattacks temporarily repulsed the enemy with showers of hand grenades, but minutes later the coal-scuttle helmets could again be seen darting up the wadis.

At 2:30 P.M. on February 16, Drake on Garet Hadid radioed the 3rd Battalion commander on Ksaira, proposing that "you cut your way out and join me." Lieutenant Colonel John H. Van Vliet, Jr., replied promptly: "There are eight 88s between you and me." As if in confirmation, the enemy pulled onto the flat between the two hills, "unlimbered his guns and shelled our men at will," a lieutenant recalled. "We had no artillery to reply to him and he was out of range of our smaller weapons."

A few minutes later, a message from McQuillin confirmed that no cavalry would ride to the rescue: "Fight your way out. Time and place yours. Air cover will be provided. Instructions will be dropped by plane this afternoon." Two typed sheets followed in a parachute sack which landed on Ksaira rather than Garet Hadid; Van Vliet spent more than an hour decoding the prolix message and then encoding an abridged version for radio transmission to Drake. Soldiers slashed their tires with bayonets and battered surplus equipment with hammers until the hilltops echoed like a forge. A sergeant walked through the small motor pool, firing pistol bullets into every engine block. Men too gravely wounded to walk—there were sixty on Ksaira alone—were draped with canvas and left to German clemency. An officer later described how the regimental chaplain, "standing in full view of enemy snipers with his hands raised in benediction, asked the blessing of God upon the decision." Drake broadcast the code phrase to decamp—"Bust the balloon"— and hundreds of soldiers crept down the rocky slopes beneath a full moon sheathed in clouds. With one delay and another, the last troops did not leave Ksaira until nearly midnight, precluding any chance of reaching safety before daybreak.

"We marched all that night across the sand, in gulleys or dry washes, wherever we could find a path other than being silhouetted on a skyline," wrote one soldier. "Whenever the moon would come out, or a real or imagined sound was heard, we would halt and crouch down." Weak from hunger and tormented by thirst, GIs soon tossed away machine guns and mortar tubes, then ammunition, blankets, and even rifles. Columns disintegrated into noisy bands of stragglers who offered comrades with full canteens up to a thousand francs for a sip of water. Troops stumbled through the ghostly battlefields where Hightower and

Alger had fought, now strewn with dead men. Rooting through incinerated tanks, scavengers pulled out C-ration cans to lick the charred hash
and beef stew inside.

Corporal Dave Berlovich, once a Des Moines bookstore clerk, found
himself in a thicket with two comrades who insisted he travel alone.
"You're marked as a Jew, aren't you?" one man asked. Berlovich
recoiled. "Fuck no, I'm a Catholic." His father was Jewish, but Berlovich
had been raised in Iowa by his Christian mother. By the glare of a struck
match they examined his dog tag: stamped below the corporal's name
and serial number was a tiny "H"—for Hebrew—he had never noticed
before. Yanking the chain and tag from his neck, Berlovich flung them
into a thorn thicket and hurried west at a redoubled pace.

Dawn caught them all in the open, scattered across five miles of desert
west of Sidi bou Zid. Their objective, Djebel Hamra, loomed on the horizon, shrouded in mist. A column of trucks appeared on a dirt road, and
for a few sweet moments Drake's men believed that rescue was at hand.
Then troops in gray poured from beneath the canvas awnings. "Those,"
a lieutenant informed Colonel Van Vliet, "are not our vehicles."
Machine-gun fire from the left flank sent the men fleeing before a maelstrom of bullets and mortar bursts. Drake tried to rally the 400 men still
within earshot by dispatching a dozen volunteers to fight a delaying
action. The squad "gained the desired ground, a little knoll in the
desert," a witness reported, "and there they were able to hold the enemy
off for about an hour." Flanked and overrun by panzer grenadiers, the
rear guard was wiped out.

At ten A.M., Drake ordered Lieutenant William W. Luttrell to assume
command of another squad. "He took one look at me and screamed,
'Lieutenant, take those men and charge!' " Luttrell later recounted. Lacking only a saber to complete the Civil War tableau, Luttrell formed a
hasty skirmish line of frightened riflemen. "Move out!" he barked, then
watched as his little command was cut to ribbons. "They just went down
in front of me—some slow and some quick, some forward and some
backward." Luttrell survived to be taken prisoner by a Wehrmacht
sergeant with a machine pistol—"Everything is better in Germany," his
captor advised—but the scorched smell of passing machine-gun bullets
lingered in memory for the rest of his life.

Panzers finished the encirclement, herding the Americans into small
groups. "I saw that it was hopeless and put my white handkerchef on a
stick and waved it. That was that," Van Vliet reported. From the open
turret of a Tiger tank, an officer yelled at Drake, "Colonel, you surren-

der." Drake replied, "You go to hell," and turned his back until a Wehrmacht major appeared and, in perfect English, offered a seat in his scout car. He had once practiced law in Chicago, the major claimed, and would be honored by Drake's company.

The debacle was complete. Of Van Vliet's men from Djebel Ksaira, some 800 were captured, along with another 600 from Garet Hadid. A burial detail stacked the dead in a mass grave, then joined the column of American prisoners stretching east as far as the eye could see. A few hundred GIs—including the tagless, ecumenical Berlovich—reached Allied lines, many having survived a week or more on stolen eggs and fried cactus leaves. Drake's second-in-command and the only officer to escape, Lieutenant Colonel Gerald C. Line, staggered into the American camp and later wrote his wife, "I haven't found out for sure whether I am sane or insane."

For all military intents and purposes, the 168th Infantry Regiment—Iowa's finest—had been obliterated. "It is pardonable to be defeated," observed Lieutenant Luttrell, who would spend the rest of the war in a German prison, "but unpardonable to be surprised."

Their triumph at Sidi bou Zid left the Germans off balance. FRÜHLINGSWIND had been a stunning success, and the Allied abandonment of Gafsa made MORGENLUFT—Rommel's thrust in the south—superfluous. Now what?

Atrocious Allied communications security helped answer this question. Uncoded radio transmissions broadcast in the clear provided German eavesdroppers with ample evidence of Allied turmoil and intentions. Security in Ward's 1st Armored Division later was judged "unbelievably low," the worst in any American unit in Tunisia; transmissions included such bald disclosures as "If the enemy attacks again I will have to withdraw." Following Anderson's order at 10:40 A.M. on February 16 that II Corps was to forgo further counterattacks, German commanders soon knew with certainty that American troops would fight only a delaying action at Sbeïtla as part of a general retreat. With Kesselring's approval, Arnim ordered his troops on to Sbeïtla, the gateway to Kasserine Pass and the Grand Dorsal.

Rommel's staff car wheeled into Gafsa on Tuesday morning, the sixteenth. Those Tunisians not busy digging out survivors from the American demolitions looted the town with festive abandon, ripping out pipes, window frames, and sinks. Wearing his long leather duster, Rommel watched in amusement as a crowd gathered around the car chanting,

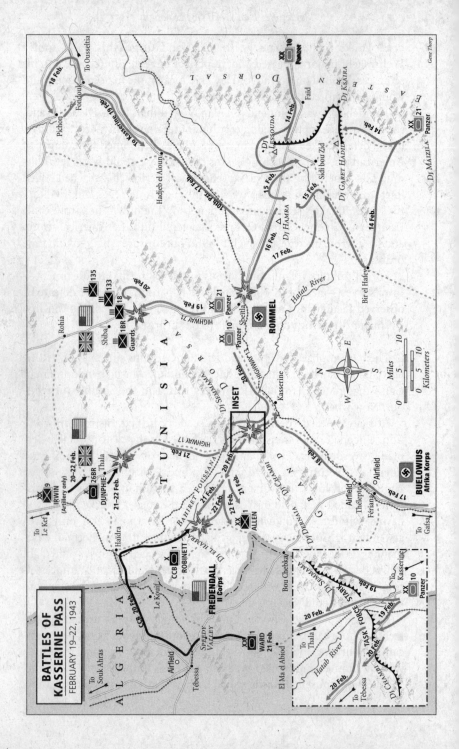

BATTLES OF
KASSERINE PASS
FEBRUARY 19–22, 1943

Gene Thorp

"Hitler! Rommel! Hitler! Rommel!" Peasants pressed forward with gifts of eggs and flapping chickens, while German soldiers divvied up cartons of Lucky Strikes found in an abandoned U.S. Army truck.

Arnim had marching orders of a sort, but what was the Desert Fox to do? Kesselring's original scheme called for the 21st Panzer Division to join Afrika Korps troops in the assault on Gafsa, but Arnim had informed Rommel this very morning that he no longer saw any reason to transfer the division. Instead, he had notions of swinging northeast from Sbeïtla to bag more American and British troops around the Ousseltia Valley. Rommel pushed his men on to the abandoned airfields at Fériana and Thélepte, but his eyes were again fixed on the western horizon and the huge depot at Tébessa. Kesselring, conferring with Hitler in East Prussia, was unavailable to referee between his ever more antagonistic commanders in Africa. The Americans were reeling, but Axis momentum now slowed perceptibly for want of a unified command and an overarching offensive vision. A ragged uncertainty took hold. To the Allies' enormous good fortune, more than two days would be wasted by bickering in the German high command.

"I had never gambled," Rommel later wrote, "never had to fear losing everything. But in the position as it was now, a rather greater risk had to be taken." The weaker force must take the longer chance. A thrust to Tébessa and then on another 140 miles to Bône would unhinge the entire Allied line and "force the British and Americans to pull back the bulk of their forces to Algeria." It could "change the entire complexion of the North African theater of war." In a message to Kesselring and Comando Supremo in Rome, he requested that both the 10th and the 21st Panzer Divisions be placed under his command for "an immediate enveloping thrust of strong forces . . . on Tébessa and the area north of it." Awaiting a reply from Rome, Rommel dined in Gafsa on couscous and mutton with a local sheikh.

Arnim disagreed, in a phone call to Rommel and in messages to Kesselring. "The terrain would be against us," he warned. Tébessa was mountainous and easily defended; such an attack would take at least two weeks, with uncertain fuel supplies and Montgomery's Eighth Army banging on the back door at Mareth. Better to veer north in a shallow envelopment to relieve the pressure building west of Tunis.

Allied intelligence detected part of this protracted debate. Thanks to Ultra, eavesdroppers heard a message from Rommel on February 17 indicating that he could hardly risk attacking Tébessa with just the fifty-two German and seventeen Italian tanks currently under his command. But other, more critical messages were not decrypted—including

Rommel's request for the two armored divisions. Once again Ultra decrypts proved misleading.

Kesselring dithered, then concluded that opportunity outweighed risk and threw his weight behind Rommel's plan in a message to Comando Supremo: "I consider it essential to continue the attack toward Tébessa." After more exasperated prodding by Rommel, who pleaded that the operation had "a chance for success only if the attack is launched without delay," approval would come from Rome at 1:30 on Friday morning. Rommel could have the two panzer divisions "to force a decisive success in Tunisia." There was a catch, however. Rather than lunging as far west as Tébessa, he was told to aim seventy miles due north of Kasserine, at Le Kef, where the roads were better and he could cut off Anderson's First Army. The envelopment would be narrowed by at least fifty miles, roughly splitting the difference between Rommel's proposal and Arnim's.

Rommel ranted at "an appalling and unbelievable piece of shortsightedness" by superiors who "lacked the guts to give a whole-hearted decision." Then, calming himself, he ordered a bottle of champagne. North or west hardly mattered. He was on the attack. Suddenly, he told his aide, he felt "like an old war horse that had heard the music again."

Not since A.D. 647, when the caliph's soldiers burned Sbeïtla and put its Byzantine inhabitants to the sword, had the little town suffered a night like that of February 16–17. "There was indescribable confusion," wrote one officer. "The road was jammed as far as one could see [with] remnants of a beaten force hurrying to the rear." Sbeïtla had already been crowded with hundreds of French colonial troops driven from Faïd Pass two weeks earlier, as well as rear-echelon American soldiers growing more and more edgy at reports of disaster in the east. Now hollow-eyed survivors from a half-dozen shattered battalions stumbled into town, enemy artillery thudding behind them. Most assumed that Rommel rather than Arnim commanded the three armored columns baying at their heels; there was a perverse thrill at being routed by the famous Desert Fox, who, one artilleryman conceded, "was slapping us around like schoolboys. It was discouraging and humiliating but, more than that, it was fantastic."

Panic built slowly. Nurses evacuating a French hospital gave away everything that could not be heaped onto a dray cart, and GIs took off with alarm clocks, letter openers, and bottles of peach brandy. At the American 77th Evacuation Hospital more than 600 burned and otherwise wounded men lay head to foot in green ward tents to avoid breathing in one another's faces. Pallid medics donated pint after pint of their own blood for transfusions until word came to "pack and run." They packed and they ran in the moonlight. Patients swaddled in Army blankets were hoisted into open trucks, lightless except for hooded lanterns on the rear bumpers. As the convoy rumbled west toward Kasserine Pass, snow dusted the olive-drab lumps in the truck beds. "Retreat," said one surgeon, "is a ghastly word." A sardonic GI supplied the perfect reply in a letter home: "Americans never retreat but *withdraw*."

Night deepened. Battle sounds drew closer. Tracer fire flicked into the olive groves three miles east of Sbeïtla. "Shooting. Have to go," a soldier scribbled in a letter, then added, "Never so scared in my life." More units fled, some with orders and many without. French officers again harnessed men to carts, horses to gun carriages, and mules to broken trucks, all of which further clogged traffic on Highway 13. Howze implored Carleton Coon and his OSS colleagues to crouch in foxholes and flip Molotov cocktails at passing Tiger tanks. "We didn't want to," Coon later reported. "It was not OSS work." Instead they played poker, using rifle cartridges for chips, and planted a few exploding mule turds. Joining the refugees was a Signal Corps pigeon platoon that had arrived in Sbeïtla on February 11 to supplement radio and telephone communications. No messages had yet been sent by wing; the handlers needed a week to settle their birds before they would home properly. Now 1,500 decidedly unsettled pigeons headed west in a swaying, cooing loft balanced on a truck bed.

At 8:30 P.M., engineers without warning blew up the pump house that fed the aqueduct to Sfax. Subsequent detonations demolished a railroad trestle east of Sbeïtla as well as road culverts and the aqueduct itself. Although most enemy tanks were still miles from Sbeïtla, the ammunition dump soon went up in a thunderous yellow roar heard across central Tunisia.

Retreating soldiers are always predisposed to believe the worst, and the men credited the blasts to enemy infiltrators. Panic that had been isolated now became general. Flight ensued. Terrified drivers tore through the narrow streets, crumpling fenders or veering into ditches. On Highway 13, vehicles raced three abreast like chariots. Arm-flapping officers tried to flag down their men only to be brushed aside, and soldiers unable to hitch a ride hied cross-country. Finding an infantry squad firing wildly into the night a young officer asked what the men were aiming at. One soldier looked up from his smoking M-1 long enough to answer, "I'll be damned if I know, Lieutenant, but everyone else is shooting." Others deepened their shame with casual cruelty. "We were next to a group of Arab houses," a reconnaissance battalion soldier later wrote. "We decided to see what the inside of one of the houses was like so we ran into it with the half-track and knocked off the corner. Five women came out of the house and went over to another." Tommies summoned to reinforce Sbeïtla fought their way through the floodtide. "Get that junk off the road," snarled a British officer, "and let an army through."

The fog of war lay thick on Orlando Ward, and had since the hostile debouchment at Faïd four days earlier. He rarely ventured from the 1st Armored Division command post, and he was hard put to conjure an accurate picture of the battlefield from the shrill dispatches filtering into his Sbeïtla cactus patch. Yet Ward remained calm, even cheerful, despite evidence that the Americans had lost two armored battalions, two infantry battalions, two artillery battalions, and sundry smaller units. Only Fredendall's order on Tuesday evening to destroy the ammunition dump "annoyed and rattled" him. The blast seemed premature, a clear signal to foe and to friend of another American retirement.

Ward was further discomposed by reports that among those stampeding west were McQuillin and many CCA troops not already dead or captured. Old Mac had been awakened at 10:45 P.M. by flares and then machine-gun fire stitching the orchards east of town. Like a chessboard knight, he hopped rearward to the sprawling Roman ruins on the western outskirts, and kept right on hopping past the tomb of the martyred saint Jucundus. Colonel Stack, the CCC commander, watched McQuillin amble past with a French horse cavalry unit, then went to find Ward. "I told General Ward," Stack recounted, "that if he thought that CCA was his front line, he was mistaken." The general radioed McQuillin and found him "some miles in the rear," Stack added. "Ward ordered McQuillin to stop the retreat of CCA and return to his original position."

At one A.M. on February 17, Ward phoned Fredendall in Speedy Valley to warn of barbarians at the gate. The spearhead of perhaps ninety panzers, including nine Tigers, had pierced the American left flank three miles east of town. Ward did not know how long his division could stand and fight.

Fredendall immediately phoned Truscott in Constantine. The II Corps commander earlier had reported that "the picture . . . does not look too good," but now his warning was dire. "[Fredendall] considered situation extremely grave, and uncertain of ability to hold," Truscott wrote, scratching notes as fast as he could. Thirty minutes later, Fredendall called back: "Fears that we have lost 1st Armored Division," Truscott scribbled. "Feels that First Army has not given credit to his reports as to gravity of situation."

Truscott had his own spy at Sbeïtla, a colonel who sent him lyrical if poetically licensed private intelligence missives. Shortly after one A.M. the colonel reported that "tanks were fighting in the moonlight in Sbeïtla, and were all around Ward's command post." Truscott now concluded that Old Ironsides would soon be overrun. Fredendall took such counsel of his fears that he soon ordered Speedy Valley abandoned for a new corps headquarters in the primary school at Le Kouif, seventeen miles northeast of Tébessa. The tunnel project was forsaken forever, its incomplete shafts left as dank monuments to an American Ozymandias.

This farrago of bad tidings had the virtue of being wrong. The enemy was near but not *that* near, certainly not with almost a hundred tanks. (And no panzer was yet within eighty arduous road miles of Speedy Valley.) Enough stalwarts had chosen to stand fast that the German advance was checked in midcareer. "Strong enemy resistance," the 21st Panzer reported after several skirmishes. With just sixty-five tanks, the panzer commander decided to await daybreak before pressing his attack. Further weakening the Axis cause, Arnim chose this moment to peel away part of the 10th Panzer Division for a thrust twenty-five miles to the northeast, where his tanks would find nothing but grief from mines and screaming sheets of Allied artillery fire.

Better yet from Ward's perspective, his division had been reunited for the first time since Northern Ireland. Finally convinced that the main Axis attack had indeed come through Faïd Pass, Anderson authorized Fredendall to shift CCB and other American units sixty miles toward Sbeïtla.

"Move the big elephants to Sbeïtla, move fast, and come shooting!" Fredendall told Robinett. In two pachydermal columns they pounded south. Ward placed CCB on his right just east of town, and across Highway 13 the remnants of CCA anchored the left. CCC provided a rearguard reserve just west of town. Robinett tromped about throughout that long Tuesday night, emplacing his tanks, clucking at the fainthearts, and displaying all the swagger of a man keen to fight. When a fretful artilleryman voiced fear that his guns had been overrun, Robinett paraphrased Sherman: "When things are going badly at the rear, go to the front—they are always better up there."

In truth, things were not so fine at the front either. CCA had buckled beyond repair, and so had the confidence of the high command. "Everything is going badly at Sbeïtla," Anderson told a French general. At 1:30 on Wednesday morning, the British commander authorized Fredendall to abandon Sbeïtla, while asking that Ward hold until the next evening so fallback fortifications could be dug at Kasserine Pass in the west and at Sbiba in the north. Fredendall protested that by the next evening Old Ironsides would be reduced to smoking scrap. Anderson agreed to compromise by setting eleven A.M. on Wednesday as the decampment hour. Before dawn, the plan changed yet again to give Fredendall more discretion, and Ward was instructed to hold at all costs until hearing otherwise.

"I have had another argument with the big boss here," Fredendall told Truscott, who now had a stenographer listening in on his phone conversations. "He wanted me to hold all day at Sbeïtla. . . . It would have been all tangled up in another dog fight. Finally I got them to agree to let me go ahead. They not only want to tell you *what* to do but *how* to do it. Anyway, I think we are going to get our tail out the door alright."

As for Drake, Fredendall added, "We have to write him off."

"Reference to Waters?" Truscott asked.

"No, we don't know a damn thing about Waters."

Fredendall's tone softened. The tunneling sounds at Speedy Valley had been supplanted by the clamor of men striking their tents and loading their trucks. His corps was in tatters, already thrown back fifty miles with 2,500 casualties and no end in sight. His career, too, seemed wrecked. For over thirty-five years he had served in uniform, built a name, earned his stars. But surely Eisenhower would need a scapegoat.

"When do you think the old man would like to have my suit?" Fredendall asked.

Truscott hesitated. "He knows that you are doing the best you can do."

"Sometimes," Fredendall said, "that is not good enough."

Ward and Robinett braced for an attack at dawn on Wednesday, February 17, but no attack came. Position, numbers, and morale lay with the Axis, yet they held back, snuffling cautiously rather than slamming into the disordered Americans. Kesselring remained in East Prussia. Arnim chased his wild goose to the northeast. Rommel ate couscous in Gafsa and drafted petitions to Comando Supremo. Although Luftwaffe squadrons battered Sbeïtla and other Allied strongholds, there was no galloping urgency. The Axis seemed afflicted with the same languor that had marked Allied movements early in the Tunisian campaign, and each passing hour permitted reinforcement and repositioning.

Ward regained his swash. "We stood in the cactus patch all morning and on into the afternoon," a sergeant told his parents. "With the glasses and then with the eye, you could see the dots of the armored fighting vehicles. The general, one of the finest men, stood on the skyline smoking a cigar, very calm, which was good on the nerves of a number of very jittery people, including me."

Fifteen minutes before noon, the attack resumed. Wehrmacht infantry advanced down Highway 13 and panzers struck CCB on the American right, where Robinett had strung a tank destroyer battalion in a picket line several miles east of town. A few crews fired on the converging panzers, but most broke for the rear; then all did. Rather than leapfrogging back by company as planned, the half-tracks "just turned and kept going,".one soldier later recalled. "Everybody was throwing out smoke pots, so it made a dramatic scene."

At 1:15 P.M., the panzers sidled toward the 2nd Battalion of the 13th Armored Regiment, whose commander, Henry Gardiner, had fought with gallantry around Tébourba nearly three months before. Gardiner's tankers still mounted the antique M-3 General Lee, but they had been given time to burrow into a wadi and to camouflage artistically with wet clay. "I counted thirty-five enemy tanks come rolling over a rise in the ground almost to the direct front, a distance of about three miles," Gardiner reported. Waiting; waiting; and then at point-blank range he cried, "Boys, let them have it!" Fire leaped from the wadi, striking fifteen panzers and destroying five. The volley "stopped the attack cold," Gardiner added.

For an hour. Then the panzers came again, angry now, with a sweeping attack around the American right five miles south of Sbeïtla. Artillery gun chiefs screamed for more ammunition, their open mouths bright red O's in faces black with grime and powder. Between shellings, men at the last pitch of exhaustion napped sitting upright. "We were all very shaky after the battle of the night before because we had little or no sleep and because we had lost quite a few men," one artilleryman recounted.

Gardiner warned Robinett that his tanks would "soon be in serious trouble." At 2:30 P.M., Ward authorized CCB to withdraw behind her two sister combat commands. For three hours Gardiner's men fought a deft rearguard battle at a cost of nine General Lees, including the battalion commander's. With his driver dead and his tank in flames, Gardiner hid until sunset, then fled west in the wake of his retreating army.

At dusk, German and Italian troops edged into Sbeïtla. It was rubble, an empty, burning, stinking place of demolished bridges and dribbling water mains. Only the Roman temples and St. Jucundus's crypt, ruins already, had escaped destruction. Robinett might have invoked another Sherman aphorism: "War is cruelty, and you cannot refine it." Darkness slipped down on the Allied column winding west into the thick forests beyond Kasserine Pass, the defile that would give this two-week sequence of battles its name. "The night was heavy with low cloud, and always that intolerable wind . . . and all the inevitable turmoil and confusion of night movement," wrote A. D. Divine. "Clouds were red with the burning of the Sbeïtla dumps."

Again the Allies had been drubbed. But in the glooming a spark kindled among those who had stood fast and fought well at the end. Pride, vengeance, anger came, yes, and a sense that enough was enough, that from this havoc a ruthless killing spirit could emerge. The war was coming inside them now. Among those trudging beneath the dark towering peaks of the Grand Dorsal was Ernie Pyle, who considered the retreat "damned humiliating" even as he wrote of the soldiers around him:

> You need feel no shame nor concern about their ability. . . . There is nothing wrong with the common American soldier. His fighting spirit is good. His morale is okay. The deeper he gets into a fight, the more of a fighting man he becomes.

Pyle was telling his readers what he knew they wanted to hear. Oddly enough, it was the truth.

"This Place Is Too Hot"

THE Grand Dorsal extends northeast to southwest for 200 miles before petering out beyond Fériana. Three gaps pierce the range in the south, connecting Tunisia's interior plateau to the Algerian highlands. The second and most dramatic of these is Kasserine Pass, twenty-five miles west of Sbeïtla, just beyond the scrofulous village of Kasserine. For millennia it has offered an invasion alley, west to east and back again. Where it is most constricted, at 2,000 feet above sea level, the pass is barely a mile wide.

Two formidable sentinels stand on the pass's flanks. Djebel Chambi on the south is Tunisia's tallest mountain at 5,064 feet, a forbidding massif that is thickly wooded almost to the crest. Djebel Semmama on the north, 4,447 feet high, turns a sheer face to the pass while offering gentler, scalable approaches from the east. The meandering Hatab River bisects the defile on a northwest-to-southeast heading; significantly, the steep-banked stream, which runs dry in summer but very wet in February, impedes movement between the northern and southern halves of the pass. Fissured with wadis and infested with cactus, Kasserine has an ambience familiar to anyone who has traveled in the American Southwest. It is a badlands.

Traveling west just beyond Kasserine village in the throat of the pass, the road forks. Highway 13, the left tine, continues westerly along the Hatab for another thirty miles to the Algerian border near Tébessa. Both road and river traverse the Bahiret Foussana, a broad valley of scattered farms, as well as zinc, lead, and phosphate mines. The Hatab terrain has been described as "a gigantic, crudely corrugated shed roof draining into a badly bent and twisted gutter." The right tine, designated Highway 17, skirts Djebel Semmama to ramble due north for thirty miles to the hilltop town of Thala and then another forty to Le Kef.

Kasserine Pass is not impregnable—nothing is, short of heaven's gate—but an Army history notes that it "offers such advantages to defense that a sufficient force could exact an exorbitant price." Fredendall's II Corps possessed a sufficient force, but unfortunately for the Americans that force was not arrayed at the pass. The remnants of Ward's 1st Armored Division had been ordered to reassemble in the uplands south of Tébessa to protect the supply dumps; the rest of the corps was scattered, as usual.

"I am holding a lot of mountain passes against armor with three and a half battalions of infantry," Fredendall told Truscott just before two P.M. on February 17. "If [the enemy] get together any place a couple of infantry battalions, they might smoke me out."

"The artillery of the 9th Division are on the way," Truscott replied.

"If you can get me a combat team of infantry—I haven't got a damn bit of reserve."

"I will do the best I can."

"I need a combat team of infantry worse than hell," Fredendall repeated. "All I have got is three and a half battalions of infantry. They are not enough."

Fredendall sounded like a man running out of tether. Eisenhower was shipping 800 soldiers daily from Casablanca—roughly a battalion a day—but few would arrive in Tunisia before the end of February. "There isn't any hope of getting a combat team up here for a number of days," Truscott said slowly. "The infantry of the 9th Division is moving just as fast as it can now."

"We can expect a little reinforcement?"

"Not a hell of a lot."

Thus the initial defense of Kasserine fell to the 19th Combat Engineer Regiment, 1,200 men singularly miscast for the task. Since arriving at the front six weeks earlier, the engineers had worked almost exclusively on road construction, except for those diverted to dig the now-abandoned tunnels at Speedy Valley. The regiment had failed to complete rifle training before shipping overseas, and only one man had ever heard shots fired in anger. The regimental arsenal included fifty-four dump trucks and half a dozen air compressors.

At nine P.M. on February 17, in chill fog and spitting rain, these ersatz infantrymen finished forming a three-mile skirmish line across the throat of the pass just west of the road fork. For the next thirty-six hours, while the Germans consolidated their winnings down the valley, they waited, lying at night like spoons in a drawer to stay warm, prey to anxiety and tactical pathos. Machine guns were badly sited, foxholes were too shallow, and barbed wire remained mostly on the spools. Nearly every man had entrenched on the floor of the pass, rather than the adjacent heights. Most commanders knew, at least in theory, that a valley could not be held without also controlling its shoulders. But, as one officer later observed, much of the American campaign in Tunisia involved "trying to draw a line between what we knew and what we did."

Just beyond the Roman ruins west of Sbeïtla, Rommel tried to draw his own line between what he wanted to do and what he had been told to do. Hands clasped behind his back, goggles perched on his visor, he studied the distant peaks of Semmama and Chambi. That way led seventy miles to Tébessa and the great supply dumps he had hoped to despoil before following the glory road to Bône. But it also offered, via Highway 17 through Thala, a backdoor route to Le Kef, the objective ordered by Comando Supremo.

A more direct and slightly shorter path to Le Kef could be had by taking Highway 71 north for eighty miles from Sbeïtla along the eastern flank of the Grand Dorsal. The enemy would certainly contest both routes. Where would the defenses be softer? Left, through Kasserine Pass, or right, directly toward Le Kef? Rommel studied the terrain with his field glasses while staff officers in slouch hats toed the ground with their double-laced desert boots.

His choice had been complicated by Arnim, who instead of giving Rommel the entire 10th Panzer had held back half the division's tanks, including the Tigers, on a thin claim of needing them in the north. While denouncing the "pigheadedness" of his two African commanders, Kesselring had yet to return from East Prussia to adjudicate their squabble. Kesselring believed the order from Comando Supremo contained enough ambiguity to permit Rommel a full attack on Tébessa before he turned toward Le Kef. But Kesselring was not here and Rommel—demonstrating an atypical obedience possibly infused with spite—chose to believe that Le Kef must be his first objective.

At 4:50 A.M. on Friday, February 19, Rommel issued his orders: the Afrika Korps was to drive west and capture Kasserine Pass; 21st Panzer would attack north on Highway 71 toward Le Kef; 10th Panzer—or as much of the division as could be mustered—would concentrate at Sbeïtla, ready to exploit whichever route seemed easier. With two roads diverging before him, Rommel would divide his force and travel both.

Even at his distant remove Fredendall recognized the vulnerability of Kasserine Pass. He peeled away a battalion from Terry Allen's 1st Division and shoved it forward to join the 19th Engineers, along with a four-gun French battery and some tank destroyers. That brought the number of defenders to 2,000. In another call to Truscott late Thursday morning, he asserted that "the 1st Armored gave them a good licking"—a triumph that existed mostly in II Corps imaginations—while asking for 120 replacement Sherman tanks. Truscott could offer fifty-two, nearly enough to outfit a battalion, and he chose not to reveal that Eisenhower had decided to hold back more than 200 other newly arrived Shermans for fear of losing them all.

At eight that evening, Fredendall phoned Colonel Alexander Stark, commander of Allen's 26th Infantry Regiment, who was south of Tébessa.

"Alex, I want you to go to Kasserine right away and pull a Stonewall Jackson. Take over up there."

Stark hesitated. "You mean tonight, General?"

"Yes, Alex, right away."

It took Stark nearly twelve hours to pick his way across the dark bowl of the Bahiret Foussana, alive with challenge—"Snafu!"—and counter-sign—"Damned right!" He arrived in the pass at 7:30 on Friday morning, just as the Germans did. Unlike the Confederate general whose military genius he was now to replicate, Stark knew little of the capacity or disposition of his troops, many of whom had never heard of him. A quick inspection of the misty pass revealed a predicament even Stonewall would have been hard put to salvage. Except for a single platoon positioned on the slopes of Djebel Semmama, all four infantry companies occupied low ground on the left side of the pass; likewise on the right, where one engineer platoon held Djebel Chambi and three companies held the flats. To shift troops from one side of the defile to the other would require a ten-mile detour to the nearest bridge over the Hatab River. Antitank mines had simply been dumped, rather than buried, on likely enemy approaches. Another 60,000 mines and 5,000 booby traps were on their way from Algeria by cargo plane and truck, but the arrival time was uncertain. Fredendall had also asked Anderson for thirty tons of barbed wire, and every platoon was pleading for sandbags, shovels, and picks.

A German attempt at dawn to seize the pass in a coup de main had been repulsed with good shooting from the French 75s; the Afrika Korps reconnaissance battalion bounced back as if brushing a hot stove. But at ten A.M., enemy artillery began falling around Stark's command tent three miles west of the Kasserine narrows. "Thirty-five to forty trucks brought up enemy infantry at 10:15," reported a staff officer. "They are making for high ground on our left."

And, soon, on the right. Wraiths in field gray scrambled up the rocky inclines, flopping to fire before scuttling on. Machine-gunners crouched behind them with tripods and ammunition boxes, lashing the pass with flails of tracer fire. American reinforcements arrived early in the afternoon, including the regimental band, a tank platoon, and three companies from the 9th Division's 39th Infantry. The badly laid mines sufficed to cripple five panzers below Djebel Chambi, and Stark's spirits lifted despite German capture of the ridgeline below Semmama's peak.

Shadows swallowed the pass when Stark received a late-afternoon visit from Brigadier Charles A. L. Dunphie, whose British 26th Armoured Brigade straddled the Thala road twenty miles behind the Americans. Stark pronounced the battle "well in hand," despite "slight difficulties with communication" from artillery shells severing his phone lines. Dunphie suspected that Stark was mistaken, a suspicion reinforced when the brigadier ventured forward 400 yards in his staff car for a personal reconnaissance and came streaking back to the tent beneath a swarm of German bullets. Enemy infiltration past U.S. lines was as obvious as it was ubiquitous. The Americans had no reserves, and, Dunphie reported, even the "position of [Stark's] own troops was vague, and in particular he could not tell me where he had laid minefields beyond the fact that they had laid all they could get hold of." In short, Dunphie concluded, Stark "had completely lost control of events. . . . I thought Stark a nice old boy—gallant but quite out of his depth." Returning to Thala at seven P.M., he reported to Anderson that conditions were "very poor at the pass." For his part, Stark dubbed Dunphie "that blockhead." Even in the face of mortal peril the cousins could not forbear their squabbling.

Stark had not yet "completely lost control of events." That would happen in the next few hours. But Anderson chose this moment to issue a stand-or-die edict effective at eight P.M.: "The army commander directs that there will be no withdrawal from the positions now held by the First Army. No man will leave his post unless it is to counterattack."

Even as this puff of gas circulated through the ranks, many a man was leaving his post, and *not* to counterattack. Enemy artillery fell with greater insistence as the night deepened. "The worst of it all was to see some of your best buddies next to you being shot down or blown up," observed an engineer corporal. "I never knew that there could possibly be so many shells in the air at one time and so many explosions near you and still come out alive." Compounding the terror was a new German weapon deployed for the first time, the Nebelwerfer, a six-barreled mortar that "stonked" targets with a half-dozen 75-pound high-explosive rounds soon known as screaming meemies or moaning minnies because the wail they made in flight was said to resemble "a lot of women sobbing their hearts out."

Night fever spread through the engineer ranks holding Stark's right. "A considerable number of men left their positions and went to the rear," an engineer officer reported. Some were corraled and herded back to the line; more simply melted into the night. Stark's left was even shakier. At 8:30 P.M., enemy patrols overran the infantry battalion command post. German infiltrators cut off the solitary company on the slopes of Djebel Semmama, then seized Point 1191, the mountain's most important ridge. Many GIs who eluded capture were subsequently robbed of their clothes and weapons by Arab brigands. "In some instances the Arabs got the drop on the men with M-1 and '03 rifles they had already obtained," a chagrined company commander told the provost marshal.

Bad as the bad night had been, the foggy morning of February 20 was worse. Rommel rose early to visit an Italian Centauro Division battalion sweeping into the pass from the southeast. At 10:30 A.M. he drove to Kasserine village, passing the bloated bodies of dead American drivers still behind the wheels of their charred vehicles. On a rail bridge spanning the Hatab River, Rommel met General Karl Buelowius, commander of the Afrika Korps, and General Fritz Freiherr von Broich, commander of the depleted and tardy 10th Panzer Division. The field marshal was displeased. Although Buelowius had ordered two grenadier battalions to resume their assault, the attack seemed sluggish. The Americans were crumbling but stubbornly refused to collapse. Unless the Germans punctured the pass *this very day*, Rommel believed, Allied reinforcements would clot the wound and prevent him from exploiting any breakthrough, particularly since the 21st Panzer had made little progress in its northward probe up Highway 71. He ordered three more battalions into action for a six-battalion attack—10th Panzer on the Axis right, Afrika Korps on the left—supported by five artillery battalions. After sharply berating Buelowius for torpor and Broich for not leading from the front—both stood glum as apprehended truants in their greatcoats and slouch hats—Rommel returned to the command post in the Kasserine train station.

The American collapse began in earnest by late morning. At 11:22 the 19th Engineers' commander, Colonel A.T.W. Moore, warned Stark by radio that enemy infantry and tanks were forcing the pass along Highway 13. An engineer major bellowed: "Forget about our equipment and just save your life." Artillery observers fled, explaining plausibly if ingloriously: "This place is too hot." Companies disintegrated into platoons, platoons into squads, squads into solitary foot soldiers chased to the rear by screaming meemies. Half an hour later, Moore radioed, "Enemy overrunning our C.P.," and bolted for high ground. He soon arrived at Stark's tent to announce that the 19th Engineers no longer existed. In fact, with 128 casualties, the regiment had been sorely hurt but not obliterated.

The "uncoordinated withdrawal," as Moore delicately called it, was mirrored on the American left. Stark ordered his artillery to fall back; French gunners, without tractors to move their 75s, wept as they spiked the guns and took to the hills. Colonel Theodore J. Conway, sent forward by Truscott to assess Stark's plight, was shocked to see troops streaming past him for the rear. Briefly, he thought of Washington on horseback in the battle of New York, whacking his fleeing Continentals with the flat of his sword in a vain effort to turn them; having neither horse nor sword, Conway joined the exodus.

Stark held until after five P.M., when grenades began detonating near his command post in the Hatab gulch. With his staff and two hapless Army cameramen who had just arrived in search of "some action shots," he hurried upriver before striking overland toward Thala. "We had to crawl," Stark later recounted, "as in some instances [German soldiers] were not more than fifteen yards away."

Casualties just among infantrymen totaled nearly 500 dead, wounded, and missing. Italian tanks drove five miles on Highway 13 toward Tébessa without seeing a trace of the Americans except for burning wreckage. At 3:35 A.M. on Sunday, February 21, precisely a week after the Axis offensive had begun, Fredendall's headquarters warned: "Enemy reliably reported in possession of heights on either side of Kasserine Pass. . . . Attack also going towards Thala on a four-thousand-yard front and has advanced about two thousand yards beyond the pass."

Kasserine Pass was lost. Anderson observed the occasion with another windy exhortation. "There is to be no further withdrawal under any excuse. . . . Fight to the last man." That, the weary Yanks agreed, simply meant the British were willing to fight to the last American.

"Order, Counter-order, and Disorder"

DEMOLITIONISTS laid slabs of guncotton through the vast dumps at Tébessa and awaited orders to fire the stores. As rumors of an approaching enemy horde flew across the Bahiret Foussana, 400 quartermaster troops scurried helter-skelter. The supply depot's arsenal consisted of two machine guns and a single 37mm cannon. Sentries paced the ancient walls and peered eastward for telltale coils of dust. A British officer marinated in the lore of Khartoum and Balaklava proposed repelling any approaching panzers with grenades flung from the parapets. Four hundred thousand gallons of gasoline in five-gallon flimsies were loaded into boxcars for evacuation, but more than a million meals' worth of rations would be abandoned if the enemy attacked. Hatchet-wielding cooks stalked like madmen through Tébessa's coops and hutches, slaughtering every chicken and rabbit rather than leave them for the Germans. The little garrison gorged on stew for breakfast.

As always in the great clash of armies, the small dramas draw the eye. Ted Roosevelt was helping the French near Ousseltia when word came that his son, Quentin—a twenty-five-year-old artillery officer, named for an uncle killed in the Great War—had been gravely wounded in a strafing near Kasserine. A Messerschmitt bullet had pierced his lung and lodged in his liver. The ambulance driver raced to three field hospitals before finding one not yet fleeing the German advance. Roosevelt wrote to his wife, Eleanor:

> On the morning of the second day he ran a temperature of 104 and they thought he was dying. They got a message through to me. I started for there after dark. I had not slept for two days and the hospital was sixty miles away, sixty miles of night driving thinking I'd find him dead.

He found him alive. Asleep on a cot in a mud-floor tent, Quentin had made the turn. "I went over and kissed him as if he were a little boy again and indeed I did feel he was our little boy," Roosevelt wrote. "I'm feeling buoyant."

Little buoyancy could be found at II Corps headquarters in the school at Le Kouif. Although Fredendall fought off despondency with occasional nips of bourbon, one officer described him sitting on the school's front steps "head in hands and giving every evidence of being both bewildered and defeated." George Marshall had once said of Fredendall, "I like that man. You can see determination all over his face." Now that face mostly showed despair; he had begun referring to his adversary as "Professor Rommel." Whistling tunelessly while staring at the map, he abruptly turned to an aide and said, "If I were back home, I'd go out and paint the garage doors. There's a lot of pleasure in painting a garage door."

Alerted to the possible abandonment of Tébessa, General Juin hurried to Le Kouif, where he found the corps commander perched on a packing crate in an empty office. Tossing his left-handed salute, Juin urged the Americans to stand fast. Surrendering Tébessa meant offering the panzers a flat, open avenue to Constantine, a strategic prize.

Fredendall shrugged. He had no reserves. His corps was reeling. He would do whatever Anderson ordered.

Juin drew himself up. "My wife and my children are in Constantine," he said in a fractured voice. "If you carry out this order, I shall remove from you the Constantine Division in order to defend Tébessa and we will get ourselves killed there."

Fredendall stirred from his crate, his lethargy momentarily dispelled. "I saw his attitude change," Juin later recounted, "and throwing his arms round my neck, he swore not to abandon Tébessa."

At least not yet. Fredendall repaired to his new bivouac, an elegant mansion owned by a Vichy mining executive. After Speedy Valley's sepulchral chill, the house seemed decadently cozy. Sitting by the oil stove in his slippers, he instructed his chief of staff, "Dabney, open up the bottle. Let's have a drink." On the evening of February 20, with Kasserine Pass gone and Professor Rommel running amok, the 1st Division artillery chief arrived after a muddy jeep ride that left his face so spattered he appeared to be wearing a plaster mask. "Reported to Fredendall who said that he had a very important mission for me but it could wait until after dinner," Brigadier General Clift Andrus recorded. "Dinner! Tablecloths, silver, waiters in white, beef—even ice cream."

"I'm going to be the goat in this," Fredendall told one of his lieutenants. That was most probable, unless he could find a substitute: Fredendall's pale eye fell on Pinky Ward. At 3:15 P.M. on Friday, he cabled Eisenhower an "eyes only" message:

Ward appears tired out, worried, and has informed me that to bring new tanks in would be the same as turning them over to the

Germans. Under these circumstances do not think he should continue in command although he has done the best he could. Need someone with two fists immediately.

While Eisenhower pondered this unsettling request in Algiers, the Allied command structure along the Grand Dorsal grew yet more convoluted. With part of the 1st Division dispatched to Bou Chebka, twenty miles southwest of Kasserine Pass, Fredendall initially gave Terry Allen the mission of commanding a large area that included French and British units. On Saturday morning, as defenses in the pass collapsed, he ordered Robinett to take over the remnants of Stark's force and to counterattack with CCB. Ward again was excluded from the chain of command.

Several hours later, Fredendall thought better of handing Rommel the remaining American tanks on a platter. In an impromptu conference over the hood of his staff car near Thala, he instead ordered Robinett to defend the approaches to Tébessa. But he seemed listless and defeated: "There is no use, Robbie, they have broken through and you can't stop them," he said, then added, "If you get away with this one, Robbie, I will make you a field marshal."

Robinett's defense of the western avenues would be "coordinated" by Brigadier Dunphie, who was blocking the northern approaches to Thala, even though Dunphie lacked compatible radios or any other means to communicate with the thousands of American troops scattered across nearly a thousand square miles. As one final twist in a very twisted plot, Anderson—surer with each hour that Fredendall's generalship was unlikely to resolve this mess—assigned his own candidate, Brigadier Cameron G. G. Nicholson, to command the British, French, and American forces now assembled south of Thala.

Fredendall retired to his wainscoted dining room to fret. Anderson's First Army headquarters was hardly more composed. "Everything was confusion there," reported one American colonel who watched a British officer slap a hysterical comrade across the face and bark, "Get hold of yourself." A British Guardsman captured the sentiment of every man in the Allied ranks: "the most perfect example of order, counter-order, and disorder that has happened in my experience."

Into the muddle stepped a man orderly in appearance, thought, and deed. General Harold Alexander had at last arrived from Cairo, ready to lead all ground forces in Tunisia, as agreed at Casablanca. Designated the 18th Army Group, his new command comprised First Army in the north and Eighth Army just entering Tunisia in the south. After visiting Eisenhower in Algiers on Monday, the fifteenth—"Your mission is the early destruction of all Axis forces in Tunisia," the commander-in-chief advised—Alexander conferred with Anderson on Thursday night and toured II Corps on Friday while his staff of seventy officers and 500 enlisted men settled in at Constantine. Officially scheduled to take over on Saturday, February 20, Alexander found the front so disorganized that he advanced his own investiture by a day. At 7:20 P.M. on Friday night, four hours after Fredendall had asked for Ward's removal, he cabled Eisenhower, "In view of situation I have assumed command." In a note to Montgomery he confessed himself "very shocked. There has been no policy and no plan. The battle area is all mixed up with British, French, and American units."

He cut a dashing figure in his red-banded cap, with his open tunic, leather jacket, and corduroy trousers tucked into Turkish knee boots. He was lean and bronzed, with deep creases at the corners of his mouth that became furrows for the tips of his mustaches, and his eyes were crinkled from a career spent squinting into the middle distance. He was the third son of the Earl of Caldeon and had been raised in patrician privilege on an immense estate at Ulster. (Once asked to cite manly virtues, he proposed "natural good manners.") Considered "able more than clever," he had aspired to become a painter and then president of the Royal Academy. Instead, he attended Sandhurst, soon becoming the youngest lieutenant colonel in the British Army and later its youngest general. His combat record over thirty years rivaled Hector's. Rudyard Kipling wrote of him, "At the worst crises he was both inventive and cordial and . . . would somehow contrive to dress the affair in high comedy." When a staff officer at Dunkirk told him, "Our position is catastrophic," Alexander was said to have replied, "I'm sorry, I don't understand long words." Most recently, as Montgomery's superior, he had helped engineer the British victory at El Alamein. Suave, phlegmatic, and immaculate—"the archetypal Edwardian hero"—he was Britain's most admired soldier and Churchill's favorite general.

Some thought him stupid. "Wellington without the wit," one biographer called him. "Intellect was not his most conspicuous asset." Despite his command of French, German, Hindi, and Urdu, Brooke and Montgomery both considered him an "empty vessel." Another British officer confessed, "I cannot imagine his ever producing a plan, let alone a *good* plan." Others were charmed by his unpretentiousness—he would tap-dance in regimental talent shows—and sangfroid. Harold Macmillan likened Alexander's mess to high table at an Oxford college, where war was "politely ignored" and conversation rambled over "the campaigns of Belisarius, the advantages of classical over Gothic architecture, or the best ways to drive pheasants in flat country."

Brilliantly slow or slowly brilliant, Alexander had arrived, he was in charge, and he was appalled. To Churchill and Brooke he wrote, "Real fault has been lack of direction from above from the very beginning." He considered Anderson a "solid soldier, rather dull." But, Alexander later observed, the First Army commander "was allowing the Germans to hurry him and he didn't control his headquarters. . . . He had lost the initiative."

Yet it was the Yanks who alarmed him more. By misfortune, the first Americans he encountered were swaggering Anglophobes, including the mercurial General Joseph W. Stilwell in Burma and now Fredendall in Tunisia. The latter was "utterly shaken," Alexander concluded, with no idea how to redeem himself; his staff was "dithery." "The poor body has a great weakness from its illness," he had said of II Corps on February 18. The troops appeared "soft, green, and quite untrained. . . . They lack the will to fight." American incapacity horrified him in those first hours and days; the impression lingered to damage Allied comity in Italy, where Alexander would serve as commander-in-chief.

"My main anxiety is the poor fighting value of the Americans," he now told London. "They simply do not know their job as soldiers and this is the case from the highest to the lowest. . . . Perhaps the weakest link of all is the junior leader, who just does not lead, with the result that their men don't really fight." In a scathing comment to an American journalist he encapsulated this failure of young officers to look after their men: "You know, your chaps don't wear the old school tie." Unless the U.S. Army shaped up by the time an invasion of Europe was launched, he warned Brooke, it "will be quite useless and play no useful part whatsoever."

Alexander's mind lacked the subtlety to envision a day when this raw clay had grown tall or to apprehend the many differences between British and American men-at-arms, so easily masked by their common language. Having participated in several catastrophic retreats himself, he should have recognized that defeat sometimes carried annealing and even salutary properties. A great sorting out was under way: the competent from the incompetent, the courageous from the fearful, the lucky from the unlucky. It would happen faster in the American Army than it had in the British. Alexander was not wholly wrong, but he was wrong.

Three separate actions unfolded during or just after the fall of Kasserine Pass. From the Allied perspective, one was bad and two were good, a ratio contravening the run of luck heretofore. They unfolded east to west in geographic as well as temporal sequence.

First, Rommel's northern thrust up Highway 17 with the 21st Panzer Division failed. As the panzers rolled toward Le Kef on Friday morning, February 19—this was the right wing of Rommel's double assault on Allied defenses—German intelligence concluded that all the troops straddling the road at Sbiba, twenty-five miles above Sbeïtla, were French and British. In fact, eight American infantry battalions drawn from the 34th and 1st Divisions and backed by artillery held the terrain east of the blacktop. "If they attack us in force we cannot hold, but by God we will," declared a 1st Division officer. Battered by British fire six miles south of Sbiba, truckborne grenadiers and twenty-five panzers veered eastward in an attempt to perforate the American flank. The German attack closed to within 600 yards of entrenched Yank infantry, then faltered; by midafternoon a dozen German tanks had been wrecked by artillery fire, and enemy corpses littered the desert. One GI likened the effect of 105mm shells on armor hulls to "taking shoe boxes and shoving them flat."

A renewed assault Saturday morning by forty panzers and two Wehrmacht infantry battalions on the American flank quickly collapsed. With Rommel's reluctant approval, the 21st Panzer backed off and dug in below Sbiba. In the reckoning that followed, French infantrymen seized half a dozen Arabs accused of spying or sabotage, stood them against the wall of a mosque, and dispatched them in a single smoking volley. A French captain strolled from body to slumped body administering the coup de grâce with a pistol bullet to the brain.

Checked on the right, Rommel turned his full attention to the left. The fall of Kasserine Pass suggested that the western, roundabout route through Thala was the easier way to Le Kef, and now the second action unspooled. Desperate to slow German momentum, Brigadier Dunphie ordered a small British rear guard down the Thala road toward Kasserine.

The result was foreordained, if valiant. At noon on February 20, tanks from the 8th Panzer Regiment slammed into the British two miles north of Kasserine Pass on Highway 17. For the next six hours, the Tommies yielded one untenable hill after another. "We were forced back, and on every ridge we left a few more of our tanks, derelict, perhaps burning," wrote one soldier. A correspondent described crewmen fleeing their burning hulks "like caterpillars dropping from a flaming nest. They run zig-zag, eyes staring white in smoke-blackened faces, strings of German machine gun fire lashing them as they go." The squadron commander, Major A. N. Beilby, strolled from tank to tank directing counterfire until shell fragments killed him. By six P.M., there were no tanks left to direct and every artillery officer lay dead with Beilby. Survivors scoured north "as hard as stiff legs and flapping revolvers in the leg holster would permit," chased by dusk-brightened tracers.

Rommel again held the initiative, but with it came a familiar conundrum: now what? From his command post near Kasserine, he studied the map, then motored through the pass to study the ground. He had twice divided his army, at Sbeïtla and at Kasserine. "I hoped to split the enemy forces far more than our own," he later explained. But now he lacked the strength to attack simultaneously north toward Thala and west toward Tébessa. Thala led north to Le Kef. But he could hardly ignore CCB and the other American forces lurking somewhere west, beyond the Bahiret Foussana, perhaps waiting to counterattack to sever the Axis path of retreat through Kasserine. Despite its grievous losses, II Corps still had 150 tanks.

A reconnaissance report at 11:25 A.M. on February 21 pushed Rommel to a decision that led to the third action in this sequence, which in turn would lead to Kasserine's finale. Twenty miles west of the pass and parallel to the Algerian border, a jagged escarpment known as Djebel el Hamra ran north to south, crossed by the packed-dirt roadbed of Highway 13. Wehrmacht scouts reported that no substantial Allied forces could be found east of el Hamra; the shallow bowl of the Bahiret Foussana was empty. Without waiting for confirmation from Luftwaffe pilots that his left flank was indeed secure, Rommel ordered the 10th Panzer to continue up Highway 17 toward Thala in his main attack; the Afrika Korps would push to el Hamra and safeguard the flank by sealing the passes from Tébessa and Bou Chebka.

The scouts were wrong. Djebel el Hamra and its lesser foothills bristled with Americans, on good ground and in formidable strength. In the south, Terry Allen held the Bou Chebka Pass with the 16th Infantry. "Well, boys," Allen announced, "this is our sector and we will fight in place." To the north, on the east face of the ridge and in a thin screen across the Bahiret Foussana, Robinett commanded eight battalions, eleven artillery batteries—nearly fifty guns—and a hodgepodge of others, including Senegalese riflemen and 700 lost souls snagged in a straggler line. Thick pines and rocky redoubts provided excellent concealment along a 4,000-yard front. From his command post near Highway 13, Robinett could see twenty miles to Kasserine Pass across a foggy plain dotted with pear orchards and cactus farms. Cocksure as ever, he *knew* the enemy would come his way. "It was," Robinett later claimed, "simply written on the ground."

Anderson on this very Saturday had reported that "American fighting value was very low"—the Yank commanders, he added, were especially "frightful." Yet a new bravado animated American ranks. Allen captured the mood in a message to Bill Darby, whose Rangers guarded against enemy infiltrators in the south: "There is a hell of a mess on our front.... Can you send me one reinforced company with a hairy-chested commander with big nuts?" Darby sent Company C, whose captain presumably possessed the requisite anatomical credentials, then told his own men, "Onward we stagger. And if the tanks come, may God help the tanks."

The tanks came, but at Robinett. General Buelowius surged forward along the Hatab's south bank at two P.M. on February 21 with forty panzers followed in trace by lorried infantry. Italian troops from the 5th Bersaglieri Battalion joined the attack, recognizable in their plumed pith helmets and distinctive running march. But within an hour, the weight of massed American howitzers began to tell. Shells burst around Axis formations tacking for cover where no cover existed. German 88s answered from the riverbank but Buelowius lacked enough guns for effective counterbattery fire. By four P.M. the attackers had drawn within range of American tanks and plunging fire from antitank guns hidden in the rocks. Even for the Afrika Korps it was too galling: at six P.M. Buelowius broke off the attack, still four miles short of Djebel el Hamra. Shades in feathers and coal-scuttle helmets backed into the dusk until searching shell fire could no longer range them. Buelowius had lost ten tanks, Robinett but one.

Repulsed on the right, Rommel ordered Buelowius to make a wide envelopment to the left. He meant to flank the Americans in the south and catch them from the rear. In darkness and teeming rain, Buelowius sidled across the mud; by first light on the twenty-second, his men were not only drenched and disorganized but lost, having wandered seven miles south of Djebel el Hamra.

Undeterred, two grenadier battalions attacked at dawn where they found themselves, just above Bou Chebka Pass. By eight A.M., five American howitzers and three lesser guns had been captured, along with thirty vehicles. The American line buckled and fell back, leaving a knobby, fog-shrouded salient known as Hill 812 covered with howling German grenadiers.

It seemed all too familiar: high hopes after a credible initial clash; an indefatigable enemy who pressed the attack; a brittle defense that fractured under stress. By chance, the Afrika Korps had struck the seam where Robinett's authority ended and Allen's began. Thirty-five miles away, the II Corps command post was feverishly packing for Constantine and Le Kef in the fear that Le Kouif would soon be overrun. Spooked by the German advances on what one Tommy dubbed Panic Sunday, officers joked about preparing their *Oflag*—prison camp—bags.

Yet something had hardened in this army. Even as violent death swept the ranks, men stood their ground. The line stiffened. The Afrika Korps was twenty-three air miles from Tébessa; it would come not an inch closer. At nine A.M. the fog lifted, exposing hundreds of grenadiers now marooned on Hill 812. Buelowius ordered two dozen panzers and the 5th Bersaglieri to push northwest at Djebel el Hamra as a diversion from his trapped infantry; the force came within two miles of the ridgeline before stalling under American fire from three sides.

"The air was full of hardware and smoke and the sounds of a real scrap," Clift Andrus later recalled. If ever a man appeared propitiously it was Andrus, the imperturbable 1st Division artillery chief known as Mr. Chips: a bemused, bespectacled figure with a pipe, a walking stick, and a small mustache.

"The most skillful and practical artillery officer I know," Allen called him, and now Andrus lived up to that praise. The Americans had many guns but no one to direct them in concert. Andrus rounded up wandering gunners and put them into the line. "Eyes at the back of their heads, whiskers, mud, and every sign of utterly exhausted men," he wrote of one battery. Told that the Americans were about to counterattack, "most of them started to cry" in sheer relief. Ax-swinging gunners felled pines on the djebel's front slope to clear fields of fire. And what fields they were. "An artilleryman's dream," Andrus reported. "The valley floor was covered with targets of every description, from tanks and eighty-eight batteries to infantry and trucks."

A single battalion, the 27th Field Artillery, fired more than 2,000 rounds, and others were nearly as prodigal. By two P.M., the milling Afrika Korps was in retreat. Soon a headlong rout of terrorized soldiers heaved eastward. Enemy dead lay like gray flagstones across the Bahiret Foussana. The 16th Infantry drove the grenadiers from Hill 812, recapturing intact every gun and vehicle lost that morning. Henry Gardiner, who again found himself in the thick of the fighting, described "one of the most exhilarating sights. . . . A column of prisoners came marching around a bend in the *wadi* with their hands held high, led by one of our tankers with a tommy gun."

An American soldier strolled through a makeshift POW cage filling a helmet with aluminum stars—rank insignia of the Italian private—then announced to Robinett that he had "captured a whole flock of Italian brigadier generals." Robinett plucked two from the pile for his own shoulders. He had been looking for stars since his promotion to general officer before Christmas.

"Lay Roughly on the Tanks"

As this action in the west played out, the final act in the Kasserine saga unfolded on Highway 17, where Rommel's main attack rolled toward Thala, past the wreckage of the exterminated British rear guard. Exhausted and spattered with mud, the field marshal had felt, in the past two days, moments of exhilaration that rivaled the happiness he had known as a young officer in the Great War. An aide described Rommel's arrival at the front early on Sunday, the twenty-first: "He suddenly appeared, just like the old days, among the very foremost infantry and tanks, in the middle of their attack, and had to hit the ground just like the riflemen when the enemy's artillery opened up!"

By midafternoon all euphoria had leached away. Rommel saw that his Afrika Korps troops, long accustomed to the freewheeling combat of the open desert, had much to learn about seizing high ground and avoiding vulnerable valleys in hill country. And the 10th Panzer, now pressing up the Thala road with a spearhead of thirty tanks, twenty guns, and thirty-five infantry half-tracks, seemed sluggish. German intelligence had expected only Americans north of Kasserine Pass, but a pesky British armor force harassed the advancing German column through midday without offering decisive battle. Of Broich and the other panzer commanders Rommel would later complain, "They did not seem to realize that they were in a race with the Allied reserves." For more than four hours, the German attack crept forward, Rommel in a staff car left of the highway and Broich on the right. Arabs in wool robes with pointed cowls flitted across the hills, stripping the dead of even their socks. Bodies lay spread-eagled, shockingly white.

The British had their own problems. Brigadier Nicholson, dispatched by Anderson to oversee Dunphie and the other defenders, failed to reach Thala until 3:15 Sunday morning, after spending six hours plowing through axle-deep mud in his Humber Box. Upon arriving, he found "no full-blooded orders" from Anderson but vague, irritating instructions to "act offensively" without risking the loss of armor that "might be wanted elsewhere." Dunphie's fifty tanks were mostly obsolete Valentines, no match for the panzers. His largest infantry unit—the 2nd Battalion of the 5th Leicestershire Regiment—had just arrived from

England and "had no conception of what was coming to them," Nicholson later noted. "I found it difficult to get a sense of urgency into them." Except for five U.S. tank destroyers who joined the fight, a British officer reported that he had been unable to rally American stragglers passing by "at speed" with—as a Yank officer observed—"the usual story of being the only survivor." All day long, hundreds of fleeing soldiers from Stark's wrecked command drifted through Thala yelling, "He's right behind us!" No one needed to ask who "he" was.

Absent full-blooded orders from Anderson, Nicholson issued his own to Dunphie: "You will ensure at all costs that the German armoured force on your front does not reach [Thala] before 1800 hours." Twelve miles south of Thala, Dunphie stopped backpedaling at four P.M. and dug in. A mile away, the enemy assault line massed on a ridge with a precision that, as one Tommy reported, "was beautiful to watch but very frightening."

With Rommel now in direct command, the panzers rumbled through the dismounted grenadiers, and the German line surged forward. Tank fire boomed across the hills. The outgunned Valentines, often suckered into betraying their positions with premature return fire, simply blew apart. After an hour of exceptional courage, Dunphie sounded retreat, minus fifteen tanks.

Back the British fell, scooting between cactus patches until they reached the ridge held by the Leicesters three miles south of Thala. "Machine gun fire could be seen snaking up the road straight for us," one officer recalled. Dunphie stood "erect in his scout car, calmly conducting the battle over the wireless" before following the last Valentine into the perimeter behind billows of man-made smoke. It was 6:30 P.M. Darkness and rain draped the battlefield.

Dunphie was a gunner by trade, and he belatedly realized his mistake in not positioning artillery closer to the front. He had almost no guns available. Thala was held by a weak French battalion and a few other reinforcements quartered in the local brothel, "empty but heavy with cheap scent." At an elevation of 3,300 feet, Thala had the feel of a highlands bastion, but holding it against a determined assault would be difficult with this feeble force. North of town the road straightened, the land flattened, and the route to Le Kef—forty miles away—lay undefended. "I felt strategic fear," Juin later confessed, "for if Rommel broke through, all of North Africa was doomed."

Almost on Dunphie's heels, an armored column led by a Valentine clanked toward the British perimeter on Highway 17. Hatless soldiers lay smoking on the fenders of these apparent stragglers. The Leicesters, whom Nicholson had just berated for their half-dug foxholes and unlaid minefields, glanced up from their digging at the familiar turret silhouette. In better light they might have seen the name *Apple Sammy* stenciled on the Valentine's flank. *Apple Sammy* had been captured at Tébourba three months earlier. "Keep away from my bloody trench," a rifleman hollered at the passing tank. "You're knocking it in."

Like Greeks from a wooden horse, grenadiers spilled off the tanks and fell on the astonished defenders. Eight panzers, plus the duplicitous *Apple Sammy*, were inside the British harbor. Germans sprinted down the Leicester trench line, heaving grenades and spraying machine-pistol fire. Tank rounds destroyed the battalion signals truck, and pleas for help went out as dead air. German crews slewed their guns in a murderous crossfire. "Hands up, come out," an accented voice called in the darkness. "Surrender to the panzers." In minutes the Leicesters were undone, and 300 stunned prisoners vanished into the night.

Two thousand yards north, Dunphie's remaining tanks sheltered in a grassy hollow just below the town. Dismounted crews had settled down for supper when "German tracers began to float over our heads," wrote one soldier. "A flare shot up into the air. . . . Six German tanks were right upon us, greenish-yellow flame flickering from their machine gun muzzles." A fuel truck exploded to lave the hollow in light, projecting weird shadows against the ridge.

"Lay roughly on the tanks!" a troop commander ordered, and for three hours a chaotic brawl surged across the tuft grass. "It was a tank fight in the dark at twenty yards' range and under," reported Dunphie. A few intrepid Tommies slapped passing panzers with "sticky bombs," grenades covered with adhesive and fuzed for five seconds. At 9:30 a headquarters clerk scribbled in the war diary: "Situation confused." Dunphie radioed Nicholson to warn that the Leicesters had been overrun and that a like fate threatened the tanks. But when he proposed pulling back to the edge of Thala, Nicholson refused: "Hold at all costs."

At all costs they held, and the cost was dear. Dunphie's original fifty tanks had been pared to twenty-one when the last German fired a last burst at midnight before skulking off; Rommel now occupied the ridge once held by the Leicesters, who now mustered forty able-bodied men, short by 800. Dunphie ordered every cook, driver, and batman in Thala to the line. Barely a mile away, Rommel—whose losses included nine panzers—massed his remaining force of fifty tanks, 2,500 infantrymen, and thirty guns. For the balance of the night "alarms were many and firing profuse," one chronicler noted, and the British braced for the death blow, which would surely come at dawn.

✳ ✳ ✳

Dawn came; the blow did not. Better still for the British, another providential American artilleryman showed up, this one with 2,200 men, forty-eight guns, and a killer's heart. Brigadier General Stafford Le Roy Irwin, artillery commander of the 9th Infantry Division, had covered 735 miles in a four-day motor march across the icy, rutted Atlas. Irwin's arrival in Thala at eight P.M. on Sunday night was "dramatic and effective," Dunphie later declared. "Irwin himself was a tonic. Artillery was the one thing we lacked and the one thing we wanted." For his part, Irwin judged the predicament at Thala "extremely critical."

A West Point classmate of Eisenhower's, Irwin was a tall, russet-haired cavalryman who had switched to artillery in 1917 because calibrating gunnery seemed more challenging than guessing the proper mix of hay and oats for horses. Witty and urbane, a Virginian, he was a skilled watercolorist who loved poetry almost as much as he loved massing fires. By first light on February 22—despite wretched maps, squally weather, and British misapprehension over the enemy's whereabouts—Irwin had emplaced his guns in a three-mile arc so that the first German shells of the morning were answered in kind. The lines were barely a thousand yards apart, and snipers discouraged forward observation, so much of the American gunnery involved blindly dumping hundreds of shells on the reverse slope of the next ridge.

It served. At seven A.M. Broich phoned Rommel, who had returned to Kasserine. The panzers had planned to attack, but now Allied shells were raining down. Also, at five A.M. the British had launched an armored sally against a salient on the German right. ("I'm sorry," the British tank commander told his men, "but we've got to go out on a forlorn hope. I doubt whether any of us will come back.") The attack had been repulsed, with seven of ten British tanks destroyed, but the raid implied unexpected fortitude. A more serious counterattack could follow. Perhaps they should wait? Rommel agreed.

The field marshal had shot his bolt. Despite captured stocks, his army was low on ammunition, with but four days' rations left, and only enough fuel to travel less than two hundred miles. Arab spies and Luftwaffe reconnaissance reported Allied reinforcements headed to Thala. After Broich's call, Rommel drove to the front. He scanned the shell-plowed terrain outside Thala, then returned to his tent in a thicket between Djebel Chambi and the Hatab River. At noon, Kesselring landed at Kasserine in his little Storch and motored to the command post in Rommel's staff car.

True to character, Kesselring felt optimistic. Early in the weekend, he had feared the offensive was sputtering. But reports filtering into his headquarters near Rome the previous night seemed satisfactory, "even promising of success." True, Arnim's refusal to send all of the 10th Panzers was "a very serious failure . . . which could not be made good again," and Kesselring had reproached him. Yet the Allies were reeling, Kesselring believed.

Rommel wasted no time in disabusing him of this notion. In an hour-long conference frequently interrupted by a jangling telephone, he insisted on "stopping the attack and withdrawing the attack group." Rommel lashed out at Arnim, the Luftwaffe, the Italians, even the "poor combat value" of his own men. His left flank was exposed to attack from the west, where the American defense "had been very skillfully executed." The assault on Thala, rescheduled for one P.M., would be postponed again. A staff officer recorded Rommel's cooler arguments:

> It appears futile to continue the attack in view of the constant reinforcing of the hostile forces, the unfavorable weather, which renders the terrain impassable off the hard roads, and because of the increasing problems caused by the mountain terrain, which is so unsuited to the employment of armored units. All this add[s] to the low strength of our organization.

"Rommel was in a depressed mood," Kesselring observed. "I noticed in him a scarcely concealed desire to go back to his army on the southern front as soon as possible. . . . I thought it best to raise his self-confidence by expressing my confidence in him, citing his former accomplishments which were achieved under much more aggravating circumstances." Montgomery's army was "still far away" and no threat. "We have the initiative," Kesselring added. "Tébessa is within easy reach."

No use. The old warhorse would not answer the bugle again. He showed "nothing of his usual passionate will to command," Kesselring noted. "Rommel was physically worn out and psychologically fatigued." The Desert Fox had "undoubtedly turned into a tired old man."

Thala would prove the high-water mark of the Axis campaign in northwest Africa. Shelling by both sides continued the rest of that rainy Monday. By sunset, American gunners had only a fifteen-minute supply of 105mm ammunition left; Irwin later deemed February 22, 1943, "the toughest day [I] experienced during World War II"—strong words from a man who would see much combat in the next two years. But the tide had swung. The reprieved Tommies at Thala chattered "as if they had been enjoying a bath after a polo match," reporter A. B. Austin wrote. "Absolute Gilbert and Sullivan."

Back in Rome, Kesselring formally authorized the withdrawal. On Monday night, Axis troops left their trenches and slipped back through Kasserine Pass, unhurried and unbowed. The 21st Panzer served as a rear guard, but there was nothing to guard against. "The enemy follows only hesitantly," the Panzer Army Africa war diary noted on February 23. "The day passes without fighting of any consequence." Broich waited near Kasserine village until the last vehicle had rolled through a gap in a freshly laid minefield and sappers had plugged the exit with a few final Teller mines. Rommel was already speeding through Gafsa on his return to Mareth in the southeast. He took a moment to write home: "I've stood up well so far to the exhausting days of battle. Unfortunately we won't be able to hold the ground we've gained for long."

The enemy follows only hesitantly. On February 22, Eisenhower sent Fredendall an unctuous cable, voicing "every confidence that under your inspiring leadership current advances of the enemy will be stopped in place and . . . your forces will, when the proper time comes, play an effective part in driving the enemy from Tunisia." That night the commander-in-chief followed up with a phone call. The "proper time" had come. Intercepted German radio traffic suggested a broad withdrawal. Fredendall would be "perfectly safe" in counterattacking immediately to catch Rommel in the open. Eisenhower was so certain of this that he offered to "assume full responsibility."

Fredendall demurred. The enemy had "one more shot in his locker." It would be wiser, he insisted, to spend another day on the defensive as a precaution. Army intelligence officers had recruited Tunisian agents to scout the enemy's movements, only to find that "the inability of most Arabs to read or write, to count accurately over twenty-five, or to tell time" limited their espionage value. No one knew exactly where Rommel was.

Hesitation gripped both II Corps and First Army. Having been knocked about for more than a week, senior commanders wanted only to put some distance between themselves and their tormentors. General Alexander remained closeted in Constantine, trying to make sense of the morass he had inherited three days before. Little effort was made to seize the initiative.

Several more convoluted command changes further impeded Allied pursuit. Eisenhower had been mulling Fredendall's request to relieve Ward, and was about to accede when he heard from Truscott that Ward had "brought order out of chaos" during the retreat. From Morocco, the commander-in-chief summoned Major General Ernest N. Harmon, one of Patton's lieutenants during TORCH. In Algiers, Eisenhower told Harmon to assume command of either II Corps or 1st Armored, whichever seemed appropriate. Harmon—a burly cavalryman once described as "a cobra without the snake charmer"—snapped, "Well, make up your mind, Ike. I can't do both." He then went to bed only to be rousted by Eisenhower, who helped lace his boots before packing him off to the Tunisian front.

At three A.M., Tuesday, February 23, Harmon arrived at Le Kouif. He was to serve as "a senior assistant" to Fredendall, who also received a pointed message from Eisenhower: "I have no thought of your replacing Ward who, it seems to me, on two occasions at least, rendered a very fine account of himself in actual battle." Slumped in a chair next to the stove, Fredendall scratched out a letter of credence introducing Harmon as a deputy corps commander authorized to oversee the 1st Armored Division and British forces. This made Harmon the eighth tactical commander of Allied forces in less than a week. "Here it is," Fredendall said. "The party is yours." Concluding that the man was drunk, Harmon stuffed the paper into his pocket and motored off to Thala in a jeep.

There he found Brigadier Nicholson little impressed by him or his letter. Nicholson politely explained that he intended "to fight this battle out"; *then* Harmon could take over. "[Harmon] was a little surprised at first but soon was cooperating whole-heartedly," Nicholson reported, adding: "We gave them a fucking bloody nose yesterday and we'll do it again this morning." Harmon growled his approval, then drove to see Ward. "Nobody goes back from here," Harmon declared.

In a Thala cellar on the morning of February 23, a breathless young officer dashed up to Nicholson and Dunphie. "The Germans have gone!" An excited murmur rippled through the command post. Cautiously, the brigadiers drove in a scout car to the sanguinary ridge once held by the Leicesters. "We could see nothing in front of us," an officer reported, except for Arab looters. Nicholson could hardly believe his force had survived. He thought of Kipling's lines:

> *Man cannot tell but Allah knows*
> *How much the other side is hurt.*

Surely Rommel still held the pass with a covering force, waiting to ambush overzealous pursuers? At 11:30 A.M., Nicholson, who later chastised himself for timidity, ordered reconnaissance forward but "not unduly to hasten." With his approval, scouts waited until three P.M. before edging toward Kasserine.

Rommel had gone and his trail was stone cold, but it took more than a day for Allied troops to cross the Grand Dorsal in numbers. "Our follow-up was slow," Harmon later conceded, "and we let them get away." Ward had graciously offered Harmon his staff, then scribbled a terse note to Beetle Smith at AFHQ headquarters. He could no longer work under Fredendall. Mutual distrust had become intolerable. Dejected and silent, reduced to two staff officers and a driver, he set up a tent near Robinett's command post to await a reply from Algiers. An aide noted that Ward "feels very low and needs rest."

Light snow fell on the American and British soldiers picking their way through Kasserine Pass on the morning of February 25. The desolate landscape was "cluttered with wrecked German and American airplanes, burned out vehicles, abandoned tanks, [and] scattered shell cases," Robinett reported. Ration tins, unfinished love letters, a pair of boxing gloves: the detritus of battles lost and won. Italian prisoners in black-plumed helmets dug graves for bodies now ripe beyond recognition; an American soldier sat guard in a jeep, chewing gum and reading a Superman comic. Severe orders were issued against looting, and the throaty sound of tommy guns echoed in the snow. Tunisians ran, or fell.

Even if Allied troops had been roused to hot pursuit, Rommel's sappers discouraged audacity. All nine bridges between Sbiba and Sbeïtla had been demolished, as had thirteen others around Kasserine. More than 43,000 German mines had been planted. East of the pass, Allied "vehicles were blowing up on the minefields in all directions," said one British officer. "A most unpleasant and windy business." Battery-operated mine detectors shorted out in the damp weather, forcing engineers armed with bayonet probes to "spread out like caddies and golfers looking for a lost ball." Soldiers also watched for the telltale sign of dismembered camels, whose flat feet usually provided enough pressure to detonate the eleven pounds of TNT in a Teller mine.

A precise tally of casualties at Kasserine remains elusive, in part because of uncertainty over the French, Italian, and Tunisian tolls. American losses exceeded 6,000 of the 30,000 men engaged in the battle. Of those, half were missing. (German records, ever precise, listed 4,026 Allied soldiers of all nationalities captured.) Fredendall's corps lost 183 tanks, 104 half-tracks, more than 200 guns, and 500 jeeps and trucks. British losses were relatively light, apart from the poor Leicesters and a few dozen tanks, and the Germans suffered fewer than 1,000 casualties, including 201 dead.

Some American units were mauled nearly beyond repair, among them the 2nd and 3rd Battalions of the 1st Armored Regiment—temporarily combined to form the understrength 23rd Battalion. The 3rd Battalion of the 6th Armored Infantry, so badly carved up at Oran during Operation RESERVIST, was again gutted at Kasserine, shrinking from 750 men to 418. Half the survivors lacked shoes, like ragamuffin Valley Forge soldiers. "Our people from the very highest to the very lowest have learned that this is not a child's game," Eisenhower told Marshall.

"The proud and cocky Americans today stand humiliated by one of the greatest defeats in our history," Harry Butcher scribbled in his diary. "There is a definite hangheadedness." From Faïd Pass to Thala, the Americans had been driven back eighty-five miles in a week, farther than at the infamous "bulge" in the Belgian Ardennes nearly two years later. At least in terms of yardage lost, Kasserine may fairly be considered the worst American drubbing of the war.

Grievous as the past ten days had been, the Allies had suffered a tactical, temporary setback rather than a strategic defeat. Rommel had failed to reach the Allied supply depots, failed to force the British First Army to withdraw from northern Tunisia, failed to gut the offensive capacity of Allied forces, who would soon make good their losses. Seasoned German soldiers proved themselves wily and ruthless, and Axis commanders demonstrated the battlefield virtue of leading from the front. But the Axis high command was more riven with rivalry and inefficiencies than even its Allied counterpart—a poor standard indeed.

Both sides had violated key principles of war to the detriment of their respective causes; they had, among other errors, failed to maintain contact with a retreating foe to exploit his derangement. The Axis had made this mistake at both Sidi bou Zid and Thala. Rommel, moreover, had violated the cardinal precept of concentration by twice dividing his force and attacking at too many places at once. Arnim had been right: the anabasis in mountainous country with a modest, footsore force *was* too ambitious, particularly without Arnim's wholehearted support.

Allied failings were painfully evident, again. Portions of five American divisions had fought around Kasserine, but almost never intact. Leaders came and leaders went, sometimes changing twice a day as if washing in and out with the tide. Strangers commanded strangers. For years, Fredendall would be castigated for the poor American showing; like several of his subordinate commanders, he was overmatched, unable to make the leap from World War I's static operations to modern mobile warfare. But Robinett made a fair point after the war: that it was "dead wrong" to blame Fredendall exclusively. "Possibly," he wrote, "one would have to search all history to find a more jumbled command structure than that of the Allies in this operation."

That error could be laid at Eisenhower's door. Even as Rommel was forcing the pass on February 20, Eisenhower summoned reporters to a press conference in Algiers and took "full responsibility for the defeat"—remarks he then placed off the record. He acknowledged underestimating French vulnerability and stretching the Allied line to the breaking point. Subsequently he expressed regret at not having insisted, in November, on subordinating French troops to the Allied chain of command, and at allowing the dispersal of American forces as far south as Gafsa. Moreover, he wrote after the war, "had I been willing at the end of November to admit temporary failure and pass to the defensive, no attack against us could have achieved even temporary success."

There were other, unacknowledged failings. He had recommended—but not demanded—that Fredendall counterattack vigorously on February 22, just as he had recommended but not demanded the concentration of the 1st Armored Division in mid-February. He expressed surprise in late February that the 37mm "squirrel rifle" and 75mm half-track "Purple Heart box" proved no match for German panzers, although these deficiencies had been recognized for months. During the "wearing and anxious" week after his trip to Sidi bou Zid, he spent so much time dictating explanations to the chiefs of staff that Marshall chided him: "I am disturbed by the thought that you feel under necessity in such a trying situation to give so much personal time to us. . . . You can concentrate on this battle with the feeling that it is our business to support you and not to harass you."

Certainly he had done some things well, even very well. He cannibalized the U.S. 2nd Armored and 3rd Infantry Divisions for reinforcements, and hurried the 9th Division artillery to its gallant rendezvous at Thala. He worked on rearming the French; redesigned American training methods; unleashed Alexander; overhauled his intelligence operation; and parried Churchill, who had sent an annoying message insisting that the Tunisian campaign be finished by March and the Sicily invasion launched in June. "We must be prepared for hard and bitter fighting," Eisenhower told the prime minister on February 17, "and the end may not come as soon as we hope."

He studied his mistakes—this practice was always one of Eisenhower's virtues—and absorbed the lessons for future battles in Italy and western Europe. And he steeled himself for the remote prospect that his first big battle might have been his last. To his son John, he wrote: "It is possible that a necessity might arise for my relief and consequent demotion. . . . It will not break my heart and it should not cause you any mental anguish. . . . Modern war is a very complicated business and governments are forced to treat individuals as pawns."

Eisenhower could take heart that for the first time—notably in the successful defense of Djebel el Hamra—American commanders showed some capacity for combined arms combat, the vital integration of armor, infantry, artillery, and other combat arms. That art, like fighting on the defensive and operating within an allied coalition, had been given short shrift in stateside training; soldiers were forced to learn where lessons always cost most, on the battlefield.

The coordination of ground and air forces remained dismal, however. Fratricide flourished despite standing orders not to fire at airplanes until fired upon. In three Allied fighter groups alone, friendly fire destroyed or damaged thirty-nine planes. And error cut both ways: disoriented B-17 Flying Fortresses on February 22 missed their intended targets in Kasserine Pass by ninety air miles, killing many Tunisians and battering the British airfield near Souk el Arba. Apologies were issued, along with a few thousand dollars in reparations.

Beyond the modest combined-arms showing, three bright gleams radiated from Kasserine's wreckage. First was the competence of American artillery at Sbiba, at Djebel el Hamra, and at Thala. Second was the mettle under fire displayed by various American commanders, among them Irwin, Robinett, Andrus, Gardiner, and Allen, and comparable mettle in British commanders. Third was the broad realization that even an adversary as formidable as Erwin Rommel was neither invincible nor infallible. He and his host could be beaten. This epiphany was not to be undervalued: *they could be beaten.* Amazingly, barely two months would elapse between the "hangheadness" of Kasserine and the triumph of total victory in Tunisia.

Demolitionists removed the guncotton and fuzes from the dumps at Tébessa. Exhausted men slept a sleep too deep even for nightmares. After ten days of cacophonous slaughter, an eerie silence fell over the battlefield, broken in the smallest hours of the morning by the hammer of typewriters in the adjutants' tents, where clerks labored all night to transform the holiest mysteries of sacrifice and fate into neat lists of the missing and the wounded and the dead.

Part Four

10. The World We Knew Is a Long Time Dead

Vigil in Red Oak

SOUTHWEST Iowa's second winter of war had passed, and hints of the second spring could be seen in the blooming crocuses and felt in the afternoon sun that ventured farther north each day. In Red Oak and Villisca and Clarinda, as in the rest of the country, war remained a bit abstract even as fragmentary reports of the first big American battle against the Germans began winging westward from Africa. Iowans knew the war vicariously, through newsreels and letters home, yet it remained a thing manifested more as an absence than as a presence. The junior college in Montgomery County had closed for lack of students. Weeds sprouted on the unused baseball diamond at American Legion Park. Nurses and young doctors had all gone off, and old Doc Reiley was persuaded to emerge from retirement to fill the gap. The Red Oak Taxicab Company hired female drivers for the first time. No one drove much, because even those with gasoline rationing cards were restricted to four gallons a week, except for farmers and other essential worthies, who got somewhat more.

Everyone soldiered on. In Red Oak, the Grand showed movies nearly every night and double features on Saturday. Kids swarmed to the Green Parrot downtown for sodas after school. J. C. Penney's shelves were often barren, but customers wandered in anyway, as if shopping were an act of imagination rather than of commerce. The Red Oak Stalking Tigers—no one fully appreciated the irony of that mascot, of course—prepared to play in the district basketball tourney. A student production of *Room for Ten* drew a big crowd to the school gymnasium. As planting season approached, a worrisome machinery shortage was eased by the state War Board's wise decision to increase Montgomery County's quota of plows and cultivators.

Even if the battlefront seemed far removed, patriotism ran deep. The Victory Day book drive had already collected 500 volumes, and schoolchildren in Red Oak, asked to buy $900 in war bonds to underwrite the purchase of one jeep for the Army, bought enough bonds to finance nine. Great War veterans planned an elaborate commemoration for March 9, 1943, the twenty-fifth anniversary of the day when Company M first went over the top to face German fire in 1918.

The first inkling of bad news from Tunisia came disguised as good news. The *Red Oak Express* of February 22 ran a front-page story by the Associated Press beneath the headline "Moore Leads Escape from Nazi Lines." Datelined "on the Tunisian Front," the article recounted how the former Boy Captain—"red-eyed, haggard, and weak from lack of food and water"—had led many in his battalion to safety from a hill surrounded by German soldiers. Everyone in Montgomery County agreed that in a tight spot Bob Moore was a *very* good man to have around. But few other details emerged over the next two weeks other than sketchy dispatches about a fight in a remote place called Kasserine.

The initial telegrams reached Red Oak on the evening of March 6; by midnight there were more than two dozen, nearly identical: "The Secretary of War desires me to express his regret that your son has been missing in action in North Africa since February 17." Townsmen in bib overalls or gabardine suits gathered on the broad portico of the Hotel Johnson, next to the Western Union office. Leaning against the double Ionic columns, they smoked and talked and listened as the courthouse clock on Coolbaugh Street chimed the hours.

Most next of kin were easy to find. Mae Stifle, a widow who had raised eight children, worked as a housekeeper at that very hotel. She got two telegrams within fifteen minutes telling her that two sons, Sergeant Frank and Private Dean, were missing; in the morning, a third telegram added her son-in-law, Darrell Wolfe, to the list. "Some people don't believe in prayer," she said, "but I pray for my boys every day." The Vern Bierbaum family also lost two sons, Cleo and Harold, *and* a son-in-law, *and* their son-in-law's brother. Both Gillespie boys were missing; their father, who ran the feed store, tucked the telegrams inside the family Bible. Those who had left the county were harder to track down, like Lois Bryson, who now worked the four-to-midnight shift installing hydraulic tubing at the Martin bomber plant in Omaha. Eventually, word reached her that her husband, Fred, was also missing. He had joined Company F in Villisca when he was seventeen.

On March 11, the *Express* printed a headline no one could dispute: "SW Iowa Is Hit Hard." The photographs of missing boys just from Red Oak filled four rows above the fold on page one. "War consciousness mounted hourly in Red Oak, stunned by the flood of telegrams this week," the article began. The busiest man in town was a boy, sixteen-year-old Billie Smaha, who delivered wires for Western Union. "They kind of dreaded me," Billie later told the *Saturday Evening Post*. "I never wore a Western Union hat because I thought that would scare them too much when I went up to the door."

Wild rumors flourished. Shenandoah, Iowa, supposedly had lost 500 men—even though barely one-quarter that number were serving in North Africa. The truth was grim enough. Clarinda had lost forty-one, Atlantic forty-six, Glenwood thirty-nine, Council Bluffs thirty-six, Shenandoah twenty-three, Villisca nine. Red Oak's toll reached forty-five, nearly a third of Company M, which altogether had lost 153 men, among them the commander and six lieutenants. Total losses for the 168th Infantry Regiment included 109 officers and 1,797 enlisted men. "There is no place to my knowledge where in this war there has been such a large group from such a comparatively small area," an Army official told the *Council Bluffs Nonpareil*.

Everyone soldiered on, again. The Great War anniversary commemoration was canceled. When letters began arriving from prison camps, it became clear that most of those missing had, blessedly, been taken prisoner. Many ended up in Stalag III-B with French, Russian, and Dutch soldiers, while officers typically went to an *Oflag* in Silesia. "Mom and Dad, I have no clothes except shirt, pants, shoes, and field jacket, and up 'til a few days ago they hadn't been off for a month," Lieutenant Duane A. Johnson of Red Oak wrote from Germany in March. "Send the food parcel first. I don't care if it's all chocolate." Letters also came from those who had narrowly escaped capture or death. "I lost everything but my rifle, new fountain pen, shovel, and my life," Sergeant Willis R. Dunn wrote his parents in Villisca. "So I'm thanking God for that."

The Ladies' Monday Club redoubled its book drive; collection boxes soon occupied all four corners of the town square. The VFW collected safety razors for the German camps. War Dads, an organization of the sort that in a later day would be called a support group, grew large and active. A speech by an Iowa college teacher who had been interned by the Germans for seven months while working in Egypt drew 900 people to the Methodist church on a Sunday night in mid-March; latecomers had to stand in the choir loft, behind the robed singers.

The telegrams kept coming. Billie Smaha stayed busy. *Life* magazine arrived to document Red Oak's misfortune; the brief article included a two-page aerial photo of the town with labels denoting the houses of those missing, captured, or dead. A *New York Herald-Tribune* reporter calculated that "if New York City were to suffer losses in the same proportion in a single action, its casualty list would include more than 17,000 names." In Red Oak, population 5,600, small plaques eventually honored the fallen at the Elks Club and the Ko-z-Aire Furnace Company, and photos of those smiling boys in smart uniforms stood on mantels and pianos all over town. At the Washington School, a teacher named Frances Worley kept an honor roll in a scrapbook; before the names of those lost she set gold stars, just like the stars she pasted on especially meritorious homework papers.

The second spring of the war came. Buds stippled the oak trees and the wild geese came back and the creek bottoms sang with life. Grass greened between the headstones that spilled down the hillside cemetery east of town. People went about their business as before, but the war was inside them now, as it would be inside a thousand other communities before peace returned. "Red Oak came as close to any town in America to knowing what the war was all about," wrote a local historian. Surely it was true.

"We Know There'll Be Troubles of Every Sort"

Rommel's army had slipped from Kasserine back across the central Tunisian plateau toward the Eastern Dorsal. As February yielded to March, the opposing lines took roughly the same shape they had held before the Valentine's Day offensive knocked the Americans nearly into Algeria. The Axis territorial gain amounted to a fragile salient in lower Tunisia; it bowed as far west as Sbeïtla and Gafsa on flat, indefensible terrain that Rommel knew he could not hold against a determined attack. Commanders on both sides recognized that a final campaign in Africa would be fought on a shrinking battlefield—for now, the eastern third of Tunisia. Here, in a ragged rectangle fifty miles wide and 300 miles long, two Allied armies would confront two Axis armies in a climactic struggle for control of the continent and the southern Mediterranean.

In the north, Arnim's Fifth Panzer Army secretly prepared to widen the bridgehead around Tunis and Bizerte by recapturing some of the territory held since early winter by Anderson's First Army. In the south, Rommel regrouped his Panzer Army Africa and pondered how to stop Montgomery's Eighth Army, which in the past four months had traveled more than a thousand miles from Egypt to begin pushing into Tunisia from western Libya.

And in the center, where II Corps remained under Anderson's tactical command, the Americans buried their dead, turned their backs to Kasserine Pass, and waited to see who would lead them forward.

Earl Van Derreer, a technical sergeant from California with the U.S. 14th Fighter Group, in his burrow at Youks les Bains, Algeria, in January 1943

LEFT: Colonel Paul McD. Robinett, seated, during passage to Northern Ireland in May 1942. Commander of the 13th Armored Regiment and later, as a brigadier general, of Combat Command B of the 1st Armored Division, Robinett was five feet four inches tall, with a cavalry strut and impressive tactical skills; he also "annoyed everyone" with his fussy and divisive arrogance.

RIGHT: Major General Orlando Ward, commander of the U.S. 1st Armored Division, in Northern Ireland shortly before leaving for North Africa. Known as "Pinky" for his once reddish hair, he was capable, ambitious, highly sensitive, and deeply suspicious of the British. (*Courtesy of the Ward family*)

A dead German soldier after the battle for Sened Station in southern Tunisia, in early February 1943

Crewmen with an American anti-tank gun watch for attacking German tanks near Sidi bou Zid, February 14, 1943, in the early hours of the Axis counteroffensive that led to Kasserine Pass.

An American M-3 tank crosses a wadi outside Sidi bou Zid on the morning of February 14, hours before the Germans completed their double envelopment of the town.

The wreckage of an American P-38 fighter near Sidi bou Zid. In the distance looms Djebel Lessouda, where John Waters was captured and Robert Moore escaped with part of his battalion.

Three battered GIs return to American lines after being trapped behind German positions for three days near Sidi bou Zid.

ABOVE: Soldiers from the 2nd Battalion of the 16th Infantry Regiment—part of Terry Allen's 1st Division—head east through Kasserine Pass on February 26, 1943, after Rommel's withdrawal.

RIGHT: Major General Ernest N. Harmon, sent by Eisenhower to Tunisia during the Kasserine Pass debacle, returned six weeks later to command the 1st Armored Division. Blunt and barrel-chested, he once was described as "a cobra without the snake charmer."

American combat engineers search for mines at the Kasserine train station, February 26, 1943. Rommel's withdrawing soldiers planted more than 43,000 mines, forcing American troops to "spread out like caddies and golfers looking for a lost ball."

Across Gumtree Road lies Djebel Orbata, where Darby led his Rangers across the hills east of El Guettar to fall on the Italians from the rear on March 20–21, 1943. (*Collection of the author*)

On March 16, 1943, on the eve of the II Corps attack on Gafsa, Eisenhower pins a third star on a buoyant Patton to mark his promotion to lieutnant general. One officer said of the new II Corps commander, "Bedizened with stars and loaded with guns, he came with Marsian speech and a song of hate."

Field Marshal Harold Alexander (*left*), commander of the new 18th Army Group, with Eisenhower (*center*) and Patton during their first collective meeting, in Fériana, on March 17, 1943, the day the American attack began on Gafsa and El Guettar

ABOVE: Lieutenant General Lesley J. McNair (*center*), commander of U.S. Army Ground Forces, at the Tunisian front on April 22, 1943, the day before he was badly wounded by a German shell.

RIGHT: Major General Walter B. "Beetle" Smith, Eisenhower's capable if irascible chief of staff, in his Algiers office, March 1943

British troops storming a position during an apparent training exercise in Tunisia

British Eighth Army soldiers moving toward the Mareth Line in southern Tunisia, March 24, 1943

An American tank destroyer battalion on reconnaissance at El Guettar on March 23, 1943, during the spoiling attack by the German 10th Panzer Division

The bodies of American soldiers killed in action brought down from the hills of northern Tunisia by mule, April 25, 1943

American artillery detonates around attacking German tanks of the 10th Panzer Division near El Guettar on April 23, 1943. After hours of savage fighting, Ted Roosevelt reported that the enemy "hesitated, turned around, and retreated. The men around me burst into cheers."

Hill 609, as soldiers from the 34th Infantry Division saw it in their approach from the west. Wind tossed the yellowing wheat on the lower slopes, making the hill undulate like a great breathing thing. (*Collection of the author*)

General Bernard L. Montgomery salutes the cheering throng in Sousse after the port town was liberated in April 1943. Once described by George Bernard Shaw as "that intensely compacted hank of steel wire," Montgomery provoked Eisenhower to complain, "I can deal with anybody except that son of a bitch."

ABOVE: Field Marshal Erwin Rommel (*third from left*) and his staff in Tunisia in early 1943, from captured German photo negatives. "Rommel, Rommel, Rommel!" Churchill had exclaimed. "What else matters but beating him?"

Major General Omar N. Bradley shortly before leaving for Africa, where he eventually succeeded Patton as commander of the U.S. II Corps. A prim, severe Missourian who was described as "the least dressed-up commander of an American army in the field since Zachary Taylor," he likened rooting Axis troops from the Tunisian hills to "hunting wild goats."

Italian prisoners captured by the 9th Infantry Division along the north coast of Tunisia, May 1, 1943

Soldiers from the 60th Infantry Regiment of the 9th Division, in the hills outside Bizerte on May 7, 1943, the day the port fell

Lieutenant Colonel Charles J. Denholm, commander of the 1st Battalion of the 16th Infantry, on May 8, 1943, hours after he and other soldiers captured at hill 523 were freed from an Italian prison ship that had been repeatedly attacked by unwitting Allied planes in the Gulf of Tunis

RIGHT: Major General Manton S. Eddy (*left*), commander of the 9th Infantry Division, and his assistant commander, Brigadier General Daniel A. Stroh, in Bizerte on May 9, 1943

BELOW: American troops along the Bizerte corniche shortly after the port fell. The town had been without running water for three months; typhus was present and cholera threatened.

LEFT: French civilians greet Allied troops with victory signs on May 10, 1943, shortly after the fall of Tunis.

BELOW: An aerial view of Bizerte, taken on May 10, 1943. After seven months of bombing, not a single building was habitable. "Bizerte was the most completely wrecked place I had ever seen," Ernie Pyle reported.

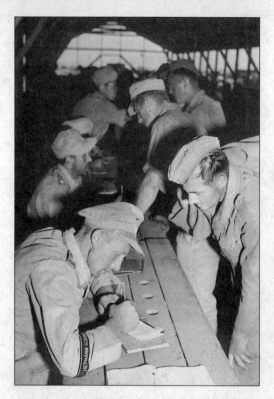

LEFT: A captured German soldier from the Hermann Göring Division fills out paperwork in a temporary Moroccan prison camp before being shipped to the United States or Britain.

BELOW: General Louis-Marie Koeltz, commander of the French XIX Corps, presents the Croix de Guerre to Terry Allen (*center*) and Ted Roosevelt for their valor in the Tunisian campaign.

General Hans-Jürgen von Arnim, commander of Axis forces in North Africa, on May 15, 1943, three days after his capture and shortly before being flown to a prison in England. Behind him is General Hans Cramer, commander of the German Afrika Korps.

American soldiers from the 34th Infantry Division march through Tunis in the victory parade on May 20, 1943. Patton complained that "our men do not put up a good show in reviews"; thousands of spectators disagreed, shrieking "Vive l'Amerique" from sidewalks and balconies.

Twenty-seven acres of headstones today fill the American military cemetery at Carthage, outside Tunis. (*Collection of the author*)

* * *

The Carthaginians of antiquity—notoriously poor losers—had often punished their defeated generals with crucifixion. Whether Eisenhower had this cautionary Tunisian precedent in mind is uncertain, though he was, it is true, a devoted student of the Punic Wars. In any case, to avoid an equivalent fate for himself he had begun looking for scapegoats while the ashes of Kasserine were still warm. In a message to Marshall he minimized his losses, asserting with some legitimacy that "this affair is only an incident" in the broader African campaign. Yet the reeling defeat and 6,000 American casualties sent morale plummeting throughout the theater; sixty ambulances had shuttled the evacuated wounded to hospitals from the Oran airfield. "It's pretty discouraging," Eisenhower's deputy Everett Hughes wrote in his diary. "I can't make heads or tails of the whole war. We have men but no organization. Who does what?" Censorship kept the home front ignorant of the full extent of Allied losses, but Eisenhower knew that soon enough the truth would out and alarm would spread.

First to go was his intelligence officer, Brigadier Eric E. Mockler-Ferryman, whom Eisenhower believed had relied excessively on Ultra to divine enemy intentions. The brigadier went quietly. "If a man is not wanted," he observed, "argument won't change the situation." Eisenhower asked London to send him a British replacement "who has a broader insight into German mentality and method." Lesser heads soon rolled, too, among them Stark's. He was sent home on March 2 and would later serve with distinction in the Pacific. McQuillin's relief came soon after Stark's. Tunisia, as Paul Robinett observed, was fast becoming "a professional graveyard, particularly for those in the upper middle part of the chain of command." Alexander strongly considered cashiering Anderson; unable to persuade Montgomery to relinquish the Eighth Army chief of staff as a replacement, he instead decided to keep Anderson but to "watch him very closely."

Orlando Ward also awaited the ax. As he told his diary, "F and I do not have enough room." "F," of course, was the crux. For months Eisenhower had handled Fredendall with the tongs appropriate for a presumed Marshall protégé, even while privately voicing regret at not sending Patton to Tunisia instead. The commander-in-chief had also, inconveniently, twice written notes commending the II Corps commander for his leadership during Kasserine, and had praised him to Marshall as a "stouthearted" battle captain worthy of a third star. If, as Moltke once claimed, a general needed to lose an entire division before becoming truly experienced, then Fredendall's seasoning was well advanced.

But reports from the front could hardly be ignored. Ernie Harmon was scathing. "He's no damned good," he told Eisenhower on February 28, on his way back to Morocco. "You ought to get rid of him." Fredendall was a "common, low son-of-a-bitch," Harmon added, "a physical and moral coward." Truscott reported that II Corps was unlikely to "ever fight well under his command." Even Alexander chimed in. "I'm sure," he told Eisenhower, "you must have a better man than *that*."

A final verdict came from an officer who had just arrived in Africa, another West Point classmate from '15 sent to help however Eisenhower deemed fit. On March 5, during a break at a command conference near Tébessa, Eisenhower asked Major General Omar N. Bradley to step onto the porch of the mansion where they were meeting.

"What do you think of the command here?" Eisenhower asked, pulling furiously on a cigarette.

"It's pretty bad," Bradley replied. "I've talked to all the division commanders. To a man they've lost confidence in Fredendall as the corps commander."

The deed was done quietly, in a brief encounter at Youks-les-Bains airfield. Fredendall would receive his third star, command of a training army in Tennessee, and a hero's welcome home. Soon enough, Eisenhower would develop the capacity to cut a throat without remorse or emollient, but not yet. Fredendall had been given a soft landing, Eisenhower told Harmon, to avoid shaking public confidence in the high command, and that certainly included himself. To Marshall he explained that Fredendall "has difficulty in picking good men" and "has shown a peculiar apathy in preparing for a big push."

Fredendall stole away from Le Kouif at 3:30 A.M. on March 7, after distributing his liquor cache to the staff. Rather than tempt fate by flying to Algiers, he chose to leave in a civilian Buick in the dead of night when no enemy fighters could find him, although "there was something wrong with the shock absorbers and we bounced all the way," his aide reported. Along the road, Fredendall and his traveling party would stop for a picnic lunch of K rations and a piquant French burgundy he had been saving.

"Glory be," Ward wrote. But the most trenchant epitaph came from Beetle Smith: "He was a good colonel before the war."

Patton was hunting boar in the Moroccan outback when a dust-caked messenger on motorcycle flagged him down with orders for the front. A few hours later, he arrived at the Maison Blanche airfield, outside

Algiers, where he and Eisenhower had a brief conference over the hood of a car. The commander-in-chief expected Patton to command II Corps for only three weeks or so before resuming his preparations for the invasion of Sicily. "Your personal courage is something you do not have to prove to me, and I want you as a corps commander—not as a casualty," Eisenhower lectured. "You must not retain for one instant any man in a responsible position where you have become doubtful of his ability to do his job. . . . I expect you to be perfectly cold-blooded about it."

Patton had been brooding over the still uncertain fate of his son-in-law—he would personally comb Djebel Lessouda for John Waters's grave—and in any case, dispassion was hardly in his nature. He "damned the Germans so violently and emotionally that tears came to his eyes three times during the short conference," Butcher reported. Eisenhower agreed that the man hated the enemy "like the devil hates holy water."

Omar Bradley, who was to become Patton's deputy, sketched an indelible portrait of his first appearance at the Le Kouif primary school:

> With sirens shrieking Patton's arrival, a procession of armored scout cars and half-tracks wheeled into the dingy square opposite the schoolhouse headquarters of II Corps at Djebel Kouif on the late morning of March 7. . . . In the lead car Patton stood like a charioteer. He was scowling into the wind and his jaw strained against the web strap of a two-starred steel helmet.

"He is indeed picturesque," Ward told his diary. One captain spoke for many young officers: "Patton sure scares the shit out of me."

Both reactions pleased him, and he wasted no time leaving his bootprints on II Corps. One definition of military morale is a will to fight that is stronger than the will to live; the Americans plainly needed inspiriting. "Bedizened with stars and loaded with guns," Robinett observed, Patton "came with Marsian speech and a song of hate." Again and again he vowed, "We will kick the bastards out of Africa." For this task, he needed officers who "can sweat, get mad, and think at the same time." And he needed men with "an adequate hatred of Germans."

They soon developed a more than adequate hatred of Patton. A flurry of orders intended to stiffen discipline caused an uproar throughout the corps. Every lieutenant was now required to prominently display his gold or silver rank insignia, known as "aiming stakes" for the propensity of enemy snipers to single out recognizable officers. Military policemen, derided as Patton's Gestapo, routinely fined drivers for improper tire pressure or low oil levels. Failure to wear leggings incurred a $15 fine—"We don't even have underwear let alone puttees," one pilot wailed—and to be without a necktie cost $10. It was said that graves registration units would not bury a man killed in action unless he was properly garbed in cravat and leg wraps. Unpolished boots and unfastened chin straps, even in the latrine, also drew fines. Every evening Patton returned to the school with an armful of confiscated knit watch caps, which he detested as slovenly accoutrements of the slipshod.

Determined and energetic, he could also be boorish and abusive, incapable of distinguishing between the demands of a disciplinarian and the caprices of a bully. "Terry, where is your foxhole?" he asked Allen during a visit to the 1st Division. When Allen pointed to a slit trench outside his tent, Patton unzipped his fly and urinated in it, signaling his contempt for passive defenses. Fidgeting and yawning during a meeting at Le Kouif with twenty officers of the Big Red One, he abruptly accused them of cowardice and demanded that the "yellow-bellies . . . get in there and do a little fighting." When Allen's chief of staff pointed out that the concussion of artillery blasts could break the neck of a soldier whose helmet was fastened, Patton erupted in a spittle-flecked tirade, barking that "when he wanted advice from a colonel he damn well would ask for it and otherwise he damn well didn't want it." After another officer had a close brush with an enemy patrol, Patton declared, "You might have gotten killed. When I want you to get killed, I will tell you."

Nicknames stuck to him like steel to a magnet: Gorgeous George, Flash Gordon, Necktie Patton, Old Chewing Gum. The most flattering, Old Blood and Guts, soon mutated into Blood and Bull, or Our Blood, His Guts. Some admired him as a force of nature—"smart, blasphemous, fit, and glamorous . . . but born in the wrong century," as one British officer put it. Most simply tried to stay out of his way, as they would shun a dangerous storm. A believer in reincarnation, he might have been an embodiment of William Tecumseh Sherman, as described by Walt Whitman: "a bit of stern open air made up in the image of a man." Bradley concluded that Patton was simply "the strangest duck I have ever known."

Morale improved, perhaps because of Patton, perhaps despite him. Beginning on March 8, II Corps was no longer part of Anderson's First Army but directly under Alexander and his 18th Army Group as part of the field marshal's reorganization. The American divisions—the 1st Armored and 1st, 9th, and 34th Infantry—coalesced in a way that had been impossible the first four months of the campaign. While forestalling any renewed German attack with thick minefields—in March, more than 12,000 antitank mines were planted every day—the divisions regrouped and trained intently for several weeks. "We've been given a wet ball on a muddy field," said Allen, who was much inclined to football metaphors. "Watch us run with it."

Ted Roosevelt recorded on March 1 that he had changed clothes for the first time since January 14. Clean pants, hot food, and timely mail did wonders for the soul. Driving from encampment to encampment in *Rough Rider,* Roosevelt shambled among the tents, shouting hail-fellow exhortations. After the men had scrubbed their filthy uniforms with gasoline and lined up for delousing, he helped pass out medals right and left, roaring approval in his foghorn voice before speeding off to another bivouac.

"I've always thought that it was nonsense to say Americans don't like medals," he wrote Eleanor. "I knew I liked them. I wanted to get them, put them on, and walk up and down in front of you and say, 'Look what a hell of a feller you've married.'"

But Roosevelt's sobriety in other letters captured the mood of many men who now understood that they were in a fight to the death for the duration. "I guess nations going to war must go through a stumbling period before they purge the incompetents," he wrote:

> I think this is a five-year war. It won't be over until another winter has passed, until we are firmly on the Continent, and until Germany is faced with still another winter. . . . Now we know too much. Now we know that the world we knew is a long time dead. We know there'll be troubles of every sort.

Patton had immediate troubles of an administrative sort, which would plague him and other American commanders to the end of the war. Problems with replacement soldiers sent to fill casualty-depleted ranks had been evident even before Kasserine. Now, as thousands more trundled into Tunisia, it was clear that the War Department was repeating the blunders of 1918, when the Army's personnel system had broken down completely.

Soldiers were viewed as interchangeable parts, like spark plugs or gaskets. As parts wore out or broke, new parts were shipped to keep units running close to full strength. Plausible in theory, this assembly-line model had several pernicious flaws. The urgent demand for replacements in mid-February led the Army to strip soldiers from the 3rd

Infantry Division and 2nd Armored Division in Morocco. Many of those transferred were capable, but few commanders could resist the chance to dump their troublemakers and bunglers, too.

Worse yet, the War Department had assumed that airpower would so lighten the infantry's burden that losses would be less than they had been in World War I. Remarkably, no one foresaw that riflemen would be chewed up much faster than, say, cooks or typists. Moreover, combat simply wore down units. Senior generals came to realize that divisions should not be left in the line longer than thirty to forty days without rest; to fill the ranks with inexperienced replacement soldiers who lacked emotional ties to their new comrades did nothing for combat efficiency.

These defects, and more, began to appear in Tunisia. Because of the urgent demand for combat replacements, many of the men shoved forward had not finished basic training, and many were physical or disciplinary derelicts. They were handled, Eisenhower's personnel chief admitted, like "sacks of wheat." One study estimated that 80 percent had not qualified in their basic weapons. Of 2,400 men sent to the 34th Division, an extraordinary number were overage and in poor physical shape. One batch of 250 men included 119 who were thirty-nine or older. Nineteen thousand trained U.S. armor force replacements would arrive in Africa, but the crying need for rear-echelon service units meant most became drivers, stevedores, and ammo handlers. Rather than trust the vagaries of Army personnel officers, savvy commanders began sending their agents to replacement depots to pick out new soldiers, one officer wrote, "somewhat as one would buy a horse."

No less worrisome was a surge in mental breakdowns. Every man exposed to extended combat had become "a bit windy of shellfire," in a British reporter's phrase. Before Kasserine, "psychiatric reactions" accounted for a fifth, and sometimes more than a third, of all battlefield evacuations. Now, in the spring of 1943, more than 1,700 men would be admitted to the psychiatric ward of a single hospital, the 95th General, and many thousands of others were showing symptoms of instability. Eisenhower worried in a memo to Patton that "an increasing number of these cases are now being reported."

First known as shell shock because of the Great War misapprehension that neuropsychiatric disorders derived mainly from concussions suffered in artillery barrages, the syndrome in Tunisia was renamed combat exhaustion, a term borrowed from the British. Soldiers also called it war fatigue or old sergeant syndrome. The Army's chief psychiatrist described a typical patient: "He appeared as a dejected, dirty, weary man.

His facial expression was one of depression, sometimes of tearfulness. Frequently his hands were trembling or jerky." By the end of the war more than 500,000 men from the Army ground forces alone would be discharged for psychiatric reasons—this despite ruthless culling during induction physicals, when 12 percent of the 15 million draftees examined were rejected as mentally unfit. For every six men wounded, another became a neuropsychiatric casualty.

Individual cases in North Africa were often poignant, sometimes horrifying. A 1st Division soldier "beat his head against our foxhole 'til his skin on his forehead was just hanging in strands. He was foaming at the mouth like a madman." A twenty-year-old infantryman, the only survivor in a truck hit by a mortar shell, loped into the night with a pair of suspenders in search of a tree from which to hang himself. Another unhinged twenty-year-old agitatedly recounted how he had positioned the bodies of two dead soldiers, one German and the other American, as shields during an artillery barrage. Men by the hundreds, then by the thousands, had tremors or paralysis in their limbs, dysfunctional bowels, vacant stares. Some tried to scoop foxholes in their hospital cots with hands and feet, tearfully whimpering that "Herman the German" was stalking through the ward.

At first, serious cases were evacuated far from the front, often to the United States or England, where they lost touch with their units, suffered a sharp loss of self-esteem, and often exaggerated their problems. An Army study concluded that commanders fostered "an attitude closely akin to the old Puritan approach toward the venereal problem—the ostrich attitude, the 'we don't discuss it' idea, or 'it just isn't so.' Unfortunately it is very much so. . . . The front-line soldier wears out in combat."

Doctors soon learned to treat patients as far forward as possible. Treatments in North Africa included electroshock; large doses of barbiturates, to induce deep sleep for two to seven days; and sodium pentothal, intended to bring repressed demons to the surface. Nearly three-quarters of treated soldiers resumed military duties in some form, but less than 2 percent returned to combat.

The lessons emerging from Tunisia were clear to Army psychiatrists: "the average soldier reached his peak effectiveness in the first ninety days of combat and was so worn out after 180 days that he was rendered useless and unable to return to military service." Another study noted that "no man is removed from combat duty until he [has] become worthless. The infantryman considers this a bitter injustice. . . . He can look forward only to death, mutilation, or psychiatric breakdown." After months of stress, of close calls, of witnessing the unspeakable, even the bravest men wondered, as one fighter squadron commander did, "Am I becoming uncourageous?" Modern combat could break any soldier.

That was not a conclusion acceptable to the U.S. Army, and it was certainly anathema to the new II Corps commander. Patton had little tolerance for human limits. In his cosmology, combat exhaustion was an illegitimate diagnosis for cowards to hide behind.

Visiting a field hospital near Fériana shortly after his arrival in Tunisia, Patton displayed the choler that would cost him his command a few months later, in Sicily, when he brutally slapped two hospitalized soldiers. Strolling from bed to bed, murmuring comfort, he asked one wounded soldier how he had been hurt. The man replied that he had been shot while trying to surrender.

Patton whirled away, his face contorted with disgust. "Serves him right," he said bitterly. "That's what he gets for giving up."

"One Needs Luck in War"

DAWN was just a gray rumor in the east on February 26 when the creak of panzer tracks carried across the sage grass and limestone hills to the farming village of Sidi Nsir. Midway between Mateur and Béja on Highway 11, City Sneer—as Allied troops inevitably called it— anchored the center of the British line, which extended seventy miles from Cap Serrat, on the north coast, to Bou Arada, below the Medjerda River valley.

The usual sunrise sounds of singing larks and lowing cows abruptly ceased at 6:30 A.M., when four German battalions slammed into the British defenders. Stucco walls disintegrated beneath an artillery barrage and the urgent staccato of machine-gun fire merged into a single prolonged burst. By late morning, thirty tanks, including fourteen Tigers— all commanded by Colonel Rudolph Lang, conqueror of Longstop Hill on Christmas Day—had flanked the British gunners and closed to within 600 yards. "Self and three men left," one lieutenant radioed. "It can't be much longer. Good-bye and cheerio."

Eight similar attacks had occurred across the British front in an offensive code-named OCHSENKOPF, or Ox Head. Local successes at Sidi Nsir and elsewhere notwithstanding, the assault was ill-conceived and would only hasten the Axis destiny in Tunisia. Originally designed by Arnim as a modest attack on Medjez-el-Bab, the plan blossomed under the fertilizing influence of Kesselring's optimism to become a major offensive intended to seize Béja and once again widen the Axis bridgehead around Tunis.

As commander of the new Army Group Africa, Rommel had just been given authority over both his own army and Arnim's, but he was informed of OCHSENKOPF almost as an afterthought. Foremost among its deficiencies, the offensive was uncoupled from the attack at Thala several days earlier, allowing the Allies time to regroup. Rommel was flabbergasted, and he railed against "the nincompoops at Comando Supremo." As one officer observed of both sides in the Tunisian campaign, "It was a small war with too many generals."

It was not the nincompoops who would die, of course, but Wehrmacht teenagers and fuzz-cheeked Tommies. For more than two weeks the fighting flared up and down the line in bursts of fine savagery. General Allfrey rushed reinforcements here and there across the V Corps front. By March 1, Lang had only five battleworthy panzers left, and his own soldiers were calling him Tank Killer.

The Germans fared somewhat better in the far north. Arnim personally surpervised a westward lunge by eight battalions, which swarmed out of their Jefna revetments past the curing bones of the dead left on Green and Bald Hills the previous November. Italian soldiers and German parachute engineers led by Rudolf Witzig, the hero of Green and Bald, deftly flanked the British and French at a mining hamlet named Sedjenane, which fell on March 3. After driving the unfledged 46th Division troops back ten miles, Arnim pushed them another ten by closing to within a few thousand yards of Djebel Abiod, the northern gateway to Béja. Anderson considered abandoning Medjez-el-Bab, on the assumption that the town's fall was "almost inevitable" if the enemy attack enveloped the British left. Alexander not only refused to give up Medjez but forbade further retreat.

Cruel mountain fighting in bitter weather followed. Sniper fire so devastated the ranks of British junior officers that platoon and company commanders—disdaining Patton's new rules for the Americans—removed their brass rank insignia, exchanged revolvers for rifles, tucked binoculars into their tunics, and tried to avoid any visible gesture that implied leadership acumen.

In the end Arnim was too weak and scattered to exploit his gains. The British line fell back twenty miles in the north, ten miles in the center, and very little in the south. That lost yardage would have to be won back, hill by bloody hill, before any drive on Tunis could resume. British casualties were heavy, including 2,500 men taken prisoner and sixteen tanks destroyed. But Arnim's losses were more grievous, because he could afford them less. Although he claimed his casualties numbered only about a thousand, the British counted 2,200 German prisoners, with perhaps as many more killed and wounded.

Moreover, nearly 90 percent of the panzers used in OCHSENKOPF were destroyed or disabled. The bridgehead had been extended, slightly, but the Axis line was thin and brittle. The offensive accomplished little other than to infuriate Rommel and discomfit Anderson.

"It was not a happy period," Anderson later acknowledged. "Things went wrong too often."

Rommel was still seething at the nincompoops as his scout car labored in a nimbus of golden dust up a corkscrew mountain road at two P.M. on March 5. The beautiful failure at Thala—how close they had come to real victory!—lay ten days and two hundred miles behind. Now he was back where he felt most comfortable, in the desert, with his Afrika Korps, scanning the eastern horizon for the dusty spoor of Montgomery's army. This was splendid country, a dominion of refracted light and arid space, far different from the fatherland, different even from Kasserine. He had stopped brooding long enough to admire the irrigated orchards and greening wheat fields and exclaim: "What a colony this would make for us Germans!"

From the crest of this nameless ridge, marked on the map as Hill 715, the turquoise Mediterranean shimmered twenty miles due north. Libya lay seventy miles to the east, but the British were much closer, perhaps fifteen miles, in a sinewy line that stretched north to south before Médenine, a verdant market town fed by a dozen roads from every compass point including the Saharan south. "The world could be so beautiful for all men," Rommel had written to Lu two days before. "There is so much that could be done—especially here in Africa with its wide-open spaces."

Yes, this would have made a fine colony; but the field marshal knew it was not fated, not for the Germans and certainly not for the Italians, though they coveted the land even more. He had again urged abandoning this corner of Tunisia and the Mareth defensive line behind him, shortening the perimeter he and Arnim held from 400 miles to 100. But the nincompoops would not agree, and while they stroked their chins in Berlin and Rome, he intended to strike.

Operation CAPRI was a spoiling attack, designed to wreck Eighth Army's assembly areas and forestall the British offensive everyone knew would soon come. If CAPRI failed—and already OCHSENKOPF in the north had forced a two-day delay—"the end of the army in Africa would be close," Rommel warned. There was "no point in harboring any illusions." On the plain below, 31,000 men with 215 guns and 135 tanks—including the 10th, 15th, and 21st Panzer Divisions—jostled forward for the attack set to begin at dawn. Tank crews kicked a soccer ball around within sight of British pickets in a show of unconcern.

Concern was warranted. If "things went wrong too often" for Anderson in the north, now they went spectacularly right for Montgomery in the south. Since the capture of Tripoli on January 23, little fighting had occurred on Eighth Army's front, other than halfhearted skirmishes intended to distract Rommel during Kasserine. Deliberate at best, Montgomery had intended to take another month before forcing his way into central Tunisia with a set-piece assault on the Mareth Line.

But Ultra decrypts in late February revealed Rommel's intended attack at Médenine. In a redemption for British intelligence after the sour disappointment of Kasserine, Allied eavesdroppers soon knew the precise size, location, and timing of CAPRI. Montgomery stopped plodding and rushed his army forward to reinforce the single division exposed as his Médenine vanguard. Forewarned, he was now forearmed, with 300 British tanks, 817 artillery and antitank guns, twice Rommel's air strength, and three seasoned divisions entrenched along a twenty-five-mile front.

Thick mist lingering after a rainy night masked the panzers as they spilled from their wadis at six A.M. on March 6. British troops were just tucking into their sausages and tea when a canopy of Nebelwerfer shells screamed overhead. The German attack went badly from the beginning. Commanders in the 21st Panzer fell for the ruse of bully beef tins laid out to simulate a minefield five miles west of Médenine. Swerving left, they veered beneath the frowning British guns and offered their flanks to stabbing volleys that left a dozen tanks in flames—all within view of Rommel on his height. 15th Panzer two miles north and 10th Panzer two miles south fared no better against the bristle of antitank guns. "It is an absolute gift," Montgomery wrote, "and the man must be mad." By ten A.M. the armored attack had stalled. Surviving panzers "wandered rather vaguely," the British 201st Guards Brigade reported, looking for defilade from the steel sleeting through their ranks.

Gunfire faded to a mutter. Then a second assault at 2:30 P.M. offered 10,000 Axis infantrymen the dubious honor of a more prominent role in the attack. A Coldstream Guardsman reported:

A great many little figures appeared over the distant crest, all in formation. With a shriek and a thud the entire corps artillery came down. . . . When the smoke cleared, other little figures appeared with stretchers.

One Highlanders history called it a "wonderful shoot," with field-gray troops "dropping like ninepins." Montgomery, who kept a photo of Rommel above his desk, saw little to impress him in this attack. "The Marshal has made a balls of it. I shall write letters," he sniffed, and retired to his trailer to do precisely that.

Médenine was "the first perfect battle," a British major exulted. Thirty thousand artillery and antitank shells had gutted the Afrika Korps without British tanks ever leaving the sideline. Montgomery's losses were a trifling 130. Rommel suffered 635 casualties, mostly German, and the destruction of fifty-two tanks, more than a third of his armored force. Scots Guard patrols that night slipped across the battlefield to blow up crippled panzers before they could be recovered, leaving behind fragments "none of which was larger than a card table."

Rommel had ventured forward during the day before returning to his bivouac on Hill 715. The slaughter had been so lopsided, the battle so plainly anticipated by the British, that the field marshal suspected treachery, perhaps from the Italians, a suspicion Kesselring came to share. Neither ever imagined that the Allies were decoding his mail. "This operation was pointless from the moment it turned out that we had not taken the enemy by surprise," Rommel said. "A great gloom settled over us all."

Now came another slap, this one from the Berlin high command, which that night again rejected the field marshal's plea to radically contract the Axis line. "To withdraw both armies into one cramped bridgehead around Tunis and Bizerte would spell the beginning of the end," Hitler decreed.

If hardly unexpected, the decision was devastating. For the army group to remain in Africa was "now plain suicide," Rommel declared. By the time he worked his way down Hill 715 on March 7, he had decided the moment had come to take his long-deferred sick leave in the Austrian Alps. No one wanted him in Tunisia, certainly not those running the war at Comando Supremo. "During the drive back to headquarters," his command diary recorded, "C in C [commander-in-chief] decides to begin his health cure right now—at once." He spent a day saying goodbye to his Africans: a pale, thin figure yellowed by jaundice, his face and neck splotched with angry boils. "C in C makes emotional farewell," his aide wrote. "The whole thing stinks."

"I hadn't seen him for some weeks and was shocked at how unwell he looked," his reconnaissance commander, Hans von Luck, later recounted. "He was visibly weak . . . and completely worn out." Campaign maps were strewn around his trailer, memento mori of his lost cause. Rommel stood and shook hands. Tears flooded his eyes. "The tears of a great man now cast down," Luck added, "moved me as much as anything I saw in the war."

At 7:50 A.M. on March 9, he boarded a plane at Sfax for the flight to Rome. For over a month, his departure remained secret from the Allies, and they kept swatting at his ghost; but he never set foot in Africa again. "He was gradually consumed by the fire which glowed within him," wrote his chief of staff. Even Kesselring's optimism dimmed. Médenine was "the last trump in our Tunisian hand," he subsequently concluded. "We could no longer hope to keep the war out of Europe and away from Germany for another year. One needs luck in war. Rommel without doubt had been deserted by his lucky star for quite some time."

Over tea during a visit to Hitler's secret command post in the Ukraine, Rommel futilely urged the Führer to shrink the Tunisian bridgehead to a defensible inner keep. Hitler dismissed the notion with a rant. "If the German people are incapable of winning the war," the Führer declared, "then they can rot." To his young son, Rommel confided, "Sometimes you feel that he's not quite normal."

"Dear General Arnim," Rommel wrote on March 12:

A further withdrawal of forces is not approved for the present. . . . I am only sorry that the Führer has refused my urgent request to be allowed to return immediately to Africa. He has ordered me to begin my course of medical treatment at once. My thoughts and concern are now as before with Africa. Long live the Führer!

He was doomed and he knew it, and so too was the unspeakable cause he had served. "Our star was in decline," Rommel later wrote. The glory was gone forever. He told his son, "I've fallen from grace."

On Friday, March 12, as Rommel lamented his plight, Eisenhower wrote his own son at West Point: "I have observed very frequently that it is not the man who is so brilliant [who] delivers in time of stress and strain, but rather the man who can keep on going indefinitely, doing a good straightforward job."

A "good straightforward job" was now called for, and in this homely requisite the Americans found their genius. If the winter campaign in North Africa had revealed Eisenhower's infirmities, just as it revealed

those of his army, spring would elicit strengths of character and competence in both the man and the host he commanded. Eisenhower had
been naive, sycophantic, unsure of his judgment, insufficiently vigorous,
and a more titular than actual commander. The U.S. Army had been
sloppy, undisciplined, cavalier, insufficiently vigorous, and a more titular than actual army. These traits did not abruptly slough away, molting
into brilliances of generalship and élan. But new martial lineaments
emerged, and they became the stuff of victory and liberation.

After months of sailing with the wind in his face, Eisenhower now
found a fresh breeze at his back. His health returned. Alexander and Patton shouldered many of his battlefield burdens. Axis weakness and the
weight of Allied material strength became increasingly evident. The
praise he craved was forthcoming—from Churchill, who publicly
extolled his "selflessness of character and disdain of purely personal
advancement," and from President Roosevelt, who sent word: "Tell Ike
that not only I, but the whole country is proud of the job he has done.
We have every confidence in his success." With his equilibrium restored
and his job apparently secure, Eisenhower's leadership ripened with the
season.

"I have caught up with myself and have things on a fairly even keel,"
he assured Marshall in early March. He sensed the power of a few fixed
ideas compellingly preached, and these became tenets of the armies he
commanded, even if sometimes practiced more in the breach than the
observance. Foremost was Allied unity. "German propaganda is trying to
convince the world that [the] British and Americans are at each other's
throats in this theater," he told Alexander in a handwritten note. "We'll
show them." He also radiated certitude of victory, which he saw in raw
terms: good triumphing over evil after a struggle to rival the primordial
brawl of angels. "We have bitter battling ahead, even in Tunisia," he
wrote an old friend on March 21. "Beyond this is the more serious, long-
termed prospect of getting at the guts of the enemy and tearing them
out." To his brother Edgar he asserted, "We're going to clear the Axis out
of Africa—and that's something!"

He was busier than ever, but more focused. "Political questions are
not plaguing me as much as formerly," he told Edgar. He announced
that visitors to Algiers were unwelcome unless vital to victory. "American Legion commanders, princes, and others of that stripe are nothing
but a deadly bore," he wrote Marshall. "I am cutting everybody off my
list [who] has not something specific to do with winning the war." He
took a personal interest in fielding better mine detectors, better tank
sights, even better colored smoke for battlefield signaling.

Endearingly modest, he retained the homespun authenticity that was part of his charisma; men would do much to evoke that remarkable grin. "Eisenhower's genius seems to be that of a good chairman," the reporter Philip Jordan, once a harsh critic, told his diary in the weeks after Kasserine. "I have changed my views of this man: he *has* something." To a former schoolteacher in Abilene, who had once had trouble distinguishing between the six Eisenhower boys, the commander-in-chief wrote on March 5: "I was third in line and the homeliest of the lot, if that will assist your memory." The award of his fourth star, he told his son John, "doesn't amount to a tinker's damn in the winning of this war—and that is all that concerns me." Whatever his relationship with Kay Summersby, he clearly pined for Mamie. "I miss her so much that every letter from her is worth more than anything else to me."

More and more of his time was spent on HUSKY, the invasion of Sicily tentatively scheduled for a fair moon in mid-June, and he now looked over the horizon toward the next campaign, as a commander-in-chief must do. He formed a secret group called Force 141—the number was that of a meeting room in the Hôtel St. Georges—to draft and redraft nine separate plans for the assault. "HUSKY planning is most involved and difficult . . . [and] presents intricacies and difficulties that cause me a lot of headaches," he told Marshall. He scrutinized lessons from TORCH regarding landing craft, shipping schedules, paratrooper operations, and a hundred other elements.

With one eye on Sicily, he kept the other on Tunisia. Perhaps his chief contribution in the spring campaign was to ensure that the matériel needed to finish the job was at hand. After the war a belief would take root that the successes of the American Army were attributable to overwhelming material superiority—brute strength—while setbacks could be chalked up to poor generalship. But modern war was a clash of systems: political, economic, and military. The engine of an enemy's destruction could be built only by effectively integrating forces that ranged from industrial capacity to national character to educational systems that produced men able to organize global war.

"The battle," Rommel famously observed, "is fought and decided by the quartermasters before the shooting begins." The shooting had begun months before in northwest Africa, but now the quartermasters truly came into their own. The prodigies of American industrial muscle and organizational acumen began to tell. In Oran, engineers built an assembly plant near the port and taught local workers in English, French, and Spanish how to put together a jeep from a box of parts in nine minutes. That plant turned out more than 20,000 vehicles. Another new factory nearby assembled 1,200 railcars, which were among 4,500 cars and 250 locomotives ultimately added to North African rolling stock.

In late January, Eisenhower had pleaded with Washington for more trucks. Less than three weeks later, a special convoy of twenty ships sailed from Norfolk, New York, and Baltimore with 5,000 two-and-a-half-ton trucks, 2,000 cargo trailers, 400 dump trucks, 80 fighter planes, and, for ballast, 12,000 tons of coal, 16,000 tons of flour, 9,000 tons of sugar, 1,000 tons of soap, and 4,000 submachine guns, all of which arrived in Africa on March 6. "It was," an Army account noted with justifiable pride, "a brilliant performance."

In World War I, more than half of all supplies for American forces were obtained abroad, including nearly all artillery and airplanes. In this war, almost everything would be shipped from the United States, including immense tonnages sent to the Russians, British, French, and other allies. The demands of modern combat were unprecedented. Although a latter-day infantry division was half the size of its Great War predecessor, it typically used more than twice as much ammunition—111 tons on an average fighting day. In Africa, total supply requirements amounted to thirteen tons per soldier each month.

Can do. From late February to late March, 130 ships sailed from the United States for Africa with 84,000 soldiers, 24,000 vehicles, and a million tons of cargo. Although the U.S. II Corps lost more armor at Kasserine than the Germans had massed at the beginning of the battle, those losses were replaced immediately. Other matériel appeared just as fast, including 500 miles of extra communications wire shipped to the front from Algiers less than a day after it was requested. When Patton requested—no, demanded—new shoes for his entire corps, 80,000 pairs arrived almost overnight. So much ammunition arrived in Tunisia that it was stacked in pyramids and thatched with branches to simulate an Arab village.

The Americans' "genius lay in creating resources rather than in using them economically," a British study observed astutely. Room was found in cargo holds for countless crates of Coca-Cola, to the disbelief of British logisticians. A train supposedly hauling rations to Béja for 50,000 men was found upon arrival to carry one sack of flour, a case of grapefruit juice, a boxcar of crackers, and sixteen boxcars of peanut butter. Truck chassis and truck cabs were loaded on different ships and dispatched to different ports if not different continents; so were artillery projectiles and artillery charges, radios and radio batteries, and many other components whose utility is rarely improved by divorce. Quays became so cluttered with arriving cargo that ships could not even load ballast for the return trip home and began carrying it with them on the outbound voyage. Inventories were confused beyond computation: not until the summer of 1944 would the Army be able to tally with some confidence precisely what had been shipped to North Africa.

"The American Army does not solve its problems," one general noted, "it overwhelms them." There was prodigal ineconomy—of time, of motion, of *stuff*—but beyond the extravagance lay a brisk ability to get the job done. After Kasserine, American aviation engineers built five new airfields around Sbeïtla—in seventy-two hours. More than one hundred fields in all would be built during the Tunisian campaign. The enemy would not be "solved" in Tunisia. He would be overwhelmed.

The German military had pioneered modern military logistics, but as the war entered its forty-third month Wehrmacht victualers could not keep pace with the Allies on all fronts simultaneously. With so much effort devoted to the Eastern Front, and with the overmatched German navy occupied elsewhere, supply lines to North Africa depended heavily on the Italian fleet.

That was a flimsy reed. One-third of the Italian merchant fleet had been interned when Rome entered the war; by September 1942, half of the remainder was at the bottom of various seas. Then things got worse. From the beginning of TORCH to May 1943, the Italians would lose 243 ships and boats on the Tunisian run—most to Allied air attack—with another 242 damaged. The Sicilian Channel was described by one German officer as a "roaring furnace," and to Italian sailors it became "the death route," the most dangerous sea passage in the world. Italian captains often feigned engine trouble to avoid it; the skipper of one transport carrying 600 mules for the Wehrmacht's 334th Division headed out three times, turned back three times, and never did reach Africa.

Ships not yet sunk were often immobilized for lack of fuel. Allied bombers battered Italian shipyards so relentlessly that at any given moment two-thirds of all escort vessels were unfit for service. Enthusiasm for "the Germans' war" dwindled with each new casualty list, and Italians increasingly worried over the dolorous prospect of defending their homeland.

As spring advanced, nights grew shorter, offering less cover to those sneaking across the Mediterranean. The heavily armed, shallow-draft vessels known as Siebel ferries gave some relief, and ninety had braved the furnace by late January. But German logisticians calculated that they needed four times that number, and steel shortages kept the ferry fleet small. Before his departure, Rommel warned that "to create the build-up necessary for a defense against a major attack" in Africa would require shipping 140,000 tons of supplies each month; that was double the amount received in January and February combined, even before Allied interdiction intensified. By contrast, the Allies in March moved 220,000 tons just through the ports around Oran.

Other woes also plagued German logisticians. The relentless Allied air raids so unnerved Arab dockworkers that stevedores had to be imported from Hamburg. The ports being damaged, more and more supplies had to be hauled by a fleet of 200 Ju-52 transport planes, but each plane carried less than two tons. Trains used to move matériel within Tunisia required coal imported from Europe; as supplies dwindled, crews turned to local lignite, which greatly reduced locomotive efficiency. When even lignite grew scarce, the only alternative was a feeble mixture of oil cakes and sediment from the olive harvest. Cheap Tunisian wine was distilled into a thin fuel.

These tribulations stirred mild interest in the German high command and at Comando Supremo, where, as one account noted, "paper divisions had the strength of real ones, . . . ships and convoys were never sunk, and . . . armies, at least on paper, were always up to strength." Even as the Allies crumpled at Kasserine, an inspection team from Berlin reported that if Axis ships kept sinking at the current rate none would remain afloat by early summer. Alarms from Africa grew shrill. Arnim warned that "if no supplies reach us, all will be up in Tunisia by 1 July." The Axis bridgehead, he added, was becoming "a fortress without ammunition and rations."

In Berlin and Rome promises were issued and broken, re-issued and re-broken. Without stripping the other battlefronts or resurrecting the Italian navy, little could be done. Even less *was* done. "Hitler wanted to be stronger than mere facts, to bend them to his will," Kesselring's chief of staff observed. "All attempts to make him see reason only sent him into a rage."

"The Devil Is Come Down"

THE soft whir of a film projector silenced the British officers in Montgomery's mess. Setting down their tea mugs, the men pivoted their canvas chairs toward an army blanket hung as a makeshift screen. The familiar supper smell of bully beef and biscuits was overpowered by the stink of sweat-stained khaki and ripe cardigans. Brilliant white flashes limned the jagged rim of the wadi sheltering the command post, and the grumble of artillery carried on the evening airs beneath a waxing moon.

Then the movie began. Artillery booms and flashes on the screen mingled with the real thing until they were almost indistinguishable: a celluloid depiction of the battle of El Alamein five months earlier was superimposed on tonight's opening barrage of Eighth Army's assault against the Mareth Line. But it was the film that held the men rapt. Churchill himself had sent this print of *Desert Victory*, a sixty-five-minute documentary that had become a worldwide propaganda sensation in the two weeks since its London premiere. Montgomery had seen the movie already, on March 16, but now, four nights later, he seemed no less entranced as he watched again, "a wee bugger in a black beret"—as a Scottish soldier described him—reliving the greatest triumph of British arms since Waterloo. His vulpine face, whitened with reflected images from the screen, hardly moved except for faint twitches of his thin black mustache.

There was Rommel, seen in captured German footage, sporting his leather duster and goggles. Then Monty himself, that "intensely compacted hank of steel wire," in George Bernard Shaw's arch phrase. Tankers stacked their shells, medics unfolded their stretchers. Then: sappers wriggle forward to snip the wire, and gun chiefs squint at their watches before shouting the command: *Fire!* The terrible cannonade turns night to noon. Infantrymen in baggy shorts surge forward, their rifles held at port arms. Bayonets thrust. Pipes keen. Then it's over, except for the final flickering frames of dead Germans blackening in the sun and POWs scuffing toward their cages as Eighth Army pushes west. The Union Jack flaps over Tobruk on November 13, then Benghazi a week later, then Tripoli on January 23—way stations to Médenine and the current line at Mareth. "Pursuit," the narrator asserts, "was relentless."

The leader slapped round and round on the spinning reel as the officers shambled back to their bivouacs. They had a battle to fight, not just one to relive, and so far it was not going especially well. Montgomery stood and stretched to his full five foot seven—perhaps a bit taller in chukka boots—before returning to his caravan. He loved the film. "It is first class," he wrote Alexander. As one reporter noted, "He was thoroughly enjoying this conqueror business."

Bernard Law Montgomery was a bishop's son who had passed a "lonely and loveless" childhood in remote Tasmania, dreaming of greatness and believing himself born to conquer. Near the photo of Rommel above his desk was a copy of Drake's prayer before the attack on Cádiz in

1587, entreating God for "the true glory." There lay Montgomery's quest: the true glory. He was ascetic and fussy, a teetotaling, Bible-reading maverick who cited Cromwell and Moses among his favorite great captains and who had opened a commanders' seminar on El Alamein a few weeks earlier by forbidding not only smoking but coughing. (Churchill, upon hearing Montgomery boast that abstinence made him "100 percent fit," replied that he both drank and smoked and was "*200* percent fit.") Hardened in the trenches—he had been badly wounded at Ypres—he was hardened more by the early death of a wife he adored. "One only loves once," he told Alexander, "and now it is finished."

A line from the Book of Job was among his favorites: "Yet man is born unto trouble, as the sparks fly upward." He was a master of organization and training, of the set battle, of the theatrics of command. "Kill Germans, even padres—one per week and two on Sundays," he told his soldiers. Not a man among the 200,000 in Eighth Army doubted that he was their leader, or that he would be stingy in spending their lives. That was something. A majority of his forty-three infantry battalions came from Commonwealth or allied armies, and he had enough political moxie to avoid prodigality with other nations' troops. After taking command in Egypt in mid-August 1942 under Alexander's indulgent supervision, Montgomery had whipped Rommel first at Alam Halfa, then a second, decisive time at El Alamein. That British attack on October 23, with more than a thousand tanks, cracked the much weaker Axis defenders across a forty-mile front. "The sheer weight of British resources made up for all blunders," one account noted. Twelve days later, Rommel was in the full retreat that had led to southern Tunisia. Until Alamein, the British Army had been mostly winless; his victory in Egypt gave new life to Churchill's government and to empire, at a cost of 13,560 British casualties but with more than twice as many exacted from his enemies. Church bells had pealed in Britain for the first time in three years. Fan letters arrived at Montgomery's bivouac by the thousands, including some marriage proposals, and soldiers rushed to glimpse his passing car as if he were a film star, which now he was. "We all trust him to win," one brigadier said. As a redeeming virtue, that too was something.

And yet. Sparks flew up around Montgomery. He was puerile, petty, and egocentric, bereft of irony, humility, and a sense of proportion. It would not suffice for him to succeed; others must fail. "If he admitted to an error, it was always minor, and served, like a touch of black in a color scheme, to throw up his general infallibility," the historian Correlli Barnett would write after the war. Acknowledging the "chaos of his temperament," his biographer Ronald Lewin described a kindliness and intermittent humanity marred by ruthlessness, intolerance, and sheer lack of empathy; a marvelous capacity for ignoring the inessential, combined with a purblind insensitivity about the obvious; a deep but unsophisticated Christianity; a panache, a burning ambition, above all an individuality—such were the gifts which both good and bad fairies brought to Montgomery's cradle.

He disdained the French—"quite useless except to guard aerodromes"—and especially the Americans, to whom he would be miserably yoked for the duration of the war. Montgomery dismissed Eisenhower, whom he had met in Britain just long enough to rebuke for lighting a cigarette, in four words: "Good chap, no soldier!" After their second meeting, soon to occur near Mareth, he would embroider his assessment of the commander-in-chief in a letter to Brooke: "He knows nothing whatever about how to make war or to fight battles; he should be kept right away from all that business if we want to win this war." Before ever seeing the U.S. Army, he proclaimed that "the real trouble with the Americans is that the soldiers won't fight. They haven't got the light of battle in their eyes."

Montgomery was perhaps most controversial among his own countrymen. He deemed Anderson "quite unfit to command an army." First Army as a whole was worthless. "The party in Tunisia is a complete dog's-breakfast," he declared, "and there is an absence of good chaps over there." He quipped that he intended to "drive the Germans and the First Army back into the sea." A senior British general considered him "a thoroughly disloyal subordinate."

Swaggering into Tunisia, Montgomery and his army were also thoroughly overconfident. He envisioned a grand sweep to Tunis, with more laurels and church bells awaiting him. "We will roll up the whole show from the south," he told Alexander. Churchill tartly noted: "Indomitable in retreat, invincible in advance, insufferable in victory." Yet the army lumbered like "a dray horse on a polo field," in Correlli Barnett's phrase, despite an enthusiasm for the amphetamine benzedrine, which was issued in tens of thousands of tablets "to all Eighth Army personnel" on Montgomery's order.

Contrary to the *Desert Victory* mythology, pursuit after Alamein was hardly "relentless." Rommel had escaped with the core of his army despite a fifteenfold British advantage in tanks, an artillery superiority of twelve to one, and an intimate knowledge of Axis weakness thanks to Ultra and other intelligence. Eighth Army had hugged the ancient Pirate

Coast across Libya much closer than it hugged the retreating Axis. That lollygagging had allowed Rommel time to drub the Americans at Kasserine, return to Médenine for a drubbing of his own, then slip away again. "Once Monty had his reputation," charged the British air marshal Arthur Coningham, "he would never risk it again."

Now another chance to bag the enemy army obtained, thanks to a stand-or-die order from the Axis high command.

This time the last ditch was to be dug at Mareth, a line of fortifications stretching twenty-two miles between the Mediterranean and the rugged Matmata Hills in the south. For centuries, the narrow coastal gap had been the main portal into southern Tunisia for trans-Saharan caravans carrying slaves and ivory. It was said that traveling merchants seized by Berber highwaymen were forced to drink vats of hot water to flush out any gold they had swallowed.

Although Hitler had vacillated before ordering Mareth held, Kesselring—ignoring Rommel's skepticism—considered the position a suitable place to begin converting Tunisia into "one vast fortress." A retreat farther up the Tunisian coast, toward Gabès or Sfax, might allow the merger of Alexander's two armies; it would also shorten Allied bombing runs to Tunis and Bizerte. Under orders issued by Comando Supremo on March 17, Mareth was "to be defended to the last." With Rommel gone to Europe, Arnim would command the Axis army group that comprised his own Fifth Panzer Army in the north and Panzer Army Africa, renamed First Italian Army, in the south. The latter included remnants of the Afrika Korps among its 50,000 Germans and 35,000 Italians, and was commanded by General Giovanni Messe, who for the past two years had led the Italian expeditionary corps in Russia.

Built by the French in the 1930s to thwart Italian aggression from the east, the Mareth Line by an odd turn was now garrisoned by twenty-two Italian battalions backed and flanked—"corseted"—by ten German infantry battalions and the 15th Panzer Division with thirty-two functioning tanks. Wadis were scarped into antitank ditches—more than a hundred feet wide and twenty feet deep in places. Thick plaits of barbed wire screened the front, which was four miles deep and seeded with 170,000 mines. Twenty-five decrepit French blockhouses marked the line, some with concrete walls ten feet thick. The Axis flank to the west beyond the hills was protected by *chotts*—desert salt lakes—and was marked on French maps as *terrain chaotique*.

These engineering nuances were known to the Allies, of course. Anglo-American intelligence possessed not only the Mareth blueprints

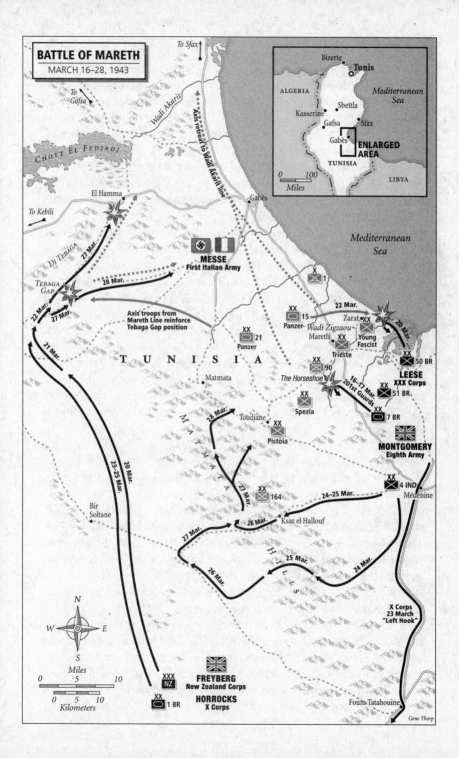

BATTLE OF MARETH
MARCH 16–28, 1943

To Sfax

To Gafsa

Wadi Akarit

To Kebili

CHOTT EL FEDJADJ

El Hamma

27 Mar.

DJ TEBAGA

28 Mar.

TEBAGA GAP

22 Mar.

27 Mar.

21 Mar.

20 Mar.

23–25 Mar.

Bir Soltane

Axis troops from Mareth Line reinforce Tebaga Gap position

T U N I S I A

Matmata

M A T M A T A

28 Mar.

Toudjane

27 Mar.

27 Mar.

26 Mar.

Ksar el Hallouf

26 Mar.

Gabès

MESSE
First Italian Army

XX 15 Panzer-

XX 21 Panzer

XX 90

The Horseshoe

XX Spezia

XX Pistoia

XX 164

Wadi Zigzaou
Mareth

XX Trieste

Young Fascist

16–17 Mar
201st Guards

24–25 Mar.

25 Mar.

24 Mar.

H I L L S

X 1

22 Mar.

Zarat

XX 20 Mar.

XX 50 BR

LEESE
XXX Corps

XX 51 BR

XX 7 BR

MONTGOMERY
Eighth Army

XX 4 IND
Médenine

X Corps
23 March
"Left Hook"

Foum Tatahouine

N
W   E
S

Miles
0   5   10

Kilometers
0   5   10

XXX NZ

FREYBERG
New Zealand Corps

XX 1 BR

HORROCKS
X Corps

Gene Thorp

Enlarged area inset

Bizerte

Tunis

ALGERIA

Mediterranean Sea

Sbeïtla

Kasserine

Gafsa

Sfax

Gabès

ENLARGED AREA

TUNISIA

LIBYA

0   100
Miles

Mediterranean Sea

but also the former French commander, who, Beetle Smith reported, was indulged in Algiers with six aides—"one for himself and five for his wife. The five were always borrowing ham and bacon and sugar for Madame." On March 12, Alexander offered his assessment of enemy intentions at Mareth in a lilting if ambiguous message drawn from the twelfth chapter of Revelation: "The devil is come down unto you, having great wrath, because he knoweth that he hath but a short time."

Montgomery knew his Bible and he believed he also knew his enemy. Eighth Army outnumbered the 85,000-man First Italian Army by more than two to one. The disparity in heavy weapons was even more lopsided, including a five-to-one tank advantage, 743 to 142. With a sense of infallibility stoked by the rout at Médenine, Montgomery considered the Italians simply too weak to withstand his horde, corseting be damned. He dispatched his New Zealand Corps, with roughly one-quarter of his combat force, on a looping expedition to the west, where by a series of secret night marches they were to negotiate the *terrain chaotique* before falling on the enemy's rear with 26,000 men and 150 tanks, wreaking havoc and despair. But the main blow, code-named PUGILIST GALLOP, would be a frontal attack by his XXX Corps just a few miles from the coast on a pinched front of 1,200 yards; once a hole was torn in the enemy line, the X Corps would plunge through in an ecstasy of exploitation. "When I give a party, it is a good party," Montgomery assured his men on attack eve. "And this is going to be a good party."

The party had begun badly. In preliminary jostling intended to improve British positions four nights before the main attack, two Guards battalions on the night of March 16 struck an enemy salient ten miles from the coast, on the road from Médenine to Mareth. The attackers included the 6th Grenadier Guards and the 3rd Coldstreams, newly arrived from Syria with heavy Hebron coats and tasseled fly switches. Their objective, a curvy cluster of hills rising 600 feet above the plain and known as the Horseshoe, was said to be "lightly held" by "one or two isolated machine gun posts."

In fact, it was defended by 6,500 stone-cold killers from the German 90th Light Division and was part of a four-mile front bristling with more than fifty guns. Two grenadier battalions infested the Horseshoe proper, and Axis engineers had made good use of the three months allowed them to improve the Mareth defenses. After a British artillery barrage of 24,000 shells that did little but irk the defenders, the moonlit Guardsmen surged forward with much hoarse whispering and nervous nibbling of cookies stuffed in their pockets. Within minutes they were mired in unsuspected minefields of unprecedented density. German parachute flares floated over the line like tiny suns, exposing the men to a hellish crossfire. After some nasty bayonet work in the bottom of a wadi, the Guardsmen fell back, leaving the Horseshoe littered with bloody Hebron coats and fly switches that would switch no more. "It was my first contact with sudden death, and I couldn't credit my senses," one survivor reported. A German officer cadged cigarettes from British prisoners in exchange for cold coffee and black bread. "For you the war is over," he told them, "but I must go on."

The Coldstreams suffered 159 casualties, the Grenadiers 363, including twenty-seven of thirty-four officers. "Well I am still alive and that is more than I dared hope twelve hours ago," the Coldstream padre wrote. "Our attack was a complete failure." It was, one of Montgomery's lieutenants admitted, "the most damnable thing." Enemy casualties were fewer than 200. Burial squads trying to retrieve sixty-nine British bodies from one especially morbid acre found that they first had to remove more than 700 mines.

A lesser man might have reconsidered his scheme for a frontal attack against such formidable defenses. Not Montgomery. Unfazed, he proclaimed that these preliminary operations "as a whole were a great success." Distracted with planning for Sicily, he seemed so disengaged from PUGILIST GALLOP that Major General J. S. "Crasher" Nichols, commander of the division ordered to spearhead the attack, was "left largely to his own devices," according to an official British account of the battle. The result was a valorous attack of regrettable ineptitude using a solitary infantry brigade reinforced by a solitary regiment of Valentine tanks, most armed with the impotent 2-pounder popgun.

Of such battles are myths made and empires lost. As Montgomery and his officers watched their movie on March 20, 300 guns from the Royal Artillery unleashed 36,000 rounds. Most fell on the Young Fascist Division investing the point of attack, eight miles north of the earlier Guards foray and within smell of the briny Mediterranean. Infantrymen capered forward in the bright moonlight "as if they were going to a picnic," one witness reported. An officer holding a hurricane lamp led minesweeping Scorpion tanks through choking dust toward the Wadi Zigzaou. They found a steep-banked freshet with water eight feet deep in places and protected by a parallel antitank ditch fanged with concrete dragons' teeth.

The medieval flavor of this battlefield was reinforced by the appearance of "thug patrols," British squads carrying scaling ladders, which they laid over the antitank ditch for riflemen to scoot across into the labyrinth of trenches and breastworks on the far side. Valentine crews at midnight dumped into the wadi dozens of fascines, dense bundles of sticks intended to give purchase to the tank tracks. Other Tommies trotted forward with tape to mark paths through the mine belts, or formed human ladders for their comrades to surmount the wadi banks.

So far, so good. Then the lead Valentine foundered in the mucky Zigzaou, blocking the only vehicle crossing. The tanks' hot exhaust ignited the fascines; soon roaring bonfires added their illumination to the Very lights and dusty moonbeams. Four tanks managed to negotiate the wadi on a hastily built bypass, but a fifth stalled, blocking the gap cut in a minefield.

By first light on March 21, portions of four infantry battalions had gained a shallow bridgehead: a mile wide and half a mile deep. But with aircraft hampered by foul weather, even 300 guns could not, as one general had advised, "pound the objectives to powder and render the defenders imbecile." Italian gunnery intensified in daylight, enfilading the wadi with sheets of fire. German grenadiers and artillery soon reinforced the Young Fascists. Casualties soared. Tommies spent the day trying to winkle defenders out of their pillboxes and waiting for darkness so the Valentines could again force a passage across the wadi. British engineers managed to build only one of three planned crossings over the Zigzaou. "Soon a vague feeling spread from soldier to soldier that something is wrong," one witness reported, "that someone is making a hash of things."

In the small hours of March 22, forty-two Valentines were able to cross the wadi, but their tracks chewed up the delicate causeway and no antitank guns or other vehicles could follow. Thick overcast limited air support, and a cloudburst swelled the Zigzaou, further undoing the engineers' handiwork. Ammo carriers plodded forward with their heavy green boxes, and litter bearers shuttled to and from the rear without ever bothering to fold their stretchers. "My operations progressing well," Montgomery cabled Alexander at 11:45 A.M. on the twenty-second. "Suggest you announce that my operations are proceeding satisfactorily and according to plan."

One hour and fifty-five minutes after this inanity went out, the 7,000-man 15th Panzer Division counterattacked in three columns from an assembly area seven miles northwest of Wadi Zigzaou. Thirty tanks and two infantry battalions slammed into the bridgehead, gripping the British in such an intimate embrace that despite fairing weather Allied pilots hesitated to fire for fear of killing their own. Panzers methodically obliterated one strong point after another, grinding in the slit trenches. Soon thirty-five Valentines were reduced to smoking hulks. The Zigzaou's seething ravine became an abattoir, with bodies beached on the mud or floating heavily in the stream. As shrapnel frothed the water around them, bare-chested Sikh sappers toiled to repair the causeway with steel mesh and duckboards amid the improbable battle cry of "More fascines!"

"Crowds of men wounded and unwounded flitted like wraiths through the haze," the correspondent Jack Belden wrote. "Some crawled. Some stumbled. Some marched erect." *Most*, in fact, crawled, often toward the rear on hands and knees in single file across fifty yards of steel-swept no-man's-land. Snatches of incongruous conversation drifted above the shell fire. "Organization," a voice called in the gloaming. "That's the trouble."

By nightfall the bridgehead was all but gone. The 50th Division's 151st Brigade alone had 600 casualties. A drift to the rear continued. Someone *had* made a hash of things.

Montgomery disliked being awakened even for good news and not since Alamein had aides dared disturb his repose. But there was no sugaring this pill. At two A.M. on Tuesday, March 23, he was roused with word that his XXX Corps commander, General Oliver W. H. Leese, needed to see him. The huge, toothy Leese met Montgomery in the latter's cramped map lorry, ten miles southeast of the battlefield. The 50th Division had pulled nearly all surviving troops back across the Zigzaou, Leese reported. A follow-on British thrust had been canceled. Casualties were heavy. The attack had failed.

Montgomery kept his composure until Leese left with orders to return in the morning. The Eighth Army chief of staff, Brigadier Francis "Freddie" de Guingand, found his commander tousled and stunned amid the tacked-up maps, his normally impassive countenance now dissolved with worry. For the first time in ten months, Eighth Army was withdrawing. The infernal rumble of artillery rattled the lorry—"a whole night being shelled like hell," De Guingand later recalled. In a small voice Montgomery asked, "What am I to do, Freddie?"

The answer lay on the map, and within two hours Montgomery had found it, along with his composure. The Matmata Hills—a "jagged purple coxcomb" drenched with the scent of wildflowers, as one soldier wrote—

extended at a right angle from the Mareth Line, roughly paralleling the Mediterranean coast for a hundred miles. Only the narrow Tebaga Gap pierced the range, fifty crow-flying miles west of Mareth, and only through this pass could the Axis defenses be outflanked. It was in that direction that Montgomery had dispatched his New Zealand Corps more than a week earlier with orders to turn the enemy line. The circuitous 200-mile expedition took the Kiwis past the arid land of the Troglodytes, an ancient people who lived like moles in subterranean hovels and whose strange language Herodotus had likened to the cry of a bat. The cavalcade also drove through a locust plague of biblical intensity: millions of insects borne on a hot, southwesterly wind pelted windshields and tank turrets. But by midafternoon on March 21, the corps vanguard had pressed into Tebaga Gap.

Alerted by Luftwaffe reconnaissance, General Messe and his lieutenants knew of this flanking peril; alerted by Ultra, the British knew they knew. Wehrmacht legions sidled westward, first the 164th Division, then eventually the 21st and 15th Panzer Divisions. A promising Kiwi attack on the night of the twenty-first took 850 prisoners at a cost of only sixty-five casualties. But then lethargy and caution, those handmaidens of battlefield stalemate, prevented quick exploitation before Axis reinforcements arrived in force. A golden chance to fall on the enemy rear was lost.

No matter. Montgomery had regained his vim. At 4:30 A.M. on March 23, he alerted the New Zealand Corps to a complete change of plans. Rather than serve as a sideshow, the Kiwis would deliver the main blow. Three divisions under General Leese would remain on the coast to occupy enemy defenders at Mareth. But reinforcements would add weight to the New Zealand attack, and Lieutenant General Brian Horrocks, who had waited in vain with his X Corps to crash through a Leese-made hole at Mareth, would assume command of this new, left-hook assault, code-named SUPERCHARGE II. "Am sending Horrocks to take charge," Montgomery added in his predawn message. "Am sure you will understand."

One man who did not understand was the New Zealanders' legendary commander, Lieutenant General Bernard C. Freyberg. English-born but raised in New Zealand, Freyberg had been a dentist before finding his true calling as warrior of Homeric strength and courage. Known as Tiny to his troops, he had a skull the size of a medicine ball, with a pushbroom mustache and legs that extended like sycamore trunks from his khaki shorts. In the Great War, he had won the Victoria Cross on the Somme, served as a pallbearer for his great friend Rupert Brooke, and emerged so seamed by shrapnel that when Churchill once persuaded him to display his wounds the count reached twenty-seven. More were to come. Oarsman, boxer, swimmer of the English Channel, he had been medically retired for "aortic incompetence" in the 1930s before being summoned back to uniform. No greater heart beat in British battle dress. Churchill a month earlier had proclaimed Freyberg "the salamander of the British empire," an accolade that raised Kiwi hackles—"Wha' in 'ell's a 'sallymander'?"—until the happy news spread that the creature mythically could pass through fire unharmed. "Simple as a child and as cunning as a Maori dog," Freyberg was both superstitious—he refused, for example, to look at a new moon through glass—and literate. In his raspy voice he enjoyed reciting Mrs. Bennet's gleeful prattle in *Pride and Prejudice* upon learning that her daughter Lizzy is to marry the rich Mr. Darcy: "Ten thousand a year! Oh, Lord! What will become of me? I shall go distracted!"

The Salamander was displeased at being supplanted by Horrocks, who was six years younger as well as junior in grade. Freyberg seemed "grim, firm, and not at all forthcoming," the British official history recorded, while Horrocks "felt embarrassed and was annoyed too." Montgomery sought to make amends for his offense by sending each man a bottle of brandy, while De Guingand addressed all messages to "my dear Generals" and jokingly referred to them as "Hindenburg and Ludendorff."

Montgomery set aside thoughts of Tunis and Sicily long enough to concoct a plan worthy of his reputation. Insisting that SUPERCHARGE II go forward as quickly as possible, he also proposed an unusual late-afternoon attack out of the southwest: at that hour, the sinking sun would blind Axis defenders. After a frantically busy night of creeping forward and digging in, by dawn on March 26 some 40,000 attackers and 250 tanks lay hidden near an old Roman wall that stretched four miles across Tebaga Gap. From their camouflaged holes, the men watched the sun march across the African sky until it was directly behind them. Officers played chess in their slit trenches to while away the hours.

Then, at 3:30 P.M., low waves of British and American bombers attacked Axis targets marked with red and blue artillery smoke shells. Thirty minutes later, the Royal Artillery erupted in a thundering cannonade as a providential sandstorm further blinded the defenders. At precisely 4:15 P.M. the first tanks surged from their revetments, with shrieking Maori riflemen clinging to their hulls. One Kiwi commander recounted:

> The infantry climbed out of their pits—where there had been nothing visible there were now hundreds of men who shook out

into long lines and followed on five hundred yards behind the tanks. At 4:23 P.M. the barrage lifted a hundred yards—an extraordinary level line of bursting shells—tanks and infantry closed to it, and the assault was on.

Through the gap they poured, the forward edge of the advancing ranks marked with swirling orange smoke for the benefit of Allied pilots. "Speed up, straight through, no halting," officers called. Two German battalions buckled and collapsed. On one particularly bloody hill, a brigadier reported "dead and mangled Germans everywhere, more than I had seen in a small area since the Somme in 1916." British tank commanders heaved grenades from their open hatches and Maoris pelted the fleeing enemy troops with stones when their ammunition ran out. To the east, Gurkhas from the 4th Indian Division went baying into battle "not unlike hounds finding the scent."

By nightfall, the attack had penetrated four miles into the pass. Tanks "trundled as snails feeling their way" in the darkness until midnight, when the rising moon emerged from the clouds to reveal the extraordinary spectacle of British and German forces hurrying side by side toward the vital road junction of El Hamma at the head of Tebaga Gap.

It was a race the Germans won, if only temporarily. In the early morning of March 27 an improvised antitank screen of eleven guns—as crudely effective as a dropped portcullis—delayed the British for more than a day three miles south of El Hamma. That was long enough. By the time the blockade was flanked, General Messe had adroitly pulled back his forces from both Mareth and Tebaga Gap toward another fortified gap at Wadi Akarit, sixty miles north. "Like a black snake squirming over the ground we could see the lorries and guns of the German tail making their escape," a disappointed British soldier reported. "Once again . . . a clever escape."

Montgomery had won a battle but not a resounding victory, and certainly not the war. Three German divisions, with the help of Italian cannon fodder, had thwarted three British corps for a fortnight. True, the price was dear, and this Axis army could hardly afford heavy casualties. Seven thousand Axis prisoners were taken in the Mareth actions, a third of them German; the cost to Eighth Army totaled 4,000, including 600 casualties in the breakthrough at Tebaga Gap. After the battle a single British private was seen leading several hundred Italian prisoners, who chattered like parrots; asked if he needed help escorting them to their cages, the young soldier answered, "Oh, Lord, no! They trust me."

"It was the most enjoyable battle I have ever fought," Montgomery exulted. Perhaps so, although local legend attributed the severe five-year drought that began in 1943 to Montgomery's imprecations on the land. Yet Eighth Army had forced the outer gate to begin its inexorable march up Tunisia's east coast toward Tunis. That was plain, and every sensible German and Italian officer knew that the two Axis armies now faced mortal peril from the two Allied armies.

Yet Eighth Army still seemed to lack an instinct for the jugular. In boxing terms, it was a poor finisher. General Freyberg ordered his advance squadrons to bypass Gabès on the morning of March 29 and give chase on the coastal road—ordered this only to learn that at that very moment the spearhead commander was accepting the keys to the city from the Gabès mayor. The 4th Indian Division, already delayed a critical twelve hours by a horrendous traffic jam, was forced to wait at Gabès while the 51st Highlanders donned their kilts for a proper march-through with pipers. Again pursuit languished. "The enemy does not follow," the 90th Light Division war diary noted. The retreating Axis soldiers had time to pilfer tables, mirrors, women's dresses, even pianos. The British had to settle for six captured railcars full of German sausage.

Some of Montgomery's admirers considered his mid-battle switch from a frontal assault to the sweeping left hook among the boldest decisions in his glorious career. Yet a more imaginative plan at the outset, enforced by a more attentive commander, might have made Mareth the decisive battle it could have been. "We never lost the initiative, and we made the enemy dance to our tune the whole time," Montgomery claimed on March 31. That assertion was questionable. He had violated his own wise precept "to concentrate all your forces and give a mighty crack." He also had underestimated the resourcefulness of his enemy; the technical requirements of fighting in hill country; and the difficulty of crossing a stoutly defended watercourse, the Zigzaou. That boded ill for Eighth Army after years in the desert: the army and its commander would encounter more hills in northern Tunisia and *many* more in Italy, along with innumerable rivers. Major General Francis Tuker, the 4th Indian Division commander, concluded, "There was, in Eighth Army, an apparent lack of purpose at this time."

In the months after Mareth, Montgomery acknowledged that the failure of his coastal attack had required him to recast his entire plan. There was no shame in deft improvisation, to be sure. But soon he was asserting that the left wing had always been designated to deliver the fatal blow. By the end of the war he even seemed to believe it, having perhaps persuaded himself through repetition. Perhaps the high bar of infallibility demanded no miscues, no false starts, no desperate two A.M. wailing about what to do now. As they cleared Gabès for the long, last march toward Tunis, his men gathered themselves for the sort of war—one with mountains and rivers and allies—that would confront them for the duration.

11. Over the Top

"Give Them Some Steel!"

A<small>N</small> old Arab song warned:

> *Gafsa is miserable,*
> *Its water is blood,*
> *Its air is poison.*
> *You may live there a hundred years*
> *Without making a friend.*

Miserable it was, a flyspecked phosphate camp of 10,000 souls. Jugurtha, who led the Numidian revolt against Rome in the second century B.C., once hid his treasury here because the town was so remote. After changing hands four times in the past three months, Gafsa had become even more wretched; the budding groves of pomegranates and apricots could hardly redeem the misery of war. As Montgomery prepared to give battle 120 miles southeast at Mareth, General Alexander had ordered the Americans to liberate Gafsa yet again. The attack was code-named Operation WOP, in homage to the 7,000 Centauro Division soldiers occupying the town and nearby hills. GIs composed their own tribute, a ribald ditty titled "The Third Time We Took Gafsa."

If seizing Gafsa seemed insufficiently ambitious for Patton's II Corps, which had swelled to 88,473 men—precisely the size of Sherman's army in Carolina at the end of the Civil War—the modesty of the assignment reflected Alexander's disdain for American fighting prowess. Alexander had two strategic options. He could use II Corps and Anderson's First Army to drive a wedge between the Axis forces across the Eastern Dorsal, isolating Arnim's army in the north from the First Italian Army in the south; each would in turn be ground between the Allied millstones. Or, he could squeeze Axis troops into a shrinking bridgehead around Tunis, with Montgomery's Eighth Army crushing the enemy to pulp.

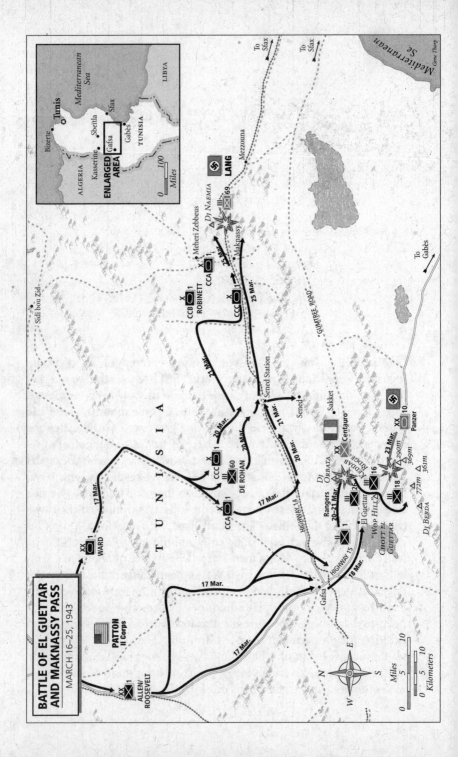

BATTLE OF EL GUETTAR
AND MAKNASSY PASS

MARCH 16–25, 1943

PATTON II Corps

ALLEN/ROOSEVELT 1
WARD 1

TUNISIA

17 Mar.

17 Mar.

17 Mar.

17 Mar.

Gafsa

HIGHWAY 15

HIGHWAY 14

18 Mar.

El Guettar

Rangers 20–21 Mar.

1

"Wop Hill"

CHOTT EL GUETTAR

Dj BERDA

72m

361m

Dj ORBATA

Kreddab Ridge

16

18

290m

369m

23 Mar.

Centauro

Sakket

Sened

Sened Station

17 Mar.

20 Mar.

20 Mar.

21 Mar.

20 Mar.

21 Mar.

CCA 1

DE ROHAN 60

CCC 1

21 Mar.

"GUMTREE ROAD"

Panzer 10

To Gabès

CCB 1

ROBINETT

CCC 1

25 Mar.

CCA 1

22 Mar.

Meheri Zebbeus

Maknassy

Dj NAEMIA

LANG

69

To Sfax

To Sfax

Mezzouna

Sidi bou Zid

Gene Thorp

Mediterranean Sea

ENLARGED AREA

ALGERIA

Bizerte
Tunis

Mediterranean Sea

Sbeïtla
Kasserine

Sfax

Gafsa
Gabès

TUNISIA

LIBYA

0   100
Miles

N

W   E

S

Miles
0   5   10

Kilometers
0   5   10

Alexander chose the latter course. The inexperienced Americans, he believed, could not withstand the panzer counterattacks sure to follow any attempt to split the bridgehead. "I do *not* want the Americans getting in the way," Montgomery privately told Alexander. Instead, he added, the cousins should "get the road ready for me to use" by lifting mines and fixing potholes.

Montgomery was insufferable, as usual, but Alexander's decision was defensible in the wake of Kasserine: the memory of terrified Yanks scorching up the Thala road remained vivid. With Eisenhower's concurrence, he twice warned Patton to avoid "pitched, indecisive battles" where "we might get into trouble." Alexander considered Patton "a dashing steed," but he did not want him dashing into Montgomery's path. Patton would be kept on a tighter rein than Montgomery and even Anderson. Allen's 1st Division was ordered to "assist the advance of the British Eighth Army from the south" by building a supply dump in Gafsa and protecting Montgomery's left flank as he drove toward Sfax and then Tunis. Only scouts would venture southeast of Gafsa toward Gabès, although if things went well Ward's 1st Armored Division might later push on due east through Sened Station to Maknassy. Of Patton's four divisions, the greenest pair—the 34th and 9th—would remain in reserve.

Patton was incensed at being relegated to a weak supporting role, but he swallowed his pride and prepared to attack. Word of his third star had arrived on March 12. "I am a lieutenant general," he told his diary. "Now I want, and will get, four stars." A day later, as if recalculating the azimuth of his character, he added, "I am just the same since I am a lieutenant general." No man felt a more vivid kinship with the great captains of yore, and Patton now likened the Gafsa offensive to Stonewall Jackson's flank attack in support of Longstreet at the Second Battle of Manassas in 1862. Tromping about in high brown boots and a fleece-lined coat, he told his commanders he wanted "to see more dead bodies, American as well as German." To his troops he declaimed:

> Fortunately for our fame as soldiers, our enemy is worthy of us. The German is a war-trained veteran—confident, brave, and ruthless. We are brave. We are better-equipped, better fed, and in the place of his blood-glutted Woten, we have with us the God of Our Fathers Known of Old. . . . If we die killing, well and good, but if we fight hard enough, viciously enough, we will kill and live. Live to return to our family and our girl as conquering heroes—men of Mars.

He was rolling now. On March 16 Patton summoned all staff officers to his dank command post in a shot-up Fériana hotel. With a scowl made even fiercer by the cold sore erupting on his upper lip, he announced: "Gentlemen, tomorrow we attack. If we are not victorious, let no one come back alive." He excused himself, then retired to pray. To Bea he wrote, "I am always a little short of breath before a match."

That night, military policemen wielding flashlights hooded with red cellophane waved the convoys down rain-slick Highway 15 on the forty-five-mile approach march to Gafsa. The floor of each vehicle was sand-bagged, to absorb mine blasts. Arab tents on the hillsides glittered like cobwebs in the dim moonlight. "The hardest thing a general has to do," Patton told his diary, "is to wait for the battle to start after all the orders are given." At eleven P.M. he heard the rumble of artillery. "Well, the battle is on," he scribbled. "I am taking off my shoes to go to bed."

There was no battle, although the American press in its eagerness to forget Kasserine would tout Operation WOP as if it *were* Second Manassas. Twelve hundred Italians and a German reconnaissance battalion slipped away to the east at dawn, unmolested by Ward's CCA, which was delayed by heavy rain and failed to sever the escape road to Sened Station as planned. Ted Roosevelt waited on a low ridge while bombers plastered Gafsa and scouts drove sheep over the road to test for mines. After hours of listening to confused voices crackle from the radio, Roosevelt impatiently bolted forward. *Rough Rider* led a convoy of jeeps—"like a small flotilla of ships bumping through the wadis," one witness wrote—into Gafsa to find the enemy gone. By 12:30 P.M. the town was declared secure.

"The Dagoes beat it," Patton wrote. He and Allen, who wore riding breeches and a field jacket, drove down from Fériana to find only stunned civilians emerging from their cellars. An old woman in black wailed on a broken balcony, her grief sweeping across the ruined town. A month of Axis occupation and the morning's bombardment had finished the destruction begun by American demolitionists during the Kasserine retreat. Italian and Arab pillagers had wrecked nearly every house belonging to Gafsa's 500 French residents and 800 Jews—smashing furniture, tearing doors from their hinges, and stealing rugs, faucets, and bathtubs. Cattle and camels had been driven off; not for months had date caravans arrived in the *fondouk,* and the grain market in the Halle aux Grains stood forlornly empty. Items not stolen or smashed had been thrown down cisterns, including family photo albums. After the previous Axis occupation, French troops had shot Arab looters and left their bodies in the square; now they began rounding up the usual suspects again.

Within hours, the Americans had once more made the town theirs. Chaplains celebrated a mass to honor St. Patrick's holy day. Later in the week, Patton claimed as his headquarters the yellow brick gendarmerie with its blue tile floor. In an abandoned mine shaft, soldiers on patrol discovered ore cars, which they rode down the tracks like a roller coaster, shrieking in merriment. Madame LaZonga and her "daughters" soon returned from Tébessa to reopen the bordello, contributing to venereal disease rates in Tunisia that had reached 34 cases per 1,000 white soldiers and a staggering 451 per 1,000 black soldiers. Patton ordered the brothel off-limits to U.S. units, but French colonial troops offered to rent their helmets and tunics as disguises. The II Corps provost marshal and intelligence chief both reported that when asked by a sentry if he was out of uniform, one patron in a kepi answered, "No, suh, ah sure isn't. I'se a Moroccan."

Patton knew the value of publicity, and he wasted no time wooing the correspondents who trailed him to Gafsa. Charming and voluble, he hosted press dinners featuring Viennese steak and good coffee; each hack received a dessert pack of cigarettes and a roll of Life Savers. A radio report broadcast to the United States just before midnight on March 17 told listeners: "If any American officer ever had the will to win, that man is Lieutenant General George S. Patton. He certainly won the first round today. . . . Apparently the Nazis saw him coming and ran."

But even Patton could hardly persuade himself that this was the campaign of a Stonewall Jackson. "The great and famous battle of Gafsa has been fought and won," he sarcastically informed his diary. To reporters he said, "I'd feel happier if I knew where the Germans were. As long as I know where they are I don't mind how hard they fight." Already frustration had set in. On the evening of March 17 he called Terry Allen and snapped, "You should have kept going until you found somebody to fight."

On the nineteenth, as Montgomery prepared to attack Mareth, Alexander modified his orders to the Americans. Patton was to extend his two-pronged offensive to the east. After seizing Sened Station, Ward's tanks and an infantry regiment were to press on twenty miles to Maknassy, then dispatch raiders to shoot up a Luftwaffe airfield across the Eastern Dorsal at Mezzouna. Farther south, Allen's Big Red One would edge into the hills beyond Gafsa. Darby's 1st Ranger Battalion had already captured El Guettar, a palmy oasis ten miles southeast of Gafsa on Highway 15. Italian troops melted into the rugged djebels along a gravel track dubbed Gumtree Road, which ultimately led a hundred miles to Sfax.

No one who met him ever doubted that Bill Darby was born to command other men in the dark of night. He exuded certainty, one officer said, "that he could lead anyone into combat and bring them back safely." Handsome and good-humored, he often joked that he hailed from an Arkansas family so poor that his father had slopped the children at a hog trough. Except for minor missions at Arzew in November and at Sened in February, his battalion had seen little fighting, and many bored Rangers had transferred to conventional units for fear the war was passing them by. Some had sold their British mountain boots in Algeria to pay for wine or harlots. Now they would regret it, because Terry Allen had a dark-of-night mission for them. After falling back from Gafsa, several thousand Italians had occupied an impregnable defile in the hills east of El Guettar. A frontal assault by the Big Red One down Gumtree Road would cost hundreds of casualties, and American units veering southeast on the paved road to Gabès would also expose a flank to enemy artillery from the same defile. Isn't there some way, Allen had asked Darby, to loop behind them without attacking into the teeth of Italian defenses?

On the evening of March 20, a serpentine column of 500 Rangers and seventy mortarmen veered northeast off Highway 15 three miles outside El Guettar. They had taped their dog tags to prevent clinking and blackened their skin with dirt and spit. Up the scree they tramped, stumbling over unseen obstacles on an unblazed trail. More than a thousand boots scraped the rock with a soft hiss that one soldier likened to "the sighing of the sea."

For ten miles they snaked over the fissured shoulder of Djebel Orbata, a 3,700-foot bluff looming above Gumtree Road. They crossed flumes and saddles; to scale the sandstone cliffs, they clasped wrists to form human chains. Their hands were bloodied, their fatigues shredded. At one A.M., the moon rose. Among those struggling to keep up was a bald, middle-aged socialite named Ralph M. Ingersoll, who had been managing editor of *Fortune* and *The New Yorker,* and then general manager of Time, Inc. Now he was just another footsore engineer lieutenant.

> No one will ever believe how beautiful it was on that march after the moon came out [he wrote]. . . . The deep valleys, the jagged peaks, the play of moonlight and shadow in the gorges, the delicate translucent puffs of clouds that drifted slowly across the edge of the moon as it rose higher and arched across the sky—all these were themes in a symphony in gray and silver tones. . . . Going over the

saddle of a hill, you could see the line of men for several hundred yards ahead, winding down the hillside, figures in soft silver armor.

By first light on the twenty-first, Ingersoll and the mortarmen had fallen behind; the night seemed less enchanting after more sweaty miles lugging the heavy tubes. But the Rangers were where they wanted to be: a thousand yards above Gumtree Road, overlooking the sleeping Centauro encampment. The Italians in the narrow gorge had left their flank unguarded. Some Rangers dozed while awaiting the attack order, and when Darby woke them they "scrambled to their feet . . . rubbing fists in their eyes like sleepy children." He studied the tents and trenchworks below, then announced, "Okay, men, let's have a shoot." The Rangers fixed bayonets and scuttled down the hill. "You wait and see," another soldier murmured, "they won't bring no prisoners back."

The brisk bugle notes of "Charge" echoed along the sierra, now aglow with the ferrous tints of dawn. Morning shadows limned the valley with blue piping. "Give them some steel!" Darby cried. The Rangers clattered forward in a whooping semicircle. Bullets scythed the Italian officers' mess, set for a breakfast no one would eat. Soldiers in their underwear poured from the tents, flushed by grenades. "Nice shooting," Darby called over the radio. "We need a little cold steel over there on the hill mass to the south. . . . They are making a nuisance of themselves up there." Ingersoll arrived in time to hear mortar rounds belch from their tubes. Rangers kneeling behind the rocks reminded him of soldiers in a Civil War print shooting along "a tumbledown stone fence in Virginia instead of Tunisia."

Along the valley's north wall, white flags began to flap. Prisoners *were* taken, and an Italian-speaking Ranger chaplain persuaded more to surrender. Blue smoke draped the valley, thick with "odors of hot guns and dust stirred from the muzzle blasts," one Ranger reported. Dead Italians littered the camp, their waxy faces frozen in surprise. A few German artillery rounds replied, but by noon the fight was over. The delayed arrival of the heavy mortars had allowed some Italians to escape up the road, but many others, in ragged overcoats patched with coarse twine, were captured. Between the Rangers and Allen's troops, now pressing up Gumtree Road, the prisoner haul exceeded a thousand.

Kitchen trucks drove up with a barrel of hot stew, which the men ladled into their canteen cups or helmets. By four P.M., the Rangers were back in their bivouac. Allen's three infantry regiments continued forward along a fifteen-mile crescent southeast of El Guettar before digging in for the night.

"Few Germans in front of II Corps," Patton's intelligence officer, Monk Dickson, reported. "Rommel [sic] probably will attack us with whatever he has left after dealing with Eighth Army. Probably not earlier than 24 March."

In five days, the Americans had covered seventy-five miles, taking Gafsa, El Guettar, and Sened Station, while reclaiming more than 2,000 square miles of territory—at a cost of fifty-seven battle casualties. "It's all going like maneuvers," Terry Allen mused. "It can't be right."

Ted Roosevelt woke on Tuesday, March 23, to the harsh cough of machine-gun fire. Flipping the blanket from his bedroll, he sat up with the creaky deliberation of a fifty-six-year-old man nursing a bum knee, arthritic joints, and a fibrillating heart. He had kept his boots on for the scant warmth they offered. For months he had been miserably cold, "the cold of the desert," he called it. To Eleanor he had written three days earlier: "There's but one thought I keep to me: Aren't we too old to be called on to grapple with the enemy? Should not flaming youth leap into the breach—shouldering us aside—so that we can sit in the sun?"

Leaning on a cane, he stumped up the ridge with his gamecock hobble. He could tell by the high rate of fire that the machine guns were German; their sound now mingled with the answering chatter from American weapons. A sentry barked the password challenge—"Three?"—and was answered with the countersign: "Strikes!" Moonlight coated the landscape in quicksilver, and fog drifted across the desert pan below. But a rosy glow in the east showed that dawn was coming fast. Gun flashes rippled like heat lightning. Roosevelt found the 18th Infantry Regiment's command post on Hill 336—"Wop Hill"—and lowered himself into a chest-deep slit trench.

"The battlefield lay at my feet, a circular plain about seven miles in diameter," he would write Eleanor two days later. "I could see it all." The American line formed a fifteen-mile fishhook. The 1st Division's three regiments—16,000 men—occupied Keddab Ridge from north to south. The 26th Infantry held the north flank near Gumtree Road, on Roosevelt's left. Part of the 16th Infantry and a battalion from the 18th Infantry held the center. A few hundred yards to his right, the ridge petered out in a narrow valley bisected by Highway 15, which ran from El Guettar eight miles in the rear past the American line and on toward Gabès over the horizon. Across the highway to the south, the land lifted again and the American line resumed. Only a few hours earlier, Roosevelt had dispatched two battalions from the 18th Infantry to extend the line onto the lower slopes of 3,000-foot Djebel Berda. On ground so rugged that guns had to be winched into position, the battalions tied in with Darby's Rangers, whose entrenchments swung to the west and provided the long American shank with its barbed hook.

The chink of tools caught Roosevelt's attention. Soldiers were furiously hacking slit trenches out of the rocky ground, regardless of the ants and scorpions infesting the ridgeline. Small white-petaled daisies covered the slope, straining toward the rising sun. The Big Red One had planned to attack this morning, under yet another change of orders from Alexander. Eighth Army's difficulties at Mareth had caused Montgomery to reconsider his contempt for the Americans. Just three days before, he had dismissed the Yanks in his diary as "complete amateurs." Now he needed their help.

Patton was asked to threaten the Axis flank by attacking down Highway 15 toward Gabès. During the night, American artillery had moved forward to provide covering fire for Allen's infantry even as intelligence reports warned that panzers were moving toward II Corps for a possible spoiling attack. From the swelling thunder of guns and the shells now snapping overhead, Roosevelt could guess that the enemy had stolen a march and struck first. Under orders from Kesselring, who recognized that an American thrust down the Gabès highway would trap the First Italian Army at Mareth, Arnim dispatched the strongest of his three armored divisions—the storied 10th Panzer—to counterattack before Patton moved.

A voice carried up Hill 336. "Here they come!" Roosevelt peered into the dust and glare, his weak eyes watering at the strain. The terrain along the Gabès road was brutally open, offering little cover other than tuft grass and a few olive trees. Then suddenly, as if materializing from the dust itself, the panzers appeared: a fleet in rectangular formation bulling up the highway. Hundreds of Wehrmacht infantrymen clattered from trucks behind the tanks, then trotted forward with their rifles at port arms. To one officer the apparition resembled "a huge iron fort moving down the valley."

Sheaves of orange fire leaped from the front edge of the formation. "The enemy tanks numbered in three digits," one sergeant later recalled, "but no one had the heart to count them." Roosevelt had the heart, fibrillating or not: on his right flank, before smoke obscured the enemy echelons, he counted twenty-four panzers breaking toward the gap traced by Highway 15. There were, in fact, more, although the entire 10th Panzer was down to fifty-seven tanks and a comparable number of armored cars and half-tracks. Two other armored prongs veered toward the American left, followed by grenadiers and a flatbed Volkswagen hauling extra ammunition. Bellowing encouragement above the battle din, Roosevelt ordered another tank destroyer battalion forward from Gafsa and then radioed commands to his artillerymen. Waves of gull-winged Stukas attacked the ridge, swooping so low that officers emptied their pistols skyward before diving for cover. "I felt I could reach up my hand and grasp them," Roosevelt later told Eleanor. The panzers churned out banks of white smoke to hide themselves and the grenadiers. Soon even the sun vanished. "The plain," Roosevelt reported, "became a smoky, dusty dream."

On the American left flank, smoke and dust were the least of it. By eight A.M., two U.S. artillery battalions—the 32nd and the 5th—were in mortal peril after being caught in the exposed forward positions they had occupied in anticipation of attacking rather than being attacked. "Many human silhouettes coming over a ridge in front," one platoon leader reported. For reasons uncertain—simple confusion was always possible—the II Corps staff had also ordered the 1st Division to cancel plans for stacking extra ammunition with the guns; true to character, the division mostly ignored the corps order, but shells ran short anyway. Gunners sloshed cans of water to cool their glowing barrels while others struggled from the rear with ninety-six-pound rounds on their shoulders. Darting among shallow folds on the battlefield, German soldiers barked, "*Hitler kommt!* Surrender!" Artillerymen fired a few final point-blank salvos, spiked their guns with grenades, and fought in retreat as riflemen.

Two infantry battalions to the left of Roosevelt's command post also fared poorly. Panzers slammed into the 3rd Battalions of both the 18th and 16th Infantry Regiments, grinding slit trenches beneath their tracks. Both units gave ground and retreated across Keddab Ridge before stiffening at a broad wadi behind the American line; the hand-to-hand fighting was as brutal as that on Longstop Hill three months earlier. One company—K of the 18th—kept the grenadiers at bay with synchronized showers of hand grenades and shouts of "Come on, you Hun bastards!" By late morning, the company had tossed 1,300 grenades and suffered more than sixty casualties. In a small oasis near the wadi, Terry Allen—hair disarranged, necktie long ripped off—summoned reinforcements from Gafsa and supplies from as far away as Tébessa. As the sound of German tank fire drew near, a staff officer proposed moving the division command post. "I will like hell pull out," Allen answered, "and I'll shoot the first bastard who does."

Desperate as the fight was along Keddab Ridge, it was the southern German thrust down Highway 15 that most imperiled the 1st Division.

Not far from Roosevelt's perch, the 601st Tank Destroyer Battalion anchored the segment of American line overlooking the road. Thirty panzers struck so quickly that one company buckled and fell back with heavy losses while another, also mauled, fought until its ammunition racks were empty. German tanks poured into the gap and had nearly broken through to turn the American flank when Company A opened fire at 2,200 yards; the 75mm volley staggered the panzers, which veered south only to mire in boggy ground and a minefield along a dry lake bed. Fire intensified from both the tank destroyers and Allen's artillery. With each hit, the men on the ridgeline roared their approval, none louder than leather-lunged Roosevelt. By midmorning the panzers had seen enough of the gap the Americans now called Death Valley. "They hesitated, turned around, and retreated," Roosevelt reported. "The men around me burst into cheers."

Twenty-four of thirty-six guns from the 601st were lost. Collectively, the battalion had fired nearly 3,000 75mm shells and almost 50,000 machine-gun rounds. The unit commander, to whom Patton had sent word that "I expect him to die if there is an attack," survived to notify Allen that his battalion no longer existed. Lost, too, were seven new M-10 guns from the 899th Tank Destroyer Battalion, which rushed into battle from Gafsa only to be ambushed on the valley floor at ten A.M. ("Gallant but green," Roosevelt commented after watching the sally.) Yet the 10th Panzer had been cut up even worse. American artillery, tank destroyers, and mines knocked out thirty-seven enemy tanks; some were towed away by German salvage teams, but others burned furiously. The enemy retreated eastward to regroup. American soldiers huzzahed themselves hoarse.

The first act was over, but the Germans never settled for simple one-act dramas. Allen and Roosevelt tidied up the line. Wounded men thrashed on their stretchers. More guns hurried forward. Nineteen U.S. jeeps, harried by Stukas and long-range artillery, sped to the rear for more ammunition; thirteen made it back, wallowing like overloaded scows beneath crates of bullets and shells.

With sirens screaming from his motorcycle escort, Patton drove up from Fériana—not before taking time to berate a soldier for being ill-shaven and legging-less, although he had just left the line to fetch more ammunition. Patton had wondered where the Germans were. Now he knew. "I want to fight the champ," he said. "If you lose, you've lost to the champ and it's no disgrace. If you win, you're the new champ."

At three P.M., a British radio intercept team working with II Corps deciphered a transmission from a 10th Panzer reconnaissance unit. Six German battalions would renew the attack at four P.M. At 3:45 another intercepted message warned: "*Angriff bis 1640 verschoben.*" The attack had been postponed until 4:40 to allow German artillery to reposition. Patton deemed the intelligence urgent enough to warn his subordinates in uncoded messages of the imminent assault and then the brief delay. At 4:15 Allen ordered his signalers to broadcast a message over a 10th Panzer radio frequency: "What the hell are you guys waiting for? We have been ready since four P.M. Signed, First Division." Patton, who had arrived at the division's command post, shook his head. "Terry, when are you going to learn to take this damned war seriously?"

Patton's uncoded warnings and Allen's taunt alerted the Germans to their security lapses, and 10th Panzer soon changed its codes. "We couldn't read German mail for quite a long time after that," Allen's intelligence officer later acknowledged. The British were furious at the American indiscretion, but for now the Yanks stood ready. At 4:45 two grenadier battalions, a motorcycle battalion, an artillery battalion, and two panzer battalions with some fifty tanks appeared on the lip of Highway 15, just over two miles from Keddab Ridge. Patton and Allen moved up to join Roosevelt in his slit trench on Hill 336, as if, one officer suggested, watching "an opera from a balcony seat."

This time the panzers hung back, milling in a miasma of brown dust beyond range of the tank destroyers. A. J. Liebling likened the tanks' balky advance to "diffident fat boys coming across the floor at a party to ask for the next dance, stopping at the slightest excuse, going back and then coming on again." The German grenadiers showed no such hesitation: straight for the American line they marched. The crackle of small arms and the deeper boom of heavy guns grew in fury. "The men walked upright, moved slowly, and made no attempt at concealment or maneuver," one battalion commander later reported. "We cut them down at fifteen hundred yards. It was like mowing hay."

American gunners for the first time had experimented with ricochet fire—deliberately skittering their shells across the ground through enemy formations, with devastating results. Now they used a "scissors and search" pattern: some tubes adjusted their fire from longer ranges to shorter, others reversed the pattern. They swept the battlefield with steel as multiple sprinklers water a garden. Darby watched from Djebel Berda in the south as American time-fuze artillery shells—set to burst a few feet above the ground—rained on the enemy formations. "Eerie black smoke of the time shells showed that they were bursting above the heads of the

Germans," he wrote. "There was no running, just a relentless forward lurching of bodies."

The fight descended into something between war and manslaughter. Roosevelt, who had ordered the time-fuze barrage, thought the battle "seemed unreal." Gaps appeared in the grenadier ranks. The faces and uniforms of those still standing turned brown with grit as if the doomed men had already begun returning, earth to earth, dust to dust. Roosevelt later wrote:

> Just in front of me were four hundred men, a German unit. We took them under fire and they went to ground behind some sand dunes. The artillery went after them with time shells, air burst. In no time they were up running to the rear. Black bursts over their head, khaki figures reeling and falling.

Enemy soldiers bunched behind one hill in such numbers that the formation seemed to spread like a shadow. Then Allied artillery found the reverse slope. "The battalion broke from cover and started to run for another wadi in the rear," reported Clift Andrus. "But none ever reached it." At 6:45 P.M. an 18th Infantry observation post reported: "Our artillery crucified them." Shells fell at seven-yard intervals across the retreating shot-torn ranks. "My God," Patton murmured to Roosevelt, "it seems a crime to murder good infantry like that."

Survivors rejoined the panzers to withdraw eastward in the haze and long shadows. How many men the Germans lost remains uncertain, but the 10th Panzer Division, already badly reduced before the battle, was essentially halved again. An Ultra message on March 25 listed twenty-six serviceable tanks in a unit that now was a panzer division in name only. Allen's losses for the week totaled 417, half of them on March 23, and two dozen guns. The American Army had won a signal victory, defeating a veteran German armored division that had terrorized opponents in Poland, France, Russia, and Tunisia. "The first solid, indisputable defeat we inflicted on the German army in the war," Omar Bradley called it. True, El Guettar had been a defensive battle, fought from entrenchments without the brio of the armored sweep Patton so longed to lead. True, too, poor habits persisted—of security, indiscipline, and that annoying tendency to charge into enemy kill sacks. Yet the 1st Division had demonstrated agility—quickly shifting from thrust to parry in the face of the German spoiling attack—as well as fortitude and stunning firepower. "The Hun will soon learn to dislike that outfit," Eisenhower predicted in a congratulatory message.

Ted Roosevelt, who embodied the division's temperament for better and for worse, was awarded the Distinguished Service Cross. "I never expect to see anything like this again, a battle played at my feet," he wrote Eleanor. But he did, fifteen months later, at a place called Utah Beach, where he would win the Medal of Honor for the same cool leadership he had demonstrated on Keddab Ridge.

But the last word goes to a young soldier killed in the final exchanges at El Guettar. His unfinished letter home, found next to his body, began: "Well, folks, we stopped the best they had."

"Search Your Soul"

FORTY miles northeast, a battle of comparable intensity and consequence was brewing as the left tine of Patton's two-pronged offensive sent Axis troops reeling across the Eastern Dorsal.

Orlando Ward's attack had begun well enough, despite a gully-washing flash flood that swept away tents and rifles on a three-foot wall of water. With more than 20,000 troops—the 60th Infantry Regiment had joined Ward's 1st Armored Division—he also commanded 277 tanks, nearly half of them Shermans. Sened Station fell on March 21, soon followed by the nearby hilltop hamlet of Sened, where a garrison of 542 Italians defied a "surrender or be annihilated" ultimatum until the first cannonade provoked a frantic wagging of white flags. At dawn on March 22, scouts discovered that Maknassy, twenty miles east, had been abandoned. Ward's troops began pouring into the town later that morning.

Then he stopped, and in that decision lay deep trouble. Under Alexander's March 19 plan, Ward was to occupy Maknassy and remain there except for launching Operation BUSTER, a battalion-sized tank raid on the German airfield at Mezzouna, fifteen miles east on the road to Sfax. As he drove down Highway 14 into Maknassy that Monday morning, the twenty-second, Ward considered his options. Irrigation had converted the desert here into a vast citrus and olive orchard. Maknassy was a pleasing farm center, with date palms and shuttered shops lining a single paved street 300 yards long. Five miles east of town, the groves ended and the flat terrain rose abruptly to a snaggle-toothed ridgeline several hundred feet high; beyond this modest escarpment lay Mezzouna and the open coastal plain.

A French liaison officer had urged Ward to grab the heights quickly or risk "very serious and costly fighting." But little intelligence was available. Ward did not know that only a few Italian companies held the Highway 14 gap, or that German reinforcements were hurrying forward. With orders anchoring him in Maknassy, he felt little incentive to seize the high ground or risk pointless casualties; only thirty-one Americans had been killed or wounded in getting this far. Just the day before, Patton had urged Ward "to use more drive" and to personally hug the front lines. Although fuming in his diary that "Ward simply dawdled all day" in occupying Maknassy, Patton chose not to go forward himself. Rather, he sent a staff officer, who concurred in Ward's decision to fully assemble his forces before moving on the hills. Ward collected field glasses from staff officers and distributed them among his tank commanders. It was the sort of gesture at which he excelled.

Ward also had other worries. The 60th Infantry, on loan from the 9th Infantry Division, had not distinguished itself. The regiment seemed sluggish, and there had been friction with Ward's tankers. Colonel Frederick J. de Rohan, the regimental commander, was dueling with his executive officer for the unit's loyalty. "The regiment was divided right down the middle," one officer later recalled. Some officers had the gall to sign a petition requesting De Rohan's removal. Moreover, a War Department inspector reported that malaria had plagued the regiment since the landings at Port Lyautey, with 468 cases tallied and insufficient stocks of quinine to treat them.

Then there was the Robinett problem. In the month since Kasserine, Ward's trust in his CCB commander had evaporated. "Robby has let his ambition run away with him and is cutting my throat," Ward wrote his wife in late February. Even Robinett's staff officers considered him disloyal for his habit of disparaging Ward and undermining him with the II Corps staff; one officer pronounced Robinett "a little dictator." Ward lamented the "consummate conceit and selfishness" of a man who had become "a terrible thorn in my side." He seethed, but confrontation was not his way. He also recognized that whatever demons of ambition possessed Robinett, he was among the most tactically competent tank officers in the U.S. Army. "Robinett personification of 'I,'" Ward confided to his diary on March 9. "He is most difficult, but able." Eisenhower, too, had taken notice. In a "Dear Pink" letter to Ward on March 12, the commander-in-chief cited reports that "Robinett was exceedingly difficult to handle. Don't ever be afraid to use the iron inside the glove, if it has to be done." Eisenhower had his own grievance to nurse: Robinett's critique of the Army's deficiencies, written privately to Marshall after the Tébourba debacle in December, had finally reached Algiers. Now the commander-in-chief, too, was seething, perhaps because the criticisms were legitimate even if the out-of-channels tattling was not. In a note to Marshall, Eisenhower called Robinett "a puzzling man." Notwithstanding Robinett's combat record, the best of any frontline commander, he added: "I will never recommend him for promotion until he learns to control his tongue. He seems intelligent but entirely without judgment, except in a tactical sense."

Finally, Ward had his Patton problem. "George Patton is taking over with a vim," Ward had written Eisenhower. "Personally, I am a new man." That enthusiasm was not reciprocated by the new corps commander, who told his diary, a week after replacing Fredendall, that "1st Armored is timid." On March 18, he wrote Bea, ominously, "I may have to relieve a general." Ward's finer qualities—professionalism, penetrating intelligence, decency—impressed Patton not at all. "Ward has not done well," he scribbled after Maknassy fell. "No drive." Patton became increasingly shrill, demanding that Ward "get up off his ass."

In a phone call one evening the corps commander grew incensed when Ward mentioned his good fortune in losing no officers in combat that day. "Goddammit, Ward, that's not fortunate. That's bad for the morale of the enlisted men," Patton snapped. "I want you to get more officers killed."

Ward was dumbfounded. "Are you serious?"

"Yes, goddammit, I'm serious. I want you to put some officers out as observers well up front and keep them there until a couple get killed."

Characteristically, Ward looked for a silver lining. In his diary on March 22 he wrote: "Patton impatient but fair."

Alexander's new orders to II Corps on March 22—the revision that prompted Terry Allen's plan to attack from El Guettar, preempted when 10th Panzer attacked him first—set in train an ordeal no soldier in Old Ironsides could have foreseen. To further threaten the Axis flank, 1st Armored was directed to continue eastward. Having just chosen not to seize the Maknassy heights, Ward received instructions from Patton to capture the hills that very night. Patton made clear that this was the opportunity every true swashbuckler craved: a chance to rampage through the enemy rear with 300 tanks.

At 11:30 P.M., after a thirty-minute bombardment by three dozen guns, two infantry battalions broke cover from the orchards east of Maknassy and scuttled across half a mile of moonlit grassland. By 3:30 on Tuesday morning, one battalion—the 1st of the 6th Armored Infantry—had seized its hilltop objective against feeble opposition. The other battalion—the 3rd of the 60th Infantry—was stopped cold. Mines and machine-gun fire pinned the men to the exposed slopes of Djebel Naemia, an L-shaped ridge overlooking Highway 14 in the throat of the pass. Shortly after sunrise, the battalion commander warned Ward that he faced at least an entrenched enemy battalion.

He was actually facing only eighty German infantrymen—the remnants of Rommel's former *Begleitkompanie*, his personal bodyguard—and a few engineers. With primitive ferocity that dispirited an American force ten times their size, the Germans pelted their attackers with bullets, stones, and a cascade of dislodged boulders. A single 88mm gun was used both to repel the attackers and to dissuade Italians trying to surrender. At noon Ward renewed the attack, this time with tanks. Four Shermans impaled themselves on mines, but American momentum nearly carried the pass until another steel-and-stone counterattack threw the Yanks back.

Having forfeited surprise and audacity at the outset, Ward then compounded his tactical sins: he failed to strike with sufficient strength. This was poor tank country—the broken ground of the hills funneled armor into the vulnerable roadbed, and the rocky terrain made tanks throw their tracks. But Ward had used only two of his six infantry battalions in the initial assault. With every hour, the defenders grew stronger. Now the Americans faced none other than Colonel Rudolf Lang, who had been personally ordered by Arnim to take command on the Maknassy heights. Eager to avenge his failed attack on Béja during OCHSENKOPF, Lang arrived Tuesday morning to find Italian soldiers scampering to the rear. After ordering the 88mm crew to "use all means . . . to prevent even one single additional man or vehicle from moving toward the east," Lang—soaked in sweat, eyes glowing with anticipated glory—loped into the pass to rally a defense that was soon celebrated in Wehrmacht lore as a German Thermopylae.

Eight Tigers helped. *Gefreiter*s cheered as the monstrous tanks lumbered up the highway from Mezzouna. Long-range artillery also arrived, along with nineteen smaller panzers and portions of two grenadier battalions. Soon Lang had 350 German defenders to face a reinforced armored division. As for his timorous allies, he later reported: "Although they were strong in numbers it was no longer possible to depend upon the Italian troops. Those who did not run away as soon as the enemy attacked, surrendered."

A third American attack, at dusk on the twenty-third, failed with heavy losses, including the 3rd Battalion commander, who was shot in the leg. That night German flares drenched the slopes with cold light; at each new starburst a thousand men fell flat as one, moving no more than marble men would move until the magnesium hissed out. Red and orange tracers poked the terrain from every angle like heated needles, and snipers sidled through the shadows. Luftwaffe pilots dropped strings of butterfly bombs, antipersonnel explosives with yellow wings that revolved to arm the detonator. They "floated to earth like colored lanterns strung in a row," one soldier noted. "It was beautiful and uncomfortable."

Ward attacked again at seven o'clock Wednesday morning with eight battalions, including tanks. Enemy pickets let the American scouts close to within twenty yards before cutting them down with grenades that ignited the tuft grass. Some fled the fire, while others tried to smother the flames with field jackets and were shot dead. Leaving his command post three miles west of Maknassy, Ward worked his way under artillery fire to the narrow-gauge rail tracks that snaked along Highway 14 at the base of Djebel Naemia. Men by the hundreds crouched in culverts or ditches, or straggled through the orchards.

He worked the lines, rallying his troops. "Come on! Come on! It's not hurting you!" he cried. "We've got to make that rise in the ground directly to the front." Some followed; most did not. Mortar and machine-gun fire soon drove every man to ground again. Mines stopped an American tank attack on the right flank. A more sweeping envelopment—also on the right, where Ward thought he saw sufficient defilade to shield his Shermans from German antitank fire—failed, too. There was no defilade, only counterattacking panzers. Repeated attacks by four U.S. infantry battalions gained hardly an inch.

Casualties piled up by the score, then by the hundreds. Apathy stole over the battlefield, and no amount of hectoring could budge the men from their burrows. In a captured enemy diary, U.S. intelligence officers found an entry that spoke for both sides:

> Here one can find out what it means to spend a whole day with one's nose in the dust. This is a miserable place; not a tree, not a shrub around; just a little grass, and the rest is sand, stone, and lime. . . . We are grimy from head to foot.

A 1st Armored supply officer observed: "This here is a shootin' gallery, and we is the ducks." Nonplussed, Ward watched the fighting from a sheltered hillock near the highway before returning to his command post early in the afternoon.

Patton had again spent the day with Allen's division, reveling in its repulse of the panzers at El Guettar. Upon returning to his own command post, still in the dank Fériana schoolhouse, he wolfed down his supper and started a letter to Bea. At seven P.M., a staff officer, Lieutenant Colonel Russell F. Akers, brought the latest reports from Maknassy. In forty-eight hours Ward had made no progress. "What's wrong with that goddam 1st Armored Division?" Patton fumed. Akers suggested, somewhat unjustly, that the stalemate reflected Ward's tendency to lurk fifteen miles behind the front lines. Patton picked up a field phone. "Get me General Ward," he snapped, then slammed down the receiver and returned to his letter. The phone rang with Ward on the line.

"Pink, you got that hill yet?" Patton listened for less than ten seconds before interrupting. "I don't want any goddam excuses. I want you to get out there and get that hill. You lead the attack personally. Don't come back 'til you've got it." He again slammed down the receiver.

Before going to bed, Patton wrote in his diary: "Now my conscience hurts me for fear I have ordered him to his death."

Ward stood with the pallid dignity of a man consigned to the gallows. He eased a helmet over the remaining strands of his once-red hair, picked up a carbine, and at eight P.M. headed back toward Djebel Naemia.

He stopped first at the 6th Infantry command post, in a malodorous tent tucked into the trees east of Maknassy. There on a litter he saw Lieutenant Colonel William B. Kern, the regiment's 1st Battalion commander, who had fought so ably from Oran to Kasserine; a machine-gun bullet had destroyed his right eye. Dusted with sulfa powder and sedated with morphine, Kern was bound for a field hospital in the rear. Ward patted his shoulder and pressed on.

More than 2,000 men in three 6th Infantry battalions were to attack shortly after midnight. To catch the enemy off guard, no advance artillery barrage would be fired. Ward moved to the front of the 2nd Battalion, clutching his carbine as the troops stifled their surprise at seeing a major general take the point. At 12:30 on Thursday morning, March 25, the column set off for Djebel Naemia, a hulking black presence to the northeast. Twelve hundred yards from the ridge, the column divided, with one company angling left and two others, led by Ward, skirting the right flank. Rifle fire chattered from the redoubt ahead. Ward paused to harangue a faltering sergeant. "Sergeant, could you go back home and face your mother, sweetheart, and friends, and tell them that you did your duty to your country and your comrades, and look them in the eye? No, you couldn't," Ward said. "The thing for you to do is to move forward." The sergeant moved forward.

But not far. German crossfire sent the battalion scurrying for cover. Ward ran with eight men across the first and then the second of three knolls on Djebel Naemia's south face. His carbine jammed and he tossed it aside. "Damn it, men," he yelled to the cowering figures behind him. "You're not going to let a 51-year-old man run your tongues out? Let's get up that hill." Ward's aide, Captain Ernest C. Hatfield, wondered whether the general was deliberately seeking martyrdom.

The third knoll was too much. "The machine gun fire was terrific and was grazing the ground about twenty inches high while other machine guns were firing about forty inches off the ground," Hatfield later reported. A bullet slammed into the leg of a dispatch runner lying between Ward and Hatfield. A shell fragment clipped the corner of Ward's eye and the bridge of his nose. Blood quickly masked his face, spreading in a crimson bib down the front of his fatigues.

By first light, the attack had stalled. A few men reached Naemia's crest; German mortars drove them off. Ward crawled down the hill at seven A.M. to direct tank fire at German strong points, but an hour later the exhausted battalions pulled back and dug in a thousand yards from the ridge. Wounded soldiers flooded the aid stations. Ward ordered the attack suspended, then rode to Maknassy in an ambulance with a boy who had lost a foot and another who was missing half his face.

Robinett and Omar Bradley were at the division command post when Ward arrived at eleven A.M. His appearance shocked them. Dried blood and sulfa powder caked his face. Scratches and purple bruises covered his legs and hands. A machine-gun bullet had traced a line across the back of his field jacket "as if he had been swiped with a red-hot poker," Robinett observed. While a doctor patched the eye wound, Hatfield brought a cup of tea from the field kitchen. Asked how he felt, Ward replied, "Damned inadequate."

In Fériana later that day, Patton read the latest dispatches from the fighting front before sitting down to scribble another letter home. In his jagged, canted hand he told Bea, "I think I have made a man of Ward."

Two days later, on the twenty-seventh, Patton appeared at the division command post to pin a Silver Star on Ward's chest. The corps commander was "calm, pleasant, and logical," Ward noted in his diary. But in a scathing private meeting before the ceremony, Patton accused Ward of indolence and excessive dependence on his staff. "I have little confidence in Ward or in the 1st Armored Division," Patton wrote in his diary the next day. "Ward lacks force. The division has lost its nerve and is jumpy. I fear that all our troops want to fight without getting killed."

The stalemate east of Maknassy showed no sign of breaking, particularly after Patton shifted some tanks from Old Ironsides to Terry Allen's force in the south. In a message to the division, Ward decried "skulking and straggling. . . . Search your soul," he urged, "and make the enemy pay with his life for threatening the life of our country."

Yet his own days in Tunisia were numbered. By early April, the division's losses since the recapture of Sened Station would reach 304 killed in action, 1,265 wounded, 116 missing, and forty tanks destroyed—with little to show for them but Patton's ingratitude. Although the division would claim 2,000 enemy killed or wounded, and another 960 captured—plus another 2,000 captured by the 1st Armored troops attached to Allen—those figures were certainly inflated. Eisenhower wrote Marshall that Ward "has not been fully able to recover from initial shocks and exhibit the necessary sturdiness of purpose." He lacked "the necessary veneer of callousness."

There was truth in that. Ward had a delicacy ill-suited to a job requiring iron resolve and lead-from-the-front vigor. Even Colonel Lang, watching the Americans from the other side of Djebel Naemia, had been surprised by their timid initial approach to the Maknassy heights; a more forceful attack, he concluded, could have shortened the Tunisian campaign by weeks. In his view, the Americans appeared reluctant to risk heavy casualties in a decisive battle, preferring to crush their foes with material superiority even if that meant extending the fight. There was truth in that assessment too.

A letter from Alexander to Patton on April 1 sealed Ward's fate. "With some diffidence," the army group commander had concluded that "Ward is not the best man to command the American 1st Armored Division." (Alexander was less diffident in a private note to Brooke, pronouncing Ward "quite useless.") Patton immediately asked Eisenhower to recall Ernie Harmon, who had returned to Morocco after his brief duty with II Corps at Kasserine. Averse to direct confrontations with his peers, Patton delegated the hatchet work to Omar Bradley. "Look, Brad, you're a friend of Pink Ward's," he said over breakfast. "Go up there and tell him why I've got to let him go."

A few hours later Bradley arrived at Ward's command post in the Maknassy orchard. He had been a year junior to Ward at West Point and in the same cadet company; he believed the firing unjust. In concocting a plan designed mainly to accommodate Montgomery, then changing it repeatedly, Alexander had hardly demonstrated brilliance. As for Patton, he had provided more snarling criticism than useful tactical advice or infantry reinforcements. Ward had been unlucky, Bradley believed. But luck in war was a general's one indispensable virtue.

In his tent, Ward greeted Bradley with a serene smile, as if expecting the news. Patton had decided to make a change, Bradley said without mentioning Alexander's letter. There would surely be important work for Ward at home or in another theater. Harmon would arrive within a day to take over. Nearly in tears, Bradley shook hands and hurried back to Fériana. Ward said little.

"Bradley gave me order for my relief," he wrote in his diary. "He much upset, more than I." In a handwritten note to the division he announced: "The undersigned hereby relinquishes command of this splendid division to Major General Harmon. I beg you to render unto him the splendid support and loyalty that you have given me."

Harmon would arrive on April 5, strafed en route by Messerschmitts and then by Patton, who, upon being asked whether he wanted Harmon to attack or defend, roared in reply, "What have you come here for, asking me a lot of goddamned stupid questions? Get the hell out of here and get on with what I told you to do, or I'll send you back to Morocco!" Ward waited in Maknassy with his bag and his bedroll. He saluted his successor and said, "The party is all yours, Harmon."

If outwardly gracious, Ward churned inside. He resented the British, Fredendall, Eisenhower, and Patton, whom he considered overrated as a tank commander. Had things gone better in Tunisia, he believed he might have been chief of staff someday. Other indignities would nettle him in coming days. Robinett sent a generous if hypocritical farewell message offering "my deepest gratitude to you for your many tolerances" and admitting, "Frankly, I am tired and need a change of pasture." Eisenhower in Algiers was pleasant even while telling Ward he was "not mean enough." Mark Clark privately tried to prevent Ward from receiving the Distinguished Service Cross for his valor on Djebel Naemia. A board reviewing the case concluded that "the facts do not warrant the award of the DSC"—beyond the less exalted Silver Star already awarded—and, Clark wrote Eisenhower, "I concur in that recommendation." Ward received the DSC anyway.

Ward was a good soldier—his conscience, as he so often said, was clear—and he accepted all slights with equanimity. "My record, I am afraid, has dubbed me stupid and brave," he confided to a friend. "It probably takes a stupid man to get himself into such fixes." By mid-April he would be home in Denver. There was indeed important work for him, first as commander of the Army's tank destroyer and field artillery schools, and then as commander of another armored division, which would seize Munich in April 1945. In the American Army few relieved commanders got a second chance to lead men in combat; Ward was an exception because he was exceptional. But first he had to do penance for his virtues as well as his sins.

"Ward was too sensitive, both to criticism from his immediate superior and to the loss of his friends and subordinates on the battlefield," Eisenhower wrote Marshall. "In all else he seems tops."

Night Closes Down

WITH the Americans unable to reach the enemy's rear through the Maknassy heights, Alexander revised his orders to Patton for a third time. At noon on March 25—as Ward was having his bloody eye doctored and Montgomery prepared to launch his left hook at Mareth—II Corps was told to shift the weight of its attack to the south. The 9th Infantry Division would join Allen's 1st Division in cutting a hole through enemy defenses southeast of El Guettar so that tanks drawn from Ward's 1st Armored could lunge down Highway 15 toward Gabès. The offensive was designed to harass German forces facing Montgomery by again threatening to split the Axis armies and trap the Mareth defenders from behind.

As ordered by Patton, Allen shortly before midnight on the twenty-fifth pulled Darby's Rangers and two battalions of the 18th Infantry Regiment off Djebel Berda on the extreme southern flank of the American line. They were happy to leave: a frenzied German counterattack the previous evening had driven them back 2,000 yards. The Rangers returned to Gafsa to loll in the hot springs and play volleyball; the 18th Infantry looped north to Gumtree Road and now anchored the left flank of Allen's division, which occupied a nine-mile front north of Highway 15. The 9th Division shuffled forward to take the positions south of the highway vacated by Darby and the 18th.

If any gods were watching from their djebel eyries and saw disaster brewing, they declined to intervene on behalf of the mortals in olive drab. Patton's plan, concocted in response to Alexander's hasty change of orders, was badly flawed. German infiltrators now occupied the highest ground on Djebel Berda, including a key promontory designated Hill 772;

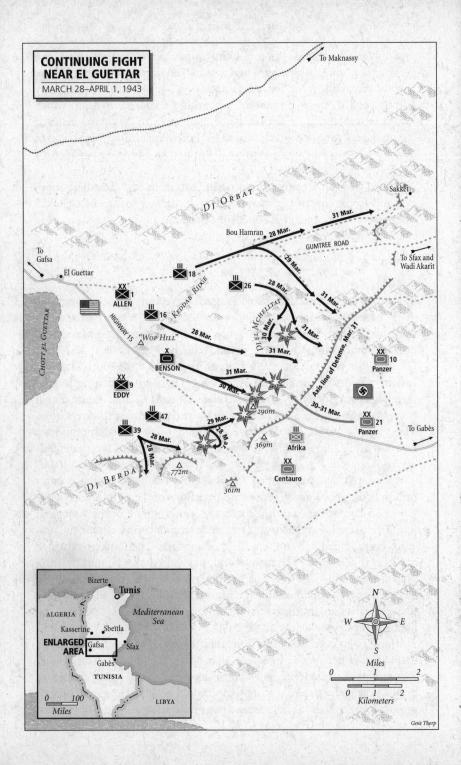

CONTINUING FIGHT NEAR EL GUETTAR

MARCH 28–APRIL 1, 1943

To Maknassy

DJ. ORBAT

Sakket

Bou Hamran

31 Mar.

28 Mar.

29 Mar.

GUMTREE ROAD

To Sfax and Wadi Akarit

To Gafsa

El Guettar

|||18

KEDDAB RIDGE

|||26

28 Mar.

31 Mar.

XX 1 ALLEN

|||16

28 Mar.

"WOP HILL"

DJ. EL MCHELLTAT

30 Mar.

31 Mar.

31 Mar.

Axis line of Defense, Mar. 31

XX 10 Panzer

HIGHWAY 15

X BENSON

31 Mar.

30 Mar.

290m

30–31 Mar.

XX 9 EDDY

|||47

29 Mar.

28 Mar.

369m

|||Afrika

XX 21 Panzer

To Gabès

|||39

28 Mar.

28 Mar.

28 Mar.

772m

361m

XX Centauro

DJ. BERDA

Bizerte

Tunis

ALGERIA

Kasserine

Sbeïtla

Mediterranean Sea

ENLARGED AREA

Gafsa

Sfax

Gabès

TUNISIA

LIBYA

0   100

Miles

N

W   E

S

Miles

0   1   2

0   1   2

Kilometers

Gene Thorp

they could see virtually every American movement. Instead of first securing this pinnacle and the connecting ridges, the Americans chose to skirt
them in a hell-for-leather attack by the two infantry divisions on either
side of Highway 15.

Moreover, the 9th Division was short-handed, ill-informed, and
poorly equipped for the battle ahead. Of the division's three infantry regiments, one—the 60th—had been diverted to Ward's quixotic fight at
Maknassy and another—the 39th—had spent most of the past five
months on guard duty in Algeria. Delays in moving forward postponed
the attack a day, until Sunday, March 28; as always, the Germans used
the extra time wisely. The 9th Division's bespectacled commander,
Major General Manton S. Eddy, whose domed forehead and chin wattles
gave him the mien of a "big galoot who looks like a country school
teacher," was in fact energetic and imaginative; to encourage military
discipline, he had once issued a three-day pass to a private for saluting an
empty staff car. But his troops had neither heavy artillery, nor armored
bulldozers, nor sufficient compasses, nor experience in attacking fortified ramparts.

An intelligence estimate based on reports from departing 1st Division
officers posited that the ground was "but lightly held by the Germans,"
or by Italians who would quail at the sight of American bayonets. That
was wrong. Poor maps, based on 1903 French survey sheets, implied that
the topography ahead was mostly flat. That, too, was wrong. Though
badly reduced in the failed March 23 attack, the 10th Panzer and Italian
Centauro Divisions had regrouped, and now had the benefit of fighting
defensively in a badlands terrain of box canyons and knife-blade ridges.
Particular care was lavished on fortifying Hill 369. A steep massif two
miles south of the highway; it rose 500 feet above the desert, with a
greater presence than its modest height suggested. For a command post,
German engineers excavated five dugouts from the solid rock; each was
ten feet square and roofed with tile and dirt. Machine guns occupied
three forty-foot knolls north of the hill facing the road, while infantrymen infested trenches carved from the talus. Ten 75mm antitank guns
were sited around the hill, backed by three even deadlier 100mm guns
spaced 100 yards apart. After dark, Wehrmacht trucks drove forward
with cans of muscatel for the defenders.

Hill 369 prevented all travel down Highway 15, and it was the 9th Division's objective. Uncoiling from wadis at the base of Djebel Berda, a column of four U.S. battalions marched east at 3:30 A.M. on March 28. A
medical officer described dawn "lighting up the opposite mountain

range in gold and purple and black, with a brilliant blue sky." That was the last pretty thing many of those men saw. At 5:35 A.M. Germans firing pistol flares and machine guns ambushed the 2nd Battalion of the 47th Infantry, which had unwittingly veered south into a hilly labyrinth. Within fifteen minutes Company E alone, on the point, lost 179 men. Surrendering officers tied handkerchefs to their carbine muzzles. Those who continued to fight, died. "The last I saw of him," a lieutenant later reported of one rifleman, "he was laying on the ground holding his intestines in both hands." Troops in field gray rounded up 242 prisoners, including the battalion commander, eight other officers, and Eisenhower's junior aide, who had been sent to the front for seasoning. An American patrol later found only stiffened bodies and a sweet stench rising from the crepuscular wadis. Shaking his fist and pulling on his pipe, the 47th Infantry commander stalked through his command post, muttering, "You sons of bitches. You sons of bitches."

Worse yet, another battalion had also wandered off course and was so thoroughly lost that not a word was heard from it for thirty-six hours. The two remaining battalions in the assault attacked what they presumed was Hill 369 but was in fact Hill 290, a lesser eminence a mile closer to the highway and not shown on the map. The hill held, and German artillery, guided to the centimeter by observers on Djebel Berda, combed the wadis with fire. Men burrowed into any depression they could find, urinating in canteen cups and defecating in helmets. The wounded pleaded for help, mimicked by English-speaking Germans trying to lure medics into the open. One soldier later wrote in his diary: "Just lay in my hole and beat the dirt with my fists."

Alexander visited II Corps and professed satisfaction despite all this. Patton's fury, however, knew no bounds. He gave Eddy a tongue-lashing that stunned the division commander. "In all my career I've never been talked to as Patton talked to me this morning," he told one of his colonels. "I may be relieved of command." Eddy kept his job but was shaken enough to throw good money after bad. He ordered a single battalion, the 2nd of the 39th Infantry, to advance down Highway 15 and take Hill 369 in a dawn assault.

Off they went again, this time in trucks, somehow persuaded that the Germans were weary from a long day of winning and that only Italian stragglers waited to be routed. With a slamming of tailgates and rattling of equipment, the men clambered from the trucks at first light on March 30, only to again mistake unmapped Hill 290 for Hill 369. A single star shell inaugurated the enemy ambuscade, followed by the usual machine-gun hellfire. The battalion broke. Most fled back down the asphalt highway; others not dead or captured hid until darkness let them slip away the next night.

North of Highway 15, things had hardly gone better for Allen's 1st Division. The 18th Infantry advanced several miles down Gumtree Road on the left flank, but otherwise all progress was measured in yards or inches. The wedge of land between Gumtree and the highway was soon stained white with artillery splashes and trussed in endless skeins of Signal Corps wire. The 26th Infantry surgeon's diary for March 29 reported: "Snipers and machine gunners had every wadi covered and our casualties were terrific until everybody decided to hole up until dark. . . . We baked in the hot sun from 11:30 A.M. until dark." Daylight evacuations were fatal, and the wounded bled to death or died of shock waiting for nightfall.

Darkness brought its own misery. "You fight all day here in the desert and what's the end of it?" one GI wrote. "Night just closes down over you and chokes you." A dispatch from the 26th Infantry reduced the battle to four words: "This place is hell." A two-battalion attack by the 16th Infantry, abutting the 9th Division, went nowhere and cost 105 casualties in ten minutes. One officer reported that Allen "fussed and fumed, lit one cigarette after another, [and] was beside himself." Some even said his stutter returned.

Late on March 29, Alexander revised the American attack plan a fourth time: an armored spearhead drawn from the 1st Armored Division was to bull through the enemy defenses down Highway 15. Given Axis fortifications, this scheme had little chance of success, and it is uncertain how much time Alexander had taken to study the ground. His order included precise instructions on how to deploy the American battalions. Patton replied with a huffy message to army group headquarters:

> I feel that I must respectfully call General Alexander's attention to the fact that in the United States Army we tell officers what to do, not how to do it, that to do otherwise suggests lack of confidence in the officer. . . . I feel that for the honor and prestige of the U.S. Army I must protest.

With Patton's protest delivered and his honor redeemed, the attack went forward at noon on March 30 with seven battalions under Colonel Clarence C. Benson, who until that morning had never met several of his subordinate commanders. "From a hundred wadis and ditches tanks began to debouch onto the center of the valley," the correspondent Alan

Moorehead wrote, ". . . as though one was looking at a battle fleet steaming into action over a green, flat sea—a wonderful sight." Whip antennae swayed to the rhythm of the pitching tanks. Dark ranks of infantrymen rose from their holes to trail the Shermans. After a 5,000-yard running start on a half-mile front, Benson's juggernaut ran into a minefield and then blistering fire from German guns in a feral patch the Americans now called the Hot Corner. Puffing on his corncob pipe 300 yards back, Benson soon realized that the enemy had been reinforced, first with Afrika Korps grenadiers and then with the 21st Panzer Division.

"I saw tanks hit by shells burst into flames," correspondent John D'Arcy-Dawson reported. "The turret was thrown back and small figures leaped to the ground, running between falling shells toward jeeps which bounded forward to pick them up." Moorehead added: "Ambulances began to stream back from the other direction. Over everything sounded the same quick staccato coughing of the guns." With five tanks in flames, Benson retreated. Trying to chivvy the enemy from their works, he warned, was "like digging potatoes."

At 12:30 the next afternoon, Benson Force tried again, but made just modest headway before the fuming guns drove them back minus another eight tanks. Grim councils of war followed. "We seem to be stuck everywhere," Patton told his diary on March 31.

The Axis line drew back two miles in the north and a mile in the south, then held fast. A two-battalion attack on Hill 772—belatedly recognized as the battlefield linchpin—failed, with grievous losses. "Nasty grim mountain fighting," Patton told Eisenhower. On April Fool's Day, Alexander ordered another change—his fifth—reinstating the original plan for two infantry divisions to pry open a gap for the tanks. Weary dogfaces continued to gnaw at the djebels but to little profit. The 9th Division log for April 2 acknowledged: "No movement of any importance during the day."

Tens of thousands of mortar and artillery rounds fell on both sides. The 9th Division would expend more than a million rounds of rifle and machine-gun ammunition at El Guettar. The 47th Infantry added another seventy-five stretcher bearers to the regiment's original sixteen; the 39th Infantry added sixty. Even the squeal of ambulance brakes at night drew fire. The dead were stacked like sawed logs in a truckbed and hauled to Gafsa for burial.

In little more than a week of fighting, the 9th Division suffered 1,812 casualties—more than 10 percent of the division. Five of six battalion commanders were lost. Casualties in the 47th Infantry alone totaled 868, more than a quarter of the regiment. Eddy later considered El Guettar the division's toughest battle of World War II, not to be eclipsed by combat in Sicily and Normandy. The 1st Division's losses approached 1,300. Stanhope Mason, the Big Red One's operations officer and eventual chief of staff, also deemed El Guettar the "most severe battle of the three years of warfare," a remarkable assessment for a division whose destiny led to such killing fields as Sicily, Normandy, and Aachen.

The stuck-everywhere period lasted a week. Nearly every man now felt the deep weariness that Ernie Pyle called "cell-by-cell exhaustion." II Corps had done what was asked, luring two panzer divisions and more away from Eighth Army's front. Montgomery had broken through at Mareth, captured Gabès, and now besieged the enemy at Wadi Akarit on the coast, due east of the Americans. But that was cold comfort. As hopes faded for a breakthrough to the sea, a peevish frustration took hold— "everybody ordering everybody else," as one major put it. Ted Roosevelt wrote Eleanor: "We let the opportunity get away."

Patton took it badly. His choler turned to rage on Thursday morning, April 1, when his favorite aide, Captain Richard N. Jenson, died in an air raid while visiting Benson's command post, four miles east of El Guettar. Eight Stukas attacked out of the sun, killing three men, wounding Brigadier Dunphie—the British hero of Thala—and just missing Bradley with a bomb that detonated fifteen feet from his slit trench. The concussion killed Jenson instantly. "Every bone in his body was broken and the skin wasn't scratched," one officer reported.

Patton stood on the portico of the Gafsa gendarmerie as Jenson's body arrived in the rear seat of a jeep. He drove immediately to the town cemetery, where twenty other dead boys lay wrapped in mattress covers awaiting burial. New crosses and Stars of David were stacked in a nearby tent. Tears coursing down his cheeks, Patton uncovered Jenson's face, kissed him on the forehead, and snipped a lock of hair, which he saved for the dead man's mother. After kneeling to pray, Patton rose and without a word drove back to his office.

"Forward troops have been continuously bombed all morning," he wrote an hour later in a scathing report to the Allied high command. "Total lack of air cover for our units has allowed German air force to operate almost at will."

At 10:45 P.M. Thursday, the New Zealander who commanded the Allied tactical air forces, Air Vice Marshal Arthur Coningham, replied in a message so widely distributed that even the Pentagon historian's office received a copy. Patton's complaint was "inaccurate and exaggerated," a "false cry of wolf," the waspish Coningham wrote. Noting that 353 Allied fighters had flown on April 1—more than two-thirds of them over II Corps—he added that Patton's message "was first assumed to be seasonal 1st April joke. . . . It can only be assumed that 2nd Corps personnel concerned are not battleworthy in terms of present operations."

Coningham's condescension and conclusions were offensive; his facts, however, were fundamentally sound. By no longer attempting to provide a permanent air umbrella over Allied troops, British and American squadrons could now concentrate on Axis airfields, shipping, and other rear-echelon targets, where the havoc they wrought was vast but mostly invisible to the ground forces. The number of Luftwaffe sorties had peaked at 370 on February 24, dwindling since then to fewer than seventy-five a day. The slow, vulnerable Stuka was nearly extinct and was making its final battlefield appearances.

None of that mattered to Patton, whose convulsive fury at the insult tripped alarm bells in Algiers. At Eisenhower's insistence, Coningham issued a twenty-seven-word retraction, notifying all the original recipients that his message was "to be withdrawn and cancelled." At noon on April 3, the two most senior Allied airmen in North Africa, Air Marshal Sir Arthur W. Tedder and Lieutenant General Carl Spaatz, arrived in Gafsa on an appeasement mission. Patton had just finished pounding the desk in outrage when three Focke-Wulf fighters roared over Gafsa at 200 feet, spitting bright yellow needles from their wings. After strafing the streets, the planes returned for a final bombing run, during which a melon-sized fragment blew through the conference room where the generals were now sprawled on the floor. Plaster tumbled from the walls as Patton dashed outside to empty his revolvers at the fleeing bandits. Dusting himself off, Tedder asked how such a flamboyant demonstration had been arranged. "I'll be damned if I know," Patton replied, "but if I could find the sonsabitches who flew those planes, I'd mail each one of them a medal."

Coningham arrived the next day on his own peace sortie. The helmeted Patton sat behind his desk, stern as a hanging judge. Voices were raised, fists thumped. "Pardon my shouting," Patton shouted, "but I too have pride and will not stand for having Americans called cowards. . . . If I had said half what you said, I would now be a colonel and on my way home."

Coningham subsequently issued an effusive apology. Patton responded with a gallant message, telling the New Zealander, "To me you exemplify in their most perfect form all the characteristics of the fighting gentle-man." Still he stewed. Singling out two particularly irritating British units, he told his diary, "I hope the Boches beat the complete life out of the 128th Brigade and 6th Armored Division. I am fed up with being treated like a moron by the British. . . . Ike must go."

How intense his animus had become that he could, however fleet-ingly, wish in a single breath for the destruction of his closest allies and the downfall of his closest friend.

If choler infected the American camp, so did an even deeper and darker emotion. Ernie Pyle now noticed in the troops "the casual and workshop manner in which they talked about killing. They had made the psychological transition from their normal belief that taking human life was sinful, over to a new professional outlook where killing was a craft." The American combat soldier had finally learned to hate.

> His blood was up. He was fighting for his life, and killing then
> for him was as much a profession as writing was for me. He wanted
> to kill individually or in vast numbers. . . . The front-line soldier
> wanted [the war] to be terminated by the physical process of his
> destroying enough Germans to end it. He was truly at war. The rest
> of us, no matter how hard we worked, were not.

What Rommel called *Krieg ohne Hass,* war without hate, had prevailed in the desert for more than two years. If more myth than battlefield reality—no armies bent on mutual annihilation can avoid malice—a perverse chivalry *had* obtained, producing "a clean, straight, dispassion-ate war with no Gestapo, no politics, no persecuted civilians, no ruined homes," as one correspondent romanticized it. The British in 1942 even felt obliged to institute hate training by stressing enemy brutality and spattering slaughterhouse blood around assault training courses.

The Americans were less imaginative but just as ineffective. Various exhortations had touted the virtue of antipathy. "You are going to get killing mad eventually—why not now?" Lieutenant General Lesley J. McNair, chief of Army ground forces, had urged in a national radio address in November. A training memorandum from AFHQ in Algiers urged commanders to "teach their men to hate the enemy—to want to kill by any means." Patton told his corps in mid-March, "We must be eager to kill."

But the infliction of nearly 6,000 casualties in three weeks—including

845 dead—did what no speechifying could do. "Perhaps these American troops will suddenly get their blood up and find their feet," Alexander wrote Brooke on April 3. "I say 'perhaps' because, unlike us, they are a mercurial people and are either up or down."

The blood *was* up in these mercurial people. They were further inflamed by wide-eyed atrocity tales of Germans bayoneting prisoners. At El Guettar "we really learned to hate," a sergeant in the 26th Infantry later wrote. "The hatred for the Krauts carried through to the rest of the Tunisian campaign, Sicily, France, Belgium, through Germany, into the Harz mountains, and Czechoslovakia." An officer in the 6th Infantry concluded, "A soldier is not effective until he has learned to hate. When he lives for one thing, to kill the enemy, he becomes of value."

"They lost too many friends," Pyle observed with his usual penetrating simplicity. "Soon it was killing that animated them."

A very thin membrane separates the sanctioned rancor of war from sheer barbarism, and in North Africa shooting at Arabs became a sport in some units. Troops convinced themselves that the natives were either in cahoots with the enemy or subhuman; they were called wogs—the slang came from the British, who rated Tunisian Arabs a "serious menace"—and they lived in "woggeries."

"We became ruthless with the Arab," a 1st Division soldier wrote. "If we found them where they were not to be, they were open game, much as rabbits in the States during hunting season." Another soldier explained: "Here Arabs live all over. Some we shoot on sight, some we search, and some we make a deal with to buy eggs and chickens." Soldiers boasted of using natives for marksmanship practice, daring one another to shoot an Arab coming over a hill like a target in an arcade. Others fired at camels to see the riders bucked off, or shot at the feet of Arab children "to watch them dance in fear," as one 34th Division soldier recounted.

At a training camp in Algeria, sentries were told they could fire on anyone "dressed in white and not promptly responding to the password." Natives suspected of espionage or sabotage were usually turned over to the French for summary justice, but not always. "We made them dig their graves," one 1st Division soldier reported. "We lined them up and shot them." British commandos near Green Hill in the north burned woggeries whose inhabitants were suspected of aiding the Germans. "It is not pleasant to stand round blazing huts while women and children scream outside," one witness acknowledged.

After Kasserine, during a move from Sbiba toward Fondouk, "I saw men from another outfit shoot Arabs just to watch them jump and fall," Edward Boehm later recounted. Boehm was a lieutenant from Montana, with Battery C of the 185th Field Artillery. "I could hear them yell and laugh each time and there was nothing I could do about it. . . . I saw them do it, like you're shooting gophers. I could hear them: 'Wow, I got one!' Those guys were murderers."

Such atrocities were committed by a very small percentage of American troops, but provost marshal and judge advocate files reflected a disturbing indiscipline. When a truck convoy bound for II Corps with replacement troops stopped for lunch in Affreville, Algeria, some soldiers got drunk on local wine and started firing at Arabs along Highway 4. One private shot dead a man on his donkey, wounded a second, and then killed another before boasting that he "got three out of five Arabs." Given a dishonorable discharge, he was sentenced to twenty years at hard labor.

But other crimes went unavenged. On March 31, Giraud sent Eisenhower a letter citing incidents "in which U.S. and British troops have molested, assaulted, and killed natives." Several weeks later, a secret AFHQ memorandum reported that Giraud's chief of staff "again called our attention to a situation which has come up repeatedly in the past month. This is the continuing cases of rape in the forward areas . . . against Arab women." Another internal AFHQ memo regarding "crimes committed by American troops in the forward areas" reported that an additional military police battalion had been dispatched to keep order.

Some of the most appalling incidents involved depredations in the northern Algerian village of Le Tarf, seven miles from the Tunisian border. In mid-April, drunken troops from an American engineering company reportedly terrorized Le Tarf for two days. Witness statements in a French investigative document sent to AFHQ recounted gang rapes of six Arab women, all of them named, including a thirty-year-old suffering from typhus, a forty-five-year-old widow, a fifty-year-old, and a fifty-five-year-old and her daughter-in-law. A fifteen-year-old and a forty-year-old widowed mother reported escaping after a chase by predatory soldiers. Several Arab men alleged being beaten with rifle butts and fists.

"The people of the district, European as well as native, are now living in fear of the daily occurrences caused by the troops," a local official wrote. A French investigator reported visiting the American company, which had bivouacked two miles up the road; he was assured that the unit in question was not involved. If American authorities examined the French allegations—and AFHQ files indicate that at least a preliminary investigation was launched—their findings have vanished. During World War II, 140 U.S. soldiers were executed for murder and rape, but if justice was meted out for the ravaging of Le Tarf, the records remain silent.

"I Had a Plan . . . Now I Have None"

T ED Roosevelt was among the first to sense the enemy's withdrawal.
"It has a soft feel up and down the front this morning," he wrote on
Tuesday, April 6. At Wadi Akarit, fifty miles east of the 1st and 9th Division front, Eighth Army had attacked the new Axis line with a tank
advantage of 462 to 25. The "apocalyptic hurricane of steel and fire," as
General Messe described the British assault, took more than 5,000 Italian
prisoners, so many as to constitute a nuisance; they were used as foot-
stools by Tommies scrambling out of the antitank ditches. Messe told
Arnim he could hold until Wednesday night, but only by flinging "the
last man into the furnace." Instead, most of the surviving troops—
including nearly every German—slipped away to the north after dark on
Tuesday, while those facing the Americans also fell back before their
escape route was severed. *Non è stata una bella battaglia,* Messe
lamented: this was not a good battle.

It was not especially good for the British, either. Eighth Army suffered
600 dead and 2,000 wounded, yet still failed to annihilate the enemy or
prevent his flight. On Tuesday night, Alexander issued his sixth and final
change of orders to the Americans: II Corps was to attack in the morning
without regard to armor losses, in a last attempt to ram the Axis flank.
On a paper scrap torn from a notebook, Patton scratched a message in
his runic cursive for Colonel Benson: "Attack and destroy the enemy; act
aggressively. GSP, Jr."

They swung at air. As the enemy melted away, Hill 772 and Djebel
Berda finally fell. So did Hill 369, after a ferocious U.S. artillery bombardment. Soon the desert along Highway 15 was covered with "American tanks, half-tracks, mobile guns, jeeps, [and] trucks, surging eastward
in line abreast like a Spanish fleet, with pennants and flags flying." A
thousand prisoners were seized, bringing the total captured by II Corps
at El Guettar to 4,700. But only one in ten was German, and the bulk of
the enemy army was only a dusty pall on the northeast horizon. In his
diary Patton wrote: "*Sic Transit Gloria Mundi.*"

The Maknassy heights also fell, finally, and American pursuers had a
bit more luck near Mezzouna and along Gumtree Road. Colonel Lang
got away, but a half-dozen U.S. tanks raked a German rearguard convoy, and marauding Allied fighter-bombers tormented the retreating
columns. Among those caught in the open was the 10th Panzer Division
operations officer, Colonel Claus von Stauffenberg, a tall, brilliant aris-
tocrat who during duty in the Soviet Union was so alienated by German
barbarism that after arriving in Africa in February he had quietly begun

agitating for a military coup to oust Hitler. On Wednesday afternoon, fighters strafed Count Stauffenberg's staff car with 20mm cannon fire. Gravely wounded, he was rushed to a field hospital in Sfax, where his right hand was amputated at the wrist and tossed into the garbage still wearing a ring; surgeons also removed his left eye and took two shattered fingers from his left hand. Evacuated to Italy, Stauffenberg was placed on a hospital train bound for Munich. His long recuperation gave him time to concoct the bomb plot that nearly killed Hitler on July 20, 1944.

Within an hour or two of Stauffenberg's wounding, American scouts and British Eighth Army troops spied one another across the desert for the first time. "Hello, Limeys!" the Yanks shouted, notwithstanding that the troops so hallooed were Indian. No matter: the army of the west and the army of the east had joined, despite a five-month Axis campaign to keep them apart. As other British and American troops met, they seemed unlikely kinsmen. Two weeks at El Guettar had reduced the Americans' uniforms to tatters and the men wearing them to scarecrows. Two years in Africa had made the bleached and bronzed British resemble "Ay-rabs in jeeps," as the Yanks called them, garbed in a heterogeneous array of khaki shorts, short-sleeve blouses or bare backs, and headgear that ranged from berets to burnooses.

That first meeting produced handshakes and broad grins but few memorable utterances. "This is certainly a pleasant surprise," a British sergeant said amiably. To which Private Perry Searcy of Kentucky replied, "Well, it's good to see somebody besides a Nazi."

The cousins were together, and no enemy would sunder them again.

Eisenhower was jubilant. "We are at last operating on a single battle line and have placed the enemy in a position that, to say the least, is highly embarrassing for him," he wrote to his son, John. "I have been aiming for this for a long time and, frankly, I must say that I experience a definite feeling of happiness and delight."

Success in Tunisia reinforced Eisenhower's conviction in the righteousness of the Allied cause, a theme he articulated most ardently to his closest correspondents with robust, primitive patriotism. "My single passion is to do my full duty in helping to smash the disciples of Hitler," he told John. Although his men fought—as all men at arms fight—primarily for one another, Eisenhower saw other, "priceless things for which we are fighting."

It seems to me [he wrote in early April] that in no other war in history has the issue been so distinctly drawn between the forces of

arbitrary oppression on the one side and, on the other, those con-
ceptions of individual liberty, freedom, and dignity, under which
we have been raised in our great Democracy. . . . I do have the feeling of a crusader in this war.

He was just as fervent in championing Allied unity, which he considered the keystone of imminent victory in Tunisia and the eventual larger
victory beyond. "We are establishing a pattern for complete unity in Allied
effort—ground, air, navy—that will stand the Allied nations in good stead
throughout the remainder of this war," he wrote to General A. D. Surles at
the War Department. Again and again he reiterated "my policy of refusing
to permit any criticism couched along nationalistic lines."

Enforcing this policy was not easy. Proximity to the British had only
deepened the latent Anglophobia of many American generals—Patton,
Clark, and Bradley among them. If the British were more circumspect in
their disdain, the Yanks suspected with good cause that they were being
patronized. "The only way in which we can get things really tidied up,"
Air Marshal Tedder wrote on March 26, "is by showing the Americans
the right way to do things and letting them see where they are wrong."
Alexander concurred, telling Montgomery three days later: "I have taken
infinite trouble with them—and mind you one has to deal very carefully
with them because they are not one of us. . . . I have grave doubts that
these soldiers are really doing their duty as we understand it."

Even Eisenhower had to swallow hard. On March 30 he flew to the
Eighth Army command post south of Gabès to confer with Montgomery.
Both men followed their public display of conviviality with private binges
of character assassination. "His high-pitched accent and loud talking
would drive me mad," Montgomery complained to Alexander. "I should
say he was good probably on the political line; but he obviously knows
nothing whatever about fighting." For his part, Eisenhower warned Marshall that Montgomery "will never willingly make a single move until he is
absolutely certain of success." The hostility—and it had just begun—was
aggravated by Montgomery's juvenile demand that he be sent an American B-17 Flying Fortress for his personal use: he had occupied Sfax ahead
of schedule and thus won a gentleman's wager with Beetle Smith. "Montgomery to Eisenhower. Entered Sfax 0830 this morning. Please send
Fortress," he cabled on April 10. The plane was sent (it would crash three
months later), but the commander-in-chief seethed. "Goddam it, I can
deal with anybody except that son of a bitch," he complained. Montgomery was "a thorn in my side, a thorn in my side."

As if to compensate for such forbidden sentiments, Eisenhower proselytized like a man possessed by the true faith. "Every subordinate throughout the hierarchy of command will execute the orders he receives without even pausing to consider whether that order emanated from a British or American source," he decreed. In a conference with Alexander and Patton, he confided that he did not think of himself "as an American but as an ally." Patton told his diary, "Ike is more British than the British."

Yet in his ecumenical zeal, Eisenhower neglected the role his country-men were to play in the last act of the Tunisian drama. II Corps officers had long speculated that the British intended to have Anderson's First Army capture Bizerte and Montgomery's Eighth Army capture Tunis. Those suspicions were confirmed when Alexander's staff unveiled a plan for the endgame that excluded II Corps except for the 9th Division, on the assumption that it would be too hard to supply British and American forces simultaneously around the shrinking Axis bridgehead. "Both Pat-ton and I were speechless with rage," Bradley later wrote. "But since we were under strict orders from Ike to do what Alexander told us to do, we raised no objections."

Incapable of holding his tongue for long, Patton sent Bradley to Algiers in late March for a private talk with his old West Point classmate. Eisenhower seemed unaware of the British plan and, in Bradley's view, not terribly interested. Bradley offered several arguments: that leaving three experienced American divisions on the sidelines was tactically fool-ish; that seconding the 9th Division meant returning to the bad habit of mixing national units; that the United States and its army had earned the right to be in on the kill.

"This war's going to last a long time, Ike. There'll be a lot more Amer-icans in it before we're through," Bradley added. "Until you give us the chance to show what we can do in a sector of our own, with an objective of our own, under our own command, you'll never know how good or bad we really are."

Eisenhower nodded and studied the wall map in his St. Georges office. That afternoon he cabled Alexander, urging "a real effort to use the II U.S. Corps right up to the bitter end of the campaign." Over the next two weeks a new plan evolved in which part of the American force—but not the 1st Division, and only half of 1st Armored—would capture Bizerte. Demonstrating his skills as a staff courtier, Eisenhower deftly took credit for the revision. Alexander's original plan "seemed to me a bit on the slow, methodical side," he wrote Marshall, "and, in addition, appeared to contemplate the eventual pinching out of the U.S. II Corps. . . . Alexander sees eye to eye with me."

To Patton on April 5, Eisenhower wrote: "General Alexander has told me that your corps is *not* to be pinched out of the coming campaign."

Well laid though the plans were, they would not survive contact with the enemy. The greatest threat yet to Eisenhower's vision of Allied comity had begun to unfold in a dusty village called Fondouk.

One final chance remained to intercept the fugitive remnant of General Messe's army before it reached the sanctuary of the Tunis defenses.

Midway between El Guettar and Tunis, the Marguellil River threaded a narrow pass through the Eastern Dorsal where Fondouk—a few adobe hovels and a mosque—straddled Highway 3 as it sliced toward Kairouan twenty miles to the northeast. Less than a thousand yards wide, the defile was bracketed on the north by a stony pinnacle named Djebel Rhorab and on the south by an equally stony escarpment named Djebel Haouareb. The shallow river wandered in muddy braids through the pass within the steep-banked wadi it had worn. Prickly pear and drooping olives dappled the 300-foot hills; so, in the splendor of a North African April, did marigolds, and crimson poppies like blood pooling on the rocks.

Germans infested these slopes, and had for months. They had blasted gun positions from the shale and built bivouac dens in the cliffs, appointed with stoves, beds, and occasional crucifixes. Gunners registered their artillery on the open approaches from the west and calibrated their mortars on all the dead spaces below the ridges. Fields of fire were nearly perfect. The defenders included two battalions of the 999th Africa Division, whose ranks were filled with court-martialed soldiers considered "suitable for rehabilitation" by fire. Many were convicted black marketeers, demoted officers, or *Schwarzschlächter,* "black butchers," who had illegally slaughtered livestock for food. Forbidden to wear national emblems, they sported no breast or cap eagles, no cockades or collar patches, no belt buckle insignia of *"Gott Mit Uns."* Discounting the formidable rehabilitative powers of German sergeants, British intelligence considered the units inferior.

This was a mistake, as American troops could attest. One halfhearted effort had already been made in late March to force Fondouk Pass. In harmony with the II Corps demonstrations at Maknassy and El Guettar, which were intended to siphon Axis forces from Montgomery's front, Patton on March 25 had ordered the 34th Infantry Division to "go out in that area and make a lot of noise, but don't try to capture anything." The division's three infantry regiments—the 168th, 133rd, and 135th—had

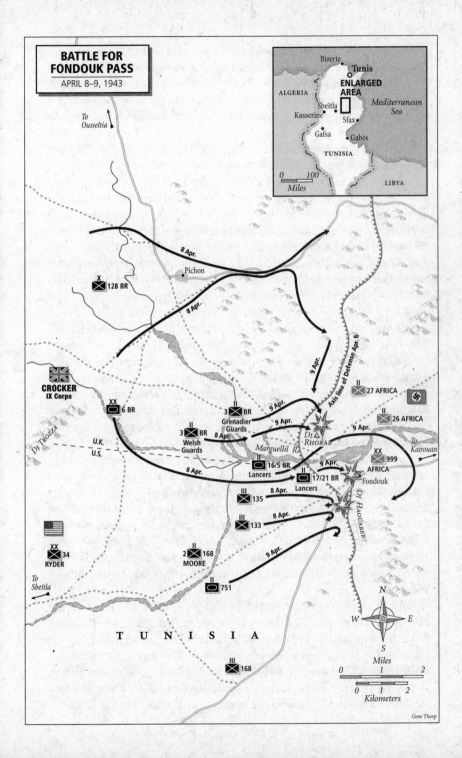

BATTLE FOR FONDOUK PASS
APRIL 8–9, 1943

ENLARGED AREA

Bizerte · Tunis ✪
ALGERIA
Sbeïtla · Sfax ·
Kasserine · · Sfax
Gafsa · · Gabès
TUNISIA
LIBYA
Mediterranean Sea

0 — 100
Miles

To Ousseltia

8 Apr.
Pichon
8 Apr.

X 128 BR

CROCKER
IX Corps

XX 6 BR

Dj. Trozza

U.K. / U.S.

9 Apr.

3 BR

3 BR
Welsh Guards

Grenadier Guards
8 Apr.
9 Apr.

Marguellil R.

8 Apr.
16/5 BR Lancers

9 Apr.
17/21 BR Lancers

Axis line of Defense Apr. 8

27 AFRICA

26 AFRICA

9 Apr.

Dj. Rhorab

XX 999 AFRICA

To Kairouan

Fondouk

Dj. Haouareb

135
8 Apr.

133
8 Apr.

XX 34 RYDER

2 168 MOORE

751
9 Apr.

168

T U N I S I A

To Sbeïtla

N
W · E
S

Miles
0 — 1 — 2

Kilometers
0 — 1 — 2

Gene Thorp

finally been reunited, and a homebody strain of Iowa and Minnesota still ran through them. But rough handling at Kasserine left residual scars both physical and psychic. In a March 11 message to his officers, Major General Ryder, the tall Kansan who commanded the 34th, decried "this military creeping paralysis present in our division" and the want of "offensive spirit."

The first foray at Fondouk had proved Ryder's point. Moving forward on a night so impenetrable—"dark as a stack of black cats," one soldier said—that a guide with a lit cigarette walked ten feet in front of each vehicle, the division attacked with four battalions on a 3,000-yard front at six A.M. on March 27. By midafternoon, after struggling uphill beneath the frowning guns, the assault stalled 500 yards short of Djebel Haouareb. German machine guns roared through the next night, spitting lime-green tracers so thick that soldiers claimed to have read a newspaper by the light. A renewed attack on the morning of the twenty-eighth collapsed, as did various infantry maneuvers over the next three days. At the 15th Evacuation Hospital near Sbeïtla, every square inch of the admissions tent, four ward tents, both surgical tents, and the evacuation tent was covered with bleeding boys from Fondouk, and nurses turned away more ambulances. As Patton had requested, the division made a lot of noise and captured nothing, at a cost of 527 casualties. Most losses fell on the star-crossed 168th Infantry, just replenished after the Sidi bou Zid debacle. Now its ranks needed filling again.

Belatedly, Alexander realized that only a much bigger force could crack the Fondouk gap. Caution and conventionality—jabs, short hooks, and frontal assaults—had characterized the six weeks of his generalship in Tunisia. Nearly 90,000 Americans had been used to peck at the Eastern Dorsal in three different spots, while a comparable force in Anderson's First Army had mostly sat on its haunches for the past month. Just as Colonel Lang had concluded that a more forceful American attack at Maknassy heights would have unhinged the defenders there, so senior Axis commanders came to believe that the African campaign could have ended a month sooner had Alexander struck a quicker, bolder blow at Fondouk.

Now he tried to make amends. The 34th Division would join with the British IX Corps and French troops, more than tripling the Fondouk force. Infantrymen would prise open the gap along the Marguellil River, allowing the British 6th Armoured Division to sweep onto the coastal plain toward Kairouan. Messe's army, fleeing Montgomery and Patton in the south, was to be intercepted and destroyed before it merged with Arnim's Fifth Panzer Army in the north.

At eleven A.M. on Tuesday, April 6, trailing a banner of dust, Lieu-tenant General John Crocker arrived at Ryder's camouflaged tent in an orchard nine miles southeast of Fondouk. The British corps commander had arrived in Africa a few weeks earlier with a reputation that had grown steadily since his capable command of a tank brigade in France in 1940. Direct and sane, Crocker nevertheless harbored prejudices against the Americans. Some were trivial: he was credited with a caustic bon mot—"How green is our ally"—and he disliked the common Yank habits of eating only with a fork and smoking at table. More important, he con-sidered U.S. forces so weighted with equipment that it "handicapped their strategic mobility." American officers tended to be "very ignorant and the staff had little idea of how to operate forces." Americans also seemed given to fantasy, retrospectively elevating the Kasserine debacle into a victory. To his wife a few weeks earlier, Crocker had written that in dealing with Americans "it is necessary to watch your step and wrap any-thing that one has to say which is the least critical or which savours of advice in the most tactful language." They were "a queer lot with many nice ones. . . . So far as soldiering is concerned, believe me, the British have nothing at all to learn from them."

It was regrettable that Crocker thought so, because his plan for Fon-douk was flawed. Earlier in the week, he had proposed seizing Djebel Rhorab in the north with the British 128th Infantry Brigade, while Ryder's men attacked in the south toward Djebel Haouareb, scene of their recent repulse. Now, however, fifteen officers in Ryder's stuffy tent huddled around a large map mounted on plywood—colored paper squares represented the various battalions—to find that Crocker had amended the scheme in hopes of accelerating the armored push toward Kairouan. Djebel Rhorab was only weakly held, Crocker asserted, so British infantrymen would initially swing farther north, "denying" the hill to the enemy but not actually occupying it until the American attack was well under way. American artillery could blanket the hill with smoke shells, but not with high explosives lest they hit the arriving British troops.

Ryder was stunned. Just a week earlier, his division had been blistered with fire from Rhorab, which jutted to within 500 yards of Crocker's proposed avenue for the American attack. Surely the Germans had since reinforced an already formidable position. "I had a plan based on our conference of a few days ago," Ryder replied evenly, "but now I have none." He pointed out the vulnerability of his troops, which would face galling fire from both north and east. Crocker waved away these objec-tions. Speed and maneuver would overwhelm the thin defenses. Ryder stared at Crocker with pursed lips, then shrugged. Eisenhower's orders seemed clear enough: subordinates were to salute and carry on, disregarding nationality.

Now another officer spoke up, *en français*. General Louis-Marie Koeltz, commander of the French XIX Corps, knew this ground from personal heartache. The Germans had routed his troops here in January to capture the high ground they now occupied. In his sky-blue uniform and gold-spackled red kepi, Koeltz pointed out that the American approaches were "entirely flat and completely exposed except for a row of cacti." His own reconnaissance showed that a frontal attack would fail. Blue eyes flashing, tidy mustache twitching in his ruddy face, Koeltz added, "We could take out Djebel Rhorab from the north, because in this region the infantry could be supported by tanks." The rolling terrain and dense olive groves there would offer attackers more cover than the naked ground approaching Djebel Haouareb.

Crocker listened politely, then reaffirmed his plan. "My intervention had no effect," Koeltz later said. "Having to express myself in French, I may not have been well understood."

It went badly, of course. Fatalism settled over the 34th Division, which collectively bought $26 million in life insurance that spring, mostly on the eve of the Fondouk offensive. Chaplains stayed busy hearing confessions or ministering to the doubtful. A head count at church services one Sunday in April tallied almost 7,000 worshippers, nearly half the division. In a handwritten note, Alexander told Eisenhower that troops in the 34th Division "seem reasonably confident about tomorrow's operation, and I do hope it will go well." To Brooke, however, he pronounced them "soft, green, and quite untrained. . . . Is it surprising then that they lack the will to fight?"

As the 135th Infantry commander later conceded, no officer in the division favored this attack, "but no one was saying so to the others." British planning was derided as "brittle and axiomatic . . . inflexible." Ryder had been wary of the British since the invasion of Algiers and now, unjustly, he believed that they "wished to win the war with American troops and matériel." At Fondouk, that meant expending the 34th Division so the 6th Armoured could bust through to Kairouan unscathed.

Perhaps, Ryder mused, the division could tiptoe past Djebel Rhorab before dawn. He successfully petitioned Crocker for permission to advance his attack from 5:30 A.M. on April 8 to three A.M. His men laced toilet paper in their helmet nets so they might see one another in the dark, while rehearsing the challenge—"Grocery?"—and countersign—

"Store." They picked at a final meal of hardtack and "thousand-bone" oxtail soup, then nibbled the single slice of white bread served each man for dessert. At eight P.M. on Wednesday night, the regiments packed into trucks for assembly areas west of Fondouk. A half-ton truck for carrying out the dead trailed the convoy, bold white letters on its side proclaiming: "The Stuka Valley Hearse—Death Rides with Us."

At 2:30, in a shallow wadi, each rifleman dumped his overcoat and collected two extra bandoliers of ammunition. Colonel Ray C. Fountain, a former federal bankruptcy referee in Des Moines who now commanded the 133rd Infantry, informed his officers: "I have been told that there will be tremendous aerial bombing support which will flatten everything—something we haven't seen to date."

There would be no bombing, tremendous or otherwise. Poor communications and confusion over the new attack time led to cancellation of the air strikes. As the two assault regiments pressed forward on a two-mile front, a battalion on the far left got lost in the darkness, veered into the river bottoms, and so completely undid Ryder's timing that not until 5:30, the original H-hour, did the assault begin in earnest.

They found themselves in the beaten zone almost immediately. "A wave of flying dust and steel and lead was always before us," one soldier recalled. Daylight revealed 6,000 American infantrymen creeping through tuft grass too short to hide a cat. "We were like a pea on a plate," a sergeant reported. At 7:30, as plunging fire from Rhorab on the left and Haouareb straight ahead intensified, orders came to pull back 2,000 yards for another bombing raid that never materialized. By the time the troops moved forward again the Germans had their range. Gales of artillery swept the field; machine-gun rounds snipped the long-stemmed poppies, and antitank shells ricocheted end over end through the cactus like a buzzsaw. "We continued to move forward toward the enemy, standing erect like the British regulars charging up Bunker Hill," a young officer wrote.

Not for long. By noon all forward movement had stopped, 700 yards from Djebel Haoureb. Frantic men scraped at the dirt with bayonets and mess-kit lids, then lay motionless except to flick away the hot shell fragments burning through their twill uniforms. "The mere raising of an eyebrow attracted enemy fire," one sergeant in the 135th Infantry reported.

It never got better, not for two days. Tanks rumbled up in the early afternoon to inspirit the infantrymen, but instead attracted more fire. Within minutes four Shermans were flaming and the rest pulled back. Renewed attack orders at three P.M. went unheeded; the men "did little more than look up . . . and dig a little deeper," a lieutenant noted. Fifteen more tanks arrived at five P.M., but no rifleman would follow them, and soon another half-dozen burning hulls brightened the valley's long shadows.

General Crocker was fixated on when to unleash the 6th Armoured Division toward Kairouan, and he persuaded himself that perhaps Djebel Rhorab had been neutralized or even abandoned. It had not. By midafternoon, enemy skirmishers halted British infantrymen more than a mile from the crest. Throughout the next day—April 9—a Guards battalion fought a ferocious "boulder-to-boulder" battle that left every officer in two British companies dead or wounded. At 3:30 P.M., thirty-four hours after the Allied attack began, Djebel Rhorab fell. More than one hundred German prisoners were captured, but a like number escaped. The Welsh Guards' losses alone totaled 114, a hefty price for a hill considered inconsequential.

A hard night for Ryder's men had been succeeded by another hard day. "The hill looked bigger than ever," a lieutenant in the 133rd Infantry wrote of Djebel Haouareb. In the American ranks, "not a soul could be seen moving." Troops went to ground and would not rise except to skulk rearward on various pretexts. "There was no cover or concealment," a company commander in the 135th Infantry reported. "Mortar and artillery fire was so heavy that the dust cloud formed by the shell fragments looked like a smoke screen." Three American tank attacks outran all artillery and infantry cover, and were forced to beat a quick retreat. One battalion commander asked to be arrested rather than press the fight another hour; his request was granted. Acts of valor were as conspicuous for their singularity as for their gallantry. "We are going to get on top of that mountain and brew tea on the backs of those dead Germans," one private bellowed. His platoon leader replied, "Private, you are now a sergeant. Let's go."

They went—but there would be no tea-brewing, not yet. Alexander himself broke the impasse by ordering Crocker to crash the pass with an armored spearhead, the faltering Americans be damned. Word filtered down the ranks that the "gap must be forced . . . like a covey of partridges flying over the guns." "Goodbye," one squadron commander told a comrade. "I shall never see you again. We shall all be killed."

Not all, but enough, including the prescient commander. No sooner had the 17th/21st Lancers pressed forward a few hundred yards—the unit's heritage included an alarmingly similar charge at Balaklava in 1854—than the lead Sherman radioed: "There's a hell of a minefield in front. It looks about three hundred yards deep. Shall I go on?" The reply came immediately: "Go on. Go on at all costs." Mines ripped the front ranks, and fifteen German antitank guns took most of the rest. Crews spilling from their flaming turrets were machine-gunned before they touched the ground. Thirty-two tanks were lost. Two surviving Shermans clattered to the rear with dazed Tommies clinging to the hulls. Some men were burned so badly that their smoldering battle dress set fire to blankets in the armored carriers hauling them to an aid station.

Foolhardy or not—tank men would debate the matter for years—the audacious assault won through. Another squadron, the 16th/5th Lancers, followed on, veering to the left along a narrow, navigable lane that angled into the Marguellil wadi. "The tank rocked like a tug in the high sea," a British captain wrote. "On we went, engines revving, Browning rattling, guns crashing, being flung backwards and forwards and from side to side." Bulling through the fenny bottoms, the tanks began to emerge late Friday afternoon more than a mile beyond Fondouk village. American infantrymen trailing far behind on the southern slopes were amazed to see the Tommies pause to build tea-brewing fires in the lee of their Shermans even while shrapnel rattled off the hulls. The unhinged enemy—seven Axis battalions eventually fought at Fondouk, including the rehabilitated though much reduced convicts—slipped away at dusk through the wheat and wildflowers. Others remained at their guns, stone dead and half-buried in spent brass. "Their faces were as smooth and white as marble statues," one Yank lieutenant recalled.

Once again, the breakthrough came too late. The retreating Italians in Messe's army had tramped past Kairouan on the night of April 8–9, silhouetted against the domes and minarets. Feeling little pressure from Montgomery or Patton, the Germans trundled through the next night, looting local hotels of linen, cutlery, and mattresses as they went. After learning that remnants of the 10th and 21st Panzer Divisions lurked somewhere ahead, Crocker chose to lay up for the night rather than push into the coastal plain in darkness. By ten o'clock on Saturday morning, April 10, more than a hundred British Shermans had cleared Fondouk Pass to grab 650 prisoners and destroy fourteen enemy tanks. But the bulk of the enemy army escaped to the north in another of those tawny dust clouds that receded just beyond artillery range.

That evening Kairouan fell, and Allied troops marched through the five gates piercing her crenellated walls. "Lovely fluted domes looked like white velvet on a scarlet carpet, so thick were the poppies in the fields beneath them," wrote the correspondent Philip Jordan. A British sergeant offered a less romantic view of the city, though it dated to A.D. 671 and was considered the fourth holiest in all Islam: "To us it looked just the usual wog town." Arabs stared impassively from shops in the labyrinthine souk, but French children handed sprays of pink mimosa to the liberators, and Jews wept with joy at being told they could remove their yellow stars. Tommies pinned the discarded stars to their own caps or handed out matches so the Jews could burn them.

Burial details combed the Fondouk battlefield to collect the dead before looters stripped them; grave robbers had become so bold that chaplains carried carbines. The British had lost thirty-nine tanks and an uncertain number of men in addition to the Welsh Guard casualties on Djebel Rhorab. "Always that terrible, torpid stench of burned flesh," wrote the Reverend G. P. Druitt, chaplain of the 16th/5th Lancers. He had just removed a charred corpse from a wrecked Sherman. "It seems to hang in one's nostrils for days."

American losses in the past three days totaled 439, including more than one hundred killed in action. Wrapped in white mattress covers, the dead were lined up for trucking to another new cemetery. "It is only by the grace of God that I am here to write this today," a soldier in the 135th Infantry told his parents in Minnesota. In the evacuation hospital, surgeons worked all night, steam rising from each incision in the cold air. The stoicism of British tankers particularly impressed the medicos. "You couldn't make them complain even when you had to strip the burned skin off their hands and faces," the 109th Medical Battalion reported. Among the wounded Americans was Robert Moore, commander of the 2nd Battalion of the 168th Infantry, who had been tossed from a slit trench by the German bomb that killed his radio operator. Temporarily blind and deaf, Moore was evacuated to the rear where a soldier who had known him in Villisca described him a week later as "still very dazed and shaky . . . a sad and worried man. He spoke several times of his wife Dorothy and of daughter Nancy and wondered if he would ever see them again."

A great opportunity had been lost. Messe's troops closed on the Tunis bridgehead at Enfidaville, forty miles south of the capital and the most formidable position occupied by the Axis since the loss of El Alamein five months earlier. Now the Tunisian campaign would become a siege. How long it would last was anyone's guess, and the setting wanted only battering rams and boiling oil dumped from the ramparts to complete the medieval ambiance. Fondouk had been an ugly battle for the Allies, particularly after the frustrations of Mareth, Médenine, El Guettar, Maknassy, and Wadi Akarit. Alexander's strategy had been plodding, Crocker's tactics impoverished, American battleworthiness suspect. A bad plan was badly executed, and the long stern chase up the Tunisian littoral had come up short despite the capture of 6,000 Germans and 22,000 Italians in the past month.

Yes, a great opportunity had been lost, but there was always time for recriminations. Crocker fired first. In an ill-advised philippic to a group of officers visiting from Algiers on Sunday morning, April 11, he declared that "all commanders from Major General Ryder downwards in the 34th U.S. Division were too far in the rear of the troops they commanded" and that leadership "by junior officers was very weak indeed." Holding the 34th wholly responsible for the failures at Fondouk, he recommended it be withdrawn from combat duty for retraining in the rear "under British guidance." One of the visiting American generals, Harold R. Bull, was so alarmed at Crocker's "severe and caustic" comments that he immediately flew back to Algiers to warn Eisenhower.

Worse yet, Crocker or someone close to him had fed similar remarks to four war correspondents. Dispatches soon published in the United States suggested that "Rommel" had again made fools of the Allies. *Time* magazine reported in its April 19 issue that Fondouk was "downright embarrassing" for the Americans and had "afforded a sharp comparison between British and U.S. troops. . . . All day the British worked their way efficiently along the ridges; all day the U.S. troops tentatively approached but never stormed the first of their heights."

Ryder declined to rise to the bait, saying only, "The British were damn good." But bad feelings percolated through all ranks. Crocker's battle plan was likened to the Light Brigade's charge or the costly British frontal assault against General Andrew Jackson at New Orleans in January 1815. "I do not believe the British know any more about how to fight an armored division or how it should be organized than we do," said Ernie Harmon, the new commander of the 1st Armored Division. Chaplain Druitt of the 16th/5th Lancers evinced little Christian charity in telling his diary that the Yanks "have failed to take their objective as usual. . . . It is infuriating. We're missing the bus completely owing to the American failure." A British gunner passing an American convoy flipped an obscene gesture and barked, "Going to fuck up another front, I suppose?" And Tommies at mess sang a new ditty:

> *Our cousins regret they're unable to stay*
> *For the Germans are giving them hell.*

Eisenhower was both depressed and angry. The undeniable defects in American combat skills, while hardly as irredeemable as British caricatures suggested, left him feeling as low as "whale tracks at the bottom of the sea," Patton reported. The failure of military censors to suppress the damaging reports in *Time* and elsewhere so infuriated the commander-in-chief that he briefly advocated sacking his censorship chief. But he took no action against Crocker. To Patton and Bradley, he wondered aloud whether his orders to American commanders to accommodate the British "had been taken so literally that they had been too meek in acquiescing without argument to orders from above, which they felt involved use of poor tactics." Ryder's supposed "soft-heartedness" in refusing to cashier incompetent subordinates also bewildered him. And Eisenhower was not above a little petty spite. "Ike says Alex isn't as good as he thinks he is," his deputy Everett Hughes wrote in his diary. "He is up against some real fighting now."

There was irony in all this carping, visible only from the high ground of history. On average nearly a thousand Axis prisoners were tramping into Anglo-American cages every day. Allied forces were about to secure their fifth great battlefield conquest in a year, with a triumph that would join Midway, El Alamein, Guadalcanal, and Stalingrad as a milepost on the road to victory. More than 200,000 Axis troops were now penned like sheep in a Tunisian fold measuring roughly fifty by eighty miles, just large enough to bury two enemy armies. An entire continent would soon be reclaimed and an entire sea, the Mediterranean, converted into an Anglo-American lake. If American troops still seemed callow at times, one need only consider how far they had come since the bumblings of TORCH and imagine how far they would go once the greatest industrial power on earth had fully flung itself into total war.

That Eisenhower felt dispirited simply affirmed Wellington's maxim that "nothing except a battle lost can be half so melancholy as a battle won." To Marshall, he wrote: "I realize that the seeds of discord between ourselves and our British allies were sown, on our side, as far back as when we read our little red school history books." There was sense in that, just as there was in Eisenhower's prediction that "this war is not going to be won until we are in the heart of Europe." Between now and then, however many months or years it took, the task of keeping the Allied coalition unified in pursuit of a common goal would remain among the great military challenges of modern history. Chauvinism, vainglory, frustration, and grief—all these were centrifugal forces, pushing the alliance apart. As Eisenhower had only begun to appreciate, unity required perpetual vigilance and the skills of a master diplomat.

As for the troops at Fondouk, they glanced at the windrows of corpses in their white shrouds and looked away. Yesterday had never happened.

There was only tomorrow, and the killing required tomorrow in order to reach the next day. Sergeant Samuel Allen, Jr., a former college student who had led his own swing band in the palmy days of peace, tried to explain in a letter home the flinty nihilism that made young men at war seem so old when they contemplated the dead.

"We have found that it is best to forget about those friends, not to talk about them," he wrote. "They don't even exist."

12. THE INNER KEEP

Hell's Corner

ONE hundred thousand strong, the Americans pounded north on four trunk roads beginning Sunday, April 11, as the Allies maneuvered to attack the Tunisian bridgehead. Dust whitened the convoys, giving the troops a spectral pallor despite their sunburns and the grit that blackened every frayed collar. They needed haircuts and shaves and baths, but more than anything they needed rest. The veterans—and most of them now qualified—possessed what Lincoln had inelegantly called "the tired spot that can't be got at." Ernie Pyle, who was with them as usual, wrote: "They were dead weary, as a person could tell even when looking at them from behind. Every line and sag of their bodies spoke their inhuman exhaustion. . . . They were young men, but the grime and whiskers and exhaustion made them look middle-aged." A sergeant wrote to his family in Iowa: "It'll soon be five months that a pup tent has been our home. Five months since I've even so much as sat at a table while eating."

North they pounded for 150 miles, another vehicle roaring by every thirty-seven seconds around the clock, precisely as planned, 30,000 vehicles all told, on highways that had carried Carthaginian elephants, Roman chariots, and Byzantine chargers. The desert fell behind. Once again, they were back in the northern hills where many had fought in November and December. The mid-April wheat was thigh high. Rock roses and ladies' fingers bloomed along the roads, and poppies spread like flame on the slopes in "hilarious, shouting bands of color." Gorgeous banks of blue convolvulus resembled wood smoke in the middle distance, or, to the jaded eye, a foaming mortar barrage. Hawthorne budded. Apples blossomed. The songs of cuckoos spilled from the thickets.

God's bounty meant nothing to these men. Beneath the vernal landscape every soldier now saw topography, just as a pathologist can see the skull beneath a scalp. A streambed was not a streambed but defilade; pastures were not pastures but exposed fields of fire. Laurel thickets became ambush sites, and every grove of cork trees might hide a German 88. No soldier could look at this corrupted terrain without feeling that it had become sinister and deeply personal.

Not even a Tunisian spring could hide the battle scars. Refugees trudged on the road shoulders, floured by the dust of the passing trucks. Only rubble remained where for centuries there had been towns with names like Sidi bou Zid and Sbeïtla and Medjez-el-Bab. Once-pretty Béja, with its rambling walls and hilltop Byzantine towers, was posted with yellow signs warning all pilgrims of typhus.

To Béja they were headed, or near it, as part of the grand scheme for the coup de grâce devised by Eisenhower and Alexander. The plan went like this: More than 300,000 Allied troops in some twenty divisions, with 1,400 tanks and as many artillery tubes, would attack in three main groups along a 140-mile arc that extended from Enfidaville south of Tunis to the Mediterranean coast west of Bizerte. Montgomery's Eighth Army would strike from the south with six divisions, angling for the capital while also preventing the Axis from converting Cap Bon—a large, stony peninsula east of Tunis—into an African Bataan that could hold out for months. From the southwest, roughly parallel to the Medjerda River valley, Anderson's First Army would attack toward Tunis with six British and three French divisions. And on the far left flank of the Allied line, the Americans would drive on Bizerte from the west with four U.S. divisions and three French battalions known collectively as the Corps Franc d'Afrique. "We have got them just where we want them," Alexander told his men, "with their backs to the wall."

Getting the Allied divisions where *they* were wanted had required settling several fraternal squabbles. Influenced by Crocker, Alexander had intended to banish the U.S. 34th Division from the line for extensive retraining even as he acceded to Eisenhower's request that II Corps participate in the kill. He also was reluctant to commit all of the 1st Armored Division, "owning to its present low state of morale and training." Also, Allen's 1st Infantry Division was to withdraw to prepare for HUSKY, the invasion of Sicily.

Patton howled. The Americans now had 467,000 troops in northwest Africa, more than 60 percent of the Anglo-American army. Most were earmarked for HUSKY or were part of the immense Yankee logistical apparatus. But Alexander proposed taking the Tunisian laurels with a force almost wholly British. "Frankly, I am not happy," Patton wrote Alexander on April 11. If the U.S. Army appeared to be "acting in a minor role, the repercussions might be unfortunate." A day later he wrote again, proposing that the 34th Division be kept with II Corps to "restore its soul" and warning that because it was a National Guard unit "its activities assume local interest of great political significance." In other words: congressmen from Iowa and Minnesota would react poorly to any humiliation of their boys by British officers. At Patton's request, Bradley carried this second letter to Alexander's headquarters in Haïdra. "Give me the division," Bradley told the field marshal, "and I'll promise you they'll take and hold their very first objective."

Intrigued, Alexander brushed off his staff's objections and told Bradley, "Take them, they're yours." After further negotiation, all four American divisions in II Corps were to be included in the attack: American logisticians had demonstrated that they could supply U.S. troops without disrupting the British lines to Anderson's army, in part by using 5,000 trucks to stock dumps near Béja and by hiring *balancelles*—fishing smacks—to ship ammunition from Bône. Patton had also objected to again subsuming II Corps into Anderson's command after it had been reporting directly to Alexander for more than a month. Anderson did little to woo back the estranged Yanks when, upon reviewing their plans for capturing Bizerte, he flicked his swagger stick at the map and said, "Just a childish fancy, just a childish fancy." ("I'll make that son of a bitch eat those words," Ernie Harmon later vowed; Patton informed his diary, "I would rather be commanded by an Arab.") Again Alexander acquiesced, authorizing the II Corps commander to appeal any disagreeable order from Anderson directly to Alexander. Running counter to the usual rigidity of combat etiquette, this arrangement was not merely unorthodox but even improper.

So the Yanks were coming, lots of them, although British troops still constituted nearly two-thirds of Alexander's army group. If in his quest to transcend chauvinism Eisenhower remained aloof from issues of national honor, Marshall did not. Citing a "marked fall in prestige of American troops," he warned Eisenhower on April 14, "Please watch this very closely." The need to prove that U.S. troops were the battlefield equals of any—a compulsion dating to World War I—remained a powerful force in the American military psyche.

The actors had taken their positions. Now the curtain was set to rise for the last time in Africa. Two brawny Allied armies would attack two eviscerated Axis armies, with the British angling from the south and southwest, and the Americans driving from the west.

On April 18, II Corps officially relieved British troops around Béja. But when the U.S. command post went up in tents on a farm two miles

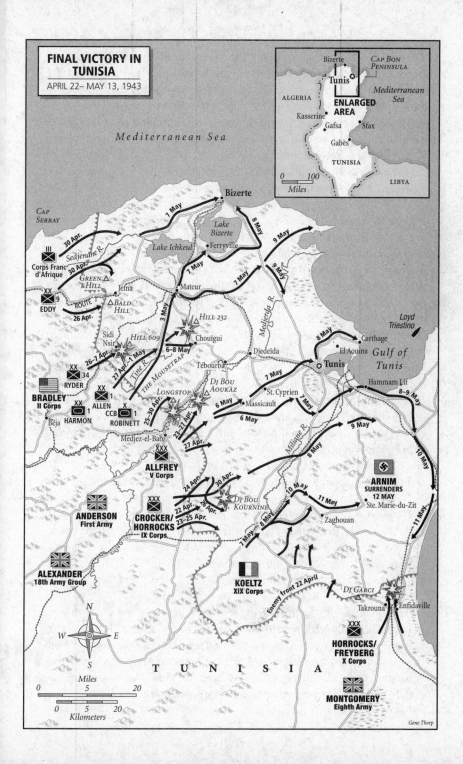

FINAL VICTORY IN TUNISIA

APRIL 22– MAY 13, 1943

ENLARGED AREA

Bizerte
Cap Bon Peninsula
Tunis
ALGERIA
Mediterranean Sea
Kasserine
Gafsa
Sfax
Gabès
TUNISIA
LIBYA

0   100
Miles

Mediterranean Sea

Bizerte

CAP SERRAT

7 May

Lake Bizerte

8 May

9 May

30 Apr.

Sedjenane R.

Lake Ichkeul

Ferryville

III
Corps Franc d'Afrique

30 Apr.

7 May

9 May

GREEN HILL

Jefna

Mateur

7 May

9 May

XX 9
EDDY

ROUTE

BALD HILL

26 Apr.

3 May

Loyd Triestino

HILL 232

Chouïgui

Medjerda R.

8 May

Carthage

El Aouina

Gulf of Tunis

Sidi Nsir

HILL 609

6–8 May

26-7 Apr.

THE MOUSETRAP

27 Apr.–1 May

Djedeïda

Tébourba

Tunis

XX 34
RYDER

Tine R.

Dj Bou Aoukàz

7 May

St. Cyprien

Hammam Lif

8–9 May

BRADLEY
II Corps

XX 1
ALLEN

LONGSTOP

6 May

Massicault

7 May

CCB
X
ROBINETT

25–30 Apr.

23-27 Apr.

6 May

XX 1
HARMON

Béja

Medjez-el-Bab

27 Apr.

9 May

10 May

24 Apr.

30 Apr.

XXX
ALLFREY
V Corps

Dj Bou Kournine

8 May

ARNIM
SURRENDERS
12 MAY
Ste. Marie-du-Zit

ANDERSON
First Army

22 Apr.

23-25 Apr.

26 Apr.

10 May

11 May

Miliane R.

Zaghouan

11 May

XXX
CROCKER/
HORROCKS
IX Corps

7 May

8 May

ALEXANDER
18th Army Group

Enemy front 22 April

Dj Garci

KOELTZ
XIX Corps

Takrouna

Enfidaville

N
W   E
S

HORROCKS/
FREYBERG
X Corps

Miles
0   5   20

Kilometers
0   5   20

T U N I S I A

MONTGOMERY
Eighth Army

Gene Thorp

northwest of town, one man was conspicuously absent: G. S. Patton, Jr. As Eisenhower had long intended, Patton had quietly surrendered the corps command in order to complete preparations for Sicily, now less than three months away. In forty-three days he had become a national hero, fought the best German tank forces to a draw, and gone far toward building a reputation as "our greatest fighting general," in Franklin Roosevelt's phrase. Yet—as perhaps even he realized—his tenure had been checkered at best. For all Patton's melodramatics, his influence on the esprit and discipline of II Corps was marginal. Even when allowances are made for the restrictions imposed by Alexander, he had demonstrated little tactical flair at El Guettar, Maknassy, or the first Fondouk. Sweeping envelopments by rampaging tanks, he was discovering, were nearly as rare in this war as they had been in the last.

Despite Eisenhower's praise for "the outstanding example of leadership you have given us all," Patton would leave Tunisia with his thirst for glory unslaked. His frustration can be seen in his orders to inflate the estimates of damage inflicted on Axis forces by II Corps: padding the body count, this would be called in a later war. According to three accounts left by senior staff officers, Patton disputed the initial assessments of enemy losses. "It wasn't 'colorful' enough—didn't make the operation look big enough," Lieutenant Colonel Russell F. Akers, Jr., the corps assistant operations officer, privately told Bradley's aide after the war. "Result: we doubled figures on equipment damaged, destroyed, or captured intact." Patton's chief intelligence officer, Monk Dickson, recorded the following conversation in mid-April:

Patton: Your estimates of enemy killed and wounded are absurd. We handed them ten times that many casualties.
Dickson: Sir, we counted all their graves that we could find, interrogated both medical and combat people, and checked their rolls. . . . Experienced soldiers are hard to kill.
Patton: Add another cipher to both totals.
Dickson: Sir, I can not conscientiously do it.

The II Corps after-action report sent to Algiers asserted that 800 German graves had been counted on the road from Gafsa to Gabès. Enemy equipment that II Corps claimed was destroyed on the ground and from the air between March 15 and April 10 included 128 tanks, 850 other vehicles, and 300 artillery tubes and machine guns—numbers that are certainly inflated, whether or not at Patton's behest. Because the final report was still in preparation when Patton left, Akers added, the departing commander "gave me his signature on a piece of paper, which I traced onto the stencil when it had been cut."

As he left Gafsa, Patton picked a bouquet of nasturtiums and laid them on Dick Jenson's grave. Nearly 800 other American boys were buried there with the young captain. He wept at the sight, never bad behavior in a general. His final diary entry before he left Tunisia was vintage Patton:

> As I gain in experience I do not think more of myself but less of others. Men, even so-called great men, are wonderfully weak and timid. They are too damned polite. War is very simple, direct, and ruthless. It takes a simple, direct, and ruthless man to wage war.

On Thursday morning, April 22, Patton's successor arrived by jeep on the crest of a leafy hill outside Béja. He was a bespectacled six-footer, with a high, convex forehead and thin hair that had been graying since his cadet days. Now he was fifty, just. The jut of his jaw was often mistaken for a sign of pugnacity; in fact, a boyhood skating accident had shattered his teeth and left him with a lifelong reluctance to smile for photographers lest they make, as he put it, a "permanent record of that jumbled mess." He wore a tatty field jacket and canvas leggings, making him "the least dressed-up commander of an American army in the field since Zachary Taylor, who wore a straw hat," one witness observed. Unscrolling the map of northern Tunisia that he carried under his arm, he clipped it to an easel, then turned to the small band of correspondents who had come to take his measure and hear his plan.

Omar Nelson Bradley had moved to center stage; there he would remain for the duration and beyond. He descended from hardscrabble Missouri farmers and one itinerant schoolteacher, his father. Eisenhower had contributed a generous accolade for his classmate's yearbook entry at West Point: "True merit is like a river, the deeper it is, the less noise it makes." Like Patton, Bradley could be simple, direct, and ruthless, but the similarities ended there. Profanity offended him and he had never even tasted alcohol until the age of thirty-three; his teetotaling wife, Mary, flew into a rage at the spectacle of intoxication—hardly rare on Army posts. His cultivated image of homespun humility—he was "the G.I. General"—was not so much wrong as incomplete; he also possessed an intolerant rectitude and a capacity for dissimulation that in lesser men might devolve into deceit. Hunting was his great passion—when he was stationed at Fort Benning he often tramped into the Georgia swamp before breakfast to shoot the heads off water moccasins; in Tunisia he settled for rocks tossed into the air by his aides. He had a born infantryman's feel for terrain, with a detailed mental map of every significant swale and ridge from Béja to Bizerte. Of the fifty-nine members of the West Point class of 1915 who became generals—'15 was "the class that stars fell on"—Bradley had been first to win the rank. Arabs, assuming that "Omar" was a Muslim name, were pleased that one of their own had achieved such stature in the American Army. Patton wryly complained that Bradley was simply "too damned sound."

With map unfurled on the easel and pointer in hand, Bradley quickly explained the impending campaign in his flat, sodbuster twang. "He laid down his schedule with no more panache than a teacher outlining the curriculum for the new semester," recalled A. J. Liebling, among those squatting at his feet. Mateur was the key to Bizerte. The 9th Division would take the far left flank along the sea—skirting Green and Bald Hills, where the British had found so much trouble. The other two U.S. infantry divisions—the 1st and 34th—would attack farther south, through Sidi Nsir and the hill country below it. The 1st Armored Division would exploit any breakthrough onto the coastal plain leading to Bizerte.

Bradley neglected to mention that his first act as corps commander—even before he repealed Patton's necktie directive—had been to disobey a direct order from Eisenhower. In a patronizing "Dear Brad" message on April 16, the commander-in-chief noted that "the southern portion of your sector appears to be reasonably suited for tank employment and it is in that area that you will be expected to make your main effort." This proposed route, through the narrow Tine River valley, was such an obvious German ambush site that II Corps had dubbed it the Mousetrap. Certain that such an attack invited disaster, Bradley simply ignored the proposal and ordered his commanders to avoid the Mousetrap. He likened the job ahead to "hunting wild goats." By hugging the high ground—"djebel hopping," he called it—troops were to avoid the vulnerable bottlenecks that had cost so many lives in the past five months. The attack would take time; there were many djebels to hop and many goats to hunt. Axis sappers had spent months fortifying the hills with pneumatic drills, concrete, countless mines, and six artillery battalions. In the II Corps sector, the enemy now mustered an estimated 12,000 infantry troops, and that number would more than triple in the next two weeks.

Bradley took a few questions, climbed back into his jeep, and vanished down the hill. Reduced to half a page with a single map, his battle concept was sent to the British V Corps, which abutted the American zone on the south. General Allfrey studied it and then shook his head. "This chap Bradley," he was reported as saying, "obviously knows nothing about commanding a corps."

Although the endgame was just beginning on the ground, it had been under way for weeks in the air. Overwhelming Allied air superiority might be hard to see from the bottom of a slit trench at Béja, but it was all too visible to the Axis wretches caught in Allied bombsights. Thousands of tons of high explosives had been dropped on ports, airfields, and marshaling yards across northeast Tunisia, Sicily, and southern Italy, with thousands more to come. Bizerte had been hit so hard that not a single structure in the city was habitable. "We attacked Bizerte with the intention of blotting it off the map," said one Army Air Forces general. That was not boast but fact. Raids on Tunis concentrated on docks and airfields, but the pummeling still killed 752 civilians and wounded more than a thousand; pinpoint accuracy was out of reach for B-17s flying at 23,000 feet through flak so heavy the route became known, bitterly, as the Milk Run. A single raid on Palermo blew up an ammunition ship, sank seven other freighters, and generated waves powerful enough to toss two coastal lighters onto the quay; the port was immobilized for weeks. In another raid, three Italian destroyers ferrying a panzer battalion to Tunisia were sunk. Six men survived to tell the tale.

Allied minelayers north and east of Tunisia became so proficient that Axis vessels were forced to cross the Sicilian Straits through a single swept channel a mile wide and forty miles long. Ultra eavesdropping revealed ship manifests and sailing times in such detail that Allied targeteers could select their prey on the basis of which cargo they most wished to see on the Mediterranean floor any given day. A solitary, pathetic scow carrying fuel or tank shells might draw fifty attacking planes. American aircrews calculated that on average twenty-eight tons of bombs sufficed to sink a midsized merchantman; a typical formation of eighteen Flying Fortresses dropped twice that tonnage, and crews came off the target singing "It's Better to Give Than to Receive" over their intercoms. In March alone, more than three dozen Axis ships had been sunk on the Tunisian run, and with them nearly half the military cargo and fuel intended for Arnim's forces.

Consequently, Kesselring turned to air transport more and more. By early April, 200 or more flights a day—organized in wave-skimming convoys called *Pulks*—carried men and matériel to Africa. The Allies responded, beginning on April 5, with Operation FLAX, a series of ruthless fighter sweeps and bombing raids. On their first FLAX mission, U.S.

pilots bushwacked fifty Ju-52 transports and their escorts; in what was described as a "general air mêlée," seventeen German aircraft were shot down at a cost of two American planes. Bombers also dropped nearly 11,000 twenty-pound fragmentation bombs on targets in Bizerte and Italy. By day's end, Luftwaffe losses reached thirty planes in the air and many more on the ground.

Worse was to come. On April 18, Palm Sunday, four squadrons of the American 57th Fighter Group—the Black Scorpions, the Fighting Cocks, the Exterminators, and the Yellow Diamonds—joined a Spitfire squadron over Cap Bon for the final patrol of the day. Sixty fighters were "spaced up into the sky like a flight of stairs, each line of four planes abreast making a step," according to a contemporary account by Richard Thruelsen and Elliott Arnold. "The bottom of this flight was at four thousand feet. The Spits, at the top, were at fifteen thousand feet." Purple shadows were stretching across Cap Bon when the pilots suddenly spotted several V-formations of Ju-52s and six-engine Me-323s six miles off the coast. "They were flying the most beautiful formation I've ever seen," one pilot said later. "It seemed like a shame to break it up."

Splitting into pairs, the marauders attacked from the right rear, quickly disarranging the perfect Vs and picking off the stragglers. A pilot described his first victim: "A short burst left his port engine burning. The flame trailed the whole length of the plane. The center or nose engine was also on fire." Blazing planes cartwheeled into the violet water or crashed on the Tunisian beach. "The sea turned red and a great circle of debris bobbed in an oily scum," a witness reported. "From the beaches rose the tall black columns of a dozen funeral pyres."

Thirty-eight Luftwaffe planes were destroyed. Twenty more were shot down the next morning, then another thirty-nine on April 22, including many carrying cargoes of fuel that burned like winged hellfire during the languid, corkscrew descent into the Mediterranean. In less than three weeks, FLAX destroyed 432 Axis aircraft at a cost of thirty-five Allied planes; the losses included more than half the German air transport fleet. A flyboy cockiness invested Allied airfields. "If Kesselring goes on making mistakes like this, we're not going to get much of a reputation," Air Marshal Tedder observed. At Göring's insistence, Axis flights took place only in darkness; with spring days ever longer, there were only about sixty sorties each night to bring Arnim supplies and reinforcements.

Although a quarter-million Axis men crowded the bridgehead, only one-third of them were genuine combat troops. Most others were noncombatants from the Italian logistical tail that had been organized for

an army with pretensions to a vast colonial empire, or rear-echelon soldiers from divisions destroyed in Rommel's long retreat across Africa's
northern rim. Reduced to fewer than a hundred guns, the Italian army
"was in agony," one general observed. Arab black-marketeers did a brisk
business in safe-conduct passes sold to Italians keen on slipping across
no-man's-land. Allied pilots and artillerymen papered the Axis ranks
with propaganda sheets encouraging defection and dissent; these were the
initial barrages of nearly 4 billion leaflets—equivalent to 4,000 truckloads—that would be printed in the Mediterranean in the next two years.

Axis reserves were still ferried to Tunis at a rate of about 2,000 men
each day, but most frontline units were beyond reconstitution. The 15th
and 21st Panzer Divisions had roughly 5,600 men each, while the 90th
Light Africa was down to 6,000 and the 164th Light Africa numbered
only 3,000. The Italian Centauro and Spezia Divisions had been obliterated, and three others had been reduced, collectively, to eleven scarecrow
battalions. General Messe warned that "the repulse of a large-scale
enemy attack is impossible with the amount of ammunition on hand."
By late April, a Luftwaffe anti-aircraft unit had trouble scrounging the
thirty-five gallons of fuel a day it needed for its radar sets. A German staff
officer noted that "an armored division without petrol is little better
than a heap of scrap iron"; an armored division without tanks was even
less. The Axis armor fleet numbered fewer than 150 tanks, barely a tenth
the Allied force. The 15th Panzer had four tanks fit for battle. Arnim
rejected several counterattack proposals as pointless "butting at the
mountains." When a senior officer visiting from Berlin accused Army
Group Africa of "squinting over its shoulder," Arnim tartly replied that
he was "squinting for ships."

As early as December, the German high command had discreetly considered what transport would be needed for a complete evacuation of the
Tunisian bridgehead, but those contingency plans had been shelved in
light of Kesselring's unflagging optimism. When Kesselring later proposed a "comb-out" of extraneous personnel, Hitler refused on grounds
that selective evacuation would hurt morale. Although Allied intelligence estimated that in early April the Axis could still remove 37,000
men a day from Tunisia, not until mid-month did a limited, belated
evacuation begin of the *mangiatori*—"useless mouths." Mouths unfortunate enough to be considered essential got little to eat: an Italian soldier's
diary indicated that his daily ration comprised half a mess tin of cold
rice, a couple of potatoes, and a slice and a half of bread.

If his virtual abandonment of the African army seems daft in hind-
sight, Hitler as usual could spin a logically coherent strand within the

larger web of his lunacy. On April 8, he and Mussolini met in a castle near Salzburg to conspire. Il Duce's former strut was gone. Every Allied step closer to Tunis was a step closer to Rome. Naples and other cities in the south were being pummeled from the air. Strikes and peace demonstrations racked Turin and Milan. Depressed and feeble, Mussolini renewed his plea for a separate peace between Berlin and Moscow; the Axis could then turn full force toward the Mediterranean, holding Tunisia while falling on the enemy rear through Spain and Spanish Morocco.

Hitler dismissed this scheme. Of Mussolini's proposals, only standing fast in Tunisia interested him. After the disaster at Stalingrad, recent German successes in the Kharkov counteroffensive—three Soviet armies had been obliterated in less than a month—had revived the Führer's craving for complete victory over the hated Russians. As long as the Anglo-Americans concentrated their strength on the periphery of the Axis empire, they could not attempt major operations elsewhere. Tunisia, he told Mussolini, was shielding Italy and the rest of southern Europe. The Führer also recognized that the final loss of North Africa would further undermine Mussolini at home, perhaps fatally, imperiling both the defense of the Italian homeland and the Axis itself. Tunisia must be defended to the last ditch.

Il Duce's backbone was stiffened by Hitler's rhetoric. He agreed that the bridgehead should hold "at all costs"—that portentous phrase used so glibly by those far removed from the firing line. "Everything can happen if we persist," he told Kesselring in Rome on April 12, "and therefore we shall hold." The next day—Tuesday, the thirteenth—Arnim was told there would be no mass evacuation.

Appalled at what he called "this liquidation," Arnim later acknowledged "the greatest desire to call it quits and to ask to be relieved." Instead, he saluted the order, began cobbling together infantry battalions from his cooks and clerks, and turned to the task of digging that last ditch.

Hammering Home the Cork

As the Allied armies converged on the bridgehead, their engagements increasingly occurred simultaneously. For narrative simplicity, they may be considered one at a time, beginning with Eighth Army in the south.

Montgomery's horde swaggered toward Tunis as cocksure as a street fighter eager to put an opponent on the pavement one last time. Tommies sorted through booty abandoned by retreating Axis troops, including American swimsuits captured at Kasserine and a box of Italian regimental silverware left on the road like an oblation. A cool swank pervaded the ranks and even the muddle-headed cries of *"Vivent les Américains!"* from liberated villagers failed to prick the high spirits of an army that had its quarry's scent.

Montgomery had known since April 11 that Alexander intended First Army to make the main Allied thrust toward Tunis. Gentler terrain clearly favored an armored blow from the southwest rather than due south, where the coastal plain narrowed to a funnel barely a mile wide and frowned upon by hills that were high, steep, and twenty miles deep—"bald rock faces, gullies, and abominations," as the official British history put it. This Montgomery could accept; he had urged Alexander to "concentrate all your strength" for "*an almighty crack*" in one spot, and as requested he donated his own 1st Armoured Division and an armored car regiment to First Army toward that end.

But Montgomery was not a man to relinquish laurels easily, particularly to those he considered his military inferiors, which included virtually everyone. "It would be all right if Anderson was any good, as he could do it all," he wrote in his diary on April 12. "But he is no good." To Alexander on April 16 he cabled: "All my troops are in first-class form and want to be in the final Dunkirk." Although, under Alexander's plan, Eighth Army was to contribute little more than a hearty feint, Montgomery still hoped to beat Anderson to the Tunisian capital by "gate crashing" the Axis bridgehead with a four-division assault on the rocky massif above Enfidaville.

It is axiomatic in mountain warfare that the second-highest crest is often worthless ground, but Eighth Army now launched a campaign to capture a chain of second-highest hills. After years in the desert, the abrupt change in topography was pleasing to the eye—for 1,800 miles these men had dreamed of green hills and wildflowers—but tactically confusing. Montgomery's increasing reliance on brute force played badly here: even overwhelming firepower had a limited effect on sloping, fissured terrain that sheltered defenders and swallowed vast tonnages of bombs and artillery shells. Eighth Army units were badly understrength after the travails of the past year, and up to one-quarter of the remaining infantrymen would be needed to haul ammunition over ground often too rugged even for mules.

Such handicaps seemed manageable to the British, because their intelligence had concluded that the Enfidaville fortifications were lightly held, with six or eight demoralized German battalions and some hapless

Italians supposedly facing the X Corps sector. (Soon that estimate of enemy forces would triple.) But Montgomery was convinced he could "bounce the enemy out of Enfidaville," just as he believed he had little to learn from the amateurs in First Army and II Corps, despite their six-month apprenticeship in Tunisian hill fighting. Now arrogance and error would reap the usual dividends.

Even the second-highest crests had substantial foothills that served as watchtowers shielding the inner keep. Among these, three miles west of Enfidaville, was Takrouna, a 600-foot limestone knob crowned with a domed mosque, an old Berber fort, and adobe houses on three levels. General Messe himself took a hand in arranging its defenses, manned by 300 Italian infantry troops. "In an endeavor to rouse the spirit of emulation," Messe later explained, "I included a platoon of Germans in the garrison." Freyberg's New Zealanders—specifically, the Maori tribesmen of his 28th Battalion—attacked this "rotting stalagmite" just before midnight on Monday, April 19. For two days, the battle scorched Takrouna's pale faces, up and down rough-hewn steps, through secret tunnels, and in and out of one blood-spattered room after another.

Reinforcements hurried forward on both sides. By Wednesday morning, there was "never a moment that the top of Takrouna was not half-hidden by shellbursts [and] tracer shells streaking in a slight arc across the valley and ricocheting crazily among the houses," one commander later wrote. Italian troops shinnying up a rope tossed grenades into a makeshift Maori dressing station full of wounded soldiers, prompting reprisals that included chasing enemy soldiers over the precipice at bay-onet point and tossing two prisoners after them. "One of those grim moments," an official New Zealand account conceded, "when all control is lost."

"Sergeants were promoting themselves to platoon sergeants, corporals to sergeants, and so on. In many cases they were no sooner promoted than they were wounded," a battalion commander, wounded himself, later recalled. Harrowing fire reduced two Maori companies to fewer than twenty men each, and nine of twelve company commanders in the attack were killed or wounded. Takrouna finally fell—General Horrocks considered it "the most gallant feat of arms I witnessed in the course of the war"—but at a Pyrrhic price. Kiwi losses amounted to 459 men, including 34 officers. More than seven hundred prisoners were captured, three-quarters of them Italian.

But that was it: this far and no farther. A simultaneous attack by the 4th Indian Division against Djebel Garci, five miles to the west, captured a few tactically insignificant acres at a loss of another 500 men. Both valor and bloodlust equaled those on Takrouna. A Gurkha platoon commander, who had suffered a dozen wounds to his head alone, played dead before rejoining his men in the dark to renew the attack. "My hands being cut about and bloody," he recounted, "I had to ask one of my platoon to take my pistol out of my holster and to put it in my hand." Gurkhas—short, swarthy Nepalese warriors said to tire only when strolling across flat ground—reportedly took no prisoners, delighted in decapitating enemies with their long, curved *kukri* blades, and calculated Axis losses by the number of enemy wristwatches adorning Gurkha arms at the end of any fight. But they met their match on Garci, where knives and stones supplemented rifles and artillery. "In the darkness men grappled and slew each other," an Indian witness reported. "Every gain drew a counterattack from desperate men pledged to hold the heights at all costs."

For the first time, the enemy seemed willing en masse to fight to the last cartridge. A new, homicidal desperation fired the battlefield, stoked by the savage intimacy of boulder-to-boulder combat and the Axis recognition that the next step back would put them in the sea. Men grew gray for lack of sleep. Stretcher bearers stumbled up and stumbled back, their legs rubbery and palms blistered raw. By April 22, Axis shelling seemed heavier than ever and the Tommies lay low all day to "wait for the enemy to get over his ill temper," one commander said. A Scots officer reported that his Highlanders had stopped carrying bagpipes into battle because the pipers were invariably hit and pipes themselves had grown too dear, at £80 a set. News of Eighth Army's difficulties elicited an uncharitable schadenfreude in the Allied ranks. "Let's radio Monty," Bradley quipped, "and see if he wants us to send him a few American advisers to show his desert fighters how to get through those hills."

Weary and distracted by preparations for HUSKY, Montgomery now threatened to make a bad situation worse with an abrupt change of plans. If his men could not force their way through the hills, he would fling them up the narrow coastal road in an effort to reach Bou Ficha and then Tunis. After issuing orders to suspend the mountain attacks and prepare for a frontal assault up Highway 1, Montgomery flew to Cairo for three more days of Sicily planning. He returned on Easter Monday, the twenty-sixth, with a raging case of tonsillitis, to find his subordinates—particularly the division commanders Bernard Freyberg and Francis Tuker—in surly rebellion at a plan that appeared to put the army commander's personal ambition ahead of tactical prudence. Irritated and feverish, Montgomery took to his caravan bed. "The big issues are so vital that we have got to force this through here," he croaked. Horrocks threw up his hands in exasperation. "Of course we can break through," he snapped before storming from the trailer. "But there won't be much left of your fine Eighth Army when we have done it." Montgomery just grunted as the door slammed.

Even the most irresistible force occasionally encounters an immovable object, and for Montgomery Enfidaville was that object. After years of fighting and the months-long tramp across Africa, Eighth Army had "rather a sad and stale air," a British intelligence officer later wrote. Montgomery and his staff "appeared to have lost interest. They never liked mountains." A positioning attack to seize a ridgeline between Takrouna and the coast road foreshadowed the calamity to come if Montgomery persisted with his plan. The green 56th Division entered the line on April 26 after a grueling 3,300-mile overland trip from Iraq, and immediately suffered a battalion commander killed and the division commander badly wounded. The spooked survivors stampeded as if they meant to run all the way back to Kirkuk. "As they went up the slope I saw them waver, turn, and retreat," an artillery officer later recalled. "It was only the second time I had seen our infantry running; the first was at Mareth. . . . It reminded me of the infantry in open order advancing on the first day of the Somme."

Another Somme was the last thing the British Army needed, and to his credit Montgomery recognized the futility of persisting with this approach. "Am not, repeat *not* happy about present plan for finishing off this business," he cabled Alexander at six P.M. on April 29. "Can you possibly come and see me tomorrow?" He was ready to let Anderson carry the fight by transferring two more divisions to First Army; the move would eliminate Eighth Army from the race for Tunis and essentially end its role in the African campaign. Such was war. Glory would have to be won in other fights on other fields. While waiting for Alexander to arrive, Montgomery dashed off a private note to Brooke in London. "I could almost burst into tears at the tragedy of the whole thing," he wrote. "I have no doubt we shall put it right in the end, but we have lost a great opportunity, and we have lost a lot of good chaps.

"I sometimes feel," he added, "I am beginning to need a short rest."

As usual in Tunisia, Montgomery's criticism was less a meditation on his own army's performance than a churlish broadside at Anderson and First Army. He dismissed Anderson's plan for capturing Tunis as "a partridge drive" with "all the seeds of failure." Rather than concentrating that almighty crack at a single vulnerable point in the enemy's thin line, First Army was dispersing its power in multiple attacks across a forty-mile front. If the French in the south and Americans in the north were included, that frontage stretched to ninety miles.

The merit of Montgomery's appraisal soon became clear, which of course afforded him satisfaction in direct proportion to Anderson's misery. The latter's plan had little nuance. Among other failings, he had inadequately exploited Allied airpower: having planned haphazardly, he frittered away his overwhelming strength in seventy different air attacks on forty-four separate targets. Yet with three armored and ten infantry divisions at his disposal, Anderson came to the reasonable conclusion that the fuel-starved Germans would be unable to parry multiple thrusts.

Operation VULCAN was just that: multiple thrusts. First, the IX Corps of General Crocker—fresh from the Fondouk unpleasantness—would attack on the British right to draw enemy forces from Allfrey's V Corps on the left. Then, sixteen hours later, Allfrey would thunder toward Tunis down the Medjerda valley, where Anderson rightly believed "the enemy's vitals" could be found. Finally, a day later, the Americans on the far left flank would begin their surge toward Bizerte, although they were not expected to actually reach it. Even less was expected from the French XIX Corps, wedged between the British First and Eighth Armies as a sop to Allied unity. Anderson intended to destroy Arnim's Fifth Panzer Army before wheeling south to take the First Italian troops from the rear as they faced Montgomery. The offensive was to last nine days. "We are going to annihilate finally the armies of von Arnim and Rommel—all of us together," he told his troops, still flailing at the Desert Fox's long shadow.

Kenneth Anderson was incapable of making a plan without diffidence—that "queer thing human nature" kept intruding—and VULCAN was no exception. "The plan's all right, but will the troops fight?" he asked General Evelegh. The 78th Division commander, whose men had been fighting and dying since those first grim weeks in November, hardly knew how to answer. At length he replied stiffly, "One can only plan in the expectation that they will."

The Germans struck first, as they so often did, with a spoiling attack code-named FLIEDERBLÜTE—Lilac Blossom—and timed by Kesselring for the night of April 20 as a birthday tribute to Hitler. Five battalions from the Hermann Göring Division, first formed as a state police unit in 1933, attacked south of Medjez-el-Bab with tanks from the 10th Panzer. Singing as they advanced, the enemy nevertheless achieved enough surprise that one British artillery officer in his tent, annoyed at the racket, hollered, "Go away, James, and stop making so much noise." But dawn exposed the attackers to galling machine-gun and artillery fire that tore great gaps in their ranks. By nightfall on the twenty-first, the line had been restored, with 450 Germans captured and thirty-three panzers destroyed. British losses were modest, and Anderson's timetable for VULCAN was undisturbed but for a four-hour delay in a single division.

Crocker launched his corps with a great belching of guns at 3:40 A.M. on Thursday, the twenty-second. By late the next day—Good Friday— he had shoved the 6th Armoured Division into the breach, punching ten miles through the German line and rousing hopes of a rampage to the sea. But the attack stalled. Murderous antitank fire and Wehrmacht counterattacks at a scabrous hill called Djebel Bou Kournine led to stalemate. The British 1st Armoured Division ended up almost where it had started, and other advances were limited to a few hard miles. A Tommy at Bou Kournine wrote:

> Men have begun drifting back in small groups, most of them badly shaken. They talk of crawling up sheer precipices to find every level expanse swept by machine gun fire; of wounded rolling all the way to the bottom; of tripwire mines and boobytraps on handgrip ledges; of areas automatically illuminated on approach by flares and bulbs, immediately drawing fire; of premature rifle shots from stumbling men, supposed to have given the game away; and of walls and caves and all sorts of cunning defensive devices on the summit, piled round the dead of previous assaults.

On April 26, Anderson ordered IX Corps to halt the futile, costly attack. Search parties scuffed through the ripening wheat at night, feeling with their feet for corpses; they soon stopped, having discovered that German sappers often mined fallow fields and then sowed grain so that the new crop would camouflage their handiwork. Wounded men filled the aid stations, their faces blued by starlight and shock. General Crocker joined them the next day, after being struck in the chest by debris from a new British antitank weapon; eager to show his troops that the gadget could penetrate a captured Tiger, he had instead set fire to a grainfield and put himself in the hospital. There he would remain for the rest of the campaign.

So it was up to Allfrey and V Corps. As planned, on the night of April 21 three battalions from Medjez-el-Bab had crept through the barley and olives to a staging area north of the Medjerda. They went to ground before dawn in gullies near the hamlet of Chassart Teffaha. Each man lay motionless in the scorching sun all the next day, alone with his thoughts and a clear view of the objective looming two miles to the northeast:

Longstop Hill. As in late December, Longstop barred all traffic through the Medjerda valley and would have to be captured before any tank column could push up Highway 50 to Tébourba and Tunis beyond. Unredeemed even by April marigolds and gauzy sunlight, the double-peaked hill seemed more sinister than ever. Skeletons in moldering uniforms sat in the crevices where they had died during the Christmas battles, as if, one British general later wrote, "the ghosts of good soldiers gathered to watch."

Allfrey's attack opened at eight P.M. on the twenty-second, with a cannonade answered weirdly by a spring storm that whipped through from the north in a spectacular lightning display. Four hundred tubes roared from gun pits around Medjez, and the infantrymen rose from their holes to scramble up the lower slopes. "The flashes of those guns, we hoped, were visible in Tunis as a sign of the wrath to come," BBC correspondent Howard Marshall reported. "Stripped to the waist, the gunners kept up their stream of fire while our infantry advanced close behind the barrage." The imperturbable Alexander was among those watching through field glasses from a Medjerda meadow, "like a crowd of spectators watching climbers on the face of the Eiger." Magnesium flares and artillery detonations illuminated tiny dots ascending the slope, followed at a distance by the slightly larger dots that were pack mules. These periodically broke in terror for the bottom: "fractious, four-legged children of Satan," a soldier-turned-muleteer called them.

Good Friday dawned with the attack behind schedule and the assault battalions exposed. A reporter in Medjez noted that "the whole ridge seemed on fire." Djebel el Ahmera—the western peak of the double-crested pinnacle belatedly discovered at Christmas—was to be seized by the 8th Battalion of the Argyll and Sutherland Highlanders on the theory that the Scots would find inspiration in terrain so like home. Instead, German gunners shortly after noon caught the command group in an open field, and their barrage slaughtered the battalion staff and its pipe major.

Heatstroke felled many of those the German shells missed. Soon half the battalion was down. The other half was exhausted, but enraged after a Wehrmacht prisoner whipped out a concealed machine pistol and gunned down several Jocks before being riddled with bullets himself. For the next several days, few prisoners were taken. "The Argylls had been roused to a state of berserk fury," observed Major J. T. McK. Anderson, who would win the Victoria Cross for his heroics at Longstop. "We just had a hate—at the Germans, the hill, and everything." Major Anderson's bayonet charge with thirty howling comrades finally captured el Ahmera;

with the piper dead, the men settled for a windy harmonica player. But Longstop's second crest—Djebel el Rhar, every bit as recalcitrant as it had been in December—fell only on Easter Monday, after British tanks crawled toward the summit. "The hill was an infernal sight, smoking and reeking," a reporter wrote. Three hundred grenadiers were permitted to surrender, their Zeiss binoculars and tins of beef tongue immediately seized as spoils of war.

Longstop had fallen, this time for good, but V Corps was running out of steam as surely as IX Corps had in the south. The Argylls had been reduced by two-thirds. More than five hundred men of the British 1st Infantry Division were killed, or wounded, or went missing in a Good Friday assault along the right bank of the Medjerda, and 329 more were lost the next day in just two battalions. Twenty-nine of forty-five tanks reinforcing the infantrymen were destroyed or damaged; they were among 252 British tanks the Germans claimed in the last ten days of April.

Nowhere in Africa was the fighting more ferocious than on Djebel Bou Aoukaz—the Bou—a 700-foot hogback ridge four miles from Longstop and across the Medjerda. Three Guards battalions attacked the Bou and its spurs for more than a week while the Germans "threw everything but their cap badges at us." Day after day the rush of artillery and the cackle of machine guns rocked the hill; soldiers lay at night in their slit trenches with their pathetic parapets, hand-built of scree, inhaling the "pungent scent of rosemary and evergreen torn by shell splinters and freshened by the rain." When grenade supplies ran out the Tommies tossed rocks at the enemy, "just to keep them on the move." Bodies in the Bou's ripening fields were marked with rifles stuck bayonet-first in the ground, with a soupbowl helmet hung from the butt; the gravediggers sent to collect the fallen one night reported that a hay field had sprouted "a forest of rifles." By the end of April, the 1st Irish Guards had been reduced to eighty men including a stretcher bearer who would eventually lose his wounded leg to a surgeon's knife but for now hobbled up and back, declaring, "I have no time for the gangrene." The 5th Grenadier Guards suffered almost 300 casualties in holding one ridge, including thirteen of sixteen officers, under shelling of such intensity that one lieutenant was reduced to observing: "There is no doubt about it: they are very keen to get this hill."

The hill remained in British hands, but the rest of the bridgehead still belonged to the enemy. By April 29, both Alexander and Anderson recognized that the V Corps offensive had stalled. Allfrey had advanced six miles in an arc on either side of the Medjerda, roughly the same distance gained by Crocker's corps, but he was still twenty-five miles from Tunis.

The next day—Friday, the thirtieth—Anderson told Eisenhower that First Army in the past week had suffered 3,500 casualties, including roughly 900 killed. VULCAN had cost one man for every three yards gained. Many companies were reduced to fewer than two dozen soldiers of all ranks.

If British losses were heavy, so were German and Italian, and there was always consolation in that. Arnim now had sixty-nine functioning panzers in all of Africa. His reserves consisted of a single depleted tank battalion.

But still there was no Allied breakthrough, only heartache and death. Anderson rejected a truce proposal from the Hermann Göring Division to collect the dead, and at night the chinking of shovels from surreptitious burial details could be heard across the fields and orchards of the no-man's-land. A British chaplain who found a long-dead Guardsman near the Bou later described trying to inter the man quickly before dawn. "One arm was sticking straight up," the chaplain wrote. "We couldn't get it in the shallow grave. Every time we forced it down, it jumped up again, a gleaming white hand in the darkness.

"It is terribly hard to break a dead man's arm."

"Count Your Children Now, Adolf!"

WITH both British armies brought to a standstill, the final drive in the Tunisian campaign may fairly be said to have begun with the Americans. Omar Bradley's initial assault in the north was no less frustrating than those of the British—and certainly no more valorous. But once started the attack was never stopped, even when daily progress was measured in inches, and the drive that began Good Friday can be seen as a continuous, two-week victory march to the sea that finally brought the U.S. Army battle honors fairly won.

"We are sitting in an old busted farmhouse, writing by candlelight," Terry Allen wrote Mary Fran on April 22. His black hair tousled, cigarette dangling from his lips, he wore the same frayed green shirt and trousers he had worn at Gafsa and El Guettar, now so mended by his orderly that the ensemble looked more like a quilt than a uniform. The aluminum stars on his shoulders were still those plucked from an Italian private two months ago. Even candlelight could not soften the tension in Allen's face or erase the crow's-feet etched deeper than ever around his eyes. Having turned fifty-five on April 1, he looked older. He had been to mass to pray for himself and his men, including those whom he inevitably had ordered to their deaths. "I'm hoping and praying that my scheme of maneuver is OK," he wrote. "The strain is rather tough and I'll be glad when this mess is over."

The guns finished his thought. Searing white flashes leaped from the pits and rippled along the ridgelines like heat lightning. The barrage, A. B. Austin wrote, "[filled] the hollows with light. It was if the hill waves really were pitching and rolling." A single 105mm howitzer firing at its maximum rate could lob 4,000 pounds of shells in an hour over a 43,000-square-yard area; American gunners now massed more than 300 guns, spitting eleven tons of steel each minute. The shells were fitted with new radar sensors that made the rounds detonate forty feet or so above the target, for optimal killing dispersion. After every concentration the gunners whooped, "Count your children now, Adolf!"

The infantry surged forward in Friday's first light, "a long, slow line of dark-helmeted forms silhouetted in the flash," Ernie Pyle wrote. As Eddy's 9th Division swept across a broad, twenty-eight-mile front on the left flank, Bradley threw the heft of his attack against the right with the 34th and 1st Infantry Divisions and the 6th Armored Infantry Regiment forming a thirteen-mile crescent on a northeasterly vector. The Big Red One shook out three regiments abreast, each with a two-mile frontage, lurching toward hills designated only by their height in meters, plucked from a map—350, 407, 400, 469, 575, 394, 346, 444. Ten enemy battalions awaited the assault, backed by Tigers. Guns boomed, mortars crumped, great gouts of orange and red streaked the hilltops, and smoke lay in dirty banks across the battlefield.

Within two hours they were in trouble if not in perdition itself, and Allen's prayers appeared to have gone unheard. Hill 350, looming above the southwest entrance to the Mousetrap, proved especially grievous for the 2nd Battalion of the 18th Infantry, which suffered 224 casualties on Good Friday alone. Her sister battalion, the 3rd, tallied another 138 assaulting Hill 407 two miles to the north; the commander wept at his losses. In the division center, artillery fell short for a long hour, inadvertently killing or wounding seventy men in the 16th Infantry. Soldiers found every slope seeded with antipersonnel mines, many of the kind known as Castrators or Bouncing Bettys because they sprang belt-high before detonating. In one company of the 26th Infantry, all the officers and the first sergeant were killed or wounded. A soldier in the 26th, hearing agonized shrieks from a wounded comrade, later reported: "I rolled over to him and he looked at me and pleaded, 'Help me. Please shoot me.'" The boy soon died, unassisted.

Into this maelstrom on Friday morning rode a short, sharp-featured visitor from Washington who promptly concluded that the troops lacked the requisite passion for closing with the enemy. Lieutenant General Lesley J. McNair had come to Tunisia to assess American battleworthiness, for which he was responsible as commander of U.S. Army ground forces. Unsociable, enigmatic, and half-deaf, a blue-eyed Scot from Minnesota, McNair had been the youngest American general in France in 1917. An artillerist and accomplished mathematician who carried a slide rule as other men carried pipes or Bibles, he liked to describe himself as a simple "pick-and-shovel man," but one associate likened him to "a Presbyterian pulpit speaker—all irony and intellect." "You may do the wrong thing," McNair often advised, "but do *something*."

Now McNair did something, and it was indeed the wrong thing. Arriving at Allen's "old busted farmhouse" at five A.M., he strode past the steaming manure pile in the courtyard, gulped down a cup of coffee, then argued bitterly with Ted Roosevelt—who showed up in *Rough Rider*—over the prudence of a three-star general's continuing closer to the battlefront. Undeterred, McNair eluded the officer assigned to escort him and pressed forward in a jeep with a large three-star placard on the bumper, bouncing toward the sound of the guns. After sweeping through the 26th Infantry on the left flank, he sped south to the 16th Infantry, grousing that "nowhere did I find anything other than 100 percent lethargy. There was not a bit of fight in the entire outfit."

McNair grew more liverish that afternoon, when he found much of the 2nd Battalion pinned down behind a hill and soldiers braying at him to "get the jeep the hell out of the area." Muttering at this "sorry picture of a fighting outfit" and ignoring more advice to stay back, McNair climbed the ridgeline to an artillery observation post, where he opened a large map to study the terrain. A dozen German shells landed harmlessly behind him before the thirteenth burst with a fierce crack on the crest, killing a company first sergeant. One steel fragment sliced through the rear lip of McNair's helmet, slowing enough so that it lodged in his skull instead of penetrating his brain; another gouged an eight-inch gash in his neck and shoulder, severing an artery. As blood soaked his open map, McNair observed, "I miscalculated my defilade." Rushed by jeep to the division clearing station for treatment with plasma and sulfa—the general grumbled when a surgeon scissored away his $16 tailored shirt—he was then hauled by Dodge ambulance over a camel track to an evacuation hospital north of Béja. Bradley soon appeared to pin a Purple Heart—accidentally upside down—on McNair's pajamas. Flown to a hospital in Oran before evacuation to Washington, McNair continued to complain that "American soldiers are not fighting."

That was untrue—a damned lie, really. Some 500 U.S. soldiers would be killed in Tunisia during Easter week, with another 2,000 wounded; no Pentagon calumny could diminish their sacrifice. While Allen's men struggled in the south to advance a few thousand yards a day, on the left flank General Eddy's 23,000 troops—his own 9th Division and 4,000 from the Corps Franc d'Afrique—pushed forward in vegetation so dense the men often had to crawl.

The 47th Infantry bulled through the sword grass along Highway 7 until Green and Bald Hills loomed into view. Charred wreckage from the three failed British attacks on the Jefna fortifications littered the roadbed and lower slopes. Rather than launch yet another frontal assault, the 47th began to gnaw at the German fringes on the morning of the twenty-third, demonstrating and distracting while her two sister regiments looped north to outflank the enemy in terrain long considered impassable.

Impassable it proved to be, at least at first. Division von Manteuffel—5,000 Axis soldiers in nine battalions—held the twenty-mile front between Jefna and the sea in fortifications so deep that some bunkers required ladders to enter. The 39th Infantry's attack north of Highway 7 started poorly when a German patrol bushwacked and captured 150 men, including the regimental commander, Colonel J. Trimble Brown. Less than an hour later, an intrepid captain, who had seen Brown and his band led away after surrendering their rings and watches, counterattacked with Company G, killing or wounding forty-five Germans, freeing the prisoners, and saving the day if not Colonel Brown's battle plans, which unfortunately disappeared with the fleeing enemy. Shortly before midnight Eddy relieved Brown, who collected his bag and bedroll before heading to the rear.

So it went day after day. Savage fighting raged across more nameless hills—432, 438, 513, 382—at such close quarters that soldiers struggled to stay awake for fear their snores would attract grenades. Peaks were captured and lost, captured again and lost again. Fog hugged the hollows, making them even more opaque and sinister. One officer likened the terrain to "being led into a dark theater after the movie had started." American gunners shattered enemy counterattacks with barrages of white phosphorus shells dumped so near to friendly lines that GIs stumbled out of the smoke with chemical specks burning holes in their uniforms. Muezzins' calls to prayer from hilltop mosques drew gunfire from skittish troops convinced that the criers were signaling the Germans. Taking no chances, U.S. counterintelligence agents created a zone "free from Arabs" by forcibly evacuating a 400-square-mile swath east of Béja.

Eddy's victualers procured 350 mules and fifty tons of fodder to haul supplies where no jeep could travel, and each pack train returned with dead boys trussed over the saddles.

The enemy held fast to Green and Bald, but north of Highway 7 the line slowly bent back. By April 27, the 39th Infantry was two miles north of Green Hill and threatening to envelope the entire Jefna redoubt. The 60th Infantry—though still licking its wounds from Maknassy a month earlier—pressed even farther east on the other side of the Sedjenane River; by month's end the regiment would cover twelve miles, almost half the distance to Bizerte. The Corps Franc d'Afrique edged along the coast with three battalions of men considered too politically volatile for the main French army; among the commanders were a reputed Spanish admiral, a Jewish doctor, and an anti-Vichy colonel who had been jailed in Morocco for helping Patton during TORCH. But most colorful by far was a company of *goums*, Moroccan tribesmen in filthy robes and sandals cut from old tires. As conventional soldiers the "goons"—as the Americans inevitably called them—were hopeless, routinely raiding Arab villages and carrying off native women. Still, they had their uses, particularly when word spread among the enemy that *goums* received a bounty for every ear collected, reportedly flicking them onto the paymaster's table as if counting off ten-franc notes. Many an Axis corporal slept with his cap pulled low. Silently the *goums* returned from their midnight raids with sandbags full of what may have been dried figs, though GIs eager to trade for souvenirs preferred to believe they were Axis ears.

"One more hill!" the American officers told their men each morning, always with the ironic inflection required when comrades lie to one another. Every captured pinnacle brought better artillery observation and thus a better opportunity to pulverize the next ridge with well-aimed fire. The infantry—having learned the hard lessons of El Guettar and Maknassy—maneuvered around the flanks to force the enemy back yet again.

"One more hill!" It was not true, not yet, but every man could sense truth beneath the fiction.

No hill loomed larger than the flattop called Djebel Tahent locally but better known to the Americans as Hill 609. Arnim's troops had retreated half a dozen miles across the II Corps front only to dig in deeper than ever, and by Monday, April 26, Bradley recognized that 609 was the linchpin of Axis defenses. Three miles northeast of Sidi Nsir on the American right, 609 dominated the countryside by virtue of its height and location: almost two thousand feet above sea level, it frowned down on all direct approaches from Béja to Mateur. A desolate mesa 800 yards long and 500 yards wide crowned the hill, which was dramatically faced with fifty-foot limestone cliffs on the south and east. From the summit, a man with a telescope could pick out individual house windows in Mateur twelve miles away and the hazy smudge of Bizerte another twenty miles beyond.

Except for a small olive grove 500 yards from the southern slope, the terrain offered little cover to attackers, while the limestone palisades provided countless knobs and crevices to hide defenders. Storks nested in fissures that formed natural chimneys up the cliff walls; machine guns now nested in scree at the base. Wind tossed the yellowing wheat on the lower slopes, making the hill undulate like a great breathing thing. Neighboring heights—461, 490, 531, 455—provided intertwined fields of fire manned largely by Barenthin Regiment soldiers drawn from the Wehrmacht's parachute and glider schools, who, in Alexander's assessment, were "perhaps the best German troops in Africa."

Anderson proposed simply ignoring the hill. In a phone call to Bradley's Béja command post on Tuesday morning, the British commander advised: "Never mind the enemy opposing you at Sidi Nsir. When you have him on a hilltop, try always to get around him. I don't want you only to push the enemy back, but to get behind him and capture him before he can establish a bridgehead around Bizerte." Almost as an afterthought, Anderson requested the transfer of an American infantry regiment to reinforce the stalled First Army farther south.

Bradley was appalled, and privately concluded that Anderson was "in far over his head as an army commander." In a hastily arranged rendezvous that afternoon at Allen's battered farmhouse, Bradley clipped his map to an easel and explained to Anderson why 609 could not be wished away. The Big Red One had made enough progress to have an exposed left flank just a couple of miles southwest of the hill, from where German gunners had now begun to flay Allen's troops with fire. The 1st Division was more than two thousand men understrength, including a shortfall of sixty officers; new lieutenants received a fifteen-minute orientation lecture, then were shoved straight into the line. Allen lacked the muscle to bull ahead against the five enemy battalions on his front without risking a catastrophic counterattack from Hill 609 that would roll up his left wing. Furthermore, bypassing the hill meant returning to the vulnerable valleys and again drawing fire from every hilltop *Gefreiter* with a mortar tube. "All this depends upon our taking Hill 609," Bradley concluded.

Allen nodded vigorously, head swiveling to keep the cigarette smoke

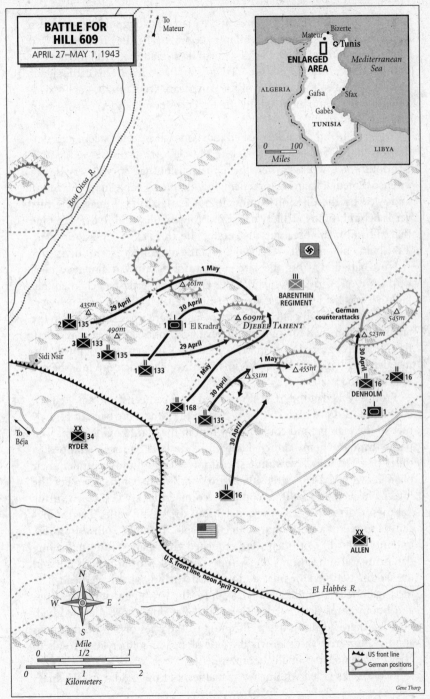

BATTLE FOR HILL 609

APRIL 27–MAY 1, 1943

To Mateur

ENLARGED AREA

Mateur • Bizerte
⊙ Tunis

ALGERIA

Gafsa •
• Sfax
Gabès •

TUNISIA

Mediterranean Sea

LIBYA

0   100
Miles

Bou Oissa R.

△ 461m

1 May

III
BARENTHIN REGIMENT

29 April

435m
△
2 ☒ 135

30 April

1 ☒ 1 El Kradra

△ 609m
DJEBEL TAHENT

German counterattacks

△ 545m

490m
△

3 ☒ 133

3 ☒ 135

29 April

1 ☒ 133

1 May

30 April

△ 523m

30 April

2 ☒ 16

Sidi Nsir

△ 531m

1 May

△ 455m

1 ☒ 16
DENHOLM

2 ☒ 168

1 ☒ 135

2 ☒ 1

30 April

To Béja

XX
RYDER 34

30 April

1 May

3 ☒ 16

XX
ALLEN 1

U.S. front line, noon April 27

El Habbés R.

N
W   E
S

Mile
0   1/2   1

0   1   2
Kilometers

🔺🔺🔺 US front line

⬡ German positions

Gene Thorp

from his eyes. Anderson squinted at the map for a long minute, then also nodded. As for the loan of an infantry regiment, Bradley refused. "We'd like to help you, but you're asking me to do something I will not agree to without direct orders from Ike." To his staff he added, "This campaign is too important to the prestige of the American Army to take such risks." Eisenhower soon concurred, telling his corps commander, "Stand your ground, Brad."

To seize the hill, Bradley turned to troops whose self-esteem and reputation may have been the lowest in the U.S. Army. Since the fiasco at Fondouk three weeks earlier, the 34th Division had spent every day in intense remedial training, practicing night attacks, tank-infantry tactics, and—led by the division commander, Charles Ryder—marching fifty yards behind rolling artillery barrages. Now Bradley told Ryder: "Get me that hill and you'll break up the enemy's defenses clear across our front. Take it and no one will ever again doubt the toughness of your division."

Nine battalions from the 34th swept toward Sidi Nsir along a 6,000-yard front on April 27. A mendacious German deserter had claimed that Hill 609 was held by only a war-worn rear guard, which could be overrun by a determined platoon of fifty men. "There was excitement in the air and the tone was for an immediate attack," one captain later recalled. But Ryder recognized that what he called the "checkerboard of interlocking defenses" required that his men reduce the adjacent hills before attacking 609 itself.

Troops picked at their C rations, filled their canteens, and smoked last cigarettes. At dusk, each soldier tied a white cloth to the back of his helmet so the man behind could follow him in the dark. Engineers marked paths through enemy minefields with white tape or rocks wrapped in toilet paper. Every few minutes, platoon leaders huddled under their blankets with red-lensed flashlights to check their compasses. "For the love of heaven and hell," a company commander's voice called in the darkness, "get going." As they edged into the killing zone, the ripping-canvas sound of a German machine gun split the night, joined by a second and third. "Our men were crouched gray shapes, running, falling flat, firing, running again," one witness reported. Mortar rounds burst in the saddles between the hills, and yellow flares blossomed overhead. The men again fell flat, still as death except for the writhing wounded. Mines and booby traps detonated with a short, flat pop; more men writhed. "We lay there awaiting dawn, listening to the cries of a wounded man about a hundred yards down the side slope," a soldier later recalled. "[He] weakened and finally became silent."

Two attacks failed with heavy casualties, but by midday on Wednesday, April 28, Hills 435 and 490 had fallen between Sidi Nsir and 609. Four German counterattacks were repulsed. All day the valleys rumbled with artillery fire; the crack of shells splitting rock carried from the hilltops. Hundreds of men fell sick in apparent reaction to Atabrine, a synthetic antimalaria drug dubbed "yellow magic" and recently distributed in lieu of quinine, the world supply of which Japan controlled almost exclusively. Many would have preferred malaria. Weak and nauseated, they vomited down the front of their uniforms and fouled their trousers with uncontrollable diarrhea before rising on command in Thursday's wee hours to stumble forward again.

Fog muffled every footstep as the 3rd Battalion of the 135th Infantry advanced 2,000 yards from Hill 490 to El Kradra, an Arab hamlet beneath the south wall of 609. Watching at first light, Drew Middleton reported that he could trace "the path of these soldiers through the wheat just as you would follow the path of Pickett's charge through the summer wheat at Gettysburg." But an attack against Hill 531 on the right was thrown back—the defenders wired together bundles of "potato masher" grenades and dropped them on GIs scaling the escarpment— and delays on the other flank left the battalion at El Kradra vulnerable to a German counterattack. Muzzle flashes erupted across the face of 609 like "tiny sparks, and the wind brought us the angry chatter of a machine gun," Middleton noted. In disarray, the battalion retreated 400 yards from the village to shelter in the olives. Fleas from the village huts so tormented some men that they stripped to their shoes, helmets, and ammunition belts, then dunked their infested uniforms in gasoline. Hundreds of shells crashed across the crest of Hill 609—"it resembles an erupting volcano," one soldier said—but the Germans held fast and the American momentum ebbed.

Ryder's troubles at 609 had increasingly discomfited Terry Allen, who complained that his 16th Infantry was catching "unshirted hell" in artillery and mortar salvoes fired from the hill. At two P.M. on April 28, he had ordered all three 1st Division regiments to halt until the 34th Division could better protect his left flank. In a querulous phone call to Ryder, Allen asked how much longer the 34th needed to capture Hill 606.

"Don't you mean Hill 609?" Ryder replied.

"No, I mean Hill 606. My division artillery has put enough fire on that hill to knock it down three meters."

Another morning of inactivity on Thursday was more than Allen could bear. The corps' casualties in the offensive now exceeded 2,400 men, and nearly half of those came in the Big Red One; while enemy losses were uncertain, only 400 prisoners had been captured since Good

Friday. The 34th Division had been reduced to firing white phosphorus shells into the bunchgrass around 609 so that sharpshooters could pick off Germans flushed by the flames. Convinced that his own division's fortunes were being dragged down by Ryder's failure, Allen on Thursday stopped pacing long enough to order the 16th Infantry forward again. The unit was to seize Hill 523, another fortified butte a mile due east of 609. Allen proceeded despite trenchant protests from the regimental commander, Colonel George A. Taylor, who considered the attack rash.

Impatience cost Allen dearly. In a moonless drizzle shortly after midnight on Friday, April 30, the 1st Battalion of the 16th Infantry crossed a wheat field from the south, climbed Hill 523, and by 4:45 A.M. had captured eleven Germans while killing or routing several dozen more. But dawn brought a quick reversal: in the gray light, figures in coal-scuttle helmets darted through a nearby earthquake fissure to surround the hill. The subsequent mêlée with Barenthin Regiment troops was "more like a street fight than a battle at any distance," one survivor reported. "We couldn't call for artillery because the forces were so close." The brawl, he added, disintegrated into "fist fights, coupled with grenades."

When the crack of artillery finally carried to Colonel Taylor's command post, a clerk noted in his log that "the sound is sweet to our ears"—then realized that those were German guns. Ted Roosevelt ordered a tank company up the hill, but mines and 47mm fire destroyed three Shermans in a narrow draw—the lead tank took more than two dozen hits—and others were repulsed short of the crest. Through breaks in the smoke, the bitter end could be seen from a nearby observation post, which at noon reported to Taylor: "The Heinies are all over that hill." By 12:30 the Germans had marched away more than 150 prisoners, including the battalion commander, Lieutenant Colonel Charles J. Denholm; another hundred dead and wounded Americans were left behind. In the next twenty-four hours, Hill 523 was to change hands three more times.

Hill 609 would change hands only once, finally. Despite skepticism from his armor commanders—"No one in his right mind would consider putting tanks in mountains," one colonel warned—Bradley persuaded Ryder to order seventeen Shermans up the west slope at dawn on April 30. Clouds of infantrymen trailed behind, often grabbing the skirt of a tank with one hand while firing their rifles with the other. "God bless all of you," a company commander from the 133rd Infantry told his men. "We must succeed or die trying." Some did die: Private First Class Edward S. Kopsa of Grundy Center, Iowa, fell with a shell wound so gaping that his heart could be seen beating. "Tell my mother," Kopsa said, and the beating stopped. But within two hours, the tanks had covered almost a mile, machine guns rattling and main guns roaring. The reek of gunpowder saturated air that was already full of primitive shrieks and cries for help. By midafternoon, American soldiers had scrambled up a goat trail to gain the summit, where they winkled the defenders from their breastworks. Additional battalions enveloped the hill from both flanks, and among the first reinforcements to top the crest were Iowans from the 2nd Battalion of the 168th Infantry, including Company F of Villisca and Company E of Shenandoah. Feeble German counterattacks on May Day were shattered with artillery and automatic-weapons fire, and all along the line scouts reported enemy forces retreating or surrendering.

"Jerries approach our troops, some run, some fall on their faces, most of them are weary, haggard, wild-eyed, terrified men who swing arms above heads," the 16th Infantry reported. "A panorama of defeat, as vehicles, mules, and men walk toward the [GIs] with white flags fluttering." Others feigned surrender with white-flag ruses—Staff Sergeant Clarence T. Storm, whose wife worked in the Villisca five-and-dime, was among those killed by such treachery—and the GIs' disdain for the enemy grew murderous. "For twenty-four hours," Bradley noted, "few prisoners came in from the 34th Division's front."

The summit of 609 resembled hell's half-acre, a fire-scoured wasteland of spent brass, bloody bandages, and, oddly, family photos, as if those about to die had pulled them from their wallets for a last farewell. The dead Germans in their rock redoubts reminded one soldier of Civil War photos showing bloated corpses along the rail fences at Antietam. The tabletop "was literally covered with bodies," another wrote. "The stench was terrible." Although the hill was "pitted with shell craters, thick as currants in cake," few holes were deeper than six inches: solid rock underlay the thin soil. After futilely trying to bury the dead in these shallow craters, GIs tossed them into earthquake rifts and a bulldozer plowed them over. "Those who went through it," wrote Ernie Pyle, "would seriously doubt that war could be any worse than those two weeks of mountain fighting."

The 34th Division had redeemed itself, although such fine notions seemed vacant in the immediate aftermath. Ryder put his losses at 324 men. The American dead were hauled from the hill in truck beds. "All you could see," an artilleryman later remembered, "was their shoes hanging off the tail gate." Across the valley, a staff officer in the 16th

Infantry summoned a lieutenant preparing to lead a patrol back up Hill 523. "I don't believe I would take any prisoners on 523."

"No," the lieutenant agreed, "no prisoners will be taken."

But except for dead men and Colonel Denholm's map, the hill was empty. The enemy was gone. As Bradley had foreseen, the capture of Hill 609 unhinged enemy defenses across the entire front, from the Mediterranean to the Mousetrap. American troops bayed in pursuit. A reporter watching from 609 wrote, "At our feet every road was thronged with troops, guns, and supplies, pouring northward."

Outside Béja, Bradley sat on a metal stool in his tent, reading dispatches. He studied the map on the easel, now crisscrossed with blue and red crayon marks showing an enemy in full retreat and pursuers close behind. He was in good humor, chuckling often and, as his aide later recounted, "smoothing the sparse gray hair on his head and thinking aloud." Fresh reports arrived from the 9th Division in the north, the 34th and 1st in the south, and the 1st Armored Division, preparing to blow down the Tine valley on two mine-cleared routes named Broadway and Riley Street. The enemy appeared to be falling back as much as fifteen miles to the far side of Mateur. When another dispatch noted signs of a possible counterattack, Bradley nodded.

"Let 'em come," he said. "We want to kill Germans."

Mateur fell on May 3, three days ahead of Alexander's estimate. The 91st Reconnaissance Battalion entered the deserted town from the south and west at 11:30 A.M. just as German demolitionists blew up the last bridge across the Tine to the east; by early evening, Army engineers had a new span in place. A dozen roads and rail lines converged at Mateur, and its capture ended any Axis hope of concentrating against the British, who were still struggling in the Medjerda valley twenty miles to the south.

The land here flattened out before rising again in a final set of foothills that cradled two large lakes between Mateur and Bizerte. Swallows scissored the brilliant air, rich with the odors of manure and fresh-cut hay, and poplars marched along the road shoulders in perfect ranks. In a white manor house flanked by cypresses, troops found a biography of Bismarck open on the desk; soon they surmised that the mansion for months had served as General Hasso von Manteuffel's division headquarters. American scouts sat on a knoll overlooking the Tine, singing "Moonlight on the River Colorado." Others got drunk in a Mateur wine cellar, and the 1st Armored commander ordered them shot at sunset. "General," a staff colonel urged him, "I think we ought to let the men live until sunrise. It's customary." General Harmon reluctantly agreed, and on reflection commuted the sentence. Wounded Americans and captured Germans shared a farmhouse aid station near Mateur, "smoking, cursing, or grimacing." A GI who arrived by ambulance with a bullet in his lung gestured at a column of prisoners and murmured, "Tell the sons of bitches to go to hell."

Many thousands had retreated to the last bastion, the Lake Ichkeul hills. American gunners, wearing Barbasol shave cream as sunblock and head nets against the swarming flies, plastered them with artillery that ignited the dry grass. "Arab shacks and straw burned with great fury, sending clouds of smoke into the air," an officer noted. A company of Shermans from the 13th Armored Regiment was sent to overrun trenches sheltering a German rear guard. "Some of the enemy were buried alive when the side of the trenches collapsed under the weight of the medium tanks," another officer reported. "Others were mowed down by the tankers' machine guns." Commanders urged them forward. "Here is our chance," Eddy told the 9th Division. "Don't let it slip away—push on!" Harmon ordered his tank crews to drive "like shit through a tin goose."

The 1st Armored Division had been held on a very short leash for weeks, and its hour was about to arrive. The terrain now favored a pursuit by Old Ironsides' 200 tanks, and Alexander scheduled the final assault on Bizerte for May 6, at the same time as a massive attack by First Army to break through to Tunis. Once again, though, the German defenses looked formidable, with antitank gunners on the approaches to Bizerte said to be "dug in to their eyebrows." Hamilton Howze, who had returned to a line unit after Ward's departure, later wrote: "In the time of waiting I confess I found out what fear is: it is a monkey's paw that squeezes your liver in a heavy grip." On a visit to Harmon's command post southwest of Mateur, Bradley stood in a grainfield scanning the countryside. "Can you do it?" he asked Harmon.

"Yes, but it's going to be expensive," Harmon replied. "I'd guess fifty tanks to finish the job."

"Go ahead. It'll cost us less in the long run if we cut him to pieces quickly."

Yet Harmon nursed his own doubts. If the 34th Division had been the Army's most troubled combat unit before the victory at Hill 609, Old Ironsides after Kasserine and Maknassy was a close second. Harmon had spent his month in command trying to rebuild what he deemed "a cry-baby outfit," still fractured by divided loyalties to Ward and Robinett and "honeycombed with dissension." But he had alienated many with his brusque approach, exemplified by a memo in mid-April that casti-gated the division for "lack of discipline, lack of system, and a general sloppy appearance." And at dusk on April 13 he had summoned every officer to the slopes of Djebel Lessouda, where the charred wreckage from Sidi bou Zid lay scattered in the shadows. Harmon delivered a shrill rebuke, which, in Robinett's description, "damned all past perfor mance of duty, sparing none." He concluded with a raspy warning: "The division will get to Mateur, but maybe you won't." Some men had the temerity to boo; most trudged off in dejection. "His speech was not very well received," a lieutenant later wrote. "We all went to bed that night very much hurt."

Now they had reached Mateur; but the biggest prize still lay ahead, in Bizerte. On May 5 Harmon drove to Robinett's headquarters and led the CCB commander into an open field for a private conversation. With his massive skull and barrel chest, Harmon towered over his pint-sized sub-ordinate. "Will the damned tanks fight?" he demanded.

"Damned right they will fight, as some are doing now," Robinett snapped. "They have always fought and will fight again." Never content to leave well enough alone, he then berated Harmon for questioning "the courage of these men." Harmon turned on his heel and returned to his jeep, while a furious Robinett tromped back to the tent and composed a message to all ranks: "Towards the rear anonymous individuals have said that we are 'not battle worthy.' This insult to our glorious dead and to you, the courageous living, shall not be forgotten nor left uncontested."

After that unpromising prelude, Harmon held a final planning con-ference for his lieutenants at the division command post a few hours later. The attack was set for first light the next morning, Thursday, May 6, with CCB in the vanguard. But Robinett's behavior during the past month continued to gnaw at Harmon. Robinett "seems to think only in terms of defense and is definitely casualty conscious," Harmon privately informed the War Department. "I do not feel that he has the qualities of leadership that are necessary in an armored division." Six months of combat had worn him down. As he watched Robinett drive away from the conference toward his own command post, Harmon muttered to himself: "Hell, that fellow isn't going to fight for me tomorrow." The judgment was harsh and probably wrong, but Harmon's mind was made up. Summoning his driver, he raced after Robinett to relieve him of command.

Harmon had nearly overtaken the jeep on the poplar-shaded road when the rush of German artillery split the air. A shell exploded a few feet behind Robinett, shredding his left leg and flinging him and his driver from their seats. More rounds crashed through the trees as soldiers appeared from the CCB encampment and bundled their wounded commander into an ambulance, which zigzagged through shell fire to the camouflaged command tent around the next bend.

Minutes later, Harmon pushed aside the canvas flaps and walked in "looking hard as rock." A glance at the mangled leg told Harmon that Robinett's war was over. Robinett looked up with glassy eyes. He had already relinquished command of CCB to Colonel Benson. In an hour he would be driven to the field hospital in Béja, vomiting in agony; a regimental band waited to serenade him with "The Missouri Waltz." A flight to Algeria and evacuation to the United States would be followed by many months of medical rehabilitation and a lasting hitch in his bantam strut.

"You are about to win a great victory," Robinett told Harmon thickly before stretcher bearers carried him to the ambulance, "and I only regret that I cannot be present to share the battle with my men."

Harmon shook his head. "Poor bastard," he muttered, then turned and strode from the tent.

Tunisgrad

THE most intense artillery barrage ever seen in Africa erupted in gusts of white flame at three A.M. on May 6. More than 400 Royal Artillery guns cut loose simultaneously on targets along Highway 5, five miles south of the Medjerda River. Here First Army had concentrated for the great lunge on Tunis, now code-named Operation STRIKE. "The muzzle flashes lit up the gun pits with a dancing yellow light, and the shells, tearing overhead at a rate of five or six hundred a minute, burst a few seconds later on the opposite slope like the flowering of a field of ruby tulips," a young officer wrote.

Determined to bury the enemy beneath "stunning weights of metal," gunners plotted one shell for every six feet of enemy frontage. (At El Alamein, the figure had been one shell for every thirty feet.) Shells shrieked "over our heads in an endless stream, so close, it seemed that you could almost strike a match on them," a witness declared. After half an hour the barrage lifted momentarily, then fell with redoubled vigor, marching eastward by 100 yards every three minutes. Seventy-two suspected enemy artillery batteries that had been pinpointed by gun flashes or aerial surveillance received lavish attention: each hostile battery was hammered on three occasions with two-minute concentrations by as many as thirty-two guns. The effect was "a roof of shells . . . destroying every living thing that moves." More than a few inanimate targets were also destroyed, including, as a scout sorrowfully reported, an oak vat containing 8,000 gallons of red Tunisian wine.

Behind the guns at 5:40 A.M. came the planes, again with a bombardment unprecedented on the continent. More than 2,000 Allied sorties would be flown this Thursday, beating a path from Medjez-el-Bab to Tunis. Fighters and bombers so thick they eclipsed the rising sun concentrated on a four-mile square around Massicault and St. Cyprien along Highway 5. Insult followed injury: clouds of propaganda pamphlets warned enemy survivors that they had been duped by "Rommel" and left to die alone in Africa.

Well before dawn, the infantry had surged forward on a 3,000-yard front, guided by a Bofors gun that fired three red tracers on a fixed line every five minutes. At Alexander's insistence, First Army had been reinforced with two divisions and a Guards brigade from Montgomery's horde. They had arrived more than 30,000 strong from Enfidaville over the past few days, fire-blackened tea tins banging against their yellow fenders; although headlights were authorized for the move, after years of blackout not one vehicle in five had working bulbs. No fraternal love was lost between the mountain tribe and the desert tribe—the two British armies were "as different as chalk from cheese," General Horrocks conceded—and Tommies in the 78th Division went so far as to paint signs on their vehicles: "We have no connection with the Eighth Army." But the added weight lent irresistible momentum to Anderson's attack, and by daybreak the British 4th Division and the 4th Indian Division had pried a gap two miles wide through enemy defenses.

Four tank battalions rushed through. Defenders not killed by artillery or air attack died at their posts or broke for the rear, tossing aside their rifles as they ran. Despite advance knowledge from intercepted radio messages about where the British would likely attack, Arnim was powerless; the Fifth Panzer Army had been reduced to fewer than seventy tanks, little ammunition, and even less fuel. By eleven A.M., British armor had penetrated 5,000 yards beyond the gap, with light losses. Anderson initially had proposed having his tankers linger to mop up stragglers, but Alexander overruled him. The tanks were to "drive with all speed and energy on Tunis," Alexander ordered. "The rapier," he later explained, "was to be thrust into the heart."

"The whole valley before us became a heaving sea of flame," wrote the American journalist John MacVane. "Over a dozen roads and trails, plumes of floury dust rose from the columns of vehicles." The stink of cordite and crushed wheat was nauseating enough to bring some men to their knees. Through "a thick pall of smoke and dust resembling ground mist," drivers bumped along in second gear, navigating by compass heading. The correspondent Alan Moorehead described seeing Alexander racing forward "at almost reckless speed, both his hands tight on the wheel and his face whitened like a baker's boy with white dust."

Allied eavesdroppers intercepted German radio messages sending medics into the line as riflemen; the walking wounded soon were ordered to join them. Another message, from Arnim's quartermaster, requested that no more ammunition be dispatched from Italy because there was no fuel with which to distribute it in Africa. A third message reported that the 15th Panzer Division had been "laid low.... Its bulk must be considered as annihilated." As German resistance disintegrated, the British vanguard was urged to press on with a prearranged code word: "Butter." Soon radios across the front were chirping: "Butter, butter, butter." By dusk, two armored divisions had reached Massicault, eight miles beyond the infantry and a day's march from Tunis. On a hilltop west of the capital a British colonel reported, "I can see the lily-white walls of that blasted city."

Eighteen Royal Navy destroyers patrolled the Sicilian Straits to prevent any last-moment Axis decampment. The ships' superstructures had been painted an unmistakable royal red after three accidental bombings by overzealous Allied planes. All waters within five miles of the Tunisian coast were declared a free-fire zone, and Eisenhower's naval chief soon reduced his order of the day to seven words: "Sink, burn, and destroy. Let nothing pass."

The righteous wrath of such orders fell heavily on 464 American and British prisoners-of-war embarked on the freighter *Loyd Triestino* for passage to Italian stockades. Marched through the wrecked docks of Tunis on the night of May 5, each man before boarding received a quarter-loaf of sour bread, a tablespoon of canned meat, eight prunes, and a scoop of Red Cross macaroni. Among the Yanks were Lieutenant Colonel Denholm and the 150 men from the 16th Infantry who had been captured on Hill 523. German guards confiscated the prisoners' cash— always tendering a proper receipt in return—and limited their interrogations to wistful queries about whether captured Axis troops were being sent to camps in Canada or the United States. The 3,000-ton scow cast off at five A.M. on May 6, slowly steaming from a harbor so crowded with the protruding masts of sunken ships that one prisoner thought it looked "almost like a forest."

Three hours later the first Allied planes attacked, sinking a destroyer escort and driving *Triestino* to a cove sheltered by cliffs on Cap Bon's northwest shore. Terrified prisoners cowered in the dank hold as near misses opened seams in the hull and cannon fire riddled the upper decks. German anti-aircraft crews answered, and after a second attack blue smoke draped the listing vessel. Suffering from dysentery and limited to three filthy heads on the exposed weather deck, the men ripped up planks in the hold so they could defecate into the bilge. "The air," Denholm later reported, "was very bad."

With his ship slowly sinking, the Italian captain hauled anchor and wallowed back toward Tunis early on May 7. A third Allied attack put a bomb into the forecastle; it was a dud. More marauders swarmed above the ship as she neared Tunis harbor, with each near miss bringing frenzied shouts from the soldiers locked in the hold. "The ship seemed to jump out of the water, then settle back with a kind of quiver, which wasn't good," a lieutenant later recalled. "Not one of us doubted the transport was going to sink. We began beating the cage and yelling to be released." A fourth attack was too much for the thirty Italian crewmen, who "went completely to pieces," cut away the lifeboats, and—"hopping around like fleas"—dove into the water after them. The crewless captain steered for La Goulette, a fishing village below Carthage, and beached the *Triestino* on an even keel several hundred yards from shore. He and the German gunners freed the howling prisoners and then rowed off in the remaining lifeboat.

At least half a dozen more attacks occurred through the long afternoon. Only poor marksmanship and extraordinary good fortune spared the ship: more than one hundred bombs fell and every one missed except the dud. Tommies struck the Italian flag and Denholm's men laid out large red crosses on the weather deck with upholstery ripped from the ship's saloon. Pilots either failed to see the warnings or considered them a ruse; the attacks continued, forcing the men back into the fetid hold. A crude raft was launched toward La Goulette, but the wind blew it seaward. That night several Tommies swam ashore seeking help, and an intrepid Frenchman in a motorboat carried a plea to approaching Allied forces to stop the attacks. At last *Triestino*'s ordeal was over. Denholm reported more than four thousand cannon and machine-gun holes in her hull. Miraculously, only one man had been killed, three wounded.

* * *

Harmon's 1st Armored surged east in a light rain on the late afternoon of May 6. CCA angled toward Ferryville on the southwest shore of Lake Bizerte, while CCB sliced due east to control the roads between Bizerte and Tunis. German antitank guns were rooted out one by one; having predicted the loss of fifty tanks, Harmon in the event lost forty-seven. North of the two lakes, Eddy's 9th Division clattered down Highway 11 with orders from Bradley to "get the hell into Bizerte" and prevent sabotage of the port.

By Friday morning the enemy was reeling, leaving a wake of incinerated vehicles and charred German corpses. The reporter A. B. Austin recorded that "the women of Tindja and Ferryville were loading their perambulators with the bright, brassy German shell-cases. Flower vases? Umbrella stands?" A U.S. tank commander rumbled into Ferryville playing the *William Tell* Overture on his ocarina over the radio network. Cheering crowds waved tricolors at both the passing Shermans and Harold V. Boyle of the Associated Press, who stood in a jeep, waving and declaiming: "Vote for Boyle / Son of toil / Honest Hal / The Ay-rab's pal!" More cheers followed, and the slogan "Vote for Boyle!" became a standard greeting from the curbside throngs to baffled troops trailing the vanguard. Also puzzling was an enigmatic graffito soldiers began noticing on walls and road signs. Of uncertain origin, as ambiguous as it was ubiquitous, the phrase would follow them to the heart of Germany two years later. It read: "Kilroy was here."

With the 9th Division headed for Bizerte and 1st Armored tanks effectively cutting the Axis bridgehead in half, the Big Red One had little to do in the Tine River valley eight miles south of Mateur, and there lay trouble. Terry Allen was a fighting man with a compulsion to fight; inactivity was his bane. Ordered by Bradley to hold in place and prevent a counterattack by the Barenthin Regiment across the Tine, Allen on the night of May 5 concocted a plan to root enemy troops from the hills east of the river. His 18th Infantry Regiment commander opposed the scheme; so did Ted Roosevelt and several senior staff officers who argued at eleven P.M. that if left unmolested the Barenthin troops would feign a counterattack and withdraw east to flatter terrain. Allen wavered, prayed over the matter, and at midnight ordered the attack forward.

At 4:20 A.M. on May 6, the 18th Infantry surged from the Tine across Highway 55 and up the grain-gilded slope marked on Army maps as Hill 232. By 5:30 a flanking battalion was lost in the dark and several assault companies had been pinned down by scything machine-gun and mortar fire. "Bullets were singing all around now," Private Max B. Siegel of the

3rd Battalion told his diary. "Our boys were not doing so good. Many were hit and calling for medics. . . . I seen a few boys running back. I tried to keep low." Engineers finished bridging the Tine at seven A.M. but the span collapsed with a great crack after only four tanks had crossed. The 3rd Battalion commander stumbled back with fewer than three dozen shocked, silent men. Others lay motionless in the wheat until nightfall, to avoid drawing artillery fire. By four P.M. all battalions and tanks had splashed back across the Tine. Losses in the 18th Infantry totaled 282 men. The Barenthin slipped away in the night.

Allen was chastened, and even loyalists doubted his judgment. "My bloody foolish commander," complained Lieutenant Colonel John T. Corley, who in a storied combat career would win the Distinguished Service Cross twice and the Silver Star eight times. "We got the shit beat out of us. . . . It's the vanity of the commander. He wanted to be in on the kill."

Early on Friday afternoon, Bradley and Eisenhower arrived in the leafy glen west of the Tine where the 1st Division had moved its head-quarters. A warm drizzle slicked the roads, and camouflage netting billowed in the breeze. A shot-up farmhouse across the swale had served as a German supply dump, and the yard was strewn with gray tunics and Afrika Korps sun helmets. This was Eisenhower's third trip to the front since the Good Friday offensive began, and Harry Butcher thought he resembled "a hen setting on a batch of eggs . . . wondering if they will ever break the shell." He had approved the final plan for Sicily on May 3, and now awaited concurrence from the combined chiefs in London and Washington. With more time to devote to the endgame in Tunisia, he had seen a great deal that was heartening. "We are learning something every day," he wrote a friend, "and in general do not make the same mistakes twice." While admitting to Marshall only the slightest need for rest—"When this affair is all cleared up, I am going to take a twenty-four-hour leave where no one in the world will be able to reach me"—to Butcher he proposed getting "good and drunk when Tunisia is in the bag."

In truth he was sleeping badly, often waking at four A.M. to pace and fret, puffing through a pack of cigarettes before breakfast. Although victory in Africa approached, there was still much to unsettle a commander. "The fighting since April 23 has had a definite influence on our thinking and calculations," he wrote Marshall. "Even the Italian, defending mountainous country, is very difficult to drive out, and the German is a real problem." The portents were unmistakable, for Sicily and whatever battlefields lay beyond. "The Tunisian fight appears to offer a good indication of what we can expect when we meet the German in defensive positions," Eisenhower added, "especially where the terrain is favorable to him."

But only to his closest confidants did Eisenhower acknowledge the deeper impact of his extended stay at the front. Here, where the consequences of combat were most vivid, the weight of command felt heaviest. To his brother Arthur he wrote of visiting "the desperately wounded" and of seeing "bodies rotting on the ground and smell[ing] the stench of decaying human flesh." He had ordered so many men to their deaths, thousands upon thousands, with many thousands yet to die. He sought refuge in duty and *pro patria* resolve, as commanders must. "Far above my hatred of war is the determination to smash every enemy of my country, especially Hitler and the Japs," he told Arthur. He also immersed himself in nitty-gritty decisions concerning supply and personnel, as if his own willful intercession in minutiae could hurry the war to its end. That very week, he had proposed the Army quartermaster design a better winter uniform of "very rough wool, because such material does not show the dirt." To Marshall on Wednesday he noted, "We have discovered that our older men—that is the 50- to 55-year-old fellow—does not wear out *physically* as quickly as might be imagined."

Now the fifty-five-year-old Terry Allen stumbled from his tent, where he had been roused from a dead sleep on the ground. He looked not only worn out but catatonic, and he spoke in monosyllables. His eyes were glazed, his hair mussed. As Eisenhower and Bradley slipped on their reading glasses to study the map, Allen tersely described the previous night's attack on Hill 232. Casualties were high. Some companies were hardly bigger than platoons. His men were tired after months of combat.

Eisenhower peered over his spectacles. The British, he pointed out, had chased Rommel across the desert for several months from El Alamein to the Mareth Line, with little water or rest. They, he added, had "taken it." Allen replied irrelevantly that his unit in the Great War had attacked every day for weeks. The conference ended. Allen tossed a weary salute as the two generals left. "How much better it would have been if Allen had been thoroughly cheerful, buoyant, and aggressive," Butcher scribbled in his diary.

Eisenhower shrugged off the unfortunate encounter. "I found the II Corps in wonderful spirit. The 1st Division has suffered a great deal of attrition," he wrote Marshall a few hours later. But Bradley seethed. The attack on Hill 232 was "a foolish one and undertaken without authorization," he later declared. While Allen was among the Army's most competent leaders—Alexander would go so far as to tell Drew Middleton he "was the finest division commander he had encountered in two wars"—Bradley found him "the most difficult man with whom I have ever had to work," an incorrigible rebel "fiercely antagonistic to any echelon above that of division." He was disturbed by Allen's truculent independence and the Big Red One's self-absorption—the "Holy First," some called it—particularly because the 1st Division was expected to play a pivotal role in Sicily.

For his part, Allen privately considered Bradley "a phony Abraham Lincoln." Two men could hardly have been more dissimilar: the abstemious, restrained, cerebral corps commander and the carousing, emotional, impetuous division commander. But Bradley had both the rank and the commander-in-chief's ear—Eisenhower had just recommended him for a third star—and this boded ill for Allen. "From that point forward," Bradley later wrote of the Tine River debacle, "Terry was a marked man in my book."

As Eisenhower and Bradley drove back to the new II Corps headquarters below Hill 609, Lieutenant Colonel Charley P. Eastburn radioed the 9th Division command post. "Believe road to Bizerte wide open," said Eastburn, commander of the 894th Tank Destroyer Battalion. "Request permission to proceed and occupy the town." The reply from Eddy came swiftly: "Go ahead. Good luck." Mustering three companies, including more than a dozen tanks, Eastburn forded a creek past a demolished bridge, then wheeled back onto Highway 11. Shortly before four P.M. the cavalcade rattled past the stone gateposts at Bizerte's western edge.

They entered a dead city. The ancient port of 70,000 souls lay empty, gutted by more than two dozen 4,000-pound bombs and many tons of lesser explosives. "Bizerte was the most completely wrecked place I had ever seen," Ernie Pyle wrote. Italianate houses lay disemboweled, their porticos smashed. Charred palm trunks, stripped of fronds, lined the corniche. Shops had been bombed and then looted, and a stench of rot and plaster dust hung in the rain. The town had been without running water for three months. Typhus was here and cholera threatened.

Warehouses and shipyards lay in rubble. Bombs had wrenched a 100-ton crane from its foundation, tossing it across a dry dock. All that remained of a large Catholic church was three scorched walls and debris heaped in the nave. "You walked through the great stone front door, right out under the open sky again," a soldier recalled. To escape the bombing, German soldiers had retired months before to tents west of town; in recent days, they had returned to blow up the remaining docks, power plants, and even fishing smacks that Allied bombers missed.

As Colonel Eastburn paused in the downtown shambles to ask a drunk Frenchman for directions to city hall, machine-gun bullets abruptly ricocheted off the pavement and 88mm shells cracked overhead. Muzzle flashes from German rearguard troops winked in the rubble 500 yards across a shipping channel originally dug by Phoenician colonists to connect the salt lagoon of Lake Bizerte with the Mediterranean.

Eastburn's Shermans returned fire with a smoky roar; other gunners hammered away at the Wehrmacht snipers infesting rooftops and a steeple. More Frenchmen popped from their cellars to toast the liberators with upraised wine bottles, huzzahing each tank volley even as slabs of stucco sheared from the walls and sniper bullets pinged about. "Quite ridiculous," a British liaison officer muttered. "Quite ridiculous." In the Café de la Paix, a soldier banged out "It's a Long Way to Tipperary" on a tuneless upright despite the bark of a Sherman main gun down the street. "Everybody was standing up straight at attention, partly humming, partly singing because nobody knew all the words," according to one account. "This café was part of another planet."

By dawn, the last Germans had died or fled. The Corps Franc d'Afrique was trucked forward to Bizerte for the honor of formally capturing the town. Behind the French procession, American soldiers followed in a jeep, with a busty mannequin liberated from a lingerie shop. The men belted out a new barracks ballad that eventually would reach two hundred stanzas, all of them salacious:

> *Dirty Gertie from Bizerte,*
> *Hid a mousetrap 'neath her skirtie,*
> *Made her boyfriend's finger hurtie . . .*

A few miles to the east, scouts reported "hundreds of vehicles being burned on the flats, while overhead the sky was brilliant with tracer ammo being fired in anticipation of surrender." Harmon's Shermans rolled to the edge of the Gulf of Tunis, took aim at a few Germans trying to escape by barge or skiff, and blew them out of the water. The end was near.

Tunis fell at 3:30 P.M. on May 7, almost as Eastburn entered Bizerte. The Derbyshire Yeomanry and 11th Hussars, drawn respectively from the First and Eighth Armies, raced into the city so fast that Royal Air Force fighters mistook the vanguard for fleeing Germans and attacked three times. Snipers fought a bitter delaying action downtown, puncturing the tires on British armored scout cars; reduced to their rims, the vehicles rattled across the cobblestones in a blaze of sparks. Unlike Bizerte, much of Tunis beyond the wrecked port remained unscathed and many of the city's 180,000 residents had remained through the occupation. Delirious French throngs now capered through the rainy capital, tossing flower garlands at the liberators or spraying them with scent from atomizer bottles. French vigilantes chased departing Germans with muskets and horse pistols, singing the "Marseillaise."

"The streets were full of civilian traffic. Astonished Germans were seen on the pavements, walking out with their girlfriends," a Rifle Brigade commander later wrote. "The populace was screaming itself hoarse in true French style. . . . To the enormous amusement of the battalion, I was embraced from behind by a highly colored French female of ample proportions and acquiescent tendencies." Tommies found Wehrmacht officers drinking schnapps at the Majestic Hotel bar or awaiting shaves from an Arab barber. Muffled explosions rumbled from garages along Rue el Jebbar as Germans grenaded their cars; others roared through the streets like gangsters on the lam with tires squealing and guns blazing. "Get out your weapons, boys," one sergeant ordered. "Jerry's still obstinate." Tracers crisscrossed the boulevards, and Shermans fired point-blank at suspected redoubts. Hussars reported capturing the city's collaborationist governor, "complete with Buick and girlfriend," and above the roar of one firefight a Cockney voice bellowed, "Stop that shooting, you bloody fools. It's one of ours."

East of the city, near the white chapel where St. Louis had died of plague while leading the last Crusade in 1270, columns of black smoke billowed from burning fuel dumps. Wehrmacht soldiers spiked their big guns and piled small arms to be crushed by panzer tracks. At El Aouina airfield the only thing still functioning was a windsock.

Into the city came "endless streams of lorries pouring ahead three abreast, full of exuberant troops. . . . Men were singing and shouting." General Barré, the first French general to fire on the Germans in Tunisia, was given the honor of marching into the capital at the head of his troops. Logisticians and camp followers trailed closely: vengeful Frenchmen, jubilant Jews, souvenir hunters, quartermasters reserving the best buildings for their bosses, and journalists who enraged Anderson by describing the capture of Tunis as a "left hook by Eighth Army." "Cannot this pernicious rivalry be stopped?" he cabled Eisenhower. "We are all one army and working for one cause." ("God," Everett Hughes told his diary, "I wish we could forget our egos for a while.")

Ten teams from a counterintelligence unit known as S Force also swept through town carrying a list of 130 targets, including the suspected Gestapo and SS headquarters at, respectively, 168 and 172 Avenue de Paris, and a house on Rue Abdelhouab used to train Arab saboteurs. Also warranted for arrest were scores of civilians, whose descriptions and purported offenses were equally vague: "Scarzini, Italian dentist," on Avenue Bab Djedid, for instance, and "Ramdam, a Tunisian egg merchant," in La Goulette.

For months, Eisenhower had worried that Axis troops would convert the Cap Bon peninsula into a diehard redoubt. But once Bizerte and Tunis fell, fuel shortages and Allied alacrity prevented Arnim from regrouping. Bradley's soldiers cut the last Bizerte-Tunis road at daylight on May 9, effectively ending American combat operations in Tunisia. Now there was nothing to do but smoke out renegades and escort prisoners to their cages. German officers under a flag of truce asked Harmon for terms; in reply, he quoted Grant at Fort Donelson: "Unconditional surrender. We propose to move immediately upon your works." For good measure he added, "We will kill all who try to get away."

Few tried. Soon every American truck and jeep sported a German helmet as a hood ornament. "Winning in battle is like winning at poker or catching lots of fish," Pyle wrote. "It's damned pleasant and it sets a man up."

II Corps casualties in the preceding two weeks had exceeded 4,400, nearly half falling on Allen's 1st Division. Enemy dead in the final fortnight were estimated at 3,000 in the American sector, with another 41,000 captured. Booty included 30,000 small arms—almost enough to corduroy the roads, as Sheridan had done with Confederate muskets near Appomattox. The wheezy declamations that commanders had issued earlier in the campaign now yielded to eloquent brevity; Bradley's two-word cable to Eisenhower on May 9 read simply: "Mission accomplished."

For the British farther south, the end was less tidy, although the Axis troops still holding the Enfidaville line lacked enough gasoline to fall back forty miles on Cap Bon unless they abandoned their heavy weapons. Kesselring at his headquarters in Rome ordered U-boats to haul fuel and matériel to Tunisia—each could carry twenty tons—but only one reached the African coast, where the skipper failed to find a suitable beach for his cargo of ammunition. On the night of May 8, German commanders signaled Axis ships lying offshore to jettison their fuel barrels, wanly hoping that a few would drift to shore on the tide. An announcement from Berlin that remaining Axis troops "will be withdrawn in small boats" brought derisive hoots from the German and Allied camps alike. Alexander's intelligence officer repeated Churchill's bon mot of 1940, when a German invasion of England had been expected: "We are waiting, so are the fishes."

The jig was up. The Fifth Panzer Army, which had occupied the northern swath of bridgehead from Tunis to Bizerte, recorded a last entry in its war diary at 3:23 P.M. on May 8: "The mass of our tanks and artillery is destroyed. No ammunition, no fuel left. Intention: fight to the last round. . . . In loyal performance of duty, the last fighters of the Fifth Panzer Army greet the homeland and our Führer. Long live Germany." The 90th Light Division ordered troops to smash all equipment, including wristwatches.

At Hammam Lif, a coastal resort ten miles southeast of Tunis, British tanks and infantrymen with fixed bayonets swept through six parallel streets on May 9, cleaning out snipers. The fighting surged up and down staircases and across rose gardens in the milky dawn. More than a dozen tanks outflanked the enemy with a bold sally along the strand, "kicking up waves like a steamboat as they circled through the water," one journalist reported. Two other squadrons bulled through town, turrets swiveling from side to side, as Arab mourners in a funeral cortège scattered into the alleys and giddy Frenchmen sprang from their cellars to offer the Tommies wine and pastry. In the blue-and-white summer palace of the bey of Tunis, a British lieutenant found the assembled Tunisian cabinet in the wrecked throne room. The bey soon emerged from an inner chamber and, with the sangfroid of a host welcoming guests to tea, politely inquired after the health of the British king and his queen. Perfectly well, thank you, the lieutenant assured him, then ordered the bey arrested for collaboration. Much keening was heard from the royal concubines, but his bodyguards, resplendent in scarlet and black, surrendered their weapons without protest and then looted the palace.

Like Terry Allen on the Tine, Montgomery had found consignment to the periphery a deeply frustrating fate. On the night of May 10 he launched his 56th Division against Zaghouan, twenty miles northwest of Enfidaville; the attack cost nearly 400 British casualties, a setback as unfortunate as it was unnecessary. On Tuesday the eleventh, Cap Bon was cleared, and Axis resistance dwindled to isolated pockets in the tortured hills above Enfidaville. In a dozen liberated towns, jubilant French civilians unfurled their tricolors and draped the Tommies with honeysuckle. On May 12, for the first time since November, soldiers were allowed to build campfires; Sherwood Rangers celebrated with victory cocktails made of equal parts gin, wine, whiskey, and condensed milk. "Looking back on the last six months," a captain wrote to his father, "it seems as if one has been holding one's breath, and you have just let it go for the first time." A Grenadier Guard on the evening of May 12 described "the plain dotted with points of light, each reflecting dimly the shape of a Sherman tank; the tramp of feet as the Germans marched away to imprisonment; the sea shining in the moonlight; and the hills resounding as the Germans who were still at liberty fired their remaining ammo dumps."

On Cap Bon, Anderson turned to General Horrocks and said, "I have waited a long, long time for this."

The prisoners came by the hundreds, then the thousands, then the tens of thousands; eventually there were more than 200,000, waving white flags made of mosquito netting or their underwear. They came in neat columns of field gray, singing "Lili Marlene" with that annoying German trick of clipping the last note of each line. They came as a bedraggled mob of *mangiatori,* singing sad Neapolitan ballads, or in sauntering platoons of Italian paratroopers, overcoats draped on their shoulders like the jackets of boulevardiers on the Via Veneto. They came in dun-colored Afrika Korps trucks with palm tree insignia stenciled on the tailgates; or in alcohol-burning buses piled high with baggage and pet dogs; or in chauffeured Mercedes sedans, colonels and generals dressed in gorgeous uniforms with Iron Crosses at their throats and boots so beautifully buffed that, one GI said, "you would have thought the bastards were going to a wedding."

"Germans were everywhere," Ernie Pyle reported. "It made me a little light-headed." Many surrendering soldiers were light-headed, too: with drink. A Derbyshire Yeomanry patrol on May 9 reported: "Found nineteen German officers dining off champagne. Champagne rather dry." Others groveled, waving handkerchiefs and sweetly yoo-hooing, "British Tommy! British Tommy!" Lacking a sword to present in surrender, a military hospital commander handed his captors a case of dental instruments. As Barenthins and Manteuffels and Hermann Görings shuffled to their cages, GI guards issued orders in a hybrid tongue of English and Yiddish, then sang their own song:

Are ve not der Supermen?
Ya, ve iss der Supermen, super-dooper Supermen . . .

A few escaped, in dinghies or by lashing themselves to the undercarriages of the last overloaded Axis planes to leave. Ultra eventually disclosed that only 632 men were evacuated in the final days; Allied sailors netted another 700 at sea, including a German platoon that had cut down telegraph poles "on which," a Grenadier Guards account noted, "they sat astride and began to paddle hopefully" toward Italy. Stragglers from the 15th Panzer Division across the Medjerda River were persuaded to surrender by a couple of well-placed warning shots; finding the water too deep to wade, the men were ferried into custody on the dray horses of Arab farmers, who charged the Germans fifty francs per trip.

Into the stockades they swarmed—"the *Herrenvolk* like chickens in a yard," A. D. Divine wrote. To each new batch of prisoners, General Koeltz, the French corps commander, proclaimed, "The anguished of yesterday salute the vanquished of today!" Among the booty seized by King's Dragoon Guards were instruments from the 21st Panzer Division band, including a piano with all but two of its eighty-eight keys intact. German musicians serenaded the camps with "Roll Out the Barrel," and Wehrmacht officers organized songfests and soccer leagues and vaudeville troupes with costumes improvised from camouflage netting.

As recently as May 5, Eisenhower had assured Marshall that "the Axis cannot have more than a total of 150,000 men in Tunisia." That was wrong by nearly half; the surrendering host included acres of rear-echelon troops and Italian colonial officials. Within a week the prison population would grow to 225,000 and beyond, stuffed into camps built to hold 70,000. For reasons ranging from shipping shortfalls to poor delousing facilities on the piers of New York, the Allied system for transporting prisoners to Algeria and Morocco, and then to Britain or the United States, had showed signs of strain even before Tunis collapsed. Now things got much worse.

Carefully calibrated guard-to-prisoner ratios—one for every twenty Italians and three for every twenty Germans—were immediately scrapped; even so, the hordes eventually required 8,600 guards, equivalent to half a division. Prisoners were shoehorned into boxcars without latrines or sufficient water for the tortuous trip across Africa. One GI described Italian troops in trucks "packed together like sardines, urinating and vomiting." Liberty ships became prison barges, with life rafts improvised from empty oil drums, but many prisoners were also crammed onto Algerian coasters, where they were tormented by thieving

Senegalese guards and overwatched by French officers who nibbled chocolate on the bridge and tossed morsels to the lunging men below.

For some, that was the least of it. U.S. Army provost marshals documented at least twenty-one Axis prisoners shot dead in the summer of 1943, some by American guards, others by French colonial guards; some accidentally, others trying to escape, and a few under circumstances never adequately explained. An Army investigation of mistreatment in French camps also documented Italian prisoners forced to work fourteen-hour days as railroad laborers. Among other allegations: "constant threat of attempted sodomy by Arab guards"; "no blankets for three months . . . forty men without shoes for three months . . . eleven men in a cell with one window. Arabs and children spat through the window and threw stones." Italian prisoners who managed to escape "prefer anything, even death, to being returned to the French," the investigators added. "At Camp #131, when 58 prisoners were ordered returned to the care of the French, men groveled on the ground, begging that Americans intercede and refuse their return. One asked to be shot. Finally had to be forced into French buses." A British general also observed French jailors "using their prisoners to clear minefields, while we consider it contrary to international law. They don't worry too much about feeding them either."

Neither starvation, nor mine-clearing, nor spittle, nor sodomy would befall the Axis generals, only the ignominy of defeat in a bad cause. In late April and early May, certain senior officers had conveniently fallen ill with maladies that required their return to Germany for treatment; among the invalids were division commanders Friedrich Weber and Hasso von Manteuffel. A few were also ordered home or otherwise escaped. But the Allies bagged more than a dozen generals. Four from the Wehrmacht and two from the Luftwaffe surrendered to II Corps. They were fed C rations and beans on May 10 before being ushered into Bradley's intelligence tent—known as the Playhouse—where Monk Dickson plied them with whiskey and cigars during a long chat around a plywood mapboard. The commander of the 15th Panzer reportedly wept as he observed, "The Americans have fought like sportsmen."

The biggest fish were caught farther south. At 11:15 A.M. on May 12, Mussolini authorized the capitulation of the First Italian Army. He offered Giovanni Messe the consolation of promotion to field marshal, then added in a message: "As the aims of your resistance can be considered achieved, your Excellency is free to accept an honorable surrender." Dickering followed, with white-flag emissaries dispatched to coax terms from the British, who offered the choice of unconditional surrender or annihilation. Ten minutes before the British deadline, Messe struck his colors. Taken into custody, he complained bitterly about the small size of his prison-camp tent. One witness described him slumped in the back seat of a staff car, "heavy and stern. He had tried standing up in his car and saluting as his captured countrymen marched past, but soon got tired and sat down again and let the endless stream of Italian soldiers go their way without a nod of recognition."

With fuel scavenged from a barrel found washed up on the beach, Arnim and his coterie had retreated to remote Ste.-Marie-du-Zit, twenty miles north of Enfidaville, where they camped with General Hans Cramer and the remnants of the Afrika Korps. Hitler's orders to "fight to the last bullet" had provoked animated theological discussions. "What does the last bullet mean in a modern war?" Arnim asked his staff. As Gurkha riflemen swarmed over the next hill on May 12, Arnim decided it meant the last tank shell, which had long been expended. White flags sprouted across the encampment. Cramer sent a final radio message informing Berlin that the Afrika Korps "has fought itself to the condition where it can fight no more." Arnim personally put a torch to Rommel's trailer, which the Desert Fox had bequeathed him in April, and dispatched a bullet-headed colonel to find the British headquarters.

He soon returned with Generals Allfrey and Tuker—commanding, respectively, the British V Corps and 4th Indian Division—in his staff car. Hundreds of Wehrmacht soldiers stared impassively, their heads swiveling as the British commanders climbed from the car and walked through the camp. In a narrow ravine, Arnim and Cramer stood erect outside the last intact Afrika Korps caravan, still camouflaged with artfully arranged branches. Both German generals wore long-waisted tunics with green breeches, high-peaked caps, and polished riding boots. Especially compared to Tuker—who sported threadbare drill trousers and scuffed desert boots, and who impishly introduced himself as "General von Tucher"—Arnim looked as if he had "turned out for a Potsdam parade, spotless and immaculate," one witness said.

Declining to use his capable English, Arnim spoke French to inform the British that he "could not alter Hitler's orders" by surrendering all remaining forces in North Africa. Allfrey brusquely promised to "blow them off the map," and gave Arnim fifteen minutes to pack for prison. All personal weapons were to be surrendered immediately. "He took this badly," Allfrey later recalled, "pulling out his automatic and throwing it down in a temper." Tuker cheerfully demanded his pocket knife, which Arnim, now "very red in the face," tossed on a table with a clatter. As his staff officers formed ranks at a right angle to the caravan, Arnim delivered a brief speech, his voice cracking, then walked down the formation to offer handshakes and *Heils.*

"He then got in his car and stood up in front, saluting his men as he was driven off," Allfrey recalled. "I did not like the man . . . and was glad to see his back." Down the valley the car sped with a British escort before turning onto the Tunis road, past the charred ruins of a once-mighty army and the tramping columns of prisoners, who tossed stiff-armed salutes and chanted, "Von Arnim! Von Arnim!" He was flown to Algiers and a camp erected on a muddy soccer field. Eisenhower snubbed Arnim by refusing him an audience, thus establishing a precedent of not speaking to a German general until the final surrender at Reims two years later. A British lieutenant colonel commandeered Arnim's limousine—a Steyer Daimler said to have twenty-eight forward and six reverse gears— while the surviving trailer was shipped to India for display as a curiosity during charity fund-raisers. As for Arnim, a GI bard composed a quatrain that perfectly captured the scorn Allied soldiers now felt for their conquered foe:

> *Jürgen T. von Arnim wore an iron-plated monocle*
> *But he could not see behind him—now wasn't that ironicle?*
> *He fought a rear-guard action and he did it very bitterly*
> *With booby traps and Teller mines and gallant sons of Iterly.*

His petulant refusal to surrender the final forces mattered little; the Axis army had imploded. At 1:16 P.M. on Thursday, May 13, Alexander sent Churchill a message of singular grace: "Sir, it is my duty to report that the Tunisian campaign is over. All enemy resistance has ceased. We are masters of the North African shores."

EPILOGUE

Roses perfumed the morning air in Tunis on Thursday, May 20, 1943. A brilliant sun climbed through a cloudless sky, and shadows melted to narrow black stains on the pavement. By eleven A.M., the temperature in the shade was ninety-two degrees—"too damn hot to cuss," one soldier wrote—but crowds six deep lined Avenue Maréchal Gallieni and the broad, palmy Avenue Jules Ferry for the victory parade that would end the North African campaign. Children squirmed to the front or shinnied up trees. Sidewalk vendors peddled little French, British, and American flags. An anticipatory hum ran through the throng "like a jolly football crowd," Harold Macmillan told his diary. "Every street was packed; every window in every house was packed; every roof was packed."

Shortly before noon, the massed pipes and drums of the Scottish regiments hove into view with a great wheezing of bags and swishing of tartans. In stately half step the pipers advanced to the still empty reviewing stand, then wheeled in a countermarch to take positions across the boulevard, skirling for all they were worth. The clack of hobnails on pavement followed, and an honor guard of immensely tall Grenadier Guards marched into position with, an American officer reported, "the same precision and utter indifference as to what was going on around them as they used to show while changing the guard at Buckingham Palace." Heat soon began to thin the Grenadier ranks as those weak with dysentery dropped to one knee or abruptly heeled over. The regimental sergeant major "used all his cunning to remove each sick man in turn without any spectator becoming aware of it," the Guards historians noted.

A convoy of limousines and open sedans pulled up to the reviewing platform. In riding breeches and knee boots, clutching a swagger stick, his arms akimbo, Eisenhower took his place in the front row next to the immaculately vacuous General Giraud. The commander-in-chief's principal lieutenants—Cunningham, Alexander, Tedder, Anderson—arrayed themselves behind him. Macmillan and Robert Murphy occupied a final rank, beaming and waving in their tropical suits like civil servants on holiday. Lesser lights filled lesser platforms on the flanks. Bradley and Patton were relegated to a peripheral bleacher crowded with minor French bureaucrats; Patton sourly noted that he was assigned a spot next to a "very large French ecclesiastic with a purple sash around his middle, which was probably necessary to support his well-developed stomach and also act as a background for a tremendous cross with an amethyst in it."

At noon, the crowd's mood darkened momentarily when booming gunfire was mistaken for an air raid, but the cannonade simply signaled the start of the parade. Redoubled cheers greeted the Foreign Legion band, which tramped past in white hats and red epaulets, playing a suitably martial march, and the appearance of a color guard triggered an ecstasy of saluting across the reviewing stands. General Juin followed at the head of the French troops, a contingent deliberately inflated to impress Arabs and other suspected disloyalists. For more than an hour they marched past ten abreast, a vivid comic-opera procession of képis and berets, turbans and peaked caps, scarlet pantaloons and wasp-waisted blue tunics. Crimson-cloaked spahis stood in the stirrups of their white chargers, saluting with upraised sabers. Algerians and Moroccans and Senegalese *tirailleurs* padded past, some shod and some not. Behind them came shambling, bearded *goums* in striped robes—their leather pouches provoked nudges from GIs determined to believe that each sack held a cache of enemy ears—and high-stepping Legionnaires whose ranks were full of blond Germans and Poles.

After the French came the Americans. A band crashed through "The Stars and Stripes Forever," and the 34th Division's 135th Infantry Regiment—chosen for their valor at Hill 609 to represent all American infantrymen—swept past, rubber-soled shoes clapping softly on the pavement. The men had burned their vermin-infested combat uniforms and now wore new, olive-drab wool blouses, buttoned at the collar with the sleeves rolled down. Steel helmets half hid their faces. General Harmon thought the troops shuffled like "Arkansas backwoodsmen," and Patton complained that "our men do not put up a good show in reviews. I think that we still lack pride in being soldiers, and we must develop it." Thousands of spectators disagreed. From the sidewalks and the balconies came shrieks of "*Vive l'Amérique!*" and young men dashed into the street to pump the hands of their liberators.

Then pipers, again. The faint strains of "Flowers of the Forest" trailed the last Americans, and the British wheeled into view, almost 14,000 men arrayed nine abreast and led by General Evelegh. Each marcher had received instructions as meticulous as a battle plan, including the commandment: "Brasses will be polished." They were gleaming. The men wore shorts and knee socks, with berets or forage caps, and their blouses were open at the throat and rolled to the elbow to give an effect of sinewy limbs and tanned faces. Macmillan beamed at the "swinging striding outstepping men," and an American colonel admitted that "the British made much the better show." On they came, nine by nine by nine, Maoris and Aussies and Sikhs and Coldstreams, a precise twenty yards separating each contingent. Commanders snapped a smart "eyes-right" salute as they clapped past the main reviewing stand, and great flocks of Spitfires and Flying Fortresses roared overhead, wagging their wings in homage.

The parade straggled to a merciful finish with yet another refrain of "Glory of the Trumpets" and Sherman tanks clanking behind the British infantry. As the last gun tubes and limbers passed the reviewing stands, hoarse spectators shinnied down from the trees and emptied the balconies. Hundreds of Italian prisoners-of-war who had been paroled to watch the parade—cheering each new formation with manic enthusiasm—complained bitterly as guards herded them back behind barbed wire. Eisenhower and his lieutenants climbed into their cars for the short trip to the resident-general's mansion, where Juin would host a luncheon for seventy people sitting at one long table; afterward, they would meet the new bey, uncle of the ousted collaborator, in a ceremony described by Harry Butcher as "complete with gold throne, eunuchs, and native Tunisian troops." Patton and Bradley, still miffed at their exclusion from the main reviewing stand, headed back to Algeria to resume training for Sicily. The parade, Patton grumbled, had been "a goddamned waste of time."

Even after two and a half hours in the molten sun Eisenhower showed no sign of wilting. A reporter described him as "lean, bronzed, and loose-limbed. He was happy as a schoolboy . . . taking the salutes as the units passed. When the parade drew to an end he smoked, laughed, and joked with the various leaders."

In truth, he had been peevish and distracted, notwithstanding the gleeful announcement from his West Point classmates that they were renaming him Ikus Africanus. "All the shouting about the Tunisian campaign leaves me utterly cold," he confided to Marshall. The concept of a victory parade appalled him, and he had tried without success to convert the event into a sober commemoration of the dead. He still slept badly. If he seemed jolly, jolliness was among the many masks the commander-in-chief had learned to wear.

No soldier in Africa had changed more—grown more—than Eisenhower. He continued to pose as a small-town Kansan, insisting that he was "too simple-minded to be an intriguer or [to] attempt to be clever," and he retained the winning traits of authenticity, vigor, and integrity. He had displayed admirable grace and character under crushing strain. But he was hardly artless. Naïveté provided a convenient screen for a man who was complex, shrewd, and sometimes Machiavellian. The Darlan affair had taught him the need to obscure his own agency in certain events even as he shouldered responsibility for them. The failings of Fredendall and other deficient commanders had taught him to be tougher, even ruthless, with subordinates. And he had learned the hardest lesson of all: that for an army to win at war, young men must die.

"One of the fascinations of the war was to see how Americans developed their great men so quickly," a British general later observed. None more than Eisenhower. In the fall of 1942, the general continued, he had been "a well-trained and loyal subordinate" to his more experienced British colleagues. Now he was a commander. His son, John, later wrote: "Before he left for Europe in 1942, I knew him as an aggressive, intelligent personality." North Africa transformed him "from a mere person to a personage . . . full of authority, and truly in command."

Even as victory was claimed and commemorated, a few loose ends remained to tie up.

The tiny Mediterranean island of La Galite was liberated by a battle flotilla sailing from Bône; a British naval officer reported that a shipboard ceremony with the islanders was repeatedly interrupted "by the need to salvage firstly the delegates' hats, which they kept throwing into the air and the wind blew into the sea, and secondly the mayor, who fell overboard." Allied salvage crews combed Tunisia for scrap and abandoned Axis matériel, but reported finding "not a great deal of value. Most of the weapons have been effectively rendered useless." Mine-clearing occupied thousands of engineers, and mines would continue killing civilians and soldiers, including Colonel Richard R. Arnold, Kay Summersby's fiancé. Arnold died in an explosion at Sedjenane on June 6. Sixty years later, Tunisian authorities were still digging up an average of fifty unexploded bombs, shells, and mines every month.

The French high command wasted no time embarking on what the OSS secretly described as "a ruthless campaign against Moslems and, to a lesser extent, Italians" in Tunisia. The six-month Axis occupation had won widespread Arab allegiance with effective propaganda, anti-Semitic edicts, and economic measures, including some land redistribution and a doubling of wages, paid with stolen Bank of France notes. In retribution for suspected Arab perfidy during the occupation, "a general reign of terror was instituted, in which arbitrary arrests and torture of Moslems became frequent occurrences," the OSS disclosed. Detention camps on the island of Djerba allegedly held 3,000 Arabs, with beatings, killings, and mass executions reported; gendarmes and other rogue officials were "running amuck in the interior and . . . beating and imprisoning personal enemies." Among other reparations, French officials demanded 25 million francs from Arabs in Sidi bou Zid to compensate French farmers whose land had been plundered. Such actions were contrary to united nations ideals, the OSS observed, and served "to discredit not only the French authorities but U.S. and British prestige as well."

Preoccupied with the imminent invasion of Sicily, Eisenhower and his lieutenants paid little attention, and most Allied troops could not have cared less. Recuperation before the next campaign absorbed every man, and the days were spent sleeping, fishing with hand grenades in Lake Bizerte, and, soon, training. Among some, a powerful nostalgia took root. Even discerning men like Spaatz and Tedder soon romanticized northwest Africa as war at its best: a facile, unencumbered campaign of human proportions fought by a doughty band of brothers.

Gimlet-eyed GIs and Tommies had no such illusions. Irony and cynicism infested the ranks. "I am Jesus' little lamb," soldiers told one another, "yes, by Jesus Christ I am." Ernie Pyle had already seen enough misery to ask darkly, "When you figure how many boys are going to get killed, what's the use anyway?" However realistic they were about war, the troops nurtured other fantasies, including the conviction that many units had done their bit and would now go home. "Dame Rumor with her thousand tongues is running wild through all the camps in Africa," one soldier warned. The arrival of many new troops in Tunisia fed the belief that veterans would at least get home leave. Among the newcomers was the 3rd Infantry Division, now commanded by Lucian Truscott; the division's ranks included a baby-faced farm boy from Texas with a fifth-grade education, an addiction to dice, and an affection for the Army because "they let you sleep until 5:30." Private First Class Audie L. Murphy, not yet nineteen and weighing in at 110 pounds, would become the most decorated American combat soldier in history, but not even the appearance of his like would free most troops from compulsory service for the duration.

Charles Ryder was so alarmed at his men's self-delusion that he assembled all officers and sergeants on a hill near Mateur in mid-May, and told them:

> There are many rumors out there that the 34th Division [troops have] fought their battles, done their time, and are going back to the States. But, gentlemen, I am here to tell you today that the 34th Division will not go back until the war is over. . . . As this war goes on it will get progressively worse and there will be progressively harder objectives to take, and more casualties as the German lines tighten. We shall fight in Europe, and we shall find that in comparison, the Tunisian campaign was but a maneuver with live ammunition.

It was the truth, and the truth hurt enough for one soldier to quip, "Ol' General Ryder's so homely that probably his wife doesn't care whether he gets back or not."

Most of their leaders, too, would go on to the Italian campaigns, or northern France, or both. They included Eisenhower, Bradley, Patton, Clark, Alexander, and Montgomery; they would face, again, Kesselring and Rommel. For some, however, the end in Africa effectively ended their hour on the stage. Among them was Anderson, who graciously wrote Eisenhower on May 12: "It will ever remain one of the proudest memories of my life, whatever the future may hold in store, that I have been so intimately connected with the U.S. Army." The future held little for Anderson. Vilified beyond redemption by Montgomery and others, he returned to a knighthood in England but was stripped of his army command before Normandy. He ended his career as a postwar governor of Gibraltar.

Among those who did go home was Robert Moore, hardly recognizable as the erstwhile Boy Captain since his wounding at Fondouk. Moore's orders assigned him to training duty in Georgia. Of the men in Company F, whom he had led out of Villisca two years earlier, "there sure are not many of us left," he wrote his family on May 12. "Not more than seven or eight of the original outfit. It will be a happy day when I see you all, won't it?"

July 15, 1943, was happy indeed. Moore stepped from the Burlington No. 6 in Villisca at 9:30 A.M., clutching the camel-hide briefcase his men had given him as a farewell gift. Into his arms leaped his seven-year-old daughter, Nancy; a newspaper photographer captured the moment in a picture that would win the Pulitzer Prize. Fire bells rang to announce the homecoming and American flags lined Third Avenue in front of the family drugstore. Bob Moore was to serve honorably for the rest of the war and beyond, remaining in the Iowa National Guard until retiring as a brigadier general in 1964, a year before the drugstore closed. When he died in 1991, the mourners at his funeral sang "The Battle Hymn of the Republic" and told stories about how young Bob had once led his battalion to safety through German lines during the battle of Kasserine Pass. The message board outside the Presbyterian church read simply: "Old soldiers never die."

Young ones do, and in North Africa they had died by the thousands. Allied casualties in TORCH and the subsequent Tunisian campaign exceeded 70,000; if laid head to toe they would have stretched eighty miles, from the Algerian border to Tunis. The toll included 38,000 British—two-thirds in First Army and one-third in Eighth Army—of whom more than 6,200 were killed in action and 10,600 were missing or captured. French casualties exceeded 19,400, half of whom were dead or missing. When French Algerian units returned to their hometowns beginning in mid-May, the troops lined the main streets for a roll call. Each man answered until the name of a dead comrade was called. Then, reporter John D'Arcy-Dawson wrote, a deep voice replied, *"Mort!"* The drums rolled, while the spectators removed their hats, and the women bowed and crossed themselves.

To more than a thousand American casualties in TORCH were added 18,221 more from mid-November to mid-May. These included 2,715 killed in action, nearly 9,000 wounded, and more than 6,500 missing. As always, infantrymen took the brunt. (Although infantry units accounted for 14 percent of the U.S. Army's overseas strength in the war, they suffered 70 percent of the casualties.) The 34th Division alone sustained more than 4,000 dead, wounded, and missing—one-quarter of Ryder's force—and Allen's 1st Division suffered nearly as many.

Some units were simply shattered. The 1st Battalion of the 6th Armored Infantry, which arrived for TORCH with 734 men, incurred 455 casualties in the next six months, or 62 percent. The battalion's A Company had four commanders in that half year, an indication of how the campaign devoured junior officers. Leadership losses also decimated British ranks: of six battalion commanders involved in the first dash to Tunis in November, the last still in command was killed by one of the final shells fired in May. Similarly, the 8th Argylls had suffered forty-nine officer casualties since landing at Bougie, 150 percent of the battalion's officer allotment.

Axis casualties remain uncertain. Confusion on both sides of the line in the campaign's final month resulted in contradictory tallies of prisoners captured, graves counted, and wounded soldiers treated. The German dead in Tunisia have been estimated at more than 8,500, with 3,700 Italians also killed. Combat wounded typically outnumber the dead by a factor of three or four, so an additional 40,000 to 50,000 Axis wounded can be surmised.

Ambiguity also shrouded the number of German and Italian prisoners of war. Allied records in late May listed 238,243 unwounded prisoners in custody, including nearly 102,000 Germans. Arnim thought the total prisoner count closer to 300,000—he, of course, among them—while Rommel's former chief of staff put the German figure alone at roughly 166,000. A quarter million appears to be a reasonable estimate of those captured. Goebbels privately called the fall of North Africa a "second Stalingrad," telling his diary, "Our losses there are enormous." True enough, although half as many German divisions were destroyed as at Stalingrad, and prison camps in Tunisia bulged with rear-echelon dregs.

Yet for one side the campaign had ended in humiliation and disaster; for the other, in triumph and hosannahs. Whatever the precise tally of Axis casualties, the number of enemy armies obliterated was certain— two—and so was the number of enemy soldiers still fighting in North Africa: zero.

At a price of 70,000 casualties "one continent had been redeemed," in Churchill's phrase. But more than territory could be claimed. The gains were most profound for the Americans, in their first campaign against the Wehrmacht. Four U.S. divisions now had combat experience in five variants of Euro-Mediterranean warfare: expeditionary, amphibious, mountain, desert, and urban. Troops had learned the importance of terrain, of combined arms, of aggressive patrolling, of stealth, of massed armor. They now knew what it was like to be bombed, shelled, and machine-gunned, and to fight on. They provided Eisenhower with a blooded hundred thousand, "high-grade stock from which we must breed with the utmost rapidity," as one general urged.

Still, they had far to go. Truscott worried at "too much satisfaction with a mediocre performance," and a tendency by some commanders to gloss over deficiencies. Bradley believed the campaign "showed American soldiers unwilling to close with the enemy—that was his greatest worry," reported Truscott, who added, "Why not at least be honest with

ourselves?" Some lessons—such as the critical choreography between
tankers and riflemen—were soon forgotten and would have to be
relearned for the usual fee in blood. North Africa, the historian Eric
Larrabee once noted, provided "a place to be lousy in, somewhere to let
the gift for combat and command be discovered."

It was also a place where many things that flowered later in the war
first germinated. Some were soul-stirring, such as the return of France to
the confederation of democracies. Some were distressing: the anglophobia of Bradley, Patton, and others; Alexander's contempt for American martial skills; and various feuds, tiffs, and spats. More profound was
a subtle shift in the balance of power within the Anglo-American
alliance; the United States was dominant now, by virtue of power and
heft, with consequences that would extend not only beyond the war but
beyond the century.

It was the discovery of those "gifts for combat and command" that
remains most beguiling sixty years later. "There are three things that
make a man fight," Ryder observed. "One is pride in himself, another is
pride in his organization, and the third is hate. The 34th has all of them."
A terrible beauty, then, born in Africa. Most Yanks had arrived in
Morocco and Algeria convinced that they were fighting someone else's
war; now they were fully vested, with a stake of their own. Drew Middleton noted that after Tunisia "the war has become a grudge fight, a personal matter."

Many felt a new clarity about the war and about themselves. "There's
nothing over here to fog your vision of right and wrong," an Iowa boy
wrote his parents. A corporal in the 13th Armored Regiment, formerly a
haberdasher in New York, told his girlfriend: "In years to come, after it is
all a distant memory, I'll be able to hold my head as high as the next
man's and my eyes level." And they were incorrigibly optimistic. "We
didn't know how to think about losing," wrote one soldier, a former
shoe salesman. "We didn't have the temper of mind which encompassed
the loss of the war." A British major who had accompanied the Yanks
since their first landings in Morocco concluded that the Americans "are
unlike anyone else in the speed with which they put things right, if and
when they are ordered, persuaded, or led to do so."

Africa provided affirmations of duty, of camaraderie, and of survival,
even if articulated in the sarcastic idiom of the dogface. "I am not willing
to die," a sergeant wrote his sister. "Dead, I would be of no further use to
the government." Yet sometimes the cynicism sloughed away, revealing
what every man was really fighting for: the right to go home. One soldier

wrote: "We all feel we've got something to fight for and something to live for, and we go along every day with the hope and the prayer on our lips that we can soon be on our journey home."

Africa was the first step on that long journey. "There was, for the first time in the war, a real lifting of spirits," Churchill later wrote. Less than a year earlier, the Axis had been advancing inexorably on all fronts; Rommel's drive into Egypt had filled the Cairo rail stations with refugees while panicky British diplomats burned documents in their gardens. Now only in the U-boat campaign did the Axis retain anything like a sustained offensive, and that was waning: the first Allied convoy to complete passage of the Mediterranean since 1941 left Gibraltar on May 17 and reached Alexandria without loss nine days later.

Hitler had lost the strategic initiative, forever. Even Kesselring sensed an insuperable momentum in the Allied camp. "It was in Tunisia," he later observed, "that the superiority of your air force first became evident." A Swiss newspaper reported that in Berlin people were "walking around as though hit in the head." The blow was more painful in Italy, which had lost its colonies and its self-delusions. As Allied bombing intensified, the Fascists seemed increasingly impotent. A German general in Rome reported in May that "in Europe there is at present only one Italian armored battalion, equipped with totally obsolete French tanks, ready for action in Sicily. . . . If the enemy has an initial success, the fatalism so prevalent at present will lead to the most disquieting results." Mussolini was said to be so unnerved that he could eat only milk and rice.

Yet Tunis—like Stalingrad, El Alamein, Midway, and Guadalcanal—lay on the outer rim of the Axis empire. In the winter of 1942–43, the Germans had transferred seventeen divisions from western Europe to the Eastern Front, an act suggesting that the campaign in North Africa had done little to influence the titanic struggle waged by the Russians (although the Mediterranean action proved a serious drain on the German air force). Hitler would assert in early July that the battle in Tunisia had "succeeded in postponing the invasion of Europe by six months," while also keeping Italy in the Axis camp and forestalling a sudden Allied thrust over the Alps through the Brenner Pass.

As the historian Michael Howard has noted, the Führer overestimated Allied capabilities: not even Patton dreamed of driving the length of Italy to abruptly appear in Munich. But the campaign *had* bought the Axis some time by keeping the Mediterranean closed an extra half year; by straining Allied shipping and constraining strategic planning; by sucking

Allied troops and supplies into the Mediterranean and away from any cross-Channel expedition; and, most ominously, by giving Kesselring months to begin reinforcing the Reich's southern flank.

The protracted campaign in Tunisia certainly delayed other European operations, beginning with HUSKY. There was nothing for it but to soldier on. "War is a burden to be carried on a steep and bloody road," Marshall observed, "and only strong nerves and determined spirits can endure to the end."

And what if Tunis had fallen in that first heady rush in November? The invasion of Sicily and then the Italian mainland would likely have been accelerated by months, perhaps allowing the capture of Rome in 1943. But Allied shipping and airpower limitations make it hard to conclude that D-day at Normandy could have been mounted much earlier than June 6, 1944—or rather, mounted successfully.

It remains far from clear that such an acceleration, even if possible, would have been prudent. If TORCH provided one benefit above others, it was to save Washington and London from a disastrously premature landing in northern Europe. Given the dozens of Wehrmacht divisions waiting behind the Atlantic Wall, France would have been a poor place to be lousy in. TORCH had been a great risk—"the purest gamble America and Britain undertook during the war," the official U.S. Army Air Forces history concluded—but it deferred the even greater gamble of a cross-Channel invasion until the odds improved.

For now, the victors celebrated their victory. For the Anglo-Americans, Churchill wrote Eisenhower, the triumph was "an augury full of hope for the future of the world. Long may they march together, striking down the tyrants and oppressors of mankind."

Many shared his sentiment. "Together we had all faced death on a number of occasions and this experience had created between us a bond which could never be taken away," a British captain in the 78th Division wrote. "We had gone to the brink and come back."

Among those who had not come back was a young American stretcher bearer, Caleb Milne, who was killed by a mortar round on May 11 while giving first aid to a wounded soldier. In a final, prescient letter to his mother, Milne described the Tunisian campaign as

> a vivid, wonderful world so full of winter and spring, warm rain and cold snow, adventures and contentments, good things and bad. How often you will have me near you when wood smoke drifts across the wind, or the first tulips arrive, or the sky darkens in a

summer storm. . . . Think of me today, and in the days to come, as I am thinking of you *this minute,* not gone or alone or dead, but part of the earth beneath you, part of the air around you, part of the heart that must not be lonely.

Kilroy had been here, and now he prepared to move on. Beyond Tunis harbor, just over the horizon, another continent waited.

NOTES

To provide an individual citation for every fact in this book would result in an extraordinarily cumbersome and pedantic ream of notes. I have instead grouped the sources relevant to particular passages of the text; the intent is to provide explicit attribution, as well as a guide for readers seeking additional source material. The bibliography also gives further information regarding the sources cited.

The following abbreviations appear in the endnotes and bibliography.

AAF   Army Air Forces
AAFinWWII   W. F. Craven and J. L. Cate, eds., *The Army Air Forces in World War II*, vol. II
AAR   after action report
AD   armored division
AFHQ micro   Allied Forces Headquarters microfilm, NARA RG 331
AFHRA   Air Force Historical Research Agency
ag   adjutant general
AR   armored regiment
ASEQ   Army Service Experiences Questionnaire, MHI
Bde   brigade
Bn   battalion
CARL   Combined Arms Research Library, Fort Leavenworth, Kansas
CBH   Chester B. Hansen diary, MHI
CCS   Combined Chiefs of Staff
CEOH   U.S. Army Corps of Engineers, Office of History
Chandler   Alfred Chandler, ed., *The Papers of Dwight David Eisenhower: The War Years*, vol. II
CINCLANT   Commander-in-Chief, Atlantic Fleet
CMH   U.S. Army Center of Military History, Fort McNair, Washington, D.C.
Co   company
Col U OHRO   Columbia University Oral History Research Office
corr   correspondence
CSI   Combat Studies Institute, Fort Leavenworth, Kansas
CT   combat team
DDE Lib   Dwight D. Eisenhower Presidential Library
Destruction   I.S.O. Playfair and C.J.C. Molony, *The Mediterranean and the Middle East*, vol. IV
diss   dissertation
Div   division
DSC   Distinguished Service Cross
E   entry
ETO   European Theater of Operations

FA field artillery
FCP Forrest C. Pogue, background material for *The Supreme Commander*
FDR Lib Franklin D. Roosevelt Presidential Library
FMS Foreign Military Studies, MHI
FRUS *Foreign Relations of the United States: The Conferences at Washington, 1941–1942, and Casablanca, 1943*
GCM Lib George C. Marshall Library, Lexington, Va.
GSP George S. Patton, Jr., Papers
Hansen draft of Omar Bradley's *A Soldier's Story*, C. B. Hansen, MHI
HKH Henry Kent Hewitt Papers
ID infantry division
inf infantry
Intel intelligence
Iowa GSM Iowa Gold Star Museum, Fort Dodge, Iowa
IWM Imperial War Museum, London
JAG judge advocate general
JCS Joint Chiefs of Staff
lib library
LHC Liddell Hart Centre for Military Archives, King's College, London
LKT Jr. Lucian K. Truscott, Jr.
LOC MS Div Library of Congress Manuscript Division
Med Mediterranean
MCC Mina Curtiss Collection
MHI U.S. Army Military History Institute, Carlisle, Pa.
MWC Mark Wayne Clark
micro microfilm
MP military police
MRC FDM McCormick Research Center, First Division Museum, Cantigny, Ill.
msg message
mss manuscript
MTOUSA Mediterranean Theater of Operations, United States Army
N Af North Africa
NARA National Archives and Records Administration, College Park, Md.
NATOUSA North African Theater of Operations, United States Army
n.d. no date
NHC Naval Historical Center, Washington, D.C.
NSA National Security Agency
NWAf George F. Howe, *Northwest Africa: Seizing the Initiative in the West*
NWC Lib National War College Library
OCMH Office of the Chief of Military History
OCNO Office of the Chief of Naval Operations
OCS Office of the Chief of Staff
OH oral history
OSS Office of Strategic Services
OW Orlando Ward Papers
Para parachute
PMR Paul McD. Robinett papers
PP-pres Papers, Pre-presidential
PRO Public Record Office, Kew, England
qm quartermaster
Regt regiment
RG record group

RN   Royal Navy
ROHA   Rutgers University Oral History Archives of World War II
SEM   Samuel Eliot Morison Office Files
SM   Sidney T. Matthews Papers
SOOHP   Senior Officer Oral History Program
S.P.   self-published
td   tank destroyer
TdA   Terry de la Mesa Allen Papers
Three Years   Harry C. Butcher, *My Three Years with Eisenhower*
TR   Theodore Roosevelt III Papers
ts   typescript
USAF   U.S. Air Force
USAF HRC   U.S. Air Force Historical Research Center
USMA Arch   U.S. Military Academy Archives, West Point
USAWWII   *United States Army in World War II*
USN   U.S. Navy
USNAd   "U.S. Naval Administration in World War II"
USNI OHD   U.S. Naval Institute, Oral History Department, Annapolis, Md.
UTEP   University of Texas at El Paso
UT-K   University of Tennessee, Knoxville, Center for the Study of War and Society
WD   War Department
WTF   Western Task Force
WWII   World War II
YU   Yale University Library, Manuscripts and Archives

PROLOGUE

PAGE

1   *Twenty-seven acres*: Author visits, Sept. 1996, Apr. 2000; "North Africa American Cemetery," n.d., American Battle Monuments Commission.

3   *No large operation*: AAFinWWII, 41 ("*the degree of strategic surprise*"); Siegfried Westphal, *The German Army in the West*, 131 ("*to the last man*").

4   "*There is a soul*": William T. Sherman, *Memoirs*, 387.
   North Africa is where: Mina Curtiss, ed., *Letters Home*, 65 ("*It is a very, very horrible war*"); James Tobin, *Ernie Pyle's War*, 89 ("*killing is a craft*"); A. B. Austin, *Birth of an Army*, 133 ("*The last war*").

5   *September 1, 1939*: Gerhard L. Weinberg, *A World at Arms: A Global History of World War II*, 894, 57; Martin Gilbert, *The Second World War*, 14–19 ("*Take a good look*"). Weinberg estimates total war-related deaths at 60 million.
   "*The small countries*": Winston S. Churchill, *Their Finest Hour*, 24.
   France was not small: *Destruction*, 116; Gilbert, 90 ("*First they were too cowardly*"); Mark M. Boatner III, *The Biographical Dictionary of World War II*, 421 ("*They call me only*"); NWAf, 16–17.

6   *Pétain so pledged*: Gilbert, 100 ("*Whatever happens*"), 130 ("*The war is won*"), 137 (*RAF pilots shot down*), 151 ("*Whither thou goest*"); Marvin A. Kreidberg and Merton G. Henry, *History of Military Mobilization in the United States Army, 1775–1945*, 674–75; Norman Gelb, *Desperate Venture*, 72 ("*our eyelids*").

7   *Hitler faced*: Gilbert, 135 ("*we are on the march*"), 194–99, 246–47, 272, 277 ("*the single most decisive act*"), 304; Weinberg, 260, 264–72; Churchill, *The Grand Alliance*, 606, 608 ("*the sleep of the saved*").

8   *Two years, three months*: Gelb, 25 ("*more unready for war*"); Christopher R. Gabel, *The U.S. Army GHQ Maneuvers of 1941*, 8; James A. Huston, *The Sinews of War:*

Army Logistics, 1775–1953, 411; Richard M. Ketchum, *The Borrowed Years, 1938–1941*, 544 (*"reconstruction of a dinosaur"*).

That task had started: Ketchum, 645; Lee B. Kennett, *G.I.: The American Soldier in World War II*, 19–22, 29; Ralph Stein and Harry Brown, *It's a Cinch, Private Finch!* (*"Do you like girls?"* and *"at least below the rank of major"*); Roy R. Grinker and John P. Siegel, *War Neuroses in North Africa*.

9   *Jeremiads derided*: Roger Barry Fosdick, "A Call to Arms," diss, 1985; *Time*, Aug. 18, 1941, 36.

Equipment and weaponry: Marvin Jensen, *Strike Swiftly: The 70th Tank Battalion*, 6 (*"tanks are dear"*); Doris Kearns Goodwin, *No Ordinary Time*, 51 (*"The idea of huge armies"*); David Brinkley, *Washington Goes to War*, 57; Alexander M. Bielakowski, "Calmer Heads Will Prevail," paper, Society for Military History, Apr. 2000; Alexander M. Bielakowski, "The Role of the Horse in Modern Warfare as Viewed in the Interwar U.S. Army's *Cavalry Journal*," *Army History*, summer–fall 2000, 20.

10   *To lead the eventual host*: Mark A. Stoler, *George C. Marshall: Soldier-Statesman of the American Century*, 93; Gabel, 116; Charles E. Kirkpatrick, "Orthodox Soldiers: Army Formal Schools Between the Two World Wars," paper, March 1990; Richard W. Stewart, "The Red Bull Division," *Army History*, winter 1993, 1; letter, L. J. McNair to C. Brewer, Nov. 15, 1943, NARA RG 165, Director of Plans and Ops, corr, box 1229; E. J. Kahn, Jr., "Education of an Army," *New Yorker*, Oct. 14, 1944, 28; Joseph W. A. Whitehorne, *The Inspectors General of the United States Army, 1903–1939*, 440 (*stained with scandal*).

Yet slowly the giant stirred: Geoffrey Perret, *There's a War to Be Won: The United States Army in World War II*, 29 (*$9 billion*), 31; Gilbert, 240 (*amputation saws*).

But where?: Louis Morton, "Germany First: The Basic Concept of Allied Strategy in World War II," in Kent Roberts Greenfield, ed., *Command Decisions*, 3–38 (*"the problem confronting us"*); Maurice Matloff and Edwin M. Snell, *Strategic Planning for Coalition Warfare, 1941–1942*, USAWWII, 27, 44, 113; Ray S. Cline, *Washington Command Post: The Operations Division*, USAWWII, 56; Gilbert, 286 (*"life, liberty, independence"*).

11   *The American idea*: Gelb, *Desperate Venture*, 70 (*"Through France"*); Cline, 156; John Slessor, *The Central Blue*, 434 (*"go for him bald-headed"*); Arthur Bryant, *The Turn of the Tide*, 353 (*"wanted revenge"*).

Direct, concentrated attack: Russell F. Weigley, *The American Way of War*, 313 (for an enlightening critique of the U.S. strategic tradition see Brian M. Linn, "The American Way of War Revisited," *Journal of Military History*, April 2002, 501); Maurice Matloff, *Strategic Planning for Coalition Warfare, 1943–1944*, USAWWII, 11; Matloff and Snell, 156; memo, DDE, Chandler, vol. I, 66 (*"We've got to go"*).

As the new chief: Matloff, 12; Leo J. Meyer, "The Decision to Invade North Africa," in Greenfield, ed., *Command Decisions*, 134; Samuel Eliot Morison, *The Two-Ocean War*, 222; Field Marshal Viscount Alanbrooke, OH, FCP, Jan. 28, 1947, MHI (*"We shall be pushed out"*); Alex Danchev and Daniel Todman, eds., *War Diaries, 1939–1945, Field Marshal Lord Alanbrooke*, 281–82; Richard W. Steele, *The First Offensive*, 171, 231; Benjamin A. Dickson, "G-2 Journal: Algiers to the Elbe," ts, n.d., MHI, 9 (*some skeptics*); Dwight D. Eisenhower, *Crusade in Europe*, 43; Gilbert, 283; Frederick E. Morgan, ts, n.d., cited in FCP, MHI (*"He recoiled in horror"*); Robert E. Sherwood, *Roosevelt and Hopkins: An Intimate Biography*, 591; GCM, OH, Forrest C. Pogue, Oct. 5, 1956, GCM Lib (*"Bodies floating in the Channel"*); GCM, OH, July 25, 1949, SM, MHI (*"sacrifice play"*).

13   *Whereas the dominant American strategic impulse*: Morton, "Germany First," 34; Meyer, "The Decision to Invade North Africa," 132; Weigley, 328; Michael

Howard, *The Mediterranean Strategy in the Second World War*, 14–17; Matloff and Snell, 55; Gelb, 96 (*"This has all along"*).

14   *The American military disagreed*: Matloff and Snell, 104 (*"indirect contribution"*); Gelb, 89 (*"will not result in removing"*).

   To many American officers: William C. Frierson, "Preparations for TORCH," Dec. 1945, vol. I, Historical Division, WD Special Staff, CMH 2–3.7 AD, 22; Eric Larrabee, *Commander in Chief*, 436 (*"After England Failed"*).

   Following another visit: Stoler, *The Politics of the Second Front*, 55–56; Matloff and Snell, 214, 231, 268–72, 276; Albert C. Wedemeyer, *Wedemeyer Reports!*, 158 (*"Scotch bagpipe band"*); msg, WD to AFHQ, Nov. 4, 1942, NARA RG 492, MTOUSA, box 1388; Walter Bedell Smith, OH, May 8, 1947, FCP, MHI (*often had to rely on the British*); Morison, *History of the United States Naval Operations in World War II*, vol. IX, *Sicily-Salerno-Anzio*, 4 (*war could last a decade*); GCM, OH, July 25, 1949, SM, MHI (*would have to field at least 200 divisions*).

15   *Other factors also influenced*: Walter Scott Dunn, Jr., *Second Front Now 1943*; Gilbert, 322, 350 (*Operation WATCHTOWER*), 335 (*"I am going on to Suez"*).

16   *By chance, the bad news*: Danchev and Todman, eds., 268–69, 286 (*Cromwell's death mask*); Gilbert, 335 (*"What can we do"*); Arthur Layton Funk, *The Politics of Torch*, 86; Meyer, 143; Matloff and Snell, 283; *NWAf*, 14.

   The president had made: Howard, *Grand Strategy*, vol. IV, xxi (*"defeat of Germany"*); Danchev and Todman, eds., 250 (*"The prospects of success"*), 275 (*"to play baccarat"*); Charles Bolte, OH, Oct. 17, 1973, Maclyn Burg, DDE Lib, OH 395, 51–52 (*Army logisticians*); Eisenhower, *Crusade in Europe*, 41; Meyer, 135–39 (*7,000 landing craft*); Matloff and Snell, 104 (*"persuasive rather than rational"*), 241 (*only 20,000*); Cline, 150 (*at least 600,000*), 157 (*"Who is responsible"*).

17   *Roosevelt had saved*: Forrest C. Pogue, *George C. Marshall: Ordeal and Hope, 1939–1942*, 330 (*"We failed to see"*); *Three Years*, 29 (*"blackest day"*); Matloff and Snell, 190 (*"thrashing around"*), 298 (*"a blessing in disguise"*), 310–11; Cline, 160; Funk, 86–92; minutes, CCS, July 25, 1942, 10:30 A.M., NARA RG 218, JCS records, box 325; Churchill, *The Hinge of Fate*, 449–51; *NWAf*, 15.

CHAPTER 1: PASSAGE
A Meeting with the Dutchman

21   *A few minutes past ten A.M.*: John Clagett, "Admiral H. Kent Hewitt, U.S. Navy," *Naval War College Review*, XXVIII, summer/fall 1975, 2 (*"squeezed the tar"*); note, July 24, 1943, HKH, LOC MS Div., box 1 (*turkey trot*); George Sessions Perry, "Why Don't They Write About Hewitt?" *Saturday Evening Post*, Dec. 16, 1944, 22; Louis Mountbatten, OH, n.d., HKH, NHC, box 6 (*"a fat, bedraggled figure"*); HKH, n.d., Col U OHRO, CNOF-0334, NHC, box 20; Thaddeus V. Tuleja, "Admiral H. Kent Hewitt," in Stephen Howarth, ed., *Men of War: Great Naval Leaders of World War II*, 315–16; HKH, "Reminiscences of a World War II Admiral," ts, n.d., NHC, box 21, 170–206; John T. Mason, ed., *The Atlantic War Remembered*, 160–63.

22   *In April 1942*: DDE to T. Troubridge, Oct. 13, 1942, NARA RG 407, E 427, AG Office, WWII Ops Reports, box 203 (*"The object of the operations"*); Matloff and Snell, 291.

   Through a tiny window: Brinkley, 117 (*if the military*); William D. Leahy, *I Was There*, 98; James B. Stack, OH-317, DDE Lib.; Alfred Goldberg, *The Pentagon: The First Fifty Years*, 175.

   The plane settled: Associated Press article, in *New York Sun*, Jan. 30, 1943, HKH, LOC MS Div, box 9, folder 6 (*"You do everything"*); "Amphibious Training Command," #145, USNAd, NHC, VII-26; William S. Biddle, "Amphibious Training of

American Troops in Great Britain," lecture, Fort Hood, 1943, William S. Biddle Papers, MHI; Kenneth Macksey, *Crucible of Power: The Fight for Tunisia, 1942–1943*, 48 (*imaginary ocean*); Ken Ford, *Battleaxe Division*, 6.

23   *Would the eight*: "Reminiscences of a World War II Admiral," 170–206; Michael Howard, *Grand Strategy*, 112; C.B.A. Behrens, *Merchant Shipping and the Demands of War*, 367–68; F.H. Hinsley, *British Intelligence in the Second World War*, vol. 2, 470; Walter Karig, *Battle Report: The Atlantic War*, 167; Disney note, HKH, LOC MS Div, box 2, folder 6.

  The staff car crawled: *New York Times*, Oct. 21, 1942, 1; *Washington Evening Star*, Oct. 21, 1942, 1 (*"there aren't any nylon stockings"*); Goodwin, 394.

26   *The car pulled up*: Quartermaster report, n.d., NARA RG 319, OCMH, box 231 (*among the secret cargoes*).

  Since Roosevelt's final decision: Theodore J. Conway, SOOHP, Robert F. Ensslin, Sept. 1977, MHI; Leahy, 136 (*"pig-headed"*).

  First, he insisted: Greenfield, ed., 149; FDR to Churchill, in Aug. 31, 1942, memo, E. King to GCM, NARA RG 218, JCS, box 325 (*"I am reasonably sure"*); James MacGregor Burns, *Roosevelt: The Soldier of Freedom*, 290 (*public opinion in North Africa*); Larrabee, 424.

27   *There was skepticism*: Harold Macmillan, *The Blast of War*, 160 (*"where all good Americans"*); Churchill to FDR, Sept. 14, 1942, NARA RG 218, JCS, box 225; Danchev and Todman, eds., 316 (*wait a full month*).

  The second vital issue: Matloff and Snell, 287; minutes, CCS meeting, Aug. 28, 1942, NARA RG 218, JCS, box 225 (*"take great risks"*); Andrew Browne Cunningham, *A Sailor's Odyssey*, 470; Eisenhower, *Crusade in Europe*, 79.

  But General Marshall: Howard, *Grand Strategy*, 124, 127; *NWAf*, 26; *Destruction*, 124; msg, War Cabinet, Joint Intelligence Sub-Committee, Aug. 7, 1942, NARA RG 165, Plans and Ops, General Records, corr, box 1229; Bernard Fergusson, *The Watery Maze*, 197 (*drawstring*); General Lord Ismay, *The Memoirs of General Lord Ismay*, 261; MWC, OH, May 19, 1948, G. F. Howe, NARA RG 319, OCMH, box 228; minutes, CCS meeting, Aug. 28, 1942, NARA RG 218, JCS, box 225 (*"only bring ridicule"*).

28   *Roosevelt agreed*: FDR to Churchill, Aug. 31, 1942, NARA RG 492, MTOUSA records, box 1388; Danchev and Todman, eds., 315 (*"a much wiser plan"*); Eisenhower, *Crusade in Europe*, 80 (*"realm of the probable"*).

29   *On September 5*: GCM, OH, Oct. 5, 1956, FCP, GCM Lib; GCM, OH, July 25, 1949, SM, MHI.

  At the White House: William Seale, *The President's House*, vol. II, 976; Hewitt, Col U OHRO, copy at NHC, Hewitt papers, box 20.

  Even as he shook Patton's hand: HKH to GSP, Sept 1, 1942, HKH, LOC MS Div, box 2, folder 5 (*"By all means"*); HKH, OH, Jan. 23, 1951, G. F. Howe, NARA RG 319, OCMH, box 228 (*Army planners proposed*); Ismay, 265 (*"bunch of rattlesnakes"*); "Amphibious Training Command," #145, USNAd, NHC, VII-8 (*"failure to cooperate"*); Eisenhower, *Crusade in Europe*, 82 (*Eisenhower's personal warrant*); Carlo D'Este, *Patton: A Genius for War*, 422 (*"Don't scare the Navy"*); Warren Tute, *The North African War*, 152; *NWAf*, 43.

30   *At precisely two*: "FDR Day by Day, Oct. 21, 1942," Secret Service records, box 4, FDR Lib; diary, Oct. 21, 1942, GSP, LOC MS Div. (*"Come in"*).

  "Well, gentlemen": Ladislas Farago, *Patton: Ordeal and Triumph*, 195 (*"conqueror or a corpse"*); John S. D. Eisenhower, *Allies: Pearl Harbor to D-Day*, 63 (*"cigarette-holder gesture"*); Larrabee, 486.

31   *But TORCH had its own hazards*: Morison, *The Two-Ocean War*, 223; S.L.A. Marshall, *World War I*, 192.

For his part, Roosevelt: Henry L. Stimson and McGeorge Bundy, *On Active Service in Peace and War*, 425, 416; diary, Oct. 21, 1942, GSP, LOC MS Div (*how to moor*); Clagett, "Admiral H. Kent Hewitt," 72 (*"just dropped off"*).

Gathering the Ships

33 *An unholy din rolled*: "Commander in Chief, Atlantic Fleet," vol. I, USNAd, 391; Morison, *Operations in North African Waters*, vol. II, *History of United States Naval Operations in World War II*, 48; *Soldier Stevedores*, Signal Corps Film Bulletin #32, NARA Films, RG 111, Chief Signal Officer; William Reginald Wheeler, ed., *The Road to Victory*, 35.

Into the holds: Richard M. Leighton and Robert W. Coakley, *Global Logistics and Strategy: 1940–1943*, 465; Frierson, "Preparations for 'Torch,'" vol. 1, 63 (*$100,000 in gold coins*); memo, Aug. 23, 1942, LKT Jr. Papers, GCM Lib, box 9 (*flyswatters*); msg, Oct. 18, 1942, NARA RG 338, General Records ETO, 7th Army Awards, box 1 (*Purple Hearts*).

In theory, only 800 people: Oscar W. Koch, *G-2: Intelligence for Patton*, 4; 12th Air Force doc., Oct. 17, 1942, Lauris Norstad Papers, Air Campaign in Naf, DDE Lib, box 6 (*"I am your friend"*); C. L. Strong, "Allo, Maroc," *Bell Telephone Magazine*, Sept. 1943; "Commander in Chief, Atlantic Fleet," vol. I, USNAd, 384; John H. Waller, *The Unseen War in Europe*, 252 (*"Behold"*).

34 *Quartermasters had*: Quartermaster report, n.d., NARA RG 319, OCMH, box 231 (*"Do not open"*); "Chemical Warfare Policy, Operation TORCH," Sept. 10, 1942, AFHQ G-3, and memo, "chemical warfare policy," W. B. Smith, Sept. 27, 1942, both in NARA, AFHQ micro, R-83-F (*"most unlikely"*). The use of chemical weapons appears never to have been seriously considered. See Brooks E. Kleber and Dale Birdsell, *The Chemical Warfare Service: Chemicals in Combat*, 87–93.

Using a Michelin: Jack F. Wilhm et al., "Armor in the Invasion of North Africa," Armored School, 18; M. T. Wordell and E. N. Seiler, *Wildcats over Casablanca*, 19 (*Baedekers*); Lucian K. Truscott, Jr., *Command Missions*, 33; Alfred M. Beck et al., *The Corps of Engineers: The War Against Germany*, 63; "Catalogue of Standard Ordnance Items," vol. I, in "Kasserine Pass Battles," vol. II, pt. 3, CMH.

All cargo was: Leighton and Coakley, 443; Carl E. Bledsoe, report, Oct. 15, 1942, NARA RG 165, Plans and Ops, Gen'l Records, corr, box 1228; "Commander in Chief, Atlantic Fleet," vol. I, USNAd, 391; John Erbes, "Hell on Wheels Surgeon," ts, n.d., USMA Arch, 11.

35 *On this disorderly Thursday*: Blumenson, *The Patton Papers, 1940–1945*, 92, 94–95; Farago, 194; D'Este, *Patton*, 425; Wheeler, ed., 10 (*Aeneid*).

It was a fair self-assessment: Rick Atkinson, introduction to GSP, *War as I Knew It*, xi–xxii; Mark M. Boatner III, *The Biographical Dictionary of World War II*, 413.

36 *"Give me generals"*: Mountbatten, OH, n.d., HKH, NHC, box 6; Larrabee, 486; diary, Oct. 21, 1942, GSP, LOC MS Div.

His command for TORCH: Matloff and Snell, 317; E. N. Harmon with Milton MacKaye and William Ross MacKaye, *Combat Commander*, 69 (*"put iron in their souls"*); D'Este, *Patton*, 422, 426–27 (*"had been ordered into arrest"* and *"If you don't succeed"*).

In a dinner toast: Harry H. Semmes, *Portrait of Patton*, 81; Henry Gerard Phillips, *The Making of a Professional: Manton S. Eddy, USA*, 84; James H. Doolittle with Carroll V. Glines, *I Could Never Be So Lucky Again*, 299; Harmon, *Combat Commander*, 69; Martin Blumenson, *Patton: The Man Behind the Legend, 1885–1945*, 64.

37 *On Friday morning, October 23*: "Reminiscences of Rear Adm. Joshua W. Cooper," USNI OHD, John T. Mason, 1975 (*"If you have any doubts"*); Morison, *Operations in North African Waters*, 43.

   As the hour of departure: Frierson, "Preparations for 'Torch,'" vol. I, 23.

   More usually: Wheeler, ed., 224–25; Albert E. Cowdrey, *Fighting for Life: American Military Medicine in World War II*, 165–67 (*Recent experience*).

38 *No less dramatic*: GCM to AFHQ, Oct. 8, 1942, NARA RG 492, MTOUSA records of the special staff, box 1385; "W.R.P.," "Mission to Morocco," *Navy*, Nov. 1958, 7; Charles F. Marsh, ed., *The Hampton Roads Communities in World War II*, 259; Bertram B. Fowler, "Twelve Desperate Miles," *Saturday Evening Post*, Aug. 28, 1943, 14; Wheeler, ed., 73.

   All the confusion: Walter T. Kerwin, Jr., SOOHP, D. A. Doehle, MHI, 1980 (*"a sweltering inferno"*); general courts-martial offense ledger sheets, NARA RG 153, Office of the Judge Advocate General, boxes 17–19; "Amphibious Training Command," #145, USNAd, IX-34; Steve Kluger, *Yank: The Army Weekly*, 58; Lee B. Kennett, *G.I.: The American Soldier in World War II*, 32.

39 *Naughty Norfolk*: J. Blan van Urk, "Norfolk—Our Worst War Town," *American Mercury*, Feb. 1943, 1944 (*"solid block of beer joints"* and *"give me a concentration camp"*); Phyllis A. Hall, "Crisis at Hampton Roads: The Problems of Wartime Congestion, 1942–1944," *Virginia Magazine of History and Biography*, July 1993, 405 (*"girlie trailers"*); Marvin W. Schlegel, *Conscripted City: Norfolk in World War II*, 193 (*massacre white citizens*).

   Sober and otherwise: Owen C. Bolstad, *Dear Folks: A Dog-Faced Infantryman in World War II*, 9; Edwin Hubert Randle, *Safi Adventure*, 20.

   Eight to twelve officers shared: Robert Wallace, "Africa, We Took It and Liked It," *Saturday Evening Post*, Jan. 16, 1943, 20.

40 *From this very anchorage*: James R. Reckner, *Teddy Roosevelt's Great White Fleet*, 23; "Commander in Chief, Atlantic Fleet," vol. I, USNAd, 383 (*"previously seen salt water"*); A. Russell Buchanan, *The United States and World War II*, vol. I, 148.

   Patton settled into: Diary, Oct. 21 and 23, 1942, GSP, LOC MS Div.; Fred Ayer, Jr., *Before the Colors Fade*, 116.

41 *"generals so bold"*: NWAf, 44; Farago, 194; D'Este, *Patton: A Genius for War*, 885n.

   Shortly before seven: "U.S. Atlantic Fleet, Amphibious Force—Action Report," NARA RG 407, E 427, box 24490. For an interesting antecedent, see Thucydides, "Launching of the Sicilian Expedition," *History of the Peloponnesian War*, Rex Warner trans., 427–9.

   The dawn was bright: Bruce Catton, *A Stillness at Appomattox*, 56 (*bright and blowing*); Ch'ên T'ao, "Turkestan," *The Jade Mountain: A Chinese Anthology*, Witter Bynner, trans., 14 (*into the rooms*).

Rendezvous at Cherchel

42 *It began with a single light*: Frederick C. Painton, "Secret Mission to North Africa," *Reader's Digest*, May 1943, 1; Godfrey B. Courtney, "Clark's Secret Mission," in Louis L. Snyder, ed., *Masterpieces of War Reporting: The Great Moments of World War II*, 205–206 (*"got to get off"*); N.L.A. Jewell, *Secret Mission Submarine*, 21; E. Alexander Powell, *In Barbary*, 309; A. J. Redway, "Admiral Jerauld Wright: The Life and Recollections of a Supreme Allied Commander," NHC, WWII CF Indiv Pers, box 674; Joseph E. Persico, *Roosevelt's Secret War*, 200–205.

43 *an odd choice*: F. W. Winterbotham, *The Ultra Secret*, 90 (*among the few Americans*); Nigel Hamilton, *Master of the Battlefield: Monty's War Years, 1942–1944*, 154 (*a secret so profound*).

That Eisenhower had entrusted: Carl W. McCardle, "Mark W. Clark," *These Are the Generals*, 90–91 (*Contraband*); Blumenson, *Mark Clark*, 51, 54 ("*nine dittos*"), 248–5 ("*The more stars*"); Mark W. Clark, *Calculated Risk*, 49 ("*When the soup*"); Blumenson, *The Patton Papers, 1940–1945*, 87 ("*He seems to me*"); D'Este, *Bitter Victory*, 55 ("*evil genius*").

44   *The voyage to Cherchel*: Funk, 164; *Three Years*, 146 ("*happy as a boy*"); David Alvarez, *Secret Messages*, 62, 93, 97, 152, 184, 166–67, 170–71; Mary S. Lovell, *Cast No Shadow*, 147; H. Montgomery Hyde, *Cynthia*, 147; Anthony Cave Brown, *The Last Hero: Wild Bill Donovan*, 229; Peter Tompkins, *The Murder of Admiral Darlan*, 20 ("*an ornament of Harry's*"); Kenneth Pendar, *Adventure in Diplomacy*, 11 ("*so many Alices*"); R. Harris Smith, *OSS*, 39; Leon Borden Blair, "Amateurs in Diplomacy: The American Vice Consuls in North Africa, 1941–1943," *Historian*, Aug. 1973, 607.

45   *Only a howling dog*: Redway, 236; Clark, 79; Richard Livingstone, "Mark Clark's Secret Landing," in Basil Liddell Hart, ed., *History of the Second World War*, vol. 3, 1200; Tompkins, 47 ("*What sort of army*").

     Murphy was too excited: Robert Murphy, *Diplomat Among Warriors*, 2, 70, 74, 102 ("*nobody ever pays*"), 107; Pendar, 18 ("*gaiety*"); Charles de Gaulle, *The Complete War Memoirs of Charles de Gaulle*, 314; Macmillan, *War Diaries: The Mediterranean, 1943–1945*, 69.

46   *At six A.M. General Mast*: Boatner, 349; L. James Binder, *Lemnitzer, A Soldier for His Time*, 82–83.

     For more than four hours: Eisenhower, *Crusade in Europe*, 87; Blumenson, *Mark Clark*, 82; Binder, 83–84 ("*Where are these*").

47   *Perhaps lies*: Most participants in this celebrated episode wrote accounts, sometimes elaborated in the telling. Among the most reliable is Teissier's "Notes sur la Mission du General Clark en Afrique du Nord," quoted in Waller, *The Unseen War in Europe*, 256; Murphy, 119; Binder, 82–88; "The French-American meeting of the Messelmoun," OSS Files, NARA RG 226, E 99, box 39; William L. Langer, *Our Vichy Gamble*, 329; Renée Gosset, *Conspiracy in Algiers*, 45; Redway, 236; *Three Years*, 154; Clark, 85–88; Mason, ed., 201.

On the Knees of the Gods

49   *As Hewitt's Task Force*: Churchill, *The Hinge of Fate*, 539; Michael Howard and John Sparrow, *The Coldstream Guards, 1920–1946*, 108 ("*only the boiling white foam*").

     Eight distinct deception plans: George Juskalian, author interview, Feb. 25, 2000; Charles Cruickshank, *Deception in World War II*, 38–44; Mason, ed., 194 (*platoon of reporters*).

50   *Like Hewitt's ships*: "North African Operation, Convoys, Plans," n.d., NARA RG 319, OCMH, box 231; *Tank Destroyer Forces World War II*, 19; "Glossary for Use of U.S. Army Forces," Sept. 1942, NARA RG 407, E 427, "Pre-Invasion Planning," box 24348.

     The loading at British ports: Leo J. Meyer, "Strategy and Logistical History: Mediterranean Theater of Operations," CMH, 2.37 CC1, II-31; Frierson, "Preparations for 'Torch,'" vol. I, 26; "History of Planning, ASF [Army Service Forces]," 1946, CMH, 3-2.2 AA, 86.

     The cable stirred: Frierson, "Preparations for 'Torch,'" vol. I, 37; "History of Planning, ASF," CMH, 86; Joseph Bykofsky and Harold Larson, *The Transportation Corps: Operations Overseas*, 143.

     Few of the 72,000: "What to Do Aboard a Transport," 260; Francis J. Vojta, *The Gopher Gunners: A History of Minnesota's 151st Field Artillery*, 141 (*Belgravia Riding Academy*); Guy Ramsey, *One Continent Redeemed*, 20; A. D. Malcolm, *History of the Argyll & Sutherland Highlanders 8th Battalion, 1939–47*, 74; Wallace,

"Africa, We Took It and Liked It"; Robert J. Berens, *Citizen Soldier*, 42; William F. Beekman, "A Diary of World War II," ts, n.d., Iowa GSM.

51 *For the officers*: Henry E. Gardiner, ts, n.d., USMA Arch, 78 (*"Blouses were worn"*); Monro MacCloskey, *Torch and the Twelfth Air Force*, 84 (*"Bath, sahib?"*); Juskalian, author interview, Feb. 25, 2000; letter, TR to Eleanor, Oct. 26, 1942, TR, LOC, box 9. (Ted Roosevelt was alternately known as TR, Jr., and TR, III; he was in fact the third successive Roosevelt male to bear the name. See Edmund Morris, *Theodore Rex*, 46, 766.)

52 *Below the waterline*: Kluger, *Yank: The Army Weekly*, 16; Mina Curtiss, ed., *Letters Home*, 102; Howard and Sparrow, 108; Jensen, 24.

Troops caught nibbling: Oswald Jett, "As I Saw the War," ts, n.d., ASEQ, 1st AD, 47th Medical Bn, MHI; Harry P. Abbott, *The Nazi "88" Made Believers*, 25; Bolstad, 70; Wilbur C. Darnell, author interview, Oct. 19, 1999; "Historical Record of the 19th Engineer Regiment, Oct. 1942–Oct. 1943," NARA RG 407, E 427, box 19248 (*"became quite wild"*).

Morale suffered: G. R. Grandage, "Operation TORCH: Invasion of North Africa," ts, IWM, 87/16/1 (*nothing stronger than ginger ale*); "Morale report for period 19–26 November 1942," Center Task Force, NARA RG 407, E 427, AG, NAf-Med, box 239 (*"sorry sons of bitches"* and *"I hate myself"*).

"To make a good army": Barbara W. Tuchman, *Sand Against the Wind: Stilwell and the American Experience in China, 1911–1945*, 204; Russell A. Gugeler, ts (unpublished Ward biography), OW, MHI, x-18, x-27; George F. Howe, *The Battle History of the 1st Armored Division*, 16; Hamilton H. Howze, *A Cavalryman's Story*, 37; Hamilton H. Howze, OH, Russell A. Gugeler, Aug. 1976, OW, MHI (*"None of the division"*).

53 *Twenty months earlier*: Charles E. Heller and William A. Stofft, eds., *America's First Battles, 1776–1965*, 238; Homer Ankrum, *Dogfaces Who Smiled Through Tears*, 22–34.

54 *after nine false alarms*: Vojta, 124; Brinkley, 36; Ankrum, 32 (*"World War II is a battle"*).

Ten months later: Benjamin F. Caffey, Jr., OH, Feb. 1950, SM, MHI; Ann Larson, ed., "The History and Contribution to American Democracy of Volunteer 'Citizen Soldiers' of Southwest Iowa, 1930–1945," 22; John H. Hougen, *The Story of the Famous 34th Infantry Division*.

Among those who survived: Robert R. Moore, Jr., author interview, June 13, 2000; *Omaha World-Herald*, Nov. 9, 1997, 1.

55 *Fourteen years later, Bob Moore*: "Induction of Company F," memo, Iowa GSM; author visit, southwest Iowa, Oct. 1999; *Villisca* (Iowa) *Review*, Feb. 20, 1941.

56 *Then the time*: Dave Berlovich, author interview, Oct. 19, 1999; *Clarinda* (Iowa) *Herald-Journal*, March 3, 1941; *Red Oak* (Iowa) *Express*, March 3, 1941; Larson, ed., 42.

And in Villisca: Villisca Review, Feb. 27 and March 6, 1941.

57 *"Everyone was excited"*: Curtiss, ed., 102; William O. Darby with William H. Baumer, *Darby's Rangers: We Led the Way*, 7; Ramsey, 20; S.W.C. Pack, *Invasion North Africa, 1942*, 10; Drew Middleton, *Our Share of Night*, 167 (*"Chinese flag"*); "North Africa," NARA RG 338, Records of US Army Commands, WTF, box 1; Morison, *Operations in North African Waters*, 175n (*"First Families of Virginia, in bathrobes"*).

Shortly after sunset: Gardiner, ts, n.d., USMA Arch, 78; letter, TR to Eleanor, Oct. 30, 1942, TR, LOC, box 9.

A Man Must Believe in His Luck

57 *Known as TUXFORD*: DDE msg, Oct. 21, 1942, NARA RG 218, Records of JCS, box 325; Richard McMillan, *Mediterranean Assignment*, 316; Winston G. Ramsey,

ed., "The War in Gibraltar," *After the Battle*, No. 21, 1978, 1; Alden Hatch, *General Ike*, 128 (*"thick as logs"*); Michael J. McKeough and Richard Lockridge, *Sgt. Mickey and General Ike*, 46 (*"ten shillings"*).

58   *The Snoopers had*: "Interviews on Four Aspects of the Air Campaign in Africa," July 1943, Office of Asst. Chief of Air Staff, Intel, NARA RG 334, NWC Lib, box 14; Ramsey, ed., "The War in Gibraltar," 1 (*windsocks*); "A Study of Gibraltar," July 1941, NARA RG 407, E 427, 1st AD, 601-2.10.

   Late in the afternoon: Paul W. Tibbetts, Jr., *The Tibbetts Story*, 107; *AAFinWWII*, 66.

   Staff cars pulled up: Carleton E. Coon, ts, n.d., NARA RG 226, OSS, box 39, folder 8 (*"General Howe"*); msg, NARA RG 407, E 427, "Pre-Invasion Planning," box 24350.

   Eisenhower left the guest suite: Raymond H. Croll Papers, ts, n.d., MHI, 97–98; Tute, 155; Ramsey, ed., "The War in Gibraltar."

59   *Eisenhower's brisk stroll*: Larrabee, 412 (*"worth an army corps"*); Kenneth S. Davis, *Experience of War*, 285 (*"good and right in the moral sense"*); Arthur Coningham, OH, FCP, Feb. 14, 1947, MHI (*"Ike has the qualities"*).

   In his rapid rise: Boatner, 152; Larrabee, 415, 419 (*"far more complicated"*), 420, 421 (*P. D. Eisenhauer*); Stephen E. Ambrose, *The Supreme Commander: The War Years of General Dwight D. Eisenhower*, 15 (*"lot of big talk"*), 17, 97 (*"not very sure of himself"*).

60   *His capacity for hard work*: Chronology, Chandler, vol. V; Ambrose, *The Supreme Commander*, 104; Larrabee, 420 (*"contrived"*); Ambrose, *Eisenhower: Soldier, General of the Army, President-Elect, 1890–1952*, 202; DDE to GCM, Oct. 20, 1942, Chandler, vol. I, 629 (*"Whenever"*); DDE to GCM, Chandler, vol. I, 591 (*"I find"*); DDE to Vernon E. Prichard, Aug. 27, 1942, Chandler, vol. I, 505 (*"Fake reputations"*).

   As D-Day for TORCH: DDE to C. K. Gailey, Jr., Oct. 12, 1942, Chandler, vol. I, 608; Ambrose, *Eisenhower*, 178; DDE, *Crusade in Europe*, 65 (*"sober, even fearful"*).

61   *Inside Gibraltar*: Photograph, Ramsey, ed., "The War in Gibraltar," 1; DDE to HKH, Nov. 3, 1942, HKH, correspondence, NHC, box 1 (*"Dear Kent"*).

   On November 6: msg, Nov. 6, 1942, NARA RG 492, MTOUSA, box 1388; "Memorandum to General Eisenhower," Oct. 29, 1942, DDE Lib, PP-pres, box 153; GCM to DDE, Nov. 5, 1942, NARA RG 492, MTOUSA, box 1388 (*"orders to defend"*); Murphy, 121; Harry C. Butcher diary, DDE Lib, PP-pres, box 165, 164 (*"big and little"*).

   On November 7: Three Years, 165–67; DDE to GCM, Nov. 7, 1942, Chandler, 669.

62   *Not until reconnaissance planes*: War diary, German naval staff, NARA RG 334, NWC Lib, box 645; diary, Hellmuth Greiner, NARA RG 319, OCMH, box 225; *NWAf*, 186 (*"I await a ruthless"*).

   At daybreak on Saturday: "Torpedoing and Salvage of USS *Thomas Stone*," Jan. 26, 1943, NARA RG 407, box 24487; AAR, 39th CT, NARA RG 407, E 427, box 7501; Jensen, 26; Joseph B. Mittelman, *Eight Stars to Victory*, 56; Phillips, *El Guettar*, 43; AAR, 39th CT, NARA RG 407, E 427, box 7501.

64   *Some hours passed*: André Beaufre, "General Giraud's Escape," *History of the Second World War*, vol. 3, Basil Liddell Hart, ed., 1198 (*field glasses*); Kenneth S. Davis, *Dwight D. Eisenhower: Soldier of Democracy*, 357; Clark, 96; DDE to H. H. Giraud, Nov. 4, 1942, Chandler, vol. I, 656 (*phony London letterhead*).

   Giraud was intrepid: Sept. 19, 1942, NARA RG 331, AFHQ micro, R-78-D (*"Surrounded"*); Brown, *The Last Hero*, 240; Davis, *Dwight D. Eisenhower*, 346 ("Allez, mes enfants!"); David Hunt, *A Don at War*, 154; Murphy, 180 (*porcelain cat*); Macmillan, *War Diaries*, 68 (*"so stately"*), 71; Butcher diary, DDE Lib, A-221 (*"Papa Snooks"*).

65   *The general's greatest genius*: Beaufre, 1197; G. Ward Price, *Giraud and the African Scene*, 45.

        Now he was in: Clark, *Calculated Risk*, 96-98; Eisenhower, *Crusade in Europe*, 100; GCM to DDE, Nov. 1 and 6, 1942, NARA RG 492, MTOUSA, box 1388 (*10 million francs*); Binder, 97; Morison, *Operations in North African Waters*, 186; Davis, *Dwight D. Eisenhower*, 357; DDE to GCM, Oct. 29, 1942, Chandler, vol. I, 640; *Three Years*, 171 ("*Old gentleman*"); DDE to GCM, Nov. 7, 1942, Chandler, 668 ("*I'm weary*").

66   *Dinner at Government House*: Murphy, 180; Tompkins, 112; *Three Years*, 171 ("*We would like*").

        Giraud took his leave: Ambrose, *Eisenhower*, 203 ("*airplane accident*"); S. W. Roskill, *The War at Sea, 1939–1945*, vol. II, 320; John S. D. Eisenhower, *Allies*, 176 (*a few moments of meditation*); Pack, *Invasion North Africa*, 26; Davis, *Dwight D. Eisenhower*, 354; DDE to GCM, Oct. 29, 1942, Chandler, vol. I, 642 ("*I fear nothing*"); DDE to GCM, Oct. 20, 1942, Chandler, vol. I, 628 ("*To a certain extent*").

CHAPTER 2: LANDING
"*In the Night, All Cats Are Grey*"

69   *Two hundred and thirty*: "History of Third Port, TC," NARA RG 407, 270/64/28/7, 10; Powell, *In Barbary*, 322.

        The plan was British: RESERVIST planning memo, Aug. 17, 1942, NARA RG 94, special file, 6–8. 1311/42; Churchill, *The Hinge of Fate*, 534 ("*in the night, all cats*"); AAR, n.d., "Reservist" file, SM, MHI.

70   *To command RESERVIST*: John Laffin, *British VCs of World War 2*, 25; Leo Disher, "HMS *Walney*," in John A. Parris, Jr., and Ned Russell, *Springboard to Berlin*, 93 ("*Rain, darkness*"), 102 ("*the opportunity I have been waiting for*"). Disher's firsthand account is brilliant.

        Peters worried the Americans: Richard Lamb, *Churchill As War Leader*, 172 ("*showed how a frontal assault*"); Susan H. Godson, *Viking of Assault: Admiral John Lesslie Hall, Jr., and Amphibious Warfare*, 9; Fergusson, 182 ("*defenders must be drenched*"); Field order #1, Oct. 11, 1942, 26th Inf, MRC FDM; MWC, "Memorandum to General Eisenhower," Oct. 13, 1942, DDE, PP-pres, box 153 ("*a Trojan horse*"); Roskill, 327.

71   *Convinced that Peters planned*: AAR, NARA RG 407, "Special Files," box 24486; A. C. Bennett to CINC U.S. Fleet, Nov. 30, 1942, NARA RG 38, OCNO, box 786.

        Another American admiral: "Reminiscences of Vice Adm. Bernhard H. Bieri," 1997, USNI OHD, 112 ("*I can't take your advice*"); Paul McDonald Robinett, *Armor Command*, 32; MWC, "Memorandum to General Eisenhower," Oct. 13, 1942, DDE, PP-pres, box 153 ("*If these craft*"); unmailed letter, OW to PMR, n.d., OW, MHI.

        The honor of storming: "Historical and Pictorial Review," 6th Inf yearbook, 1941, MHI; Howze, OH, Gugeler, Aug. 1976, OW, MHI ("*finest assignment*").

72   *The overloaded cutters*: Disher, in Parris and Russell, 102, 109 ("*without firing a shot*"); memo, Leland L. Rounds to William Donovan, July 13, 1944, "Torch Report," NARA RG 226, E 99, OSS files, box 40; L. L. Rounds, OH, Oct. 21, 1948, SM, MHI; Anthony Cave Brown, ed., *The Secret War Report of the OSS*, 145; "Awards of Medals for Gallantry During Attack on Oran Harbour," Admiralty AAR, PRO, 1/11915.

        At one minute: AAR, Wallace Moseley, RN, Nov. 17, 1942, NARA RG 38, OCNO, CINCLANT, box 2; Disher, in Parris and Russell, 111; Marvin P. Clemons, ASEQ, 1st AD, MHI (*former coal mine brakeman*).

73 *Peters, Duncan, and fifteen*: *Walney* account: AAR, T. H. Troubridge, RN, Nov. 13, 1942, NARA RG 407, special file, 6–8. 1311/42; AAR, Wallace Moseley, RN, Nov. 17, 1942, NARA RG 38, OCNO, CINCLANT, box 2; AAR, RN, n.d., SM, MHI; Disher, in Parris and Russell, 93–125; Pack, *Invasion North Africa, 1942*, 87; AAR, RN, "Assault on Oran," Dec. 27, 1942, NARA RG 331, AFHQ micro, R-16-A; David Rame, *Road to Tunis*, 61–62 (*"wire through cheese"*); NWAf, 203; *Destruction*, 148.

75 Hartland *fared*: *Hartland* account: AAR, John M. Gill, USN, "Operations of U.S. Naval Forces, Center Task Force," Nov. 30, 1942, NARA RG 38, OCNO, box 786; "Awards of Medals for Gallantry During Attack on Oran Harbour," Admiralty, PRO, 1/11915.

    A mile to the west: Ernie Pyle, *Here Is Your War*, 22 (*"Them dead men"*); Disher, in Parris and Russell, 123; memo, E. B. Howard to DDE, Nov. 18, 1942, NARA RG 407, E 427, box 3165.

76 *Men paddled*: "Awards of Medals for Gallantry," Admiralty, PRO, 1/11915; AAR, Gill; AAR, G. D. Dickey, USN, "Operations of U.S. Naval Forces, Center Task Force," Nov. 30, 1942, NARA RG 38, OCNO, box 786; Paul Auphan and Jacques Moral, *The French Navy in World War II*, 226.

    French marines rounded up: "History of 3rd Battalion, 6th Armored Infantry," NARA RG 407; AAR, Wallace D. Moseley, RN, Admiralty, PRO, 1/11915; AAR, Gill; Auphan and Moral, 226–27; AAR, A. B. Cunningham, RN, "Operation TORCH—Report of Proceedings," March 30, 1943; NWAf, 204; AAR, RN, n.d., SM, MHI (*"contributed to the half-hearted manner"*); DDE to B. B. Somervell, Nov. 18, 1942, NARA RG 492, MTOUSA, records of special staff, box 1381; Edward Ellsberg, *No Banners, No Bugles*, 49, 71, 133.

77 *Corpses bobbed*: Andrew T. McNamara, *Quartermaster Activities of II Corps*, 28; William A. Carter, "Carter's War," ts, 1983, CEOH, III-8; William F. Powers, OH, Herbert Hart, Aug. 1985, CEOH; John G. Rosta, OH, G. Kurt Piehler and Mark Rybak, ROHA, 1997; memo, II Corps QM, Nov. 30, 1942, NARA RG 331, AFHQ micro, R-73-D.

    Ostensibly to avoid: memo, A. B. Cunningham, Dec. 18, 1942, Admiralty 1/11915, PRO (*"silence is the best policy"*); Rame, 60 (*hatless buccaneer*); Laffin, 26; "Reminiscences of Rear Adm. George W. Bauernschmidt," 1991, USNI OHD (*pilotage fees*).

    Eisenhower eventually accepted: Butcher diary, DDE Lib, A-174; A. J. Redway, "Admiral Jerauld Wright," ts, 1995, NHC, 269; "Reminiscences of Vice Adm. Bernhard H. Bieri," 1997, USNI OHD (*"going to get that fellow"*); diary, Nov. 15, 1942, OW, MHI; Gugeler, OW, MHI, x-35.

In Barbary

78 *Faint odors*: John P. Downing, *At War with the British*, 68; H. R. Knickerbocker et al., *Danger Forward*, 38 (*"sumptuous as a condemned man's"*); NWAf, 192–93; "History of the 26th Infantry in the Present Struggle," part IV, n.d., MRC FDM; Bill Sabin, "The Loves and Lives of 13008634," ts, UT-K, MS-1881, box 20, 9 (*"Sure I'm scared"*); Rame, 7 (*"Looks as if"*).

    Under the plan: NWAf, 192–93. (Many U.S. Army units in North Africa were organized into regimental combat teams and battalion combat teams, usually by adding engineers and other support units to the infantry or armored core. At the risk of oversimplification, I generally retain the traditional regimental and battalion nomenclature.)

79 *The largest contingent*: James J. Altieri, "Darby's Rangers: An Illustrated Portrayal of the Original Rangers," 1977, Louis F. Lisko Papers, Rangers, ASEQ, MHI;

David W. Hogan, Jr., *Raiders or Elite Infantry?* 18; Milton Lehman, "The Rangers Fought Ahead of Everybody," *Saturday Evening Post*, July 15, 1946, 15; James Altieri, *The Spearheaders*, 122 (*"Be bloody thankful"*).

Two companies: William O. Darby and W. H. Dammer, "U.S. Rangers," lecture, Oct. 27, 1944, Army and Navy Staff College; Anders Kjar Arnbal, *The Barrel-Land Dance Hall Rangers*, 11; "Reminiscences of Walter C. W. Ansel," 1972, USNI OHD, 3–111 (*"For King and country!"*); Altieri, *The Spearheaders*, 129; Darby, *Darby's Rangers*, 19–21; Jerome Joseph Haggerty, "A History of the Ranger Battalions in World War II," 115; Knickerbocker et al., 45 (*The mayor of Arzew*); Ramsey, 30.

80 *On the weather deck*: Stanley J. Grogan, "Memorandum for Mr. McCloy," n.d., NARA RG 165, E 418, Director of Plans and Ops, box 1228; A. J. Liebling, "Find 'Em, Fix 'Em, and Fight 'Em," *New Yorker*, Apr. 24, 1943, 221; C. M. Eymer, ts, MRC FDM, Allen 1989.124, box 392; Consuelo Allen, author interview, Sept. 21, 2000; Knickerbocker et al., 38.

81 *Terry de la Mesa Allen*: William Frye, " 'Terrible Terry' of the 1st Division Is Getting Tougher as He Goes Along," *Kansas City Star*, June 17, 1943 (*name swaggered*); Franklyn A. Johnson, *One More Hill*, 9; Robert John Rogers, "A Study of Leadership in the First Infantry Division During World War II," master's thesis, 1965, 8; Thomas W. Dixon, "Terry Allen," *Army*, Apr. 1978, 57.

The drowsy interwar years: obituary, *New York Times*, Sept. 13, 1969 (*"the fightingest man"*); "How Major Allen Beat Cowboy Champ in 300-Mile Race," *Brooklyn Daily Eagle*, Dec. 31, 1922; *San Antonio Light*, Jan. 20, 1952.

Less successful: Rogers, "A Study of Leadership," 8 (*"most indifferent student"*); Terry de la Mesa Allen Papers, MS 307, S.L.A. Marshall Military History Collection, UTEP; "Gen. Marshall Smashing Army's Caste System in Quest for Best Leaders," *St. Louis Post-Dispatch*, Dec. 19, 1940.

82 *With war, the rioters*: Robert A. Hewitt, SOOHP, Earl D. Bevan, 1982, MHI (*kept a list in a safe*); Robert W. Porter, Jr., SOOHP, John N. Sloan, 1981, MHI; "Gen. Marshall Smashing Army's Caste System in Quest for Best Leaders," *St. Louis Post-Dispatch*, Dec. 19, 1940.

After receiving: C. M. Eymer, ts, MRC FDM, Allen 1989.124, box 392; Stanhope Brasfield Mason, "Reminiscences and Anecdotes of World War II," 1988, ts, MRC FDM; GCM to TdA, July 30, 1942, GCM Papers, Pentagon office corr, GCM Lib, box 56, folder 17 (*"Be on your guard"*); DDE to TdA, "Morals and Conduct," Oct. 10, 1942, AFHQ micro, R-73-D, box 115 (*a tart memorandum*).

Proud, self-absorbed: Downing, 51; Porter, SOOHP, MHI (*"You should forget"*); letter, TdA to Mary Frances, Oct. 23, 1942, TdA, MHI.

83 *Chaos awaited him*: Ford, 6; Stephen V. Ralph, "The Operations of the 2nd Battalion, 16th Infantry in the Invasion of North Africa," 1947, MRC FDM, 13; AAR, "Naval Commander Centre Task Force, Operation TORCH," Dec. 27, 1942, NARA AFHQ micro, RN Operations, R 16-A; Howe, *The Battle History of the 1st Armored Division*, 32; MacCloskey, 83 (*"Men, this is what"*).

Linguists holding bullhorns: Mason, 26; Knickerbocker et al., 24–25; John K. Waters, SOOHP, William C. Parnell III, 1980, MHI, 166 (*"Okay, boys"*).

Some fired: Derrill M. Daniel, "Landings at Oran, Gela and Omaha Beaches," 1947, Armed Forces Staff College, 9 (*"They're not shooting"*); Gerald Astor, *The Greatest War*, 259 (*"half the grapevines"*); Ralph, 15 (*fled down the road*).

84 *Confusion and error*: Malcolm Marshall, ed., *Proud Americans of World War II*, 24 (*"Tank coming!"*); Paul K. Skogsberg, "The North African Campaigns," ASEQ, 1st Reconnaissance Troop, MHI, 21 (*ran him through*); Abbott, 28 (*"Everything's all right"*); Parris and Russell, 87 (*"The French die hard"*).

Terry Allen had seen worse: Liebling, "Find 'Em, Fix 'Em, and Fight 'Em," 221;

letter, TdA to Associated Press, July 23, 1947, TdA, MHI (*"a mountebank"*); "Peppery General; Well Known Here, Changes His Branch of Service in New Assignment of Duty," *Kansas City Star,* Jan. 4, 1942; Frye, "Terrible Terry," *Kansas City Star,* June 17, 1943 (*"A soldier doesn't fight"*).

Using a flashlight: Henry C. Wolfe, AAR, "Pre-Invasion Planning," Dec. 1942, NARA RG 407, E 427, box 24348; Frye, "Terrible Terry" (*"I believe"*); Knickerbocker et al., 45.

85 *At Beach Y*: George Juskalian, author interview, Feb. 25, 2000; TR to Eleanor, Nov. 11, 1942, TR, LOC.

Bookmakers in the 1st Division: Quentin Reynolds, *The Curtain Rises,* 214; GCM to TdA, June 5, 1942, GCM Papers, Pentagon corr, GCM Lib, box 56, folder 17; Downing, 34 (*"Goddam it"*).

Handsome he was not: Maxwell Hamilton, "Junior in Name Only," *Retired Officer,* June 1981, 28 (*"the most disreputable-looking"*); GCM to TdA, June 5, 1942, GCM Papers, Pentagon corr, GCM Lib, box 56, folder 17 (*"rare courage"*); Michael Pearlman, *To Make Democracy Safe for America,* 249.

86 *His father, the twenty-sixth*: Hamilton, 29, 31 (*"never amount"*); Pearlman, 250–51; Edward J. Renehan, Jr., *The Lion's Pride,* 210, 226; Linda Donn, *The Roosevelt Cousins,* 99.

Now Roosevelt was ashore: Pearlman, 251; TR to Eleanor, Oct. 20, Oct. 30, Nov. 11, 1942, Jan. 16, 1943, TR, LOC (*"little, scarcely seen shapes"*).

The French counterattacked: Tank Destroyer Forces World War II, 20; Karig, 213; Robinett, *Armor Command,* 56.

87 *"Soldier, what"*: William M. Lee, ASEQ, n.d., 26th Inf, MHI (*"Come on, follow me"*); Mrs. Theodore Roosevelt, Jr., *Day Before Yesterday,* 440; Renehan, 66.

VILLAIN

87 *One final element*: "Parachutist's combat equipment," 2nd Bn/503rd Para Inf, "Air Campaign in N Af," DDE Lib, box 6; "Partial Planning File, First United States' Use of Parachute Operations in Connection with TORCH," 1942, MHI Lib (*Slips of rice paper*).

88 *The objective of Operation VILLAIN*: "Operation TORCH: The Dispatch of Aircraft from the United Kingdom by Eighth Air Force," Sept. 14, 1944, Historical Section, U.S. Strategic Air Forces in Europe, NARA RG 407, E 427, Pre-Invasion Planning, box 24351; Lowell Rooks, II Corps chief of staff, cited in MWC, "Memorandum to General Eisenhower," Oct. 7, 1942, DDE Lib, PP-pres, box 153 (*"no material difference"*); MWC, OH, SOOHP, F. S. Rittgers, Jr., 1972, MHI (*"The British just want"*).

The 2nd Battalion: William Pelham Yarborough, *Bail Out over North Africa,* 31; John C. Warren, *Airborne Missions in the Mediterranean, 1942–1945,* 8–9; "Administrative History, 60th Troop Carrier Group," AFHRA, NARA micro, R-B 0155-0157 (*"distracted conversation"*).

Clark had approved: Eighth Air Force msg, AFHRA, NARA micro, R-A 5857; Lloyd G. Wilson, "The Operations of the 509th Parachute Battalion in North Africa"; William Breuer, *Geronimo: American Paratroopers in World War II,* 34 (*"Dear God"*).

89 *After takeoff*: Warren, 7; AAR, Gordon H. Browne, NARA RG 226, OSS, E 99, boxes 39–40.

90 *The sun rose*: AAR, Carleton S. Coon, NARA RG 226, E 99, OSS, box 39, folder 8 (*banging their fists*); Maurice Tugwell, *Airborne to Battle: A History of Airborne Warfare, 1918–1971,* 141.

Airborne once again: Gerard M. Devlin, *Paratrooper!*, 138; Wilson, "The Operations of the 509th Parachute Battalion in North Africa," 1947, 10; AAR, William P. Yarborough, Nov. 13, 1942, NARA RG 407, E 427, AG, WWII Operations Reports, box 234; "Administrative History, 60th Troop Carrier Group," AFHRA, NARA micro, R-B 0155–0157.

91   *Most of Raff's*: Breuer, 41; "USAF Airborne Operations, World War II and Korea," 1962, USAF Historical Division, MHI, 5; Warren, 13.

To the Last Man

91   *Viewed from the great*: Powell, 280 (*"resounded to the groans"*); R.H.W.S. Hastings, *The Rifle Brigade in the Second World War, 1939–1945*, 209 (*"white-walled city"*); Tompkins, 11 (*"reclining woman"*).

93   *So it was*: Murphy, 120–28 (*"I am convinced"*); Anthony Clayton, *Three Marshals of France*, 70; Tompkins, 70 (*"chloroform the city"*), 90 (*"painful search"*).

94   *"I am happy to say"*: Langer, 346; Murphy, 127–30; Kingsbury Smith, "Unrevealed Facts About Robert Murphy," *American Mercury*, Nov. 1944, 528 (*"We are coming by invitation"*).
        Murphy described: François Kersaudy, *Churchill and De Gaulle*, 222; Leahy, 48 (*Popeye*); Murphy, 127–30; Lamb, 211 (*"a bad man"*).

95   *By a coincidence*: Russell Brooks, "The Unknown Darlan," *U.S. Naval Institute Proceedings*, Aug. 1955, 879; Boatner, 117; Tompkins, 65; Eisenhower, *Crusade in Europe*, 105 (*"If I could meet"*); Murphy, 118, 129 (*"I have known"*).
        For fifteen minutes: Pendar, AAR, Jan. 3, 1945, NARA RG 226, E 99, OSS, box 40 (*"The necessary"*); Murphy, 131 (*"Giraud is not"*).

96   *The insurrection*: Funk, 212 (*"This isn't just"*), 218–20; Pendar, *Adventure*, 108–109 (Pirates of Penzance); AAR, "Narrative of Captain Frederick Brown," July 17, 1945, NARA RG 26, E 99, OSS, box 40; msg, Nov. 8, 1942, NARA RG 38, OCNO, Office of Naval Intel., box 1 (*"France and her honor"*).
        Regrettably, the Allies: Bolstad, 31, 63; Leslie W. Bailey, "The Operations of the 3rd Battalion, 135th Infantry at Algiers," 1948, 11; *NWAf*, 243.

97   *The lights of Algiers*: AAR, A. B. Russell, RN, "Operation Terminal," Nov. 11, 1942, SM, MHI; Leslie W. Bailey, *Through Hell and High Water*, 52.
        Then, on his fourth: AAR, A.F.C. Layard, in Bolstad, 225.
        Badly shaken: Richard Collier, *The War in the Desert*, 14 (*"light out like stripey-assed baboons"*); Tute, 177; Auphan and Moral, 222; Layard, 225; Bailey, *Through Hell and High Water*, 46.

98   *Fancourt sounded the recall*: John MacVane, *Journey into War*, 59; H. L. St. J. Fancourt, "Report of Commanding Officer, Force TERMINAL," Nov. 11, 1942, SM, MHI (*"The morale effect of a destroyer"*).

99   *Even with the ship gone*: Bailey, *Through Hell and High Water*, 49; "A Partial History, 135th Infantry Regiment," n.d., Iowa GSM; "Regimental History, 135th Infantry," NARA RG 407.
        Then the unmistakable creak: Hougen, *The Story of the Famous 34th Infantry Division*; Kenneth Maitland Davies, *To the Last Man*, 97; *NWAf*, 244; Bolstad, 95.
        Thirty-three thousand: Richard F. Kinden, "The Road to Fort McGregor and the Long Way Home," ts, IWM, 84/50/1 (*"I should have thought"*); Pack, 64 (*"testing for salt"*).

100   *Finding the right beach*: Jack Marshall, "Tales of a Timid Commando," ts, n.d., ASEQ, 34th ID, MHI; AAR, "Company B, 168th Inf," Nov. 1942, Iowa GSM; Ankrum, 122 (*"I'm sorry to tell you"*); AAR, RN, Inshore Squadron, H.M.S.

Bulolo, Dec. 8, 1942, NARA AFHQ micro, RN Ops., R-17-A; Morison, *Operations in North African Waters,* 206; AAR, "5 Corps Lessons From TORCH," Nov. 26, 1942, NARA RG 334, NWC Lib, box 472.

Outnumbered five to one: Marshall, "Tales of a Timid Commando" (*"Why don't you"*); Macksey, *Crucible of Power: The Fight for Tunisia, 1942–1943,* 71 (*"French families"*); Benjamin Caffey, OH, Feb. 1950, SM, MHI; Middleton, *Our Share of Night,* 175 (*enterprising wine merchant*).

On the far western fringe: David Scott Daniell, *History of the East Surrey Regiment,* vol. IV, 151; Middleton, 175 (*"You gentlemen"*).

101 *The 168th Infantry: NWAf,* 236; Robert R. Moore, AAR, "Record of Events from 14 Oct. 1942 to Armistice, Nov. 1942," Iowa GSM; "The Tunisian Campaign," 34th Div., Dec. 13, 1943, NARA RG 407, E 427, 334–0.3 (*"not prepared"*); letter, Moore to family, Dec. 2, 1942 (*"I got my helmet creased"*); *Red Oak Express,* Feb. 22, 1943; *Des Moines Sunday Register,* July 18, 1943 (*"I thought the fight"*); Bill Roth, "The Longest Days of a G.I.," ts, n.d., Iowa GSM; 168th Inf Regt, pamphlet, Iowa GSM.

"Glory Enough for Us All"

103 *The stars had once again:* U.S.S. *Brooklyn* war diary, Nov. 7, 1942, SEM, NHC, box 15.

More than 100: The Landings in North Africa, 16 (*"reeling drunk"*); Morison attributes the "Chinese laundry" line to Robert C. Giffen, *Operations in North African Waters,* 48; Kreidberg and Henry, 678; Astor, 252.

A gale born south of Iceland: Erbes, "Hell on Wheels Surgeon," ts, USMA Arch, 11; Robert E. Coffin, "Operation TORCH: A Perilous Preview," *Army,* Nov. 1992, 42 (*"I can't believe a ship"*); Philip G. Cochran, OH, 1975, USAF HRC, 418; Fitzhugh L. Palmer, Jr., "The Old Indispensables," *Proceedings,* Aug. 1976, 61.

For Hewitt, the storm: Alfred M. Gruenther to GSP, Oct. 13, 1942, NARA RG 218, CCS 381, section 1–1a, box 325; Dickson, "G-2 Journal: Algiers to the Elbe," ts, MHI, 21; AFHQ msg, Nov. 7, 1942, NARA RG 492, MTOUSA, box 1388 (*"Very poor"*).

104 *"I hope to God":* Mountbatten, OH, n.d., HKH, NHC, box 6.

The choice: diary, Oct. 28, 30, 1942, GSP, LOC Ms Div, box 2, folder 13.

"We are to be congratulated": Blumenson, *Patton: The Man Behind the Legend,* 168; Farago, 9, 13 (*"Some goddam fool"*).

105 *Despite their early antipathy:* Blumenson, *Patton: The Man Behind the Legend,* 112, 121 (*"War is the only place"*); DDE to GSP, Jr., Oct. 13, 1942, Chandler, 618; *NWAf,* 44–45; "Reminiscences of Rear Adm. Elliott B. Strauss," 1989, USNI OHD (*"when things get overturned"*).

In the smallest hours: weather reports, HKH, correspondence, NHC, box 1; Tuleja, "Admiral H. Kent Hewitt," in Howarth, ed., 319–20.

Hewitt studied: Clagett, "Admiral H. Kent Hewitt, U.S. Navy," 76 (*"velvet"*).

A solitary banana boat: AAR, "Trip of Honduran SS *Contessa,*" March 22, 1943, in Wheeler, ed., 76.

106 *With new urgency:* Harmon, *Combat Commander,* 81; Franklyn E. Dailey, Jr., *Joining the War at Sea, 1939–1945,* 137 (*"resembled a fraternity house"*); memo, HQ Task Force A, Oct. 10, 1942, NARA micro, Western Task Force, AFHQ G-3, R-24-C (*first-day battle casualities*); Harry McK. Roper, "Report on Observations Made as Observer with Task Force Brushwood," n.d., NARA RG 337, Observer Reports, box 52; AAR, Hewitt, March 1943, NARA RG 218, JCS, CCS 381, section 1–1a, box 325 (*wetted down*); Morison, *Operations in North African Waters,* 71 (*"pretend they're Japs"*).

Commanders with an impulse: F.E.M. Whiting, correspondence, 1972, USNI OHD ("Ense petit"); Morison, *Operations in North African Waters*, 92 ("*glory enough*"); Emily Morison Beck, ed., *Sailor Historian: The Best of Samuel Eliot Morison*, 205 ("*gangway for a fighting ship*").

Patton napped: Patton directive, Oct. 14, 1942, NARA RG 165, Office of the Director of Plans and Operations, General Records, corr, box 1229 ("*Get off that damned beach*"); GCM to DDE, n.d., NARA RG 492, MTOUSA, box 1387 ("*avoid firing*"); NWAf, 45, 70 ("*superiority complex*").

On the darkened bridge: msg, NARA RG 319, OCMH, box 229 ("*We come, among*"); AFHQ msg, NARA RG 218, JCS, box 325 ("Vive"); Farago, 17 ("Mes amis").

107   *"God's most favorite"*: Hatch, *George Patton: General in Spurs*, 138.

Only rebels: Brooks, "Casablanca—The French Side of the Fence," *Proceedings*, Sept. 1951, 909; "Memorandum for Colonel Donovan," OSS AAR, Jan. 1943, NARA RG 226, E 99, box 40 (*scheme by Moroccan Jews*); "TORCH Report," Sept. 6, 1944, NARA RG 226, E 99, OSS, box 40 (*Leroy the Badger*); AAR, Émile Béthouart, NARA RG 226, E 99, OSS, box 40 ("*a juvenile enthusiasm*"); letter, Auguste Paul Noguès to G. F. Howe, n.d., NARA RG 319, OCMH, box 225.

After that, nothing: Macmillan, *The Blast of War*, 197 ("*No-Yes*"); AAR, Michel Despax, July 15, 1944, NARA RG 226, E 99, OSS, box 40 (*his mistress's bed*); AAR, Béthouart; letter, Noguès to Howe; Philip H. Bagby, "D-Day in Casablanca," *American Foreign Service Journal*, March 1945, 16 (*Senegalese soldiers*); NWAf, 95.

108   *"The sky is dark"*: letter, Dave Murdock, *Arizona Republic*, Dec. 6, 1942, MCC, YU. Soldier letters collected by Mina Curtiss frequently indicate the date and newspaper or magazine in which the correspondence was published.

The lieutenant was deceived: Morison, "The Approach to Fedala," ts, n.d., SEM, NHC, box 16 ("*One plot showed*"); "Commander in Chief, Atlantic Fleet," 1946, vol. I, USNAd, 426 ("*center of Times Square*").

Despite this irrefutable evidence: 3rd ID, "Brushwood Final Report," Dec. 8, 1942, NARA micro, AFHQ G-3 Operations, R-24-C; "Commander in Chief, Atlantic Fleet," 1946, vol. I, USNAd, 426 ("*as though one switch*"); AAR, U.S. Atlantic Fleet Amphibious Force, n.d., NARA RG 407, E 427, box 24430; Morison, "The Approach to Fedala," ts, n.d., SEM, NHC, box 16; Truscott, *Command Missions*, 93 ("*To be perfectly honest*").

109   *Destroyers tacked*: "Operations, 3rd Bn., 60th Combat Team, 8–11 Nov. 1942," NARA RG 407, E 427, box 7540; Ernest D. Whitehead, Sr., *World War II: An Ex-Sergeant Remembers*, 33 (*impaled his thigh*); Wallace, "Africa, We Took It and Liked It," 20; Randle, *Safi Adventure*, 27 ("*Don't harass*").

Then the loadmasters bellowed: AAR, U.S.S. *Charles Carroll*, n.d., U.S. Atlantic Fleet Amphibious Force, NARA RG 407, E 427, box 24490.

At Fedala, the first wave: "Commander in Chief, Atlantic Fleet," 1946, vol. I, USNAd, 430 ("*indescribable confusion*"); "CSI Battlebook 3-A: Operation TORCH," CSI, 53; AAR, J. T. Hagglove, "Report of Operation at Fedala," U.S.S. *Leonard Wood*, Nov. 28, 1942, NARA RG 407, E 427, Box 24490; "Commander in Chief, Atlantic Fleet," 1946, vol. I, USNAd, 436; Kerwin, SOOHP, MHI, 123 (*scavenging life jackets*).

111   *Eighty miles north*: Truscott, *Command Decisions*, 97; Mittelman, 48 ("*like a yacht race*"); AAR, *Henry T. Allen*, n.d., SEM, NHC, box 16; "Western Task Force: Attack on Mehdia and Port Lyautey Airdrome," 1945, ts, 2–3.7 AEI, CMH.

The third and final: Karl Baedeker, *The Mediterranean*, 109; Justin McGuinness, *Footprint Morocco Handbook*, 203; Oscar Koch, ts, n.d., MHI (*picture postcards*); lecture, Louis Ely, Feb. 5, 1943, SEM, NHC (*Jew's Cliff*).

To seize Safi port: AAR, 47th Infantry, n.d., NARA RG 407, E 427, box 7514; Karig, 184 (*"sawed-off"*); SEM, NHC, box 4, folder 2; George Bastedo, "K Goes to Africa," ts, n.d., in Chester H. Jordan file, 3rd Bn, 47th Inf, ASEQ, MHI; Randle, *Safi Adventure*, appendix A (*"Violent, rapid"*).

112 *The usual muddle*: Harmon, 84 (*stretched a huge net*); "Commander in Chief, Atlantic Fleet," 1946, vol. I, USNAd, 408.

  Machine-gun rounds: lecture, C. G. Richardson, "The Attack on Safi," Aug. 20, 1943, NARA RG 334, NWC Lib, box 164.

113 *Unsettled, the troops*: James Adams, "Observer's Report on Landing Operations of Task Force BLACKSTONE," Jan. 1943, NARA RG 337, E 15A, box 52 (*They flopped*); Bastedo, "K Goes to Africa"; Wilhm et al., "Armor in the Invasion of North Africa."

  Three more waves: Adams, "Observer's Report" (*"A soldier would snake"*); Randle, *Safi Adventure*, 45, 58.

  By early afternoon: Mittelman, 65; Erbes, "Hell on Wheels Surgeon," 15 (*"with a welder's torch"*).

  It was all too much: "Official Report Submitted by Commander of the Safi Garrison," Nov. 14, 1942, NARA RG 338, Fifth Army, box 1; *NWAf*, 109.

114 *Eisenhower had trusted*: *Three Years*, 173–76; DDE to GCM, Nov. 8, 1942, Chandler, 673 (*"Everything appears"*).

  Besides that: DDE to John S. D. Eisenhower, Oct. 13, 1942, Chandler, vol. I, 617.

  "this business of warfare": *Three Years*, 176–77; DDE to W. B. Smith, Nov. 9, 1942, Chandler, 678 (*"That I do not believe"*).

115 *"Worries of a Commander"*: DDE memo, Nov. 8, 1942, Chandler, 675.

CHAPTER 3: BEACHHEAD
A Sword in Algiers

116 *This was war*: Martha Gellhorn, quoted in Paul Fussell, *Doing Battle: The Making of a Skeptic*, 298 (*"our condition"*); Matthew Arnold, "Dover Beach."

  East of the Algerian: *Destruction*, 144; *The Landings in North Africa*, 13; "5 Corps Lessons from TORCH," extract from letter, Nov. 26, 1942, NARA RG 334, NWC Lib, box 472 (*"all very friendly"*).

117 *Lieutenant Colonel Edward J. Doyle*: letter, John O'Daniel to OW, Jan. 1951, NARA RG 319, OCMH, box 225; Berens, 36–37 (*Ignoring orders* and *"at the beach"*).

  Luftwaffe pilots: *The Landings in North Africa*, 104; *Baltimore Sun*, Dec. 17, 1942; Karig, 220; Morison, *Operations in North African Waters*, 213.

  Pleasing as such retaliatory: AAR, Jan. 3, 1945, NARA RG 226, E 99, OSS, box 40; Pendar, 112.

118 *In Juin's limousine*: Charles W. Ryder, OH, March 1949, SM, MHI (*"I will go anywhere"*); Murphy, 132.

  A bugler perched: AAR, July 17, 1945, and Jan. 3, 1945, NARA RG 226, E 99, OSS, box 40 (*"I don't like blood"*); Pendar, 114; Hougen, *The Story of the Famous 34th Infantry Division* (*hunting trophies*); Ryder, OH, March 1949, SM, MHI (*"Are you"*); AAR, C. W. Ryder, Nov. 19, 1942, NARA RG 407, E 427, AG, box 244; Murphy, 133.

119 *At dawn on Monday*: Roskill, 325; Fergusson, 213; S.W.C. Pack, *Invasion North Africa 1942*, 80 (*"Everyone lie down!"*).

  So, too, did General Giraud: Langer, 350 (*"his presence"*); DDE to GCM, Nov. 9, 1942, Chandler, 680 (*"stupid Frogs"*).

120 *The authorities in Vichy*: Langer, 356 (*"a rebel chief and a felon"*); memo, J.J. McCloy to L. J. McNair, March 31, 1943, NARA RG 165, Plans and Ops, box 1230; Funk, 234; Tompkins, 116 (*uniform had gone missing*).

Three hours later: Murphy, 135 (*"messes things"*); Darryl F. Zanuck, *Tunis Expedition*, 39, 48.

The Hôtel St. Georges: Baedeker, 221; Middleton, 191 (*spinsters touring*).

121 *Clark found General Ryder*: Berens, 38 (*"shoot their butts off"*); "Record of Events," Feb. 22, 1943, NARA RG 338, Fifth Army, box 1, 1–13; Clark, *Calculated Risk*, 108.

"We have work": Clark, *Calculated Risk*, 108–13; "Record of Events" (*"All my associates"*); Langer, 352 (*"Pétain is nothing"*); log, Nov. 10, 1942, Jerauld Wright Papers, LOC, box 2 (*"That is your decision"*); Murphy, 138 (*"Would you mind"*).

122 *The Americans retreated*: Murphy, 138 (*Clark's tacit threat*); Funk, 243 (*"in the name"*); Tompkins, 121 (*"J'accepte"*); "Record of Events," 13.

He immediately: Alan Moorehead, *The End in Africa*, 61 (*"He appeared"*); Funk, 240 (*"I issued"*); Tompkins, 123 (*"I am lost"*); "Record of Events," 13; Morison, *Operations in North African Waters*, 217; Dickson, "G-2 Journal: Algiers to the Elbe," 29 (*"Mon Admiral, by order"*).

123 *At Gibraltar, Eisenhower thumbed*: Chandler, 679 (*"War brings"*); Butcher diary, Nov. 8 (*"good assassin"*) and 13 (*"in a neutral country"*), DDE Lib, PP-pres, box 165.

124 *But it was Oran*: DDE to GCM, Nov. 9, 1942, Chandler, 680 (*"My biggest"*).

A Blue Flag over Oran

124 *American soldiers had converged*: Field Order #1, Oct. 11, 1942, 26th Inf., MRC FDM (*Brooklyn, Brockton*).

Terry Allen and a larger portion: Rame, 16 (*"scrofulous"*); author interview, Eston White; Downing, 92 (*When the mule*).

125 *A wounded soldier lay*: Downing, 89 (*"Don't kick"*); Fred W. Hall, Jr., "A Memoir of World War II," ts, 1997, Eisenhower Center, University of New Orleans (*"The fallen wire"*).

St. Cloud was a buff-tinted: NWAf, 220n; AAR, Leland L. Rounds, July 13, 1944, NARA RG 226, E 99, OSS, box 40; Field Order #1, intel. annex, Oct. 11, 1942, 26th Inf., MRC FDM (*"second- or third-class"*); Rame, 16.

At 3:30 P.M., the battalion: Marshall, ed., *Proud Americans*, 31–40 (*"Keep going, Mac"*); Robert W. Baumer, *Before Taps Sounded*, 64.

126 *Now French artillerymen*: Marshall, ed., 26 (*"Please, please,"*), 31 (*"Stop!"*), 35 (*goats stampeded*).

Night slipped down: Russell F. Akers, OH, July 27, 1949, SM, MHI.

By seven A.M. on November 9: Parris and Russell, 193; Rame, 28–31.

"I'm going to put": Rame, 29; Knickerbocker et al., 46.

127 *At that moment*: Rogers, "A Study of Leadership in the First Infantry Division During World War II," 14, 16; "Nothing Stopped the Timberwolves," *Saturday Evening Post*, Aug. 17, 1946, 20; Frye, " 'Terrible Terry' of the 1st Division Is Getting Tougher as He Goes Along."

Standing beneath a fig tree: John K. Waters, SOOHP, 1980, William C. Parnell III, MHI, 683; Mason, "Reminiscences and Anecdotes of World War II," MRC FDM; "A Factual Situation and Operations Report on the Combat Operations of the 1st Infantry Division," n.d., TdA, MHI (*"There will not be"*); "Terry Allen and the First Division in North Africa and Sicily," n.d., TdA, MHI; Ramsey, 55 (*"I just couldn't do it"*).

128 *The circumvention of St. Cloud*: Rogers, 15; Knickerbocker et al., 50 (*"You will not talk"*); Rame, 40; Howe, *The Battle History of the 1st Armored Division*, 45 (*flood the port*). (George Marshall later sent FDR a copy of Allen's field order no. 3 as a model of brevity.)

    Festive crowds: Joseph S. Frelinghuysen, *Passages to Freedom*, 26; letter, William B. Kern to PMR, Jan. 1950, NARA RG 319, OCMH.

129 *For more than five hours*: "18th Infantry, Draft Regimental History," n.d., Stanhope Mason Collection, MRC FDM; Lida Mayo, *The Ordnance Department: On Beachhead and Battlefront*, 117 (*a large blue pennant*).

    Beyond the killed: NWAf, 227, 228n; Observer Report, #41, March 5, 1943, NARA RG 337, Box 52 (*Allen and Roosevelt also relieved*); author interview, Juskalian, Feb. 25, 2000.

    The liberators immediately: McNamara, 22 ; Pyle, *Here Is Your War*, 83 (*"to make them feel"*); Waters, SOOHP, 171; Edward J. Josowitz, *An Informal History of the 601st Tank Destroyer Battalion*, 7 (*threw a jolly party*); Pearlman, 249; author interview, Juskalian.

    Almost 37,000 men now occupied: Howe, *The Battle History of the 1st Armored Division*, 47 (*"Everything is rosy"*); DDE to W. B. Smith, Nov. 10, 1942, Chandler, 686 (*"rush and rush"*).

"An Orgy of Disorder"

130 *Casablanca provided*: Landings in North Africa, 27–39; Auphan and Moral, 230–36; Morison, *Operations in North African Waters*, 93–114 (*"fire-away Flannagan"*).

    hardly a syllable: Three Years, 182.

    Hewitt considered: New York Sun, Jan. 30, 1943, HKH, LOC Ms. Div., box 9, folder 6; Clagett, "Admiral H. Kent Hewitt, U.S. Navy," part 2, 83; U.S.S. *Brooklyn* war diary, Nov. 8, 1942, SEM, NHC, box 15 (*"Have noticed"*).

131 *Within ten minutes*: Brooks, "Casablanca—The French Side of the Fence," 909.

    The Jean Bart: AAR, Carl E. Bledsoe, Jan. 27, 1943, NARA RG 337, E 15A, box 51; Mason, 181; Godson, 51.

    The commander of the French: Auphan and Moral, 230; Tompkins, 162–65 (*black cassock* and *wives and children*).

132 *French shells*: AAR, R. E. Ingersoll, "TORCH Operation, Comments and Recommendations," March 1, 1943, NARA RG 407, E 427, "Special Files," box 24486; AAR, USN, "Participation in Operation TORCH Action off Casablanca," Nov. 19, 1942, NARA RG 407, E 427, "Special Files," box 24488; Landings in North Africa, 35; "Signal Communication in the North African Campaign," ts, 1945, *Tactical Communication in World War II*, Part I, Historical Section, Office of the Chief Signal Officer, MHI, 17.

    concussion: HKH, "Reminscences of a World War II Admiral," ts, NHC, box 21; letter, Edward S. Johnston to SEM, Apr. 1947, SEM, NHC, box 16; Farago, 35–36 (*"I hope you have"*); Blumenson, *The Patton Papers, 1940–1945*, 103, 105 (*"I was on"*).

133 *Hewitt was too busy*: Landings in North Africa, 37; Morison, *Operations in North African Waters*, 100–101 (*"grasshopper with a rock"*), 104; "Reminiscences of Rear Adm. Joshua W. Cooper," OH, John T. Mason, 1975, USNI OHD (*galley trash can*); AAR, Daniel F. Seacord, U.S.S. *Ludlow*, n.d., NHC; Harley Cope, "Play Ball, Navy!" *Proceedings*, Oct. 1943, 1131.

    Four miles: AAR, "Aircraft Operations During the Execution of TORCH," CINCLANT, March 30, 1943, NARA RG 38, OCNO, WWII Action, box 3; Wordell and Seiler, 133 (*Scotch tape*).

134 *Patched and vengeful*: C. T. Booth and M. T. Wordell, OH Dec. 4, 1942, NARA RG 334, E 315, NWC Lib, box 476 (*"The first pass"*); Wordell and Seiler, 93.

    The air attacks and weight: "Commander in Chief, Atlantic Fleet," ts, 1946, vol. I, USNAd, 449; Wordell and Seiler, 93 (*"heeled over"*); Auphan and Moral, 233; *Landings in North Africa*, 35–36; Morison, *Operations in North African Waters*, 107.

    The most operatic death: AAR, translated from French Naval Historical Service, n.d., in *Ludlow* file, NHC; Auphan and Moral, 233; *Landings in North Africa*, 36; Collier, 146 (*Terrified pigs*).

135 *Of the French ships*: AAR, "Aircraft Operations During the Execution of TORCH," CINCLANT, March 30, 1943, NARA RG 38, OCNO, WWII Action, box 3; Wordell and Seiler, 93 (*sweeping, ceremonial turn*); letter, C. V. August, *Chicago News*, Jan. 28, 1943, MCC, YU (*bathed in champagne*).

    Diehard French officers: Ellsberg, 271 (*"We Come"*); Tompkins, 165.

    Patton finally reached: letters, Edward S. Johnston to S. E. Morison, April–May 1947, SEM, NHC, box 16 (*"I cannot stomach"*); D'Este, *Patton*, 435.

136 *That would be*: Blumenson, *Patton: The Man Behind the Legend*, 128 (*"orgy of disorder"*); Observer Report #37, Feb. 10, 1943, NARA RG 337, box 52 (*"Had the landings"*); "Western Task Force: The Attack on Fedala," n.d., War Department, CMH, 2–3.7 WE; "Signal Communication in the North African Campaign," ts, 1945, *Tactical Communication in World War II*, Part I, Historical Section, Office of the Chief Signal Officer, MHI, 59; Kenneth G. Crawford, *Report on North Africa*, 45; letter, Arthur R. Wilson to GCM, Dec. 12, 1942, NARA RG 165, E 13, OCS, box 106; Joseph A. Watters, "The Invasion of North Africa at Fedala and Casablanca," ts, n.d., ASEQ, 3rd ID, MHI; *Three Years*, 148.

    While trapped: Hatch, *George Patton: General in Spurs*, 138 (*"I wish"*); Charles R. Codman, *Drive*, 22; Harry H. Semmes, "George S. Patton, Jr.'s Psychology of Leadership," *Army*, Jan.–Feb. 1955, 1 (*"words of fire"*); Harmon, 94 (*useful rumor*).

137 *Five French infantry battalions*: Wilhm et al., 71; "History of Regimental Landing Group 30," March 30, 1943, NARA RG 407, E 427, box 245 (*"Rendezvous!"*); "Western Task Force: The Attack on Fedala"; decoration affidavits, Mackenzie E. Porter, Robert D. Henriques, NARA RG 338, 7th Army Awards, box 2; William Ellsworth, OH, n.d., SM, MHI (*"For God's sake stop"*); Coffin, "Operation TORCH: A Perilous Preview," 42; Donald G. Taggart, ed., *History of the Third Infantry Division*, 23.

    A white handkerchief: "History of Regimental Landing Group 30" (*offered water*).

    Patrols pushing: Morison, *Operations in North African Waters*, 65 (*"the greatest setback"*).

    Rommel was still: William Ellsworth, OH, n.d., SM, MHI; Franklin M. Reck, *Beyond the Call of Duty*, 27 (*"Good day, my friends!"*); Taggart, ed., 20; Morison, *Operations in North African Waters*, 86, 110; *NWAf*, 128; Farago, 39 (*"determined to slug it out"*).

138 *The fight would be*: "Commander in Chief, Atlantic Fleet," ts, 1946, vol. I, USNAd, 443; letter, Arthur R. Wilson to GCM, Dec. 12, 1942, NARA RG 165, E 13, OCS, box 106; Farago, 200 (*"My theory"*); Codman, 35 (*Patton strolled*); Blumenson, *The Patton Papers, 1940–1945*, 106 (*"God was"*).

    God withdrew: Wilson to GCM, Dec. 12, 1942 (*"calmest day"*); Beck et al., 77; *Landings in North Africa*, 76; Garrison H. Davidson, OH, John T. Greenwood, 1980, CEOH, 172 (*"Let's do it"*).

    Shore parties lacked: Bykofsky and Larson, 160; "Amphibious Training Command," ts, n.d., USNAd, VII-36, 58; "Signal Communication in the North

African Campaigns," in *Tactical Communications in World War II*, part 1, 1945, MHI, 24; Leo J. Meyer, "Strategy and Logistical History: Mediterranean Theater of Operations," ts, n.d., CMH, 2.37 CC1, III-15; Earl Burton, "The Invasion of North Africa," in Armed Forces Series, vol. 2, 1992.

139 *A company of 113*: "Commander in Chief, Atlantic Fleet," 1946, ts, vol. I, USNAd, 431 (*"bring order"*); *History of 67th Armored Regiment*, 67; Taggart, ed., 23; "CSI Battlebook 3-A: Operation TORCH," CSI, ADA 151 625 (*"full of metal"*); decoration citation, Walter J. Burns, 204th MP Co., NARA RG 338, Fifth Army, A 47-A-3948, box 56.

Two hours later: H. Essame, *Patton: A Study in Command*, 55 (*"flay the idle"*); Blumenson, *The Patton Papers, 1940–1945*, 108 (*"nasty blue"* and *"beach was a mess"*).

140 *One officer quoted Patton*: Codman, 21.

Scourging would not: Taggart, ed., 29; Watters, ASEQ, MHI; Forrest K. Kleinman, "The Bizarre Battle for Casablanca," *Army*, Aug. 1997, 38; GSP to DDE, Nov. 14, 1942; "Western Task Force: The Attack on Fedala," 60.

"Today has been bad": Blumenson, *The Patton Papers, 1940–1945*, 109; DDE to GSP, Nov. 10, 1942, Chandler, 684.

Battle for the Kasbah

141 *Of the nine major*: LKT Jr. to MWC, Sept. 12, 1942, LKT Jr. Papers, GCM Lib, box 9 (*"should not be"*); Farago, 29; GCM to DDE, Oct. 5, 1942, NARA RG 492, MTOUSA, box 1386 (*"noon Dog Day"*).

"Beloved Wife": LKT Jr. to Sarah, Oct. 22, 1942, LKT Jr. Papers, GCM Lib; Lucian K. Truscott, Jr., *Twilight of the Cavalry*, xiii–xv; John K. Waters, SOOHP, William C. Parnell III, 1980, MHI; Boatner, 574; Truscott, *Command Missions*, 71; Theodore J. Conway, SOOHP, Robert F. Ensslin, 1977, I-22; diary, Oct. 15, 1942, GSP, LOC, box 2, folder 13 (*"I am just"*).

Truscott's opening gambit: Author visit, April 2000; P. M. Hamilton, OH, Nov. 30, 1949, SM, MHI; P. M. Hamilton, OH, July 1945, "Western Task Force: Attack on Mehdia and the Port Lyautey Airdrome," ts, 1945, CMH, 2–3.7 AEI; Reck, 44.

143 *The failed diplomatic*: "Western Task Force: Attack on Mehdia," 27; "Commander in Chief, Atlantic Fleet," 1946, ts, vol. I, USNAd, 416 (*"with cold steel"*); AAR, Carl E. Bledsoe, Jan. 27, 1943, NARA RG 337, E 15A, box 51 (*"absolutely dumbfounded"*).

144 *Nightfall made matters worse*: Semmes, 121; "Western Task Force: Attack on Mehdia," 63.

On the broad: Truscott, *Command Missions*, 113–14.

The troops ducked: LKT Jr. to GSP, Nov. 12, 1942, LKT Jr. Papers, GCM Lib, box 9 (*"halfway to Bermuda"*).

Like Patton, Truscott concluded: Farago, 29–30 (*"disaster against"*); Peter Andrews, "A Place to Be Lousy In," *American Heritage*, Dec. 1991, 100 (*Truscott suspected*); Truscott, *Command Missions*, 97–98 (*"One of the first lessons"*).

145 *Yet only luck*: Semmes, 125; Semmes, reply to Armored School queries, Dec. 1949, SM, MHI; Truscott, *Command Missions*, 118 (*"not a cheerful one"*).

At first light: AAR, Gordon Browne, n.d., OSS files, NARA RG 226, E 99, box 39 ("Tout va bien"); "Western Task Force: Attack on Mehdia," 4; msg, GCM, Oct. 2, 1942, NARA RG 492, MTOUSA, Special Staff, box 1385 (*"rivet attention"*); Malvergne Silver Star documentation, NARA RG 338, Fifth Army, box 56; Roul Tunley, "A Frenchman Returns," *Sea Power*, Jan. 1945, 13; AAR, Co C, 15th Engineer Combat Bn, n.d., NARA RG 407, E 427, 9th ID, box 7455.

146 *Dallas yawed wildly*: R. Brodie, Jr., OH, June 19, 1951, SM, MHI; *NWAf*, 165; Morison, *Operations in North African Waters*, 131.

Two hours later: "Western Task Force: Attack on Mehdia," 122; "Adventures by Men of the 60th Infantry Regiment in WWII," ts, 1993, MHI, 9; Mittelman, 72; Truscott, *Command Missions*, 120 (*"a beautiful sight"*); Frederic A. Henney, "Combat Engineers in North Africa: The Capture of Port Lyautey," *Military Engineer*, Jan. 1944, 1; *Landings in North Africa*, 53 ("Beau Geste").

147   *Enemy resistance*: NWAf, 164, 170 (*"a brightly colored pageant"*); "Western Task Force: Attack on Mehdia," 96; Semmes, 139; Truscott, *Command Missions*, 123 (*"Our parley"*).

      The three-day fight: AAR, LKT Jr., Dec. 15, 1942, AFHQ G-3, NARA micro R-24-C; AAR, "Trip of Honduran SS *Contessa*," March 22, 1943, in Wheeler, ed., *The Road to Victory*, 76; Fowler, "Twelve Desperate Miles," 14.

148   *In a final twist*: AAFinWWII, 77; Astor, 282 (*"war hysteria"*).

"It's All Over for Now"

148   *Gray with fatigue*: Clagett, "Admiral H. Kent Hewitt, U.S. Navy," 72, 75.

      Hewitt resumed: AAR, "Report on Operation TORCH by Capt. A. G. Shepard," Jan. 9, 1943, NARA RG 38, OCNO, WW II Action Reports, box 3; "Aircraft Operations during the execution of TORCH," March 30, 1943, CINCLANT, NARA RG 38, OCNO, box 3 (*"No more Jean Bart"*); Morison, *Operations in North African Waters*, 163; HKH, comment on Jan. 1950 Morison volume, HKH, NHC, box 1 (*"Come a little closer"*).

149   *For Patton, enough was enough*: DDE to GSP, Oct. 13, 1942, NARA RG 492, MTOUSA Special Staff, AFHQ, box 1383; "Western Task Force: The Attack on Fedala," n.d., CMH, 2–3.7 WE.

      At two A.M., about the time: 3rd ID field artillery officer, OH, n.d., SM, MHI; Codman, 40 (*"Unless the French navy"*); Blumenson, *The Patton Papers, 1940–1945*, 109 (*"Staff wanted me"*).

      At dawn, the guns: Arthur R. Wilson to GCM, Dec. 12, 1942, NARA RG 165, E 13, OCS, classified general correspondence, box 106 (*"Report whether"*); Wordell and Seiler, 162 (*"Boys, it's all"*).

150   *Franco-American amity*: Brooks, "Casablanca—The French Side of the Fence," 909 (*"Chicago, I give up!"*); Taggart, ed., 30.

      At the Miramar: Geoffrey Keyes, OH, Feb. 15, 1950, SM, MHI.

      "They drank $40 worth": GSP to Henry Stimson, Dec. 7, 1942, Blumenson, *The Patton Papers, 1940–1945*, 112; Morison, *Operations in North African Waters*, appendix II, 285; HKH, "Reminiscences," 230.

      The conquest of Morocco: NWAf, 173; Blumenson, *The Patton Papers, 1940–1945*, 110 (*"We are in"*), 114 (*"If you adhere"*).

151   *Press dispatches*: Blumenson, *The Patton Papers, 1940–1945*, 107 (*"I realize"*), 111, 116, 119.

      After leaving: "Report on Material and Logistics, Commander Task Force 34," n.d., NARA RG 407, E 427, "Special Files," box 24486; AAR, "Report on Operation TORCH by Capt. A. G. Shepard," Jan. 9, 1943, NARA RG 38, OCNO, WW II Action Reports, box 3; Wilhm et al., "Armor in the Invasion of North Africa," 47; HKH, "Reminiscences," 230.

152   *And yet*: AAR, "Report on Operation TORCH by Capt. A. G. Shepard," Jan. 9, 1943, NARA RG 38, OCNO, WWII Action Reports, box 3; NWAf, 175; war diary, German naval staff, Nov. 1942, NARA RG 334, NWC Lib, box 645 (*"Go after them"*).

      "Good lads": letter, E. S. Johnston to SEM, Apr. 1947, SEM, NHC, box 16; Wordell and Seiler, 173; John Ellis, *Brute Force: Allied Strategy and Tactics in the Second World War*, 528.

Blackout drapes: Davidson, OH, 182; Codman, 47; author visit, April 2000.
  At 7:48 P.M., the festivities: Davidson, OH, 182.

153 *The German submarine U-173*: "Reminiscences of Vice Admiral Charles Wellborn, Jr.," 1972, USNI OHD (*"you could see"*); "Report on Material and Logistics, Commander Task Force 34," n.d., NARA RG 407, E 427, "Special Files," box 24486; AAR, "Report on Operation TORCH by Capt. A. G. Shepard," Jan. 9, 1943, NARA RG 38, OCNO, WWII Action Reports, box 3; Morison, *Operations in North African Waters*, 169; Clay Blair, *Hitler's U-Boat War*, vol. II, 110; uboat.net/boats/u173.htm.
  The "goosing": U.S.S. *Brooklyn* war diary, Nov. 11, 2156 hrs., SEM, NHC, box 15.
  Hewitt was furious: HKH, ts, n.d., comments on SEM, *Operations in North African Waters*, Jan. 1950 edition, HKH, NHC, box 1 (*"extreme reluctance"*).

154 *For more than an hour*: HKH to USN, June 16, 1950, HKH, NHC, box 1; HKH, "Reminiscences"; Morison, *Operations in North African Waters*, 171.
  Finally, he could continue: AAR, "Report on Operation TORCH by Capt. A. G. Shepard," Jan. 9, 1943, NARA RG 38, OCNO, WWII Action Reports, box 3.
  Hewitt slumped: HKH, OH, G. F. Howe, Jan. 23, 1951, NARA RG 319, 2–3.7, box 228; HKH, ts, n.d., comments on SEM, *Operations in North African Waters*, Jan. 1950 edition, HKH, NHC, box 1.
  As dusk sifted: Blair, *Hitler's U-Boat War*, vol. I, 473, and vol. II, 111; Morison, *Operations in North African Waters*, 171; uboat.net/boats/u130.htm.
  Each hit home: AAR, *Hugh L. Scott*, Nov. 18, 1942, and "U.S. Atlantic Fleet, Amphibious Force, Action Report," both in NARA RG 407, E 427, box 24490.

155 *Her two sisters*: *Landings in North Africa*, 78; letter, E. S. Johnston to SEM, Apr. 1947, SEM, NHC, box 16 (*"The damned fools"*); msg, L. B. Ely to HKH, Nov. 12, 2025 hrs., HKH, NHC, box 1; Codman, 48.
  Fifteen hundred survivors: "United States Navy Medical Department at War, 1941–1945," vol. I, part 3, ts, n.d., USNAd, 673; Albert W. Kenner, "Medical Service in the North African Campaign," *Military Review*, Feb. 1944, 5; Harry McK. Roper, "Report on Observations Made as Observer with Task Force Brushwood," n.d., NARA RG 337, Observer Reports, box 52; Blumenson, *The Patton Papers, 1940–1945*, 168 (*"pieces of bacon"*); Charles M. Wiltse, *Medical Service in the Mediterranean and Minor Theaters*, 119, 121.

156 *Friday's dawn brought*: AAR, NARA RG 407, E 427, U.S. Atlantic Fleet Amphibious Force, box 24430.
  Soldiers looking seaward: Blair, vol. II, 201; "Comments of Admiral H. Kent Hewitt, USN, on *Operations in North African Waters* (original edition), 26 Feb. 1947"; HKH to SEM, March 13, 1947; HKH to J. L. Hall, March 13, 1947, all in HKH, NHC, box 1.
  General Clark's arrest of Darlan: "Record of Events," Feb. 22, 1943, NARA RG 338, Fifth Army, box 1, 25–28 (*"Not once"*); Murphy, 142 ("Merde!").

157 *At noon on November 13*: *Three Years*, 190; DDE to W. B. Smith, Nov. 11, 1942, Chandler, 693; DDE to Churchill, Nov. 11, 1942, Chandler, 689; DDE to GCM, Nov. 11, 1942, Chandler, 692.

158 *At the St. Georges*: Funk, 248 (*a coward*).
  Eisenhower sighed: DDE to GCM, Nov. 9 and 11, 1942, Chandler, 680, 692; DDE to MWC, Nov. 12, 1942, Chandler, 698; DDE to W. B. Smith, Nov. 12, 1942, Chandler, 701; "Record of Events," Feb. 22, 1943, NARA RG 338, Fifth Army, box 1; letter, Noguès to G. F. Howe, Jan. 1950, NARA RG 319, OCMH, 2–3.7 CC1, box 225.
  Eisenhower shook hands: DDE to MWC, Nov. 11, 1942, Chandler, 699 (*"When you are away"*); Clark, 123 (*"Now we can"*).

159 *Sixty years after* TORCH: *NWAf*, 173; *Destruction*, 154.

The number of French killed: De Gaulle, 353; Marcel Vigneras, *Rearming the French*, 18; DDE to W. B. Smith, Nov. 16, 1942, Chandler, 718 (*eighteen French battalions*); Butcher diary, A-4, Nov. 25, DDE Lib, PP-pres, box 166 (*"remain embittered"*).

TORCH *had lured*: Milton Viorst, *Hostile Allies: FDR and Charles de Gaulle*, 123 (*"It's not very pretty"*); DDE to W. B. Smith, Nov. 12, 1942, Chandler, 702 (*"We are just"*).

The war's momentum: Roy Jenkins, *Churchill: A Biography*, 702–703.

160 *"habits of peace"*: W.G.F. Jackson, *The Battle for North Africa*, 396.

"For God's sake": DDE to W. B. Smith, Nov. 12, 1942, Chandler, 702; Leahy, 137 (*the White House*).

CHAPTER 4: PUSHING EAST
"We Live in Tragic Hours"

163 *At two A.M. on November 8*: Twelve Apostles summary, n.d., NARA RG 226, E 99, OSS files, box 39 (*with his Spanish maids*); Tompkins, 141–42 (*"They had better"*); Boatner, 155; Cunningham, 186 (*the Monk*), 221; Philip Jordan, *Jordan's Tunis Diary*, 132 (*"fashion plate gone seedy"*); Alan Moorehead, *The End in Africa*, 82 (*"Hurry"*).

There was no need: Ralph Bennett, *Ultra and Mediterranean Strategy*, 190 (*"panther's leap"*); *Kriegstagebuch*, 90th Panzer Armee Korps, Nov. 16–30, 1942, NARA RG 319, OCMH, box 225; Volkmar Kühn, *German Paratroops in World War II*, 158–61; Paul Carell, *The Foxes of the Desert*, 311; Loerzer, "Negotiations with . . . Estéva," n.d., FMS, #D-040, 2 (*low, intimidating pass*).

164 *French troops ringed*: Paul Deichmann, "Mission of OB Süd . . . in North Africa After the Allied Landing," n.d., FMS, #D-067, 6; Cunningham, 226; NARA RG 319, OCMH, "Background Papers to NW Africa," box 222.

Hitler had learned: Kühn, *German Paratroops in World War II*, 158; Walter Warlimont, *Inside Hitler's Headquarters, 1939–1945*, 271; Anthony Martienssen, *Hitler and His Admirals*, 147; msg, Hitler to Mussolini, Nov. 20, 1942, NARA RG 319, OCMH, 2-3.7, box 225 (*"Yours in"*).

Already 230: Horst Boog et al., *Germany and the Second World War*, vol. VI, *The Global War*, 793–94 (*"cornerstone of our conduct"*).

165 *On Tuesday, November 10*: Walter Nehring, "The First Phase of the Battle in Tunisia," 1947, FMS, #D-147, 29; Franz Kurowski, *The History of the Fallschirm Panzerkorps Hermann Göring*, 109; Kühn, 160; Gardiner, memoir, ts, 1970, USMA Arch, 84.

Weak as the German vanguard: Blumenson, *Kasserine Pass*, 35, 37 (*"I count on everyone"*); Brooks, "The Unknown Darlan," 879 (*"November 8, we fight everybody"*); Auphan and Moral, 251 (*"The enemy is the German"*).

On November 12: *Kriegstagebuch*, Nov. 16, 1942, 2130 hrs, 90th Panzer Armee Korps, Nov. 16, 1942, NARA RG 319, OCMH, box 225 (*"only nodding"*); Robinett, *Armor Command*, 73 (*"After forty years"*); NARA RG 319, OCMH, "Background Papers to NW Africa," box 222; Blumenson, *Kasserine Pass*, 38 (*"I shall be known"*).

Sadly, yes: Bennett, 191; *Kriegstagebuch*, Nov. 16–30, 1942, 90th Panzer Armee Korps, NARA RG 319, OCMH, box 225 (*"cannot read"*); Carell, 311 (*marched four abreast*); Albert Kesselring, "The War in the Mediterranean," part II, "The Fighting in Tunisia and Tripolitania," n.d., FMS, #T-3 P1, 7; AAR, Bayerlein, Apr. 19, 1943, NARA RG 319, OCMH, 2-3.7, box 225; Deichmann, 18; "Account of Marjorie Springs," n.d., NARA RG 226, E 99, OSS, box 39 (*newly fashionable goose step*); Nigel Nicholson and Patrick Forbes, *The Grenadier Guards in the War of 1939–1945*, vol. II, 339.

166 *Soon enough, Derrien*: Tompkins, 145; Auphan and Moral, 269; Kühn, *Rommel in the Desert*, 181–84.

    A French court: Morison, *Operations in North African Waters*, 241 (*"national unworthiness"*); Cunningham, 226 (*"it is an honor"*); Tompkins, 145; Auphan and Moral, 284–85 (*Derrien, too*); Clayton, *Three Marshals of France*, 73.

    "We live in tragic hours": Blumenson, *Kasserine Pass*, 42.

    Conviviality reigned: Kesselring, FMS, T-3 P1, part II, 6; Kesselring, *The Memoirs of Field-Marshal Kesselring*, 8–9; Macksey, *Kesselring: The Making of the Luftwaffe*, 155–56; Boatner, 271.

167 *On November 10*: Macksey, 143 (*poison gas*); Kühn, *German Paratroops in World War II*, 172 (*"drop of water"*).

    The Allies had achieved: Siegfried Westphal, *The German Army in the West*, 121; Lowell Bennett, *Assignment to Nowhere: The Battle for Tunisia*, 101; H. A. Jacobsen and J. Rohwer, eds., *Decisive Battles of World War II: The German View*, 212.

A Cold Country with a Hot Sun

167 *Five hundred and sixty*: Hinsley, *British Intelligence in the Second World War*, vol. II, 475; Middleton, *Our Share of Night*, 169 (*"Those squareheads"*); Freeland A. Daubin, Jr., "The Battle of Happy Valley," Apr. 1948, ts, Armored School Advanced Officers Class, 9 (*"that all of the Germans"*).

    Town mayors donned: Gardiner, memoir, ts, 1970, USMA Arch, 79 (version also in PMR, "Tank Commander," ts, n.d., GCM Lib., box 20); Moorehead, 73; Ralph Bennett, 225; Robert H. Welker, "G.I. Jargon: Its Perils and Pitfalls," *Saturday Review of Literature*, Oct. 1944, 7; Harmon, *Combat Commander*, 107 (*reparations*).

168 *British troops dominated*: Austin, 10 (*"Edwardian motoring veil[s]"*); Howard and Sparrow, 109; "History, HQ Detachment, 109th Medical Bn, 34th ID," Feb. 1942–Nov. 1943, NARA RG E 427, box 9618; Moorehead, 91 (*fishmongers in striped sweaters*); A.A.C.W. Brown, "364 Days Overseas Service," ts, 1981, IWM, 81/33/1; letter, Dan Rupert, May 22, 1943, MCC, YU; Jordan, 46.

    For the Yanks: Oswald Jett, ASEQ, "As I Saw the War," ts, 1988, 1st AD, 47th Medical Bn, 287; Laurence R. Robertson, ASEQ, ts, n.d., 1st AD, MHI, 164; Powell, *In Barbary*, 102; Randle, *Safi Adventure*, 138; Frelinghuysen, 27.

    Eastward the caissons: Rame, 81–82 (*"hanging like red lamps"*); Peter Schrijvers, *The Crash of Ruin*, 44.

    At dusk they bivouacked: Liebling, *Mollie & Other Pieces*, 31; Robertson, ASEQ, 1st AD, MHI, 164; Bolstad, 105 (*"Gas!"*); letter, Virginia Samsell, n.d., MCC, YU (*burro named Rommel*).

169 *Pilfering by the locals*: Jensen, 51; Mayo, 120; Ralph G. Martin, *The GI War, 1941–1945*, 41; Hilary St. George Saunders, *The Red Beret*, 81; Howe, *The Battle History of the 1st Armored Division*, 51 (*"If they"*); McNamara, 30 (*"useless, worthless, illiterate"*).

    At dawn, the promenade: letter, Jack Pardekooper, Jan. 1943, MCC, YU (*"Every town over here"*); letter, Joseph T. Dawson, Nov. 21, 1942, MRC FDM (*"The sky is almost"*); Rame, 88 (*"She'll be"*).

    Thanks to Ultra's decipherment: Hinsley, vol. II, 466–67, 488–89 (*"low category"* and *"probable scale"*).

170 *There was much talk*: Frierson, "Preparations for TORCH," 1945, vol. I, CMH 2-3.7 AD, 46 (*primarily to the British*); Yarborough, SOOHP, 1975, MHI, 26; Howe, *The Battle History of the 1st Armored Division*, 51–54.

Proverbially: Eisenhower, *Crusade in Europe*, 119 (*"were not clearly understood"*); DDE to E. N. Eisenhower, Nov. 16, 1942, Chandler, 724.

"I get so impatient": DDE to W. B. Smith, Nov. 11, 12, and 16, 1942; DDE to E. N. Eisenhower, Nov. 16, 1942, all in Chandler, 693, 703, 724.

171 *Nor was he yet*: Hinsley, *British Intelligence in the Second World War*, abridged ed., 256, 263, 267; Jackson, *The Battle for North Africa*, 399.

Perhaps the biggest: Leighton and Coakley, 438; Beck et al., 63; Meyer, "Strategy and Logistical History: Mediterranean Theater of Operations," vol. I, II–40; AAR, Henry C. Wolfe, Dec. 12, 1942, NARA RG 407, E 427, "Pre-Invasion Planning," box 24348; Jordan, 40 (*"Inevitably there was chaos"*).

Ordnance officers wandered: Mayo, 119; Meyer, "Strategy and Logistical History," vol. I, IV–7; Lunsford E. Oliver, "In the Mud and Blood of Tunisia," *Collier's*, Apr. 17, 1943, 11; DDE to GCM, Nov. 30, 1942, Chandler, 779; Field Marshal the Viscount Alexander of Tunis, "The African Campaign from El Alamein to Tunis," *London Gazette*, Feb. 3, 1948, 865.

Even success: Russell F. Akers, OH, July 27, 1949, SM, MHI.

173 *This muddle greeted*: DDE to Anderson, Nov. 12, 1942, DDE Lib, PP-pres, box 5 (*"I applaud"*); Parris and Russell, 155 (*"The German"*).

Anderson had been born in India: CBH, Apr. 18–22, 1943, MHI (*"grinning preoccupation"*); Gregory Blaxland, *The Plain Cook and the Great Showman*, 28–29, 106, 167 (*"jutting chin"*); Jordan, 44 (*"moderately successful surgeon"*), 61.

One British general: David Fraser, *And We Shall Shock Them*, 251 (*"plain cook"*); "Personal Diary of Lt. Gen. C. W. Allfrey, the Tunisian Campaign," Feb. 7, 1943, Allfrey Collection, LHC (*Sunshine*); Chandler, 778n (*GROUCH*); Boatner, 9; Jordan, 137; DDE to GCM, Oct. 10, 1942, Chandler, vol. I, 628 (*"he studies"*); K.A.N. Anderson to DDE, Dec. 23, 1948, DDE Lib, PP-pres, box 5 (*"a queer sort"*); Anderson to DDE, Jan. 19, 1944, DDE Lib, PP-pres, box 5 (*"good medicine"*).

174 *Anderson's most ambitious*: "General Anderson's Plan, 19 September 1942," Kenneth Anderson file, DDE Lib, box 5; "Possible Variations to Plan Y," First Army, Nov. 7, 1942, PRO, WO 175/50; *NWAf*, 277.

A battalion of the Royal West Kent: AAR, Inshore Squadron, H.M.S *Bulolo*, Dec. 8, 1942, NARA, AFHQ micro, RN Operations, R 17-A.

Two bombs hit: David Rolf, *The Bloody Road to Tunis*, 34 (*"swimming frantically"*); AAR, Inshore Squadron, H.M.S. *Bulolo*, Dec. 8, 1942, NARA, AFHQ micro, RN Operations, R 17-A (*lowered boats without orders*); Pack, *Passage to Africa*, 102.

175 *Most soldiers and sailors*: Roskill, 337; Macksey, *Crucible of Power*, 87.

Things went better: Baedeker, 301; Saunders, 80 (*"I'll have"*); *NWAf*, 278.

Unfortunately, Bône: "At the Front in North Africa," U.S. Army Signal Corps, 16mm; Moorehead, 81; Meyer, IV–13; Cyril Ray, *Algiers to Austria*, 8; Rame, 280 (*"In this force"*).

Having chased Napoleon: Shelby Foote, *The Civil War*, vol. III, 29; *Destruction*, 169; Ray, 9, 32; AAR, 26th Armoured Bde, PRO, WO 175/211; Howe, *The Battle History of the 1st Armored Division*, 54; George Forty, *Tank Action*, 110.

176 *"had no appeal"*: Blaxland, 91.

And then, they were in Tunisia: Parris and Russell, 209; Marshall, *Over to Tunis*, 45 (*"cold country"*); R.L.V. ffrench Blake, *A History of the 17th/21st Lancers, 1922–1959*, 91, 113 (*"The most important thing"*); Liebling, 38; Gustav A. Mueller, ASEQ, ts, n.d., 13th AR, 1st AD, 249.

177 *To protect Anderson's*: Edson D. Raff, *We Jumped to Fight*, 74, 79; William A. Carter, "Carter's War," ts, n.d., CEOH, IV-6; William F. Powers, OH, Aug. 1985, Herbert Hart, CEOH, 45 (*"stamped the hell"*).

But most of the Allied force: Ray, 55; Ford, 46 (*said to be feuding*); Robinett, *Armor Command*, 77 (*Santa Claus*); Daniell, *The Royal Hampshire Regiment*, vol. 3, 89.

With Anderson's approval: AAR, "Operation of 1st Bn., Parachute Regiment," E.W.C. Flavell, and S Company report, Jan. 18, 1943, in Lt. Gen. Sir Charles Walter Allfrey Collection, LHC, 3/4; J. Hill, "Operation TORCH," *Army Quarterly and Defence Journal*, Jan. 1946, 177 (*all 3,000*); Macksey, *Crucible of Power*, 93 ("*non-existent preponderance*").

178 *They cheered again*: J.R.T. Hopper, "Figures in a Fading Landscape," ts, 1995, IWM, 97/3/1.

Then Stuka dive-bombers: Hill, "Operation TORCH," *Army Quarterly and Defense Journal*, Jan. 1946, 177; AAR, 1st Derbyshire Yeomanry, n.d., PRO 175/293; Saunders, 83–86; Blaxland, 105 (*local enthusiasm faded*); Lowell Bennett, 123.

Medjez-el-Bab

178 "*Whoever has Medjez-el-Bab*": Kühn, *German Paratroops in World War II*, 162 ("*master of all Tunisia*"); Austin, 31 (*tobacco and salt*); Baedeker, 329; Homer, *The Iliad*, trans. Robert Fagles, 160.

179 *Medjez-el-Bab's strategic value*: author visits, Sept. 1996, Apr. 2000; Moorehead, 71.

At this bucolic place: Kriegstagebuch, Division Lederer, Nov. 17 and 20, 1942, NARA RG 319, OCMH, box 225 ("*throw the enemy back*"); Kühn, *German Paratroops in World War II*, 162; "Notes by Major Burckhardt on Tactics in Africa," NARA RG 407, E 427, "Pre-Invasion Planning," box 24348; Wilhelm Knoche, "Meine Erlebnisse im Tunesien-Feldzug," FMS, D-323, 12, 19–20 ("*Think what's at stake*"); Kesselring, *Memoirs*, 142.

180 *At four A.M. on November 19*: Hill, "Operation TORCH," 177; AAR, "Operations of 1st Bn., Parachute Regiment," Jan. 18, 1943, Allfrey Collection, LHC, 3/4.

Barré passed word: AAR, 1st Derbyshire Yeomanry, n.d., PRO, WO 175/293; AAR, First Army, PRO, WO 175/50.

181 *An apricot dawn*: Knoche, 28; Edward A. Raymond, "Some Battle Lessons," *Field Artillery Journal*, Feb. 1944, 104 ("*The war*").

West of town: Hill, "Operation Torch," 177 ("*guns of all calibers*" and "*gun teams had worked*").

The balance of the day: Howard A. Smith, Jr., "Among Those Baptized," *Field Artillery Journal*, Apr. 1944, 214 ("*Poor buggers*"); James Lucas, *Panzer Army Africa*, 143.

182 *By late afternoon*: NWAf, 287; DDE, "Commander-in-Chief's Dispatch, North African Campaign, 1942–1943," 19; Raymond, 104; Knoche, 29, 31; Kühn, *German Paratroops in World War II*, 168; Lucas, 143.

This disagreeable news: Howe, *The Battle History of the 1st Armored Division*, 52 (*Anderson had resisted*); NWAf, 291.

183 *Neither side*: Liebling, 3; Lowell Bennett, 130 ("*a funny sort of front*").

But Axis forces: Kriegstagebuch, 90th Panzer Armee Korps, Nov. 22, 1942, NARA RG 319, OCMH, box 225 ("*There is no time*"); Hinsley, *British Intelligence in the Second World War*, abridged ed., 270; AAR, 17th/21st Lancers, PRO, WO 175/292 ("*Alice*"); Anderson to DDE, Nov. 16, 1942, NARA, AFHQ micro, R-5-C; W. S. Chalmers, *Full Cycle: The Biography of Admiral Sir Bertram Home Ramsay*, 151 ("*Huns are beating*").

Never hesitant to play: John Kennedy, *The Business of War*, 274 ("*like a peacock*"); Jenkins, *Churchill: A Biography*, 681 ("*not as good fighters*"); Danchev and Todman, eds., 243 ("*totally unfit*").

184 *Eisenhower maintained*: DDE to H. H. Arnold, Nov. 21, 1942, Chandler, 751; memo, DDE, Nov. 22, 1942, Chandler, 761 (*"It would be wrong"*); Hinsley, *British Intelligence in the Second World War,* abridged ed., 263, 270 (25,000); DDE to W. B. Smith, Nov. 18, 1942, Chandler, 734 (*"If we don't"*).

Most disheartening: Anthony Farrar-Hockley, "The Follow-up to TORCH," Basil Liddell Hart, ed., *History of the Second World War,* vol. 3, 1228.

Allied fighters, by contrast: NWAf, 293; Richard G. Davis, *Carl A. Spaatz and the Air War in Europe,* 139; AAFinWWII, 121 (*"rather appalling"*), 127; DDE to GCM, Nov. 22, 1942, Chandler, 759; asst. G-3 inspection report to AFHQ, Dec. 1942, NARA, AFHQ micro, R-5C.

Troops learned to their sorrow: Warren, 14; Charles Messenger, *The Tunisian Campaign,* 13 (*crew chiefs sat*); John S. D. Eisenhower, 204; Tibbits, 119 (*crews wielded*); L. F. Ellis, *Welsh Guards at War,* 27 (*"a loving type of mud"*).

185 *On November 24*: W. J. Jervois, *The History of the Northamptonshire Regiment: 1934–1948,* 119; NWAf, 302.

The other prong: ibid.; Ray, 12–13; Farrar-Hockley, 1228; Lucas, 144; Macksey, *Crucible of Power,* 94; Ford, 17.

Fat Geese on a Pond

187 *With both brigades*: Rolf, 36 (*"Armor for Tunis!"*); AAR, "Operations of 1st Bn., Parachute Regiment," Jan. 18, 1943, Allfrey Collection, LHC, 3/4; Saunders, 88 (*"great ebony warriors"*); Waters, SOOHP, 1980, MHI (*"tank-infested"*); Blaxland, 104, 108.

son of a Baltimore banker: Waters, SOOHP, 54, 66.

Waters's fifty-four light tanks: Arthur Robert Moore, ASEQ, ts, 1993, 1st AD; Forty, *United States Tanks of World War II in Action,* 42–51; Daubin, 6 (*"squirrel rifle"* and *"hat box"*).

188 *The battalion rolled*: Waters, SOOHP, 611 (*"I'm scared to death"*); Daubin, 16 (*"three-day growth"*); Howe, *The Battle History of the 1st Armored Division,* 66.

Farther north: ffrench Blake, 93 (*"sent up a stream"*).

But it was on: Waters, SOOHP, 611 (*"Right in front of me"*); Robinett, *Armor Command,* 65, Daubin, 6–19.

189 *Seventeen Stuarts*: Daubin, 19 (*"fat geese"*); Waters, SOOHP, 611; Rudolph Barlow, OH, n.d., SM, MHI; Lowell Bennett, 197 (*"bounced off like peas"*); Hans Jürgen von Arnim, "Recollections of Tunisia," 1951, trans. Janet E. Dewey, FMS, #C-098, CMH, 20; Rame, 156 (*shot down or crushed*); Forty, *United States Tanks of World War II in Action,* 47, 49; Howe, *The Battle History of the 1st Armored Division,* 67; Boog et al., 805.

191 *Panicky, exaggerated reports*: Nehring, "The First Phase of the Battle in Tunisia," FMS, #D-147, MHI (*"tear open one tactical hole"*); Kriegstagebuch, 90th Panzer Armee Korps, Nov. 25, 1942, NARA RG 319, OCMH, box 225; Ulrich Bürker, "Einsatz Der 10. Panzer Division in Tunisien, II. Teil," Dec. 1947, FMS, #D-310, 10; Lucas, 136 (*preparing to burn*).

Kesselring voiced sympathy: Kesselring, "The War in the Mediterranean, Part II, The Fighting in Tunisia and Tripolitania," FMS, #T-3, P1, MHI, 13 (*"made a beautiful mess"*); Kesselring, *Memoirs,* 143.

Smiling Albert's assurances: Chandler, 778n (DIZZY and INCUR); Nicholson and Forbes, 265; Kennett, 122 (*"never had any bringing up"*).

192 *The key to the door*: Charles Hendricks, "A Time of Testing: U.S. Army Engineers in the Tunisia Campaign of World War II," paper, Oct. 1999, Colloquium on Military Fortifications and Infrastructure in Tunisia; DDE to GSP, Nov. 26, 1942,

Chandler, 774 (*"At this moment"*); DDE to W. B. Smith, Nov. 27, 1942, Chandler, 777 (*"I believe"*).

CHAPTER 5: *PRIMUS IN CARTHAGO*
"Go for the Swine with a Blithe Heart"

194 *From the tall windows*: Raymond H. Croll, ts, n.d., MHI, 116; CBH, Feb. 1942, MHI; minutes, commander-in-chief staff conference, Oct. 26, 1942, NARA RG 331, AFHQ micro, R-79-D (*had intended to move*).
"How weary I am": DDE to MWC, Nov. 20, 1942, and Nov. 21, 1942, Chandler, 745, 750.
He was hardly: Croll, 99, 116.
195 *Eisenhower's own office: Three Years*, 199.
A few days before leaving: DDE to MWC, Nov. 20, 1942, Chandler, 744; Robert Murphy, Col U OHRO, David C. Berliner, OH-224, Oct. 12, 1972, 6–7; "History of AFHQ, Part One, Aug.–Dec. 1942," n.d., NARA RG 331, box 63 (*400 offices*); Butcher diary, DDE Lib, A-43 (*as much meat*); "Tactical Communication in World War II," part 1, "Signal Communication in the North African Campaigns," 1945, Historical Section, Office of the Chief Signal Officer, MHI, 54 (*"reasonable estimate"*); Hansen, 3/40 (*"huge, chairborne force"*); Dickson, "G-2 Journal: Algiers to the Elbe," n.d., MHI, 30 (*"never were so few"*); Jordan, 180 (*"it's worth fifty divisions"*).
Algiers already showed: Croll, 116 (*electric razors*); Moorehead, 65; MacVane, *Journey into War*, 85 (*"I am married"*); Rame, 206; both in NARA RG 338, Fifth Army awards and decorations, A 47-A-3948, box 56 (*"Valor, Patience"*).
196 *Oranges*: Carter, "Carter's War," ts, 1983, CEOH, III-2, III-14; Lowell Bennett, 295; Jensen, 50.
Indiscipline overwhelmed: AAR, Dec. 28, 1942, Center Task Force, Staff JAG, NARA RG 407, E 427, AG, WWII Ops Reports, box 244; AAR, II Corps JAG, Dec. 22, 1942, and AAR, HQ II Corps, JAG, Sept. 9, 1943, both in NARA RG 338, II Corps JAG, box 157.
There was folderol: DDE, *Crusade in Europe*, 128 (*Eisenhower was a Jew*); Milton S. Eisenhower, *The President Is Calling*, 145 (*"Ike"*); Butcher diary, Nov. 25, 1942, DDE Lib (*Clark gave*); DDE to GCM, Nov. 21, 1942, and DDE to MWC, Nov. 21, 1942, Chandler, 748; John D'Arcy-Dawson, *Tunisian Battle*, 66 (*correspondents advised*).
"After leaving where we were": Dale Allen Hawley, *New York Herald Tribune*, July 3, 1943, MCC, YU.
197 *In a message on November 22*: Chandler, 767n; Butcher diary, DDE Lib, A-50 (*"Go for the swine"*); DDE to MWC, Nov. 19, 1942, Chandler, 740; DDE to W. B. Smith, Nov. 18, 1942, Chandler, 736.
In truth, he spent: DDE to W. B. Smith, Nov. 18, 1942, Chandler, 732.
No distraction tormented: DDE to W. B. Smith, Nov. 9, 1942, Chandler, 677 (*"these Frogs"*); DDE, "Commander-in-Chief's Dispatch, North African Campaign," 17 (*"morbid sense of honor"*); DDE to GCM, Feb. 4, 1943, Chandler, 937 (*"volatile"*); Kennedy, 282 (*"a dog about religion"*).
But the commander-in-chief lacked: CCS, "Minutes of Meeting," Jan. 15, 1943, 1430, NARA RG 218, "Records of U.S. JCS," box 195 (*132 desertions*); Wallace, "Africa, We Took It and Liked It," 20; "The Reminiscences of Rear Adm. George W. Bauernschmidt," 1991, USNI OHD, appendix B, 9 (*French supply requests*).
198 *More distracting*: Crawford, *Report on North Africa*, 83 (*"like a Tammany scan-*

dal"); Milton Eisenhower, 137 (*"fighting Nazis"*); *Three Years,* 192 (*"stinking skunk"*); Chandler, 739n (*"We are fighting"*); Langer, 368.

Darlan's repressive actions: MacVane, *On the Air in World War II,* 121; Macmillan, *The Blast of War,* 184; Middleton, 242; Tompkins, 132, 136, 139 (*hoarded coffee*).

Eisenhower averted: DDE to GSP, Nov. 26, 1942, Chandler, 775; DDE to GCM, Nov. 17, 1942, Chandler, 729; DDE to CCS, Nov. 14, 1942, Chandler, 708; DDE to W. B. Smith, Nov. 14, 1942, Chandler, 712.

Roosevelt had authorized: Three Years, 206 (*"I am but a lemon"*).

199 *All this was folderol:* Ramsey, 111 (*"For Christ's sake"*); Omar N. Bradley and Clay Blair, *A General's Life,* 133; Hanson Baldwin, *New York Times,* March 29, 1969, 1 (*"best damn lieutenant colonel"*); Piers Brendon, *Ike: His Life and Times,* 96 (*"fatchist"*); Macmillan, *The Blast of War,* 174 (*"I'm no reactionary!"*).

At the end: Hatch, *General Ike,* 130; McKeough and Lockridge, 51, 61; Merle Miller, *Ike the Soldier,* 435; *Three Years,* 199, 206.

Even an officer as strong: DDE to GCM, Nov. 17, 1942, Chandler, 731; Kay Summersby Morgan, *Past Forgetting,* 110 (*"lonely man"*); DDE to H. H. Arnold, Nov. 21, 1942, Chandler, 751.

200 *He regretted, too:* DDE to GCM, Nov. 30, 1942, Chandler, 781; Ismay, *Memoirs,* 289; Bryant, 527, 528, 534 (*"far too busy"*); *Three Years,* 201 (*"The whole thing"*).

The low moan: Ramsey, 236; Paul Semmens, "The Hammer of Hell," ts, n.d., CMH, 94; *Three Years,* 306, 200.

To his son: DDE to John S. D. Eisenhower, Nov. 20, 1942, Chandler, 747 (*"I hope"*); Morgan, 101; Davis, *Dwight D. Eisenhower: Soldier of Democracy,* 399.

"The Dead Salute the Gods"

201 *no roasted peacock:* Daubin, "The Battle of Happy Valley"; AAR, T. A. Seely, includes OH w/ J. K. Waters, Dec. 29, 1942, NARA RG 337, Observer Reports, #46, box 52; Rame, 120 (*"swallows diving"*); Fergusson, 96 (*"Like all things German"*); Charles W. Eineichner, ASEQ, Rangers, MHI (*"any weapon we had"*); "Lessons of the Tunisian Campaign, 1942–3, British Forces," n.d., NARA RG 492, MTOUSA, box 56.

On the rare occasions: Tank Destroyer Forces World War II, 22; Howe, *Battle History of the 1st Armored Division,* 69; Rame, 138; Robert S. Cameron, "Americanizing the Tank," diss, Temple Univ., 1994, 772 (*any airborne object*); Robert A. Brand, ASEQ, 16th Inf, MHI; Relman Morin, *Dwight D. Eisenhower: A Gauge of Greatness,* 81 (*"WEFT"*).

202 *Despite such demoralizing episodes:* H. B. Latham to G. F. Howe, June 13, 1950, NARA RG 319, OCMH, box 228; AAR, T. A. Seely, NARA RG 337, Observer Reports, #46, box 52.

Before dawn on November 26: NWAf, 300–301; author visit, Apr. 2000; Howe, *Battle History of the 1st Armored Division,* 68; Daubin, 1–29; Waters, SOOHP, 611 (*"a beautiful column"*).

203 *The approaching Mk IV:* ffrench Blake, *A History of the 17th/21st Lancers, 1922–1959,* 97; Belton Y. Cooper, *Death Traps,* 25.

From the ridge: Daubin, 1–29 (*"long searing tongues"*); minutes, "Meeting of the Subcommittee on Armored Vehicles of the National Research Council," June 1943, 9; John Ellis, *On the Front Lines,* 153 (*"like a finger"*).

Wreathed in gray smoke: Messenger, 21 (*"snapped like a cap pistol"* and *"power-driven grindstone"*); Daubin, 1–29.

204 *"Our losses,":* Kriegstagebuch, Nov. 26, 1942, Div. Lederer, NARA RG 319, OCMH, box 225.

205 *"The Americans had done well"*: ffrench Blake, 97.
Ten *miles south*: Parris and Russell, 223–24 (*eggs and a beefsteak*); Middleton, 209 (*"dusty and empty"*).
Tucked into an oxbow: author visit, Apr. 2000; Blaxland, 111; Robinett, *Armor Command*, 75 (*"haunting memory"*).
The Surreys were spread: Jordan, 237 (*twelve hours*); Daniell, *History of the East Surrey Regiment*, vol. IV, 153–57; Lowell Bennett, 212–15; Ford, 27–28 (*"My good man"*); Middleton, 215 (*"We'll be in Tunis"*); war diary, XC Panzer Corps, Nov. 27, 1942, NARA RG 319, OCMH, box 225.
206 *There was not a moment*: Gardiner, ts, 1970, USMA Arch, 84–86; Gerald Linderman, *The World Within War*, 58; *Destruction*, 177.
207 *For two miles*: Gordon A. Baker, *Iron Knights: The United States 66th Armored Regiment*, 136 (*"looked like a damned cathedral"*); Gardiner, "We Fought at Kasserine," *Armored Cavalry Journal*, March/Apr. 1948, 8.
Perfectly camouflaged: Gardiner, ts, USMA Arch, 84–86 (*"horribly wounded"*); Jervois, 119–22; Howe, *Battle History of the 1st Armored Division*, 72–73 (*"fought in each other's presence"*); Robinett, *Armor Command*, 75–76; AAR, n.d., PMD, LOC, box 6; Linderman, 25 (*"burns like twenty haystacks"*); Lowell Bennett, 298 (*"As soon as I get well"*).
208 *British soldiers, stone deaf*: Middleton, 209–10 (*"When they reached"* and *"sixpence for a Spitfire"*); ffrench Blake, 98; Jordan, 65 (*"a pack of lies"*); Rame, 141 (*"The dead salute"*).
Toward midnight: Jervois, 121 (*recognized as witless*); *Destruction*, 177.
209 *Regrettably, this decision*: AAR, 5th FA Bn, Nov. 13, 1942–Jan. 18, 1943, and 5th FA Bn journal and operations report, Nov. 20, 1942–March 1, 1943, and letter, R. N. Tyson to Clift Andrus, Dec. 3, 1942, all in NARA RG 407, E 427, box 5879; Robinett, *Armor Command*, 71 (*"looked like street lights"*); Frelinghuysen, 27–38 (*"Frederic Remington painting"*); 10th Panzer Div., intel report, Dec. 17, 1942, NARA RG 319, OCMH, box 227.
210 *Dawn on November 29*: Jervois, 122; Middleton, 211 (*"Drag ass"*); Frelinghuysen, 41–45 (*"People who fight a war"*).
211 *The southern prong*: Malcolm, 89–91 (*"no more menacing"*); author visit, Apr. 2000; Ray, 14–15; Austin, 19, 35.
212 *Both presumptions*: Carell, 313 (*"a Tunisian Verdun"*); Jean-Yves Nasse, *Green Devils: German Paratroops, 1939–1945*, 72–74; James E. Mrazek, *The Fall of Eben Emael*, 180–91.
The Argylls stopped: Malcolm, 91–95 (*"Look, George"* and *"If only I had"*); *Kriegstagebuch*, Nov. 28, 1942, NARA RG 319, OCMH, box 225; Lucas, *Panzer Army Africa*, 147; NWAf, 308n; Ford, 22; Richard Doherty, *Only the Enemy in Front*, 7, 35; Blaxland, 117 (*"gaunt and gangling figure"*).
214 *The commandos departed*: Jack A. Marshall, ASEQ, 34th Div, 168th Inf, "The Battle That Wasn't," ts, n.d., MHI; Jack A. Marshall, "Tales of a Timid Commando," ts, n.d., author's possession (*"a tall, Dracula-like figure"*); AAR, 1st Commando troops, n.d., C. W. Allfrey Collection, LHC, 3/5/3; Jordan, 88–93; "British Commandos," Aug. 1942, Military Intelligence Service, WD, 7; Fussell, *Wartime*, 284 (*"Never give the enemy"*); H. Marshall, *Over to Tunis*, 82 (*"ant in a hairbrush"*); Lowell Bennett, 99; *Kriegstagebuch*, Div von Broich, Dec. 1, 1942, NARA RG 319, OCMH, box 225 (*"decimated in a short fire fight"*); Coon, *A North Africa Story*, 68 (*"tall, Dracula-like figure"*); Hougen, *The Story of the Famous 34th Infantry Division*.
216 *Five hundred and thirty*: AAR, "Report by Lt. Col. J. D. Frost, MC," 2nd Bn, the Parachute Regiment, n.d., PRO, WO 175/56; John Frost, *Nearly There*, 1; Frost, *A*

Drop Too Many, 74 (*"We were not"*); Robert Peatling, *Without Tradition: 2 Para, 1941–1945,* 73–87 (*"traveling circus"* and *"a medieval look"*); Warren, 17; Saunders, 93–99; Tugwell, 144.

At five P.M. *the 180 men: Destruction,* 177n; *NWAf,* 309; Rame, 179 (*"Dr. Livingston"*); *AAFinWWII,* 87.

"Jerry Is Counterattacking!"

217 *In late November:* chronology, Chandler, vol. v, 99; *Three Years,* 204–208 (*"Boy Scout trip"*).

the shocking news: Auphan and Moral, 255–66 (*"Scuttle!"*); Cunningham, 158, 255–65; Jean-Paul Pallud, "The French Navy at Toulon," *After the Battle,* 1992, 1 (*"The ship is sunk!"*); De Gaulle, *Memoirs,* 359; Boatner, 301; *Three Years,* 203–204.

Of greater concern: DDE to GCM, Nov. 30, 1942, Chandler, 700 (*"apparently imbued"*); Clark, *Calculated Risk,* 134 (*"the Anderson setup"*); Eisenhower, *Crusade in Europe,* 48 (*"nothing is more difficult"*).

218 *Some things about the war:* Hinsley, *British Intelligence in the Second World War,* vol. II, 487 (*exceeded 850*), 491; DDE to GCM, Nov. 30, 1942, Chandler, 779; *Three Years,* 208; Abbott, 64 (*"There'll be Stukas"*).

To Eisenhower's surprise: Huston, 478 (*U.S. Army doctrine* and *Regulations had prohibited*); Chandler, 968n (*until 1941*); Dickson, "G-2 Journal: Algiers to the Elbe," MHI, 44 (*"only way to hurt a Kraut"*); *NWAf,* 480 (*"Purple Heart box"*); Linderman, 25 (*Ronsons*); Cameron, "Americanizing the Tank," 764; Jensen, 60 (*"light every time"*); Robinett, *Armor Command,* 157 (*"rat racing"*).

219 *"My immediate aim":* DDE to GCM, Nov. 30, 1942, Chandler, 779.

Even as this pretty delusion: Ulrich Bürker, "Einsatz der 10. Panzer Division in Tunisien," Dec. 1947, FMS, #D-310, MHI, 15; Boog et al., 805 (*"definite change"* and *"play for time"*); *NWAf,* 310; Lucas, 151; Ralph Bennett, 194; Heinz Pomtow, "The Campaign in Tunisia," FMS, #3-A, NARA RG 319, OCMH, box 225; 10th Panzer Div, "Combat Report of the Tébourba Engagement, 1–4 December 1942," n.d., PMR, LOC Ms Div box 4; Kühn, *German Paratroops in World War II,* 174 (*only thirty German*).

From decrypted German messages: Hinsley, *British Intelligence in the Second World War,* vol. II, 504 (*"special priority signal"*); Ford, 31 (*"All around us"*); Rame, 164–65 (*"incandescent, enormous"*). Rame was the nom de plume of A. D. Divine.

220 *Fischer's tanks had closed:* war diary, Blade Force, Dec. 1–2, 1942, PRO, WO 175/179; "At the Front in North Africa with the U.S. Army," NARA RG 111, Office of the Chief Signal Officer, No. 1001, Dec. 1942; AAR, 78th Div, Dec. 2, 1942, PRO, WO 175/168.

221 *Two German infantry groups:* 10th Panzer Div., "Combat Report of the Tébourba Engagement, 1–4 December 1942" (*"Not the slightest interest"*); *NWAf,* 315–16 (*the Americans retreated*); R. N. Tyson to Clift Andrus, Dec. 3, 1942, NARA RG 407, E 427, box 5879.

They came running: Moorehead, 90 (*"Keep clear"*); Nicholson and Forbes, 263 (*"Thank God"*).

The CCB commander: "Register of Graduates," class of 1913, USMA, 1989 ed.; Robinett, *Armor Command,* 87; Rame, 153.

222 *Robinett was delighted:* "Comments on *Kasserine Pass,*" PMR, MHI, 4 (*"Always do whatever"*), 12; Martin M. Philipsborn, Jr., Papers, MHI; Abbott, 51; Robinett, *Armor Command,* 77–80; Robinett biographical sketch, 1945, CMH; McCurtain

Scott, OH, March 1976, Russell Gugeler, OW, MHI (*"fussy"*); "Personal Diary of Lt. Gen. C. W. Allfrey, the Tunisian Campaign," Feb. 15, 1943, LHC (*"all talk and grouse"*).

Robinett arrived: corr, Philip G. Walker to PMR, Aug. 9, 1950, PMR, LOC, box 4 (*bitter objections* and *"appeared to be watching"*); NWAf, 317; 10th Panzer Div., "Combat Report of the Tébourba Engagement, 1–4 December 1942"; Abbott, 51 (*"demoralizers"*); Jordan, 96 (*"The most intrepid chaps"*); Oliver, "In the Mud and Blood of Tunisia," 11 (*"The boys stuck"*).

223 *Now the noose:* Howe, *Battle History of the 1st Armored Division,* 78; Robinett, *Armor Command,* 80–82; Nehring, "The First Phase of the Battle in Tunisia," 1947, FMS #D-147, MHI, 37; Rame, 169; Linderman, 254 (*"hammers of the devil"*).

Robinett had seen: PMR, "The Axis Offensive in Central Tunisia, Feb. 1943," n.d., PMR, LOC; Robinett, *Armor Command,* 77.

General Fischer himself: 10th Panzer Div., "Combat Report of the Tébourba Engagement, 1–4 December 1942."

Fischer also deployed: Nehring, FMS #D-147, 27 (*"decisive"*), 37; Egon Kleine and Volkmar Kühn, *Tiger: The History of a Legendary Weapon, 1942–1945,* 8; Kühn, *Rommel in the Desert,* 178.

224 *From a range:* AAR, 2nd Hampshires, Dec. 31, 1942, 78th Div. appendix, PRO, WO 175/168; Daniell, *The Royal Hampshire Regiment,* vol. III, 91–98; Bryan Perrett, *Against All Odds,* 153 (*"The situation"*).

If Wednesday: M. J. Barton, "The Hampshire Regiment at Tébourba, 1942," *Army Quarterly and Defence Journal,* Apr. 1944, 57–63; 10th Panzer Div, "Combat Report of the Tébourba Engagement, 1–4 December 1942" (*"Indications are"*); Blaxland, 126 (*"It was Dunkirk"*).

"Commander is dissatisfied": First Army, command post files, n.d., PRO, WO 175/56.

225 *Too late:* situation report to K.A.N. Anderson, Dec. 4, 1942, First Army, PRO, WO 175/50; K.A.N. Anderson, "Operations in North West Africa," *London Gazette,* 1946; Jordan, 75 (*"Bollocks!"*); Messenger, 24 (*"Looking back"*).

At noon: 10th Panzer, "Combat Report," Dec. 4, 1942; AAR, Philip G. Walker to PMR, Aug. 9, 1950, PMR, LOC, box 4 (*"But for occasional curses"*); Daniell, *The Royal Hampshire Regiment,* 98; Jordan, 76 (*"One night in Glasgow"*).

At a field hospital: ffrench Blake, 102; Gardiner, ts, USMA Arch, 95 (*"illuminated by candlelight"*).

226 *Several miles to the east:* Moynihan, ed., 67 (*"with delicate respect"*).

The East Surreys had departed: Daniell, *History of the East Surrey Regiment,* 157; Daniell, *The Royal Hampshire Regiment,* 91; NWAf, 320n; Nehring, 37; 10th Panzer, "Combat Report," Dec. 4, 1942; Jordan, 69 (*"There is an air"*).

"The coordination of tank attacks": PMR to GCM, Dec. 8, 1942, NARA RG 165, E 13, box 106; Robinett, *Armor Command,* 85 (*"had not foreseen"*).

227 *"My dear C-in-C":* Anderson to DDE, Dec. 5, 1942, DDE Lib, PP-pres, box 5.

"There was abroad": ibid; Anderson, "Operations in North West Africa"; Anderson to DDE, n.d., PRO, WO 175/50 (*"enemy has already"*); Anderson to DDE, Dec. 6, 1942, PRO, WO 175/50 (*"wheezy French lorries"*).

Fischer and his 10th Panzer Division: CCB Operations Report, Dec. 6, 1942, NARA RG 319, OCMH, box 229; corr, W. B. Kern to PMR, "Account of the Battle Between U.S. and German Forces near El Bathan," Apr. 25, 1950, NARA RG 319, OCMH, box 229 (*a single man*); Robinett, *Armor Command,* 88–91 (*terrified .50-caliber gunner*).

As the battalion commander: 27th Armored FA Bn, "Battalion History," n.d.,

PMR Papers, GCM Lib, box 12 (*"For Christ's sake"*); Howe, *Battle History of the 1st Armored Division,* 85; *NWAf,* 328.

228 *Help had been ordered*: Erbes, "Hell on Wheels Surgeon," 31 (*"charge up the valley"*); AAR, Philip G. Walker, n.d., PMR, LOC, box 4 (*"Shells were cutting"*); CCB Operations Report, Dec. 6, 1942; Howe, *Battle History of the 1st Armored Division,* 87; Robinett, *Armor Command,* 93.

    Rain began: Martin Philipsborn, "Intelligence Report for Period 1 Dec. to 11 Dec. 1942," CCB, NARA RG 319, OCMH, box 229 (*"total effect was in fact terrifying"*).

229 *Latrine rumors*: Lowell Bennett, 205 (*poison gas*), 132 (*"Beware"*); Daniell, *History of the East Surrey Regiment,* vol. IV, 157; E.W.C. Flavell, "Operations of 1st Bn., Parachute Regiment," Dec. 7 and 10, 1942, C.W. Allfrey Collection, LHC, 3/4; Butcher diary, DDE Lib, A-100 (*burned an entire Arab village*); Rame, 146 (*"like an escaping murderer"*); T. J. Camp, ed., "Tankers in Tunisia," 34; AAR, 2nd Bn, 13th AR, n.d., PMR, LOC, box 6; letter, Thomas Riggs to parents, June 25, 1943, PMR, LOC, box 4 (*like repelled like*); Fussell, *The Great War and Modern Memory,* 124 (*a potential reliquary*).

230 *"In an attack"*: Fuller quoted in S.L.A. Marshall, *Men Against Fire,* 71; asst. G-3 inspection report to AFHQ, n.d., NARA AFHQ micro, R 5-C; First Army to AFHQ, Dec. 8–9, 1942, AFHQ micro, R 5-C (*"Reason is"*).

    Even before Eisenhower's reply: Juin, OH, Dec. 5, 1948, SM, MHI (*Juin stalked off*); Louis Koeltz, *Une Campagne Que Nous Avons Gagnée Tunisie,* 83–84.

    Omens and auguries: "Operations Report," CCB, Dec. 10, 1942, NARA RG 319, OCMH, box 229; Howe, *Battle History of the 1st Armored Division,* 91.

231 *At eight a.m.*: Nicholson and Forbes, *265* ("Tank Boche!"); Robinett, *Armor Command,* 96–100.

    Holding a poor map: W. H. Hatcher to PMR, Oct. 13, 1949, PMR, LOC, box 4 (*futile effort to blind*); AAR, 10th Panzer, "The Tank Battle of Cactus Hill in the Area to the Southwest of Tébourba," PMR, LOC, box 4; Robinett, *Armor Command,* 100–104 (*"ground was alive"* and *"You have ruined me!"*).

232 *He had indeed*: AAR, G. E. Lynch, March 5, 1943, NARA RG 337, Observer Reports, box 52, #21; "From Beer Beach to Kasserine Pass: The Story of the 175th Field Artillery Battalion," NARA RG 407, E 427, box 9542; AAR, J. Wedderburn Maxwell, 78th (U.K.) Div, in 175th FA Bn, War Diary, NARA RG 407, E 427, box 9542; *NWAf,* 332; Robinett, *Armor Command,* 104 (*"new terrors into the minds"*); Howe, *Battle History of the 1st Armored Division,* 92 (*reasoned pleas*); Rame, 197–98 (*"Turn the column"* and *stuffed bedrolls*).

233 *At 1:30 a.m.*: Oliver, "In the Mud and Blood of Tunisia," 11 (*"I never felt so bad"*); James Scott Stapel, ts, 1988, ASEQ, 1st AD (*thermite grenades*); Butcher diary, DDE Lib, A-85, A-93 (*Eisenhower also considered*); Gugeler, ts, OW, MHI, x-39; Mayo, 121; *NWAf,* 332; Anderson, "Operations in North West Africa" (*"crippling loss"*); Robinett, *Armor Command,* 109; AAR, "Operations of Company C, 701st TD Battalion, 3 Oct. 1942 to 24 Jan. 1943," NARA RG 407, E 427, box 23699; DDE to K.A.N. Anderson, Dec. 14, 1942, Chandler, 841 (*no longer combat worthy*).

234 *"The faults were clear"*: Rame, 202.

    Other deficiencies: Robinett, *Armor Command,* 109; GSP to GCM, Dec. 21, 1942, NARA RG 165, E 13, chief of staff classified correspondence, box 106 (*live goats*); Howe, *Battle History of the 1st Armored Division,* 95 (*training ammunition*); *NWAf,* 332n.

235 *"We are having our troubles"*: Robert H. Ferrell, ed., *The Eisenhower Diaries,* 83.

CHAPTER 6: A COUNTRY OF DEFILES
Longstop

237 *For eleven days*: Johnson, *One More Hill*, 25; Jack Belden, *Still Time to Die*, 219 (*"standing on a window ledge"*); Nicholson and Forbes, 266, 271 ("Fabriqué à Paris!" and *"family of Arabs living"*); Parris and Russell, 249 (*"one bloody great mine"*).

By December, 180,000 American troops: Matloff, 52; DDE memo, Dec. 15, 1942, Chandler, 842; Zanuck, 102, 117 (*pulverized dates*); L. Bennett, 237; letter, Harold Gottlieb, 32nd Bombardment Sq., in Annette Tapert, *Lines of Battle: Letters from American Servicemen, 1941–1945* (*"No shave, no bath"*); "Memorial Booklet, 2nd Lt. Robert Maurice Mullen, Co. A, 18th Inf., 1st Div.," MRC FDM, 1988.32, box 206 (*"Thanks for giving me"*); Robinett, *Armor Command*, 113 (*bathrobes*).

238 *"There are none"*: quoted in Tobin, 80.

The lull allowed: Downing, *At War with the British*, 111, 135, 140 (*"old-fashioned workingmen"*); Donald McB. Curtis, *The Song of the Fighting First*, MRC FDM, 67 (*"We've eaten British compo"*).

239 *Across the killing fields*: Boog et al., 806; Samuel W. Mitcham, Jr., "Arnim," in Correlli Barnett, ed., *Hitler's Generals*, 335–41; *Destruction*, 187.

Defense meant fortifications: "French Policy Toward Arabs, Jews and Italians in Tunisia," OSS, Research and Analysis Branch, Dec. 1943, NARA RG 334, E 315, NWC Lib, box 895 (*"Equipped with tools"*); war crimes testimony, Heinz Schweiger, June 1945, NARA RG 153, JAG, file 3-32, box 2 (*Others were press-ganged*); war diary, V Corps, Dec. 27, 1942, and intel summary, early December, PRO, WO 175/82; "Information Gathered from the 20th to the 23rd December 1942," II Corps Miscellaneous Papers, n.d., NARA RG 407, E 427, box 3163; "18th Infantry, Draft Regimental Wartime History," Stanhope Mason Collection, MRC FDM, 22; Dorothy Stannard, *Tunisia*, 259.

240 *"This means a most un-Christian Christmas"*: Anderson to DDE, Dec. 16, 1942, First Army files, PRO, WO 175/50; also, NARA, AFHQ micro, R-188-D; Anderson to DDE, Dec. 15, 1942, Chandler, 841n; Anderson dispatch, "Operations in North West Africa."

241 *Longstop offered*: author visit, Apr. 2000; John Horsfall, *The Wild Geese Are Flighting*, 26 (*"so foul, broken, blasted"*); Ray, 35 (*"a country of defiles"*).

Had the British spent: AAR, 1st Guards Bde, Jan. 9, 1943, PRO, WO 175/86; *Destruction*, 188; Howard and Sparrow, 113; E. R. Hill, "The Coldstream at Longstop Hill," *Army Quarterly and Defence Journal*, July 1944, 175 (*"We failed to realize"*).

242 *As required by the unwritten rules*: Hill, "The Coldstream at Longstop Hill"; AAR, 1st Guards Bde, Jan. 9, 1943, PRO, WO 175/86; Middleton, 232 (*Muzzle flashes reddened*); NWAf, 339–41; Perrett, *At All Costs*, 156; Messenger, 28–29; Horsfall, 153; AAR, 2nd Coldstream Guards, Dec. 23–25, 1942, PRO, WO 175/487.

An hour passed: S-1 journal, 1/18th Inf., Dec. 22–25, 1942 (*"Brooklyn"*), and 1st Guards Bde, Operations Order No. 1, Dec. 22, 1942, NARA RG 407, E 427, box 5351; Saunders, 111 (*"Blackpool beach"*); "Report of Longstop Hill Engagement, Tunisia," 18th Inf, March 20, 1943, NARA RG 407, E 427, box 5936.

243 *The relief in combat*: NWAf, 341–43; AAR, 1st Guards Bde, Jan. 9, 1943, PRO, WO 175/186; Howard and Sparrow, 113 (*hiked in squelching boots*); Hill, "The Coldstream at Longstop Hill," 175; Rame, 207 (*"Good King Wenceslas"*).

Dawn on Longstop: Marshall, ed., *Proud Americans of World War II*, 51–55 (*"They just appeared"*).

Along the hill crest: Austin, 127, 131 (*"like a boy"* and *"leaping with light"*);

Ellis, *On the Front Lines,* 69; "18th Infantry, Draft Regimental Wartime History," Stanhope Mason Collection, MRC FDM, 21 (*"mud would foul your rifle"*).

244 *Pinned in a cactus*: Porter, SOOHP, 259; Linderman, 243 (*"white chrysanthemum"*); Marshall, ed., *Proud Americans,* 55.

   The Coldstreams had just finished: AAR, 1st Guards Bde, Jan. 9, 1943; PRO, WO 175/186; "Report of Longstop Hill Engagement, Tunisia," 18th Inf, March 20, 1943, NARA RG 407, E 427, box 5936; Ray, 29; Ellis, 98 (*"bored indifference"*), 71 (*"the release of fear"*); Moynihan, ed., 67 (*some already green*); Nicholson and Forbes, 269 (*even for mules*); Messenger, 29 (*bogged down 5,000 yards*); Hill, "The Coldstream at Longstop Hill," 175.

245 *A lull persisted*: Parris and Russell, 256 (*"guns flashed"*).

   From that pinnacle: AAR, V Corps, Dec. 24, 1942, PRO, WO 175/82 (*"in our possession"*); Hill, "The Coldstream at Longstop Hill," 175; NWAf, 342 (*"never been appreciated"*).

   The rain slowed: Marshall, ed., *Proud Americans,* 55 (*"Get this man out!"* and *handing out razor blades*); D'Arcy-Dawson, 52; Edward A. Raymond, "Long Toms in Action," *Field Artillery Journal,* Nov. 1943, 803 (*"Muddy Christmas"*).

246 *Eisenhower had yet*: Ambrose, *Eisenhower: Soldier, General of the Army, President-Elect, 1890–1952,* 215; chronology, Chandler, vol. V, 102; United Press article, Feb. 27, 1943, James R. Webb Collection, DDE Lib; DDE to Ira C. Eaker, Dec. 6, 1942, Chandler, 808 (*wicked dagger*); Eisenhower, *Crusade in Europe,* 124; McKeough and Lockridge, 85.

   He suspected: Three Years, 210; CCS to DDE, Chandler, vol. II, 793n (*"Losses in"*); DDE to Churchill, Dec. 5, 1942, Chandler, 802 (*"this battle"*); DDE to T. T. Handy, Dec. 7, 1942, Chandler, 811 (*"every recognized"*); Butcher diary, DDE Lib, A-96 (*"Engage and wear"*); Foote, *The Civil War,* vol. 3, 739 (*Grant's casualties*).

247 *"Through all this"*: memo, DDE, Dec. 10, 1942, Chandler, 824.

   Shortly after noon: Baedeker, 301; Rame, 102 (*"cubes of frozen moonlight"*); Raff, 60; Powell, *In Barbary,* 252.

   Even as they neared: NWAf, 337; Butcher diary, A-99; DDE, "Commander-in-Chief's Dispatch, North African Campaign," 22 (*all rail loadings*); "History of Planning Division, ASF," ts, 1946, CMH, 3-2.2; Kreidberg and Henry, 649 (*twice as many*); *Destruction,* 385; Harry L. Coles and Albert K. Weinberg, *Civil Affairs: Soldiers Become Governors,* 51 (*"Stop sending stockings"*); GCM to DDE, Dec. 23, 1942, NARA, AFHQ micro, R-49-M, Supreme Allied Commander's Secretariat (*"Do not discuss"*).

248 *Increasingly, the strain showed*: John S. D. Eisenhower, *Allies,* 210; *Three Years,* 218 (*"a caged tiger"*); GCM to Elmer Davis, Dec. 13, 1942, NARA RG 165, E 13, OCS correspondence, box 106 (*"I am very"*); GCM to John Dill, Dec. 5, 1942, Chandler, 793n (*Privately the chief*); William D. Hassett, *Off the Record with F.D.R.,* 145 (*"Why are they so slow?"*).

   The strain on Eisenhower: Three Years, 212 (*"Those are your troubles"*); Howze, *A Cavalryman's Story,* 52 (*"Tell everybody here"*); Butcher diary, Nov. 27, 1942, DDE Lib, A-99 (*"Damned if I'm not"*), A-106;

   Following an overnight stop: Robinett, *Armor Command,* 113 (*"greatly depressed"*); Three Years, 227–228 (*"ordered trials"* and *offered to resign*); Butcher diary, A-112; First Army log, Dec. 24, 1942, PRO, WO 175/50 (*"Decision was made"* and *"Due to continual rain"*).

"They Shot the Little Son of a Bitch"

250 *Algiers on Christmas Eve*: Renée Gosset, *Conspiracy in Algiers*, 130; Mario Faivre, *We Killed Darlan*, 122; Tompkins, 185 (*Mousse d'Islam*); Parris and Russell, 193; Robert M. Marsh, ASEQ, 81st Reconn., 1st AD, 1989, MHI; A.A.C.W. Brown, "364 Days Overseas Service," 1981, IWM, 81/33/1; R. Priestly, 2nd Bn, Para Regt, ts, IWM, 83/24/1; Paul K. Skogsberg, "The North African Campaigns," ASEQ, ts, n.d., 1st Reconn. Troop, 1st ID, 25; Fussell, *Wartime*, 186 (*"White Mistress"*).

Morale officers: "History of Special Service Section," II Corps, n.d., NARA RG 407, E 427, box 3236 (*"extremely bad discipline"* and *"at high tension"*); Gale A. Mathers, "The Special Service Office in the European Theater," Aug. 30, 1943, NARA RG 407, E 427, box 3236 (*"I have seen cases"*); Crawford, 172.

251 *The Little Fellow*: Howard and Sparrow, 109; MacVane, *On the Air in World War II*, 143 (*"His small blue eyes"*); Clark, *Calculated Risk*, 128; MWC, SOOHP, Forest S. Rittgers, Jr., 1972–73, MHI (*"You know, the Little Fellow"*); Murphy, 143 (*"There are four plots"*).

One would suffice: Tompkins, 185–87; Gosset, 130; Faivre, 125–26; Murphy msg to State Dept., Dec. 24, 1942, NARA, AFHQ micro, R-226-B; Ambrose, *Ike's Spies*, 49–50; Anthony Verrier, *Assassination in Algiers*, 226.

252 *Half a mile away*: MWC, SOOHP, MHI (*"They shot"*).

A voluble mob: Murphy, 143; Clark, *Calculated Risk*, 128–30 (*"a troublesome boil"*); Boatner, 119; William H. Lee, memo, AFHQ, Dec. 24, 1942, OW, MHI; Marsh, ASEQ; MacVane, *Journey into War*, 134; MacVane, *On the Air in World War II*, 157 (*"never seen happier faces"*).

253 *Eisenhower had insisted*: "Tactical Communications in World War II," part 1, *Signal Communication in the North African Campaign*, 1945, Historical Section, Office of the Chief Signal Officer, MHI, 92 (*he remained beyond reach*); First Army log, Dec. 24, 1942, PRO, WO 175/50 (*"most serious thing"*); Juin, OH, Dec. 5, 1948, SM, MHI; Anderson to Brooke, Dec. 25, 1942, PRO, WO 175/56; "Record of Events and Documents from the Date That Lieutenant General Mark W. Clark Entered into Negotiations with Admiral Jean Francois Darlan Until Darlan Was Assassinated," Feb. 22, 1943, NARA RG 338, Fifth Army, box 1 (*"Have just returned"*); Davis, *Dwight D. Eisenhower: Soldier of Democracy*, 401; *Three Years*, 229 (*ended one problem*).

Badly reduced: Rudolf Lang, "Battles of Kampfgruppe Lang in Tunisia," 1947, FMS, #D-173, MHI.

254 *More than a hundred*: AAR, 1st Guards Bde, Jan. 9, 1943, PRO, WO 175/186; "Report of Longstop Hill Engagement, Tunisia," 18th Inf, March 20, 1943, NARA RG 407, E 427, box 5936; Howard and Sparrow, 116; "18th Infantry, Draft Regimental Wartime History," MRC FDM, 24; Marshall, ed., *Proud Americans*, 55 (*"We will fight to the last"*).

The right flank: Linderman, 284 (*"sick kittens"*); Nicholson and Forbes, 269 (*"a few scraggy chickens"*).

255 *Word soon circulated*: NWAf, 343; Hill, "The Coldstream at Longstop Hill," 175; Downing, 145.

Longstop belonged to the Germans: Arnim, "Recollections of Tunisia," FMS #C-098, MHI; Operations Bulletin No. 2, May 31, 1943, HQ, NW African Air Forces, NARA RG 334, NWC Lib, box 132 (*4,000-pound bomb*).

Of the Tommies and Yanks: Intel. Summary No. 89, 1st Guards Bde, May 15, 1943, PRO, WO 175/186 (*oddly unmolested*); Nicholson and Forbes, 271 (*"a cheesegrater"*); William G. Chamberlin, ASEQ, 32nd FA Bn, 1st ID, n.d.; Johnson, *One More Hill*, 27–28 (*"Objective lost"*).

"This Is the Hand of God"

256 *For a man*: McKeough and Lockridge, 63; DDE to Berthe Darlan, Dec. 25, 1942, Chandler, 861 (*"You have"*); Morgan, 98, 101 (*"God rest ye merry"*).

The investigation: MacVane, *On the Air in World War II*, 158; Moorehead, *The End in Africa*, 58; Faivre, 131 (*"I have brought to justice"*); Tompkins, 195–97 (*coffin*); Verrier, 249 (*"surprised to be shot"*).

As his assassin: "Darlan funeral," Signal Corps, 35mm, B&W, NARA, ADC 1002; Curt Riess, ed., *They Were There*, 530 (*"Not a tear"*); Butcher diary, DDE Lib, A-121; Tompkins, 191 (*bared halberds*).

257 *As the funeral*: United Press account, *New York Times*, Dec. 27, 1942; *New York Times*, Dec. 28, 1942; "Funeral for Admiral Darlan—Record of Events," Dec. 26, 1942, NARA, AFHQ micro, R-204-F (*"all sidearms"*).

The requiem mass: Cunningham, OH, Feb. 12, 1947, Forrest C. Pogue, MHI (*"Go ahead"*).

It was over: "Darlan funeral," Signal Corps, 35mm, B&W, NARA, ADC 1002; "Funeral for Admiral Darlan—Record of Events," Dec. 26, 1942, NARA, AFHQ micro, R-204-F (*"the following errors"*).

The procession wound: Gosset, 130; De Gaulle, *Memoirs*, 381 (*"the long disease"*); Macmillan, *The Blast of War*, 167 (*"Once bought"*); Hunt, 153 (*"fell like a stone"*).

258 *Finger-pointing*: Fergusson, 148 (*"a cup of tea"*); *Three Years*, 239 (*"Is there anyone here"*); Jordan, 139 (*"Arab"*); D'Este, *Bitter Victory*, 55 (*"You will find the Americans"*).

Yet a harsher: Larrabee, 436 (*"our Italians"*); Alexander G. Clifford, *The Conquest of North Africa, 1940–1943*, 405 (*"gifted amateurs"*); W.R.C. Penney, ts, n.d., LHC (*"crashing bores"*); Fergusson, 148 (*"The British cope"*).

259 *"The plain facts"*: AAR, 1st Guards Bde, Jan. 9, 1943, PRO, WO 175/86.

To Major General Terry Allen: Dixon, "Terry Allen," 57 (*"Please always remember"*); GCM to TdA, July 30, 1942, GCM Lib, Pentagon correspondence, box 56, folder 17; Baumer, 68, 117 (*"all that stuff"*); Pyle, *Here Is Your War*, 187 (*"like vermin"*).

Yet as the weeks: Dixon, "Terry Allen," 57; Steven Clay, *Blood and Sacrifice: The History of the 16th Infantry Regiment*, 27 (read in mss); Curtis, 42; Liebling, "Find 'Em, Fix 'Em, and Fight 'Em," 221 (*"like whiskey"*); Pyle, *Here Is Your War*, 188 (*"Is this a private war"*); Robert W. Porter, SOOHP, John N. Sloan, 1981, MHI, 260; S.L.A. Marshall, *Men Against Fire*, 161 (*"A man fights"*).

260 *The last straw*: Porter, SOOHP, 259–60 (*"I can't understand"*); "Terry Allen and the First Division," MHI; D'Este, *Bitter Victory*, 274.

good men dared: Sherwood, xvii.

The bottom of the year: DDE to CCS, Dec. 26, 1942, Chandler, 868 (*"severest disappointment"*); "directive for commander-in-chief, Allied Expeditionary Force," Aug. 13, 1942, NARA RG 218, JCS records, box 325.

261 *An enormous siege*: Bennett, *Ultra and Mediterranean Strategy*, 196; Ellis, *On the Front Lines*, 36; "Commander-in-Chief's Dispatch, North African Campaign, 1942–1943," 51. (Eisenhower came to believe that quick victory in Tunisia would have put Allied troops in the Po River Valley in northern Italy by winter 1943.)

For now, there were deficiencies: Allerton Cushman, AGF Observer Report, March 29, 1943, NARA RG 165, E 418, Director of Plans and Ops, box 1228 (*"The German army"*); Stanley J. Grogan, "Memorandum for Mr. McCloy," n.d., NARA RG 165, E 418, box 1228 (*"More than discipline"*); John P. Lucas, Observer Report, Apr. 28, 1943, NARA RG 165, E 13, OCS classified general correspondence, box 106 (*"not leading their men well"*).

262 *They had seen things*: Marshall, "The Battle That Wasn't," ASEQ, 34th Inf Div, MHI (*"cracked porcelain surface"*); Michael D. Doubler, *Closing with the Enemy*, 253, 293; Linderman, 212 (*"questers"*); John C. McManus, *The Deadly Brotherhood: The American Combat Soldier in World War II*, 282 (*"Twins, we feel"*).

    "Things have not gone well": Anderson to Brooke, Dec. 25, 1942, PRO, WO 175/56.

CHAPTER 7: CASABLANCA
The Ice-Cream Front

265 *At 10:30 P.M.*: "President's Trip to Casablanca," Guy H. Spaman to Frank J. Wilson, June 26, 1945, FDR Lib, Secret Service records, box 4; George E. Durno, "Flight to Africa: A Chronicle of the Casablanca Conference Between President Roosevelt and Prime Minister Churchill," n.d., FDR Lib, 200-2-U; Hassett, 127, 142, 146; Leahy, 143; Raymond W. Copson, "Summit at Casablanca," *American History*, Apr. 2002, 60.

    With a steamy sigh: Seale, vol. II; Michael F. Reilly, *Reilly of the White House*, 136–47; Goodwin, 366; Sherwood, 665.

266 *A kind of Roman camp*: AAR, 1st Armored Signal Batt, Sept 18, 1943, NARA RG 165, director for plans and ops, corr, box 1230; Wordell and Seiler, 281.

267 *Fragrant with begonias*: Reilly, 150; Austin, 71; Durno, 63, 66, 68; msg to DDE, Jan. 10, 1943, NARA, AFHQ micro, "Casablanca Conference," R-49-M; Donald E. Houston, *Hell on Wheels: The 2nd Armored Division*, 143 (*"Hail to the Chief"*); Macmillan, *The Blast of War*, 194; memo, Arthur R. Wilson, Dec. 10, 1942, NARA RG 407, E 427, box 246 (*George Washington*).

    Overseeing this feverish activity: Austin, 71 (*"Every other four-wheeler"*); Semmes, *Portrait of Patton*, 132; Patton, *War As I Knew It*, 35; Codman, 76 (*"absolutely steady"*); Crawford, *Report on North Africa*, 26 (*"the Ice-Cream Front"*).

    Patton was miserable: Farago, 222 (*huge Packard*); A. G. Shepard, "Report on Operation TORCH," Commander in Chief, U.S. Atlantic Fleet, serial 0014, NARA RG 38, OCNO, box 3; Robinett, *Armor Command*, 110 (*"Where are the Germans"*); Blumenson, *Patton*, 174–75 (*"Top Dog"*); John Field, "Patton of the Armored Force," *Life*, Nov. 30, 1942, 113; Blumenson, *The Patton Papers, 1940–1945*, 163 (*"kill someone"*).

268 *Patton discharged*: Blumenson, *The Patton Papers, 1940–1945*, 175, 123, 150.

    Arriving from London: Pendar, *Adventure in Diplomacy*, 140 (*"working up mud"*); Thomas B. Buell, *Master of Sea Power: A Biography of Fleet Admiral Ernest J. King*, 253; Pogue, *George C. Marshall: Organizer of Victory, 1943–1945*, 18 (*dire warnings*).

269 *Churchill and his entourage*: Lord Moran, *Churchill: Taken from the Diaries of Lord Moran*, 85 (*silk vest and nothing else*); Ismay, *Memoirs*, 284–85 (*"we were clever enough"*); Bryant, 434, 485; Kennedy, 280; W. Averell Harriman and Elie Abel, *Special Envoy to Churchill and Stalin, 1941–1946*, 180 (*"Any fool can see"*); Goodwin, 301 (*"big English bulldog"*).

    "at the conference": Matloff and Snell, 379 (*"the British will have a plan"*); Roger Parkinson, *A Day's March Nearer Home*, 14; "The Reminiscences of Walter C. W. Ansel," 1972, USNI OHD, 3–124; Ian Jacob diary, quoted in Bryant, 540 (*"dark hole"*); Moran, 78 (*"the control of the Mediterranean"*); D'Este, *Bitter Victory: The Battle for Sicily*, 38 (*"dripping of water"*); Lord Tedder, *With Prejudice*, 390; Macmillan, *War Diaries: The Mediterranean, 1943–1945*, 8.

270 *Operation SATIN envisioned*: The AAF in Northwest Africa, 29; "Memorandum of Conference at Advanced Allied Force Headquarters," Jan. 21, 1943, NARA, AFHQ micro, R-187-D; *Three Years*, 236.

271 *SATIN was bold*: NWAf, 350; Roskill, 433 (*437,000 soldiers*); CCS msg, Jan. 1943, NARA RG 218, JCS records, box 325 (*"The Allied forces"*); "Diary Covering the Activities of General Fredendall and Supporting Players," Jan. 3, 1943, James R. Webb Collection, DDE Lib (*"II Corps is to be bait"*).

    Eisenhower and his staff: memo, AFHQ G-4, Jan. 15, 1943, NARA, AFHQ micro, R-188-D (*"logistically out of hand"*); "Record of Conference Held by C-in-C Allied Force," Jan. 10, 1943, NARA, AFHQ micro, R-188-D (*"fatal to do nothing"*).

    Eisenhower made several moves: "History of Allied Force Headquarters," 1945, MTOUSA Historical Section, NARA RG 407, E 427, 95ALI-0.1, boxes 142–43; Theodore J. Conway, SOOHP, Sept. 1977, Robert F. Ensslin, MHI; Ambrose, *Eisenhower: Soldier, General of the Army, President-Elect, 1890–1952*, 226; Akers, OH, July 27, 1949, SM, MHI; D. Clayton James, with Anne Sharp Wells, *A Time for Giants*, 153 (*"begged and pleaded"*); Butcher diary, DDE Lib, A-8 (*"Clark admitted"*), A-127 (*"Ike doesn't think Clark"*), A-157, A-194 (*"manure pile"* and lectured him); Danchev and Todman, eds., 356 (*"very ambitious and unscrupulous"*).

272 *"I bless the day"*: DDE to GCM, Nov. 11, 1942, Chandler, 690.

    At fifty-nine: "Outline History of II Corps," n.d., NARA RG 407, E 427, box 3112; Robert H. Berlin, *U.S. Army World War II Corps Commanders*, 5; *These Are the Generals*, 227 (*"very soldierly little fellow"*); Benjamin S. Persons, *Relieved of Command*, 27; "World War II Generals," 1945, WD, USMA Lib.

273 *Thirty-five years later*: letter, James Webb to family, Apr. 20, 1943, OW, MHI (*a conviction that neither*); Leland L. Rounds, OH, Oct. 21, 1948, SM, MHI; "Leland L. Rounds: His Tale, July 13, 1944," OSS files, NARA RG 226, E 99, box 39 (*"Lay off"*).

    Orders issued from: Curtis, "The Song of the Fighting First," ts, 1988, MRC FDM, 56; Carter, "Carter's War," ts, n.d., CEOH, III-13.

    Truscott found him: Kirkpatrick, "Orthodox Soldiers: Army Formal Schools Between the Two World Wars," 10; Truscott, *Command Missions*, 144 (*"outspoken in his opinions"*); Fredendall to LKT Jr., Jan. 22, 1943, 1050 hrs. and 1345 hrs., LKT Jr., GCM Lib, box 9, folder 5.

    Fredendall also harbored: "Diary Covering the Activities of General Fredendall," Oct. 7, 1942, "Log of Our Transatlantic Flight," James R. Webb Collection, DDE Lib; James, *A Time for Giants*, 95 (*"Ike is the best"*); Dickson, "G-2 Journal," MHI, 35.

274 *Lloyd Fredendall's chosen avenue*: Rame, 214 (*Solomon the Eunuch*); Baedeker, 315; Miller, *Ike the Soldier*, 472; G-1 report, HQ II Corps, Feb. 14, 1943, NARA RG 492, MTOUSA, box 263; Carter, "Carter's War," III-13 (*"Fredendall's kindergarten"*); Dickson, "G-2 Journal," 37 (*"surrounded by children"*); "Diary Covering the Activities of General Fredendall," Jan. 25, 1943, James R. Webb Collection, DDE Lib (*"woods are stiff"*).

    Tébessa's high plateau: "Diary Covering the Activities of General Fredendall," Jan. 8 (*"cold as a snake"*), Jan. 9 (*bulletproof Cadillac*), and Jan. 11 (*"Everyone is freezing"*), 1943, James R. Webb Collection, DDE Lib; Austin, 77 (*"lumber camp"*); Pyle, *Here Is Your War*, 301 (*in his canvas chair*).

    Day and night: blueprint, 19th Engineer Regt, NARA RG 407, E 427, box 19248; "Historical Record of the 19th Engineer Regiment," Oct. 1942–Oct. 1943, NARA RG 407, box 19248; "II Corps Engineer Section Journal," Jan. 21–March 1943,

NARA RG 407, E 427, box 3234; "Diary Covering the Activities of General Fredendall," Jan. 25, 1943, James R. Webb Collection, DDE Lib.

275 *Some officers believed*: Truscott, *Command Missions*, 146; MacVane, *Journey into War*, 195 (*"Some of ours"*); Waters, SOOHP, MHI, 175–76, 202 (*some questioned*); Carter, "Carter's War," CEOH, IV-15 (*"We had no proper"*).

    Suspected Tunisian collaborators: "History of the 26th Infantry in the Present Struggle," MRC FDM, 5/19, 6/13; Raff, 194–95 (*"Of the thirty-nine"*).

276 *Ted Roosevelt, who had been peeled*: TR to Eleanor, Jan. 16 and Feb. 2, 1943, TR, LOC, box 9; Cameron, "Americanizing the Tank," 761; "Journal for the 3rd Battalion," 26th Infantry, Feb. 1943, MRC FDM (*"everything but the Rising Sun"*).

    Among the most active: AAR, "Account of Carleton S. Coon," NARA RG 226, E 99, OSS, box 39, folders 8, 34, 39, 75, 85 (*"mule turds"*); Coon, *A North African Story*, 68 (*"rogues and cutthroats"*), 76 (*"one Arab and one cow"*), 79; George C. Chalou, ed., *The Secrets War: The Office of Strategic Services in World War II*, 20 (*"Bad-Eyes Brigade"*); *The Overseas Targets: War Report of the OSS*, vol. 2, 19–20 (*"This use of hostages"*); Brown, *The Last Hero: Wild Bill Donovan*, 266, 269 (*"Captain Retinitis"*).

277 *"It is still"*: TR to Eleanor, Feb. 6, 1943, TR, LOC, box 9.

    So were the tens: Pyle, "Our Soldiers in Tunisia Learn the Agony of War," ts, n.d., AAR, 26th Inf, NARA RG 407, E 427, box 5942; Mayo, 135; article, Gault MacGowan, *New York Sun*, Dec. 8, 1942 (*Army grub*); letter, Raymond Dreyer to family, March 10, 1943, MCC, YU (*Life Savers*); letter, Joseph T. Dawson to family, Apr. 26, 1943, Dawson Collection, MRC FDM (*"We often wonder"*); Abbott, 64 (*"Tunisian deer"*); Lawrence J. Starr, ASEQ, 135th Inf, 34th ID, MHI; Houston, 139; *History 67th Armored Regiment*, 71.

    Dysentery, parasites: Wilson, "The Operations of the 509th Parachute Battalion in North Africa," 1948; Hamilton H. Howze, "The Battle of Sidi bou Zid," lecture, n.d., Cavalry School, MHI (*"Stuka time"*); D'Arcy-Dawson, 95 (*"Messerstorks"*); Ray, 34 (*250 Allied casualties*); Ford, 44 (*Evelegh ordered*); Austin, 77.

278 *"Never out of artillery range"*: Lawrence J. Starr, ASEQ, 135th Inf, 34th ID, MHI (*"An old man at twenty"*); *Tank Destroyer Forces World War II*, 24; Liebling, 66 (*"old man with chilblains"*); Robinett, *Armor Command*, 139 (*"Lay it on them!"*); Abbott, 83 (*"Mother, please"*).

    "I should have": diary, Nov. 10, 1942, OW, MHI; Robinett, *Armor Command*, 28 (*"I would either go"*).

    Known as Dan: author interviews, Edith Ward Spalding, Oct. 2000, Robin Ward Yates, Sept. 2000, and John Ward Yates, August 2001; obituary, *Assembly*, March 1973; Gugeler, ts, n.d. (unpublished Ward biography), OW, MHI, I-11, III-1, V-4, VII-13, IX-4, IX-22; David A. Shugart, "On the Way: The U.S. Field Artillery in the Inter-War Period," paper, Apr. 2000, Society for Military History, 5; W. B. Smith to OW, July 1943, OW, MHI; OW to 8th AD cadre, March 3, 1942, OW, MHI.

279 *Ward had two peculiarities*: Gugeler, IX-16; diary, Nov. 8, 1942, Jan. 15, 20, 27, 1943, OW, MHI.

"The Touch of the World"

280 *The Emperor of the West*: logs, FRUS; Reilly, 152; Elliott Roosevelt, *As He Saw It*, 71 (*"Winnie is"*).

    Preserving the status quo: Austin, 73 (*"Business: Chiefs of Staff"*); Sherwood, 676 (*"Ike seems jittery"*); Eisenhower, *Crusade in Europe*, 133, 135; Frederick E. Morgan, OH, n.d., FCP, MHI (*how such a man*).

281 *He spoke without notes*: Chandler, 906n; *FRUS*, Jan. 15, 1943, 569 (*"might be a good division"*), 567 (*"At first operations"*).

   Watching this performance: Bryant, 17, 552 (*"shooting his tongue"*); Boatner, 63; Danchev and Todman, eds., xv (*"I flatly disagree"*); David Fraser, *Alanbrooke*, 92–93, 297; Kennedy, 291.

282 *did not distract*: Danchev and Todman, eds., 352 (*"ridiculous plan"*), 351 (*"Eisenhower as a general"*).

   Now Brooke pounced: msg no. COS (W) 430, British chiefs of staff, Jan. 5, 1943, Watson Notes, GCM Lib; *FRUS*, 567, 574, 577; Bryant, 548; *NWAf*, 353; Hinsley, *British Intelligence in the Second World War*, vol. II, 579 (*Ultra decrypt today*).

   Eisenhower tried to regroup: *FRUS*, 567–69 (*"any necessary adjustments"*); *Three Years*, 236 (*"Fredendall's plan"*); "Minutes of Meeting," CCS, Jan. 15, 1943, NARA RG 218, JCS records, box 195.

283 *British and American chiefs*: Kent Roberts Greenfield, *American Strategy in World War II: A Reconsideration*, 31; Howard, *Grand Strategy*, vol. IV, 245; Morison, *The Two-Ocean War*, 241; Behrens, 328; Francis Tuker, *Approach to Battle*, 319 (*It is axiomatic*).

   No sooner had Eisenhower: *FRUS*, 539 (*"final victory"*); memo, British chiefs of staff, Jan. 2, 1943, NARA RG 165, E 422, box 54; "Minutes of Meeting," JCS, Jan. 16, 1943, 1700 hrs., NARA RG 218, box 169; Matloff, 24 (*Eisenhower's own planners*).

284 *All of which argued*: *FRUS*, 539, 570, 572, 573; Clark, *Calculated Risk*, 50 (*"Why stick your head"*); Leighton and Coakley, 673.

   As Brooke had listened: Bryant, 545; Pogue, *George C. Marshall: Organizer of Victory, 1943–1945*, 7; Ernest J. King and Walter Muir Whitehill, *Fleet Admiral King*, 413 (*"old crustacean"*); Buell, xi, 11, 75 (*foghorn voice*), 78–79 (*bibulous and lecherous*); GCM, OH, Oct. 5, 1956, Forrest Pogue, GCM Lib (*"Albion perfidious"*); C. E. Lambe, OH, Feb. 26, 1947, FCP, MHI (*"his eye on the Pacific"*).

   King threw a rock: "Minutes of Meeting," JCS, Jan. 16, 1943, 1700 hrs., NARA RG 218, box 169 (*"do not seem"*); *FRUS*, 547, 549; Mary H. Williams, ed., *Chronology, 1941–1945*, *USAWWII*, 81–97; Leighton and Coakley, 662, 663n (*only 15 percent*); Mansoor, *The GI Offensive in Europe*, 47–48 (*virtually all U.S. Marines*); Matloff and Snell, 157 (*at least three times*), 357–60.

285 *No matter*: *FRUS*, 553, 555; Albert C. Wedemeyer, *Wedemeyer Reports!*, 165 (*secretly tape-recorded*), 158; "Minutes of Meeting," JCS, Jan. 16, 1943, 0930 hrs., NARA RG 218, box 169 (*"If we subscribed"*).

   Brooke recorded his assessment: Danchev and Todman, eds., 360.

   Casablanca lay: Gugeler, ts, MHI, X-53 (*"too terrible"*); *Three Years*, 243 (*"neck is in a noose"*); Butcher diary, DDE Lib, A-176; Eisenhower, *Crusade in Europe*, 136–37; Danchev and Todman, eds., 363 (*"deficient of experience"*); Sherwood, 689 (*"The President told General Marshall"*); D'Este, *Eisenhower: A Soldier's Life*, 623 (read in mss) (*"what I'm going to do with Tunisia"*); Roosevelt, *As He Saw It*, 79 (*"What's your guess?"*); Blumenson, *The Patton Papers, 1940–1945*, 154 (*"He thinks his thread"*).

286 *Brooke's deputy*: Kennedy, 273 (*"He is difficult enough"*); Codman, 76; Durno, 73 (*"You Are My Sunshine"*); Reilly, 155; Harmon, *Combat Commander*, 109 (*"Corporal of the guard!"*).

287 *Mornings, he lounged*: Sherwood, 688; Roosevelt, *As He Saw It*, 102; Macmillan, *The Blast of War*, 194; Kersaudy, 240 (*"Come and see"*); Ismay, OH, Dec. 17 and Dec. 20, 1946, FCP, MHI (*"Very well"*); Frederick E. Morgan, OH, n.d., FCP, MHI (*"to view with contempt"*); Charles F. A. Portal, OH, Feb. 7, 1947, FCP, MHI (*"We don't get paid"*).

   Roosevelt also found: Roosevelt, *As He Saw It*, 94; Codman, 76; Powell, *In Barbary*.

A state dinner: FRUS, 832 (*effects of teetotalism*), 608 (*"there just aren't going"*).
288 *Around and around*: "Minutes of Meeting," CCS, Jan. 16, 1943, 1030 hrs., NARA RG 218, JCS records, box 195 (*"how Germany is to be defeated"*).
There it was: "Minutes of a meeting at the White House on Thursday, Jan. 7, 1943, at 1500," NARA RG 165, E 422, box 54; FRUS, 594–96, 597 (*"not interested in occupying Italy"*); Trumbull Higgins, *Soft Underbelly*, 47; "Minutes of Meeting," CCS, Jan. 18, 1943, 1030 hrs., NARA RG 218, JCS records, box 195.
289 *After two stormy hours*: Danchev and Todman, eds., 362 (*"It is no use"*).
"We lost our shirts": Wedemeyer, 191–92.
290 *Besides, the president*: Signal Corps film, ADC-979 and ADC-465, NARA; Walter Logan, United Press account, Jan. 21, 1943; Durno, 74 (*"Roadsides were a panorama"*); Reilly, 160 (*To distract curious*), 155 (*"The Heinies know"*); Harmon, 109; Blumenson, *The Patton Papers, 1940–1945*, 157 (*"bunch of cheap detectives"*); Clark, *Calculated Risk*, 149 (*"Negro troops who"*); Whitehead, 35–37; "President's Trip to Casablanca," Guy H. Spaman to Frank J. Wilson, June 26, 1945, FDR Lib, Secret Service records, box 4 (*no bullets*); Harriman and Abel, 181 (*trained on the docile troops*).
Rumors that FDR: Houston, 144 (*"Anything is possible"*); Durno, 75–79; Logan, UP account, Jan. 21, 1943; Blumenson, *The Patton Papers, 1940–1945*, 158 (*"says India is lost"*); *Three Years*, 283 (*"hoped to die"*).
291 *The distant roar*: "Minutes of Meeting," CCS, Jan. 19, 1943, 1600 hrs., NARA RG 218, JCS records, box 195; Austin, 71–72 (*"We'll need"*); John S.D. Eisenhower, *Allies*, 238 (*"petit De Gaulle"*), 244; Tompkins, 230 (*"a self-seeker"*); Codman, 72, 80 (*"Uncle Sam"*); Murphy, 170, 174–76; Roosevelt, *As He Saw It*, 74, 91 (*"a dud"*); De Gaulle, 387, 392; Anthony Eden, *The Memoirs of Anthony Eden, Earl of Avon*, 421; Leahy, 144; Pendar, 151 (*Jeanne d'Arc*); Moran, 88; FRUS, 694; Harmon, 109; Signal Corps film, ADC-979 and ADC-465, NARA; Churchill, *The Hinge of Fate*, 682; Sherwood, 685 (*entire Secret Service detail*); Reilly, 158.
292 *But here they were*: Signal Corps film, ADC-979 and ADC-465, NARA; Price, 190; MacVane, *Journey into War*, 180–83; Davis, *Experience of War*, 379; Sherwood, 688 (*"a very warlike look"*); Jordan, *Jordan's Tunis Diary*, 153 (*"Peter Pan"*); Parris and Russell, 277 (*"I was born"*).
293 *As the generals*: FRUS, 726 (*"unprecedented in history"*), 822; Macmillan, *The Blast of War*, 203; Price, 191; Middleton, 254; Harriman and Abel, 186 (*"the privilege"*); Moorehead, 119 (*"It was all rather embarrassing"*).
"I think we have all": FRUS, 727; Copson, "Summit at Casablanca" (*"storm and ruin"*).
294 *No one scrutinizing*: Sherwood, 687, 696 (*"popped into my mind"*); FRUS, 635 (*"the united nations"*); "Minutes of a meeting at the White House on Thursday, Jan. 7, 1943, at 1500," NARA RG 165, E 422, box 54; Wedemeyer, 187 (*"compel the Germans"*).
What was done was done: Robert Dallek, *Franklin D. Roosevelt and American Foreign Policy, 1932–1945*, 373; Howard, *Grand Strategy*, vol. IV, 282–85; Anne Armstrong, *Unconditional Surrender*, 13–14 (*Third Punic War* and *none of the fifteen*).
295 *The reporters had their story*: MacVane, *Journey into War*, 180–83; Austin, 73 (*"What's your paper, eh?"*); Middleton, 254 (*"the touch of the world"*).

The Sinners' Concourse

295 *while the hacks*: Harriman and Abel, 191 (*For four hours*); Moran, 89; Churchill, *The Hinge of Fate*, 694 (*"most elaborately organized brothels"*); "Minutes of Meet-

ing," Jan. 15, 1943, 1000 hrs., NARA RG 218, JCS records, box 169 (*"refuse any invitation"*); Sherwood, 694; Pendar, 135.

Their refuge: "Moses Taylor Villa," NARA RG 338, Fifth Army files, box 262; Durno, 26; Bryant, 563; Pendar, 136, 140, 145 (*nervous breakdown*).

296 *Looming above La Saadia*: Moran, 90 (*"paralyzed legs dangling"*); Churchill, *Hinge of Fate*, 695; Pendar, 148–49.

They sat in reverent silence: FRUS, 535; Powell, *In Barbary*, 428, 436 (*Sinners' Concourse*); Pendar, 148–49 (*"ain't no war"*); Marvine Howe, "In Marrakesh," *New York Times*, March 3, 2002; Larrabee, 39.

297 *But what should happen*: Morison, *History of United States Naval Operations in World War II*, vol. IX: *Sicily-Salerno-Anzio*, 7 (*"Where do we go"*); GCM, OH, Oct. 29, 1956, FCP, GCM Lib (*"chrome steel baseboards"*); "Minutes of Meeting," JCS, Jan. 20, 1943, 0900 hrs., NARA RG 218, box 169; Lamb, 222 (*"Nothing in the world"*).

The compromises at Anfa: Behrens, 331; Greenfield, *American Strategy*, 92 (*"I note that the Americans"*); Morton Yarmon, "The Administrative and Logistical History of the ETO," part IV, "TORCH and the European Theater of Operations," 1946, CMH, 8.31 AA, 117; Vigneras, 31, 38; Abraham Friedman, "Operation TORCH: The Dispatch of Aircraft from the United Kingdom by Eighth Air Force," Sept. 14, 1944, Historical Section, U.S. Strategic Air Forces in Europe, NARA RG 407, E 427, box 24351, 15–16; Slessor, 448.

298 *Many months would also pass*: Armstrong, 154 (*"putrefying albatross"*); Parkinson, 70; Greenfield, *American Strategy*, 9; Thomas Fleming, *The New Dealers' War: F.D.R. and the War Within World War II*, 184–85; Warlimont, 316; Howard, *Grand Strategy*, vol. IV, 284 (*"a word of encouragement"*).

A sense of companionship: Murphy, 168 (*"a reluctant tail"*); Christopher Hitchens, "The Medals of His Defeat," *Atlantic Monthly*, Apr. 2002, 118 (*wariness*); Danchev and Todman, eds., 364 (*"charming people"*); "Minutes of Meeting," copy #61, CCS, NARA RG 218, JCS records, box 195 (*some pencil turned*); George Q. Flynn, *The Mess in Washington: Manpower Mobilization in World War II*, 207 (*a great waterman*); Harriman and Abel, 191 (*"the old order could not last"*).

299 *Dinner at La Saadia*: Pendar, 149–58 (*"I am the pasha"* and *"Don't tell me"*); Roosevelt, *As He Saw It*, 119; Churchill, *The Hinge of Fate*, 695; Moran, 90 (*"I love these Americans"*); Harriman and Abel, 191–92; Larrabee, 39.

CHAPTER 8: A BITS AND PIECES WAR
"Goats Set Out to Lure a Tiger"

301 *The almond trees*: Robinett, *Armor Command*, 152–55 (*panniers heaped* and *grave markers*); Moorehead, 109 (*veiled women peered*); Henry E. Gardiner, ts, n.d., USMA Arch, 120 (*its brakes stuck*).

As a first line of defense: Anthony Clayton, *Three Marshals of France*, 74 (*"British senior officers"*); Adrian Clements Gore, "This Was the Way It Was," ts, 1987, IWM, 90/29/1 (*"a comic-opera soldier"*).

303 *The French possessed almost no*: Truscott, *Command Missions*, 135; Anderson, "Operations in North West Africa," June 7, 1943, *London Gazette*; Ankrum, 207, 225; Liebling, *Mollie & Other War Pieces*, 92 (*"goats set out"*); msg, Advance AFHQ to AFHQ, Feb. 3 and 4, 1943, NARA, AFHQ micro, R-100-D, 319.1 (*"somewhat discouraged"*).

"This past week": "Memo for diary," Jan. 19, 1943, Chandler, 909; *Three Years*, 242–43 (*"one of the world's greatest"*), 244, 245 (*"Mud is a silly alibi"*), 250; DDE to J. T. McNarney, Jan. 19, 1943, Chandler, 914 (*"There is no use"*).

The abrupt scuttling: DDE to GCM, Jan. 30, 1943, Chandler, 932 (*"We must *keep"*); DDE to CCS, Feb. 3, 1943, Chandler, 934 (*"offensively defensive"*); Butcher diary, Jan. 18, 1943, DDE Lib, A-161 (*"I don't want anything"*).

304 *In this the Germans:* NWAf, 377; memo, DDE to W. B. Smith, Jan. 11, 1943, and memo, L. W. Rooks to W. B. Smith, Feb. 11, 1943, NARA AFHQ micro, R-71 Special (*"no action can be taken"*); Rame, 221 (*"retiring from crest to crest"*); Anderson, "Operations in North West Africa" (*"not hopeful"*).

General Anderson ordered: NWAf, 378, 382; "Report of Ousseltia Valley Campaign, 19–29 January 1943," CCB, 1st AD, Feb. 12, 1943, NARA RG 407, E 427, 601-CCB-0.3 (*"An excellent example"*); Rame, 218–19 (*"a lake of morning mist"*); "The French Army of North Africa in the Tunisian Campaign," lecture, 1943, Fort Hood, William S. Biddle Papers, MHI; Howe, *The Battle History of the 1st Armored Division,* 111–13; Truscott, *Command Missions,* 138 (*400 Germans*).

305 *French casualties:* NWAf, 382, 386n, 387; "Report of Liaison Officer on French Troops," Jan. 24, 1943, LKT Jr. Papers, GCM Lib, box 9, folder 5 (*"French can no longer"*); memo, DDE, Jan. 19, 1943, Chandler, 909; "Personal Diary of Lt. Gen. C. W. Allfrey, the Tunisian Campaign," Jan. 13, 1943, Allfrey Collection, LHC; Anderson, "Operations in North West Africa"; G-1 report, HQ II Corps, Feb. 14, 1943, NARA RG 492, MTOUSA, box 263; Eisenhower, *Crusade in Europe,* 489; DDE to Anderson, Jan. 26, 1943, Chandler, 922.

He had no sooner: Three Years, 244–45, 255; DDE to W. B. Smith, Jan. 26, 1943, Chandler, 923 (*"barracks used by our soldiers"*); DDE to T. Handy, Jan. 28, 1943, Chandler, 927 (*"As much as we preach"*).

306 *Orlando Ward, who ostensibly commanded:* Gugeler, ts, OW, MHI, X-62; diary, Jan. 23, 28, 1943, OW, MHI; Truscott, *Command Missions,* 142; NWAf, 387–88; Fredendall to LKT Jr, phone transcript, Jan. 24, 1943, LKT Jr. Papers, GCM Lib, box 9, folder 5 (*"Remember that force"*); Howze, OH, Aug. 1976, Russell Gugeler, OW, MHI; "Report of Operation, 27 January–3 February 1943," 1st AD, NARA RG 407, E 427, box 14767; Knickerbocker et al., 59, 82 (*"bits and pieces"*).

307 *General von Arnim duly noted:* author visit, April 2000; Carell, 333 (*"my nightmare"*); Wilson, "The Operations of the 509th Parachute Battalion in North Africa"; James B. Carvey, "Faïd Pass," *Infantry Journal,* Sept. 1944, 8.

308 *That was about to change:* Howze, "The Battle of Sidi bou Zid," lecture, n.d., Cavalry School, MHI (*"Do not fire"*); Akers, OH, July 27, 1949, SM, MHI; Truscott, *Command Missions,* 150; Hansen, 2/80 (*"the most important point"*); Blumenson, "Kasserine Pass, 30 January–22 February 1943," in Heller and Stofft, eds., 245.

Prompt, decisive action: "Narrative of Events from 23 January 1943 to 26 February," CCA, 1st AD, NARA RG 407, E 427, 601-CCA-0.3, box 14767; Blumenson, *Kasserine Pass,* 108.

McQuillin's nickname: R. E. McQuillin, Army biographical files, MHI; Robert Simons, OH, July 1976, Gugeler, OW, MHI (*"As a man he was"*); Howze, OH, Aug. 1976, OW, MHI.

309 *Having granted the enemy:* A. N. Stark, Jr., Army biographical files, MHI; author interviews, George Juskalian, Feb. 25, 2000 (*"It was nerve-racking"*), and Paul F. Gorman, Feb. 7, 2000; Akers, OH, July 27, 1949, G. F. Howe, SM, MHI; Truscott, *Command Missions,* 148; Blumenson, *Kasserine Pass,* 109; Raphael L. Uffner, "Recollections of World War II with the First Infantry Division," ts, n.d., MRC FDM, 245–50 (*"strongly rejected"*); "History of the 26th Infantry in the Present Struggle," MRC FDM, 7/1–2; Robinett, *Armor Command,* 143.

Truscott and Ward drove: author visit, Apr. 2000; Jordan, *Jordan's Tunis Diary,* 175 (*"that half-world"*); Truscott, *Command Missions,* 148–49.

310 *The American force:* "History of the 26th Infantry in the Present Struggle," 7/1–2; Laurence P. Robertson, ts, 1988, ASEQ, 1st AR, 1st AD, MHI (also, earlier draft in

Laurence Robertson papers, USMA Arch); "Narrative of Events from 23 January 1943 to 26 February," CCA, 1st AD, NARA RG 407, E 427, 601-CCA-0.3, box 14767; G. C. Kelleher, Army biographical files, MHI; Uffner, 250 (*French toast*).

For *Company H*: Robertson, ts, MHI, 184 (*"The velocity"* and *heavy black bread*); Truscott, *Command Missions*, 149; Uffner, 248; "Catalogue of Standard Ordnance Items, Volume I," in "Kasserine Pass Battles," vol. II, part 3, CMH.

311 *The failed counterattack*: "Narrative of Events from 23 January 1943 to 26 February," CCA, 1st AD, NARA RG 407, E 427, box 14767; OW to McQuillin, Jan. 31, 1943, 2115 hrs., NARA RG 407, E 427 (*"I am counting on you"*); "History of the 26th Infantry in the Present Struggle," 7/2–3 (*"held their fire"*); NWAf, 393–94; E. C. Smith, Feb. 14, 1943, MCC, YU (*"shook us"*); AAR, CCA, Feb. 1, 1943, and S-2 report, CCA, Feb. 1, 1943, NARA RG 407, E 427, box 14767.

Faïd Pass was gone: NWAf, 392 (*scathing message*), 394n (*more than 900*); Heller and Stofft, eds., 246 (*McQuillin bitterly*); Hansen, 2/80 (*"To retake it"*); Howe, *The Battle History of the 1st Armored Division*, 135; Rudolf Lang, "Battles of Kampfgruppe Lang in Tunisia," 1947, FMS, D-173; Carell, 331 (*"It will soon be over"*).

"This Can't Happen to Us"

312 *Fredendall's attention*: Liebling, *Mollie & Other War Pieces*, 76 (*"draw the pucker string"*); NWAf, 392–96.

Infantrymen from the 1st Battalion: Edwin L. Powell, Jr., OH, 1982, Lynn L. Sims, CEOH, 102–107 (*"Sunday School picnic"*); author interview, Aurelio Barron, Oct. 19, 1999 (*"All down the road"*); "History of the 168th Infantry," Jan. 31, 1942, NARA RG 407, E 427, boxes 9575–77; Rame, 229; Rolf, 79 (*"It was the most terrible thing"*); AAFinWWII, 142; Lauren E. McBride, "The Battle of Sened Station," *Infantry Journal*, Apr. 1945, 30 (*"Maimed and twisted"*).

313 *Three different colonels*: Stewart, "The 'Red Bull' Division: The Training and Initial Engagements of the 34th Infantry Division, 1941–43," 1; Dennis B. Dray, "Regimental Commander of the 168th Infantry, Colonel Thomas Davidson Drake: Battle of Sened and Sidi bou Zid, Tunisia," ts, Nov. 1977, Iowa Military Academy, Iowa GSM; memo, Jan. 12, 1943, in William F. Beekman, "A Diary of World War II as Observed Through the Eyes, Ears, and Mind of Bill Beekman," ts, n.d., Iowa GSM (*"Neither will good table manners"*); Green and Gauthier, eds., 76 (*Quack-Quack*).

314 *As his 1st Battalion huddled*: Thomas D. Drake, "Factual Account of Operations, 168th Infantry," Apr. 1945, Charles W. Ryder Collection, DDE Lib, container 4; Ankrum, 174; Curtiss, ed., 276.

But first, Sened Station: Drake, "Factual Account of Operations, 168th Infantry"; "History of the 168th Infantry," NARA RG 407, E 427, Moynihan, ed., 57.

a cakewalk: author interview, Aurelio Barron (*"Go on up there!"*); Ankrum, 174 (*"all those bees"*); Hougen, *The Story of the Famous 34th Infantry Division*; McBride, "The Battle of Sened Station" (*"I saw his canteen"*); Drake, "Factual Account of Operations, 168th Infantry" (*"Men were dying everywhere"*).

315 *At midafternoon*: Berens, 5, 47 (*"Kill them all!"*); "168th African History," in "168th Infantry Publications," Iowa GSM; Rame, 235.

Fredendall was considerably less charmed: NWAf, 397 (*contradictory orders*); "Historical Record, HQ," March 1, 1943, CCD, NARA RG 407, E 427, 601-CCD 0.3 (*"Too much time"*); Carter, "Carter's War," CEOH, IV-13 (*"There has been a breakthrough!"*); Drake, "Factual Account of Operations, 168th Infantry"; Camp, ed., 55 (*"A sort of hysteria"*); Powell, OH, CEOH, 110 (*"hightailing it"*); letter, James McGuinness to parents, May 23, 1943, Co. F, 168th Inf, World War II Letters, 1940–1946, Western Historical Manuscript Collection, University of Missouri–Columbia, Missouri (*"Some of the fellows"*).

316 *The American attack was spent*: "History of the 168th Infantry," NARA RG 407, E 427 (*"Your outfit"*); AAR, 1st AD, Jan. 27–Feb. 3, 1943, "Kasserine Pass Battles," vol. I, part I, CMH (*"no decisive objective"*); Howe, *The Battle History of the 1st Armored Division*, 129; NWAf, 398; Ankrum, 174.

317 *"One of the things that gives me"*: DDE to Fredendall, Feb. 4, 1943, Chandler, 939; Truscott, *Command Missions*, 150 (*Fredendall was too rash*); *Three Years*, 254 (*"futile rushing around"*); diary, Feb. 8, 10, 1943, OW, MHI (*"spherical SOB"*).

   As recently as February 1: "Meeting, 1000 hours, 1 Feb. 1943," NARA, AFHQ micro, R-188-D; NWAf, 399.

   "We could not help wondering": "701st Tank Destroyer Battalion: North African Campaign Diary, B Company," 1943, MHI.

"The Mortal Dangers That Beset Us"

317 *At eight A.M. on February 12*: David Irving, *The Trail of the Fox*, 267.

318 *The trailer door*: Fritz Krause, "Studies on the Mareth Position," n.d., FMS, D-046, MHI, 9 (*"My dear young friend"*); Kesselring, "The War in the Mediterranean," part II, "The Fighting in Tunisia and Tripolitania," 49–50 (*"The very last armored"*); Forty, *The Armies of Rommel*, 176; B. H. Liddell Hart, ed., *The Rommel Papers*, 394 (*"It's two years"*).

   "Rommel, Rommel, Rommel!": Bryant, 450 (*"What else matters"*); Boatner, 461; Matthew Cooper, *The German Army, 1939–1945*, 352; Charles Douglas-Home, *Rommel*, 110; Macksey, *Kesselring: The Making of the Luftwaffe*, 101; Kesselring, "The War in the Mediterranean," part II, "The Fighting in Tunisia and Tripolitania," 49–50 (*"one good division"*); James J. Sadkovich, "Of Myths and Men: Rommel and the Italians in North Africa, 1940–1942," *International History Review*, May 1991, 284; Bruce Allen Watson, *Exit Rommel*, 56, 158–59 (*"fugitive leading"*).

319 *"Day and night"*: Liddell Hart, ed., *The Rommel Papers*, 390–91; Bennett, *Ultra and Mediterranean Strategy*, 373–74; Krause, "Studies on the Mareth Position," 9 (*"a broken man"*).

   Rommel understood: NWAf, 370, 372; Field Marshal the Viscount Alexander of Tunis, "The African Campaign from El Alamein to Tunis," 1948, supplement to *London Gazette*, 868; Anderson, "Operations in North West Africa."

320 *Yet Rommel's German units*: "Rommel to Tunisia," NARA RG 319, OCMH, box 227; war diary, Panzer Army Africa, Feb. 3–4 and Feb. 10–17, 1943, in "Kasserine Pass Battles," vol. I, part 1, CMH; Hellmuth Greiner diary notes, Feb. 16, 1943, and personnel report, Panzer Armee Afrika, Feb. 1, 1943, NARA RG 319, OCMH, box 225; Kesselring, "Final Commentaries on the Campaign in North Africa, 1941–1943," 1949, FMS, #C-075, 17 (*"hypnotic influence"*); NWAf, 370.

   True, Rommel's army included: Boog et al., 801n (*350,000 Axis men*); NWAf, 371; Anderson, "Operations in North West Africa."

   Rommel increasingly blamed: Domenico Petracarro, "The Italian Army in Africa, 1940–1943: An Attempt at Historical Perspective," *War & Society*, Oct. 1991, 103 (*tied bandannas*); Enno von Rinteln, "The Italian Commmand and Armed Forces in the First Half of 1943: Their Situation, Intentior.s, and Measures," 1947, FMS, #T-1a, trans. Janet E. Dewey, MHI (*"was in agony"*); Westphal, *The German Army in the West*, 130; Kesselring, "Italy as a Military Ally," n.d., FMS, #C-015, 9 (*"three fashionable passions"*); war diary, Panzer Army Africa, Feb. 11, 1943, in "Kasserine Pass Battles," vol. I, part 1, CMH.

321 *In these and other matters*: Arnim, "Recollections of Tunisia," 48–49 (*"sober cal-*

culations" and *"a second Stalingrad"*); Greiner diary notes, Feb. 16 (*"house of cards"*) and March 10, 1943 (*brigade of homosexuals*), and personnel report, Panzer Armee Afrika, Feb. 1, 1943, NARA RG 319, OCMH, box 225; Jackson, *The Battle for North Africa*, 415; *Destruction*, 274.

talk of decampment: Kesselring, "Final Commentaries on the Campaign in North Africa, 1941–1943," 28, 31; Kesselring, *Memoirs*, 143, 149; Warlimont, 310, 284 (*restricted rations*).

to avoid a similar diet: Alexander, "The African Campaign from El Alamein to Tunis," 868; *Destruction*, 273, 283–84; OKW to Comando Supremo, Jan. 19, 1943, NARA RG 319, OCMH, box 225; Irving, *The Trail of the Fox*, 253 (*English dictionary*); Liddell Hart, ed., *The Rommel Papers*, 397 (*"break up the American"*).

322 *Kesselring agreed*: Irving, 266–67 (*"We are going to go"*); *NWAf*, 206–207; war diary, Fifth Panzer Army, Feb. 8, 1943, in "Kasserine Pass Battles," vol. I, part 1, CMH (*"weaken the American"*); war report, Panzer Army Africa, Jan. 16 to Feb. 12, 1943.

323 *The front remained*: Pyle, *Here Is Your War*, 154; Dickson, "G-2 Journal," MHI, 37; Oswald Jett, "As I Saw the War," ts, n.d., ASEQ, 47th Medical Bn, 1st AD, MHI, 287 (*Army chaplain*); war diary, 27th Armored FA, Feb. 11, 1943, PMR, GCM Lib, box 12 (*Clubmobile*).

II Corps had suffered: Waters, SOOHP, 690; William H. Simpson, AGF Observer Report, Apr. 1943, NARA RG 165, E 418, Director of Plans and Ops, box 1229 (*130 charged with absence*); Ankrum, 179–80 (*"Hell, no"*); Hougen, *The Story of the Famous 34th Infantry Division*; William Petroski, "Fifty Years Later, Defeat by Rommel Still Clear," March 21, 1993, *Des Moines Sunday Register* (*"We had never heard of them"*); Heller and Stofft, eds., 247.

Quiescence at the front: Everett S. Hughes diary, Feb. 10, 1943, "Allied High Command" micro, reel 5, David Irving collection, MHI (original in LOC Ms Div) (*"too complicated to be placed"*); G-3 memo, Feb. 8, 1943, NARA RG 331, AFHQ micro, R-188-D (*Allied intelligence concluded*); Hinsley, *British Intelligence in the Second World War*, 274; Ralph Bennett, 373–74.

324 *Commanders in Tunisia*: Statement, P. C. Hains, III, 1st AR, in AAR, 2nd Bn, 168th Inf, "Kasserine Pass Battles," vol. 1, part 1 (*seven possible*); Robinett, *Armor Command*, 152 (*"He sucked in his breath"*), 155, 160; Robinett, "Among the First," ts, PMR, GCM Lib, box 22, 366–70 (*"The conference"*); Martin Philipsborn, Jr., and Milton Lehman, "The Untold Story of Kasserine Pass," *Saturday Evening Post*, Feb. 14, 1948, 23 (*"We can't win"*).

Daubed it was: *NWAf*, 402–403; Leon F. Lavoie et al., "The First Armored Division at Faïd-Kasserine," 1949, Armored School Advanced Course, 22 (*"The generals of three nations"*).

Nor were commanders certain: "Diary Covering the Activities of General Fredendall and Supporting Players, Dec. '42–March '43," James R. Webb Collection, DDE Lib (*"They seemed to expect"*); Gugeler, ts, OW, MHI, x-66; E.C. Hatfield, diary, Feb. 6, 1943, OW, MHI (*"angry and disappointed"*); Howze, SOOHP, MHI; Howze, OH, Gugeler, OW, MHI (*"infuriated, insulted"*).

325 *The greatest insult arrived*: Jackson, 430; *NWAf*, 400; Gugeler, ts, OW, MHI, x-72 (*"It's wrong"*).

Fredendall had visited Sbeïtla: Peter C. Hains, III, OH, May 1991, David W. Hogan, MHI (*"Good God"*); Blumenson, *Kasserine Pass*, 122; Andrews, "A Place to Be Lousy In," 100; Gugeler, ts, OW, MHI, x-73; Howze, OH, Gugeler, OW, MHI (*"Neither he nor I"*).

326 *Orders were orders*: Howe, *The Battle History of the 1st Armored Division*, 141; Ankrum, 182 (*"isn't that much barbed wire"*), 183 (*"How would you hear rocks"*), 186 (*"Poppycock!"*); AAR, 2nd Bn, 168th Inf Regt, Feb. 3–16, 1942, Iowa GSM;

Waters, SOOHP, 189–90 (*"Waters, I've got orders"* and *"General McQuillin, let me ask"*).

327 *There was nothing for it*: AAR, 168th Inf Regt, Feb. 27, 1943, Iowa GSM; AAR, 3rd Bn, 168th Inf Regt, n.d., Iowa GSM; AAR, 2nd Bn, 168th Inf Regt, Feb. 3–16, 1942, Iowa GSM (*"killed at once"* and *"when I want prisoners taken"*); Robertson, ts, ASEQ, 1st AR, 1st AD, MHI.

"A Good Night for a Mass Murder"

327 *As commander-in-chief*: Chandler, vol. I, 604n (*far greater powers*); Danchev and Todman, eds., 365 (*neither "the tactical"* and *"We were pushing"*); Miller, *Ike the Soldier*, 464; DDE to GCM, Feb. 8, 1943, Chandler, 942–46 (*"popular impression"*); *Three Years*, 258 (*"burning inside"*).

329 *Upon hearing the news: Three Years*, 260; Hughes diary, Jan. 24, 1943, MHI (*"Ike is doomed"*).

　　that *woman*: Miller, 469; Morgan, *Past Forgetting*, 111; Irving, *The War Between the Generals: Inside the Allied High Command*, 47–48; Hughes diary, Feb. 12, 1943, MHI (*"Maybe Kay"*).

330 *Skibereen was behind the wheel*: chronology, Chandler, vol. V, 105; D. D. Eisenhower, *At Ease: Stories I Tell to Friends*, 259 (*"taking too many trips"*); Charles M. Thomas, diary fragment, Feb. 13, 1943, possession of Roger Cirillo (*"I never knew the wind and sand"*).

　　"In one respect only": Truscott, *Command Missions*, 153; Blumenson, *Kasserine Pass*, 124; Eisenhower, *Crusade in Europe*, 141 (*"the divisions have"*).

331 *Fifteen minutes later*: Michael J. King, "Rangers: Selected Combat Operations in World War II," 1985, CSI, 15; Altieri, "Darby's Rangers," 1945, Ranger Book Committee; Jerome Joseph Haggerty, "A History of the Ranger Battalions in World War II," Ph.D. diss, 1982, Fordham University, 120; Altieri, *The Spearheaders*, 197 (*"We've got to leave our mark"*), 206 (*"good night for a mass murder"*); Patrick O'Donnell, *Beyond Valor*, 33–35 (*at least one wounded prisoner*).

　　Anderson walked in: Akers, OH, SM, MHI; Dickson obituary, *Assembly*, Sept. 1978; B. A. Dickson, "statement of service," Benjamin A. Dickson Collection, USMA Arch, box 3; Blumenson, *Kasserine Pass*, 125.

332 *"Rommel can be expected"*: Dickson, "G-2 Journal: Algiers to the Elbe," 38–43 (*"alarmist and a pessimist"*); Dickson, OH, Dec. 13, 1950, G. F. Howe, SM, MHI.

　　For over two hours: Porter, SOOHP, MHI; Hinsley, *British Intelligence in the Second World War*, 583–85, 757; Dickson, "G-2 Journal: Algiers to the Elbe," 38–43; Robert A. Hewitt, OH, n.d., G. F. Howe, SM, MHI (*"General disposition of forces"*); John H. Thompson, "Kasserine Fiasco Laid to British," *Chicago Tribune*, Feb. 1948; DDE to GCM, Feb. 15, 1943, Chandler, 955 (*"as good as could be made"*), 956 (*"seems keen and fit"*).

333 *An urgent phone call*: PMR to DDE, Sept. 12, 1967 (*"hoped to win"*), and DDE to PMR, Sept. 15, 1967, Robinett Papers, MHI; Robinett, "Among the First," ts, PMR, GCM Lib, box 22, 366–70 (*"Only a question"* and *"The yielding of ground"*); Robinett, *Armor Command*, 160–62 (*"only evidence"* and *"Now that General Eisenhower"*); Eisenhower, *Crusade in Europe*, 142.

334 *Another cactus patch*: Gugeler, ts, OW, MHI, x-77; Truscott, *Command Missions*, 153; Peter C. Hains, III, OH, Apr. 26, 1951, G. F. Howe, SM, MHI; "The Battle of Sidi bou Zid," n.d., PMR, LOC, box 6.

　　Eisenhower had sensed: diary, Feb. 13, 1943, OW, MHI (*"Ike would swap"*); Eisenhower, *Crusade in Europe*, 142; Eisenhower, *At Ease*, 259–60 (*"Get your mine fields out"*); CCA, "Narrative of Events from 23 January 1943 to 26 February," 1st

AD, NARA RG 407, E 427, 601-CCA-0.3, box 14825 (*"listened to a description"*); "The Battle of Sidi bou Zid," n.d., PMR, LOC, box 6.

335 *He stepped from:* D'Este, *Eisenhower: A Soldier's Life*, 641mss (*"We do not pray"*); Blumenson, *Kasserine Pass*, 139 (*"General, what will we do"*); John S.D. Eisenhower, *Allies*, 269 (*"I think you're going"*).

A week later: DDE to GCM, Feb. 21, 1943, Chandler, 970 (*"a delicate matter"*); Hinsley, *British Intelligence in the Second World War*, vol. II, 583–86, 757–59 (*"A-day"*), 761–62; G-2 records, II Corps, Feb. 13, 14, 1943, NARA RG 338, II Corps, box 9 (*"Urgent. Absolute priority"* and *"Rommel has been reported"*); "The Battle of Sidi bou Zid," n.d., PMR, LOC, box 6; Waters, SOOHP, 193 (*"My error"*); NWAf, 411.

336 *A cold drizzle:* "History of the 26th Infantry in the Present Struggle," 6/13; Robertson, ts, ASEQ, 1st AR, 1st AD, MHI; letter, W. Bruce Pirnie, Jr., to Amon G. Carter, June 16, 1943, OW, MHI (*"seemed sort of silly"*); msg, DDE to AGWAR, Feb. 13, 1943, 1013 hrs., NARA RG 331, AFHQ micro, G-3 Forward, Constantine, R-99-D, 319.1 (*"Axis cannot risk"*)

CHAPTER 9: KASSERINE
A Hostile Debouchment

339 *A brief, howling sandstorm:* Hudel and Robinett, "The Tank Battle at Sidi bou Zid," in "Kasserine Pass Battles," n.d., vol. I, part 1, CMH; Lucas, *Panzer Army Africa*, 165; AAR, "Narrative of Events from 23 January 1943 to 26 February," CCA, 1st AD, NARA RG 407, E 427, 601-CCA-0.3; *Tätigkeitsbericht*, 10th Panzer Div., 14–22 Feb. 1943, NARA RG 319, OCMH, box 225; James E. Hagan, ASEQ, n.d., Co G, 3rd Bn, 1st Armored Regt; Ankrum, 186 (*"Krupp Iron Works"*); Howze, "The Battle of Sidi bou Zid," lecture, MHI.

340 *Three miles east:* letter, W. Bruce Pirnie, Jr., to Amon G. Carter, June 16, 1943, OW, MHI (*"really changed the sound"*); Waters, SOOHP, 204, 213 (*"If you can't fire"*); NWAf, 408, 412.

One after another: Howe, *The Battle History of the 1st Armored Division*, 145–46; David W. Hazen, "Role of the Field Artillery in the Battle of Kasserine Pass," master's thesis, 1973, U.S. Army Command and General Staff College, 43 (*somehow forgotten in the confusion*); Thomas E. Hannum, "The 30 Years of Army Experience," ASEQ, ts, n.d., Co A, 91st Armored FA, MHI (*"We didn't know exactly"*); Robert G. Bond, "Induction into the Armed Service," ASEQ, ts, n.d., 1st AD, MHI; Howze, "The Battle of Sidi bou Zid"; William H. Balzer, ASEQ, ts., n.d., 1st Armored Regt, MHI (*"All around me comrades"*); 443rd CA Battalion history, and letter, Werner L. Larson to G. F. Howe, 1951, NARA RG 319, OCMH, box 229; Wiltse, 126 (*"lost his sense of direction"*); John T. Jones, Jr., ASEQ, n.d., Co H, 3rd Bn, 1st Armored Regt.

341 *The enemy without question:* AAR, "Operations of 3rd Bn, 1st Armored Regt," Feb. 14, 1943, NARA RG 407, E 427, box 14916; Harold V. Boyle, Associated Press account of *Texas, Cavalry Journal*, March–Apr. 1943, 12 (*"smoked us up"* and *"like peas"*); Robertson, ASEQ, Co H, 1st Armored Regt, MHI (*"dryland Dunkirk"*); John B. Scheller, ASEQ, n.d., 1st Armored Regt Band, MHI (*"Take off, men!"*); Hannum, "The 30 Years of Army Experience" (*"air was full of whistles"*); Stanley J. Krekeler, ASEQ, ts, n.d., 91st Armored FA, 1st AD, MHI (*lint from camouflage nets*); Pirnie to Carter, June 16, 1943, OW, MHI (*"suddenly blossomed"*); Milo L. Green and Paul S. Gauthier, ed., *Brickbats from F Company*, 149; Howe, *The Battle History of the 1st Armored Division*, 150–53; Louis V. High-

tower, DSC citation, 1943, NARA RG 492, NATOUSA general orders; Blumenson, *Kasserine Pass,* 141–42.

343 *Of fifty-two Shermans: Kriegstagebuch,* 21st Panzer Div., 14–23 Feb., 1943, in "Kasserine Pass Battles," vol. I, part 2, CMH; Hudel and Robinett, "The Tank Battle of Sidi bou Zid."

The disaster: AAR, "1st Armored Regt., North African Campaign, Nov. 8, 1942–May 9, 1943," NARA RG 407, E 427, box 14916; Waters, SOOHP, MHI, 203–22 (*"Sir, I couldn't"*), 596 (*"There must be something"*); AAR, 2nd Bn, 168th Inf Regt, Feb. 1943, Iowa GSM; "Kasserine Pass Battles," n.d., vol. I, part 1, CMH (*"Pete, I'm going to shut"*); Balzer, ASEQ, 1st Armored Regt, MHI; Blumenson, *Kasserine Pass,* 164–65.

344 *Ten miles to the southeast:* Edgar P. Moschel, statement in "168th Inf Regt. Narrative of Action," n.d., Iowa GSM; Franklin M. Davis, Jr., "The Battle of Kasserine Pass," *American Legion,* Apr. 1965, 22 (*"It seems like"*); AAR accounts by Gerald C. Line, Thomas D. Drake, Harry P. Hoffman, in "Kasserine Pass Battles," vol. I, part 1, CMH; Hougen, *The Story of the Famous 34th Infantry Division.*

345 *Drake soon recognized:* "Narrative of Events from 23 January 1943 to 26 February," CCA; AAR, 3rd Bn, 168th Inf Regt, Feb. 8–20, 1943, Iowa GSM; letter, Thomas D. Drake to Charles W. Ryder, Oct. 4, 1944, Ryder Papers, DDE Lib, box 1 (*"fled so fast"*).

At two P.M. Drake: "Narrative of Events from 23 January 1943 to 26 February," CCA; "Brief Statement of Lt. Col. John H. Van Vliet, Jr.," in "168th Inf Regt. Narrative of Action," Iowa GSM; letter, Drake to Ryder, Oct. 4, 1944, Ryder Papers, DDE Lib., box 1; AAR account, Marvin E. Williams, 3rd Bn, 168th Inf, "Kasserine Pass Battles," vol. I, part 1, CMH; Blumenson, *Kasserine Pass,* 145.

346 *Eisenhower and Truscott:* chronology, Chandler, vol. V; Morgan, 112 (*"very tired"*); Truscott, *Command Missions,* 155–56 (*"There was no reason"*); DDE to GCM, Feb. 15, 1943, Chandler, 956 (*"I really believe"*).

The truth would soon: Hazen, 42, 48–54; William R. Betson, "Sidi bou Zid—A Case History of Failure," *Armor,* Nov.–Dec. 1982, 38; Peter Hoffman, *Stauffenberg: A Family History, 1905–1944,* 171; DDE to GCM, Feb. 15, 1943, Chandler, 956; AAR, 60th Inf Regt, Feb. 1943, NARA RG 407, E 427, box 7535.

347 *With Summersby:* Powell, *In Barbary,* 242 (*"barbarians"*); Baedeker, 290 ("Venari lavari"); Truscott, *Command Missions,* 156; Truscott aide official diary, Feb. 1943, LKT Jr. Papers, GCM Lib, box 18, folder 1.

"When you remember me": Miller, *Ike the Soldier,* 477 (*"always to do my duty"*); McKeough and Lockridge, 73 (*picked out "Taps"*).

None Returned

348 *With Anderson's decision:* Liebling, *Mollie & Other Pieces,* 67, 85; Dickson, "G-2 Journal: Algiers to the Elbe," MHI, 43; "History of the 26th Infantry in the Present Struggle," Feb. 15, 1943, MRC-FDM, 8/4–16 (*Madame LaZonga*); "Journal for the 3rd Battalion," 26th Infantry Regt, Feb. 15, 1943, MRC-FDM; Messenger, 50 (*"rather sinister darkness"*); AAR, "Account of B Company Operations at Gafsa," 19th Engineer Regt, n.d., in II Corps records, NARA RG 407, E 427, box 19248 (*wedged six tons of ammonal*); Liddell Hart, ed., *The Rommel Papers,* 400 (*The explosion also demolished*). Ammonal is composed of TNT, ammonium nitrate, and aluminum; guncotton is an ingredient of smokeless gunpowder.

The sprawling air bases: AAFinWWII, 155; AAR, "Report of Operations, XII Air Support Command," Apr. 9, 1943, NARA; Pyle, *Here Is Your War,* 176 (*large wall map*); "From Beer Beach to Kasserine Pass: The Story of the 175th Field Artillery Battalion," n.d., 34th ID, NARA RG 407, E 427, box 9542; Edwin L. Powell, Jr.,

OH, 1982, Lynn L. Sims, CEOH (*"Before I finished"*); *NWAf,* 437; AAR, 805th Tank Destroyer Battalion, "The Tunisian Campaign," Feb. 1943, NARA RG 407, E 427, box 23768; *Tank Destroyer Forces World War II,* 29.

349 *A battlefield bromide*: Charles J. Hoy, "Reconnaissance Lessons from Tunisia," *Cavalry Journal,* Nov.–Dec. 1943, 16–19; Ben Crosby, OH, March 1951, G. F. Howe, SM, MHI (*"badly used up"*); Moschel, statement in "168th Inf Regt. Narrative of Action," n.d., Iowa GSM.

Yet *a mood of benighted*: letter, Robinett to H. Gardiner, Dec. 26, 1967, PMR, GCM Lib, box 5, folder 21; First Army to II Corps, Feb. 14, 1943, 2010 hrs., NARA RG 331, AFHQ micro, AFHQ G-3 Forward, R-100-D, 319.1 (*"As regards action"*).

This hallucination: George F. Hoffman and Donn A. Starry, eds., *Camp Colt to Desert Storm: The History of U.S. Armored Forces,* 151; diary, Feb. 15, 1943, OW, MHI (*"I didn't like it much"*); Howe, *The Battle History of the 1st Armored Division,* 157; Howze, *A Cavalryman's Story,* 41, 59 (*"not contesting the order"*); Catton, *A Stillness at Appomattox,* 211; George L. Durgin, ASEQ, 2nd Bn, 1st Armored Regt, 1st AD, MHI (*"Off we went"*); Robinett, *Armor Command,* 163 (*"saluted and smiled"*).

350 *Half a mile south*: Tobin, *Ernie Pyle's War,* 15 (*"signature belch"*); Pyle, *Here Is Your War,* 167 (*"We are going to kick hell"*); Hains, OH, Apr. 26, 1951, SM, MHI.

The day was dry: Edwin H. Burba, "Battle of Sidi bou Zid," *Field Artillery Journal,* Sept. 1943, 643; Robertson, ASEQ, Co. H, 1st Armored Regt, MHI (*" 'Into the valley of death' "*); author visit, Apr. 2000.

351 *Alger had been told*: "The Attack on Sidi bou Zid," 2nd Bn, 1st Armored Regt, "by officers of the battalion while POWs," n.d., James D. Alger Collection, USMA Arch; "Record of Events," 2nd Bn appendix to AAR, 1st Armored Regt, North African campaign, Nov. 8, 1942–May 9, 1943, NARA RG 407, E 427, box 14916; Howze, "The Battle of Sidi bou Zid"; Howe, *The Battle History of the 1st Armored Division,* 159; *NWAf,* 419–21; war diary, 10th Panzer Div., Feb. 15, 1943, "Kasserine Pass Battles," vol. I, part 2; "G-3 Journal" and message traffic, 1st AD, Feb. 15, 1943, NARA RG 407, E 427, box 14767 (*"Tanks now approaching"* and *"Keep your eye peeled"*); letter, T. Riggs to parents, June 25, 1943, PMR LOC, box 4.

No sooner did: Rame, *Road to Tunis,* 247–48 (*"like a bright diamond"* and *"within a matter of minutes"*); Pyle, *Here Is Your War,* 170 (*"Brown geysers"*).

352 *The killing was confined*: Lavoie et al., "The First Armored Division at Faïd-Kasserine"; Macksey, *Crucible of Power,* 149–153 (*electric blue*); Macksey, *Tank Versus Tank,* performance chart, 107; Ellis, *On the Front Lines,* 117 (*"it takes ten minutes"*); "Record of Events," 2nd Bn appendix to AAR, 1st Armored Regt, North African campaign, Nov. 8, 1942–May 9, 1943, NARA RG 407, E 427, box 14916 (*"None returned"*).

"As dusk began": R. E. McQuillin, comments on draft of *Northwest Africa: Seizing the Initiative in the West,* n.d., NARA RG 319, OCMH, box 228; Balzer, ASEQ, 1st Armored Regt, MHI (*"I found myself"*); Howe, *The Battle History of the 1st Armored Division,* 163–65 (*"We might have walloped"*); *NWAf,* 415; DDE, "Commander-in-Chief's Dispatch, North African Campaign, 1942–1943," 35; Krekeler, ASEQ, 91st Armored FA, MHI; Anderson to DDE, Feb. 15, 1943, 1743 hrs, NARA RG 331 micro, AFHQ G-3 Forward, R-99-D, 319.1 (*"dangerously dispersed"*); Tobin, 82 (*"awful nights"*).

"Sometimes That Is Not Good Enough"

353 *The immolation*: Des Moines Sunday Register, July 18, 1943, 1; AAR, 2nd Bn, 168th Inf Regt, Feb. 3–19, 1943, "Kasserine Pass Battles," vol. I, part 1, CMH; Austin, 87 (*"Message okay"*).

At 10:30 P.M.: AAR, 2nd Bn, 168th Inf Regt, Feb. 15–16, 1943, Iowa GSM *("so close")*; Norland Norgaard, AP dispatch in *Red Oak Express*, Feb. 22, 1943, 1; *Des Moines Sunday Register*, July 18, 1943, 1; "An American Story: The Life and Times of a Midlands Family," *Omaha World-Herald*, Nov. 9, 1997, 1; Hougen, *The Story of the Famous 34th Infantry Division*; NWAf, 424; Eugene L. Daniels, DSC citation, NATOUSA Gen'l. Order 66, July 30, 1943, NARA RG 492.

354 *Drake's ordeal*: AAR account, Marvin E. Williams, 3rd Bn, 168th Inf, "Kasserine Pass Battles," vol. I, part 1, CMH *("Besieged")*; letter, Drake to Ryder, Oct. 4, 1944, Ryder Papers, DDE Lib, box 1; *Tätigkeitsbericht*, 10th Panzer Div., Feb. 16, 1943, NARA RG 319, OCMH, box 225; AAR, "168th Inf Regiment Narrative of Action," Iowa GSM; Blumenson, *Kasserine Pass*, 196; *Kriegstagebuch*, 21st Panzer Div., Feb. 17, 1943, "Kasserine Pass Battles," vol. I, part 2, CMH; Robert L. Owen, ts, Jan. 19, 1993, "Kasserine Pass file," Iowa GSM; AAR accounts, G. C. Line, T. D. Drake, "Kasserine Pass Battles," vol. I, part 1, CMH; "Brief Statement of Lt. Col. John H. Van Vliet, Jr.," in "168th Inf Regt. Narrative of Action," Iowa GSM; AAR, Harry P. Hoffman, 3rd Bn, 168th Inf Regt, Iowa GSM.

355 *A few minutes later*: H. P. Hoffman, G. C. Line, T. D. Drake accounts, "Kasserine Pass Battles," vol. I, part 1, CMH; Van Vliet account, "168th Inf Regt. Narrative of Action," Iowa GSM; Larson, ed., "The History and Contribution to American Democracy of Volunteer 'Citizen Soldiers' of Southwest Iowa, 1930–1945," 57–58; AAR, 3rd Bn, 168th Inf Regt, Feb. 16–17, 1943, Iowa GSM.

"We marched": Bill Roth, "The Longest Days of a G.I.," n.d., Iowa GSM *("Whenever the moon")*; Larson, ed., 61–63; author interview, Dave Berlovich, Oct. 19, 1999 *("You're marked")*.

356 *Dawn caught them*: author interviews, Clifton J. Warner, Ross W. Cline, Oct. 19, 1999; AAR, 3rd Bn, 168th Inf Regt, Feb. 17, 1943, Iowa GSM; Drake, in "Kasserine Pass Battles," vol. I, part 1 *("gained the desired ground")*; William Walling Luttrell, "A Personal Account of the Experiences as a German Prisoner of War," ts, n.d., Iowa GSM *("He took one look")*; Van Vliet account, "168th Inf Regt. Narrative of Action," Iowa GSM; letter, Drake to Ryder, Oct. 4, 1944, Ryder Papers, DDE Lib, box 1 *("You go to hell")*; Blumenson, *Kasserine Pass*, 199; Roth, "The Longest Days of a G.I."; *Kriegstagebuch*, 21st Panzer Div., Feb. 17, 1943, "Kasserine Pass Battles," vol. I, part 2, CMH; NWAf, 424; Larson, ed., 61–63, 66–67; letter, Gerald C. Line to wife, March 2, 1943, Iowa GSM, #1999.25.2 *("sane or insane")*.

357 *Their triumph at Sidi bou Zid*: "Signal Communication in the North African Campaigns," 1945, Historical Section, Special Activities Branch, Office of the Chief Signal Officer, "Tactical Communication in World War II, Part 1," MHI, 166 *("unbelievably low")*; Philipsborn report to Robinett, CCB, 1st AD, Feb. 16, 1943, NARA RG 407, E 427; Howe, "American Signal Intelligence in Northwest Africa and Western Europe," 1980, U.S. Cryptologic History, series IV, WWII, vol. I, NARA RG 457, NSA files, SRH 391, box 114, 29–30; war diary, Panzer Army Afrika, Feb. 16, 1943, "Kasserine Pass Battles," vol. I, part 2, (mislabeled "Fifth Panzer Army"), CMH; *Destruction*, 292; NWAf, 425–26.

Rommel's staff car: Liddell Hart, ed., *The Rommel Papers*, 398–400 *("Hitler! Rommel!")*; Messenger, 50.

359 *Arnim had*: Liddell Hart, ed., *The Rommel Papers*, 400 *("I had never gambled")*; war diary, Panzer Army Afrika, Feb. 18, 1943, "Kasserine Pass Battles," vol. I, part 2, CMH; Irving, *The Trail of the Fox*, 270; Arnim, "Recollections of Tunisia," FMS, C-098, 55; minutes of conference with Kesselring, Arnim, et al., war diary, 10th Panzer Div, Feb. 15, 1943, "Kasserine Pass Battles," vol. I, part 2.

Allied intelligence detected: Hugh Skillen, *Spies of the Airwaves*, 274; Bennett, *Ultra and Mediterranean Strategy*, 206–207.

360 *Kesselring dithered*: war diary, Panzer Army Afrika, Feb. 18, 19, 1943, "Kasserine Pass Battles," vol. I, part 2, CMH; *NWAf*, 440; Liddell Hart, ed., *The Rommel Papers*, 402 (*"appalling and unbelievable"*), 411 (*"old war horse"*).

    Not since A.D. 647: Blumenson, *Kasserine Pass*, 178; Robinett, *Armor Command*, 165–66 (*"indescribable confusion"*); Howze, "The Battle of Sidi bou Zid"; Schrijvers, 63 (*"slapping us around"*).

    Panic built slowly: Martin, 47; Cowdrey, 117 (*"a ghastly word"*); Roberta Love Tayloe, *Combat Nurse: A Journal of World War II*, 39; letter, unsigned, Feb. 23, 1943, MCC, YU (*"Americans never retreat"*).

361 *Night deepened*: letter, unsigned, Feb. 17, 1943, MCC, YU (*"Shooting. Have to go"*); "Account of Carleton S. Coon," NARA RG 226, OSS records, E 99, box 39, folder 8 (*"We didn't want to"*); "Signal Communication in the North African Campaigns," 1945, Historical Section, Special Activities Branch, Office of the Chief Signal Officer, "Tactical Communication in World War II, Part 1," MHI, 100, 164 (*pigeon platoon*).

    At 8:30 P.M.: Howe, *The Battle History of the 1st Armored Division*, 172; Philipsborn report to Robinett, CCB, 1st AD, Feb. 16, 1943, NARA RG 407, E 427; *NWAf*, 432; letter, R. I. Stack to G. F. Howe, March 8, 1951, NARA RG 319, OCMH, box 226; Rame, 253; Ankrum, 221 (*"I'll be damned"*); Robert M. Marsh, ASEQ, ts, notes to G. F. Howe, Sept. 23, 1952, 81st Reconnaissance Bn, 1st AD, MHI (*"We were next"*); Oswald Jett, ASEQ, "As I Saw the War," ts, n.d., 47th Medical Bn, 1st AD, MHI, 287 (*"Get that junk"*).

362 *The fog of war*: McCurtain Scott, OH, March 1976, Gugeler, OW, MHI (*"annoyed and rattled"*); diary, Feb. 16, 1943, OW, MHI; Gugeler, ts, OW, MHI, x-85.

    Ward was further discomposed: CCA, "Narrative of Events from 23 January 1943 to 26 Feb.," NARA RG 407, E 427, 601-CCA-0.3, box 14825; Ben Crosby, OH, March 1951, G. F. Howe, SM, MHI; letter, R. I. Stack to G. F. Howe, March 8, 1951, NARA RG 319, OCMH, box 226 (*"I told General Ward"*); author visit, Apr. 2000; *NWAf*, 432.

    Fredendall immediately: phone memos, Feb. 16–17, 1943, LKT Jr. Papers, GCM Lib, box 9; Truscott, *Command Missions*, 159–62 (*"tanks were fighting"*); Blumenson, *Kasserine Pass*, 191; PMR, "Comments on Kasserine Pass by Martin Blumenson," PMR, MHI, 7; II Corps provost marshal journal, Feb. 19, 1943, NARA RG 407, E 427, box 3126.

363 *This farrago*: *Kriegstagebuch*, 21st Panzer Div., Feb. 16–17, 1943, "Kasserine Pass Battles," vol. I, part 2, CMH; Howe, *The Battle History of the 1st Armored Division*, 172–73; war diary, 10th Panzer Div., Feb. 17, 1943, "Kasserine Pass Battles," vol. I, part 2, CMH.

    "Move the big elephants": Robinett, *Armor Command*, 165–69 (*"When things are going badly"*); Robinett, "The Axis Offensive in Central Tunisia," lecture, n.d., PMR, LOC MS Div.

    In truth: Blumenson, *Kasserine Pass*, 192 (*"Everything is going badly"*); phone transcript, Feb. 17, 1943, 1055 hrs., LKT Jr. Papers, GCM Lib, box 9 (*"I have had"*).

364 *Ward and Robinett braced*: L. C. Gates, *The History of the 10th Foot, 1919–1950*, 135; letter, T. Riggs to parents, June 25, 1943, PMR, LOC MS Div, box 4 (*"We stood in the cactus"*).

365 *Fifteen minutes*: *Tank Destroyer Forces World War II*, 27 (*"Everybody was throwing"*); Gardiner, "We Fought at Kasserine," 8 (*"I counted thirty-five"*); Robinett, *Armor Command*, 167–75 (*"let them have it!"*); Robinett, "The Axis Offensive in Central Tunisia," lecture; n.d.; Howe, *The Battle History of the 1st Armored Division*, 175–79; *NWAf*, 434–36; CCB log, Feb. 17, 1943, NARA RG 407, E 427, 601-CCB-0.3, box 14825.

"*War is cruelty*": Foote, *The Civil War*, vol. III, 602; Rame, 252, 254 (*"The night was heavy"*); Tobin, 82 (*"You need feel"*).

"This Place Is Too Hot"

366 *Two formidable sentinels*: author visits, Sept. 1996 and Apr. 2000; *NWAf*, 348, 446 (*"gigantic, crudely corrugated"*).

367 *Kasserine Pass is not impregnable*: *NWAf*, 446 (*"offers such advantages"*); phone transcript, Feb. 17, 1943, 1340 hrs. (*"I am holding"*), and phone memo, Rooks to Truscott, Feb. 18, 1943, LKT Jr. Papers, GCM Lib, box 9; AAR, 19th Engineers, March 8, 1943, NARA RG 407, E 427, box 19248; Beck et al., 96–98 (*failed to complete*); Conway, SOOHP, MHI (*"trying to draw a line"*).

368 *Just beyond*: *NWAf*, 440–42, 453; Hoffman, *Stauffenberg*, 171; war diary, Panzer Army Afrika, Feb. 19, 1943, "Kasserine Pass Battles," vol. I, part 2; Kesselring, *Memoirs*, 151; *Destruction*, 295.

369 *Even at his distant remove*: "History of the 26th Infantry in the Present Struggle," MRC FDM, 8/14–16 (*"pull a Stonewall Jackson"*); phone transcript, Feb. 18, 1943, 1022 hrs., LKT Jr. Papers, GCM Lib, box 9; Heller and Stofft, eds., 255–57 (*hold back more than 200*); letter, Stark to OW, Jan. 28, 1951, OW, MHI; "Historical Record of the 19th Engineer Regiment," Oct. 1942–Oct. 1943, NARA RG 407, E 427, box 19248; AAR, 2nd Bn, 19th Engineers, RG 407, box 19248; author interview, Hans von Luck, May 1994, Hamburg; Hans von Luck, *Panzer Commander*, 113; war diary, Afrika Korps, Feb. 19, 1943, "Kasserine Pass Battles," vol. I, part 2.

370 *And, soon, on the right*: Davis, "The Battle of Kasserine Pass," 22; "History of the 26th Infantry in the Present Struggle," MRC FDM, 8/19; *NWAf*, 451.

  Shadows swallowed: memo, Charles A. L. Dunphie, forwarded to G. F. Howe from Cabinet Office historical section, Sept. 11, 1951, NARA RG 319, OCMH, box 229 (*"out of his depth"*); "Report of Operations," II Corps, May 2, 1943, "Kasserine Pass Battles," vol. 1, part 2, CMH (*"well in hand"*); letter, Stark to OW, Jan. 28, 1951, OW, MHI (*"that blockhead"*); "History of the 26th Infantry," MRC FDM, 8/21.

371 *Even as this puff*: diary, Charles M. Thomas, Co. C, 19th Engineers, possession of Roger Cirillo (*"The worst of it all"*); letter, George F. Hertz, published in *Iowa City Daily Iowan*, May 19, 1943, MCC, YU; Ellis, *On the Front Lines*, 89 (*"women sobbing"*).

  Night fever spread: AAR, 19th Engineers, March 8, 1943, NARA RG 407, E 427, box 19248 (*"A considerable number of men"*); "History of the 26th Infantry," MRC FDM, 8/22; *NWAf*, 452; "Historical Record of the 19th Engineer Regiment," Oct. 1942–Oct. 1943, NARA RG 407, box 19248; II Corps provost marshal journal, report from William A. Seitz, Co. A, 26th Inf, n.d., NARA RG 407, E 427, box 3126 (*"In some instances"*).

  Bad as the bad night: *NWAf*, 454–55; Hoffman, *Stauffenberg*, 171.

372 *The American collapse*: "History of the 26th Infantry," MRC FDM, 8/24–25; diary, C. M. Thomas, possession of Roger Cirillo (*"Forget about"*); Blumenson, *Kasserine Pass*, 249–52; "Historical Record of the 19th Engineer Regiment," Oct. 1942–Oct. 1943, NARA RG 407, E 427, box 19248 (*"This place is too hot"*).

  The "uncoordinated withdrawal": AAR, 19th Engineer Regt, March 8, 1943, NARA RG 407, E 427, box 19248; "History of the 26th Infantry," MRC FDM, 8/22–25 (*French gunners* and *"action shots"* and *"Fight to the last man"*); Blumenson, *Kasserine Pass*, 255 (*Casualties just among infantrymen*); *NWAf*, 455; Conway, SOOHP, MHI (*Washington on horseback*); letter, Stark to OW, Jan. 28, 1951, OW, MHI (*"We had to crawl"*).

"Order, Counter-order, and Disorder"

373 *Demolitionists laid*: Rame, 263 (*slabs of guncotton*); McNamara, 57; "Tébessa Tableaux," ts; n.d., Samuel L. Meyers Papers, MHI (*slaughtering every chicken*).
As always in the great clash: letter, TR to Eleanor, Feb. 24, 1943, TR, LOC; Renehan, 234; Roosevelt, *Day Before Yesterday*, 441.
Little buoyancy: Mason, "Reminiscences and Anecdotes of World War II," MRC FDM (*"head in hands"*); *These Are the Generals*, 227 (*"I like that man"*); James R. Webb, "First Waltz with Rommel," ts, n.d., James R. Webb Papers, DDE Lib, box 1 (*"If I were back home"*); Michael Carver, ed., *The War Lords: Military Commanders of the Twentieth Century*, 603 (*"I saw his attitude change"*); Blumenson, *Kasserine Pass*, 280.

374 *Fredendall repaired*: "Diary Covering the Activities of General Fredendall and Supporting Players, Dec. '42-March '43," James R. Webb Collection, DDE Lib (*"Dabney, open up the bottle"*); Clift Andrus, notes on Omar Bradley's *A Soldier's Story*, n.d., MRC FDM (*"Dinner!"*).
"I'm going to be": Hal Boyle, "Brass Seen at Fault at Kasserine Pass," Associated Press, Feb. 11, 1948, NARA RG 319, OCMH, box 225; Fredendall to DDE, Feb. 19, 1943, DDE Lib, PP-pres, box 42 (*"Ward appears tired"*).

375 *While Eisenhower pondered*: NWAf, 457–58; Robinett, *Armor Command*, 175–77; Robinett, "The Axis Offensive in Central Tunisia, Feb. 1943," lecture; Robinett, letter to G. F. Howe, March 4, 1952, PMR, LOC MS Div., box 4; letter, Philipsborn to G. F. Howe, Feb. 18, 1952, PMR, LOC MS Div., box 4 (*"There is no use"*); Dunphie memo, forwarded to G. F. Howe from Cabinet Office historical section, Sept. 11, 1951, NARA RG 319, OCMH, box 229; Porter, SOOHP, MHI (*"Get hold"*); letter, F.A.V. Copland-Griffiths to A. F. Smith, March 19, 1943, 1st Guards Bde, PRO WO 175/186 (*"the most perfect example"*).
Into the muddle: Alexander, "The African Campaign from El Alamein to Tunis," 869; DDE to Alexander, Feb. 7, 1943, NARA RG 331, AFHQ micro, R-5-C; Blaxland, 160; Alexander to DDE, Feb. 19, 1943, 1920 hrs., Alexander files, DDE Lib, box 3, folder 8; Alexander to Montgomery, Feb. 22, 1943, in Stephen Brooks, ed., *Montgomery and the Eighth Army*, 152 (*"very shocked"*).

376 *He cut a dashing*: Austin, 105; Carver, ed., *The War Lords*, 332–37 (*"natural good manners"* and *"able more than clever"*); Boatner, 4–5; Doherty, *Irish Generals*, 32, 36 (*"At the worst crises"*), 38 (*Churchill's favorite*); D'Este, *Eisenhower: A Soldier's Life*, 650 (mss) (*"Our position is catastrophic"*); Rupert Clarke, *With Alex at War*, xii–xiii; Brian Holden Reid, in John Keegan, ed., *Churchill's Generals*, 105 (*"archetypal Edwardian hero"*).
Some thought him stupid: Reid, in Keegan, ed., *Churchill's Generals*, 104 (*"Wellington without the wit"*), 108 (*"empty vessel"*), 109 (*"Intellect was not"*); Rolf, 25; Clarke, *With Alex at War*, xii (*tap dancing*); Dominick Graham and Shelford Bidwell, *Tug of War: The Battle for Italy, 1943–1945*, 36 (*"the campaigns of Belisarius"*).

377 *Brilliantly slow*: Alexander, OH, n.d., G. F. Howe, SM, MHI (*"solid soldier"* and *"allowing the Germans"*); Hamilton, 166 (*"The poor body"*); *Destruction*, 304 (*"Real fault"* and *"My Main anxiety"*); "Reminiscences of Hanson Weightman Baldwin," OH, 1976, John T. Mason, Jr., USNI OHD (*"old school tie"*); Reid, in Keegan, ed., 114 (*"quite useless"*).

378 *First, Rommel's northern thrust*: war diary, 10th Panzer Div., Feb. 19, 1943, "Kasserine Pass Battles," vol. I, part 2, CMH; Benjamin Caffey, OH, Feb. 1950, G. F. Howe, SM, MHI; NWAf, 452–53; Johnson, *One More Hill*, 37 (*"If they attack*

us"); Howard and Sparrow, 119; "18th Infantry, Draft Regimental Wartime History," Stanhope Mason Collection, MRC FDM; Camp, ed., 23 (*"taking shoe boxes"*).

A renewed assault: author interview, Clem Miller, Jan. 4, 2000; author interviews, Edward Boehm, Nov. 26, 1999, and Jan. 4, 2000; Edward Boehm, "My Autobiography in WWII," ts, 1997, possession of Roger Cirillo, 36; "The Fragrance of Spring Was Heavy in the Air," account of 185th FA Bn, *Trail Tales*, Boone County (Iowa) Historical Society, No. 35, 1979, 37; Vernon Hohenberger, "Retracing My Footsteps in World War II," ts, n.d., Iowa GSM, 37; "The Tunisian Campaign, 34th Division," Iowa GSM, 5.

Checked on the right: AAR, 10th Bn, The Rifle Brigade, PRO, WO 175/518; *Destruction*, 297; Davis, "The Battle of Kasserine Pass," 22 (*"like caterpillars dropping"*); *The Rifle Brigade in the Second World War, 1939–1945*, 217; Austin, 90; D.G.A., "With Tanks to Tunis," *Blackwoods*, June 1945, 399 (*"We were forced"* and *"as hard as stiff legs"*); ffrench Blake, 118.

379 *Rommel again held*: Liddell Hart, ed., *The Rommel Papers*, 405; *NWAf*, 458, 460; Robinett, "Comments on *Kasserine Pass* by Martin Blumenson," PMR, MHI, 13, 16.

A reconnaissance report: author visit, Apr. 2000; *NWAf*, 461.

The scouts were wrong: Stanhope Mason and F. W. Gibb, OH, Apr. 26, 1951, G. F. Howe, SM, MHI; letter, Joseph T. Dawson to brother, Feb. 21, 1943, Dawson Collection, MRC FDM (*"this is our sector"*); Hazen, 104; Steven Clay, *Blood and Sacrifice: The History of the 16th Infantry Regiment from the Civil War Through the Gulf War*, 33 (mss); Edwin L. Powell, Jr., OH, 1982, Lynn L. Sims, CEOH, 130; Robinett, *Armor Command*, 181; letter, Philipsborn to G. F. Howe, Feb. 18, 1953, with PMR comments, PMR, LOC MS Div, box 4 (*"simply written on the ground"*).

380 *Anderson on this very Saturday*: "Personal Diary of Lt. Gen. C. W. Allfrey, the Tunisian Campaign (with 5 Corps)," Feb. 21, 23, 1943, Allfrey Collection, LHC (*"American fighting value"*); Haggerty, "A History of the Ranger Battalions in World War II," Ph.D. diss, 121 (*"a hairy-chested commander"*); Altieri, *The Spearheaders*, 236 (*"Onward we stagger"*).

The tanks came: Robinett, *Armor Command*, 183; *NWAf*, 462–64; Howe, *Battle History of the 1st Armored Division*, 191; "Combat Command B, Operations Report, Bahiret Foussana Valley, 20–25 February, 1943," "Kasserine Pass Battles," vol. I, part 2, CMH; II Corps, "report of operations," May 2, 1943, "Kasserine Pass Battles," vol. I, part 2, CMH; Clay, 35 (mss); Macksey, *Crucible of Power*, 166.

Repulsed on the right: *NWAf*, 463–64; Robinett, "The Axis Offensive in Central Tunisia, Feb. 1943," lecture, LOC MS Div.

Undeterred, two grenadier battalions: Robinett, *Armor Command*, 185; Andrus, notes on Omar Bradley's *A Soldier's Story*, n.d., MRC FDM; Clay, 35 (mss); Robinett, "The Axis Offensive in Central Tunisia, Feb. 1943," lecture, LOC; Robinett, "Comments on *Kasserine Pass* by Martin Blumenson," PMR, MHI, 13; Blumenson, *Kasserine Pass*, 279; Rolf, 139 (*Panic Sunday*).

381 *Yet something had hardened*: Andrus, notes on Omar Bradley's *A Soldier's Story*, n.d., MRC FDM (*"air was full"* and *"An artilleryman's dream"*); Andrus biographical file, compiled by Albert H. Smith, MHI (*"most skillful and practical"*).

A single battalion: "Combat Command B, Operations Report, Bahiret Foussana Valley, 20–25 February, 1943," "Kasserine Pass Battles," vol. I, part 2, CMH; Gardiner, "We Fought at Kasserine," 8 (*"A column of prisoners"*); Robinett, *Armor Command*, 187 (*"captured a whole flock"*).

"Lay Roughly on the Tanks"

382 *As this action in the west*: Messenger, 54; Irving, *The Trail of the Fox,* 274 (*"He suddenly"*).

    By midafternoon all euphoria: AAR, 2nd Bn, 19th Engineers, May 20, 1943, NARA RG 407, E 427, box 19248; Liddell Hart, ed., *The Rommel Papers,* 405 (*"They did not seem"*); 10th Panzer Div. intelligence report, "Re: the advance of the 10th Panzer Division through the Faïd Pass to Thala," Feb. 25, 1943, NARA RG 319, OCMH, box 225; Hoffman, *Stauffenberg,* 172.

    The British had: Cameron Nicholson, "The Battle of Kasserine, February 1943," Nicholson collection, IWM, micro DS/MISC 7, 4 (*"no full-blooded orders"* and *"I found it difficult"*); Dunphie memo, forwarded to G. F. Howe from Cabinet Office historical section, Sept. 11, 1951, NARA RG 319, OCMH, box 229; memo, S. L. Irwin to P. M. Robinett, June 23, 1949, NARA RG 319, OCMH, box 229 (*"usual story"*); Nigel Nicholson, *Alex: The Life of Field Marshal Earl Alexander of Tunis,* 176 (*"He's right behind us"*).

383 *Absent full-blooded orders*: Dunphie memo; Blaxland, 163 (*"beautiful to watch"*); ffrench Blake, 119; *NWAf,* 465; D.G.A., "With Tanks to Tunis," 399 (*"erect in his scout car"*).

    Dunphie was a gunner: Dunphie memo; Nicholson, *Alex,* 176 (*"empty but heavy"*); author visit, Apr. 2000; Herman Walter Wright Lange, "Rommel at Thala," *Military Review,* Sept. 1961, 72.

    Almost on Dunphie's heels: war diary, 2/5 Leicestershire Regiment, Feb. 1943, PRO WO 175/513; Blaxland, 163; C. Nicholson, "The Battle of Kasserine"; ffrench Blake, 119; Hastings, 219 (*"Keep away"*); Macksey, *Crucible of Power,* 169; *Tätigkeitbericht,* 10th Panzer Div., Feb. 21, 1943, NARA RG 319, OCMH, box 225.

384 *Two thousand yards*: D.G.A., "With Tanks to Tunis" (*"German tracers"*); Dunphie memo (*"tank fight in the dark"*); AAR, F Battery, 12 (HAC) Regt, RHA, appendix C, and "The Battle of Thala (North Africa) with F Bty 12th (HAC) Regt," RHA, appendix E (*"Lay roughly"*), and war diary, "Operations of Nickforce, 20–23 Feb. 1943," appendix D, all in Nicholson collection, micro, DS/MISC 7, IWM; Irwin memo to Robinett, June 23, 1949; war diary, 2/5 Leicestershire Regiment, Feb. 1943, PRO WO 175/513; Hastings, 219 (*"alarms were many"*); Watson, 143; Heller and Stofft, eds., 259; Blumenson, *Kasserine Pass,* 270, 275.

385 *Dawn came*: Dunphie memo (*"Irwin himself"*); memo, Irwin to Robinett, June 23, 1949 (*"extremely critical"*); Irwin, OH, Jan. 1950, G. F. Howe, SM, MHI; AAR, "Thala Engagement, 21–24 Feb. 1943," 9th ID artillery, n.d., NARA RG 407, E 427, box 7424; AAR, 60th FA, n.d., NARA RG 407, E 427, box 7471; Phillips, *Sedjenane: The Pay-off Battle,* 28; Phillips, *The Making of a Professional: Manton S. Eddy, USA,* 91; William C. Westmoreland, *A Soldier Reports,* 20.

    It served: Blumenson, *Kasserine Pass,* 275; Austin, 91 (*"I'm sorry"*).

    The field marshal had shot: *NWAf,* 469; Liddell Hart, ed., *The Rommel Papers,* 406–407.

    True to character: Kesselring, "The Events in Tunisia," 1949, FMS, #D-066, MHI, 5–10; AAR, Panzer Army Africa, Feb. 22, 1943, NARA RG 319, OCMH, box 225 (*It appears futile*); Watson, 169; Kesselring, "The War in the Mediterranean, Part II, The Fighting in Tunisia and Tripolitania," FMS, #T-3 P1, 38.

386 *Thala would prove*: "Narrative of Events, Thala Engagement, 21–24 Feb. 1943," 9th ID artillery, March 4, 1943, "Kasserine Pass Battles," vol. I, part 1, CMH; Robinett, "Comments on *Kasserine Pass,*" PMR, MHI (*"toughest day"*); Austin, 93 (*"Gilbert and Sullivan"*); Kesselring, "Final Commentaries on the Campaign in North Africa," FMS, #C-075, MHI, appendix, 14; AAR, Panzer Army Africa, Feb. 23,

1943, NARA RG 319, OCMH, box 225 (*"The enemy follows"*); Hoffman, 172; Liddell Hart, ed., 408 (*"I've stood up"*).

387 *On February 22*: DDE to Frendendall, Feb. 22, 1943, Chandler, 980 (*"every confidence"*); Eisenhower, *Crusade in Europe*, 145 (*"perfectly safe"*); Hinsley, *British Intelligence in the Second World War*, vol. II, 592–93; Howe, "American Signal Intelligence in Northwest Africa," U.S. Cryptologic History, series IV, vol. 1, NARA RG 457, NSA files, SRH 391, box 114, 29–30; memo, B. A. Dixon, II Corps G-2, Apr. 19, 1943, NARA RG 407, E 427, box 3163 (*"inability of most Arabs"*).

   Several more convoluted: AAR, 1st AD, "Report of Operations, Bahiret Foussana Valley," Feb. 23, 1943, "Kasserine Pass Battles," vol. I, part 2, CMH; Blumenson, *Kasserine Pass*, 282; Robinett, "Comments on *Kasserine Pass*," PMR, MHI, 15; Gugeler, x-104; DDE to Fredendall, Feb. 22, 1943, Chandler, 982; Harmon, *Combat Commander*, 50 (*"cobra without"*), 112 (*"make up your mind"*), 116 (*"Nobody goes back"*); "Report of Gen. Harmon on taking command II Corps as deputy," n.d., LKT Jr. Papers, GCM Lib, box 9; C. Nicholson, "The Battle of Kasserine," 9 (*"to fight this battle out"*); Harmon, OH, Sept. 1952, G. F. Howe, SM, MHI (*Concluding that the man* and *"a fucking bloody nose"*).

388 *In a Thala cellar*: letter, F.A.V. Copland-Griffiths to A. F. Smith, March 19, 1943, 1st Guards Bde, PRO WO 175/186 (*"The Germans have gone!"*); C. Nicholson, "The Battle of Kasserine," 9 (*"Man cannot tell"*); war diary, "Operations of Nickforce," Feb. 23, 1943, 1130 hrs (*"not unduly"*).

389 *"Our follow-up was slow"*: Harmon, OH, Sept. 1952, G. F. Howe, SM, MHI; Harmon, *Combat Commander*, 50, 111–16; Nicholson, "The Battle of Kasserine," 9; Robinett, "Comments on *Kasserine Pass* by Martin Blumenson," PMR, MHI, 15; Hatfield diary, Feb. 23, 1943, OW, MHI (*"feels very low"*).

   Light snow fell: Robinett, *Armor Command*, 195 (*"cluttered with wrecked"*); Parris and Russell, 293, 296 (*chewing gum*); diary, C. M. Thomas; "Personal Diary of Lt. Gen. C. W. Allfrey," Feb. 23, 1943 (*orders were issued*); AAR, "The Tunisian Campaign, 34th Division," 5.

   Even if Allied troops: "G-2 Report on Tunisian Campaign," 34th ID, June 12, 1943, Iowa GSM; "Report of Engineer Operations, II Corps, 15 March to 10 April 1943," NARA RG 338, box 147; letter, F.A.V. Copland-Griffiths to A. F. Smith, March 19, 1943, 1st Guards Bde, PRO WO 175/186 (*"vehicles were blowing up"*); Hendricks, "A Time of Testing: U.S. Army Engineers in the Tunisian Campaign of World War II," lecture, 7; Ralph Ingersoll, *The Battle Is the Pay-off*, 112 (*"like caddies"*); Howze, *A Cavalryman's Story*, 61; Beck et al., 106; Charles S. Schwartz, "The Field Operations of a Maintenance Battalion," ts, n.d., ASEQ, in papers of W. L. Rossie, 1st AD, MHI.

   A precise tally: Heller and Stofft, eds., 261; *NWAf*, 477–78; "Office, Division Inspector, 1st AD," Feb. 23, 1943; *Destruction*, 302; DDE to GCM, Feb. 24, 1943, Chandler, 984 (*"not a child's game"*).

390 *"The proud and cocky"*: *Three Years*, 268; *NWAf*, 479; Ellis, *Brute Force*, 253; Gugeler, x-99; Robinett, "Comments on *Kasserine Pass*," 14 (*"one would have to search"*).

391 *That error could be laid*: *Three Years*, 265 (*"full responsibility"*); Eisenhower, *Crusade in Europe*, 146 (*"had I been willing"*).

   There were other: *Three Years*, 244; DDE to GCM, Feb. 24, 1943, Chandler, 984 (*expressed surprise*); Eisenhower, *Crusade in Europe*, 148; Chandler, 958n (*"I am disturbed"*).

   Certainly he had done: DDE to L. R. Fredendall, Feb. 22, 1943, Chandler, 981; DDE to Churchill, Feb. 17, 1943, Chandler, 960 (*"We must be prepared"*); DDE to J.S.D. Eisenhower, Feb. 19, 1943, Chandler, 965 (*"It is possible"*).

392 *Fratricide flourished*: Semmens, "The Hammer of Hell," 122; Paul L. Williams, "Report of Operations, XII Air Support Campaign," Apr. 9, 1943; Eisenhower, *Crusade in Europe*, 145; Richard G. Davis, *Carl A. Spaatz and the Air War in Europe*, 199. *the hammer of typewriters*: Ingersoll, 31.

CHAPTER 10:
THE WORLD WE KNEW IS A LONG TIME DEAD
Vigil in Red Oak

395 *Southwest Iowa's second winter*: Red Oak (Iowa) *Express*, Villisca (Iowa) *Review, Clarinda* (Iowa) *Herald-Journal, Council Bluffs Nonpareil*, Feb.–Apr. 1943; Larson, ed., "The History and Contribution to American Democracy of Volunteer 'Citizen Soldiers' of Southwest Iowa, 1930–1945," 43; author visit, southwest Iowa, Oct. 1999; "Red Oak, Iowa, Has 23 Boys Missing in Action in North Africa," *Life*, May 3, 1943, 26; Milton Lehman, "Red Oak Hasn't Forgotten," *Saturday Evening Post*, Aug. 17, 1946, 14 (*American Legion Park* and *female drivers* and "*They kind of dreaded me*"); 168th Infantry Publications," Iowa GSM.

397 *When letters began arriving*: Red Oak (Iowa) *Express*, Apr. 26, 1943 ("*Send the food parcel first*"); Villisca (Iowa) *Review*, March 18, 1943 ("*I lost everything*"); memo, Jan. 2, 1945, and repatriated POW statements, Apr. 1945, NARA RG 153, Office of the JAG, box 2, files 3-2 and 3-8; letter, Drake to Ryder, Oct. 4, 1944, Ryder Papers, DDE Lib; Lehman, "Red Oak Hasn't Forgotten" (*Ko-z-Aire Furnace Company* and *she set gold stars*); Larson, ed., 43 ("*Red Oak came as close*").

"We Know There'll Be Troubles of Every Sort"

399 *The Carthaginians of antiquity*: Powell, *In Barbary*, 64; DDE to GCM, Feb. 21, 1943, Chandler, 971 ("*this affair*"); Jordan, 201; E. Hughes diary, March 6, 1943, "Allied High Command," Irving collection, MHI, reel 5 ("*pretty discouraging*").
   First to go: E. A. Mockler-Ferryman, ts, n.d., LHC, 129–35 ("*If a man is not wanted*"); DDE to Brooke, Feb. 20, 1943, Chandler, 969 ("*broader insight*"); "History of the 26th Infantry in the Present Struggle," 9/3, MRC FDM, box 301; Robinett, "The Axis Offensive in Central Tunisia, Feb. 1943," lecture ("*professional graveyard*"); Alexander, OH, G. F. Howe, SM, MHI ("*watch him*").
   Orlando Ward also awaited: diary, March 4, 1943, OW, MHI; Butcher diary, DDE Lib, A-250 (*voicing regret*); DDE to Fredendall, Feb. 20 and March 2, 1943, Chandler, 969 and 1002; Persons, 2; Harmon, *Combat Commander*, 120 ("*no damned good*"); Harmon, OH, Sept. 1952, G. F. Howe, SM, MHI ("*common, low*"); Blumenson, ed., *The Patton Papers, 1940–1945*, 177 ("*coward*"), 181; Truscott, *Command Missions*, 173; Alexander, OH, SM, MHI ("*I'm sure*").

400 *A final verdict came*: Bradley, *A Soldier's Story*, 42; Hansen, 3/70; letter, Harmon to G. F. Howe, Oct. 16, 1952, NARA RG 319, OCMH (*soft landing*); DDE to GCM, March 3 and 4, 1943, Chandler, 1006–1007; "Diary covering the activities of Gen. Fredendall," James R. Webb Collection, DDE Lib ("*something wrong*"); Rolf, 165 ("*Glory be*"); W. B. Smith, OH, May 12, 1947, G. F. Howe, SM, MHI ("*a good colonel*").
   Patton was hunting boar: Garrison H. Davidson, OH, 1980, John T. Greenwood, CEOH, 189; DDE to GCM, March 11, 1943, Chandler, 1022; memo, DDE to GSP Jr., March 6, 1943, Chandler, 1010; Hatch, 149; *Three Years*, 273 ("*tears came to his eyes*" and "*like the devil*").

401 *"With sirens shrieking"*: Bradley, *A Soldier's Story,* 43; Gugeler, x-127 (*"pic-turesque"*); Skillen, 284 (*"scares the shit"*).

   Both reactions pleased him: Paul Wanke, "American Military Psychiatry and Its Role Among Ground Forces in World War II," *Journal of Military History,* Jan. 1999, 141; Robinett, *Armor Command,* 204; observer report, team #3, n.d., NARA RG 165, Director of Plans and Ops, corr, box 1229 (*"can sweat"*); Blumenson, *Patton,* 183.

   They soon developed: Ingersoll, 20, 28; Thomas E. Hannum, "The Thirty Years of Army Experience," ts, n.d., ASEQ, 91st Armored FA, 1st AD, MHI; Downing, 188; Philip G. Cochran, OH, 1975, USAF HRC, 88 (*"don't even have underwear"*); Josowitz, *An Informal History of the 601st Tank Destroyer Battalion*; Bradley, *A Soldier's Story,* 44.

402 *Determined and energetic*: Blumenson, *Patton,* 183; Mason, "Reminiscences and Anecdotes of World War II," ts, 1988, MRC FDM, 64–67, 130–31 (*"yellow-bellies"*); Carter, "Carter's War," CEOH, VI-18; Gardiner, ts, USMA Arch, 137; W.R.C. Penney, ts, n.d., LHC (*"smart, blasphemous"*); Foote, vol. 3, 395 (*"stern open air"*); Bradley and Blair, *A General's Life,* 99 (*"strangest duck"*).

   Morale improved: memo to AFHQ chief engineer, March 9, 1943, NARA, AFHQ micro, R-90-F; Robert John Rogers, "A Study of Leadership in the First Infantry Division During World War II," master's thesis, 1965, Fort Leavenworth, 21 (*"Watch us run"*); TR to Eleanor, March 2, 6, 11, and 20, 1943, TR, LOC, box 9.

403 *Soldiers were viewed*: Robert R. Palmer et al., *The Procurement and Training of Ground Combat Troops,* 170, 175, 181–83 (*"as one would buy"*); Kreidberg and Henry, 647; letter, J. L. Devers to L. J. McNair, Feb. 4, 1944, NARA RG 165, Director of Plans and Ops, corr, box 1230; Taggart, ed., 41; Houston, 145; Harmon, "Notes on Combat Experience During the Tunisian and African Campaigns," in "Kasserine Pass Battles," vol. II, part 3; report, Walton H. Walker, June 29, 1943, NARA 165, E 418, box 1229 (*"sacks of wheat"*); "Activities of the G-1 Section During the Tunisian Campaign," 34th ID, n.d., Iowa GSM; memo, from 5th Replacement Bn to II Corps, Apr. 12, 1943, NARA RG 492, MTO, special staff, box 1043; T. J. Camp, ed., 15; report #42, March 13, 1943, NARA RG 337, Observer Reports, box 52; "Lessons of the Tunisian Campaign, 1942–3, British Forces," n.d., NARA RG 492, MTOUSA, box 56.

404 *No less worrisome*: Russell Hill, *Desert Conquest,* 235 (*"a bit windy"*); Donald Vining, ed., *American Diaries of World War II,* 53; Cowdrey, 137–44; Grinker and Spiegel, 234; DDE to GSP Jr., Apr. 12, 1943, NARA RG 94, II Corps, box 3161 (*"increasing number"*).

   First known as shell shock: "Casualties, Wounded, and Wounds, 1946–7," G-3 Section, Army Field Forces, NARA RG 337, file 704, series 10, box 46 (*"the ostrich attitude"*); Wanke, 127–46; Doubler, 243–44; McManus, 67 (*"beat his head"*); Grinker and Spiegel, 14–16, 31, 38, 59, 63, 71, 232–34; Philip G. Cochran, OH, USAF HRC, 106 (*"Am I becoming uncourageous?"*).

406 *Visiting a field hospital*: Parris and Russell, 299.

"One Needs Luck in War"

406 *Dawn was just*: Daniell, *The Royal Hampshire Regiment,* vol. 3, 103–105; "155th Field Battery at Béja," *Field Artillery Journal.*

   Eight similar attacks: NWAf, 502–509 (*"nincompoops"*); *Destruction,* 327–28; Ray, 41; Rommel, *Krieg Ohne Hass,* 363–64; McCurtain Scott, OH, March 1976, R. Gugeler, OW, MHI (*"too many generals"*).

407 *not the nincompoops*: Daniell, *History of the East Surrey Regiment,* vol. 4, 161; Austin, 97–98; Forty, *Tank Action: From the Great War to the Gulf,* 119; Parris and Russell, 268; Kühn, *Rommel in the Desert,* 196; Kleine and Kühn, *Tiger: The History of a Legendary Weapon, 1942–1945; Destruction,* 328n (*"Tank Killer"*).

The Germans fared: NWAf, 505; *Destruction,* 327; Alexander, "The African Campaign from El Alamein to Tunis," 870–71 (*"almost inevitable"*); Anderson, "Operations in North West Africa."

Cruel mountain fighting: Parris and Russell, 264–65; Gates, 138–43; R. Priestly, ts, n.d., 2nd Bn, Para Regt, IWM, 83/24/1; Perrett, *At All Costs,* 159; NWAf, 508; Anderson, "Operations in North West Africa" (*"not a happy period"*).

408 *Rommel was still seething*: Liddell Hart, ed., *The Rommel Papers,* 414–16; Irving, *The Trail of the Fox,* 280–84 (*"What a colony"*).

Yes, this would have made: Liddell Hart, ed., *The Rommel Papers,* 414 (*"end of the army"*); Macksey, *Tank Versus Tank,* 119 (*kicked a soccer ball*); NWAf, 514–19; *Destruction,* 322–26.

409 *But Ultra decrypts*: Hinsley, *British Intelligence in the Second World War,* vol. 2, 283; Bennett, *Ultra and Mediterranean Strategy,* 210, 379.

Thick mist lingering: Blaxland, 189; Rolf, 162; Irving, 282; *Destruction,* 325 (*"wandered rather vaguely"*); D. C. Quilter, ed., *"No Dishonorable Name,"* 159 (*"A great many"*); Ian C. Cameron, *History of the Argyll & Sutherland Highlanders 7th Battalion,* 80 (*"wonderful shoot"*); Hamilton, 169 (*"I shall write letters"*).

410 *"the first perfect battle"*: Clifford, 400; letter, A.J.A. Weir to parents, June 1943, IWM, 67/258/1 (*"larger than a card table"*); Bernard Ireland, *The War in the Mediterranean, 1940–1943,* 198; Kesselring, *Memoirs,* 152; Greiner diary, March 10, 1943, NARA RG 319, OCMH, box 225; Liddell Hart, ed., *The Rommel Papers,* 415–16 (*"great gloom"*).

If hardly unexpected: Liddell Hart, ed., 416 (*"plain suicide"*), 422; Irving, *The Trail of the Fox,* 283 (*"During the drive"* and *"whole thing stinks"*), 288 (*"fallen from grace"*); Hans von Luck, *Panzer Commander,* 114; author interview, Hans von Luck, Hamburg, May 1994; Westphal, 127 (*"gradually consumed"*); Kesselring, "The War in the Mediterranean, Part II, The Fighting in Tunisia and Tripolitania," 42 (*"last trump"*); Ronald Lewin, *Rommel as Military Commander,* 209 (*"not quite normal"*); Rommel to Arnim, March 12, 1943, NARA RG 319, OCMH, box 226.

411 *"I have observed"*: DDE to J.S.D. Eisenhower, March 12, 1943, Chandler, 1028.

412 *After months of sailing*: Chandler, 961n (*"selflessness of character"*); *Three Years,* 280 (*"Tell Ike"*).

"I have caught up": DDE to GCM, Alexander et al., Chandler, 860, 1020, 1049, 1052, 1018.

He was busier: DDE to Edgar Eisenhower, GCM, et al., Chandler, 1018, 1024, 1009, 1050, 862; Jordan, 197 (*"Eisenhower's genius"*).

413 *More and more*: DDE to GCM, et al., Chandler, 1033, 1036, 860.

Rommel famously observed: Martin Van Creveld, *Supplying War,* 201; 601st Ordnance Bn, unit history, MHI; *Logistical History of NATOUSA/MTOUSA,* n.d., NARA RG 407, E 427, AG, WWII operations reports, 95-AL1-4, box 203; Bykofsky and Larson, 148; quartermaster memo, n.d., NARA RG 319, OCMH, box 225; Leighton and Coakley, 475 (*"brilliant"*).

414 *In World War I*: lecture, B. B. Somervell, "Army Service Forces," Aug. 9, 1943, NARA RG 334, NWC Lib, L-1-43, box 167; Kreidberg and Henry, 649; memo, North African logistics, n.d., NARA RG 319, OCMH, box 225.

Can do: Leighton and Coakley, 485; Ellis, *Brute Force: Allied Strategy and Tactics in the Second World War,* 298 (*II Corps lost more armor*); "Signal Communication in the North African Campaigns," from "Tactical Communications in World War II," part I, Historical Section, Chief Signal Officer, MHI, 120 (*500 miles*); McNamara, 60 (*new shoes*); *Logistical History of NATOUSA/ MTOUSA,* 82.

> *The Americans' "genius":* Behrens, 333, 313 (*"creating resources"*); Kennett, 93; McNamara, 70; letter, Carter B. Magruder to LeRoy Lutes, March 21, 1943, NARA RG 319, OCMH, Ordnance Dept., box 596; "History of Planning Division, Army Service Forces," 1946, CMH, 3-2.2 AA, 87.

415 *"The American Army":* Ellis, *Brute Force,* 525 (*"overwhelms them"*); Donald Davison, "Aviation Engineers in the Battle of Tunisia," 1943, 12; Beck et al., 90.

> *The German military:* Leighton and Coakley, 14; Cooper, *The German Army, 1933–1945,* 362; Bragadin, 245–47 (*"roaring furnace"*); Friedrich Weber, "Battles of 334th Division and of Group Weber," n.d., FMS, #D-215, MHI.

> *Ships not yet sunk:* Howard, *Grand Strategy,* vol. 4, 349–50; Warlimont, "High Level Decisions—The Tunisian Campaign," Feb. 1951, FMS, #C-092a, MHI, 19; *NWAf,* 368, 499n, 513fn, 682; Liddell Hart, ed., *The Rommel Papers,* 417 (*"to create the build-up"*).

416 *Other woes:* NWAf, 366; AAR, Wehrmacht transportation officer, Apr. 1–May 4, 1943, NARA RG 319, OCMH, box 225 (*lignite*); Arnim, "Recollections of Tunisia," FMS, C-098, MHI, 62 (*oil cakes*), 84.

> *These tribulations:* Lucas, *Panzer Army Africa,* 173 (*"paper divisions"*); Bennett, *Ultra and Mediterranean Strategy,* 373–74; *Destruction,* 274 (*"if no supplies"*); Warlimont, "High Level Decisions," Feb. 1951, FMS, #C-092a, MHI, 33–34 (*"a fortress"*); Cooper, 368 (*"Hitler wanted"*).

"The Devil Is Come Down"

416 *The soft whir:* Desert Victory; Brian Horrocks, *A Full Life,* 148; Brooks, ed., 176; D'Este, *Bitter Victory,* 99 (*"wee bugger"*); Fred Majdalany, *The Battle of El Alamein,* 150; Hill, *Desert Conquest,* 252–61 (*"this conqueror business"*).

417 *Bernard Law Montgomery:* Majdalany, 37–38 (*"lonely and loveless"*); Tute, 194; Hamilton, 142; Boatner, 372–74; John North, ed., *The Alexander Memoirs, 1940–1945,* 17 (*"One only loves"*).

418 *the Book of Job:* Doherty, *Irish Generals,* 29; W. P. Lunn-Rockliffe, "The Tunisian Campaign," *Army Quarterly and Defence Journal,* Apr.–May 1969, 109, and June–July, 1969, 228; Rolf, 26 (*"Kill Germans"*); Alan F. Wilt, *War from the Top,* 197; Gilbert, 372; Barnett, *The Desert Generals,* 268 (*"sheer weight of British resources"*); Charles D. McFetridge, "In Pursuit: Montgomery After Alamein," *Military Review,* June 1994, 54; Chalmers, 158; Hamilton, 169 (*"trust him"*).

> *And yet:* Barnett, *The Desert Generals,* 236; Carver, ed., *The War Lords,* 501 (*"a kindliness"*).

419 *He disdained:* Hamilton, *Master of the Battlefield,* 163 (*"quite useless"*), 177, 206; D'Este, *Bitter Victory,* 107n (*"Good chap"*); Brooks, ed., 194, 131, 175 (*"quite unfit"*), 150; Macksey, *The Tank Pioneers,* 186; F. E. Morgan, OH, n.d., FCP, MHI (*"thoroughly disloyal"*).

> *Swaggering into Tunisia:* Boatner, 372; Ellis, *Brute Force,* 284; Ellis, *On the Front Lines,* 261; Clarke, 81 (*"We will roll"*); Barnett, *The Desert Generals,* 274 (*"dray horse"*); report on benzedrine sulfate, "Military Reports on the United Nations," No. 2, Jan. 15, 1943, WD, Military Intelligence Service, NARA RG 334, NWC Lib, box 585.

> *Contrary to:* Ellis, *Brute Force,* 265, 286; Coningham, OH, Feb. 14, 1947, FCP, MHI (*"Once Monty"*).

420 *This time:* msg to Rommel, Jan. 27, 1943, NARA RG 319, OCMH, box 225; Stan-

nard, ed., 287 (*vats of hot water*); Kesselring, T-3 P1, 33; Krause, "Studies on the Mareth Position," FMS, #D-046; *Destruction*, 331–33; John W. Gordon, *The Other Desert War: British Special Forces in North Africa, 1940–1943*, 163.

These engineering nuances: W. B. Smith, OH, May 8, 1947, FCP, MHI (*"one for himself"*); Alexander, "The African Campaign from El Alamein to Tunis," 873.

422 *Montgomery knew*: *Destruction*, 333–34; NWAf, 525–30; Nicholson and Forbes, 298 (*"When I give"*).

The party had begun: Howard and Sparrow, 129–38 (*"lightly held"*); Quilter, ed., 161; A. C. Elcomb, "The Battle of Mareth," *Army Quarterly and Defence Journal*, Oct. 1973, 44; Fred Telford, ts, n.d., 3rd Bn, Coldstream Guards, IWM, 97/41/1 (*"It was my first contact"* and *"For you the war"*); *Destruction*, 335; NWAf, 531; Messenger, 75; Rolf, 170–71 (*"I am still alive"* and *"the most damnable thing"*).

423 *A lesser man*: Howard and Sparrow, 133 (*"a great success"*); *Destruction*, 332–34 (*"left largely"*).

As Montgomery and his officers: Belden, 219–24 (*"someone is making"*); W.A.T. Synge, *The Story of the Green Howards, 1939–1945*; Lewin, *The Life and Death of the Afrika Korps*, 191 (*"to a picnic"*); NWAf, 531–33; *Destruction*, 338–41; Elcomb, 44–55; Tuker, 291 (*"pound the objectives"*), 295; G. R. Stevens, *Fourth Indian Division*, 209; *The Tiger Kills*, 162; B. H. Liddell Hart, *The Tanks*, 249; Macksey, *Crucible of Power*, 216; Fritz Bayerlein, "Memorandum for the War Diary," May 5, 1943, NARA RG 319, OCMH, box 225.

425 *Montgomery disliked*: Hamilton, 193–95 (*"What am I"*); Rolf, 171; Francis de Guingand, *Operation Victory*, 250–55; Charles Richardson, *Send for Freddie*, 117.

The answer lay: Clifford, 401 (*"jagged purple coxscomb"*); Howard Kippenberger, *Infantry Brigadier*, 277; Powell, *In Barbary*, 123; Tuker, 299; H. Marshall, *Over to Tunis*, 100; Hastings, 201.

426 *Alerted by Luftwaffe reconnaissance*: msg, Messe to Arnhem, March 25, 1943, NARA RG 319, OCMH, box 226; Hinsley, *British Intelligence in the Second World War*, vol. 2, 284–85; *Destruction*, 341–44; NWAf, 533; Doherty, *A Noble Crusade: The History of Eighth Army, 1941–45*, 129.

One man: W. G. Stevens, *Freyberg, V.C., The Man, 1939–1945*, 36, 47, 54–56, 60; Lewin, *Montgomery as Military Commander*, 170; Boatner, 167; Dan Davin essay on Freyberg in Carver, ed., *The War Lords*, 582–95 (*"cunning as a Maori dog"*).

427 *The Salamander was displeased*: *Destruction*, 344; De Guingand, 258.

Montgomery set aside: "Direct Air Support in the Battle of El Hamma," AAF Informational Intelligence Summary, 43–36, July 10, 1943, NARA RG 334, NWC Lib, box 13; *Destruction*, 348–54; Kippenberger, 282–84.

428 *Through the gap*: Stewart, ed., 182 (*"Speed up"*); Kippenberger, 289 (*"dead and mangled"*), 280 (*"They trust me"*); T. M. Lindsay, *Sherwood Rangers*, 79, 83 (*"Like a black snake"*); Liddell Hart, *The Tanks*, 251; Tuker, 306 (*"trundled as snails"*); Bisheshwar Prasad, ed., *The North African Campaign, 1940–43, Official History of the Indian Armed Forces*, 502–505; Messenger, 91 (*"not unlike hounds"*); Lewin, *Montgomery as Military Commander*, 173; Brooks, ed., 211; NWAf, 537; Horrocks, 155.

429 *"It was the most enjoyable battle"*: Brooks, ed., 185; Stannard, ed., 287 (*drought*); D. McCorquodale et al., *History of the King's Dragoon Guards, 1938–1945*, 221; bomb damage assessment, Operations Bulletin No. 2, May 31, 1943, NW African AF, NARA RG, NWC Lib, box 132; Rolf, 190 (*donned their kilts*); Dudley Clarke, *The Eleventh at War*, 288–95.

Some of Montgomery's admirers: Doherty, 130–35; Hamilton, 208; Tuker, 307 (*"lack of purpose"*); essay on Montgomery by Michael Carver, in Keegan, ed.,

Churchill's Generals; "Montgomery and the Battle of Mareth. Talk with Christopher Buckley," Nov. 24, 1946, LHC, 11/1946/12 (*through repetition*).

431 *An old Arab song*: Stannard, ed., 279; Baedeker, 385; author visit, Apr. 2000; *NWAf*, 541; Parris and Russell, 301.

    If seizing Gafsa: "Report on Operation, 15 March–10 Apr. 1943," II Corps, CARL, N-2652A; Bradley and Blair, 141; Nicholson, *Alex*, 177 ("*I do* not *want*"), 180 ("*dashing steed*"); DDE to GCM, March 29, 1943, Chandler, 1059; Alexander, OH, SM, MHI.

433 *Patton was incensed*: Blumenson, *The Patton Papers, 1940–1945*, 187–90 ("*Fortunately for our fame*"); *NWAf*, 545; Howze, *A Cavalryman's Story*, 64 ("*more dead bodies*"); Bradley, *A Soldier's Story*, 52.

434 *That night, military policemen*: "History of the 26th Infantry in the Present Struggle," n.d., MRC FDM, box 301, 9–18; Blumenson, *The Patton Papers, 1940–1945*, 191 ("*The hardest thing*"); AAR, "Report of Operations 1st AD, Maknassy, 12 March–10 Apr., 1943," NARA RG 407, E 427, box 14767; letter, TdA to G. F. Howe, Apr. 16, 1951, NARA RG 319, OCMH, box 229; Hansen, 4/33; James Wellard, *The Man in a Helmet*, 77 ("*small flotilla of ships*").

    "*The Dagoes beat it*": Blumenson, *The Patton Papers, 1940–1945*, 193, 191; Bradley and Blair, 142; Liebling, *Mollie & Other War Stories*, 67, 85; Pyle, *Here Is Your War*, 231–33; MacVane, *Journey into War*, 231–34; Martin, *The GI War*, 52; Yarborough, 90; Knickerbocker et al., 66; diary, CBH, March 26, 28, 1943, MHI; Marshall, ed., *Proud Americans*, 66 (*ore cars*); Dickson, "G-2 Journal," MHI, 53 ("*a Moroccan*"); Ellis, *On the Front Lines*, 274 (*venereal disease*); II Corps, provost marshal journal, 1943, NARA RG 407, E 427, box 3126 ("*No, suh*"); Carter, "Carter's War," CEOH, IV-44.6.

435 *Patton knew the value*: D'Arcy-Dawson, 177 (*Viennese steak*); Blumenson, *The Patton Papers, 1940–1945*, 191–92 ("*If any American*"); MacVane, *Journey into War*, 232; Porter, SOOHP, MHI, 276–78 ("*You should*").

    On the nineteenth: *NWAf*, 550, 557; author visit, Apr. 2000; Knickerbocker et al., 67.

436 *No one who met him*: Michael J. King, *William Orlando Darby: A Military Biography*, 17, 46; King, "Rangers: Selected Combat Operations in WWII"; Arnbal, 27.

    On the evening: Altieri, *Darby's Rangers: An Illustrated Portrayal*; Lehman, "The Rangers Fought Ahead of Everybody," 28; Darby, *Darby's Rangers: We Led the Way*, 71; Boatner, 250; Ingersoll, 115–16 ("*sighing of the sea*"), 147–70 ("*rubbing fists in their eyes*"); King, "Rangers: Selected Combat Operations in WWII," 19–20; Arnbal, 61–62 ("*odors of hot guns*").

437 *Kitchen trucks*: Liebling, "Find 'Em, Fix 'Em, and Fight 'Em," Apr. 24, 1943, 221, and May 1, 1943, 24; II Corps G-2 incident report, March 22, 1943, in 9th ID records, NARA RG 407, E 427, box 7334 ("*Few Germans*"); Dixon, "Terry Allen," 57.

438 "*There's but one thought*": TR to Eleanor, March 20, 25, Apr. 11, 1943, TR, LOC, box 9; AAR, 1st ID, n.d., in DSC documentation packet, TR, LOC, box 39; Sam Carter, "The Operations of the 1st Battalion, 18th Infantry, at El Guettar," 1948, Fort Benning, Infantry School, 19; *NWAf*, 560–64.

439 *The chink*: author visit, Apr. 2000; "The African Campaign from El Alamein to Tunis," 874–76; Marshall, ed., *Proud Americans*, 72, 79; Hamilton, 206 ("*complete amateurs*"); Skillen, 298; Gustav von Vaerst, "Operations of the Fifth Panzer Army in Tunisia," n.d., FMS #D-001, 6–10; Carter, "The Operations of the 1st

Battalion, 18th Infantry," 19 (*"huge iron fort"*); Raymond, "Slugging It Out," *Field Artillery Journal*, Jan. 1944, 14 (*"no one had the heart"*); Milton M. Thornton and R. G. Emery, "Try the Reverse Slope," *Infantry Journal*, Feb. 1944, 8; author interview, Eston White, Feb. 2000.

440 *On the American left*: Arnim, "Recollections of Tunisia," FMS #C-098, 82; *Tank Destroyer Forces World War II*, 30–32; Andrus, notes on *A Soldier's Story*, MRC FDM; Mason, "Reminiscences and Anecdotes of World War II," MRC FDM, 81, 135; Carter, "The Operations of the 1st Battalion, 18th Infantry at El Guettar," 20–22; Riess, ed., 553; Arnold J. Heidenheimer, *Vanguard to Victory: History of the 18th Infantry*; Clay, *Blood and Sacrifice*, 8/37–39 (mss); Marshall, ed., *Proud Americans*, 77–78, 83, 85–86; Blumenson, *The Patton Papers, 1940–1945*, 224 (*"Hun bastards"*); Liebling, "Find 'Em, Fix 'Em, and Fight 'Em," Apr. 24, 1943, 221, and May 1, 1943, 24 (*"I will like hell"*).

    Desperate as the fight: "TD Combat in Tunisia," Jan. 1944, Tank Destroyer School, MHI; Porter, SOOHP, MHI, 276 (*"I expect him"*); Mason, "Reminiscences and Anecdotes," 82–3; AAR, 899th TD Bn, "Unit History, 1943," NARA RG 407, E 427, box 23879; Christopher R. Gabel, "Seek, Strike, and Destroy: U.S. Army Tank Destroyer Doctrine in World War II," 1985, CSI, 38; Raymond, "Slugging It Out," 14; *NWAf*, 560.

441 *With sirens screaming*: *Tank Destroyer Forces World War II*, 31–32; Hansen, 4/57 (*"I want"*).

442 *At three P.M.*: "G-2 Report, Battle of El Guettar," G-2 Miscellaneous Papers, II Corps, NARA RG 407, E 427, box 3164; Thomas E. Bennett, "Gafsa–El Guettar," 1st ID log, March 23, 1943, possession of Roger Cirillo; "A Summary of the El Guettar Offensive," TdA, MHI; Skillen, 297, 299; Hinsley, *British Intelligence in the Second World War*, 286; Koch, 22; Rogers, "A Study of Leadership in the First Infantry Division During World War II," 27 (*"Terry, when"*).

    Patton's uncoded warnings: Porter, SOOHP, 1981, MHI, 282 (*alerted the Germans*); *NWAf*, 562–63; AAR, 899th TD Bn, "Unit History, 1943," NARA RG 407, E 427, box 23879.

    This time the panzers: Liebling, "Find 'Em, Fix 'Em, and Fight 'Em" (*"diffident fat boys"*); "TD Combat in Tunisia"; V. R. Rawie, 5th FA commander, quoted in Andrus biographical file, MHI (*ricochet fire*); Mason, "Reminiscences and Anecdotes," 87 (*"scissors and search"*); Darby, *Darby's Rangers*, 76; TR to Eleanor, March 25, Apr. 11, 1943, TR, LOC, box 9; Andrus, notes on *A Soldier's Story*, MRC FDM; Hansen, 4/41A (*"it seems a crime"*).

443 *Survivors rejoined*: Phillips, *El Guettar: Crucible of Leadership*, 4; Skillen, 299; *NWAf*, 564n; II Corps operations report, n.d., GSP, LOC MS Div., box 10; Carter, "The Operations of the 1st Battalion, 18th Infantry at El Guettar"; II Corps, G-3 journal, March 1943, NARA RG 407, E 427, box 3175 (*"Hun will soon"*); Bradley and Blair, 144 (*"indisputable defeat"*); Drew Middleton, "The Battle Saga of a Tough Outfit," *New York Times Magazine*, Apr. 8, 1945, 8 (*"Well, folks"*).

"Search Your Soul"

444 *Orlando Ward's attack*: II Corps, G-3 journal, March 1943, NARA RG 407, E 427, box 3175; AAR, "Report of Operations 1st AD, Maknassy, 12 March–10 Apr. 1943," NARA RG 407, E 427, box 14767; Johnson, *One More Hill*, 46; "Adventures by Men of the 60th Infantry Regiment in WWII," 1993, MHI.

    Then he stopped: memo, Jean Bouley to Robinett, Aug. 1, 1949, PMR, LOC, box 4 (*"very serious and costly"*); Howe, "American Signal Intelligence in Northwest Africa and Western Europe," U.S. Cryptologic History, series IV,

WWII, vol. I, 1980, NARA RG 457, NSA files, SRH 391, box 114, 35; *NWAf,* 552; Vaerst, "Operations of the Fifth Panzer Army in Tunisia," 12–13; Blumenson, *The Patton Papers, 1940–1945,* 196; Camp, ed., "Tankers in Tunisia," 32, author visit, Apr. 2000.

445 *Ward also had:* Theodore J. Conway, SOOHP, Sept. 1977, Robert F. Ensslin, MHI, ii-39 (*"regiment was divided"*); Phillips, *The Making of a Professional: Manton S. Eddy, USA,* 112; observer report #41, March 5, 1943, NARA RG 337, Observer Reports, box 52 (*malaria*).

  the Robinett problem: Gugeler, ts, OW, MHI, x-113; diary, Feb.–March, 1943, OW, MHI; Edwin A. Russell, OH, May 15, 1950, SM, MHI (*"little dictator"*); DDE to OW, March 12, 1943, OW, MHI (*"difficult to handle"*); PMR to DDE, Apr. 12, 1943, PMR, LOC, box 4; DDE to GCM, March 3, 1943, OW, MHI (*"puzzling man"*)

446 *his Patton problem:* OW to DDE, March 7, 1943, Chandler, 1027n; Blumenson, *The Patton Papers, 1940–1945,* 188, 193, 197; Hansen, 4/96; McCurtain Scott, OH, March 1976, OW, MHI (*"Goddamit, Ward"*); diary, March 22, 1943, OW, MHI (*"Patton impatient"*).

  Alexander's new orders: AAR, "Report of Operations 1st AD, Maknassy, 12 March–10 Apr 1943," NARA RG 407, E 427, box 14767; AAR, CCC, 1st AD, March–Apr. 1943, NARA; *NWAf,* 553–55; author visit, Apr. 2000.

447 *He was actually facing:* Lang, "Report on the Fighting of *Kampfgruppe* Lang," part II, 1947, FMS, #D-166, MHI; *Kriegstagebuch V,* Fifth Panzer Army, March 23–24, 1943, NARA RG 319, OCMH, box 226; Kleine and Kühn, *Tiger;* Carell, 350.

  A third American attack: letter, T. Riggs to parents, June 25, 1943, PMR, LOC, box 4 (*"beautiful and uncomfortable"*); William S. McElhenny, 1st AD, ts, n.d., OW, MHI, box 1 (*"Come on!"*); AAR, 1st Bn, 6th Armored Inf; AAR, 60th Inf, March 22–24, NARA RG 407, E 427, box 7535; Camp, ed., "Tankers in Tunisia," 15; G-2 summary No. 6, Apr. 2, 1943, II Corps, "Report on Operation, 15 March–10 Apr., 1943," CARL, N-2652A (*"Here one can find"*); Robertson, ASEQ, ts, n.d., 1st AD, 288 (*"shootin' gallery"*).

449 *Patton had again:* letter, R. F. Akers, Jr., to C. B. Hansen, Jan. 12, 1951, CBH, MHI (*"Pink, you got"*); war diaries, 1943, CBH, MHI, 8-A, S-10; Blumenson, *The Patton Papers, 1940–1945,* 197 (*"my conscience"*).

  Ward stood: diary, E. C. Hatfield, March 24, 1943, OW, MHI; AAR, E. C. Hatfield, 1st AD, March 27, 1943, OW, MHI, box 1 (*"Sergeant could you"*); AAR, CCC, NARA 407, E 427, 601-CCC-0.3, March–Apr. 1943; *NWAf,* 556; Robinett, *Armor Command,* 209; CBH, 1943, MHI; Scott, OH, OW, MHI (*"Damned inadequate"*); Blumenson, *The Patton Papers, 1940–1945,* 198 (*"made a man"*).

450 *Two days later:* diary, March 27, 1943, OW, MHI; Blumenson, *The Patton Papers, 1940–1945,* 199.

451 *The stalemate:* OW to "All Personnel, 1st AD," March 27, 1943, PMR, GCM Lib, box 12 (*"Search your soul"*); AAR, "Report of Operations, 1st AD, Maknassy, 12 March–10 Apr. 1943," NARA RG 407, E 427, box 14767; *NWAf,* 575; DDE to GCM, Apr. 3 and 24, 1943, Chandler, 1066, 1101.

  There was truth: Blumenson, *The Patton Papers, 1940–1945,* 221; Lang, "Report on the Fighting of *Kampfgruppe* Lang," MHI; Gugeler, ts, OW, MHI, X-138 (*"With some diffidence"*), 141 (*"Look, Brad"*); Rolf, 199 (*"quite useless"*); OW note, Apr. 4, 1943, OW, MHI; diary, Apr. 4, 1943, OW, MHI (*"Bradley gave"*).

452 *Harmon would arrive:* Harmon, *Combat Commander,* 123–25 (*"stupid questions"* and *"party is all yours"*); E. N. Harmon, OH, Sept. 15, 1952, SM, MHI.

  If outwardly gracious: OW, OH, May 5, 1957, FCP, MHI (*chief of staff*); PMR to OW, Apr. 20, 1943, PMR, GCM Lib, box 12 (*"deepest gratitude"*); OW, DSC awards packet, NARA RG 338, Fifth Army, A 47-A-3948, box 56.

Ward was a good soldier: OW to L. E. Oliver, Sept. 27, 1943, OW, MHI ("*My record*"); Boatner, 599; DDE quoted in GCM to OW, May 5, 1943, Pentagon office correspondence, GCM Lib, box 90, folder 4 ("*too sensitive*").

Night Closes Down

453 *With the Americans*: AAR, II Corps, "Report on Operation, 15 March–10 April 1943," CARL, N-2652A; Knickerbocker et al., 94; S-1 log, 18th Inf, NARA RG 407, E 427, box 5941; Carter, "The Operations of the 1st Battalion, 18th Infantry at El Guettar," 23; Arnbal, 75; *NWAf*, 564–69.

455 *Moreover, the 9th Division*: AAR, "Report on Operation Conducted by 9th ID, Southern Tunisia, 26 March–8 Apr. 1943," NARA RG 407, E 427, box 7326; D. T. Kellett, "El Guettar: Victory or Stalemate?," *Military Review*, July 1951, 18; AAR, 39th Inf Regt, NARA RG 407, E 427, box 7501; Carter, "Carter's War," IV-44; Phillips, *The Making of a Professional*, 76, 80, 97 ("*big galoot*"); "Hold Fast," 1945 booklet on 9th ID; Knickerbocker et al., 71; Doubler, 294–95.

An intelligence estimate: AAR, "Report on Operation Conducted by 9th ID"; "Report on Defense of Hills 260 [*sic*] and 369," May 23, 1943, II Corps engineers, NARA RG 338, box 147 (*five dugouts*); Heinz Werner Schmidt, *With Rommel in the Desert*, 266; author visit, Apr. 2000.

Hill 369 prevented: AAR, 47th Inf, n.d., NARA RG 407, E 427, box 7514; AAR, 9th ID, n.d., NARA RG 407, E 427, box 7348; Phillips, *El Guettar*, 24–31 ("*lighting up*"), 37 ("*You sons*"); David E. Gillespie, ed., *History of the Forty-Seventh Infantry Regiment*; AAR, 10th Panzer Div., March 27, 1943, NARA RG 319, OCMH, box 225; Mittelman, 93-101.

456 *Worse yet*: AAR, "Report on Operation Conducted by 9th ID"; Randle, "The General and the Movie," *Army*, Sept. 1971; Parris and Russell, 310; William M. Lee, ASEQ, n.d., 26th Inf Regt, 1st ID, MHI; Johnson, *One More Hill*, 55 ("*Just lay in my hole*"); AAR, 47th Inf, n.d., NARA RG 407, E 427, box 7514.

Alexander visited: AAR, II Corps, CARL N-2652A (*professed satisfaction*); Phillips, *El Guettar*, 38 ("*In all my career*"), 43–47; Mittelman, 101.

457 *North of Highway 15*: Marion Hunt and Duane R. Sneddeker, "Over Here, Over There," *Gateway Heritage*, winter 1993, 48 ("*We baked*"); AAR, 1st ID, "Gafsa–El Guettar," March 31, 1943, possession of Roger Cirillo; author interview, Albert H. Smith, Jan. 24, 2000; "History of the 26th Infantry in the Present Struggle," FDM MRC, box 301, 9/62–81; Martin, *The GI War*, 56 ("*Night just closes down*"); Mason, "Reminiscences and Anecdotes," 54 ("*fussed and fumed*"), 136.

Late on March 29: AAR, "Report on Operation, 15 March–10 Apr. 1943," II Corps, CARL, N-2652A; *NWAf*, 569–71 (*a fourth time*); Kellett, 18 (*little chance of success*); Blumenson, *The Patton Papers, 1940–1945*, 200 ("*I feel*").

With Patton's protest: C. C. Benson, "Some Tunisian Details," *Field Artillery Journal*, Jan. 1944, 2; Moorehead, 136–37 ("*From a hundred wadis*"); D'Arcy-Dawson, 187 ("*I saw tanks hit*"); "Unit History, 1943," 899th TD Bn, NARA RG 407, E 427, box 23879; *NWAf*, 571; AAR, "Report on Operation Conducted by 9th ID," March 30, 1943; Wellard, 80; Blumenson, *The Patton Papers, 1940–1945*, 202 ("*We seem*").

458 *The Axis line drew back*: GSP to DDE, March 29, 1943, Patton files, DDE Lib, PP-pres, box 91 ("*Nasty, grim*"); AAR, 9th ID, Apr. 2, 1943, NARA RG 407, E 427, box 7348; AAR, 9th ID surgeon, n.d., NARA RG 407, E 427, box 7348; AAR, "Report on Operation Conducted by 9th ID"; *NWAf*, 575; Phillips, *El Guettar*, 70; Randle, *Safi Adventure*, 216; Mason, "Reminiscences and Anecdotes," 69 ("*most severe*").

459 *The stuck-everywhere period*: Linderman, 256 ("*cell-by-cell*"); Howe, *The Battle*

History of the 1st Armored Division, 217 (*"everybody ordering"*); TR to Eleanor, Apr. 8, 1943, TR, LOC, box 9.

Patton took it badly: Blumenson, *The Patton Papers, 1940–1945,* 204–205; CBH, Apr. 1, 1943, MHI; Bradley and Blair, *A General's Life,* 147; Bradley, *A Soldier's Life,* 63; Butcher diary, DDE Lib, PP-pres, box 166, A-314 (*"Every bone"*); Hansen, 4/79; Pyle, *Here Is Your War,* 232.

"Forward troops": Coningham, Patton messages, DDE Lib, PP-pres, box 91; daily intel report, Sunset No. 47, Feb. 20, 1943 and Sunset No. 49, n.d., NSA files, NARA RG 457, SRS 1869, box 1; Tedder, 410–11; Laurence S. Kuter, "Goddammit, Georgie!," *Air Force Magazine,* Feb. 1973, 51; D'Este, *Patton,* 483; Blumenson, *The Patton Papers, 1940–1945,* 207–208, 211 (*"I hope the Boches"*); Bradley, *A Soldier's Story,* 63–64; Carter, "Carter's War," CEOH, IV–42.

461 *If choler infected*: Pyle, *Here Is Your War,* 241–42.

What Rommel called: Clifford, 390 (*"clean, straight"*); Ellis, *On the Front Lines,* 17 (*slaughterhouse blood*); L. J. McNair, "The Struggle Is for Survival," radio address, Nov. 11, 1942, *Vital Speeches of the Day,* 111; training memorandum #22, AFHQ through II Corps G-3, "History of the 26th Infantry in the Present Struggle," MRC FDM, box 301, 9/36; GSP Jr., "order of the day," "History of the 26th Infantry in the Present Struggle," MRC FDM, box 301, 9/35.

nearly 6,000 casualties: "Report on Operation, 15 March–10 Apr. 1943," II Corps, CARL, N-2652A; D'Este, *Bitter Victory,* 62 (*"Perhaps these American"*); G-2 summary #7, Apr. 19, 1943, II Corps, NARA RG 407, E 427, box 7334; Samuel D. Spivey, *A Doughboy's Narrative,* 73 (*"we really learned"*); "History of the 26th Infantry in the Present Struggle," MRC FDM, box 301, 10/24; Herschel H. Husinpiller, "Armored Infantry in Africa," ts, n.d., Fort Benning Infantry School Library, 7 (*"A soldier is not"*); Parris and Russell, 308–310; Pyle, *Here Is Your War,* 106 (*"They lost"*).

462 *A very thin membrane*: "Intelligence at HQ First Army, Nov. 1942–May 1943," ts, May 23, 1943, National Archives of Canada, RG 24, vol. 01, intelligence 10719 (*"serious menace"*); William E. Faust, ASEQ, ts, 1990, 1st ID, Divarty HHQ, MHI, 39 (*"We became ruthless"*); letter, printed in *Minneapolis Tribune,* Apr. 11, 1943, MCC-YU (*"Here Arabs live"*); Thomas A. Kindre, OH, 1994, G. Kurt Piehler, ROHA; Tom Gendron, OH, 1977, 1st ID, Michael Corley, possession of Paul Gorman; Howard D. Ashcraft, *As You Were,* 10, 17 (*"to watch them dance"*).

At a training camp: Schrijver, 118; "History of the 26th Infantry in the Present Struggle," MRC FDM, box 301, 9/90; McManus, 67 (*"We made them dig"*); D'Arcy-Dawson, 107, 125, 133 (*"It is not pleasant"*).

After Kasserine: author interviews, Edward Boehm, Nov. 26, 1999, and Jan. 4, 2000; Edward Boehm, "My Autobiography During World War II," ts, 1997, possession of Roger Cirillo.

463 *Such atrocities*: inspector general report, July 13, 1943, NARA RG 492, MTOUSA, records of the special staff, box 2011 (*"three out of five"*).

But other crimes: "Historical Report of the Provost Marshal Section of the Atlantic Base Section," Oct. 5, 1942, to May 31, 1943, NARA RG 492, provost marshal general, box 2228; Giraud letter in memo, Apr. 3, 1943, NARA RG 331, AFHQ micro, R-204-F; memo, J. C. Holmes, chief, AFHQ liaison section to G-1 (personnel), May 3, 1943, NARA RG 331, AFHQ micro, R-204-F; memo, NATO provost marshal to G-1, May 6, 1943, NARA RG 331, AFHQ micro, R-204-F.

Some of the most appalling: "Report of the Battalion Chief of Leon Tenneroni," Bône, Apr. 21, 1943, in "Inspections and Investigations by Inspectors General and Other Officers & Reports Of [*sic*]," vol. II, serial #8, HQ NATO, June 6, 1943, to CG, 8th AAF, "Report of Security Investigation," NARA RG 492, MTO, Records of the Special Staff, box 1043; "History of the 98th Engineer (General Service) Regiment," Aug. 17, 1941–May 1944, NARA RG 407, E 427, Engineers, box 19556; WWII U.S. Army executions, JAG, history branch office, U.S. force, ETO, 8-3.5 AA, v. 1; memo, "comparison of executions during WWI and WWII," U.S. Army JAG to undersecretary of war, Apr. 22, 1946, author's possession.

"I Had a Plan . . . Now I Have None"

464 *"a soft feel"*: TR to Eleanor, Apr. 6, 1943, TR, LOC, box 9; *Destruction,* 374–75 (*"last man"* and "Non è stata").

   It was not especially good: Adrian Stewart, *Eighth Army's Greatest Victories,* 189; Jackson, *Alexander of Tunis as Military Commander,* 189; Benson, "Some Tunisian Details," 2 (*"Attack and destroy"*).

   They swung at air: Wellard, 80 (*"abreast like a Spanish fleet"*); AAR, "The El Guettar Operation, Intelligence Report," Benson Force, n.d., NARA RG 407, E 427, box 3126; Blumenson, *The Patton Papers, 1940–1945,* 213; *NWAf,* 577; "Report on Operation, 15 March–10 Apr. 1943," II Corps, CARL, N-2652A; Hoffman, *Stauffenberg,* 177–80; Boatner, 534.

465 *Within an hour*: Parkinson, 89 (*"Hello, Limeys!"*); Gordon, 169; Hill, *Desert Conquest,* 272 (*"somebody besides a Nazi"*), 300.

   Eisenhower was jubilant: DDE to John S. D. Eisenhower, Apr. 8, 1943, Chandler, 1083; DDE to E. E. Hazlett, Jr., Apr. 7, 1943, Chandler, 1081 (*"It seems"*).

466 *He was just*: DDE to A. D. Surles, Apr. 6, 1943, Chandler, 1080; DDE to GSP, Apr. 5, 1943, Chandler, 1073 (*"my policy"*).

   Proximity to the British: Tedder, 406 (*"The only way"*); Lewin, *Montgomery as Military Commander,* 178; Brooks, ed., 157–72, 191; Butcher diary, DDE Lib, PP-pres, box 166, A-282; "Reminiscences of Hanson Weightman Baldwin," 1976, John T. Mason, USNI OHD, 4–375 (*"anybody except that son of a bitch"*); Morgan, *Past Forgetting,* 115 (*"a thorn in my side"*).

   As if to compensate: DDE to GSP, Apr. 5, 1943, Chandler, 1073; Blumenson, *The Patton Papers, 1940–1945,* 220, 218.

467 *Yet in his ecumenical*: B. A. Dickson, OH, Dec. 13, 1950, SM, MHI; Bradley and Blair, *A General's Life,* 144–45 (*"speechless"*); Bradley, *A Soldier's Story,* 59 (*"This war's"*); DDE to Alexander, March 23, 1943, Chandler, 1056; DDE to GCM, March 29, 1943, Chandler, 1059; DDE to GSP, Apr. 5, 1943, Chandler, 1074 (*"your corps"*).

468 *One final chance*: author visit, Apr. 2000; "G-2 Report on Tunisian Campaign," June 12, 1943, 34th ID, Iowa GSM; Vaerst, "Operations of the Fifth Panzer Army in Tunisia," MHI, 18; Arnim, "Recollections of Tunisia," MHI, 91; Forty, *The Armies of Rommel,* 177; Carell, 340; Blaxland, 219 (*powers of German sergeants*).

   This was a mistake: Ryder, OH, Feb. 21, 1950, G. F. Howe, SM, MHI (*"go out in that area"*); "The Tunisian Campaign, 34th ID," Dec. 13, 1943, NARA RG 407, E 427, 334-0.3; msg "to all officers of the 34th Div., 11 March 1943," 201 file, Charles W. Ryder papers, DDE Lib, box 2 (*"creeping paralysis"*); Clem Miller, *Some Things You Never Forget,* 109; Davies, 103–107; Hougen, *The Story of the Famous 34th Infantry Division*; AAR, 109th Medical Bn, n.d., in "109th Med Publications," Iowa GSM.

470 *Belatedly, Alexander realized*: Nehring, FMS, MS #T-3, vol. 3a, MHI; Macksey, *Crucible of Power,* 229, 257.

471 *At eleven A.M.*: Macksey, *The Tank Pioneers,* 186–91 (*"watch your step"*); Hansen, 3–66; Blaxland, 211; Liddell Hart, "Notes for History, Talk with Crocker," July 9, 1943, LHC, 11/1943/46; AAR, IX Corps, n.d., PRO, WO 175/97.

It was regrettable: "The Tunisian Campaign, 34th ID," Dec. 13, 1943, NARA RG 407, E 427, 334-0.3; Ryder, OH, SM, MHI; Caffey, OH, Feb. 1950 SM, MHI (*"I had a plan"*); *NWAf*, 583–85; *Destruction*, 377–80; Harold G. Bull, OH, Sept. 21, 1950, SM, MHI.

472 *Now another officer*: Louis-Marie Koeltz, "Memo on meeting held April 6, 1943, at the command post of General Ryder," 1950, trans. for author by Claudia Brown, NARA RG 319, OCMH, box 225; Robinett, *Armor Command,* 126; Alexander, OH, SM, MHI; letter, J. T. Crocker, Sept. 8, 1950, and memo, Gordon H. A. MacMillan, n.d., both in memo, H. B. Latham, Cabinet Office Historical Section, to G. F. Howe, Sept. 25, 1950, NARA RG 319, OCMH, box 229.

It went badly: JAG, 34th ID, "Historical Report on Activities," June 30, 1943, Iowa GSM; "Chaplain's Report on the Tunisian Campaign," 34th ID, n.d., NARA RG 407, E 427, box 9417; Alexander to DDE, Apr. 7, 1943, Alexander files, DDE Lib, box 3, folder 8 (*"reasonably confident"*); D'Este, *Bitter Victory,* 62 (*"soft, green"*); Robert Ward, OH, Nov. 30, 1950, G. F. Howe, SM, MHI (*"no one was saying"*); Hansen, 3/60-6 (*"brittle and axiomatic"*); Ryder, OH, Feb, 21, 1950, SM, MHI (*"wished to win"*).

Perhaps, Ryder mused: "The Tunisian Campaign, 34th ID," Dec. 13, 1943, NARA RG 407, 334-0.3; Virgil Craven, "The Operation of Company I, 133rd Infantry, in the Attack at Fondouk Gap," 1950, Fort Benning Infantry School, 6, 9–19; Bailey, *Through Hell and High Water,* 90; Ankrum, 250, 243; Austin, 114; D.G.A., "With Tanks to Tunis," 399; Green and Gauthier, ed., 154; letter, Ray C. Fountain, *Des Moines Tribune,* Aug. 5, 1943, Iowa GSM.

473 *There would be no bombing*: "Proposed Mission Against Fondouk Gap, Tunisia, On 7 April 1943," Feb. 7, 1951, Air University Lib, NARA RG 319, OCMH, box 228; Davis, *Carl A. Spaatz and the Air War in Europe,* 207; log, Co C, 1st Bn, 133rd Infantry Regt, Iowa GSM (*"A wave of flying dust"*); Miller, *Some Things You Never Forget,* 111 (*"a pea on a plate"*); Roland Anderson, "The Operations of the 135th Infantry Regiment in the Vicinity of Fondouk el Okbi," 1948, Fort Benning Infantry School; Bailey, *Through Hell and High Water,* 90 (*"We continued"*); letter, Robert P. Miller to G. F. Howe, Jan. 14, 1951, NARA RG 319, OCMH, box 229; Craven, "The Operations of Company I," 10–19 (*"did little more"*); Robert Ward, OH, Nov. 30, 1950, G. F. Howe, SM, MHI; author interview, Paul Calder, Nov. 8, 1999; Ankrum, 238 (*"the mere raising"*).

474 *General Crocker was fixated*: AAR, letter, 1st Guards Bde, Apr. 21, 1943, PRO, WO 175/186; Ellis, *Welsh Guards at War,* 114–21; *NWAf*, 588 (*even abandoned*); Blaxland, 221 (*boulder-to-boulder*).

A hard night: Craven, "The Operations of Company I," 19, 22 (*"hill looked bigger than ever"* and *asked to be arrested*); "Narrative History, North African–Tunisian Campaign, 133rd Inf Regt.," June 7, 1943, NARA RG 407, E 427, box 9549; letter, Donald C. Landon to G. F. Howe, Jan. 17, 1951, NARA RG 319, OCMH, box 228; Richard F. Wilkinson, ts, n.d., in AAR, Co C, 1st Bn, 133rd Inf Regt, Iowa GSM (*"brew tea"*).

They went—but: Alexander, "The African Campaign from El Alamein to Tunis," 877–79; ffrench Blake, *A History of the 17th/21st Lancers, 1922–1959,* 133 (*"We shall all"*); Moorehead, 145; C. N. Barclay, *History of the 16th/5th The Queen's Royal Lancers, 1925 to 1961,* 88–91 (*set fire to blankets* and *"The tank rocked"*); "Combat Report," 3rd Co (German) 334th Mobile Bn, NARA RG 319, OCMH, box 225; Anderson, "The Operations of the 135th Infantry Regiment"; AAR, 16th/5th Lancers, Apr. 9–10, 1943, PRO, WO 175/291; Bailey, *Through Hell and High Water,* 96 (*"as smooth and white"*).

475 *The retreating Italians*: *Kriegstagebuch* V, Fifth Panzer Army, Apr. 9, 1943, NARA

RG 319, OCMH, box 226; *NWAf,* 588–90; *Destruction,* 382; Jordan, 226; Rolf, 215 (*"usual wog town"*); author visit, Apr. 2000; D'Arcy-Dawson, 199–201; Austin, 117; Hansen, 41/116; diary, G. P. Druitt, Apr. 1943, IWM, 96/38/1.

476 *American losses:* "The Tunisian Campaign, 34th ID," Dec. 13, 1943, NARA RG 407, E 427, 334-0.3; Bolstad, 135 (*"It is only"*); Ankrum, 253, 256; AAR, Co C, 109th Medical Bn, n.d., Iowa GSM (*"You couldn't make"*); Green and Gauthier, ed., 154; letter, Robert R. Moore to Dorothy, Nancy Jo, May 12, 1943, possession of Robert R. Moore, Jr.

A great opportunity: NWAf, 591–92; letter, J. T. Crocker, Sept 8, 1950, and memo, Gordon H. A. MacMillan, n.d. (*"all commanders"*), both in memo, H. B. Latham, Cabinet Office Historical Section, to G. F. Howe, Sept. 25, 1950, NARA RG 319, OCMH, box 229; Bull, OH, Sept. 21, 1950, SM, MHI (*"severe and caustic"*); *Time,* Apr. 19, 1943, 28.

477 *Ryder declined:* Richard Wilson, "The Gallant Fight of the 34th Division," 1943, *Des Moines Register and Tribune;* Charles Werterbaker, account of Fondouk, *Time,* May 24, 1943; Bailey, *Through Hell and High Water,* 100; E. N. Harmon to H. G. Bull, Apr. 1943, Harmon papers, MHI (*"I do not believe"*); diary, G. P. Druitt, Apr. 1943, IWM, 96/38/1; Macksey, *Crucible of Power,* 261; Schrijvers, *The Crash of Ruin* (*"Our cousins regret"*).

Eisenhower was both: Butcher diary, DDE Lib, PP-pres, box 166, A 306, 307, 308, 313 (*"whale tracks"* and *advocated sacking*); Hughes diary, May 1, 1943, MHI, R-5 (*"Ike says"*); DDE to GCM, Apr. 5, 1943, Chandler, 1073; DDE to MWC, March 29, 1943, Chandler, 1062; Mina Curtiss, ed., *Letters Home,* 61 (*"We have found"*).

CHAPTER 12: THE INNER KEEP
Hell's Corner

480 *One hundred thousand:* "Operations of II Corps, Northern Tunisia, 23 Apr.–9 May," NARA RG 407, E 427, box 3113; Pyle, *Here Is Your War,* 247 (*"dead weary"*); Vining, ed., 71; letter, Raymond Dreyer, May 18, 1943, in *Fenton* (Iowa) *Reporter,* July 1, 1943, MCC, YU (*"five months"*); Moorehead, 153 (*"hilarious, shouting bands"*); H. Marshall, *Over to Tunis,* 46 (*convolvulus resembled wood smoke*).

481 *Not even a Tunisian spring:* Meyer, "Strategy and Logistical History: Mediterranean Theater of Operations," n.d., vol. I, CMH, X-16; *NWAf,* 604–605; CBH, Apr. 1943, MHI.

To Béja: To Bizerte with the II Corps, 4–9; *NWAf,* 599–601; *Destruction,* 398; Alexander memo, Apr. 21, 1943, NARA, AFHQ micro, R-6-C (*"We have got"*).

Getting the Allied divisions: C. S. Sugden, XVIII Army Group, to AFHQ G-3, Apr. 7, 1943, NARA RG 331, AFHQ micro, R-6-C (*"present low state"*); Morton Yarmon, "The Administrative and Logistical History of the ETO: IV, TORCH and the ETO," March 1946, Historical Division, U.S. Army Forces, ETO, CMH, 8.31 AA v. 4, 97 (*467,000 troops*); GSP to Alexander, Apr. 11 and 12, 1943, GSP, LOC, box 32; Bradley and Blair, 150 (*"Take them"*); Mayo, 142; Harmon, *Combat Commander,* 130 (*"just a childish fancy"*); Blumenson, *The Patton Papers,* 1940–1945, 218 (*"I would rather"*); Pogue, *George C. Marshall: Organizer of Victory,* 1943–1945, 189 (*"marked fall"*), 191 (*battlefield equals*).

482 *On April 18:* Patton, *War As I Knew It,* introduction by Rick Atkinson, xi (*"fighting general"*); letter, Akers to C. B. Hansen, Jan. 12, 1951, Hansen papers, MHI (*"we doubled figures"*); Dickson, "G-2 Journal," MHI, 59 (*"Your estimates"*);

Hansen, 4/121 (*Patton disputed*); "Report on Operation Conducted by II Corps, U.S. Army, Tunisia," Apr. 10, 1943, Arthur S. Nevins Papers, MHI; AAR, II Corps, "Report on Operation," etc., "Statistical Data Corrected to Include 2 May 1943," CARL, N-2652 A.

485 *As he left*: Blumenson, *The Patton Papers, 1940–1945*, 221.

 On Thursday morning: Bradley and Blair, 25, 35, 50, 58, 159; Liebling, 89 (*"least dressed-up"*); Bradley, *A Soldier's Story*, 29; Fletcher Pratt, *Eleven Generals: Studies in American Command*, 300, 314; B. A. Dickson, OH, SM, MHI; Davis, *Dwight D. Eisenhower: Soldier of Democracy*, 413 (*"too damned sound"*).

486 *With map unfurled*: Liebling, 89; DDE to Bradley, Apr. 16, 1943, Chandler, 1093; Bradley and Blair, 155; Martin, *The G.I. War, 1941–1945*, 57 (*"hunting wild goats"*); Hansen, 5/60A (*"djebel hopping"*), 5/27 (*"This chap Bradley"*); "Operations of II Corps, Northern Tunisia, 23 Apr.–9 May," NARA RG 407, E 427, box 3113.

487 *Although the endgame*: Donald Davison, "Aviation Engineers in the Battle of Tunisia," June 1943, AAF School of Applied Tactics, Orlando, MHI, 13, 28; "Statement by Brig. Gen. Laurence S. Kuter," May 22, 1943, Pentagon, NARA RG 319, background *To Bizerte with II Corps*, 2-3.7 BA, box 103 (*"We attacked Bizerte"*); Operations Bulletin No. 2, May 31, 1943, HQ, NW African AF, NARA RG 334, NWC Lib, box 132 (*killed 752 civilians*); "Interview on Four Aspects of the Air Campaign in Africa," July 5, 1943, Office of Assistant Chief of Air Staff, Intel., NARA RG 334, NWC Lib, box 14; *Destruction*, 412; Carell, 351.

 Allied minelayers: Bragadin, 242–43; "Reports Received by U.S. War Department on Use of Ultra in the European Theater, WWII," NARA RG 457, NSA files, SRH-037, 12; *The AAF in Northwest Africa*, Wings at War, No. 6, Center for Air Force History, 59–60 (*twenty-eight tons of bombs*); letter, R. Bruce Graham, Feb. 28, 1943, MCC, YU (*"It's Better to Give"*); *Destruction*, 416–17.

 Kesselring turned to air transport: "Operations Bulletin No. 1," Apr. 30, 1943, HQ NW NAAF, NARA RG 334, NWC Lib, box 132; Ulrich Buchholz, "Supply by Air of the Enlarged Bridgehead of Tunis," 1947, FMS, #D-071, MHI; *Destruction*, 415–16.

488 *Worse was to come*: Richard Thruelsen and Elliott Arnold, *Mediterranean Sweep: Air Stories from El Alamein to Rome*, 86–93; *Destruction*, 601; Buchholz, "Supply by Air," FMS, #D-071; MacCloskey, 166; DDE, "Commander-in-Chief's Dispatch," 44; Davis, *Carl A. Spaatz and the Air War in Europe*, 196; Roderic Owen, 205; Tedder, 205 (*"If Kesselring goes on"*); *Destruction*, 416.

 Although a quarter-million: Hinsley, *British Intelligence in the Second World War*, vol. 2, 611; Rinteln, "The Italian Command and Armed Forces in the First Half of 1943" (*"was in agony"*); Lucas, *Panzer Army Africa*, 176; "P.W.B. Combat Propaganda," Sept. 2, 1943, AFHQ, Wallace Carroll Papers, LOC MS Div, box 3; "Psychological Warfare in the Mediterranean Theater," Aug. 1945 report to War Dept., Naples, MHI; Wallace Carroll, *Persuade or Perish*, 158.

489 *Axis reserves*: *Destruction*, 603, 604n, 542; Hinsley, *British Intelligence in the Second World War*, vol. II, 612; First Italian Army to OKH, Apr. 14, 1943, NARA RG 319, OCMH, box 225 (*"the repulse"*); Ellis, *Brute Force*, 255 (*"armored division without petrol"*); Macksey, *Crucible of Power*, 271 (*"squinting for ships"*); Hinsley, *British Intelligence in the Second World War*, abridged ed., 5; *Destruction*, 360, 403.

 the German high command: Warlimont, 307–308, 313 (mangiatori); Kesselring, *Memoirs*, 155; CCS to Joint Staff Mission and DDE, Apr. 7, 1943, DDE Lib, PP-pres, box 91; *Destruction*, 384 (*daily ration*).

 If his virtual abandonment: NWAf, 601–602; *Destruction*, 409, 393–94.

490 *Il Duce's backbone*: Arnim, "Recollections of Tunisia," 71, 66 (*"the greatest desire"*).

Hammering Home the Cork

490 *As the Allied armies*: Lindsay, 85–87; *The Tiger Kills*, 179–80; C.R.B. Knight, *Historical Record of the Buffs*, 176.

491 *Montgomery had known*: *Destruction*, 397–402 (*"bald rock faces"*); Hamilton, 233–36 (*"if Anderson"*); Lewin, *Montgomery as Military Commander*, 177–82; Macksey, *Crucible of Power*, 241, 271; *The Tiger Kills*, 184–90; Lindsay, 89; Stevens, *Fourth Indian Division*, 233; Tuker, 338, 346 (*fortifications were lightly held*); Prasad, ed., 511.

492 *Even the second-highest*: author visit, Apr. 2000; Lewin, *Montgomery as Military Commander*, 180 (*"rotting stalagmite"*); John Laffin, "The Battle of Takrouna," *After the Battle* 12, 1976, 48; I. McL. Wards, *Takrouna*, 3–27 (*"One of those grim moments"*); Kippenberger, 305–11 (*"never a moment"*); Horrocks, 163; Hill, *Desert Conquest*, 291.

   But that was it: Prasad, ed., 511–12; *The Tiger Kills*, 184 (*"My hands"*); Hill, *Desert Conquest*, 265; Montgomery to Brooke, Apr. 12, 1943, quoted in Brooks, ed., 206; Macksey, *Crucible of Power*, 272 (*"In the darkness"*).

493 *For the first time*: Kippenberger, 313–14 (*"wait for the enemy"*); Bradley, *A Soldier's Story*, 90 (*"Let's radio"*).

   Weary and distracted: *Destruction*, 441–42; G. R. Stevens, 245 (*surly rebellion*); Horrocks, 164 (*"Of course we can"*).

494 *Even the most irresistible*: Hunt, 176 (*"rather a sad"*); David Williams, *The Black Cats at War: The Story of the 56th (London) Division T.A., 1939–1945*; Macksey, *Crucible of Power*, 287; Messenger, 111 (*"It was only"*); Hamilton, 236–38; Brooks, ed., 222 (*"short rest"*).

   As usual in Tunisia: Hamilton, 216 (*"partridge drive"*); Brooks, ed., 209; Davis, *Carl A. Spaatz and the Air War in Europe*, 208–209 (*seventy different air attacks*); Messenger, 102; Macksey, *Crucible of Power*, 277; Blaxland, 227 (*"The plan's all right"*); Nicholson and Forbes, 318–19.

495 *The Germans struck*: Anderson, "Operations in North West Africa"; Kurowski, 118; Horsfall, 167 (*"Go away, James"*).

496 *Crocker launched*: *Destruction*, 434; *NWAf*, 612; Messenger, 103–104; Ellis, *On the Front Lines*, 75 (*"Men have begun"*).

   On April 26: Anderson, "Operations in North West Africa"; George E. Wrockloff, "Land Mines," n.d., NARA RG 334, NWC Lib, ANSCOL S-1-43, W-89, box 169; Macksey, *The Tank Pioneers*, 191; Hastings, 229.

   So it was up to Allfrey: Malcolm, 118; Ray, 50; *Destruction*, 436 (*"ghosts of good soldiers"*); Marshall, *Over to Tunis*, 124–25; Skillen, 327 (*"like a crowd"*); Horsfall, 98 (*"children of Satan"*), 140.

497 *Good Friday dawned*: D'Arcy-Dawson, 213–14; Perret, *At All Costs*, 159–66; Alexander to Montgomery, March 29, 1943, in Brooks, ed., 189; Middleton, 269; Malcolm, 118; Ray, 52; Austin, 132; Daniell, *History of the East Surrey Regiment*, vol. IV, 171; Jordan, 237 (*"an infernal sight"*); Messenger, 105 (*"the whole ridge"*); P. Royle, ts, n.d., IWM, 66/305/1 (*Zeiss binoculars*).

498 *Longstop had fallen*: *Destruction*, 437; *NWAf*, 611–13; AAR, 1st Bn Irish Guards, Apr. 27–30, 1943, PRO, WO 175/488; G. E. Thurbon, ts, n.d., IWM, 94/8/1; D.J.L. Fitzgerald, *History of the Irish Guards in the Second World War* (*"threw everything"* and *"no time for the gangrene"*); Nicolson and Forbes, 321–30 (*"pungent scent"*); Marshall, *Over to Tunis*, 134–35 (*"a forest of rifles"*).

   The hill remained: Anderson, "Operations in North West Africa"; *Three Years*, 292 (*3,500 casualties*); *NWAf*, 613; G. P. Druitt, ts, n.d., IWM, 96/38/1 (*"One arm was sticking"*).

"Count Your Children Now, Adolf!"

499 *"We are sitting"*: Baumer, 122; Bradley, *A Soldier's Story*, 81.

500 *The guns finished*: Austin, 120 (*"the hollows"*); Arthur R. Harris, "The Bigger They Are the Harder They Fall," *Field Artillery Journal*, May–June 1938, 228; *NWAf*, 614; Hannum, "The 30 Years of Army Experience," ASEQ, 91st Armored FA, 1st AD, MHI, 38–40 (*"Count your children"*).

The infantry surged: Tobin, 95 (*"long, slow line"*); *NWAf*, 621–23; Johnson, *One More Hill*, 63–64; Eston White, author interview, Feb. 2000; log, "16th Infantry, Béja-Mateur Campaign," Apr. 25, 1943, NARA RG 407, E 427, box 5919; John W. Baumgartner et al., "History of the 16th Infantry, 1798–1946," 28; "History of the 26th Infantry in the Present Struggle," MRC FDM, 10/26–74; Spivey, 76 (*"Please shoot me"*).

Into this maelstrom: Kahn, "Education of an Army," *New Yorker*, Oct. 14, 1944, 28, and Oct. 21, 1944, 34; G. Perret, *There's a War to Be Won: The United States Army in World War II*, 70; Larrabee, 119 (*"a Presbyterian pulpit speaker"*); Boatner, 353.

501 *Now McNair did something*: McNair diary, visit to North Africa, Apr. 15–May 3, 1943, NARA RG 337, HQS, commanding general, box 1 (*"nowhere did I find"*); Clay, *Blood and Sacrifice*, 167 (mss); CBH, Apr. 23–25, 1943, MHI; Kahn, "Education of an Army"; John Kelley, interview by Michael Corley, 1977, possession of Paul Gorman (*argued bitterly*); Hall, "A Memoir of World War II"; Charles T. Horner, Jr., "The General's First Purple Heart," ts, n.d., ASEQ, 16th Inf Regt, 1st ID, MHI (*"get the jeep"*); Hansen, 5/52 (*upside down*); Clark, *Calculated Risk*, 168 (*"American soldiers"*).

502 *That was untrue: Three Years*, 292; Phillips, *Sedjenane*, 27, 57, 67.

Impassable it proved to be: AAR, "Report on the Operation Conducted by the 9th Infantry Division in Northern Tunisia, 11 Apr.–8 May 1943," NARA RG 407, E 427, box 7326; AAR, 47th Inf Regt, NARA RG 407, E 427, box 7514; AAR, 60th Inf Regt, NARA RG 407, E 427, box 7535; AAR, 9th ID artillery, NARA RG 407, E 427, box 7424; *NWAf*, 615–20; Mittelman, 106–14.

So it went: Phillips, *Sedjenane*, 86, 104 (*"a dark theater"*), 111; Mittelman, 106–14; "The Fragrance of Spring Was Heavy in the Air," *Trail Tales*, 1979, Boone Co. (Iowa) History Society, Iowa GSM; "G-2 report, II Corps, Battle for Bizerte," Annex B, counter-intelligence section, May 13, 1943, NARA RG 407, E 427, box 3126 (*"free from Arabs"*); "Adventures by Men of the 60th Infantry Regiment in WWII," 1993, MHI, 20–22.

503 *The enemy held fast*: Bradley, *A Soldier's Story*, 89; Liebling, *Mollie & Other Pieces* 9; Mittelman, 106; Howard and Sparrow, 118; D'Arcy-Dawson, 134; William E. Faust, ASEQ, ts, 1st ID artillery, 1990, MHI, 42, 50.

No hill loomed: author visit, Apr. 2000; Anderson, "Operations in North West Africa"; Alexander, "The African Campaign from El Alamein to Tunis" (*"best German troops"*).

504 *Anderson proposed*: Bradley, 86–87 (*"Never mind"*), Bradley and Blair, 157 (*"far over his head"*); *To Bizerte with the II Corps*, 16; CBH, May 1, 1943, MHI; "G-3 Report, Tunis Operation," 1st ID, Apr. 28–30, 1943, NARA RG 407, E 427, box 5759; "History of the 26th Infantry in the Present Struggle," MRC FDM, chapter 10; CBH, May 1, 1943 (*"This campaign is too important"*).

506 *To seize the hill*: Caffey, OH, SM, MHI; Bradley, 85 (*"Get me that hill"*); letter, Robert P. Miller to G. F. Howe, Jan. 14, 1951, NARA RG 319, OCMH, box 225; Arnold N. Brandt, "The Operations of the 1st Battalion, 135th Infantry at Hills 609 and 531," 1948 (*"There was excitement"*); Ryder, OH, SM, MHI; Berens, 62; Bailey, *Through Hell and High Water*, 106; Green and Gauthier, 120–24 (*"For the*

love of heaven" and *"crouched gray shapes"*); Pyle, *Here Is Your War*, 254 (*rocks wrapped*); Bolstad, 140 (*"We lay there awaiting dawn"*).

Two attacks failed: NWAf, 631; *To Bizerte with the II Corps*, 18–21; AAR, "Operations Following the Battle of Fondouk," 1st Bn, 133rd Inf Regt, June 30, 1943, Iowa GSM; Ankrum, 277–81; Bolstad, 140; AAR, Co C, 1st Bn, 133rd Inf Regt, Apr. 30, 1943, Iowa GSM; Mickey C. Smith and Dennis Worthen, "Soldiers on the Production Line," *Pharmacy in History*, 1995, 183; Riess, ed., 543; Middleton, 275 (*"wheat at Gettysburg"*); "The Tunisian Campaign, 34th Div.," Dec. 1943, Iowa GSM; "Report of Action on Hill 609, 135th Inf Regt.," June 30, 1943, Iowa GSM; Leslie W. Bailey, "An Infantry Battalion in Attack," Iowa GSM; Robert Ward, OH, Nov. 30, 1950, G. F. Howe, SM, MHI; Johnson, *One More Hill*, 65 (*"erupting volcano"*); Bolstad, 138–40; C. Miller, *Some Things You Never Forget*, 123–24.

507 *Ryder's troubles*: T. Allen, "A Factual Summary of the Combat Operations of the 1st Infantry Division," 28 (*"unshirted hell"*); Curtis, *The Song of the Fighting First*, 98 (*"Hill 606"*); "Terry Allen and the First Division in North Africa and Sicily," Allen papers, MHI; *NWAf*, 633, 636; Green and Gauthier, 129 (*white phosphorus*); letter, Allen to G. F. Howe, n.d., NARA RG 319, OCMH, box 229; letter, G. A. Taylor to G. F. Howe, Nov. 22, 1950, NARA RG 319, OCMH, box 228 (*considered the attack rash*); letter, C. J. Denholm to G. F. Howe, Dec. 13, 1950, NARA RG 319, OCMH, box 228.

508 *Impatience cost*: Clay, 167–69 (mss); Robert E. Cullis, "We Learn in Combat," *Infantry Journal*, June 1944, 31 (*"more like a street fight"*); AAR, Co H, 3rd Bn, 1st Armored Regt, Apr. 30, 1943, NARA RG 407, E 427, box 14916; Robert V. Maraist and Peter C. Hains, "Conference on North African Operations," transcript, June 16, 1943, Fort Knox, SM, MHI; log, "16th Inf., Beja-Mateur Campaign," Apr. 30, 1943, NARA RG 407, E 427, box 5919 (*"Heinies are all over"*).

Hill 609 would change hands: Maraist and Hains, transcript, SM, MHI (*"No one"*); Ankrum, 274 (*"God bless all of you"*), 276 (*"Tell my mother"*); B. A. Dickson, OH, SM, MHI; Bradley, 87; AAR, "Operations of This Company While on Detached Service," Co I, 1st AR, May 14, 1943, possession of Roger Cirillo; AAR, "Operations Following the Battle of Fondouk," 1st Bn, 133rd Inf Regt, June 30, 1943, Iowa GSM; Hougen, *The Story of the Famous 34th Infantry Division*; Larson, ed., 84–86.

509 *"Jerries approach"*: log, "16th Inf., Beja-Mateur Campaign," May 1, 1943 (*"A panorama"*); Robert R. Moore quoted in *Villisca* (Iowa) *Review*, n.d., Iowa GSM (*killed by such treachery*); Robert R. Moore, "Tunisian Stand," ts, Oct. 1943, NARA RG 319, OCMH, box 103; "The Tunisian Campaign, 34th Division," Dec. 1943, Iowa GSM; Brandt, "The Operations of the 1st Battalion, 135th Infantry at Hills 609 and 531"; Ankrum, 282; Bradley, 94 (*"few prisoners"*); "Dennis Frederick Neal, Soldier," ts, n.d., Iowa GSM, 68 (*"literally covered"*); "German Tanks Trapped," *Times* (London), May 5, 1943 (*"thick as currants in cake"*); Pyle, *Here Is Your War*, 259 (*"Those who went"*).

Ryder put his losses: "The Tunisian Campaign, 34th Division," Dec. 1943, Iowa GSM; Marshall, ed., *Proud Americans*, 96 (*"shoes hanging"*); log, "16th Inf., Beja-Mateur Campaign," May, 1, 1943 (*"no prisoners will be taken"*); "German Tanks Trapped," *Times* (London), May 5, 1943 (*"At our feet"*).

510 *Outside Béja*: CBH, May 1, 1943, MHI (*"smoothing the sparse gray hair"*).

Mateur fell on May 3: AAR, "Report of Operations, 23 Apr.–9 May," 1st AD, NARA RG 407, E 427, box 14767; Hoy, "The Last Days in Tunisia," *Cavalry Journal*, Jan.–Feb. 1944, 8; *NWAf*, 645; *To Bizerte with the II Corps*, 36.

The land here: Austin, 138–39 (*Bismarck*); Fred H. Salter, *Recon Scout*, 76–85;

Harmon, *Combat Commander*, 132 (*"let the men live"*); Middleton, 282 (*"Tell the sons of bitches"*).

511   *Many thousands had retreated*: Hannum, "The Thirty Years of Army Experience," ASEQ, 91st Armored FA, 1st AD, 40; Gardiner, ts, USMA Arch, 134; unsigned narrative of Mateur-Bizerte action, ts, n.d., PMR, GCM Lib, box 12 (*"Arab shacks"*); L. P. Robertson, ASEQ, 1st AR, MHI, 343 (*"a tin goose"*), 347 (*"Some of the enemy"*); msg, Eddy to 9th ID and Corps Franc d'Afrique, Apr. 29, 1943, NARA RG 407, E 427, box 7334 (*"Here is our chance"*).

    The 1st Armored Division: Howze, "Tank Action," ts, 1943, Ward papers, MHI (*"monkey's paw"*); Bradley, 92 (*"Can you do it?"*).

    Yet Harmon nursed: letter, E. N. Harmon to G. F. Howe, Oct. 16, 1952, NARA RG 319, OCMH, box 225 (*"crybaby outfit"*); Harmon memo, Apr. 14, 1943, in "History of the 91st Armored FA Battalion" (*"lack of discipline"*); Robinett, "Among the First," PMR, GCM Lib, box 28, 474–75 (*"damned all past performance"*); Robert Simons, OH, July 1976, OW, MHI (*the temerity to boo*); S. J. Krekeler, ASEQ, ts, n.d., 91st Armored FA, 1st AD, 92.

512   *Now they had reached*: Robinett, *Armor Command*, 227 (*"Will the damned"*); Robinett memo to CCB, May 5, 1943, PMR, GCM Lib, box 12 (*"Towards the rear"*).

    After that unpromising prelude: letter, Harmon to WD G-1, May 23, 1943, Harmon papers, MHI; Harmon, OH, Sept. 16, 1952, SM, MHI (*"Hell, that fellow"*); Robinett, *Armor Command*, 228–29 (*"looking hard"*).

Tunisgrad

513   *The most intense*: Blaxland, 252; Middleton, 287; Anderson, "Operations in North West Africa"; Nicholson, *Alex*, 190 (*"The muzzle flashes"*).

    Determined to bury: Tuker, 367–69 (*"stunning weights"*); *Destruction*, 450–51; Stevens, *Fourth Indian Division*, 251–53; Marshall, *Over to Tunis*, 118 (*"you could almost"*); "Military Reports of the United Nations," Sept. 15, 1943, Military Intelligence Division, WD, NARA RG 334, box 585; Messenger, 113–14 (*"a roof of shells"*).

514   *Behind the guns*: "Report on Participation of the Allied Air Force in the North Africa Campaign, Apr. 11–May 14, 1943," n.d., NARA RG 319, 2-3.7 BA, box 103; NWAf, 649.

    Well before dawn: Tuker, 367; Stevens, 249; Horrocks, 168 (*"chalk from cheese"*).

    Four tank battalions: Anderson, "Operations in North West Africa"; NWAf, 645–49; North, ed., 38–39 (*"into the heart"*).

515   *"The whole valley"*: MacVane, *On the Air in World War II*, 180; Blaxland, 252; Daniell, *History of the East Surrey Regiment*, vol. IV, 173; "Military Reports of the United Nations," Sept. 15, 1943, Military Intelligence Division, WD, NARA RG 334, box 585 (*"thick pall"*); Nicholson, *Alex*, 191 (*"baker's boy"*).

    Allied eavesdroppers: Skillen, 333 (*medics*); Ernst Schnarrenberger, "Situation of the Fortification of Tunis," March 1947, FMS, D-005; Hinsley, *British Intelligence in the Second World War*, vol. 2, 615; *Kriegstagebuch* V, Fifth Panzer Army, May 6, 1943, RG 319, OCMH, box 226 (*"laid low"*); *Destruction*, 450; Nicholson and Forbes, 334 (*"Butter"*), 335 (*"I can see the lily-white walls"*); Roskill, 441; Cunningham, 529 (*"Sink, burn"*).

    The righteous wrath: letter, Charles J. Denholm to G. F. Howe, Feb. 20, 1951, NARA RG 319, OCMH, box 229; R. W. Porter, Jr., "Report of Interrogation of Recaptured American Soldiers," May 11, 1943, 1st ID, NARA RG 407, E 427, box 3161; letter, Floyd F. Youngman to parents, June 4, 1943, in Curtiss, ed., *Letters*

Home, 291 (*"like a forest"*); *AAFinWWII*, 193; William Munday, "Prison Ship Escapes," *Tunis Telegraph*, May 10, 1943, in Downing, *At War with the British*, photo; Hill, *Desert Conquest*, 318; Edwin V. Westrate, *Forward Observer*, 167 (*"hopping around"*); Dawson, *Tunisian Battle*, 240–45; *NWAf*, 650; Craven and Cate, eds., 193 (*more than one hundred*).

517 *Harmon's 1st Armored*: Bradley, *A Soldier's Story*, 93; *NWAf*, 650, 653; Austin, 151 (*"perambulators"*); Phillips, *Sedjenane*, 136; Dickson, "G-2 Journal," MHI, 64; Crawford, 138; Berens, 69–70; Ohio Historical Society web site, www.ohiohistory.org/etcetera/exhibits/kilroy.

With the 9th Division: "18th Infantry, Draft Regimental Wartime History," Stanhope Mason Collection, MRC FDM; Allen, "A Factual Summary of the Combat Operations of the 1st ID," TdA papers, MHI; Mason, "Reminiscences and Anecdotes," MRC FDM.

the 18th Infantry surged: AAR, "Operations of 18th Inf in Mateur Sector," n.d., includes 1st, 2nd, 3rd Bn reports, NARA RG 407, E 427, box 5937; Vining, ed., 72–73 (*"Bullets were singing"*); Mason, "Reminiscences and Anecdotes of WWII," MRC FDM; "18th Infantry, Draft Regimental Wartime History," Stanhope Mason Collection, MRC FDM; Allen, "A Factual Summary of the Combat Operations of the 1st ID," TdA papers, MHI; "G-3 Report, Tunis Operation," 1st ID, May 5–6, 1943, NARA RG 407, E 427, box 5759; Knickerbocker et al., 80; John T. Corley, OH, n.d., possession of Paul Gorman, 39–40 (*"bloody foolish"*).

518 *Early on Friday afternoon*: *Three Years*, 289 (*"hen"*); DDE to CCS et al., Chandler, 1100, 1108, 1113, 1118; Butcher diary, DDE Lib, A-349 (*"good and drunk"*).

he was sleeping badly: *Three Years*, 310; DDE to GCM et al., Chandler, 1104, 1114, 1115, 1148.

519 *Now the fifty-five-year-old*: *Three Years*, 298; Butcher diary, DDE Lib, A-365 (*"How much better"*).

Eisenhower shrugged off: DDE to GCM, May 6, 1943, Chandler, 1118; Hansen, 5/46 (*"most difficult"*), 5/134 (*"Holy First"*); Middleton, "The Saga of a Tough Outfit," *New York Times Magazine*, Apr. 8, 1945, 8 (*"the finest division commander"*); Bradley, 93–94; D'Este, *Bitter Victory*, 271 (*"phony Abraham Lincoln"*); Bradley and Blair, 158 (*"marked man"*).

520 *As Eisenhower and Bradley*: letter, C. P. Eastburn to OCMH, June 6, 1947, NARA RG 319, OCMH, box 103.

a dead city: interrogation report, Anatole Cordonier, chief naval engineer, Bizerte, by 9th ID, May 7, 1943, NARA RG 407, E 427, box 7334; Pyle, *Here Is Your War*, 281 (*"Bizerte was"*); letter, Donald Peel, May 16, 1943, ASEQ, 9th ID, MHI (*"You walked through"*); "Statement by BG Laurence S. Kuter," Pentagon, May 22, 1943, NARA RG 319, 2-3.7 BA, box 103; Clifford, 439; letter, Thomas Riggs to parents, June 25, 1943, PMR, LOC, box 4.

521 *As Colonel Eastburn*: letter, Eastburn to OCMH, June 6, 1947; Stannard, ed., 173; Curtiss, ed., 63; Austin, 152 (*"Quite ridiculous"*); Martin, 59 (*"Everybody was standing"*).

By dawn, the last Germans: Phillips, *Sedjenane*, 133; Abbott, 90; Berens, 70; Howe, *The Battle History of the 1st Armored Division*, 247 (*"hundreds of vehicles"*); Gardiner, ts, USMA Arch, 150.

Tunis fell at 3:30 P.M.: Clarke, *The Eleventh at War*, 299–300; AAR, 1st Derbyshire Yeomanry, PRO, WO 175/293; *Destruction*, 452; J.R.T. Hopper, "Figures in a Fading Landscape," ts, 1995, IWM, 97/3/1.

522 *"The streets were full"*: F. Stephens, "Collapse in Tunis," *Military Review*, Apr. 1945, 69 (*"Astonished Germans"* and *"complete with Buick"*); Blaxland, 256; MacVane, *On the Air in World War II*, 185–86 (*"Stop that shooting"*); Jordan, 254 (*"Get

out your weapons"); Powell, *In Barbary*, 17; D'Arcy-Dawson, 235; Noel F. Busch, "The Fall of Tunis," *Life*, May 1943, 35 (*a windsock*).

Into the city: Marshall, *Over to Tunis*, 149 (*"Men were singing"*); Blumenson, *Kasserine Pass*, 317–18; Hastings, 232; Anderson to DDE, May 10, 1943, PP-pres, DDE Lib, box 5 (*"pernicious rivalry"*); Hughes diary, May 7, 1943, "Allied High Command," MHI, micro, R-5 (*"our egos"*); "S Force Operation Instruction No. 1," Apr. 1943, "Special Preparation Capture of Tunis 1943," NARA RG 331, AFHQ micro, R-81I; "Intelligence at HQ First Army, Nov. 1942–May 1943," May 23, 1943, ts, National Archives of Canada, RG 24, vol. 01, Intelligence 10719.

523 *For months, Eisenhower had worried*: Harmon, *Combat Command*, 138; Parris and Russell, 346 (*"we will kill"*); Jensen, 73–74; Pyle, *Here Is Your War*, 277 (*"Winning in battle"*).

    II Corps casualties: *To Bizerte with the II Corps*, 51–52; "Operation of II Corps, Northern Tunisia, 23 Apr.–9 May 1943," NARA RG 407, E 427, box 3113; Bradley and Blair, 159.

    For the British: Richard Feige, "Relationship Between Operations and Supply in Africa," 1947, FMS #D-125, MHI, 11; Webster Anderson, "Organization and Functioning of the Petroleum Section, AFHQ," Aug. 10, 1943, NARA RG 334, NWC Lib, box 162; *Destruction*, 423; Hunt, 181–82 (*"We are waiting"*); *Kriegstagebuch* V, Fifth Panzer Army, NARA RG 319, OCMH, box 226; Nicholson and Forbes, 343 (*wristwatches*).

524 *At Hammam Lif*: Clifford, 443; Ellis, *Welsh Guards at War*, 123; Parris and Russell, 354 (*"like a steamboat"*); Howard and Sparrow, 142; Nicholson and Forbes, 339; Blaxland, 257; Quilter, ed., 54.

    Like Terry Allen on the Tine: Messenger, 117–18; Blaxland, 259; ffrench Blake, 148; Lindsay, 91; P. Royle, ts, n.d., IWM, 66/305/1 (*"Looking back"*); Nicholson and Forbes, 343–44 (*"dotted with points"*); Horrocks, 172 (*"I have waited"*).

525 *The prisoners came*: John Mayo, OH, ASEQ, 1987, 1st AR, MHI; film, "At the Front in North Africa with the U.S. Army," Dec. 1942, NARA RG 111, Office of the Chief Signal Officer, #1001; AAR, 16th/5th Lancers, May 12, 1943, PRO, WO 175/291; Martin, 59–60 (*"going to a wedding"*).

    "Germans were everywhere": Pyle, *Here Is Your War*, 273; Robert M. Marsh, ASEQ, 1989, ts, 81st Reconnaissance Bn, 1st AD; Nicholson and Forbes, 341 (*"Champagne rather dry"*), 285 (*"British Tommy!"*); Howard and Sparrow, 141 (*dental instruments*); Jensen, 75; Linderman, 331.

526 *A few escaped*: Luck, *Panzer Commander*, 122; Hinsley, *British Intelligence in the Second World War*, abridged edition, 292; "Commander-in-Chief's Dispatch," 48; Nicholson and Forbes, 342 (*"they sat astride"*); Clarke, *The Eleventh at War*, 303; Rame, 291–94; "Personal Diary of Lt. Gen. C. W. Allfrey, the Tunisian Campaign," May 12, 1943, LHC (*"The anguished of yesterday"*); McCorquodale et al., 235; Austin, 153; letter, Raymond Dreyer, *Fenton* (Iowa) *Reporter*, Nov. 4, 1943, MCC, YU.

    As recently as May 5: DDE to GCM, May 5, 1943, Chandler, 1114 (*"the Axis cannot"*), 1146n; memos, MTOUSA, May 1943, NARA RG 492, Records of the Office of the Commanding General, box 56.

    Carefully calibrated: memo, B. M. Sawbridge to W. B. Smith, July 1943, MTOUSA, NARA RG 492, Office of the Commanding General, box 332; Schrijvers, 51 (*"like sardines"*); Kurowski, 121.

527 *For some*: "Records Relating to Prisoners," MTOUSA, NARA RG 492, Provost Marshal General, box 2245; "Observation of Provost Marshal Activities in Oran Area," "memo for Gen. Dillon," Nov. 25, 1943, MTOUSA, NARA RG 492, box 2209; Penney, ts, LHC (*"using their prisoners"*).

Neither starvation: Destruction, 445–46; *NWAf,* 662; Hansen, 5/104; Parris and Russell, 348 (*"fought like sportsmen"*).

The biggest fish: Destruction, 458–59; Hunt, 181; Parris and Russell, 357 (*"He had tried"*).

528 *With fuel scavanged*: Arnim, "Recollections of Tunisia," 113–15; Carell, 353; Destruction, 457–58.

He soon returned: Stevens, *Fourth Indian Division,* 255; Tuker, 374–78; D'Arcy-Dawson, 245–46 (*"a Potsdam parade"*); Allfrey diary, May 12, 1943, LHC (*"He took this badly"*); Eisenhower, *Crusade in Europe,* 157 (*snubbed Arnim*); J.B.A. Glennie, ts, 1988, in papers of R. de L. King, IWM, 96/29/1 (*a Steyer Daimler*); Martin, 51 (*"an iron-plated monocle"*); Destruction, 459.

EPILOGUE

530 *Roses perfumed*: Signal Corps footage, NARA film, ADC-1113 and ADC-2407; Bailey, 119; letter, Joe Farley, n.d., MCC, YU (*"too damn hot"*); Macmillan, *War Diaries,* 88–91 (*"football crowd"*).

Shortly before noon: Gardiner, ts, USMA Arch, 151–52 (*"same precision"*); Nicholson and Forbes, 349; diary, May 20, 1943, GSP, LOC, box 2, folder 13 (*"French ecclesiastic"*).

531 *At noon, the crowd's mood*: Three Years, 312; Moorehead, 65; Hougen, *The Story of the Famous 34th Infantry Division*; Bailey, *Through Hell and High Water,* 119.

After the French: Bailey, 119 (*"Arkansas backwoods men"*); diary, May 20, 1943, GSP, LOC, box 2, folder 13 (*"lack pride"*); Harmon, *Combat Commander,* 141; Davies, 110–11.

532 *Then pipers*: memo, 24th Guards to 1st Irish Guards, May 17, 1943, PRO, WO 175/488 (*"Brasses will"*); Macmillan, *War Diaries,* 90–91; Gardiner, ts, USMA Arch, 151–52 (*"much the better show"*).

The parade straggled: Nicholson, *Alex,* 193 (*"Hundreds of Italians"*); Nicholson and Forbes, 349; Macmillan, *War Diaries,* 91–92; Three Years, 313; Bradley, *A Soldier's Story,* 109 (*"waste of time"*).

Even after two and a half: McMillan, *Mediterranean Assignment,* 319 (*"lean, bronzed"*); Three Years, 310, 312; DDE to GCM, May 13, 1943, Chandler, 1129; DDE to Fox Conner, Aug. 21, 1942, Chandler, vol. I, 485 (*"too simple-minded"*); D.K.R. Crosswell, *The Chief of Staff: The Military Career of General Walter Bedell Smith,* 151; F. E. Morgan, OH, FCP, MHI (*"One of the fascinations"* and *"a well-trained"*); Larrabee, 427 (*"Before he left"*).

533 *The tiny Mediterranean island*: Roskill, 444 (*"salvage firstly"*); memo, B.M. Archibald, AFHQ G-3, to G-4, July 15, 1943, NARA RG 331, micro, R-141-C (*"not a great deal"*); *Register of Graduates and Former Cadets,* USMA, 1998 (*Arnold*); lecture, Col. Mohamed Ali El Bekri, May 14, 2001, Army-Navy Club, Washington, D.C. (*Sixty years later*).

534 *The French high command*: "French Policy Toward Arabs, Jews, and Italians in Tunisia," Dec. 1943, OSS, Research and Analysis Branch, NARA RG 334, E 315, NWC Lib, box 895.

Preoccupied with the imminent invasion: Miller, *Some Things You Never Forget,* 126; "History of the 168th Infantry," Iowa GSM; Davies, 111; Carver, ed., *The War Lords,* 572; Fussell, *Wartime,* 264 (*"I am Jesus' little lamb"*), 139 (*"When you figure how many"*); letter, Joe Spring, PM, n.d., in MCC, YU (*"Dame Rumor"*); Harold B. Simpson, *Audie Murphy, American Soldier,* 18, 47, 66–67; Kennett, 136–37; "Dennis Frederick Neal, Soldier," ts, n.d., Iowa GSM, 72–73 (*"There are many rumors"* and *"Ol' General Ryder's"*).

535 *Most of their leaders*: Anderson to DDE, May 12, 1943, Anderson file, DDE Lib, PP-pres, box 5; Boatner, 9; "World War II War Hero Fights Final Battle," Apr. 1991 newspaper clipping, no citation, Iowa GSM; "An American Story: The Life and Times of a Midlands Family," Nov. 9, 1997, *Omaha World-Herald*, 1; letter, Robert R. Moore to family, May 12, 1943; author interview, Robert R. Moore, Jr., June 2000.

536 *Young ones do*: *Destruction*, 460; *NWAf*, 675; D'Arcy-Dawson, 24 (*"Mort!"*); letter, Joseph T. Dawson to family, June 1, 1943, J. T. Dawson Collection, MRC FDM; Doubler, 240; Blaxland, 253 (six battalion commanders), 265.

537 *Axis casualties*: Blaxland, 265; Messenger, 120; *Destruction*, 460; Arnim, "Recollections of Tunisia," MHI, 115; Westphal, 124; Kühn, *German Paratroops in World War II*, 179; Parkinson, 104.

   "one continent": Churchill, *The Hinge of Fate*, 780; Doubler, 13; Gelb, 320; "The Administrative and Logistical History of the ETO," vol. 4, March 1946, CMH, 124 (*"high-grade stock"*).

   Truscott worried: Truscott, *Command Missions*, 192; Larrabee, 436 (*"a place to be lousy"*).

538 *It was the discovery*: Richard Wilson, "The Gallant Fight of the 34th Division in the North African Campaign," 1943, *Des Moines Register and Tribune*, Iowa GSM (*"three things"*); Middleton, "We'll Take 'Em Apart and Then Get Home," *New York Times Magazine*, July 18, 1943, 8 (*"grudge fight"*); letter, Stephen Dinning, *Des Moines Register and Tribune*, March 21, 1943, MCC, YU (*"There's nothing over here"*); letter, Bernard Kessel, n.d., MCC, YU (*"In years to come"*); letter, n.d., submitted by James D. Buckley, MCC, YU (*"We didn't know"*); Essame, 55 (*"unlike anyone else"*).

   "I am not willing": letter, Ray Salibury to sister, July 6, 1943, in Tapert, ed., *Lines of Battle*; letter, anonymous, Apr. 1943, *Minneapolis Tribune*, MCC, YU (*"We all feel"*).

539 *Africa was the first step*: Gelb, 319; Bryant, 419; Warlimont, 277–78; Churchill, *The Hinge of Fate*, 779.

   Hitler had lost: "An Interview with General Field Marshal Albert Kesselring," May 1946, *World War II German Military Studies*, vol. 3, ETHIN 72, MHI (*"It was in Tunisia"*); Kesselring, *Memoirs*, 157; Gelb, 320 (*"walking around"*); "Estimate of the Present Combat Value of the Italian Armed Forces," May 6, 1943, NARA RG 319, OCMH, box 226 (*"only one Italian"*); Howard, *Grand Strategy*, vol. 4, 338 (*milk and rice*).

   Yet Tunis—like Stalingrad: Goodwin, 437; Warlimont, 314 (*"postponing the invasion"*); Howard, *Grand Strategy*, vol. 4, 337, 355.

540 *The protracted campaign*: Fraser, *Alanbrooke*, 336; Roger Barry Fosdick, "A Call to Arms: The American Enlisted Soldier in World War II," Ph.D. diss, 1985, Claremont Graduate School, 22 (*"War is a burden"*); Bennett, *Ultra and Mediterranean Strategy*, 371; Mansoor, *The GI Offensive in Europe*, 85; AAFinWWII, 50 (*"the purest gamble"*); Churchill, *The Hinge of Fate*, 778.

   "Together we had all faced death": P. Royle, ts, IWM, 66/305/1, 77; Caleb Milne, n.d., in Tapert, ed., *Lines of Battle* (*"a vivid, wonderful world"*).

SOURCES

BOOKS

The AAF in Northwest Africa. Washington, D.C.: Center for Air Force History, 1992.

Abbott, Harry P. *The Nazi "88" Made Believers.* Dayton, Oh.: Otterbein Press, 1946.

Adams, Henry H. *1942: The Year That Doomed the Axis.* New York: Warner, 1973.

Altieri, James J. *Darby's Rangers: An Illustrated Portrayal of the Original Rangers.* Durham, N.C.: Ranger Book Committee, 1945.

———. *The Spearheaders.* Indianapolis: Bobbs-Merrill, 1960.

Alvarez, David. *Secret Messages: Codebreaking and American Diplomacy, 1930–1945.* Lawrence, Kan.: University Press of Kansas, 2000.

Ambrose, Stephen E. *Eisenhower: Soldier, General of the Army, President Elect, 1890–1952. Volume 1.* New York: Simon & Schuster, 1983.

———. *The Supreme Commander: The War Years of General Dwight D. Eisenhower.* New York: Doubleday, 1970.

Ambrose, Stephen E., and Richard H. Immerman. *Ike's Spies: Eisenhower and the Espionage Establishment.* Garden City, N.Y.: Doubleday, 1981.

Ankrum, Homer. *Dogfaces Who Smiled Through Tears.* Lake Mills, Ia.: Graphic Publishing, 1987.

Armstrong, Anne. *Unconditional Surrender.* New Brunswick, N.J.: Rutgers University Press, 1961.

Arnbal, Anders Kjar. *The Barrel-Land Dance Hall Rangers.* New York: Vantage Press, 1993.

Ashcraft, Howard D. *As You Were: Cannon Company, 34th Infantry Division, 168th Infantry Regiment.* Richmond, Va.: Ashcraft Enterprises, 1990.

Astor, Gerald. *The Greatest War: Americans in Combat, 1941–1945.* Novato, Calif.: Presidio, 1999.

Auphan, Paul, and Jacques Mordal. *The French Navy in World War II.* Trans. A.C.J. Sabalot. Annapolis: United States Naval Institute, 1959.

Austin, A. B. *Birth of an Army.* London: Victor Gollancz, 1943.

Ayer, Fred, Jr. *Before the Colors Fade.* Dunwoody, Ga.: Norman S. Berg, 1971.

Baedeker, Karl. *The Mediterranean.* New York: Scribners, 1911.

Bailey, Leslie W. *Through Hell and High Water.* New York: Vantage, 1994.

Baily, Charles M. *Faint Praise: American Tanks and Tank Destroyers During World War II.* Hamden, Conn.: Archon, 1983.

Barber, Laurie, and John Tonkin-Covell. *Freyberg: Churchill's Salamander.* London: Hutchinson, 1990.

Barclay, C. N. *History of the 16th/5th The Queen's Royal Lancers.* Aldershot: Gale & Polden, 1963.

Barnett, Correlli. *The Desert Generals.* New York: Viking, 1961.

———, ed. *Hitler's Generals.* New York: Quill/William Morrow, 1989.

Baumer, Robert W. *Before Taps Sounded.* S.P., 2000.

Baumgartner, John W., ed. *The 16th Infantry Regiment.* De Quoin, Ill.: Cricket Press, 1999.

Beaufre, André. *1940: The Fall of France.* New York: Knopf, 1968.

Beck, Alfred M., et al. *The Corps of Engineers: The War Against Germany. U.S. Army in World War II.* Washington, D.C.: Center of Military History, 1985.

Beck, Emily Morison, ed. *Sailor Historian: The Best of Samuel Eliot Morison.* Boston: Houghton Mifflin, 1977.

Beckett, Frank. *"Prepare to Move": With the 6th Armoured Division in Africa and Italy.* Grimsby, U.K.: S.P., 1994.

Beebe, Gilbert W., and Michael E. DeBakey. *Battle Casualties: Incidence, Mortality, and Logistic Considerations.* Springfield, Ill.: Charles C. Thomas, 1952.

Beesly, Patrick. *Very Special Intelligence.* New York: Ballantine, 1977.

Behrendt, Hans-Otto. *Rommel's Intelligence in the Desert Campaign.* London: William Kimber, 1985.

Behrens, C.B.A. *Merchant Shipping and the Demands of War.* London: Her Majesty's Stationery Office, 1955.

Belden, Jack. *Still Time to Die.* New York: Harper, 1944.

Bellafaire, Judith L., ed. *The U.S. Army and World War II: Selected Papers from the Army's Commemorative Conferences.* Washington, D.C.: U.S. Army Center of Military History, 1998.

Bennett, Lowell. *Assignment to Nowhere: The Battle for Tunisia.* New York: Vanguard Press, 1943.

Bennett, Ralph. *Ultra and Mediterranean Strategy.* New York: William Morrow, 1989.

Berens, Robert J. *Citizen Soldier.* Ames, Ia.: Sigler, 1995.

Berlin, Robert H. *U.S. Army World War II Corps Commanders.* Fort Leavenworth, Kan.: Combat Studies Institute, 1989.

Bidwell, Shelford. *Artillery Tactics, 1939–1945.* London: Almark, 1976.

———. *The Royal Horse Artillery.* London: Leo Cooper, 1973.

Binder, L. James. *Lemnitzer: A Soldier for His Time.* Washington, D.C.: Brassey's, 1997.

Bingham, J.K.W., and Werner Haupt. *North African Campaign, 1940–1943.* London: Macdonald, 1968.

Blair, Clay. *Hitler's U-Boat War: The Hunted, 1942–1945.* New York: Modern Library, 1998.

———. *Hitler's U-Boat War: The Hunters, 1939–1942.* New York: Random House, 1996.

Blaker, Gordon A. *Iron Knights: The United States 66th Armored Regiment.* Shippensburg, Pa.: Burd Street Press, 1999.

Blaxland, Gregory. *The Plain Cook and the Great Showman.* London: William Kimber, 1977.

Blumenson, Martin. *Kasserine Pass.* New York: Jove Books, 1983.

———. *Mark Clark.* New York: Congdon & Weed, 1984.

———. *Patton: The Man Behind the Legend, 1985–1945.* New York: William Morrow, 1985.

———. *The Patton Papers, 1940–1945.* New York: Da Capo Press, 1996.

Boatner, Mark M., III. *The Biographical Dictionary of World War II.* Novato, Calif.: Presidio, 1999.

Bolstad, Owen C. *Dear Folks: A Dog-Faced Infantryman in World War II.* S.P.: 1993.

Boog, Horst, et al. *Germany and the Second World War.* Vol. VI: *The Global War.* Trans. Ewald Osers et al. New York: Oxford University Press, 2001.

Bradley, Omar N. *A Soldier's Story.* New York: Henry Holt, 1951.

Bradley, Omar N., and Clay Blair. *A General's Life.* New York: Simon & Schuster, 1983.

Bragadin, Marc'Antonio. *The Italian Navy in World War II.* Trans. Gale Hoffman. Annapolis: U.S. Naval Institute, 1957.

Brendon, Piers. *Ike: His Life and Times.* New York: Harper & Row, 1986.

Breuer, William B. *Geronimo: American Paratroopers in World War II.* New York: St. Martin's Press, 1989.

Brinkley, David. *Washington Goes to War*. New York: Ballantine, 1989.

Brokaw, Tom. *The Greatest Generation*. New York: Random House, 1998.

Brooks, Stephen, ed. *Montgomery and the Eighth Army*. London: Army Records Society, 1991.

Brown, Anthony Cave. *Bodyguard of Lies*. New York: Harper & Row, 1975.

———. *The Last Hero: Wild Bill Donovan*. New York: Times Books, 1982.

———, ed. *The Secret War Report of the OSS*. New York: Berkley, 1976.

Bryant, Arthur. *The Turn of the Tide*. London: Collins, 1957.

Buchanan, A. Russell. *The United States and World War II*. Vol. I. New York: Harper & Row, 1946.

Buell, Thomas B. *Master of Sea Power: A Biography of Fleet Admiral Ernest J. King*. Boston: Little, Brown, 1980.

Burdick, Charles B. *Germany's Military Strategy and Spain in World War II*. Syracuse, N.Y.: Syracuse University Press, 1968.

Burns, James MacGregor. *Roosevelt: The Soldier of Freedom*. New York: Harcourt Brace Jovanovich, 1970.

Butcher, Harry C. *My Three Years with Eisenhower*. New York: Simon & Schuster, 1946.

Butler, J.R.M. *Grand Strategy*. Vol. II, *History of the Second World War*. London: Her Majesty's Stationery Office, 1971.

Bykofsky, Joseph, and Harold Larson. *The Transportation Corps: Operations Overseas. U.S. Army in World War II*. Washington, D.C.: Office of the Chief of Military History, 1957.

Bynner, Witter, trans. *The Jade Mountain: A Chinese Anthology*. New York: Vintage, 1972.

Cameron, Ian C. *History of the Argyll & Sutherland Highlanders 7th Battalion*. London: Thomas Nelson, 1946.

Cardinell, Robert B., ed. *Adventures by Men of the 60th Infantry Regiment in WWII*. Winter Park, Fla.: 1993.

Carell, Paul. *The Foxes of the Desert*. Trans. Mervyn Savill. New York: Bantam, 1972.

Carmichael, Thomas N. *The Ninety Days*. New York: Bernard Geis Associates, 1971.

Carroll, Wallace. *Publish or Perish*. Boston: Houghton Mifflin, 1948.

Carver, Michael. *Out of Step: Memoirs of a Field Marshal*. London: Hutchinson, 1989.

———, ed. *The War Lords: Military Commanders of the Twentieth Century*. Boston: Little, Brown, 1976.

Catton, Bruce. *A Stillness at Appomattox*. New York: Doubleday, 1953.

———. *The War Lords of Washington*. New York: Harcourt, Brace, 1948.

Chalmers, W. S. *Full Cycle: The Biography of Admiral Sir Bertram Home Ramsay*. London: Hodder & Stoughton, 1959.

Chalou, George C., ed. *The Secrets War: The Office of Strategic Services in World War II*. Washington, D.C.: National Archives and Records Administration, 1992.

Chandler, Alfred, ed. *The Papers of Dwight David Eisenhower: The War Years*. Vols. 1, 2, 5. Baltimore: Johns Hopkins Press, 1970.

Chant, Christopher. *The Encyclopedia of Code Names of World War II*. London: Routledge & Kegan Paul, 1986.

Chase, Patrick J. *Seek, Strike, Destroy: The History of the 894th Tank Destroyer Battalion in World War II*. Baltimore: Gateway Press, 1995.

Churchill, Winston S. *The Second World War*. Vol. II: *Their Finest Hour*; vol. III: *The Grand Alliance*; vol. IV: *The Hinge of Fate*. Boston: Houghton Mifflin, 1949, 1950, 1951.

Clardy, Andrea, ed. *Gordon Gammack: Columns from Three Wars*. Ames, Ia.: Iowa State University Press, 1979.

Clark, J. J., with Clark G. Reynolds. *Carrier Admiral*. New York: David McKay, 1967.

Clark, Mark W. *Calculated Risk*. New York: Harper & Brothers, 1950.

Clarke, Dudley. *The Eleventh at War*. London: Michael Joseph, 1952.

Clarke, Rupert. *With Alex at War*. Barnsley, U.K.: Leo Cooper, 2000.

Clay, Steve. *Blood and Sacrifice: The History of the 16th Infantry Regiment from the Civil War Through the Gulf War*. La Grange Park, Ill.: Cantigny Military History, 2000.

Clayton, Anthony. *Three Marshals of France*. London: Brassey's, 1992.

Clifford, Alexander G. *The Conquest of North Africa, 1940–1943*. Boston: Little, Brown, 1943.

Cline, Ray S. *Washington Command Post: The Operations Division. U.S. Army in World War II*. Washington, D.C.: Department of the Army, 1951.

Coates, John Boyd, Jr., ed. *Orthopedic Surgery in the Mediterranean Theater of Operations. U.S. Army in World War II*. Washington, D.C.: Office of the Surgeon General, 1957.

Codman, Charles R. *Drive*. Boston: Little, Brown, 1957.

Coffey, Thomas M. *Hap*. New York: Viking, 1982.

Coggins, Jack. *The Campaign for North Africa*. New York: Doubleday, 1980.

Cohen, Eliot A., and John Gooch. *Military Misfortunes: The Anatomy of Failure in War*. New York: Vintage, 1991.

Coles, Harry L., and Albert K. Weinberg. *Civil Affairs: Soldiers Become Governors. U.S. Army in World War II*. Washington, D.C.: Office of the Chief of Military History, 1964.

Collier, Richard. *The War in the Desert*. New York: Time-Life Books, 1977.

Colville, John. *The Fringes of Power: Downing Street Diaries, 1939–1955*. London: Hodder & Stoughton, 1985.

Commager, Henry Steele. *The Story of the Second World War*. Washington, D.C.: Brassey's, 1991.

Coon, Carleton S. *A North African Story*. Ipswich, Mass.: Gambit, 1980.

Cooper, Belton Y. *Death Traps*. Novato, Calif.: Presidio, 1998.

Cooper, Matthew. *The German Army, 1933–1945*. Lanham, Md.: Scarborough House, 1990.

Cowdrey, Albert E. *Fighting for Life: American Military Medicine in World War II*. New York: Free Press, 1994.

Craven, Wesley Frank, and James Lea Cate, ed. *The Army Air Forces in World War II*. Vol. II: *Europe: Torch to Pointblank*. Chicago: University of Chicago Press, 1949.

Crawford, Kenneth G. *Report on North Africa*. New York: Farrar & Rinehart, 1943.

Cressman, Robert J. *The Official Chronology of the U.S. Navy in World War II*. Annapolis: Naval Institute Press, 2000.

Crosswell, D.K.R. *The Chief of Staff: The Military Career of General Walter Bedell Smith*. New York: Greenwood, 1991.

Crowley, T. T., and G. C. Burch. *Eight Stars to Victory: Operations of the First Engineers' Combat Battalion in World War II*. 1947.

Cruickshank, Charles. *Deception in World War II*. New York: Oxford University Press, 1980.

Cunningham, Andrew Browne. *A Sailor's Odyssey*. New York: E. P. Dutton, 1951.

Curtis, Donald McB. *The Song of the Fighting First*. S.P., 1988.

Curtiss, Mina, ed. *Letters Home*. Boston: Little, Brown, 1944.

Dailey, Franklyn E., Jr. *Joining the War at Sea, 1939–1945*. Wilbraham, Mass.: Dailey International, 1998.

Dallek, Robert. *Franklin D. Roosevelt and American Foreign Policy, 1932–1945*. New York: Oxford University Press, 1979.

Danchev, Alex, and Daniel Todman, eds. *War Diaries 1939–1945, Field Marshal Lord Alanbrooke*. Berkeley and Los Angeles: University of California Press, 2001.

Daniell, David Scott. *History of the East Surrey Regiment*. Vol. IV, *1920–1952*. London: Ernest Benn, 1957.

———. *The Royal Hampshire Regiment*. Vol. 3, *1918–1954*. Aldershot, U.K.: Gale & Polden, 1955.

Darby, William O., and William H. Baumer. *Darby's Rangers: We Led the Way*. Novato, Calif.: Presidio, 1980.

D'Arcy-Dawson, John. *Tunisian Battle*. London: Macdonald, 1943.

Davies, Kenneth Maitland. *To the Last Man*. St. Paul, Minn.: Ramsey County Historical Society, 1982.

Davis, Kenneth S. *Dwight D. Eisenhower: Soldier of Democracy*. New York: Konecky, 1945.

———. *Experience of War*. New York: Doubleday, 1965.

Davis, Richard G. *Carl A. Spaatz and the Air War in Europe*. Washington, D.C.: Center for Air Force History, 1993.

Dear, I.C.B., ed. *The Oxford Companion to World War II*. Oxford, U.K.: Oxford University Press, 1995.

De Belot, Raymond. *The Struggle for the Mediterranean, 1939–1945*. Trans. James A. Field, Jr. Princeton: Princeton University Press, 1951.

De Gaulle, Charles. *The Complete War Memoirs of Charles de Gaulle*. New York: Simon & Schuster, 1964.

De Guingand, Francis. *Operation Victory*. New York: Scribner's, 1947.

D'Este, Carlo. *Bitter Victory: The Battle for Sicily, July–August 1943*. New York: Harper-Perennial, 1991.

———. *Eisenhower: A Soldier's Life*. New York: Henry Holt, 2002.

———. *Patton: Genius for War*. New York: HarperPerennial, 1996.

Detwiler, Donald S. *World War II German Military Studies*, vol. XIV. New York: Garland, 1979.

Devlin, Gerard M. *Paratrooper*. New York: St. Martin's Press, 1979.

Doherty, Richard. *Irish Generals*. Belfast: Appletree Press, 1993.

———. *A Noble Crusade: The History of Eighth Army, 1941–45*. Rockville Centre, N.Y.: Sarpedon, 1999.

———. *Only the Enemy in Front*. London: BCA, 1994.

Donn, Linda. *The Roosevelt Cousins*. New York: Knopf, 2001.

Doolittle, James H., with Carroll V. Glines. *I Could Never Be So Lucky Again*. New York: Bantam, 1991.

Doubler, Michael D. *Closing with the Enemy*. Lawrence, Kan.: University Press of Kansas, 1994.

Douglas-Home, Charles. *Rommel*. New York: Saturday Review Press, 1973.

Downing, John P. *At War with the British*. Daytona Beach, Fla.: J. P. Downing, 1980.

Dunn, Walter Scott, Jr. *Second Front Now, 1943*. Tuscaloosa: University of Alabama Press, 1980.

Dupuy, Trevor Nevitt. *Land Battles: North Africa, Sicily and Italy*. New York: Franklin Watts, 1962.

Eden, Anthony. *The Memoirs of Anthony Eden, Earl of Avon*. 3 vols. London: Cassell, 1960.

Eisenhower, David. *Eisenhower at War, 1943–1945*. New York: Random House, 1986.

Eisenhower, Dwight D. *At Ease: Stories I Tell to Friends*. New York: Doubleday, 1967.

———. *Crusade in Europe*. Baltimore: Johns Hopkins Press, 1997.

Eisenhower, John S. D. *Allies: Pearl Harbor to D-Day*. New York: Doubleday, 1982.

Eisenhower, Milton S. *The President Is Calling*. New York: Doubleday, 1974.

Ellis, John. *Brute Force: Allied Strategy and Tactics in the Second World War*. New York: Viking, 1990.

———. *On the Front Lines*. London: John Wiley, 1991.

Ellis, L. F. *Welsh Guards at War*. Aldershot, U.K.: Gale and Polden, 1946.

Ellsberg, Edward. *No Banners, No Bugles*. New York: Dodd, Mead, 1955.

Essame, H. *Patton: A Study in Command*. New York: Scribners, 1974.

Faivre, Mario. *We Killed Darlan*. Trans. Douglas W. Alden. Manhattan, Kan.: Sunflower University Press, 1975.

Farago, Ladislas. *Patton: Ordeal and Triumph*. New York: Ivan Obolensky, 1964.

Fergusson, Bernard. *The Watery Maze*. New York: Holt, Rinehart, 1961.

Ferrell, Robert H., ed. *The Eisenhower Diaries*. New York: Norton, 1981.

ffrench Blake, R.L.V. *A History of the 17th/21st Lancers, 1922–1959*. London: Macmillan, 1962.

Fitzgerald, D.J.L. *History of the Irish Guards in the Second World War*. Aldershot, U.K.: Gale and Polden, n.d.

Fleming, Thomas. *The New Dealers' War: F.D.R. and the War Within World War II*. New York: Basic Books, 2001.

Flower, Desmond, and James Reeve, eds. *The War, 1939–1945*. New York: Da Capo, 1997.

Flynn, George Q. *The Mess in Washington: Manpower Mobilization in World War II*. Westport, Conn.: Greenwood Press, 1979.

Foote, Shelby. *The Civil War*. Vol. 3. New York: Viking, 1986.

Ford, Ken. *Battleaxe Division*. Stroud, U.K.: Sutton, 1999.

Foreign Relations of the United States: The Conferences at Washington, 1941–1942, and Casablanca, 1943. Washington, D.C.: U.S. Government Printing Office, 1968.

Forty, George. *The Armies of George S. Patton*. London: Arms and Armour, 1996.

———. *The Armies of Rommel*. London: Arms and Armour, 1997.

———. *M4 Sherman*. Poole, U.K.: Blandford, 1987.

———. *Tank Action: From the Great War to the Gulf*. Stroud, U.K.: Sutton, 1996.

———. *United States Tanks of World War II in Action*. Poole, U.K.: Blandford, 1983.

Fraser, David. *Alanbrooke*. New York: Atheneum, 1982.

———. *And We Shall Shock Them*. London: Hodder & Stoughton, 1983.

———. *Knight's Cross: A Life of Field Marshal Erwin Rommel*. New York: HarperCollins, 1993.

Frelinghuysen, Joseph S. *Passages to Freedom*. Manhattan, Kan.: Sunflower University Press, 1990.

Frost, John. *A Drop Too Many*. London: Buchan & Enright, 1982.

———. *Nearly There*. London: Leo Cooper, 1991.

Fuller, J.F.C. *The Second World War, 1939–45*. New York: HarperCollins, 1993.

Funk, Arthur Layton. *The Politics of Torch*. Lawrence, Kan.: University Press of Kansas, 1974.

Fussell, Paul. *Doing Battle: The Making of a Skeptic*. Boston: Back Bay, 1998.

———. *The Great War and Modern Memory*. New York: Oxford University Press, 1977.

———. *Wartime*. New York: Oxford University Press, 1989.

Gabel, Christopher R. *The U.S. Army GHQ Maneuvers of 1941*. Washington, D.C.: Center of Military History, 1991.

Gates, L. C. *The History of the Tenth Foot, 1919–1950*. Aldershot, U.K.: Gale & Polden, 1953.

Gelb, Norman. *Desperate Venture*. New York: William Morrow, 1992.

———. *Ike and Monty*. New York: William Morrow, 1994.

Gilbert, Martin. *The Second World War*. New York: Henry Holt, 1989.

Gillespie, David E., ed. *History of the Forty-seventh Infantry Regiment*. S.P., 1946.

Godson, Susan H. *Viking of Assault: Admiral John Lesslie Hall, Jr., and Amphibious Warfare*. Washington, D.C.: University Press of America, 1982.

Goldberg, Alfred. *The Pentagon: The First Fifty Years*. Washington, D.C.: Office of the Secretary of Defense, Historical Office, 1992.

Goodwin, Doris Kearns. *No Ordinary Time*. New York: Touchstone, 1995.

Gordon, John W. *The Other Desert War: British Special Forces in North Africa, 1940–1943*. New York: Greenwood Press, 1987.

Gosset, Renée. *Conspiracy in Algiers*. Trans. Nancy Hecksher. New York: The Nation, 1945.

Graham, Dominick, and Shelford Bidwell. *Tug of War: The Battle for Italy, 1943–1945*. New York: St. Martin's, 1986.

Green, Milo L., and Paul S. Gauthier. *Brickbats from F Company*. Corning, Ia.: Gauthier Publishing, 1982.

Greenfield, Kent Roberts. *American Strategy in World War II: A Reconsideration*. Baltimore: Johns Hopkins Press, 1963.

———, ed. *Command Decisions*. New York: Harcourt Brace, 1959.

The Grenadier Guards, 1939–1945. Aldershot, U.K.: Gale and Polden, 1946.

Grinker, Roy R., and John P. Spiegel. *War Neuroses in North Africa*. U.S. Army, 1943.

Gropman, Alan, ed. *The Big "L": American Logistics in World War II*. Washington, D.C.: National Defense University Press, 1997.

Hamilton, Nigel. *Master of the Battlefield: Monty's War Years, 1942–1944*. New York: McGraw-Hill, 1983.

Harmon, E. N., with Milton MacKaye and William Ross MacKaye. *Combat Commander*. Englewood Cliffs, N.J.: Prentice-Hall, 1970.

Harriman, W. Averell, and Elie Abel. *Special Envoy to Churchill and Stalin, 1941–1946*. New York: Random House, 1975.

Harrison, Gordon A. *Cross-Channel Attack*. U.S. Army in World War II. Washington, D.C.: Office of the Chief of Military History, 1951.

Hart, Scott. *Washington at War: 1941–1945*. Englewood Cliffs, N.J.: Prentice-Hall, 1970.

Hassett, William D. *Off the Record with F.D.R., 1942–1945*. New Brunswick, N.J.: Rutgers University Press, 1958.

Hastings, R.H.W.S. *The Rifle Brigade in the Second World War, 1939–1945*. Aldershot, U.K.: Gale & Polden, 1950.

Hatch, Alden. *General Ike*. New York: Holt, 1952.

———. *George Patton: General in Spurs*. New York: Curtis Books, 1950.

Heavey, William F. *Down Ramp! The Story of the Army Amphibian Engineers*. Washington, D.C.: Infantry Journal Press, 1947.

Heckstall-Smith, Anthony. *The Fleet That Faced Both Ways*. London: Anthony Blond, 1963.

Heidenheimer, Arnold J. *Vanguard to Victory: History of the 18th Infantry*. Aschaffenburg, Germany: 1954.

Heller, Charles E., and William A. Stofft, eds. *America's First Battles, 1776–1965*. Lawrence, Kan.: University Press of Kansas, 1986.

Hewes, James E., Jr. *From Root to McNamara: Army Organization and Administration, 1900–1963*. Washington, D.C.: U.S. Army Center of Military History, 1975.

Higgins, Trumbull. *Soft Underbelly*. New York: Macmillan, 1968.

Hill, Russell. *Desert Conquest*. New York: Knopf, 1943.

Hinsley, F. H. *British Intelligence in the Second World War*. Volume 2. New York: Cambridge University Press, 1981.

———. *British Intelligence in the Second World War*, abridged ed. New York: Cambridge University Press, 1993.

History of 47th Infantry Regiment. 1946.

History 67th Armored Regiment. Brunswick, West Germany: Georg Westermann, 1945.

Hofmann, George F., ed., and Donn A. Starry. *Camp Colt to Desert Storm: The History of U.S. Armored Forces*. Lexington, Ky.: University Press of Kentucky, 1999.

Hoffman, Peter. *Stauffenberg: A Family History, 1905–1944*. New York: Cambridge University Press, 1995.

Hogan, David W., Jr. *Raiders or Elite Infantry?* Westport, Conn.: Greenwood Press, 1992.

———. *U.S. Army Special Operations in World War II*. Washington, D.C.: U.S. Army Center of Military History, 1992.

Hogg, Ian. *Tank Killing*. London: Sidgwick & Jackson, 1996.

Hold Fast! Munich, West Germany: F. Bruckmann, 1945.

Horrocks, Brian. *A Full Life*. London: Leo Cooper, 1974.

Horsfall, John. *The Wild Geese Are Flighting*. Kineton, U.K.: Roundwood, 1976.

Hougen, John H. *The Story of the Famous 34th Infantry Division*. San Angelo: S.P., 1949.

Houston, Donald E. *Hell on Wheels: The 2nd Armored Division*. Novato, Calif.: Presidio, 1977.

Howard, Michael. *Grand Strategy*. Vol. IV, *August 1942–September 1943*. London: Her Majesty's Stationery Office, 1972.

———. *The Mediterranean Strategy in the Second World War*. London: Greenhill, 1993.

Howard, Michael, and John Sparrow. *The Coldstream Guards, 1920–1946.* London: Oxford University Press, 1951.

Howarth, Stephen, ed. *Men of War: Great Naval Leaders of World War II.* London: Weidenfeld & Nicholson, 1992.

Howe, George F. *The Battle History of the 1st Armored Division.* Nashville: Battery Press, 1979.

———. *Northwest Africa: Seizing the Initiative in the West. U.S. Army in World War II.* Washington, D.C.: Center of Military History, 1991.

Howze, Hamilton H. *A Cavalryman's Story.* Washington, D.C.: Smithsonian Institution Press, 1996.

Hunnicutt, R. P. *Sherman: A History of the American Medium Tank.* Belmont, Calif.: Taurus, 1978.

———. *Stuart: A History of the American Light Tank,* vol. 1. Novato, Calif.: Presidio, 1992.

Hunt, David. *A Don at War.* London: Frank Cass, 1990.

Huston, James A. *The Sinews of War: Army Logistics, 1775–1953.* Washington, D.C.: U.S. Army, 1966.

Hyde, H. Montgomery. *Cynthia.* London: Hamish Hamilton, 1965.

Icks, Robert J. *Famous Tank Battles.* Garden City, N.Y.: Doubleday, 1972.

Ingersoll, Ralph. *The Battle Is the Pay-off.* New York: Harcourt, Brace, 1943.

Ireland, Bernard. *The War in the Mediterranean, 1940–1943.* London: Arms and Armour, 1993.

Irving, David. *The Trail of the Fox.* New York: Thomas Congdon, 1977.

———. *The War Between the Generals.* London: Allen Lane, 1981.

Ismay, General Lord. *The Memoirs of General Lord Ismay.* New York: Viking, 1960.

Jackson, W.G.F. *Alexander of Tunis as Military Commander.* London: B. T. Batsford, 1971.

———. *The Battle for North Africa.* New York: Mason/Charter, 1975.

Jacobsen, Hans-Adolf, and Jürgen Rohwer. *Decisive Battles of World War II: The German View.* Trans. Edward Fitzgerald. New York: G.P. Putnam's, 1965.

James, D. Clayton, with Anne Sharp Wells. *A Time for Giants: Politics of the American High Command in World War II.* New York: Franklin Watts, 1987.

Jenkins, Roy. *Churchill: A Biography.* New York: Farrar, Straus, 2001.

Jensen, Marvin. *Strike Swiftly! The 70th Tank Battalion.* Novato, Calif.: Presidio, 1977.

Jervois, W. J. *The History of the Northamptonshire Regiment: 1934–1948.* Aylesbury, U.K.: Regimental History Committee, 1953.

Jewell, N.L.A. *Secret Mission Submarine.* Chicago: Ziff-Davis, 1944.

Johnson, David E. *Fast Tanks and Heavy Bombers: Innovation in the U.S. Army, 1917–1945.* Ithaca, N.Y.: Cornell University Press, 1998.

Johnson, Franklyn A. *One More Hill.* New York: Funk & Wagnalls, 1949.

Jones, Vincent. *Operation Torch.* New York: Ballantine, 1972.

Jordan, Kenneth N., Sr. *Yesterday's Heroes.* Atglen, Pa.: Schiffer, 1996.

Jordan, Philip. *Jordan's Tunis Diary.* London: Collins, 1943.

Josowitz, Edward L. *An Informal History of the 601st Tank Destroyer Battalion.* S.P., 1945.

Karig, Walter. *Battle Report: The Atlantic War.* New York: Rinehart, 1946.

Keegan, John, ed. *Churchill's Generals.* New York: Grove Weidenfeld, 1991.

Kennedy, John. *The Business of War.* London: Hutchinson, 1957.

Kennett, Lee B. *G.I.: The American Soldier in World War II.* New York: Scribner's, 1987.

Kersaudy, François. *Churchill and De Gaulle.* New York: Atheneum, 1982.

Kesselring, Albert. *The Memoirs of Field-Marshal Kesselring.* London: Greenhill, 1997.

Ketchum, Richard M. *The Borrowed Years, 1938–1941: America on the Way to War.* New York: Random House, 1989.

King, Ernest J., and Walter Muir Whitehill. *Fleet Admiral King: A Naval Record.* New York: Norton, 1952.

King, Michael J. *William Orlando Darby: A Military Biography*. Hamden, Conn.: Archon, 1981.

Kippenberger, Howard. *Infantry Brigadier*. London: Oxford University Press, 1949.

Kirkpatrick, Charles E. *An Unknown Future and a Doubtful Present: Writing the Victory Plan of 1941*. Washington, D.C.: Center of Military History, 1990.

Kleber, Brooks E., and Dale Birdsell. *The Chemical Warfare Service: Chemicals in Combat*. Washington, D.C.: Center of Military History, 1990.

Kleine, Egon, and Volkmar Kühn. *Tiger: The History of a Legendary Weapon, 1942–1945*. Trans. David Johnston. Winnipeg: J. J. Fedorowicz Publishing, 1989.

Kluger, Steve. *Yank: The Army Weekly*. New York: St. Martin's Press, 1991.

Knickerbocker, H. R., et al. *Danger Forward: The Story of the First Division in World War II*. Atlanta: Albert Love Enterprises, 1947.

Knight, C.R.B. *The Buffs*. London: Medici Society, 1951.

Koch, Oscar W., with Robert G. Hays. *G-2: Intelligence for Patton*. Philadelphia: Army Times Publishing, 1971.

Koeltz, Louis. *Une Campagne Que Nous Avons Gagnée Tunisie*. Paris: Hachette, 1959.

Kozaczuk, Wladyslaw. *Enigma*. University Publications of America, 1984.

Kreidberg, Marvin A., and Merton G. Henry. *History of Military Mobilization in the United States Army, 1975–1945*. Washington, D.C.: Department of the Army, 1955.

Kreis, John F., ed. *Piercing the Fog: Intelligence and Army Air Forces Operations in WWII*. Washington, D.C.: Air Force History and Museum Program, 1996.

Kühn, Volkmar. *German Paratroops in World War II*. Trans. H. A. and A. J. Barker. London: Ian Allan, 1978.

———. *Rommel in the Desert*. Trans. David Johnston. West Chester, Pa.: Schiffer Publishing, 1991.

Kurowski, Franz. *The History of the Fallschirm Panzerkorps Hermann Göring*. Trans. David Johnston. Winnipeg: J. J. Fedorowicz, 1995.

Laffin, John. *British VCs of World War 2*. London: Suton, 1997.

Lamb, Richard. *Churchill as War Leader*. New York: Carroll & Graf, 1991.

The Landings in North Africa. Washington, D.C.: Naval Historical Center, 1993.

Langer, Willam L. *Our Vichy Gamble*. New York: Knopf, 1947.

L'Armée Française dans la Campagne de Tunisie. Tunis: J. Aloccio, 1944.

Larrabee, Eric. *Commander in Chief*. New York: Touchstone, 1987.

Leahy, William D. *I Was There*. New York: Whittlesey House, 1950.

Leasor, James. *War at the Top*. London: Michael Joseph, 1959.

Leighton, Richard M., and Robert W. Coakley. *Global Logistics and Strategy: 1940–1943*. *U.S. Army in World War II*. Washington, D.C.: Center of Military History, 1995.

Levine, Alan J. *The War Against Rommel's Supply Lines, 1942–1943*. Westport, Conn.: Praeger, 1999.

Lewin, Ronald. *The Life and Death of the Afrika Korps*. London: B. T. Batsford, 1977.

———. *Montgomery as Military Commander*. New York: Stein and Day, 1971.

———. *Rommel as Military Commander*. New York: Barnes & Noble, 1998.

———. *Ultra Goes to War*. New York: McGraw-Hill, 1978.

———, ed. *The War on Land: The British Army in World War II*. New York: William Morrow, 1970.

Liddell Hart, B. H. *The Other Side of the Hill*. London: Cassell, 1951.

———, ed. *The Rommel Papers*. Trans. Paul Findlay. New York: Collectors Reprints, 1995.

———. *The Tanks*. New York: Praeger, 1959.

Liddell Hart, Basil, ed. *History of the Second World War*. Vol. 3. London: Purnell, 1966.

Liebling, A. J. *Mollie & Other Pieces*. New York: Schocken, 1989.

Linderman, Gerald. *The World Within War*. New York: Free Press, 1997.

Lindsay, T. M. *Sherwood Rangers*. London: Burrup, Mathieson, 1952.

Logistical History of NATOUSA/MTOUSA. Naples, Italy: U.S. War Department, 1945.

Lovell, Mary S. *Cast No Shadow*. New York: Pantheon, 1992.

Lucas, James. *Panzer Army Africa*. San Rafael, Calif.: Presidio, 1977.

———. *Storming Eagles: German Airborne Forces in World War II*. London: Arms and Armour, 1988.

Lyon, Peter. *Eisenhower: Portrait of the Hero*. Boston: Little, Brown, 1974.

MacCloskey, Monro. *Torch and the Twelfth Air Force*. New York: Richards Rosen, 1971.

MacDonald, Charles B. *The Mighty Endeavor*. New York: Oxford University Press, 1969.

Macksey, Kenneth. *Commando*. Chelsea, Mich.: Scarborough House, 1990.

———. *Crucible of Power: The Fight for Tunisia, 1942–1943*. London: Hutchinson, 1969.

———. *Kesselring: The Making of the Luftwaffe*. New York: David McKay, 1978.

———. *Military Errors of World War Two*. London: Cassell, 1998.

———. *The Tank Pioneers*. London: Jane's, 1981.

———. *Tank Versus Tank*. Topsfield, Mass.: Salem House, 1988.

Macmillan, Harold. *The Blast of War, 1939–1945*. New York: Harper, 1967.

———. *War Diaries: Politics and War in the Mediterranean, 1943–1945*. New York: St. Martin's, 1984.

MacVane, John. *Journey into War: War and Diplomacy in North Africa*. New York: Appleton-Century, 1943.

———. *On the Air in World War II*. New York: Morrow, 1979.

Majdalany, Fred. *The Battle of El Alamein*. Philadelphia: J. B. Lippincott, 1965.

Malcolm, A. D. *History of the Argyll & Sutherland Highlanders 8th Battalion*. London: Thomas Nelson and Sons, 1949.

Mansoor, Peter R. *The GI Offensive in Europe*. Lawrence, Kan.: University Press of Kansas, 1999.

Marolda, Edward J. *FDR and the U.S. Navy*. New York: St. Martin's Press, 1998.

Marsh, Charles F. *The Hampton Roads Communities in World War II*. Chapel Hill: University of North Carolina Press, 1951.

Marshall, Howard. *Over to Tunis*. London: Eyre and Spottiswoode, 1943.

Marshall, Malcolm, ed. *Proud Americans*. S.P., 1994

Marshall, S.L.A. *Men Against Fire*. Alexandria, Va.: Byrrd Enterprises, 1961.

———. *World War I*. Boston: Houghton Mifflin, 1987.

Martienssen, Anthony. *Hitler and His Admirals*. New York: E. P. Dutton, 1949.

Martin, Ralph G. *The GI War, 1941–1945*. Boston: Little, Brown, 1967.

Maslowski, Peter. *Armed with Cameras: The American Military Photographers of World War II*. New York: Free Press, 1993.

Mason, John T., Jr., ed. *The Atlantic War Remembered*. Annapolis: Naval Institute Press, 1990.

Masterman, J. C. *The Double-Cross System in the War of 1939 to 1945*. New Haven: Yale University Press, 1972.

Matloff, Maurice. *Strategic Planning for Coalition Warfare, 1943–1944*. U.S. Army in World War II. Washington, D.C.: Center of Military History, 1994.

Matloff, Maurice, and Edwin M. Snell. *Strategic Planning for Coalition Warfare, 1941–1942*. U.S. Army in World War II. Washington, D.C.: Office of the Chief of Military History, 1953.

Mayo, Linda. *The Ordnance Department: On Beachhead and Battlefront*. U.S. Army in World War II. Washington, D.C.: Office of the Chief of Military History, 1968.

McCorquodale, D., et al. *History of the King's Dragoon Guards*. Glasgow, 1946.

McGuinness, Justin. *Morocco Handbook*. Bath, England: Footprint, 1999.

McIntosh, Elizabeth P. *Sisterhood of Spies: The Women of the OSS*. Annapolis: Naval Institute Press, 1998.

McKeough, Michael, and Richard Lockridge. *Sgt. Mickey and General Ike.* New York: Putnam's, 1946.

McLachlan, Donald. *Room 39: A Study in Naval Intelligence.* New York: Atheneum, 1968.

McManus, John C. *The Deadly Brotherhood: The American Combat Soldier in World War II.* Novato, Calif.: Presidio, 1998.

McMillan, Richard. *Mediterranean Assignment.* Garden City, N.Y.: Doubleday, Doran, 1943.

McNamara, Andrew T. *Quartermaster Activities of II Corps.* Fort Lee, Va.: U.S. Army, 1955.

Mellor, William Bancroft. *Patton: Fighting Man.* New York: Putnam's, 1946.

Melton, George E. *Darlan.* Westport, Conn.: Praeger, 1998.

Messenger, Charles. *The Tunisian Campaign.* Shepperton, U.K.: Ian Allan, 1982.

Middleton, Drew. *Our Share of Night.* New York: Viking, 1946.

Miller, Clem. *Some Things You Never Forget.* Superior, Wisc.: Savage Press, 1996.

Miller, Merle. *Ike the Soldier: As They Knew Him.* New York: G. P. Putnam's, 1987.

Millet, Alan R., and Williamson Murray. *Military Effectiveness.* Vol. III, *The Second World War.* Boston: Allen & Unwin, 1988.

Mittelman, Joseph B. *Eight Stars to Victory.* Washington, D.C.: Ninth Infantry Division Association, 1948.

Montgomery, Viscount of Alamein. *El Alamein to the River Sangro.* London: Barrie & Jenkins, 1973.

Montgomery County, Iowa, 50th Anniversary, World War II Military History. Montgomery County Sesquicentennial Commission, 1995.

Moorehead, Alan. *The End in Africa.* London: Hamish Hamilton, 1943.

Moran, Lord. *Churchill Taken from the Diaries of Lord Moran.* Boston: Houghton Mifflin, 1966.

Morgan, Kay Summersby. *Past Forgetting.* New York: Simon & Schuster, 1976.

Morin, Relman. *Dwight D. Eisenhower: A Gauge of Greatness.* Associated Press, 1969.

Morison, Samuel Eliot. *History of United States Naval Operations in World War II.* Volume II, *Operations in North African Waters.* Boston: Little, Brown, 1950.

———. *History of United States Naval Operations in World War II.* Volume IX, *Sicily-Salerno-Anzio.* Boston: Little, Brown, 1954.

———. *The Two-Ocean War.* New York: Galahad Books, 1997.

Moynihan, Michael, ed. *People at War, 1939–1945.* Trowbridge: David & Charles, 1989.

Mrazek, James E. *The Fall of Eben Emael.* S.P., 1970.

Munoz, Antonio J. *Lions of the Desert: Arab Volunteers in the German Army.* Bayside, N.Y.: Axis Europa.

Murphy, Robert. *Diplomat Among Warriors.* New York: Doubleday, 1964.

Murray, Williamson, and Allan R. Millet, eds. *Military Innovation in the Interwar Period.* Cambridge, U.K.: Cambridge University Press, 1996.

Nasse, Jean-Yves. *Green Devils: German Paratroops, 1939–45.* Trans. W. Mühlberger, G. Schubert, and Jean-Pierre Villaume. Paris: Histoire & Collections, 1997.

The New Yorker Book of War Pieces. New York: Schocken Books, 1947.

Nicholas, H. G., ed. *Washington Despatches, 1941–45.* Chicago: University of Chicago Press, 1981.

Nicholson, Nigel. *Alex: The Life of Field Marshal Earl Alexander of Tunis.* New York: Atheneum, 1973.

Nicholson, Nigel, and Patrick Forbes. *The Grenadier Guards in the War of 1939–1945.* Volume II. Aldershot, U.K.: Gale & Polden, 1949.

North, John, ed. *The Alexander Memoirs, 1940–1945.* London: Cassell, 1962.

O'Donnell, Patrick K. *Beyond Valor.* New York: Free Press, 2001.

O'Neill, Richard. *Suicide Squads.* London: Salamander, 1981.

The Overseas Targets: War Report of the OSS. Volume 2. New York: Walker, 1976.

Overy, Richard. *Why the Allies Won*. New York: W. W. Norton, 1997.

Owen, Roderic. *Tedder*. London: Collins, 1952.

Pack, S.W.C. *Invasion North Africa, 1942*. New York: Scribners, 1978.

Palmer, Robert R., et al. *The Procurement and Training of Ground Combat Troops. U.S. Army in World War II*. Washington, D.C.: Department of the Army, 1948.

Parkinson, Roger. *A Day's March Nearer Home*. New York: David McKay, 1974.

Parris, John A., Jr., and Ned Russell, with Leo Disher and Phil Ault. *Springboard to Berlin*. New York: Thomas Y. Crowell, 1943.

Parton, James. *"Air Force Spoken Here": General Ira Eaker and the Command of the Air*. Bethesda, Md.: Adler & Adler, 1986.

Patton, George S., Jr. *War as I Knew It*. Boston: Houghton Mifflin, 1995.

Paul, William Pratt, ed. *History of the Argyll & Sutherland Highlanders 6th Battalion*. London: Thomas Nelson and Sons, 1949.

Pearlman, Michael. *To Make Democracy Safe for America*. Urbana: University of Illinois Press, 1984.

Peatling, Robert. *Without Tradition: 2 Para, 1941–1945*. S.P., 1994.

Pendar, Kenneth. *Adventure in Diplomacy*. New York: Dodd, Mead, 1945.

Perkins, Norris H. *North African Odyssey*. Portland, Ore.: Four Mountain Productions, 1995.

Perkins, Norris H., and Michael E. Rogers. *Roll Again Second Armored*. S.P., 1988.

Perret, Geoffrey. *There's a War to Be Won*. New York: Ballantine, 1991.

Perrett, Bryan. *Against All Odds*. London: Arms and Armour Press, 1995.

———. *At All Costs*. London: Arms and Armour Press, 1993.

———. *Through Mud and Blood*. London: Robert Hale, 1975.

Persico, Joseph E. *Roosevelt's Secret War: FDR and World War II Espionage*. New York: Random House, 2001.

Persons, Benjamin S. *Relieved of Command*. Manhattan, Kan.: Sunflower University Press, 1997.

Phillips, Henry Gerard. *El Guettar: Crucible of Leadership*. Penn Valley, Calif.: S.P., 1991.

———. *The Making of a Professional: Manton S. Eddy, USA*. Westport, Conn.: Greenwood, 2000.

———. *Sedjenane: The Pay-off Battle*. Penn Valley, Calif.: S.P., 1993.

Piekalkiewicz, Janusz. *Rommel and the Secret War in North Africa, 1941–1943*. Trans. Edward Force. West Chester, Pa.: Schiffer, 1992.

Pimlott, John, ed. *Rommel in His Own Words*. London: Greenhill, 1994.

Playfair, I.S.O., and C.J.C. Molony. *The Mediterranean and Middle East*. Vol. IV, *The Destruction of the Axis Forces in Africa. History of the Second World War*. London: Her Majesty's Stationery Office, 1966.

Playfair, I.S.O., et al. *The Mediterranean and Middle East*. Vol. III, *British Fortunes Reach Their Lowest Ebb. History of the Second World War*. London: Her Majesty's Stationery Office, 1960.

Pogue, Forrest C. *George C. Marshall: Ordeal and Hope, 1939–1942*. New York: Viking, 1966.

———. *George C. Marshall: Organizer of Victory, 1943–1945*. New York: Viking, 1973.

Powell, E. Alexander. *In Barbary*. New York: Century, 1926.

Powell, Geoffrey. *The Green Howards*. London: Hamish Hamilton, 1968.

Prasad, Bisheshwar, ed. *Official History of the Indian Armed Forces in the Second World War: The North African Campaign, 1940–1943*. New Delhi: Combined Inter-Services Historical Section, 1956.

Pratt, Fletcher. *Eleven Generals: Studies in American Command*. New York: William Sloane, 1949.

Price, G. Ward. *Giraud and the African Scene*. New York: Macmillan, 1944.

Pyle, Ernie. *Here Is Your War.* New York: Henry Holt, 1943.

Quilter, D. C., ed. *"No Dishonourable Name."* London: William Clowes and Sons, N.d.

Raff, Edson D. *We Jumped to Fight.* New York: Eagle Books, 1944.

Rame, David. *Road to Tunis.* New York: Macmillan, 1944.

Ramsey, Guy. *One Continent Redeemed.* Garden City, N.Y.: Doubleday, Doran, 1943.

Randle, Edwin Hubert. *Ernie Pyle Comes Ashore and Other Stories.* Clearwater, Fla.: Eldnar Press, 1972.

———. *Safi Adventure.* Clearwater, Fla.: Eldnar Press, 1969.

Ray, Cyril. *Algiers to Austria: A History of 78 Division in the Second World War.* London: Eyre & Spottiswoode, 1952.

Reck, Franklin M. *Beyond the Call of Duty.* New York: Thomas Y. Crowell, 1944.

Reckner, James R. *Teddy Roosevelt's Great White Fleet.* Annapolis: Naval Institute Press, 1988.

Register of Graduates and Former Cadets. West Point, N.Y.: United States Military Academy, 1998.

Reilly, Michael F. *Reilly of the White House.* New York: Simon & Schuster, 1947.

Renehan, Edward J., Jr. *The Lion's Pride.* New York: Oxford University Press, 1998.

Reynolds, Quentin. *The Curtain Rises.* New York: Random House, 1944.

Richardson, Charles. *Send for Freddie.* London: William Kimber, 1987.

Riess, Curt, ed. *They Were There.* New York: G. P. Putnam's Sons, 1944.

Roberts, G.P.B. *From the Desert to the Baltic.* London: William Kimber, 1987.

Robinett, Paul McDonald. *Armor Command.* Washington, D.C.: McGregor & Werner, 1958.

Rolf, David. *The Bloody Road to Tunis.* London: Greenhill, 2001.

Rommel, Erwin. *Krieg Ohne Hass.* West Germany: Heidenheimer, 1950.

Roosevelt, Elliott. *As He Saw It.* New York: Duell, Sloan & Pearce, 1946.

Roosevelt, Mrs. Theodore, Jr. *Day Before Yesterday.* New York: Doubleday, 1959.

Roskill, S. W. *The War at Sea, 1939–1945.* Vol. II. London: Her Majesty's Stationery Office, 1956.

The Royal Fusiliers: History of the 2nd Battalion. Aldershot, U.K.: Gale & Polden, 1946.

Ruge, Friedrich. *Der Seekrieg.* Trans. M. G. Saunders. Annapolis: United States Naval Institute, 1957.

Rutherford, Ward. *Kasserine: Baptism of Fire.* New York: Ballantine, 1970.

Sainsbury, Keith. *The North African Landings, 1942: A Strategic Decision.* London: Davis-Poynter, 1976.

Salter, Fred H. *Recon Scout.* Kalispell, Mont.: Scott, 1994.

Saunders, Hilary St. George. *The Red Beret.* Nashville: Battery Press, 1985.

Schlegel, Marvin W. *Conscripted City: Norfolk in World War II.* Norfolk, Va.: War History Commission, 1951.

Schmidt, Heinz Warner. *With Rommel in the Desert.* New York: Bantam, 1979.

Schrijvers, Peter. *The Crash of Ruin: American Combat Soldiers in Europe During World War II.* New York: New York University Press, 1998.

Seale, William. *The President's House.* Vol. II. Washington, D.C.: White House Historical Association, 1986.

Semmes, Harry H. *Portrait of Patton.* New York: Appleton-Century-Crofts, 1955.

Sherman, William T. *Memoirs.* Da Capo Press, 1984.

Sherwood, Robert E. *Roosevelt and Hopkins: An Intimate History.* New York: Harper & Brothers, 1948.

Simpson, B. Mitchell III. *Admiral Harold R. Stark: Architect of Victory, 1939–1945.* Columbia, S.C.: University of South Carolina Press, 1989.

Simpson, Harold B. *Audie Murphy, American Soldier.* Hillsboro, Tex.: Hill Junior College Press, 1975.

Skillen, Hugh. *Spies of the Airwaves.* United Kingdom: S.P., 1989.

Slessor, John. *The Central Blue.* New York: Prager, 1957.

Smith, R. Harris. *OSS.* Berkeley: University of California Press, 1972.

Snyder, Louis L., ed. *Masterpieces of War Reporting: The Great Moments of World War II.* New York: Julian Messner, 1962.

Spears, Edward. *Assignment to Catastrophe.* New York: A. A. Wyn, 1955.

Spivak, Marcel, and Armand Léoni. *Les Forces Françaises Dans la Lutte Contre l'Axe en Afrique.* Volume II. *La Campagne de Tunisie, 1942–1943.* Ministère de la Défense: 1985.

Spivey, Samuel D. *A Doughboy's Narrative.* Albany, Ga.: S.P., 1995.

Stafford, David. *Roosevelt and Churchill: Men of Secrets.* Woodstock, N.Y.: Overlook, 1999.

Stannard, Dorothy. *Tunisia.* Singapore: APA Insight Guides, 1995.

Stanton, Shelby L. *Order of Battle: U.S. Army, World War II.* Novato, Calif.: Presidio Press, 1984.

Statistical Review World War II. Washington, D.C.: War Department, U.S. Army Service Forces, 1946.

Steele, Richard W. *The First Offensive, 1942: Roosevelt, Marshall and the Making of American Strategy.* Bloomington: Indiana University Press, 1973.

Stein, Ralph, and Harry Brown. *It's a Cinch, Private Finch!* New York: Whittlesey House, 1943.

Stevens, G. R. *Fourth Indian Division.* Toronto: McLaren and Son, 1948.

Stevens, W. G. *Freyberg, VC, the Man.* Wellington, N.Z.: Reed, 1965.

Stewart, Adrian. *Eighth Army's Greatest Victories.* London: Leo Cooper, 1999.

Stilwell, Joseph. *The Stilwell Papers.* London: MacDonald, 1949.

Stimson, Henry L., and McGeorge Bundy. *On Active Service in Peace and War.* New York: Harper, 1948.

St. John, Philip A. *Thirty-Fourth Infantry Division.* Paducah, Ky.: Turner Publishing, 1989.

Stoler, Mark. *George C. Marshall: Soldier-Statesman of the American Century.* New York: Twayne, 1989.

———. *The Politics of the Second Front.* Westport, Conn.: Greenwood, 1977.

Stouffer, Samuel A., et al. *The American Soldier: Combat and Its Aftermath.* Vol. II. Princeton: Princeton University Press, 1949.

Strong, Kenneth. *Intelligence at the Top.* New York: Doubleday, 1969.

Synge, W.A.T. *The Story of the Green Howards, 1939–1945.* Richmond, U.K.: Green Howards, 1952.

Taggart, Donald G., ed. *History of the Third Infantry Division.* Nashville: Battery Press, 1987.

Tank Destroyer Forces World War II. Paducah, Ky.: Turner Publishing, 1992.

Tapert, Annette, ed. *Lines of Battle.* New York: Times Books, 1987.

Tayloe, Roberta Love. *Combat Nurse: A Journal of World War II.* Santa Barbara, Calif.: Fithian Press, 1988.

Tedder, Lord. *With Prejudice.* Boston: Little, Brown, 1966.

These Are the Generals. New York: Knopf, 1943.

Thompson, R. W. *Churchill and the Montgomery Myth.* New York: M. Evans, 1967.

Thruelsen, Richard, and Elliott Arnold. *Mediterranean Sweep.* New York: Duell, Sloan and Pearce, 1944.

Tibbetts, Paul W., Jr., with Clair Stebbins and Harry Franken. *The Tibbetts Story.* New York: Stein & Day, 1978.

The Tiger Kills. London: His Majesty's Stationery Office, 1944.

Tobin, James. *Ernie Pyle's War.* Lawrence, Kan.: University Press of Kansas, 1997.

To Bizerte with the II Corps. Washington, D.C.: War Department Historical Division, 1943.

Tompkins, Peter. *The Murder of Admiral Darlan.* New York: Simon & Schuster, 1965.

Truscott, Lucian K., Jr. *Command Missions.* New York: E. P. Dutton, 1954.

———. *The Twilight of the U.S. Cavalry.* Lawrence, Kan.: University Press of Kansas, 1989.

Tuchman, Barbara W. *Sand Against the Wind: Stilwell and the American Experience in China, 1911–45.* London: Papermac, 1991.

Tugwell, Maurice. *Airborne to Battle: A History of Airborne Warfare, 1918–1971.* London: William Kimber, 1971.

Tuker, Francis. *Approach to Battle.* London: Cassell, 1963.

Tute, Warren. *The North African War.* New York: Two Continents, 1976.

Urban, Matt. *The Matt Urban Story.* Holland, Mich.: S.P., 1989.

Van Creveld, Martin. *Supplying War.* Cambridge, U.K.: Cambridge University Press, 1977.

Verney, G. L. *The Desert Rats.* London: Hutchinson, 1954.

Verrier, Anthony. *Assassination in Algiers.* New York: W. W. Norton, 1990.

Vigneras, Marcel. *Rearming the French.* Washington, D.C.: Office of the Chief of Military History, Department of the Army, 1957.

Vining, Donald, ed. *American Diaries of World War II.* New York: Pepys Press, 1982.

Viorst, Milton. *Hostile Allies: FDR and Charles de Gaulle.* New York: Macmillan, 1965.

Vojta, Francis J. *The Gopher Gunners of Minnesota: A History of Minnesota's 151st Field Artillery.* S.P., 1995.

Von Luck, Hans. *Panzer Commander.* New York: Praeger, 1989.

Von Mellenthin, F. W. *Panzer Battles.* Trans. H. Betzler. Ed. L.C.F. Turner. Norman, Okla.: University of Oklahoma Press, 1956.

Waller, John H. *The Unseen War in Europe.* New York: Random House, 1996.

The War in North Africa. West Point, N.Y.: Department of Military Art and Engineering, USMA, 1947.

The War in North Africa: The Allied Invasion. West Point, N.Y.: Department of Military Art and Engineering, USMA, 1950.

Wards, I. McL. *Takrouna.* Wellington, N.Z.: Department of Internal Affairs, 1951.

Warlimont, Walter. *Inside Hitler's Headquarters, 1939–1945.* Trans. R. H. Barry. Novato, Calif.: Presidio, 1964.

Warren, John C. *Airborne Missions in the Mediterranean, 1942–1945.* USAF Historical Division, Research Studies Institute, Air University, 1955.

Watson, Bruce Allen. *Exit Rommel: The Tunisian Campaign, 1942–1943.* Westport, Conn.: Praeger, 1999.

Wedemeyer, Albert C. *Wedemeyer Reports!* New York: Henry Holt, 1958.

Weigley, Russell F. *The American Way of War.* Bloomington: Indiana University Press, 1977.

Weinberg, Gerhard L. *A World at Arms.* Cambridge, U.K.: Cambridge University Press, 1995.

Wellard, James. *The Man in a Helmet.* London: Eyre & Spottiswoode, 1947.

Westmoreland, William C. *A Soldier Reports.* New York: Doubleday, 1976.

Westphal, Siegfried. *The German Army in the West.* London: Cassell, 1951.

Westrate, Edwin V. *Forward Observer.* Philadelphia: Blakiston, 1944.

Weygand, Maxime. *Recalled to Service.* Trans. E. W. Dickes. London: William Heinemann, 1952.

What to Do Aboard a Transport. New York: H. Wolff, 1943.

Wheeler, William Reginald, ed. *The Road to Victory: A History of the Hampton Roads Port of Embarkation in World War II.* Newport News: Yale University Press, 1946.

Whitehead, Ernest D. *World War II: An Ex-Sergeant Remembers.* Kearney, Neb.: Morris Publishing, 1996.

Whitehorne, Joseph W. A. *The Inspectors General of the United States Army, 1903–1939.* Washington, D.C.: Office of the Inspector General, 1998.

Whiting, Charles. *Bradley.* New York: Ballantine Books, 1971.

———. *Kasserine: The Anatomy of a Slaughter.* Scarborough House, 1984.

———. *Patton.* New York: Ballantine, 1970.

Williams, David. *The Black Cats at War: The Story of the 56th (London) Division T.A., 1939–1945.* London: Imperial War Museum, 1995.

Wilson, John B. *Maneuver and Firepower.* Washington, D.C.: U.S. Army Center of Military History, 1998.

Wilt, Alan F. *War from the Top.* Bloomington: Indiana University Press, 1990.

Wiltse, Charles M. *The Medical Department: Medical Service in the Mediterranean and Minor Theaters. U.S. Army in World War II.* Washington, D.C.: Center of Military History, 1987.

Winterbotham, F. W. *The Ultra Secret.* New York: Harper & Row, 1974.

Wise, James Waterman, ed. *Very Truly Ours: Letters from America's Fighting Men.* New York: Dial Press, 1943.

Wordell, M. T., and E. N. Seiler. *Wildcats over Casablanca.* Boston: Little, Brown, 1943.

Yarborough, William Pelham. *Bailout over North Africa.* Williamstown, N.J.: Phillips, 1979.

Young, Gordon R., ed. *The Army Almanac.* Harrisburg, Pa.: Stackpole, 1959.

Zanuck, Darryl F. *Tunis Expedition.* New York: Random House, 1943.

PERIODICALS

Allard, Dean. "The U.S. Navy Comes Ashore in the Med." *Naval History* 11, no. 5 (Sept.–Oct. 1997): 45+.

"Allen and His Men." *Time* 42, no. 6 (9 Aug. 1943): 30+.

Andrews, Peter. "A Place to Be Lousy In." *American Heritage* 42, no. 8 (Dec. 1991): 100+.

Bagby, Philip H. "D-Day in Casablanca." *American Foreign Service Journal* (March 1945): 16+.

Barton, M. J. "The Hampshire Regiment at Tebourba, 1942." *The Army Quarterly and Defence Journal* (April 1944): 57–63.

"Battle Casualties." *Infantry Journal* (Sept. 1949): 18–26.

Beaufre, Andre. "General Giraud's Escape." *History of the Second World War* 3 (1966): 1197+.

Benson, C. C. "Some Tunisian Details." *Field Artillery Journal* 34, no. 1 (Jan. 1944): 2+.

Betson, William R. "Sidi Bou Zid—A Case History of Failure." *Armor* (Nov.–Dec. 1982): 38+.

Bielakowski, Alexander M. "The Role of the Horse in Modern Warfare as Viewed in the Interwar U.S. Army's *Cavalry Journal.*" *Army History* (summer–fall 2000), 20+.

Blair, Leon Borden. "Amateurs in Diplomacy: The American Vice Consuls in North Africa 1941–1943." *Historian* 34, no. 4 (Aug. 1943): 607+.

Blumenson, Martin. "Bradley-Patton: World War II's 'Odd Couple.'" *Army* 35, no. 12 (Dec. 1985): 56+.

———. "Will 'Ultra' Rewrite History?" *Army* 28, no. 8 (Aug. 1978): 43+.

Boyle, Harold V. Untitled account of Kasserine Pass. *Cavalry Journal* (Mar.–Apr. 1943): 12+.

Brooks, Russell. "Casablanca—The French Side of the Fence." *U.S. Naval Institute Proceedings* 77, no. 9 (Sept. 1951): 909+.

———. "The Unknown Darlan." *U.S. Naval Institute Proceedings* (Aug. 1955): 879+.

Burba, Edwin H. "Battle of Sidi bou Zid." *Field Artillery Journal* 33, no. 9 (Sept. 1943): 643+.

———. "Sidi bou Zid to Sbeïtla." *Field Artillery Journal* 34, no. 1 (Jan. 1944): 8+.

Busch, Noel F. "The Fall of Tunis." *Life* (May 1943): 35+.

Bush, Richard D. "Forward Observation in Africa." *Field Artillery Journal* 33, no. 10 (Oct. 1943): 771+.

Carver, R.M.P. "Tanks into Tunis." *Royal Armoured Corps Journal* 4, no. 1 (Jan 1950): 18+.

Carvey, James B. "Faid Pass." *Infantry Journal* (Sept. 1944): 8+.

Chandler, Harry W. "91st Reconnaissance Squadron in Tunisia." *Cavalry Journal* 53, no. 2 (March–April 1944): 14+.

Clagett, John. "Admiral H. Kent Hewitt, U.S. Navy." *Naval War College Review* 28, part 1 (summer 1975); part 2, fall 1975: 72+.

Coffin, Robert E. "Operation Torch: A Perilous Preview." *Army* 42, no. 11 (Nov. 1992): 42+.

Collier, Cameron D. "Tiny Miracle: The Proximity Fuze." *Naval History* (July–Aug. 1999): 43+.

Combs, Sydney. "Night Fighting." *Field Artillery Journal* 34, no. 2 (Feb. 1944): 99+.

Cope, Harley. "Play Ball, Navy!" *U.S. Naval Institute Proceedings* 69 (Oct. 1943): 1311+.

Copson, Raymond W. "Summit at Casablanca." American History, vol. XXXVII, no. 1 (Apr. 2002): 60+.

Courtney, Godfrey B. "General Clark's Secret Mission." *Life* 13, no. 26 (28 Dec. 1942): 75+.

Cullis, Robert E. "We Learn in Combat." *Infantry Journal* (June 1944): 31+.

"D.G.A." "With Tanks to Tunisia." *Blackwoods* (June 1945): 399+.

Darnell, Donald P. "Brigadier General Theodore Roosevelt, Jr., Earned the Medal of Honor at Utah Beach." *World War II* (May 1995): 18+.

Davis, Franklin M., Jr. "The Battle of Kasserine Pass." *American Legion Magazine* (April 1965): 22+.

Denno, Bryce F. "Eight-Ball Cannoneers." *Field Artillery Journal* (Jan 1983): 12+.

Dixon, Thomas W. "Terry Allen." *Army* (April 1978): 57+.

Elcomb, A. C. "The Battle of Mareth—March 1943." *Army Quarterly and Defence Journal*, (Oct. 1973).

Ellmann, Gilbert A. "Panther vs. Panzer." *Military Review* 34, no. 5 (Aug. 1944): 21+.

Farrar-Hockley, Anthony. "The Follow-up to TORCH." *History of the Second World War*, vol. 3 (1966): 1224+.

Fernand-Laurent, J. C. "The Truth About Toulon." *Colliers* 3, no. 19 (8 May 1943): 11+.

Field, John. "Patton of the Armored Force." *Life* 13, no. 22 (30 Nov. 1942): 113+.

Fowler, Bertram B. "Twelve Desperate Miles." *Saturday Evening Post* 216, no. 9 (28 Aug. 1943): 14+.

"The Fragrance of Spring Was Heavy in the Air." *Trail Tales,* no. 35 (Boone County, Iowa, Historical Society: 1979).

Gardiner, Henry E. "We Fought at Kasserine." *Armored Cavalry Journal* (March–April 1948): 8+.

Greenwood, John T. "The U.S. Army and Amphibious Warfare During World War II." *Army History,* no. 27 (summer 1993): 1+.

Hains, Peter C., III. "Tanks in Tunisia." *Cavalry Journal* 52, no. 3 (July–Aug. 1943): 10+.

Hall, Phyllis A. "Crisis at Hampton Roads: The Problems of Wartime Congestion, 1942–1944." *Virginia Magazine of History and Biography* 101, no. 3 (July 1993): 405+.

Hamilton, Maxwell. "Junior in Name Only." *Retired Officer* (June 1981): 28+.

"Hampton Roads: Greatest Naval Base of the Western World." *Life* 11 (1 Sept 1941): 58+.

Harris, Arthur R. "The Bigger They Are the Harder They Fall." *Field Artillery Journal* (May–June 1939): 229+.

Henney, Frederic A. "Combat Engineers in North Africa: The Capture of Port Lyautey." *Military Engineer* 36, no. 219 (Jan. 1944): 1+.

Hewitt, H. Kent. "The Landing in Morocco, November 1942." *U.S. Naval Institute Proceedings* 78, no. 11 (Nov. 1952): 1243+.

Hill. E. R. "Epic Fights—The Coldstream at Longstop Hill." *Army Quarterly and Defence Journal* (July 1944): 175+.

Hill, J. "Operation 'TORCH.'" *Army Quarterly and Defence Journal* (Jan. 1946): 177+.

Hitchens, Christopher. "The Medals of His Defeats." *Atlantic* 289, no. 4 (Apr. 2002): 118+.

Hoffman, Jon T. "The Legacy and Lessons of Operation TORCH." *Marine Corps Gazette* 76, no. 12 (Dec. 1992): 60+.

Howze, Hamilton H. "Artillery Tank Support." *Field Artillery Journal* 33, no. 10 (Oct. 1943): 779+.

Hoy, Charles J. "The Last Days in Tunisia." *Cavalry Journal* 53, no. 1 (Jan.–Feb. 1944): 8+.

———. "Mechanics of Battlefield Reconnaissance." *Cavalry Journal* 53, no. 3 (May–June 1944): 24+.

———. "Reconnaissance Lessons from Tunisia." *Cavalry Journal* 52, no. 6 (Nov.–Dec. 1943): 16+.

Hunt, Marion, and Duane R. Sneddeker. "Over Here, Over There." *Gateway Heritage* 13, no. 3 (winter 1993): 48+.

Jensen, Marvin G. "An Independent Tank Battalion in World War II." *Armor* 108, no. 3 (May–June 1999): 27+.

Johnstone, Carl M., Jr. "Up Forward." *Field Artillery Journal* 33, no. 10 (Oct. 1943): 776+.

Kahn, E. J., Jr. "Education of an Army." *New Yorker* 20, no. 35 (14 Oct. 1944): 28+, and no. 36 (21 Oct. 1944): 34+.

Kellett, Donald T. "The Action at Robaa." *Infantry Journal* 63 (Sept. 1948): 12+.

———. "El Guettar: Victory or Stalemate?" *Military Review* 31, no. 4 (July 1951): 17+.

Kennedy, David M. "Victory at Sea." *Atlantic Monthly* (March 1999): 51+.

Kenner, Albert W. "Medical Service in the North African Campaign." *Military Review* 12, no. 11 (Feb. 1944): 5+.

Kerr, B. H. "Tunisia's Burma Road." *Field Artillery Journal* 33, no. 10 (Oct. 1943): 785+.

Kirkpatrick, Charles E. "Joint Planning for Operation TORCH." *Parameters* (summer 1991): 73+.

Kleinman, Forrest K. "The Bizarre Battle for Casablanca." *Army* 47, no. 8 (Aug. 1997): 38+.

Knight, Ridgeway B. "General Clark's Secret Mission to Algeria on Oct. 21, 1942." *American Service Journal* (March 1943): 122+.

Kuter, Laurence S. "Goddammit, Georgie!" *Air Force Magazine* 56, no. 2 (Feb. 1973): 51+.

Laffin, John. "The Battle of Takrouna." *After the Battle* 12 (1976): 48+.

Lange, Herman W. W. "Rommel at Thala." *Military Review* 41 (September 1961): 72+.

Larkey, Kenneth. "The Effect of Time Shell." *Field Artillery Journal* (March–April 1940): 145+.

Larson, William B. "Hill 223." *Infantry Journal* 55 (Sept. 1944): 23+.

Lehman, Milton. "The Rangers Fought Ahead of Everybody." *Saturday Evening Post* (15 June 1946): 28+.

———. "Red Oak Hasn't Forgotten." *Saturday Evening Post* 219, no. 7 (17 Aug. 1946): 14+.

Levi, Julian. "The Psychiatric Toll of Warfare." *Fortune* 28, no. 6 (Dec. 1943): 140+.

Liddell Hart, Basil. "Operation TORCH." *History of the Second World War* 3 (1966): 1205+.

Liebling, A. J. "Find 'Em, Fix 'Em, and Fight 'Em." *New Yorker* 19, no. 10 (24 April 1943): 221+, and no. 11 (1 May 1943): 24+.

Lindley, Ernest K., and Edward Weintal. "How We Dealt with Spain." *Harper's* (Dec. 1944): 22+.

Livingston, Richard. "Mark Clark's Secret Landing." *History of the Second World War* 3 (1966): 1199+.

"Lone U.S. Tank Slugs It Out with the Nazis." *Cavalry Journal* 52, no. 2 (March–April 1943): 12+.

Lunn-Rockliffe, W. P. "The Tunisian Campaign." *Army Quarterly and Defence Journal* 98 (April–May 1969): 109+, and (June–July 1969): 228+.

MacLean, French L. "German General Officer Casualties in World War II." *Military Review* 70, no. 4 (April 1990): 45+.

Martin, O. W. "Armored Artillery at Sened Station." *Field Artillery Journal* 33, no. 8 (Aug. 1943): 569+.

McBride, Lauren E. "The Battle of Sened Station." *Infantry Journal* (April 1945): 30+.

McFetridge, Charles D. "In Pursuit: Montgomery After El Alamein." *Military Review* 74, no. 6 (June 1994): 54–69.

McKenney, Janice. "More Bang for the Buck in the Interwar Army: The 105-mm. Howitzer." *Military Affairs* (April 1978): 80.

McNair, Lesley J. "The Struggle Is for Survival." *Vital Speeches of the Day* 9, no. 4 (Dec. 1942): 111+.

"McNair, Trainer of the Troops." *Time* 40, no. 26 (28 Dec 1942): 37+.

Meyer, Sam. "The Strange Fame of *Thomas Stone*." *Naval History* (summer 1988): 46+.

Middleton, Drew. "The Battle Saga of a Tough Outfit." *New York Times Magazine* (8 April 1945): 8+.

———. " 'We'll Take 'Em Apart and Then Get Home.' " *New York Times Magazine* (18 July 1943): 8+.

Muller, F. M. "2nd Armored Division Combat Loading, Morocco." *Armored Cavalry Journal* 56 (July–Aug. 1947): 2+.

"Nothing Stopped the Timberwolves." *Saturday Evening Post* (17 Aug. 1946): 20+.

Oliver, Lunsford E. "In the Mud and Blood of Tunisia." *Collier's* (17 April 1943): 10+.

Ormerod, C. B. "British Tank Attack at Fondouk Pass." *Cavalry Journal* 52, no. 3 (July–Aug. 1943).

Page, Douglas J. "El Guettar: March 25–April 8, 1943." *Field Artillery Journal* 33, no. 9 (Sept. 1943): 645+.

Painton, Frederick C. "Secret Mission to North Africa." *Reader's Digest* (May 1943): 1+.

Pallud, Jean-Paul. "The French Navy at Toulon." *After the Battle* 76 (1992): 1+.

Palmer, Fitzhugh L., Jr. "The Old Indispensables." *U.S. Naval Institute Proceedings* (Aug. 1976): 61+.

Perry, George Sessions. "Why Don't They Write About Hewitt?" *Saturday Evening Post* (16 Dec. 1944): 22+.

Petracarro, Domenico. "The Italian Army in Africa 1940–1943: An Attempt at Historical Perspective." *War and Society* 9, no. 2 (Oct. 1991): 103+.

Philipsborn, Martin, Jr., and Milton Lehman. "The Untold Story of Kasserine Pass." *Saturday Evening Post* (14 Feb 1948): 23+.

Rance, A. J. "Corps Artillery—How It Was Employed." *Field Artillery Journal* 33, no. 12 (Dec. 1943): 886+.

Raymond, Edward A. "France Fights Again." *Field Artillery Journal* 33, no. 5 (May 1943): 381+.

———. "Long Toms in Action." *Field Artillery Journal* 33, no. 11 (Nov. 1943): 803+.

———. "Slugging It Out." *Field Artillery Journal* 34, no. 1 (Jan. 1944): 14+.

———. "Some Battle Lessons." *Field Artillery Journal* 34, no. 2 (Feb. 1944): 104+.

"Red Oak, Iowa, Has 23 Boys Missing in Action in North Africa." *Life* 14, no. 18 (3 May 1943): 26+.

Sadkovich, James J. "Of Myths and Men: Rommel and the Italians in North Africa, 1940–1942." *International History Review* 13, no. 2 (May 1991): 284+.

Sahlin, Arvid W. "A Hell of a Place for a Farm Boy." *Naval History* 6, no. 4 (winter 1992): 57+.

"Sedjenane-Bizerte: April 8–May 7, 1943." *Field Artillery Journal* 33, no. 10 (Oct. 1943): 783+.

Semmes, Harry H. "General George S. Patton, Jr.'s Psychology of Leadership." *Armor* 64, no. 1 (Jan.–Feb. 1955): 1+.

Slocum, A. N., Jr. "The Armored Division in Exploitation." *Military Review* 24, no. 10 (Jan. 1945): 49+.

Smith, Howard A., Jr. "Among Those Baptized." *Field Artillery Journal* 34, no. 4 (April 1944): 214+.

Smith, Kingsbury. "Unrevealed Facts About Robert Murphy." *American Mercury* 59, no. 251 (Nov. 1944): 528+.

Smith, Mickey C., and Dennis Worthen. "Soldiers on the Production Line." *Pharmacy in History* 37 (1995): 183+.

Stephens, F. "Collapse in Tunisia." *Military Review* 25, no. 1 (April 1945): 69+.

Stewart, Richard W. "The 'Red Bull' Division: The Training and Initial Engagements of the 34th Infantry Division, 1941–43." *Army History*, no. 25 (winter 1993): 1+.

Strong, C. L. "Allo, Moroc." *Bell Telephone Magazine* (Sept. 1943).

Strong, Evert E. "Thala Engagement." *Field Artillery Journal* 33, no. 8 (Aug. 1943): 573+.

Thompson, P. W. "Close Support in Tunisia." *Field Artillery Journal* 33, no. 7 (July 1943): 489+.

Thornton, Milton M., and R. G. Emery. "Try the Reverse Slope." *Infantry Journal* (Feb. 1944): 8+.

Tunley, Roul. "A Frenchman Returns." *Sea Power* 5, no. 1 (Jan. 1945): 13+.

Van Urk, J. Blan. "Norfolk—Our Worst War Town." *American Mercury* 56, no. 230 (Feb. 1943): 144+.

"W.R.P." "Mission to Morocco." *Navy* 1, no. 7 (Nov. 1958): 7+.

Wallace, Robert. "Africa, We Took It and Liked It." *Saturday Evening Post* 215, no. 29 (16 Jan. 1943): 20+, and no. 30 (23 Jan. 1943): 16+.

Wanke, Paul. "American Military Psychiatry and Its Role Among Ground Forces in World War II." *Journal of Military History* 63, no. 1 (Jan. 1999): 127+.

"The War in Gibraltar." *After the Battle* 21 (1978): 1+.

Welker, Robert H. "GI Jargon: Its Perils and Pitfalls." *Saturday Review of Literature* (Oct. 1944): 7+.

Wesbrook, Stephen D. "The Railey Report and Army Morale, 1941: Anatomy of a Crisis." *Military Review* 60, no. 6 (June 1980): 11+.

Young, Leilyn M. "Rangers in a Night Operation." *Military Review* 24, no. 4 (July 1944): 64+.

Newspapers

"37 in Company Missing in Africa." *Red Oak* (Iowa) *Express,* 11 March 1943: 1.

Alexander, Field Marshal the Viscount. "The African Campaign from El Alamein to Tunis." *London Gazette,* 3 Feb. 1948.

"An American Story: The Life and Times of a Midlands Family." *Omaha* (Neb.) *World-Herald,* 9 Nov. 1997: 1.

Blair, William M. "Non-Stop Air Armada of Allies Flew 1,400 Miles to North Africa." *New York Times,* 10 Jan. 1943: 1.

Bracker, Milton. "Rangers Toughen but Are Still Boys." *New York Times,* 6 March 1943.

Buttry, Stephen. "An American Story." *Omaha* (Neb.) *Sunday World-Herald,* 9 Nov. 1997: 1.

Clifton, C. C. "How Iowans Fought in Africa." *Des Moines Sunday Register,* 18 July 1943: 1.

De Luce, Daniel. "All the Fight Knocked Out of Germans." *Washington Post,* 13 May 1943: 1.

Frye, William. " 'Terrible Terry' of the 1st Division Is Getting Tougher as He Goes Along." *Kansas City Star,* 17 June 1943.

"Gen. Marshall Smashing Army's Caste System in Quest for Best Leaders." *St. Louis Post-Dispatch,* 19 Dec. 1940: C1.

"German Tanks Trapped." *Times of London,* 5 May 1943: 1

"How Major Allen Beat Cowboy Champ in 300-Mile Race." *Brooklyn Daily Eagle,* 31 Dec. 1922.

Howe, Marvine. "In Marrakesh." *New York Times,* 3 March 2002.

Kluckhorn, Frank L. "Tunisian Resistance Ends in Rout of Germans." *New York Times,* 12 May 1943: 1.

Middleton, Drew. "The Battle Saga of a Tough Outfit." *New York Times Magazine,* 8 April 1945: 8+.

Munday, William. "Prison Ship Escapes." *Tunis Telegraph.* 10 May 1943: 1.

Norgaard, Noland. "Major Moore Escapes from Nazi Lines." *Red Oak* (Iowa) *Express,* 22 Feb. 1943: 1.

Petroski, William. "50 Years Later, Defeat by Rommel Still Clear." *Des Moines Sunday Register,* 21 March 1993: 1B.

Thompson, John H. "Kasserine Fiasco Laid to British." *Chicago Tribune,* Feb. 1948.

Vogel, Steve. "The Battle of Arlington: How the Pentagon Got Built." *Washington Post,* 26 Apr 1999: 1.

Wilson, Richard. "The Gallant Fight of the 34th Division in the North African Campaign." *Des Moines Register and Tribune,* 1943.

I also draw extensively on issues of the following Iowa newspapers from February through March 1941: *Clarinda Herald-Journal; Council Bluffs Nonpareil; Red Oak Express; Sioux City Journal; Villisca Review.*

Manuscripts

"18th Infantry Draft Regimental Wartime History." MRC FDM.

"701st Tank Destroyer Battalion: North African Campaign Diary." MHI.

"The Administrative History of the Eighth Fleet." N.d., NHC, World War II Command File, Fleets.

Anderson, K.A.N. "Operations in North West Africa, 8 November 1942 to 13 May 1943." 1946. *London Gazette.*

Anderson, Roland. "The Operations of the 135th Infantry Regiment in the Vicinity of Fondouk el Okbi." 1948. Fort Benning, Ga. Infantry School.

Bailey, Leslie W. "The Operations of the 3rd Battalion, 135th Infantry at Algiers, North Africa, 7 November–10 November, 1942." 1948. Fort Benning, Ga. Infantry School.

"Battle Analysis of the Battle of Sidi bou Zid, 14 February 1943." 1984. CSI.

Baumgartner, John W., et al. "History of the 16th Infantry, 1798–1946."

Bielakowski, Alexander M. "Calmer Heads Will Prevail: The Interwar U.S. Cavalry and the Issue of Mechanization." Paper delivered before the Society for Military History, April 2000.

Blumenson, Martin, et al. "Airborne Operations." 1964. CMH.

Boehm, Edward. "My Autobiography During World War II." 1997.

Brandt, Arnold N. "The Operations of the 1st Battalion, 135th Infantry at Hills 609 and 531." 1948. Fort Benning, Ga. Infantry School.

"British Commandos." 1942. War Department, Military Intelligence Service.

Buchholz, Ulrich. "Supply by Air of the Enlarged Bridgehead of Tunis." 1947. U.S. Army European Command. FMS D-071.

Bürker, Ulrich. "Commitment of the 10th Panzer Division in Tunisia." 1947. U.S. Army European Command. FMS, D-174.

———. "Einsatz der 10. Panzer-Division in Tunesien." Part II. 1947. U.S. Army European Command. FMS, D-310.

Cairns, Bogardus S. "Employment of Armor in the Invasion of Oran." 1946. Fort Leavenworth, Kan. CARL N-2253.26.

Cameron, Robert S. "Americanizing the Tank: U.S. Army Administration and Mechanized Development Within the Army, 1917–1943." Ph.D diss., Temple University, 1994.

Camp, T. J., ed. "Tankers in Tunisia." 1943. Fort Knox, Ky. Armored Replacement Training Center.

Carter, Sam. "The Operations of the 1st Battalion, 18th Infantry at El Guettar." 1948. Fort Benning, Ga.: Infantry School.

Carter, William A. "Carter's War." 1983. CEOH.

Cochran, Alexander S. "Chickens or Eggs? Operations TORCH and HUSKY and U.S. Army Amphibious Doctrine." Paper for Fourteenth Naval History Symposium, Sept. 1999.

———. "Constructing a Military Coalition from Materials at Hand: The Case of Allied Force Headquarters." Paper delivered before the Society for Military History Conference, 1999.

———. "Crisis at AFHG: Ike, Kasserine, and Coalition Command." Comments presented at Society for Military History annual meeting, Apr. 2002.

Craven, Virgil. "The Operations of Company I, 133rd Infantry, in the Attack at Fondouk Gap." 1950. Fort Benning, Ga. Infantry School.

Daniel, Derrill M. "Landings at Oran, Gela and Omaha Beaches." 1947. Norfolk, Va. Armed Forces Staff College.

Daubin, Freeland A., Jr. "The Battle of Happy Valley." 1948. Fort Knox, Ky. Armored School. MHI.

Davidson, Garrison H. "Grandpa Gar: The Saga of One Soldier as Told to His Grand-children." 1979. USMA Arch.

Davison, Donald. "Aviation Engineers in the Battle of Tunisia." 1943. Orlando, Fla. Army Air Forces School of Applied Tactics. MHI.

Deichmann, Paul. "Mission of OB Süd with the Auxiliary Battle Command in North Africa." N.d. U.S. Army European Command. FMS, D-067.

Dickson, Benjamin A. "G-2 Journal: Algiers to the Elbe." Unpublished memoir, N.d. MHI. (A version of this material may also be found in USMA Arch.)

Dray, Dennis B. "Regimental Commander of the 168th Infantry, Colonel Thomas David-son Drake: Battle of Sened and Sidi bou Zid, Tunisia." 1977. Iowa GSM.

Drea, Edward J. "Unit Reconstitution: A Historical Perspective." 1983. CSI.

Durno, George E. "Flight to Africa: A Chronicle of the Casablanca Conference Between President Roosevelt and Prime Minister Churchill in January, 1943." N.d. FDR Lib.

Eckhard, Christian. "Considerations at Supreme Headquarters Concerning the Overall Conduct of the War in North Africa After the Allied Landing." 1947. U.S. Army Euro-pean Command. FMS, D-145.

———. "OKW Reaction to the Allied Landing in North Africa." 1947. U.S. Army Euro-pean Command. FMS, D-145.

———. "Study of the Situation in the High Command of the Wehrmacht." 1947. U.S. Army European Command. FMS, D-066.

Edwards, Harry W. "A Different War: Marines in Europe and North Africa." 1994. Marines in World War II Commemorative Series.

Erbes, John. "Hell on Wheels Surgeon." N.d. John Erbes Collection, USMA Arch.

Feige, Richard. "Relationship Between Operations and Supply in Africa." 1947. U.S. Army European Command. FMS, D-125.

"The First Phase of the Engagements in Tunisia." Part I. N.d. U.S. Army European Com-mand. FMS, D-086.

Fosdick, Roger Barry. "A Call to Arms: The American Enlisted Soldier in World War II." Ph.D. diss., Claremont Graduate School, 1985.

Fountain, Ray C. "Notes on the Movement and Actions of the 133rd Infantry." N.d. Iowa GSM.

Friedman, Abraham. "Operation TORCH: The Dispatch of Aircraft from the United King-dom by Eighth Air Force." 1944. U.S. Strategic Air Forces in Europe, Historical Section.

Frierson, William C. "The Pentagon." 1944. CMH.

———. "Preparations for 'TORCH.'" 2 vols. 1945. CMH.

Gabel, Christopher R. "Seek, Strike, and Destroy: U.S. Army Tank Destroyer Doctrine in World War II." 1985. CSI.

Gardiner, Henry E. "Tank Commander." Unpublished memoir. 1956. Paul M. Robinett Papers. GCM Lib. (A version of this material may also be found in USMA Arch.)

Gause, Alfred. "Army Group Africa." 1953. U.S. Army European Command. FMS, D-385.

Gugeler, Russell A. Unpublished biography of Orlando Ward. N.d. Orlando Ward Papers. MHI.

Haggerty, Jerome Joseph. "A History of the Ranger Battalions in World War II." Ph.D. diss., Fordham University, 1982.

Hayes, Harold G. "Operations on Signal Intelligence Gained from North African Theater of Operations." 1943. NARA, NSA SRH-409.

Hazen, David W. "Role of the Field Artillery in the Battle of Kasserine Pass." Master's thesis, U.S. Army Command and General Staff College, 1973.

Hendricks, Charles. "A Time of Testing: U.S. Army Engineers in the Tunisia Campaign of World War II." Colloquium on Military Fortifications and Infrastructure in Tunisia. 1999. CMH.

Hewitt, H. Kent. "Reminiscences of a World War II Admiral." N.d. NHC.

"History of Allied Force Headquarters." 3 vols. 1945. MTOUSA Historical Section.

"History of Planning Division, Army Service Forces." 1946. CMH.

"History of the 26th Infantry in the Present Struggle" N.d. MRC FDM.

House, Jonathan M. "Toward Combined Arms Warfare: A Survey of 20th-Century Tactics, Doctrine, and Organization." 1984. CSI.

Howe, George F. "Allied and Axis Command in the Mediterranean." Delivered to American Historical Society meeting, Chicago, Dec. 1950.

———. "American Signal Intelligence in Northwest Africa and Western Europe." 1980. United States Cryptologic History, World War II, vol. 1. NSA.

Howze, Hamilton H. "Tank Action," 1943. OW, MHI.

Hudel, Major, and Paul McD. Robinett. "The Tank Battle at Sidi bou Zid." MHI.

Husinpiller, Herschel H. "Armored Infantry in Africa." N.d. Fort Benning, Ga. Infantry School. MHI.

Huston, James A. "Airborne Operations." 1955. CMH.

Jarrett, G. B. "Ordnance: The Theme Song of Military History." N.d. MHI.

"Kasserine Pass Battles." 7 vols. N.d. CMH.

Kern, W. B. "Account of French near Fondouk El Okbi on January 16, 1943." N.d. PMR, GCM Lib.

———. "Account of the Battle Between U.S. and German Forces near El Bathan," 1950. PMR, LOC.

Kesselring, Albert. "Concluding Remarks on the Mediterranean Campaign." N.d. U.S. Army European Command. FMS, C-104.

———. "The Events in Tunisia." 1949. U.S. Army European Command. FMS, D-066.

———. "Final Commentaries on the Campaign in North Africa, 1941–1943." 1949. U.S. Army European Command. FMS, C-075.

———. "Italy as a Military Ally." N.d. U.S. Army European Command. FMS, C-015.

———. "The War in the Mediterranean Area, Part I." N.d. U.S. Army European Command. FMS T-3.

———. "The War in the Mediterranean, Part II: The Fighting in Tunisia and Tripolitania." N.d. U.S. Army European Command. FMS, T-3.

King, Michael J. "Rangers: Selected Combat Operations in World War II." 1985. CSI.

Kirkpatrick, Charles E. "Filling the Gaps: Reevaluating Officer Professional Education in the Inter-war Army, 1920–1940." Paper, 1989.

———. "Orthodox Soldiers: Army Formal Schools Between the Two World Wars." Paper. 1990.

Knoche, Wilhelm. "Meine Erlebnisse im Tunesien-Feldzug." 1998. U.S. Army European Command. FMS, D-323.

Krause, Fritz. "Decision to Occupy the Mareth Line." N.d. U.S. Army European Command. FMS, D-012.

———. "Studies on the Mareth Position." N.d. U.S. Army European Command. FMS, D-046.

Lang, Rudolf. "Battles of Kampfgruppe Lang in Tunisia." 1947. US. Army European Command. FMS, D-173.

———. "Report on the Fighting of Kampfgruppe Lang." Part II. N.d. U.S. Army European Command. FMS, D-166.

Lange, Herman Walter Wright. "The Battle of Thala." Thesis. George Washington University, 1966.

Larson, Ann, ed. "The History and Contribution to American Democracy of Volunteer 'Citizen Soldiers' of Southwest Iowa, 1930–1945." 1981. National Endowment of the Humanities.

Lavoie, Leon F., et al. "The First Armored Division at Faid-Kasserine." 1949. Fort Knox, Ky. Armored School. MHI.

Loerzer, A. D. "Verhandlung Mit dem Stellvertreter von General Barré und dem Residenten von Tunis Admiral Estéva." N.d. U.S. Army European Command. FMS, D-040.

"Logistics in World War II: Final Report of the Army Service Forces." 1947. Washington, D.C. War Department.

Marshall, Jack A. "The Battle That Wasn't." N.d. ASEQ, 34th ID, MHI.

McKinney, Leonard L. "Portable Flame Thrower Operations in World War II." 1949. Washington, D.C. Office of the Chief, Chemical Corps. MHI.

Meyer, Leo J. "Strategy and Logistical History: Mediterranean Theater of Operations." 1962. CMH.

Millett, John D. "Overseas Movement of the First Infantry Division and the First Armored Division." 1993. CMH.

Moore, Robert R. "Tunisian Stand." N.d. NARA RG 319, OCMH, Box 103.

Mortensen, Daniel R. "A Pattern for Joint Operations: World War II Close Air Support North Africa." 1987. Washington, D.C. Office of Air Force History and CMH.

Nehring, Walter. "The Development of the Situation in North Africa." 1947. U.S. Army European Command. FMS, D-120.

———. "The First Phase of the Battle in Tunisia." 1947. U.S. Army European Command. FMS, D-147.

Nicholson, Cameron. "The Battle of Kasserine, February 1943." N.d. Microfilm. IWM.

"The Ninth Infantry Division: Adventures by Men of the 60th Infantry Regiment in WWII." 1993. MHI.

Ochsner, Herman. "History of German Chemical Warfare in World War II." 1949. Washington, D.C. Historical Office of the Chief of the Chemical Corps.

"A Partial History, 135th Infantry Regiment." N.d. Iowa GSM.

Phillips, Edwin Allen. "Destroyer Experiences in the Atlantic and Pacific in World War II." NHC.

Prigge, Christopher N. "Crossed Sabers in Steel: The Evolution of World War II Mechanized Cavalry Doctrine." Paper delivered at Society for Military History meeting, April 2000.

"Proposed Mission Against Fondouk Gap, Tunisia, on 7 April 1943." 1951. Air University Library, Historical Division.

"Psychological Warfare in the Mediterranean Theater." Part I. 1945. Naples, Italy. U.S. Army MTO.

Ralph, Stephen V. "The Operations of the 2nd Battalion, 16th Infantry in the Invasion of North Africa." 1947. Fort Benning, Ga. Infantry School.

"Reports Received by U.S. War Department on Use of Ultra in the European Theater, World War II." NARA. NSA, SRH-037.

Robinett, Paul M. "Among the First." N.d. GCM Lib.

Rogers, Robert John. "A Study of Leadership in the First Infantry Division During World War II." Master's thesis. Fort Leavenworth, Kan., 1965.

Schnarrenberger, Ernst. "Report on My Activities as Commander of Rear Area of Army of North Africa." 1947. U.S. Army European Command. FMS, D-072.

———. "Situation of the Fortification of Tunis." 1947. U.S. Army European Command. FMS, D-005.

Semmens, Paul. "The Hammer of Hell: Forward Area Antiaircraft Artillery at Kasserine Pass and the Remagen Bridge." N.d. CMH.

Shugart, David A. "On the Way: The U.S. Field Artillery in the Inter-War Period." Paper delivered at Society for Military History meeting, April 2000.

"Signal Communication in the North African Campaigns." Part 1, "Tactical Communication in World War II." 1945. Office of the Chief Signal Officer, Historical Section. MHI.

"The Story of the Embarkation of the 1st Infantry Division." N.d. CARL, N-6172.

"Strategy and Logistical History, Mediterranean Theater of Operations." Unpublished volume in Army "Green Series." NARA RG 319, OCMH, boxes 257–58.

TD Combat in Tunisia. 1944. U.S. Army Tank Destroyer School. MHI.

"Terry Allen and the First Division in North Africa and Sicily." N.d. TdA, MHI.

Toppe, Alfred. "Desert Warfare: German Experiences in World War II." 1991. CSI.

"U.S.A.F. Airborne Operations, World War II and Korean War." March 1962. USAF Historical Division.

Uffner, Raphael L. "Recollections of World War II with the First Infantry Division." 1991. MRC FDM.

"United States Naval Administration in World War II."1946. Amphibious Training Command. No. 145. NHC.

———. Commander in Chief, Atlantic Fleet. Vol. 1.

———. COMNAVEU. Vols 1–2, N.d. NHC.

———. United States Navy Medical Department at War, 1941–1945. Vol. 1, Part 3, N.d. NHC.

Von Arnim, Hans J. T. "Recollections of Tunisia." Trans. Janet E. Dewey. 1951. U.S. Army European Command. FMS, C-098.

———. "Tunisian Operations." Trans. Janet E. Dewey. 1951. U.S. Army European Command. FMS, C-094.

Von Liebenstein, Kurt. "The Drive via Gafsa Against Kasserine Pass." 1947. U.S. Army European Command. FMS, D-124.

———. "Operations of the 164th Light Africa Division." N.d. U.S. Army European Command. FMS, D-315.

Von Rinteln, Enno. "The Italian Command and Armed Forces in the First Half of 1943." Trans. Janet E. Dewey. 1947. U.S. Army European Command. FMS, T-1a.

Von Vaerst, Gustav. "Operations of the Fifth Panzer Army in Tunisia." N.d. U.S. Army European Command. FMS, D-001.

Wade, Gary. "World War II Division Commanders." N.d. CSI.

Warlimont, Walter. "High Level Decisions—Tunisian Campaign." Trans. Janet E. Dewey. 1951. U.S. Army European Command. FMS, C-092a.

Webb, James R. "First Waltz with Rommel." N.d. Webb papers, DDE Lib, box 1.

Weber, Friedrich. "Battles of 334th Division and of Group Weber." N.d. U.S. Army European Command. FMS, D-215.

Werner, Christoph Wilhelm. "The Battles of the Hermann Göring Division in Tunisia From January to 12 May 1943." 1947. U.S. Army European Command. FMS, D-085.

"Western Task Force: Landing Operations at Safi." N.d. Washington D.C. War Department, Historical Division. CMH.

"Western Task Force: The Attack on Fedala." N.d. Washington, D.C. War Department, Historical Division. CMH.

"Western Task Force: The Attack on Mehdia and the Port Lyautey Airdrome." 1945. Washington, D.C. War Department, Historical Division. CMH.

Wilhm, Jack F. et al. "Armor in the Invasion of North Africa." 1950. Fort Knox, Ky. Armored School. MHI.

Wilson, Lloyd G. "The Operations of the 509th Parachute Battalion in North Africa." 1948. Fort Benning, Ga. Infantry School. MHI.

"World War II, A Brief History." 1946. Washington, D.C. Office of the Provost Marshal General.

Yarmon, Morton. "The Administrative and Logistical History of the ETO: IV, TORCH and the European Theater of Operations." 1946. Historical Division, U.S. Army Forces, European Theater. CMH.

Papers, Letters, Collections, Personal Narratives, and Diaries

Dwight D. Eisenhower Presidential Library, Abilene, Kan.: files for Harold R. L. Alexander; Terry Allen; Kenneth Anderson; Harry C. Butcher; Lloyd Fredendall; Operation TORCH; George S. Patton, Jr.; Charles W. Ryder; James R. Webb

Eisenhower Center, University of New Orleans: Fred W. Hall, Jr.

George C. Marshall Foundation Research Library, Lexington, Va.: George F. Howe Papers; George C. Marshall Papers; Paul M. Robinett Papers; Lucian K. Truscott, Jr., Papers; Reginald Winn Collection

Imperial War Museum, London: A.A.C.W. Brown, "364 Days Overseas Service"; G. P. Druitt diary; Charles Gairdner diary; J.B.A. Glennie, narrative in papers of R. de L. King; Adrian Clements Gore, "This Was the Way It Was"; G. R. Grandage, "Operation TORCH"; J.R.T. Hopper, "Figures in a Fading Landscape"; H. M. Jones, narrative; Richard F. Kinden, "The Road to Fort McGregor and the Long Way Home"; W. D. McClure, diary; Cameron Nicholson Collection; A. G. Oakley diaries; R. Priestly papers; P. Royle, narrative; K. Shirley Smith, diary; R. C. Taylor, "Seven Sunrays"; Fred Telford, narrative; G. E. Thubron, narrative; A.J.A. Weir, letters; J. K. Windeatt, "Very Ordinary Soldier"

Iowa Gold Star Museum, Fort Dodge, Iowa: Leslie W. Bailey, "An Infantry Battalion in Attack"; William F. Beekman, "A Diary of World War II as Observed Through the Eyes, Ears and Mind of Bill Beekman"; Eugene L. Daniel papers; Vernon Hohenberger, "Retracing My Footsteps in World War II"; Lester Kness, "An Iowa Soldier Remembers Patton"; William Walling Luttrell, "A Personal Account of the Experiences as a German Prisoner of War"; Edgar P. Moschel, "168th Inf Regiment Narrative of Action"; Dennis F. Neal, "Dennis Frederick Neal, Soldier"; Robert L. Owen, typescript on 168th Infantry Regiment band at Kasserine Pass; Bill Roth, "The Longest Days of a G.I."; John H. Van Vliet, Jr., typescript

Library of Congress, Manuscript Division, Washington, D.C.: Wallace Carroll Papers; H. Kent Hewitt Papers; Samuel Eliot Morison Papers; George S. Patton, Jr., Papers; Paul M. Robinett Papers; Theodore Roosevelt, Jr., Papers; Jerauld Wright Papers

Liddell Hart Centre for Military Archives, King's College, London: Charles Walter Allfrey Collection; B. H. Liddell Hart Collection; E. E. Mockler-Ferryman papers; William Ronald Campbell Penney Collection

McCormick Research Center, First Division Museum, Cantigny, Ill.: Clift Andrus, notes on *A Soldier's Story*; Joseph T. Dawson Collection; Stanhope Brasfield Mason, "Reminiscences and Anecdotes of World War II"; Robert Maurice Mullen, "Memorial Booklet"; Jean Gordon Peltier diary; Raphael L. Uffner Papers

Naval Historical Center, Washington, D.C.: H. Kent Hewitt Papers; Samuel Eliot Morison Office Files

Norwich University, Norwich, Vt.: Ernest Harmon Papers

U.S. Army Military History Institute, Carlisle, Pa.: Terry de la Mesa Allen Papers; William S. Biddle Papers; Robert W. Black Collection; Roy C. Brewer Papers; Raymond H. Croll Papers; William J. Donovan Papers; Chester B. Hansen Papers; Ernest B. Harmon Papers; David Irving Collection (microfilm transcription of Everett Hughes's diaries, "Allied High Command"); Oscar Koch Papers; Louis F. Lisko Papers; John P. Lucas Papers; Samuel L. Myers Papers; Martin M. Philipsborn Papers; Oscar S. Reeder Papers; Robert I. Stack Papers; Orlando Ward Papers

Diaries and personal narratives contained in MHI Army Service Experiences Questionnaire: 1st Armored Division (William H. Balzar; Robert G. Bond; Harold F. Blodgett; Thomas E. Hannum; William A. Heslep; Oswald Jett; Howard F. Kenney; Stanley J. Krekeler; Robert M. Marsh; John Mayo; Arthur Robert Moore; Gustav A. Mueller; James Rhoden Pritchard; Laurence P. Robertson; James Scott Stapel; Ernest A. Wells)

    1st Infantry Division (William E. Faust; Charles T. Horner, Jr.; George J. Koch; William M. Lee; Paul K. Skogsberg; Andrew C. Wright)

    3rd Infantry Division (Joseph A. Watters)

    9th Infantry Division (George Bastedo; Donald Peel)

    60th Troop Carrier Group (Robert L. Miley)

U.S. Military Academy, West Point, N.Y.: James D. Alger Collection; Benjamin A. Dickson Collection; Henry E. Gardiner Papers; Will Lang Collection

University of Missouri at Columbia, Western Historical Manuscript Collection: James McGuinness letter

University of Tennessee at Knoxville: Bill Sabin Papers

University of Texas at El Paso Library, S.L.A. Marshall Military History Collection: Terry de la Mesa Allen Papers

Yale University Library, New Haven, Conn.: Mina Curtiss Collection

Author Interviews

Consuelo Allen; Aurelio Barron; Dave Berlovich; Edward Boehm; Paul H. Calder; Frank B. Clay; Ross W. Cline; Wilbur C. Darnell; Paul F. Gorman; George Juskalian; Jack A. Marshall; Clem Miller; Robert R. Moore, Jr.; John D. Nelson; William W. Quinn; Albert H. Smith; Hans von Luck; Edith Ward Spalding; Clifton J. Warner; Eston White; John Ward Yates; Robin Ward Yates

Interview and Oral History Transcripts

Columbia University, Oral History Research Office, New York: Mark W. Clark; H. Kent Hewitt; Lyman Lemnitzer; Robert Murphy

Dwight D. Eisenhower Presidential Library, Abilene, Kan.: Ray W. Barker; Charles Bolte; LeRoy Lutes; James B. Stack

George C. Marshall Library, Lexington, Va.: Forrest C. Pogue interview: George C. Marshall

Library of Congress, Washington, D.C.: Paul M. Robinett papers: Walter Nehring

McCormick Research Center, First Division Museum, Cantigny, Ill.: Harley Reynolds; John Hall Thompson

National War College Library, NARA, RG 334: John S. Allard; Webster Anderson; C.T. Booth; Charles Hoy; M.T. Wordell

Rutgers University, Oral History Archives of World War II, New Brunswick, N.J.: Walter Bruyere, III; Thomas A. Kindre; John G. Rosta

U.S. Air Force Historical Research Center, Maxwell Air Force Base, Ala.: Philip G. Cochran

U.S. Army Corps of Engineers, Office of History, Alexandria, Va.: Garrison H. Davidson; Herbert W. Ehrgott; Henry J. Hoeffer; Harry O. Paxson; Edwin L. Powell, Jr.; William F. Powers

U.S. Army Military History Institute, Carlisle, Pa: *Russell A. Gugeler interviews*: Jacob Devers; Hamilton H. Howze; McCurtain Scott; Robert Simons

    Sidney Matthews Papers: Russell F. Akers; Leo S. Bachmann; Rudolph Barlow; R. Brodie, Jr.; Harold G. Bull; Benjamin F. Caffey, Jr.; Ben Crosby; Frederic P. Culbert; Benjamin A. Dickson; Leon Dostert; Hobart Gay; Frederick W. Gibbs; Henri Giraud;

Peter C. Hains, III; Pierpont M. Hamilton; Ernest N. Harmon; Robert A. Hewitt; LeRoy Irwin; Alphonse Juin; Geoffrey Keyes; George C. Marshall; Stanhope Mason; John W. O'Daniel; Edwin A. Russell; Charles W. Ryder; Harry H. Semmes; Walter Bedell Smith; Alexander Stark; Kenneth D. W. Strong

Forrest Pogue interviews: Field Marshal Viscount Alanbrooke; Arthur Coningham; Lord Cuningham of Hyndhope; Charles de Gaulle; Benjamin A. Dickson; James Gault; Hastings L. Ismay; Albert Kenner; C. E. Lambe; Frederick E. Morgan; Viscount Mountbatten of Burma; Viscount Portal of Hungerford; Walter Bedell Smith; Orlando Ward

Senior Officer Oral History Program: Mark W. Clark; Theodore J. Conway; Harry H. Critz; Ira C. Eaker; William P. Ennis, Jr.; Hobart R. Gay; Peter C. Hains, III; John A. Heintges; Robert A. Hewitt; Hamilton Howze; Walter T. Kerwin, Jr.; Robert W. Porter, Jr.; Elwood R. Quesada; John K. Waters; Albert C. Wedemeyer; William P. Yarborough

U.S. Army Office of the Chief of Military History, Washington, "Background Papers to NW Africa," NARA, RG 319, boxes 220–231: Harold Alexander; Terry Allen; Mark W. Clark; John T. Crocker; Robert E. Cullis; Francis De Guingand; Charles J. Denholm; H. Kent Hewitt; Gordon H. A. MacMillan; Robert P. Miller; Leland L. Rounds; Charles W. Ryder; R. I. Stack; Robert Ward

U.S. Naval Institute, Annapolis, Md.: Walter Ansel; Hanson Weightman Baldwin; George W. Bauernschmidt; Bernhard H. Bieri; Joshua W. Cooper; George C. Dyer; Ralph K. James; Jackson K. Parker; U.S. Grant Sharp; Elliott B. Strauss; Edward K. Walker; Charles Wellborn, Jr.; F.E.M. Whiting

Motion Pictures

From National Archives, RG 111, Office of the Chief Signal Officer
Allied Offensive in North Africa. Film Bulletin No. 51
At the Front in North Africa with the U.S. Army. No. 1001, Dec. 1942
Soldier Stevedores. Film Bulletin No. 32
Tunisian Victory: An Official Record. No. 1012
Signal Corps silent B&W footage:
ADC 1; ADC 246; ADC 2407; ADC 1113; ADC 979; ADC 465; ADC 1002; ADC 998
From British Army Film & Photographic Unit / Royal Air Force Film Production Unit
Desert Victory. 1943

Miscellany

"The Attack on Sidi bou Zid." Narrative composed by officers, 2nd Battalion, 1st Armored Regiment, while prisoners of war, n.d. James D. Alger Collection, USMA Arch.
Biddle, William S. "Amphibious Training of American Troops in Great Britain in Preparation for North African Landing Operation." Lecture, Fort Hood, Tex., 1943. MHI.
———. "The French Army of North Africa in the Tunisian Campaign." Lecture, Fort Hood, Tex., 1943. MHI.
Cirillo, Roger. Lecture, Hannibal Club. May 14, 2001. Washington, D.C.
Darby, William O. "U.S. Rangers." Lecture, Army and Navy Staff College. Oct. 27, 1944. MHI.
Dunphie, Charles. Memo on Thala, N.d. NARA RG 319, OCMH, box 229.
Dunton, D. H. "Air Service Organization and Functioning in NATOUSA." Lecture, Army and Navy Staff College. 2 Sept. 1943. NARA, RG 334, NWC Lib.
El Bekri, Mohamed Ali. Lecture, Hannibal Club. May 14, 2001. Washington, D.C.
"French Policy Toward Arabs, Jews and Italians in Tunisia." OSS, Research and Analysis Branch, Dec. 1943. NARA RG 334, NWC Lib., box 895.

Grahl, Charles H. "Biennial Report of the Adjutant General of the State of Iowa." Des Moines: Office of the Adjutant General, 1940. Iowa GSM.

Howze, Hamilton H. "The Battle of Sidi bou Zid." Lecture, U.S. Army Cavalry School, n.d. MHI.

Maraist, Robert V., and Peter C. Hains. Transcript, "Conference on North African Operations." Fort Knox, Ky., 16 June 1943. SM, MHI.

Matejka, Jerry V. "Communication Plans: Basic, Joint and Combined." Lecture, Army-Navy Staff College, 19 Aug. 1943. NARA RG 334, NWC Lib, box 167.

"Partial Planning File, First United States' Use of Parachute Troops in Connection with TORCH," n.d. MHI Library.

Pirnie, W. Bruce, Jr. Letter about Sidi bou Zid, to Amon G. Carter, publisher of *Fort Worth Star Telegram*, 16 June 1943. OW, MHI.

Richardson, C. G. "The Attack on Safi." Lecture, Army and Navy Staff College. 20 Aug. 1943. NARA RG 334, NWC Lib, box 164.

Robinett, Paul M. "The Axis Offensive in Central Tunisia, Feb. 1943," n.d., LOC.

———. "Memorandum Notes." Army War College seminar, Nov. 1951, Army War College Studies, Z-R55.

Seacord, Daniel F. *"Ludlow."* Account, U.S.S. *Ludlow.* NHC, 1979.

Somervell, Brehon. "Army Service Forces." Lecture, Army-Navy Staff College, 9 Aug. 1943. NARA RG 334, NWC Lib, box 167.

"Statement of Brig. Gen. Laurence C. Kuter." Pentagon, 22 May 1943. NARA RG 319, box 103.

U.S. Army Military History Institute, Carlisle, Pa.: Army Service Experiences Questionnaires for 1st Infantry Division; 1st Armored Division; 3rd Infantry Division; 9th Infantry Division; 34th Infantry Division; Rangers; II Corps.

Interviews by Michael Corley with John T. Corley, Tom Gendron, John Kelley (1977, possession of Paul Gorman); thedropzone.org, interviews by Patrick K. O'Donnell with Leo Inglesby, Carl Lehmann.

ACKNOWLEDGMENTS

I was born in occupied Munich in 1952 and spent my early childhood in occupied Austria as the son of an American Army officer. That perhaps explains a lifelong fascination with World War II—how *did* we find ourselves in central Europe, and why? But my professional passion for the subject was enflamed in the mid-1990s when, as the Berlin bureau chief for *The Washington Post*, I covered a succession of fiftieth-anniversary commemorations, from the landings at Normandy to the final surrender of Germany. Walking the battlefields at Anzio and Arnhem, Salerno and the Bulge, and listening to veterans recount their tales made two things clear: this was the greatest story of the twentieth century, and like all great stories, it was bottomless. There was more to write; there will always be more to write. The armies that liberated Europe in 1944 and 1945 had a cumulative history, as did the officers and men who composed those armies, and no comprehensive understanding of the victory of May 1945 is possible without understanding the earlier campaigns in Africa and Italy. Hence, the Liberation Trilogy.

Any twenty-first-century author writing about World War II owes an incalculable debt to those of the twentieth century, and I gratefully acknowledge mine. Among the hundreds of volumes consulted for this work, a special recognition is owed the 114-volume *U.S. Army in World War II*, the official history informally known as the Green Series. I have also profited from the official British *History of the Second World War*, as well as innumerable regimental and division histories, personal memoirs, historical analyses, and scholarly studies. The compendium is large, and now one book larger.

Out of conviction that the ground itself has a great deal to say, I traveled to Tunisia in September 1996 and April 2000; to Morocco in April 2000; and to El Alamein, Egypt, in May 1996. To further steep myself I visited Volgograd (formerly Stalingrad), Moscow, the Seelow Heights east of Berlin, and other battlefields in Italy, France, Germany, Belgium, Luxembourg, and the Netherlands from 1994 to 2001. I also interviewed many veterans. But the core of this narrative is drawn from primary, contemporaneous sources—diaries, letters, records official and unofficial, after-action reports, unpublished memoirs, original maps—a surprising number of which have not previously been used in comprehensive accounts of the war. For help in tracking down these many thousands of documents I am deeply grateful for the professionalism and patience of a hundred or more historians and archivists.

At the National Archives in College Park, Maryland, I thank John W. Carlin, Archivist of the United States; Michael J. Kurtz; Richard Boylan; Timothy Mulligan; and especially Timothy K. Nenninger, who is also president of the Society for Military History. As chief of modern military records, Tim has been an extraordinary guide in the deep woods of federal archives. He was also kind enough to read the galleys and to offer suggestions. This would be a lesser book without him.

The U.S. Army's Military History Institute at Carlisle Barracks, Pennsylvania, is a national treasure beyond value, and in my seventeen visits there since 1998 I have accumulated a large debt to the recently retired director, Lt. Col. Edwin M. Perry, and to John Slonaker; Dennis J. Vetock; Richard J. Sommers; Louise Arnold-Friend; Nancy Baylor; Pamela Cheney; James T. Baughman; Richard L. Baker; Stanley Lanque, Randy Hackenburg, and especially the chief archivist, David A. Keough.

The U.S. Army Center of Military History has also been a trove of documents, photographs, and expertise. Thanks to Brig. Gen. John Sloan Brown, the chief of military history, and to the chief historian, Jeffrey J. Clarke, who generously read the galleys. I am also grateful to Robert K. Wright, Jr.; Mary L. Haynes; Jim Knight; R. Cody Phillips; Charles Hendricks; and Geraldine K. Harcarik.

Thomas J. Mann in the Library of Congress reading room and Frederick Bauman, Jr., in the manuscript division were very helpful.

The Robert McCormick Research Center at the First Division Museum, in Cantigny, Illinois, is among the finest unit archives in the world, and I appreciate the help of the executive director of the Cantigny First Division Foundation, John Votaw; Andrew E. Woods; and Eric Gillespie; as well as the encouragement of the McCormick Tribune Foundation.

The Iowa Gold Star Museum at Fort Dodge has many unique records of the 34th Infantry Division, and I thank the director, Jerry L. Gorden; Richard A. Moss, secretary/treasurer of the 34th Infantry Division Association; and curator Mike Vogt.

At the West Point Library, I'm grateful to the special collections director, Alan Aimone; associate director Suzanne Christoff; and manuscripts curator Susan Lintelman.

I am grateful for assistance from the U.S. Army War College at Carlisle Barracks, Pennsylvania, and particularly to the former commandant, Maj. Gen. Robert H. Scales, Jr.; the former academic dean, Col. Jeffrey D. McCausland; and professors Samuel J. Newland; Adolf Carlson; J. Boone Bartholomees, Jr.; and Barrie E. Zais.

Mickey Russell, a historian in the Air Force Historical Research Agency at Maxwell Air Force Base, Alabama, and Sue Goodman, chief of the reference branch at the Air University Library, were particularly helpful.

At the Naval Historical Center in Washington I appreciate the help of Kathy Lloyd and Michael Walker in operational archives, and Glenn Helm in the Navy Department Library. Similarly, at the U.S. Naval Institute in Annapolis, Maryland, I thank the director of oral history, Paul Stillwell; publisher Thomas F. Marfiak; and Ann Hassinger.

At the Combat Studies Institute in Fort Leavenworth, Kansas, the director, Col. Lawyn C. Edwards, and Lt. Col. Steven Clay were helpful, and I appreciate the assistance of the staff of the Combined Arms Research Library.

The George C. Marshall Foundation Research Library in Lexington, Virginia, is another national treasure. Thanks to Thomas E. Camden, the former museum and research library director; archivist Aaron Haberman; and the foundation president, Albert J. Beveridge III.

I also owe debts to Jane Yates, archivist at the Citadel Archives and Museum in South Carolina; Rebecca A. Ratcliff, historian in residence at the National Security Agency at Fort Meade, Maryland; Boyd L. Dastrup, command historian at the U.S. Army Field Artillery School at Fort Sill, Oklahoma; William F. Atwater, director of the U.S. Army Ordnance Museum, and Peter S. Kindsvatter, command historian at the U.S. Army Ordnance Center and School, at Aberdeen Proving Ground, Maryland; Van Roberts of the U.S. Army Infantry School Library at Fort Benning, Georgia; Martin K. Gordon of the U.S. Army Corps of Engineers' office of history at Fort Belvoir, Virginia; Robert S. Cameron of the U.S. Army Armor Center at Fort Knox, Kentucky; and Claude Watkins of American Ex-Prisoners of War.

Among the university archivists and librarians who have been helpful, I would like to thank Christine Weideman at the Yale University library; Thomas F. Burdett, curator of the S.L.A. Marshall Military History Collection at the University of Texas at El Paso; Phynessa McCurry at the University of Tennessee at Knoxville; Krista Ainsworth, special collections librarian at Norwich University; William T. Stolz of the Western Historical Manuscript Collection at the University of Missouri in Columbia; Alexander S. Cochran, professor of military strategy at the National War College; and Sandra Stewart Holyoak and Shaun Illingworth of the Rutgers University Oral History Archives of World War II.

At the Franklin D. Roosevelt Library in Hyde Park, New York, Robert Parks was helpful; I am also endebted to the staff of the Dwight D. Eisenhower Library in Abilene, Kansas.

In London, I am grateful for the assistance of Simon Robbins and the Department of Documents staff, as well as to the trustees of the Imperial War Museum; the archives staff of the Public Record Office in Kew; and to Patricia J. Methven, director of archive services, and Elizabeth Selby, archives assistant, at the Liddell Hart Centre for Military Archives at King's College.

I would like to acknowledge the encouragement and generous support of the Association of the United States Army, particularly from Gen. Gordon R. Sullivan, USA (ret.), the association president and former Army chief of staff;

Lt. Gen. Theodore G. Stroup, Jr., USA (ret.); and Lt. Gen. Thomas G. Rhame, USA (ret.).

I owe a very large debt to AUSA's director of operational and strategic studies, Roger Cirillo, a retired Army lieutenant colonel and a historian whose knowledge of World War II rivals that of anyone alive. Roger has been unstinting in giving time, advice, and material from his vast personal archive.

Grateful acknowledgement is made of permission to quote various materials, including:

The Trustees of the Liddell Hart Centre for Military Archives for material from the collections of Brigadier E. E. Mockler Ferryman; Maj. Gen. William Ronald Campbell Penney; Lieutenant General Sir Charles Walter Allfrey; and B. H. Liddell Hart.

Robin Ward Yates for excerpts from Orlando Ward's diary, letters, and other personal material; Robert Moore for excerpts from Robert R. Moore's letters and other papers; Jack A. Marshall for excerpts from his memoirs; Mrs. D. Fawkes for excerpts from the papers of Maj. A.J.A. Weir; Stephen Telford for excerpts from the papers of Fred Telford; Capt. P. Royle for excerpts from his papers; the family of Gen. Sir Cameron Nicholson for excerpts from his papers; Lady Belinda Milbank for excerpts from the papers of Adrian Gore.

In instances where current copyright holders could not be located, or where permissions arrived too late to be noted in this edition, I will gladly include acknowledgements in future editions.

Among others who have provided encouragement or practical assistance are three retired generals who served as chiefs of Army history: William A. Stofft, Harold Nelson, and Jack Mountcastle. Thanks also to Col. David R. Kiernan, USA (ret.), director of strategic communications at MPRI; Ray Callahan of the University of Delaware; Col. Steve Robinette, USA (ret.); John Ward Yates; Gen. Montgomery C. Meigs; and Carla Cohen and Barbara Meade, owners of that fine port in a storm, Politics & Prose bookstore.

My professional home for nearly two decades, *The Washington Post*, has long tolerated my impulse to heed W. H. Auden's dictum that we were put on this earth to make things. I thank Donald E. Graham; Bo Jones; Leonard Downie, Jr.; and Steve Coll. I'm deeply grateful for the friendship and support of several *Post* colleagues: Fred Hiatt, David Maraniss, Margaret Shapiro, Bob Woodward, Stephen C. Fehr, Robert G. Kaiser; Barton Gellman, and Jeff Leen, who cast his fine critical eye over the manuscript.

My friend and agent, Rafe Sagalyn, was there when I needed him, as he always has been. So too was my friend and counselor, Lewis Libby. Alice Crites showed ingenuity and persistence as a researcher, and Rush Atkinson tracked down many of the photographs that enhance this book. Gene Thorp, a master cartographer, demonstrated patience exceeded only by his great competence. Claudia Brown and Ronald R. Duquette helped with some French translations.

The publisher, Henry Holt and Company, has been supportive in every conceivable way. My greatest debt and deepest gratitude goes to the president and publisher, John Sterling, who edited my previous books and who shared the vision of this one. I am again the lucky beneficiary of his peerless sense of structure, character, and language, as well as his publishing acumen. Thanks also to the exceptional efforts of Elizabeth Stein, Jolanta Benal, Kenn Russell, Maggie Richards, Elizabeth Shreve, Christine Ball, and others in the Holt family.

All this assistance notwithstanding, any errors of fact or judgment are solely my responsibility.

Finally, some debts are too profound for adequate expression. To Jane, Rush, and Sarah, who endured years of preoccupation with North Africa, I ask the same indulgence as we turn to Italy and beyond.

Rick Atkinson
Washington, D.C.
June 15, 2002

INDEX

The initials DDE refer to Dwight David Eisenhower; page numbers in *italics* refer to maps.

ABOUT THE AUTHOR

RICK ATKINSON is a former staff writer and assistant managing editor of the *Washington Post*, and the best-selling author of *The Long Gray Line* and *Crusade*. His many awards include the Pulitzer Prize. He lives in Washington, D.C.

AN EXCERPT FROM

The Day of Battle

THE WAR IN SICILY AND ITALY,

1943-1944

VOLUME TWO OF THE LIBERATION TRILOGY

Rick Atkinson

PROLOGUE

SHE could be heard long before she was seen on that foggy Tuesday morning, May 11, 1943. Through the mist swaddling lower New York Bay sounded a deep bass A, two octaves and two notes below middle C, not so much blown as exhaled from the twin seven-foot whistles on the forward funnel, specially tuned to be audible ten miles away without discomfiting passengers at the promenade rail. Her peacetime paints—red, white, and black—had vanished beneath coats of pewter gray, although only after a spirited protest by camouflage experts who preferred a dappled pattern of blues and greens, called the Western Approaches scheme, to better befuddle enemy U-boats trying to fix her speed, bearing, and identity. Not that anyone glimpsing the famous triple stacks, the thousand-foot hull, or the familiar jut of her regal prow could doubt who she was. Gray paint had also been slathered over her name, but she remained, in war as in peace, the *Queen Mary*.

She slid past Ambrose Light at 8:30 A.M., precisely five days, twenty hours, and fifty minutes after leaving Gourock, Scotland. Escorting U.S. Navy destroyers peeled away to seaward. Like her antebellum colors, the *Queen*'s prewar finery was long gone, stripped and stored in a New York warehouse: the six miles of Wilton carpet, the two hundred cases of bone china and crystal, the wine cabinets and humidors that had provided fourteen thousand bottles and five thousand cigars on a typical crossing in the palmy days of peace. For this voyage, designated WW #21W, she had been transformed into a prison ship. Carpenters had removed any belowdecks fitting that could be used as a weapon, while installing alarm bells, locks, sandbagged machine-gun redoubts, and coiled barbed wire around dining and exercise areas. Now from deep in the hold came the drone of five thousand German prisoners, bagged in the North African campaign just ending and held in Scottish cages before being tendered to the *Queen* in Gourock. Three hundred British soldiers stood watch below; any guard inclined to befriend the enemy was advised, "Remember their barbarities." In truth, five days of violent zigzagging across the North Atlantic had rendered the barbarians docile. This lot, bound for a constellation of camps in the American Southwest, more than tripled the German POW population in the United States, which eventually would reach 272,000. To reduce heating bills, most camps sat south of 40 degrees north latitude; some commandants fed their prisoners bacon and eggs, encouraged camp pets and piano lessons, and permitted the Germans to order curtains from a Sears, Roebuck catalogue. That, too, encouraged docility.

But it was on the upper decks that the *Queen Mary*'s larger purpose on this voyage could be found. The secret passenger manifest listed the United Kingdom's most senior war chiefs, including commanders of the British army, navy, and air force, bound for Washington, D.C., and TRI-DENT, the code name for a two-week Anglo-American conference on war strategy. Officers crowded the rails as the ship glided through the Verrazano Narrows, peering into the fog in a vain effort to glimpse the Manhattan skyline seven miles north; they settled instead for dim views of Coney Island to starboard and Staten Island's Fort Wadsworth to port. Stewards and subalterns scurried about, sorting piles of luggage and tagging those bound for the White House with red slips bearing a large "W"—including two dozen bags belonging to a certain "Air Commodore Spencer." Secret documents were collected and filed in locked boxes stacked in the former children's playroom on the promenade deck, while classified wastepaper smoldered in an incinerator improvised from a bathtub in mezzanine suite number 105.

To mislead potential spies lurking in Scottish ports, great pains had been taken to obscure the details of this voyage. The ship's print shop in Gourock had engraved menus in Dutch to suggest that the mysterious traveler to New York was Wilhelmina, exiled queen of the Netherlands. Workmen also installed wheelchair ramps and handrails, and counterintelligence rumormongers in dockyard pubs let slip that the *Queen Mary* was being dispatched to pick up President Franklin D. Roosevelt for a secret visit to Britain. But all pretense ended shortly after nine A.M. The ship's great screws turned a final turn, the iron anchor sank with a rattle and a mighty splash, and Air Commodore Spencer strolled on deck, "looking well and fat and pink," and eager to get on with the war.

Like the *Queen Mary*, Winston S. Churchill was simply too obtrusive to disguise, "the largest human being of our time," as one contemporary concluded. There was the Havana cigar, of course, said to be long as a trombone and one of the eight he typically smoked in a day. The familiar moon face glowered beneath the furrowed pate he had taken to rubbing with a scented handkerchief. This morning, after leaving a £10 tip for the *Queen*'s service staff, he swapped the casual "siren suit" worn through much of the voyage for the uniform of the Royal Yacht Squadron. The effect had been likened to that of "a gangster clergyman who has gone on the stage." The previous night Churchill had celebrated both his imminent arrival in America and the third anniversary of his premiership with the sort of feast that recalled not only the *Queen*'s prewar luxury but the sun-never-sets Empire itself: croûte au pot à l'ancienne, petite sole meunière, pommes Windsor, and baba au rhum, all washed down with a magnum of Mumm's Cordon Rouge, 1926.

"We are all worms," Churchill once intoned, "but I do believe I am a glow-worm." Who could dispute it? For three years he had fought the good fight, at first alone and then with the mighty alliance he had helped construct. He had long warned minions that he was to be awakened at night only if Britain were invaded; that alarum never sounded. His mission in this war, he asserted, was "to pester, nag and bite"—a crusade that Roosevelt, who would receive thirteen hundred telegrams from Churchill during the war, knew all too well. "Temperamental like a film star and peevish like a spoilt child," the prime minister's army chief wrote of him; his wife, Clementine, added, "I don't argue with Winston. He shouts me down. So when I have anything important to say I write a note to him."

"In great things he is very great," said the South African statesman and field marshal Jan Smuts, "in small things not great." Certainly the small things engaged him, from decrying a shortage of playing cards for soldiers, to setting the grain ration for English poultry farmers, to reviewing all proposed code words for their martial resonance. (He sternly forbad WOEBETIDE, JAUNDICE, APÉRITIF, and BUNNYHUG). Yet his greatness in great things obtained. It was perhaps best captured by an admirer's seven-word encomium: "There is no defeat in his heart."

Sea voyages always reinvigorated Churchill, and none more than WW #21W. The prime minister's traveling party privately dubbed him "Master," and he had worked them hard each day, from cipher clerks to field marshals, preparing studies and the memoranda he called "prayers" for the TRIDENT meetings set to start on Wednesday. Typist dictationists worked in shifts on a specially designed silent Remington, taking down dispatches and minutes he mumbled through billowing cigar smoke. (His diction was further impeded by his lifelong struggle with the letter "s.") He stamped especially urgent documents with the decree "action this day," then retired for another hand of bezique—played with multiple decks from which all cards below seven were removed—and another tot of brandy, or champagne, or his favorite whiskey, Johnnie Walker Red. He had insisted on mounting a machine gun in his lifeboat. If the

Queen were torpedoed, he declared, "I won't be captured. The finest way to die is in the excitement of fighting the enemy. . . . You must come with me in the boat and see the fun." At times he seemed weighted with cares—"all hunched up and scowling at his plate"—and he rebuked those unblessed with his fluency by reading aloud from Fowler's *Modern English Usage* on the "wickedness of splitting infinitives and the use of 'very' instead of 'much.'" Yet more often he was in high spirits: discussing seamanship with the captain on the bridge, watching films like *The Big Shot* and *All Through the Night* in the lounge, or chuckling at stories swapped over supper in his cabin with his confederates. Particularly pleasing was a Radio Berlin report that placed him in the Middle East, supposedly attending a conference with Roosevelt. "Who in war," he asked, "will not have his laugh amid the skulls?"

Churchill had proposed inspiriting his American cousins by storming ashore in Manhattan's Battery Park, then promenading up Broadway. "One can always do what one wants if it takes people by surprise," he explained. "There is not time for plotters to develop their nefarious plans." Alas, the U.S. Secret Service disagreed, and instead three anonymous launches wallowed across the gray harbor toward the *Queen Mary* from Tompkinsville, on Staten Island. Waiting on the docks was Harry Hopkins, the president's closest counselor, with the *Ferdinand Magellan,* a seven-car presidential train pointed toward Washington.

As Churchill stepped into the lead launch, the *Queen's* entire company stood at the rails and cheered him off, their huzzahs trailing him to shore, where he disembarked and tossed a farewell wave before clambering onto the waiting train. They also knew, as they stood baying into the fog, that there was no defeat in his heart.

Packed into the *Magellan* baggage car with the suitcases and document crates was a thick sheaf of maps that had covered the walls of a makeshift war room next to Churchill's cabin on the *Queen Mary.* Replicating the campaign maps in the subterranean Cabinet War Rooms beneath Great George Street in London, the sheets depicted—with pushpins and lengths of colored yarn—the battle lines on a dozen combat fronts around the globe on this Tuesday, the 1,349th day of the Second World War. The struggle that had begun in September 1939 was more than half over; yet if both commanders and commanded intuited that they were nearer the end than the beginning, they also sensed that less than half the butcher's bill had been paid in a bloodletting that ultimately would claim sixty million lives: one life every three seconds for six years. They also knew that if the Allied powers—led by the United States,

Britain, and the Soviet Union—now possessed the strategic initiative, the Axis powers of Germany, Italy, and Japan still held the real estate, including six thousand miles of European coastline and the entire eastern littoral of Asia. This the maps made all too clear.

The exception to Axis territorial hegemony was Africa, a campaign now in its final hours. Seven months earlier, in November 1942, Anglo-American troops had landed in Morocco and Algeria, sweeping aside weak forces of the collaborationist Vichy French government, then wheeling east for a forced march into Tunisia through the wintry Atlas Mountains. There they joined cause with the British Eighth Army, which, after a hard-won victory at El Alamein in Egypt, had pushed west across the crown of Africa. A succession of battles lost and won against two German-Italian armies raged across Tunisia, a country the size of the state of Georgia; particularly galling was the drubbing at Kasserine Pass in February 1943, which had cost six thousand U.S. casualties and, in terms of yardage lost, would remain the worst American defeat of the war. Yet superior air power, naval power, artillery, and the combined weight of the Allied armies had trapped and crushed the Axis forces, which would formally surrender on Thursday, May 13. The booty included a quarter million Axis prisoners, among them the scruffy vanguard now queued up in the *Queen Mary*'s hold for delousing.

Victory in North Africa—exhilarating, unqualified victory—also gave the Allies control of the fine ports and airfields from Casablanca to Alexandria. It forestalled Axis threats to Middle East oil fields, reopened the Suez Canal for the first time since 1941—saving two months' sailing time for convoys going out to India from Britain, since they no longer had to circumnavigate Africa—and exposed the wide southern flank of occupied Europe to further Allied attack. The triumph in North Africa also coincided with victory in the North Atlantic. Ferocious depredations by German submarine wolfpacks had abruptly declined, thanks to improved electronic surveillance and because cryptologists had cracked German naval radio codes, allowing Allied warplanes and ships to pinpoint and destroy the marauders. Germany would lose forty-seven U-boats in May, triple the number sunk in March, and more than 3,500 Allied merchant ships would cross the Atlantic in the summer of 1943 without a sinking; a year earlier, the Allies had lost a ship every eight hours. The German submariner casualty rate during the war, 75 percent, would exceed that of every other service arm in every other nation.

Elsewhere in this global war, the ebb and flow of battle was less decisive. In the Pacific, Japan had been driven from Guadalcanal and Papua; Japanese reinforcements had been badly whipped in the Bismarck Sea in

February; and American forces on this very day, May 11, were landing on Attu in the Aleutians, a far-corner fight that would obliterate the Japanese garrison of 2,500 at a cost of more than a thousand U.S. lives. American fighter pilots on April 18, again thanks to a timely radio intercept, ambushed and killed Admiral Isokoru Yamamoto, architect of the sneak attack on Pearl Harbor. Yet Japan held firm in Burma, and still occupied ports, coastal cities, and much farmland in China, as well as Pacific islands from the Kuriles to the central Solomons. Tokyo had embraced a defensive strategy of attrition and stalemate in hopes of breaking the Allies' will and keeping the Soviet Union out of the Pacific war.

On the Eastern Front, the war retained the immensely sanguinary character that had prevailed since Adolf Hitler invaded the Soviet Union in June 1941. Here, too, the tide had turned against the Axis, which less than a year earlier had invested the suburbs of Leningrad and Stalingrad and stood but a few hours' drive from the Caspian Sea. The Germans had lost thirty divisions since January, most of them at Stalingrad or in Tunisia, a loss equivalent to one eighth of Hitler's total order of battle; tank numbers had dropped in the past three months from 5,500 to 3,600. A Soviet counteroffensive recaptured Kursk, Rostov, and the entire eastern shore of the Sea of Azov. Joseph Goebbels, propaganda minister for the Third Reich, described the Führer's despair in his diary on May 9: "He is absolutely sick of the generals. . . . All generals lie, he says. All generals are disloyal. All generals are opposed to National Socialism."

And yet: the Red Army remained more than three hundred miles from Germany's eastern border, facing two thirds of the Wehrmacht's combat strength. Hitler still commanded three hundred German divisions, plus ninety more from satellite armies. The pummeling of German industry and cities with vast bomber fleets showed promise but had had skimpy results so far, in part because much of America's airpower had been diverted from British bases to Africa. All of continental Europe, except for neutral Spain, Portugal, Switzerland, and Sweden, remained under the Axis boot, from the Bay of Biscay to the River Donetz, and from the North Cape to Sicily. Some 1.3 million forced laborers toiled in German factories, while another quarter million slaved on Atlantic Wall fortifications along the vulnerable west coast in France and the Low Countries; countless others deemed worthless or dangerous were herded into concentration or extermination camps, including a quarter million French, of whom only 35,000 would survive.

The next Anglo-American blow—after victory in North Africa—had been decided five months earlier, in Casablanca at the last big strategy conference. Operation HUSKY was summarized in twenty-one words by the Combined Chiefs of Staff, the amalgamation of American and British commanders who directed the war for Roosevelt and Churchill: "An attack against Sicily will be launched in 1943 with the target date as the period of the favorable July moon." The largest island in the Mediterranean lay only a hundred miles from Tunis, off the toe of the Italian boot, and its invasion would provide a postscript to the African campaign. American strategists had been leery of waging war in the Mediterranean since even before the November 1942 landings in northwest Africa; Roosevelt triggered that campaign by siding with Churchill and overruling his own generals, who argued that Allied power should instead be concentrated in Britain for a direct lunge across the English Channel toward Berlin. The American high command at Casablanca agreed to support HUSKY because the capture of Sicily would further safeguard Mediterranean shipping and perhaps divert Axis strength from the Soviet front; it would also provide air bases for bombing Italy and other targets in occupied Europe, and might cause weak-kneed Rome to abandon the war by abrogating its "Pact of Steel" with Berlin, formalized in May 1939.

Beyond Sicily, however, there was no plan, no grand strategy, no consensus on what to do with the immense Allied army now concentrating in the Mediterranean. For this reason, the TRIDENT conference had been convened in Washington. Churchill had harbored ambitions of a campaign on mainland Italy for nearly a year; in early April he petitioned Roosevelt to go beyond Sicily, which he decried as "a modest and even petty objective for our armies . . . Great possibilities are open in this theatre." Knocking Italy from the war "would cause a chill of loneliness over the German people, and might be the beginning of their doom." Sensing Yankee reluctance, he had warned Harry Hopkins on May 2 of "serious divergences beneath the surface" of Allied comity; privately, he told King George VI of his determination to battle the "Pacific First" advocates in Washington, where many demanded a stronger American effort against Tokyo.

"We did not come here with closed minds or rigid plans," Churchill had dictated during the passage from Gourock in preparing his opening argument for the TRIDENT talks. His musings, pecked on that silent Remington across 10 Downing Street stationery, included, "Objective 1: Get Italy out of the war," and "Never forget there are 185 German divisions against the Russians. . . . We are not at present in contact with *any*." And the heart of the matter: if Sicily fell "by the end of August, what should these [Anglo-American] troops do in the seven or eight months between this and a first possible BOLERO [the staging in Britain for a cross-Channel invasion of western Europe]? We cannot afford to have idle armies while the Russians are bearing such a disproportionate weight."

Beneath his brass lay a supplication. Forty-five months of war had stretched Britain as far as she would stretch. More than 12 percent of the British population now served in the armed forces; with national mobilization nearly complete, severe manpower shortages loomed if the war dragged on, particularly if it required storming the glacis of Festung Europa across the Channel. British battle deaths already exceeded 100,000, with thousands more missing, 20,000 merchant mariners lost, and another 45,000 dead in the United Kingdom from German air raids.

Salvation lay here, in America. The green and feeble U.S. Army of just a couple years earlier now exceeded six million, led by a thousand generals, seven thousand colonels, and 343,000 lieutenants. The Army Air Forces since mid-1941 had grown 3,500 percent, the Army Corps of Engineers 4,000 percent. A Navy that counted eight aircraft carriers after Pearl Harbor would have fifty, large and small, by the end of 1943. More cargo vessels would be built this year in the United States—a Liberty ship now took just fifty days, from keel laying to launch—than existed in the entire British merchant fleet. Just today, perhaps as a subtle reminder to Churchill before his arrival, Roosevelt had publicly announced that "production of airplanes by the United States"—86,000 in 1943—"now exceeds that of all other nations combined." Of $48 billion in war supplies provided by the United States to its allies, two thirds would go to Britain.

The first eighteen months of war for the United States had been characterized by inexperience, insufficiency, and, all too often, ineptitude. A long seasoning, still unfinished, was required, a sorting out: of strong from weak, effective from ineffective, and, as always, lucky from unlucky. That sorting and seasoning continued in combat units and among those who commanded them. *The New York Times's* veteran military correspondent, Hanson Baldwin, after a long trip through the war zone had concluded on this Tuesday morning's front page that "the greatest American problem is leadership: the Army so far has failed to produce a fraction of the adequate officer leadership needed." As for the average GI, Baldwin added, he "is not mentally tough or sufficiently determined. Part of his heart is in it, but only part."

Yet at home, where the productive capacity of the American industrial base approached full mobilization, the process was more advanced. The country had heaved itself from the ways of peace to the ways of war, galvanized as never before and perhaps never again. A final automobile had emerged from American production lines on February 10, 1942; supplanting it in 1943 would be thirty thousand tanks—more than three per hour around the clock, and more in a year than Germany would build from 1939 to 1945. The Rudolph Wurlitzer Company now made compasses and de-icers instead of pianos and accordions, International Silver turned out Browning automatic rifles rather than tableware, and various lipstick, typewriter, and hubcap manufacturers produced, respectively, cartridge cases, machine guns, and helmets. Similar conversions occurred throughout the economy, which this year would also make 6 million rifles, 98,000 bazookas, 648,000 trucks, 33 million sets of soldiers' cotton drawers, 61 million pairs of wool socks. And on, and on, and on.

So, too, had the war infiltrated every kitchen, every closet, every medicine cabinet. Sugar, tires, and gasoline had been rationed first, followed by nearly everything else, from shoes to coffee. "Use it up, wear it out, make it do, or do without" became a consumer mantra. Plastic buttons replaced brass; zinc pennies supplanted copper. To save fifty million tons of wool annually, the government outlawed vests, cuffs, patch pockets, and wide lapels; hemlines rose, pleated skirts vanished, and an edict requiring a 10 percent reduction in the cloth used for women's bathing suits led to the bikini. Regulation L-85, issued by the War Production Board, not only rationed natural fibers but also limited fabric colors to those approved by the Dyestuff Advisory Committee, including honor gold, valor red, and gallant blue.

German prisoners might order curtains from Sears, Roebuck but the catalog no longer offered saxophones, copper kettles, or plows. A bobby pin shortage forced hairdressers to improvise with toothpicks, while paint-on hosiery replaced vanished silk with the likes of "Velva Leg Film Liquid Stockings." Nationwide, the speed limit was thirty-five miles per hour, known as "victory speed." A government campaign to salvage toothpaste tubes—sixty tubes contained enough tin to solder all the electrical connections in a B-17 bomber—resulted in 200 million collected in sixteen months. "Bury a Jap with scrap," posters urged, and elaborate charts informed Americans that 10 old pails held sufficient steel for a mortar, 10 old stoves equaled one scout car, and 252 lawn mowers would make an anti-aircraft gun.

But all those recycled mowers and toothpaste tubes, all the warships and planes and wool socks, would pay off only if they were flung into the proper battles, in the proper campaigns, guided by a proper, war-winning strategy. And such a strategy did not yet exist.

No place in America had been more transformed by war than Washington, which the *Ferdinand Magellan* entered from the northeast with a hypnotic clack-clack-clacking shortly after six P.M. "The once sleepy southern city of charm and grace on the Potomac has burgeoned into the frenzied capital of the world," fumed the *Washington Times-Herald*. "Lobbyists, propagandists, experts of every species, wealthy industrialists, social climbers, inventors, ladies of uneasy virtue and pickpockets infest the city."

To this panoply now were added a prime minister and his retinue of more than a hundred generals, admirals, clerks, bodyguard detectives, and Royal Marines. At 6:45 P.M., a convoy of limousines rolled from the White House grounds and turned south. Seven Secret Service agents sat in squad cars along the route, including an agent posted at the top of an inconspicuous ramp on Fourteenth Street, which sloped to a subterranean rail spur under the Bureau of Engraving and Printing. As the train lurched to a stop in a squeal of brakes, the limousines pulled onto the platform. Lifted from the lead vehicle and placed in a waiting wheelchair, Franklin Roosevelt scanned the *Magellan*'s rear passenger compartment. His gray pallor, the wattled neck, the bagged and hazy eyes, all the fretful symptoms of stress and age seemed to vanish at the sight of Churchill clumping forward in his improbable yacht squadron uniform. The president beamed, the prime minister beamed, and the conclave that would search for that war-winning strategy to save the world was under way.

But first the visitors must be settled, and this was no simple task. "If the war lasts much longer, Washington is going to bust right out of its pants," *Life* magazine had warned in January. Five months later, the busting was well advanced. The city's twelve thousand hotel rooms were always booked, forcing some visitors to find shelter as far away as Philadelphia. Houseboat colonies sprouted on the Potomac River, and sprawling hamlets of shabby temporary houses, known as demolishables, spread through the District of Columbia and its suburbs. There would be no houseboat or demolishable for the British delegation, of course: Churchill took a suite at the White House, and the rest of the delegation was shoehorned into the Statler Hotel, the Wardman Park, the British embassy, and various other hostels and private houses. Sixteen Royal Marines marched off to a U.S. Army barracks, sweating miserably in the clinging humidity that entitled British diplomats in Washington to "tropical post pay."

Churchill could sense that the country had indeed changed since his previous visit eleven months earlier, and so had its capital. The Pentagon, which in 1942 was still under construction across the river in Hell's Bottom, now stood complete as not only the world's largest office building, but also "the largest feeding operation under one roof in the world" (55,000 meals a day for 35 cents each). All those well-fed, poorly housed War Department bureaucrats were busier than ever. One wit proposed a new government motto—"Exhaustion is not enough"—and on Pennsylvania Avenue a makeshift information center for visiting contractors and businessmen was known as "the Madhouse." This month, the War Manpower Commission had announced plans to induct twelve thousand men into the military every day for the rest of the year, with childless married men called to the colors for the first time and those with children certain to be drafted soon. Perhaps not coincidentally, the FBI director, J. Edgar Hoover, disclosed that his agents had arrested more than five hundred draft dodgers in twenty cities, with warrants outstanding on three thousand others.

Among other signs of these frenzied times: thirty-five "rumor clinics" had been established across the country "to investigate malicious and meaningless rumors," which would be vetted by college professors—apparently immune to scuttlebutt—whose findings would be reported in local newspapers. There was such a crying need for lathe operators, machinists, and leather workers that some help-wanted ads even solicited "White or Colored"; a government press release urgently seeking skilled typists for the war effort contained forty-six errors on a single page. The Office of War Information reported that a recent plea for fine blond hair—used in weather instruments and optical equipment—had resulted in such a cascade of golden tresses that no further donations were needed.

Amid the mania and the melodrama, one notable addition had been made to the Washington landscape four weeks before Churchill's arrival. He could have seen it from his White House digs, looking past the fading azaleas and beyond the Washington Monument to a grove of cherry trees framing the Tidal Basin. There, the memorial to Thomas Jefferson had been dedicated, an elegant neoclassical temple sheltering a nineteen-foot statue of the third president—temporarily cast in plaster, because the War Production Board needed the bronze. Jefferson's manifesto, chiseled in marble, summarized perfectly the animating sentiment of the men who would begin meeting tomorrow in search of a path that could carry them to war's end: "I have sworn upon the altar of God eternal hostility against every form of tyranny over the mind of man."

They got to work at 2:30 P.M. on Wednesday, May 12, in Roosevelt's oval study, a snug hideaway above the Blue Room. Nautical paintings and etchings decorated the walls, and a bear skin covered the floor. The president sat in his armless wheelchair greeting Churchill and the ten other men—mostly from the Combined Chiefs—who joined that first session. Roosevelt's massive desk, positioned away from the windows by the Secret Service, held a blue lamp, four cloth toy donkeys, a stack of books, an inkpot, a medicine bottle, a small clock shaped like a ship's wheel, and a bronze bust of the First Lady, which had somehow escaped the scrap collectors.

Five months earlier, American strategists had left the Casablanca conference convinced they had been outfoxed by the British, who were better prepared and had been unified in their determination to continue the Mediterranean strategy begun with the invasion of North Africa. To avoid another humiliation, the Yanks before TRIDENT had bombarded the British with position papers; they also drafted more than thirty studies on various war policies and doubled the size of the U.S. delegation. In searching for "a grand design by which to reach the heartland of Europe" in decisive battle, American planners scrutinized potential portals to the continent, from the Iberian peninsula and southern France to Italy, Greece, and Turkey. Still, almost to a man they favored the most direct route across the English Channel.

The president's brain trust also worked hard to overcome what many considered the biggest obstacle to American strategic hegemony: Roosevelt himself, and his evident willingness to be swayed by Churchill's honeyed oratory. "The man from London . . . will have his way with our Chief, and the careful and deliberate plans of our staff will be overridden," the secretary of war, Henry Stimson, told his diary on May 10. "I feel very troubled about it." The U.S. Joint Chiefs had conferred with Roosevelt at the White House three days earlier and had wrung from him a vow to press the British for commitment to a cross-Channel invasion of Europe. Driving home the point, a Joint Chiefs memo reiterated the Pentagon's "antipathy to an invasion of the Italian mainland," while warning that the British "are traditionally expert at meeting the letter while avoiding the spirit of commitments." Roosevelt replied with a three-word scribble across the margin that echoed Churchill's minute on the *Queen Mary*: "No closed minds."

In this charged milieu, "the man from London" spoke. North Africa was done, Sicily was near. "What should come next?" Churchill asked. The Allies had "the authority and prestige of victory" and must "grasp the fruits of our success." Following his typed notes, he laid out his arguments: Russia fighting 185 German divisions; Allies currently fighting none; Italy ripe for the plucking.

The prime minister had used the phrase "soft underbelly" in a cable to

Roosevelt in November 1942, meaning the supposedly vulnerable southern flank of Axis Europe. Privately, to his military advisers this week, Churchill added, "We want them to agree to the exploitation of HUSKY and the attack on the underbelly taking priority." Now he pressed the point. "Need we invade the soil of Italy, or could we crush her by air attack? Would Germany defend Italy?" Answering himself, Churchill said it was imperative "to use our great armies to attack Italy" rather than leave them idle after Sicily. If Hitler rallied to defend his Fascist partner, Benito Mussolini, that many fewer German troops could fight the Russians. The prime minister did not believe a defeated Italy would present an economic burden to the Allies, nor did he even concede "that an occupation of Italy would be necessary."

There it was, the British strategy in a Mediterranean nutshell. Roosevelt replied immediately. Churchill's argument was vivid but unpersuasive. "Where do we go from Sicily?" the president asked, again echoing the prime minister. Some twenty-five Allied divisions—with roughly fifteen thousand men each—would muster in the Mediterranean by the end of Operation HUSKY and "these must be kept employed." But he had "always shrunk from the thought of putting large armies in Italy," a diversion that could "result in attrition for the United Nations and play into Germany's hands." Better to continue staging a mighty host in Britain. The subsequent invasion, a knockout punch aimed at the German homeland, "should be decided upon definitely as an operation for the spring of 1944." Finishing, the president smiled and gave the casual toss of the head that one admirer called his "cigarette-holder gesture."

This impasse persisted the next morning when the Combined Chiefs—the half dozen heads of the American and British armies, navies, and air forces—met without Roosevelt and Churchill in the Federal Reserve Building, a severe rectilinear edifice with a pillared portico facing Constitution Avenue. The scent of roses and fresh cut grass seeped past the rigid sentries into the wainscoted room used by the board of governors; here, the U.S. delegation presented an eleven-paragraph memo entitled "Global Strategy of the War." Point 3 held the crux: "It is the opinion of the United States chiefs of staff that a cross-Channel invasion of Europe is necessary to an early conclusion of the war with Germany."

A tall, austere man with sandy hair gone gray carried forward the American argument. General George C. Marshall, the Army chief of staff, knew his mind on this issue even as he fretted over the president's susceptibility to British blandishments. Marshall was a clean-desk man, famously convinced that "no one ever had an original idea after three o'clock in the afternoon," and he disdained orthodoxy, sycophants, and the telephone. To Churchill he was "the greatest Roman of them all"; a British general described him as "a little aloof, dignified, above the battle, unbuyable. . . . I never saw him show his feelings in any way." In fact, Marshall possessed a molten temper. He demanded that subordinates "expunge the bunk, complications, and ponderosities" from the nation's war effort, and his signature query, accompanied by the unblinking gaze of those ice-blue eyes, could terrify lieutenants and lieutenant generals alike: "Are you confident that you've thought this through?" Aside from horseback riding, gardening was his sole civil diversion; "the pride of his heart," according to his wife, remained the compost pile outside his Virginia home.

Invading Italy, Marshall said, "would establish a vacuum in the Mediterranean" that sucked troops and matériel away from a cross-Channel attack. Operations after Sicily "should be limited to the air offensive" or risk "a prolonged struggle" in the Mediterranean, which was "not acceptable to the United States."

Arguments spilled from those thirty War Department studies: eliminating Italy from the war could bring more burden than benefit, since precious Allied shipping would be needed to feed the Italian civilian population. Germany would recoup the twelve million tons of coal currently provided Rome each year, as well as the rolling stock now needed to supply Italy. The "soft underbelly" in general lacked sufficient ports to support the huge Allied armies needed to plunge into central Europe. American planners considered the British beguiled by "side-shows," "periphery-pecking," and "unremunerative scatterization." (That last must have disheartened every lover of the language regardless of strategic creed.) Privately, the Yanks suspected that Britain's fixation on the Mediterranean reflected both traditional imperial interests and faint-hearted reluctance to again risk the horrific casualties incurred on the Western Front a generation earlier.

"Mediterranean operations," Marshall added, "are highly speculative as far as ending the war is concerned."

Listening attentively was General Sir Alan Brooke, chief of the Imperial General Staff, whose sharp-featured countenance did not betray his private assessment of Marshall: "a big man and a very great gentleman who inspired trust, but did not impress me by the ability of his brain." Brooke's brain was able enough, though he tended to dismiss as purblind those uncommitted to his own vision. At fifty-nine, with round shoulders and dark, pomaded hair, he could be petulant—"very liverish," in his phrase; this state was perhaps the handmaiden to exhaustion after four years of war with the Germans and, not infrequently, with Churchill. "When I thump the table and push my face towards him what does he do?" the prime minister said. "Thumps the table harder and glares back at me." Brooke calculated that each month battling Churchill "is a year off my life"; in a letter to a friend he added, "It is the night work after dinner till 1 a.m. with him that kills me." The ninth and youngest child of an expatriate Anglo-Irish baronet, Brooke had been born and raised in France, a history that bestowed on him both a native fluency and a lifelong dread of the nickname Froggie. He nurtured homely passions for birds and for wildlife photography, in which he was a pioneer. If Marshall had his compost pile, Brooke had Southeran's shop in Sackville Street, where he would sit transfixed in his red uniform braces, scrutinizing ornithological plates. On the *Queen Mary* he had put aside *Birds of the Ocean* long enough to note in his diary, with handwriting as vertical and jagged as the Irish coastline: "Running a war seems to consist in making plans and then ensuring that all those destined to carry [them] out don't quarrel with each other instead of the enemy."

Now he quarreled with Marshall, albeit without raising his voice. The eleven-paragraph U.S. strategic memo was answered with a thirty-one-paragraph British countersalvo. Point 5 encapsulated Britain's thesis: "The main task which lies before us this year in the European theater is the elimination of Italy. If we could achieve this, it is our opinion that we should have gone a very long way towards defeating Germany."

Brooke pressed the point with staccato precision. Germany currently kept thirty-five divisions in France and the Low Countries, with another ten, available as reinforcements, in the Fatherland; attacking Italy would divert some of these German troops and weaken defenses against an eventual Allied cross-Channel attack, which might not be feasible until 1945 or 1946 anyway. If Italy collapsed, German soldiers would have to replace the forty-three Italian divisions occupying the Balkans and the seven others bivouacked in southern France. Without Italian allies, Berlin was unlikely to fight south of the Po Valley in northern Italy. "Our total commitment on the Italian mainland in the event of a collapse," a British staff memo estimated, "will not exceed nine divisions."

A stack of studies, bound in red leather folders, further advanced the British cause. "If Italy collapses, the Germans cannot hold Italy *and* the Balkans, and they will concentrate everything they can on the defence of the latter." The Mediterranean offered such enticing opppportunities that "we shall have every chance of breaking the Axis and of bringing the war with Germany to a successful conclusion in 1944."

But, Brooke warned his American colleagues, unless the fight was carried into Italy after the capture of Sicily "no possibility of an attack into France would arise." Indeed, "to cease Mediterrranean operations on the conclusion of HUSKY would lengthen the war."

Momentary silence fell on the room as the session ended. The allies were miles apart, still, and mutually suspicious. "Your people have no intention of ever crossing the Channel," one American planner had told his British counterpart. Admiral Ernest J. King, the irascible U.S. chief of naval operations, subsequently advised his fellow chiefs, "We ought to divert our forces to the Pacific."

At Marshall's suggestion they adjourned with a scraping of chairs and ambled next door to the Public Health Building. Lunch awaited them in the map room, where strategic thrust and parry momentarily yielded to small talk and the benign clink of cutlery. That night Brooke confided to his diary, "I am thoroughly depressed."

Washington lacked the isolated tranquillity that had distinguished Casablanca five months earlier. Endless meetings, often three or more a day, were followed by endless social obligations, including four consecutive nights of black-tie affairs. For all its sophisticated war paint, the capital remained a provincially convivial place, eager to please and a-twitter at hosting such distinguished battle captains.

Fans at a Washington Nationals baseball game applauded wildly at the appearance of a pair of genuine field marshals in the box seats. Bing Crosby and Kate Smith sang between innings as the visitors tried to divine the difference between home plate and a home run. At one dinner party, each arriving guest reached into a top hat—one for ladies, another for gentlemen—and drew a slip on which was printed the name of a famous lover in history. Table seating then was determined by uniting the paramours: Helen with Paris, Cleopatra with Antony, Chloe with Daphnis, Heloïse with Abelard. Also intimate, if less risqué, was a private showing at the White House of a new U.S. Army Signal Corps film, *The Battle of Britain*; doughty Royal Air Force pilots climbed into their cockpits, Spitfires tangled with Focke Wulfs, mortally wounded planes heeled over in smoky spirals. Churchill sat transfixed by the spectacle, the flickering projector light reflecting off the tears that coursed down his plump cheeks. Only the Washington heat remained inhospitable, forcing some wilting Brits to desperate measures: the wife of the economist John Maynard Keynes was found perched, entirely nude, before the open door of a Westinghouse refrigerator in the Georgetown house where the couple was staying.

To escape both official Washington and social Washington, Marshall bundled the Combined Chiefs onto a pair of transport planes for a weekend in southeast Virginia. Landing at Langley Field, the men squeezed into eight waiting Army staff cars and motored up Route 17 for a tour of the Yorktown battlefield, where the British professed—amid guffaws—not to recall "the name of that chap who did so badly here" in 1781. Then it was on to Williamsburg, the meticulously restored former colonial capital.

If Washington had been a-twitter, Williamsburg seethed with excitement at the visitation. Lawns had been trimmed, hedges clipped, honeysuckle cropped. At the Williamsburg Inn, linen and china emerged from wartime storage crates, and the silver was polished and repolished. Carpenters built a new table to seat thirteen diners and adjusted the floodlights to illuminate the dogwoods. Someone managed to circumvent government restrictions on Freon to procure the only two tanks of refrigerant south of Richmond: the inn would be pleasingly air conditioned.

John D. Rockefeller, Jr., who had financed Williamsburg's resurrection, got wind of the visit and assigned various servants to oversee dinner preparations. Appalled to learn that inferior cream might be used to make the ice cream, Rockefeller ordered a fresh urn dispatched from his estate at Pocantico Hills in New York, along with select fruits and cheeses, while his private club in Manhattan prepared fresh terrapin à la Maryland, which required two days of simmering. Terrapin, cream, fruit, cheese, and a consignment of sherry all were tucked into the upper berth of a Pullman car at Penn Station by an overburdened butler, who staggered off the train in Richmond four hours later and continued with his bounty to Williamsburg by limousine.

Shortly before five P.M. on Saturday, May 15, the convoy of chiefs turned off Queen Street onto Duke of Gloucester Street before stopping at the old Capitol building, where they were greeted by a black doorman in colonial livery. Having admired the rubbed woodwork and the portrait of young George Washington, they strolled to the Raleigh Tavern for finger sandwiches and cinnamon toast in the Daphne Room, washed down with tea and highballs. Then it was on to the inn, where fires crackled in the twin lobby hearths—economy be damned—and bourbon juleps were served in goblets made by a local silversmith. Dinner, at 8:15, included Rockefeller's menu, plus crabmeat cocktail, Virginia ham, beaten biscuits, and a 1929 Heidsieck Dry Monopole champagne. All agreed that the strawberry ice cream was divine.

After coffee and brandy, Marshall rousted the visitors for a midnight excursion to the colonial governor's palace, brilliantly lighted with hundreds of candles in each room and throughout the gardens. Admiral Sir Dudley Pound, the First Sea Lord, lost his way in the topiary maze and called for help from the other chiefs, who rushed to the rescue only to get lost themselves, with much boyish chortling.

Sunday morning, after breakfast on the terrace, the chiefs played croquet on the lawn or went swimming in borrowed trunks. Brooke, who was mulling whether to spend £1,500 for a forty-five-volume set of *Gould's Birds,* tromped off with his field glasses in search of catbirds and hairy woodpeckers. Before heading to the airfield for the return flight, the high command filed into Bruton Parish Church, where ushers escorted them to General Washington's pew. Parishioners jammed the sanctuary, clogging the twin transept aisles with folding chairs after the pews filled. Dudley Pound, who was suffering from an unsuspected brain tumor and had but a few months to live, had been asked to read the scripture. Stepping to the lectern, he thumbed to the sixth chapter of Matthew and sang out, "Consider the lilies of the field, how they grow; they toil not, neither do they spin." Pound finished in a strong voice:

> *Take therefore no thought for the morrow: for the morrow shall take thought for the things of itself. Sufficient unto the day is the evil thereof.*

While the chiefs went south, Roosevelt and Churchill headed north. With Eleanor Roosevelt and Harry Hopkins also in the limousine, and a motorcycle escort clearing the road, the motorcade rolled up Massachusetts Avenue before angling out of the capital on Wisconsin Avenue toward the presidential retreat called Shangri-La—later renamed Camp David—in the Catoctin Mountains of central Maryland. Spying a billboard for Barbara Fritchie Candy, Roosevelt recited a couplet from John Greenleaf Whittier's ballad about the legendary Civil War heroine who defied passing rebel troops by waving the Stars and Stripes from her window.

> *"Shoot, if you must, this old gray head,*
> *But spare your country's flag," she said.*

To the president's amazement, Churchill then "gabbled the whole poem," all sixty lines—"She leaned far out on the window-sill, / And shook it forth with a royal will." Soon the Roosevelts and Hopkins were punctuating the prime minister's cadences with the refrain: "Shoot, if you must . . ."

For three days they unbent in the serene glades of Shangri-La, napping in the log cabins, angling for brook trout, discussing the hot tramp of Confederate troops through these hills toward Gettysburg eighty years earlier. Another guest, Roosevelt's daughter, Anna, wrote her husband on May 14 that Churchill "picks his teeth all through dinner and uses snuff liberally. The sneezes which follow the latter practically rock the foundations of the house. . . . I admired his snuff box and found it was one that had once belonged to Lord Nelson." Often the president sat by a window with his beloved stamp collection; when Churchill's pleas grew too insistent for more tanks or more planes, more this or more that, Roosevelt would cut him short by holding a stamp specimen to the light and murmuring, "Isn't this a beauty from Newfoundland?" On other occasions, to relieve the president from the "Winston hours," an aide would summon Roosevelt to an imaginary phone call.

They had much in common besides their ultimate responsibility for saving the world. They shared passions for secrecy, skulduggery, and military history. Roosevelt "loved the military side of events," one subordinate wrote, "and liked to hold them in his own hand," while Churchill seemed to fancy himself the reincarnation of his famous ancestor the Duke of Marlborough, the victor over the French at Blenheim in 1704. Despite his current resistance to Churchill's Italian gambit, the president had his own "diversionist tendencies" and harbored a fascination for the Mediterranean nearly as lurid as the prime minister's. Neither ever forgot, or tried to forget, the agony that war had brought to so many. (Marshall routinely sent Roosevelt brilliantly colored graphics detailing the latest combat casualty figures, "so that it would be quite clear.") Certainly the president's admiration and affection for Churchill ran deep. "Isn't he a wonderful old Tory to have on our side?" he once asked.

And yet: Churchill could draw near and no nearer. Convivial and charming, Roosevelt at his core remained opaque, mysterious, unknowable in what one aide called "his heavily forested interior." Trying to follow his thought process, Henry Stimson said, was "very much like chasing a vagrant beam of sunshine around an empty room." Seldom did he issue orders; rather, he intimated that he "wished to have things done." No politician ever was better at resolving problems by ignoring them; Roosevelt could elevate inaction to an art form. Yet on more than twenty occasions he rejected the advice of his military brain trust to follow his own instincts, as he had done in deciding to invade North Africa the previous November. "Not a tidy mind," one British observer noted, and the American chiefs could only agree. "The president," Eleanor once said, "never 'thinks'! He *decides*."

He reduced his own political philosophy to two nouns: democrat and Christian. A bit more nuanced were his inalienable Four Freedoms—of speech, of worship, from want, and from fear—which he had articulated in the State of the Union message of January 1941. Months earlier, he had begun to dream about the postwar world, and if he kept Churchill at arm's length it was partly because his vision did not include the restoration of colonial empires. Surely he had spoken from the heart in telling the prime minister, "It is fun to be in the same decade with you." Yet there was also cold conviction in Roosevelt's observation to his son Elliott: "Britain is on the decline."

America was ascendant, and Roosevelt had reason to hope that his countrymen possessed the stamina to remake a better world: a forthcoming Roper opinion poll, secretly slipped to the White House on Thursday, revealed that more than three quarters of those surveyed agreed that the United States should play a larger global role after the war. Nearly as many believed that the country should "plan to help other nations get on their feet," and more than half concurred that Americans should "take an active part in some sort of an international organization with a court and police force strong enough to enforce its decisions." The president found it equally heartening that 70 percent approved of his war leadership and two thirds favored him for reelection in 1944 if the world was still at war.

But if Britain was on the decline, so was Roosevelt personally, as he no doubt realized. Those who had seen him at Casablanca were dismayed at how frail he now looked, and all the pretty stamps in Newfoundland could not fully restore him. "Something at once attractive and pathetic in this man," a British diplomat wrote in his diary. "The great torso, the huge and splendid head, the magnificent frame, immobile, anchored to a sofa or a chair, carried from room to room." Roosevelt said little about his health, other than to grouse over a recurrent sinus condition. It was just another secret to keep.

Negotiations resumed at 10:30 A.M. on Monday. Camaraderie and good fun promptly popped like soap bubbles, and for three days the deadlock persisted as the military chiefs haggled. Brooke and his British colleagues renounced both imperial designs in the Mediterranean and any peripheral strategems; rather, they argued, an Italian campaign "in the spirit of the chase" would exploit a Sicilian victory, unhinge Rome, and unbalance Berlin. The Americans refused to concede, and declared that no U.S. ground or naval forces would be released for combat beyond Sicily. Marshall, whose beetling brows gave him a stern Old Testament look, reminded the chiefs "that in North Africa a relatively small German force" had fought an irksome rearguard campaign for six months; a German decision to fight in Italy "might make intended operations extremely difficult and time consuming."

Nearly three dozen aides and staff officers hovered behind the chiefs, rifling through documents or pulling out those red leather folders to prove this point or dispute that assertion. By 4:30 on Wednesday afternoon, Marshall had reached his limit. The chiefs were scheduled to meet Roosevelt and Churchill at the White House in two hours; to confess that the high command remained at loggerheads would likely mean ceding strategic planning to the president and prime minister, a prospect horrifying to every man in epaulets. Marshall proposed that the room be cleared except for the chiefs. The supernumeraries filed out; ninety minutes later, the door reopened, and on the mahogany table lay an agreement.

It was a curious compromise, because compromise it was. A cross-Channel attack would be launched—the target date was fifty weeks away: on May 1, 1944—"to secure a lodgement on the Continent from which further offensive operations can be carried out." To help assemble the twenty-nine divisions required for such an invasion, soon to be codenamed OVERLORD, four American and three British divisions would be transferred from the Mediterranean after the Sicilian campaign to staging bases in Britain. As for the Med, the Allied commander-in-chief in North Africa, General Dwight D. Eisenhower, was instructed to plan whatever operations following the conquest of Sicily seemed "best calculated to eliminate Italy from the war and to contain the maximum number of German forces." The chiefs calculated that Eisenhower eventually would be left with 27 divisions and 3,600 aircraft to continue his war against the soft underbelly, although a direct invasion of Italy was not specified.

The baby had been cut in half, a solution perhaps satisfying to the disputants but rarely auspicious for the baby. As the officers collected their papers and snapped shut their briefcases, a grumble of thunder rolled across Washington. Rain soon lashed the city from the west, breaking the heat.

TRIDENT had another week to run. If the central disagreement had been finessed, a dozen other issues required resolution, from shipping allocations to operations in the Pacific. The social round also continued without mercy. At a reception on the South Lawn of the White House, the Marine Band played Stephen Foster airs and "The Battle Hymn of the Republic" while guests sipped iced coffee and stared beyond the fence at tourists who stared back. During a British embassy luncheon on May 22, Churchill, fortified with whiskey, declared that he expected "England and the United States to run the world. . . . Why be apologetic about Anglo-Saxon superiority?" The bemused vice president, Henry A. Wallace, accused the prime minister of advocating "Anglo-Saxondom *über Alles.*" Churchill waved away the charge. "We Anglo-Saxons"—he pronounced it *schaxons*—"are the only ones who really know how to run the show." Poor Brooke left the luncheon to get a haircut and tumbled down fourteen stone steps; battered and bruised, he found consolation in the purchase of two rare bird books discovered in a local shop.

Rarely content and never quiescent, Churchill now threatened to overplay his hand. He kept Roosevelt up until 2:30 in the morning of Monday, May 24. (After TRIDENT, the exhausted president would flee to his Hyde Park estate and sleep ten hours for three consecutive nights.) Later that day the prime minister sought to repudiate the compromise reached by the chiefs, on the ground that it failed to specifically advocate an invasion of Italy. He also raised the notion of a continued attack into Yugoslavia and Greece. To Lord Moran, his personal physician, Churchill added, "Have you noticed that the president is a very tired man? His mind seems closed. He seems to have lost his wonderful elasticity. . . . I cannot let the matter rest where it is."

Harry Hopkins warned Churchill to do just that or risk an ugly rupture; even Roosevelt complained that the prime minister was acting like a "spoiled boy." Chastened, Churchill agreed instead to fly from Washington to Algiers to confer with Eisenhower, taking in tow both a scuffed-up Brooke and a grumpy Marshall, who likened himself to "a piece of baggage." Hopkins told Moran, "We have come to avoid controversy with Winston. We find he is too much for us." The physician agreed that Churchill "is so taken up with his own ideas that he is not interested in what other people think."

Still, the sweep of his rhetoric proved a tonic, as it had so many times before. At noon on a bright Wednesday, a joint session of Congress convened in the House of Representatives, joined by the British ambassador's son, a young subaltern who had lost both legs in North Africa and who was wheeled into the House gallery by his tall, stooped father. Churchill had spent nearly ten hours the previous day dictating speech drafts to his long-suffering typists, and he now stood at the podium, grasping the lapels of his dark suit, rolling his vowels and reminding free men everywhere that the road was long, but the cause was righteous. "War is full of mysteries and surprises. A false step, a wrong direction, an error in strategy, discord or lassitude among the Allies, might soon give the common enemy power to confront us," he said. "It is in the dragging-out of the war at enormous expense, until the democracies are tired or bored or split, that the main hopes of Germany and Japan must now reside."

After fifty minutes he finished, as he often finished, by taking flight:

> By singleness of purpose, by steadfastness of conduct, by tenacity and endurance—such as we have so far displayed—by this and only by this can we discharge our duty to the future of the world and to the destiny of man.

Roosevelt had remained at the White House to avoid crowding Churchill in the limelight. He listened to the speech on the radio he kept in the left drawer of his big desk. "Winston writes beautifully," the president told his secretary, "and he's a past master at catch phrases."

The conference sputtered to an end without the wistful sense of brotherhood that had characterized Casablanca. Mutual confidence remained a sometime thing; the ideal of an epoch when good men dared to trust one another was still imperfectly realized. They were tired of arguing, tired of shouldering the burdens they shouldered, tired of the whole catastrophe. They knew the hard time had come, and that it would require hard men.

For the Americans, the first leg of the century's most grueling race had come to an end, its emblem the Afrika Korps prisoners now trudging into camps in Kansas and Oklahoma. That leg, from Pearl Harbor through the capture of Tunisia, had required spunk and invention, unity and organizational acumen. Now the long middle leg of the race was about to begin, of uncertain duration, over an undetermined course, and few doubted that new virtues would be needed: endurance, impenitence, an obdurate will.

For the first time, the Allied high command had met with a clear sense that the war, at least in Europe, would be won—someday, somehow. "The mellow light of victory begins to play over the entire expanse of the world war," as Churchill would tell the House of Commons in June. During the conference, daily reports of U-boat sinkings affirmed that the tide in that particular struggle had turned, dramatically and irreversibly. The joint communiqué drafted for TRIDENT by Roosevelt and Churchill evinced a bluff optimism while proferring a few white lies, such as the assertion that "there has been a complete meeting of minds" about all theaters, including "the war in the Mediterranean."

Despite this glossing over, a plan now existed where there had been no plan. The British had succeeded in keeping the war centered in the Mediterranean, at least for a year, and in making the elimination of Italy from the Axis partnership an immediate goal. Churchill had again thwarted the American impulse to muscle up in the Pacific theater at the expense of the Atlantic (although, in the event, the U.S. war against Tokyo would be prosecuted almost as furiously as the European struggles). Assistance to China would continue, and Allied bomber fleets would grow ever larger, until they literally blackened the skies over Germany and eventually Japan. The British had made extravagant claims— "over-egged the pudding," as one critic put it—to overcome Yankee skepticism by asserting that Germany was unlikely to fight hard for mainland Italy; that the long-term Allied commitment in Italy was likely to call for only nine divisions and to require no substantial occupation; and that a hard fight in the Mediterranean could end the war in 1944. All of these prophesies proved false.

The Americans had managed to put brakes on the Mediterranean campaign: seven divisions would decamp for Britain in the fall, and no additional reinforcements would be sent south. They also extracted a pledge that the Allies would invade western France by a specific date. The deal, Roosevelt told an aide, was "the best I could get at this time." Neither the president nor his warlords had answered the legitimate British questions about how, if the plug were pulled in the Mediterranean, German forces would be engaged during the many months until OVERLORD could be mounted in France; or how the Russians would be mollified if the Anglo-Americans took a powder for those many months; or whether it would not be prudent to draw Axis forces from the Atlantic wall by making Berlin reinforce its southern flank.

The Allies had a plan where there had been no plan, but whether it was a good plan remained to be seen. Certainly it was vague. How Italy should be knocked out was left to the theater commander, General Eisenhower, and the concomitant goal of containing "the maximum number of German forces" implied a war of attrition and opportunism rather than a clear strategic objective.

The dispatch of Allied armies to North Africa and now to Sicily had created its own momentum, its own logic. In an effort to square the circle, a slightly cockeyed strategic scheme emerged that would guide the Anglo-Americans until the end of the war: a relentless pounding of Festung Europa from the air and from the *southern* flank, setting the stage for a cross-Channel invasion aimed at Berlin. Whether a meaningful Mediterranean campaign could be waged without endless entanglement, and whether the enemy reacted as Allied strategists hoped he would react, remained to be seen.

Perhaps the greatest achievement of the men meeting at TRIDENT was not the sketching of big arrows on a map but rather the affirmation of their humanity. This was their true common language: the shared values of decency and dignity, of tolerance and respect. Despite the petty bickering and intellectual fencing, a fraternity bound them on the basis of who they were, what they believed, and why they fought. It could be glimpsed, like one of Brooke's beautiful birds, in Churchill's gentle draping of a blanket on Roosevelt's shoulders, and in their grim determination to wage war without liking it.

At four P.M. on Tuesday, May 25, precisely two weeks after his arrival, Churchill strode down the narrow corridors of the West Wing to the Oval Office. His departure by flying boat from the Potomac off Gravelly Point was set for the next morning, his luggage was packed, his farewells were bid or soon would be bid. The code name for the morning flight had been repeatedly amended in the past forty-eight hours from WATSON to REDCAR to STUDENT, and the prime minister, evidently finding none of those words suitably warlike, had lobbied in vain to get it changed again, to NEPTUNE.

Roosevelt sat in the armless wheelchair. Sunshine flooded the Rose Garden outside the French doors. Bulletproof glass had been installed in the windows facing south, but the president had rejected several of the more hysterical security proposals, including machine guns on the terrace and air locks on the outer doors to thwart a poison gas attack. With Churchill at his side, he gave a nod and an aide opened the office door to admit 150 reporters for the 899th press conference of Roosevelt's presidency.

"We are awfully glad to have Mr. Churchill back here," he told the scribes after they had shuffled in. "Considering the size of our problems, these discussions have been done in practically record time." Roosevelt swiveled toward the prime minister. "I think that he will be willing to answer almost—with stress on the *almost*—any question."

"Mr. Prime Minister," a reporter said, "can you tell us generally about the plans for the future, probably beginning with Europe?"

"Our plans for the future," Churchill replied, "are to wage this war until unconditional surrender is procured from all those who have molested us, and this applies equally to Asia and to Europe."

Roosevelt beamed. "I think that word 'molestation' or 'molesting' is one of the best examples of your habitual understatement that I know."

The reporters tittered. "I am curious to know," another asked, "what you think is going on in Hitler's mind?" The titter turned to boisterous laughter.

"Appetite unbridled, ambition unmeasured—all the world!" the prime minister said. "There is no end of the appetite of this wicked man. I should say he repents now that he did not curb his passion before he brought such a portion of the world against him and his country."

"Do you care to say anything about Mussolini and Italy?"

Churchill scowled. "I think they are a softer proposition than Germany."

On it went, query and response, and the reporters were so beguiled that by the end they had interrupted with laughter twenty-one times.

The Allies had no intent of keeping Italian territory after the war, or of matching Axis barbarities, Churchill added. "We shall not stain our name by an inhuman act." As for the Italian people, they "have sinned—erred—by allowing themselves to be led by the nose by a very elaborate tyranny." But they "will have their life in the new Europe."

Churchill rose to his full five feet, seven inches. "We are the big animal now," he said, "shaking the life out of the smaller animal, and he must be given no rest, no chance to recover."

The door opened and the reporters reluctantly began to file out. Seizing the moment with unsuspected agility, the prime minister climbed up onto his chair, tottered unsteadily for a moment, then stood above the popping flashbulbs and the grinning president and the applauding scribes, flashing the V-for-victory sign with his stubby fingers, over and over again.